List of the Elements with Their Atomic Symbols and Atomic Weights

Name	Symbol	Atomic Number	Atomic Weight	Name	Symbol	Atomic Number	Atomic Weight
Actinium	Ac	89	227.028	Meitnerium	Mt	109	(268)
Aluminum	Al	13	26.9815	Mendelevium	Md	101	(258)
Americium	Am	95	(243)	Mercury	Hg	80	200.59
Antimony	Sb	51	121.76	Molybdenum	Mo	42	95.94
Argon	Ar	18	39.948	Neodymium	Nd	60	144.24
Arsenic	As	33	74.9216	Neon	Ne	10	20.1797
Astatine	At	85	(210)	Neptunium	Np	93	237.048
Barium	Ba	56	137.327	Nickel	Ni	28	58.693
Berkelium	Bk	97	(247)	Niobium	Nb	41	92.9064
Beryllium	Be	4	9.01218	Nitrogen	N	7	14.0067
Bismuth	Bi	83	208.980	Nobelium	No	102	(259)
Bohrium	Bh	107	(264)	Osmium	Os	76	190.23
Boron	B	5	10.811	Oxygen	O	8	15.9994
Bromine	Br	35	79.904	Palladium	Pd	46	106.42
Cadmium	Cd	48	112.411	Phosphorus	P	15	30.9738
Calcium	Ca	20	40.078	Platinum	Pt	78	195.08
Californium	Cf	98	(251)	Plutonium	Pu	94	(244)
Carbon	C	6	12.011	Polonium	Po	84	(209)
Cerium	Ce	58	140.115	Potassium	K	19	39.0983
Cesium	Cs	55	132.905	Praseodymium	Pr	59	140.908
Chlorine	Cl	17	35.4527	Promethium	Pm	61	(145)
Chromium	Cr	24	51.9961	Protactinium	Pa	91	231.036
Cobalt	Co	27	58.9332	Radium	Ra	88	226.025
Copernicium	Cn	112	(285)	Radon	Rn	86	(222)
Copper	Cu	29	63.546	Rhenium	Re	75	186.207
Curium	Cm	96	(247)	Rhodium	Rh	45	102.906
Darmstadtium	Ds	110	(271)	Roentgenium	Rg	111	(272)
Dubnium	Db	105	(262)	Rubidium	Rb	37	85.4678
Dysprosium	Dy	66	162.50	Ruthenium	Ru	44	101.07
Einsteinium	Es	99	(252)	Rutherfordium	Rf	104	(261)
Erbium	Er	68	167.26	Samarium	Sm	62	150.36
Europium	Eu	63	151.965	Scandium	Sc	21	44.9559
Fermium	Fm	100	(257)	Seaborgium	Sg	106	(266)
Fluorine	F	9	18.9984	Selenium	Se	34	78.96
Francium	Fr	87	(223)	Silicon	Si	14	28.0855
Gadolinium	Gd	64	157.25	Silver	Ag	47	107.868
Gallium	Ga	31	69.723	Sodium	Na	11	22.9898
Germanium	Ge	32	72.61	Strontium	Sr	38	87.62
Gold	Au	79	196.967	Sulfur	S	16	32.066
Hafnium	Hf	72	178.49	Tantalum	Ta	73	180.948
Hassium	Hs	108	(269)	Technetium	Tc	43	(98)
Helium	He	2	4.00260	Tellurium	Te	52	127.60
Holmium	Ho	67	164.930	Terbium	Tb	65	158.925
Hydrogen	H	1	1.00794	Thallium	Tl	81	204.383
Indium	In	49	114.818	Thorium	Th	90	232.038
Iodine	I	53	126.904	Thulium	Tm	69	168.934
Iridium	Ir	77	192.22	Tin	Sn	50	118.710
Iron	Fe	26	55.847	Titanium	Ti	22	47.88
Krypton	Kr	36	83.80	Tungsten	W	74	183.84
Lanthanum	La	57	138.906	Uranium	U	92	238.029
Lawrencium	Lr	103	(260)	Vanadium	V	23	50.9415
Lead	Pb	82	207.2	Xenon	Xe	54	131.29
Lithium	Li	3	6.941	Ytterbium	Yb	70	173.04
Lutetium	Lu	71	174.967	Yttrium	Y	39	88.9059
Magnesium	Mg	12	24.3050	Zinc	Zn	30	65.39
Manganese	Mn	25	54.9381	Zirconium	Zr	40	91.224

Fundamentals of General, Organic, and Biological
Chemistry

Seventh Edition

John McMurry
Cornell University

David S. Ballantine
Northern Illinois University

Carl A. Hoeger
University of California, San Diego

Virginia E. Peterson
University of Missouri, Columbia

PEARSON

Boston   Columbus   Indianapolis   New York   San Francisco   Upper Saddle River
Amsterdam   Cape Town   Dubai   London   Madrid   Milan   Munich   Paris   Montréal   Toronto
Delhi   Mexico City   São Paulo   Sydney   Hong Kong   Seoul   Singapore   Taipei   Tokyo

Library of Congress Cataloging-in-Publication Data

Fundamentals of general, organic, and biological chemistry/John McMurry...[et al.].—7th ed.
   p. cm.
  Includes bibliographical references and index.
   ISBN-13: 978-0-321-75083-9 (alk. paper)
   ISBN-10: 0-321-75083-7 (alk. paper)
  1. Chemistry.   I. McMurry, John.
   QD31.3.M355 2013
   540—dc23

                       2011044000

Editor in Chief: Adam Jaworski
Executive Editor: Jeanne Zalesky
Senior Marketing Manager: Jonathan Cottrell
Assistant Editor: Lisa R. Pierce
VP/Executive Director, Development: Carol Trueheart
Development Editor: Erica Pantages Frost
Media Producer: Ashley Eklund
Editorial Assistant: Lisa Tarabokjia
Marketing Assistant: Nicola Houston
Managing Editor, Chemistry and Geosciences: Gina M. Cheselka
Project Manager, Production: Wendy Perez
Full Service/Compositor: PreMediaGlobal
Full Service Project Manager: Jared Sterzer
Senior Technical Art Specialist: Connie Long
Illustrations: Precision Graphics
Design Manger: Derek Bacchus
Interior and Cover Design: Gary Hespenheide
Photo Manager: Maya Melenchuk
Photo Researcher: Eric Schrader
Text Permissions Manager: Beth Wollar
Text Permissions Researcher: Sheri Gilbert
Operations Specialist: Jeffrey Sargent
Cover Photo Credit: *Close-up of eye*: Don Hammond/Design Pics, Inc. / Alamy;
fireworks: Patrakov Fedor / Shutterstock

Credits and acknowledgments borrowed from other sources and reproduced, with permission, in this textbook appear on page C-1 and xxii.

1 2 3 4 5 6 7 8 9 10—CRK—15 14 13 12 11

ISBN-10: 0-321-75083-7; ISBN-13: 978-0-321-75083-9

About the Authors

John McMurry, educated at Harvard and Columbia, has taught approximately 17,000 students in general and organic chemistry over a 30-year period. A professor of chemistry at Cornell University since 1980, Dr. McMurry previously spent 13 years on the faculty at the University of California at Santa Cruz. He has received numerous awards, including the Alfred P. Sloan Fellowship (1969–71), the National Institute of Health Career Development Award (1975–80), the Alexander von Humboldt Senior Scientist Award (1986–87), and the Max Planck Research Award (1991).

David S. Ballantine received his B.S. in Chemistry in 1977 from the College of William and Mary in Williamsburg, VA, and his Ph.D. in Chemistry in 1983 from the University of Maryland at College Park. After several years as a researcher at the Naval Research Labs in Washington, DC, he joined the faculty in the Department of Chemistry and Biochemistry of Northern Illinois University, where he has been a professor since 1989. He was awarded the Excellence in Undergraduate Teaching Award in 1998 and has been departmental Director of Undergraduate Studies since 2008. In addition, he is the coordinator for the Introductory and General Chemistry programs and is responsible for supervision of the laboratory teaching assistants.

Carl A. Hoeger received his B.S. in Chemistry from San Diego State University and his Ph.D. in Organic Chemistry from the University of Wisconsin, Madison in 1983. After a postdoctoral stint at the University of California, Riverside, he joined the Peptide Biology Laboratory at the Salk Institute in 1985, where he ran the NIH Peptide Facility while doing basic research in the development of peptide agonists and antagonists. During this time he also taught general, organic, and biochemistry at San Diego City College, Palomar College, and Miramar College. He joined the teaching faculty at University of California, San Diego, in 1998. Dr. Hoeger has been teaching chemistry to undergraduates for over 20 years, where he continues to explore the use of technology in the classroom; his current project involves the use of videopodcasts as adjuncts to live lectures. In 2004, he won the Paul and Barbara Saltman Distinguished Teaching Award from UCSD. He is deeply involved with the General Chemistry program at UCSD and also shares partial responsibility for the training and guidance of teaching assistants in the Chemistry and Biochemistry departments.

Virginia E. Peterson received her B.S. in Chemistry in 1967 from the University of Washington in Seattle and her Ph.D. in Biochemistry in 1980 from the University of Maryland at College Park. Between her undergraduate and graduate years she worked in lipid, diabetes, and heart disease research at Stanford University. Following her Ph.D. she took a position in the Biochemistry Department at the University of Missouri in Columbia and is now Professor Emerita. When she retired in 2011 she had been the Director of Undergraduate Advising for the department for 8 years and had taught both senior capstone classes and biochemistry classes for nonscience majors. Although retired, Dr. Peterson continues to advise undergraduates and teach classes. Awards include both the college-level and the university-wide Excellence in Teaching Award and, in 2006, the University's Outstanding Advisor Award and the State of Missouri Outstanding University Advisor Award. Dr. Peterson believes in public service and in 2003 received the Silver Beaver Award for service from the Boy Scouts of America.

Brief Contents

Contents

Features

Preface

This textbook and its related digital resources provide students in the allied health sciences with a needed background in chemistry and biochemistry while offering a general context for chemical concepts to ensure that students in other disciplines gain an appreciation of the importance of chemistry in everyday life.

To teach chemistry all the way from "What is an atom?" to "How do we get energy from glucose?" is a challenge. Throughout our general chemistry and organic chemistry coverage, the focus is on concepts fundamental to the chemistry of living things and everyday life. In our biochemistry coverage we strive to meet the further challenge of providing a context for the application of those concepts in biological systems. Our goal is to provide enough detail for thorough understanding while avoiding so much detail that students are overwhelmed. Many practical and relevant examples are included to illustrate the concepts and enhance student learning.

The material covered is ample for a two-term introduction to general, organic, and biological chemistry. While the general and early organic chapters contain concepts that are fundamental to understanding the material in biochemistry, the later chapters can be covered individually and in an order that can be adjusted to meet the needs of the students and the duration of the course.

The writing style is clear and concise and punctuated with practical and familiar examples from students' personal experience. Art work, diagrams, and molecular models are used extensively to provide graphical illustration of concepts to enhance student understanding. Since the true test of knowledge is the ability to apply that knowledge appropriately, we include numerous worked examples that incorporate consistent problem-solving strategies.

Regardless of their career paths, all students will be citizens in an increasingly technological society. When they recognize the principles of chemistry at work not just in their careers but in their daily lives, they are prepared to make informed decisions on scientific issues based on a firm understanding of the underlying concepts.

New to This Edition

The major theme of this revision is *making connections*, which is accomplished in a variety of ways:

- **NEW and updated *Chemistry in Action* boxes** highlight and strengthen the connections between general, organic, and biological chemistry.
- **NEW *Mastering Reactions* boxes** discuss, in some depth, the "how" behind a number of organic reactions.
- **NEW in-chapter questions specifically related to *Chemistry in Action* applications and *Mastering Reactions*** reinforce the connection between the chapter content and practical applications.
- **NEW Concept Maps** added to certain chapters, draw connections between general, organic, and biological chemistry—in particular those chapters dealing with intermolecular forces, chemical reactions and energy, acid–base chemistry, and relationships between functional groups, proteins, and their properties.
- **NEW and updated Concept Links offer** visual reminders for students that indicate when new material builds on concepts from previous chapters. **Updated questions in the End of Chapter section build on Concept Links** and require students to recall information learned in previous chapters.
- **NEW and updated end-of-chapter (EOC) problems:** approximately 20–25% of the end-of-chapter problems have been revised to enhance clarity.
- **All Chapter Goals tied to EOC problem sets:** chapter summaries include a list of EOC problems that correspond to the chapter goals for a greater connection between problems and concepts.

- **Chapters 1 and 2** have been restructured to place a greater emphasis on building math skills.
- **Chapter 6 (Chemical Reactions)** has been reorganized into two chapters: Chapter 5 (Classification and Balancing of Chemical Reactions) and Chapter 6 (Chemical Reactions: Mole and Mass Relationships) to allow student to narrow their focus; Chapter 5 focuses on the qualitative aspect of reactions, while Chapter 6 focuses on calculations.

Organization

General Chemistry: Chapters 1–11 The introduction to elements, atoms, the periodic table, and the quantitative nature of chemistry (Chapters 1 and 2) is followed by chapters that individually highlight the nature of ionic and molecular compounds (Chapters 3 and 4. The next three chapters discuss chemical reactions and their stoichiometry, energies, rates, and equilibria (Chapters 5, 6, and 7). Topics relevant to the chemistry of life follow: Gases, Liquids, and Solids (Chapter 8); Solutions (Chapter 9); and Acids and Bases (Chapter 10). Nuclear Chemistry (Chapter 11) closes the general chemistry sequence.

Organic Chemistry: Chapters 12–17 These chapters concisely focus on what students must know in order to understand biochemistry. The introduction to hydrocarbons (Chapters 12 and 13) includes the basics of nomenclature, which is thereafter kept to a minimum. Discussion of functional groups with single bonds to oxygen, sulfur, or a halogen (Chapter 14) is followed by a short chapter on amines, which are so important to the chemistry of living things and drugs (Chapter 15). After introducing aldehydes and ketones (Chapter 16), the chemistry of carboxylic acids and their derivatives (including amides) is covered (Chapter 17), with a focus on similarities among the derivatives. More attention to the mechanisms by which organic reactions occur and the vernacular used to describe them has been incorporated into this edition.

Biological Chemistry: Chapters 18–29 Rather than proceed through the complexities of protein, carbohydrate, lipid, and nucleic acid structure before getting to the roles of these compounds in the body, structure and function are integrated in this text. Protein structure (Chapter 18) is followed by enzyme and coenzyme chemistry (Chapter 19). With enzymes introduced, the central pathways and themes of biochemical energy production can be described (Chapter 20). If the time you have available to cover biochemistry is limited, stop with Chapter 20 and your students will have an excellent preparation in the essentials of metabolism. The following chapters cover carbohydrate chemistry (Chapters 21 and 22), then lipid chemistry (Chapters 23 and 24). Next we discuss nucleic acids and protein synthesis (Chapter 25) and genomics (Chapter 26). The last three chapters cover protein and amino acid metabolism (Chapter 27), the function of hormones and neurotransmitters, and the action of drugs (Chapter 28), and provide an overview of the chemistry of body fluids (Chapter 29).

Chapter by Chapter Changes

COVERAGE OF GENERAL CHEMISTRY

The major revisions in this section involve reorganization or revision of content to strengthen the connections between concepts and to provide a more focused coverage of specific concepts. In order to reinforce the relationship between topics, Concept Maps have been included in several chapters to illustrate the connections between concepts.

Specific changes to chapters are provided below:

Chapter 1

- Chapters 1 and 2 from the sixth edition have been combined; a greater emphasis is placed on math skills. Goals were revised and updated to reflect the combined chapter.

- The concept of homogeneous and heterogeneous mixtures is introduced (previously in Chapter 9).
- There are several new references to the Application boxes (now titled *Chemistry in Action*), both in the text and in the problems. Four Application boxes were updated to provide more current connections to everyday life and the health fields.

Chapter 2

- Chapter 3 from the sixth edition has become Chapter 2 in the seventh edition: Atoms and the Periodic Table.
- Information on the periodic table has been updated (the 117th element has been discovered, no longer considered a metalloid; 112th element has been named).
- Application boxes (*Chemistry in Action*) have been modified to enhance clarity, relevance to the student, and connection to the text.

Chapter 3

- Chapter 3 in this edition was Chapter 4 in the sixth edition: Ionic Compounds.
- There is a new Application (*Chemistry in Action*) box titled "Ionic Liquids."
- Changes have been made to the boxes to enhance clarity, relevance to the student, and connection to the text.

Chapter 4

- Chapter 4 in this edition was Chapter 5 in the sixth edition: Molecular Compounds.
- Section 11 (Characteristics of Molecular Compounds) has been moved; it is now Section 5.

Chapter 5

- Chapter 5 in this edition, Classification and Balancing of Chemical Reactions, is a portion of Chapter 6 from the sixth edition (6e Sections 6.1–6.2 and 6.8–6.13).
- There are several new references to the Application (*Chemistry in Action*) boxes, both in the text and in the problems.

Chapter 6

- Chapter 6 in this edition, Chemical Reactions: Mole and Mass Relationships, is a portion of Chapter 6 from the sixth edition (6e Sections 6.3 – 6.7).
- There are several new references to the Applications boxes, both in the text and in the problems.
- A new concept map has been added, relating topics in Chapters 3 and 4 to topics in Chapters 5 and 6 and to topics in Chapters 7 and 10.

Chapter 7

- An explanation of bond energies has been added to show how the energy of chemical reactions is related to the covalent bonds in reactants and products.
- Bond and reaction energies in units of both kcal and kJ have been consistently included.
- A new concept map has been added at the end of chapter that shows how energy, rates, and equilibrium are related.
- There is a new *Chemistry in Action* application box titled "Coupled Reactions."

Chapter 8

- Section 8.11 (Intermolecular Forces) has been moved to Section 8.2 to help students make the connection between these forces and the physical states and properties of matter that are discussed in the subsequent sections.
- Chemistry in Action application boxes have been revised to strengthen the connection with chapter content.
- There is a new Concept Map relating molecular shape and polarity (Chapter 4) and the energy of chemical and physical changes (Chapter 7) to intermolecular forces and the physical states of matter.

Chapter 9

- Section 9.7 (Units of Concentration) has been reorganized to add mass/mass units and improve connections between units.
- A new Concept Map has been added to show the relationship between intermolecular forces (Chapter 8) and the formation of solutions and between concentration units of molarity and mole/mass relationships of reactions in solution.

Chapter 10

- Section 10.4 (Water as Both Acid and Base) and Section 10.6 (Dissociation of Water) have been combined to strengthen the connection between these concepts.
- Section 10.11 (Buffer Solutions) and Section 10.12 (Buffers in the Body) have been combined to strengthen the connection between these concepts and reduce redundancy of content in later chapters.
- Content in the *Chemistry in Action* application boxes has been combined and revised to strengthen connections between concepts and practical applications.
- New Concept Map has been added to show the relationships between strong/weak electrolytes (Chapter 9) and the extent of formation of H^+ and OH^- ions in acid/base solutions, and between equilibrium (Chapter 7) and strong/weak acids.

Chapter 11

- One *Chemistry in Action* application box was eliminated and others were revised to strengthen the connections between chapter content and practical applications.

COVERAGE OF ORGANIC CHEMISTRY

A major emphasis in this edition was placed on making the fundamental reactions that organic molecules undergo much clearer to the reader, with particular attention on those reactions encountered again in biochemical transformations. Also new to this edition is the expanded use and evaluation of line-angle structure for organic molecules, which are so important when discussing biomolecules. Most of the Application boxes (*Chemistry in Action*) have been updated to reflect current understanding and research. A number of instructors have asked for an increased discussion of the mechanisms of organic reactions; however, since many that teach this class did not want it to be integrated directly into the text we developed a completely new feature titled *Mastering Reactions*. This boxed feature discusses in relative depth the "how" behind a number of organic reactions. We have designed *Mastering Reactions* so that they may be integrated into an instructor's lecture or simply left out with no detriment to the material in the text itself.

Other specific changes to chapters are provided below:

Chapter 12

- There is a new feature box called *Mastering Reactions* that explains curved-arrow formalism used in organic mechanisms.
- There is a functional group scheme map that will aid in classifying functional groups.
- Table 1 has been substantially reworked to include line structures and sulfur compounds.

Chapter 13

- Sixth edition section 13.7 has been converted into a *Mastering Reactions* box (How Addition Reactions Occur). The content of *Mastering Reactions* box includes expanded discussion of Markovnikov's Rule.
- Chapter 13 now includes in-text references to *Chemistry in Action* boxes, including in-text problems related to them. There are also several cross-references to the *Mastering Reactions* boxes.

Chapter 14

- The language used to describe the classification of alcohols has been adjusted to make it clearer for the reader.
- A *Mastering Reactions* box (How Eliminations Occur) has been added. Discussion of Zaitsev's Rule and its mechanistic explanation are included.

Chapter 15

- A new *Chemistry in Action* box (Knowing What You Work With: Material Safety Data Sheets) has been added.

Chapter 16

- A *Mastering Reactions* box (Carbonyl Additions) has been added, with an emphasis on hemiacetal and acetal formation.
- The discussion of formation of cyclic hemiacetals and acetals has been adjusted to make it more clear to the reader.

Chapter 17

- The colors used in many of the illustrations were corrected and/or modified to allow students to easily follow which atoms come from which starting materials in the formation and degradation of the various carboxylic acid derivatives.

Chapter 18

- There are new references to the Chemistry in Action boxes, both in the text and in the problems.
- There is an expanded discussion of isoelectric points.
- There is a new Concept Map illustrating the organizing principles of protein structure, types of proteins, and amino acids.

Chapter 19

- There is an expanded discussion of minerals, including a new table.
- A clarification of the definition of uncompetitive inhibition (previously noncompetitive inhibition) has been added.

Chapter 20

- A new Concept Map relating biochemical energy to chemical energy concepts discussed in earlier chapters has been added.
- Energy calculations are in both kcalories and kjoules.
- The discussion of "uncouplers" has been integrated into the text.

Chapter 21

- A new *Chemistry in Action* box was added, combining and updating concepts from earlier applications discussing aspects of dietary carbohydrates.
- Many ribbon molecules were made clearer by floating the model on white rather than black backgrounds.
- A new worked example was added to clarify how to analyze a complex molecule for its component structures.

Chapter 22

- The text discussion was made more readable by reducing the jargon present in this chapter.
- The discussion of glucose metabolism in diabetes and metabolic syndrome was freshened.

Chapter 23

- The discussion of cholesterol and bile acids was moved from Chapter 28 to this chapter.
- Dietary and obesity statistics were updated.
- Text information about medical uses of liposomes was added.

Chapter 24

- Jargon was removed and concepts were clarified by a more thorough explanation of reactions.
- A clearer explanation of how triacylglycerides are digested, absorbed, and moved through the body to destination cells was added.
- The discussion of energy yields from fat metabolism was extended for clarity.

Chapter 25

- The retrovirus information has been updated to focus on retroviruses in general.
- The influenza information focuses on the nature of the common influenza viruses and new research directions.

Chapter 26

- This chapter, Genomics, was Chapter 27 in the sixth edition. It has been updated to reflect the current state of genome mapping.
- The *Chemistry In Action* box, DNA Fingerprinting, has been updated to include PCR fingerprinting.

Chapter 27

- This chapter, Protein and Amino Acid Metabolism, was Chapter 28 in the sixth edition.
- Changes have been made to enhance clarity, relevance to the student, and connection to the text.

Chapter 28

- The chapter is now focused only on the messenger aspect of these peptides, amino acid derivatives, and steroids.
- Discussions were made clearer by spelling-out terms instead of defining abbreviations.
- The steroid-abuse section was revamped to increase relevance and enhance clarity for the student.

Chapter 29

- Changes were made to enhance clarity, relevance to the student, and connection to the text.

KEY FEATURES

Focus on Learning

Worked Examples Most Worked Examples include an **Analysis** section that precedes the **Solution**. The Analysis lays out the approach to solving a problem of the given type. When appropriate, a **Ballpark Estimate** gives students an overview of the relationships needed to solve the problem and provides an intuitive approach to arrive at a rough estimate of the answer. The Solution presents the worked-out example using the strategy laid out in the Analysis and, in many cases, includes expanded discussion to enhance student understanding. When applicable, following the Solution there is a Ballpark Check that compares the calculated answer to the Ballpark Estimate and verifies that the answer makes chemical and physical sense.

Worked Example **1.11** Factor Labels: Unit Conversions

A child is 21.5 inches long at birth. How long is this in centimeters?

ANALYSIS This problem calls for converting from inches to centimeters, so we will need to know how many centimeters are in an inch and how to use this information as a conversion factor.

BALLPARK ESTIMATE It takes about 2.5 cm to make 1 in., and so it should take two and a half times as many centimeters to make a distance equal to approximately 20 in., or about 20 in. $\times$ 2.5 $=$ 50 cm.

SOLUTION

STEP 1: **Identify given information.** Length $=$ 21.5 in.

STEP 2: **Identify answer and units.** Length $=$?? cm

STEP 3: **Identify conversion factor.** 1 in. $=$ 2.54 cm $\rightarrow \dfrac{2.54 \text{ cm}}{1 \text{ in.}}$

STEP 4: **Solve.** Multiply the known length (in inches) by the conversion factor so that units cancel, providing the answer (in centimeters). $21.5 \text{ in.} \times \dfrac{2.54 \text{ cm}}{1 \text{ in.}} = 54.6 \text{ cm (Rounded off from 54.61)}$

BALLPARK CHECK How does this value compare with the ballpark estimate we made at the beginning? Are the final units correct? 54.6 cm is close to our original estimate of 50 cm.

Key Concept Problems are integrated throughout the chapters to focus attention on the use of essential concepts, as do the **Understanding Key Concepts problems** at the end of each chapter. Understanding Key Concepts problems are designed to test students' mastery of the core principles developed in the chapter. Students thus have an opportunity to ask "Did I get it?" before they proceed. Most of these Key Concept Problems use graphics or molecular-level art to illustrate the core principles and will be particularly useful to visual learners.

KEY CONCEPT PROBLEM 6.4

What is the molecular weight of cytosine, a component of DNA (deoxyribonucleic acid)? (black $=$ C, blue $=$ N, red $=$ O, white $=$ H.)

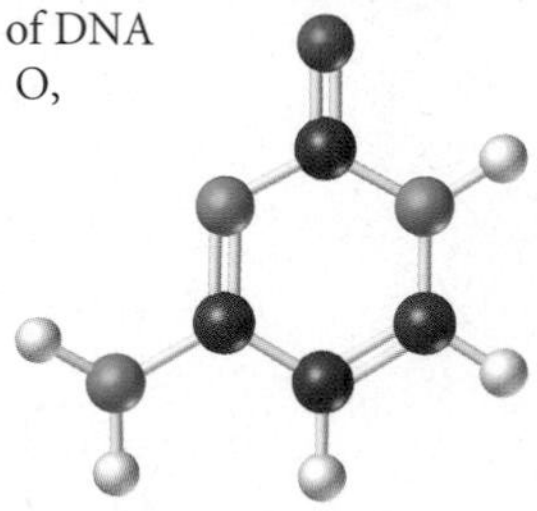

Cytosine

Problems The problems within the chapters, for which brief answers are given in an appendix, cover every skill and topic to be understood. One or more problems follow each Worked Example and others stand alone at the ends of sections.

PROBLEM 1.18
Write appropriate conversion factors and carry out the following conversions:
(a) 16.0 oz = ? g   (b) 2500 mL = ? L   (c) 99.0 L = ? qt

PROBLEM 1.19
Convert 0.840 qt to milliliters in a single calculation using more than one conversion factor.

More Color-Keyed, Labeled Equations It is entirely too easy to skip looking at a chemical equation while reading the text. We have used color extensively to call attention to the aspects of chemical equations and structures under discussion, a continuing feature of this book that has been judged to be very helpful.

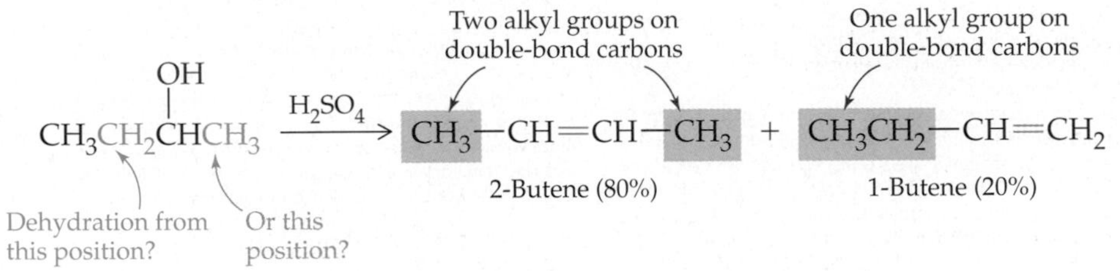

$$CH_3CH_2CHCH_3 \xrightarrow{H_2SO_4} CH_3{-}CH{=}CH{-}CH_3 \ + \ CH_3CH_2{-}CH{=}CH_2$$

OH (on second carbon)

Two alkyl groups on double-bond carbons

One alkyl group on double-bond carbons

2-Butene (80%)   1-Butene (20%)

Dehydration from this position?   Or this position?

Key Words Every key term is boldfaced on its first use, fully defined in the margin adjacent to that use, and listed at the end of the chapter. These are the terms students must understand to continue with the subject at hand. Definitions of all Key Words are collected in the Glossary.

Focus on Relevancy

Chemistry is often considered to be a difficult and tedious subject. But when students make a connection between a concept in class and an application in their daily lives, the chemistry comes alive, and they get excited about the subject. The applications in this book strive to capture student interest and emphasize the relevance of the scientific concepts. The use of relevant applications makes the concepts more accessible and increases understanding.

Applications—now titled *Chemistry in Action*—are both integrated into the discussions in the text and set off from the text. Each boxed application provides sufficient information for reasonable understanding and, in many cases, extends the concepts discussed in the text in new ways. The boxes end with a cross-reference to end-of-chapter problems that can be assigned by the instructor.

CHEMISTRY IN ACTION

Anemia – A Limiting Reagent Problem?

Anemia is the most commonly diagnosed blood disorder, with symptoms typically including lethargy, fatigue, poor concentration, and sensitivity to cold. Although anemia has many causes, including genetic factors, the most common cause is insufficient dietary intake or absorption of iron.

Hemoglobin (abbreviated Hb), the iron-containing protein found in red blood cells, is responsible for oxygen transport throughout the body. Low iron levels in the body result in decreased production and incorporation of Hb into red blood cells. In addition, blood loss due to injury or to menstruation in women increases the body's demand for iron in order to replace lost Hb. In the United States, nearly 20% of women of child-bearing age suffer from iron-deficiency anemia compared to only 2% of adult men.

The recommended minimum daily iron intake is 8 mg for adult men and 18 mg for premenopausal women. One way to ensure sufficient iron intake is a well-balanced diet that includes iron-fortified grains and cereals, red meat, egg yolks, leafy green vegetables, tomatoes, and raisins. Vegetarians should pay extra attention to their diet, because the iron in fruits and vegetables is not as readily absorbed by the body as the iron

▲ Can cooking in cast iron pots decrease anemia?

in meat, poultry, and fish. Vitamin supplements containing folic acid and either ferrous sulfate or ferrous gluconate can decrease iron deficiencies, and vitamin C increases the absorption of iron by the body.

However, the simplest way to increase dietary iron may be to use cast iron cookware. Studies have demonstrated that the iron content of many foods increases when cooked in an iron pot. Other studies involving Ethiopian children showed that those who ate food cooked in iron cookware were less likely to suffer from iron-deficiency anemia than their playmates who ate similar foods prepared in aluminum cookware.

See Chemistry in Action Problems 6.59 and 6.60 at the end of the chapter.

NEW Feature box in this edition—*Mastering Reactions* include How Addition Reactions Occur, How Elimination Reactions Occur, and Carbonyl Additions and discuss how these important organic transformations are believed to occur. This new feature allows instructors to easily introduce discussions of mechanism into their coverage of organic chemistry.

MASTERING REACTIONS

Organic Chemistry and the Curved Arrow Formalism

Starting with this chapter and continuing on through the remainder of this text, you will be exploring the world of organic chemistry and its close relative, biochemistry. Both of these areas of chemistry are much more "visual" than those you have been studying; organic chemists, for example, look at how and why reactions occur by examining the flow of electrons. For example, consider the following reaction of 2-iodopropane with sodium cyanide:

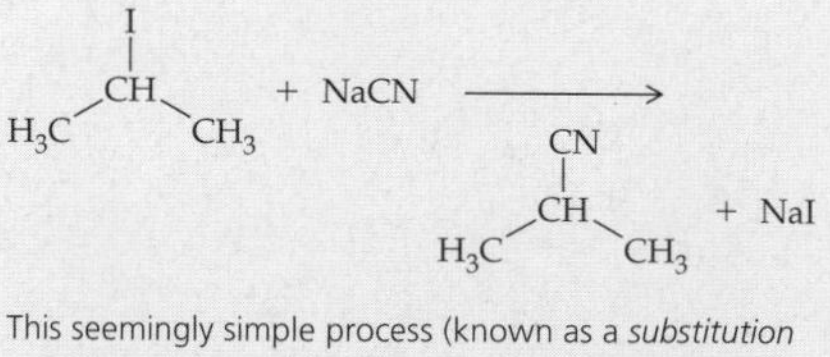

This seemingly simple process (known as a *substitution reaction*, discussed in Chapter 13) is not adequately described by the equation. To help to understand what may really be going on, organic chemists use what is loosely described as "electron pushing" and have adopted what is known as *curved arrow formalism* to represent it. The movement of electrons is depicted using curved arrows, where the number of electrons corresponds to the head of the arrow. Single-headed arrows represent movement of one electron, while a double-headed arrow indicates

The convention is to show the movement *from* an area of high electron density (the start of the arrow) *to* one of lower electron density (the head of the arrow). Using curved arrow formalism, we can examine the reaction of 2-iodopropane with sodium cyanide in more detail. There are two distinct paths by which this reaction can occur:

Path 1

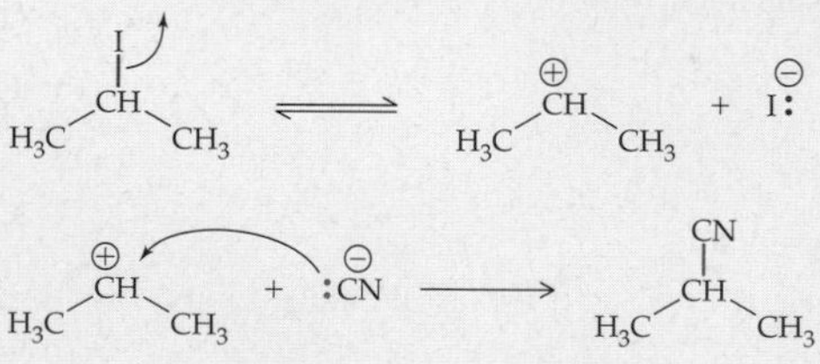

Path 2

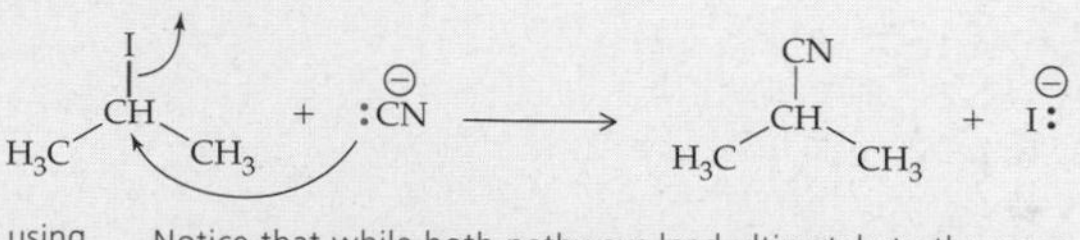

Notice that while both pathways lead ultimately to the same product, the curved arrow formalism shows us that they have significantly different ways of occurring. Although it is not important right now to understand which of the two paths

Focus on Making Connections

This can be a difficult course to teach. Much of what students are interested in lies in the last part of the course, but the material they need to understand the biochemistry is found in the first two-thirds. It is easy to lose sight of the connections among general, organic, and biological chemistry, so we use a feature—**Concepts to Review**—to call attention to these connections. From Chapter 4 on, the Concepts to Review section at the beginning of the chapter lists topics covered in earlier chapters that form the basis for what is discussed in the current chapter.

We have also retained the successful Concept Link icons and Looking Ahead notes.

Concept Link icons ▶▶▶ are used extensively to indicate places where previously covered material is relevant to the discussion at hand. These links provide cross-references and also serve to highlight important chemical themes as they are revisited.

LOOKING AHEAD ▶▶▶ notes call attention to connections between just-covered material and discussions in forthcoming chapters. These notes are designed to illustrate to the students why what they are learning will be useful in what lies ahead.

NEW Concept Maps are used to illustrate and reinforce the connections between concepts discussed in each chapter and concepts in previous or later chapters.

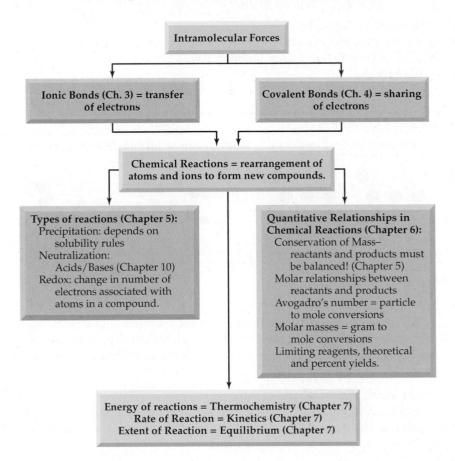

Focus on Studying

End of Chapter Section

Summary: Revisiting the Chapter Goals

The Chapter Summary revisits the Chapter Goals that open the chapter. Each of the questions posed at the start of the chapter is answered by a summary of the essential information needed to attain the corresponding goal.

SUMMARY: REVISITING THE CHAPTER GOALS

1. What are the basic properties of organic compounds? Compounds made up primarily of carbon atoms are classified as organic. Many organic compounds contain carbon atoms that are joined in long chains by a combination of single (C—C), double (C=C), or triple (C≡C) bonds. In this chapter, we focused primarily on *alkanes*, hydrocarbon compounds that contain only single bonds between all C atoms (*see Problems 29, 31, 32*).

is represented by lines and the locations of C and H atoms are understood (*see Problems 22–24, 44, 45, 48, 49–51*).

5. What are alkanes and cycloalkanes, and how are they named? Compounds that contain only carbon and hydrogen are called *hydrocarbons*, and hydrocarbons that have only single bonds are called *alkanes*. A *straight-chain alkane* has all its carbons connected in a row, a *branched-chain alkane* has a

Key Words

All of the chapter's boldface terms are listed in alphabetical order and are cross-referenced to the page where it appears in the text.

Understanding Key Concepts

The problems at the end of each chapter allow students to test their mastery of the core principles developed in the chapter. Students have an opportunity to ask "Did I get it?" before they proceed.

UNDERSTANDING KEY CONCEPTS

12.22 How many hydrogen atoms are needed to complete the hydrocarbon formulas for the following carbon backbones?

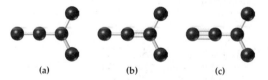

(a) (b) (c)

12.23 Convert the following models into condensed structures (black = C; white = H; red = O):

12.25 Convert the following models into line drawings and identify the functional groups in each:

(a) (b)

12.26 Give systematic names for the following alkanes:

Chemistry in Action and Mastering Reactions Problems

Each boxed application and feature throughout the text ends with a cross-reference to end-of-chapter problems. These problems help students test their understanding of the material and, more importantly, help students see the connection between chemistry and the world around them.

General Questions and Problems

These problems are cumulative, pulling together topics from various parts of the chapter and previous chapters. These help students synthesize the material just learned while helping them review topics from previous chapters.

Acknowledgments

Although this text is now in its seventh edition, each revision has aspired to improve the quality and accuracy of the content and emphasize its relevance to the student users. Achieving this goal requires the coordinated efforts of a dedicated team of editors and media experts. Without them, this textbook would not be possible.

On behalf of all my coauthors, I would like to thank Adam Jaworski (Editor in Chief) and Jeanne Zalesky (Executive Editor) for building an excellent team for this project. Thanks also to Jared Sterzer (Production Manager), Wendy Perez (Project Manager), Eric Schrader (Photo Researcher), Lisa Tarabokjia (Editorial Assistant), and Connie Long (Art Specialist) for their attention to detail as we moved forward. Erica Frost, our developmental editor, deserves special recognition for providing invaluable feedback—her painstaking perusal of each chapter and her eye for details have contributed greatly to the accessibility and relevance of the text. Very special thanks also to Lisa Pierce, Assistant Editor, who patiently guided the process and worked closely with us—thank you for your flexibility and dedication to the success of this project.

The value of this text has also been enhanced by the many individuals who have worked to improve the ancillary materials. Particular thanks to Susan McMurry for her efforts to ensure the accuracy of the answers to problems provided in the text and her revisions of the solutions manuals. Thanks to Ashley Eklund, Miriam Adrianowicz, and Lauren Layn for their work on the media supplements. Thanks also to Margaret Trombley, Kristin Mayo, and Damon Botsakos for their efforts to expand and improve Mastering Chemistry.

Finally, thank you to the many instructors and students who have used the sixth edition and have provided valuable insights and feedback to improve the accuracy of the current edition. We gratefully acknowledge the following reviewers for their contributions to the seventh edition.

Accuracy Reviewers of the Seventh Edition

Sheikh Ahmed, *West Virginia University*
Danae R. Quirk Dorr, *Minnesota State University, Mankato*
Karen Ericson, *Indiana University-Purdue University, Fort Wayne*
Barbara Mowery, *York College of Pennsylvania*
Susan Thomas, *University of Texas, San Antonio*
Richard Triplett, *Des Moines Area Community College*

Reviewers of the Seventh Edition

Francis Burns, *Ferris State University*
Lisa L. Crozier, *Northeast Wisconsin Technical Center*
Robert P. Dixon, *Southern Illinois University, Edwardsville*
Luther Giddings, *Salt Lake Community College*
Arlene Haffa, *University of Wisconsin, Oshkosh*
L. Jaye Hopkins, *Spokane Community College*
Mohammad Mahroof, *Saint Cloud State University*
Gregory Marks, *Carroll University*
Van Quach, *Florida State University*
Douglas Raynie, *South Dakota State University*

Reviewers of the Previous Editions

Sheikh Ahmed, *West Virginia University*
Stanley Bajue, *CUNY-Medgar Evers College*
Daniel Bender, *Sacramento City College*
Dianne A. Bennett, *Sacramento City College*
Alfredo Castro, *Felician College*
Gezahegn Chaka, *Louisiana State University, Alexandria*
Michael Columbia, *Indiana University-Purdue University, Fort Wayne*
Rajeev B. Dabke, *Columbus State University*
Danae R. Quirk Dorr, *Minnesota State University, Mankato*

Pamela S. Doyle, *Essex County College*
Marie E. Dunstan, *York College of Pennsylvania*
Karen L. Ericson, *Indiana University-Purdue University, Fort Wayne*
Charles P. Gibson, *University of Wisconsin, Oshkosh*
Clifford Gottlieb, *Shasta College*
Mildred V. Hall, *Clark State Community College*
Meg Hausman, *University of Southern Maine*
Ronald Hirko, *South Dakota State University*
L. Jaye Hopkins, *Spokane Community College*
Margaret Isbell, *Sacramento City College*
James T. Johnson, *Sinclair Community College*
Margaret G. Kimble, *Indiana University-Purdue University Fort Wayne*
Grace Lasker, *Lake Washington Technical College*
Ashley Mahoney, *Bethel University*
Matthew G. Marmorino, *Indiana University, South Bend*
Diann Marten, *South Central College, Mankato*
Barbara D. Mowery, *York College of Pennsylvania*
Tracey Arnold Murray, *Capital University*
Andrew M. Napper, *Shawnee State University*
Lisa Nichols, *Butte Community College*
Glenn S. Nomura, *Georgia Perimeter College*
Douglas E. Raynie, *South Dakota State University*
Paul D. Root, *Henry Ford Community College*
Victor V. Ryzhov, *Northern Illinois University*
Karen Sanchez, *Florida Community College, Jacksonville-South*
Mir Shamsuddin, *Loyola University, Chicago*
Jeanne A. Stuckey, *University of Michigan*
John Sullivan, *Highland Community College*
Deborah E. Swain, *North Carolina Central University*
Susan T. Thomas, *University of Texas, San Antonio*
Yakov Woldman, *Valdosta State University*

The authors are committed to maintaining the highest quality and accuracy and look forward to comments from students and instructors regarding any aspect of this text and supporting materials. Questions or comments should be directed to the lead co-author.

David S. Ballantine
dballant@niu.edu

Resources in Print and Online

Name of Supplement	Available in Print	Available Online	Instructor or Student Supplement	Description
MasteringChemistry® (www.masteringchemistry.com)		✓	Supplement for Instructors and Students	MasteringChemistry from Pearson has been designed and refined with a single purpose in mind: to help educators create those moments of understanding with their students. The Mastering platform delivers engaging, dynamic learning opportunities—focused on your course objectives and responsive to each student's progress—that are proven to help students absorb course material and understand difficult concepts. By complementing your teaching with our engaging technology and content, you can be confident your students will arrive at those moments—moments of true understanding. The seventh edition will feature 20 new general, organic, and biological (GOB) specific tutorials, totaling over 100 GOB tutorials.
Instructor Resource Manual (isbn: 0321765427)	✓	✓	Supplement for Instructors	The manual features lecture outlines with presentation suggestions, teaching tips, suggested in-class demonstrations, and topics for classroom discussion.
Test Item File (isbn: 0321765435)	✓	✓	Supplement for Instructors	This has been updated to reflect the revisions in this text and contains questions in a bank of more than 2,000 multiple-choice questions.
Instructor Resource Center on DVD (isbn: 0321776119)		✓	Supplement for Instructors	This DVD provides an integrated collection of resources designed to help you make efficient and effective use of your time. The DVD features art from the text, including figures and tables in PDF format for high-resolution printing, as well as pre-built PowerPoint™ presentations. The first presentation contains the images, figures, and tables embedded within the PowerPoint slides, while the second includes a complete, modifiable, lecture outline. The final two presentations contain worked in-chapter sample exercises and questions to be used with Classroom Response Systems. This DVD also contains animations, as well as the TestGen version of the Test Item File, which allows you to create and tailor exams to your needs.
Study Guide and Full Solutions Manual (isbn: 032177616X) Study Guide and Selected Solutions Manual (isbn: 0321776100)	✓		Supplement for Students	**Study Guide and Full Solutions Manual** and **Study Guide and Selected Solutions Manual**, both by Susan McMurry. The selected version provides solutions only to those problems that have a short answer in the text's Selected Answer Appendix. Both versions explain in detail how the answers to the in-text and end-of-chapter problems are obtained. They also contain chapter summaries, study hints, and self-tests for each chapter.
Chemistry and Life in the Laboratory: Experiments, 6e (isbn: 0321751604)	✓		Supplement for Laboratory	***Chemistry and Life in the Laboratory*, sixth edition**, by Victor L. Heasley, Val J. Christensen ,Gene E. Heasley. Written specifically to accompany any fundamentals of general, organic and biological chemistry text, this manual contains 34 comprehensive and accessible experiments specifically for GOB students.
Catalyst: The Pearson Custom Laboratory Program for Chemistry		✓	Supplement for Laboratory	This program allows you to custom-build a chemistry lab manual that matches your content needs and course organization. You can either write your own labs using the Lab Authoring Kit tool or you can select from the hundreds of labs available at http://www.pearsonlearningsolutions.com/custom-library/catalyst. This program also allows you to add your own course notes, syllabi, or other materials.

Personalized Coaching and Feedback At Your Fingertips

MasteringChemistry®

MasteringChemistry™ has been designed and refined with a single purpose in mind: to help educators create that moment of understanding with their students. The Mastering platform delivers engaging, dynamic learning opportunities—focused on your course objectives and responsive to each student's progress—that are proven to help students absorb course material and understand difficult concepts.

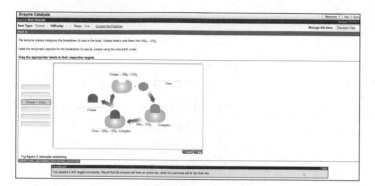

NEW! Chemistry Tutorials

MasteringChemistry® self-paced tutorials are designed to coach students with hints and feedback specific to their individual misconceptions. For the Seventh Edition, new tutorials have been created to guide students through the most challenging General, Organic, and Biological Chemistry topics and help them make connections between different concepts.

Unmatched Gradebook Capability

MasteringChemistry is the only system to capture the step-by-step work of each student in your class, including wrong answers submitted, hints requested, and time taken on every step. This data powers an unprecedented gradebook.

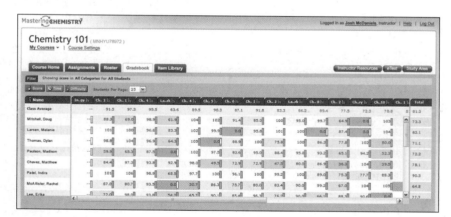

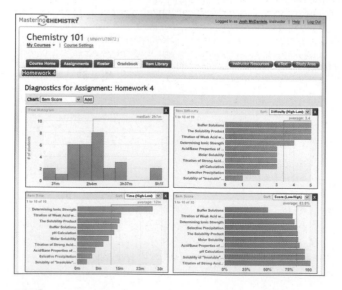

Gradebook Diagnostics

Instructors can identify at a glance students who are having difficulty with the color-coded gradebook. With a single click, charts summarize the most difficult problems in each assignment, vulnerable students, grade distribution, and even score improvement over the course.

Extend Learning Beyond The Classroom

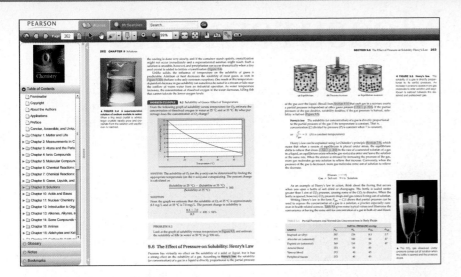

Pearson eText

Pearson eText gives students access to the text whenever and wherever they can access the Internet. The eText pages look exactly like the printed text and include powerful interactive and customization functions.

- Students can create notes, highlight text in different colors, create bookmarks, zoom, click hyperlinked words and phrases to view definitions, and view in single-page or two-page view.
- Students can link directly to associated media files, enabling them to view an animation as they read the text.
- It is possible to perform a full-text search and have the ability to save and export notes.

Instructors can share their notes and highlights with students and can also hide chapters that they do not want their students to read.

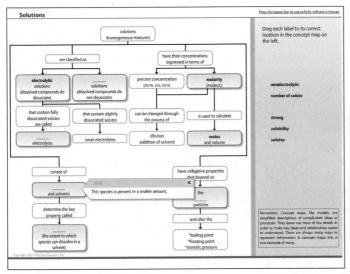

NEW! Concept Map problems

These interactive maps help students synthesize material they learned in previous chapters and demonstrate their understanding of interrelatedness of concepts in general, organic, and biological chemistry.

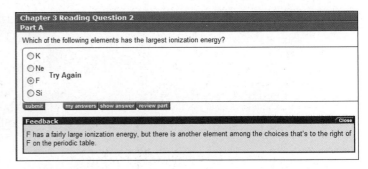

Reading Quizzes

Chapter-specific quizzes and activities focus on important, hard-to-grasp chemistry concepts.

Matter and Measurements

CONTENTS

◄ Increasing our knowledge of the chemical and physical properties of matter depends on our ability to make measurements that are precise and accurate.

CHAPTER GOALS

1. **What is matter and how is it classified?**
   THE GOAL: Be able to discuss the properties of matter, describe the three states of matter, distinguish between mixtures and pure substances, and distinguish between elements and compounds.

2. **How are chemical elements represented?**
   THE GOAL: Be able to name and give the symbols of common elements.

3. **What kinds of properties does matter have?**
   THE GOAL: Be able to distinguish between chemical and physical properties.

4. **What units are used to measure properties, and how can a quantity be converted from one unit to another?**
   THE GOAL: Be able to name and use the metric and SI units of measurement for mass, length, volume, and temperature and be able to convert quantities from one unit to another using conversion factors.

5. **How good are the reported measurements?**
   THE GOAL: Be able to interpret the number of significant figures in a measurement and round off numbers in calculations involving measurements.

6. **How are large and small numbers best represented?**
   THE GOAL: Be able to interpret prefixes for units of measurement and express numbers in scientific notation.

7. **What techniques are used to solve problems?**
   THE GOAL: Be able to analyze a problem, use the factor-label method to solve the problem, and check the result to ensure that it makes sense chemically and physically.

8. **What are temperature, specific heat, density, and specific gravity?**
   THE GOAL: Be able to define these quantities and use them in calculations.

Earth, air, fire, water—the ancient philosophers believed that all matter was composed of these four fundamental substances. We now know that matter is much more complex, made up of nearly 100 naturally occurring fundamental substances, or elements, in millions of unique combinations. Everything you see, touch, taste, and smell is made of chemicals formed from these elements. Many chemicals occur naturally, but others are synthetic, including the plastics, fibers, and medicines that are so critical to modern life. Just as everything you see is made of chemicals, many of the natural changes you see taking place around you are the result of *chemical reactions*—the change of one chemical into another. The crackling fire of a log burning in the fireplace, the color change of a leaf in the fall, and the changes that a human body undergoes as it grows and ages are all results of chemical reactions. To understand these and other natural processes, you must have a basic understanding of chemistry.

As you might expect, the chemistry of living organisms is complex, and it is not possible to understand all concepts without a proper foundation. Thus, the general plan of this book is to gradually increase in complexity, beginning in the first 11 chapters with a grounding in the scientific fundamentals that govern all of chemistry. In the following six chapters, we look at the nature of the carbon-containing substances, or *organic chemicals*, that compose all living things. In the final 12 chapters, we apply what we have learned in the first part of the book to the study of biological chemistry.

We begin in Chapter 1 with an examination of the states and properties of matter and an introduction to the systems of measurement that are essential to our understanding of matter and its behavior.

1.1 Chemistry: The Central Science

Chemistry is often referred to as "the central science" because it is crucial to nearly all other sciences. In fact, as more and more is learned, the historical dividing lines between chemistry, biology, and physics are fading, and current research is more interdisciplinary. Figure 1.1 diagrams the relationship of chemistry and biological chemistry to other fields of scientific study. Whatever the discipline in which you are most interested, the study of chemistry builds the necessary foundation.

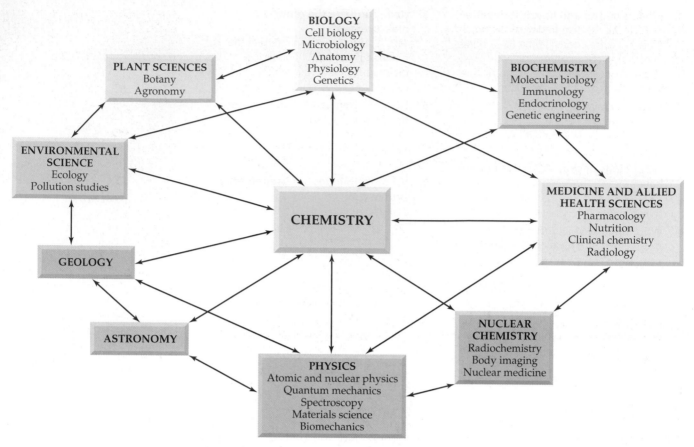

▲ **Figure 1.1**
Some relationships between chemistry—the central science—and other scientific and health-related disciplines.

Chemistry The study of the nature, properties, and transformations of matter.

Matter The physical material that makes up the universe; anything that has mass and occupies space.

Scientific Method The systematic process of observation, hypothesis, and experimentation used to expand and refine a body of knowledge.

Property A characteristic useful for identifying a substance or object.

Physical change A change that does not affect the chemical makeup of a substance or object.

Chemical change A change in the chemical makeup of a substance.

Chemistry is the study of matter—its nature, properties, and transformations. **Matter**, in turn, is a catchall word used to describe anything physically real—anything you can see, touch, taste, or smell. In more scientific terms, matter is anything that has mass and volume. As with our knowledge of all the other sciences, our knowledge of chemistry has developed by application of a process called the **scientific method** (see Chemistry in Action on p. 8). Starting with observations and measurements of the physical world, we form hypotheses to explain what we have observed. These hypotheses can then be tested by more observations and measurements, or experiments, to improve our understanding.

How might we describe different kinds of matter more specifically? Any characteristic that can be used to describe or identify something is called a **property**; size, color, and temperature are all familiar examples. Less familiar properties include *chemical composition*, which describes what matter is made of, and *chemical reactivity*, which describes how matter behaves. Rather than focus on the properties themselves, however, it is often more useful to think about *changes* in properties. Changes are of two types: *physical* and *chemical*. A **physical change** is one that does not alter the chemical makeup of a substance, whereas a **chemical change** is one that *does* alter a substance's chemical makeup. The melting of solid ice to give liquid water, for instance, is a physical change because the water changes only in form but not in chemical makeup. The rusting of an iron bicycle left in the rain, however, is a chemical change because iron combines with oxygen and moisture from the air to give a new substance, rust.

Table 1.1 lists some chemical and physical properties of several familiar substances—water, table sugar (sucrose), and baking soda (sodium bicarbonate). Note in Table 1.1 that the changes occurring when sugar and baking soda are heated are chemical changes, because new substances are produced.

TABLE 1.1 Some Properties of Water, Sugar, and Baking Soda

Water	Sugar (Sucrose)	Baking Soda (Sodium Bicarbonate)
Physical properties		
Colorless liquid	White crystals	White powder
Odorless	Odorless	Odorless
Melting point: 0 °C	Begins to decompose at 160 °C, turning black and giving off water.	Decomposes at 270 °C, giving off water and carbon dioxide.
Boiling point: 100 °C	—	—
Chemical properties		
Composition:*	Composition:*	Composition:*
11.2% hydrogen	6.4% hydrogen	27.4% sodium
88.8% oxygen	42.1% carbon	1.2% hydrogen
	51.5% oxygen	14.3% carbon
		57.1% oxygen
Does not burn.	Burns in air.	Does not burn.

Compositions are given by mass percent.

▲ **Burning of potassium in water is an example of a chemical change.**

PROBLEM 1.1

Identify each of the following as a physical change or a chemical change:

(a) Grinding of a metal   **(b)** Fruit ripening

(c) Wood burning   **(d)** A rain puddle evaporating

1.2 States of Matter

Matter exists in three forms: solid, liquid, and gas. A **solid** has a definite volume and a definite shape that does not change regardless of the container in which it is placed; for example, a wooden block, marbles, or a cube of ice. A **liquid**, by contrast, has a definite volume but an indefinite shape. The volume of a liquid, such as water, does not change when it is poured into a different container, but its shape does. A **gas** is different still, having neither a definite volume nor a definite shape. A gas expands to fill the volume and take the shape of any container it is placed in, such as the helium in a balloon or steam formed by boiling water (Figure 1.2).

Solid A substance that has a definite shape and volume.

Liquid A substance that has a definite volume but assumes the shape of its container.

Gas A substance that has neither a definite volume nor a definite shape.

◀ **Figure 1.2**
The three states of matter—solid, liquid, and gas.

(a) Ice: A solid has a definite volume and a definite shape independent of its container.

(b) Water: A liquid has a definite volume but a variable shape that depends on its container.

(c) Steam: A gas has both variable volume and shape that depend on its container.

State of matter The physical state of a substance as a solid, liquid, or gas.

Change of state The conversion of a substance from one state to another—for example, from liquid to gas.

Many substances, such as water, can exist in all three phases, or **states of matter**—the solid state, the liquid state, and the gaseous state—depending on the temperature. The conversion of a substance from one state to another is known as a **change of state**. The melting of a solid, the freezing or boiling of a liquid, and the condensing of a gas to a liquid are familiar to everyone.

Worked Example 1.1 Identifying States of Matter

▶▶▶ The symbol °C means degrees Celsius and will be discussed in Section 1.13.

Formaldehyde is a disinfectant, a preservative, and a raw material for the manufacturing of plastics. Its melting point is $-92\ °C$ and its boiling point is $-19.5\ °C$. Is formaldehyde a gas, a liquid, or a solid at room temperature ($25\ °C$)?

ANALYSIS The state of matter of any substance depends on its temperature. How do the melting point and boiling point of formaldehyde compare with room temperature?

SOLUTION
Room temperature ($25\ °C$) is above the boiling point of formaldehyde ($-19.5\ °C$), and so the formaldehyde is a gas.

PROBLEM 1.2
Acetic acid, which gives the sour taste to vinegar, has a melting point of $16.7\ °C$ and a boiling point of $118\ °C$. Predict the physical state of acetic acid when the ambient temperature is $10\ °C$.

1.3 Classification of Matter

The first question a chemist asks about an unknown substance is whether it is a pure substance or a mixture. Every sample of matter is one or the other. Water and sugar alone are pure substances, but stirring some sugar into a glass of water creates a *mixture*.

Pure substance A substance that has a uniform chemical composition throughout.

Mixture A blend of two or more substances, each of which retains its chemical identity.

Homogeneous mixture A uniform mixture that has the same composition throughout.

Heterogeneous mixture A non-uniform mixture that has regions of different composition.

▶▶▶ We'll revisit the properties of mixtures in Section 9.1 when we discuss solutions.

What is the difference between a pure substance and a mixture? One difference is that a **pure substance** is uniform in its chemical composition and its properties all the way down to the microscopic level. Every sample of water, sugar, or baking soda, regardless of source, has the composition and properties listed in Table 1.1. A **mixture**, however, can vary in both composition and properties, depending on how it is made. A **homogeneous mixture** is a blend of two or more pure substances having a uniform composition at the microscopic level. Sugar dissolved in water is one example. You cannot always distinguish between a pure substance and a homogeneous mixture just by looking. The sugar–water mixture *looks* just like pure water but differs on a molecular level. The amount of sugar dissolved in a glass of water will determine the sweetness, boiling point, and other properties of the mixture. A **heterogeneous mixture**, by contrast, is a blend of two or more pure substances having non-uniform composition, such as a vegetable stew in which each spoonful is different. It is relatively easy to distinguish heterogeneous mixtures from pure substances.

Another difference between a pure substance and a mixture is that the components of a mixture can be separated without changing their chemical identities. Water can be separated from a sugar–water mixture, for example, by boiling the mixture to drive off the steam and then condensing the steam to recover the pure water. Pure sugar is left behind in the container.

Element A fundamental substance that cannot be broken down chemically into any simpler substance.

▶▶▶ Elements are explored in the next section of this chapter (Section 1.4).

Pure substances are themselves classified into two groups: those that can undergo a chemical breakdown to yield simpler substances and those that cannot. A pure substance that cannot be broken down chemically into simpler substances is called an **element**. Examples include hydrogen, oxygen, aluminum, gold, and sulfur. At the time this book was printed, 118 elements had been identified, although only 91 of these occur naturally. All the millions of other substances in the universe are derived from them.

Any pure material that *can* be broken down into simpler substances by a chemical change is called a **chemical compound**. The term *compound* implies "more than one" (think "compound fracture"). A chemical compound, therefore, is formed by combining two or more elements to make a new substance. Water, for example, can be chemically changed by passing an electric current through it to produce hydrogen and oxygen. In writing this chemical change, the initial substance, or **reactant** (water), is written on the left; the new substances, or **products** (hydrogen and oxygen), are written on the right; and an arrow connects the two parts to indicate a chemical change, or **chemical reaction**. The conditions necessary to bring about the reaction are written above and below the arrow.

Chemical compound A pure substance that can be broken down into simpler substances by chemical reactions.

Reactant A starting substance that undergoes change during a chemical reaction.

Product A substance formed as the result of a chemical reaction.

Chemical reaction A process in which the identity and composition of one or more substances are changed.

▶▶▶ We will discuss how chemical reactions are represented in more detail in Section 1.6, and how reactions are classified in Chapter 5.

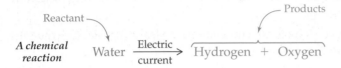

The classification of matter into mixtures, pure compounds, and elements is summarized in Figure 1.3.

Figure 1.3
◄ A scheme for the classification of matter.

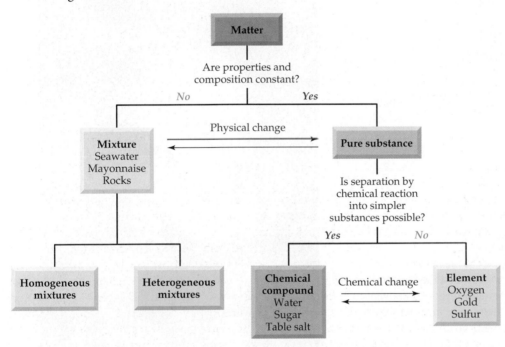

Worked Example 1.2 Classifying Matter

Classify each of the following as a mixture or a pure substance. If a mixture, classify it as heterogeneous or homogeneous. If a pure substance, identify it as an element or a compound.

(a) Vanilla ice cream   **(b)** Sugar

ANALYSIS Refer to the definitions of pure substances and mixtures. Is the substance composed of more than one kind of matter? Is the composition uniform?

SOLUTION

(a) Vanilla ice cream is composed of more than one substance—cream, sugar, and vanilla flavoring. The composition appears to be uniform throughout, so this is a homogeneous mixture.

(b) Sugar is composed of only one kind of matter—pure sugar. This is a pure substance. It can be converted to some other substance by a chemical change (see Table 1.1), so it is not an element. It must be a compound.

PROBLEM 1.3

Classify each of the following as a mixture or a pure substance. If a mixture, classify it as heterogeneous or homogeneous. If a pure substance, identify it as an element or a compound.

(a) Concrete   **(b)** The helium in a balloon   **(c)** A lead weight   **(d)** Wood

PROBLEM 1.4

Classify each of the following as a physical change or a chemical change:

(a) Dissolving sugar in water

(b) Producing carbon dioxide gas and solid lime by heating limestone

(c) Frying an egg

(d) The conversion of salicylic acid to acetylsalicylic acid (see the following Chemistry in Action)

▶▶▶ Prostaglandins are discussed in Section 24.9.

CHEMISTRY IN ACTION

Aspirin—A Case Study

Acetylsalicylic acid, more commonly known as aspirin, is perhaps the first true wonder drug. It is used as an analgesic to reduce fevers and to relieve headaches and body pains. It possesses anticoagulant properties, which in low doses can help prevent heart attacks and minimize the damage caused by strokes. But how was it discovered, and how does it work? The "discovery" of aspirin is a combination of serendipity and a process known as the scientific method: observation, evaluation of data, formation of a hypothesis, and the design of experiments to test the hypothesis and further our understanding.

The origins of aspirin can be traced back to the ancient Greek physician Hippocrates in 400 B.C., who prescribed the bark and leaves of the willow tree to relieve pain and fever. His knowledge of the therapeutic properties of these substances was the result of systematic observations and the evaluation of folklore—knowledge of the common people obtained through trial and error. The development of aspirin took another step forward in 1828 when scientists isolated a bitter-tasting yellow extract, called salicin, from willow bark. Experimental evidence identified salicin as the active ingredient responsible for the observed medical effects. Salicin could be easily converted by chemical reaction to salicylic acid (SA), which by the late 1800s was being mass-produced and marketed. SA had an unpleasant taste, however, and often caused stomach irritation and indigestion.

Further experiments were performed to convert salicylic acid to a substance that retained the therapeutic activity of SA, but without the unpleasant side effects. The discovery of acetylsalicylic acid (ASA), a derivative of SA, has often been attributed to Felix Hoffman, a chemist working for the Bayer pharmaceutical labs, but the first synthesis of ASA was actually reported by a French chemist, Charles Gerhardt, in 1853. Nevertheless, Hoffman obtained a patent for ASA in 1900, and Bayer marketed the new drug, now called aspirin, in water-soluble tablets.

▲ *Hippocrates.* **The ancient Greek physician prescribed a precursor of aspirin found in willow bark to relieve pain.**

But, how does aspirin work? Once again, experimental data provided insights into the therapeutic activity of aspirin. In 1971, the British pharmacologist John Vane discovered that aspirin suppresses the body's production of prostaglandins, which are responsible for the pain and swelling that accompany inflammation. The discovery of this mechanism led to the development of new analgesic drugs.

Research continues to explore aspirin's potential for preventing colon cancer, cancer of the esophagus, and other diseases.

See Chemistry in Action Problem 1.96 at the end of the chapter.

🔑 **KEY CONCEPT PROBLEM 1.5**

In the image below, red spheres represent element A and blue spheres represent element B. Identify the process illustrated in the image as a chemical change or a physical change. Explain your answer.

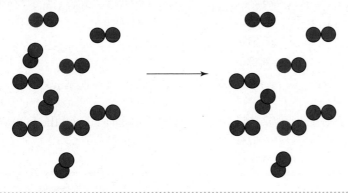

1.4 Chemical Elements and Symbols

As of the date this book was printed, 118 chemical elements have been identified. Some are certainly familiar to you—oxygen, helium, iron, aluminum, copper, and gold, for example—but many others are probably unfamiliar—rhenium, niobium, thulium, and promethium. Rather than write out the full names of elements, chemists use a shorthand notation in which elements are referred to by one- or two-letter symbols. The names and symbols of some common elements are listed in Table 1.2, and a complete alphabetical list is given inside the front cover of this book.

Note that all two-letter symbols have only their first letter capitalized, whereas the second letter is always lowercase. The symbols of most common elements are the first one or two letters of the elements' commonly used names, such as H (hydrogen) and Al (aluminum). Pay special attention, however, to the elements grouped in the last column to the right in Table 1.2. The symbols for these elements are derived from their original Latin names, such as Na for sodium, once known as *natrium*. The only way to learn these symbols is to memorize them; fortunately, they are few in number.

Only 91 of the elements occur naturally; the remaining elements have been produced artificially by chemists and physicists. Each element has its own distinctive properties, and just about all of the first 95 elements have been put to use in some way that takes advantage

▶▶▶ We will discuss the creation of new elements by nuclear bombardment in Chapter 11.

TABLE **1.2** Names and Symbols for Some Common Elements

Elements with Symbols Based on Modern Names						Elements with Symbols Based on Latin Names	
Al	Aluminum	**Co**	Cobalt	**N**	Nitrogen	**Cu**	Copper (*cuprum*)
Ar	Argon	**F**	Fluorine	**O**	Oxygen	**Au**	Gold (*aurum*)
Ba	Barium	**He**	Helium	**P**	Phosphorus	**Fe**	Iron (*ferrum*)
Bi	Bismuth	**H**	Hydrogen	**Pt**	Platinum	**Pb**	Lead (*plumbum*)
B	Boron	**I**	Iodine	**Rn**	Radon	**Hg**	Mercury (*hydrargyrum*)
Br	Bromine	**Li**	Lithium	**Si**	Silicon	**K**	Potassium (*kalium*)
Ca	Calcium	**Mg**	Magnesium	**S**	Sulfur	**Ag**	Silver (*argentum*)
C	Carbon	**Mn**	Manganese	**Ti**	Titanium	**Na**	Sodium (*natrium*)
Cl	Chlorine	**Ni**	Nickel	**Zn**	Zinc	**Sn**	Tin (*stannum*)

TABLE 1.3 Elemental Composition of the Earth's Crust and the Human Body*

Earth's Crust		Human Body	
Oxygen	46.1%	Oxygen	61%
Silicon	28.2%	Carbon	23%
Aluminum	8.2%	Hydrogen	10%
Iron	5.6%	Nitrogen	2.6%
Calcium	4.1%	Calcium	1.4%
Sodium	2.4%	Phosphorus	1.1%
Magnesium	2.3%	Sulfur	0.20%
Potassium	2.1%	Potassium	0.20%
Titanium	0.57%	Sodium	0.14%
Hydrogen	0.14%	Chlorine	0.12%

Mass percent values are given.

Chemical formula A notation for a chemical compound using element symbols and subscripts to show how many atoms of each element are present.

▶▶▶ We'll learn more about the structure of atoms and how they form compounds in Chapter 2.

of those properties. As indicated in Table 1.3, which shows the approximate elemental composition of the earth's crust and the human body, the naturally occurring elements are not equally abundant. Oxygen and silicon together account for nearly 75% of the mass in the earth's crust; oxygen, carbon, and hydrogen account for nearly all the mass of a human body.

Just as elements combine to form chemical compounds, symbols are combined to produce **chemical formulas**, which show by subscripts how many *atoms* (the smallest fundamental units) of each element are in a given chemical compound. For example, the formula H_2O represents water, which contains 2 hydrogen atoms combined with 1 oxygen atom. Similarly, the formula CH_4 represents methane (natural gas), and the formula $C_{12}H_{22}O_{11}$ represents table sugar (sucrose). When no subscript is given for an element, as for carbon in the formula CH_4, a subscript of "1" is understood.

H_2O	CH_4	$C_{12}H_{22}O_{11}$
2 H atoms	1 C atom	12 C atoms
1 O atom	4 H atoms	22 H atoms
		11 O atoms

PROBLEM 1.6
Match the names of the elements described below (a–f) with their elemental symbols (1–6).
(a) Sodium, a major component in table salt
(b) Tungsten, a metal used in light bulb filaments
(c) Strontium, used to produce brilliant red colors in fireworks
(d) Titanium, used in artificial hips and knee-replacement joints
(e) Fluorine, added to municipal water supplies to strengthen tooth enamel
(f) Tin, a metal used in solder

(1) W **(2)** Na **(3)** Sn **(4)** F **(5)** Ti **(6)** Sr

PROBLEM 1.7
Identify the elements represented in each of the following chemical formulas, and tell the number of atoms of each element:
(a) NH_3 (ammonia) **(b)** $NaHCO_3$ (sodium bicarbonate)
(c) C_8H_{18} (octane, a component of gasoline) **(d)** $C_6H_8O_6$ (vitamin C)

1.5 Elements and the Periodic Table

The symbols of the known elements are normally presented in a tabular format called the **periodic table**, as shown in Figure 1.4 and the inside front cover of this book. We will have much more to say about the periodic table and how it is numbered later, but will note for now that it is the most important organizing principle in chemistry. An enormous amount of information is embedded in the periodic table, information that gives chemists the ability to explain known chemical behavior of elements and to predict new behavior. The elements can be roughly divided into three groups: *metals*, *nonmetals*, and *metalloids* (sometimes called *semimetals*).

Periodic table A tabular format listing all known elements.

▶▶▶ The organization of the periodic table will be discussed in Chapter 2.

1A 1	2A 2	3B 3	4B 4	5B 5	6B 6	7B 7	8B 8	8B 9	8B 10	1B 11	2B 12	3A 13	4A 14	5A 15	6A 16	7A 17	8A 18
1 H 1.00794																	2 He 4.00260
3 Li 6.941	4 Be 9.01218											5 B 10.81	6 C 12.011	7 N 14.0067	8 O 15.9994	9 F 18.9984	10 Ne 20.1797
11 Na 22.98977	12 Mg 24.305											13 Al 26.98154	14 Si 28.0855	15 P 30.9738	16 S 32.066	17 Cl 35.4527	18 Ar 39.948
19 K 39.0983	20 Ca 40.078	21 Sc 44.9559	22 Ti 47.88	23 V 50.9415	24 Cr 51.996	25 Mn 54.9380	26 Fe 55.847	27 Co 58.9332	28 Ni 58.69	29 Cu 63.546	30 Zn 65.39	31 Ga 69.72	32 Ge 72.61	33 As 74.9216	34 Se 78.96	35 Br 79.904	36 Kr 83.80
37 Rb 85.4678	38 Sr 87.62	39 Y 88.9059	40 Zr 91.224	41 Nb 92.9064	42 Mo 95.94	43 Tc (98)	44 Ru 101.07	45 Rh 102.9055	46 Pd 106.42	47 Ag 107.8682	48 Cd 112.41	49 In 114.82	50 Sn 118.710	51 Sb 121.757	52 Te 127.60	53 I 126.9045	54 Xe 131.29
55 Cs 132.9054	56 Ba 137.33	57 *La 138.9055	72 Hf 178.49	73 Ta 180.9479	74 W 183.85	75 Re 186.207	76 Os 190.2	77 Ir 192.22	78 Pt 195.08	79 Au 196.9665	80 Hg 200.59	81 Tl 204.383	82 Pb 207.2	83 Bi 208.9804	84 Po (209)	85 At (210)	86 Rn (222)
87 Fr (223)	88 Ra 226.0254	89 †Ac 227.0278	104 Rf (261)	105 Db (262)	106 Sg (266)	107 Bh (264)	108 Hs (269)	109 Mt (268)	110 Ds (271)	111 Rg (272)	112 Cn (285)	113 (284)	114 (289)	115 (288)	116 (292)	117 (293)	118 (294)

58 Ce 140.12	59 Pr 140.9077	60 Nd 144.24	61 Pm (145)	62 Sm 150.36	63 Eu 151.965	64 Gd 157.25	65 Tb 158.9254	66 Dy 162.50	67 Ho 164.9304	68 Er 167.26	69 Tm 168.9342	70 Yb 173.04	71 Lu 174.967
90 Th 232.0381	91 Pa 231.0399	92 U 238.0289	93 Np 237.048	94 Pu (244)	95 Am (243)	96 Cm (247)	97 Bk (247)	98 Cf (251)	99 Es (252)	100 Fm (257)	101 Md (258)	102 No (259)	103 Lr (262)

Metals · Metalloids · Nonmetals

▲ **Figure 1.4**
The periodic table of the elements.
Metals appear on the left, nonmetals on the right, and metalloids in a zigzag band between metals and nonmetals. The numbering system is explained in Section 2.4.

Ninety-four of the currently known elements are metals—aluminum, gold, copper, and zinc, for example. **Metals** are solid at room temperature (except for mercury), usually have a lustrous appearance when freshly cut, are good conductors of heat and electricity, and are malleable rather than brittle. That is, metals can be pounded into different shapes rather than shattering when struck. Note that metals occur on the left side of the periodic table.

Eighteen elements are **nonmetals**. All are poor conductors of heat and electricity. Eleven are gases at room temperature, six are brittle solids, and one is a liquid. Oxygen and nitrogen, for example, are gases present in air; sulfur is a solid found in large underground deposits. Bromine is the only liquid nonmetal. Note that nonmetals occur on the right side of the periodic table.

Only six elements are **metalloids**, so named because their properties are intermediate between those of metals and nonmetals. Boron, silicon, and arsenic are examples. Pure silicon has a lustrous or shiny surface, like a metal, but it is brittle, like a nonmetal, and its electrical conductivity lies between that of metals and nonmetals. Note that metalloids occur in a zigzag band between metals on the left and nonmetals on the right side of the periodic table.

Metal A malleable element, with a lustrous appearance, that is a good conductor of heat and electricity.

Nonmetal An element that is a poor conductor of heat and electricity.

Metalloid An element whose properties are intermediate between those of a metal and a nonmetal.

(a)

(b)

(c)

▲ **Metals: Gold, zinc, and copper.**
(a) Known for its beauty, gold is very unreactive and is used primarily in jewelry and in electronic components. (b) Zinc, an essential trace element in our diets, has industrial uses ranging from the manufacture of brass, to roofing materials, to batteries. (c) Copper is widely used in electrical wiring, in water pipes, and in coins.

(a)

(b)

(c)

▲ **Nonmetals: Nitrogen, sulfur, and iodine.**
(a) Nitrogen, (b) sulfur, and (c) iodine are essential to all living things. Pure nitrogen, which constitutes almost 80% of air, is a gas at room temperature and does not condense to a liquid until it is cooled to −328 °C. Sulfur, a yellow solid, is found in large underground deposits in Texas and Louisiana. Iodine is a dark violet crystalline solid that was first isolated from seaweed.

(a)

(b)

▲ **Metalloids: Boron and silicon.**
(a) Boron is a strong, hard metalloid used in making the composite materials found in military aircraft. (b) Silicon is well known for its use in making computer chips.

Those elements essential for human life are listed in Table 1.4. In addition to the well-known elements carbon, hydrogen, oxygen, and nitrogen, less familiar elements such as molybdenum and selenium are also important.

TABLE 1.4 Elements Essential for Human Life*

Element	Symbol	Function
Carbon	C	These four elements are present in all living organisms
Hydrogen	H	
Oxygen	O	
Nitrogen	N	
Arsenic	As	May affect cell growth and heart function
Boron	B	Aids in the use of Ca, P, and Mg
Calcium*	Ca	Necessary for growth of teeth and bones
Chlorine*	Cl	Necessary for maintaining salt balance in body fluids
Chromium	Cr	Aids in carbohydrate metabolism
Cobalt	Co	Component of vitamin B_{12}
Copper	Cu	Necessary to maintain blood chemistry
Fluorine	F	Aids in the development of teeth and bones
Iodine	I	Necessary for thyroid function
Iron	Fe	Necessary for oxygen-carrying ability of blood
Magnesium*	Mg	Necessary for bones, teeth, and muscle and nerve action
Manganese	Mn	Necessary for carbohydrate metabolism and bone formation
Molybdenum	Mo	Component of enzymes necessary for metabolism
Nickel	Ni	Aids in the use of Fe and Cu
Phosphorus*	P	Necessary for growth of bones and teeth; present in DNA/RNA
Potassium*	K	Component of body fluids; necessary for nerve action
Selenium	Se	Aids vitamin E action and fat metabolism
Silicon	Si	Helps form connective tissue and bone
Sodium*	Na	Component of body fluids; necessary for nerve and muscle action
Sulfur*	S	Component of proteins; necessary for blood clotting
Zinc	Zn	Necessary for growth, healing, and overall health

*C, H, O, and N are present in most foods. Other elements listed vary in their distribution in different foods. Those marked with an asterisk are macronutrients, essential in the diet at more than 100 mg/day; the rest, other than C, H, O, and N, are micronutrients, essential at 15 mg or less per day.

LOOKING AHEAD ▶▶▶ The elements listed in Table 1.4 are not present in our bodies in their free forms. Instead, they are combined into many thousands of different chemical compounds. We will talk about some compounds formed by metals in Chapter 3 and compounds formed by nonmetals in Chapter 4.

PROBLEM 1.8
The six metalloids are boron (B), silicon (Si), germanium (Ge), arsenic (As), antimony (Sb), and tellurium (Te). Locate them in the periodic table, and tell where they appear with respect to metals and nonmetals.

PROBLEM 1.9
Locate the element Hg (discussed in the Chemisty in Action on p. 15) in the periodic table. Is it a metal, nonmetal, or metalloid? What physical and chemical properties contribute to the toxicity of mercury and compounds containing mercury?

1.6 Chemical Reactions: An Example of Chemical Change

If we take a quick look at an example of a chemical reaction, we can reinforce some of the ideas discussed in the previous sections. The element *nickel* is a hard, shiny metal, and the compound *hydrogen chloride* is a colorless gas that dissolves in water to give a solution called *hydrochloric acid*. When pieces of nickel are added to hydrochloric acid in a test tube, the nickel is slowly eaten away, the colorless solution turns green, and a gas bubbles out of the test tube. The change in color, the dissolving of the nickel, and the appearance of gas bubbles are indications that a chemical reaction is taking place, as shown in Figure 1.5.

Overall, the reaction of nickel with hydrochloric acid can be either written in words or represented in a shorthand notation using symbols to represent the elements or compounds involved as reactants and products, as shown below.

Reactants ———   ——— Products

Nickel + Hydrochloric acid $\longrightarrow$ Nickel (II) chloride + Hydrogen

[Ni + 2 HCl $\longrightarrow$ NiCl$_2$ + H$_2$]

(a)   (b)   (c)

▲ **Figure 1.5**

Reactants and products of a chemical reaction.

(a) The reactants: The flat dish contains pieces of nickel, an element that is a typical lustrous metal. The bottle contains hydrochloric acid, a solution of the chemical compound hydrogen chloride in water. These reactants are about to be combined in the test tube. (b) The reaction: As the chemical reaction occurs, the colorless solution turns green when water-insoluble nickel metal slowly changes into the water-soluble chemical compound nickel (II) chloride. Gas bubbles of the element hydrogen are produced and rise slowly through the green solution. (c) The product: Hydrogen gas can be collected as it bubbles from the solution. Removal of water from the solution leaves behind the other product, a solid green chemical compound known as nickel (II) chloride.

1.7 Physical Quantities

Physical quantity A physical property that can be measured.

Unit A defined quantity used as a standard of measurement.

Our understanding of matter depends on our ability to measure the changes in physical properties associated with physical and chemical change. Mass, volume, temperature, density, and other physical properties that can be measured are called **physical quantities** and are described by both a number and a **unit** of defined size:

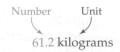

Number   Unit

61.2 kilograms

CHEMISTRY IN ACTION

Mercury and Mercury Poisoning

Mercury, the only metallic element that is liquid at room temperature, has fascinated people for millennia. Egyptian kings were buried in their pyramids along with containers of mercury, alchemists during the Middle Ages used mercury to dissolve gold, and Spanish galleons carried loads of mercury to the New World in the 1600s for use in gold and silver mining. Even its symbol, Hg, from the Latin *hydrargyrum,* meaning "liquid silver," hints at mercury's uniqueness.

Much of the recent interest in mercury has concerned its toxicity, but there are some surprises. For example, the mercury compound Hg_2Cl_2 (called *calomel*) is nontoxic and has a long history of medical use as a laxative, yet it is also used as a fungicide and rat poison. Dental amalgam, a solid alloy of approximately 50% elemental mercury, 35% silver, 13% tin, 1% copper, and trace amounts of zinc, has been used by dentists for many years to fill tooth cavities, with little or no adverse effects except in individuals with a hypersensitivity to mercury. Yet exposure to elemental mercury *vapor* for long periods leads to mood swings, headaches, tremors, and loss of hair and teeth. The widespread use of mercuric nitrate, a mercury compound employed to make the felt used in hats, exposed many hatters of the eighteenth and nineteenth centuries to toxic levels of mercury. The eccentric behavior displayed by hatters suffering from mercury poisoning led to the phrase "mad as a hatter."

Why is mercury toxic in some forms but not in others? It turns out that the toxicity of mercury and its compounds is related to solubility. Only soluble mercury compounds are toxic, because they can be transported through the bloodstream to all parts of the body, where they react with different enzymes and interfere with various biological processes. Elemental mercury and insoluble mercury compounds become toxic only when converted

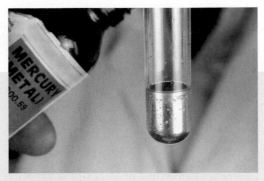

▲ **Elemental Mercury, a liquid at room temperature, forms many toxic compounds.**

into soluble compounds, reactions that are extremely slow in the body. Calomel, for example, is an insoluble mercury compound that passes through the body long before it is converted into any soluble compounds. Mercury alloys were considered safe for dental use because mercury does not evaporate readily from the alloys and it neither reacts with nor dissolves in saliva. Mercury vapor, however, remains in the lungs when breathed, until it is slowly converted into soluble compounds. Soluble organic forms of mercury can be particularly toxic. Trace amounts are found in nearly all seafood, but some larger species such as king mackerel and swordfish contain higher levels of mercury. Because mercury can affect the developing brain and nervous system of a fetus, pregnant women are often advised to avoid consuming them.

Recent events have raised new concerns regarding the safe use of mercury in some other applications. Perhaps the most controversial example is the use of thimerosal, an organic mercury compound, as a preservative in flu vaccines. While there is anecdotal evidence suggesting a link between thimerosal and autism in children, most scientific data seem to refute this claim. In response to these concerns, preservative-free versions of the influenza vaccine are available for use in infants, children, and pregnant women.

See Chemistry in Action Problem 1.97 at the end of the chapter.

The number alone is not much good without a unit. If you asked how much blood an accident victim had lost, the answer "three" would not tell you much. Three drops? Three milliliters? Three pints? Three liters? (By the way, an adult human has only 5–6 liters of blood.)

Any physical quantity can be measured in many different units. For example, a person's height might be measured in inches, feet, yards, centimeters, or many other units. To avoid confusion, scientists from around the world have agreed on a system of standard units, called by the French name *Système International d'Unites* (International System of Units), abbreviated *SI*. **SI units** for some common physical quantities are given in Table 1.5. Mass is measured in *kilograms* (kg), length is measured in *meters* (m), volume is measured in *cubic meters* (m^3), temperature is measured in *kelvins* (K), and time is measured in *seconds* (s, not sec).

SI units are closely related to the more familiar *metric units* used in all industrialized nations of the world except the United States. If you compare the SI and metric units shown in Table 1.5, you will find that the basic metric unit of mass is the *gram* (g) rather than the kilogram (1 g = 1/1000 kg), the metric unit of volume is the *liter* (L) rather than the cubic meter (1 L = 1/1000 m^3), and the metric unit of temperature

SI units Units of measurement defined by the International System of Units.

TABLE 1.5 Some SI and Metric Units and Their Equivalents

Quantity	Si Unit (Symbol)	Metric Unit (Symbol)	Equivalents
Mass	Kilogram (kg)	Gram (g)	1 kg = 1000 g = 2.205 lb
Length	Meter (m)	Meter (m)	1 m = 3.280 ft
Volume	Cubic meter (m³)	Liter (L)	1 m³ = 1000 L = 264.2 gal
Temperature	Kelvin (K)	Celsius degree (°C)	See Section 1.13
Time	Second (s)	Second (s)	—

is the *Celsius degree* (°C) rather than the kelvin. The meter is the unit of length, and the second is the unit of time in both systems. Although SI units are now preferred in scientific research, metric units are still used in some fields. You will probably find yourself working with both.

In addition to the units listed in Table 1.5, many other widely used units are derived from them. For instance, units of *meters per second* (m/s) are often used for *speed*—the distance covered in a given time. Similarly, units of *grams per cubic centimeter* (g/cm³) are often used for *density*—the mass of substance in a given volume. We will see other such derived units in future chapters.

One problem with any system of measurement is that the sizes of the units often turn out to be inconveniently large or small for the problem at hand. A biologist describing the diameter of a red blood cell (0.000 006 m) would find the meter to be an inconveniently large unit, but an astronomer measuring the average distance from the earth to the sun (150,000,000,000 m) would find the meter to be inconveniently small. For this reason, metric and SI units can be modified by prefixes to refer to either smaller or larger quantities. For instance, the SI unit for mass—the kilogram—differs by the prefix *kilo-* from the metric unit gram. *Kilo-* indicates that a kilogram is 1000 times as large as a gram:

$$1 \text{ kg} = (1000)(1 \text{ g}) = 1000 \text{ g}$$

Small quantities of active ingredients in medications are often reported in *milligrams* (mg). The prefix *milli-* shows that the unit gram has been divided by 1000, which is the same as multiplying by 0.001:

$$1 \text{ mg} = \left(\frac{1}{1000}\right)(1 \text{ g}) = (0.001)(1 \text{ g}) = 0.001 \text{ g}$$

▶▶▶ The use of exponents is reviewed in Section 1.10.

A list of prefixes is given in Table 1.6, with the most common ones displayed in color. Note that the exponents are multiples of 3 for *mega-* (10^6), *kilo-* (10^3), *milli-* (10^{-3}), *micro-* (10^{-6}), *nano-* (10^{-9}), and *pico-* (10^{-12}). The prefixes *centi-*, meaning 1/100, and *deci-*, meaning 1/10, indicate exponents that are not multiples of 3. *Centi-* is seen most often in the length unit *centimeter* (1 cm = 0.01 m), and *deci-* is used most often in clinical chemistry, where the concentrations of blood components are given in milligrams per deciliter (1 dL = 0.1 L). These prefixes allow us to compare the magnitudes of different numbers by noting how the prefixes modify a common unit.

For example,

$$1 \text{ meter} = 10 \text{ dm} = 100 \text{ cm} = 1000 \text{ mm} = 1{,}000{,}000 \text{ } \mu\text{m}$$

Such comparisons will be useful when we start performing calculations involving units in Section 1.12. Note also in Table 1.6 that numbers having five or more digits to the right of the decimal point are shown with thin spaces every three digits for convenience—0.000 001, for example. This manner of writing numbers is becoming more common and will be used throughout this book.

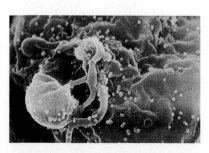

▲ The HIV-1 virus particles (in green) budding from the surface of a lymphocyte have an approximate diameter of 0.000 000 120 m.

TABLE **1.6** Some Prefixes for Multiples of Metric and SI Units			
Prefix	**Symbol**	**Base Unit Multiplied By***	**Example**
mega	M	$1{,}000{,}000 = 10^6$	1 megameter (Mm) $= 10^6$ m
kilo	k	$1000 = 10^3$	1 kilogram (kg) $= 10^3$ g
hecto	h	$100 = 10^2$	1 hectogram (hg) $= 100$ g
deka	da	$10 = 10^1$	1 dekaliter (daL) $= 10$ L
deci	d	$0.1 = 10^{-1}$	1 deciliter (dL) $= 0.1$ L
centi	c	$0.01 = 10^{-2}$	1 centimeter (cm) $= 0.01$ m
milli	m	$0.001 = 10^{-3}$	1 milligram (mg) $= 0.001$ g
micro	μ	$0.000\ 001 = 10^{-6}$	1 micrometer (μm) $= 10^{-6}$ m
nano	n	$0.000\ 000\ 001 = 10^{-9}$	1 nanogram (ng) $= 10^{-9}$ g
pico	p	$0.000\ 000\ 000\ 001 = 10^{-12}$	1 picogram (pg) $= 10^{-12}$ g
femto	f	$0.000\ 000\ 000\ 000\ 001 = 10^{-15}$	1 femtogram (fg) $= 10^{-15}$ g

*The scientific notation method of writing large and small numbers (for example, 10^6 for 1,000,000) is explained in Section 1.10.

> **PROBLEM 1.10**
> Give the full name of the following units and express the quantities in terms of the basic unit (for example, 1 mL = 1 milliliter = 0.001 L):
> **(a)** 1 cm   **(b)** 1 dg   **(c)** 1 km   **(d)** 1 μs   **(e)** 1 ng

1.8 Measuring Mass, Length, and Volume

The terms *mass* and *weight*, though often used interchangeably, really have quite different meanings. **Mass** is a measure of the amount of matter in an object, whereas **weight** is a measure of the gravitational pull that the earth, moon, or other large body exerts on an object. Clearly, the amount of matter in an object does not depend on location. Whether you are standing on the earth or standing on the moon, the mass of your body is the same. On the other hand, the weight of an object *does* depend on location. Your weight on earth might be 140 lb, but it would only be 23 lb on the moon because the pull of gravity there is only about one-sixth as great.

At the same location, two objects with identical masses have identical weights; that is, gravity pulls equally on both. Thus, the *mass* of an object can be determined by comparing the *weight* of the object to the weight of a known reference standard. Much of the confusion between mass and weight is simply due to a language problem: We speak of "weighing" when we really mean that we are measuring mass by comparing two weights. Figure 1.6 shows a two-pan balance in which the mass of objects are measured by comparison with the known masses of standard materials, such as brass weights.

Mass A measure of the amount of matter in an object.

Weight A measure of the gravitational force that the earth or other large body exerts on an object.

◄ **Figure 1.6**
The two-pan balance is used to measure the mass of objects, such as the pennies on the left pan, by comparing them with the mass of standard objects, such as the brass weights on the right pan.

One kilogram, the SI unit for mass, is equal to 2.205 lb—too large a quantity for many purposes in chemistry and medicine. Thus, smaller units of mass such as the gram, milligram (mg), and microgram (μg), are more commonly used. Table 1.7 shows the relationships between metric and common units for mass.

The meter is the standard measure of length, or distance, in both the SI and metric systems. One meter is 39.37 inches (about 10% longer than a yard), a length that is much too large for most measurements in chemistry and medicine. Other, more commonly used measures of length are the *centimeter* (cm; 1/100 m) and the *millimeter* (mm; 1/1000 m). One centimeter is a bit less than half an inch—0.3937 inch to be exact. A millimeter, in turn, is 0.03937 inch, or about the thickness of a dime. Table 1.8 lists the relationships of these units.

Volume is the amount of space occupied by an object. The SI unit for volume—the cubic meter, m^3—is so large that the liter (1 L = 0.001 m^3 = 1 dm^3) is much more commonly used in chemistry and medicine. One liter has the volume of a cube 10 cm (1 dm) on edge and is a bit larger than one U.S. quart. Each liter is further divided into

TABLE 1.7 Units of Mass

Unit	Equivalent	Unit	Equivalent
1 kilogram (kg)	= 1000 grams = 2.205 pounds	1 ton	= 2000 pounds = 907.03 kilograms
1 gram (g)	= 0.001 kilogram = 1000 milligrams = 0.035 27 ounce	1 pound (lb)	= 16 ounces = 0.454 kilogram = 454 grams
1 milligram (mg)	= 0.001 gram = 1000 micrograms	1 ounce (oz)	= 0.028 35 kilogram = 28.35 grams
1 microgram (μg)	= 0.000 001 gram = 0.001 milligram		= 28,350 milligrams

TABLE 1.8 Units of Length

Unit	Equivalent
1 kilometer (km)	= 1000 meters = 0.6214 mile
1 meter (m)	= 100 centimeters = 1000 millimeters = 1.0936 yards = 39.37 inches
1 centimeter (cm)	= 0.01 meter = 10 millimeters = 0.3937 inch
1 millimeter (mm)	= 0.001 meter = 0.1 centimeter
1 mile (mi)	= 1.609 kilometers = 1609 meters
1 yard (yd)	= 0.9144 meter = 91.44 centimeters
1 foot (ft)	= 0.3048 meter = 30.48 centimeters
1 inch (in)	= 2.54 centimeters = 25.4 millimeters

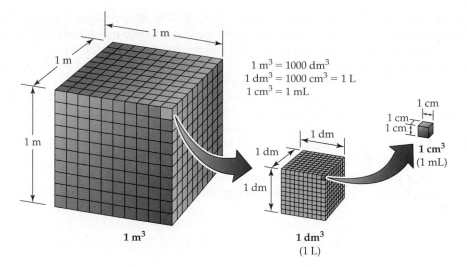

$$1 \ m^3 = 1000 \ dm^3$$
$$1 \ dm^3 = 1000 \ cm^3 = 1 \ L$$
$$1 \ cm^3 = 1 \ mL$$

1 m³

1 dm³
(1 L)

1 cm³
(1 mL)

◄ **Figure 1.7**
A cubic meter is the volume of a cube 1 m on edge. Each cubic meter contains 1000 cubic decimeters (liters), and each cubic decimeter contains 1000 cubic centimeters (milliliters). Thus, there are 1000 mL in a liter and 1000 L in a cubic meter.

TABLE 1.9 Units of Volume

Unit	Equivalent
1 cubic meter (m³)	= 1000 liters
	= 264.2 gallons
1 liter (L)	= 0.001 cubic meter
	= 1000 milliliters
	= 1.057 quarts
1 deciliter (dL)	= 0.1 liter
	= 100 milliliters
1 milliliter (mL)	= 0.001 liter
	= 1000 microliters
1 microliter (µL)	= 0.001 milliliter
1 gallon (gal)	= 3.7854 liters
1 quart (qt)	= 0.9464 liter
	= 946.4 milliliters
1 fluid ounce (fl oz)	= 29.57 milliliters

1000 *milliliters* (mL), with 1 mL being the size of a cube 1 cm on edge, or 1 cm³. In fact, the milliliter is often called a *cubic centimeter* (cm³ or cc) in medical work. Figure 1.7 shows the divisions of a cubic meter, and Table 1.9 shows the relationships among units of volume.

1.9 Measurement and Significant Figures

How much does a tennis ball weigh? If you put a tennis ball on an ordinary bathroom scale, the scale would probably register 0 lb (or 0 kg if you have a metric scale). If you placed the same tennis ball on a common laboratory balance, however, you might get a reading of 54.07 g. Trying again by placing the ball on an expensive analytical balance like those found in clinical and research laboratories, you might find a mass of 54.071 38 g. Clearly, the precision of your answer depends on the equipment used for the measurement.

Every experimental measurement, no matter how precise, has a degree of uncertainty to it because there is always a limit to the number of digits that can be determined. An analytical balance, for example, might reach its limit in measuring mass to the fifth decimal place, and weighing the tennis ball several times might produce

▲ The tennis ball weighs 54.07 g on this common laboratory balance, which is capable of determining mass to about 0.01 g.

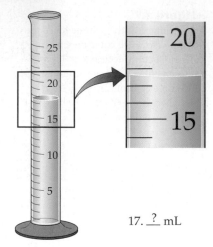

slightly different readings, such as 54.071 39 g, 54.071 38 g, and 54.071 37 g. Also, different people making the same measurement might come up with slightly different answers. How, for instance, would you record the volume of the liquid shown in Figure 1.8? It is clear that the volume of liquid lies between 17.0 and 18.0 mL, but the exact value of the last digit must be estimated.

To indicate the precision of a measurement, the value recorded should use all the digits known with certainty, plus one additional estimated digit that is usually considered uncertain by plus or minus 1 (written as ±1). The total number of digits used to express such a measurement is called the number of **significant figures**. Thus, the quantity 54.07 g has four significant figures (5, 4, 0, and 7), and the quantity 54.071 38 g has seven significant figures. *Remember*: All but one of the significant figures are known with certainty; the last significant figure is only an estimate accurate to ±1.

17. _?_ mL

▲ **Figure 1.8**
What is the volume of liquid in this graduated cylinder?

Significant figures The number of meaningful digits used to express a value.

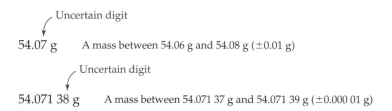

Deciding the number of significant figures in a given measurement is usually simple, but it can be troublesome when zeros are involved. Depending on the circumstances, a zero might be significant or might be just a space-filler to locate the decimal point. For example, how many significant figures does each of the following measurements have?

94.072 g	Five significant figures (9, 4, 0, 7, 2)
0.0834 cm	Three significant figures (8, 3, 4)
0.029 07 mL	Four significant figures (2, 9, 0, 7)
138.200 m	Six significant figures (1, 3, 8, 2, 0, 0)
23,000 kg	*Anywhere* from two (2, 3) to five (2, 3, 0, 0, 0) significant figures

The following rules are helpful for determining the number of significant figures when zeros are present:

RULE 1: Zeros in the middle of a number are like any other digit; they are always significant. Thus, 94.072 g has five significant figures.

RULE 2: Zeros at the beginning of a number are not significant; they act only to locate the decimal point. Thus, 0.0834 cm has three significant figures, and 0.029 07 mL has four.

RULE 3: Zeros at the end of a number and *after* the decimal point are significant. It is assumed that these zeros would not be shown unless they were significant. Thus, 138.200 m has six significant figures. If the value were known to only four significant figures, we would write 138.2 m.

RULE 4: Zeros at the end of a number and *before* an implied decimal point may or may not be significant. We cannot tell whether they are part of the measurement or whether they act only to locate the unwritten but implied decimal point. Thus, 23,000 kg may have two, three, four, or five significant figures. Adding a decimal point at the end would indicate that all five numbers are significant.

Often, however, a little common sense is useful. A temperature reading of 20 °C probably has two significant figures rather than one, because one significant figure would imply a temperature anywhere from 10 °C to 30 °C and would be of little use. Similarly, a volume given as 300 mL probably has three significant figures. On the other hand, a figure of 150,000,000 km for the distance between the earth and the sun has only two or three significant figures because the distance is variable. We will see a better way to deal with this problem in the next section.

One final point about significant figures: some numbers, such as those obtained when counting objects and those that are part of a definition, are *exact* and effectively have an unlimited number of significant figures. Thus, a class might have *exactly* 32 students (not 31.9, 32.0, or 32.1), and 1 foot is defined to have *exactly* 12 inches.

Worked Example **1.3** Significant Figures of Measurements

How many significant figures do the following measurements have?

(a) 2730.78 m   (b) 0.0076 mL   (c) 3400 kg   (d) 3400.0 m²

ANALYSIS All nonzero numbers are significant; the number of significant figures will then depend on the status of the zeros in each case. (Hint: which rule applies in each case?)

SOLUTION

(a) Six (rule 1)   (b) Two (rule 2)
(c) Two, three, or four (rule 4)   (d) Five (rule 3)

▲ The number of seats in this auditorium is an exact number with an unlimited number of significant figures.

PROBLEM 1.11
How many significant figures do the following measurements have?
(a) 3.45 m   (b) 0.1400 kg
(c) 10.003 L   (d) 35 cents

 KEY CONCEPT PROBLEM 1.12

How would you record the temperature reading on the following Celsius thermometer? How many significant figures do you have in your answer?

1.10 Scientific Notation

Rather than write very large or very small numbers in their entirety, it is more convenient to express them using *scientific notation*. A number is written in **scientific notation** as the product of a number between 1 and 10, times the number 10 raised to a power. Thus, 215 is written in scientific notation as 2.15×10^2:

$$215 = 2.15 \times 100 = 2.15(10 \times 10) = 2.15 \times 10^2$$

Notice that in this case, where the number is *larger* than 1, the decimal point has been moved *to the left* until it follows the first digit. The exponent on the 10 tells how many places we had to move the decimal point to position it just after the first digit:

$$215. = 2.15 \times 10^2$$

Decimal point is moved two places to the left, so exponent is 2.

Scientific notation A number expressed as the product of a number between 1 and 10, times the number 10 raised to a power.

To express a number *smaller* than 1 in scientific notation, we have to move the decimal point *to the right* until it follows the first digit. The number of places moved is the negative exponent of 10. For example, the number 0.002 15 can be rewritten as 2.15×10^{-3}:

$$0.002\ 15 = 2.15 \times \frac{1}{1000} = 2.15 \times \frac{1}{10 \times 10 \times 10} = 2.15 \times \frac{1}{10^3} = 2.15 \times 10^{-3}$$

$$0.002\ 15 = 2.15 \times 10^{-3}$$

Decimal point is moved three places to the right, so exponent is −3.

To convert a number written in scientific notation to standard notation, the process is reversed. For a number with a *positive* exponent, the decimal point is moved to the *right* a number of places equal to the exponent:

$$3.7962 \times 10^4 = 37,962$$

Positive exponent of 4, so decimal point is moved to the right four places.

For a number with a *negative* exponent, the decimal point is moved to the *left* a number of places equal to the exponent:

$$1.56 \times 10^{-8} = 0.000\ 000\ 015\ 6$$

Negative exponent of −8, so decimal point is moved to the left eight places.

Scientific notation is particularly helpful for indicating how many significant figures are present in a number that has zeros at the end but to the left of a decimal point. If we read, for instance, that the distance from the earth to the sun is 150,000,000 km, we do not really know how many significant figures are indicated. Some of the zeros might be significant, or they might merely act to locate the decimal point. Using scientific notation, however, we can indicate how many of the zeros are significant. Rewriting 150,000,000 as 1.5×10^8 indicates two significant figures, whereas writing it as 1.500×10^8 indicates four significant figures. Scientific notation is not ordinarily used for numbers that are easily written, such as 10 or 175, although it is sometimes helpful in doing arithmetic.

▶▶▶ Rules for doing arithmetic with numbers written in scientific notation are reviewed in Appendix A.

Worked Example 1.4 Significant Figures and Scientific Notation

There are 1,760,000,000,000,000,000,000 molecules of sucrose (table sugar) in 1 g. Use scientific notation to express this number with four significant figures.

ANALYSIS Because the number is larger than 1, the exponent will be positive. You will have to move the decimal point 21 places to the left.

SOLUTION
The first four digits—1, 7, 6, and 0—are significant, meaning that only the first of the 19 zeros is significant. Because we have to move the decimal point 21 places to the left to put it after the first significant digit, the answer is 1.760×10^{21}.

▲ How many molecules are in this 1 g pile of table sugar?

Worked Example 1.5 Scientific Notation

The rhinovirus responsible for the common cold has a diameter of 20 nm, or 0.000 000 020 m. Express this number in scientific notation.

ANALYSIS The number is smaller than 1, and so the exponent will be negative. You will have to move the decimal point eight places to the right.

SOLUTION
There are only two significant figures, because zeros at the beginning of a number are not significant. We have to move the decimal point 8 places to the right to place it after the first digit, so the answer is 2.0×10^{-8} m.

Worked Example **1.6** Scientific Notation and Unit Conversions

A clinical laboratory found that a blood sample contained 0.0026 g of phosphorus and 0.000 101 g of iron.

(a) Give these quantities in scientific notation.

(b) Give these quantities in the units normally used to report them—milligrams for phosphorus and micrograms for iron.

ANALYSIS Is the number larger or smaller than 1? How many places do you have to move the decimal point?

SOLUTION

(a) 0.0026 g phosphorus $= 2.6 \times 10^{-3}$ g phosphorus

0.000 101 g iron $= 1.01 \times 10^{-4}$ g iron

(b) We know from Table 1.6 that $1 \text{ mg} = 1 \times 10^{-3}$ g, where the exponent is -3. Expressing the amount of phosphorus in milligrams is straightforward because the amount in grams (2.6×10^{-3} g) already has an exponent of -3. Thus, 2.6×10^{-3} g $= 2.6$ mg of phosphorus.

$$(2.6 \times 10^{-3} \text{ g})\left(\frac{1 \text{ mg}}{1 \times 10^{-3} \text{ g}}\right) = 2.6 \text{ mg}$$

We know from Table 1.6 that $1 \text{ } \mu g = 1 \times 10^{-6}$ g where the exponent is -6. Expressing the amount of iron in micrograms thus requires that we restate the amount in grams so that the exponent is -6. We can do this by moving the decimal point six places to the right:

$$0.000\ 101 \text{ g iron} = 101 \times 10^{-6} \text{ g iron} = 101 \text{ } \mu g \text{ iron}$$

PROBLEM 1.13

Convert the following values to scientific notation:

(a) 0.058 g   **(b)** 46,792 m   **(c)** 0.006 072 cm   **(d)** 345.3 kg

PROBLEM 1.14

Convert the following values from scientific notation to standard notation:

(a) 4.885×10^4 mg   **(b)** 8.3×10^{-6} m   **(c)** 4.00×10^{-2} m

PROBLEM 1.15

Rewrite the following numbers in scientific notation as indicated:

(a) 630,000 with five significant figures

(b) 1300 with three significant figures

(c) 794,200,000,000 with four significant figures

1.11 Rounding Off Numbers

It often happens, particularly when doing arithmetic on a pocket calculator, that a quantity appears to have more significant figures than are really justified. For example, you might calculate the gas mileage of your car by finding that it takes 11.70 gallons of gasoline to drive 278 miles:

$$\text{Mileage} = \frac{\text{Miles}}{\text{Gallons}} = \frac{278 \text{ mi}}{11.70 \text{ gal}} = 23.760\ 684 \text{ mi/gal (mpg)}$$

Although the answer on a calculator has eight digits, your calculated result is really not as precise as it appears. In fact, as we will see below, your answer is good to only three significant figures and should be **rounded off** to 23.8 mi/gal.

How do you decide how many digits to keep? The full answer to this question is a bit complex and involves a mathematical treatment called *error analysis*, but for many purposes, a simplified procedure using just two rules is sufficient:

Rounding off A procedure used for deleting nonsignificant figures.

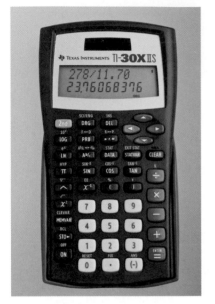

▲ Calculators often display more digits than are justified by the precision of the data.

RULE 1: In carrying out a multiplication or division, the answer cannot have more significant figures than either of the original numbers. This is just a common-sense rule if you think about it. After all, if you do not know the number of miles you drove to better than three significant figures (278 could mean 277, 278, or 279), you certainly cannot calculate your mileage to more than the same number of significant figures.

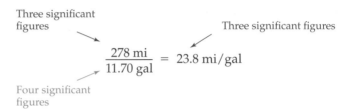

Three significant figures

Three significant figures

$$\frac{278 \text{ mi}}{11.70 \text{ gal}} = 23.8 \text{ mi/gal}$$

Four significant figures

RULE 2: In carrying out an addition or subtraction, the answer cannot have more digits after the decimal point than either of the original numbers. For example, if you have 3.18 L of water and you add 0.013 15 L more, you now have 3.19 L. Again, this rule is just common sense. If you do not know the volume you started with past the second decimal place (it could be 3.17, 3.18, or 3.19), you cannot know the total of the combined volumes past the same decimal place.

Volume of water at start ⟶ 3.18? ?? L ⟵ Two digits after decimal point
Volume of water added ⟶ + 0.013 15 L ⟵ Five digits after decimal point
Total volume of water ⟶ 3.19? ?? L ⟵ Two digits after decimal point

If a calculation has several steps, it is generally best to round off at the end after all the steps have been carried out, keeping the number of significant figures determined by the least precise number in your calculations. Once you decide how many digits to retain for your answer, the rules for rounding off numbers are straightforward:

RULE 1: If the first digit you remove is 4 or less, drop it and all following digits. Thus, 2.4271 becomes 2.4 when rounded off to two significant figures because the first of the dropped digits (a 2) is 4 or less.

RULE 2: If the first digit you remove is 5 or greater, round the number up by adding a 1 to the digit to the left of the one you drop. Thus, 4.5832 becomes 4.6 when rounded off to two significant figures because the first of the dropped digits (an 8) is 5 or greater.

Worked Example **1.7** Significant Figures and Calculations: Addition/Subtraction

Suppose that you weigh 124 lb before dinner. How much will you weigh after dinner if you eat 1.884 lb of food?

ANALYSIS When performing addition or subtraction, the number of significant figures you report in the final answer is determined by the number of digits in the least precise number in the calculation.

SOLUTION
Your after-dinner weight is found by adding your original weight to the weight of the food consumed:

$$
\begin{array}{r}
124 \quad \text{lb} \\
\underline{1.884 \text{ lb}} \\
125.884 \text{ lb (Unrounded)}
\end{array}
$$

Because the value of your original weight has no significant figures after the decimal point, your after-dinner weight also must have no significant figures after the decimal point. Thus, 125.884 lb must be rounded off to 126 lb.

Worked Example 1.8 Significant Figures and Calculations: Multiplication/Division

To make currant jelly, 13.75 cups of sugar was added to 18 cups of currant juice. How much sugar was added per cup of juice?

ANALYSIS For calculations involving multiplication or division, the final answer cannot have more significant figures than either of the original numbers.

SOLUTION
The quantity of sugar must be divided by the quantity of juice:

$$
\frac{13.75 \text{ cups sugar}}{18 \text{ cups juice}} = 0.763\,888\,89 \ \frac{\text{cup sugar}}{\text{cup juice}} \text{ (Unrounded)}
$$

The number of significant figures in the answer is limited to two by the quantity 18 cups in the calculation and must be rounded to 0.76 cup of sugar per cup of juice.

PROBLEM 1.16
Round off the following quantities to the indicated number of significant figures:
(a) 2.304 g (three significant figures)
(b) 188.3784 mL (five significant figures)
(c) 0.008 87 L (one significant figure)
(d) 1.000 39 kg (four significant figures)

PROBLEM 1.17
Carry out the following calculations, rounding each result to the correct number of significant figures:
(a) 4.87 mL + 46.0 mL   **(b)** 3.4 × 0.023 g
(c) 19.333 m − 7.4 m   **(d)** 55 mg − 4.671 mg + 0.894 mg
(e) 62,911 ÷ 611

1.12 Problem Solving: Unit Conversions and Estimating Answers

Many activities in the laboratory and in medicine—measuring, weighing, preparing solutions, and so forth—require converting a quantity from one unit to another. For example: "These pills contain 1.3 grains of aspirin, but I need 200 mg. Is one pill enough?" Converting between units is not mysterious; we all do it every day. If you run 9 laps around a 400-meter track, for instance, you have to convert between the distance unit "lap" and the distance unit "meter" to find that you have run 3600 m (9 laps times

▲ Currency exchange between the US$ and Euros is another activity that requires a unit conversion.

400 m/lap). If you want to find how many miles that is, you have to convert again to find that 3600 m = 2.237 mi.

The simplest way to carry out calculations involving different units is to use the **factor-label method**. In this method, a quantity in one unit is converted into an equivalent quantity in a different unit by using a **conversion factor** that expresses the relationship between units:

$$\text{Starting quantity} \times \text{Conversion factor} = \text{Equivalent quantity}$$

As an example, we learned from Table 1.8 that 1 km = 0.6214 mi. Writing this relationship as a fraction restates it in the form of a conversion factor, either kilometers per mile or miles per kilometer.

Since 1 km = 0.6214 mi, then:

Conversion factors between kilometers and miles $\dfrac{1 \text{ km}}{0.6214 \text{ mi}} = 1$ or $\dfrac{0.6214 \text{ mi}}{1 \text{ km}} = 1$

Note that this and all other conversion factors are numerically equal to 1 because the value of the quantity above the division line (the numerator) is equal in value to the quantity below the division line (the denominator). Thus, multiplying by a conversion factor is equivalent to multiplying by 1 and so does not change the value of the quantity being multiplied:

These two quantities are the same. $\dfrac{1 \text{ km}}{0.6214 \text{ mi}}$ or $\dfrac{0.6214 \text{ mi}}{1 \text{ km}}$ These two quantities are the same.

The key to the factor-label method of problem solving is that units are treated like numbers and can thus be multiplied and divided (though not added or subtracted) just as numbers can. When solving a problem, the idea is to set up an equation so that all unwanted units cancel, leaving only the desired units. Usually, it is best to start by writing what you know and then manipulating that known quantity. For example, if you know there are 26.22 mi in a marathon and want to find how many kilometers that is, you could write the distance in miles and multiply by the conversion factor in kilometers per mile. The unit "mi" cancels because it appears both above and below the division line, leaving "km" as the only remaining unit.

$$26.22 \text{ mi} \times \frac{1 \text{ km}}{0.6214 \text{ mi}} = 42.20 \text{ km}$$

Starting quantity   Conversion factor   Equivalent quantity

The factor-label method gives the right answer only if the equation is set up so that the unwanted unit (or units) cancel. If the equation is set up in any other way, the units will not cancel and you will not get the right answer. Thus, if you selected the incorrect conversion factor (miles per kilometer) for the above problem, you would end up with an incorrect answer expressed in meaningless units:

$$\text{Incorrect } 26.22 \text{ mi} \times \frac{0.6214 \text{ mi}}{1 \text{ km}} = 16.29 \frac{\text{mi}^2}{\text{km}} \text{ Incorrect}$$

The main drawback to using the factor-label method is that it is possible to get an answer without really understanding what you are doing. It is therefore best when solving a problem to first think through a rough estimate, or *ballpark estimate*, as a check on your work. If your ballpark estimate is not close to the final calculated solution, there is a misunderstanding somewhere and you should think the problem through again. If, for example, you came up with the answer 5.3 cm³ when calculating the volume of a human cell, you should realize that such an answer could not possibly be right. Cells are too tiny to be distinguished with the naked eye, but a volume of 5.3 cm³ is about the size

---

Factor-label method A problem-solving procedure in which equations are set up so that unwanted units cancel and only the desired units remain.

Conversion factor An expression of the numerical relationship between two units.

of a walnut. The Worked Examples 1.11, 1.12, and 1.13 at the end of this section show how to estimate the answers to simple unit-conversion problems.

The factor-label method and the use of ballpark estimates are techniques that will help you solve problems of many kinds, not just unit conversions. Problems sometimes seem complicated, but you can usually sort out the complications by analyzing the problem properly:

STEP 1: Identify the information given, including units.

STEP 2: Identify the information needed in the answer, including units.

STEP 3: Find the relationship(s) between the known information and unknown answer, and plan a series of steps, including conversion factors, for getting from one to the other.

STEP 4: Solve the problem.

BALLPARK CHECK Make a ballpark estimate at the beginning and check it against your final answer to be sure the value and the units of your calculated answer are reasonable.

Worked Example 1.9 Factor Labels: Unit Conversions

Write conversion factors for the following pairs of units (use Tables 1.7–1.9):

(a) Deciliters and milliliters

(b) Pounds and grams

ANALYSIS Start with the appropriate equivalency relationship and rearrange to form conversion factors.

SOLUTION

(a) Since 1 dL = 0.1 L and 1 mL = 0.001 L, then 1 dL = $(0.1\ L)\left(\dfrac{1\ mL}{0.001\ L}\right)$ =

100 mL. The conversion factors are

$$\frac{1\ dL}{100\ mL} \quad \text{and} \quad \frac{100\ mL}{1\ dL}$$

(b) $\dfrac{1\ lb}{454\ g}$ and $\dfrac{454\ g}{1\ lb}$

Worked Example 1.10 Factor Labels: Unit Conversions

(a) Convert 0.75 lb to grams.

(b) Convert 0.50 qt to deciliters.

ANALYSIS Start with conversion factors and set up equations so that units cancel appropriately.

SOLUTION

(a) Select the conversion factor from Worked Example 1.9(b) so that the "lb" units cancel and "g" remains:

$$0.75\ \cancel{lb} \times \frac{454\ g}{1\ \cancel{lb}} = 340\ g$$

(b) In this, as in many problems, it is convenient to use more than one conversion factor. As long as the unwanted units cancel correctly, two or more conversion factors can be strung together in the same calculation. In this case, we can convert first between quarts and milliliters, and then between milliliters and deciliters:

$$0.50\ \cancel{qt} \times \frac{946.4\ \cancel{mL}}{1\ \cancel{qt}} \times \frac{1\ dL}{100\ \cancel{mL}} = 4.7\ dL$$

Worked Example **1.11** Factor Labels: Unit Conversions

A child is 21.5 inches long at birth. How long is this in centimeters?

ANALYSIS This problem calls for converting from inches to centimeters, so we will need to know how many centimeters are in an inch and how to use this information as a conversion factor.

BALLPARK ESTIMATE It takes about 2.5 cm to make 1 in., and so it should take two and a half times as many centimeters to make a distance equal to approximately 20 in., or about 20 in. $\times$ 2.5 = 50 cm.

SOLUTION

STEP 1: **Identify given information.**	Length = 21.5 in.
STEP 2: **Identify answer and units.**	Length = ?? cm
STEP 3: **Identify conversion factor.**	1 in. = 2.54 cm $\rightarrow \dfrac{2.54 \text{ cm}}{1 \text{ in.}}$
STEP 4: **Solve.** Multiply the known length (in inches) by the conversion factor so that units cancel, providing the answer (in centimeters).	$21.5 \text{ in.} \times \dfrac{2.54 \text{ cm}}{1 \text{ in.}} = 54.6 \text{ cm}$ (Rounded off from 54.61)

BALLPARK CHECK How does this value compare with the ballpark estimate we made at the beginning? Are the final units correct? 54.6 cm is close to our original estimate of 50 cm.

Worked Example **1.12** Factor Labels: Concentration to Mass

A patient requires an injection of 0.012 g of a pain killer available as a 15 mg/mL solution. How many milliliters of solution should be administered?

ANALYSIS Knowing the amount of pain killer in 1 mL allows us to use the concentration as a conversion factor to determine the volume of solution that would contain the desired amount.

BALLPARK ESTIMATE One milliliter contains 15 mg of the pain killer, or 0.015 g. Since only 0.012 g is needed, a little less than 1.0 mL should be administered.

▲ **How many milliliters should be injected?**

SOLUTION

STEP 1: **Identify known information.**	Dosage = 0.012 g Concentration = 15 mg/mL
STEP 2: **Identify answer and units.**	Volume to administer = ?? mL
STEP 3: **Identify conversion factors.** Two conversion factors are needed. First, g must be converted to mg. Once we have the mass in mg, we can calculate mL using the conversion factor of mL/mg.	$1 \text{ mg} = .001 \text{ g} \Longrightarrow \dfrac{1 \text{ mg}}{0.001 \text{ g}}$ $15 \text{ mg/mL} \Longrightarrow \dfrac{1 \text{ mL}}{15 \text{ mg}}$
STEP 4: **Solve.** Starting from the desired dosage, we use the conversion factors to cancel units, obtaining the final answer in mL.	$(0.012 \text{ g})\left(\dfrac{1 \text{ mg}}{0.001 \text{ g}}\right)\left(\dfrac{1 \text{ mL}}{15 \text{ mg}}\right) = 0.80 \text{ mL}$

BALLPARK CHECK Consistent with our initial estimate of a little less than 1 mL.

Worked Example **1.13** Factor Labels: Multiple Conversion Calculations

Administration of digitalis to control atrial fibrillation in heart patients must be carefully regulated because even a modest overdose can be fatal. To take differences between patients into account, dosages are sometimes prescribed in micrograms per kilogram of body weight ($\mu g/kg$). Thus, two people may differ greatly in weight, but both will receive the proper dosage. At a dosage of 20 $\mu g/kg$ body weight, how many milligrams of digitalis should a 160 lb patient receive?

ANALYSIS Knowing the patient's body weight (in kg) and the recommended dosage (in $\mu g/kg$), we can calculate the appropriate amount of digitalis.

BALLPARK ESTIMATE Since a kilogram is roughly equal to 2 lb, a 160 lb patient has a mass of about 80 kg. At a dosage of 20 $\mu g/kg$, an 80 kg patient should receive 80 $\times$ 20 μg, or about 1600 μg of digitalis, or 1.6 mg.

SOLUTION

STEP 1: Identify known information.

STEP 2: Identify answer and units.

STEP 3: Identify conversion factors. Two conversions are needed. First, convert the patient's weight in pounds to weight in kg. The correct dose can then be determined based on μg digitalis/kg of body weight. Finally, the dosage in μg is converted to mg.

STEP 4: Solve. Use the known information and the conversion factors so that units cancel, obtaining the answer in mg.

Patient weight = 160 lb
Prescribed dosage = 20 μg digitalis/kg body weight
Delivered dosage = ?? mg digitalis

$$1 \text{ kg} = 2.205 \text{ lb} \rightarrow \frac{1 \text{ kg}}{2.205 \text{ lb}}$$

$$1 \text{ mg} = (0.001 \text{ g})\left(\frac{1 \mu g}{10^{-6} \text{ g}}\right) = 1000 \ \mu g$$

$$160 \ \text{lb} \times \frac{1 \ \text{kg}}{2.205 \ \text{lb}} \times \frac{20 \ \mu g \text{ digitalis}}{1 \ \text{kg}} \times \frac{1 \text{ mg}}{1000 \ \mu g}$$
$$= 1.5 \text{ mg digitalis (Rounded off)}$$

BALLPARK CHECK Close to our estimate of 1.6 mg.

PROBLEM 1.18

Write appropriate conversion factors and carry out the following conversions:

(a) 16.0 oz = ? g   (b) 2500 mL = ? L   (c) 99.0 L = ? qt

PROBLEM 1.19

Convert 0.840 qt to milliliters in a single calculation using more than one conversion factor.

PROBLEM 1.20

One international nautical mile is defined as exactly 6076.1155 ft, and a speed of 1 knot is defined as one international nautical mile per hour. What is the speed in meters per second of a boat traveling at a speed of 14.3 knots? (Hint: what conversion factor is needed to convert from feet to meters? From hours to seconds?)

PROBLEM 1.21

Calculate the dosage in milligrams per kilogram body weight for a 135 lb adult who takes two aspirin tablets containing 0.324 g of aspirin each. Calculate the dosage for a 40 lb child who also takes two aspirin tablets.

1.13 Temperature, Heat, and Energy

All chemical reactions are accompanied by a change in **energy**, which is defined in scientific terms as *the capacity to do work or supply heat* (Figure 1.9). Detailed discussion of the various kinds of energy will be included in Chapter 7, but for now we will look at the various units used to describe energy and heat, and how heat energy can be gained or lost by matter.

   Temperature, the measure of the amount of heat energy in an object, is commonly reported either in Fahrenheit (°F) or Celsius (°C) units. The SI unit for reporting temperature, however, is the *kelvin* (K). (Note that we say only "kelvin," not "degrees kelvin".)

   The kelvin and the celsius degree are the same size—both are 1/100 of the interval between the freezing point of water and the boiling point of water at atmospheric pressure.

Energy The capacity to do work or supply heat.

Temperature The measure of the amount of heat energy in an object.

Thus, a change in temperature of 1 °C is equal to a change of 1 K. The only difference between the Kelvin and Celsius temperature scales is that they have different zero points. The Celsius scale assigns a value of 0 °C to the freezing point of water, but the Kelvin scale assigns a value of 0 K to the coldest possible temperature, sometimes called *absolute zero*, which is equal to −273.15 °C. Thus, 0 K = −273.15 °C, and +273.15 K = 0 °C. For example, a warm spring day with a temperature of 25 °C has a Kelvin temperature of 298 K (for most purposes, rounding off to 273 is sufficient):

$$\text{Temperature in K} = \text{Temperature in °C} + 273.15$$

$$\text{Temperature in °C} = \text{Temperature in K} - 273.15$$

For practical applications in medicine and clinical chemistry, the Fahrenheit and Celsius scales are used almost exclusively. The Fahrenheit scale defines the freezing point of water as 32 °F and the boiling point of water as 212 °F, whereas 0 °C and 100 °C are the freezing and boiling points of water on the Celsius scale. Thus, it takes 180 Fahrenheit degrees to cover the same range encompassed by only 100 celsius degrees, and a Celsius degree is therefore exactly 180/100 = 9/5 = 1.8 times as large as a Fahrenheit degree. In other words, a change in temperature of 1.0 °C is equal to a change of 1.8 °F. Figure 1.10 gives a comparison of all three scales.

Converting between the Fahrenheit and Celsius scales is similar to converting between different units of length or volume, but is a bit more complex because two corrections need to be made—one to adjust for the difference in degree size and one to adjust for the different zero points. The degree-size correction is made by using the relationship 1 °C = (9/5) °F and 1 °F = (5/9) °C. The zero-point correction is made by remembering that the freezing point is higher by 32 on the Fahrenheit scale than on the Celsius scale. These corrections are incorporated into the following formulas, which show the conversion methods:

Celsius to Fahrenheit: $\quad °F = \left(\dfrac{9\,°F}{5\,°C} \times °C \right) + 32\,°F$

Fahrenheit to Celsius: $\quad °C = \dfrac{5\,°C}{9\,°F} \times (°F - 32\,°F)$

▲ **Figure 1.9**
The reaction of aluminum with bromine releases energy in the form of heat.
When the reaction is complete, the products undergo no further change.

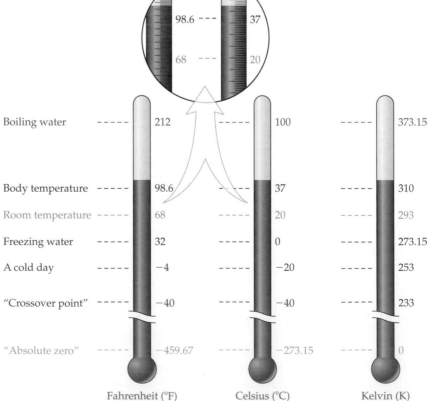

▶ **Figure 1.10**
A comparison of the Fahrenheit, Celsius, and Kelvin temperature scales.
One Fahrenheit degree is 5/9 the size of a kelvin or a celsius degree.

CHEMISTRY IN ACTION

Temperature–Sensitive Materials

Wouldn't it be nice to be able to tell if the baby's formula bottle is too hot without touching it? Or to easily determine if the package of chicken you are buying for dinner has been stored appropriately? Temperature-sensitive materials are already being used in these and other applications. Although these materials have been used previously in many popular "fads," like mood rings or clothes that changed color at different temperatures, more practical applications are emerging.

Most current applications use substances known as thermochromic materials that change color as their temperature increases, and they change from the liquid phase to a semi-crystalline ordered state. These "liquid crystals" can be incorporated into plastics or paints and can be used to monitor the temperature of the products or packages in which they are incorporated. For example, some meat packaging now includes a temperature strip that darkens when the meat is stored above a certain temperature, which makes the meat unsafe to eat. Some beverage containers turn color to indicate when the beverage has reached its optimal temperature for consumption. Hospitals and other medical facilities now routinely use strips that, when

placed under the tongue or applied to the forehead, change color to indicate the patient's body temperature. In the future, we may even see road signs that change color to warn us of dangerous icy road conditions.

See Chemistry in Action Problems 1.98 and 1.99 at the end of the chapter.

Energy is represented in SI units by the unit *joule* (J; pronounced "jool"), but the metric unit *calorie* (cal) is still widely used in medicine. In most of this text we will present energy values in both units of calories and joules. One calorie is the amount of heat necessary to raise the temperature of 1 g of water by 1 °C. A *kilocalorie* (kcal), often called a *large calorie (Cal)* or *food calorie* by nutritionists, equals 1000 cal:

$$1000 \text{ cal} = 1 \text{ kcal} \qquad 1000 \text{ J} = 1 \text{ kJ}$$
$$1 \text{ cal} = 4.184 \text{ J} \qquad 1 \text{ kcal} = 4.184 \text{ kJ}$$

Not all substances have their temperatures raised to the same extent when equal amounts of heat energy are added. One calorie raises the temperature of 1 g of water by 1 °C but raises the temperature of 1 g of iron by 10 °C. The amount of heat needed to raise the temperature of 1 g of a substance by 1 °C is called the **specific heat** of the substance. It is measured in units of $\text{cal}/(\text{g} \cdot {}^\circ\text{C})$.

> **Specific heat** The amount of heat that will raise the temperature of 1 g of a substance by 1 °C.

$$\text{Specific heat} = \frac{\text{calories}}{\text{grams} \times {}^\circ\text{C}}$$

Specific heats vary greatly from one substance to another, as shown in Table 1.10. The specific heat of water, $1.00 \text{ cal}/(\text{g} \cdot {}^\circ\text{C})$ (or 4.184 J/g °C) is higher than that of most other substances, which means that a large transfer of heat is required to change the temperature of a given amount of water by a given number of degrees. One consequence is that the human body, which is about 60% water, is able to withstand changing outside conditions.

Knowing the mass and specific heat of a substance makes it possible to calculate how much heat must be added or removed to accomplish a given temperature change, as shown in Worked Example 1.15.

$$\text{Heat (cal)} = \text{Mass (g)} \times \text{Temperature change } (^\circ\text{C}) \times \text{Specific heat}\left(\frac{\text{cal}}{\text{g} \cdot {}^\circ\text{C}}\right)$$

TABLE 1.10 Specific Heats of Some Common Substances		
Substance	**Specific Heat** [cal/g °C];	[J/g °C]
Ethanol	0.59;	2.5
Gold	0.031;	0.13
Iron	0.106;	0.444
Mercury	0.033;	0.14
Sodium	0.293;	1.23
Water	1.00;	4.18

Worked Example 1.14 Temperature Conversions: Fahrenheit to Celsius

A body temperature above 107 °F can be fatal. What does 107 °F correspond to on the Celsius scale?

ANALYSIS Using the temperature (in °F) and the appropriate temperature conversion equation we can convert from the Fahrenheit scale to the Celsius scale.

BALLPARK ESTIMATE Note in Figure 1.10 that normal body temperature is 98.6 °F, or 37 °C. A temperature of 107 °F is approximately 8 °F above normal; since 1 °C is nearly 2 °F, then 8 °F is about 4 °C. Thus, the 107 °F body temperature is 41 °C.

SOLUTION

STEP 1: **Identify known information.**

STEP 2: **Identify answer and units.**

STEP 3: **Identify conversion factors.** We can convert from °F to °C using this equation.

STEP 4: **Solve.** Substitute the known temperature (in °F) into the equation.

Temperature $= 107\ °F$

Temperature $= ??\ °C$

$$°C = \frac{5\ °C}{9\ °F} \times (°F - 32\ °F)$$

$$°C = \frac{5\ °C}{9\ °F} \times (107\ °F - 32\ °F) = 42\ °C^*$$

(Rounded off from 41.666 667 °C)

BALLPARK CHECK Close to our estimate of 41 °C.

*It is worth noting that the 5/9 conversion factor in the equation is an exact conversion, and so does not impact the number of significant figures in the final answer.

Worked Example 1.15 Specific Heat: Mass, Temperature, and Energy

Taking a bath might use about 95 kg of water. How much energy (in calories and Joules) is needed to heat the water from a cold 15 °C to a warm 40 °C?

ANALYSIS From the amount of water being heated (95 kg) and the amount of the temperature change (40 °C − 15 °C = 25 °C), the total amount of energy needed can be calculated by using specific heat $[1.00\ cal/(g \cdot °C)]$ as a conversion factor.

BALLPARK ESTIMATE The water is being heated 25 °C (from 15 °C to 40 °C), and it therefore takes 25 cal to heat each gram. The tub contains nearly 100,000 g (95 kg is 95,000 g), and so it takes about 25 × 100,000 cal, or 2,500,000 cal, to heat all the water in the tub.

SOLUTION

STEP 1: **Identify known information.**

STEP 2: **Identify answer and units.**

STEP 3: **Identify conversion factors.** The amount of energy (in cal) can be calculated using the specific heat of water (cal/g · °C), and will depend on both the mass of water (in g) to be heated and the total temperature change (in °C). In order for the units in specific heat to cancel correctly, the mass of water must first be converted from kg to g.

STEP 4: **Solve.** Starting with the known information, use the conversion factors to cancel unwanted units.

Mass of water $= 95\ kg$

Temperature change $= 40\ °C - 15\ °C = 25\ °C$

Heat $= ??\ cal$

Specific heat $= \dfrac{1.0\ cal}{g \cdot °C}$

$1\ kg = 1000\ g \rightarrow \dfrac{1000\ g}{1\ kg}$

$$95\ kg \times \frac{1000\ g}{kg} \times \frac{1.00\ cal}{g \cdot °C} \times 25\ °C = 2,400,000\ cal$$

$$= 2.4 \times 10^6\ cal\ (or\ 1.0 \times 10^7\ J)$$

BALLPARK CHECK Close to our estimate of 2.5×10^6 cal.

1.14 Density and Specific Gravity

One further physical quantity that we will take up in this chapter is **density**, which relates the mass of an object to its volume. Density is usually expressed in units of grams per cubic centimeter (g/cm³) for solids and grams per milliliter (g/mL) for liquids. Thus, if we know the density of a substance, we know both the mass of a given volume and the volume of a given mass. The densities of some common materials are listed in Table 1.11.

Density The physical property that relates the mass of an object to its volume; mass per unit volume.

$$\text{Density} = \frac{\text{Mass (g)}}{\text{Volume (mL or cm}^3)}$$

Although most substances contract when cooled and expand when heated, water behaves differently. Water contracts when cooled from 100 °C to 3.98 °C, but below this temperature it begins to *expand* again. The density of liquid water is at its maximum of 1.0000 g/mL at 3.98 °C but decreases to 0.999 87 g/mL at 0 °C. When freezing occurs, the density drops still further to a value of 0.917 g/cm³ for ice at 0 °C. Since a less dense substance will float on top of a more dense fluid, ice and any other substance with a density less than that of water will float in water. Conversely, any substance with a density greater than that of water will sink in water.

Knowing the density of a liquid is useful because it is often easier to measure a liquid's volume rather than its mass. Suppose, for example, that you need 1.50 g of

▲ The Galileo thermometer contains several weighted bulbs which rise or fall as the density of the liquid changes with temperature.

TABLE **1.11** Densities of Some Common Materials at 25 °C			
Substance	**Density***	**Substance**	**Density***
Gases		Solids	
Helium	0.000 194	Ice (0 °C)	0.917
Air	0.001 185	Gold	19.3
		Human fat	0.94
Liquids		Cork	0.22–0.26
Water (3.98 °C)	1.0000	Table sugar	1.59
Urine	1.003–1.030	Balsa wood	0.12
Blood plasma	1.027	Earth	5.54

*Densities are in g/cm³ for solids and g/mL for liquids and gases.

Specific gravity The density of a substance divided by the density of water at the same temperature.

▲ **Figure 1.11**
A hydrometer for measuring specific gravity.
The instrument has a weighted bulb at the end of a calibrated glass tube. The depth to which the hydrometer sinks in a liquid indicates the liquid's specific gravity.

ethanol. Rather than use a dropper to weigh out exactly the right amount, it would be much easier to look up the density of ethanol (0.7893 g/mL at 20 °C) and measure the correct volume (1.90 mL) with a syringe or graduated cylinder. Thus, density acts as a conversion factor between mass (g) and volume (mL).

$$1.50 \; \text{g ethanol} \times \frac{1 \; \text{mL ethanol}}{0.7893 \; \text{g ethanol}} = 1.90 \; \text{mL ethanol}$$

For many purposes, ranging from winemaking to medicine, it is more convenient to use *specific gravity* than density. The **specific gravity** (sp gr) of a substance (usually a liquid) is simply the density of the substance divided by the density of water at the same temperature. Because all units cancel, specific gravity is unitless:

$$\text{Specific gravity} = \frac{\text{Density of substance (g/mL)}}{\text{Density of water at the same temperature (g/mL)}}$$

At typical temperatures, the density of water is very close to 1 g/mL. Thus, the specific gravity of a substance is numerically equal to its density and is used in the same way.

The specific gravity of a liquid can be measured using an instrument called a *hydrometer*, which consists of a weighted bulb on the end of a calibrated glass tube, as shown in Figure 1.11. The depth to which the hydrometer sinks when placed in a fluid indicates the fluid's specific gravity: the lower the bulb sinks, the lower the specific gravity of the fluid.

In medicine, a hydrometer called a *urinometer* is used to indicate the amount of solids dissolved in urine. Although the specific gravity of normal urine is about 1.003–1.030, conditions such as diabetes mellitus or a high fever cause an abnormally high urine specific gravity, indicating either excessive elimination of solids or decreased elimination of water. Abnormally low specific gravity is found in individuals using diuretics—drugs that increase water elimination.

Worked Example 1.16 Density: Mass-to-Volume Conversion

What volume of isopropyl alcohol (rubbing alcohol) would you use if you needed 25.0 g? The density of isopropyl alcohol is 0.7855 g/mL at 20 °C.

ANALYSIS The known information is the mass of isopropyl alcohol needed (25.0 g). The density (0.7855 g/mL) acts as a conversion factor between mass and the unknown volume of isopropyl alcohol.

BALLPARK ESTIMATE Because 1 mL of isopropyl alcohol contains only 0.7885 g of the alcohol, obtaining 1 g of alcohol would require almost 20% more than 1 mL, or about 1.2 mL. Therefore, a volume of about 25 × 1.2 mL = 30 mL is needed to obtain 25 g of alcohol.

SOLUTION

STEP 1: **Identify known information.**

Mass of rubbing alcohol = 25.0 g
Density of rubbing alcohol = 0.7855 g/mL

STEP 2: **Identify answer and units.**

Volume of rubbing alcohol = ?? mL

STEP 3: **Identify conversion factors.** Starting with the mass of isopropyl alcohol (in g), the corresponding volume (in mL) can be calculated using density (g/mL) as the conversion factor.

Density = g/mL → 1/density = mL/g

STEP 4: **Solve.** Starting with the known information, set up the equation with conversion factors so that unwanted units cancel.

$$25.0 \; \text{g alcohol} \times \frac{1 \; \text{mL alcohol}}{0.7855 \; \text{g alcohol}} = 31.8 \; \text{mL alcohol}$$

BALLPARK CHECK Our estimate was 30 mL.

CHEMISTRY IN ACTION

A Measurement Example: Obesity and Body Fat

According to the U.S. Centers for Disease Control and Prevention, the U.S. population is suffering from a fat epidemic. Over the last 25 years, the percentage of adults 20 years or older identified as obese increased from 15% in the late 1970s to nearly 33% in 2008. Even children and adolescents are gaining too much weight: The number of overweight children in all age groups increased by nearly a factor of 3, with the biggest increase seen among teenagers (from 5% to 18.1%). Of particular concern is the fact that 80% of children who were overweight as teenagers were identified as obese at age 25. Obesity increases the risk for many adverse health conditions, including type 2 diabetes and heart disease.

How do we define obesity, however, and how is it measured? Obesity is defined by reference to *body mass index* (BMI), which is equal to a person's mass in kilograms divided by the square of his or her height in meters. BMI can also be calculated by dividing a person's weight in pounds by the square of her or his height in inches multiplied by 703. For instance, someone 5 ft 7 in. (67 inches; 1.70 m) tall weighing 147 lb (66.7 kg) has a BMI of 23:

$$\text{BMI} = \frac{\text{weight (kg)}}{[\text{height (m)}]^2}, \text{ or } \frac{\text{weight (lb)}}{[\text{height (in.)}]^2} \times 703$$

A BMI of 25 or above is considered overweight, and a BMI of 30 or above is obese. By these standards, approximately 61% of the U.S. population is overweight. Health professionals are concerned by the rapid rise in obesity in the United States because of the link between BMI and health problems. Many reports have documented the correlation between health and BMI, including a recent study on more than 1 million adults. The

▲ **A person's percentage body fat can be estimated by measuring the thickness of the fat layer under the skin.**

lowest death risk from any cause, including cancer and heart disease, is associated with a BMI between 22 and 24. Risk increases steadily as BMI increases, more than doubling for a BMI above 29.

An individual's percentage of body fat is most easily measured by the skinfold-thickness method. The skin at several locations on the arm, shoulder, and waist is pinched, and the thickness of the fat layer beneath the skin is measured with calipers. Comparing the measured results to those in a standard table gives an estimation of percentage body fat. As an alternative to skinfold measurement, a more accurate assessment of body fat can be made by underwater immersion. The person's underwater body weight is less than her or his weight on land because water gives the body buoyancy. The higher the percentage of body fat, the more buoyant the person and the greater the difference between land weight and underwater body weight. Checking the observed buoyancy on a standard table then gives an estimation of body fat.

See Chemistry in Action Problems 1.100 and 1.101 at the end of the chapter.

Weight (lb)

Height	110	115	120	125	130	135	140	145	150	155	160	165	170	175	180	185	190	195	200
5'0"	21	22	23	24	25	26	27	28	29	30	31	32	33	34	35	36	37	38	39
5'2"	20	21	22	23	24	25	26	27	27	28	29	30	31	32	33	34	35	36	37
5'4"	19	20	21	21	22	23	24	25	26	27	27	28	29	30	31	32	33	33	34
5'6"	18	19	19	20	21	22	23	23	24	25	26	27	27	28	29	30	31	31	32
5'8"	17	17	18	19	20	21	21	22	23	24	24	25	26	27	27	28	29	30	30
5'10"	16	17	17	18	19	19	20	21	22	22	23	24	24	25	26	27	27	28	29
6'0"	15	16	16	17	18	18	19	20	20	21	22	22	23	24	24	25	26	26	27
6'2"	14	15	15	16	17	17	18	19	19	20	21	21	22	22	23	24	24	25	26
6'4"	13	14	15	15	16	16	17	18	18	19	19	20	21	21	22	23	23	24	24

Body Mass Index (numbers in boxes)

▲ The specific gravity of urine, measured by a urinometer, is used to diagnose conditions such as diabetes.

PROBLEM 1.26
A sample of pumice, a porous volcanic rock, weighs 17.4 grams and has a volume of 27.3 cm³. If this sample is placed in a container of water, will it sink or will it float? Explain.

PROBLEM 1.27
Chloroform, once used as an anesthetic agent, has a density of 1.474 g/mL. What volume would you use if you needed 12.37 g?

PROBLEM 1.28
The sulfuric acid solution in an automobile battery typically has a specific gravity of about 1.27. Is battery acid more dense or less dense than pure water?

SUMMARY: REVISITING THE CHAPTER GOALS

1. What is matter and how is it classified? *Matter* is anything that has mass and occupies volume—that is, anything physically real. Matter can be classified by its physical state as *solid, liquid,* or *gas*. A solid has a definite volume and shape, a liquid has a definite volume but indefinite shape, and a gas has neither a definite volume nor a definite shape. Matter can also be classified by composition as being either *pure* or a *mixture*. Every pure substance is either an *element* or a *chemical compound*. Elements are fundamental substances that cannot be chemically changed into anything simpler. A chemical compound, by contrast, can be broken down by chemical change into simpler substances. Mixtures are composed of two or more pure substances and can be separated into component parts by physical means (*see Problems 40–45, 96, 103*).

2. How are chemical elements represented? Elements are represented by one- or two-letter symbols, such as H for hydrogen, Ca for calcium, Al for aluminum, and so on. Most symbols are the first one or two letters of the element name, but some symbols are derived from Latin names—Na (sodium), for example. All the known elements are commonly organized into a form called the *periodic table*. Most elements are *metals*, 18 are *nonmetals*, and 6 are *metalloids* (*see Problems 29–31, 48–57, 96, 102, 103*).

3. What kinds of properties does matter have? A *property* is any characteristic that can be used to describe or identify something: *physical* properties can be seen or measured without changing the chemical identity of the substance (that is, color, melting point), while *chemical* properties can only be seen or measured when the substance undergoes a *chemical change*, such as a chemical reaction (*see Problems 37–39, 42–44, 47, 97, 102, 103*).

4. What units are used to measure properties, and how can a quantity be converted from one unit to another? A property that can be measured is called a *physical quantity* and is described by both a number and a label, or *unit*. The preferred units are either those of the International System of Units (*SI units*) or the *metric system*. Mass, the amount of matter an object contains, is measured in *kilograms* (kg) or *grams* (g). Length is measured in *meters* (m). Volume is measured in *cubic meters* (m³) in the SI system and in *liters* (L) or *milliliters* (mL) in the metric system. Temperature is measured in *kelvins* (K) in the SI system and in *degrees celsius* (°C) in the metric system. A measurement in one unit can be converted to another unit by multiplying by a *conversion factor* that expresses the exact relationship between the units (*see Problems 58–63, 72–82, 100, 101, 104, 105, 107–109, 121*).

5. How good are the reported measurements? When measuring physical quantities or using them in calculations, it is important to indicate the exactness of the measurement by *rounding off* the final answer using the correct number of *significant figures*. All but one of the significant figures in a number is known with certainty; the final digit is estimated to ±1 (*see Problems 32–35, 64–71, 104, 112*).

6. How are large and small numbers best represented? Measurements of small and large quantities are usually written in *scientific notation* as the product of a number between 1 and 10, times a power of 10. Numbers greater than 10 have a positive exponent, and numbers less than 1 have a negative exponent. For example, $3562 = 3.562 \times 10^3$, and $0.003\ 91 = 3.91 \times 10^{-3}$ (*see Problems 64–71, 75, 82, 108*).

7. What techniques are used to solve problems? Problems are best solved by applying the *factor-label method*, in which units can be multiplied and divided just as numbers can. The idea is to set up an equation so that all unwanted units cancel, leaving only the desired units. Usually it is best to start by identifying the known and needed information, then decide how to convert the known information to the answer, and finally check to make sure the answer is reasonable both chemically and physically (*see Problems 76–82, 101, 106, 107, 109, 110–112, 114, 115, 118–123*).

8. What are temperature, specific heat, density, and specific gravity? *Temperature* is a measure of how hot or cold an object is. The *specific heat* of a substance is the amount of heat necessary to raise the temperature of 1 g of the substance by 1 °C (1 cal/g °C or 4.184 J/g °C). Water has an unusually high specific heat, which helps our bodies to maintain an even temperature. *Density*, the physical property that relates mass to volume, is expressed in units of grams per milliliter (g/mL) for a liquid or grams per cubic centimeter (g/cm³) for a solid. The *specific gravity* of a liquid is the density of the liquid divided by the density of water at the same temperature. Because the density of water is approximately 1 g/mL, specific gravity and density have the same numerical value (*see Problems 32, 36, 42, 43, 83–89, 90–95, 98, 99, 106, 109, 113, 118–120, 122, 123*).

KEY WORDS

Change of state, *p. 6*

Chemical change, *p. 4*

Chemical compound, *p. 7*

Chemical formula, *p. 10*

Chemical reaction, *p. 7*

Chemistry, *p. 4*

Conversion factor, *p. 26*

Density, *p. 33*

Element, *p. 6*

Energy, *p. 29*

Factor-label method, *p. 26*

Gas, *p. 5*

Heterogeneous mixture, *p. 6*

Homogeneous mixture, *p. 6*

Liquid, *p. 5*

Mass, *p. 17*

Matter, *p. 4*

Metal, *p. 11*

Metalloid, *p. 11*

Mixture, *p. 6*

Nonmetal, *p. 11*

Periodic table, *p. 11*

Physical change, *p. 4*

Physical quantity, *p. 14*

Product, *p. 7*

Property, *p. 4*

Pure substance, *p. 6*

Reactant, *p. 7*

Rounding off, *p. 24*

Scientific Method, *p. 4*

Scientific notation, *p. 21*

SI units, *p. 15*

Significant figures, *p. 20*

Solid, *p. 5*

Specific gravity, *p. 34*

Specific heat, *p. 31*

State of matter, *p. 6*

Temperature, *p. 29*

Unit, *p. 14*

Weight, *p. 17*

UNDERSTANDING KEY CONCEPTS

The problems in this section are intended as a bridge between the Chapter Summary and the Additional Problems that follow. Primarily visual in nature, they are designed to help you test your grasp of the chapter's most important principles before attempting to solve quantitative problems. Answers to all Key Concept problems are at the end of the book following the appendixes.

1.29 The six elements in blue at the far right of the periodic table are gases at room temperature. The red elements in the middle of the table are the so-called coinage metals. Identify each of these elements using the periodic table inside the front cover of this book.

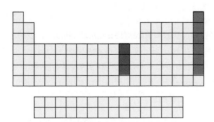

1.30 Identify the three elements indicated on the following periodic table and tell which is a metal, which is a nonmetal, and which is a metalloid.

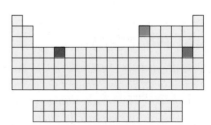

1.31 The radioactive element indicated on the following periodic table is used in smoke detectors. Identify it, and tell whether it is a metal, a nonmetal, or a metalloid.

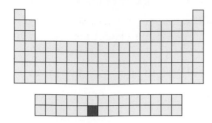

1.32 (a) What is the specific gravity of the following solution?

(b) How many significant figures does your answer have?

(c) Is the solution more dense or less dense than water?

1.33 Assume that you have two graduated cylinders, one with a capacity of 5 mL (a) and the other with a capacity of 50 mL (b). Draw a line in each showing how much liquid you would add if you needed to measure 2.64 mL of water. Which cylinder do you think is more precise? Explain.

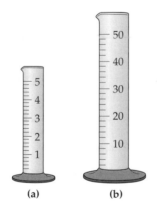

1.34 State the length of the pencil depicted in the accompanying figure in both inches and centimeters using appropriate numbers of significant figures.

1.35 Assume that you are delivering a solution sample from a pipette. Figures (a) and (b) show the volume level before and after dispensing the sample, respectively. State the liquid level (in mL) before and after dispensing the sample, and calculate the volume of the sample.

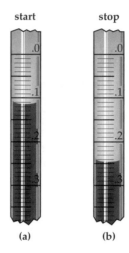

1.36 Assume that identical hydrometers are placed in ethanol (sp gr 0.7893) and in chloroform (sp gr 1.4832). In which liquid will the hydrometer float higher? Explain.

ADDITIONAL PROBLEMS

These exercises are divided into sections by topic. Each section begins with review and conceptual questions, followed by numerical problems of varying levels of difficulty. Many of the problems dealing with more difficult concepts or skills are presented in pairs, with each even-numbered problem followed by an odd-numbered one requiring similar skills. The final section consists of unpaired General Questions and Problems that draw on various parts of the chapter and, in future chapters, may even require the use of concepts from previous chapters. Answers to all even-numbered problems are given at the end of the book following the appendixes.

CHEMISTRY AND THE PROPERTIES OF MATTER

1.37 What is the difference between a physical change and a chemical change?

1.38 Which of the following is a physical change and which is a chemical change?

(a) Boiling water

(b) Decomposing water by passing an electric current through it

(c) Exploding of potassium metal when placed in water

(d) Breaking of glass

1.39 Which of the following is a physical change and which is a chemical change?

(a) Making lemonade (lemons + water + sugar)

(b) Frying eggs

(c) Burning a candle

(d) Whipping cream

(e) Leaves changing color

STATES AND CLASSIFICATION OF MATTER

1.40 Name and describe the three states of matter.

1.41 Name two changes of state, and describe what causes each to occur.

1.42 Sulfur dioxide is a compound produced when sulfur burns in air. It has a melting point of $-72.7\ °C$ and a boiling point of $-10\ °C$. In what state does it exist at room temperature (298 K)? (refer to Figure 1.10).

1.43 Butane (C_4H_8) is an easily compressible gas used in cigarette lighters. It has a melting point of $-138.4\ °C$ and a boiling point of $-0.5\ °C$. Would you expect a butane lighter to work in winter when the temperature outdoors is 25 °F? Why or why not? (refer to Figure 1.10).

1.44 Classify each of the following as a mixture or a pure substance:

(a) Pea soup   (b) Seawater

(c) The contents of a propane tank

(d) Urine   (e) Lead

(f) A multivitamin tablet

1.45 Which of these terms, (i) mixture, (ii) solid, (iii) liquid, (iv) gas, (v) chemical element, (vi) chemical compound, applies to the following substances at room temperature?

(a) Gasoline   (b) Iodine

(c) Water   (d) Air

(e) Blood   (f) Sodium bicarbonate

(g) Gaseous ammonia   (h) Silicon

1.46 Hydrogen peroxide, often used in solutions to cleanse cuts and scrapes, breaks down to yield water and oxygen:

$$\text{Hydrogen peroxide} \longrightarrow \text{Water} + \text{Oxygen}$$

(a) Identify the reactants and products.

(b) Which of the substances are chemical compounds, and which are elements?

1.47 When sodium metal is placed in water, the following change occurs:

$$\text{Sodium} + \text{Water} \longrightarrow \text{Hydrogen} + \text{Sodium hydroxide}$$

(a) Identify the reactants and products.

(b) Which of the substances are elements, and which are chemical compounds?

ELEMENTS AND THEIR SYMBOLS

1.48 Describe the general properties of metals, nonmetals, and metalloids.

1.49 What is the most abundant element in the earth's crust? In the human body? List the name and symbol for each.

1.50 What are the symbols for the following elements?

(a) Gadolinium (used in color TV screens)

(b) Germanium (used in semiconductors)

(c) Technetium (used in biomedical imaging)

(d) Arsenic (used in pesticides)

(e) Cadmium (used in rechargeable batteries)

1.51 Supply the missing names or symbols for the elements in the spaces provided:

(a) N _____   (b) K _____

(c) Cl _____   (d) _____ Calcium

(e) _____ Phosphorus   (f) _____ Manganese

1.52 Correct the following statements.

(a) The symbol for bromine is BR.

(b) The symbol for manganese is Mg.

(c) The symbol for carbon is Ca.

(d) The symbol for potassium is Po.

1.53 Correct the following statements.

(a) Carbon dioxide has the formula CO2.

(b) Carbon dioxide has the formula Co_2.

(c) Table salt, NaCl, is composed of nitrogen and chlorine.

1.54 The amino acid glycine has the formula $C_2H_5NO_2$. Which elements are present in glycine? What is the total number of atoms represented by the formula?

1.55 Glucose, a form of sugar, has the formula $C_6H_{12}O_6$. Which elements are included in this compound, and how many atoms of each are present?

1.56 Write the formula for ibuprofen: 13 carbons, 18 hydrogens, and 2 oxygens.

1.57 Given the physical properties of the following elements classify each one as a metal, nonmetal, or metalloid:

(a) a hard, shiny, very dense solid that conducts electricity

(b) a brittle, gray solid that conducts electricity poorly

(c) a brown, crystalline solid that does not conduct electricity

(d) a colorless, odorless gas

PHYSICAL QUANTITIES: DEFINITIONS AND UNITS

1.58 What is the difference between a physical quantity and a number?

1.59 What are the units used in the SI system to measure mass, volume, length, and temperature? In the metric system?

1.60 Give the full name of the following units:

(a) cc   (b) dm   (c) mm

(d) nL   (e) mg   (f) m^3

1.61 Write the symbol for the following units:

(a) nanogram   (b) centimeter

(c) microliter   (d) micrometer

(e) milligram

1.62 How many picograms are in 1 mg? In 35 ng?

1.63 How many microliters are in 1 L? In 20 mL?

SCIENTIFIC NOTATION AND SIGNIFICANT FIGURES

1.64 Express the following numbers in scientific notation with the correct number of significant figures:

(a) 9457   (b) 0.000 07

(c) 20,000,000,000 (four significant figures)

(d) 0.012 345   (e) 652.38

1.65 Convert the following numbers from scientific notation to standard notation:

(a) 5.28×10^3 (b) 8.205×10^{-2}

(c) 1.84×10^{-5} (d) 6.37×10^4

1.66 How many significant figures does each of the following numbers have?

(a) 237,401   (b) 0.300   (c) 3.01

(d) 244.4   (e) 50,000   (f) 660

1.67 How many significant figures are there in each of the following quantities?

(a) Distance from New York City to Wellington, New Zealand, 14,397 km

(b) Average body temperature of a crocodile, 25.6 °C

(c) Melting point of gold, 1064 °C

(d) Diameter of an influenza virus, 0.000 01 mm

(e) Radius of a phosphorus atom, 0.110 nm

1.68 The diameter of the earth at the equator is 7926.381 mi.

(a) Round off the earth's diameter to four significant figures, to two significant figures, and to six significant figures.

(b) Express the earth's diameter in scientific notation.

1.69 Round off each of the numbers in Problem 1.67 to two significant figures, and express them in scientific notation.

1.70 Carry out the following calculations, express each answer to the correct number of significant figures, and include units in the answers.

(a) 9.02 g + 3.1 g   (b) 88.80 cm + 7.391 cm

(c) 362 mL − 99.5 mL

(d) 12.4 mg + 6.378 mg + 2.089 mg

1.71 Carry out the following calculations, express the answers to the correct numbers of significant figures, and include units in the answers.

(a) $5280 \dfrac{\text{ft}}{\text{mi}} \times 6.2$ mi

(b) 4.5 m × 3.25 m

(c) $2.50 \text{ g} \div 8.3 \dfrac{\text{g}}{\text{cm}^3}$

(d) 4.70 cm × 6.8 cm × 2.54 cm

UNIT CONVERSIONS AND PROBLEM SOLVING

1.72 Carry out the following conversions:

(a) 3.614 mg to centigrams

(b) 12.0 kL to megaliters

(c) 14.4 μm to millimeters

(d) 6.03×10^{-6} cg to nanograms

(e) 174.5 mL to deciliters

(f) 1.5×10^{-2} km to centimeters

1.73 Carry out the following conversions. Consult Tables 1.7–1.9 as needed.

(a) 56.4 mi to kilometers and to megameters

(b) 2.0 L to quarts and to fluid ounces

(c) 7 ft 2.0 in. to centimeters and to meters

(d) 1.35 lb to kilograms and to decigrams

1.74 Express the following quantities in more convenient units by using SI unit prefixes:

(a) 9.78×10^4 g   (b) 1.33×10^{-4} L

(c) 0.000 000 000 46 g   (d) 2.99×10^8 cm

1.75 Fill in the blanks to complete the equivalencies either with appropriate units prefixes or with the appropriate scientific notation. The first blank is filled in as an example.

(a) 125 km = 1.25×10^5 m

(b) 6.285×10^3 mg = _____?_____ kg

(c) 47.35 dL = 4.735 × _____?_____ mL

(d) 67.4 cm = 6.7×10^{-4} _____?_____

1.76 The speed limit in Canada is 100 km/h.

(a) How many miles per hour is this?

(b) How many feet per second?

1.77 The muzzle velocity of a projectile fired from a 9 mm handgun is 1200 ft/s.

(a) How many miles per hour is this?

(b) How many meters per second?

1.78 The diameter of a red blood cell is 6×10^{-6} m.

    (a) How many centimeters is this?

    (b) How many red blood cells are needed to make a line 1 cm long? 1 in. long?

1.79 The Willis Tower in Chicago has an approximate floor area of 418,000 m^2. How many square feet of floor space is this?

1.80 A normal value for blood cholesterol is 200 mg/dL of blood. If a normal adult has a total blood volume of 5 L, how much total cholesterol is present?

1.81 The recommended daily dose of calcium for an 18-year-old male is 1200 mg. If 1.0 cup of whole milk contains 290 mg of calcium and milk is his only calcium source, how much milk should an 18-year-old male drink each day?

1.82 The white blood cell concentration in normal blood is approximately 12,000 cells/mm^3 of blood. How many white blood cells does a normal adult with 5 L of blood have? Express the answer in scientific notation.

ENERGY, HEAT, AND TEMPERATURE

1.83 The boiling point of liquid nitrogen, used in the removal of warts and in other surgical applications, is -195.8 °C. What is this temperature in kelvins and in degrees Fahrenheit? (3.74 J/g °C)

1.84 Diethyl ether, a substance once used as a general anesthetic, has a specific heat of 0.895 cal/(g °C). How many calories and how many kilocalories of heat are needed to raise the temperature of 30.0 g of diethyl ether from 10.0 °C to 30.0 °C? How many Joules and kiloJoules?

1.85 Aluminum has a specific heat of 0.215 cal/(g °C). When 25.7 cal (108.5 J) of heat is added to 18.4 g of aluminum at 20.0°, what is the final temperature of the aluminum?

1.86 Calculate the specific heat of copper if it takes 23 cal (96 J) to heat a 5.0 g sample from 25 °C to 75 °C.

1.87 The specific heat of fat is 0.45 cal/(g·°C) (1.9 J/g °C) and the density of fat is 0.94 g/cm^3. How much energy (in calories and joules) is needed to heat 10 cm^3 of fat from room temperature (25 °C) to its melting point (35 °C)?

1.88 A 150 g sample of mercury and a 150 g sample of iron are at an initial temperature of 25.0 °C. If 250 cal (1050 J) of heat is applied to each sample, what is the final temperature of each? (See Table 1.10.)

1.89 When 100 cal (418 J) of heat is applied to a 125 g sample, the temperature increases by 28 °C. Calculate the specific heat of the sample and compare your answer to the values in Table 1.10. What is the identity of the sample?

DENSITY AND SPECIFIC GRAVITY

1.90 Aspirin has a density of 1.40 g/cm^3. What is the volume in cubic centimeters of a tablet weighing 250 mg?

1.91 Gaseous hydrogen has a density of 0.0899 g/L at 0 °C. How many liters would you need if you wanted 1.0078 g of hydrogen?

1.92 What is the density of lead (in g/cm^3) if a rectangular bar measuring 0.500 cm in height, 1.55 cm in width, and 25.00 cm in length has a mass of 220.9 g?

1.93 What is the density of lithium metal (in g/cm^3) if a cube measuring 0.82 cm $\times$ 1.45 cm $\times$ 1.25 cm has a mass of 0.794 g?

1.94 Ethanol produced by fermentation has a specific gravity of 0.787 at 25 °C. What is the volume of 125 g of ethanol at this temperature? (The density of water at 25 °C is 0.997 g/mL.)

1.95 Ethylene glycol, commonly used as automobile antifreeze, has a specific gravity of 1.1088 at room temperature (25 °C). What is the mass of 1.00 L of ethylene glycol at this temperature?

CHEMISTRY IN ACTION

1.96 The active ingredient in aspirin, acetylsalicylic acid (ASA), has the formula $C_9H_8O_4$ and melts at 140 °C. Identify the elements and how many atoms of each are present in ASA. Is it a solid or a liquid at room temperature? [*Aspirin—A Case Study, p. 8*]

1.97 Calomel (Hg_2Cl_2) is not toxic but methyl mercury chloride (CH_3HgCl) is highly toxic. What physical property explains this difference in toxicity? [*Mercury and Mercury Poisoning, p. 15*]

1.98 A thermochromic plastic chip included in a shipping container for beef undergoes an irreversible color change if the storage temperature exceeds 28 °F. What is this temperature on the Celsius and Kelvin scales? [*Temperature-Sensitive Materials, p. 31*]

1.99 A temperature-sensitive bath toy undergoes several color changes in the temperature range from 37 °C to 47 °C. What is the corresponding temperature range on the Fahrenheit scale? [*Temperature-Sensitive Materials, p. 31*]

1.100 Calculate the BMI for an individual who is

    (a) 5 ft 1 in. tall and weighs 155 lb

    (b) 5 ft 11 in. tall and weighs 170 lb

    (c) 6 ft 3 in. tall and weighs 195 lb

    Which of these individuals is likely to have increased health risks? [*A Measurement Example: Obesity and Body Fat, p. 35*]

1.101 Liposuction is a technique for removing fat deposits from various areas of the body. How many liters of fat would have to be removed to result in a 5.0 lb weight loss? The density of human fat is 0.94 g/mL. [*A Measurement Example: Obesity and Body Fat, p. 35*]

GENERAL QUESTIONS AND PROBLEMS

1.102 The most recently discovered element is number 117, Ununseptium. Based on its location in the periodic table, classify it as a metal, nonmetal, or metalloid and discuss the physical properties (physical state, conductivity, etc.) you would expect it to exhibit.

1.103 A white solid with a melting point of 730 °C is melted. When electricity is passed through the resultant liquid, a brown gas and a molten metal are produced. Neither the metal nor the gas can be broken down into anything simpler by chemical means. Classify each—the white solid, the molten metal, and the brown gas—as a mixture, a compound, or an element.

1.104 Refer to the pencil in Problem 1.34. Using the equivalent values in Table 1.8 as conversion factors, convert the length measured in inches to centimeters. Compare the calculated length in centimeters to the length in centimeters measured using the metric ruler. How do the two values compare? Explain any differences.

1.105 Gemstones are weighed in carats, where 1 carat = 200 mg exactly. What is the mass in grams of the Hope diamond, the world's largest blue diamond, at 44.4 carats?

1.106 The relationship between the nutritional unit for energy and the metric unit is 1 Calorie = 1 kcal.

(a) One donut contains 350 Calories. Convert this to calories and joules.

(b) If the energy in one donut was used to heat 35.5 kg of water, calculate the increase in temperature of the water (in °C).

1.107 Drug dosages are typically prescribed in units of milligrams per kilogram of body weight. A new drug has a recommended dosage of 9 mg/kg.

(a) How many mgs would a 130 lb woman have to take to obtain this dosage?

(b) How many 125 mg tablets should a 40 lb child take to receive the recommended dosage?

1.108 A clinical report gave the following data from a blood analysis: iron, 39 mg/dL; calcium, 8.3 mg/dL; cholesterol, 224 mg/dL. Express each of these quantities in grams per deciliter, writing the answers in scientific notation.

1.109 The Spirit of America Goodyear blimp has a volume of 2.027×10^5 ft^3.

(a) Convert this volume to L.

(b) When in operation it is filled with helium gas. If the density of helium at room temperature is 0.179 g/L, calculate the mass of helium in the blimp.

(c) What is the mass of air occupying the same volume? The density of air at room temperature is 1.20 g/L.

1.110 Approximately 75 mL of blood is pumped by a normal human heart at each beat. Assuming an average pulse of 72 beats per minute, how many milliliters of blood are pumped in one day?

1.111 A doctor has ordered that a patient be given 15 g of glucose, which is available in a concentration of 50.00 g glucose/1000.0 mL of solution. What volume of solution should be given to the patient?

1.112 Reconsider the volume of the sample dispensed by pipette in Problem 1.35. Assuming that the solution in the pipette has a density of 0.963 g/mL, calculate the mass of solution dispensed in the problem to the correct number of significant figures.

1.113 Today, thermometers containing mercury are used less frequently than in the past because of concerns regarding the toxicity of mercury and because of its relatively high melting point (−39 °C). This means that mercury thermometers cannot be used in very cold environments because the mercury is a solid under such conditions. Alcohol thermometers, however, can be used over a temperature range from −115 °C (the melting point of alcohol) to 78.5 °C (the boiling point of alcohol).

(a) What is the effective temperature range of the alcohol thermometer in °F?

(b) The densities of alcohol and mercury are 0.79 g/mL and 13.6 g/mL, respectively. If the volume of liquid in a typical laboratory thermometer is 1.0 mL, what mass of alcohol is contained in the thermometer? What mass of mercury?

1.114 In a typical person, the level of blood glucose (also known as blood sugar) is about 85 mg/100 mL of blood. If an average body contains about 11 pints of blood, how many grams and how many pounds of glucose are present in the blood?

1.115 A patient is receiving 3000 mL/day of a solution that contains 5 g of dextrose (glucose) per 100 mL of solution. If glucose provides 4 kcal/g of energy, how many kilocalories per day is the patient receiving from the glucose?

1.116 A rough guide to fluid requirements based on body weight is 100 mL/kg for the first 10 kg of body weight, 50 mL/kg for the next 10 kg, and 20 mL/kg for weight over 20 kg. What volume of fluid per day is needed by a 55 kg woman? Give the answer with two significant figures.

1.117 Chloral hydrate, a sedative and sleep-inducing drug, is available as a solution labeled 10.0 gr/fluidram. What volume in milliliters should be administered to a patient who is meant to receive 7.5 gr per dose? (1 gr = 64.8 mg ; 1 fluidram = 3.72 mL)

1.118 When 1.0 tablespoon of butter is burned or used by our body, it releases 100 kcal (100 food Calories or 418. 4 kJ) of energy. If we could use all the energy provided, how many tablespoons of butter would have to be burned to raise the temperature of 3.00 L of water from 18.0 °C to 90.0 °C?

1.119   An archeologist finds a 1.62 kg goblet that she believes to be made of pure gold. When 1350 cal (5650 J) of heat is added to the goblet, its temperature increases by 7.8 °C. Calculate the specific heat of the goblet. Is it made of gold? Explain.

1.120   In another test, the archeologist in Problem 1.119 determines that the volume of the goblet is 205 mL. Calculate the density of the goblet and compare it with the density of gold (19.3 g/mL), lead (11.4 g/mL), and iron (7.86 g/mL). What is the goblet probably made of?

1.121   Sulfuric acid (H_2SO_4, density $= 1.83$ g/mL) is produced in larger amounts than any other chemical: 2.01×10^{11} lb worldwide in 2004. What is the volume of this amount in liters?

1.122   Imagine that you place a piece of cork measuring 1.30 cm $\times$ 5.50 cm $\times$ 3.00 cm in a pan of water and that on top of the cork you place a small cube of lead measuring 1.15 cm on each edge. The density of cork is 0.235 g/cm^3 and the density of lead is 11.35 g/cm^3. Will the combination of cork plus lead float or sink?

1.123   At a certain point, the Celsius and Fahrenheit scales "cross," and at this point the numerical value of the Celsius temperature is the same as the numerical value of the Fahrenheit temperature. At what temperature does this crossover occur?

Atoms and the Periodic Table

CONTENTS

◄ These basaltic columns at the Devil's Post-pile National Monument in northern California are one example of repeating patterns that can be found in nature.

1. **What is the modern theory of atomic structure?**
   THE GOAL: Be able to explain the major assumptions of atomic theory.

2. **How do atoms of different elements differ?**
   THE GOAL: Be able to explain the composition of different atoms according to the number of protons, neutrons, and electrons they contain.

3. **What are isotopes, and what is atomic weight?**
   THE GOAL: Be able to explain what isotopes are and how they affect an element's atomic weight.

4. **How is the periodic table arranged?**
   THE GOAL: Be able to describe how elements are arranged in the periodic table, name the subdivisions of the periodic table, and relate the position of an element in the periodic table to its electronic structure.

5. **How are electrons arranged in atoms?**
   THE GOAL: Be able to explain how electrons are distributed in shells and subshells around the nucleus of an atom, how valence electrons can be represented as electron-dot symbols, and how the electron configurations can help explain the chemical properties of the elements.

Chemistry must be studied on two levels. In the previous chapter we dealt with chemistry on the large-scale, or *macroscopic*, level, looking at the properties and transformations of matter that we can see and measure. Now we are ready to look at the sub-microscopic, or atomic level, studying the behavior and properties of individual atoms. Although scientists have long been convinced of their existence, only within the past 20 years have powerful new instruments made it possible to see individual atoms. In this chapter, we will look at modern atomic theory and how the structure of atoms influences macroscopic properties.

2.1 Atomic Theory

Take a piece of aluminum foil, and cut it in two. Then, take one of the pieces and cut *it* in two, and so on. Assuming that you have extremely small scissors and extraordinary dexterity, how long can you keep dividing the foil? Is there a limit, or is matter infinitely divisible into ever smaller and smaller pieces? Historically, this argument can be traced as far back as the ancient Greek philosophers. Aristotle believed that matter could be divided infinitely, while Democritus argued (correctly) that there is a limit. The smallest and simplest bit that aluminum (or any other element) can be divided and still be identifiable as aluminum is called an **atom**, a word derived from the Greek *atomos*, meaning "indivisible."

Atom The smallest and simplest particle of an element.

Chemistry is founded on four fundamental assumptions about atoms and matter, which together make up modern **atomic theory**:

Atomic theory A set of assumptions proposed by the English scientist John Dalton to explain the chemical behavior of matter.

- All matter is composed of atoms.
- The atoms of a given element differ from the atoms of all other elements.
- Chemical compounds consist of atoms combined in specific ratios. That is, only whole atoms can combine—one A atom with one B atom, or one A atom with two B atoms, and so on. The enormous diversity in the substances we see around us is based on the vast number of ways that atoms can combine with one another.
- Chemical reactions change only the way that atoms are combined in compounds. The atoms themselves are unchanged.

Atoms are extremely small, ranging from about 7.4×10^{-11} m in diameter for a hydrogen atom to 5.24×10^{-10} m for a cesium atom. In mass, atoms vary from 1.67×10^{-24} g for hydrogen to 3.95×10^{-22} g for uranium, one of the heaviest naturally occurring atoms. It is difficult to appreciate just how small atoms are, although it might help if you realize that a fine pencil line is about 3 million atoms across and that even the smallest speck of dust contains about 10^{16} atoms. Our current understanding

▶▶▶ We will further explore the topics of chemical compounds in Chapters 3 and 4, and chemical reactions in Chapters 5 and 6.

TABLE **2.1** A Comparison of Subatomic Particles				
		Mass		
Name	Symbol	(Grams)	(amu)	Charge (Charge Units)
Proton	p	$1.672\,622 \times 10^{-24}$	$1.007\,276$	$+1$
Neutron	n	$1.674\,927 \times 10^{-24}$	$1.008\,665$	0
Electron	e^-	$9.109\,328 \times 10^{-28}$	$5.485\,799 \times 10^{-4}$	-1

Subatomic particles Three kinds of fundamental particles from which atoms are made: protons, neutrons, and electrons.

Proton A positively charged subatomic particle.

Neutron An electrically neutral subatomic particle.

Electron A negatively charged subatomic particle.

Atomic mass unit (amu) A convenient unit for describing the mass of an atom; 1 amu = $\frac{1}{12}$ the mass of a carbon-12 atom.

▲ The relative size of a nucleus in an atom is the same as that of a pea in the middle of this stadium.

Nucleus The dense, central core of an atom that contains protons and neutrons.

▶ **Figure 2.1**

The structure of an atom.
Protons and neutrons are packed together in the nucleus, whereas electrons move about in the large surrounding volume. Virtually all the mass of an atom is concentrated in the nucleus.

of atomic structure is the result of many experiments performed in the late 1800s and early 1900s (see Chemistry in Action on p. 48).

Atoms are composed of tiny **subatomic particles** called *protons, neutrons,* and *electrons.* A **proton** has a mass of $1.672\,622 \times 10^{-24}$ g and carries a positive ($+$) electrical charge; a **neutron** has a mass similar to that of a proton ($1.674\,927 \times 10^{-24}$ g) but is electrically neutral; and an **electron** has a mass that is only $1/1836$ that of a proton ($9.109\,328 \times 10^{-28}$ g) and carries a negative ($-$) electrical charge. In fact, electrons are so much lighter than protons and neutrons that their mass is usually ignored. Table 2.1 compares the properties of the three fundamental subatomic particles.

The masses of atoms and their constituent subatomic particles are so small when measured in grams that it is more convenient to express them on a *relative* mass scale. That is, one atom is assigned a mass, and all others are measured relative to it. The process is like deciding that a golf ball (46.0 g) will be assigned a mass of 1. A baseball (149 g), which is $149/46.0 = 3.24$ times heavier than a golf ball, would then have a mass of about 3.24; a volleyball (270 g) would have a mass of $270/46.0 = 5.87$; and so on.

The basis for the relative atomic mass scale is an atom of carbon that contains 6 protons and 6 neutrons. Such an atom is assigned a mass of exactly 12 **atomic mass units** (**amu**; also called a *dalton* in honor of the English scientist John Dalton, who proposed most of atomic theory as we know it), where 1 amu = $1.660\,539 \times 10^{-24}$ g. Thus, for all practical purposes, both a proton and a neutron have a mass of 1 amu (Table 2.1). Hydrogen atoms are only about $\frac{1}{12}$th as heavy as carbon atoms and have a mass close to 1 amu, magnesium atoms are about twice as heavy as carbon atoms and have a mass close to 24 amu, and so forth.

Subatomic particles are not distributed at random throughout an atom. Rather, the protons and neutrons are packed closely together in a dense core called the **nucleus**. Surrounding the nucleus, the electrons move about rapidly through a large, mostly empty volume of space (Figure 2.1). Measurements show that the diameter of a nucleus is only about 10^{-15} m, whereas that of the atom itself is about 10^{-10} m. For comparison, if an atom were the size of a large domed stadium, the nucleus would be approximately the size of a small pea in the center of the playing field.

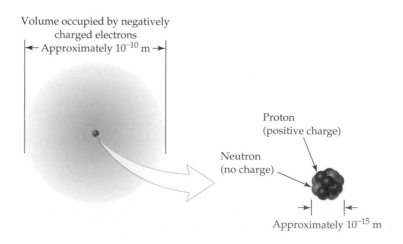

Volume occupied by negatively charged electrons
← Approximately 10^{-10} m →

Proton (positive charge)

Neutron (no charge)

← Approximately 10^{-15} m →

The structure of the atom is determined by an interplay of different attractive and repulsive forces. Because unlike charges attract one another, the negatively charged electrons are held near the positively charged nucleus. But because like charges repel one another, the electrons also try to get as far away from one another as possible, accounting for the relatively large volume they occupy. The positively charged protons in the nucleus also repel one another, but are nevertheless held together by a unique attraction called the *nuclear strong force*, which we will discuss further in Chapter 11.

| Electrons repel one another | Protons repel one another | Protons and electrons attract one another |

Worked Example 2.1 Atomic Mass Units: Gram-to-Atom Conversions

How many atoms are in a small piece of aluminum foil with a mass of 0.100 g? The mass of an atom of aluminum is 27.0 amu.

ANALYSIS We know the sample mass in grams and the mass of one atom in atomic mass units. To find the number of atoms in the sample, two conversions are needed, the first between grams and atomic mass units and the second between atomic mass units and the number of atoms. The conversion factor between atomic mass units and grams is $1 \text{ amu} = 1.660\ 539 \times 10^{-24}$ g.

BALLPARK ESTIMATE An atom of aluminum has a mass of 27.0 amu; since $1 \text{ amu} \sim 10^{-24}$ g, the mass of a single aluminum atom is very small ($\approx 10^{-23}$ g). A very *large* number of atoms, therefore, (10^{22} ?) is needed to obtain a mass of 0.100 g.

SOLUTION

STEP 1: Identify known information.

Mass of aluminum foil $= 0.100$ g

1 Al atom $= 27.0$ amu

STEP 2: Identify unknown answer and units.

Number of Al atoms $= ?$

STEP 3: Identify needed conversion factors. Knowing the mass of foil (in g) and the mass of individual atoms (in amu) we need to convert from atoms/amu to atoms/g.

$1 \text{ amu} = 1.660\ 539 \times 10^{-24}$ g

$$\rightarrow \frac{1 \text{ amu}}{1.660\ 539 \times 10^{-24} \text{ g}}$$

STEP 4: Solve. Set up an equation using known information and conversion factors so that unwanted units cancel.

$$(0.100 \text{ g})\left(\frac{1 \text{ amu}}{1.660\ 539 \times 10^{-24} \text{ g}}\right)\left(\frac{1 \text{ Al atom}}{27.0 \text{ amu}}\right)$$

$$= 2.23 \times 10^{21} \text{ Al atoms}$$

BALLPARK CHECK Our estimate was 10^{22}, which is within a factor of 10.

PROBLEM 2.1

What is the mass in grams of 150×10^{12} iron atoms, each having a mass of 56 amu?

PROBLEM 2.2

How many atoms are in each of the following?

(a) 1.0 g of hydrogen atoms, each of mass 1.0 amu

(b) 12.0 g of carbon atoms, each of mass 12.0 amu

(c) 23.0 g of sodium atoms, each of mass 23.0 amu

PROBLEM 2.3

What pattern do you see in your answers to Problem 2.2? (We will return to this very important pattern in Chapter 6.)

PROBLEM 2.4

The atoms in the gold foil used in Rutherford's experiments have an estimated radius of 1.44×10^{-10} m (see Chemistry in Action on p. 48). If we assume that the radius of the nucleus of a gold atom is 1.5×10^{-15} m, what fraction of the volume of the atom is occupied by the nucleus? (Volume $= 4/3 \pi r^3$)

CHEMISTRY IN ACTION

Are Atoms Real?

Chemistry rests on the premise that matter is composed of the tiny particles we call atoms. Every chemical reaction and every physical law that governs the behavior of matter is explained by chemists in terms of atomic theory. But how do we know that atoms are real and not just an imaginary concept? And how do we know the structure of the atom? The development of our understanding of atomic structure is another example of the scientific method at work.

Dalton's atomic theory was originally published in 1808, but many prominent scientists dismissed it. Over the next century, however, several unrelated experiments provided insight into the nature of matter and the structure of the atom. Nineteenth-century investigations into electricity, for example, demonstrated that matter was composed of charged particles—rubbing a glass rod with a silk cloth would generate "static electricity," the same phenomenon that shocks you when you walk across a carpet and then touch a metal surface. It was also known that passing electricity through certain substances, such as water, decomposed the compounds into their constituent elements (hydrogen and oxygen, in the case of water). Several hypotheses were proposed to explain the nature and origin of these charged particles, but our current understanding of atomic structure developed incrementally from several key experiments.

Experiments performed in 1897 by J. J. Thomson demonstrated that matter contained negatively charged particles that were 1000 times lighter than H^+, the lightest positively charged particles found in aqueous solution, and that the mass-to-charge ratio of these particles was the same regardless of the material used to produce the particles (Section 6.10 and Chapter 10). This result implied that atoms were not the smallest particles of matter but that they could be divided into even smaller particles. In 1909, Robert Millikan determined that the charge associated with the "electron," as these particles were now called, was 1.6×10^{-19} coulombs.

But where did the electron fit in the overall structure of matter? The pieces to this puzzle fell into place as a result of experiments performed in 1910 by Ernest Rutherford. He bombarded a gold foil with positively charged "alpha" particles emitted from radium during radioactive decay. The majority of these particles

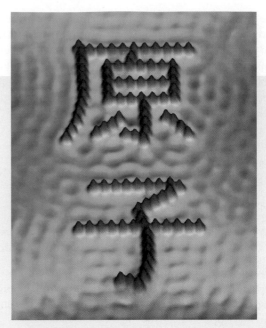

▲ STM image of the Kanji characters for "atom" formed by iron atoms (radius = 126 pm) deposited on a copper metal surface.

passed straight through the foil, but a small fraction of them were deflected, and a few even bounced back. From these results, Rutherford deduced that an atom consists mostly of empty space (occupied by the negatively charged electrons) and that most of the mass and all of the positive charges are contained in a relatively small, dense region that he called the "nucleus."

We can now actually "see" and manipulate individual atoms through the use of a device called a *scanning tunneling microscope*, or STM. With the STM, invented in 1981 by a research team at the IBM Corporation, magnifications of up to 10 million have been achieved, allowing chemists to look directly at atoms. The accompanying photograph shows a computer-enhanced representation of iron atoms that have been deposited on a copper surface.

Most present uses of the STM involve studies of surface chemistry, such as the events accompanying the corrosion of metals and the ordering of large molecules in polymers. Work is also underway using the STM to determine the structures of complex biological molecules, such as immunoglobulin G and streptavidin.

See Chemistry in Action Problems 2.84 and 2.85 at the end of the chapter.

2.2 Elements and Atomic Number

Atomic number (Z) The number of protons in atoms of a given element; the number of electrons in atoms of a given element.

Atoms of different elements differ from one another according to how many protons they contain, a value called the element's **atomic number (Z)**. Thus, if we know the number of protons in an atom, we can identify the element. Any atom with 6 protons, for example, is a carbon atom because the atomic number for carbon is 6 ($Z = 6$).

Atoms are neutral overall and have no net charge because the number of positively charged protons in an atom is the same as the number of negatively charged electrons. Thus, the atomic number also equals the number of electrons in every atom of a given element. Hydrogen, $Z = 1$, has only 1 proton and 1 electron; carbon, $Z = 6$, has 6 protons and 6 electrons; sodium, $Z = 11$, has 11 protons and 11 electrons; and so on, up to the element with the largest known atomic number $(Z = 118)$. In a periodic table, elements are listed in order of increasing atomic number, beginning at the upper left and ending at the lower right.

The sum of the protons and neutrons in an atom is called the atom's **mass number (A)**. Hydrogen atoms with 1 proton and no neutrons have mass number 1, carbon atoms with 6 protons and 6 neutrons have mass number 12, sodium atoms with 11 protons and 12 neutrons have mass number 23, and so on. Except for hydrogen, atoms generally contain at least as many neutrons as protons and frequently contain more. There is no simple way to predict how many neutrons a given atom will have.

Mass number (A) The total number of protons and neutrons in an atom.

Worked Example 2.2 Atomic Structure: Protons, Neutrons, and Electrons

Phosphorus has the atomic number $Z = 15$. How many protons, electrons, and neutrons are there in phosphorus atoms, which have mass number $A = 31$?

ANALYSIS The atomic number gives the number of protons, which is the same as the number of electrons, and the mass number gives the total number of protons plus neutrons.

SOLUTION
Phosphorus atoms, with $Z = 15$, have 15 protons and 15 electrons. To find the number of neutrons, subtract the atomic number from the mass number:

Mass number — (sum of protons and neutrons)　　　Atomic number (number of protons)

$$31 - 15 = 16 \text{ neutrons}$$

Worked Example 2.3 Atomic Structure: Atomic Number and Atomic Mass

An atom contains 28 protons and has $A = 60$. Give the number of electrons and neutrons in the atom, and identify the element.

ANALYSIS The number of protons and the number of electrons are the same and are equal to the atomic number Z, 28 in this case. Subtracting the number of protons (28) from the total number of protons plus neutrons (60) gives the number of neutrons.

SOLUTION
The atom has 28 electrons and $60 - 28 = 32$ neutrons. The list of elements inside the front cover shows that the element with atomic number 28 is nickel (Ni).

PROBLEM 2.5
Use the list inside the front cover to identify the following elements:
(a) $A = 186$, with 111 neutrons
(b) $A = 59$, with 21 neutrons
(c) $A = 127$, with 75 neutrons

PROBLEM 2.6
The cobalt used in cancer treatments has $Z = 27$ and $A = 60$. How many protons, neutrons, and electrons are in these cobalt atoms?

2.3 Isotopes and Atomic Weight

All atoms of a given element have the same number of protons, equal to the atomic number (Z) characteristic of that element. But, different atoms of an element can have different numbers of neutrons and therefore different mass numbers. Atoms with identical atomic numbers but different mass numbers are called **isotopes**. Hydrogen, for example, has three isotopes. The most abundant hydrogen isotope, called *protium*, has no neutrons and thus has a mass number of 1. A second hydrogen isotope, called *deuterium*, has one neutron and a mass number of 2; and a third isotope, called *tritium*, has two neutrons and a mass number of 3. Tritium is unstable and does not occur naturally in significant amounts, although it can be made in nuclear reactors.

Isotopes Atoms with identical atomic numbers but different mass numbers.

▶▶▶ We will see that isotopes of the same element have the same *chemical* behavior (Chapter 5), but very different *nuclear* behavior (Chapter 11).

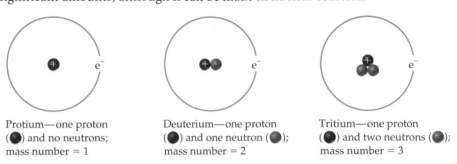

Protium—one proton (●) and no neutrons; mass number = 1

Deuterium—one proton (●) and one neutron (●); mass number = 2

Tritium—one proton (●) and two neutrons (●); mass number = 3

A specific isotope is represented by showing its mass number (A) as a superscript and its atomic number (Z) as a subscript in front of the atomic symbol, for example, $^{A}_{Z}X$, where X represents the symbol for the element. Thus, protium is $^{1}_{1}H$, deuterium is $^{2}_{1}H$, and tritium is $^{3}_{1}H$.

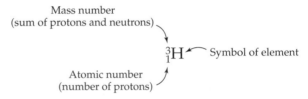

Mass number (sum of protons and neutrons)

$^{3}_{1}H$ ← Symbol of element

Atomic number (number of protons)

Unlike the three isotopes of hydrogen, the isotopes of most elements do not have distinctive names. Instead, the mass number of the isotope is given after the name of the element. The $^{235}_{92}U$ isotope used in nuclear reactors, for example, is usually referred to as uranium-235, or U-235.

▶▶▶ We will discuss nuclear reactors in Section 11.11.

Most naturally occurring elements are mixtures of isotopes. In a large sample of naturally occurring hydrogen atoms, for example, 99.985% have mass number $A = 1$ (protium) and 0.015% have mass number $A = 2$ (deuterium). Therefore, it is useful to know the *average* mass of the atoms in a large sample, a value called the element's **atomic weight**. For hydrogen, the atomic weight is 1.008 amu. Atomic weights for all elements are given on the inside of the front cover of this book.

Atomic weight The weighted average mass of an element's atoms.

To calculate the atomic weight of an element, the individual masses of the naturally occurring isotopes and the percentage of each must be known. The atomic weight can then be calculated as the sum of the masses of the individual isotopes for that element, or

$$\text{Atomic weight} = \Sigma \left[(\text{isotopic abundance}) \times (\text{isotopic mass}) \right]$$

where the Greek symbol Σ indicates the mathematical summing of terms.

Chlorine, for example, occurs on earth as a mixture of 75.77% Cl-35 atoms (mass = 34.97 amu) and 24.23% Cl-37 atoms (mass = 36.97 amu). The atomic weight is found by calculating the percentage of the mass contributed by each isotope. For chlorine, the calculation is done in the following way (to four significant figures), giving an atomic weight of 35.45 amu:

Contribution from ^{35}Cl: $(0.7577)(34.97 \text{ amu}) = 26.4968 \text{ amu}$

Contribution from ^{37}Cl: $(0.2423)(36.97 \text{ amu}) - \underline{8.9578 \text{ amu}}$

Atomic weight $= 35.4546 = 35.45$ amu

(rounded to four significant figures)

The final number of significant figures in this case (four) was determined by the atomic masses. Note that the final rounding to four significant figures was not done until *after* the final answer was obtained.

Worked Example 2.4 Average Atomic Mass: Weighted-Average Calculation

Gallium is a metal with a very low melting point—it will melt in the palm of your hand. It has two naturally occurring isotopes: 60.4% is Ga-69 (mass $=$ 68.9257 amu), and 39.6% is Ga-71 (mass $=$ 70.9248 amu). Calculate the atomic weight for gallium.

ANALYSIS We can calculate the average atomic mass for the element by summing up the contributions from each of the naturally occurring isotopes.

BALLPARK ESTIMATE The masses of the two naturally occurring isotopes of gallium differ by 2 amu (68.9 and 70.9 amu). Since slightly more than half of the Ga atoms are the lighter isotope (Ga-69), the average mass will be slightly less than halfway between the two isotopic masses; estimate $=$ 69.8 amu.

SOLUTION

STEP 1: Identify known information.	Ga-69 (60.4% at 68.9257 amu) Ga-71 (39.6% at 70.9248 amu)
STEP 2: Identify the unknown answer and units.	Atomic weight for Ga (in amu) $= ?$
STEP 3: Identify conversion factors or equations. This equation calculates the average atomic weight as a weighted average of all naturally occurring isotopes.	Atomic weight $= \Sigma \left[(\text{isotopic abundance}) \times (\text{isotopic mass}) \right]$
STEP 4: Solve. Substitute known information and solve.	Atomic weight $= (0.604) \times (68.9257 \text{ amu}) = 41.6311 \text{ amu}$ $+ (0.396) \times (70.9248 \text{ amu}) = 28.0862 \text{ amu}$ Atomic weight $= 69.7 \text{ amu}$ (3 significant figures)
	BALLPARK CHECK Our estimate (69.8 amu) is close!

Worked Example 2.5 Identifying Isotopes from Atomic Mass and Atomic Number

Identify element X in the symbol $^{194}_{78}\text{X}$, and give its atomic number, mass number, number of protons, number of electrons, and number of neutrons.

ANALYSIS The identity of the atom corresponds to the atomic number—78.

SOLUTION
Element X has Z $=$ 78, which shows that it is platinum. (Look inside the front cover for the list of elements.) The isotope $^{194}_{78}\text{Pt}$ has a mass number of 194, and we can subtract the atomic number from the mass number to get the number of neutrons. This platinum isotope therefore has 78 protons, 78 electrons, and $194 - 78 = 116$ neutrons.

PROBLEM 2.7
Potassium (K) has two naturally occurring isotopes: K-39 (93.12%; mass $=$ 38.9637 amu) and K-41 (6.88%; 40.9618 amu). Calculate the atomic weight for potassium. How does your answer compare with the atomic weight given in the list inside the front cover of this book?

PROBLEM 2.8
Bromine, an element present in compounds used as sanitizers and fumigants (for example, ethylene bromide), has two naturally occurring isotopes, with mass numbers 79 and 81. Write the symbols for both, including their atomic numbers and mass numbers.

PROBLEM 2.9
An element used to sanitize water supplies has two naturally occurring isotopes with mass numbers of 35 and 37, and 17 electrons. Write the symbols for both isotopes, including their atomic numbers and mass numbers.

2.4 The Periodic Table

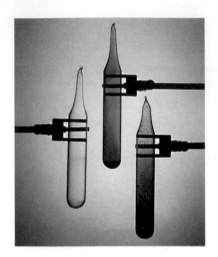

▲ Samples of chlorine, bromine, and iodine, one of Döbereiner's triads of elements with similar chemical properties.

Ten elements have been known since the beginning of recorded history: antimony (Sb), carbon (C), copper (Cu), gold (Au), iron (Fe), lead (Pb), mercury (Hg), silver (Ag), sulfur (S), and tin (Sn). It is worth noting that the symbols for many of these elements are derived from their Latin names, a reminder that they have been known since the time when Latin was the language used for all scholarly work. The first "new" element to be found in several thousand years was arsenic (As), discovered in about 1250. In fact, only 24 elements were known up to the time of the American Revolution in 1776.

As the pace of discovery quickened in the late 1700s and early 1800s, chemists began to look for similarities among elements that might make it possible to draw general conclusions. Particularly important was Johann Döbereiner's observation in 1829 that there were several *triads*, or groups of three elements, that appeared to have similar chemical and physical properties. For example, lithium, sodium, and potassium were all known to be silvery metals that react violently with water; chlorine, bromine, and iodine were all known to be colored nonmetals with pungent odors.

Numerous attempts were made in the mid-1800s to account for the similarities among groups of elements, but the great breakthrough came in 1869 when the Russian chemist Dmitri Mendeleev organized the elements in order of increasing mass and then grouped elements into columns based on similarities in chemical behavior. His table is a forerunner of the modern periodic table, introduced previously in Section 1.5 and shown again in Figure 2.2. The table has boxes for each element that give the symbol, atomic number, and atomic mass of the element:

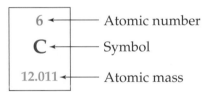

Period One of the 7 horizontal rows of elements in the periodic table.

Group One of the 18 vertical columns of elements in the periodic table.

Main group element An element in one of the 2 groups on the left or the 6 groups on the right of the periodic table.

Transition metal element An element in one of the 10 smaller groups near the middle of the periodic table.

Inner transition metal element An element in one of the 14 groups shown separately at the bottom of the periodic table.

Beginning at the upper left corner of the periodic table, elements are arranged by increasing atomic number into seven horizontal rows, called **periods**, and 18 vertical columns, called **groups**. When organized in this way, *the elements in a given group have similar chemical properties.* Lithium, sodium, potassium, and the other elements in group 1A behave similarly. Chlorine, bromine, iodine, and the other elements in group 7A behave similarly, and so on throughout the table.

Note that different periods (rows) contain different numbers of elements. The first period contains only 2 elements, hydrogen and helium; the second and third periods each contain 8 elements; the fourth and fifth periods each contain 18; the sixth and seventh periods contain 32. Note also that the 14 elements following lanthanum (the *lanthanides*) and the 14 following actinium (the *actinides*) are pulled out and shown below the others.

Groups are numbered in two ways, both shown in Figure 2.2. The 2 large groups on the far left and the 6 on the far right are called the **main group elements** and are numbered 1A through 8A. The 10 smaller groups in the middle of the table are called the **transition metal elements** and are numbered 1B through 8B. Alternatively, all 18 groups are numbered sequentially from 1 to 18. The 14 groups shown separately at the bottom of the table are called the **inner transition metal elements** and are not numbered.

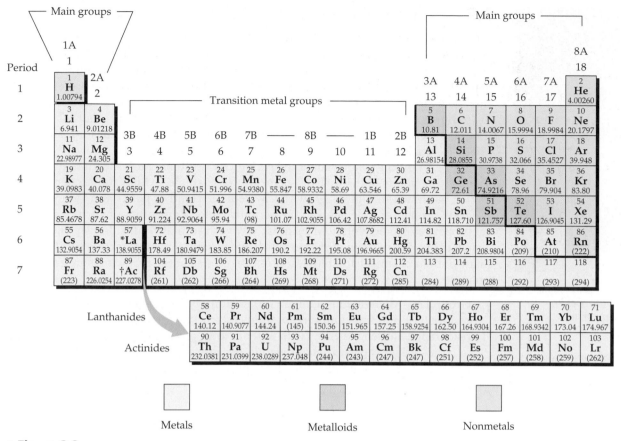

▲ **Figure 2.2**

The periodic table of the elements.

Each element is identified by a one- or two-letter symbol and is characterized by an *atomic number*. The table begins with hydrogen (H, atomic number 1) in the upper left-hand corner and continues to the yet unnamed element with atomic number 118. The 14 elements following lanthanum (La, atomic number 57) and the 14 elements following actinium (Ac, atomic number 89) are pulled out and shown below the others.

Elements are organized into 18 vertical columns, or *groups*, and 7 horizontal rows, or *periods*. The 2 groups on the left and the 6 on the right are the *main groups*; the 10 in the middle are the *transition metal groups*. The 14 elements following lanthanum are the *lanthanides*, and the 14 elements following actinium are the *actinides*; together these are known as the *inner transition metals*. Two systems for numbering the groups are explained in the text.

Those elements (except hydrogen) on the left-hand side of the black zigzag line running from boron (B) to tellurium (Te) are *metals* (yellow), those elements to the right of the line are *nonmetals* (blue), and most elements abutting the line are *metalloids* (purple).

PROBLEM 2.10

Locate aluminum in the periodic table, and give its group number and period number.

PROBLEM 2.11

Identify the group 1B element in period 5 and the group 2A element in period 4.

PROBLEM 2.12

There are five elements in group 5A of the periodic table. Identify them, and give the period of each.

▲ Sodium, an alkali metal, reacts violently with water to yield hydrogen gas and an alkaline (basic) solution.

Alkali metal An element in group 1A of the periodic table.

2.5 Some Characteristics of Different Groups

To see why the periodic table has the name it does, look at the graph of atomic radius versus atomic number in Figure 2.3. The graph shows an obvious *periodicity*—a repeating rise-and-fall pattern. Beginning on the left with atomic number 1 (hydrogen), the sizes of the atoms increase to a maximum at atomic number 3 (lithium), then decrease to a minimum, then increase again to a maximum at atomic number 11 (sodium), then decrease, and so on. It turns out that the maxima occur for atoms of group 1A elements—Li, Na, K, Rb, Cs, and Fr—and the minima occur for atoms of the group 7A elements.

There is nothing unique about the periodicity of atomic radii shown in Figure 2.3. The melting points of the first 100 elements, for example, exhibit similar periodic behavior, as shown in Figure 2.4, with a systematic trend of peaks and valleys as you progress through the elements in the periodic table. Many other physical and chemical properties can be plotted in a similar way with similar results. In fact, the various elements in a given group of the periodic table usually show remarkable similarities in many of their chemical and physical properties. Look at the following four groups, for example:

- **Group 1A—Alkali metals:** Lithium (Li), sodium (Na), potassium (K), rubidium (Rb), cesium (Cs), and francium (Fr) are shiny, soft metals with low melting points. All react rapidly (often violently) with water to form products that are highly alkaline, or basic—hence the name *alkali metals*. Because of their high reactivity, the alkali metals are never found in nature in the pure state but only in combination with other elements.

▶ **Figure 2.3**
A graph of atomic radius in picometers (pm) versus atomic number shows a periodic rise-and-fall pattern.
The maxima occur for atoms of the group 1A elements (Li, Na, K, Rb, Cs, Fr, in red); the minima occur for atoms of the group 7A elements (blue). Accurate data are not available for the group 8A elements.

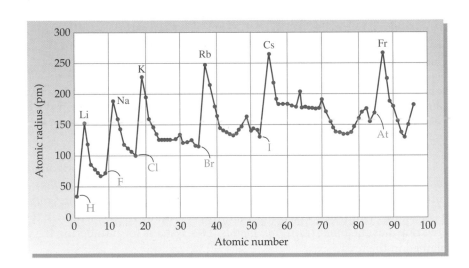

▶ **Figure 2.4**
A graph of melting point versus atomic number shows periodic properties similar to the trend in Figure 2.3.
While the maxima and minima are not as sharp as in Figure 2.3, the change in melting points of the elements still show a similar periodic trend.

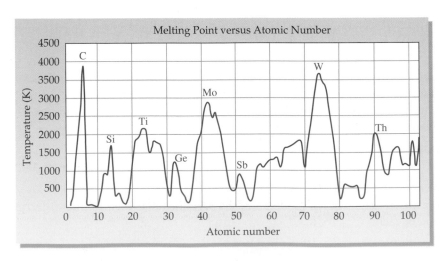

- **Group 2A—Alkaline earth metals:** Beryllium (Be), magnesium (Mg), calcium (Ca), strontium (Sr), barium (Ba), and radium (Ra) are also lustrous, silvery metals, but are less reactive than their neighbors in group 1A. Like the alkali metals, the alkaline earths are never found in nature in the pure state.

- **Group 7A—Halogens:** Fluorine (F), chlorine (Cl), bromine (Br), iodine (I), and astatine (At) are colorful and corrosive nonmetals. All are found in nature only in combination with other elements, such as with sodium in table salt (sodium chloride, NaCl). In fact, the group name **halogen** is taken from the Greek word *hals*, meaning salt.

- **Group 8A—Noble gases:** Helium (He), neon (Ne), argon (Ar), krypton (Kr), xenon (Xe), and radon (Rn) are colorless gases. The elements in this group were labeled the "noble" gases because of their lack of chemical reactivity—helium, neon, and argon don't combine with any other elements, whereas krypton and xenon combine with a very few.

Although the resemblances are not as pronounced as they are within a single group, *neighboring* elements often behave similarly as well. Thus, as noted in Section 1.5 and indicated in Figure 2.2, the periodic table can be divided into three major classes of elements—*metals, nonmetals,* and *metalloids* (metal-like). Metals, the largest category of elements, are found on the left side of the periodic table, bounded on the right by a zigzag line running from boron (B) at the top to astatine (At) at the bottom. Nonmetals are found on the right side of the periodic table, and six of the elements adjacent to the zigzag boundary between metals and nonmetals are metalloids.

Alkaline earth metal An element in group 2A of the periodic table.

Halogen An element in group 7A of the periodic table.

Noble gas An element in group 8A of the periodic table.

▶▶▶ The reason for the similarity in chemical properties of elements within each group will be explained in Section 2.8.

LOOKING AHEAD ▶▶▶ Carbon, the element on which life is based, is a group 4A nonmetal near the top right of the periodic table. Clustered near carbon are other elements often found in living organisms, including oxygen, nitrogen, phosphorus, and sulfur. We will look at the subject of *organic chemistry*—the chemistry of carbon compounds—in Chapters 12–17, and move on to *biochemistry*—the chemistry of living things—in Chapters 18–29.

PROBLEM 2.13

Identify the following elements as metals, nonmetals, or metalloids:

(a) Ti   **(b)** Te

(c) Se   **(d)** Sc

(e) At   **(f)** Ar

PROBLEM 2.14

Locate **(a)** krypton, **(b)** strontium, **(c)** nitrogen, and **(d)** cobalt in the periodic table. Indicate which categories apply to each: (i) metal, (ii) nonmetal, (iii) transition element, (iv) main group element, (v) noble gas.

PROBLEM 2.15

Heavier elements were formed in stars by the fusion of hydrogen and helium nuclei (see Chemistry in Action on p. 56). How many He-4 nuclei would be needed to form a Fe-56 nucleus? What additional particles would be needed?

🔑 KEY CONCEPT PROBLEM 2.16

Identify the elements whose nuclei are shown below. For each, tell its group number, its period number, and whether it is a metal, nonmetal, or metalloid.

● Neutron

● Proton

      (a)   **(b)**

CHEMISTRY IN ACTION

The Origin of Chemical Elements

Astronomers believe that the universe began some 15 billion years ago in an extraordinary moment they call the "big bang." Initially, the temperature must have been inconceivably high, but after 1 second, it had dropped to about 10^{10} K and subatomic particles began to form: protons, neutrons, and electrons. After 3 minutes, the temperature had dropped to 10^9 K, and protons began fusing with neutrons to form helium nuclei, $^4_2$He.

Matter remained in this form for many millions of years, until the expanding universe had cooled to about 10,000 K and electrons were then able to bind to protons and to helium nuclei, forming stable hydrogen and helium atoms.

The attractive force of gravity acting on regions of higher-than-average density of hydrogen and helium atoms slowly produced massive local concentrations of matter and ultimately formed billions of galaxies, each with many billions of stars. As the gas clouds of hydrogen and helium condensed under gravitational attraction and stars formed, their temperatures reached 10^7 K, and their densities reached 100 g/cm³. Protons and neutrons again fused to yield helium nuclei, generating vast amounts of heat and light.

Most of these early stars probably burned out after a few billion years, but a few were so massive that, as their nuclear fuel diminished, gravitational attraction caused a rapid contraction leading to still higher core temperatures and higher densities—up to 5×10^8 K and 5×10^5 g/cm³. Under such extreme conditions, larger nuclei were formed, including carbon, oxygen, silicon, magnesium, and iron. Ultimately, the stars underwent a gravitational collapse resulting in the synthesis of still heavier

▲ **"Light echoes" illuminate dust around the supergiant star V838 monocerotis, as seen from the Hubble telescope.**

elements and an explosion visible throughout the universe as a *supernova*.

Matter from exploding supernovas was blown throughout the galaxy, forming a new generation of stars and planets. Our own sun and solar system formed about 4.5 billion years ago from matter released by former supernovas. Except for hydrogen and helium, all the atoms in our bodies and our entire solar system were created more than 5 billion years ago in exploding stars. We and our world are made from the ashes of dying stars.

See Chemistry in Action Problems 2.86 and 2.87 at the end of this chapter.

2.6 Electronic Structure of Atoms

Why does the periodic table have the shape it does, with periods of different length? Why are periodic variations observed in atomic radii and in so many other characteristics of the elements? And why do elements in a given group of the periodic table show similar chemical behavior? These questions occupied the thoughts of chemists for more than 50 years after Mendeleev, and it was not until well into the 1920s that the answers were established. Today, we know that *the properties of the elements are determined by the arrangement of electrons in their atoms.*

Our current understanding of the electronic structure of atoms is based on the now accepted *quantum mechanical model*, developed by Austrian physicist Erwin Schrödinger in 1926. One of the fundamental assumptions of the model is that electrons have both particle-like and wave-like properties, and that the behavior of electrons can be described using a mathematical equation called a wave function. One consequence of this assumption is that electrons are not perfectly free to move about in an atom. Instead, each electron is restricted to a certain region of space within the atom, depending on the energy level of the electron. Different electrons have different amounts of energy and thus occupy different regions within the atom.

Furthermore, the energies of electrons are *quantized*, or restricted to having only certain values.

To understand the idea of quantization, think about the difference between stairs and a ramp. A ramp is *not* quantized because it changes height continuously. Stairs, by contrast, *are* quantized because they change height only by a fixed amount. You can climb one stair or two stairs, but you cannot climb 1.5 stairs. In the same way, the energy values available to electrons in an atom change only in steps rather than continuously.

The wave functions derived from the quantum mechanical model also provide important information about the location of electrons in an atom. Just as a person can be found by giving his or her address within a state, an electron can be found by giving its "address" within an atom. Furthermore, just as a person's address is composed of several successively narrower categories—city, street, and house number—an electron's address is also composed of successively narrower categories—*shell, subshell,* and *orbital,* which are defined by the quantum mechanical model.

The electrons in an atom are grouped around the nucleus into **shells**, roughly like the layers in an onion, according to the energy of the electrons. The farther a shell is from the nucleus, the larger it is, the more electrons it can hold, and the higher the energies of those electrons. The first shell (the one nearest the nucleus) can hold only 2 electrons, the second shell can hold 8, the third shell can hold 18, and the fourth shell can hold 32 electrons.

Shell number:	1	2	3	4
Electron capacity:	2	8	18	32

Within shells, electrons are further grouped into **subshells** of four different types, identified in order of increasing energy by the letters *s, p, d,* and *f.* The first shell has only one subshell, of the *s* type. The second shell has two subshells: an *s* subshell and a *p* subshell. The third shell has an *s,* a *p,* and a *d* subshell. The fourth shell has an *s,* a *p,* a *d,* and an *f* subshell. Of the four types, we will be concerned mainly with *s* and *p* subshells because most of the elements found in living organisms use only these. A specific subshell is symbolized by writing the number of the shell, followed by the letter for the subshell. For example, the designation 3*p* refers to the *p* subshell in the third shell. Note that the number of subshells in a given shell is equal to the shell number. For example, shell number 3 has 3 subshells.

Finally, within each subshell, electrons are grouped into **orbitals**, regions of space within an atom where the specific electrons are most likely to be found. There are different numbers of orbitals within the different kinds of subshells. A given *s* subshell has only 1 orbital, a *p* subshell has 3 orbitals, a *d* subshell has 5 orbitals, and an *f* subshell has 7 orbitals. Each orbital can hold only two electrons, which differ in a property known as *spin*. If one electron in an orbital has a clockwise spin, the other electron in the same orbital must have a counterclockwise spin. The configuration of shells, subshells, and orbitals is summarized in the figure below.

Shell number:	1	2	3	4
Subshell designation:	*s*	*s , p*	*s , p , d*	*s , p , d , f*
Number of orbitals:	1	1 , 3	1 , 3 , 5	1 , 3 , 5 , 7

Different orbitals have different shapes and orientations, which are described by the quantum mechanical model. Orbitals in *s* subshells are spherical regions centered about the nucleus, whereas orbitals in *p* subshells are roughly dumbbell-shaped regions (Figure 2.5). As shown in Figure 2.5(b), the three *p* orbitals in a given subshell are oriented at right angles to one another.

The overall electron distribution within an atom is summarized in Table 2.2 and in the following list:

- The first shell holds only 2 electrons. The 2 electrons have different spins and are in a single 1*s* orbital.

▲ Stairs are *quantized* because they change height in discrete amounts. A ramp, by contrast, is not quantized because it changes height continuously.

Shell (electron) A grouping of electrons in an atom according to energy.

Subshell (electron) A grouping of electrons in a shell according to the shape of the region of space they occupy.

Orbital A region of space within an atom where an electron in a given subshell can be found.

▶ **Figure 2.5**

The shapes of *s* and *p* orbitals.
(a) The *s* orbitals and **(b)** the *p* orbitals. The three *p* orbitals in a given subshell are oriented at right angles to one another. Each orbital can hold only two electrons.

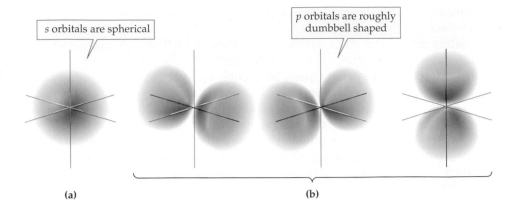

s orbitals are spherical

p orbitals are roughly dumbbell shaped

(a)

(b)

- The second shell holds 8 electrons. Two are in a 2*s* orbital, and 6 are in the three different 2*p* orbitals (two per 2*p* orbital).
- The third shell holds 18 electrons. Two are in a 3*s* orbital, 6 are in three 3*p* orbitals, and 10 are in five 3*d* orbitals.
- The fourth shell holds 32 electrons. Two are in a 4*s* orbital, 6 are in three 4*p* orbitals, 10 are in five 4*d* orbitals, and 14 are in seven 4*f* orbitals.

Worked Example 2.6 Atomic Structure: Electron Shells

How many electrons are present in an atom that has its first and second shells filled and has 4 electrons in its third shell? Name the element.

ANALYSIS The number of electrons in the atom is calculated by adding the total electrons in each shell. We can identify the element from the number of protons in the nucleus, which is equal to the number of electrons in the atom.

SOLUTION
The first shell of an atom holds 2 electrons in its 1*s* orbital, and the second shell holds 8 electrons (2 in a 2*s* orbital and 6 in three 2*p* orbitals). Thus, the atom has a total of $2 + 8 + 4 = 14$ electrons and must be silicon (Si).

PROBLEM 2.17
How many electrons are present in an atom in which the first and second shells and the 3*s* subshell are filled? Name the element.

PROBLEM 2.18
An element has completely filled $n = 1$ and $n = 2$ shells and has 6 electrons in the $n = 3$ shell. Identify the element and its major group (i.e., main group, transition, etc.). Is it a metal or a nonmetal? Identify the orbital in which the last electron is found.

TABLE 2.2 Electron Distribution in Atoms

SHELL NUMBER:	1	2	3	4
Subshell designation:	*s*	*s , p*	*s , p , d*	*s , p , d , f*
Number of orbitals:	1	1 , 3	1 , 3 , 5	1 , 3 , 5 , 7
Number of electrons:	2	2 , 6	2 , 6 , 10	2 , 6 , 10 , 14
Total electron capacity:	2	8	18	32

2.7 Electron Configurations

The exact arrangement of electrons in an atom's shells and subshells is called the atom's **electron configuration** and can be predicted by applying three rules:

RULE 1: Electrons occupy the lowest-energy orbitals available, beginning with 1*s* and continuing in the order shown in Figure 2.6a. Within each shell, the orbital energies increase in the order *s, p, d, f.* The overall ordering is complicated, however, by the fact that some "crossover" of energies occurs between orbitals in different shells above the 3*p* level. For example, the 4*s* orbital is lower in energy than the 3*d* orbitals, and is therefore filled first. The energy level diagram can be used to predict the order in which orbitals are filled, but it may be hard to remember. The schematic in Figure 2.6b may also be used and is easier to remember.

RULE 2: Each orbital can hold only two electrons, which must be of opposite spin.

RULE 3: Two or more orbitals with the same energy—the three *p* orbitals or the five *d* orbitals in a given shell, for example—are each half-filled by one electron before any one orbital is completely filled by addition of the second electron.

Electron configurations of the first 20 elements are shown in Table 2.3. Notice that the number of electrons in each subshell is indicated by a superscript. For example, the notation $1s^2\,2s^2\,2p^6\,3s^2$ for magnesium means that magnesium atoms have 2 electrons in the first shell, 8 electrons in the second shell, and 2 electrons in the third shell.

8 electrons in second shell

2 electrons in first shell

2 electrons in third shell

Mg (atomic number 12): $1s^2\,2s^2\,2p^6\,3s^2$

Electron configuration The specific arrangement of electrons in an atom's shells and subshells.

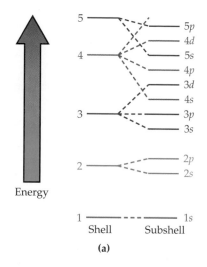

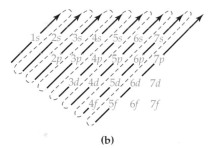

▲ **Figure 2.6**
Order of orbital energy levels.
(a) An energy-level diagram shows the order in which orbitals will be filled within each shell. Above the 3*p* level, there is some crossover of energies among orbitals in different shells.
(b) A simple scheme to remember the order in which the orbitals are filled.

	Element	Atomic Number	Electron Configuration
	TABLE 2.3 Electron Configurations of the First 20 Elements		
H	Hydrogen	1	$1s^1$
He	Helium	2	$1s^2$
Li	Lithium	3	$1s^2\,2s^1$
Be	Beryllium	4	$1s^2\,2s^2$
B	Boron	5	$1s^2\,2s^2\,2p^1$
C	Carbon	6	$1s^2\,2s^2\,2p^2$
N	Nitrogen	7	$1s^2\,2s^2\,2p^3$
O	Oxygen	8	$1s^2\,2s^2\,2p^4$
F	Fluorine	9	$1s^2\,2s^2\,2p^5$
Ne	Neon	10	$1s^2\,2s^2\,2p^6$
Na	Sodium	11	$1s^2\,2s^2\,2p^6\,3s^1$
Mg	Magnesium	12	$1s^2\,2s^2\,2p^6\,3s^2$
Al	Aluminum	13	$1s^2\,2s^2\,2p^6\,3s^2\,3p^1$
Si	Silicon	14	$1s^2\,2s^2\,2p^6\,3s^2\,3p^2$
P	Phosphorus	15	$1s^2\,2s^2\,2p^6\,3s^2\,3p^3$
S	Sulfur	16	$1s^2\,2s^2\,2p^6\,3s^2\,3p^4$
Cl	Chlorine	17	$1s^2\,2s^2\,2p^6\,3s^2\,3p^5$
Ar	Argon	18	$1s^2\,2s^2\,2p^6\,3s^2\,3p^6$
K	Potassium	19	$1s^2\,2s^2\,2p^6\,3s^2\,3p^6\,4s^1$
Ca	Calcium	20	$1s^2\,2s^2\,2p^6\,3s^2\,3p^6\,4s^2$

As you read through the following electron configurations, check the atomic number and the location of each element in the periodic table (Figure 2.2). See if you can detect the relationship between electron configuration and position in the table.

- **Hydrogen ($Z = 1$):** The single electron in a hydrogen atom is in the lowest-energy, $1s$, level. The configuration can be represented in either of two ways:

$$\textbf{H} \quad 1s^1 \quad \text{or} \quad \frac{\uparrow}{1s^1}$$

In the written representation, the superscript in the notation $1s^1$ means that the $1s$ orbital is occupied by one electron. In the graphic representation, the $1s$ orbital is indicated by a line and the single electron in this orbital is shown by an up arrow ($\uparrow$). A single electron in an orbital is often referred to as being *unpaired*.

- **Helium ($Z = 2$):** The two electrons in helium are both in the lowest-energy, $1s$, orbital, and their spins are *paired*, as represented by up and down arrows ($\uparrow\downarrow$):

$$\textbf{He} \quad 1s^2 \quad \text{or} \quad \frac{\uparrow\downarrow}{1s^2}$$

- **Lithium ($Z = 3$):** With the first shell full, the second shell begins to fill. The third electron goes into the $2s$ orbital:

$$\textbf{Li} \quad 1s^2\,2s^1 \quad \text{or} \quad \frac{\uparrow\downarrow}{1s^2} \; \frac{\uparrow}{2s^1}$$

Because [He] has the configuration of a filled $1s^2$ orbital, it is sometimes substituted for the $1s^2$ orbital in depictions of electron pairing. Using this alternative shorthand notation, the electron configuration for Li is written $[\text{He}]\,2s^1$.

- **Beryllium ($Z = 4$):** An electron next pairs up to fill the $2s$ orbital:

$$\textbf{Be} \quad 1s^2\,2s^2 \quad \text{or} \quad \frac{\uparrow\downarrow}{1s^2} \; \frac{\uparrow\downarrow}{2s^2} \quad \text{or} \quad [\text{He}]\,2s^2$$

- **Boron ($Z = 5$), Carbon ($Z = 6$), Nitrogen ($Z = 7$):** The next three electrons enter the three $2p$ orbitals, one at a time. Note that representing the configurations with lines and arrows gives more information than the alternative written notations because the filling and pairing of electrons in individual orbitals within the p subshell is shown.

$$\textbf{B} \quad 1s^2\,2s^2\,2p^1 \quad \text{or} \quad \frac{\uparrow\downarrow}{1s^2} \; \frac{\uparrow\downarrow}{2s^2} \; \underbrace{\frac{\uparrow}{}\,\frac{}{}\,\frac{}{}}_{2p^1} \quad \text{or} \quad [\text{He}]\,2s^2\,2p^1$$

$$\textbf{C} \quad 1s^2\,2s^2\,2p^2 \quad \text{or} \quad \frac{\uparrow\downarrow}{1s^2} \; \frac{\uparrow\downarrow}{2s^2} \; \underbrace{\frac{\uparrow}{}\,\frac{\uparrow}{}\,\frac{}{}}_{2p^2} \quad \text{or} \quad [\text{He}]\,2s^2\,2p^2$$

$$\textbf{N} \quad 1s^2\,2s^2\,2p^3 \quad \text{or} \quad \frac{\uparrow\downarrow}{1s^2} \; \frac{\uparrow\downarrow}{2s^2} \; \underbrace{\frac{\uparrow}{}\,\frac{\uparrow}{}\,\frac{\uparrow}{}}_{2p^3} \quad \text{or} \quad [\text{He}]\,2s^2\,2p^3$$

- **Oxygen ($Z = 8$), Fluorine ($Z = 9$), Neon ($Z = 10$):** Electrons now pair up one by one to fill the three $2p$ orbitals and fully occupy the second shell:

$$\textbf{O} \quad 1s^2\,2s^2\,2p^4 \quad \text{or} \quad \frac{\uparrow\downarrow}{1s^2} \; \frac{\uparrow\downarrow}{2s^2} \; \underbrace{\frac{\uparrow\downarrow}{}\,\frac{\uparrow}{}\,\frac{\uparrow}{}}_{2p^4} \quad \text{or} \quad [\text{He}]\,2s^2\,2p^4$$

$$\textbf{F} \quad 1s^2\,2s^2\,2p^5 \quad \text{or} \quad \frac{\uparrow\downarrow}{1s^2} \; \frac{\uparrow\downarrow}{2s^2} \; \underbrace{\frac{\uparrow\downarrow}{}\,\frac{\uparrow\downarrow}{}\,\frac{\uparrow}{}}_{2p^5} \quad \text{or} \quad [\text{He}]\,2s^2\,2p^5$$

$$\textbf{Ne} \quad 1s^2\,2s^2\,2p^6 \quad \text{or} \quad \frac{\uparrow\downarrow}{1s^2} \; \frac{\uparrow\downarrow}{2s^2} \; \underbrace{\frac{\uparrow\downarrow}{}\,\frac{\uparrow\downarrow}{}\,\frac{\uparrow\downarrow}{}}_{2p^6}$$

At this point, we may use the shorthand notation [Ne] to represent the electron configuration for a completely filled set of orbitals in the second shell.

- **Sodium to Calcium ($Z = 11 - 20$):** The pattern seen for lithium through neon is seen again for sodium ($Z = 11$) through argon ($Z = 18$) as the $3s$ and $3p$ sub-shells fill up. For elements having a third filled shell, we may use $[Ar]$ to represent a completely filled third shell. After argon, however, the first crossover in subshell energies occurs. As indicated in Figure 2.6, the $4s$ subshell is lower in energy than the $3d$ subshell and is filled first. Potassium ($Z = 19$) and calcium ($Z = 20$) therefore have the following electron configurations:

$$\textbf{K} \quad 1s^2\,2s^2\,2p^6\,3s^2\,3p^6\,4s^1 \text{ or } [Ar]4s^1 \quad \textbf{Ca} \quad 1s^2\,2s^2\,2p^6\,3s^2\,3p^6\,4s^2 \text{ or } [Ar]4s^2$$

Worked Example 2.7 Atomic Structure: Electron Configurations

Show how the electron configuration of magnesium can be assigned.

ANALYSIS Magnesium, $Z = 12$, has 12 electrons to be placed in specific orbitals. Assignments are made by putting 2 electrons in each orbital, according to the order shown in Figure 2.6.

- The first 2 electrons are placed in the $1s$ orbital ($1s^2$).
- The next 2 electrons are placed in the $2s$ orbital ($2s^2$).
- The next 6 electrons are placed in the three available $2p$ orbitals ($2p^6$).
- The remaining 2 electrons are both put in the $3s$ orbital ($3s^2$).

SOLUTION
Magnesium has the configuration $1s^2\,2s^2\,2p^6\,3s^2$ or $[Ne]3s^2$.

Worked Example 2.8 Electron Configurations: Orbital-Filling Diagrams

Write the electron configuration of phosphorus, $Z = 15$, using up and down arrows to show how the electrons in each orbital are paired.

ANALYSIS Phosphorus has 15 electrons, which occupy orbitals according to the order shown in Figure 2.6.

- The first 2 are paired and fill the first shell ($1s^2$).
- The next 8 fill the second shell ($2s^2\,2p^6$). All electrons are paired.
- The remaining 5 electrons enter the third shell, where 2 fill the $3s$ orbital ($3s^2$) and 3 occupy the $3p$ subshell, one in each of the three p orbitals.

SOLUTION

$$\text{P} \quad \underset{1s^2}{\uparrow\downarrow} \quad \underset{2s^2}{\uparrow\downarrow} \quad \underset{2p^6}{\underbrace{\uparrow\downarrow \; \uparrow\downarrow \; \uparrow\downarrow}} \quad \underset{3s^2}{\uparrow\downarrow} \quad \underset{3p^3}{\underbrace{\uparrow \; \uparrow \; \uparrow}}$$

PROBLEM 2.19
Write electron configurations for the following elements. (You can check your answers in Table 2.3.)

(a) C   **(b)** P   **(c)** Cl   **(d)** K

PROBLEM 2.20
For an atom containing 33 electrons, identify the incompletely filled subshell, and show the paired and/or unpaired electrons in this subshell using up and down arrows.

⚷ KEY CONCEPT PROBLEM 2.21

Identify the atom with the following orbital-filling diagram.

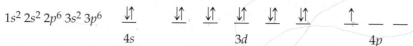

$$1s^2\,2s^2\,2p^6\,3s^2\,3p^6 \quad \underset{4s}{\uparrow\downarrow} \qquad \underset{3d}{\underbrace{\uparrow\downarrow \;\; \uparrow\downarrow \;\; \uparrow\downarrow \;\; \uparrow\downarrow \;\; \uparrow\downarrow}} \qquad \underset{4p}{\underbrace{\uparrow \; \_\_ \; \_\_}}$$

2.8 Electron Configurations and the Periodic Table

How is an atom's electron configuration related to its chemical behavior, and why do elements with similar behavior occur in the same group of the periodic table? As shown in Figure 2.7, the periodic table can be divided into four regions, or *blocks*, of elements according to the electron shells and subshells occupied by *the subshell filled last*.

- The main group 1A and 2A elements on the left side of the table (plus He) are called the **s-block elements** because an *s* subshell is filled last in these elements.
- The main group 3A–8A elements on the right side of the table (except He) are the **p-block elements** because a *p* subshell is filled last in these elements.
- The transition metals in the middle of the table are the **d-block elements** because a *d* subshell is filled last in these elements.
- The inner transition metals detached at the bottom of the table are the **f-block elements** because an *f* subshell is filled last in these elements.

Thinking of the periodic table as outlined in Figure 2.7 provides a simple way to remember the order of orbital filling shown previously in Figure 2.6. Beginning at the top left corner of the periodic table, the first row contains only two elements (H and He) because only two electrons are required to fill the *s* orbital in the first shell, $1s^2$. The second row begins with two *s*-block elements (Li and Be) and continues with six *p*-block elements (B through Ne), so electrons fill the next available *s* orbital (2*s*) and then the first available *p* orbitals (2*p*). The third row is similar to the second row, so the 3*s* and 3*p* orbitals are filled next. The fourth row again starts with 2 *s*-block elements (K and Ca) but is then followed by 10 *d*-block elements (Sc through Zn) and 6 *p*-block elements (Ga through Kr). Thus, the order of orbital filling is 4*s* followed by the first available *d* orbitals (3*d*) followed by 4*p*. Continuing through successive rows of the periodic table gives the entire filling order, identical to that shown in Figure 2.6.

$$1s \rightarrow 2s \rightarrow 2p \rightarrow 3s \rightarrow 3p \rightarrow 4s \rightarrow 3d \rightarrow 4p \rightarrow 5s \rightarrow$$
$$4d \rightarrow 5p \rightarrow 6s \rightarrow 4f \rightarrow 5d \rightarrow 6p \rightarrow 7s \rightarrow 5f \rightarrow 6d \rightarrow 7p$$

But why do the elements in a given group of the periodic table have similar properties? The answer emerges when you look at Table 2.4, which gives electron configurations for elements in the main groups 1A, 2A, 7A, and 8A. Focusing only on the

s-Block element A main group element that results from the filling of an *s* orbital.

p-Block element A main group element that results from the filling of *p* orbitals.

d-Block element A transition metal element that results from the filling of *d* orbitals.

f-Block element An inner transition metal element that results from the filling of *f* orbitals.

▶ **Figure 2.7**
The blocks of elements in the periodic table correspond to filling the different types of subshells.
Beginning at the top left and going across successive rows of the periodic table provides a method for remembering the order of orbital filling: $1s \rightarrow 2s \rightarrow 2p \rightarrow 3s \rightarrow 3p \rightarrow 4s \rightarrow 3d \rightarrow 4p$, and so on.

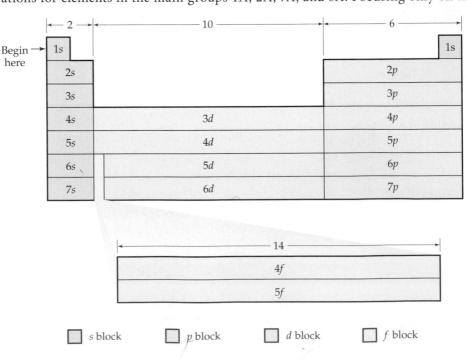

Table 2.4 Valence-Shell Electron Configurations for Group 1A, 2A, 7A, and 8A Elements

Group	Element	Atomic Number	Valence-Shell Electron Configuration
1A	Li (lithium)	3	$2s^1$
	Na (sodium)	11	$3s^1$
	K (potassium)	19	$4s^1$
	Rb (rubidium)	37	$5s^1$
	Cs (cesium)	55	$6s^1$
2A	Be (beryllium)	4	$2s^2$
	Mg (magnesium)	12	$3s^2$
	Ca (calcium)	20	$4s^2$
	Sr (strontium)	38	$5s^2$
	Ba (barium)	56	$6s^2$
7A	F (fluorine)	9	$2s^2\,2p^5$
	Cl (chlorine)	17	$3s^2\,3p^5$
	Br (bromine)	35	$4s^2\,4p^5$
	I (iodine)	53	$5s^2\,5p^5$
8A	He (helium)	2	$1s^2$
	Ne (neon)	10	$2s^2\,2p^6$
	Ar (argon)	18	$3s^2\,3p^6$
	Kr (krypton)	36	$4s^2\,4p^6$
	Xe (xenon)	54	$5s^2\,5p^6$

electrons in the outermost shell, or **valence shell**, *elements in the same group of the periodic table have similar electron configurations in their valence shells.* The group 1A elements, for example, all have one **valence electron**, ns^1 (where n represents the number of the valence shell: $n = 2$ for Li; $n = 3$ for Na; $n = 4$ for K; and so on). The group 2A elements have two valence electrons (ns^2); the group 7A elements have seven valence electrons ($ns^2\,np^5$); and the group 8A elements (except He) have eight valence electrons ($ns^2\,np^6$). You might also notice that the group numbers from 1A through 8A give the numbers of valence electrons for the elements in each main group. It is worth noting that the valence electrons are those in the outermost shell—not necessarily in the orbitals that were filled last!

What is true for the main group elements is also true for the other groups in the periodic table: atoms within a given group have the same number of valence electrons and have similar electron configurations. *Because the valence electrons are the most loosely held, they are the most important in determining an element's properties.* Similar electron configurations thus explain why the elements in a given group of the periodic table have similar chemical behavior.

Valence shell The outermost electron shell of an atom.

Valence electron An electron in the valence shell of an atom.

LOOKING AHEAD ▶▶▶   We have seen that elements in a given group have similar chemical behavior because they have similar valence electron configurations, and that many chemical properties exhibit periodic trends across the periodic table. The *chemical* behavior of nearly all the elements can be predicted based on their position in the periodic table, and this will be examined in more detail in Chapters 3 and 4. Similarly, the *nuclear* behavior of the different isotopes of a given element is related to the configuration of the nucleus (that is, the number of neutrons and protons) and will be examined in Chapter 11.

Worked Example 2.9 Electron Configurations: Valence Electrons

Write the electron configuration for the following elements, using both the complete and the shorthand notations. Indicate which electrons are the valence electrons.

(a) Na   (b) Cl   (c) Zr

ANALYSIS Locate the row and the block in which each of the elements is found in Figure 2.7. The location can be used to determine the complete electron configuration and to identify the valence electrons.

SOLUTION

(a) Na (sodium) is located in the third row and in the first column of the s-block. Therefore, all orbitals up to the 3s are completely filled, and there is one electron in the 3s orbital.

$$\text{Na: } 1s^2\, 2s^2\, 2p^6\, \underline{3s^1} \quad \text{or} \quad [\text{Ne}]\, \underline{3s^1} \quad \text{(valence electrons are underlined)}$$

(b) Cl (chlorine) is located in the third row and in the fifth column of the p-block.

$$\text{Cl: } 1s^2\, 2s^2\, 2p^6\, \underline{3s^2\, 3p^5} \quad \text{or} \quad [\text{Ne}]\, \underline{3s^2\, 3p^5}$$

(c) Zr (zirconium) is located in the fifth row and in the second column of the d-block. All orbitals up to the 4d are completely filled, and there are 2 electrons in the 4d orbitals. Note that the 4d orbitals are filled after the 5s orbitals in both Figures 2.6 and 2.7.

$$\text{Zr: } 1s^2\, 2s^2\, 2p^6\, 3s^1\, 3p^6\, 4s^2\, 3d^{10}\, 4p^6\, \underline{5s^2\, 4d^2} \quad \text{or} \quad [\text{Kr}]\, \underline{5s^2\, 4d^2}$$

Worked Example 2.10 Electron Configurations: Valence-Shell Configurations

Using n to represent the number of the valence shell, write a general valence-shell configuration for the elements in group 6A.

ANALYSIS The elements in group 6A have 6 valence electrons. In each element, the first two of these electrons are in the valence s subshell, giving ns^2, and the next four electrons are in the valence p subshell, giving np^4.

SOLUTION
For group 6A, the general valence-shell configuration is $ns^2\, np^4$.

Worked Example 2.11 Electron Configurations: Inner Shells versus Valence Shell

How many electrons are in a tin atom? Give the number of electrons in each shell. How many valence electrons are there in a tin atom? Write the valence-shell configuration for tin.

ANALYSIS The total number of electrons will be the same as the atomic number for tin $(Z = 50)$. The number of valence electrons will equal the number of electrons in the valence shell.

SOLUTION
Checking the periodic table shows that tin has atomic number 50 and is in group 4A. The number of electrons in each shell is

Shell number:	1	2	3	4	5
Number of electrons:	2	8	18	18	4

As expected from the group number, tin has 4 valence electrons. They are in the 5s and 5p subshells and have the configuration $5s^2\, 5p^2$.

PROBLEM 2.22

Write the electron configuration for the following elements, using both the complete and the shorthand notations. Indicate which electrons are the valence electrons.

(a) F   (b) Al   (c) As

PROBLEM 2.23

Identify the group in which all the elements have the valence-shell configuration ns^2.

PROBLEM 2.24

For chlorine, identify the group number, give the number of electrons in each occupied shell, and write its valence-shell configuration.

🔑 KEY CONCEPT PROBLEM 2.25

Identify the group number, and write the general valence-shell configuration (for example, ns^1 for group 1A elements) for the elements indicated in red in the following periodic table.

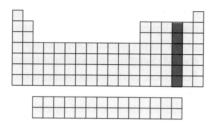

2.9 Electron-Dot Symbols

Valence electrons play such an important role in the behavior of atoms that it is useful to have a method for including them with atomic symbols. In an **electron-dot symbol**, dots are placed around the atomic symbol to indicate the number of valence electrons present. A group 1A atom, such as sodium, has a single dot; a group 2A atom, such as magnesium, has two dots; a group 3A atom, such as boron, has three dots; and so on.

Table 2.5 gives electron-dot symbols for atoms of the first few elements in each main group. As shown, the dots are distributed around the four sides of the element symbol, singly at first until each of the four sides has one dot. As more electron dots are added they will form pairs, with no more than two dots on a side. Note that helium differs from other noble gases in having only two valence electrons rather than eight. Nevertheless, helium is considered a member of group 8A because its properties resemble those of the other noble gases and because its highest occupied subshell is filled ($1s^2$).

Electron-dot symbol An atomic symbol with dots placed around it to indicate the number of valence electrons.

TABLE 2.5 Electron-Dot Symbols for Some Main Group Elements

1A	2A	3A	4A	5A	6A	7A	NOBLE GASES
H·							He:
Li·	·Be·	·Ḃ·	·Ċ·	·N̈:	·Ö:	·F̈:	:N̈e:
Na·	·Mg·	·Äl·	·Si·	·P̈:	·S̈:	·Cl̈:	:Är:
K·	·Ca·	·Ġa·	·Ġe·	·Äs:	·S̈e:	·Br̈:	:K̈r:

KEY WORDS

Alkali metal, *p. 54*

Alkaline earth metal, *p. 55*

Atom, *p. 45*

Atomic mass unit (amu), *p. 46*

Atomic number (Z), *p. 48*

Atomic theory, *p. 45*

Atomic weight, *p. 50*

d-Block element, *p. 62*

Electron, *p. 46*

Electron configuration, *p. 59*

Electron-dot symbol, *p. 65*

f-Block element, *p. 62*

Group, *p. 52*

Halogen, *p. 55*

Inner transition metal element, *p. 52*

Isotopes, *p. 50*

Main group element, *p. 52*

Mass number (A), *p. 49*

Neutron, *p. 46*

Noble gas, *p. 55*

Nucleus, *p. 46*

Orbital, *p. 57*

p-Block element, *p. 62*

Period, *p. 52*

Proton, *p. 46*

s-Block element, *p. 62*

Shell (electron), *p. 57*

Subatomic particles, *p. 46*

Subshell (electron), *p. 57*

Transition metal element, *p. 52*

Valence electron, *p. 63*

Valence shell, *p. 63*

UNDERSTANDING KEY CONCEPTS

2.29 Where on the following outline of a periodic table do the indicated elements or groups of elements appear?

(a) Alkali metals   (b) Halogens

(c) Alkaline earth metals   (d) Transition metals

(e) Hydrogen   (f) Helium

(g) Metalloids

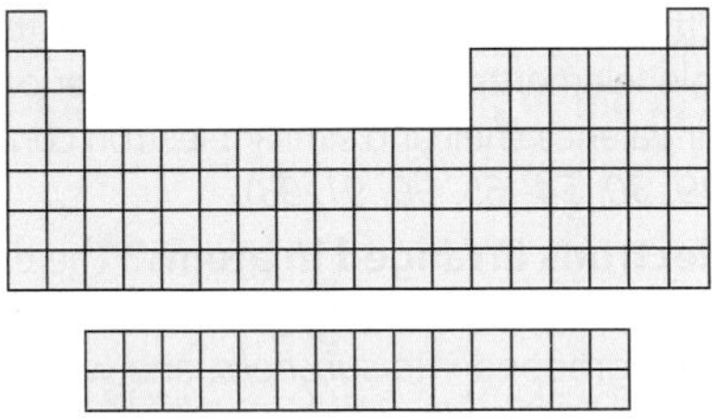

2.30 Is the element marked in red on the following periodic table likely to be a gas, a liquid, or a solid? What is the atomic number of the element in blue? Name at least one other element that is likely to be similar to the element in green.

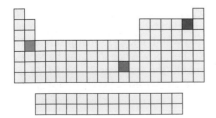

2.31 Use the blank periodic table below to show where the elements matching the following descriptions appear.

(a) Elements with the valence-shell electron configuration $ns^2\,np^5$

(b) An element whose third shell contains two p electrons

(c) Elements with a completely filled valence shell

2.32 What atom has the following orbitial-filling diagram?

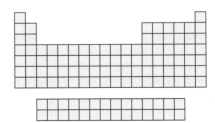

2.33 Use the orbitial-filling diagram below to show the electron configuration for As:

$$1s^2\,2s^2\,2p^6\,3s^2\,3p^6 \quad \underline{\quad} \quad \underline{\quad}\ \underline{\quad}\ \underline{\quad}\ \underline{\quad}\ \underline{\quad} \quad \underline{\quad}\ \underline{\quad}\ \underline{\quad}$$

$$ 4s \qquad\qquad 3d \qquad\qquad 4p$$

ADDITIONAL PROBLEMS

ATOMIC THEORY AND THE COMPOSITION OF ATOMS

2.34 What four fundamental assumptions about atoms and matter make up modern atomic theory?

2.35 How do atoms of different elements differ?

2.36 Find the mass in grams of one atom of the following elements:

(a) Bi, atomic weight 208.9804 amu

(b) Xe, atomic weight 131.29 amu

(c) He, atomic weight 4.0026 amu

2.37 Find the mass in atomic mass units of the following:

(a) 1 O atom, with a mass of 2.66×10^{-23} g

(b) 1 Br atom, with a mass of 1.31×10^{-22} g

2.38 What is the mass in grams of 6.022×10^{23} N atoms of mass 14.01 amu?

2.39 What is the mass in grams of 6.022×10^{23} O atoms of mass 16.00 amu?

2.40 How many O atoms of mass 15.99 amu are in 15.99 g of oxygen?

2.41 How many C atoms of mass 12.00 amu are in 12.00 g of carbon?

2.42 What are the names of the three subatomic particles? What are their approximate masses in atomic mass units, and what electrical charge does each have?

2.43 Where within an atom are the three types of subatomic particles located?

2.44 Give the number of neutrons in each naturally occurring isotope of argon: argon-36, argon-38, argon-40.

2.45 Give the number of protons, neutrons, and electrons in the following isotopes:

(a) Al-27 (b) $^{28}_{14}\text{Si}$

(c) B-11 (d) $^{115}_{47}\text{Ag}$

2.46 Which of the following symbols represent isotopes of the same element?

(a) $^{19}_{9}X$ (b) $^{19}_{10}X$

(c) $^{21}_{9}X$ (d) $^{21}_{12}X$

2.47 Give the name and the number of neutrons in each isotope listed in Problem 2.46.

2.48 Write the symbols for the following isotopes:

(a) Its atoms contain 6 protons and 8 neutrons.

(b) Its atoms have mass number 39 and contain 19 protons.

(c) Its atoms have mass number 20 and contain 10 electrons.

2.49 Write the symbols for the following isotopes:

(a) Its atoms contain 50 electrons and 70 neutrons.

(b) Its atoms have $A = 56$ and $Z = 26$.

(c) Its atoms have $A = 226$ and contain 88 electrons.

2.50 There are three naturally occurring isotopes of carbon, with mass numbers of 12, 13, and 14. How many neutrons does each have? Write the symbol for each isotope, indicating its atomic number and mass number.

2.51 One of the most widely used isotopes in medical diagnostics is technicium-99m (the *m* indicates that it is a *metastable* isotope). Write the symbol for this isotope, indicating both mass number and atomic number.

2.52 Naturally occurring copper is a mixture of 69.17% Cu-63 with a mass of 62.93 amu and 30.83% Cu-65 with a mass of 64.93 amu. What is the atomic weight of copper?

2.53 Naturally occurring lithium is a mixture of 92.58% Li-7 with a mass of 7.016 amu and 7.42% Li-6 with a mass of 6.015 amu. What is the atomic weight of lithium?

THE PERIODIC TABLE

2.54 Why does the third period in the periodic table contain eight elements?

2.55 Why does the fourth period in the periodic table contain 18 elements?

2.56 Americium, atomic number 95, is used in household smoke detectors. What is the symbol for americium? Is americium a metal, a nonmetal, or a metalloid?

2.57 What subshell is being filled for the metalloid elements?

2.58 Answer the following questions for the elements from scandium through zinc:

(a) Are they metals or nonmetals?

(b) To what general class of elements do they belong?

(c) What subshell is being filled by electrons in these elements?

2.59 Answer the following questions for the elements from cerium through lutetium:

(a) Are they metals or nonmetals?

(b) To what general class of elements do they belong?

(c) What subshell is being filled by electrons in these elements?

2.60 For (a) rubidium (b) tungsten, (c) germanium, and (d) krypton, which of the following terms apply? (i) metal, (ii) nonmetal, (iii) metalloid (iv) transition element, (v) main group element, (vi) noble gas, (vii) alkali metal, (viii) alkaline earth metal.

2.61 For (a) calcium, (b) palladium, (c) carbon, and (d) radon, which of the following terms apply? (i) metal, (ii) nonmetal, (iii) metalloid (iv) transition element, (v) main group element, (vi) noble gas, (vii) alkali metal, (viii) alkaline earth metal.

2.62 Name an element in the periodic table that you would expect to be chemically similar to sulfur.

2.63 Name an element in the periodic table that you would expect to be chemically similar to potassium.

2.64 What elements in addition to lithium make up the alkali metal family?

2.65 What elements in addition to fluorine make up the halogen family?

ELECTRON CONFIGURATIONS

2.66 What is the maximum number of electrons that can go into an orbital?

2.67 What are the shapes and locations within an atom of s and p orbitals?

2.68 What is the maximum number of electrons that can go into the first shell? The second shell? The third shell?

2.69 What is the total number of orbitals in the third shell? The fourth shell?

2.70 How many subshells are there in the third shell? The fourth shell? The fifth shell?

2.71 How many orbitals would you expect to find in the last subshell of the fifth shell? How many electrons would you need to fill this subshell?

2.72 How many electrons are present in an atom with its $1s$, $2s$, and $2p$ subshells filled? What is this element?

2.73 How many electrons are present in an atom with its $1s$, $2s$, $2p$, $3s$, $3p$, and $4s$ subshells filled and with two electrons in the $3d$ subshell? What is this element?

2.74 Use arrows to show electron pairing in the valence p subshell of

   (a) Sulfur

   (b) Bromine

   (c) Silicon

2.75 Use arrows to show electron pairing in the $5s$ and $4d$ orbitals of

   (a) Rubidum

   (b) Niobium

   (c) Rhodium

2.76 Determine the number of unpaired electrons for each of the atoms in Problems 2.74 and 2.75.

2.77 Without looking back in the text, write the electron configurations for the following:

   (a) Titanium $Z = 22$ **(b)** Phosphorus, $Z = 15$

   (c) Argon, $Z = 18$ **(d)** Lanthanum, $Z = 57$

2.78 How many electrons does the element with $Z = 12$ have in its valence shell? Write the electron-dot symbol for this element.

2.79 How many valence electrons do group 4A elements have? Explain. Write a generic electron-dot symbol for elements in this group.

2.80 Identify the valence subshell occupied by electrons in beryllium and arsenic atoms.

2.81 What group in the periodic table has the valence-shell configuration $ns^2\,np^3$?

2.82 Give the number of valence electrons and draw electron-dot symbols for atoms of the following elements:

   (a) Kr   **(b)** C

   (c) Ca   **(d)** K

   (e) B   **(f)** Cl

2.83 Using n for the number of the valence shell, write a general valence-shell configuration for the elements in group 6A and in group 2A.

CHEMISTRY IN ACTION

2.84 What is the advantage of using a scanning tunneling microscope rather than a normal light microscope? [*Are Atoms Real? p. 48*]

2.85 For the Kanji character in the lower portion of the figure on p. 48: (a) How wide is the character in terms of iron atoms? (b) Given the radius of an iron atom is 126 pm, calculate the width of this character in centimeters. [*Are Atoms Real? p. 48*]

2.86 What are the first two elements that are made in stars? [*The Origin of Chemical Elements, p. 56*]

2.87 How are elements heavier than iron made? [*The Origin of Chemical Elements, p. 56*]

2.88 Which type of electromagnetic energy in the following pairs is of higher energy? [*Atoms and Light, p. 66*]

   (a) Infrared, ultraviolet

   (b) Gamma waves, microwaves

   (c) Visible light, X rays

2.89 Why do you suppose ultraviolet rays from the sun are more damaging to the skin than visible light? [*Atoms and Light, p. 66*]

GENERAL QUESTIONS AND PROBLEMS

2.90 What elements in addition to helium make up the noble gas family?

2.91 Hydrogen is placed in group 1A on many periodic charts, even though it is not an alkali metal. On other periodic charts, however, hydrogen is included with group 7A even though it is not a halogen. Explain. (Hint: draw electron-dot symbols for H and for the 1A and 7A elements.)

2.92 Tellurium ($Z = 52$) has a *lower* atomic number than iodine ($Z = 53$), yet it has a *higher* atomic weight (127.60 amu for Te versus 126.90 amu for I). How is this possible?

2.93 What is the atomic number of the yet-undiscovered element directly below francium (Fr) in the periodic table?

2.94 Give the number of electrons in each shell for lead.

2.95 Identify the highest-energy occupied subshell in atoms of the following elements:

   (a) Iodine   **(b)** Scandium

   (c) Arsenic   **(d)** Aluminum

2.96   What is the atomic weight of naturally occurring bromine, which contains 50.69% Br-79 of mass 78.92 amu and 49.31% Br-81 of mass 80.91 amu?

2.97   **(a)** What is the mass (in amu and in grams) of a single atom of Carbon-12?

   (b) What is the mass (in grams) of 6.02×10^{23} atoms of Carbon-12?

   (c) Based on your answer to part (b), what would be the mass of 6.02×10^{23} atoms of Sodium-23?

2.98   An unidentified element is found to have an electron configuration by shell of 2 8 18 8 2. To what group and period does this element belong? Is the element a metal or a nonmetal? How many protons does an atom of the element have? What is the name of the element? Write its electron-dot symbol.

2.99   Germanium, atomic number 32, is used in building semiconductors for microelectronic devices, and has an electron configuration by shell of 2 8 18 4.

   (a) Write the electronic configuration for germanium.

   (b) In what shell and orbitals are the valence electrons?

2.100   Tin, atomic number 50, is directly beneath germanium (Problem 2.99) in the periodic table. What electron configuration by shell would you expect tin to have? Is tin a metal or a nonmetal?

2.101   A blood sample is found to contain 8.6 mg/dL of Ca. How many atoms of Ca are present in 8.6 mg? The atomic weight of Ca is 40.08 amu.

2.102   What is wrong with the following electron configurations?

   (a) Ni $1s^2\, 2s^2\, 2p^6\, 3s^2\, 3p^6\, 3d^{10}$

   (b) N $1s^2\, 2p^5$

   (c) Si $1s^2\, 2s^2\, 2p\ \underline{\uparrow\downarrow}\ \underline{\ \ }\ \underline{\ \ }$

   (d) Mg $1s^2\, 2s^2\, 2p^6\, 3s\ \underline{\uparrow\uparrow}$

2.103   Not all elements follow exactly the electron-filling order described in Figure 2.7. Atoms of which elements are represented by the following electron configurations?

   (a) $1s^2\, 2s^2\, 2p^6\, 3s^2\, 3p^6\, 3d^5\, 4s^1$

   (b) $1s^2\, 2s^2\, 2p^6\, 3s^2\, 3p^6\, 3d^{10}\, 4s^1$

   (c) $1s^2\, 2s^2\, 2p^6\, 3s^2\, 3p^6\, 3d^{10}\, 4s^2\, 4p^6\, 4d^5\, 5s^1$

   (d) $1s^2\, 2s^2\, 2p^6\, 3s^2\, 3p^6\, 3d^{10}\, 4s^2\, 4p^6\, 4d^{10}\, 5s^1$

2.104   What similarities do you see in the electron configurations for the atoms in Problem 2.103? How might these similarities explain their anomalous electron configurations?

2.105   Based on the identity of the elements whose electron configurations are given in Problem 2.103, write the electron configurations for the element with atomic number $Z = 79$.

2.106   What orbital is filled last in the most recently discovered element 117?

CHAPTER 3

Ionic Compounds

◄ Stalagmites and stalactites, such as these in a cave in the Nangu Stone Forest in China, are composed of the ionic compounds calcium carbonate, $CaCO_3$, and magnesium carbonate, $MgCO_3$.

CONCEPTS
TO REVIEW

A. The Periodic Table
(Sections 2.4 and 2.5)

B. Electron Configurations
(Sections 2.7 and 2.8)

1. **What is an ion, what is an ionic bond, and what are the general characteristics of ionic compounds?**
   THE GOAL: Be able to describe ions and ionic bonds, and give the general properties of compounds that contain ionic bonds.

2. **What is the octet rule, and how does it apply to ions?**
   THE GOAL: Be able to state the octet rule, and use it to predict the electron configurations of ions of main group elements. (◀◀ B.)

3. **What is the relationship between an element's position in the periodic table and the formation of its ion?**
   THE GOAL: Be able to predict what ions are likely to be formed by atoms of a given element. (◀◀ A, B.)

4. **What determines the chemical formula of an ionic compound?**
   THE GOAL: Be able to write formulas for ionic compounds, given the identities of the ions.

5. **How are ionic compounds named?**
   THE GOAL: Be able to name an ionic compound from its formula or give the formula of a compound from its name.

6. **What are acids and bases?**
   THE GOAL: Be able to recognize common acids and bases.

There are more than 19 million known chemical compounds, ranging in size from small *diatomic* (two-atom) substances like carbon monoxide, CO, to deoxyribonucleic acid (DNA), which can contain several *billion* atoms linked together in a precise way. Clearly, there must be some force that holds atoms together in compounds; otherwise, the atoms would simply drift apart and no compounds could exist. The forces that hold atoms together in compounds are called *chemical bonds* and are of two major types: *ionic bonds* and *covalent bonds*. In this chapter, we look at ionic bonds and at the substances formed by them. In the next chapter, we will look at covalent bonds.

All chemical bonds result from the electrical attraction between opposite charges—between positively charged nuclei and negatively charged electrons. As a result, the way that different elements form bonds is related to their different electron configurations and the changes that take place as each atom tries to achieve a more stable electron configuration.

3.1 Ions

A general rule noted by early chemists is that metals, on the left side of the periodic table, tend to form compounds with nonmetals, on the right side of the table. The alkali metals of group 1A, for instance, react with the halogens of group 7A to form a variety of compounds. Sodium chloride (table salt), formed by the reaction of sodium with chlorine, is a familiar example. The names and chemical formulas of some other compounds containing elements from groups 1A and 7A include:

Potassium iodide, KI   Added to table salt to provide the iodide ion that is needed by the thyroid gland

Sodium fluoride, NaF   Added to many municipal water supplies to provide fluoride ion for the prevention of tooth decay

Sodium iodide, NaI   Used in laboratory scintillation counters to detect radiation (See Section 11.8)

The compositions and the properties of these alkali metal–halogen compounds are similar. For instance, the two elements always combine in a 1:1 ratio: one alkali metal atom for every halogen atom. Each compound has a high melting point (all are over 500 °C); each is a stable, white, crystalline solid; and each is soluble in water.

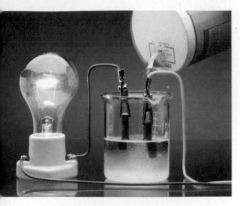

▲ **A solution of sodium chloride in water conducts electricity, allowing the bulb to light.**

Ion An electrically charged atom or group of atoms.

Cation A positively charged ion.

Anion A negatively charged ion.

Furthermore, a water solution containing each compound conducts electricity, a property that gives a clue to the kind of chemical bond holding the atoms together.

Electricity can only flow through a medium containing charged particles that are free to move. The electrical conductivity of metals, for example, results from the movement of negatively charged electrons through the metal. But what charged particles might be present in the water solutions of alkali metal–halogen compounds? To answer this question, think about the composition of atoms. Atoms are electrically neutral because they contain equal numbers of protons and electrons. By gaining or losing one or more electrons, however, an atom can be converted into a charged particle called an **ion**.

The *loss* of one or more electrons from a neutral atom gives a *positively* charged ion called a **cation** (**cat**-ion). As we saw in Section 2.8, sodium and other alkali metal atoms have a single electron in their valence shell and an electron configuration symbolized as ns^1, where n represents the shell number. By losing this electron, an alkali metal is converted to a positively charged cation.

A sodium *atom*, Na **A sodium *cation*, Na^+**

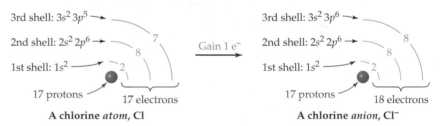

Conversely, the *gain* of one or more electrons by a neutral atom gives a *negatively* charged ion called an **anion** (**an**-ion). Chlorine and other halogen atoms have ns^2np^5 valence electrons and can easily gain an additional electron to fill out their valence subshell, thereby forming negatively charged anions.

A chlorine *atom*, Cl **A chlorine *anion*, Cl^-**

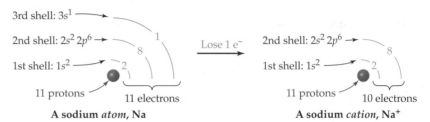

The symbol for a cation is written by adding the positive charge as a superscript to the symbol for the element; an anion symbol is written by adding the negative charge as a superscript. If one electron is lost or gained, the charge is +1 or −1 but the number 1 is omitted in the notation, as in Na^+ and Cl^-. If two or more electrons are lost or gained, however, the charge is ±2 or greater and the number *is* used, as in Ca^{2+} and N^{3-}.

PROBLEM 3.1

Magnesium atoms lose two electrons when they react. Write the symbol of the ion that is formed. Is it a cation or an anion?

PROBLEM 3.2

Sulfur atoms gain two electrons when they react. Write the symbol of the ion that is formed. Is it a cation or an anion?

KEY CONCEPT PROBLEM 3.3

Write the symbol for the ion depicted here. Is it a cation or an anion?

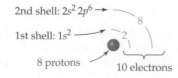

3.2 Periodic Properties and Ion Formation

The ease with which an atom loses an electron to form a positively charged cation is measured by a property called the atom's **ionization energy**, defined as the energy required to remove one electron from a single atom in the gaseous state. Conversely, the ease with which an atom *gains* an electron to form a negatively charged anion is measured by a property called **electron affinity**, defined as the energy released on adding an electron to a single atom in the gaseous state.

Ionization energy The energy required to remove one electron from a single atom in the gaseous state.

Electron affinity The energy released on adding an electron to a single atom in the gaseous state.

$$\text{Ionization energy} \quad \text{Atom} + \text{Energy} \xrightarrow{\text{Gain e}^-} \text{Cation} + \text{Electron}$$
(energy is added)

$$\text{Electron affinity} \quad \text{Atom} + \text{Electron} \xrightarrow{\text{Lose e}^-} \text{Anion} + \text{Energy}$$
(energy is relased)

The relative magnitudes of ionization energies and electron affinities for elements in the first four rows of the periodic table are shown in Figure 3.1. Because ionization energy measures the amount of energy that must be *added* to pull an electron away from a neutral atom, the small values shown in Figure 3.1 for alkali metals (Li, Na, K) and other elements on the left side of the periodic table mean that these elements lose an electron easily. Conversely, the large values shown for halogens (F, Cl, Br) and noble gases (He, Ne, Ar, Kr) on the right side of the periodic table mean that these elements do not lose an electron easily. Electron affinities, however, measure the amount of energy *released* when an atom gains an electron. Although electron affinities are small compared to ionization energies, the halogens nevertheless have the largest values and therefore gain an electron most easily, whereas metals have the smallest values and do not gain an electron easily:

Alkali metal
$\Big\{$
Small ionization energy—electron easily lost
Small electron affinity—electron not easily gained
Net result: Cation formation is favored

Halogen
$\Big\{$
Large ionization energy—electron not easily lost
Large electron affinity—electron easily gained
Net result: Anion formation is favored

You might also note in Figure 3.1 that main group elements near the *middle* of the periodic table—boron ($Z = 5$, group 3A) carbon ($Z = 6$, group 4A), and nitrogen ($Z = 7$, group 5A)—neither lose nor gain electrons easily and thus do not form ions easily. In the next chapter, we will see that these elements tend not to form ionic bonds but form covalent bonds instead.

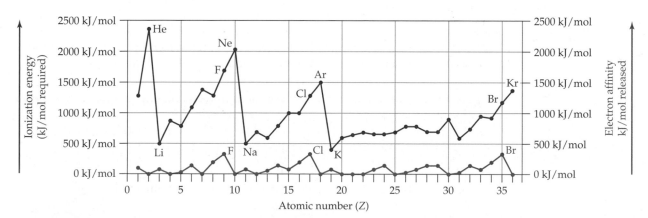

▲ **Figure 3.1**
Relative ionization energies (red) and electron affinities (blue) for elements in the first four rows of the periodic table.
Those elements having a value of zero for electron affinity do not accept an electron. Note that the alkali metals (Li, Na, K) have the lowest ionization energies and lose an electron most easily, whereas the halogens (F, Cl, Br) have the highest electron affinities and gain an electron most easily. The noble gases (He, Ne, Ar, Kr) neither gain nor lose an electron easily.

Because alkali metals such as sodium tend to lose an electron, and halogens such as chlorine tend to gain an electron, these two elements (sodium and chlorine) will react with each other by transfer of an electron from the metal to the halogen (Figure 3.2). The product that results—sodium chloride (NaCl)—is electrically neutral because the positive charge of each Na^+ ion is balanced by the negative charge of each Cl^- ion.

▶ **Figure 3.2**
(a) Chlorine is a toxic green gas, sodium is a reactive metal, and sodium chloride is a harmless white solid. (b) Sodium metal burns with an intense yellow flame when immersed in chlorine gas, yielding white sodium chloride "smoke."

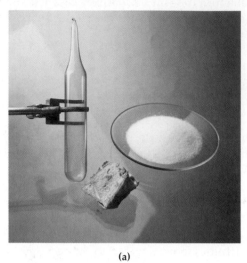

(a)   (b)

Worked Example 3.1 Periodic Trends: Ionization Energy

Look at the periodic trends in Figure 3.1, and predict where the ionization energy of rubidium is likely to fall on the chart.

ANALYSIS Identify the group number of rubidium (group 1A), and find where other members of the group appear in Figure 3.1.

SOLUTION
Rubidium (Rb) is the alkali metal below potassium (K) in the periodic table. Since the alkali metals Li, Na, and K all have ionization energies near the bottom of the chart, the ionization energy of rubidium is probably similar.

Worked Example 3.2 Periodic Trends: Formation of Anions and Cations

Which element is likely to lose an electron more easily, Mg or S?

ANALYSIS Identify the group numbers of the elements, and find where members of those groups appear in Figure 3.1.

SOLUTION
Magnesium, a group 2A element on the left side of the periodic table, has a relatively low ionization energy, and loses an electron easily. Sulfur, a group 6A element on the right side of the table, has a higher ionization energy, and loses an electron less easily.

PROBLEM 3.4
Look at the periodic trends in Figure 3.1, and predict approximately where the ionization energy of xenon is likely to fall.

PROBLEM 3.5
Which element in the following pairs is likely to lose an electron more easily?
(a) Be or B   (b) Ca or Co   (c) Sc or Se

PROBLEM 3.6
Which element in the following pairs is likely to gain an electron more easily?
(a) H or He   (b) S or Si   (c) Cr or Mn

3.3 Ionic Bonds

When sodium reacts with chlorine, the product is sodium chloride, a compound completely unlike either of the elements from which it is formed. Sodium is a soft, silvery metal that reacts violently with water, and chlorine is a corrosive, poisonous, green gas (Figure 3.2a). When chemically combined, however, they produce our familiar table salt containing Na^+ ions and Cl^- ions. Because opposite electrical charges attract each other, the positive Na^+ ion and negative Cl^- ion are said to be held together by an **ionic bond**.

When a vast number of sodium atoms transfer electrons to an equally vast number of chlorine atoms, a visible crystal of sodium chloride results. In this crystal, equal numbers of Na^+ and Cl^- ions are packed together in a regular arrangement. Each positively charged Na^+ ion is surrounded by six negatively charged Cl^- ions, and each Cl^- ion is surrounded by six Na^+ ions (Figure 3.3). This packing arrangement allows each ion to be stabilized by the attraction of unlike charges on its six nearest-neighbor ions, while being as far as possible from ions of like charge.

Ionic bond The electrical attractions between ions of opposite charge in a crystal.

◄**Figure 3.3**
The arrangement of Na^+ and Cl^- ions in a sodium chloride crystal. Each positively charged Na^+ ion is surrounded by six negatively charged Cl^- ions, and each Cl^- ion is surrounded by six Na^+ ions. The crystal is held together by ionic bonds—the attraction between oppositely charged ions.

Because of the three-dimensional arrangement of ions in a sodium chloride crystal, we cannot speak of specific ionic bonds between specific pairs of ions. Rather, there are many ions attracted by ionic bonds to their nearest neighbors. We therefore speak of the whole NaCl crystal as being an **ionic solid** and of such compounds as being **ionic compounds**. The same is true of all compounds composed of ions.

Ionic solid A crystalline solid held together by ionic bonds.

Ionic compound A compound that contains ionic bonds.

3.4 Some Properties of Ionic Compounds

Like sodium chloride, ionic compounds are usually crystalline solids. Different ions vary in size and charge, therefore, they are packed together in crystals in different ways. The ions in each compound settle into a pattern that efficiently fills space and maximizes ionic bonding.

Because the ions in an ionic solid are held rigidly in place by attraction to their neighbors, they cannot move about. Once an ionic solid is dissolved in water, however, the ions can move freely, thereby accounting for the electrical conductivity of these compounds in solution.

The high melting points and boiling points observed for ionic compounds are also accounted for by ionic bonding. The attractive force between oppositely charged particles is extremely strong, and the ions need to gain a large amount of energy by being heated to high temperatures for them to loosen their grip on one another. Sodium chloride, for example, melts at 801 °C and boils at 1413 °C; potassium iodide melts at 681 °C and boils at 1330 °C.

▲ **The melting point of sodium chloride is 801 °C.**

Despite the strength of ionic bonds, ionic solids shatter if struck sharply. A blow disrupts the orderly arrangement of cations and anions, forcing particles of like electrical charge closer together. The close proximity of like charges creates repulsive energies that split the crystal apart.

Ionic compounds dissolve in water if the attraction between water and the ions overcomes the attraction of the ions for one another. Compounds like sodium chloride are very soluble in water and can be dissolved to make solutions of high concentration. Do not be misled, however, by the ease with which sodium chloride and other familiar ionic compounds dissolve in water. Many other ionic compounds, such as magnesium hydroxide or barium sulfate, are not water-soluble, because the attractive forces between these ions and water is not sufficient to overcome the ionic attractions in the crystals.

PROBLEM 3.7
Consider the ionic liquids described in the Chemistry in Action below. How are the properties of these ionic liquids different from other common ionic substances?

CHEMISTRY IN ACTION

Ionic Liquids

Imagine a substance that could help solve the problems of nuclear waste, make solar energy more efficient, revolutionize the development of biomass-based renewable energies, serve as a solvent for enzyme-based biochemical transformations, and act as a major component in a spinning-liquid mirror telescope stationed on the moon. Ionic liquids can do all that—and more! When discussing ionic substances, most of us think of hard, crystalline materials like common table salt (see Chemistry in Action, p. 83), with high melting points. But ionic liquids have very different properties, including low melting points, high viscosity, low-to-moderate electrical conductivity, and low volatility, which make them suitable for the widely varied uses described previously.

Although the details of the discovery of ionic liquids are in dispute, one of the first *room temperature ionic liquids* (or RTILs), ethylammonium nitrate, was synthesized in 1914 by Paul Walden. Most RTILs developed since then consist of a bulky, asymmetric organic cation (see Organic Chemistry in Chapters 12–19), combined with a variety of anions. The bulky cations cannot pack together in an ordered fashion, and so these substances do not condense into a solid at ambient temperatures. Rather, they tend to form highly viscous liquids that exhibit low volatility, ideal properties for a large-diameter spinning liquid mirror in a low-pressure environment like the moon. The viscous liquid can be covered with a thin metallic film that will form a parabolic reflective surface to collect long-wavelength infrared light. And the cost of the spinning-liquid mirror is about 1% of a conventional lens, which must be ground and polished.

The bulky cations also provide unique solvent properties, enabling them to dissolve substances that are not very soluble in more conventional solvents. Their low volatility also makes them attractive as "green," or environmentally friendly, solvents. Consider the practice of using biomass as a fuel source. One common approach is to convert sugar or starch (from corn, beets, or cane sugar) into ethanol by the process of fermentation. But the major component of these and most other plants is cellulose. Cellulose is a polymer (see Chemistry in Action on pp. 118 and 538) composed of many sugars joined together in a long chain. Cellulose is chemically similar to starch but is neither highly soluble in most solvents nor subject to fermentation. RTILs, however, such as that illustrated in the figure below, can be used to dissolve cellulose at moderate temperatures and facilitate its breakdown into simple fermentable sugars. At a volume of nearly 700 billion tons of the earth's biomass, cellulose represents an important renewable energy source. The ability to convert cellulose into fuel will certainly help meet our expanding energy needs.

See Chemistry in Action Problems 3.80 and 3.81 at the end of the chapter.

Benzylmethylimidazolium chloride

◀ **Pine wood fibers dissolving in an ionic liquid solvent consisting of benzyl methyl imidazolium chloride, whose structural formula is shown.**

3.5 Ions and the Octet Rule

We have seen that alkali metal atoms have a single valence-shell electron, ns^1. The electron-dot symbol X· is consistent with this valence electron configuration. Halogens, having seven valence electrons, ns^2np^5, can be represented using :Ẍ· as the electron-dot symbol. Noble gases can be represented as :Ẍ:, since they have eight valence electrons, ns^2np^6. Both the alkali metals and the halogens are extremely reactive, undergoing many chemical reactions and forming many compounds. The noble gases, however, are quite different. They are the least reactive of all elements.

Now look at sodium chloride and similar ionic compounds. When sodium or any other alkali metal reacts with chlorine or any other halogen, the metal transfers an electron from its valence shell to the valence shell of the halogen. Sodium thereby changes its valence-shell electron configuration from $2s^22p^63s^1$ in the atom to $2s^22p^6(3s^0)$ in the Na^+ ion, and chlorine changes from $3s^23p^5$ in the atom to $3s^23p^6$ in the Cl^- ion. *As a result, both sodium and chlorine gain noble gas electron configurations, with 8 valence electrons.* The Na^+ ion has 8 electrons in the $n = 2$ shell, matching the electron configuration of neon. The Cl^- ion has 8 electrons in the $n = 3$ shell, matching the electron configuration of argon.

$$\underset{1s^2\,2s^2\,2p^6\,3s^1}{Na} \; + \; \underset{1s^2\,2s^2\,2p^6\,3s^2\,3p^5}{Cl} \; \longrightarrow \; \underset{\underbrace{1s^2\,2s^2\,2p^63s^0}_{\substack{\text{Neon}\\\text{configuration}}}}{Na^+} \; + \; \underset{\underbrace{1s^2\,2s^2\,2p^6\,3s^2\,3p^6}_{\substack{\text{Argon}\\\text{configuration}}}}{Cl^-}$$

$$Na· \; + \; ·\overset{..}{\underset{..}{Cl}}: \; \longrightarrow \; Na^+ \; + \; :\overset{..}{\underset{..}{Cl}}:^-$$

Evidently there is something special about having 8 valence electrons (filled s and p subshells) that leads to stability and lack of chemical reactivity. In fact, observations of many chemical compounds have shown that main group elements frequently combine in such a way that each winds up with 8 valence electrons, a so-called *electron octet*. This conclusion is summarized in a statement called the **octet rule**:

Octet rule Main group elements tend to undergo reactions that leave them with 8 valence electrons.

Put another way, main group *metals* tend to lose electrons when they react so that they attain an electron configuration like that of the noble gas just *before* them in the periodic table, and reactive main group *nonmetals* tend to gain electrons when they react so that they attain an electron configuration like that of the noble gas just *after* them in the periodic table. In both cases, the product ions have filled s and p subshells in their valence electron shell.

Worked Example 3.3 Electron Configurations: Octet Rule for Cations

Write the electron configuration of magnesium ($Z = 12$). Show how many electrons a magnesium atom must lose to form an ion with a filled shell (8 electrons), and write the configuration of the ion. Explain the reason for the ion's charge, and write the ion's symbol.

ANALYSIS Write the electron configuration of magnesium as described in Section 2.7 and count the number of electrons in the valence shell.

SOLUTION
Magnesium has the electron configuration $1s^22s^22p^63s^2$. Since the second shell contains an octet of electrons ($2s^22p^6$) and the third shell is only partially filled ($3s^2$), magnesium can achieve a valence-shell octet by losing the 2 electrons in the

3s subshell. The result is formation of a doubly charged cation, Mg^{2+}, with the neon configuration:

$$Mg^{2+} \quad 1s^2 2s^2 2p^6 \text{ (Neon configuration, or } [\,Ne\,])$$

A neutral magnesium atom has 12 protons and 12 electrons. With the loss of 2 electrons, there is an excess of 2 protons, accounting for the $+2$ charge of the ion, Mg^{2+}.

Worked Example 3.4 Electron Configurations: Octet Rule for Anions

How many electrons must a nitrogen atom, $Z = 7$, gain to attain a noble gas configuration? Write the electron-dot and ion symbols for the ion formed.

ANALYSIS Write the electron configuration of nitrogen, and identify how many more electrons are needed to reach a noble gas configuration.

SOLUTION

Nitrogen, a group 5A element, has the electron configuration $1s^2 2s^2 2p^3$. The second shell contains 5 electrons $(2s^2 2p^3)$ and needs 3 more to reach an octet. The result is formation of a triply charged anion, N^{3-}, with 8 valence electrons, matching the neon configuration:

$$N^{3-} \quad 1s^2 2s^2 2p^6 \quad \text{(Neon configuration)} \quad :\ddot{\underset{..}{N}}:^{3-}$$

PROBLEM 3.8
Write the electron configuration of potassium, $Z = 19$, and show how a potassium atom can attain a noble gas configuration.

PROBLEM 3.9
How many electrons must an aluminum atom, $Z = 13$, lose to attain a noble gas configuration? Write the symbol for the ion formed.

🔑 **KEY CONCEPT PROBLEM 3.10**

Which atom in the reaction depicted here gains electrons, and which loses electrons? Draw the electron-dot symbols for the resulting ions.

$$X\!: \;+\; \cdot\ddot{Y}\cdot \;\longrightarrow\; ?$$

3.6 Ions of Some Common Elements

The periodic table is the key to understanding and remembering which elements form ions and which do not. As shown in Figure 3.4, atoms of elements in the same group tend to form ions of the same charge. The metals of groups 1A and 2A, for example, form only $+1$ and $+2$ ions, respectively. The ions of these elements

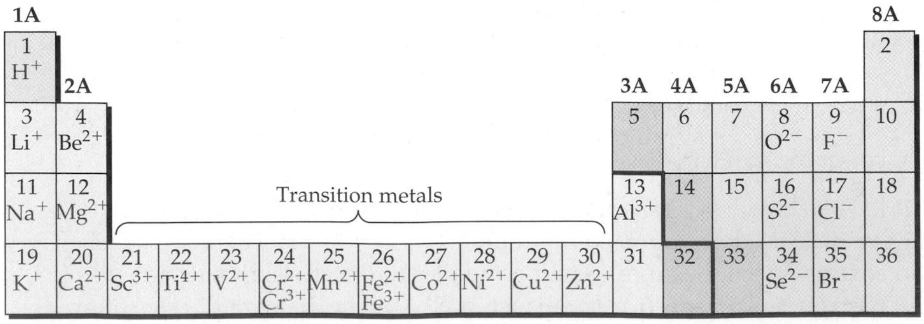

▶ **Figure 3.4**
Common ions formed by elements in the first four periods.
Ions important in biological chemistry are shown in red.

all have noble gas configurations as a result of electron loss from their valence s subshells. (Note in the following equations that the electrons being lost are shown as products.)

Group 1A: $M \cdot \rightarrow M^+ + e^-$
(M = Li, Na, K, Rb, or Cs)

Group 2A: $M \colon \rightarrow M^{2+} + 2e^-$
(M = Be, Mg, Ca, Sr, Ba, or Ra)

Four of these ions, Na^+, K^+, Mg^{2+}, and Ca^{2+}, are present in body fluids, where they play extremely important roles in biochemical processes.

The only group 3A element commonly encountered in ionic compounds is aluminum, which forms Al^{3+} by loss of three electrons from its valence s and p subshells. Aluminum is not thought to be an essential element in the human diet, although it is known to be present in some organisms.

The first three elements in groups 4A (C, Si, Ge) and 5A (N, P, As) do not ordinarily form cations or anions, because either too much energy is required to remove an electron or not enough energy is released by adding an electron to make the process energetically favorable. The bonding of these elements is largely covalent and will be described in the next chapter. Carbon, in particular, is the key element on which life is based. Together with hydrogen, nitrogen, phosphorus, and oxygen, carbon is present in all the essential biological compounds that we will be describing throughout the latter half of this book.

The group 6A elements, oxygen and sulfur, form large numbers of compounds, some of which are ionic and some of which are covalent. Their ions have noble gas configurations, achieved by gaining two electrons:

Group 6A: $\cdot \ddot{\text{O}} \cdot + 2\,e^- \longrightarrow \colon \ddot{\text{O}} \colon^{2-}$

$\ddot{\text{S}} \cdot + 2\,e^- \longrightarrow \colon \ddot{\text{S}} \colon^{2-}$

The halogens are present in many compounds as ions formed by gaining one electron:

Group 7A: $\cdot \ddot{\text{X}} \colon + e^- \longrightarrow \colon \ddot{\text{X}} \colon^-$
(X = F, Cl, Br, I)

Transition metals lose electrons to form cations, some of which are present in the human body. The charges of transition metal cations are not as predictable as those of main group elements, however, because many transition metal atoms can lose one or more d electrons in addition to losing valence s electrons. For example, iron $(\dots 3s^2 3p^6 3d^6 4s^2)$ forms Fe^{2+} by losing two electrons from the $4s$ subshell and also forms Fe^{3+} by losing an additional electron from the $3d$ subshell. Looking at the electron configuration for iron shows why the octet rule is limited to main group elements: transition metal cations generally do not have noble gas configurations because they would have to lose *all* their d electrons.

Important Points about Ion Formation and the Periodic Table:

- **Metals form cations by losing one or more electrons.**
    - Group 1A and 2A metals form +1 and +2 ions, respectively (for example, Li^+ and Mg^{2+}) to achieve a noble gas configuration.
    - Transition metals can form cations of more than one charge (for example, Fe^{2+} and Fe^{3+}) by losing a combination of valence-shell s electrons and inner-shell d electrons.

- **Reactive nonmetals form anions by gaining one or more electrons to achieve a noble gas configuration.**
    - Group 6A nonmetals oxygen and sulfur form the anions O^{2-} and S^{2-}.
    - Group 7A elements (the halogens) form −1 ions; for example, F^- and Cl^-.

- **Group 8A elements (the noble gases) are unreactive.**
- **Ionic charges of main group elements can be predicted using the group number and the octet rule.**
  - For 1A and 2A metals: cation charge = group number
  - For nonmetals in groups 5A, 6A, and 7A: anion charge = 8 − (group number)

Worked Example 3.5 Formation of Ions: Gain/Loss of Valence Electrons

Which of the following ions is likely to form?

(a) S^{3-} (b) Si^{2+} (c) Sr^{2+}

ANALYSIS Count the number of valence electrons in each ion. For main group elements, only ions with a valence octet of electrons are likely to form.

SOLUTION

(a) Sulfur is in group 6A, has 6 valence electrons, and needs only 2 more to reach an octet. Gaining 2 electrons gives an S^{2-} ion with a noble gas configuration, but gaining 3 electrons does not. The S^{3-} ion is, therefore, unlikely to form.

(b) Silicon is a nonmetal in group 4A. Like carbon, it does not form ions because it would have to gain or lose too many electrons (4) to reach a noble gas electron configuration. The Si^{2+} ion does not have an octet and will not form.

(c) Strontium, a metal in group 2A, has only 2 outer-shell electrons and can lose both to reach a noble gas configuration. The Sr^{2+} ion has an octet and, therefore, forms easily.

PROBLEM 3.11
Is molybdenum more likely to form a cation or an anion? Why?

PROBLEM 3.12
Write symbols, both with and without electron dots, for the ions formed by the following processes:

(a) Gain of 2 electrons by selenium   (b) Loss of 2 electrons by barium

(c) Gain of 1 electron by bromine

PROBLEM 3.13
By mass, seawater contains 3.5% NaCl, or table salt (see Chemistry in Action, p. 83). If one liter of seawater contains 35 g of NaCl, how many gallons of water must be evaporated to produce one pound of NaCl?

3.7 Naming Ions

Main group metal cations in groups 1A, 2A, and 3A are named by identifying the metal, followed by the word "ion," as in the following examples:

$$K^+ \qquad\qquad Mg^{2+} \qquad\qquad Al^{3+}$$
Potassium ion   Magnesium ion   Aluminum ion

It is sometimes a little confusing to use the same name for both a metal and its ion, and you may occasionally have to stop and think about what is meant. For example, it is common practice in nutrition and health-related fields to talk about sodium or potassium in the bloodstream. Because both sodium and potassium *metals* react violently with water, however, they cannot possibly be present in blood. The references are to dissolved sodium and potassium *ions*.

Transition metals, such as iron or chromium, and many metals found in the *p*-block, such as tin and lead, can form more than one type of cation. To avoid confusion, a method is needed to differentiate between ions of these metals. Two systems are used. The first is an old system that gives the ion with the smaller charge the word ending *-ous* and the ion with the larger charge the ending *-ic*.

CHEMISTRY IN ACTION

Salt

If you are like most people, you feel a little guilty about reaching for the salt shaker at mealtime. The notion that high salt intake and high blood pressure go hand in hand is surely among the most highly publicized pieces of nutritional lore ever to appear.

Salt has not always been held in such disrepute. Historically, salt has been prized since the earliest recorded times as a seasoning and a food preservative. Words and phrases in many languages reflect the importance of salt as a life-giving and life-sustaining substance. We refer to a kind and generous person as "the salt of the earth," for instance, and we speak of being "worth one's salt." In Roman times, soldiers were paid in salt; the English word "salary" is derived from the Latin word for paying salt wages (*salarium*).

Salt is perhaps the easiest of all minerals to obtain and purify. The simplest method, used for thousands of years throughout the world in coastal climates where sunshine is abundant and rainfall is scarce, is to evaporate seawater. Though the exact amount varies depending on the source, seawater contains an average of about 3.5% by mass of dissolved substances, most of which is sodium chloride. It has been estimated that evaporation of all the world's oceans would yield approximately *4.5 million cubic miles* of NaCl.

Only about 10% of current world salt production comes from evaporation of seawater. Most salt is obtained by mining the vast deposits of *halite*, or *rock salt*, formed by evaporation of ancient inland seas. These salt beds vary in thickness up to hundreds of meters and vary in depth from a few meters to thousands of meters below the earth's surface. Salt mining has gone on for at least 3400 years, and the Wieliczka mine in Galicia, Poland, has been worked continuously from A.D. 1000 to the present.

What about the link between dietary salt intake and high blood pressure? Although sodium is a macronutrient that we need—it plays a critical role in charge balance and ion transport in cell membranes—too much sodium has been linked to both hypertension and kidney ailments. The recommended daily intake (RDI) for sodium is 2300 mg, which translates to roughly 4 g of salt. However, the average adult in most industrialized countries consumes over twice this amount, with most of it coming from processed foods.

What should an individual do? The best answer, as in so many things, is to use moderation and common sense. People with hypertension should make a strong effort to lower their

▲ **In many areas of the world, salt is still harvested by evaporation of ocean or tidal waters.**

☐ 5% added while cooking

☐ 6% added while eating

☐ 12% from natural sources

☐ 77% from processed and prepared foods

sodium intake; others might be well advised to choose unsalted snacks, monitor their consumption of processed food, and read nutrition labels for sodium content.

See Chemistry in Action Problem 3.82 at the end of the chapter.

The second is a newer system in which the charge on the ion is given as a Roman numeral in parentheses right after the metal name. For example:

	Cr^{2+}	Cr^{3+}
Old name:	Chrom*ous* ion	Chrom*ic* ion
New name:	Chromium(II) ion	Chromium(III) ion

We will generally emphasize the new system in this book, but it is important to understand both systems because the old system is often found on labels of commercially supplied chemicals. The small differences between the names in either system illustrate the importance of reading a name very carefully before using a chemical. There are significant differences between compounds consisting of the same two elements but having different charges on the cation. In treating iron-deficiency anemia, for example, iron(II) compounds are preferable because the body absorbs them considerably better than iron(III) compounds.

The names of some common transition metal cations are listed in Table 3.1. Notice that the old names of the copper, iron, and tin ions are derived from their Latin names (*cuprum, ferrum,* and *stannum*).

TABLE 3.1 Names of Some Transition Metal Cations

Element	Symbol	Old Name	New Name
Chromium	Cr^{2+}	Chromous	Chromium(II)
	Cr^{3+}	Chromic	Chromium(III)
Copper	Cu^+	Cuprous	Copper(I)
	Cu^{2+}	Cupric	Copper(II)
Iron	Fe^{2+}	Ferrous	Iron(II)
	Fe^{3+}	Ferric	Iron(III)
Mercury	$*Hg_2^{2+}$	Mercurous	Mercury(I)
	Hg^{2+}	Mercuric	Mercury(II)
Tin	Sn^{2+}	Stannous	Tin(II)
	Sn^{4+}	Stannic	Tin(IV)

*This cation is composed of two mercury atoms, each of which has an average charge of +1.

Anions are named by replacing the ending of the element name with *-ide*, followed by the word "ion" (Table 3.2). For example, the anion formed by fluor*ine* is the fluor*ide* ion, and the anion formed by sul*fur* is the sul*fide* ion.

TABLE 3.2 Names of Some Common Anions

Element	Symbol	Name
Bromine	Br^-	Bromide ion
Chlorine	Cl^-	Chloride ion
Fluorine	F^-	Fluoride ion
Iodine	I^-	Iodide ion
Oxygen	O^{2-}	Oxide ion
Sulfur	S^{2-}	Sulfide ion

PROBLEM 3.14

Name the following ions:

(a) Cu^{2+} (b) F^- (c) Mg^{2+} (d) S^{2-}

PROBLEM 3.15

Write the symbols for the following ions:

(a) Silver(I) ion   (b) Iron(II) ion   (c) Cuprous ion   (d) Telluride ion

PROBLEM 3.16

Ringer's solution, which is used intravenously to adjust ion concentrations in body fluids, contains the ions of sodium, potassium, calcium, and chlorine. Give the names and symbols of these ions.

3.8 Polyatomic Ions

Ions that are composed of more than one atom are called **polyatomic ions**. Most polyatomic ions contain oxygen and another element, and their chemical formulas include subscripts to show how many of each type of atom are present. Sulfate ion, for example, is composed of 1 sulfur atom and 4 oxygen atoms and has a -2 charge: SO_4^{2-}. The atoms in a polyatomic ion are held together by covalent bonds of the sort discussed in the next chapter, and the entire group of atoms acts as a single unit. A polyatomic ion is charged because it contains a total number of electrons different from the total number of protons in the combined atoms.

The most common polyatomic ions are listed in Table 3.3. Note that the ammonium ion, NH_4^+, and the hydronium ion, H_3O^+, are the only cations; all the others are anions. These ions are encountered so frequently in chemistry, biology, and medicine that there is no alternative but to memorize their names and formulas. Fortunately, there are only a few of them.

Polyatomic ion An ion that is composed of more than one atom.

TABLE 3.3 Some Common Polyatomic Ions

Name	Formula	Name	Formula
Hydronium ion	H_3O^+	Nitrate ion	NO_3^-
Ammonium ion	NH_4^+	Nitrite ion	NO_2^-
Acetate ion	$CH_3CO_2^-$	Oxalate ion	$C_2O_4^{2-}$
Carbonate ion	CO_3^{2-}	Permanganate ion	MnO_4^-
Hydrogen carbonate ion (bicarbonate ion)	HCO_3^-	Phosphate ion	PO_4^{3-}
Chromate ion	CrO_4^{2-}	Hydrogen phosphate ion (biphosphate ion)	HPO_4^{2-}
Dichromate ion	$Cr_2O_7^{2-}$	Dihydrogen phosphate ion	$H_2PO_4^-$
Cyanide ion	CN^-	Sulfate ion	SO_4^{2-}
Hydroxide ion	OH^-	Hydrogen sulfate ion (bisulfate ion)	HSO_4^-
Hypochlorite ion	OCl^-	Sulfite ion	SO_3^{2-}

Note in Table 3.3 that several pairs of ions—CO_3^{2-} and HCO_3^-, for example—are related by the presence or absence of a hydrogen ion, H^+. In such instances, the ion with the hydrogen is sometimes named using the prefix *bi-*. Thus, CO_3^{2-} is the carbonate ion, and HCO_3^- is the bicarbonate ion; similarly, SO_4^{2-} is the sulfate ion, and HSO_4^- is the bisulfate ion.

PROBLEM 3.17

Name the following ions:

(a) NO_3^-

(b) CN^-

(c) OH^-

(d) HPO_4^{2-}

PROBLEM 3.18

Which of the biologically important ions (see Chemistry in Action, p. 86) belong to Group 1A? To Group 2A? To the transition metals? To the halogens?

CHEMISTRY IN ACTION

Biologically Important Ions

The human body requires many different ions for proper functioning. Several of these ions, such as Ca^{2+}, Mg^{2+}, and HPO_4^{2-}, are used as structural materials in bones and teeth in addition to having other essential functions. Although 99% of Ca^{2+} is contained in bones and teeth, small amounts in body fluids play a vital role in transmission of nerve impulses. Other ions, including essential transition metal ions such as Fe^{2+}, are required for specific chemical reactions in the body. And still others, such as K^+, Na^+, and Cl^-, are present in fluids throughout the body.

In order to maintain charge neutrality in solution, the total negative charge (from anions) must balance the total positive charge (from cations). Several monatomic anions, and several polyatomic anions, especially HCO_3^- and HPO_4^{2-}, are present in body fluids where they help balance the cation charges. Some of the most important ions and their functions are shown in the accompanying table.

See Chemistry in Action Problems 3.83, 3.84, and 3.85 at the end of the chapter.

Some Biologically Important Ions

Ion	Location	Function	Dietary source
Ca^{2+}	Outside cell; 99% of Ca^{2+} is in bones and teeth as $Ca_3(PO_4)_2$ and $CaCO_3$	Bone and tooth structure; necessary for blood clotting, muscle contraction, and transmission of nerve impulses	Milk, whole grains, leafy vegetables
Fe^{2+}	Blood hemoglobin	Transports oxygen from lungs to cells	Liver, red meat, leafy green vegetables
K^+	Fluids inside cells	Maintain ion concentrations in cells; regulate insulin release and heartbeat	Milk, oranges, bananas, meat
Na^+	Fluids outside cells	Protect against fluid loss; necessary for muscle contraction and transmission of nerve impulses	Table salt, seafood
Mg^{2+}	Fluids inside cells; bone	Present in many enzymes; needed for energy generation and muscle contraction	Leafy green plants, seafood, nuts
Cl^-	Fluids outside cells; gastric juice	Maintain fluid balance in cells; help transfer CO_2 from blood to lungs	Table salt, seafood
HCO_3^-	Fluids outside cells	Control acid–base balance in blood	By-product of food metabolism
HPO_4^{2-}	Fluids inside cells; bones and teeth	Control acid–base balance in cells	Fish, poultry, milk

3.9 Formulas of Ionic Compounds

Since all chemical compounds are neutral, it is relatively easy to figure out the formulas of ionic compounds. Once the ions are identified, all we need to do is decide how many ions of each type give a total charge of zero. Thus, the chemical formula of an ionic compound tells the ratio of anions and cations.

If the ions have the same charge, only one of each ion is needed:

$$K^+ \text{ and } F^- \text{ form } KF$$
$$Ca^{2+} \text{ and } O^{2-} \text{ form } CaO$$

This makes sense when we look at how many electrons must be gained or lost by each atom in order to satisfy the octet rule:

$$K\cdot + \cdot \ddot{\underset{\cdot\cdot}{F}}: \longrightarrow K^+ + :\ddot{\underset{\cdot\cdot}{F}}:^-$$
$$\cdot Ca\cdot + \cdot \ddot{\underset{\cdot\cdot}{O}}\cdot \longrightarrow Ca^{2+} + :\ddot{\underset{\cdot\cdot}{O}}:^{2-}$$

If the ions have different charges, however, unequal numbers of anions and cations must combine in order to have a net charge of zero. When potassium and oxygen combine, for example, it takes two K^+ ions to balance the -2 charge of the O^{2-} ion. Put another way, it takes two K atoms to provide the two electrons needed in order to complete the octet for the O atom:

$$2\,K\cdot \;+\; \cdot \ddot{O} \cdot \;\longrightarrow\; 2\,K^+ \;+\; :\ddot{O}:^{2-}$$

$$2\,K^+ \quad \text{and} \quad O^{2-} \quad \text{form} \quad K_2O$$

The situation is reversed when a Ca^{2+} ion reacts with a Cl^- ion. One Ca atom can provide two electrons; each Cl atom requires only one electron to achieve a complete octet. Thus, there is one Ca^{2+} cation for every two Cl^- anions:

$$\cdot Ca\cdot \;+\; 2\,\cdot \ddot{\underset{..}{Cl}}: \;\longrightarrow\; Ca^{2+} \;+\; 2\,:\ddot{\underset{..}{Cl}}:^{-}$$

$$Ca^{2+} \quad \text{and} \quad 2Cl^- \quad \text{form} \quad CaCl_2$$

It sometimes helps when writing the formulas for an ionic compound to remember that, when the two ions have different charges, the number of one ion is equal to the charge on the other ion. In magnesium phosphate, for example, the charge on the magnesium ion is +2 and the charge on the polyatomic phosphate ion is −3. Thus, there must be 3 magnesium ions with a total charge of $3 \times (+2) = +6$, and 2 phosphate ions with a total charge of $2 \times (-3) = -6$ for overall neutrality:

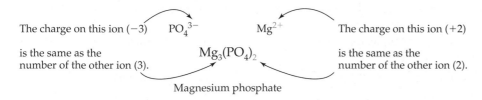

The charge on this ion (−3) $PO_4{}^{3-}$ Mg^{2+} The charge on this ion (+2)

is the same as the $Mg_3(PO_4)_2$ is the same as the
number of the other ion (3).   number of the other ion (2).

Magnesium phosphate

The formula of an ionic compound shows the lowest possible ratio of atoms in the compound and is thus known as a *simplest formula*. Because there is no such thing as a single neutral *particle* of an ionic compound, however, we use the term **formula unit** to identify the smallest possible neutral *unit* (Figure 3.5). For NaCl, the formula unit is 1 Na^+ ion and 1 Cl^- ion; for K_2SO_4, the formula unit is 2 K^+ ions and 1 $SO_4{}^{2-}$ ion; for CaF_2, the formula unit is 1 Ca^{2+} ion and 2 F^- ions; and so on.

Formula unit The formula that identifies the smallest neutral unit of an ionic compound.

One formula unit = $(+1) + (-1) = 0$ One formula unit = $(+2) + (2)(-1) = 0$

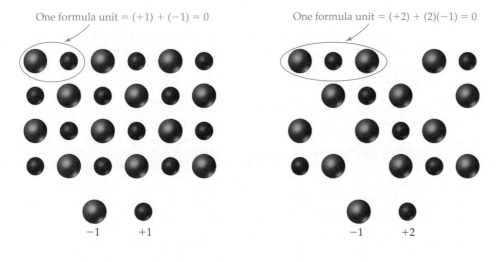

−1   +1   −1   +2

Figure 3.5
Formula units of ionic compounds.
The sum of charges on the ions in a formula unit equals zero.

Once the numbers and kinds of ions in a compound are known, the formula is written using the following rules:

- List the cation first and the anion second; for example, NaCl rather than ClNa.
- Do not write the charges of the ions; for example, KF rather than K^+F^-.
- Use parentheses around a polyatomic ion formula if it has a subscript; for example, $Al_2(SO_4)_3$ rather than Al_2SO_{43}.

Worked Example **3.6** Ionic Compounds: Writing Formulas

Write the formula for the compound formed by calcium ions and nitrate ions.

ANALYSIS Knowing the formula and charges on the cation and anion (Figure 3.4), we determine how many of each are needed to yield a neutral formula for the ionic compound.

SOLUTION
The two ions are Ca^{2+} and NO_3^-. Two nitrate ions, each with a -1 charge, will balance the $+2$ charge of the calcium ion.

$$Ca^{2+} \qquad \text{Charge} = 1 \times (+2) = +2$$
$$2NO_3^- \qquad \text{Charge} = 2 \times (-1) = -2$$

Since there are 2 ions, the nitrate formula must be enclosed in parentheses:

$$Ca(NO_3)_2 \qquad \text{Calcium nitrate}$$

PROBLEM 3.19
Write the formulas for the ionic compounds that silver(I) forms with each of the following:

(a) Iodide ion   **(b)** Oxide ion   **(c)** Phosphate ion

PROBLEM 3.20
Write the formulas for the ionic compounds that sulfate ion forms with the following:

(a) Sodium ion   **(b)** Iron(II) ion   **(c)** Chromium(III) ion

PROBLEM 3.21
The ionic compound containing ammonium ion and carbonate ion gives off the odor of ammonia, a property put to use in smelling salts for reviving someone who has fainted. Write the formula for this compound.

PROBLEM 3.22
An *astringent* is a compound that causes proteins in blood, sweat, and other body fluids to coagulate, a property put to use in antiperspirants. Two safe and effective astringents are the ionic compounds of aluminum with sulfate ion and with acetate ion. Write the formulas of both.

🔑 KEY CONCEPT PROBLEM 3.23

Three ionic compounds are represented on this periodic table—red cation with red anion, blue cation with blue anion, and green cation with green anion. Give a likely formula for each compound.

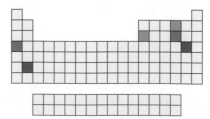

🔑 KEY CONCEPT PROBLEM 3.24

The ionic compound calcium nitride is represented here. What is the formula for calcium nitride, and what are the charges on the calcium and nitride ions?

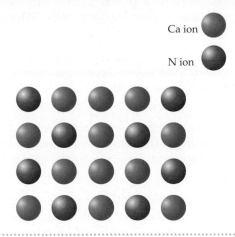

Ca ion

N ion

3.10 Naming Ionic Compounds

Just as in writing formulas for ionic compounds, these compounds are named by citing first the cation and then the anion, with a space between words. There are two kinds of ionic compounds, and the rules for naming them are slightly different.

Type I: Ionic compounds containing cations of main group elements (1A, 2A, aluminum). Since the charges on these cations do not vary, we do not need to specify the charge on the cation as discussed in Section 3.7. For example, NaCl is sodium chloride and $MgCO_3$ is magnesium carbonate.

Type II: Ionic compounds containing metals that can exhibit more than one charge. Since some metals, including the transition metals, often form more than one ion, we need to specify the charge on the cation in these compounds. Either the old (-ous, -ic) or the new (Roman numerals) system described in Section 3.7 can be used. Thus, $FeCl_2$ is called iron(II) chloride (or ferrous chloride), and $FeCl_3$ is called iron(III) chloride (or ferric chloride). Note that we do *not* name these compounds iron *di*chloride or iron *tri*chloride—once the charge on the metal is known, the number of anions needed to yield a neutral compound is also known and does not need to be included as part of the compound name. Table 3.4 lists some common ionic compounds and their uses.

TABLE 3.4 Some Common Ionic Compounds and Their Applications

Chemical Name (Common Name)	Formula	Applications
Ammonium carbonate	$(NH_4)_2CO_3$	Smelling salts
Calcium hydroxide (hydrated lime)	$Ca(OH)_2$	Mortar, plaster, whitewash
Calcium oxide (lime)	CaO	Lawn treatment, industrial chemical
Lithium carbonate ("lithium")	Li_2CO_3	Treatment of bipolar disorder
Magnesium hydroxide (milk of magnesia)	$Mg(OH)_2$	Antacid
Magnesium sulfate (Epsom salts)	$MgSO_4$	Laxative, anticonvulsant
Potassium permanganate	$KMnO_4$	Antiseptic, disinfectant*
Potassium nitrate (saltpeter)	KNO_3	Fireworks, matches, and desensitizer for teeth
Silver nitrate	$AgNO_3$	Antiseptic, germicide
Sodium bicarbonate (baking soda)	$NaHCO_3$	Baking powder, antacid, mouthwash, deodorizer
Sodium hypochlorite	$NaOCl$	Disinfectant; active ingredient in household bleach
Zinc oxide	ZnO	Skin protection, in calamine lotion

Antiseptics and disinfectants can also be harmful/toxic to non-harmful microorganisms, but are used specifically to prevent infection from harmful microorganisms.

LOOKING AHEAD ▶▶▶ Because the formula unit for an ionic compound must be neutral, we can unambiguously write the formula from the name of the compound, and vice versa. As we shall see in Chapter 4, covalent bonding between atoms can produce a much greater variety of compounds. The rules for naming covalent compounds must be able to accommodate multiple combinations of elements (for example, CO and CO_2).

Worked Example **3.7** Ionic Compounds: Formulas Involving Polyatomic Ions

Magnesium carbonate is used as an ingredient in Bufferin (buffered aspirin) tablets. Write its formula.

ANALYSIS Since magnesium is a main group metal, we can determine its ionic compound formula by identifying the charges and formulas for the anion and the cation, remembering that the overall formula must be neutral.

SOLUTION
Look at the cation and the anion parts of the name separately. Magnesium, a group 2A element, forms the doubly positive Mg^{2+} cation; carbonate anion is doubly negative, CO_3^{2-} Because the charges on the anion and cation are equal, a formula of $MgCO_3$ will be neutral.

Worked Example **3.8** Ionic Compounds: Formulas and Ionic Charges

Sodium and calcium both form a wide variety of ionic compounds. Write formulas for the following compounds:

(a) Sodium bromide and calcium bromide
(b) Sodium sulfide and calcium sulfide
(c) Sodium phosphate and calcium phosphate

ANALYSIS Using the formulas and charges for the cations and the anions (from Tables 3.2 and 3.3), we determine how many of each cation and anion are needed to yield a formula that is neutral.

SOLUTION
(a) Cations = Na^+ and Ca^{2+}; anion = Br^-: NaBr and $CaBr_2$
(b) Cations = Na^+ and Ca^{2+}; anion = S^{2-}: Na_2S and CaS
(c) Cations = Na^+ and Ca^{2+}; anion = PO_4^{3-}: Na_3PO_4 and $Ca_2(PO_4)_2$

Worked Example **3.9** Naming Ionic Compounds

Name the following compounds, using Roman numerals to indicate the charges on the cations where necessary:

(a) KF   **(b)** $MgCl_2$ **(c)** $AuCl_3$ **(d)** Fe_2O_3

ANALYSIS For main group metals, the charge is determined from the group number, and no Roman numerals are necessary. For transition metals, the charge on the metal can be determined from the total charge(s) on the anion(s).

SOLUTION
(a) Potassium fluoride. No Roman numeral is necessary because a group 1A metal forms only one cation.
(b) Magnesium chloride. No Roman numeral is necessary because magnesium (group 2A) forms only Mg^{2+}.

(c) Gold(III) chloride. The 3 Cl^- ions require a +3 charge on the gold for a neutral formula. Since gold is a transition metal that can form other ions, the Roman numeral is necessary to specify the +3 charge.

(d) Iron(III) oxide. Because the 3 oxide anions (O^{2-}) have a total negative charge of -6, the 2 iron cations must have a total charge of +6. Thus, each is Fe^{3+}, and the charge on each is indicated by the Roman numeral (III).

PROBLEM 3.25

The compound Ag_2S is responsible for much of the tarnish found on silverware. Name this compound, and give the charge on the silver ion.

PROBLEM 3.26

Name the following compounds:

(a) SnO_2 **(b)** $Ca(CN)_2$ **(c)** Na_2CO_3

(d) Cu_2SO_4 **(e)** $Ba(OH)_2$ **(f)** $Fe(NO_3)_2$

PROBLEM 3.27

Write formulas for the following compounds:

(a) Lithium phosphate   **(b)** Copper(II) carbonate

(c) Aluminum sulfite   **(d)** Cuprous fluoride

(e) Ferric sulfate   **(f)** Ammonium chloride

 KEY CONCEPT PROBLEM 3.28

The ionic compound, formed between chromium and oxygen is shown here. Name the compound, and write its formula.

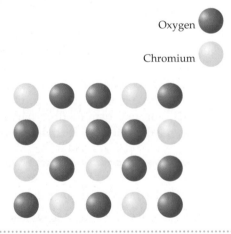

Oxygen

Chromium

3.11 H⁺ and OH⁻ Ions: An Introduction to Acids and Bases

Two of the most important ions we will be discussing in the remainder of this book are the hydrogen cation (H^+) and the hydroxide anion (OH^-). Since a hydrogen *atom* contains one proton and one electron, a hydrogen *cation* is simply a proton. When an acid dissolves in water, the proton typically attaches to a molecule of water to form the hydronium ion (H_3O^+), but chemists routinely use the H^+ and H_3O^+ ions interchangeably. A hydroxide anion, by contrast, is a polyatomic ion in which an oxygen atom is covalently bonded to a hydrogen atom. Although much of Chapter 10 is devoted to the chemistry of H^+ and OH^- ions, it is worth taking a preliminary look now.

◀◀◀ In Chapter 10 we will look at the chemical behavior of acids and bases and their importance in many areas of chemistry.

Acid A substance that provides H^+ ions in water;

Base A substance that provides OH^- ions in water

The importance of the H^+ cation and the OH^- anion is that they are fundamental to the concepts of *acids* and *bases*. In fact, one definition of an **acid** is a substance that provides H^+ ions when dissolved in water; for example, HCl, HNO_3, H_2SO_4, H_3PO_4. One definition of a **base** is a substance that provides OH^- ions when dissolved in water; for example, NaOH, KOH, $Ba(OH)_2$.

Hydrochloric acid (HCl), nitric acid (HNO_3) sulfuric acid (H_2SO_4), and phosphoric acid (H_3PO_4) are among the most common acids. When any of these substances is dissolved in water, H^+ ions are formed along with the corresponding anion (Table 3.5).

TABLE 3.5 Some Common Acids and the Anions Derived from Them

Acids		Anions	
Acetic acid	CH_3COOH	Acetate ion	*CH_3COO^-
Carbonic acid	H_2CO_3	Hydrogen carbonate ion (bicarbonate ion) Carbonate ion	CO_3^{2-}
Hydrochloric acid	HCl	Chloride ion	Cl^-
Nitric acid	HNO_3	Nitrate ion	NO_3^-
Nitrous acid	HNO_2	Nitrite ion	NO_2^-
Phosphoric acid	H_3PO_4	Dihydrogen phosphate ion Hydrogen phosphate ion Phosphate ion	$H_2PO_4^-$ HPO_4^{2-} PO_4^{3-}
Sulfuric acid	H_2SO_4	Hydrogen sulfate ion Sulfate ion	HSO_4^- SO_4^{2-}

*Sometimes written $C_2H_3O_2^-$ or as $CH_3CO_2^-$.

Different acids can provide different numbers of H^+ ions per acid molecule. Hydrochloric acid, for instance, provides one H^+ ion per acid molecule; sulfuric acid can provide two H^+ ions per acid molecule; and phosphoric acid can provide three H^+ ions per acid molecule.

▶▶▶ The behavior of polyprotic acids, or acids that provide more than one H^+ ion per acid molecule, will be discussed in more detail in Chapter 10.

Sodium hydroxide (NaOH; also known as *lye* or *caustic soda*), potassium hydroxide (KOH; also known as *caustic potash*), and barium hydroxide $[Ba(OH)_2]$ are examples of bases. When any of these compounds dissolves in water, OH^- anions go into solution along with the corresponding metal cation. Sodium hydroxide and potassium hydroxide provide one OH^- ion per formula unit; barium hydroxide provides two OH^- ions per formula unit, as indicated by its formula, $Ba(OH)_2$.

PROBLEM 3.29

Which of the following compounds are acids, and which are bases? Explain.

(a) HF   (b) $Ca(OH)_2$ (c) LiOH   (d) HCN

🔑 **KEY CONCEPT PROBLEM 3.30**

One of these pictures represents a solution of HCl, and one represents a solution of H_2SO_4. Which is which?

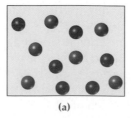
(a)

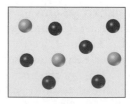
(b)

CHEMISTRY IN ACTION

Osteoporosis

Bone consists primarily of two components, one mineral and one organic. About 70% of bone is the ionic compound *hydroxyapatite,* $Ca_{10}(PO_4)_6(OH)_2$, called the *trabecular,* or spongy, bone. This mineral component is intermingled in a complex matrix with about 30% by mass of fibers of the protein *collagen,* called the *cortical,* or compact, bone. Hydroxyapatite gives bone its hardness and strength, whereas collagen fibers add flexibility and resistance to breaking.

Total bone mass in the body increases from birth until reaching a maximum in the mid-30s. By the early 40s, however, an age-related decline in bone mass begins to occur in both sexes. Bone density decreases, and the microarchitecture of bones is disrupted, resulting in weakening of bone structure, particularly in the wrists, hips, and spine. Should this thinning of bones become too great and the bones become too porous and brittle, a clinical condition called *osteoporosis* can result. Osteoporosis is, in fact, the most common of all bone diseases, affecting approximately 25 million people in the United States. Approximately 1.5 million bone fractures each year are caused by osteoporosis, at an estimated health-care cost of $14 billion.

Although both sexes are affected by osteoporosis, the condition is particularly common in postmenopausal women, who undergo bone loss at a rate of 2–3% per year over and above that of the normal age-related loss. The cumulative lifetime bone loss, in fact, may approach 40–50% in women versus 20–30% in men. It has been estimated that half of all women over age 50 will have an osteoporosis-related bone fracture at some point in their life. Other risk factors, in addition to sex,

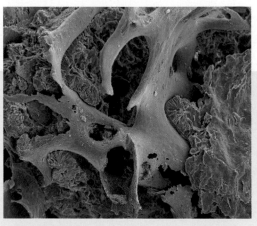

▲ **Normal bone is strong and dense; a bone affected by osteoporosis, shown here, is weak and spongy in appearance.**

include being thin, being sedentary, having a family history of osteoporosis, smoking, and having a diet low in calcium.

No cure exists for osteoporosis, but treatment for its prevention and management includes estrogen-replacement therapy for postmenopausal women as well as several approved medications called *bisphosphonates* that bind to the calcium in bone, slowing down bone loss by inhibiting the action of *osteoclasts,* or cells that break down bone tissue. Calcium supplements are also recommended, as is appropriate weight-bearing exercise. In addition, treatment with sodium fluoride is under active investigation and shows considerable promise. Fluoride ion reacts with hydroxyapatite to give *fluorapatite,* in which OH^- ions are replaced by F^-, increasing both bone strength and density.

$$Ca_{10}(PO_4)_6(OH)_2 + 2\ F^- \longrightarrow Ca_{10}(PO_4)_6F_2$$

Hydroxyapatite   Fluorapatite

See Chemistry in Action Problems 3.86 and 3.87 at the end of the chapter.

SUMMARY: REVISITING THE CHAPTER GOALS

1. What is an ion, what is an ionic bond, and what are the general characteristics of ionic compounds? Atoms are converted into *cations* by the loss of one or more electrons and into *anions* by the gain of one or more electrons. Ionic compounds are composed of cations and anions held together by *ionic bonds,* which result from the attraction between opposite electrical charges. Ionic compounds conduct electricity when dissolved in water, and they are generally crystalline solids with high melting points and high boiling points (*see Problems 33, 35, 38–41, 80, 81, 95–97*).

2. What is the octet rule, and how does it apply to ions? A valence-shell electron configuration of 8 electrons in filled *s* and *p* subshells leads to stability and lack of reactivity, as typified by the noble gases in group 8A. According to the *octet rule,*

atoms of main group elements tend to form ions in which they have gained or lost the appropriate number of electrons to reach a noble gas configuration (*see Problems 42–49, 88, 89*).

3. What is the relationship between an element's position in the periodic table and the formation of its ion? Periodic variations in *ionization energy,* the amount of energy that must be supplied to remove an electron from an atom, show that metals lose electrons more easily than nonmetals. As a result, metals usually form cations. Similar periodic variations in *electron affinity,* the amount of energy released on adding an electron to an atom, show that reactive nonmetals gain electrons more easily than metals. As a result, reactive nonmetals usually form anions. The ionic charge can be predicted from the group number and the octet rule. For main group metals, the charge on the cation is equal to the group number. For nonmetals, the charge on the anion is equal to 8 − (group number) (*see Problems 31, 32, 36, 40, 41, 50–57, 88, 89, 96*).

4. What determines the chemical formula of an ionic compound? Ionic compounds contain appropriate numbers of anions and cations to maintain overall neutrality, thereby providing a means of determining their chemical formulas (*see Problems 36, 37, 64, 65, 68, 69, 86, 87, 90, 92, 94*).

5. How are ionic compounds named? Cations have the same name as the metal from which they are derived. Monatomic anions have the name ending -*ide*. For metals that form more than one ion, a Roman numeral equal to the charge on the ion is added to the name of the cation. Alternatively, the

ending -*ous* is added to the name of the cation with the lesser charge and the ending -*ic* is added to the name of the cation with the greater charge. To name an ionic compound, the cation name is given first, with the charge of the metal ion indicated if necessary, and the anion name is given second (*see Problems 36, 58-63, 66, 68, 70–75, 93, 94*).

6. What are acids and bases? The hydrogen ion (H^+) and the hydroxide ion (OH^-) are among the most important ions in chemistry because they are fundamental to the idea of acids and bases. According to one common definition, an *acid* is a substance that yields H^+ ions when dissolved in water, and a *base* is a substance that yields OH^- ions when dissolved in water (*see Problems 76–79, 91*).

KEY WORDS

Acid, *p. 92*

Anion, *p. 74*

Base, *p. 92*

Cation, *p. 74*

Electron affinity, *p. 75*

Formula unit, *p. 87*

Ion, *p. 74*

Ionic bond, *p. 77*

Ionic compound, *p. 77*

Ionic solid, *p. 77*

Ionization energy, *p. 75*

Octet rule, *p. 79*

Polyatomic ion, *p. 85*

UNDERSTANDING KEY CONCEPTS

3.31 Where on the blank outline of the periodic table are the following elements found?

(a) Elements that commonly form only one type of cation

(b) Elements that commonly form anions

(c) Elements that can form more than one type of cation

(d) Elements that do not readily form either anions or cations

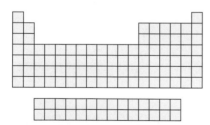

3.32 Where on the blank outline of the periodic table are the following elements found?

(a) Elements that commonly form +2 ions

(b) Elements that commonly form −2 ions

(c) An element that forms a +3 ion

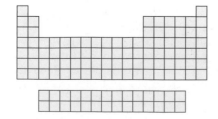

3.33 Write the symbols for the ions represented in the following drawings.

(a)   (b)   (c)   (d)

3.34 One of these drawings represents an Na atom, and one represents an Na^+ ion. Tell which is which, and explain why there is a difference in size.

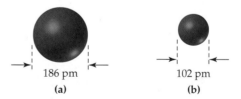

186 pm   102 pm
(a)   (b)

3.35 One of these drawings represents a Cl atom, and one represents a Cl^- ion. Tell which is which, and explain why there is a difference in size.

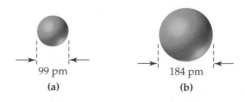

99 pm   184 pm
(a)   (b)

3.36 The elements in red in the periodic table can form cations having more than one charge. Write the formulas and names of the compounds that are formed between the red cations and the blue anions depicted in the periodic table.

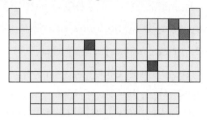

3.37 Each of these drawings (a)–(d) represents one of the following ionic compounds: $PbBr_2$, ZnS, CrF_3, Al_2O_3. Which is which?

(a)   (b)   (c)

(d)

ADDITIONAL PROBLEMS

IONS AND IONIC BONDING

3.38 Write equations for loss or gain of electrons by atoms that result in formation of the following ions:

   (a) Ca^{2+} **(b)** Au^+

   (c) F^- **(d)** Cr^{3+}

3.39 Write electronic configurations and symbols for the ions formed by the following:

   (a) Gain of 3 electrons by phosphorus

   (b) Loss of 1 electron by lithium

   (c) Loss of 2 electrons by cobalt

   (d) Loss of 3 electrons by thallium

3.40 Tell whether each statement about ions is true or false. If a statement is false, explain why.

   (a) A cation is formed by addition of one or more electrons to an atom.

   (b) Group 4A elements tend to lose 4 electrons to yield ions with a +4 charge.

   (c) Group 4A elements tend to gain 4 electrons to yield ions with a −4 charge.

   (d) The individual atoms in a polyatomic ion are held together by covalent bonds.

3.41 Tell whether each statement about ionic solids is true or false. If a statement is false, explain why.

   (a) Ions are randomly arranged in ionic solids.

   (b) All ions are the same size in ionic solids.

   (c) Ionic solids can often be shattered by a sharp blow.

   (d) Ionic solids have low boiling points.

IONS AND THE OCTET RULE

3.42 What is the *octet rule*?

3.43 Why do H and He not obey the octet rule?

3.44 Write the symbol for an ion that contains 34 protons and 36 electrons.

3.45 What is the charge of an ion that contains 21 protons and 19 electrons?

3.46 Identify the element X in the following ions, and tell which noble gas has the same electron configuration.

   (a) X^{2+}, a cation with 36 electrons

   (b) X^-, an anion with 36 electrons

3.47 Element Z forms an ion Z^{3+}, which contains 31 protons. What is the identity of Z, and how many electrons does Z^{3+} have?

3.48 Write the electron configuration for the following ions:

   (a) Rb^+ **(b)** Br^-

   (c) S^{2-} **(d)** Ba^{2+}

   (e) Al^{3+}

3.49 Based on the following atomic numbers and electronic configurations, write the symbols for the following ions:

   (a) $Z = 20$; $1s^2\,2s^2\,2p^6\,3s^2\,3p^6$

   (b) $Z = 8$; $1s^2\,2s^2\,2p^6$

   (c) $Z = 22$; $1s^2\,2s^2\,2p^6\,3s^2\,3p^6\,3d^2$

   (d) $Z = 19$; $1s^2\,2s^2\,2p^6\,3s^2\,3p^6$

   (e) $Z = 13$; $1s^2\,2s^2\,2p^6$

PERIODIC PROPERTIES AND ION FORMATION

3.50 Looking only at the periodic table, tell which member of each pair of atoms has the larger ionization energy and thus loses an electron less easily:

   (a) Li and O   **(b)** Li and Cs

   (c) K and Zn   **(d)** Mg and N

3.51 Looking only at the periodic table, tell which member of each pair of atoms has the larger electron affinity and thus gains an electron more easily:

   (a) Li and S

   (b) Ba and I

   (c) Ca and Br

3.52 Which of the following ions are likely to form? Explain.

(a) Li^{2+} (b) K^-

(c) Mn^{3+} (d) Zn^{4+}

(e) Ne^+

3.53 What is the charge on the cation formed from the following elements? For those elements that form more than one cation, indicate the ionic charges most commonly observed.

(a) Magnesium   (b) Tin

(c) Mercury   (d) Aluminum

3.54 Write the electron configurations of Cr^{2+} and Cr^{3+}.

3.55 Write the electron configurations of Co, Co^{2+} and Co^{3+}.

3.56 Would you expect the ionization energy of Li^+ to be less than, greater than, or the same as the ionization energy of Li? Explain.

3.57 (a) Write equations for the loss of an electron by a K atom and the gain of an electron by a K^+ ion.

(b) What is the relationship between the equations?

(c) What is the relationship between the ionization energy of a K atom and the electron affinity of a K^+ ion?

SYMBOLS, FORMULAS, AND NAMES FOR IONS

3.58 Name the following ions:

(a) S^{2-} (b) Sn^{2+} (c) Sr^{2+}

(d) Mg^{2+} (e) Au^+

3.59 Name the following ions in both the old and the new systems:

(a) Cr^{2+} (b) Fe^{3+} (c) Hg^{2+}

3.60 Write symbols for the following ions:

(a) Selenide ion   (b) Oxide ion

(c) Silver(I) ion

3.61 Write symbols for the following ions:

(a) Ferrous ion   (b) Tin(IV) ion

(c) Lead(II) ion   (d) Chromic ion

3.62 Write formulas for the following ions:

(a) Hydroxide ion   (b) Bisulfate ion

(c) Acetate ion   (d) Permanganate ion

(e) Hypochlorite ion   (f) Nitrate ion

(g) Carbonate ion   (h) Dichromate ion

3.63 Name the following ions:

(a) NO_2^- (b) CrO_4^{2-} (c) NH_4^+ (d) HPO_4^{2-}

NAMES AND FORMULAS FOR IONIC COMPOUNDS

3.64 Write formulas for the compounds formed by the sulfate ion with the following cations:

(a) Aluminum   (b) Silver(I)

(c) Zinc   (d) Barium

3.65 Write formulas for the compounds formed by the carbonate ion with the following cations:

(a) Strontium   (b) Fe(III)

(c) Ammonium   (d) Sn(IV)

3.66 Write the formula for the following substances:

(a) Sodium bicarbonate (baking soda)

(b) Potassium nitrate (a backache remedy)

(c) Calcium carbonate (an antacid)

(d) Ammonium nitrate (first aid cold packs)

3.67 Write the formula for the following compounds:

(a) Calcium hypochlorite, used as a swimming pool disinfectant

(b) Copper(II) sulfate, used to kill algae in swimming pools

(c) Sodium phosphate, used in detergents to enhance cleaning action

3.68 Complete the table by writing in the formula of the compound formed by each pair of ions:

	S^{2-}	Cl^-	PO_4^{3-}	CO_3^{2-}
Copper(II)	CuS			
Ca^{2+}				
NH_4^+				
Ferric ion				

3.69 Complete the table by writing in the formula of the compound formed by each pair of ions:

	O^{2-}	HSO_4^-	HPO_4^{2-}	$C_2O_4^{2-}$
K^+	K_2O			
Ni^{2+}				
NH_4^+				
Chromous				

3.70 Write the name of each compound in the table for Problem 3.68.

3.71 Write the name of each compound in the table for Problem 3.69.

3.72 Name the following substances:

(a) $MgCO_3$ (b) $Ca(CH_3CO_2)_2$

(c) $AgCN$ (d) $Na_2Cr_2O_7$

3.73 Name the following substances:

(a) $Fe(OH)_2$ (b) $KMnO_4$

(c) Na_2CrO_4 (d) $Ba_3(PO_4)_2$

3.74 Which of the following formulas is most likely to be correct for calcium phosphate?

(a) Ca_2PO_4 (b) $CaPO_4$

(c) $Ca_2(PO_4)_3$ (d) $Ca_2(PO_4)_2$

3.75 Fill in the missing information to give the correct formula for each compound:

(a) $Al_?(SO_4)_?$ (b) $(NH_4)_?(PO_4)_?$

(c) $Rb_?(SO_4)_?$

ACIDS AND BASES

3.76 What is the difference between an acid and a base?

3.77 Identify the following substances as either an acid or a base:

(a) H_2CO_3 (b) HCN

(c) $Mg(OH)_2$ (d) KOH

3.78 Write equations to show how the substances listed in Problem 3.77 give ions when dissolved in water.

3.79 Name the anions that result when the acids in Problem 3.77 are dissolved in water.

CHEMISTRY IN ACTION

3.80 Most ionic substances are solids at room temperature. Explain why the RTILs discussed in this application are liquids rather than solids. [*Ionic Liquids, p. 78*]

3.81 Ionic liquids are being evaluated for use in a moon-based spinning-liquid telescope. Which properties of ionic liquids make them particularly well-suited for this application? [*Ionic Liquids, p. 78*]

3.82 What is the RDI for sodium for adults, and what amount of table salt (in grams) contains this quantity of sodium? [*Salt, p. 83*]

3.83 Where are most of the calcium ions found in the body? [*Biologically Important Ions, p. 86*]

3.84 Excess sodium ion is considered hazardous, but a certain amount is necessary for normal body functions. What is the purpose of sodium in the body? [*Biologically Important Ions, p. 86*]

3.85 Before a person is allowed to donate blood, a drop of the blood is tested to be sure that it contains a sufficient amount of iron (men, 41 μg/dL; women, 38 μg/dL). What is the biological role of iron, and which ion of iron is involved? [*Biologically Important Ions, p. 86*]

3.86 Name each ion in hydroxyapatite, $Ca_{10}(PO_4)_6(OH)_2$; give its charge; and show that the formula represents a neutral compound. [*Osteoporosis, p. 93*]

3.87 Sodium fluoride reacts with hydroxyapatite to give fluorapatite. What is the formula of fluorapatite? [*Osteoporosis, p. 93*]

GENERAL QUESTIONS AND PROBLEMS

3.88 Explain why the hydride ion, H^-, has a noble gas configuration.

3.89 The H^- ion (Problem 3.88) is stable, but the Li^- ion is not. Explain.

3.90 Many compounds containing a metal and a nonmetal are not ionic, yet they are named using the Roman numeral system for ionic compounds described in Section 3.7. Write the chemical formulas for the following such compounds.

(a) Chromium(VI) oxide

(b) Vanadium(V) chloride

(c) Manganese(IV) oxide

(d) Molybdenum(IV) sulfide

3.91 The arsenate ion has the formula AsO_4^{3-}. Write the formula of the corresponding acid that contains this anion.

3.92 One commercially available calcium supplement contains calcium gluconate, a compound that is also used as an anticaking agent in instant coffee.

(a) If this compound contains 1 calcium ion for every 2 gluconate ions, what is the charge on a gluconate ion?

(b) What is the ratio of iron ions to gluconate ions in iron(III) gluconate, a commercial iron supplement?

3.93 The names given for the following compounds are incorrect. Write the correct name for each compound.

(a) Cu_3PO_4, copper(III) phosphate

(b) Na_2SO_4, sodium sulfide

(c) MnO_2, manganese(II) oxide

(d) $AuCl_3$, gold chloride

(e) $Pb(CO_3)_2$, lead(II) acetate

(f) Ni_2S_3, nickel(II) sulfide

3.94 The formulas given for the following compounds are incorrect. Write the correct formula for each compound.

(a) Cobalt(II) cyanide, $CoCN_2$

(b) Uranium(VI) oxide, UO_6

(c) Tin(II) sulfate, $Ti(SO_4)_2$

(d) Manganese(IV) oxide; MnO_4

(e) Potassium phosphate, K_2PO_4

(f) Calcium phosphide, CaP

(g) Lithium bisulfate, $Li(SO_4)_2$

(h) Aluminum hydroxide; $Al_2(OH)_3$

3.95 How many protons, electrons, and neutrons are in each of these ions?

(a) $^{16}O^{2-}$ (b) $^{89}Y^{3+}$ (c) $^{133}Cs^+$ (d) $^{81}Br^-$

3.96 Element X reacts with element Y to give a product containing X^{3+} ions and Y^{2-} ions.

(a) Is element X likely to be a metal or a nonmetal?

(b) Is element Y likely to be a metal or a nonmetal?

(c) What is the formula of the product?

(d) What groups of the periodic table are elements X and Y likely to be in?

3.97 Identify each of the ions having the following charges and electron configurations:

(a) X^{4+}; $[Ar]\, 4s^0 3d^3$ (b) X^+; $[Ar]\, 4s^0 3d^{10}$

(c) X^{4+}; $[Ar]\, 4s^0 3d^0$

double bond yields the Lewis structure and ball-and-stick model for vinyl chloride shown below:

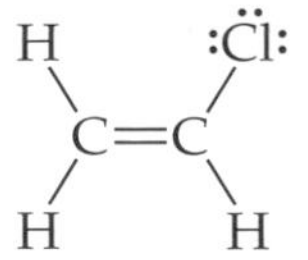

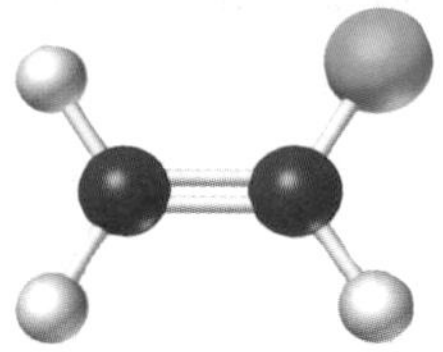

All 18 valence electrons are accounted for in 6 covalent bonds and three lone pairs, and each atom has the expected number of bonds.

Worked Example 4.8 Lewis Structures: Octet Rule and Multiple Bonds

Draw a Lewis structure for sulfur dioxide, SO_2. The connections are O—S—O.

ANALYSIS Follow the procedure outlined in the text.

SOLUTION

STEP 1: The total number of valence electrons is 18, 6 from each atom:

$$S + (2 \times O) = SO_2$$
$$6e^- + (2 + 6e^-) = 18e^-$$

STEP 2: O—S—O Two covalent bonds use 4 valence electrons.

STEP 3: :Ö—S—Ö: Adding three lone pairs to each oxygen to give each an octet uses 12 additional valence electrons.

STEP 4: :Ö—S̈—Ö: The remaining 2 valence electrons are placed on sulfur, but sulfur still does not have an octet.

STEP 5: Moving one lone pair from a neighboring oxygen to form a double bond with the central sulfur gives sulfur an octet (it does not matter on which side the S=O bond is written):

$$:\ddot{O}—\ddot{S}=\ddot{O}:$$

NOTE: The Lewis structure for SO_2 includes a single bond to one O and a double bond to the other O. It doesn't matter which O has the double bond—both structures are equally acceptable. In reality, however, the S—O bonds in this molecule are actually closer to 1.5, an average between the two possible structures we could draw. This is an example of *resonance structures*, or different Lewis structures that could be used to represent the same molecule.

▶▶▶ Aromatic compounds, a class of organic compounds discussed in Section 13.9, are an important example of resonance structures.

PROBLEM 4.8
Methylamine, CH_5N, is responsible for the characteristic odor of decaying fish. Draw a Lewis structure of methylamine.

PROBLEM 4.9
Add lone pairs where appropriate to the following structures:

(a) 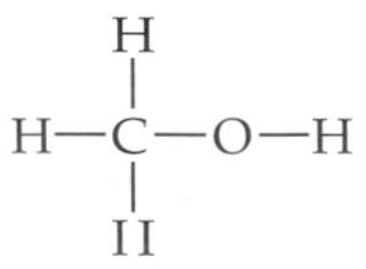
$$\begin{array}{c} H \\ | \\ H—C—O—H \\ | \\ H \end{array}$$

(b)
$$\begin{array}{c} H \\ | \\ N\equiv C—C—H \\ | \\ H \end{array}$$

(c)
$$\begin{array}{c} Cl \\ | \\ N—Cl \\ | \\ Cl \end{array}$$

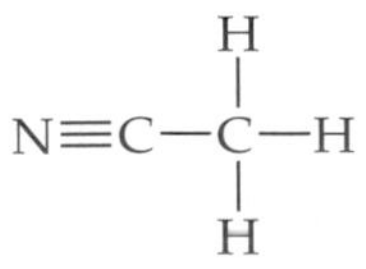

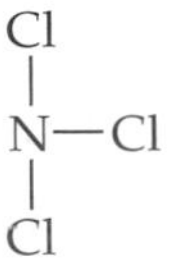

PROBLEM 4.10

Draw Lewis structures for the following:

(a) Phosgene, $COCl_2$, a poisonous gas

(b) Hypochlorite ion, OCl^-, present in many swimming pool chemicals

(c) Hydrogen peroxide, H_2O_2

(d) Sulfur dichloride, SCl_2

PROBLEM 4.11

Draw a Lewis structure for nitric acid, HNO_3. The nitrogen atom is in the center, and the hydrogen atom is bonded to an oxygen atom.

CHEMISTRY IN ACTION

CO and NO: Pollutants or Miracle Molecules?

Carbon monoxide (CO) is a killer; everyone knows that. It is to blame for an estimated 3500 accidental deaths and suicides each year in the United States and is the number one cause of all deaths by poisoning. Nitric oxide (NO) is formed in combustion engines and reacts with oxygen to form nitrogen dioxide (NO_2), the reddish-brown gas associated with urban smog. What most people do not know, however, is that our bodies cannot function without these molecules. A startling discovery made in 1992 showed that CO and NO are key chemical messengers in the body, used by cells to regulate critical metabolic processes.

The toxicity of CO in moderate concentration is due to its ability to bind to hemoglobin molecules in the blood, thereby preventing the hemoglobin from carrying oxygen to tissues. The high reactivity of NO leads to the formation of compounds that are toxic irritants. However, low concentrations of CO and NO are produced in cells throughout the body. Both CO and NO are highly soluble in water and can diffuse from one cell to another, where they stimulate production of a substance called *guanylyl cyclase*. Guanylyl cyclase, in turn, controls the production of another substance called *cyclic GMP*, which regulates many cellular functions.

Levels of CO production are particularly high in certain regions of the brain, including those associated with long-term memory. Evidence from experiments with rat brains suggests that a special kind of cell in the brain's hippocampus is signaled by transfer of a molecular messenger from a neighboring cell. The receiving cell responds back to the signaling cell by releasing CO, which causes still more messenger molecules to be sent. After several rounds of this back-and-forth communication, the receiving cell undergoes some sort of change that becomes a memory. When CO production is blocked, possibly in response to a medical condition or exposure to certain toxic metals, long-term memories are no longer stored, and those memories that previously existed are erased. When CO production is stimulated, however, memories are again laid down.

▲ **Los Angeles at sunset. Carbon monoxide is a major component of photochemical smog, but it also functions as an essential chemical messenger in our bodies.**

NO controls a seemingly limitless range of functions in the body. The immune system uses NO to fight infections and tumors. It is also used to transmit messages between nerve cells and is associated with the processes involved in learning and memory, sleeping, and depression. Its most advertised role, however, is as a *vasodilator*, a substance that allows blood vessels to relax and dilate. This discovery led to the development of a new class of drugs that stimulate production of enzymes called nitric oxide synthases (NOS). These drugs can be used to treat conditions from erectile dysfunction (Viagra) to hypertension. Given the importance of NO in the fields of neuroscience, physiology, and immunology, it is not surprising that it was named "Molecule of the Year" in 1992.

See Chemistry in Action Problems 4.89 and 4.90 at the end of the chapter.

🔑 **KEY CONCEPT PROBLEM 4.12**

The molecular model shown here is a representation of methyl methacrylate, a starting material used to prepare Lucite plastic. Only the connections between atoms are shown; multiple bonds are not indicated.

(a) What is the molecular formula of methyl methacrylate?
(b) Indicate the positions of the multiple bonds and lone pairs in methyl methacrylate.

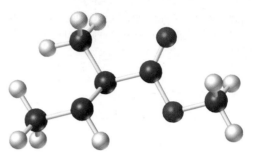

PROBLEM 4.13
Draw the Lewis dot structures for the molecules CO and NO discussed in the Chemistry in Action box on page 113. How do the Lewis structures provide insight into the reactivity of these molecules?

4.8 The Shapes of Molecules

Look back at the computer-generated drawings of molecules in the preceding section, and you will find that the molecules are shown with specific shapes. Acetylene is *linear*, water is *bent*, ammonia is *pyramid-shaped*, methane is *tetrahedral*, and ethylene is flat, or *planar*. What determines such shapes? Why, for example, are the 3 atoms in water connected at an angle of (104.5°) rather than in a straight line? Like so many properties, molecular shapes are related to the numbers and locations of the valence electrons around atoms.

Molecular shapes can be predicted by noting how many bonds and electron pairs surround individual atoms and applying what is called the **valence-shell electron-pair repulsion (VSEPR) model**. The basic idea of the VSEPR model is that the constantly moving valence electrons in bonds and lone pairs make up negatively charged clouds of electrons, which electrically repel one another. The clouds therefore tend to keep as far apart as possible, causing molecules to assume specific shapes. There are three steps to applying the VSEPR model:

STEP 1: Draw a Lewis structure of the molecule, and identify the atom whose geometry is of interest. In a simple molecule like PCl_3 or CO_2, this is usually the central atom.

STEP 2: Count the number of electron charge clouds surrounding the atom of interest. The number of charge clouds is simply the total number of lone pairs plus connections to other atoms. It does not matter whether a connection is a single bond or a multiple bond because we are interested only in the *number* of charge clouds, not in how many electrons each cloud contains. The carbon atom in carbon dioxide, for instance, has 2 double bonds to oxygen $(O{=}C{=}O)$, and thus has two charge clouds.

STEP 3: Predict molecular shape by assuming that the charge clouds orient in space so that they are as far away from one another as possible. How they achieve this favorable orientation depends on their number, as summarized in Table 4.2.

If there are only two charge clouds, as occurs on the central atom of CO_2 (2 double bonds) and HCN (1 single bond and 1 triple bond), the clouds are farthest apart when

Valence-shell electron-pair repulsion (VSEPR) model A method for predicting molecular shape by noting how many electron charge clouds surround atoms and assuming that the clouds orient as far away from one another as possible.

TABLE 4.2 Molecular Geometry Around Atoms with 2, 3, and 4 Charge Clouds

NUMBER OF BONDS	NUMBER OF LONE PAIRS	TOTAL NUMBER OF CHARGE CLOUDS	MOLECULAR GEOMETRY		EXAMPLE
2	0	2		Linear	$O{=}C{=}O$
3	0	3		Trigonal planar	$\begin{array}{c}H\\H\end{array}{>}C{=}O$
2	1			Bent	$\begin{array}{c}O\\O\end{array}{>}S{:}$
4	0	4		Tetrahedral	$H{-}\overset{\overset{H}{\mid}}{\underset{\mid}{C}}{-}H$ with H
3	1			Pyramidal	$H{-}\overset{..}{N}{-}H$ with H
2	2			Bent	$H{-}\overset{..}{O}$ with H

they point in opposite directions. Thus, both HCN and CO_2 are linear molecules, with **bond angles** of 180°:

Bond angle The angle formed by 3 adjacent atoms in a molecule.

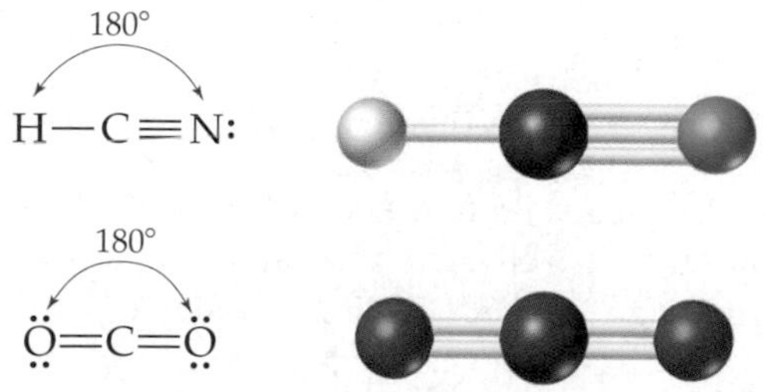

180°
H—C≡N:

These molecules are linear, with bond angles of 180°.

180°
:Ö=C=Ö:

When there are three charge clouds, as occurs on the central atom in formaldehyde (1 single bond and 1 double bond) and SO_2 (1 single bond, 1 double bond, and one lone pair), the clouds will be farthest apart if they lie in a plane and point to the corners of an equilateral triangle. Thus, a formaldehyde molecule is trigonal planar, with all bond angles near 120°. In the same way, an SO_2 molecule has a trigonal planar arrangement of its three electron clouds, but one point of the triangle is occupied by a lone pair. The connection between the 3 atoms is therefore bent rather than linear, with an O—S—O bond angle of approximately 120°:

A formaldehyde molecule is planar triangular, with bond angles of roughly 120°.

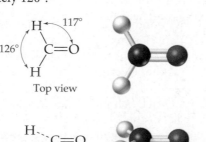

H ← 117°
126° C=O
H
Top view

H
C=O
H
Side view

An SO_2 molecule is bent, with a bond angle of approximately 120°.

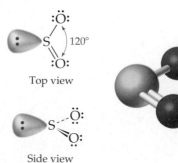

:Ö:
S 120°
:Ö:
Top view

:Ö:
S
:O:
Side view

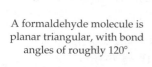

Note how the three-dimensional shapes of molecules like formaldehyde and SO_2 are shown. Solid lines are assumed to be in the plane of the paper; a dashed line recedes behind the plane of the paper away from the viewer; and a dark wedged line protrudes out of the paper toward the viewer. This standard method for showing three-dimensionality will be used throughout the rest of the book.

When there are four charge clouds, as occurs on the central atom in CH_4 (4 single bonds), NH_3 (3 single bonds and one lone pair), and H_2O (2 single bonds and two lone pairs), the clouds can be farthest apart when they extend to the corners of a *regular tetrahedron*. As illustrated in Figure 4.5, a **regular tetrahedron** is a geometric solid whose four identical faces are equilateral triangles. The central atom is at the center of the tetrahedron, the charge clouds point to the corners, and the angle between lines drawn from the center to any two corners is 109.5°.

Regular tetrahedron A geometric figure with four identical triangular faces.

▶ **Figure 4.5**
The tetrahedral geometry of an atom surrounded by four charge clouds. The atom is located at the center of the regular tetrahedron, and the four charge clouds point toward the corners. The bond angle between the center and any two corners is 109.5°.

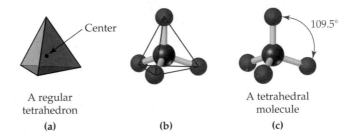

A regular tetrahedron

(a)

(b)

A tetrahedral molecule

(c)

109.5°

Center

Because valence-shell electron octets are so common, a great many molecules have geometries based on the tetrahedron. In methane (CH_4), for example, the carbon atom has tetrahedral geometry with H—C—H bond angles of exactly 109.5°. In ammonia (NH_3), the nitrogen atom has a tetrahedral arrangement of its four charge clouds, but one corner of the tetrahedron is occupied by a lone pair, resulting in an overall pyramidal shape for the molecule. Similarly, water, which has two corners of the tetrahedron occupied by lone pairs, has an overall bent shape.

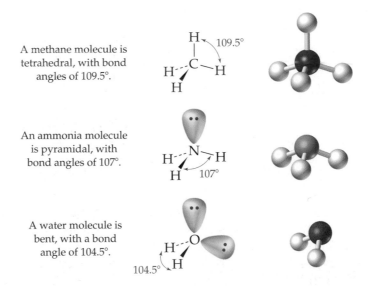

A methane molecule is tetrahedral, with bond angles of 109.5°.

An ammonia molecule is pyramidal, with bond angles of 107°.

A water molecule is bent, with a bond angle of 104.5°.

Note that the H—N—H bond angle in ammonia (107°) and the H—O—H bond angle in water (104.5°) are close to, but not exactly equal to, the ideal 109.5° tetrahedral value. The angles are diminished somewhat from their ideal value because the lone-pair charge clouds repel other electron clouds strongly and compress the rest of the molecule.

The geometry around atoms in larger molecules also derives from the shapes shown in Table 4.2. For example, each of the 2 carbon atoms in ethylene $(H_2C{=}CH_2)$ has three charge clouds, giving rise to trigonal planar geometry. It turns out that the molecule as a whole is also planar, with H—C—C and H—C—H bond angles of approximately 120°:

The ethylene molecule is planar, with bond angles of 120°.

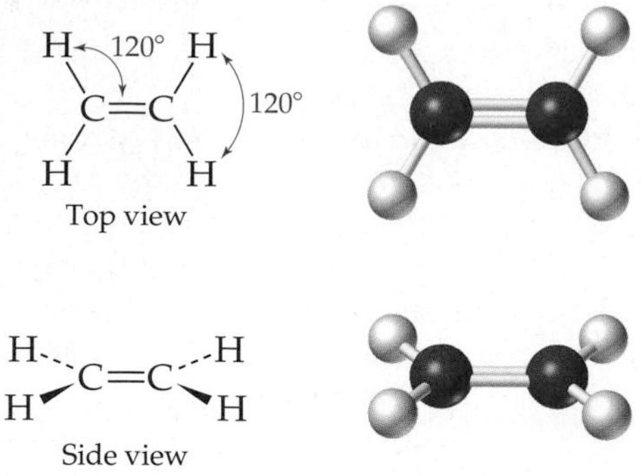

Top view

Side view

Carbon atoms bonded to 4 other atoms are each at the center of a tetrahedron, as shown here for ethane, $H_3C—CH_3$:

The ethane molecule has tetrahedral carbon atoms, with bond angles of 109.5°.

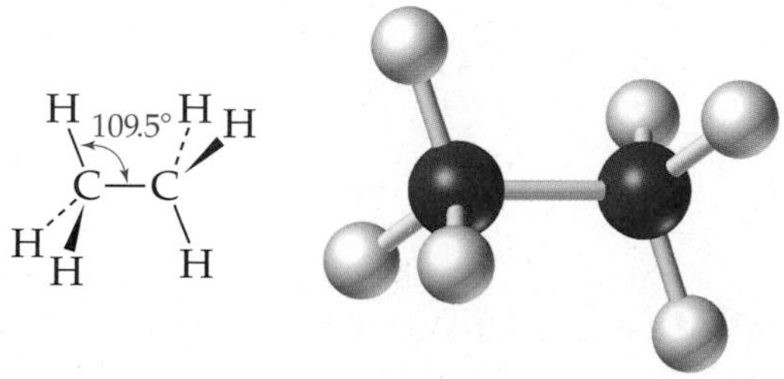

Worked Example 4.9 Lewis Structures: Molecular Shape

What shape would you expect for the hydronium ion, H_3O^+?

ANALYSIS Draw the Lewis structure for the molecular ion, and count the number of charge clouds around the central oxygen atom; imagine the clouds orienting as far away from one another as possible.

SOLUTION 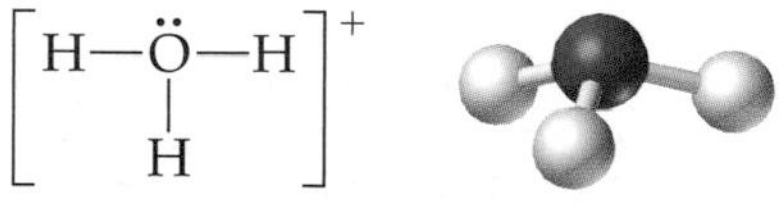
The Lewis structure for the hydronium ion shows that the oxygen atom has four charge clouds (3 single bonds and one lone pair). The hydronium ion is therefore pyramidal with bond angles of approximately 109.5°.

Worked Example 4.10 Lewis Structures: Charge Cloud Geometry

Predict the geometry around each of the carbon atoms in an acetaldehyde molecule, CH_3CHO.

ANALYSIS Draw the Lewis structure and identify the number of charge clouds around each of the central carbon atoms.

SOLUTION
The Lewis structure of acetaldehyde shows that the CH_3 carbon has four charge clouds (4 single bonds) and the CHO carbon atom has three charge clouds (2 single bonds, 1 double bond). Table 4.2 indicates that the CH_3 carbon is tetrahedral, but the CHO carbon is trigonal planar.

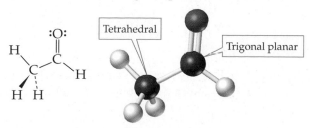

CHEMISTRY IN ACTION

VERY Big Molecules

How big can a molecule be? The answer is very, *very* big. The really big molecules in our bodies and in many items we buy are all *polymers*. Like a string of beads, a polymer is formed of many repeating units connected in a long chain. Each "bead" in the chain comes from a simple molecule that has formed chemical bonds at both ends, linking it to other molecules. The repeating units can be the same:

–a–a–a–a–a–a–a–a–a–a–a–a–

or they can be different. If different, they can be connected in an ordered pattern:

–a–b–a–b–a–b–a–b–a–b–a–b–

or in a random pattern:

–a–b–b–a–b–a–a–a–b–a–b–b–

Furthermore, the polymer chains can have branches, and the branches can have either the same repeating unit as the main chain or a different one:

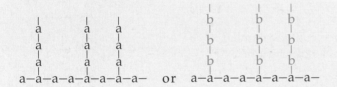

Still other possible variations include complex, three-dimensional networks of "cross-linked" chains. The rubber used in tires, for example, contains polymer chains connected by cross-linking atoms of sulfur to impart greater rigidity.

We all use synthetic polymers every day—we usually call them "plastics." Common synthetic polymers are made by connecting up to several hundred thousand smaller molecules together, producing giant polymer molecules with masses up to several million atomic mass units. Polyethylene, for example, is made by

▲ **The protective gear worn by motorcyclists (shown above), firefighters, and security forces are composed of advanced composite materials based on polymers.**

combining as many as 50,000 ethylene molecules ($H_2C\!=\!CH_2$) to give a polymer with repeating $—CH_2CH—$ units:

Many $H_2C\!=\!CH_2 \longrightarrow —CH_2CH_2CH_2CH_2CH_2CH_2—$

Ethylene   Polyethlene

The product is used in such items as chairs, toys, drain pipes, milk bottles, and packaging films. Other examples of polymers include the nylon used in clothing and pantyhose, molded hardware (nuts and bolts), and the Kevlar used in bulletproof vests (see Chemistry in Action on p. 538).

Nature began to exploit the extraordinary variety of polymer properties long before humans did. In fact, despite great progress in recent years, there is still much to be learned about the polymers in living things. Carbohydrates and proteins are polymers, as are the giant molecules of deoxyribonucleic acid (DNA) that govern many cellular processes, including reproduction, in all organisms. Nature's polymer molecules, though, are more complex than any that chemists have yet created.

▶▶ Carbohydrates are polymers composed of sugar molecules linked together in long chains (Chapter 21), while proteins are polymers of smaller molecules called amino acids (Chapter 18). DNA, a polymer of repeating nucleotide subunits, is discussed in Chapter 25.

See Chemistry in Action Problems 4.91 and 4.92 at the end of the chapter.

PROBLEM 4.14
Boron typically only forms 3 covalent bonds because it only has 3 valence electrons, but can form coordinate covalent bonds. Draw the Lewis structure for BF_4^- and predict the molecular shape of the ion.

PROBLEM 4.15
Predict shapes for the organic molecules chloroform, $CHCl_3$, and 1,1-dichloroethylene, $Cl_2C\!=\!CH_2$.

PROBLEM 4.16

Polycarbonate, also known as plexiglass, has the basic repeating unit shown below. What is the geometry of the electron clouds for the carbon atoms labeled "a" and "b" in this structure?

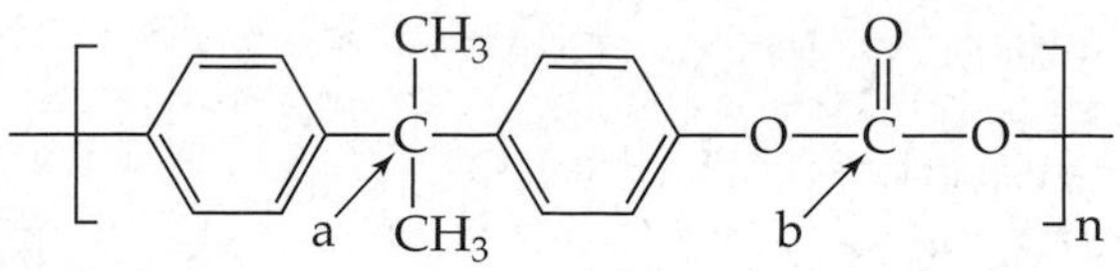

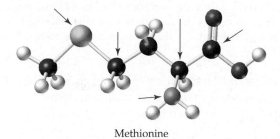

PROBLEM 4.17

Hydrogen selenide (H_2Se) resembles hydrogen sulfide (H_2S) in that both compounds have terrible odors and are poisonous. What are their shapes?

🔑 KEY CONCEPT PROBLEM 4.18

Draw a structure corresponding to the molecular model of the amino acid methionine shown here, and describe the geometry around the indicated atoms. (Remember the color key discussed in Section 4.7: black = carbon; white = hydrogen; red = oxygen; blue = nitrogen; yellow = sulfur.)

Methionine

4.9 Polar Covalent Bonds and Electronegativity

Electrons in a covalent bond occupy the region between the bonded atoms. If the atoms are identical, as in H_2 and Cl_2, the electrons are attracted equally to both atoms and are shared equally. If the atoms are *not* identical, however, as in HCl, the bonding electrons may be attracted more strongly by one atom than by the other and may be shared unequally. Such bonds are said to be **polar covalent bonds**. In hydrogen chloride, for example, electrons spend more time near the chlorine atom than near the hydrogen atom. Although the molecule as a whole is neutral, the chlorine is more negative than the hydrogen, resulting in *partial* charges on the atoms. These partial charges are represented by placing a $\delta-$ (Greek lowercase *delta*) on the more negative atom and a $\delta+$ on the more positive atom.

A particularly helpful way of visualizing this unequal distribution of bonding electrons is to look at what is called an *electrostatic potential map*, which uses color to portray the calculated electron distribution in a molecule. In HCl, for example, the electron-poor hydrogen is blue, and the electron-rich chlorine is reddish-yellow:

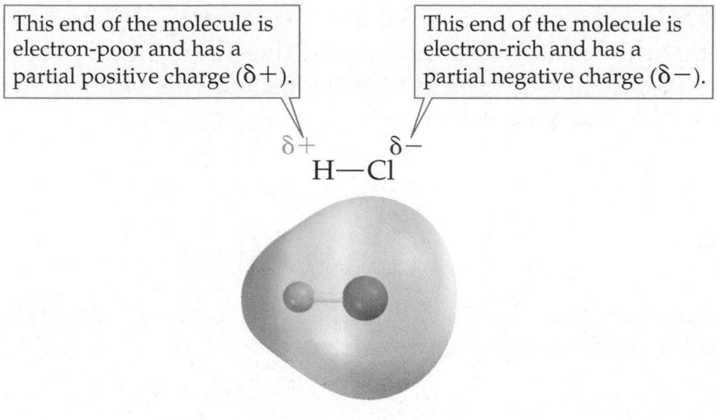

Polar covalent bond A bond in which the electrons are attracted more strongly by one atom than by the other.

This end of the molecule is electron-poor and has a partial positive charge ($\delta+$).

This end of the molecule is electron-rich and has a partial negative charge ($\delta-$).

$$\overset{\delta+}{H}-\overset{\delta-}{Cl}$$

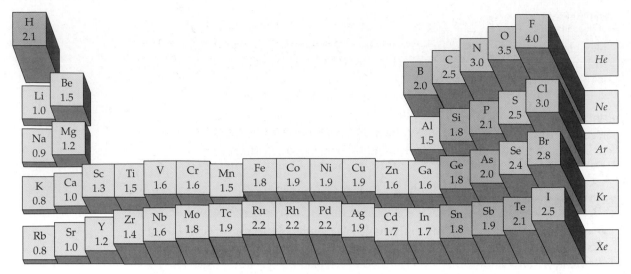

▲ **Figure 4.6**
Electronegativities of several main group and transition metal elements.
Reactive nonmetals at the top right of the periodic table are the most electronegative, and metals at the lower left are the least electronegative. The noble gases are not assigned values.

Electronegativity The ability of an atom to attract electrons in a covalent bond.

The ability of an atom to attract electrons in a covalent bond is called the atom's **electronegativity**. Fluorine, the most electronegative element, is assigned a value of 4, and less electronegative atoms are assigned lower values, as shown in Figure 4.6. Metallic elements on the left side of the periodic table attract electrons only weakly and have lower electronegativities, whereas the halogens and other reactive nonmetal elements on the upper right side of the table attract electrons strongly and have higher electronegativities. Note in Figure 4.6 that electronegativity generally decreases going down the periodic table within a group.

Comparing the electronegativities of bonded atoms makes it possible to compare the polarities of bonds and to predict the occurrence of ionic bonding. Both oxygen (electronegativity 3.5) and nitrogen (3.0), for instance, are more electronegative than carbon (2.5). As a result, both C—O and C—N bonds are polar, with carbon at the positive end. The larger difference in electronegativity values shows that the C—O bond is the more polar of the two:

Less polar ⌐   ⌐ More polar
$^{\delta+}$C⊥N$^{\delta-}$ $^{\delta+}$C⊥O$^{\delta-}$
Electronegativity   Electronegativity
difference: difference:
3.0 − 2.5 = 0.5   3.5 − 2.5 = 1.0

As a rule of thumb, electronegativity differences of less than 0.5 result in nonpolar covalent bonds, differences up to 1.9 indicate increasingly polar covalent bonds, and differences of 2 or more indicate ionic bonds. The electronegativity differences show, for example, that the bond between carbon and fluorine is highly polar covalent, the bond between sodium and chlorine is largely ionic, and the bond between rubidium and fluorine is almost completely ionic:

E.N difference		Type of bond
0 — 0.4	~	Covalent
0.5 — 1.9	~	Polar covalent
2.0 and above	~	Ionic

$^{\delta+}$C—F$^{\delta-}$ Na^{+}Cl^{-} Rb^{+}F^{-}
Electronegativity
difference: 1.5   2.1   3.2

Note, though, that there is no sharp dividing line between covalent and ionic bonds; most bonds fall somewhere between two extremes.

LOOKING AHEAD ▶▶▶ The values given in Figure 4.6 indicate that carbon and hydrogen have similar electronegativities. As a result, C—H bonds are nonpolar. We will see in Chapters 12–25 how this fact helps explain the properties of organic and biological compounds, all of which have carbon and hydrogen as their principal constituents.

Worked Example 4.11 Electronegativity: Ionic, Nonpolar, and Polar Covalent Bonds

Predict whether each of the bonds between the following atoms would be ionic, polar covalent, or nonpolar covalent. If polar covalent, which atom would carry the partial positive and negative charges?

(a) C and Br   (b) Li and Cl

(c) N and H   (d) Si and I

ANALYSIS Compare the electronegativity values for the atoms and classify the nature of the bonding based on the electronegativity difference.

SOLUTION

(a) The electronegativity for C is 2.5, and for Br is 2.8; the difference is 0.3, indicating nonpolar covalent bonding would occur between these atoms.

(b) The electronegativity for Li is 1.0, and for Cl is 3.0; the difference is 2.0, indicating that ionic bonding would occur between these atoms.

(c) The electronegativity for N is 3.0, and for H is 2.5; the difference is 0.5. Bonding would be polar covalent, with $N = \delta-$ and $H = \delta+$.

(d) The electronegativity for Si is 1.8, and for I is 2.5; the difference is 0.7. Bonding would be polar covalent, with $I = \delta-$, and $Si = \delta+$.

PROBLEM 4.19
The elements H, N, O, P, and S are commonly bonded to carbon in organic compounds. Arrange these elements in order of increasing electronegativity.

PROBLEM 4.20
Use electronegativity differences to classify bonds between the following pairs of atoms as ionic, nonpolar covalent, or polar covalent. For those that are polar, use the symbols $\delta+$ and $\delta-$ to identify the location of the partial charges on the polar covalent bond.

(a) I and Cl   (b) Li and O

(c) Br and Br   (d) P and Br

4.10 Polar Molecules

Just as individual bonds can be polar, entire *molecules* can be polar if electrons are attracted more strongly to one part of the molecule than to another. Molecular polarity is due to the sum of all individual bond polarities and lone-pair contributions in the molecule and is often represented by an arrow pointing in the direction that electrons are displaced. The arrow is pointed at the negative end and is crossed at the positive end to resemble a plus sign, $(\delta+) \longleftrightarrow (\delta-)$.

Molecular polarity depends on the shape of the molecule as well as the presence of polar covalent bonds and lone pairs. In water, for example, electrons are displaced away from the less electronegative hydrogen atoms toward the more electronegative oxygen atom so that the net polarity points between the two O—H bonds. In chloromethane, CH_3Cl, electrons are attracted from the carbon/hydrogen part of the molecule toward the electronegative chlorine atom so that the net polarity points along the C—Cl bond. Electrostatic potential maps show these polarities clearly, with electron-poor regions in blue and electron-rich regions in red.

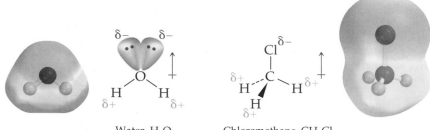

Water, H$_2$O   Chloromethane, CH$_3$Cl

Furthermore, just because a molecule has polar covalent bonds, it does not mean that the molecule is necessarily polar overall. Carbon dioxide (CO$_2$) and tetrachloromethane (CCl$_4$) molecules, for instance, have no net polarity because their symmetrical shapes cause the individual C=O and C—Cl bond polarities to cancel.

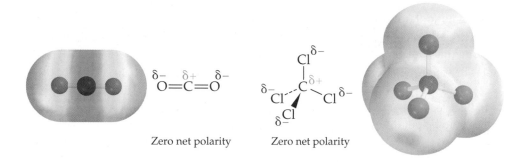

Zero net polarity   Zero net polarity

Polarity has a dramatic effect on the physical properties of molecules, particularly on melting points, boiling points, and solubilities. We will see numerous examples of such effects in subsequent chapters.

Worked Example **4.12** Electronegativity: Polar Bonds and Polar Molecules

Look at the structures of (a) hydrogen cyanide (HCN) and (b) vinyl chloride (H$_2$C=CHCl), described in Worked Examples 4.6 and 4.7, decide whether or not the molecules are polar, and show the direction of net polarity in each.

ANALYSIS Draw a Lewis structure for each molecule to find its shape, and identify any polar bonds using the electronegativity values in Figure 4.6. Then, decide on net polarity by adding the individual contributions.

SOLUTION

(a) The carbon atom in hydrogen cyanide has two charge clouds, making HCN a linear molecule. The C—H bond is relatively nonpolar, but the C≡N bonding electrons are pulled toward the electronegative nitrogen atom. In addition, a lone pair protrudes from nitrogen. Thus, the molecule has a net polarity:

(b) Vinyl chloride, like ethylene, is a planar molecule. The C—H and C=C bonds are nonpolar, but the C—Cl bonding electrons are displaced toward the electronegative chlorine. Thus, the molecule has a net polarity:

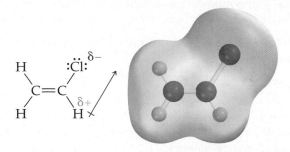

PROBLEM 4.21

Look at the molecular shape of formaldehyde (CH_2O) described on page 115, decide whether or not the molecule is polar, and show the direction of net polarity.

PROBLEM 4.22

Draw a Lewis structure for dimethyl ether (CH_3OCH_3), predict its shape, and tell whether or not the molecule is polar.

🔑 **KEY CONCEPT PROBLEM 4.23**

From this electrostatic potential map of methyllithium, identify the direction of net polarity in the molecule. Explain this polarity based on electronegativity values.

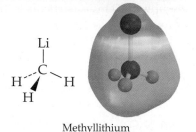

Methyllithium

4.11 Naming Binary Molecular Compounds

When two different elements combine, they form what is called a **binary compound**. The formulas of binary molecular compounds are usually written with the less electronegative element first. Thus, metals are always written before nonmetals, and a nonmetal farther left on the periodic table generally comes before a nonmetal farther right. For example,

Binary compound A compound formed by combination of two different elements.

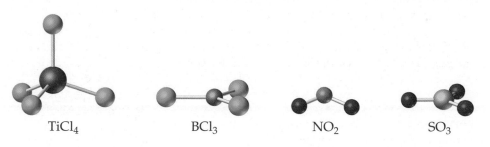

As we learned in Section 3.9, the formulas of ionic compounds indicate the number of anions and cations necessary for a neutral formula unit, which depends on the charge on each of the ions. With molecular compounds, however, many combinations of atoms are possible, since nonmetals are capable of forming multiple covalent bonds.

TABLE **4.3** Numerical Prefixes Used in Chemical Names	
Number	Prefix
1	mono-
2	di-
3	tri-
4	tetra-
5	penta-
6	hexa-
7	hepta-
8	octa-
9	nona-
10	deca-

When naming binary molecular compounds, therefore, we must identify exactly how many atoms of each element are included in the molecular formula. The names of binary molecular compounds are assigned in two steps, using the prefixes listed in Table 4.3 to indicate the number of atoms of each element combined.

STEP 1: Name the first element in the formula, using a prefix if needed to indicate the number of atoms.

STEP 2: Name the second element in the formula, using an *-ide* ending like for anions (Section 3.7), along with a prefix if needed.

The prefix *mono-*, meaning one, is omitted except where needed to distinguish between two different compounds with the same elements. For example, the two oxides of carbon are named carbon *mono*xide for CO and carbon *di*oxide for CO_2. (Note that we say *mono*xide rather than *mono*oxide.) Some other examples are:

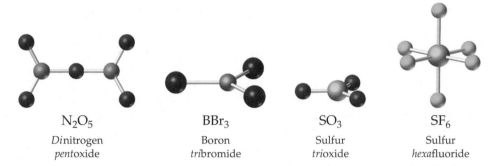

N_2O_5	BBr_3	SO_3	SF_6
*Di*nitrogen *pent*oxide	Boron *tri*bromide	Sulfur *tri*oxide	Sulfur *hexa*fluoride

Naming of molecular compounds can get complicated when more than two elements are present. This is particularly true for *organic compounds*, a class of molecular compounds composed largely of carbon (see examples in the Chemistry in Action on p. 125). The rules for naming these compounds will be discussed in later chapters.

Worked Example 4.13 Naming Molecular Compounds

Name the following compounds:

(a) N_2O_3 (b) $GeCl_4$ (c) PCl_5

SOLUTION

(a) Dinitrogen trioxide (b) Germanium tetrachloride

(c) Phosphorus pentachloride

Worked Example 4.14 Writing Formulas for Molecular Compounds

Write molecular formulas for the following compounds:

(a) Nitrogen triiodide (b) Silicon tetrachloride

(c) Carbon disulfide

SOLUTION

(a) NI_3 (b) $SiCl_4$ (c) CS_2

PROBLEM 4.24

Name the following compounds:

(a) S_2Cl_2 (b) ICl (c) ICl_3

PROBLEM 4.25

Write formulas for the following compounds:

(a) Selenium tetrafluoride (b) Diphosphorus pentoxide (c) Bromine trifluoride

PROBLEM 4.26

Geraniol, one of the components of rose oil (see the following Chemistry in Action). has the basic structure represented below. Draw the structural formula for geraniol to include any multiple bonds, and then write the condensed structure for geraniol.

$$CH_3-\underset{\underset{\displaystyle CH_3}{|}}{\overset{\overset{\displaystyle CH_3}{|}}{C}}-\underset{\underset{\displaystyle H}{|}}{\overset{\overset{\displaystyle H}{|}}{C}}-\underset{\underset{\displaystyle H}{|}}{\overset{\overset{\displaystyle H}{|}}{C}}-\underset{\underset{\displaystyle H}{|}}{\overset{\overset{\displaystyle CH_3}{|}}{C}}-\underset{\underset{\displaystyle H}{|}}{\overset{\overset{\displaystyle H}{|}}{C}}-\underset{\underset{\displaystyle H}{|}}{\overset{\overset{\displaystyle H}{|}}{C}}-OH$$

CHEMISTRY IN ACTION

Damascenone by Any Other Name Would Smell as Sweet

What's in a name? According to Shakespeare's *Romeo and Juliet,* a rose by any other name would smell as sweet. Chemical names, however, often provoke less favorable responses: "It's unpronounceable." "It's too complicated." "It must be something bad."

But why are chemical names so complicated? The reason is obvious once you realize that there are more than 19 *million* known chemical compounds. The full name of a chemical compound has to include enough information to tell chemists the composition and structure of the compound. It is as if every person on earth had to have his or her own unique name that described height, hair color, and other identifying characteristics in sufficient detail to distinguish him or her from every other person. Consider, also, that subtle differences in structure can result in significant differences in chemical or physical properties. Geraniol, for example, is used as a flavor additive in the food industry, while citronellol is used in perfumes and insect repellants, such as citronella candles. The common names for these substances are easier to remember, but their *chemical* names give us precise information about their structural differences and similarities. Geraniol ($C_{10}H_{18}O$), also known as *3,7-dimethylocta-2, 6-dien-1-ol* differs from citronellol ($C_{10}H_{20}O$ or *3,7-dimethyloct-6-en-1-ol*) by only one C — C double bond.

Unfortunately, people sometimes conclude that everything with a chemical name is unnatural and dangerous. Neither is true, of course. Acetaldehyde, for instance, is present naturally in most tart, ripe fruits and is often added in small amounts to artificial flavorings. When *pure*, however, acetaldehyde

▲ The scent of these roses contains β-damascenone, β-ionone, citronellol, geraniol, nerol, eugenol, methyl eugenol, β-phenylethyl, alcohol, farnesol, linalool, terpineol, rose oxide, carvone, and many other natural substances.

is also a flammable gas that is toxic and explosive in high concentrations.

Similar comparisons of desirable and harmful properties can be made for almost all chemicals, including water, sugar, and salt. The properties of a substance and the conditions surrounding its use must be evaluated before judgments are made. Damascenone, geraniol, and citronellol, by the way, are chemicals that contribute to the wonderful aroma of roses.

See Chemistry in Action Problems 4.93 and 4.94 at the end of the chapter.

SUMMARY: REVISITING THE CHAPTER GOALS

1. What is a covalent bond? A *covalent bond* is formed by the sharing of electrons between atoms rather than by the complete transfer of electrons from one atom to another. Atoms that share 2 electrons are joined by a *single bond* (such as C — C), atoms that share 4 electrons are joined by a *double bond* (such as C═C), and atoms that share 6 electrons are joined by a *triple* bond (such as C≡C). The group of atoms held together by covalent bonds is called a *molecule*.

Electron sharing typically occurs when a singly occupied valence orbital on one atom *overlaps* a singly occupied valence orbital on another atom. The 2 electrons occupy both overlapping orbitals and belong to both atoms, thereby bonding the atoms together. Alternatively, electron sharing can occur when a filled orbital containing an unshared, *lone pair* of electrons on one atom overlaps a vacant orbital on another atom to form a *coordinate covalent bond* (see *Problems 33–35, 40, 41, 44, 45, 89, 92*).

2. How does the octet rule apply to covalent bond formation? Depending on the number of valence electrons, different atoms form different numbers of covalent bonds. In general, an atom shares enough electrons to reach a noble gas configuration. Hydrogen, for instance, forms 1 covalent bond because it needs to share 1 more electron to achieve the helium configuration ($1s^2$). Carbon and other group 4A elements form 4 covalent bonds because they need to share 4 more electrons to reach an octet. In the same way, nitrogen and other group 5A elements form 3 covalent bonds, oxygen and other group 6A elements form 2 covalent bonds, and halogens (group 7A elements) form 1 covalent bond (see *Problems 38, 39, 50, 51, 95*).

3. What are the major differences between ionic and molecular compounds? *Molecular compounds* can be gases, liquids, or low-melting solids. They usually have lower melting points and boiling points than ionic compounds, many are water insoluble, and they do not conduct electricity when melted or dissolved (see *Problems 33, 35–37, 42, 43, 47, 99, 102, 103*).

4. How are molecular compounds represented? Formulas such as H_2O, NH_3, and CH_4, which show the numbers and kinds of atoms in a molecule, are called *molecular formulas*. More useful are *Lewis structures*, which show how atoms are connected in molecules. Covalent bonds are indicated as lines between atoms, and valence electron lone pairs are shown as dots. Lewis struc-

tures are drawn by counting the total number of valence electrons in a molecule or polyatomic ion and then placing shared pairs (bonding) and lone pairs (nonbonding) so that all electrons are accounted for (see *Problems 30, 46–66, 94–100, 104–109*).

5. What is the influence of valence-shell electrons on molecular shape? Molecules have specific shapes that depend on the number of electron charge clouds (bonds and lone pairs) surrounding the various atoms. These shapes can often be predicted using the *valence-shell electron-pair repulsion (VSEPR)* model. Atoms with two electron charge clouds adopt linear geometry, atoms with three charge clouds adopt trigonal planar geometry, and atoms with four charge clouds adopt tetrahedral geometry (see *Problems 27, 28–31, 67–72, 81, 96, 100, 109*).

6. When are bonds and molecules polar? Bonds between atoms are *polar covalent* if the bonding electrons are not shared equally between the atoms. The ability of an atom to attract electrons in a covalent bond is the atom's *electronegativity* and is highest for reactive nonmetal elements on the upper right of the periodic table and lowest for metals on the lower left. Comparing electronegativities allows prediction of whether a given bond is covalent, polar covalent, or ionic. Just as individual bonds can be polar, entire molecules can be polar if electrons are attracted more strongly to one part of the molecule than to another. Molecular polarity is due to the sum of all individual bond polarities and lone-pair contributions in the molecule (see *Problems 32, 73–84, 96, 97, 101*).

CONCEPT MAP: ELECTROSTATIC FORCES

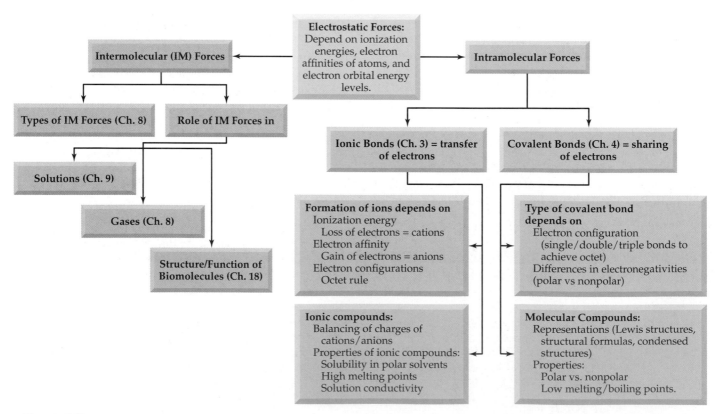

▲ **Figure 4.7**

Concept Maps. Chemistry, like most subjects, makes more sense when presented in context. When we understand the connections between concepts, or how one idea leads to another, it becomes easier to see the "big picture" and to appreciate why a certain concept is important. A concept map is one way of illustrating those connections and providing a context for what we have learned and what we will be learning in later chapters.

As you can see from the concept map in Figure 4.7, the electronic structure of atoms discussed in Chapter 2 plays a critical role in the chemical behavior of an element, specifically in terms of its tendency to form ionic compounds (Chapter 3) or molecular compounds (Chapter 4). Furthermore, the nature of the attractive forces between particles (intermolecular versus intramolecular) plays a role in the physical and chemical behavior of substances discussed in later chapters.

As we continue exploring new topics, we will expand certain areas of this concept map or add new branches as needed.

KEY WORDS

Binary compound, *p. 123*

Bond angle, *p. 115*

Bond length, *p. 100*

Condensed structure, *p. 109*

Coordinate covalent bond, *p. 106*

Covalent bond, *p. 99*

Double bond, *p. 104*

Electronegativity, *p. 120*

Lewis structure, *p. 108*

Lone pair, *p. 108*

Molecular compound, *p. 101*

Molecular formula, *p. 108*

Molecule, *p. 99*

Polar covalent bond, *p. 119*

Regular tetrahedron, *p. 116*

Single bond, *p. 104*

Structural formula, *p. 108*

Triple bond, *p. 104*

Valence-shell electron-pair repulsion (VSEPR) model, *p. 114*

UNDERSTANDING KEY CONCEPTS

4.27   What is the geometry around the central atom in the following molecular models? (There are no "hidden" atoms; all atoms in each model are visible.)

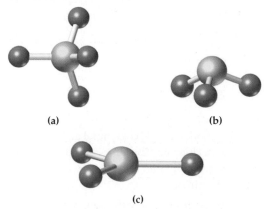

(a)

(b)

(c)

4.28   Three of the following molecular models have a tetrahedral central atom, and one does not. Which is the odd one?

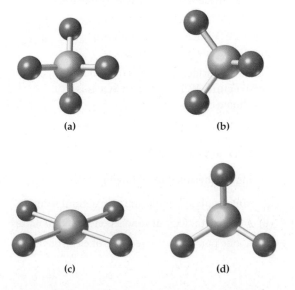

(a)

(b)

(c)

(d)

4.29   The ball-and-stick molecular model shown here is a representation of acetaminophen, the active ingredient in over-the-counter headache remedies such as Tylenol. The lines indicate only the connections between atoms, not whether the bonds are single, double, or triple (red = O, gray = C, blue = N, ivory = H).

   (a) What is the molecular formula of acetaminophen?

   (b) Indicate the positions of the multiple bonds in acetaminophen.

   (c) What is the geometry around each carbon and each nitrogen?

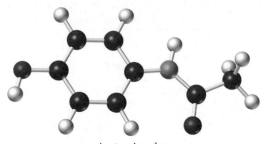

Acetaminophen

4.30   The atom-to-atom connections in vitamin C (ascorbic acid) are as shown here. Convert this skeletal drawing to a Lewis electron-dot structure for vitamin C by showing the positions of any multiple bonds and lone pairs of electrons.

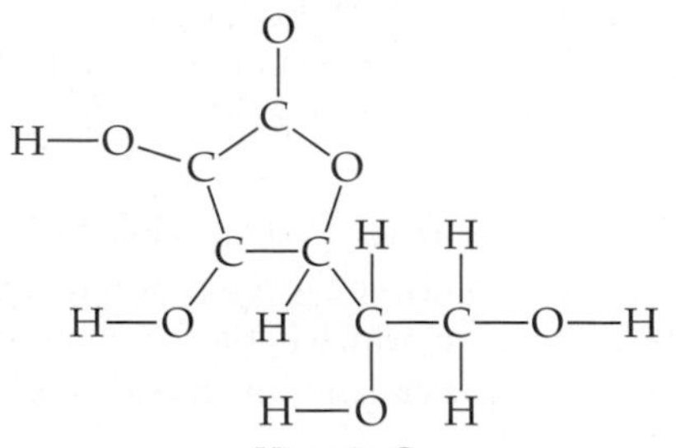

Vitamin C

4.31 The ball-and-stick molecular model shown here is a representation of thalidomide, a drug that has been approved for treating leprosy, but causes severe birth defects when taken by expectant mothers. The lines indicate only the connections between atoms, not whether the bonds are single, double, or triple (red = O, gray = C, blue = N, ivory = H).

(a) What is the molecular formula of thalidomide?

(b) Indicate the positions of the multiple bonds in thalidomide.

(c) What is the geometry around each carbon and each nitrogen?

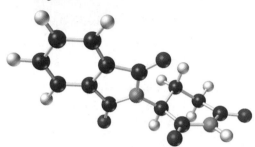

Thalidomide

4.32 Show the position of any electron lone pairs in this structure of acetamide, and indicate the electron-rich and electron-poor regions.

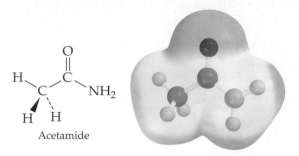

Acetamide

ADDITIONAL PROBLEMS

COVALENT BONDS

4.33 What is a covalent bond, and how does it differ from an ionic bond?

4.34 What is a coordinate covalent bond, and how does it differ from a covalent bond?

4.35 Which of the following elements would you expect to form (i) diatomic molecules, (ii) mainly covalent bonds, (iii) mainly ionic bonds, (iv) both covalent and ionic bonds? (More than one answer may apply; remember that some nonmetals can form ionic bonds with metals.)

(a) Oxygen (b) Potassium (c) Phosphorus

(d) Iodine (e) Hydrogen (f) Cesium

4.36 Identify the bonds formed between the following pairs of atoms as either covalent or ionic.

(a) Aluminum and bromine (b) Carbon and fluorine

(c) Cesium and iodine (d) Zinc and fluorine

(e) Lithium and chlorine

4.37 Write electron-dot symbols to show the number of covalent bonds and the lone pairs of electrons in the molecules that are formed by reactions between the atoms in Problem 4.36.

4.38 Look up tellurium ($Z = 52$) in the periodic table and predict how many covalent bonds it is likely to form. Explain.

4.39 Look up antimony in the periodic table ($Z = 51$). How many covalent bonds would you expect it to form? Based on this information, which of the following antimony compounds is covalent and which is ionic: $SbCl_3$ or $SbCl_5$?

4.40 Which of the following contains a coordinate covalent bond? (Hint: how many covalent bonds would you expect the central atom (underlined) to form?)

(a) $\underline{Pb}Cl_2$ (b) $\underline{Cu}(NH_3)_4^{2+}$ (c) $\underline{N}H_4^+$

4.41 Which of the following contains a coordinate covalent bond? (Hint: how many covalent bonds would you expect the central atom (underlined) to form?)

(a) $H_2\underline{O}$ (b) $\underline{B}F_4^-$ (c) $H_3\underline{O}^+$

4.42 Tin forms both an ionic compound and a covalent compound with chlorine. The ionic compound is $SnCl_2$. Is the covalent compound more likely to be $SnCl_3$, $SnCl_4$, or $SnCl_5$? Explain.

4.43 A compound of gallium with chlorine has a melting point of 77 °C and a boiling point of 201 °C. Is the compound ionic or covalent? What is a likely formula?

4.44 Nitrous oxide, N_2O, has the following structure. Which bond in N_2O is a coordinate covalent bond?

$:N\equiv N-\ddot{O}:$

Nitrous oxide

4.45 Thionyl chloride, $SOCl_2$ has the following structure. Which bond in $SOCl_2$ is a coordinate covalent bond?

$:\ddot{O}:$
$|$
$\overset{S}{\underset{:\ddot{C}l \quad \ddot{C}l:}{}}$

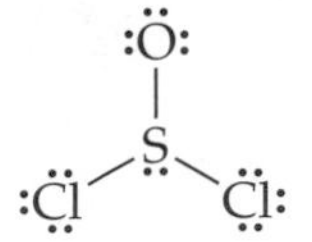

Thionyl chloride

STRUCTURAL FORMULAS

4.46 Distinguish between the following:

(a) A molecular formula and a structural formula

(b) A structural formula and a condensed structure

(c) A lone pair and a shared pair of electrons

4.47 Assume that you are given samples of two white crystalline compounds, one of them ionic and one covalent. Describe how you might tell which is which.

4.48 Determine the total number of valence electrons in the following molecules. If the molecule contains multiple bonds, indicate where the multiple bonds are located and whether they are double or triple bonds.

(a) N_2 (b) NOCl
(c) CH_3CH_2CHO (d) OF_2

4.49 Add lone pairs where appropriate to the following structures:

(a) C≡O (b) CH_3SH

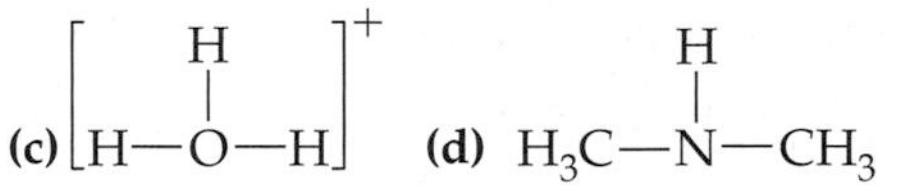

(c) $\left[H{-}\overset{\displaystyle H}{\underset{}{O}}{-}H \right]^{+}$ (d) $H_3C{-}\overset{\displaystyle H}{\underset{}{N}}{-}CH_3$

4.50 If a research paper appeared reporting the structure of a new molecule with formula C_2H_8 most chemists would be highly skeptical. Why?

4.51 Consider the following possible structural formulas for $C_3H_6O_2$. If a structure is not reasonable, explain what changes could be made to convert it to a reasonable structure.

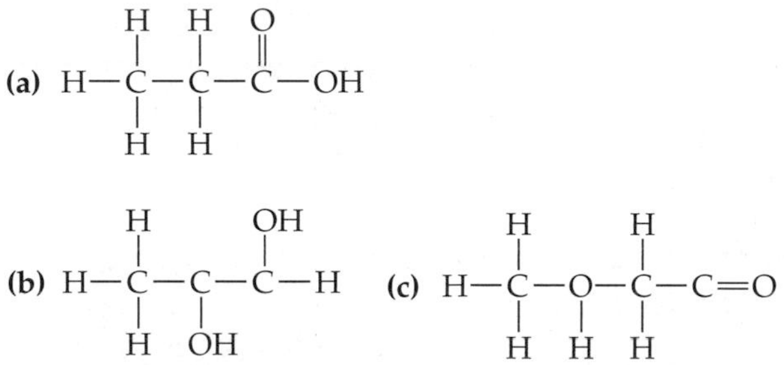

(a) H—C—C—C—OH (with H, H on first two carbons, O double bond)

(b) H—C—C—C—H (with H, H, OH, OH substituents)   (c) H—C—O—C—C=O

4.52 Convert the following Lewis structures into structural formulas in which lines replace the bonding electrons. Include the lone pairs.

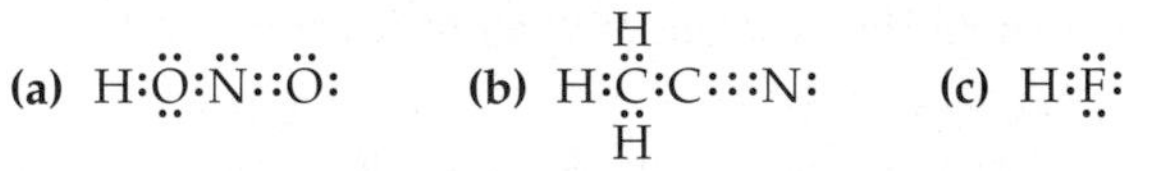

(a) H:Ö:N::Ö: (b) H:C:C:::N: (with H above and H below first C) (c) H:F:

4.53 Convert the following Lewis structure for the nitrate ion into a line structure that includes the lone pairs. Why does the nitrate ion have a −1 charge? $\left[\overset{:\ddot{O}:}{\underset{}{:\ddot{O}:N:\ddot{O}:}} \right]^{-}$

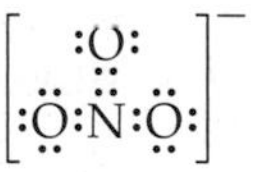

4.54 Convert the following structural formulas into condensed structures.

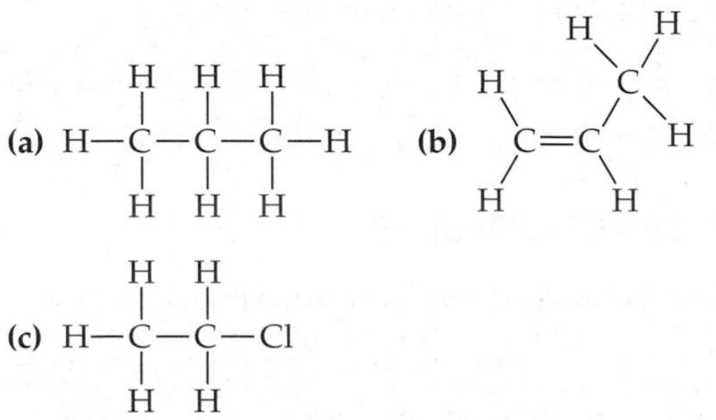

(a) H—C—C—C—H (propane with H's)   (b) $\overset{H}{\underset{H}{\diagdown}}C{=}C\overset{\diagup H}{\underset{\diagdown H}{}}$ with extra CH

(c) H—C—C—Cl (with H's)

4.55 Expand the following condensed structures into the correct structural formulas.

(a) $CH_3CH_2COCH(CH_3)_2$ (b) $CH_3CH_2COOCH_3$
(c) $CH_3CH_2OCH_2Cl$

4.56 Acetic acid is the major organic constituent of vinegar. Convert the following structural formula of acetic acid into a condensed structure similar to those shown in Problem 4.55.

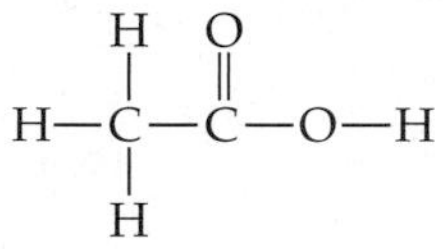

$$H{-}\overset{\displaystyle H}{\underset{\displaystyle H}{C}}{-}\overset{\displaystyle O}{\underset{}{C}}{-}O{-}H$$

DRAWING LEWIS STRUCTURES

4.57 Draw a Lewis structure for the following molecules:

(a) SF_6 (b) $AlCl_3$ (c) CS_2 (d) SeF_4
(e) $BeCl_2$ (Note: this molecule does not follow the octet rule.)
(f) N_2O_4

4.58 Draw a Lewis structure for the following molecules:

(a) Nitrous acid, HNO_2 (H is bonded to an O atom)
(b) Ozone, O_3
(c) Acetaldehyde, CH_3CHO

4.59 Ethanol, or "grain alcohol," has the formula C_2H_6O and contains an O—H bond. Propose a structure for ethanol that is consistent with common bonding patterns.

4.60 Dimethyl ether has the same molecular formula as ethanol (Problem 4.59) but very different properties. Propose a structure for dimethyl ether in which the oxygen is bonded to two carbons.

4.61 Hydrazine, a substance used to make rocket fuel, has the formula N_2H_4. Propose a structure for hydrazine.

4.62 Tetrachloroethylene, C_2Cl_4, is used commercially as a dry-cleaning solvent. Propose a structure for tetrachloroethylene based on the common bonding patterns expected in organic molecules. What kind of carbon-carbon bond is present?

4.63 Dimethyl sulfoxide, also known as DMSO, is an important organic solvent often used for drug delivery since it readily penetrates the skin. The formula for DMSO is $(CH_3)_2SO$. Draw a Lewis structure of DMSO; both C atoms are attached to the S atom.

4.64 Draw a Lewis structure for hydroxylamine, NH_2OH.

4.65 The carbonate ion, CO_3^{2-}, contains a double bond. Draw a Lewis structure for the ion and show why it has a charge of −2.

4.66 Draw a Lewis structure for the following polyatomic ions:

(a) Formate, HCO_2^{-} (b) Sulfite, SO_3^{2-}
(c) Thiocyanate, SCN^{-} (d) Phosphate, PO_4^{3+}
(e) Chlorite, ClO_2^{-} (chlorine is the central atom)

MOLECULAR GEOMETRY

4.67 Predict the geometry and bond angles around atom A for molecules with the general formulas AB_3 and AB_2E, where B represents another atom and E represents an electron pair.

4.68 Predict the geometry and bond angles around atom A for molecules with the general formulas AB_4, AB_3E, and AB_2E_2, where B represents another atom and E represents an electron pair.

4.69 Sketch the three-dimensional shape of the following molecules:

(a) Methylamine, CH_3NH_2 (b) Iodoform, CHI_3

(c) Ozone, O_3

(d) Phosphorus pentachloride, PCl_5

(e) Chloric acid, $HClO_3$

4.70 Predict the three-dimensional shape of the following molecules:

(a) SiF_4 (b) CF_2Cl_2 (c) SO_3

(d) BBr_3 (e) NF_3

4.71 Predict the geometry around each carbon atom in the amino acid alanine.

Alanine

4.72 Predict the geometry around each carbon atom in vinyl acetate, a precursor of the polyvinyl alcohol polymer used in automobile safety glass.

$$H_2C=CH-O-\overset{\overset{\displaystyle O}{\|}}{C}-CH_3$$

Vinyl acetate

POLARITY OF BONDS AND MOLECULES

4.73 Where in the periodic table are the most electronegative elements found, and where are the least electronegative elements found?

4.74 Predict the electronegativity of the yet-undiscovered element with $Z = 119$.

4.75 Look at the periodic table, and then order the following elements according to increasing electronegativity: K, Si, Be, O, B.

4.76 Look at the periodic table, and then order the following elements according to decreasing electronegativity: C, Ca, Cs, Cl, Cu.

4.77 Which of the following bonds are polar? If a bond is polar, identify the negative and positive ends of each bond by using $\delta+$ and $\delta-$.

(a) I—Br   (b) O—H

(c) C—F   (d) N—C

(e) C—C

4.78 Which of the following bonds are polar? If a bond is polar, identify the negative and positive ends of each bond by using $\delta+$ and $\delta-$.

(a) O—Cl   (b) N—Cl

(c) P—H   (d) C—I

(e) C—O

4.79 Based on electronegativity differences, would you expect bonds between the following pairs of atoms to be largely ionic or largely covalent?

(a) Be and F   (b) Ca and Cl

(c) O and H   (d) Be and Br

4.80 Arrange the following molecules in order of the increasing polarity of their bonds:

(a) HCl   (b) PH_3

(c) H_2O (d) CF_4

4.81 Ammonia, NH_3, and phosphorus trihydride, PH_3, both have a trigonal pyramid geometry. Which one is more polar? Explain.

4.82 Decide whether each of the compounds listed in Problem 4.80 is polar, and show the direction of polarity.

4.83 Carbon dioxide is a nonpolar molecule, whereas sulfur dioxide is polar. Draw Lewis structures for each of these molecules to explain this observation.

4.84 Water (H_2O) is more polar than hydrogen sulfide (H_2S). Explain.

NAMES AND FORMULAS OF MOLECULAR COMPOUNDS

4.85 Name the following binary compounds:

(a) PI_3 (b) $AsCl_3$ (c) P_4S_3

(d) Al_2F_6 (e) N_2O_5 (f) $AsCl_5$

4.86 Name the following compounds:

(a) SeO_2 (b) XeO_4

(c) N_2S_5 (d) P_3Se_4

4.87 Write formulas for the following compounds:

(a) Nitrogen dioxide   (b) Sulfur hexafluoride

(c) Bromine triiodide   (d) Dinitrogen trioxide

(e) Nitrogen triiodide   (f) Iodine heptafluoride

4.88 Write formulas for the following compounds:

(a) Silicon tetrachloride   (b) Sodium hydride

(c) Antimony pentafluoride (d) Osmium tetroxide

CHEMISTRY IN ACTION

4.89 The CO molecule is highly reactive and will bind to the Fe^{2+} ion in hemoglobin and interfere with O_2 transport. What type of bond is formed between the CO molecule and the Fe^{2+} ion? [*CO and NO: Pollutants or Miracle Molecules?*, p. 113]

4.90 What is a vasodilator, and why would it be useful in treating hypertension (high blood pressure)? [*CO and NO: Pollutants or Miracle Molecules?, p. 113*]

4.91 How is a polymer formed? [*VERY Big Molecules, p. 118*]

4.92 Do any polymers exist in nature? Explain. [*VERY Big Molecules, p. 118*]

4.93 Why are many chemical names so complex? [*Damascenone by Any Other Name, p. 125*]

4.94 Citronellol, one of the compounds found in the scent of roses, is also used in perfumes and in insect repellent products. Write the condensed formula from the structural formula of citronellol shown below. [*Damascenone by Any Other Name, p. 125*]

$$CH_3-\overset{\overset{\displaystyle CH_3}{|}}{C}=\overset{\overset{\displaystyle H}{|}}{\underset{\underset{\displaystyle H}{|}}{C}}-\overset{\overset{\displaystyle H}{|}}{\underset{\underset{\displaystyle H}{|}}{C}}-\overset{\overset{\displaystyle H}{|}}{\underset{\underset{\displaystyle H}{|}}{C}}-\overset{\overset{\displaystyle CH_3}{|}}{\underset{\underset{\displaystyle H}{|}}{C}}-\overset{\overset{\displaystyle H}{|}}{\underset{\underset{\displaystyle H}{|}}{C}}-\overset{\overset{\displaystyle H}{|}}{\underset{\underset{\displaystyle H}{|}}{C}}-OH$$

GENERAL QUESTIONS AND PROBLEMS

4.95 The discovery in the 1960s that xenon and fluorine react to form a molecular compound was a surprise to most chemists, because it had been thought that noble gases could not form bonds.

(a) Why was it thought that noble gases could not form bonds?

(b) Draw a Lewis structure of XeF_4 in which Xe is the central atom. How many electron clouds are there on the central atom?

(c) What type of bonds are the Xe—F bonds? Explain.

4.96 Acetone, a common solvent used in some nail polish removers, has the molecular formula C_3H_6O and contains a carbon-oxygen double bond.

(a) Propose two Lewis structures for acetone.

(b) What is the geometry around the carbon atoms in each of the structures?

(c) Which of the bonds in each structure are polar?

4.97 Draw the structural formulas for two compounds having the molecular formula C_2H_4O. What is the molecular geometry around the carbon atoms in each of these molecules? Would these molecules be polar or nonpolar? (Hint: there is one double bond.)

4.98 The following formulas are unlikely to be correct. What is wrong with each?

(a) CCl_3 (b) N_2H_5

(c) H_3S (d) C_2OS

4.99 Which of the compounds (a) through (d) contain ionic bonds? Which contain covalent bonds? Which contain coordinate covalent bonds? (A compound may contain more than one type of bond.)

(a) $BaCl_2$ (b) $Ca(NO_3)_2$

(c) BCl_4^- (d) $TiBr_4$

4.100 The phosphonium ion, PH_4^+, is formed by reaction of phosphine, PH_3, with an acid.

(a) Draw the Lewis structure of the phosphonium ion.

(b) Predict its molecular geometry.

(c) Describe how a fourth hydrogen can be added to PH_3.

(d) Explain why the ion has a +1 charge.

4.101 Compare the trend in electronegativity seen in Figure 4.6 (p. 120) with the trend in electron affinity shown in Figure 3.1 (p. 75). What similarities do you see? What differences? Explain.

4.102 Name the following compounds. Be sure to determine whether the compound is ionic or covalent so that you use the proper rules.

(a) $CaCl_2$ (b) $TeCl_2$ (c) BF_3

(d) $MgSO_4$ (e) K_2O (f) FeF_3

(g) PF_3

4.103 Titanium forms both molecular and ionic compounds with nonmetals, as, for example, $TiBr_4$ and TiO_2. One of these compounds has a melting point of 39 °C, and the other has a melting point of 1825 °C. Which is ionic and which is molecular? Explain your answer in terms of electronegativities of the atoms involved in each compound.

4.104 Draw a Lewis structure for chloral hydrate, known in detective novels as "knockout drops." Indicate all lone pairs.

$$Cl-\overset{\overset{\displaystyle Cl}{|}}{\underset{\underset{\displaystyle Cl}{|}}{C}}-\overset{\overset{\displaystyle O-H}{|}}{\underset{\underset{\displaystyle H}{|}}{C}}-O-H \qquad \text{Chloral hydrate}$$

4.105 The dichromate ion, $Cr_2O_7^{2-}$, has neither Cr—Cr nor O—O bonds. Draw a Lewis structure.

4.106 Oxalic acid, $H_2C_2O_4$, is a substance found in uncooked spinach leaves and other greens that can be poisonous at high concentrations (for example, in raw rhubarb leaves). If oxalic acid has a C—C single bond and the H atoms are both connected to O atoms, draw its Lewis structure.

4.107 Identify the fourth row elements represented by "X" in the following compounds.

(a) $\ddot{O}=\ddot{X}=\ddot{O}$ (b) $:\!\ddot{F}\diagdown_{\cdot\cdot}\diagup\ddot{F}\!: \atop :\ddot{X}\!:$

4.108 Write Lewis structures for molecules with the following connections, showing the positions of any multiple bonds and lone pairs of electrons.

(a) $Cl-\overset{\overset{\displaystyle O}{|}}{C}-O-\overset{\overset{\displaystyle H}{|}}{\underset{\underset{\displaystyle H}{|}}{C}}-H$ (b) $H-\overset{\overset{\displaystyle H}{|}}{\underset{\underset{\displaystyle H}{|}}{C}}-C-C-H$

4.109 Electron-pair repulsion influences the shapes of polyatomic ions in the same way it influences neutral molecules. Draw electron-dot symbols and predict the shape of the ammonium ion, NH_4^+, the sulfate ion, SO_4^{2-}, and the phosphite ion, PO_3^{3-}.

By examination, we see that only two elements, N and H, need to be balanced. Both these elements exist in nature as diatomic gases, as indicated on the reactant side of the unbalanced equation.

STEP 2: Add appropriate coefficients to balance the numbers of atoms of each element. Remember that the subscript 2 in N_2 and H_2 indicates that these are diatomic molecules (that is, 2 N atoms or 2 H atoms per molecule). Since there are 2 nitrogen atoms on the left, we must add a coefficient of 2 in front of the NH_3 on the right side of the equation to balance the equation with respect to N:

$$N_2(g) + H_2(g) \longrightarrow 2\,NH_3(g)$$

Now we see that there are 2 H atoms on the left, but 6 H atoms on the right. We can balance the equation with respect to hydrogen by adding a coefficient of 3 in front of the $H_2(g)$ on the left side:

$$N_2(g) + 3\,H_2(g) \longrightarrow 2\,NH_3(g)$$

STEP 3: Check the equation to make sure the numbers and kinds of atoms on both sides of the equation are the same.

> *On the left:* $(1 \times 2)\,N = 2\,N$ $(3 \times 2)\,H = 6\,H$
>
> *On the right:* $(2 \times 1)\,N = 2\,N$ $(2 \times 3)\,H = 6\,H$

STEP 4: Make sure the coefficients are reduced to their lowest whole-number values. In this case, the coefficients already represent the lowest whole-number values.

Worked Example 5.3 Balancing Chemical Equations

Natural gas (methane, CH_4) burns in oxygen to yield water and carbon dioxide (CO_2). Write a balanced equation for the reaction.

SOLUTION

STEP 1: Write the unbalanced equation, using correct formulas for all substances:

$$CH_4 + O_2 \longrightarrow CO_2 + H_2O \quad \text{(Unbalanced)}$$

STEP 2: Since carbon appears in one formula on each side of the arrow, let us begin with that element. In fact, there is only 1 carbon atom in each formula, so the equation is already balanced for that element. Next, note that there are 4 hydrogen atoms on the left (in CH_4) and only 2 on the right (in H_2O). Placing a coefficient of 2 before H_2O gives the same number of hydrogen atoms on both sides:

$$CH_4 + O_2 \longrightarrow CO_2 + 2\,H_2O \quad \text{(Balanced for C and H)}$$

Finally, look at the number of oxygen atoms. There are 2 on the left (in O_2) but 4 on the right (2 in CO_2 and 1 in each H_2O). If we place a 2 before the O_2, the number of oxygen atoms will be the same on both sides, but the numbers of other elements will not change:

$$CH_4 + 2\,O_2 \longrightarrow CO_2 + 2\,H_2O \quad \text{(Balanced for C, H, and O)}$$

STEP 3: Check to be sure the numbers of atoms on both sides are the same.

> *On the left:* 1 C $\qquad$ 4 H $\qquad$ $(2 \times 2)\,O = 4\,O$
>
> *On the right:* 1 C $\quad$ $(2 \times 2)\,H = 4\,H$ $\qquad$ $2\,O + 2\,O = 4\,O$
>
> $\qquad\qquad\qquad\qquad\qquad\qquad\qquad$ From CO_2 $\quad$ From 2 H_2O

STEP 4: Make sure the coefficients are reduced to their lowest whole-number values. In this case, the answer is already correct.

Worked Example 5.4 Balancing Chemical Equations

Sodium chlorate ($NaClO_3$) decomposes when heated to yield sodium chloride and oxygen, a reaction used to provide oxygen for the emergency breathing masks in airliners. Write a balanced equation for this reaction.

SOLUTION

STEP 1: The unbalanced equation is:

$$NaClO_3 \longrightarrow NaCl + O_2$$

STEP 2: Both the Na and the Cl are already balanced, with only one atom of each on the left and right sides of the equation. There are 3 O atoms on the left, but only 2 on the right. The O atoms can be balanced by placing a coefficient of 1½ in front of O_2 on the right side of the equation:

$$NaClO_3 \longrightarrow NaCl + 1½\,O_2$$

STEP 3: Checking to make sure the same number of atoms of each type occurs on both sides of the equation, we see 1 atom of Na and Cl on both sides, and 3 O atoms on both sides.

STEP 4: In this case, obtaining all coefficients in their smallest whole-number values requires that we multiply all coefficients by 2 to obtain:

$$2\,NaClO_3 \longrightarrow 2\,NaCl + 3\,O_2$$

Checking gives

On the left:	$2\,Na\ 2\,Cl\ (2 \times 3)\,O = 6\,O$
On the right:	$2\,Na\ 2\,Cl\ (3 \times 2)\,O = 6\,O$

The oxygen in emergency breathing masks comes from heating sodium chlorate.

PROBLEM 5.3

Ozone (O_3) is formed in the earth's upper atmosphere by the action of solar radiation on oxygen molecules (O_2). Write a balanced equation for the formation of ozone from oxygen.

PROBLEM 5.4

Balance the following equations:

(a) $Ca(OH)_2 + HCl \longrightarrow CaCl_2 + H_2O$

(b) $Al + O_2 \longrightarrow Al_2O_3$

(c) $CH_3CH_3 + O_2 \longrightarrow CO_2 + H_2O$

(d) $AgNO_3 + MgCl_2 \longrightarrow AgCl + Mg(NO_3)_2$

🔑 KEY CONCEPT PROBLEM 5.5

The following diagram represents the reaction of A (red spheres) with B_2 (blue spheres). Write a balanced equation for the reaction.

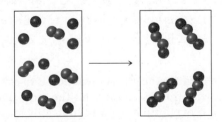

5.3 Classes of Chemical Reactions

One of the best ways to understand any subject is to look for patterns that help us categorize large amounts of information. When learning about chemical reactions, for instance, it is helpful to group the reactions of ionic compounds into three general classes: *precipitation reactions, acid–base neutralization reactions*, and *oxidation–reduction reactions*. This is not the only possible way of categorizing reactions but it is useful nonetheless. Let us look briefly at examples of each of these three reaction classes before studying them in more detail in subsequent sections.

Precipitate An insoluble solid that forms in solution during a chemical reaction.

- **Precipitation reactions** are processes in which an insoluble solid called a **precipitate** forms when reactants are combined in aqueous solution. Most precipitations take place when the anions and cations of two ionic compounds change partners. For example, an aqueous solution of lead(II) nitrate reacts with an aqueous solution of potassium iodide to yield an aqueous solution of potassium nitrate plus an insoluble yellow precipitate of lead iodide:

$$Pb(NO_3)_2\,(aq) + 2\,KI(aq) \longrightarrow 2\,KNO_3(aq) + PbI_2(s)$$

Salt An ionic compound formed from reaction of an acid with a base.

▶▶▶ See Section 3.11 for more discussion of acids and bases.

- **Acid–base neutralization reactions** are processes in which an acid reacts with a base to yield water plus an ionic compound called a **salt**. We will look at both acids and bases in more detail in Chapter 10, but you might recall for the moment that we previously defined acids as compounds that produce H^+ ions and bases as compounds that produce OH^- ions when dissolved in water. Thus, a neutralization reaction removes H^+ and OH^- ions from solution and yields neutral H_2O. The reaction between hydrochloric acid and sodium hydroxide is a typical example:

$$HCl(aq) + NaOH(aq) \longrightarrow H_2O(l) + NaCl(aq)$$

Note that in this reaction, the "salt" produced is sodium chloride, or common table salt. In a general sense, however, *any* ionic compound produced in an acid–base reaction is also called a salt. Other examples include potassium nitrate (KNO_3), magnesium bromide $(MgBr_2)$, and sodium sulfate (Na_2SO_4).

Oxidation–reduction (redox) reaction A reaction in which electrons are transferred from one atom to another.

- **Oxidation–reduction reactions**, or **redox reactions**, are processes in which one or more electrons are transferred between reaction partners (atoms, molecules, or ions). As a result of this transfer, the number of electrons assigned to individual atoms in the various reactants change. When metallic magnesium reacts with iodine vapor, for instance, a magnesium atom gives an electron to each of 2 iodine atoms, forming a Mg^{2+} ion and 2 I^- ions. The charge on the magnesium changes from 0 to +2, and the charge on each iodine changes from 0 to -1:

$$Mg(s) + I_2(g) \longrightarrow MgI_2(s)$$

Fundamentally, all reactions involving covalent compounds are classified as redox reactions, because electrons are rearranged as bonds are broken and new bonds are formed. The discussion here, however, will focus mainly on reactions involving ionic substances.

▲ **Reaction of aqueous Pb(NO₃)₂ with aqueous KI gives a yellow precipitate of PbI₂.**

Worked Example 5.5 Classifying Chemical Reactions

Classify the following as a precipitation, an acid–base neutralization, or a redox reaction.

(a) $Ca(OH)_2(aq) + 2\,HBr(aq) \longrightarrow 2\,H_2O(l) + CaBr_2(aq)$
(b) $Pb(ClO_4)_2(aq) + 2\,NaCl(aq) \longrightarrow PbCl_2(s) + 2\,NaClO_4(aq)$
(c) $2\,AgNO_3(aq) + Cu(s) \longrightarrow 2\,Ag(s) + Cu(NO_3)_2(aq)$

ANALYSIS One way to identify the class of reaction is to examine the products that form and match them with the descriptions for the types of reactions provided in this section. By a process of elimination, we can readily identify the appropriate reaction classification.

SOLUTION

(a) The products of this reaction are water and an ionic compound, or salt $(CaBr_2)$. This is consistent with the description of an acid–base neutralization reaction.

(b) This reaction involves two aqueous reactants, $Pb(ClO_4)_2$ and $NaCl$, which combine to form a solid product, $PbCl_2$. This is consistent with a precipitation reaction.

(c) The products of this reaction are a solid, $Ag(s)$, and an aqueous ionic compound, $Cu(NO_3)_2$. This does not match the description of a neutralization reaction, which would form *water* and an ionic compound. One of the products *is* a solid, but the reactants are not both aqueous compound; one of the reactants is *also* a solid (Cu). Therefore, this reaction would not be classified as a precipitation reaction. By the process of elimination, then, it must be a redox reaction.

PROBLEM 5.6

Classify each of the following as a precipitation, an acid–base neutralization, or a redox reaction.

(a) $AgNO_3(aq) + KCl(aq) \longrightarrow AgCl(s) + KNO_3(aq)$

(b) $2\,Al(s) + 3\,Br_2(l) \longrightarrow 2\,AlBr_3(s)$

(c) $Ca(OH)_2(aq) + 2\,HNO_3(aq) \longrightarrow 2\,H_2O(l) + Ca(NO_3)_2(aq)$

PROBLEM 5.7

The reaction involved in photosynthesis combines carbon dioxide and water to create simple sugars:

$$CO_2(g) + H_2O(l) \xrightarrow{\text{Sunlight}} C_6H_{12}O_6(s)$$

Balance the equation and classify the reaction.

5.4 Precipitation Reactions and Solubility Guidelines

Now let us look at precipitation reactions in more detail. To predict whether a precipitation reaction will occur upon mixing aqueous solutions of two ionic compounds, you must know the **solubilities** of the potential products—how much of each compound will dissolve in a given amount of solvent at a given temperature. If a substance has a low solubility in water, then it is likely to precipitate from an aqueous solution. If a substance has a high solubility in water, then no precipitate will form.

Solubility The amount of a compound that will dissolve in a given amount of solvent at a given temperature.

Solubility is a complex matter, and it is not always possible to make correct predictions. As a rule of thumb, though, the following solubility guidelines for ionic compounds are useful.

General Rules on Solubility

RULE 1: **A compound is probably soluble if it contains one of the following cations:**
- Group 1A cation: Li^+, Na^+, K^+, Rb^+, Cs^+
- Ammonium ion: NH_4^+

RULE 2: **A compound is probably soluble if it contains one of the following anions:**
- Halide: Cl^-, Br^-, I^- except *Ag^+*, *Hg_2^{2+}*, and *Pb^{2+}* compounds
- Nitrate (NO_3^-), perchlorate (ClO_4^-), acetate $(CH_3CO_2^-)$, sulfate (SO_4^{2-}) except *Ba^{2+}*, *Hg_2^{2+}*, and *Pb^{2+}* sulfates

If a compound does *not* contain at least one of the ions listed above, it is probably *not* soluble. Thus, Na_2CO_3 is soluble because it contains a group 1A cation, and $CaCl_2$ is soluble because it contains a halide anion. The compound $CaCO_3$, however, is probably *insoluble* because it contains none of the ions listed above. These same guidelines are presented in table form in Table 5.1.

TABLE 5.1 General Solubility Guidelines for Ionic Compounds in Water

Soluble	Exceptions
Ammonium compounds (NH_4^+)	None
Lithium compounds (Li^+)	None
Sodium compounds (Na^+)	None
Potassium compounds (K^+)	None
Nitrates (NO_3^-)	None
Perchlorates (ClO_4^-)	None
Acetates ($CH_3CO_2^-$)	None
Chlorides (Cl^-)	
Bromides (Br^-)	Ag^+, Hg_2^{2+}, and Pb^{2+} compounds
Iodides (I^-)	
Sulfates (SO_4^{2-})	Ba^{2+}, Hg_2^{2+}, and Pb^{2+} compounds

CHEMISTRY IN ACTION

Gout and Kidney Stones: Problems in Solubility

One of the major pathways in the body for the breakdown of the nucleic acids DNA and RNA is by conversion to a substance called *uric acid*, $C_5H_4N_4O_3$, so named because it was first isolated from urine in 1776. Most people excrete about 0.5 g of uric acid every day in the form of sodium urate, the salt that results from an acid–base reaction of uric acid. Unfortunately, the amount of sodium urate that dissolves in water (or urine) is fairly low—only about 0.07 mg/mL at the normal body temperature of 37 °C. When too much sodium urate is produced or mechanisms for its elimination fail, its concentration in blood and urine rises, and the excess sometimes precipitates in the joints and kidneys.

Gout is a disorder of nucleic acid metabolism that primarily affects middle-aged men (only 5% of gout patients are women). It is characterized by an increased sodium urate concentration in blood, leading to the deposit of sodium urate crystals in soft tissue around the joints, particularly in the hands and at the base of the big toe. Deposits of the sharp, needlelike crystals cause an extremely painful inflammation that can lead ultimately to arthritis and even to bone destruction.

Just as increased sodium urate concentration in blood can lead to gout, increased concentration in urine can result in the formation of one kind of *kidney stones*, small crystals that precipitate in the kidney. Although often quite small, kidney stones cause excruciating pain when they pass through the ureter, the duct that carries urine from the kidney to the bladder. In some cases, complete blockage of the ureter occurs.

Treatment of excessive sodium urate production involves both dietary modification and drug therapy. Foods such as liver, sardines, and asparagus should be avoided, and drugs such as allopurinol can be taken to lower production of sodium urate. Allopurinol functions by inhibiting the action of an enzyme called *xanthine oxidase*, thereby blocking a step in nucleic acid metabolism.

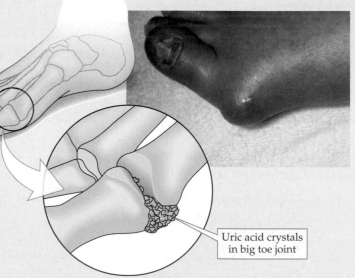

Uric acid crystals in big toe joint

▲ **Excess production of uric acid can cause gout, a painful condition characterized by the accumulation of sodium urate crystals in joints.**

See Chemistry in Action Problems 5.63 and 5.64 at the end of the chapter.

Let us try a problem. What will happen if aqueous solutions of sodium nitrate $(NaNO_3)$ and potassium sulfate (K_2SO_4) are mixed? To answer this question, look at the guidelines to find the solubilities of the two possible products, Na_2SO_4 and KNO_3. Because both have group 1A cations (Na^+ and K^+), both are water-soluble and no precipitation will occur. If aqueous solutions of silver nitrate $(AgNO_3)$ and sodium carbonate (Na_2CO_3) are mixed, however, the guidelines predict that a precipitate of insoluble silver carbonate (Ag_2CO_3) will form.

$$2\,AgNO_3(aq) + Na_2CO_3(aq) \longrightarrow Ag_2CO_3(s) + 2\,NaNO_3(aq)$$

Worked Example 5.6 Chemical Reactions: Solubility Rules

Will a precipitation reaction occur when aqueous solutions of $CdCl_2$ and $(NH_4)_2S$ are mixed?

SOLUTION

Identify the two potential products, and predict the solubility of each using the guidelines in the text. In this instance, $CdCl_2$ and $(NH_4)_2S$ might give CdS and NH_4Cl. Since the guidelines predict that CdS is insoluble, a precipitation reaction will occur:

$$CdCl_2(aq) + (NH_4)_2S(aq) \longrightarrow CdS(s) + 2\,NH_4Cl(aq)$$

PROBLEM 5.8

Predict the solubility of the following compounds:

(a) $CdCO_3$ (b) Na_2S

(c) $PbSO_4$ (d) $(NH_4)_3PO_4$

(e) Hg_2Cl_2

PROBLEM 5.9

Predict whether a precipitation reaction will occur in the following situations. If a precipitation reaction occurs, write the balanced chemical equation for the reaction.

(a) $NiCl_2(aq) + (NH_4)_2S(aq) \longrightarrow$

(b) $AgNO_3(aq) + CaBr_2(aq) \longrightarrow$

PROBLEM 5.10

In addition to kidney stone formation by sodium urate (See Chemistry in Action on p. 140), many kidney stones are formed by precipitation of oxalate by calcium. Oxalates are found in many foods, including spinach, blueberries, and chocolate. Show the balanced chemical equation for the precipitation of calcium oxalate, starting with calcium chloride $(CaCl_2)$ and sodium oxalate $(Na_2C_2O_4)$.

5.5 Acids, Bases, and Neutralization Reactions

When acids and bases are mixed in the correct proportion, both acidic and basic properties disappear because of a **neutralization reaction**. The most common kind of neutralization reaction occurs between an acid (generalized as HA), and a metal hydroxide (generalized as MOH), to yield water and a salt. The H^+ ion from the acid combines with the OH^- ion from the base to give neutral H_2O, whereas the anion from the acid (A^-) combines with the cation from the base (M^+) to give the salt:

Neutralization reaction The reaction of an acid with a base.

A neutralization reaction: $\underset{\text{Acid}}{HA(aq)} + \underset{\text{Base}}{MOH(aq)} \longrightarrow \underset{\text{Water}}{H_2O(l)} + \underset{\text{A salt}}{MA(aq)}$

The reaction of hydrochloric acid with potassium hydroxide to produce potassium chloride is an example:

$$HCl(aq) + KOH(aq) \longrightarrow H_2O(l) + KCl(aq)$$

Another kind of neutralization reaction occurs between an acid and a carbonate (or bicarbonate) to yield water, a salt, and carbon dioxide. Hydrochloric acid reacts with potassium carbonate, for example, to give H_2O, KCl, and CO_2:

$$2\,HCl(aq) + K_2CO_3(aq) \longrightarrow H_2O(l) + 2\,KCl(aq) + CO_2(g)$$

The reaction occurs because the carbonate ion (CO_3^{2-}) reacts initially with H^+ to yield H_2CO_3, which is unstable and immediately decomposes to give CO_2 plus H_2O.

We will defer a more complete discussion of carbonates as bases until Chapter 10, but note for now that they yield OH^- ions when dissolved in water just as KOH and other bases do.

$$K_2CO_3(s) + H_2O(l) \xrightarrow{\text{Dissolve in water}} 2K^+(aq) + HCO_3^-(aq) + OH^-(aq)$$

LOOKING AHEAD ▶▶▶ Acids and bases are enormously important in biological chemistry. We will see in Chapter 18, for instance, how acids and bases affect the structure and properties of proteins.

Worked Example 5.7 Chemical Reactions: Acid–Base Neutralization

Write an equation for the neutralization reaction of aqueous HBr and aqueous $Ba(OH)_2$.

SOLUTION

The reaction of HBr with $Ba(OH)_2$ involves the combination of a proton (H^+) from the acid with OH^- from the base to yield water and a salt $(BaBr_2)$.

$$2\,HBr(aq) + Ba(OH)_2(aq) \longrightarrow 2\,H_2O(l) + BaBr_2(aq)$$

PROBLEM 5.11
Write and balance equations for the following acid–base neutralization reactions:
(a) $CsOH(aq) + H_2SO_4(aq) \longrightarrow$
(b) $Ca(OH)_2(aq) + CH_3CO_2H(aq) \longrightarrow$
(c) $NaHCO_3(aq) + HBr(aq) \longrightarrow$

5.6 Redox Reactions

Oxidation–reduction (redox) reactions, the third and final category of reactions that we will discuss here, are more complex than precipitation and neutralization reactions. Look, for instance, at the following examples and see if you can tell what they have in common. Copper metal reacts with aqueous silver nitrate to form silver metal and aqueous copper(II) nitrate; iron rusts in air to form iron(III) oxide; the zinc metal container on the outside of a battery reacts with manganese dioxide and ammonium chloride inside the battery to generate electricity and give aqueous zinc chloride plus manganese(III) oxide. Although these and many thousands of other reactions appear unrelated, all are examples of redox reactions.

$$Cu(s) + 2\,AgNO_3(aq) \longrightarrow 2\,Ag(s) + Cu(NO_3)_2(aq)$$
$$2\,Fe(s) + 3\,O_2(g) \longrightarrow Fe_2O_3(s)$$
$$Zn(s) + 2\,MnO_2(s) + 2\,NH_4Cl(s) \longrightarrow$$
$$ZnCl_2(aq) + Mn_2O_3(s) + 2\,NH_3(aq) + H_2O(l)$$

Historically, the word *oxidation* referred to the combination of an element with oxygen to yield an oxide, and the word *reduction* referred to the removal of oxygen from an oxide to yield the element. Today, though, the words have taken on a much broader meaning. An **oxidation** is now defined as the loss of one or more electrons by an atom,

Oxidation The loss of one or more electrons by an atom.

and a **reduction** is the gain of one or more electrons. Thus, an oxidation–reduction reaction, or redox reaction, is one in which *electrons are transferred from one atom to another.*

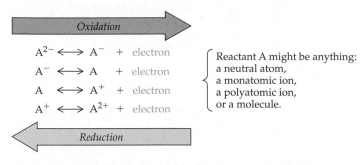

Take the reaction of copper with aqueous Ag^+ as an example, as shown in Figure 5.1. Copper metal gives an electron to each of 2 Ag^+ ions, forming Cu^{2+} and silver metal. Copper is oxidized in the process, and Ag^+ is reduced. You can follow the transfer of the electrons by noting that the charge on the copper increases from 0 to +2 when it loses 2 electrons, whereas the charge on Ag^+ decreases from +1 to 0 when it gains an electron.

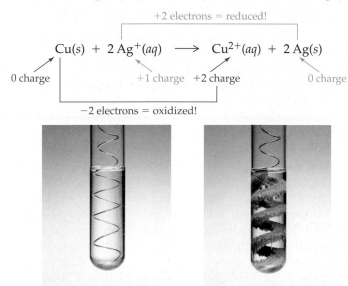

Similarly, in the reaction of aqueous iodide ion with bromine, iodide ion gives an electron to bromine, forming iodine and bromide ion. Iodide ion is oxidized as its charge increases from −1 to 0, and bromine is reduced as its charge decreases from 0 to −1.

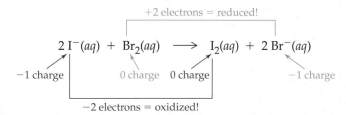

As these examples show, oxidation and reduction always occur together. Whenever one substance loses an electron (is oxidized), another substance must gain that electron (be reduced). The substance that gives up an electron and causes the reduction—the copper atom in the reaction of Cu with Ag^+ and the iodide ion in the reaction of I^- with Br_2—is called a **reducing agent**. The substance that gains an electron and causes the oxidation—the silver ion in the reaction of Cu with Ag^+ and the bromine molecule in the reaction of I^- with Br_2—is called an **oxidizing agent**. The charge on the reducing agent increases during the reaction, and the charge on the oxidizing agent decreases.

Reduction The gain of one or more electrons by an atom.

▸**Figure 5.1**
The copper wire reacts with aqueous Ag^+ ion and becomes coated with metallic silver. At the same time, copper(II) ions go into solution, producing the blue color.

Reducing agent A reactant that causes a reduction in another reactant by giving up electron to it.

Oxidizing agent A reactant that causes an oxidation by taking electrons from another reactant.

Reducing agent	Loses one or more electrons
	Causes reduction
	Undergoes oxidation
	Becomes more positive (less negative)
	(May gain oxygen atoms)
Oxidizing agent	Gains one or more electrons
	Causes oxidation
	Undergoes reduction
	Becomes more negative (less positive)
	(May lose oxygen atoms)

Among the simplest of redox processes is the reaction of an element, usually a metal, with an aqueous cation to yield a different element and a different ion. Iron metal reacts with aqueous copper(II) ion, for example, to give iron(II) ion and copper metal. Similarly, magnesium metal reacts with aqueous acid to yield magnesium ion and hydrogen gas. In both cases, the reactant element (Fe or Mg) is oxidized, and the reactant ion (Cu^{2+} or H^+) is reduced.

$$Fe(s) + Cu^{2+}(aq) \longrightarrow Fe^{2+}(aq) + Cu(s)$$
$$Mg(s) + 2\,H^+(aq) \longrightarrow Mg^{2+}(aq) + H_2(g)$$

The reaction of a metal with water or aqueous acid (H^+) to release H_2 gas is a particularly important process. As you might expect based on the periodic properties discussed in Section 3.2, the alkali metals and alkaline earth metals (on the left side of the periodic table) are the most powerful reducing agents (electron donors), so powerful that they even react with pure water, in which the concentration of H^+ is very low. This is due in part to the fact that alkali metals and alkaline earth metals have low ionization energies. Ionization energy, which is a measure of how easily an element will lose an electron, tends to decrease as we move to the left and down in the periodic table. Thus, metals toward the middle of the periodic table, such as iron and chromium, have higher ionization energies and do not lose electrons as readily; they react only with aqueous acids but not with water. Those metals near the bottom right of the periodic table, such as platinum and gold, react with neither aqueous acid nor water. At the other extreme from the alkali metals, the reactive nonmetals at the top right of the periodic table have the highest ionization energies and are extremely weak reducing agents but powerful oxidizing agents (electron acceptors). This is, again, predictable based on the periodic property of electron affinity (Section 3.2), which becomes more energetically favored as we move up and to the right in the periodic table.

We can make a few generalizations about the redox behavior of metals and nonmetals.

1. In reactions involving metals and nonmetals, metals tend to lose electrons while nonmetals tend to gain electrons. The number of electrons lost or gained can often be predicted based on the position of the element in the periodic table. (Section 3.5)
2. In reactions involving nonmetals, the "more metallic" element (farther down and/or to the left in the periodic table) tends to lose electrons, and the "less metallic" element (up and/or to the right) tends to gain electrons.

   Redox reactions involve almost every element in the periodic table, and they occur in a vast number of processes throughout nature, biology, and industry. Here are just a few examples:

- **Corrosion** is the deterioration of a metal by oxidation, such as the rusting of iron in moist air. The economic consequences of rusting are enormous: it has been estimated that up to one-fourth of the iron produced in the United States is used to replace bridges, buildings, and other structures that have been destroyed by corrosion. (The raised dot in the formula $Fe_2O_3 \cdot H_2O$ for rust indicates that one water molecule is associated with each Fe_2O_3 in an undefined way.)

▶▶▶ The relationship between formation of ions and ionization energy/electronegativity was discussed in Chapter 3.

- **Combustion** is the burning of a fuel by rapid oxidation with oxygen in air. Gasoline, fuel oil, natural gas, wood, paper, and other organic substances of carbon and hydrogen are the most common fuels that burn in air. Even some metals, though, will burn in air. Magnesium and calcium are examples.

$$CH_4(g) + 2\,O_2(g) \longrightarrow CO_2(g) + 2\,H_2O(l)$$
Methane
(natural gas)

$$2\,Mg(s) + O_2(g) \longrightarrow 2\,MgO(s)$$

- **Respiration** is the process of breathing and using oxygen for the many biological redox reactions that provide the energy required by living organisms. We will see in Chapters 21–22 that in the respiration process, energy is released from food molecules slowly and in complex, multistep pathways, but that the overall result is similar to that of the simpler combustion reactions. For example, the simple sugar glucose $(C_6H_{12}O_6)$ reacts with O_2 to give CO_2 and H_2O according to the following equation:

$$C_6H_{12}O_6 + 6\,O_2 \longrightarrow 6\,CO_2 + 6\,H_2O + Energy$$
Glucose
(a carbohydrate)

- **Bleaching** makes use of redox reactions to decolorize or lighten colored materials. Dark hair is bleached to turn it blond, clothes are bleached to remove stains, wood pulp is bleached to make white paper, and so on. The oxidizing agent used depends on the situation: hydrogen peroxide (H_2O_2) is used for hair, sodium hypochlorite (NaOCl) for clothes, and elemental chlorine for wood pulp, but the principle is always the same. In all cases, colored organic materials are destroyed by reaction with strong oxidizing agents.
- **Metallurgy,** the science of extracting and purifying metals from their ores, makes use of numerous redox processes. Worldwide, approximately 800 million tons of iron are produced each year by reduction of the mineral hematite, Fe_2O_3, with carbon monoxide.

$$Fe_2O_3(s) + 3\,CO(g) \longrightarrow 2\,Fe(s) + 3\,CO_2(g)$$

Worked Example 5.8 Chemical Reactions: Redox Reactions

For the following reactions, indicate which atom is oxidized and which is reduced, based on the definitions provided in this section. Identify the oxidizing and reducing agents.

(a) $Cu(s) + Pt^{2+}(aq) \longrightarrow Cu^{2+}(aq) + Pt(s)$

(b) $2\,Mg(s) + CO_2(g) \longrightarrow 2\,MgO(s) + C(s)$

ANALYSIS The definitions for oxidation include a loss of electrons, an increase in charge, and a gain of oxygen atoms; reduction is defined as a gain of electrons, a decrease in charge, and a loss of oxygen atoms.

SOLUTION

(a) In this reaction, the charge on the Cu atom increases from 0 to 2+. This corresponds to a loss of 2 electrons. The Cu is therefore oxidized and acts as the reducing agent. Conversely, the Pt^{2+} ion undergoes a decrease in charge from 2+ to 0, corresponding to a gain of 2 electrons for the Pt^{2+} ion. The Pt^{2+} is reduced, and acts as the oxidizing agent.

(b) In this case, the gain or loss of oxygen atoms is the easiest way to identify which atoms are oxidized and reduced. The Mg atom is gaining oxygen to form MgO; therefore, the Mg is being oxidized and acts as the reducing agent. The C atom in CO_2 is losing oxygen. Therefore, the C atom in CO_2 is being reduced, and so CO_2 acts as the oxidizing agent.

Worked Example 5.9 Chemical Reactions: Identifying Oxidizing/Reducing Agents

For the respiration and metallurgy examples discussed previously, identify the atoms being oxidized and reduced, and label the oxidizing and reducing agents.

ANALYSIS Again, using the definitions of oxidation and reduction provided in this section, we can determine which atom(s) are gaining/losing electrons or gaining/losing oxygen atoms.

SOLUTION

$$\textit{Respiration:} \quad C_6H_{12}O_6 + 6\,O_2 \longrightarrow 6\,CO_2 + 6\,H_2O$$

Because the charge associated with the individual atoms is not evident, we will use the definition of oxidation/reduction as the gaining/losing of oxygen atoms. In this reaction, there is only one reactant besides oxygen $(C_6H_{12}O_6)$, so we must determine *which* atom in the compound is changing. The ratio of carbon to oxygen in $C_6H_{12}O_4$ is 1:1, while the ratio in CO_2 is 1:2. Therefore, the C atoms are gaining oxygen and are oxidized; the $C_6H_{12}O_{16}$ is the reducing agent and O_2 is the oxidizing agent. Note that the ratio of hydrogen to oxygen in $C_6H_{12}O_6$ and in H_2O is 2:1. The H atoms are neither oxidized nor reduced.

$$\textit{Metallurgy:} \quad Fe_2O_3(s) + 3\,CO(g) \longrightarrow 2\,Fe(s) + 3\,CO_2(g)$$

The Fe_2O_3 is losing oxygen to form Fe(s); it is being reduced and acts as the oxidizing agent. In contrast, the CO is gaining oxygen to form CO_2; it is being oxidized and acts as the reducing agent.

Worked Example 5.10 Chemical Reactions: Identifying Redox Reactions

For the following reactions, identify the atom(s) being oxidized and reduced:

(a) $2\,Al(s) + 3\,Cl_2(g) \longrightarrow 2\,AlCl_3(s)$ **(b)** $C(s) + 2\,Cl_2(g) \longrightarrow CCl_4(l)$

ANALYSIS Again, there is no obvious increase or decrease in charge to indicate a gain or loss of electrons. Also, the reactions do not involve a gain or loss of oxygen. We can, however, evaluate the reactions in terms of the typical behavior of metals and nonmetals in reactions.

SOLUTION

(a) In this case, we have the reaction of a metal (Al) with a nonmetal (Cl_2). Because metals tend to lose electrons and nonmetals tend to gain electrons, we can assume that the Al atom is oxidized (loses electrons) and the Cl_2 is reduced (gains electrons).

(b) The carbon atom is the less electronegative element (farther to the left) and is less likely to gain an electron. The more electronegative element (Cl) will tend to gain electrons (be reduced).

PROBLEM 5.12

Identify the oxidized reactant, the reduced reactant, the oxidizing agent, and the reducing agent in the following reactions:

(a) $Fe(s) + Cu^{2+}(aq) \longrightarrow Fe^{2+}(aq) + Cu(s)$
(b) $Mg(s) + Cl_2(g) \longrightarrow MgCl_2(s)$
(c) $2\,Al(s) + Cr_2O_3(s) \longrightarrow 2\,Cr(s) + Al_2O_3(s)$

PROBLEM 5.13

Potassium, a silvery metal, reacts with bromine, a corrosive, reddish liquid, to yield potassium bromide, a white solid. Write the balanced equation, and identify the oxidizing and reducing agents.

PROBLEM 5.14

The redox reaction that provides energy for the lithium battery described in the Chemistry in Action on p. 147 is $2\,Li(s) + I_2(s) \rightarrow 2\,LiI(aq)$. Identify which reactant is being oxidized and which is being reduced in this reaction.

CHEMISTRY IN ACTION

Batteries

Imagine life without batteries: no cars (they do not start very easily without their batteries!), no heart pacemakers, no flashlights, no hearing aids, no laptops, no radios, no cell phones, nor thousands of other things. Modern society could not exist without batteries.

Although they come in many types and sizes, all batteries work using redox reactions. In a typical redox reaction carried out in the laboratory—say, the reaction of zinc metal with Ag^+ to yield Zn^{2+} and silver metal—the reactants are simply mixed in a flask and electrons are transferred by direct contact between the reactants. In a battery, however, the two reactants are kept in separate compartments and the electrons are transferred through a wire running between them.

The common household battery used for flashlights and radios is the *dry cell*, developed in 1866. One reactant is a can of zinc metal, and the other is a paste of solid manganese dioxide. A graphite rod sticks into the MnO_2 paste to provide electrical contact, and a moist paste of ammonium chloride separates the two reactants. If the zinc can and the graphite rod are connected by a wire, zinc sends electrons flowing through the wire toward the MnO_2 in a redox reaction. The resultant electrical current can then be used to power a lightbulb or a radio. The accompanying figure shows a cutaway view of a dry-cell battery.

$$Zn(s) + 2\,MnO_2(s) + 2\,NH_4Cl(s) \longrightarrow$$
$$ZnCl_2(aq) + Mn_2O_3(s) + 2\,NH_3(aq) + H_2O(l)$$

▲ **Think of all the devices we use every day—laptop computers, cell phones, iPods—that depend on batteries.**

Closely related to the dry-cell battery is the familiar *alkaline* battery, in which the ammonium chloride paste is replaced by an alkaline, or basic, paste of NaOH or KOH. The alkaline battery has a longer life than the standard dry-cell battery because the zinc container corrodes less easily under basic conditions. The redox reaction is:

$$Zn(s) + 2\,MnO_2(s) \longrightarrow ZnO(aq) + Mn_2O_3(s)$$

The batteries used in implanted medical devices such as pacemakers must be small, corrosion-resistant, reliable, and able to last up to 10 years. Nearly all pacemakers being implanted today—about 750,000 each year—use titanium-encased, lithium–iodine batteries, whose redox reaction is:

$$2\,Li(s) + I_2(s) \longrightarrow 2\,LiI(aq)$$

See Chemistry in Action Problems 5.65 and 5.66 at the end of the chapter.

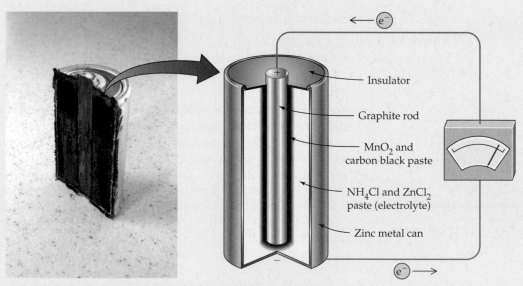

- Insulator
- Graphite rod
- MnO_2 and carbon black paste
- NH_4Cl and $ZnCl_2$ paste (electrolyte)
- Zinc metal can

▲ **A dry-cell battery. The cutaway view shows the two reactants that make up the redox reaction.**

5.7 Recognizing Redox Reactions

How can you tell when a redox reaction is taking place? When ions are involved, it is simply a matter of determining whether there is a change in the charges. For reactions involving metals and nonmetals, we can predict the gain or loss of electrons as discussed previously. When molecular substances are involved, though, it is not as obvious. Is the combining of sulfur with oxygen a redox reaction? If so, which partner is the oxidizing agent and which is the reducing agent?

$$S(s) + O_2(g) \longrightarrow SO_2(g)$$

One way to evaluate this reaction is in terms of the oxygen gain by sulfur, indicating that S atoms are oxidized and O atoms are reduced. But can we also look at this reaction in terms of the gain or loss of electrons by the S and O atoms? Because oxygen is more electronegative than sulfur, the oxygen atoms in SO_2 attract the electrons in the S—O bonds more strongly than sulfur does, giving the oxygen atoms a larger share of the electrons than sulfur. By extending the ideas of oxidation and reduction to an increase or decrease in electron *sharing* instead of complete electron *transfer*, we can say that the sulfur atom is oxidized in its reaction with oxygen because it loses a share in some electrons, whereas the oxygen atoms are reduced because they gain a share in some electrons.

A formal system has been devised for keeping track of changes in electron sharing, and thus for determining whether atoms are oxidized or reduced in reactions. To each atom in a substance, we assign a value called an **oxidation number** (or *oxidation state*), which indicates whether the atom is neutral, electron-rich, or electron-poor. By comparing the oxidation number of an atom before and after a reaction, we can tell whether the atom has gained or lost shares in electrons. Note that *oxidation numbers do not necessarily imply ionic charges*. They are simply a convenient device for keeping track of electrons in redox reactions.

The rules for assigning oxidation numbers are straightforward:

- **An atom in its elemental state has an oxidation number of 0.**

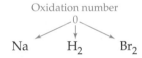

- **A monatomic ion has an oxidation number equal to its charge.**

Oxidation number	Oxidation number	Oxidation number	Oxidation number
+1	+2	−1	−2
Na^+	Ca^{2+}	Cl^-	O^{2-}

- **In a molecular compound, an atom usually has the same oxidation number it would have if it were a monatomic ion.** Recall from Chapters 3 and 4 that the less electronegative elements (hydrogen and metals) on the left side of the periodic table tend to form cations, and the more electronegative elements (oxygen, nitrogen, and the halogens) near the top right of the periodic table tend to form anions. Hydrogen and metals therefore have positive oxidation numbers in most compounds, whereas reactive nonmetals generally have negative oxidation numbers. Hydrogen is usually +1, oxygen is usually −2, nitrogen is usually −3, and halogens are usually −1:

> ▶▶▶ Electronegativity, or the propensity of an atom in a covalent bond to attract electrons, was introduced in Section 4.9.

Oxidation number A number that indicates whether an atom is neutral, electron-rich, or electron-poor.

> ▶▶▶ Review the Important Points about Ion Formation and the Periodic Table listed in Section 3.6.

For compounds with more than one nonmetal element, such as SO_2, NO, or CO_2, the more electronegative element—oxygen in these examples—has a negative oxidation number and the less electronegative element has a positive oxidation number. Thus, in answer to the question posed at the beginning of this section, combining sulfur with oxygen to form SO_2 is a redox reaction because the oxidation number of sulfur increases from 0 to +4 and that of oxygen decreases from 0 to −2.

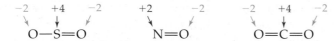

- **The sum of the oxidation numbers in a neutral compound is 0.** Using this rule, the oxidation number of any atom in a compound can be found if the oxidation numbers of the other atoms are known. In the SO_2 example just mentioned, each of the 2 O atoms has an oxidation number of −2, so the S atom must have an oxidation number of +4. In HNO_3, the H atom has an oxidation number of +1 and the strongly electronegative O atom has an oxidation number of −2, so the N atom must have an oxidation number of +5. In a polyatomic ion, the sum of the oxidation numbers equals the charge on the ion.

$$\overset{+1}{H}-\overset{-2}{O}-\overset{+5}{N}=\overset{-2}{O} \qquad \text{Total} = 1 + 5 + 3(-2) = 0$$
$$\underset{\overset{|}{\underset{O}{}}}{} \overset{-2}{}$$

Worked Examples 5.11 and 5.12 show further instances of assigning and using oxidation numbers.

Worked Example 5.11 Redox Reactions: Oxidation Numbers

What is the oxidation number of the titanium atom in $TiCl_4$? Name the compound using a Roman numeral (Section 3.10).

SOLUTION
Chlorine, a reactive nonmetal, is more electronegative than titanium and has an oxidation number of −1. Because there are 4 chlorine atoms in $TiCl_4$, the oxidation number of titanium must be +4. The compound is named titanium(IV) chloride. Note that the Roman numeral IV in the name of this molecular compound refers to the oxidation number +4 rather than to a true ionic charge.

Worked Example 5.12 Redox Reactions: Identifying Redox Reactions

Use oxidation numbers to show that the production of iron metal from its ore (Fe_2O_3) by reaction with charcoal (C) is a redox reaction. Which reactant has been oxidized, and which has been reduced? Which reactant is the oxidizing agent, and which is the reducing agent?

$$2 \, Fe_2O_3(s) + 3 \, C(s) \longrightarrow 4 \, Fe(s) + 3 \, CO_2(g)$$

SOLUTION
The idea is to assign oxidation numbers to both reactants and products and see if there has been a change. In the production of iron from Fe_2O_3, the oxidation number of Fe changes from +3 to 0, and the oxidation number of C changes from 0 to +4. Iron has thus been reduced (decrease in oxidation number), and carbon has been oxidized (increase in oxidation number). Oxygen is neither oxidized nor reduced because its oxidation number does not change. Carbon is the reducing agent, and Fe_2O_3 is the oxidizing agent.

$$\overset{+3 \quad -2}{2 \, Fe_2O_3} + \overset{0}{3 \, C} \longrightarrow \overset{0}{4 \, Fe} + \overset{+4 \, -2}{3 \, CO_2}$$

PROBLEM 5.15

What are the oxidation numbers of the metal atoms in the following compounds? Name each, using the oxidation number as a Roman numeral.

(a) VCl_3 (b) $SnCl_4$ (c) CrO_3 (d) $Cu(NO_3)_2$ (e) $NiSO_4$

PROBLEM 5.16

Assign an oxidation number to each atom in the reactants and products shown here to determine which of the following reactions are redox reactions:

(a) $Na_2S(aq) + NiCl_2(aq) \longrightarrow 2\,NaCl(aq) + NiS(s)$

(b) $2\,Na(s) + 2\,H_2O(l) \longrightarrow 2\,NaOH(aq) + H_2(g)$

(c) $C(s) + O_2(g) \longrightarrow CO_2(g)$

(d) $CuO(s) + 2\,HCl(aq) \longrightarrow CuCl_2(aq) + H_2O(l)$

(e) $2\,MnO_4^-(aq) + 5\,SO_2(g) + 2\,H_2O(l) \longrightarrow$
$\quad 2\,Mn^{2+}(aq) + 5\,SO_4^{2-}(aq) + 4\,H^+(aq)$

PROBLEM 5.17

For each of the reactions you identified as redox reactions in Problem 5.16, identify the oxidizing agent and the reducing agent.

5.8 Net Ionic Equations

In the equations we have been writing up to this point, all the substances involved in reactions have been written using their full formulas. In the precipitation reaction of lead(II) nitrate with potassium iodide mentioned in Section 5.3, for example, only the parenthetical *aq* indicated that the reaction actually takes place in aqueous solution, and nowhere was it explicitly indicated that ions are involved:

$$Pb(NO_3)_2(aq) + 2\,KI(aq) \longrightarrow 2\,KNO_3(aq) + PbI_2(s)$$

In fact, lead(II) nitrate, potassium iodide, and potassium nitrate dissolve in water to yield solutions of ions. Thus, it is more accurate to write the reaction as an **ionic equation**, in which all the ions are explicitly shown:

> **Ionic equation** An equation in which ions are explicitly shown.

An ionic equation: $Pb^{2+}(aq) + 2\,NO_3^-(aq) + 2\,K^+(aq) + 2\,I^-(aq) \longrightarrow$
$\qquad\qquad\qquad\qquad\qquad 2\,K^+(aq) + 2\,NO_3^-(aq) + PbI_2(s)$

A look at this ionic equation shows that the NO_3^- and K^+ ions undergo no change during the reaction. They appear on both sides of the reaction arrow and act merely as **spectator ions**, that is, they are present but play no role. The actual reaction, when stripped to its essentials, can be described more simply by writing a **net ionic equation**, which includes only the ions that undergo change and ignores all spectator ions:

> **Spectator ion** An ion that appears unchanged on both sides of a reaction arrow.

> **Net ionic equation** An equation that does not include spectator ions.

Ionic equation: $Pb^{2+}(aq) + 2\,\overline{NO_3^-}(aq) + 2\,\overline{K^+(aq)} + 2\,I^-(aq) \longrightarrow$
$\qquad\qquad\qquad\qquad\qquad 2\,\overline{K^+(aq)} + 2\,\overline{NO_3^-}(aq) + PbI_2(s)$

Net ionic equation: $Pb^{2+}(aq) + 2\,I^-(aq) \longrightarrow PbI_2(s)$

Note that a net ionic equation, like all chemical equations, must be balanced both for atoms and for charge, with all coefficients reduced to their lowest whole numbers. Note also that all compounds that do *not* give ions in solution—all insoluble compounds and all molecular compounds—are represented by their full formulas.

We can apply the concept of ionic equations to acid–base neutralization reactions and redox reactions as well. Consider the neutralization reaction between KOH and HNO_3:

$$KOH(aq) + HNO_3(aq) \longrightarrow H_2O(l) + KNO_3(aq)$$

Since acids and bases are identified based on the ions they form when dissolved in aqueous solutions, we can write an ionic equation for this reaction:

Ionic equation: $\overline{K^+(aq)} + OH^-(aq) + H^+(aq) + \overline{NO_3^-(aq)} \longrightarrow$
$\qquad\qquad\qquad\qquad\qquad H_2O(l) + \overline{K^+(aq)} + \overline{NO_3^-(aq)}$

Eliminating the spectator ions (K^+ and NO_3^-), we obtain the net ionic equation for the neutralization reaction:

Net ionic equation: $OH^-(aq) + H^+(aq) \longrightarrow H_2O(l)$

The net ionic equation confirms the basis of the acid–base neutralization; the OH^- from the base and the H^+ from the acid neutralize each other to form water.

Similarly, many redox reactions can be viewed in terms of ionic equations. Consider the reaction between $Cu(s)$ and $AgNO_3$ from Section 5.6:

$$Cu(s) + 2\,AgNO_3(aq) \longrightarrow 2\,Ag^+(aq) + Cu(NO_3)_2(aq)$$

The aqueous products and reactants can be written as dissolved ions:

Ionic equation: $Cu(s) + 2\,Ag^+(aq) + 2\,\cancel{NO_3^-(aq)} \longrightarrow$
$$2\,Ag(s) + Cu^{2+}(aq) + 2\,\cancel{NO_3^-(aq)}$$

Again, eliminating the spectator ions (NO_3^-), we obtain the net ionic equation for this redox reaction:

Net ionic equation: $Cu(s) + 2\,Ag^+(aq) \longrightarrow 2\,Ag(s) + Cu^{2+}(aq)$

It is now clear that the $Cu(s)$ loses 2 electrons and is oxidized, whereas each Ag^+ ion gains an electron and is reduced.

Worked Example 5.13 Chemical Reactions: Net Ionic Reactions

Write balanced net ionic equations for the following reactions:

(a) $AgNO_3(aq) + ZnCl_2(aq) \longrightarrow$
(b) $HCl(aq) + Ca(OH)_2(aq) \longrightarrow$
(c) $6\,HCl(aq) + 2\,Al(s) \longrightarrow 2\,AlCl_3(aq) + 3\,H_2(g)$

SOLUTION

(a) The solubility guidelines discussed in Section 5.4 predict that a precipitate of insoluble AgCl forms when aqueous solutions of Ag^+ and Cl^- are mixed. Writing all the ions separately gives an ionic equation, and eliminating spectator ions Zn^{2+} and NO_3^- gives the net ionic equation.

Ionic equation: $2\,Ag^+(aq) + 2\,\cancel{NO_3^-(aq)} + \cancel{Zn^{2+}(aq)} + 2\,Cl^-(aq) \longrightarrow$
$$2\,AgCl(s) + \cancel{Zn^{2+}(aq)} + 2\,\cancel{NO_3(aq)}$$

Net ionic equation: $2\,Ag^+(aq) + 2\,Cl^-(aq) \longrightarrow 2\,AgCl(s)$

The coefficients can all be divided by 2 to give:

Net ionic equation: $Ag^+(aq) + Cl^+(aq) \longrightarrow AgCl(s)$

A check shows that the equation is balanced for atoms and charge (zero on each side).

(b) Allowing the acid HCl to react with the base $Ca(OH)_2$ leads to a neutralization reaction. Writing the ions separately, and remembering to write a complete formula for water, gives an ionic equation. Then eliminating the spectator ions and dividing the coefficients by 2 gives the net ionic equation.

Ionic equation: $2\,H^+(aq) + 2\,\cancel{Cl^-(aq)} + \cancel{Ca^{2+}(aq)} + 2\,OH^-(aq) \longrightarrow$
$$2\,H_2O(l) + \cancel{Ca^{2+}(aq)} + 2\,\cancel{Cl^-(aq)}$$

Net ionic equation: $H^+(aq) + OH^-(aq) \longrightarrow H_2O(l)$

A check shows that atoms and charges are the same on both sides of the equation.

(c) The reaction of Al metal with acid (HCl) is a redox reaction. The Al is oxidized, since the oxidation number increases from $0 \rightarrow +3$, whereas the H in HCl is reduced from $+1 \rightarrow 0$. We write the ionic equation by showing the ions that are formed for each aqueous ionic species. Eliminating the spectator ions yields the net ionic equation.

Ionic equation: $6\,H^+(aq) + 6\,\cancel{Cl^-(aq)} + 2\,Al(s) \longrightarrow$
$$2\,Al^{3+}(aq) + 6\,\cancel{Cl^-(aq)} + 3\,H_2(g)$$

Net ionic equation: $6\,H^+(aq) + 2\,Al(s) \longrightarrow 2\,Al^{3+}(aq) + 3\,H_2(g)$

A check shows that atoms and charges are the same on both sides of the equation.

PROBLEM 5.18

Write net ionic equations for the following reactions:

(a) $Zn(s) + Pb(NO_3)_2(aq) \longrightarrow Zn(NO_3)_2(aq) + Pb(s)$
(b) $2\,KOH(aq) + H_2SO_4(aq) \longrightarrow K_2SO_4(aq) + 2\,H_2O(l)$
(c) $2\,FeCl_3(aq) + SnCl_2(aq) \longrightarrow 2\,FeCl_2(aq) + SnCl_4(aq)$

PROBLEM 5.19

Identify each of the reactions in Problem 5.18 as an acid–base neutralization, a precipitation, or a redox reaction.

SUMMARY: REVISITING THE CHAPTER GOALS

1. How are chemical reactions written? Chemical equations must be *balanced*; that is, the numbers and kinds of atoms must be the same in both the reactants and the products. To balance an equation, *coefficients* are placed before formulas but the formulas themselves cannot be changed (*see Problems 21–23, 26–37, 59, 60, 64, 67, 68, 71, 72, 75, 76, 79, 80*).

2. How are chemical reactions of ionic compounds classified? There are three common types of reactions of ionic compounds (*see Problems 38–50, 65, 70, 79, 81*).

  Precipitation reactions are processes in which an insoluble solid called a *precipitate* is formed. Most precipitations take place when the anions and cations of two ionic compounds change partners. Solubility guidelines for ionic compounds are used to predict when precipitation will occur (*see Problems 24, 25, 43–46, 49, 69, 76–78*).

  Acid–base neutralization reactions are processes in which an acid reacts with a base to yield water plus an ionic compound called a *salt*. Since acids produce H^+ ions and bases produce OH^- ions when dissolved in water, a neutralization reaction removes H^+ and OH^- ions from solution and yields neutral H_2O (*see Problems 37, 39, 75, 81*).

  Oxidation–reduction (redox) reactions are processes in which one or more electrons are transferred between reaction partners.

An *oxidation* is defined as the loss of one or more electrons by an atom, and a *reduction* is the gain of one or more electrons. An *oxidizing agent* causes the oxidation of another reactant by accepting electrons, and a *reducing agent* causes the reduction of another reactant by donating electrons (*see Problems 51–54, 57–62, 65, 66, 68, 82*).

3. What are oxidation numbers, and how are they used? *Oxidation numbers* are assigned to atoms in reactants and products to provide a measure of whether an atom is neutral, electron-rich, or electron-poor. By comparing the oxidation number of an atom before and after reaction, we can tell whether the atom has gained or lost shares in electrons and thus whether a redox reaction has occurred (*see Problems 51–62, 65, 66, 70–74, 82*).

4. What is a net ionic equation? The *net ionic equation* only includes those ions that are directly involved in the ionic reaction. These ions can be identified because they are found in different phases or compounds on the reactant and product sides of the chemical equation. The net ionic equation does not include *spectator ions*, which appear in the same state on both sides of the chemical equation (*see Problems 39, 47, 48, 50, 69, 76–78, 81*).

KEY WORDS

Balanced equation, *p. 134*

Chemical equation, *p. 133*

Coefficient, *p. 134*

Ionic equation, *p. 150*

Law of conservation of mass, *p. 133*

Net ionic equation, *p. 150*

Neutralization reaction, *p. 141*

Oxidation, *p. 143*

Oxidation number, *p. 148*

Oxidation–reduction (redox) reaction, *p. 138*

Oxidizing agent, *p. 143*

Precipitate, *p. 138*

Product, *p. 133*

Reactant, *p. 133*

Reducing agent, *p. 143*

Reduction, *p. 143*

Salt, *p. 138*

Solubility, *p. 139*

Spectator ion, *p. 150*

UNDERSTANDING KEY CONCEPTS

5.20 Assume that the mixture of substances in drawing (a) undergoes a reaction. Which of the drawings (b)–(d) represents a product mixture consistent with the law of conservation of mass?

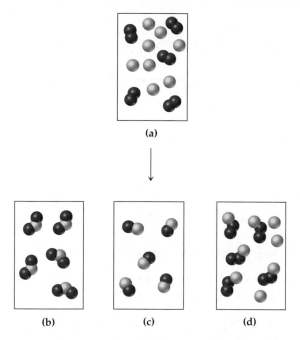

5.21 Reaction of A (green spheres) with B (blue spheres) is shown in the following diagram:

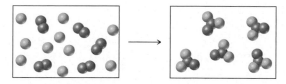

Which equation best describes the reaction?

(a) $A_2 + 2B \longrightarrow A_2B_2$

(b) $10A + 5B_2 \longrightarrow 5A_2B_2$

(c) $2A + B_2 \longrightarrow A_2B_2$

(d) $5A + 5B_2 \longrightarrow 5A_2B_2$

5.22 If blue spheres represent nitrogen atoms and red spheres represent oxygen atoms in the following diagrams, which box

represents reactants and which represents products for the reaction $2NO(g) + O_2(g) \longrightarrow 2NO_2(g)$?

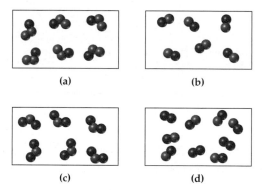

5.23 Assume that an aqueous solution of a cation (represented as red spheres in the diagram) is allowed to mix with a solution of an anion (represented as yellow spheres). Three possible outcomes are represented by boxes (1)–(3):

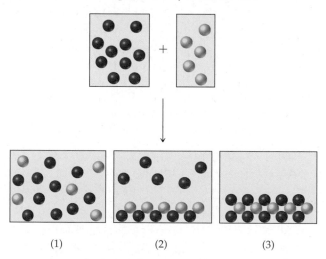

Which outcome corresponds to each of the following reactions?

(a) $2Na^+(aq) + CO_3^{2-}(aq) \longrightarrow$

(b) $Ba^{2+}(aq) + CrO_4^{2-}(aq) \longrightarrow$

(c) $2Ag^+(aq) + SO_3^{2-}(aq) \longrightarrow$

5.24 An aqueous solution of a cation (represented as blue spheres in the diagram) is allowed to mix with a solution of an anion (represented as green spheres) and the following result is obtained:

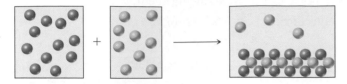

Which combinations of cation and anion, chosen from the following lists, are compatible with the observed results? Explain.

Cations: Na^+, Ca^{2+}, Ag^+, Ni^{2+}

Anions: Cl^-, CO_3^{2-}, CrO_4^{2-}, NO_3^-

5.25 A molecular view of two ionic solutions is presented right:

    (a) Which compound is most likely dissolved in beaker A: KBr, $CaCl_2$, PbI_2, Na_2SO_4?

    (b) Which compound is most likely dissolved in beaker B: Na_2CO_3, $BaSO_4$, $Cu(NO_3)_2$, $FeCl_3$?

    (c) Identify the precipitate and spectator ions for any reaction that will result when beakers A and B are mixed.

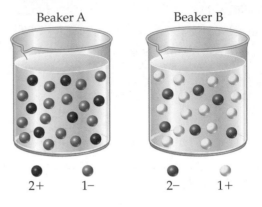

Beaker A   Beaker B

2+   1−   2−   1+

ADDITIONAL PROBLEMS

BALANCING CHEMICAL EQUATIONS

5.26 What is meant by the term "balanced equation"?

5.27 Why is it not possible to balance an equation by changing the subscript on a substance, say from H_2O to H_2O_2?

5.28 Write balanced equations for the following reactions:

    (a) Gaseous sulfur dioxide reacts with water to form aqueous sulfurous acid (H_2SO_3).

    (b) Liquid bromine reacts with solid potassium metal to form solid potassium bromide.

    (c) Gaseous propane (C_3H_8) burns in oxygen to form gaseous carbon dioxide and water vapor.

5.29 Balance the following equation for the synthesis of hydrazine, N_2H_4, a substance used as rocket fuel.

$$NH_3(g) + Cl_2(g) \longrightarrow N_2H_4(l) + NH_4Cl(s)$$

5.30 Which of the following equations are balanced? Balance those that need it.

    (a) $2\,C_2H_6(g) + 5\,O_2(g) \longrightarrow 2\,CO_2(g) + 6\,H_2O(l)$

    (b) $3\,Ca(OH)_2(aq) + 2\,H_3PO_4(aq) \longrightarrow$
$$Ca_3(PO_4)_2(aq) + 6\,H_2O(l)$$

    (c) $Mg(s) + O_2(g) \longrightarrow 2\,MgO(s)$

    (d) $K(s) + H_2O(l) \longrightarrow KOH(aq) + H_2(g)$

5.31 Which of the following equations are balanced? Balance those that need it.

    (a) $CaC_2 + 2\,H_2O \longrightarrow Ca(OH)_2 + C_2H_2$

    (b) $C_2H_8N_2 + 2\,N_2O_4 \longrightarrow 2\,N_2 + 2\,CO_2 + 4\,H_2O$

    (c) $3\,MgO + 2\,Fe \longrightarrow Fe_2O_3 + 3\,Mg$

    (d) $N_2O \longrightarrow N_2 + O_2$

5.32 Balance the following equations:

    (a) $Hg(NO_3)_2(aq) + LiI(aq) \longrightarrow$
$$LiNO_3(aq) + HgI_2(s)$$

    (b) $I_2(s) + Cl_2(g) \longrightarrow ICl_5(s)$

    (c) $Al(s) + O_2(g) \longrightarrow Al_2O_3(s)$

    (d) $CuSO_4(aq) + AgNO_3(aq) \longrightarrow$
$$Ag_2SO_4(s) + Cu(NO_3)_2(aq)$$

    (e) $Mn(NO_3)_3(aq) + Na_2S(aq) \longrightarrow$
$$Mn_2S_3(s) + NaNO_3(aq)$$

5.33 Balance the following equations:

    (a) $NO_2(g) + O_2(g) \longrightarrow N_2O_5(g)$

    (b) $P_4O_{10}(s) + H_2O(l) \longrightarrow H_3PO_4(aq)$

    (c) $B_2H_6(l) + O_2(g) \longrightarrow B_2O_3(s) + H_2O(l)$

    (d) $Cr_2O_3(s) + CCl_4(l) \longrightarrow CrCl_3(s) + COCl_2(aq)$

    (e) $Fe_3O_4(s) + O_2(g) \longrightarrow Fe_2O_3(s)$.

5.34 When organic compounds are burned, they react with oxygen to form CO_2 and H_2O. Write balanced equations for the combustion of the following:

    (a) C_4H_{10} (butane, used in lighters)

    (b) C_2H_6O (ethyl alcohol, used in gasohol and as race car fuel)

    (c) C_8H_{18} (octane, a component of gasoline)

5.35 When organic compounds are burned without enough oxygen, carbon monoxide is formed as a product instead of carbon dioxide. Write and balance the combustion reactions from Problem 5.34 using CO as a product instead of CO_2.

5.36 Hydrofluoric acid (HF) is used to etch glass (SiO_2). The products of the reaction are silicon tetrafluoride and water. Write the balanced chemical equation.

5.37 Write a balanced equation for the reaction of aqueous sodium carbonate (Na_2CO_3) with aqueous nitric acid (HNO_3) to yield CO_2, $NaNO_3$, and H_2O.

TYPES OF CHEMICAL REACTIONS

5.38 Identify each of the following reactions as a precipitation, neutralization, or redox reaction:

(a) $Mg(s) + 2\,HCl(aq) \longrightarrow MgCl_2(aq) + H_2(g)$

(b) $KOH(aq) + HNO_3(aq) \longrightarrow KNO_3(aq) + H_2O(l)$

(c) $Pb(NO_3)_2(aq) + 2\,HBr(aq) \longrightarrow$
$$PbBr_2(s) + 2\,HNO_3(aq)$$

(d) $Ca(OH)_2(aq) + 2\,HCl(aq) \longrightarrow$
$$2\,H_2O(l) + CaCl_2(aq)$$

5.39 Write balanced ionic equations and net ionic equations for the following reactions:

(a) Aqueous sulfuric acid is neutralized by aqueous potassium hydroxide.

(b) Aqueous magnesium hydroxide is neutralized by aqueous hydrochloric acid.

5.40 Write balanced ionic equations and net ionic equations for the following reactions:

(a) A precipitate of barium sulfate forms when aqueous solutions of barium nitrate and potassium sulfate are mixed.

(b) Zinc ion and hydrogen gas form when zinc metal reacts with aqueous sulfuric acid.

5.41 Identify each of the reactions in Problem 5.30 as a precipitation, neutralization, or redox reaction.

5.42 Identify each of the reactions in Problem 5.32 as a precipitation, neutralization, or redox reaction.

5.43 Which of the following substances are likely to be soluble in water?

(a) $ZnSO_4$ (b) $NiCO_3$

(c) $PbCl_2$ (d) $Ca_3(PO_4)_2$

5.44 Which of the following substances are likely to be soluble in water?

(a) Ag_2O (b) $Ba(NO_3)_2$

(c) $SnCO_3$ (d) Al_2S_3

5.45 Use the solubility guidelines in Section 5.4 to predict whether a precipitation reaction will occur when aqueous solutions of the following substances are mixed.

(a) $NaOH + HClO_4$

(b) $FeCl_2 + KOH$

(c) $(NH_4)_2SO_4 + NiCl_2$

5.46 Use the solubility guidelines in Section 5.4 to predict whether precipitation reactions will occur between the

listed pairs of reactants. Write balanced equations for those reactions that should occur.

(a) $NaBr$ and $Hg_2(NO_3)_2$

(b) $CuCl_2$ and K_2SO_4

(c) $LiNO_3$ and $Ca(CH_3CO_2)_2$

(d) $(NH_4)_2CO_3$ and $CaCl_2$

(e) KOH and $MnBr_2$

(f) Na_2S and $Al(NO_3)_3$

5.47 Write net ionic equations for the following reactions:

(a) $Mg(s) + CuCl_2(aq) \longrightarrow MgCl_2(aq) + Cu(s)$

(b) $2\,KCl(aq) + Pb(NO_3)_2(aq) \longrightarrow$
$$PbCl_2(s) + 2\,KNO_3(aq)$$

(c) $2\,Cr(NO_3)_3(aq) + 3\,Na_2S(aq) \longrightarrow$
$$Cr_2S_3(s) + 6\,NaNO_3(aq)$$

5.48 Write net ionic equations for the following reactions:

(a) $2\,AuCl_3(aq) + 3\,Sn(s) \longrightarrow 3\,SnCl_2(aq) + 2\,Au(s)$

(b) $2\,NaI(aq) + Br_2(l) \longrightarrow 2\,NaBr(aq) + I_2(s)$

(c) $2\,AgNO_3(aq) + Fe(s) \longrightarrow Fe(NO_3)_2(aq) + 2\,Ag(s)$

5.49 Complete the following precipitation reactions using balanced chemical equations:

(a) $FeSO_4(aq) + Sr(OH)_2(aq) \longrightarrow$

(b) $Na_2S(aq) + ZnSO_4(aq) \longrightarrow$

5.50 Write net ionic equations for each of the reactions in Problem 5.49.

REDOX REACTIONS AND OXIDATION NUMBERS

5.51 Where in the periodic table are the best reducing agents found? The best oxidizing agents?

5.52 Where in the periodic table are the most easily reduced elements found? The most easily oxidized?

5.53 In each of the following, tell whether the substance gains electrons or loses electrons in a redox reaction:

(a) An oxidizing agent

(b) A reducing agent

(c) A substance undergoing oxidation

(d) A substance undergoing reduction

5.54 For the following substances, tell whether the oxidation number increases or decreases in a redox reaction:

(a) An oxidizing agent

(b) A reducing agent

(c) A substance undergoing oxidation

(d) A substance undergoing reduction

5.55 Assign an oxidation number to each element in the following compounds or ions:

(a) N_2O_5 (b) SO_3^{2-}

(c) CH_2O (d) $HClO_3$

5.56 Assign an oxidation number to the metal in the following compounds:

(a) $CoCl_3$ (b) $FeSO_4$

(c) UO_3 (d) CuF_2

(e) TiO_2 (f) SnS

5.57 Which element is oxidized and which is reduced in the following reactions?

(a) $Si(s) + 2\,Cl_2(g) \longrightarrow SiCl_4(l)$

(b) $Cl_2(g) + 2\,NaBr(aq) \longrightarrow Br_2(aq) + 2\,NaCl(aq)$

(c) $SbCl_3(s) + Cl_2(g) \longrightarrow SbCl_5(s)$

5.58 Which element is oxidized and which is reduced in the following reactions?

(a) $2\,SO_2(g) + O_2(g) \longrightarrow 2\,SO_3(g)$

(b) $2\,Na(s) + Cl_2(g) \longrightarrow 2\,NaCl(s)$

(c) $CuCl_2(aq) + Zn(s) \longrightarrow ZnCl_2(aq) + Cu(s)$

(d) $2\,NaCl(aq) + F_2(g) \longrightarrow 2\,NaF(aq) + Cl_2(g)$

5.59 Balance each of the following redox reactions:

(a) $Al(s) + H_2SO_4(aq) \longrightarrow Al_2(SO_4)_3(aq) + H_2(g)$

(b) $Fe(s) + Cl_2(g) \longrightarrow FeCl_3(s)$

(c) $CO(g) + I_2O_5(s) \longrightarrow I_2(s) + CO_2(g)$

5.60 Balance each of the following redox reactions:

(a) $N_2O_4(l) + N_2H_4(l) \longrightarrow N_2(g) + H_2O(g)$

(b) $CaH_2(s) + H_2O(l) \longrightarrow Ca(OH)_2(aq) + H_2(g)$

(c) $Al(s) + H_2O(l) \longrightarrow Al(OH)_3(s) + H_2(g)$

5.61 Identify the oxidizing agent and the reducing agent in Problem 5.59.

5.62 Identify the oxidizing agent and the reducing agent in Problem 5.60.

CHEMISTRY IN ACTION

5.63 Sodium urate, the principal constituent of some kidney stones and the substance responsible for gout, has the formula $NaC_5H_3N_4O_3$. In aqueous solution, the solubility of sodium urate is only 0.067 g/L. How many grams of sodium urate could be dissolved in the blood before precipitation might occur? (The average adult has a blood capacity of about 5 L.) [*Gout and Kidney Stones, p. 140*]

5.64 Uric acid is formed in the body by the metabolism of purines. The reaction can be represented as $C_5H_4N_4$ (purine) $+ O_2 \rightarrow C_5H_4N_4O_3$ (uric acid).

(a) Balance the reaction.

(b) What type of reaction is this? [*Gout and Kidney Stones, p. 140*]

5.65 The rechargeable NiCd battery uses the following reaction:

$2\,NiO(OH) + Cd + 2\,H_2O \longrightarrow 2\,Ni(OH)_2 + Cd(OH)_2.$

Which reactant is being oxidized and which is being reduced in this reaction? [*Batteries, p. 147*]

5.66 Identify the oxidizing and reducing agents in a typical dry-cell battery. [*Batteries, p. 147*]

GENERAL QUESTIONS AND PROBLEMS

5.67 Balance the following equations.

(a) The thermite reaction, used in welding:
$Al(s) + Fe_2O_3(s) \longrightarrow Al_2O_3(l) + Fe(l)$

(b) The explosion of ammonium nitrate:
$NH_4NO_3(s) \longrightarrow N_2(g) + O_2(g) + H_2O(g)$

5.68 Lithium oxide is used aboard the space shuttle to remove water from the atmosphere according to the equation:

$$Li_2O(s) + H_2O(g) \longrightarrow LiOH(s)$$

(a) Balance the chemical equation.

(b) Is this a redox reaction? Why or why not?

5.69 Look at the solubility guidelines in Section 5.4 and predict whether a precipitate forms when $CuCl_2(aq)$ and $Na_2CO_3(aq)$ are mixed. If so, write both the balanced equation and the net ionic equation for the process.

5.70 Balance the following equations and classify each as a precipitation, neutralization, or redox reaction:

(a) $Al(OH)_3(aq) + HNO_3(aq) \longrightarrow$
$$Al(NO_3)_3(aq) + H_2O(l)$$

(b) $AgNO_3(aq) + FeCl_3(aq) \longrightarrow$
$$AgCl(s) + Fe(NO_3)_3(aq)$$

(c) $(NH_4)_2Cr_2O_7(s) \longrightarrow Cr_2O_3(s) + H_2O(g) + N_2(g)$

(d) $Mn_2(CO_3)_3(s) \longrightarrow Mn_2O_3(s) + CO_2(g)$

5.71 White phosphorus (P_4) is a highly reactive form of elemental phosphorus that reacts with oxygen to form a variety of molecular compounds, including diphosphorus pentoxide.

(a) Write the balanced chemical equation for this reaction.

(b) Calculate the oxidation number for P and O on both sides of the reaction, and identify the oxidizing and reducing agents.

5.72 The combustion of fossil fuels containing sulfur contributes to the phenomenon known as acid rain. The combustion process releases sulfur in the form of sulfur dioxide, which is converted to sulfuric acid in a process involving two reactions.

(a) In the first reaction, sulfur dioxide reacts with molecular oxygen to form sulfur trioxide. Write the balanced chemical equation for this reaction.

(b) In the second reaction, sulfur trioxide reacts with water in the atmosphere to form sulfuric acid. Write the balanced chemical equation for this reaction.

(c) Calculate the oxidation number for the S atom in each compound in these reactions.

5.73 The transition metals form compounds with oxygen in which the metals have different oxidation states. Calculate the oxidation number for the transition metal in the following sets of compounds:

(a) Mn in MnO_2, Mn_2O_3, and $KMnO_4$

(b) Cr in CrO_2, CrO_3, and Cr_2O_3.

5.74 In the Breathalyzer test, blood alcohol is determined by reaction of the alcohol with potassium dichromate:

$$16H^+(aq) + 2Cr_2O_7{}^{2-}(aq) + C_2H_5OH(aq) \longrightarrow$$
$$4Cr^{3+}(aq) + 2CO_2(g) + 11H_2O(l)$$

(a) Calculate the oxidation number of Cr in $Cr_2O_7{}^{2-}$.

(b) Calculate the oxidation number of C in C_2H_5OH and in CO_2.

(c) Identify the oxidizing agent and the reducing agent in this reaction.

5.75 Milk of magnesia is a suspension of magnesium hydroxide in water that is used to neutralize excess stomach acid. Write the balanced chemical equation for this neutralization reaction.

5.76 Iron in drinking water is removed by precipitation of the Fe^{3+} ion by reaction with NaOH to produce iron(III) hydroxide. Write the balanced chemical equation and the net ionic equation for this reaction.

5.77 Hard water contains magnesium and calcium ions (Mg^{2+}, Ca^{2+}), which can precipitate out in hot water pipes and water heaters as carbonates. Write the net ionic equation for this reaction.

5.78 Pepto-Bismol™, an antacid and antidiarrheal, contains bismuth subsalicylate, $C_7H_5BiO_4$. Some users of this product can experience a condition known as "black tongue," which is caused by the reaction of bismuth(III) ions with trace amounts of S^{2-} in saliva to form a black precipitate. Write the balanced net ionic equation for this precipitation reaction.

5.79 Iron is produced from iron ore by reaction with carbon monoxide:

$$Fe_2O_3(s) + CO(g) \longrightarrow Fe(s) + CO_2(g)$$

(a) Balance the chemical equation.

(b) Classify the reaction as a precipitation, neutralization, or redox reaction.

5.80 Balance the reaction for the synthesis of urea, commonly used as a fertilizer:

$$CO_2(g) + NH_3(g) \longrightarrow NH_2CONH_2(s) + H_2O(l)$$

5.81 Geologists identify carbonate minerals by reaction with acids. Dolomite, for example, contains magnesium carbonate, which reacts with hydrochloric acid by the following reaction:

$$MgCO_3(s) + HCl(aq) \longrightarrow MgCl_2(aq) + CO_2(g) + H_2O(l)$$

(a) Balance the reaction and write the net ionic equation.

(b) Classify the reaction as a precipitation, neutralization, or redox reaction.

5.82 Iodine, used as an antiseptic agent, can be prepared in the laboratory by the following reaction:

$$2NaI(s) + 2H_2SO_4(aq) + MnO_2(s) \longrightarrow$$
$$Na_2SO_4(aq) + MnSO_4(aq) + I_2(g) + 2H_2O(l)$$

(a) Determine the oxidation number for the Mn and I on both sides of the equation.

(b) Identify the oxidizing and reducing agents.

CHAPTER 6

Chemical Reactions: Mole and Mass Relationships

CONTENTS

◀ The amount of CO_2 and H_2O produced by the fuel combustion of airplanes and automobiles can be calculated using mole ratios and mole-to-mass conversions.

CHAPTER GOALS

1. **What is the mole, and why is it useful in chemistry?**
   THE GOAL: Be able to explain the meaning and uses of the mole and Avogadro's number.

2. **How are molar quantities and mass quantities related?**
   THE GOAL: Be able to convert between molar and mass quantities of an element or compound. (◀◀◀ A.)

3. **What are the limiting reagent, theoretical yield, and percent yield of a reaction?**
   THE GOAL: Be able to take the amount of product actually formed in a reaction, calculate the amount that could form theoretically, and express the results as a percent yield. (◀◀◀ A, B.)

When chefs prepare to cook a rice pudding, they don't count out individual grains of rice, or individual raisins, or individual sugar crystals. Rather, they measure out appropriate amounts of the necessary ingredients using more convenient units—such as cups, or tablespoons. When chemists prepare chemical reactions, they use the same approach. In this chapter we introduce the concept of the mole and how chemists use it when studying the quantitative relationships between reactants and products.

6.1 The Mole and Avogadro's Number

In the previous chapter, we learned how to use the balanced chemical equation to indicate what is happening at the molecular level during a reaction. Now, let us imagine a laboratory experiment: the reaction of ethylene (C_2H_4) with hydrogen chloride (HCl) to prepare ethyl chloride (C_2H_5Cl), a colorless, low-boiling liquid used by doctors and athletic trainers as a spray-on anesthetic. The reaction is represented as

$$C_2H_4(g) + HCl(g) \rightarrow C_2H_5Cl(g)$$

In this reaction, 1 molecule of ethylene reacts with 1 molecule of hydrogen chloride to produce 1 molecule of ethyl chloride.

How, though, can you be sure you have a 1 to 1 ratio of reactant molecules in your reaction flask? Since it is impossible to hand-count the number of molecules correctly, you must weigh them instead. (This is a common method for dealing with all kinds of small objects: Nails, nuts, and grains of rice are all weighed rather than counted.) But the weighing approach leads to another problem. How many molecules are there in 1 gram of ethylene, hydrogen chloride, or any other substance? The answer depends on the identity of the substance, because different molecules have different masses.

To determine how many molecules of a given substance are in a certain mass, it is helpful to define a quantity called *molecular weight*. Just as the *atomic weight* of an element is the average mass of the element's *atoms*, the **molecular weight (MW)** of a molecule is the average mass of a substance's *molecules*. Numerically, a substance's molecular weight (or **formula weight** for an ionic compound) is equal to the sum of the atomic weights for all the atoms in the molecule or formula unit.

For example, the molecular weight of ethylene (C_2H_4) is 28.0 amu, the molecular weight of HCl is 36.5 amu, and the molecular weight of ethyl chloride (C_2H_5Cl) is 64.5 amu. (The actual values are known more precisely but are rounded off here for convenience.)

For ethylene, C_2H_4:

$$\text{Atomic weight of 2 C} = 2 \times 12.0 \text{ amu} = 24.0 \text{ amu}$$

$$\underline{\text{Atomic weight of 4 H} = 4 \times 1.0 \text{ amu} = 4.0 \text{ amu}}$$

$$\text{MW of } C_2H_4 = 28.0 \text{ amu}$$

Molecular weight The sum of atomic weights of all atoms in a molecule.

◀◀◀ See Section 2.3 for discussion of atomic weight.

Formula weight The sum of atomic weights of all atoms in one formula unit of any compound, whether molecular or ionic.

▲ These samples of sulfur, copper, mercury, and helium each contain 1 mol. Do they all have the same mass?

For hydrogen chloride, **HCl:**

Atomic weight of H = 1.0 amu

Atomic weight of Cl = 35.5 amu

MW of HCl   = 36.5 amu

For ethyl chloride, C_2H_5Cl:

Atomic weight of 2 C = 2 × 12.0 amu = 24.0 amu

Atomic weight of 5 H = 5 × 1.0 amu = 5.0 amu

Atomic weight of Cl   = 35.5 amu

MW of C_2H_5Cl = 64.5 amu

How are molecular weights used? Since the mass ratio of 1 ethylene molecule to 1 HCl molecule is 28.0 to 36.5, the mass ratio of *any* given number of ethylene molecules to the same number of HCl molecules is also 28.0 to 36.5. In other words, a 28.0 to 36.5 *mass* ratio of ethylene and HCl always guarantees a 1 to 1 *number* ratio. *Samples of different substances always contain the same number of molecules or formula units whenever their mass ratio is the same as their molecular or formula weight ratio* (Figure 6.1).

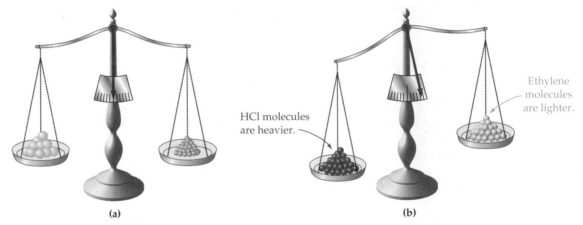

(a)   (b)

▲ **Figure 6.1**

(a) Because the yellow balls (left pan) are bigger than the green balls (right pan), you cannot get an equal number by taking equal weights. The same is true for atoms or molecules of different substances. (b) Equal numbers of ethylene and HCl molecules always have a mass ratio equal to the ratio of their molecular weights, 28.0 to 36.5.

A particularly convenient way to use this mass/number relationship for molecules is to measure amounts in grams that are numerically equal to molecular weights. If, for instance, you were to carry out your experiment with 28.0 g of ethylene and 36.5 g of HCl, you could be certain that you would have a 1 to 1 ratio of reactant molecules.

Mole The amount of a substance whose mass in grams is numerically equal to its molecular or formula weight.

Molar mass The mass in grams of 1 mole of a substance, numerically equal to molecular weight.

When referring to the vast numbers of molecules or formula units that take part in a visible chemical reaction, it is convenient to use a counting unit called a **mole**, abbreviated *mol*. One mole of any substance is the amount whose mass in grams—its **molar mass**—is numerically equal to its molecular or formula weight in amu. One mole of ethylene has a mass of 28.0 g, one mole of HCl has a mass of 36.5 g, and one mole of ethyl chloride has a mass of 64.5 g.

Just how many molecules are there in a mole? Think back to Chapter 2 where we learned to calculate the number of atoms in a sample of an element given its weight in grams, the atomic mass of the atom, and a gram/amu conversion factor. In Problem 2.2, you (hopefully!) found that a 1 gram sample of hydrogen (atomic mass 1 amu) and a 12 gram sample of carbon (atomic mass 12 amu) each contain 6.022×10^{23} atoms. One mole of any substance, therefore, contains 6.022×10^{23} formula units, a value called **Avogadro's number** (abbreviated N_A) after the Italian scientist who first recognized the importance of the mass/number relationship in molecules. Avogadro's number of formula units of any substance—that is, one mole—has a mass in grams numerically equal to the molecular weight of the substance.

Avogadro's number (N_A) The number of formula units in 1 mole of anything; 6.022×10^{23}.

$$1 \text{ mol HCl} = 6.022 \times 10^{23} \text{ HCl molecules} = 36.5 \text{ g HCl}$$

$$1 \text{ mol C}_2\text{H}_4 = 6.022 \times 10^{23} \text{ C}_2\text{H}_4 \text{ molecules} = 28.0 \text{ g C}_2\text{H}_4$$

$$1 \text{ mol C}_2\text{H}_5\text{Cl} = 6.022 \times 10^{23} \text{ C}_2\text{H}_5\text{Cl molecules} = 64.5 \text{ g C}_2\text{H}_5\text{Cl}$$

How big is Avogadro's number? Our minds cannot really conceive of the magnitude of a number like 6.022×10^{23}, but the following comparisons will give you a sense of the scale:

Amount of water in world's oceans (liters)   Age of earth in (seconds)

Population of earth

Avogadro's number: *602,200,000,000,000,000,000,000*

Distance from earth to sun (centimeters)   Average college tuition (U.S. dollars)

Worked Example 6.1 Molar Mass and Avogadro's Number: Number of Molecules

Pseudoephedrine hydrochloride ($C_{10}H_{16}ClNO$) is a nasal decongestant commonly found in cold medication. (a) What is the molar mass of pseudoephedrine hydrochloride? (b) How many molecules of pseudoephedrine hydrochloride are in a tablet that contains 30.0 mg of this decongestant?

ANALYSIS We are given a mass and need to convert to a number of molecules. This is most easily accomplished by using the molar mass of pseudoephedrine hydrochloride calculated in part (a) as the conversion factor from mass to moles and realizing that this mass (in grams) contains Avogadro's number of molecules (6.022×10^{23}).

BALLPARK ESTIMATE The formula for pseudoephedrine contains 10 carbon atoms (each one of atomic weight 12.0 amu), so the molecular weight is greater than 120 amu, probably near 200 amu. Thus, the molecular weight should be near 200 g/mol. The mass of 30 mg of pseudoepinephrine HCl is less than the mass of 1 mol of this compound by a factor of roughly 10^4 (0.03 g versus 200 g), which means that the number of molecules should also be smaller by a factor of 10^4 (on the order of 10^{19} in the tablet versus 10^{23} in 1 mol).

SOLUTION

(a) The molecular weight of pseudoephedrine is found by summing the atomic weights of all atoms in the molecule:

Atomic Weight of 10 atoms of C:	10×12.011 amu	=	120.11 amu
16 atoms of H:	16×1.00794 amu	=	16.127 amu
1 atom of Cl:	1×35.4527 amu	=	35.4527 amu
1 atom of N:	1×14.0067 amu	=	14.0067 amu
1 atom of O:	1×15.9994 amu	=	15.9994 amu

MW of $C_{10}H_{16}ClNO$ = 201.6958 amu $\longrightarrow$ 201.70 g/mol

Remember that atomic mass in amu converts directly to molar mass in g/mol. Also, following the rules for significant figures from Sections 1.9 and 1.11, our final answer is rounded to the second decimal place.

(b) Since this problem involves unit conversions, we can use the step-wise solution introduced in Chapter 1.

STEP 1: Identify known information. We are given the mass of pseudoephedrine hydrochloride (in mg).

30.0 mg pseudoephedrine hydrochloride

STEP 2: Identify answer and units. We are looking for the number of molecules of pseudoephedrine hydrochloride in a 30 mg tablet.

?? = molecules

STEP 3: Identify conversion factors. Since the molecular weight of pseudoephedrine hydrochloride is 201.70 amu, 201.70 g contains 6.022×10^{23} molecules. We can use this ratio as a conversion factor to convert from mass to molecules. We will also need to convert 30 mg to g.

$$\frac{6.022 \times 10^{23} \text{ molecules}}{201.70 \text{ g}}$$

$$\frac{.001 \text{ g}}{1 \text{ mg}}$$

STEP 4: **Solve.** Set up an equation so that unwanted units cancel.	$(30.0 \text{ mg pseudoephedrine hydrochloride}) \times \left(\dfrac{.001 \text{ g}}{1 \text{ mg}}\right) \times \left(\dfrac{6.022 \times 10^{23} \text{ molecules}}{201.70 \text{ g}}\right)$
	$= 8.96 \times 10^{19}$ molecules of pseudoephedrine hydrochloride
	BALLPARK CHECK Our estimate for the number of molecules was on the order of 10^{19}, which is consistent with the calculated answer.

Worked Example 6.2 Avogadro's Number: Atom to Mass Conversions

A tiny pencil mark just visible to the naked eye contains about 3×10^{17} atoms of carbon. What is the mass of this pencil mark in grams?

ANALYSIS We are given a number of atoms and need to convert to mass. The conversion factor can be obtained by realizing that the atomic weight of carbon in grams contains Avogadro's number of atoms (6.022×10^{23}).

BALLPARK ESTIMATE Since we are given a number of atoms that is six orders of magnitude less than Avogadro's number, we should get a corresponding mass that is six orders of magnitude less than the molar mass of carbon, which means a mass for the pencil mark of about 10^{-6} g.

SOLUTION

STEP 1: **Identify known information.** We know the number of carbon atoms in the pencil mark.	3×10^{17} atoms of carbon
STEP 2: **Identify answer and units.**	Mass of carbon $= $?? g
STEP 3: **Identify conversion factors.** The atomic weight of carbon is 12.01 amu, so 12.01 g of carbon contains 6.022×10^{23} atoms.	$\dfrac{12.01 \text{ g carbon}}{6.022 \times 10^{23} \text{ atoms}}$
STEP 4: **Solve.** Set up an equation using the conversion factors so that unwanted units cancel.	$(3 \times 10^{17} \text{ atoms})\left(\dfrac{12.01 \text{ g carbon}}{6.022 \times 10^{23} \text{ atoms}}\right) = 6 \times 10^{-6} \text{ g carbon}$
	BALLPARK CHECK The answer is of the same magnitude as our estimate and makes physical sense.

PROBLEM 6.1

Calculate the molecular weight of the following substances:

(a) Ibuprofen, $C_{13}H_{18}O_2$ (b) Phenobarbital, $C_{12}H_{12}N_2O_3$

PROBLEM 6.2

How many molecules of ascorbic acid (vitamin C, $C_6H_8O_6$) are in a 500 mg tablet?

PROBLEM 6.3

What is the mass in grams of 5.0×10^{20} molecules of aspirin $(C_9H_8O_4)$?

🔑 **KEY CONCEPT PROBLEM 6.4**

What is the molecular weight of cytosine, a component of DNA (deoxyribonucleic acid)? (black = C, blue = N, red = O, white = H.)

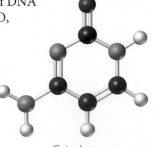

Cytosine

6.2 Gram–Mole Conversions

To ensure that we have the correct molecule to molecule (or mole to mole) relationship between reactants as specified by the balanced chemical equation, we can take advantage of the constant mass ratio between reactants. The mass in grams of 1 mol of any substance (that is, Avogadro's number of molecules or formula units) is called the **molar mass** of the substance.

Molar mass = Mass of 1 mol of substance

= Mass of 6.022×10^{23} molecules (formula units) of substance

= Molecular (formula) weight of substance in grams

In effect, molar mass serves as a conversion factor between numbers of moles and mass. If you know how many moles you have, you can calculate their mass; if you know the mass of a sample, you can calculate the number of moles. Suppose, for example, we need to know how much 0.25 mol of water weighs. The molecular weight of H_2O is $(2 \times 1.0 \text{ amu}) + 16.0 \text{ amu} = 18.0 \text{ amu}$, so the molar mass of water is 18.0 g/mol. Thus, the conversion factor between moles of water and mass of water is 18.0 g/mol:

$$0.25 \text{ mol } H_2O \times \frac{18.0 \text{ g } H_2O}{1 \text{ mol } H_2O} = 4.5 \text{ g } H_2O$$

Molar mass used as conversion factor

Alternatively, suppose we need to know how many moles of water are in 27 g of water. The conversion factor is 1 mol/18.0 g:

$$27 \text{ g } H_2O \times \frac{1 \text{ mol } H_2O}{18.0 \text{ g } H_2O} = 1.5 \text{ mol } H_2O$$

Molar mass used as conversion factor

Note that the 1 mol in the numerator is an exact number, so the number of significant figures in the final answer is based on the 27 g H_2O (2 sig figs.). Worked Examples 6.3 and 6.4 give more practice in gram–mole conversions.

Worked Example 6.3 Molar Mass: Mole to Gram Conversion

The nonprescription pain relievers Advil and Nuprin contain ibuprofen $(C_{13}H_{18}O_2)$, whose molecular weight is 206.3 amu (Problem 6.1a). If all the tablets in a bottle of pain reliever together contain 0.082 mol of ibuprofen, what is the number of grams of ibuprofen in the bottle?

ANALYSIS We are given a number of moles and asked to find the mass. Molar mass is the conversion factor between the two.

BALLPARK ESTIMATE Since 1 mol of ibuprofen has a mass of about 200 g, 0.08 mol has a mass of about $0.08 \times 200 \text{ g} = 16 \text{ g}$.

SOLUTION

STEP 1: Identify known information.   0.082 mol ibuprofen in bottle

STEP 2: Identify answer and units.   mass ibuprofen in bottle = ?? g

STEP 3: Identify conversion factor. We use the molecular weight of ibuprofen to convert from moles to grams.

1 mol ibuprofen = 206.3 g

$$\frac{206.3 \text{ g ibuprofen}}{1 \text{ mol ibuprofen}}$$

STEP 4: Solve. Set up an equation using the known information and conversion factor so that unwanted units cancel.

$$0.082 \text{ mol } C_{13}H_{18}O_2 \times \frac{206.3 \text{ g ibuprofen}}{1 \text{ mol ibuprofen}} = 17 \text{ g } C_{13}H_{18}O_2$$

BALLPARK CHECK The calculated answer is consistent with our estimate of 16 g.

CHEMISTRY IN ACTION

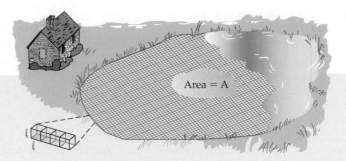

Area = A

Did Ben Franklin Have Avogadro's Number? A Ballpark Calculation

"At" length being at Clapham, where there is on the common a large pond . . . I fetched out a cruet of oil and dropped a little of it on the water. I saw it spread itself with surprising swiftness upon the surface. The oil, though not more than a teaspoonful, produced an instant calm over a space several yards square which spread amazingly and extended itself gradually . . . making all that quarter of the pond, perhaps half an acre, as smooth as a looking glass. *Excerpt from a letter of Benjamin Franklin to William Brownrigg, 1773.*

▲ **What did these two have in common? [Benjamin Franklin (left), Amedeo Avogadro (right)]**

Benjamin Franklin, author and renowned statesman, was also an inventor and a scientist. Every school-child knows of Franklin's experiment with a kite and a key, demonstrating that lightning is electricity. Less well known is that his measurement of the extent to which oil spreads on water makes possible a simple estimate of molecular size and Avogadro's number.

The calculation goes like this: Avogadro's number is the number of molecules in 1 mole of any substance. So, if we can estimate both the number of molecules and the number of moles in Franklin's teaspoon of oil, we can calculate Avogadro's number. Let us start by calculating the number of molecules in the oil.

1. The volume (V) of oil Franklin used was 1 tsp = 4.9 cm^3, and the area (A) covered by the oil was 1/2 acre = 2.0×10^7 cm^2. We will assume that the oil molecules are tiny cubes that pack closely together and form a layer only one molecule thick. As shown in the accompanying figure, the volume of the oil is equal to the surface area of the layer times the

length (l) of the side of one molecule: $V = A \times l$. Rearranging this equation to find the length then gives us an estimate of molecular size:

$$l = \frac{V}{A} = \frac{4.9 \text{ cm}^3}{2.0 \times 10^7 \text{ cm}^2} = 2.5 \times 10^{-7} \text{ cm}$$

2. The area of the oil layer is the area of the side of one molecule (l^2) times the number of molecules (N) of oil: $A = l^2 \times N$. Rearranging this equation gives us the number of molecules:

$$N = \frac{A}{l^2} = \frac{2 \times 10^7 \text{ cm}^2}{(2.5 \times 10^{-7} \text{ cm})^2} = 3.2 \times 10^{20} \text{ molecules}$$

3. To calculate the number of moles, we first need to know the mass (M) of the oil. This could have been determined by weighing the oil, but Franklin neglected to do so. Let us therefore estimate the mass by multiplying the volume (V) of the oil by the density (D) of a typical oil, 0.95 g/cm^3. (Since oil floats on water, it is not surprising that the density of oil is a bit less than the density of water, which is 1.00 g/cm^3.)

$$M = V \times D = 4.9 \text{ cm}^3 \times 0.95 \frac{\text{g}}{\text{cm}^3} = 4.7 \text{ g}$$

4. We now have to make one final assumption about the molecular weight of the oil before we complete the calculation. Assuming that a typical oil has MW = 200 amu, then the mass of 1 mol of oil is 200 g. Dividing the mass of the oil (M) by the mass of 1 mol gives the number of moles of oil:

$$\text{Moles of oil} = \frac{4.7 \text{ g}}{200 \text{ g/mol}} = 0.024 \text{ mol}$$

5. Finally, the number of molecules per mole—Avogadro's number—can be obtained by dividing the estimated number of molecules (step 2) by the estimated moles (step 4):

$$\text{Avogadro's number} = \frac{3.2 \times 10^{20} \text{ molecules}}{0.024 \text{ mol}} = 1.3 \times 10^{22}$$

The calculation is not very accurate, of course, but Ben was not really intending for us to calculate Avogadro's number when he made a rough estimate of how much his oil spread out. Nevertheless, the result is not too bad for such a simple experiment.

See Chemistry in Action Problem 6.58 at the end of the chapter.

Worked Example 6.4 Molar Mass: Gram to Mole Conversion

The maximum dose of sodium hydrogen phosphate $(Na_2HPO_4$, MW $= 142.0$ molar mass) that should be taken in one day for use as a laxative is 3.8 g. How many moles of sodium hydrogen phosphate, how many moles of Na^+ ions, and how many total moles of ions are in this dose?

ANALYSIS Molar mass is the conversion factor between mass and number of moles. The chemical formula Na_2HPO_4 shows that each formula unit contains 2 Na^+ ions and 1 HPO_4^{2-} ion.

BALLPARK ESTIMATE The maximum dose is about two orders of magnitude smaller than the molecular weight (approximately 4 g compared to 142 g). Thus, the number of moles of sodium hydrogen phosphate in 3.8 g should be about two orders of magnitude less than one mole. The number of moles of Na_2HPO_4 and total moles of ions, then, should be on the order of 10^{-2}.

SOLUTION

STEP 1: Identify known information. We are given the mass and molecular weight of Na_2HPO_4.

3.8 g Na_2HPO_4; MW $= 142.0$ amu

STEP 2: Identify answer and units. We need to find the number of moles of Na_2HPO_4, and the total number of moles of ions.

Moles of $Na_2HPO_4 = $?? mol
Moles of Na^+ ions $= $?? mol
Total moles of ions $= $?? mol

STEP 3: Identify conversion factor. We can use the molecular weight of Na_2HPO_4 to convert from grams to moles.

$$\frac{1 \text{ mol } Na_2HPO_4}{142.0 \text{ g } Na_2HPO_4}$$

STEP 4: Solve. We use the known information and conversion factor to obtain moles of Na_2HPO_4; since 1 mol of Na_2HPO_4 contains 2 mol of Na^+ ions and 1 mol of HPO_4^{2-} ions, we multiply these values by the number of moles in the sample.

$$3.8 \text{ g } Na_2HPO_4 \times \frac{1 \text{ mol } Na_2HPO_4}{142.0 \text{ g } Na_2HPO_4} = 0.027 \text{ mol } Na_2HPO_4$$

$$\frac{2 \text{ mol } Na^+}{1 \text{ mol } Na_2HPO_4} \times 0.027 \text{ mol } Na_2HPO_4 = 0.054 \text{ mol } Na^+$$

$$\frac{3 \text{ mol ions}}{1 \text{ mol } Na_2HPO_4} \times 0.027 \text{ mol } Na_2HPO_4 = 0.081 \text{ mol ions}$$

BALLPARK CHECK: The calculated answers (0.027 mol Na_2HPO_4, 0.081 mol ions) are on the order of 10^{-2}, consistent with our estimate.

PROBLEM 6.5
How many moles of ethyl alcohol, C_2H_6O, are in a 10.0 g sample? How many grams are in a 0.10 mol sample of ethyl alcohol?

PROBLEM 6.6
Which weighs more, 5.00 g or 0.0225 mol of acetaminophen $(C_8H_9NO_2)$?

PROBLEM 6.7
How would our estimate of Avogadro's number be affected if we were to assume that Benjamin Franklin's oil molecules were spherical rather than cubes (see Chemistry in Action on p. 164)? If the density of the oil was 0.90 g/mL? If the molar mass was 150 g/mol rather than 200 g/mol?

6.3 Mole Relationships and Chemical Equations

In a typical recipe, the amounts of ingredients needed are specified using a variety of units: the amount of flour, for example, is usually specified in cups, whereas the amount of salt or vanilla flavoring might be indicated in teaspoons. In chemical reactions, the appropriate unit to specify the relationship between reactants and products is the mole.

The coefficients in a balanced chemical equation tell how many *molecules*, and thus, how many *moles*, of each reactant are needed and how many molecules, and thus, moles, of each product are formed. You can then use molar mass to calculate reactant and product masses. If, for example, you saw the following balanced equation for the industrial synthesis of ammonia, you would know that 3 mol of H_2 (3 mol × 2.0 g/mol = 6.0 g) are required for reaction with 1 mol of N_2 (28.0 g) to yield 2 mol of NH_3 (2 mol × 17.0 g/mol = 34.0 g).

This number of moles   . . . reacts with this number   to yield this number of
of hydrogen . . .   of moles of nitrogen . . .   moles of ammonia.

$$3 H_2 \ + \ 1 N_2 \ \longrightarrow \ 2 NH_3$$

The coefficients can be put in the form of *mole ratios*, which act as conversion factors when setting up factor-label calculations. In the ammonia synthesis, for example, the mole ratio of H_2 to N_2 is 3:1, the mole ratio of H_2 to NH_3 is 3:2, and the mole ratio of N_2 to NH_3 is 1:2:

$$\frac{3 \text{ mol } H_2}{1 \text{ mol } N_2} \qquad \frac{3 \text{ mol } H_2}{2 \text{ mol } NH_3} \qquad \frac{1 \text{ mol } N_2}{2 \text{ mol } NH_3}$$

Worked Example 6.5 shows how to set up and use mole ratios.

Worked Example 6.5 Balanced Chemical Equations: Mole Ratios

Rusting involves the reaction of iron with oxygen to form iron(III) oxide, Fe_2O_3:

$$4 Fe(s) + 3 O_2(g) \longrightarrow 2 Fe_2O_3(s)$$

(a) What are the mole ratios of the product to each reactant and of the reactants to each other?

(b) How many moles of iron(III) oxide are formed by the complete oxidation of 6.2 mol of iron?

ANALYSIS AND SOLUTION

(a) The coefficients of a balanced equation represent the mole ratios:

$$\frac{2 \text{ mol } Fe_2O_3}{4 \text{ mol } Fe} \qquad \frac{2 \text{ mol } Fe_2O_3}{3 \text{ mol } O_2} \qquad \frac{4 \text{ mol } Fe}{3 \text{ mol } O_2}$$

(b) To find how many moles of Fe_2O_3 are formed, write down the known information—6.2 mol of iron—and select the mole ratio that allows the quantities to cancel, leaving the desired quantity:

$$6.2 \text{ mol Fe} \times \frac{2 \text{ mol } Fe_2O_3}{4 \text{ mol Fe}} = 3.1 \text{ mol } Fe_2O_3$$

Note that mole ratios are exact numbers and therefore do not limit the number of significant figures in the result of a calculation.

PROBLEM 6.8

(a) Balance the following equation, and tell how many moles of nickel will react with 9.81 mol of hydrochloric acid.

$$Ni(s) + HCl(aq) \longrightarrow NiCl_2(aq) + H_2(g)$$

(b) How many moles of $NiCl_2$ can be formed in the reaction of 6.00 mol of Ni and 12.0 mol of HCl?

PROBLEM 6.9

Plants convert carbon dioxide and water to glucose $(C_6H_{12}O_6)$ and oxygen in the process of photosynthesis. Write a balanced equation for this reaction, and determine how many moles of CO_2 are required to produce 15.0 mol of glucose.

6.4 Mass Relationships and Chemical Equations

It is important to remember that the coefficients in a balanced chemical equation represent molecule to molecule (or mole to mole) relationships between reactants and products. Mole ratios make it possible to calculate the molar amounts of reactants and products, but actual amounts of substances used in the laboratory are weighed out in grams. Regardless of what units we use to specify the amount of reactants and/or products (mass, volume, number of molecules, and so on), the reaction always takes place on a mole to mole basis. Thus, we need to be able to carry out three kinds of conversions when doing chemical arithmetic:

- **Mole to mole conversions** are carried out using *mole ratios* as conversion factors. Worked Example 6.5 at the end of the preceding section is an example of this kind of calculation.

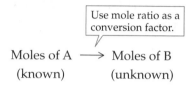

- **Mole to mass and mass to mole conversions** are carried out using *molar mass* as a conversion factor. Worked Examples 6.3 and 6.4 at the end of Section 6.2 are examples of this kind of calculation.

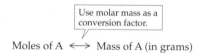

- **Mass to mass conversions** are frequently needed but cannot be carried out directly. If you know the mass of substance A and need to find the mass of substance B, you must first convert the mass of A into moles of A, then carry out a mole to mole conversion to find moles of B, and then convert moles of B into the mass of B (Figure 6.2).

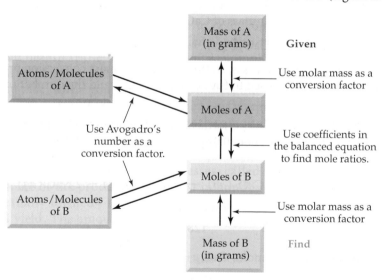

◄ **Figure 6.2**

A summary of conversions between moles, grams, and number of atoms or molecules for substances in a chemical reaction.
The numbers of moles tell how many molecules of each substance are needed, as given by the coefficients in the balanced equation; the numbers of grams tell what mass of each substance is needed.

Overall, there are four steps for determining mass relationships among reactants and products:

STEP 1: Write the balanced chemical equation.

STEP 2: Choose molar masses and mole ratios to convert the known information into the needed information.

STEP 3: Set up the factor-label expressions.

STEP 4: Calculate the answer and check the answer against the ballpark estimate you made before you began your calculations.

(c) How many grams of Mg are needed to react with 25.0 g of O_2? How many grams of MgO will result?

6.46 Titanium metal is obtained from the mineral rutile, TiO_2. How many kilograms of rutile are needed to produce 95 kg of Ti?

6.47 In the preparation of iron from hematite (Problem 6.44), how many moles of carbon monoxide are needed to react completely with 105 kg of Fe_2O_3?

6.48 The eruption of Mount St. Helens volcano in 1980 injected 4×10^8 kg of SO_2 into the atmosphere. If all this SO_2 was converted to sulfuric acid, how many moles of H_2SO_4 would be produced? How many kg?

6.49 The thermite reaction was used to produce molten iron for welding applications before arc welding was available. The thermite reaction is:

$$Fe_2O_3(s) + 2\,Al(s) \longrightarrow Al_2O_3(s) + 2\,Fe(l)$$

How many moles of molten iron can be produced from 1.5 kg of iron(III) oxide?

6.50 Pyrite, also known as fool's gold, is composed of iron disulfide, FeS_2. It is used commercially to produce SO_2 used in the production of paper products. How many moles of SO_2 can be produced from 1.0 kg of pyrite?

6.51 Diborane (B_2H_6) is a gas at room temperature that forms explosive mixtures with air. It reacts with oxygen according to the following equation:

$$B_2H_6(g) + 3\,O_2(g) \longrightarrow B_2O_3(s) + 3\,H_2O(l)$$

How many grams of diborane will react with 7.5 mol of O_2?

LIMITING REAGENT AND PERCENT YIELD

6.52 Once made by heating wood in the absence of air, methanol (CH_3OH) is now made by reacting carbon monoxide and hydrogen at high pressure:

$$CO(g) + 2\,H_2(g) \longrightarrow CH_3OH(l)$$

(a) If 25.0 g of CO is reacted with 6.00 g of H_2, which is the limiting reagent?

(b) How many grams of CH_3OH can be made from 10.0 g of CO if it all reacts?

(c) If 9.55 g of CH_3OH is recovered when the amounts in part (b) are used, what is the percent yield?

6.53 In Problem 6.43, hydrazine reacted with oxygen according to the (unbalanced) equation:

$$N_2H_4(l) + O_2(g) \longrightarrow NO_2(g) + H_2O(g)$$

(a) If 75.0 kg of hydrazine are reacted with 75.0 kg of oxygen, which is the limiting reagent?

(b) How many kilograms of NO_2 are produced from the reaction of 75.0 kg of the limiting reagent?

(c) If 59.3 kg of NO_2 are obtained from the reaction in part (a), what is the percent yield?

6.54 Dichloromethane, CH_2Cl_2, the solvent used to decaffeinate coffee beans, is prepared by reaction of CH_4 with Cl_2.

(a) Write the balanced equation. (HCl is also formed.)

(b) How many grams of Cl_2 are needed to react with 50.0 g of CH_4?

(c) How many grams of dichloromethane are formed from 50.0 g of CH_4 if the percent yield for the reaction is 76%?

6.55 Cisplatin $[Pt(NH_3)_2Cl_2]$, a compound used in cancer treatment, is prepared by reaction of ammonia with potassium tetrachloroplatinate:

$$K_2PtCl_4 + 2\,NH_3 \longrightarrow 2\,KCl + Pt(NH_3)_2Cl_2$$

(a) How many grams of NH_3 are needed to react with 55.8 g of K_2PtCl_4?

(b) How many grams of cisplatin are formed from 55.8 g of K_2PtCl_4 if the percent yield for the reaction is 95%?

6.56 Nitrobenzene $(C_6H_5NO_2)$ is used in small quantities as a flavoring agent or in perfumes, but can be toxic in large amounts. It is produced by reaction of benzene (C_6H_6) with nitric acid:

$$C_6H_6(l) + HNO_3(aq) \longrightarrow C_6H_5NO_2(l) + H_2O(l).$$

(a) Identify the limiting reagent in the reaction of 27.5 g of nitric acid with 75 g of benzene.

(b) Calculate the theoretical yield for this reaction.

6.57 Calculate the percent yield if 48.2 g of nitrobenzene is obtained from the reaction described in Problem 6.56.

CHEMISTRY IN ACTION

6.58 What do you think might be some of the errors involved in calculating Avogadro's number by spreading oil on a pond? [*Did Ben Franklin Have Avogadro's Number? p. 164*]

6.59 Dietary iron forms a 1:1 complex with hemoglobin (Hb), which is responsible for O_2 transport in the body based on the following equation:

$$Hb + 4\,O_2 \longrightarrow Hb(O_2)_4$$

How many moles of oxygen could be transported by the hemoglobin complex formed from 8 mg of dietary iron? [*Anemia—A Limiting Reagent Problem? p. 172*]

6.60 Ferrous sulfate is one dietary supplement used to treat iron-deficiency anemia. What are the molecular formula and molecular weight of this compound? How many milligrams of iron are in 250 mg of ferrous sulfate?

GENERAL QUESTIONS AND PROBLEMS

6.61 Zinc metal reacts with hydrochloric acid (HCl) according to the equation:

$$Zn(s) + 2\,HCl(aq) \longrightarrow ZnCl_2(aq) + H_2(g)$$

(a) How many grams of hydrogen are produced if 15.0 g of zinc reacts?

(b) Is this a redox reaction? If so, tell what is reduced, what is oxidized, and identify the reducing and oxidizing agents.

6.62 Batrachotoxin, $C_{31}H_{42}N_2O_6$, an active component of South American arrow poison, is so toxic that 0.05 μg can kill a person. How many molecules is this?

6.63 Lovastatin, a drug used to lower serum cholesterol, has the molecular formula of $C_{24}H_{36}O_5$.

   (a) Calculate the molar mass of lovastatin.

   (b) How many moles of lovastatin are present in a typical dose of one 10 mg tablet?

6.64 When table sugar (sucrose, $C_{12}H_{22}O_{11}$) is heated, it decomposes to form C and H_2O.

   (a) Write a balanced equation for the process.

   (b) How many grams of carbon are formed by the breakdown of 60.0 g of sucrose?

   (c) How many grams of water are formed when 6.50 g of carbon are formed?

6.65 Although Cu is not sufficiently active to react with acids, it can be dissolved by concentrated nitric acid, which functions as an oxidizing agent according to the following equation:

$$Cu(s) + 4\,HNO_3(aq) \longrightarrow$$
$$Cu(NO_3)_2(aq) + 2\,NO_2(g) + 2\,H_2O(l)$$

   (a) Write the net ionic equation for this process.

   (b) Is 35.0 g of HNO_3 sufficient to dissolve 5.00 g of copper?

6.66 The net ionic equation for the Breathalyzer test used to indicate alcohol concentration in the body is

$$16\,H^+(aq) + 2\,Cr_2O_7^{2-}(aq) + 3\,C_2H_6O(aq) \longrightarrow$$
$$3\,C_2H_4O_2(aq) + 4\,Cr^{3+}(aq) + 11\,H_2O(l)$$

   (a) How many grams of $K_2Cr_2O_7$ must be used to consume 1.50 g of C_2H_6O?

   (b) How many grams of $C_2H_4O_2$ can be produced from 80.0 g of C_2H_6O?

6.67 Ethyl alcohol is formed by enzyme action on sugars and starches during fermentation:

$$C_6H_{12}O_6 \longrightarrow 2\,CO_2 + 2\,C_2H_6O$$

If the density of ethyl alcohol is 0.789 g/mL, how many quarts can be produced by the fermentation of 100.0 lb of sugar?

6.68 Gaseous ammonia reacts with oxygen in the presence of a platinum catalyst to produce nitrogen monoxide and water vapor.

   (a) Write a balanced chemical equation for this reaction.

   (b) What mass of nitrogen monoxide would be produced by complete reaction of 17.0 g of ammonia?

6.69 Sodium hypochlorite, the primary component in commercial bleach, is prepared by bubbling chlorine gas through solutions of sodium hydroxide:

$$NaOH(aq) + Cl_2(g) \longrightarrow NaOCl(aq) + H_2O(l)$$

How many moles of sodium hypochlorite can be prepared from 32.5 g of NaOH?

6.70 Barium sulfate is an insoluble ionic compound swallowed by patients before having an X-ray of their gastrointestinal tract.

   (a) Write the balanced chemical equation for the precipitation reaction between barium chloride and sodium sulfate.

   (b) What mass of barium sulfate can be produced by complete reaction of 27.4 g of Na_2SO_4?

6.71 The last step in the production of nitric acid is the reaction of nitrogen dioxide with water:

$$NO_2(g) + H_2O(l) \longrightarrow HNO_3(aq) + NO(g)$$

   (a) Balance the chemical equation.

   (b) If 65.0 g of nitrogen dioxide is reacted with excess water, calculate the theoretical yield.

   (c) If only 43.8 g of nitric acid is obtained, calculate the percent yield.

6.72 Acetylsalicylic acid, the active ingredient in aspirin, is prepared from salicylic acid by reaction with acetic anhydride:

$$C_7H_6O_3 \quad + \quad C_4H_6O_3 \longrightarrow C_9H_8O_4 + C_2H_4O_2$$
(salicylic acid) (acetic anhydride) (acetylsalicylic acid) (acetic acid)

   (a) Calculate the theoretical yield if 47 g of salicylic acid is reacted with 25 g of acetic anhydride.

   (b) What is the percent yield if only 35 g is obtained?

6.73 Jewelry and tableware can be silver-plated by reduction of silver ions from a solution of silver nitrate. The net ionic equation is $Ag^+(aq) + e^- \longrightarrow Ag(s)$. How many grams of silver nitrate would be needed to plate 15.2 g of silver on a piece of jewelry?

6.74 Elemental phosphorus exists as molecules of P_4. It reacts with $Cl_2(g)$ to produce phosphorus pentachloride.

   (a) Write the balanced chemical equation for this reaction.

   (b) What mass of phosphorus pentachloride would be produced by the complete reaction of 15.2 g of P_4?

6.75 Lithium oxide is used aboard the space shuttle to remove water from the atmosphere according to the equation

$$Li_2O(s) + H_2O(g) \longrightarrow 2\,LiOH(s)$$

How many grams of Li_2O must be carried on board to remove 80.0 kg of water?

6.76 One of the reactions used to provide thrust for space shuttle launch involves the reaction of ammonium perchlorate with aluminum to produce $AlCl_3(s)$, $H_2O(g)$, and $NO(g)$.

   (a) Write the balanced chemical equation for this reaction.

   (b) How many moles of gas are produced by the reaction of 14.5 kg of ammonium perchlorate?

CHAPTER 7

Chemical Reactions: Energy, Rates, and Equilibrium

▲ Many spontaneous chemical reactions are accompanied by the release of energy, in some cases explosively.

CONTENTS

1. **What energy changes take place during reactions?**
   THE GOAL: Be able to explain the factors that influence energy changes in chemical reactions. (◀◀ A, B, and C)

2. **What is "free energy," and what is the criterion for spontaneity in chemistry?**
   THE GOAL: Be able to define enthalpy, entropy, and free-energy changes, and explain how the values of these quantities affect chemical reactions.

3. **What determines the rate of a chemical reaction?**
   THE GOAL: Be able to explain activation energy and other factors that determine reaction rate. (◀◀ D)

4. **What is chemical equilibrium?**
   THE GOAL: Be able to describe what occurs in a reaction at equilibrium, and write the equilibrium equation for a given reaction. (◀◀ D)

5. **What is Le Châtelier's principle?**
   THE GOAL: Be able to state Le Châtelier's principle, and use it to predict the effect of changes in temperature, pressure, and concentration on reactions.

CONCEPTS TO REVIEW

A. Energy and Heat
(Section 1.13)

B. Ionic Bonds
(Section 3.3)

C. Covalent Bonds
(Section 4.1)

D. Chemical Equations
(Section 5.1)

We have yet to answer many questions about reactions. Why, for instance, do reactions occur? Just because a balanced equation can be written it does not mean it will take place. We can write a balanced equation for the reaction of gold with water, for example, but the reaction does not occur in practice—so your gold jewelry is safe in the shower.

Balanced, but does not occur $2 \, Au(s) + 3 \, H_2O(l) \longrightarrow Au_2O_3(s) + 3 \, H_2(g)$

To describe reactions more completely, several fundamental questions are commonly asked: Is energy released or absorbed when a reaction occurs? Is a given reaction fast or slow? Does a reaction continue until all reactants are converted to products, or is there a point beyond which no additional product forms?

7.1 Energy and Chemical Bonds

There are two fundamental and interconvertible kinds of energy: *potential* and *kinetic*. **Potential energy** is stored energy. The water in a reservoir behind a dam, an automobile poised to coast downhill, and a coiled spring have potential energy waiting to be released. **Kinetic energy**, by contrast, is the energy of motion. When the water falls over the dam and turns a turbine, when the car rolls downhill, or when the spring uncoils and makes the hands on a clock move, the potential energy in each is converted to kinetic energy. Of course, once all the potential energy is converted, nothing further occurs. The water at the bottom of the dam, the car at the bottom of the hill, and the uncoiled spring no longer have potential energy and thus, undergo no further change.

In chemical compounds, the attractive forces between ions or atoms are a form of potential energy, similar to the attractive forces between the poles of a magnet. When these attractive forces result in the formation of ionic or covalent bonds between ions or atoms, the potential energy is often converted into **heat**—a measure of the kinetic energy of the particles that make up the molecule. Breaking these bonds requires an input of energy.

In chemical reactions, some of the chemical bonds in the reactants must break (energy in) so that new bonds can form in the products (energy out). If the reaction products have less potential energy than the reactants, we say that the products are *more stable* than the reactants. The term "stable" is used in chemistry to describe a substance that has little remaining potential energy and consequently little tendency to undergo further change. Whether a reaction occurs, and how much energy or heat

Potential energy Stored energy.

Kinetic energy The energy of an object in motion.

Heat A measure of the transfer of thermal energy.

SOLUTION

To find the amount of heat released (in kilocalories) by combustion of 0.35 mol of methane, we use a conversion factor of kcal/mol, and then we can convert to kilojoules using a kJ/kcal conversion factor (see Section 1.13):

$$0.35 \ \text{mol CH}_4 \times \frac{-213 \ \text{kcal}}{1 \ \text{mol CH}_4} = -75 \ \text{kcal}$$

$$-75 \ \text{kcal} \times \left(\frac{4.184 \ \text{kJ}}{\text{kcal}} \right) = -314 \ \text{kJ}$$

The negative sign indicates that the 75 kcal (314 kJ) of heat is released.

BALLPARK CHECK The calculated answer is consistent with our estimate (70 kcal or 280 kJ).

Worked Example **7.3** Heat of Reaction: Mass to Mole Conversion

How much heat is released during the combustion of 7.50 g of methane (molar mass $= 16.0 \ \text{g/mol}$)?

$$CH_4(g) + 2 \ O_2(g) \longrightarrow CO_2(g) + 2 \ H_2O(l) \quad \Delta H = -213 \frac{\text{kcal}}{\text{mol CH}_4} = -891 \frac{\text{kJ}}{\text{mol CH}_4}$$

ANALYSIS We can find the moles of methane involved in the reaction by using the molecular weight in a mass to mole conversion, and then use ΔH to find the heat released.

BALLPARK ESTIMATE Since 1 mol of methane (molar mass $= 16.0 \ \text{g/mol}$) has a mass of 16.0 g, 7.50 g of methane is a little less than 0.5 mol. Thus, less than half of 213 kcal, or about 100 kcal (418 kJ), is released from combustion of 7.50 g.

SOLUTION

Going from a given mass of methane to the amount of heat released in a reaction requires that we first find the number of moles of methane by including molar mass (in mol/g) in the calculation and then converting moles to kilocalories or kilojoules:

$$7.50 \ \text{g CH}_4 \times \frac{1 \ \text{mol CH}_4}{16.0 \ \text{g CH}_4} \times \frac{-213 \ \text{kcal}}{1 \ \text{mol CH}_4} = -99.8 \ \text{kcal}$$

or

$$7.50 \ \text{g CH}_4 \times \frac{1 \ \text{mol CH}_4}{16.0 \ \text{g CH}_4} \times \frac{-891 \ \text{kJ}}{1 \ \text{mol CH}_4} = -418 \ \text{kJ}$$

The negative sign indicates that the 99.8 kcal (418 kJ) of heat is released.

BALLPARK CHECK Our estimate was $-100 \ \text{kcal} \ (-418 \ \text{kJ})$!

Worked Example **7.4** Heat of Reaction: Mole Ratio Calculations

How much heat is released in kcal and kJ when 2.50 mol of O_2 reacts completely with methane?

$$CH_4(g) + 2 \ O_2(g) \longrightarrow CO_2(g) + 2 \ H_2O(l) \quad \Delta H = -213 \frac{\text{kcal}}{\text{mol CH}_4} = -891 \frac{\text{kJ}}{\text{mol CH}_4}$$

ANALYSIS Since the ΔH for the reaction is based on the combustion of 1 mol of methane, we will need to perform a mole ratio calculation.

BALLPARK ESTIMATE The balanced equation shows that 213 kcal (891 kJ) is released for each 2 mol of oxygen that reacts. Thus, 2.50 mol of oxygen should release a bit more than 213 kcal, perhaps about 250 kcal (1050 kJ).

SOLUTION

To find the amount of heat released by combustion of 2.50 mol of oxygen, we include in our calculation a mole ratio based on the balanced chemical equation:

$$2.50 \ \text{mol} \ O_2 \times \frac{1 \ \text{mol} \ CH_4}{2 \ \text{mol} \ O_2} \times \frac{-213 \ \text{kcal}}{1 \ \text{mol} \ CH_4} = -266 \ \text{kcal}$$

or

$$2.50 \ \text{mol} \ O_2 \times \frac{1 \ \text{mol} \ CH_4}{2 \ \text{mol} \ O_2} \times \frac{-891 \ \text{kJ}}{1 \ \text{mol} \ CH_4} = -1110 \ \text{kJ}$$

The negative sign indicates that the 266 kcal (1110 kJ) of heat is released.

BALLPARK CHECK The calculated answer is close to our estimate (-250 kcal or -1050 kJ).

CHEMISTRY IN ACTION

Energy from Food

Any serious effort to lose weight usually leads to studying the caloric values of foods. Have you ever wondered how the numbers quoted on food labels are obtained?

Food is "burned" in the body to yield H_2O, CO_2, and energy, just as natural gas is burned in furnaces to yield the same products. In fact, the "caloric value" of a food is just the heat of reaction for complete combustion of the food (minus a small correction factor). The value is the same whether the food is burned in the body or in the laboratory. One gram of protein releases 4 kcal, 1 g of table sugar (a carbohydrate) releases 4 kcal, and 1 g of fat releases 9 kcal (see Table).

▲ This frosted donut provides your body with 330 Calories. Burning this donut in a calorimeter releases 330 kcal (1380 kJ) as heat.

Caloric Values of Some Foods

Substance, Sample Size	Caloric Value (kcal, kJ)	
Protein, 1 g	4,	17
Carbohydrate, 1 g	4,	17
Fat, 1 g	9,	38
Alcohol, 1 g	7.1,	29.7
Cola drink, 12 fl oz (369 g)	160,	670
Apple, one medium (138 g)	80,	330
Iceberg lettuce, 1 cup shredded (55 g)	5,	21
White bread, 1 slice (25 g)	65,	270
Hamburger patty, 3 oz (85 g)	245,	1030
Pizza, 1 slice (120 g)	290,	1200
Vanilla ice cream, 1 cup (133 g)	270,	1130

The caloric value of a food is usually given in "Calories" (note the capital C), where 1 Cal = 1000 cal = 1 kcal = 4.184 kJ. To determine these values experimentally, a carefully dried and weighed food sample is placed together with oxygen in an instrument called a *calorimeter*, the food is ignited, the temperature change is measured, and the amount of heat given off is calculated from the temperature change. In the calorimeter, the heat from the food is released very quickly and the temperature rises dramatically. Clearly, though, something a bit different goes on when food is burned in the body, otherwise we would burst into flames after a meal!

It is a fundamental principle of chemistry that the total heat released or absorbed in going from reactants to products is the same, no matter how many reactions are involved. The body applies this principle by withdrawing energy from food a bit at a time in a long series of interconnected reactions rather than all at once in a single reaction. These and other reactions that are continually taking place in the body—called the body's *metabolism*—will be examined in later chapters.

See Chemistry in Action Problems 7.70 and 7.71 at the end of the chapter.

PROBLEM 7.1

In photosynthesis, green plants convert carbon dioxide and water into glucose $(C_6H_{12}O_6)$ according to the following equation:

$$6\,CO_2(g) + 6\,H_2O(l) \longrightarrow C_6H_{12}O_6(aq) + 6\,O_2(g)$$

(a) Estimate ΔH for the reaction using bond dissociation energies from Table 7.1. Give your answer in kcal/mol and kJ/mol. $C_6H_{12}O_6$ has five C—C bonds, seven C—H bonds, seven C—O bonds, and five O—H bonds).

(b) Is the reaction endothermic or exothermic?

PROBLEM 7.2

The following equation shows the conversion of aluminum oxide (from the ore bauxite) to aluminum:

$$2\,Al_2O_3(s) \longrightarrow 4\,Al(s) + 3\,O_2(g) \quad \Delta H = +801\,\text{kcal/mol}\,(+3350\,\text{kJ/mol})$$

(a) Is the reaction exothermic or endothermic?

(b) How many kilocalories are required to produce 1.00 mol of aluminum? How many kilojoules?

(c) How many kilocalories are required to produce 10.0 g of aluminum? How many kilojoules?

PROBLEM 7.3

How much heat is absorbed (in kilocalories and kilojoules) during production of 127 g of NO by the combination of nitrogen and oxygen?

$$N_2(g) + O_2(g) \longrightarrow 2\,NO(g) \quad \Delta H = +43\,\text{kcal/mol}\,(+180\,\text{kJ/mol})$$

PROBLEM 7.4

Once consumed, the body metabolizes alcohol (ethanol, CH_3CH_2OH; MW = 46 g/mol) to carbon dioxide and water. The balanced reaction is: $CH_3CH_2OH + 3\,O_2 \longrightarrow 2\,CO_2 + 3\,H_2O$. Using the bond energies in Table 7.1, estimate the ΔH for this reaction in kcal/mol. How does it compare to the caloric value of alcohol (in Cal/g) given in Chemistry in Action: Energy from Food on p. 185?

7.4 Why Do Chemical Reactions Occur? Free Energy

Events that lead to lower energy states tend to occur spontaneously. Water falls downhill, for instance, releasing its stored (potential) energy and reaching a lower-energy, more stable position. Similarly, a wound-up spring uncoils when set free. Applying this lesson to chemistry, the obvious conclusion is that exothermic processes—those that release heat energy—should be spontaneous. A log burning in a fireplace is just one example of a spontaneous reaction that releases heat. At the same time, endothermic processes, which absorb heat energy, should not be spontaneous. Often, these conclusions are correct, but not always. Many, but not all, exothermic processes take place spontaneously, and many, but not all, endothermic processes are nonspontaneous.

Before exploring the situation further, it is important to understand what the word "spontaneous" means in chemistry, which is not quite the same as in everyday language. A **spontaneous process** is one that, once started, proceeds on its own without any external influence. The change does not necessarily happen quickly, like a spring suddenly uncoiling or a car coasting downhill. It can also happen slowly, like the gradual rusting away of an abandoned bicycle. A *nonspontaneous process*, by contrast, takes place only in the presence of a continuous external influence. Energy must be continually expended to rewind a spring or push a car uphill. The reverse of a spontaneous process is always nonspontaneous.

As an example of a process that takes place spontaneously yet absorbs heat, think about what happens when you take an ice cube out of the freezer. The ice spontaneously

▲ Events that lead to lower energy tend to occur spontaneously. Thus, water always flows *down* a waterfall, not up.

Spontaneous process A process or reaction that, once started, proceeds on its own without any external influence.

melts to give liquid water above 0 °C, even though it *absorbs* heat energy from the surroundings. What this and other spontaneous endothermic processes have in common is *an increase in molecular disorder, or randomness.* When the solid ice melts, the H_2O molecules are no longer locked in position but are now free to move around randomly in the liquid water.

The amount of disorder in a system is called the system's **entropy**, symbolized by S and expressed in units of calories (or Joules) per mole-kelvin $[\,cal/(mol \cdot K)\,$ or $J/(mol \cdot K)\,]$. The greater the disorder, or randomness, of the particles in a substance or mixture, the larger the value of S (Figure 7.1). Gases have more disorder and therefore higher entropy than liquids because particles in the gas move around more freely than particles in the liquid. Similarly, liquids have higher entropy than solids. In chemical reactions, entropy increases when, for example, a gas is produced from a solid or when 2 mol of reactants split into 4 mol of products.

Entropy (S) A measure of the amount of molecular disorder in a system.

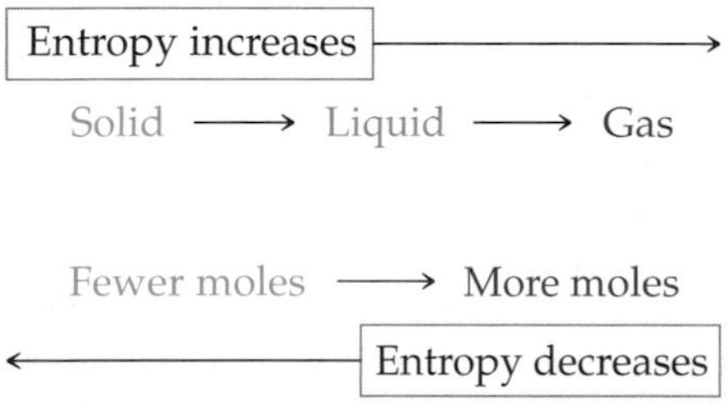

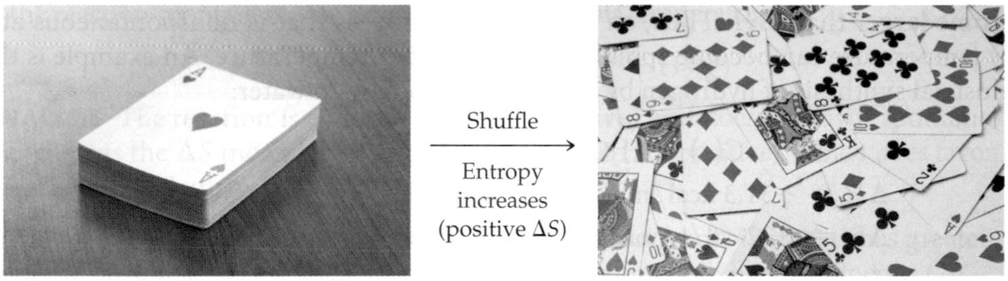

▲ **Figure 7.1**
Entropy and values of S.
A new deck of cards, neatly stacked, has more order and lower entropy than the randomly shuffled and strewn cards on the right. The value of the entropy change, ΔS, for converting the system on the left to that on the right is positive because entropy increases.

The **entropy change** for a process, ΔS, has a *positive* value if disorder increases because the process adds disorder to the system. The melting of ice to give water is an example. Conversely, ΔS has a *negative* value if the disorder of a system decreases. The freezing of water to give ice is an example.

It thus appears that two factors determine the spontaneity of a chemical or physical change: the release or absorption of heat, ΔH, and the increase or decrease in entropy, ΔS. *To decide whether a process is spontaneous, both the enthalpy change and the entropy change must be taken into account.* We have already seen that a negative ΔH favors spontaneity, but what about ΔS? The answer is that an increase in molecular disorder (ΔS positive) favors spontaneity. A good analogy is the bedroom or office that seems to spontaneously become more messy over time (an increase in disorder, ΔS positive); to clean it up (a decrease in disorder, ΔS negative) requires an input of energy, a nonspontaneous process. Using our chemical example, the combustion of a log spontaneously converts large, complex molecules like lignin and cellulose (high molecular order, low entropy) into CO_2 and H_2O (a large number of small molecules with higher entropy). For this process, the level of disorder increases, and so ΔS is positive. The reverse process—turning CO_2 and H_2O back into cellulose—does occur in photosynthesis, but it requires a significant input of energy in the form of sunlight.

When enthalpy and entropy are both favorable (ΔH negative, ΔS positive), a process is spontaneous; when both are unfavorable, a process is nonspontaneous. Clearly,

Entropy change ΔS A measure of the increase in disorder ($\Delta S = +$) or decrease in disorder ($\Delta S = -$) as a chemical reaction or physical change occurs.

Reversible reaction A reaction that can go in either direction, from products to reactants or reactants to products.

Chemical equilibrium A state in which the rates of forward and reverse reactions are the same.

Imagine the situation if you mix acetic acid and ethyl alcohol. The two begin to form ethyl acetate and water. But as soon as ethyl acetate and water form, they begin to go back to acetic acid and ethyl alcohol. Such a reaction, which easily goes in either direction, is said to be **reversible** and is indicated by a double arrow ($\rightleftharpoons$) in equations. The reaction read from left to right as written is referred to as the *forward reaction*, and the reaction from right to left is referred to as the *reverse reaction*.

Now suppose you mix some ethyl acetate and water. The same thing occurs: As soon as small quantities of acetic acid and ethyl alcohol form, the reaction in the other direction begins to take place. No matter which pair of reactants is mixed together, both reactions occur until ultimately the concentrations of reactants and products reach constant values and undergo no further change. At this point, the reaction vessel contains all four substances—acetic acid, ethyl acetate, ethyl alcohol, and water—and the reaction is said to be in a state of **chemical equilibrium**.

Since the reactant and product concentrations undergo no further change once equilibrium is reached, you might conclude that the forward and reverse reactions have stopped. That is not the case, however. The forward reaction takes place rapidly at the beginning of the reaction but then slows down as reactant concentrations decrease. At the same time, the reverse reaction takes place slowly at the beginning but then speeds up as product concentrations increase (Figure 7.6). Ultimately, the forward and reverse rates become equal and change no further.

▶ **Figure 7.6**
Reaction rates in an equilibrium reaction.
The forward rate is large initially but decreases as the concentrations of reactants drop. The reverse rate is small initially but increases as the concentrations of products increase. At equilibrium, the forward and reverse reaction rates are equal.

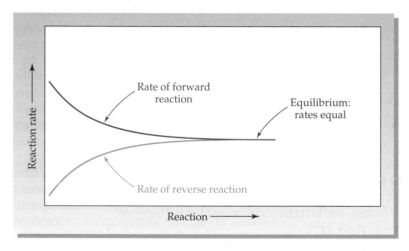

▲ When the number of people moving up is the same as the number of people moving down, the number of people on each floor remains constant, and the two populations are in equilibrium.

Chemical equilibrium is an active, dynamic condition. All substances present are continuously being made and unmade at the same rate, so their concentrations are constant at equilibrium. As an analogy, think of two floors of a building connected by up and down escalators. If the number of people moving up is the same as the number of people moving down, the numbers of people on each floor remain constant. *Individual people* are continuously changing from one floor to the other, but the *total populations* of the two floors are in equilibrium.

Note that it is not necessary for the concentrations of reactants and products at equilibrium to be equal (just as it is not necessary for the numbers of people on two floors connected by escalators to be equal). Equilibrium can be reached at any point between pure products and pure reactants. The extent to which the forward or reverse reaction is favored over the other is a characteristic property of a given reaction under given conditions.

7.8 Equilibrium Equations and Equilibrium Constants

Remember that the rate of a reaction depends on the number of collisions between molecules (Section 7.5), and that the number of collisions in turn depends on concentration, i.e., the number of molecules in a given volume (Section 7.6). For a reversible reaction, then, the rates of both the forward *and* the reverse reactions must depend on the concentration of reactants and products, respectively. When a reaction reaches equilibrium, the rates of the forward and reverse reactions are equal, and the concentrations of reactants and products remain constant. We can use this fact to obtain useful information about a reaction.

Let us look at the details of a specific equilibrium reaction. Suppose that you allow various mixtures of sulfur dioxide and oxygen to come to equilibrium with sulfur trioxide at a temperature of 727 °C and then measure the concentrations of all three gases in the mixtures.

$$2 SO_2(g) + O_2(g) \rightleftharpoons 2 SO_3(g)$$

In one experiment, we start with only 1.00 mol of SO_2 and 1.00 mol of O_2 in a 1.00 L container. In other words, the initial concentrations of reactants are 1.00 mol/L. When the reaction reaches equilibrium, we have 0.0620 mol/L of SO_2, 0.538 mol/L of O_2, and 0.938 mol/L of SO_3. In another experiment, we start with 1.00 mol/L of SO_3. When this reaction reaches equilibrium, we have 0.150 mol/L of SO_2, 0.0751 mol/L of O_2, and 0.850 mol/L of SO_3. In both cases, we see that there is substantially more product (SO_3) than reactants when the reaction reaches equilibrium, regardless of the starting conditions. Is it possible to predict what the equilibrium conditions will be for any given reaction?

As it turns out, the answer is YES! No matter what the original concentrations were, and no matter what concentrations remain at equilibrium, we find that a constant numerical value is obtained if the equilibrium concentrations are substituted into the expression

$$\frac{[SO_3]^2}{[SO_2]^2[O_2]} = \text{constant at a given T}$$

The square brackets in this expression indicate the concentration of each substance expressed as moles per liter. Using the equilibrium concentrations for each of the experiments described above, we can calculate the value and verify that it is constant:

Experiment 1. $\quad \dfrac{[SO_3]^2}{[SO_2]^2[O_2]} = \dfrac{(0.938 \text{ mol/L})^2}{(0.0620 \text{ mol/L})^2(0.538 \text{ mol/L})} = 425$

Experiment 2. $\quad \dfrac{[SO_3]^2}{[SO_2]^2[O_2]} = \dfrac{(0.850 \text{ mol/L})^2}{(0.150 \text{ mol/L})^2(0.0751 \text{ mol/L})} = 428$

At a temperature of 727 °C, the actual value of the constant is 429. Within experimental error, the ratios of product and reactant concentrations for the two experiments at equilibrium yield the same result. Numerous experiments like those just described have led to a general equation that is valid for any reaction. Consider a general reversible reaction:

$$aA + bB + \ldots \rightleftharpoons mM + nN + \ldots$$

where A, B, . . . are reactants; M, N, . . . are products; and *a, b, . . . , m, n, . . .* are coefficients in the balanced equation. At equilibrium, the composition of the reaction mixture obeys the following *equilibrium equation*, where *K* is the **equilibrium constant**.

Equilibrium constant (K) Value obtained at a given temperature from the ratio of the concentrations of products and reactants, each raised to a power equal to its coefficient in the balanced equation.

Equilibrium equation $\quad K = \dfrac{[M]^m[N]^n \cdots}{[A]^a[B]^b \cdots}$

Product concentrations
Reactant concentrations

Equilibrium constant

The equilibrium constant *K* is the number obtained by multiplying the equilibrium concentrations of the products and dividing by the equilibrium concentrations of the reactants, with the concentration of each substance raised to a power equal to its coefficient in the balanced equation. If we take another look at the reaction between sulfur dioxide and oxygen, we can now see how the equilibrium constant was obtained:

$$2\,SO_2\,(g)\;+\;O_2\,(g)\;\rightleftharpoons\;2\,SO_3\,(g)$$

$$K = \frac{[SO_3]^2}{[SO_2]^2\,[O_2]}$$

Note that if there is no coefficient for a reactant or product in the reaction equation, it is assumed to be 1. The value of K varies with temperature (25 °C) is assumed unless otherwise specified—and units are usually omitted.

For reactions that involve pure solids or liquids, these pure substances are omitted when writing the equilibrium constant expression. To explain why, consider the decomposition of limestone from Problem 7.6:

▶▶▶ The practice of omitting pure substances in the equilibrium constant expression will be utilized in Chapter 10 when we discuss equilibria involving acids and bases.

$$CaCO_3(s) \longrightarrow CaO(s) + CO_2(g)$$

Writing the equilibrium constant expression for this reaction as the concentration of products over the concentration of reactions would yield

$$K = \frac{[CaO][CO_2]}{[CaCO_3]}$$

Consider the solids CaO and $CaCO_3$. Their concentrations (in moles/L) can be calculated from their molar masses and densities at a given temperature. For example, the concentration of CaO at 25 °C can be calculated as

$$\frac{\left(3.25\,\frac{g\,CaO}{cm^3}\right)\cdot\left(\frac{1000\,cm^3}{L}\right)}{56.08\,\frac{g\,CaO}{mol\,CaO}} = 58.0\,\frac{mol\,CaO}{L}$$

The ratio of products over reactants would change if CO_2 was added to or removed from the reaction. The concentration of CaO, however, is the same whether we have 10 grams or 500 grams. Adding solid CaO will not change the ratio of products over reactants. Since the concentration of solids is independent of the amount of solid present, these concentrations are omitted and the expression for K becomes

$$K = \frac{[CaO][CO_2]}{[CaCO_3]} = [CO_2]$$

The value of the equilibrium constant indicates the position of a reaction at equilibrium. If the forward reaction is favored, the product term $[M]^m[N]^n$ is larger than the reactant term $[A]^a[B]^b$, and the value of K is larger than 1. If instead the reverse reaction is favored, $[M]^m[N]^n$ is smaller than $[A]^a[B]^b$ at equilibrium, and the value of K is smaller than 1.

For a reaction such as the combination of hydrogen and oxygen to form water vapor, the equilibrium constant is enormous (3.1×10^{81}), showing how greatly the formation of water is favored. Equilibrium is effectively nonexistent for such reactions, and the reaction is described as *going to completion*.

On the other hand, the equilibrium constant is very small for a reaction such as the combination of nitrogen and oxygen at 25 °C to give NO (4.7×10^{-31}), showing what we know from observation—that N_2 and O_2 in the air do not combine noticeably at room temperature:

$$N_2(g) + O_2(g) \rightleftharpoons 2\,NO(g) \quad K = \frac{[NO]^2}{[N_2][O_2]} = 4.7 \times 10^{-31}$$

When K is close to 1, say between 10^3 and 10^{-3}, significant amounts of both reactants and products are present at equilibrium. An example is the reaction of acetic acid with ethyl alcohol to give ethyl acetate (Section 7.7). For this reaction, $K = 3.4$.

$$CH_3CO_2H + CH_3CH_2OH \rightleftharpoons CH_3CO_2CH_2CH_3 + H_2O$$

$$K = \frac{[CH_3CO_2CH_2CH_3][H_2O]}{[CH_3CO_2H][CH_3CH_2OH]} = 3.4$$

We can summarize the meaning of equilibrium constants in the following way:

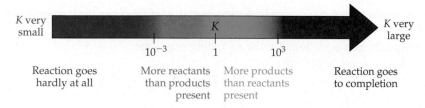

K very small			K very large
	10^{-3} 1 10^3		
Reaction goes hardly at all	More reactants than products present	More products than reactants present	Reaction goes to completion

K much smaller than 0.001   Only reactants are present at equilibrium; essentially no reaction occurs.

K between 0.001 and 1   More reactants than products are present at equilibrium.

K between 1 and 1000   More products than reactants are present at equilibrium.

K much larger than 1000   Only products are present at equilibrium; reaction goes essentially to completion.

Worked Example **7.8** Writing Equilibrium Equations

The first step in the industrial synthesis of hydrogen is the reaction of steam with methane to give carbon monoxide and hydrogen. Write the equilibrium equation for the reaction.

$$H_2O(g) + CH_4(g) \rightleftharpoons CO(g) + 3\,H_2(g)$$

ANALYSIS   The equilibrium constant K is the number obtained by multiplying the equilibrium concentrations of the products (CO and H_2) and dividing by the equilibrium concentrations of the reactants (H_2O and CH_4), with the concentration of each substance raised to the power of its coefficient in the balanced equation.

SOLUTION

$$K = \frac{[CO][H_2]^3}{[H_2O][CH_4]}$$

Worked Example **7.9** Equilibrium Equations: Calculating K

In the reaction of Cl_2 with PCl_3, the concentrations of reactants and products were determined experimentally at equilibrium and found to be 7.2 mol/L for PCl_3, 7.2 mol/L for Cl_2, and 0.050 mol/L for PCl_5.

$$PCl_3(g) + Cl_2(g) \rightleftharpoons PCl_5(g)$$

Write the equilibrium equation, and calculate the equilibrium constant for the reaction. Which reaction is favored, the forward one or the reverse one?

ANALYSIS   All the coefficients in the balanced equation are 1, so the equilibrium constant equals the concentration of the product, PCl_5, divided by the product of the concentrations of the two reactants, PCl_3 and Cl_2. Insert the values given for each concentration, and calculate the value of K.

BALLPARK ESTIMATE   At equilibrium, the concentration of the reactants (7.2 mol/L for each reactant) is higher than the concentration of the product (0.05 mol/L), so we expect a value of K less than 1.

SOLUTION

$$K = \frac{[PCl_5]}{[PCl_3][Cl_2]} = \frac{0.050 \text{ mol/L}}{(7.2 \text{ mol/L})(7.2 \text{ mol/L})} = 9.6 \times 10^{-4}$$

The value of K is less than 1, so the reverse reaction is favored. Note that units for K are omitted.

BALLPARK CHECK Our calculated value of K is just as we predicted: $K < 1$.

PROBLEM 7.13

Write equilibrium equations for the following reactions:

(a) $N_2O_4(g) \rightleftharpoons 2\,NO_2(g)$

(b) $2\,H_2S(g) + O_2(g) \rightleftharpoons 2\,S(s) + 2\,H_2O(g)$

(c) $2\,BrF_5(g) \rightleftharpoons Br_2(g) + 5\,F_2(g)$

PROBLEM 7.14

Do the following reactions favor reactants or products at equilibrium? Give relative concentrations at equilibrium.

(a) $\text{Sucrose}(aq) + H_2O(l) \rightleftharpoons \text{Glucose}(aq) + \text{Fructose}(aq)$ $K = 1.4 \times 10^5$

(b) $NH_3(aq) + H_2O(l) \rightleftharpoons NH_4^+(aq) + OH^-(aq)$ $K = 1.6 \times 10^{-5}$

(c) $Fe_2O_3(s) + 3\,CO(g) \rightleftharpoons 2\,Fe(s) + 3\,CO_2(g)$ K (at $727\,°C$) $= 24.2$

PROBLEM 7.15

For the reaction $H_2(g) + I_2(g) \rightleftharpoons 2\,HI(g)$, equilibrium concentrations at $25\,°C$ are $[H_2] = 0.0510$ mol/L, $[I_2] = 0.174$ mol/L, and $[HI] = 0.507$ mol/L. What is the value of K at $25\,°C$?

KEY CONCEPT PROBLEM 7.16

The following diagrams represent two similar reactions that have achieved equilibrium:

   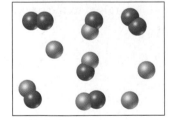

$$A_2 + B_2 \longrightarrow 2\,AB \qquad\qquad A_2 + 2B \longrightarrow 2\,AB$$

(a) Write the expression for the equilibrium constant for each reaction.

(b) Calculate the value for the equilibrium constant for each reaction.

7.9 Le Châtelier's Principle: The Effect of Changing Conditions on Equilibria

The effect of a change in reaction conditions on chemical equilibrium is predicted by a general rule called *Le Châtelier's principle:*

Le Châtelier's principle When a stress is applied to a system at equilibrium, the equilibrium shifts to relieve the stress.

The word "stress" in this context means any change in concentration, pressure, volume, or temperature that disturbs the original equilibrium and causes the rates of the forward and reverse reactions to become temporarily unequal.

We saw in Section 7.6 that reaction rates are affected by changes in temperature and concentration, and by addition of a catalyst. But what about equilibria? Are they similarly affected? The answer is that changes in concentration, temperature, and pressure *do* affect equilibria, but that addition of a catalyst does not (except to reduce the time it takes to reach equilibrium). The change caused by a catalyst affects forward and reverse reactions equally so that equilibrium concentrations are the same in both the presence and the absence of the catalyst.

Effect of Changes in Concentration

Let us look at the effect of a concentration change by considering the reaction of CO with H_2 to form CH_3OH (methanol). Once equilibrium is reached, the concentrations of the reactants and product are constant, and the forward and reverse reaction rates are equal.

$$CO(g) + 2 H_2(g) \rightleftharpoons CH_3OH(g)$$

What happens if the concentration of CO is increased? To relieve the "stress" of added CO, according to Le Châtelier's principle, the extra CO must be used up. In other words, the rate of the forward reaction must increase to consume CO. Think of the CO added on the left as "pushing" the equilibrium to the right:

$$[CO \longrightarrow]$$
$$CO(g) + 2 H_2(g) \rightleftharpoons CH_3OH(g)$$

Of course, as soon as more CH_3OH forms, the reverse reaction also speeds up, some CH_3OH converts back to CO and H_2. Ultimately, the forward and reverse reaction rates adjust until they are again equal, and equilibrium is reestablished. At this new equilibrium state, the value of $[H_2]$ is lower because some of the H_2 reacted with the added CO and the value of $[CH_3OH]$ is higher because CH_3OH formed as the reaction was driven to the right by the addition of CO. The changes offset each other, however, so that the value of the equilibrium constant K remains constant.

$$CO(g) + 2 H_2(g) \rightleftharpoons CH_3OH(g)$$

If this increases . . .   . . . then this decreases . . .   . . . and this increases . . .

. . . but this remains constant.
$$K = \frac{[CH_3OH]}{[CO] [H_2]^2}$$

What happens if CH_3OH is added to the reaction at equilibrium? Some of the methanol reacts to yield CO and H_2, making the values of $[CO]$, $[H_2]$, and $[CH_3OH]$ higher when equilibrium is reestablished. As before, the value of K does not change.

If this increases . . .

$$CO(g) + 2 H_2(g) \rightleftharpoons CH_3OH(g)$$

. . . then this increases . . .   . . . and this increases . . .

. . . but this remains constant.
$$K = \frac{[CH_3OH]}{[CO] [H_2]^2}$$

Alternatively, we can view chemical equilibrium as a *balance* between the free energy of the reactants (on the left) and the free energy of the products (on the right). Adding more reactants tips the balance in favor of the reactants. In order to restore the balance, reactants must be converted to products, or the reaction must shift to the right. If, instead, we remove reactants, then the balance is too heavy on the product side and the reaction must shift left, generating more reactants to restore balance.

▶ Equilibrium represents a balance between the free energy of reactants and products. Adding reactants (or products) to one side upsets the balance, and the reaction will proceed in a direction to restore the balance.

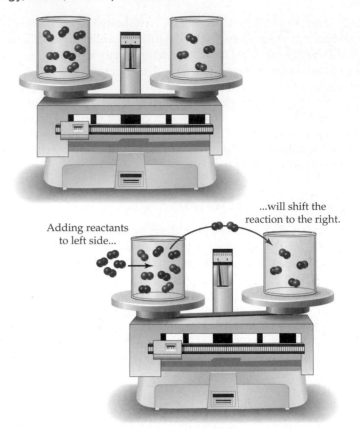

Adding reactants to left side...

...will shift the reaction to the right.

Finally, what happens if a reactant is continuously supplied or a product is continuously removed? Because the concentrations are continuously changing, equilibrium can never be reached. As a result, it is sometimes possible to force a reaction to produce large quantities of a desirable product even when the equilibrium constant is unfavorable. Take the reaction of acetic acid with ethanol to yield ethyl acetate, for example. As discussed in the preceding section, the equilibrium constant K for this reaction is 3.4, meaning that substantial amounts of reactants and products are both present at equilibrium. If, however, the ethyl acetate is removed as soon as it is formed, the production of more and more product is forced to occur, in accord with Le Châtelier's principle.

Continuously removing this product from the reaction forces more of it to be produced.

$$\underset{\text{Acetic acid}}{CH_3\overset{\displaystyle O}{\overset{\|}{C}}OH} + \underset{\text{Ethyl alcohol}}{CH_3CH_2OH} \rightleftharpoons \underset{\text{Ethyl acetate}}{CH_3\overset{\displaystyle O}{\overset{\|}{C}}OCH_2CH_3} + H_2O$$

Metabolic reactions sometimes take advantage of this effect, with one reaction prevented from reaching equilibrium by the continuous consumption of its product in a further reaction.

Effect of Changes in Temperature and Pressure

We noted in Section 7.2 that the reverse of an exothermic reaction is always endothermic. Equilibrium reactions are therefore exothermic in one direction and endothermic in the other. Le Châtelier's principle predicts that an increase in temperature will cause an equilibrium to shift in favor of the endothermic reaction so the additional heat is absorbed. Conversely, a decrease in temperature will cause an equilibrium to shift in favor of the exothermic reaction so additional heat

PROBLEM 7.17

Is the yield of SO_3 at equilibrium favored by a higher or lower pressure? By a higher or lower temperature?

$$2 SO_2(g) + O_2(g) \rightleftharpoons 2 SO_3(g) \quad \Delta H = -47 \text{ kcal/mol}$$

PROBLEM 7.18

What effect do the listed changes have on the position of the equilibrium in the reaction of carbon with hydrogen?

$$C(s) + 2 H_2(g) \rightleftharpoons CH_4(g) \quad \Delta H = -18 \text{ kcal/mol} (-75 \text{ kJ/mol})$$

(a) Increasing temperature

(b) Increasing pressure by decreasing volume

(c) Allowing CH_4 to escape continuously from the reaction vessel

PROBLEM 7.19

Another example of a coupled reaction used in the smelting of copper ore (Chemistry in Action: Coupled Reactions, p. 204) involves the following two reactions performed at 375 °C:

(1) $Cu_2O(s) \longrightarrow 2 Cu(s) + \frac{1}{2}O_2(g) \quad \Delta G \text{ (at 375 °C)} = +140.0 \text{ kJ} (+33.5 \text{ kcal})$

(2) $C(s) + \frac{1}{2}O_2(g) \longrightarrow CO(g) \quad \Delta G \text{ (at 375 °C)} = -143.8 \text{ kJ} (-34.5 \text{ kcal})$

Derive the overall reaction and calculate the net free-energy change for the coupled reaction.

SUMMARY: REVISITING THE CHAPTER GOALS

1. What energy changes take place during reactions? The strength of a covalent bond is measured by its *bond dissociation energy*, the amount of energy that must be supplied to break the bond in an isolated gaseous molecule. For any reaction, the heat released or absorbed by changes in bonding is called the *heat of reaction*, or *enthalpy change* (ΔH). If the total strength of the bonds formed in a reaction is greater than the total strength of the bonds broken, then heat is released (negative ΔH) and the reaction is said to be *exothermic*. If the total strength of the bonds formed in a reaction is less than the total strength of the bonds broken, then heat is absorbed (positive ΔH) and the reaction is said to be *endothermic* (see Problems 26–33, 40, 62, 63, 70, 71, 76–78, 80, 81, 83, 85).

2. What is "free-energy," and what is the criterion for spontaneity in chemistry? *Spontaneous reactions* are those that, once started, continue without external influence; nonspontaneous reactions require a continuous external influence. Spontaneity depends on two factors, the amount of heat absorbed or released in a reaction (ΔH) and the *entropy change* (ΔS), which measures the change in molecular disorder in a reaction. Spontaneous reactions are favored by a release of heat (negative ΔH) and an increase in disorder (positive ΔS). The *free-energy change* (ΔG) takes both factors into account, according to the equation $\Delta G = \Delta H - T\Delta S$. A negative value for ΔG indicates spontaneity, and a positive value for ΔG indicates nonspontaneity (see Problems 20–22, 25, 34–43, 46, 50, 51, 73, 84).

3. What determines the rate of a chemical reaction? A chemical reaction occurs when reactant particles collide with proper orientation and sufficient energy. The exact amount of collision energy necessary is called the *activation energy* (E_{act}). A high activation energy results in a slow reaction because few collisions occur with sufficient force, whereas a low activation energy results in a fast reaction. Reaction rates can be increased by raising the temperature, by raising the concentrations of reactants, or by adding a *catalyst*, which accelerates a reaction without itself undergoing any change (see Problems 23, 24, 44–51, 75).

4. What is chemical equilibrium? A reaction that can occur in either the forward or reverse direction is *reversible* and will ultimately reach a state of *chemical equilibrium*. At equilibrium, the forward and reverse reactions occur at the same rate, and the concentrations of reactants and products are constant. Every reversible reaction has a characteristic *equilibrium constant* (K), given by an *equilibrium equation* (see Problems 52–63, 78, 82).

For the reaction: $aA + bB + \cdots \rightleftharpoons mM + nN + \cdots$

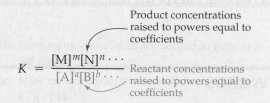

$$K = \frac{[M]^m[N]^n \cdots}{[A]^a[B]^b \cdots}$$

Product concentrations raised to powers equal to coefficients

Reactant concentrations raised to powers equal to coefficients

5. What is Le Châtelier's principle? *Le Châtelier's principle* states that when a stress is applied to a system in equilibrium, the equilibrium shifts so that the stress is relieved. Applying this principle allows prediction of the effects of changes in temperature, pressure, and concentration (see Problems 62–69, 79, 82).

---

is released. In other words, you can think of heat as a reactant or product whose increase or decrease stresses an equilibrium just as a change in reactant or product concentration does.

Endothermic reaction Favored by increase in temperature
(Heat is absorbed)

Exothermic reaction Favored by decrease in temperature
(Heat is released)

In the exothermic reaction of N_2 with H_2 to form NH_3, for example, raising the temperature favors the reverse reaction, which absorbs the heat:

$$[\longleftarrow \text{— Heat}]$$
$$N_2(g) + 3 H_2(g) \rightleftharpoons 2 NH_3(g) + \text{Heat}$$

We can also use the balance analogy to predict the effect of temperature on an equilibrium mixture; this time, we think of heat as a reactant or product. Increasing the temperature of the reaction is the same as adding heat to the left side (for an endothermic reaction) or to the right side (for an exothermic reaction). The reaction then proceeds in the appropriate direction to restore "balance" to the system.

What about changing the pressure? Pressure influences an equilibrium only if one or more of the substances involved is a gas. As predicted by Le Châtelier's principle, decreasing the volume to increase the pressure in such a reaction shifts the equilibrium in the direction that decreases the number of molecules in the gas phase and thus, decreases the pressure. For the ammonia synthesis, decreasing the volume *increases* the concentration of reactants and products, but has a greater effect on the reactant side of the equilibrium since there are more moles of gas phase reactants. Increasing the pressure, therefore, favors the forward reaction because 4 mol of gas is converted to 2 mol of gas.

$$[\text{Pressure} \longrightarrow]$$
$$\underbrace{N_2(g) + 3 H_2(g)}_{\text{4 mol of gas}} \rightleftharpoons \underbrace{2 NH_3(g)}_{\text{2 mol of gas}}$$

The effects of changing reaction conditions on equilibria are summarized in Table 7.4

TABLE 7.4 Effects of Changes in Reaction Conditions on Equilibria

Change	Effect
Concentration	Increase in reactant concentration or decrease in product concentration favors forward reaction. Increase in product concentration or decrease in reactant concentration favors reverse reaction.
Temperature	Increase in temperature favors endothermic reaction. Decrease in temperature favors exothermic reaction.
Pressure	Increase in pressure favors side with fewer moles of gas. Decrease in pressure favors side with more moles of gas.
Catalyst added	Equilibrium reached more quickly; value of K unchanged.

LOOKING AHEAD ▶▶▶ In Chapter 20, we will see how Le Châtelier's principle is exploited to keep chemical "traffic" moving through the body's metabolic pathways. It often happens that one reaction in a series is prevented from reaching equilibrium because its product is continuously consumed in another reaction.

Figure 8.1
molecular comparison of ga: quids, and solids.
) In gases, the particles feel lit traction for one another and a move about randomly. (b) In e particles are held close toget tractive forces but are free to s ver one another. (c) In solids, t articles are strongly attracted t other. They can move slightly e held in a fairly rigid arrange th respect to one another.

CHEMISTRY IN ACTION

Coupled Reactions

Living organisms are highly complex systems that use chemical reactions to produce the energy needed for daily activity. Many of these reactions occur very slowly—if at all—at normal body temperature, so organisms use several different strategies discussed in this chapter to obtain the energy they need and to function optimally. For example, the rates of slow reactions are increased by using biocatalysts, otherwise known as enzymes (Chapter 19). Le Châtelier's principle is used for regulation of critical processes, including oxygen transport (Chemistry in Action: Breathing and O_2 Transport, p. 263) and blood pH (Chemistry in Action: Buffers in the Body, p. 312). But what about reactions that do not occur spontaneously? One useful strategy is to "couple" a nonspontaneous reaction with a spontaneous one.

Coupling of reactions is a common strategy in both biochemical and industrial applications. Consider the following reaction for the recovery of copper metal from the smelting of ore containing Cu_2S:

$$Cu_2S(s) \longrightarrow 2\,Cu(s) + S(s) \quad \Delta G = +86.2\,kJ\,(+21.6\,kcal)$$

Since ΔG for this process is positive (endergonic), this reaction will not proceed spontaneously. But when the smelting process is performed at elevated temperatures in the presence of oxygen, this reaction can be "coupled" with another reaction:

$$Cu_2S(s) \longrightarrow 2\,Cu(s) + S(s) \quad \Delta G = +86.2\,kJ\,(+21.6\,kcal)$$
$$S(s) + O_2(g) \longrightarrow SO_2(g) \quad \Delta G = -300.1\,kJ\,(-71.7\,kcal)$$

$$\text{Net Reaction: } Cu_2S(s) + O_2(g) \longrightarrow 2\,Cu(s) + SO_2(g)$$
$$\Delta G = -213.9\,kJ\,(-51.1\,kcal)$$

The overall reaction has a negative ΔG (exergonic) to produce pure copper spontaneously.

Coupled Reactions in Biochemistry

An important example of coupled reactions in biochemistry is the endergonic phosphorylation of glucose (Section 22.6), which is the essential first step in the metabolism of glucose. It is combined with the hydrolysis of adenosine triphosphate (ATP) to form adenosine diphosphate (ADP), an exergonic process:

$$\text{Glucose} + HOPO_3^{2-} \longrightarrow \text{Glucose-6-phosphate} + H_2O$$
$$\Delta G = +13.8\,kJ/mol$$
$$ATP + H_2O \longrightarrow ADP + HOPO_3^{2-} + H^+ \quad \Delta G = -30.5\,kJ/mol$$

$$\text{Net Reaction: Glucose} + ATP \longrightarrow ADP + \text{Glucose-6-phosphate}$$
$$\Delta G = -16.7\,kJ/mol$$

In addition to the production of glucose-6-phosphate, which is critical for metabolic activity, any heat that is generated by the coupled reactions can be used to maintain body temperature.

See Chemistry in Action Problems 7.74 and 7.75 at the end of the chapter.

Worked Example 7.10 Le Châtelier's Principle and Equilibrium Mixtures

Nitrogen reacts with oxygen to give NO:

$$N_2(g) + O_2(g) \rightleftharpoons 2\,NO(g) \quad \Delta H = +43\,kcal/mol\,(+180\,kJ/mol)$$

Explain the effects of the following changes on reactant and product concentrations:

(a) Increasing temperature   (b) Increasing the concentration of NO

(c) Adding a catalyst

SOLUTION

(a) The reaction is endothermic (positive ΔH), so increasing the temperature favors the forward reaction. The concentration of NO will be higher at equilibrium.

(b) Increasing the concentration of NO, a product, favors the reverse reaction. At equilibrium, the concentrations of both N_2 and O_2, as well as that of NO, will be higher.

(c) A catalyst accelerates the rate at which equilibrium is reached, but the concentrations at equilibrium do not change.

CHAPTER 8

Gases, Liquids, and Solids

Change of state The change of a substance from one state of matter (gas, liquid, or solid) to another.

▶▶ You might want to reread Section 7.4 to brush up on these concepts.

CONTENTS

▶ **Figure 8.2**
Changes of state.
The changes are endothermic from bottom to top and exothermic from top to bottom. Solid and liquid states are in equilibrium at the melting point liquid and gas states are in equilibrium at the boiling point.

◀ This winter scene in Yellow National Park shows the thre of matter for water—solid (s liquid (water), and gas (steam vapor)—all present at the sa

which the changeover in behavior occurs is called the **melting point (mp)** and represents the temperature at which solid and liquid coexist in equilibrium. In the corresponding change from a liquid to a gas, the two states are in equilibrium at the **boiling point (bp)**.

The names and enthalpy changes associated with the different changes of state are summarized in Figure 8.2. Note that a solid can change directly to a gas without going through the liquid state—a process called *sublimation*. Dry ice (solid CO_2) at atmospheric pressure, for example, changes directly to a gas without melting.

Melting point (mp) The temperature at which solid and liquid are in equilibrium.

Boiling point (bp) The temperature at which liquid and gas are in equilibrium.

Worked Example 8.1 Change of State: Enthalpy, Entropy, and Free Energy

The change of state from liquid to gas for chloroform, formerly used as an anesthetic, has $\Delta H = +6.98$ kcal/mol ($+29.2$ kJ/mol) and a $\Delta S = +20.9$ cal/(mol $\cdot$ K) [$+87.4$ J/(mol $\cdot$ K)].

(a) Is the change of state from liquid to gas favored or unfavored by ΔH? by ΔS?

(b) Is the change of state from liquid to gas favored or unfavored at 35 °C?

(c) Is this change of state spontaneous at 65 °C?

ANALYSIS A process will be favored if energy is released ($\Delta H = $ negative) and if there is a decrease in disorder ($\Delta S = $ positive). In cases in which one factor is favorable and the other is unfavorable, then we can calculate the free-energy change to determine if the process is favored:

$$\Delta G = \Delta H - T\Delta S$$

When ΔG is negative, the process is favored.

SOLUTION

(a) The ΔH does NOT favor this change of state ($\Delta H = $ positive), but the ΔS does favor the process. Since the two factors are not in agreement, we must use the equation for free-energy change to determine if the process is favored at a given temperature.

(b) Substituting the values for ΔH and ΔS into the equation for free-energy change we can determine if ΔG is positive or negative at 35 °C (308 K). Note that we must first convert degrees celsius to kelvins and convert the ΔS from cal to kcal so the units can be added together.

$$\Delta G = \Delta H - T\Delta S = \left(\frac{6.98 \text{ kcal}}{\text{mol}}\right) - (308 \text{ K})\left(\frac{20.9 \text{ cal}}{\text{mol} \cdot \text{K}}\right)\left(\frac{1 \text{ kcal}}{1000 \text{ cal}}\right)$$

$$= 6.98 \frac{\text{kcal}}{\text{mol}} - 6.44 \frac{\text{kcal}}{\text{mol}} = +0.54 \frac{\text{kcal}}{\text{mol}}$$

$$\left(+0.54 \frac{\text{kcal}}{\text{mol}}\right)\left(\frac{4.184 \text{ kJ}}{\text{kcal}}\right) = +2.26 \frac{\text{kJ}}{\text{mol}}$$

Since the $\Delta G = $ positive, this change of state is not favored at 35 °C.

(c) Repeating the calculation using the equation for free-energy change at 65 °C (338 K):

$$\Delta G = \Delta H - T\Delta S = \left(\frac{6.98 \text{ kcal}}{\text{mol}}\right) - (338 \text{ K})\left(\frac{20.9 \text{ cal}}{\text{mol} \cdot \text{K}}\right)\left(\frac{1 \text{ kcal}}{1000 \text{ cal}}\right)$$

$$= 6.98 \frac{\text{kcal}}{\text{mol}} - 7.06 \frac{\text{kcal}}{\text{mol}} = -0.08 \frac{\text{kcal}}{\text{mol}} \left(\text{or} -0.33 \frac{\text{kJ}}{\text{mol}}\right)$$

Because ΔG is negative in this case, the change of state is favored at this temperature.

PROBLEM 8.1

The change of state from liquid H_2O to gaseous H_2O has $\Delta H = +9.72$ kcal/mol ($+40.7$ kJ/mol) and $\Delta S = -26.1$ cal/(mol·K) $[-109$ J/(mol·K)$]$.

(a) Is the change from liquid to gaseous H_2O favored or unfavored by ΔH? By ΔS?

(b) What is the value of ΔG (in kcal/mol and kJ/mol) for the change from liquid to gaseous H_2O at 373 K?

(c) What are the values of ΔH and ΔS (in kcal/mol and kJ/mol) for the change from gaseous to liquid H_2O?

8.2 Intermolecular Forces

What determines whether a substance is a gas, a liquid, or a solid at a given temperature? Why does rubbing alcohol evaporate much more readily than water? Why do molecular compounds have lower melting points than ionic compounds? To answer these and a great many other such questions, we need to look into the nature of **intermolecular forces**—the forces that act *between different molecules* rather than within an individual molecule.

In gases, the intermolecular forces are negligible, so the gas molecules act independently of one another. In liquids and solids, however, intermolecular forces are strong enough to hold the molecules in close contact. As a general rule, the stronger the intermolecular forces in a substance, the more difficult it is to separate the molecules, and the higher the melting and boiling points of the substance.

There are three major types of intermolecular forces: *dipole–dipole, London dispersion*, and *hydrogen bonding*. We will discuss each in turn.

Dipole–Dipole Forces

Many molecules contain polar covalent bonds and may therefore have a net molecular polarity. In such cases, the positive and negative ends of different molecules are attracted to one another by what is called a **dipole–dipole force** (Figure 8.3).

Dipole–dipole forces are weak, with strengths on the order of 1 kcal/mol (4 kJ/mol) compared to the 70–100 kcal/mol (300–400 kJ/mol) typically found for the strength of a covalent bond (see Table 7.1). Nevertheless, the effects of dipole–dipole forces are important, as can be seen by looking at the difference in boiling points between polar and nonpolar molecules. Butane, for instance, is a nonpolar molecule with a molecular weight of 58 amu and a boiling point of –0.5 °C, whereas acetone has the same molecular weight yet boils 57 °C higher because it is polar.

Intermolecular force A force that acts between molecules and holds molecules close to one another.

▶▶▶ Recall from Sections 4.9 and 4.10 that a polar covalent bond is one in which the electrons are attracted more strongly by one atom than by the other.

Dipole–dipole force The attractive force between positive and negative ends of polar molecules.

▶▶▶ Recall from Section 4.9 how molecular polarities can be visualized using electrostatic potential maps.

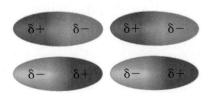

▲ **Figure 8.3**
Dipole–dipole forces.
The positive and negative ends of polar molecules are attracted to one another by dipole–dipole forces. As a result, polar molecules have higher boiling points than nonpolar molecules of similar size.

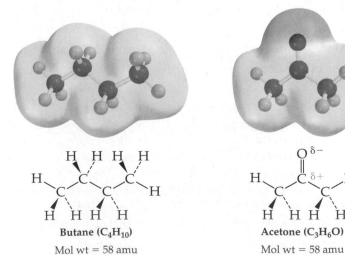

Butane (C_4H_{10})
Mol wt = 58 amu
bp = –0.5 °C

Acetone (C_3H_6O)
Mol wt = 58 amu
bp = 56.2 °C

London Dispersion Forces

Only polar molecules experience dipole–dipole forces, but all molecules, regardless of structure, experience *London dispersion forces*. **London dispersion forces** are caused by the constant motion of electrons within molecules. Take even a simple nonpolar molecule like Br_2, for example. Averaged over time, the distribution of electrons throughout the molecule is uniform, but at any given *instant* there may be more electrons at one end of the molecule than at the other (Figure 8.4). At that instant, the molecule has a short-lived polarity. Electrons in neighboring molecules are attracted to the positive end of the polarized molecule, resulting in a polarization of the neighbor and creation of an attractive London dispersion force that holds the molecules together. As a result, Br_2 is a liquid at room temperature rather than a gas.

London dispersion force The short-lived attractive force due to the constant motion of electrons within molecules.

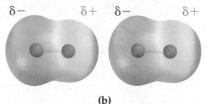

δ−   δ+   δ−   δ+

(a)   (b)

◄ **Figure 8.4**
(a) Averaged over time, the electron distribution in a Br_2 molecule is symmetrical. (b) At any given instant, however, the electron distribution may be unsymmetrical, resulting in a temporary polarity that induces a complementary polarity in neighboring molecules.

London dispersion forces are weak—in the range 0.5–2.5 kcal/mol (2–10 kJ/mol)—but they increase with molecular weight and amount of surface area available for interaction between molecules. The larger the molecular weight, the more electrons there are moving about and the greater the temporary polarization of a molecule. The larger the amount of surface contact, the greater the close interaction between different molecules.

The effect of surface area on the magnitude of London dispersion forces can be seen by comparing a roughly spherical molecule with a flatter, more linear one having the same molecular weight. Both 2,2-dimethylpropane and pentane, for instance, have the same formula (C_5H_{12}), but the nearly spherical shape of 2,2-dimethylpropane allows for less surface contact with neighboring molecules than does the more linear shape of pentane (Figure 8.5). As a result, London dispersion forces are smaller for 2,2-dimethylpropane, molecules are held together less tightly, and the boiling point is correspondingly lower: 9.5 °C for 2,2-dimethylpropane versus 36 °C for pentane.

◄ **Figure 8.5**
London dispersion forces.
More compact molecules like 2,2-dimethylpropane have smaller surface areas, weaker London dispersion forces, and lower boiling points. By comparison, flatter, less compact molecules like pentane have larger surface areas, stronger London dispersion forces, and higher boiling points.

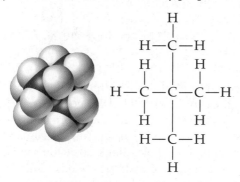

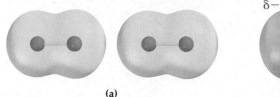

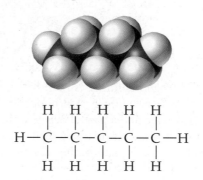

(a) 2,2-Dimethylpropane (bp = 9.5 °C)   (b) Pentane (bp = 36 °C)

Hydrogen Bonds

In many ways, hydrogen bonding is responsible for life on earth. It causes water to be a liquid rather than a gas at ordinary temperatures, and it is the primary intermolecular force that holds huge biomolecules in the shapes needed to play their essential roles in biochemistry. Deoxyribonucleic acid (DNA) and keratin (Figure 8.6), for instance, are long molecular chains that form a α-helix, held in place largely due to hydrogen bonding.

A **hydrogen bond** is an attractive interaction between an unshared electron pair on an electronegative O, N, or F atom and a positively polarized hydrogen atom bonded to

Hydrogen bond The attraction between a hydrogen atom bonded to an electronegative O, N, or F atom and another nearby electronegative O, N, or F atom.

▶ **Figure 8.6**
The α-helical structure of keratin results from hydrogen bonding along the amino acid backbone of the molecule. Hydrogen bonding is represented by gray dots in the ball and stick model on the left and red dots in the molecular structure on the right.

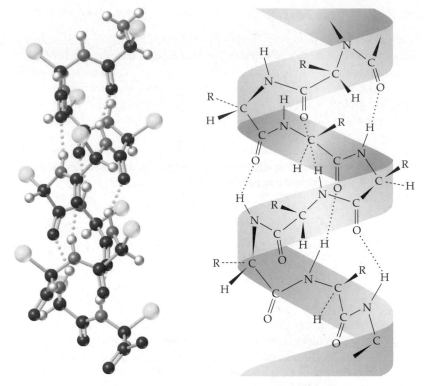

another electronegative O, N, or F. For example, hydrogen bonds occur in both water and ammonia:

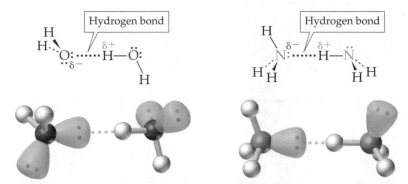

Hydrogen bonding is really just a special kind of dipole–dipole interaction. The O—H, N—H, and F—H bonds are highly polar, with a partial positive charge on the hydrogen and a partial negative charge on the electronegative atom. In addition, the hydrogen atom has no inner-shell electrons to act as a shield around its nucleus, and it is small, so it can be approached closely. As a result, the dipole–dipole attractions involving positively polarized hydrogens are unusually strong, and hydrogen bonds result. Water, in particular, is able to form a vast three-dimensional network of hydrogen bonds because each H_2O molecule has two hydrogens and two electron pairs (Figure 8.7).

▶ **Figure 8.7**
Hydrogen bonding in water.
The intermolecular attraction in water is especially strong because each oxygen atom has two lone pairs and two hydrogen atoms, allowing the formation of as many as four hydrogen bonds per molecule. Individual hydrogen bonds are constantly being formed and broken.

Hydrogen bonds can be quite strong, with energies up to 10 kcal/mol (40 kJ/mol). To see the effect of hydrogen bonding, look at Table 8.1, which compares the boiling points of binary hydrogen compounds of second-row elements with their third-row counterparts. Because NH_3, H_2O, and HF molecules are held tightly together by hydrogen bonds, an unusually large amount of energy must be added to separate them in the boiling process. As a result, the boiling points of NH_3, H_2O, and HF are much higher than the boiling points of their second-row neighbor CH_4 and of related third-row compounds.

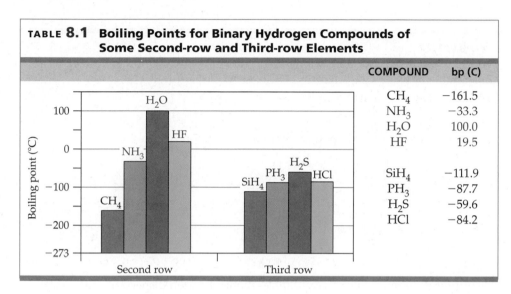

TABLE **8.1**	Boiling Points for Binary Hydrogen Compounds of Some Second-row and Third-row Elements

COMPOUND	bp (C)
CH_4	−161.5
NH_3	−33.3
H_2O	100.0
HF	19.5
SiH_4	−111.9
PH_3	−87.7
H_2S	−59.6
HCl	−84.2

A summary and comparison of the various kinds of intermolecular forces is shown in Table 8.2.

TABLE 8.2 A Comparison of Intermolecular Forces

Force	Strength	Characteristics
Dipole–dipole	Weak (1 kcal/mol, 4 kJ/mol))	Occurs between polar molecules
London dispersion	Weak (0.5–2.5 kcal/mol, 2–10 kJ/mol)	Occurs between all molecules; strength depends on size
Hydrogen bond	Moderate (2–10 kcal/mol, 8–40 kJ/mol)	Occurs between molecules with O—H, N—H, and F—H bonds

LOOKING AHEAD ▶▶▶ Dipole–dipole forces, London dispersion forces, and hydrogen bonds are traditionally called "intermolecular forces" because of their influence on the properties of molecular compounds. But these same forces can also operate between different parts of a very large molecule. In this context, they are often referred to as "noncovalent interactions." In later chapters, we will see how noncovalent interactions determine the shapes of biologically important molecules such as proteins and nucleic acids.

Worked Example 8.2 Identifying Intermolecular Forces: Polar versus Nonpolar

Identify the intermolecular forces that influence the properties of the following compounds:

(a) Methane, CH_4 (b) HCl   (c) CH_3COOH

ANALYSIS The intermolecular forces will depend on the molecular structure, what type of bonds are in the molecule (polar or non-polar), and how the bonds are arranged.

SOLUTION

(a) Since methane contains only C—H bonds, it is a nonpolar molecule; it has only London dispersion forces.

(b) The H—Cl bond is polar, so this is a polar molecule; it has both dipole–dipole forces and London dispersion forces.

(c) Acetic acid is a polar molecule with an O—H bond. Thus, it has dipole–dipole forces, London dispersion forces, and hydrogen bonds.

PROBLEM 8.2

Would you expect the boiling points to increase or decrease in the following series? Explain.

(a) Kr, Ar, Ne   (b) Cl_2, Br_2, I_2

PROBLEM 8.3

Which of the following compounds form hydrogen bonds?

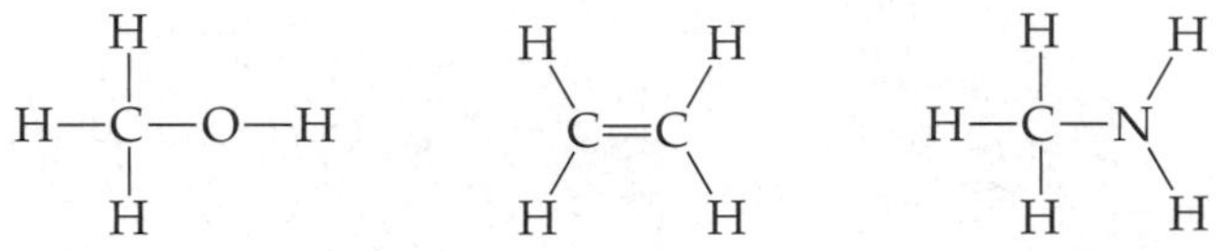

| Methyl alcohol | Ethylene | Methylamine |
| (a) | (b) | (c) |

PROBLEM 8.4

Identify the intermolecular forces (dipole–dipole, London dispersion, hydrogen bonding) that influence the properties of the following compounds:

(a) Ethane, CH_3CH_3

(b) Ethyl alcohol, CH_3CH_2OH

(c) Ethyl chloride, CH_3CH_2Cl

8.3 Gases and the Kinetic–Molecular Theory

Gases behave quite differently from liquids and solids. Gases, for instance, have low densities and are easily compressed to a smaller volume when placed under pressure, a property that allows them to be stored in large tanks. Liquids and solids, by contrast, are much more dense and much less compressible. Furthermore, gases undergo a far larger expansion or contraction when their temperature is changed than do liquids and solids.

The behavior of gases can be explained by a group of assumptions known as the **kinetic–molecular theory of gases**. We will see in the next several sections how the following assumptions account for the observable properties of gases:

Kinetic–molecular theory of gases A group of assumptions that explain the behavior of gases.

- **A gas consists of many particles, either atoms or molecules, moving about at random with no attractive forces between them.** Because of this random motion, different gases mix together quickly.

- **The amount of space occupied by the gas particles themselves is much smaller than the amount of space between particles.** Most of the volume taken up by gases is empty space, accounting for the ease of compression and low densities of gases.

- **The average kinetic energy of gas particles is proportional to the Kelvin temperature.** Thus, gas particles have more kinetic energy and move faster as the temperature increases. (In fact, gas particles move much faster than you might suspect. The average speed of a helium atom at room temperature and atmospheric pressure is approximately 1.36 km/s, or 3000 mi/hr, nearly that of a rifle bullet.)

- **Collisions of gas particles, either with other particles or with the wall of their container, are elastic; that is, the total kinetic energy of the particles is constant.** The pressure of a gas against the walls of its container is the result of collisions of the gas particles with the walls. The more collisions and the more forceful each collision, the higher the pressure.

A gas that obeys all the assumptions of the kinetic–molecular theory is called an **ideal gas**. In practice, though, there is no such thing as a perfectly ideal gas. All gases behave somewhat differently than predicted when, at very high pressures or very low temperatures, their particles get closer together and interactions between particles become significant. As a rule, however, most real gases display nearly ideal behavior under normal conditions.

8.4 Pressure

We are all familiar with the effects of air pressure. When you fly in an airplane, the change in air pressure against your eardrums as the plane climbs or descends can cause a painful "popping." When you pump up a bicycle tire, you increase the pressure of air against the inside walls of the tire until the tire feels hard.

In scientific terms, **pressure** (*P*) is defined as a force (*F*) per unit area (*A*) pushing against a surface; that is, $P = F/A$. In the bicycle tire, for example, the pressure you feel is the force of air molecules colliding with the inside walls of the tire. The units you probably use for tire pressure are pounds per square inch (psi), where 1 psi is equal to the pressure exerted by a 1-pound object resting on a 1-square inch surface.

We on earth are under pressure from the atmosphere, the blanket of air pressing down on us (Figure 8.8). Atmospheric pressure is not constant, however; it varies slightly from day to day depending on the weather, and it also varies with altitude. Due to gravitational forces, the density of air is greatest at the earth's surface and decreases with increasing altitude. As a result, air pressure is greatest at the surface: it is about 14.7 psi at sea level but only about 4.7 psi on the summit of Mt. Everest.

One of the most commonly used units of pressure is the *millimeter of mercury*, abbreviated *mmHg* and often called a *torr* (after the Italian physicist Evangelista Torricelli). This unusual unit dates back to the early 1600s when Torricelli made the first mercury *barometer*. As shown in Figure 8.9, a barometer consists of a long, thin tube that is sealed at one end, filled with mercury, and then inverted into a dish of mercury. Some mercury runs from the tube into the dish until the downward pressure of the mercury in the column is exactly balanced by the outside atmospheric pressure, which presses down on the mercury in the dish and pushes it up into the column. The height of the mercury column varies depending on the altitude and weather conditions, but standard atmospheric pressure at sea level is defined to be exactly 760 mm.

Gas pressure inside a container is often measured using an open-ended *manometer*, a simple instrument similar in principle to the mercury barometer. As shown in Figure 8.10, an open-ended manometer consists of a U-tube filled with mercury, with one end connected to a gas-filled container and the other end open to the atmosphere. The difference between the heights of the mercury levels in the two arms of the U-tube indicates the difference between the pressure of the gas in the container and the pressure of the atmosphere. If the gas pressure inside the container is less than atmospheric, the mercury level is higher in the arm connected to the container (Figure 8.10a). If the gas pressure inside the container is greater than atmospheric, the mercury level is higher in the arm open to the atmosphere (Figure 8.10b).

Pressure is given in the SI system (Section 2.1) by a unit named the *pascal* (Pa), where 1 Pa = 0.007500 mmHg (or 1 mmHg = 133.32 Pa). Measurements in pascals are becoming more common, and many clinical laboratories have made the switchover. Higher pressures are often still given in *atmospheres* (atm), where 1 atm = 760 mmHg exactly.

$$\text{Pressure units: } 1 \text{ atm} = 760 \text{ mmHg} = 14.7 \text{ psi} = 101{,}325 \text{ Pa}$$
$$1 \text{ mmHg} = 1 \text{ torr} = 133.32 \text{ Pa}$$

Ideal gas A gas that obeys all the assumptions of the kinetic–molecular theory.

Pressure (*P*) The force per unit area pushing against a surface.

▲ **Figure 8.8**
Atmospheric pressure.
A column of air weighing 14.7 lb presses down on each square inch of the earth's surface at sea level, resulting in what we call atmospheric pressure.

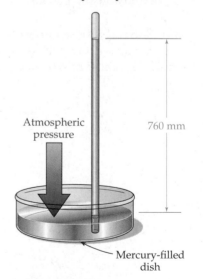

▲ **Figure 8.9**
Measuring atmospheric pressure.
A mercury barometer measures atmospheric pressure by determining the height of a mercury column in a sealed glass tube. The downward pressure of the mercury in the column is exactly balanced by the outside atmospheric pressure, which presses down on the mercury in the dish and pushes it up into the column.

▶ **Figure 8.10**
Open-ended manometers for measuring pressure in a gas-filled bulb.
(a) When the pressure in the gas-filled container is lower than atmospheric, the mercury level is higher in the arm open to the container. (b) When the pressure in the container is higher than atmospheric, the mercury level is higher in the arm open to the atmosphere.

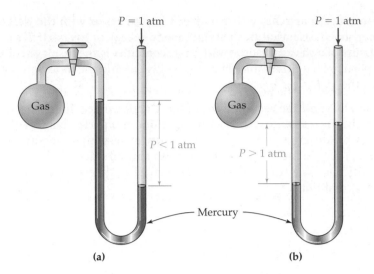

(a)   (b)

Worked Example 8.3 Unit Conversions (Pressure): psi, Atmospheres, and Pascals

A typical bicycle tire is inflated with air to a pressure of 55 psi. How many atmospheres is this? How many pascals?

ANALYSIS Using the starting pressure in psi, the pressure in atm and pascals can be calculated using the equivalent values in appropriate units as conversion factors.

SOLUTION

STEP 1: **Identify known information.**   Pressure $= 55$ psi

STEP 2: **Identify answer and units.**   Pressure $= ??$ atm $= ??$ pascals

STEP 3: **Identify conversion factors.** Using equivalent values in appropriate units, we can obtain conversion factors to convert to atm and pascals.

$$14.7 \text{ psi} = 1 \text{ atm} \rightarrow \frac{1 \text{ atm}}{14.7 \text{ psi}}$$

$$14.7 \text{ psi} = 101{,}325 \text{ Pa} \rightarrow \frac{101{,}325 \text{ Pa}}{14.7 \text{ psi}}$$

STEP 4: **Solve.** Use the appropriate conversion factors to set up an equation in which unwanted units cancel.

$$(55 \text{ psi}) \times \left(\frac{1 \text{ atm}}{14.7 \text{ psi}} \right) = 3.7 \text{ atm}$$

$$(55 \text{ psi}) \times \left(\frac{101{,}325 \text{ Pa}}{14.7 \text{ psi}} \right) = 3.8 \times 10^5 \text{ Pa}$$

Worked Example 8.4 Unit Conversions (Pressure): mmHg to Atmospheres

The pressure in a closed flask is measured using a manometer. If the mercury level in the arm open to the sealed vessel is 23.6 cm higher than the level of mercury in the arm open to the atmosphere, what is the gas pressure (in atm) in the closed flask?

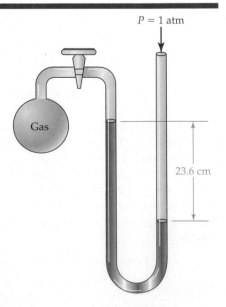

ANALYSIS Since the mercury level is higher in the arm open to the flask, the gas pressure in the flask is lower than atmospheric pressure (1 atm = 760 mmHg). We can convert the difference in the level of mercury in the two arms of the manometer from mmHg to atmospheres to determine the difference in pressure.

BALLPARK ESTIMATE The height difference (23.6 cm) is about one-third the height of a column of Hg that is equal to 1 atm (or 76 cm Hg). Therefore, the pressure in the flask should be about 0.33 atm lower than atmospheric pressure, or about 0.67 atm.

SOLUTION
Since the height difference is given in cm Hg, we must first convert to mmHg, and then to atm. The result is the difference in gas pressure between the flask and the open atmosphere (1 atm).

$$(23.6 \text{ cm Hg})\left(\frac{10 \text{ mmHg}}{\text{cm Hg}}\right)\left(\frac{1 \text{ atm}}{760 \text{ mmHg}}\right) = 0.311 \text{ atm}$$

The pressure in the flask is calculated by subtracting this difference from 1 atm:

$$1 \text{ atm} - 0.311 \text{ atm} = 0.689 \text{ atm}$$

BALLPARK CHECK This result agrees well with our estimate of 0.67 atm.

PROBLEM 8.5
The air pressure outside a jet airliner flying at 35,000 ft is about 0.289 atm. Convert this pressure to mmHg, psi, and pascals.

PROBLEM 8.6
The increase in atmospheric CO_2 levels has been correlated with the combustion of fossil fuels (see Chemistry in Action: Greenhouse Gases and Global Warming on p. 224). How would the atmospheric CO_2 levels be affected by a shift to corn-based ethanol or some other biomass-based fuel? Explain.

KEY CONCEPT PROBLEM 8.7

What is the pressure of the gas inside the following manometer (in mmHg) if outside pressure is 750 mmHg?

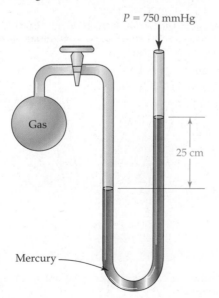

P = 750 mmHg

Gas

25 cm

Mercury

CHEMISTRY IN ACTION

Greenhouse Gases and Global Warming

The mantle of gases surrounding the earth is far from the uniform mixture you might expect, consisting of layers that vary in composition and properties at different altitudes. The ability of the gases in these layers to absorb radiation is responsible for life on earth as we know it.

The *stratosphere*—the layer extending from about 12 km up to 50 km altitude—contains the ozone layer that is responsible for absorbing harmful UV radiation. The *troposphere* is the layer extending from the surface up to about 12 km altitude. It should not surprise you to learn that the troposphere is the layer most easily disturbed by human activities and that this layer has the greatest impact on the earth's surface conditions. Among those impacts, a process called the *greenhouse effect* is much in the news today.

The greenhouse effect refers to the warming that occurs in the troposphere as gases absorb radiant energy. Much of the radiant energy reaching the Earth's surface from the sun is reflected back into space, but some is absorbed by atmospheric gases, particularly those referred to as *greenhouse gases* (GHGs)—water vapor, carbon dioxide, and methane. This absorbed radiation warms the atmosphere and acts to maintain a relatively stable temperature of 15 °C (59 °F) at the Earth's surface. Without the greenhouse effect, the average surface temperature would be about −18 °C (0 °F)—a temperature so low that Earth would be frozen and unable to sustain life.

The basis for concern about the greenhouse effect is the fear that human activities over the past century have disturbed the earth's delicate thermal balance. Should increasing amounts of radiation be absorbed, increased atmospheric heating will result, and global temperatures will continue to rise.

Measurements show that the concentration of atmospheric CO_2 has been rising in the last 150 years, from an estimated 290 parts per million (ppm) in 1850 to current levels approaching 400 ppm. The increase in CO_2 levels is largely because of the increased burning of fossil fuels and correlates with a concurrent increase in average global temperatures. The latest Assessment Report of the Intergovernmental Panel on Climate Change published in November 2007 concluded that "[W]arming of the climate system is unequivocal, as is now evident from observations of increases in global average air and ocean temperatures, widespread melting of snow and ice and rising global average sea level.... Continued GHG emissions at or above current rates would cause further warming and induce many changes in the global climate system during the 21st century that would *very likely* be larger than those observed during the 20th century."

Increased international concerns about the political and economic impacts of global climate change prompted development of the Kyoto Protocol to the United Nations Framework Convention on Climate Change (UNFCCC). Under the protocol, countries commit to a reduction in the production and emission of greenhouse gases, including CO_2, methane, and chlorofluorocarbons (CFCs). As of April 2010, 191 countries have signed and ratified the protocol. These concerns have also resulted in market pressures to develop sustainable and renewable energy sources, as well as more efficient technologies, such as hybrid electric vehicles.

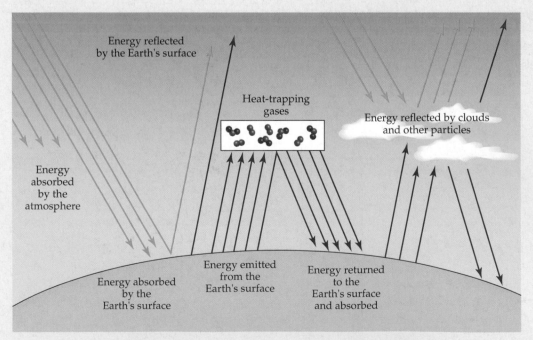

▲ Greenhouse gases (GHG) trap heat reflected from the earth's surface, resulting in the increase in surface temperatures known as global warming.

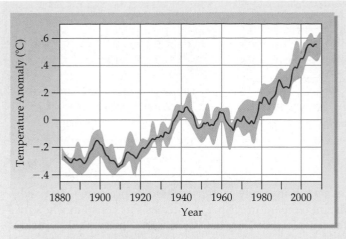

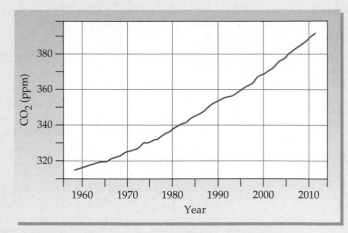

▲ **Concentrations of atmospheric CO_2 and global average temperatures have increased dramatically in the last 150 years because of increased fossil fuel use, causing serious changes in earth's climate system.**
© **NASA, GISS Surface Temperature Analysis.**

See Chemistry in Action Problems 8.100 and 8.101 at the end of the chapter.

8.5 Boyle's Law: The Relation between Volume and Pressure

The physical behavior of all gases is much the same, regardless of identity. Helium and chlorine, for example, are completely different in their *chemical* behavior, but are very similar in many of their physical properties. Observations of many different gases by scientists in the 1700s led to the formulation of what are now called the **gas laws**, which make it possible to predict the influence of pressure (P), volume (V), temperature (T), and molar amount (n) on any gas or mixture of gases. We will begin by looking at *Boyle's law*, which describes the relation between volume and pressure.

> **Gas laws** A series of laws that predict the influence of pressure (P), volume (V), and temperature (T) on any gas or mixture of gases.

Imagine that you have a sample of gas inside a cylinder that has a movable plunger at one end (Figure 8.11). What happens if you double the pressure on the gas by pushing the plunger down, while keeping the temperature constant? Since the gas particles are forced closer together, the volume of the sample decreases.

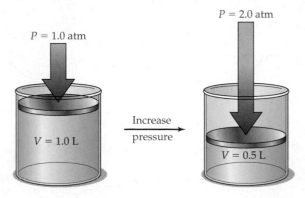

◀ **Figure 8.11**
Boyle's law.
The volume of a gas decreases proportionately as its pressure increases. For example, if the pressure of a gas sample is doubled, the volume is halved.

According to **Boyle's law**, the volume of a fixed amount of gas at a constant temperature is inversely proportional to its pressure, meaning that volume and pressure change in opposite directions. As pressure goes up, volume goes down; as pressure goes down, volume goes up (Figure 8.12). This observation is consistent with the kinetic–molecular theory. Since most of the volume occupied by gases is empty space, gases are easily compressed into smaller volumes. Since the average kinetic energy remains constant, the number of collisions must increase as the interior surface area of the container decreases, leading to an increase in pressure.

▶ **Figure 8.12**
Boyle's law.
Pressure and volume are inversely related. Graph (a) demonstrates the decrease in volume as pressure increases, whereas graph (b) shows the linear relationship between V and $1/P$.

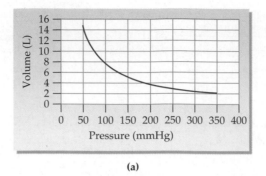

(a)

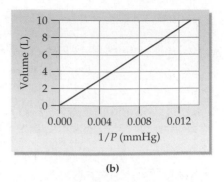

(b)

Boyle's law The volume of a gas is inversely proportional to its pressure for a fixed amount of gas at a constant temperature. That is, P times V is constant when the amount of gas n and the temperature T are kept constant. (The symbol $\propto$ means "is proportional to," and k denotes a constant value.)

$$\text{Volume } (V) \propto \frac{1}{\text{Pressure } (P)}$$

$$\text{or} \quad PV = k \quad (\text{A constant value})$$

Because $P \times V$ is a constant value for a fixed amount of gas at a constant temperature, the starting pressure (P_1) times the starting volume (V_1) must equal the final pressure (P_2) times the final volume (V_2). Thus, Boyle's law can be used to find the final pressure or volume when the starting pressure or volume is changed.

$$\text{Since} \quad P_1 V_1 = k \quad \text{and} \quad P_2 V_2 = k$$

$$\text{then} \quad P_1 V_1 = P_2 V_2$$

$$\text{so} \quad P_2 = \frac{P_1 V_1}{V_2} \quad \text{and} \quad V_2 = \frac{P_1 V_1}{P_2}$$

As an example of Boyle's law behavior, think about what happens every time you breathe. Between breaths, the pressure inside your lungs is equal to atmospheric pressure. When inhalation takes place, your diaphragm lowers and the rib cage expands, increasing the volume of the lungs and thereby decreasing the pressure inside them (Figure 8.13). Air

▶ **Figure 8.13**
Boyle's law in breathing.
During inhalation, the diaphragm moves down and the rib cage moves up and out, thus increasing lung volume, decreasing pressure, and drawing in air. During exhalation, the diaphragm moves back up, lung volume decreases, pressure increases, and air moves out.

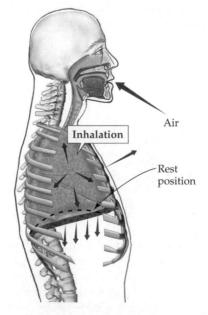

Lung volume increases, causing pressure in lungs to *decrease*. Air flows *in*.

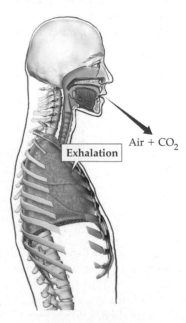

Lung volume decreases, causing pressure in lungs to *increase*. Air flows *out*.

must then move into the lungs to equalize their pressure with that of the atmosphere. When exhalation takes place, the diaphragm rises and the rib cage contracts, decreasing the volume of the lungs and increasing pressure inside them. Now gases move out of the lungs until pressure is again equalized with the atmosphere.

Worked Example 8.5 Using Boyle's Law: Finding Volume at a Given Pressure

In a typical automobile engine, the fuel/air mixture in a cylinder is compressed from 1.0 atm to 9.5 atm. If the uncompressed volume of the cylinder is 750 mL, what is the volume when fully compressed?

ANALYSIS This is a Boyle's law problem because the volume and pressure in the cylinder change but the amount of gas and the temperature remain constant. According to Boyle's law, the pressure of the gas times its volume is constant:

$$P_1V_1 = P_2V_2$$

Knowing three of the four variables in this equation, we can solve for the unknown.

◄ **A cut-away diagram of an internal combustion engine shows movement of pistons during expansion and compression cycles.**

BALLPARK ESTIMATE Since the pressure *increases* approximately 10-fold (from 1.0 atm to 9.5 atm), the volume must *decrease* to approximately 1/10, from 750 mL to about 75 mL.

SOLUTION

STEP 1: Identify known information. Of the four variables in Boyle's law, we know P_1, V_1, and P_2.

STEP 2: Identify answer and units.

STEP 3: Identify equation. In this case, we simply substitute the known variables into Boyle's law and rearrange to isolate the unknown.

STEP 4: Solve. Substitute the known information into the equation. Make sure units cancel so that the answer is given in the units of the unknown variable.

$P_1 = 1.0$ atm
$V_1 = 750$ mL
$P_2 = 9.5$ atm

$V_2 = ??$ mL

$$P_1V_1 = P_2V_2 \implies V_2 = \frac{P_1V_1}{P_2}$$

$$V_2 = \frac{P_1V_1}{P_2} = \frac{(1.0 \text{ atm})(750 \text{ mL})}{(9.5 \text{ atm})} = 79 \text{ mL}$$

BALLPARK CHECK Our estimate was 75 mL.

PROBLEM 8.8
An oxygen cylinder used for breathing has a volume of 5.0 L at 90 atm pressure. What is the volume of the same amount of oxygen at the same temperature if the pressure is 1.0 atm? (Hint: Would you expect the volume of gas at this pressure to be greater than or less than the volume at 90 atm?)

PROBLEM 8.9
A sample of hydrogen gas at 273 K has a volume of 3.2 L at 4.0 atm pressure. What is the volume if the pressure is increased to 10.0 atm? If the pressure is decreased to 0.70 atm?

PROBLEM 8.10
A typical blood pressure measured using a sphygmomanometer is reported as 112/75 (see Chemistry in Action: Blood Pressure on p. 228). How would this pressure be recorded if the sphygmomanometer used units of psi instead of mmHg?

CHEMISTRY IN ACTION

Blood Pressure

Having your blood pressure measured is a quick and easy way to get an indication of the state of your circulatory system. Although blood pressure varies with age, a normal adult male has a reading near 120/80 mmHg, and a normal adult female has a reading near 110/70 mmHg. Abnormally high values signal an increased risk of heart attack and stroke.

Pressure varies greatly in different types of blood vessels. Usually, though, measurements are carried out on arteries in the upper arm as the heart goes through a full cardiac cycle. *Systolic pressure* is the maximum pressure developed in the artery just after contraction, as the heart forces the maximum amount of blood into the artery. *Diastolic pressure* is the minimum pressure that occurs at the end of the heart cycle.

Blood pressure is most often measured by a *sphygmomanometer*, a device consisting of a squeeze bulb, a flexible cuff, and a mercury manometer. (1) The cuff is placed around the upper arm over the brachial artery and inflated by the squeeze bulb to about 200 mmHg pressure, an amount great enough to squeeze the artery shut and prevent blood flow. Air is then slowly released from the cuff, and pressure drops (2). As cuff pressure reaches the systolic pressure, blood spurts through the artery, creating a turbulent tapping sound that can be heard through a stethoscope. The pressure registered on the manometer at the moment the first sounds are heard is the systolic blood pressure.

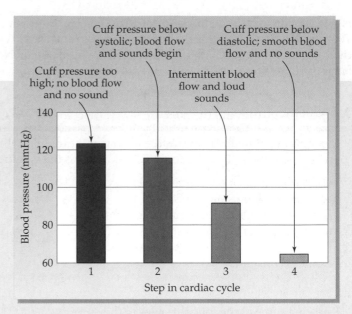

▲ The sequence of events during blood pressure measurement, including the sounds heard.

(3) Sounds continue until the pressure in the cuff becomes low enough to allow diastolic blood flow. (4) At this point, blood flow becomes smooth, no sounds are heard, and a diastolic blood pressure reading is recorded on the manometer. Readings are usually recorded as systolic/diastolic, for example, 120/80. The accompanying figure shows the sequence of events during measurement.

See Chemistry in Action Problems 8.102 and 103 at the end of the chapter.

8.6 Charles's Law: The Relation between Volume and Temperature

Imagine that you again have a sample of gas inside a cylinder with a plunger at one end. What happens if you double the sample's kelvin temperature while letting the plunger move freely to keep the pressure constant? The gas particles move with twice as much energy and collide twice as forcefully with the walls. To maintain a constant pressure, the volume of the gas in the cylinder must double (Figure 8.14).

▲ The volume of the gas in the balloon increases as it is heated, causing a decrease in density and allowing the balloon to rise.

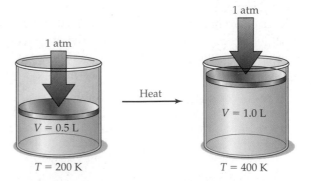

▲ **Figure 8.14**
Charles's law.
The volume of a gas is directly proportional to its kelvin temperature at constant n and P. If the kelvin temperature of the gas is doubled, its volume doubles.

According to **Charles's law**, the volume of a fixed amount of gas at constant pressure is directly proportional to its kelvin temperature. Note the difference between *directly* proportional in Charles's law and *inversely* proportional in Boyle's law. Directly proportional quantities change in the same direction: as temperature goes up or down, volume also goes up or down (Figure 8.15).

Charles's law The volume of a gas is directly proportional to its kelvin temperature for a fixed amount of gas at a constant pressure. That is, V divided by T is constant when n and P are held constant.

$$V \propto T \quad \text{(In kelvins)}$$

$$\text{or } \frac{V}{T} = k \quad \text{(A constant value)}$$

$$\text{or } \frac{V_1}{T_1} = \frac{V_2}{T_2}$$

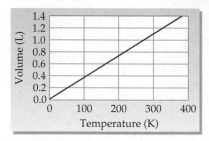

▲ **Figure 8.15**
Charles's law.
Volume is directly proportional to the kelvin temperature for a fixed amount of gas at a constant pressure. As the temperature goes up, the volume also goes up.

This observation is consistent with the kinetic–molecular theory. As temperature increases, the average kinetic energy of the gas molecules increases, as does the energy of molecular collisions with the interior surface of the container. The volume of the container must increase to maintain a constant pressure. As an example of Charles's law, think about what happens when a hot-air balloon is inflated. Heating causes the air inside to expand and fill the balloon. The air inside the balloon is less dense than the air outside the balloon, creating the buoyancy effect.

Worked Example 8.6 Using Charles's Law: Finding Volume at a Given Temperature

An average adult inhales a volume of 0.50 L of air with each breath. If the air is warmed from room temperature ($20\,°C = 293\,K$) to body temperature ($37\,°C = 310\,K$) while in the lungs, what is the volume of the air exhaled?

ANALYSIS This is a Charles's law problem because the volume and temperature of the air change while the amount and pressure remain constant. Knowing three of the four variables, we can rearrange Charles's law to solve for the unknown.

BALLPARK ESTIMATE Charles's law predicts an increase in volume directly proportional to the increase in temperature from 273 K to 310 K. The increase of less than 20 K represents a relatively small change compared to the initial temperature of 273 K. A 10% increase, for example, would be equal to a temperature change of 27 K; so a 20-K change would be less than 10%. We would therefore expect the volume to increase by less than 10%, from 0.50 L to a little less than 0.55 L.

SOLUTION

STEP 1: Identify known information. Of the four variables in Charles's law, we know T_1, V_1, and T_2.	$T_1 = 293\,K$ $V_1 = 0.50\,L$ $T_2 = 310\,K$
STEP 2: Identify answer and units.	$V_2 = ??\,L$
STEP 3: Identify equation. Substitute the known variables into Charles's law and rearrange to isolate the unknown.	$\dfrac{V_1}{T_1} = \dfrac{V_2}{T_2} \implies V_2 = \dfrac{V_1 T_2}{T_1}$
STEP 4: Solve. Substitute the known information into Charles's law; check to make sure units cancel.	$V_2 = \dfrac{V_1 T_2}{T_1} = \dfrac{(0.50\,L)(310\,K)}{293\,K} = 0.53\,L$

BALLPARK CHECK This is consistent with our estimate!

PROBLEM 8.11
A sample of chlorine gas has a volume of 0.30 L at 273 K and 1 atm pressure. What temperature (in °C) would be required to increase the volume to 1.0 L? To decrease the volume to 0.20 L?

8.7 Gay-Lussac's Law: The Relation between Pressure and Temperature

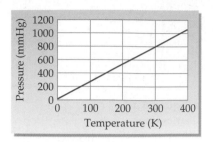

▲ **Figure 8.16**
Gay-Lussac's law.
Pressure is directly proportional to
the temperature in kelvins for a fixed
amount of gas at a constant volume. As
the temperature goes up, the pressure
also goes up.

Imagine next that you have a fixed amount of gas in a sealed container whose volume remains constant. What happens if you double the temperature (in kelvins)? The gas particles move with twice as much energy and collide with the walls of the container with twice as much force. Thus, the pressure in the container doubles. According to **Gay-Lussac's law**, the pressure of a fixed amount of gas at constant volume is directly proportional to its Kelvin temperature. As temperature goes up or down, pressure also goes up or down (Figure 8.16).

Gay-Lussac's law The pressure of a gas is directly proportional to its Kelvin temperature for a fixed amount of gas at a constant volume. That is, P divided by T is constant when n and V are held constant.

$$P \propto T \quad \text{(In kelvins)}$$

$$\text{or} \frac{P}{T} = k \quad \text{(A constant value)}$$

$$\text{or} \frac{P_1}{T_1} = \frac{P_2}{T_2}$$

According to the kinetic–molecular theory, the kinetic energy of molecules is directly proportional to absolute temperature. As the average kinetic energy of the molecules increases, the energy of collisions with the interior surface of the container increases, causing an increase in pressure. As an example of Gay-Lussac's law, think of what happens when an aerosol can is thrown into an incinerator. As the can gets hotter, pressure builds up inside and the can explodes (hence the warning statement on aerosol cans).

Worked Example 8.7 Using Gay-Lussac's Law: Finding Pressure at a Given Temperature

What does the inside pressure become if an aerosol can with an initial pressure of 4.5 atm is heated in a fire from room temperature (20 °C) to 600 °C?

ANALYSIS This is a Gay-Lussac's law problem because the pressure and temperature of the gas inside the can change while its amount and volume remain constant. We know three of the four variables in the equation for Gay-Lussac's law, and can find the unknown by substitution and rearrangement.

BALLPARK ESTIMATE Gay-Lussac's law states that pressure is directly proportional to temperature. Since the Kelvin temperature increases approximately threefold (from about 300 K to about 900 K), we expect the pressure to also increase by approximately threefold, from 4.5 atm to about 14 atm.

SOLUTION

STEP 1: Identify known information. Of the four variables in Gay-Lussac's law, we know P_1, T_1 and T_2. (Note that T must be in kelvins.)

$P_1 = 4.5 \text{ atm}$
$T_1 = 20 \,°C = 293 \text{ K}$
$T_2 = 600 \,°C = 873 \text{ K}$

STEP 2: Identify answer and units.

$P_2 = \text{?? atm}$

STEP 3: Identify equation. Substituting the known variables into Gay-Lussac's law, we rearrange to isolate the unknown.

$$\frac{P_1}{T_1} = \frac{P_2}{T_2} \implies P_2 = \frac{P_1 T_2}{T_1}$$

STEP 4: Solve. Substitute the known information into Gay-Lussac's law; check to make sure units cancel.

$$P_2 = \frac{P_1 T_2}{T_1} = \frac{(4.5 \text{ atm})(873 \text{ K})}{293 \text{ K}} = 13 \text{ atm}$$

BALLPARK CHECK Our estimate was 14 atm.

PROBLEM 8.12
Driving on a hot day causes tire temperature to rise. What is the pressure inside an automobile tire at 45 °C if the tire has a pressure of 30 psi at 15 °C? Assume that the volume and amount of air in the tire remain constant.

8.8 The Combined Gas Law

Since PV, V/T, and P/T all have constant values for a fixed amount of gas, these relationships can be merged into a **combined gas law**, which holds true whenever the amount of gas is fixed.

Combined gas law $\dfrac{PV}{T} = k$ (A constant value)

or $\dfrac{P_1V_1}{T_1} = \dfrac{P_2V_2}{T_2}$

If any five of the six quantities in this equation are known, the sixth quantity can be calculated. Furthermore, if any of the three variables T, P, or V is constant, that variable drops out of the equation, leaving behind Boyle's law, Charles's law, or Gay-Lussac's law. As a result, *the combined gas law is the only equation you need to remember for a fixed amount of gas*. Worked Example 8.8 gives a sample calculation.

Since $\dfrac{P_1V_1}{T_1} = \dfrac{P_2V_2}{T_2}$

At constant T: $\dfrac{P_1V_1}{T} = \dfrac{P_2V_2}{T}$ gives $P_1V_1 = P_2V_2$ (Boyle's law)

At constant P: $\dfrac{PV_1}{T_1} = \dfrac{PV_2}{T_2}$ gives $\dfrac{V_1}{T_1} = \dfrac{V_2}{T_2}$ (Charles's law)

At constant V: $\dfrac{P_1V}{T_1} = \dfrac{P_2V}{T_2}$ gives $\dfrac{P_1}{T_1} = \dfrac{P_2}{T_2}$ (Gay-Lussac's law)

Worked Example 8.8 Using the Combined Gas Law: Finding Temperature

A 6.3 L sample of helium gas stored at 25 °C and 1.0 atm pressure is transferred to a 2.0 L tank and maintained at a pressure of 2.8 atm. What temperature is needed to maintain this pressure?

ANALYSIS This is a combined gas law problem because pressure, volume, and temperature change while the amount of helium remains constant. Of the six variables in this equation, we know P_1, V_1, T_1, P_2, and V_2, and we need to find T_2.

BALLPARK ESTIMATE Since the volume goes down by a little more than a factor of about 3 (from 6.3 L to 2.0 L) and the pressure goes up by a little less than a factor of about 3 (from 1.0 atm to 2.8 atm), the two changes roughly offset each other, and so the temperature should not change much. Since the volume-decrease factor (3.2) is slightly greater than the pressure-increase factor (2.8), the temperature will drop slightly ($T \propto V$).

SOLUTION

STEP 1: Identify known information. Of the six variables in combined gas law we know P_1, V_1, T_1, P_2, and V_2. (As always, T must be converted from Celsius degrees to kelvins.)

$P_1 = 1.0$ atm, $P_2 = 2.8$ atm
$V_1 = 6.3$ L, $V_2 = 2.0$ L
$T_1 = 25\,°C = 298$ K

STEP 2: Identify answer and units.

$T_2 = $?? kelvin

STEP 3: Identify the equation. Substitute the known variables into the equation for the combined gas law and rearrange to isolate the unknown.

$$\frac{P_1V_1}{T_1} = \frac{P_2V_2}{T_2} \Rightarrow T_2 = \frac{P_2V_2T_1}{P_1V_1}$$

STEP 4: Solve. Solve the combined gas law equation for T_2; check to make sure units cancel.

$$T_2 = \frac{P_2V_2T_1}{P_1V_1} = \frac{(2.8\ \text{atm})(2.0\ \text{L})(298\ \text{K})}{(1.0\ \text{atm})(6.3\ \text{L})} = 260\ \text{K}(\Delta T = 2.38\,°C)$$

BALLPARK CHECK The relatively small decrease in temperature (38 °C, or 13% compared to the original temperature) is consistent with our prediction.

PROBLEM 8.13

A weather balloon is filled with helium to a volume of 275 L at 22 °C and 752 mmHg. The balloon ascends to an altitude where the pressure is 480 mmHg, and the temperature is −32 °C. What is the volume of the balloon at this altitude?

🔑 **KEY CONCEPT PROBLEM 8.14**

A balloon is filled under the initial conditions indicated below. If the pressure is then increased to 2 atm while the temperature is increased to 50 °C, which balloon on the right, (a) or (b), represents the new volume of the balloon?

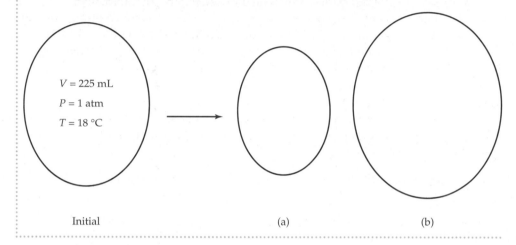

$V = 225$ mL

$P = 1$ atm

$T = 18$ °C

Initial   (a)   (b)

8.9 Avogadro's Law: The Relation between Volume and Molar Amount

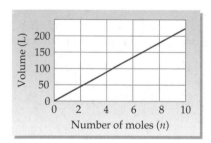

▲ **Figure 8.17**
Avogadro's law.
Volume is directly proportional to the molar amount, n, at a constant temperature and pressure. As the number of moles goes up, the volume also goes up.

Here we look at one final gas law, which takes changes in amount of gas into account. Imagine that you have two different volumes of a gas at the same temperature and pressure. How many moles does each sample contain? According to **Avogadro's law**, the volume of a gas is directly proportional to its molar amount at a constant pressure and temperature (Figure 8.17). A sample that contains twice the molar amount has twice the volume.

Avogadro's law   The volume of a gas is directly proportional to its molar amount at a constant pressure and temperature. That is, V divided by n is constant when P and T are held constant.

Volume $(V) \propto$ Number of moles (n)

or $\dfrac{V}{n} = k$ (A constant value; the same for all gases)

or $\dfrac{V_1}{n_1} = \dfrac{V_2}{n_2}$

Because the particles in a gas are so tiny compared to the empty space surrounding them, there is no interaction among gas particles as proposed by the kinetic–molecular theory. As a result, the chemical identity of the particles does not matter and the value of the constant k in the equation $V/n = k$ is the same for all gases. It is therefore possible to compare the molar amounts of *any* two gases simply by comparing their volumes at the same temperature and pressure.

Notice that the *values* of temperature and pressure do not matter; it is only necessary that T and P be the same for both gases. To simplify comparisons of gas samples, however, it is convenient to define a set of conditions called **standard temperature and pressure (STP)**, which specifies a temperature of 0 °C (273 K) and a pressure of 1 atm (760 mmHg).

At standard temperature and pressure, 1 mol of any gas (6.02×10^{23} particles) has a volume of 22.4 L, a quantity called the **standard molar volume** (Figure 8.18).

Standard temperature and pressure (STP) 0 °C (273.15 K); 1 atm (760 mmHg)

Standard molar volume of any ideal gas at STP 22.4 L/mol

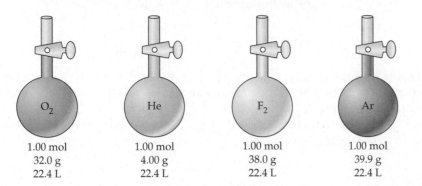

◄ Figure 8.18
Avogadro's law.
Each of these 22.4 L bulbs contains 1.00 mol of gas at 0 °C and 1 atm pressure. Note that the volume occupied by 1 mol of gas is the same even though the mass (in grams) of 1 mol of each gas is different.

O_2	He	F_2	Ar
1.00 mol	1.00 mol	1.00 mol	1.00 mol
32.0 g	4.00 g	38.0 g	39.9 g
22.4 L	22.4 L	22.4 L	22.4 L

Worked Example 8.9 Using Avogadro's Law: Finding Moles in a Given Volume at STP

Use the standard molar volume of a gas at STP (22.4 L) to find how many moles of air at STP are in a room measuring 4.11 m wide by 5.36 m long by 2.58 m high.

ANALYSIS We first find the volume of the room and then use standard molar volume as a conversion factor to find the number of moles.

SOLUTION

STEP 1: **Identify known information.** We are given the room dimensions.

Length = 5.36 m
Width = 4.11 m
Height = 2.58 m

STEP 2: **Identify answer and units.**

Moles of air = ?? mol

STEP 3: **Identify the equation.** The volume of the room is the product of its three dimensions. Once we have the volume (in m³), we can convert to liters and use the molar volume at STP as a conversion factor to obtain moles of air.

Volume $= (4.11 \text{ m})(5.36 \text{ m})(2.58 \text{ m}) = 56.8 \text{ m}^3$

$$= 56.8 \text{ m}^3 \times \frac{1000 \text{ L}}{1 \text{ m}^3} = 5.68 \times 10^4 \text{ L}$$

$$1 \text{ mol} = 22.4 \text{ L} \rightarrow \frac{1 \text{ mol}}{22.4 \text{ L}}$$

STEP 4: **Solve.** Use the room volume and the molar volume at STP to set up an equation, making sure unwanted units cancel.

$$5.68 \times 10^4 \cancel{\text{ L}} \times \frac{1 \text{ mol}}{22.4 \cancel{\text{ L}}} = 2.54 \times 10^3 \text{ mol}$$

PROBLEM 8.15
How many moles of methane gas, CH_4, are in a 1.00×10^5 L storage tank at STP? How many grams of methane is this? How many grams of carbon dioxide gas could the same tank hold?

8.10 The Ideal Gas Law

The relationships among the four variables *P, V, T,* and *n* for gases can be combined into a single expression called the **ideal gas law**. If you know the values of any three of the four quantities, you can calculate the value of the fourth.

Ideal gas law $\dfrac{PV}{nT} = R$ (A constant value)

or $PV = nRT$

Gas constant (R) The constant R in the ideal gas law, $PV = nRT$.

The constant R in the ideal gas law (instead of the usual k) is called the **gas constant**. Its value depends on the units chosen for pressure, with the two most common values being

$$\text{For } P \text{ in atmospheres:} \quad R = 0.0821 \frac{L \cdot atm}{mol \cdot K}$$

$$\text{For } P \text{ in millimeters Hg:} \quad R = 62.4 \frac{L \cdot mmHg}{mol \cdot K}$$

In using the ideal gas law, it is important to choose the value of R having pressure units that are consistent with the problem and, if necessary, to convert volume into liters and temperature into kelvins.

Table 8.3 summarizes the various gas laws, and Worked Examples 8.10 and 8.11 show how to use the ideal gas law.

TABLE 8.3 A Summary of the Gas Laws

	Gas Law	Variables	Constant
Boyle's law	$P_1V_1 = P_2V_2$	P, V	n, T
Charles's law	$V_1/T_1 = V_2/T_2$	V, T	n, P
Gay-Lussac's law	$P_1/T_1 = P_2/T_2$	P, T	n, V
Combined gas law	$P_1V_1/T_1 = P_2V_2/T_2$	P, V, T	n
Avogadro's law	$V_1/n_1 = V_2/n_2$	V, n	P, T
Ideal gas law	$PV = nRT$	P, V, T, n	R

Worked Example 8.10 Using the Ideal Gas Law: Finding Moles

How many moles of air are in the lungs of an average person with a total lung capacity of 3.8 L? Assume that the person is at 1.0 atm pressure and has a normal body temperature of 37 °C.

ANALYSIS This is an ideal gas law problem because it asks for a value of n when P, V, and T are known: $n = PV/RT$. The volume is given in the correct unit of liters, but temperature must be converted to kelvins.

SOLUTION

STEP 1: Identify known information. We know three of the four variables in the ideal gas law.

$P = 1.0 \text{ atm}$
$V = 3.8 \text{ L}$
$T = 37 °C = 310 \text{ K}$

STEP 2: Identify answer and units.

Moles of air, $n = ?? \text{ mol}$

STEP 3: Identify the equation. Knowing three of the four variables in the ideal gas law, we can rearrange and solve for the unknown variable, n. Note: because pressure is given in atm, we use the value of R that is expressed in atm:

$$PV = nRT \quad \Rightarrow \quad n = \frac{PV}{RT}$$

$$R = 0.0821 \frac{L \cdot atm}{mol \cdot K}$$

STEP 4: Solve. Substitute the known information and the appropriate value of R into the ideal gas law equation and solve for n.

$$n = \frac{PV}{RT} = \frac{(1.0 \text{ atm})(3.8 \text{ L})}{\left(0.0821 \dfrac{L \cdot atm}{mol \cdot K}\right)(310 \text{ K})} = 0.15 \text{ mol}$$

Worked Example 8.11 Using the Ideal Gas Law: Finding Pressure

Methane gas is sold in steel cylinders with a volume of 43.8 L containing 5.54 kg. What is the pressure in atmospheres inside the cylinder at a temperature of 20.0 °C (293.15 K)? The molar mass of methane (CH_4) is 16.0 g/mol.

ANALYSIS This is an ideal gas law problem because it asks for a value of P when V, T, and n are given. Although not provided directly, enough information is given so that we can calculate the value of n ($n = $ g/MW).

SOLUTION

STEP 1: Identify known information. We know two of the four variables in the ideal gas law; V, T, and can calculate the third, n, from the information provided.

$V = 43.8$ L
$T = 37\,°C = 310$ K

STEP 2: Identify answer and units.

Pressure, $P = $?? atm

STEP 3: Identify equation. First, calculate the number of moles, n, of methane in the cylinder by using molar mass (16.0 g/mol) as a conversion factor. Then use the ideal gas law to calculate the pressure.

$$n = (5.54 \text{ kg methane})\left(\frac{1000 \text{ g}}{1 \text{ kg}}\right)\left(\frac{1 \text{ mol}}{16.0 \text{ g}}\right) = 346 \text{ mol methane}$$

$$PV = nRT \quad \Rightarrow \quad P = \frac{nRT}{V}$$

STEP 4: Solve. Substitute the known information and the appropriate value of R into the ideal gas law equation and solve for P.

$$P = \frac{nRT}{V} = \frac{(346 \text{ mol})\left(0.0821\dfrac{\text{L}\cdot\text{atm}}{\text{mol}\cdot\text{K}}\right)(293 \text{ K})}{43.8 \text{ L}} = 190 \text{ atm}$$

PROBLEM 8.16

An aerosol spray can of deodorant with a volume of 350 mL contains 3.2 g of propane gas (C_3H_8) as propellant. What is the pressure in the can at 20 °C?

PROBLEM 8.17

A helium gas cylinder of the sort used to fill balloons has a volume of 180 L and a pressure of 2200 psi (150 atm) at 25 °C. How many moles of helium are in the tank? How many grams?

🔑 **KEY CONCEPT PROBLEM 8.18**

Show the approximate level of the movable piston in drawings (a) and (b) after the indicated changes have been made to the initial gas sample (assume a constant pressure of 1 atm).

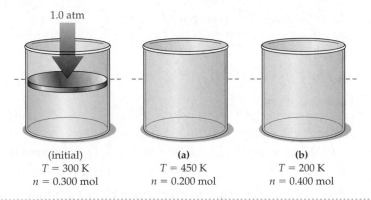

(initial)	(a)	(b)
$T = 300$ K	$T = 450$ K	$T = 200$ K
$n = 0.300$ mol	$n = 0.200$ mol	$n = 0.400$ mol

8.11 Partial Pressure and Dalton's Law

Partial pressure The contribution of a given gas in a mixture to the total pressure.

According to the kinetic–molecular theory, each particle in a gas acts independently of all others because there are no attractive forces between them and they are so far apart. To any individual particle, the chemical identity of its neighbors is irrelevant. Thus, *mixtures* of gases behave the same as pure gases and obey the same laws.

Dry air, for example, is a mixture of about 21% oxygen, 78% nitrogen, and 1% argon by volume, which means that 21% of atmospheric air pressure is caused by O_2 molecules, 78% by N_2 molecules, and 1% by Ar atoms. The contribution of each gas in a mixture to the total pressure of the mixture is called the **partial pressure** of that gas. According to **Dalton's law**, the total pressure exerted by a gas mixture (P_{total}) is the sum of the partial pressures of the components in the mixture:

Dalton's law $P_{total} = P_{gas\ 1} + P_{gas\ 2} + g$

In dry air at a total air pressure of 760 mmHg, the partial pressure caused by the contribution of O_2 is 0.21 × 760 mmHg = 160 mmHg, the partial pressure of N_2 is 0.78 × 760 mmHg = 593 mmHg, and that of argon is 7 mmHg. *The partial pressure exerted by each gas in a mixture is the same pressure that the gas would exert if it were alone.* Put another way, the pressure exerted by each gas depends on the frequency of collisions of its molecules with the walls of the container. However, this frequency does not change when other gases are present, because the different molecules have no influence on one another.

To represent the partial pressure of a specific gas, we add the formula of the gas as a subscript to P, the symbol for pressure. You might see the partial pressure of oxygen represented as P_{O_2}, for instance. Moist air inside the lungs at 37 °C and atmospheric pressure has the following average composition at sea level. Note that P_{total} is equal to atmospheric pressure, 760 mmHg.

$$P_{total} = P_{N_2} \quad + \quad P_{O_2} \quad + \quad P_{CO_2} \quad + \quad P_{H_2O}$$
$$= 573\ mmHg + 100\ mmHg + 40\ mmHg + 47\ mmHg$$
$$= 760\ mmHg$$

The composition of air does not change appreciably with altitude, but the total pressure decreases rapidly. The partial pressure of oxygen in air therefore decreases with increasing altitude, and it is this change that leads to difficulty in breathing at high elevations.

Worked Example 8.12 Using Dalton's Law: Finding Partial Pressures

Humid air on a warm summer day is approximately 20% oxygen, 75% nitrogen, 4% water vapor, and 1% argon. What is the partial pressure of each component if the atmospheric pressure is 750 mmHg?

ANALYSIS According to Dalton's law, the partial pressure of any gas in a mixture is equal to the percent concentration of the gas times the total gas pressure (750 mmHg). In this case,

$$P_{total} = P_{O_2} + P_{N_2} + P_{H_2O} + P_{Ar}$$

SOLUTION
Oxygen partial pressure (P_{O_2}):   0.20 × 750 mmHg = 150 mmHg
Nitrogen partial pressure (P_{N_2}):   0.75 × 750 mmHg = 560 mmHg
Water vapor partial pressure (P_{H_2O}): 0.04 × 750 mmHg = 30 mmHg
Argon partial pressure (P_{Ar}):   0.01 × 750 mmHg = 8 mmHg

Total pressure = 748 mmHg → 750 mmHg (rounding to 2 significant figures!)

Note that the sum of the partial pressures must equal the total pressure (within rounding error).

PROBLEM 8.19

Assuming a total pressure of 9.5 atm, what is the partial pressure of each component in the mixture of 98% helium and 2.0% oxygen breathed by deep-sea divers? How does the partial pressure of oxygen in diving gas compare with its partial pressure in normal air?

PROBLEM 8.20

Determine the percent composition of air in the lungs from the following composition in partial pressures: $P_{N_2} = 573$ mmHg, $P_{O_2} = 100$ mmHg, $P_{CO_2} = 40$ mmHg, $P_{H_2O} = 47$ mmHg; all at 37 °C and 1 atm pressure.

PROBLEM 8.21

The atmospheric pressure on the top of Mt. Everest, an altitude of 29,035 ft, is only 265 mmHg. What is the partial pressure of oxygen in the lungs at this altitude (assuming that the % O_2 is the same as in dry air)?

🔑 **KEY CONCEPT PROBLEM 8.22**

Assume that you have a mixture of He (MW = 4 amu) and Xe (MW = 131 amu) at 300 K. The total pressure of the mixture is 750 mmHg. What are the partial pressures of each of the gases? (blue = He; green = Xe)?

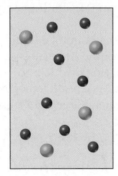

8.12 Liquids

Molecules are in constant motion in the liquid state, just as they are in gases. If a molecule happens to be near the surface of a liquid, and if it has enough energy, it can break free of the liquid and escape into the gas state, called **vapor**. In an open container, the now gaseous molecule will wander away from the liquid, and the process will continue until all the molecules escape from the container (Figure 8.19a). This, of course, is what happens during *evaporation*. We are all familiar with puddles of water evaporating after a rainstorm.

    If the liquid is in a closed container, the situation is different because the gaseous molecules cannot escape. Thus, the random motion of the molecules occasionally brings them back into the liquid. After the concentration of molecules in the gas state has increased sufficiently, the number of molecules reentering the liquid becomes equal to the number escaping from the liquid (Figure 8.19b). At this point, a dynamic equilibrium exists, exactly as in a chemical reaction at equilibrium. Evaporation and condensation take place at the same rate, and the concentration of vapor in the container is constant as long as the temperature does not change.

    Once molecules have escaped from the liquid into the gas state, they are subject to all the gas laws previously discussed. In a closed container at equilibrium, for example, the vapor molecules will make their own contribution to the total pressure of gases above the liquid according to Dalton's Law (Section 8.11). We call this contribution the **vapor pressure** of the liquid.

Vapor The gas molecules are in equilibrium with a liquid.

Vapor pressure The partial pressure of vapor molecules in equilibrium with a liquid.

▶ **Figure 8.19**
The transfer of molecules between liquid and gas states.
(a) Molecules escape from an open container and drift away until the liquid has entirely evaporated.
(b) Molecules in a closed container cannot escape. Instead, they reach an equilibrium in which the rates of molecules leaving the liquid and returning to the liquid are equal, and the concentration of molecules in the gas state is constant.

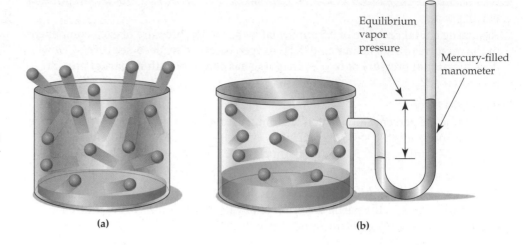

(a)　　　　(b)

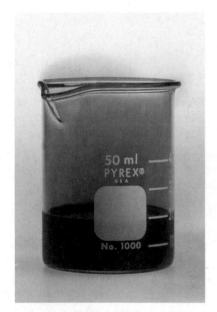

▲ **Because bromine is colored, it is possible to see its gaseous reddish vapor above the liquid.**

Normal boiling point The boiling point at a pressure of exactly 1 atmosphere.

Vapor pressure depends on both temperature and the chemical identity of a liquid. As the temperature rises, molecules become more energetic and more likely to escape into the gas state. Thus, vapor pressure rises with increasing temperature until ultimately it becomes equal to the pressure of the atmosphere. At this point, bubbles of vapor form under the surface and force their way to the top, giving rise to the violent action observed during a vigorous boil. At an atmospheric pressure of exactly 760 mmHg, boiling occurs at what is called the **normal boiling point**.

The vapor pressure and boiling point of a liquid will also depend on the intermolecular forces at work between liquid molecules. Ether molecules, for example, can engage in dipole–dipole interactions, which are weaker than the hydrogen bonds formed between water molecules. As a result, ether exhibits both lower vapor pressures and a lower boiling point than water, as seen in Figure 8.20.

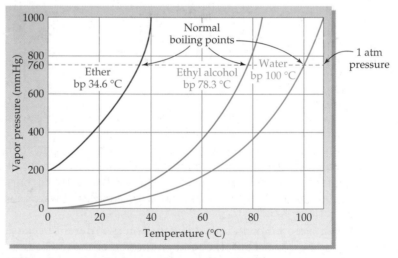

▲ **Figure 8.20**
A plot of the change of vapor pressure with temperature for ethyl ether, ethyl alcohol, and water. At a liquid's boiling point, its vapor pressure is equal to atmospheric pressure. Commonly reported boiling points are those at 760 mmHg.

If atmospheric pressure is higher or lower than normal, the boiling point of a liquid changes accordingly. At high altitudes, for example, atmospheric pressure is lower than at sea level, and boiling points are also lower. On top of Mt. Everest (29,035 ft; 8850 m), atmospheric pressure is about 245 mmHg and the boiling temperature of water is only 71 °C. If the atmospheric pressure is higher than normal, the boiling point is also higher. This principle is used in strong vessels known as *autoclaves*, in which water at high pressure is heated to the temperatures needed for sterilizing medical and dental instruments (170 °C).

Many familiar properties of liquids can be explained by the intermolecular forces just discussed. We all know, for instance, that some liquids, such as water or gasoline, flow easily when poured, whereas others, such as motor oil or maple syrup, flow sluggishly.

The measure of a liquid's resistance to flow is called its *viscosity*. Not surprisingly, viscosity is related to the ease with which individual molecules move around in the liquid and thus to the intermolecular forces present. Substances such as gasoline, which have small, nonpolar molecules, experience only weak intermolecular forces and have relatively low viscosities, whereas more polar substances such as glycerin $[C_3H_5(OH)_3]$ experience stronger intermolecular forces and so have higher viscosities.

Another familiar property of liquids is *surface tension*, the resistance of a liquid to spreading out and increasing its surface area. The beading-up of water on a newly waxed car and the ability of a water strider to walk on water are both due to surface tension.

Surface tension is caused by the difference between the intermolecular forces experienced by molecules at the surface of the liquid and those experienced by molecules in the interior. Molecules in the interior of a liquid are surrounded and experience maximum intermolecular forces, whereas molecules at the surface have fewer neighbors and feel weaker forces. Surface molecules are therefore less stable, and the liquid acts to minimize their number by minimizing the surface area (Figure 8.21).

▲ Surface tension allows a water strider to walk on water without penetrating the surface.

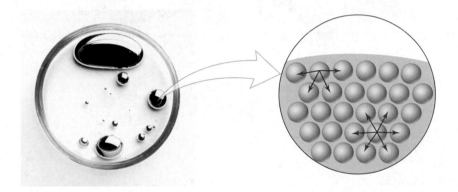

◄ **Figure 8.21**
Surface tension.
Surface tension is caused by the different forces experienced by molecules in the interior of a liquid and those on the surface. Molecules on the surface are less stable because they feel fewer attractive forces, so the liquid acts to minimize their number by minimizing surface area.

▶▶ Recall from Section 1.13 that specific heat is the amount of heat required to raise the temperature of 1g of a substance by 1 °C.

8.13 Water: A Unique Liquid

Ours is a world based on water. Water covers nearly 71% of the earth's surface, it accounts for 66% of the mass of an adult human body, and it is needed by all living things. The water in our blood forms the transport system that circulates substances throughout our body, and water is the medium in which all biochemical reactions are carried out. Largely because of its strong hydrogen bonding, water has many properties that are quite different from those of other compounds.

Water has the highest specific heat of any liquid, giving it the capacity to absorb a large quantity of heat while changing only slightly in temperature. As a result, large lakes and other bodies of water tend to moderate the air temperature and climate of surrounding areas. Another consequence of the high specific heat of water is that the human body is better able to maintain a steady internal temperature under changing outside conditions.

In addition to a high specific heat, water has an unusually high *heat of vaporization* (540 cal/g or 2.3 k J/g), meaning that it carries away a large amount of heat when it evaporates. You can feel the effect of water evaporation on your wet skin when the wind blows. Even when comfortable, your body is still relying for cooling on the heat carried away from the skin and lungs by evaporating water. The heat generated by the

▲ The moderate year-round temperatures in San Francisco are due to the large heat capacity of the surrounding waters.

chemical reactions of metabolism is carried by blood to the skin, where water moves through cell walls to the surface and evaporates. When metabolism, and therefore heat generation, speeds up, blood flow increases and capillaries dilate so that heat is brought to the surface faster.

Water is also unique in what happens as it changes from a liquid to a solid. Most substances are more dense as solids than as liquids because molecules are more closely packed in the solid than in the liquid. Water, however, is different. Liquid water has a maximum density of 1.000 g/mL at 3.98 °C but then becomes *less* dense as it cools. When it freezes, its density decreases still further to 0.917 g/mL.

As water freezes, each molecule is locked into position by hydrogen bonding to four other water molecules (Figure 8.22). The resulting structure has more open space than does liquid water, accounting for its lower density. As a result, ice floats on liquid water, and lakes and rivers freeze from the top down. If the reverse were true, fish would be killed in winter as they became trapped in ice at the bottom.

▶ **Figure 8.22**
Ice.
Ice consists of individual H_2O molecules held rigidly together in an ordered manner by hydrogen bonds. The open, cage-like crystal structure shows why ice is less dense than liquid water.

8.14 Solids

A brief look around us reveals that most substances are solids rather than liquids or gases. It is also obvious that there are many different kinds of solids. Some, such as iron and aluminum, are hard and metallic; others, such as sugar and table salt, are crystalline and easily broken; and still others, such as rubber and many plastics, are soft and amorphous.

▲ Crystalline solids, such as pyrite (left) and fluorite (right) have flat faces and distinct angles. The octahedral shape of pyrite and the cubic shape of fluorite reflect similarly ordered arrangements of particles at the atomic level.

The most fundamental distinction between solids is that some are crystalline and some are amorphous. A **crystalline solid** is one whose particles—whether atoms, ions, or molecules—have an ordered arrangement extending over a long range. This order on the atomic level is also seen on the visible level, because crystalline solids usually have flat faces and distinct angles.

Crystalline solids can be further categorized as ionic, molecular, covalent network, or metallic. *Ionic solids* are those like sodium chloride, whose constituent particles are ions. A crystal of sodium chloride is composed of alternating Na^+ and Cl^- ions ordered in a regular three-dimensional arrangement and held together by ionic bonds (see Figure 3.3). *Molecular solids* are those like sucrose or ice, whose constituent particles are molecules held together by the intermolecular forces discussed in Section 8.2. *Covalent network solids* are those like diamond (Figure 8.23) or quartz (SiO_2), whose atoms are linked together by covalent bonds into a giant three-dimensional array. In effect, a covalent network solid is one *very* large molecule.

Crystalline solid A solid whose atoms, molecules, or ions are rigidly held in an ordered arrangement.

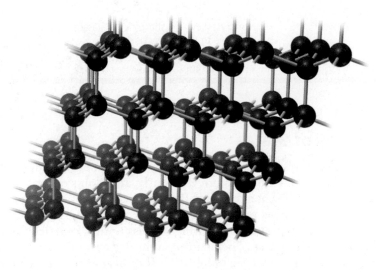

▲ **Figure 8.23**
Diamond. Diamond is a covalent network solid—one very large molecule of carbon atoms linked by covalent bonds.

Metallic solids, such as silver or iron, can be viewed as vast three-dimensional arrays of metal cations immersed in a sea of electrons that are free to move about. This continuous electron sea acts both as a glue to hold the cations together and as a mobile carrier of charge to conduct electricity. Furthermore, the fact that bonding attractions extend uniformly in all directions explains why metals are malleable rather than brittle. When a metal crystal receives a sharp blow, no spatially oriented bonds are broken; instead, the electron sea simply adjusts to the new distribution of cations.

An **amorphous solid**, by contrast with a crystalline solid, is one whose constituent particles are randomly arranged and have no ordered long-range structure. Amorphous solids often result when liquids cool before they can achieve internal order, or when their molecules are large and tangled together, as happens in many polymers. Glass is an amorphous solid, as are tar, the gemstone opal, and some hard candies. Amorphous solids differ from crystalline solids by softening over a wide temperature range rather than having sharp melting points and by shattering to give pieces with curved rather than planar faces.

Amorphous solid A solid whose particles do not have an orderly arrangement.

A summary of the different types of solids and their characteristics is given in Table 8.4.

TABLE 8.4 Types of Solids

Substance	Smallest Unit	Interparticle Forces	Properties	Examples
Ionic solid	Ions	Attraction between positive and negative ions	Brittle and hard; high mp; crystalline	NaCl, KI, $Ca_3(PO_4)_2$
Molecular solid	Molecules	Intermolecular forces	Soft; low to moderate mp; crystalline	Ice, wax, frozen CO_2, all solid organic compounds
Covalent network	Atoms	Covalent bonds	Very hard; very high mp; crystalline	Diamond, quartz (SiO_2), tungsten carbide (WC)
Metal or alloy	Metal atoms	Metallic bonding (attraction between metal ions and surrounding mobile electrons)	Lustrous; soft (Na) to hard (Ti); high melting; crystalline	Elements (Fe, Cu, Sn, . . .), bronze (CuSn alloy), amalgams (Hg+ other metals)
Amorphous solid	Atoms, ions, or molecules (including polymer molecules)	Any of the above	Noncrystalline; no sharp mp; able to flow (may be very slow); curved edges when shattered	Glasses, tar, some plastics

8.15 Changes of State

What happens when a solid is heated? As more and more energy is added, molecules begin to stretch, bend, and vibrate more vigorously, and atoms or ions wiggle about with more energy. Finally, if enough energy is added and the motions become vigorous enough, particles start to break free from one another and the substance starts to melt. Addition of more heat continues the melting process until all particles have broken free and are in the liquid phase. The quantity of heat required to completely melt a substance once it reaches its melting point is called its **heat of fusion**. After melting is complete, further addition of heat causes the temperature of the liquid to rise.

The change of a liquid into a vapor proceeds in the same way as the change of a solid into a liquid. When you first put a pan of water on the stove, all the added heat goes into raising the temperature of the water. Once the boiling point is reached, further absorbed heat goes into freeing molecules from their neighbors as they escape into the gas state. The quantity of heat needed to completely vaporize a liquid once it reaches its boiling point is called its **heat of vaporization**. A liquid with a low heat of vaporization, like rubbing alcohol (isopropyl alcohol), evaporates rapidly and is said to be *volatile*. If you spill a volatile liquid on your skin, you will feel a cooling effect as it evaporates because it is absorbing heat from your body.

It is important to know the difference between heat that is added or removed to change the *temperature* of a substance and heat that is added or removed to change the *phase* of a substance. Remember that temperature is a measure of the kinetic energy in a substance (see Section 7.1). When a substance is above or below its phase-change temperature (i.e., melting point or boiling point), adding or removing heat will simply change the kinetic energy and, hence, the temperature of the substance. The amount of heat needed to produce a given temperature change was presented previously (Section 1.13), but is worth presenting again here:

$$\text{Heat (cal or J)} = \text{Mass (g)} \times \text{Temperature change (°C)} \times \text{Specific heat} \left(\frac{\text{cal or J}}{\text{g} \times \text{°C}} \right)$$

In contrast, when a substance is at its phase-change temperature, heat that is added is being used to overcome the intermolecular forces holding particles in that phase. The temperature remains constant until *all* particles have been converted to the next phase. The energy needed to complete the phase change depends only on the amount

Heat of fusion The quantity of heat required to completely melt one gram of a substance once it has reached its melting point.

Heat of vaporization The quantity of heat needed to completely vaporize one gram of a liquid once it has reached its boiling point.

of the substance and the heat of fusion (for melting) or the heat of vaporization (for boiling).

$$\text{Heat (cal or J)} = \text{Mass (g)} \times \text{Heat of fusion}\left(\frac{\text{cal or J}}{g}\right)$$

$$\text{Heat (cal or J)} = \text{Mass (g)} \times \text{Heat of vaporization}\left(\frac{\text{cal or J}}{g}\right)$$

If the intermolecular forces are strong then large amounts of heat must be added to overcome these forces, and the heats of fusion and vaporization will be large. A list of heats of fusion and heats of vaporization for some common substances is given in Table 8.5. Butane, for example, has a small heat of vaporization since the predominant intermolecular forces in butane (dispersion) are relatively weak. Water, on the other hand, has a particularly high heat of vaporization because of its unusually strong hydrogen bonding interactions. Thus, water evaporates more slowly than many other liquids, takes a long time to boil away, and absorbs more heat in the process. A so-called *heating curve*, which indicates the temperature and state changes as heat is added, is shown in Figure 8.24.

TABLE 8.5 Melting Points, Boiling Points, Heats of Fusion, and Heats of Vaporization of Some Common Substances

Substance	Melting Point (°C)	Boiling Point (°C)	Heat of Fusion (cal/g; J/g)	Heat of Vaporization (cal/g; J/g)
Ammonia	−77.7	−33.4	84.0; 351	327; 1370
Butane	−138.4	−0.5	19.2; 80.3	92.5; 387
Ether	−116	34.6	23.5; 98.3	85.6; 358
Ethyl alcohol	−117.3	78.5	26.1; 109	200; 837
Isopropyl alcohol	−89.5	82.4	21.4; 89.5	159; 665
Sodium	97.8	883	14.3; 59.8	492; 2060
Water	0.0	100.0	79.7; 333	540; 2260

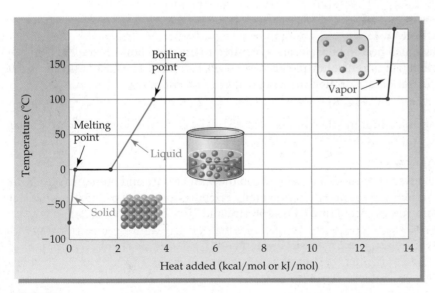

▲ **Figure 8.24**
A heating curve for water, showing the temperature and state changes that occur when heat is added.
The horizontal lines at 0 °C and 100 °C represent the heat of fusion and heat of vaporization, respectively.

Worked Example 8.13 Heat of Fusion: Calculating Total Heat of Melting

Naphthalene, an organic substance often used in mothballs, has a heat of fusion of 35.7 cal/g (149 J/g) and a molar mass of 128.0 g/mol. How much heat in kilocalories is required to melt 0.300 mol of naphthalene?

ANALYSIS The heat of fusion tells how much heat is required to melt 1 g. To find the amount of heat needed to melt 0.300 mol, we need a mole-to-mass conversion.

BALLPARK ESTIMATE Naphthalene has a molar mass of 128.0 g/mol, so 0.300 mol has a mass of about one-third this amount, or about 40 g. Approximately 35 cal or 150 J is required to melt 1 g, so we need about 40 times this amount of heat, or $(35 \times 40 = 1400 \text{ cal} = 1.4 \text{ kcal, or } 150 \times 40 = 6000 \text{ J} = 6.0 \text{ kJ})$.

SOLUTION

STEP 1: Identify known information. We know heat of fusion (cal/g), and the number of moles of naphthalene.

Heat of fusion = 35.7 cal/g, or 149 J/g
Moles of naphthalene = 0.300 mol

STEP 2: Identify answer and units.

Heat = ?? cal or J

STEP 3: Identify conversion factors. First convert moles of naphthalene to grams using the molar mass (128 g/mol) as a conversion factor. Then use the heat of fusion as a conversion factor to calculate the total heat necessary to melt the mass of naphthalene.

$(0.300 \text{ mol naphthalene}) \left(\dfrac{128.0 \text{ g}}{1 \text{ mol}} \right) = 38.4 \text{ g napthalene}$

Heat of fusion = 35.7 cal/g or 149 J/g

STEP 4: Solve. Multiplying the mass of naphthalene by the heat of fusion then gives the answer.

$(38.4 \text{ g naphthalene}) \left(\dfrac{35.7 \text{ cal}}{1 \text{ g naphthalene}} \right) = 1370 \text{ cal} = 1.37 \text{ kcal, or}$

$(38.4 \text{ g naphthalene}) \left(\dfrac{149 \text{ J}}{1 \text{ g naphthalene}} \right) = 5720 \text{ J} = 5.72 \text{ kJ}$

BALLPARK CHECK The calculated result agrees with our estimate (1.4 kcal or 6.0 kJ)

PROBLEM 8.23

How much heat in kilocalories is required to melt and boil 1.50 mol of isopropyl alcohol (rubbing alcohol; molar mass = 60.0 g/mol)? The heat of fusion and heat of vaporization of isopropyl alcohol are given in Table 8.5.

PROBLEM 8.24

How much heat in kilojoules is released by the condensation of 2.5 mol of steam? The heat of vaporization is given in Table 8.5.

PROBLEM 8.25

The physical state of CO_2 depends on the temperature and pressure (see Chemistry in Action: CO_2 as an Environmentally Friendly Solvent on p. 245). In what state would you expect to find CO_2 at 50 atm and 25 °C?

CHEMISTRY IN ACTION

CO₂ as an Environmentally Friendly Solvent

When you think of CO_2 you most likely think of the gas that is absorbed by plants for photosynthesis or exhaled by animals during respiration. You have also probably seen CO_2 in the form of dry ice, that very cold solid that sublimes to a gas. But how can CO_2 be a solvent? After all, carbon dioxide is a gas, not a liquid, at room temperature. Furthermore, CO_2 at atmospheric pressure does not become liquid even when cooled. When the temperature drops to $-78\,°C$ at 1 atm pressure, CO_2 goes directly from gas to solid (dry ice) without first becoming liquid. Only when the pressure is raised does liquid CO_2 exist. At a room temperature of $22.4\,°C$, a pressure of 60 atm is needed to force gaseous CO_2 molecules close enough together so they condense to a liquid. Even as a liquid, though, CO_2 is not a particularly good solvent. Only when it enters an unusual and rarely seen state of matter called the *supercritical state* does CO_2 become a remarkable solvent.

To understand the supercritical state of matter, consider the two factors that determine the physical state of a substance: temperature and pressure. In the solid state, molecules are packed closely together and do not have enough kinetic energy to overcome the intermolecular forces. If we increase the temperature, however, we can increase the kinetic energy so that the molecules can move apart and produce a phase change to either a liquid or a gas. In the gas state, molecules are too far apart to interact, but increasing the pressure will force molecules closer together, and, eventually, intermolecular attractions between molecules will cause them to condense into a liquid or solid state. This dependence of the physical state on temperature and pressure is represented by a *phase diagram*, such as the one shown here for CO_2.

The supercritical state represents a situation that is intermediate between liquid and gas. There is *some* space between molecules, but not much. The molecules are too far apart to be truly a liquid, yet they are too close together to be truly a gas. Supercritical CO_2 exists above the *critical point*, when the pressure is above 72.8 atm and the temperature is above $31.2\,°C$.

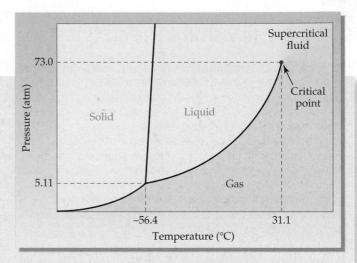

This pressure is high enough to force molecules close together and prevent them from expanding into the gas state. Above this temperature, however, the molecules have too much kinetic energy to condense into the liquid state.

Because open spaces already exist between CO_2 molecules, it is energetically easy for dissolved molecules to slip in, and supercritical CO_2 is therefore an extraordinarily good solvent. Among its many applications, supercritical CO_2 is used in the beverage and food-processing industries to decaffeinate coffee beans and to obtain spice extracts from vanilla, pepper, cloves, nutmeg, and other seeds. In the cosmetics and perfume industry, fragrant oils are extracted from flowers using supercritical CO_2. Perhaps the most important future application is the use of carbon dioxide for dry-cleaning clothes, thereby replacing environmentally harmful chlorinated solvents.

The use of supercritical CO_2 as a solvent has many benefits, including the fact that it is nontoxic and nonflammable. Most important, though, is that the technology is environmentally friendly. Industrial processes using CO_2 are designed as closed systems so that the CO_2 is recaptured after use and continually recycled. No organic solvent vapors are released into the atmosphere and no toxic liquids seep into groundwater supplies, as can occur with current procedures using chlorinated organic solvents. The future looks bright for this new technology.

See Chemistry in Action Problems 8.104 and 8.105 at the end of the chapter.

SUMMARY: REVISITING THE CHAPTER GOALS

1. What are the major intermolecular forces, and how do they affect the states of matter? There are three major types of *intermolecular forces*, which act to hold molecules near one another in solids and liquids. *Dipole–dipole forces* are the electrical attractions that occur between polar molecules. *London dispersion forces* occur between all molecules as a result of temporary molecular polarities due to unsymmetrical electron distribution. These forces increase in strength with molecular weight and with the surface area of molecules. *Hydrogen bonding*, the strongest of the three intermolecular forces, occurs between a hydrogen atom bonded to O, N, or F and a nearby O, N, or F atom (*see Problems 34–37, 116*).

2. How do scientists explain the behavior of gases? According to the *kinetic-molecular theory of gases*, the physical behavior of gases can be explained by assuming that they consist of particles moving rapidly at random, separated from other particles by great distances, and colliding without loss of energy. Gas pressure is the result of molecular collisions with a surface (*see Problems 29, 30, 40, 41, 53, 59, 68, 102, 103, 106*).

3. How do gases respond to changes in temperature, pressure, and volume? *Boyle's law* says that the volume of a fixed amount of gas at constant temperature is inversely proportional to its pressure ($P_1V_1 = P_2V_2$). *Charles's law* says that the volume of a fixed amount of gas at constant pressure is directly proportional to its Kelvin temperature ($V_1/T_1 = V_2/T_2$). *Gay-Lussac's law* says that the pressure of a fixed amount of gas at constant volume is directly proportional to its Kelvin temperature ($P_1/T_1 = P_2/T_2$). Boyle's law, Charles's law, and Gay-Lussac's law together give the *combined gas law* ($P_1V_1/T_1 = P_2V_2/T_2$), which applies to changing conditions for a fixed quantity of gas. *Avogadro's law* says that equal volumes of gases at the same temperature and pressure contain the same number of moles ($V_1/n_1 = V_2/n_2$) (*see Problems 26, 27, 32, 38–75, 107, 111, 112, 115*).

4. What is the ideal gas law? The four gas laws together give the *ideal gas law*, $PV = nRT$, which relates the effects of temperature, pressure, volume, and molar amount. At 0 °C and 1 atm pressure, called *standard temperature and pressure (STP)*, 1 mol of any gas (6.02×10^{23} molecules) occupies a volume of 22.4 L (*see Problems 76–85, 108–110, 113–115, 118, 119*).

5. What is partial pressure? The amount of pressure exerted by an individual gas in a mixture is called the *partial pressure* of the gas. According to *Dalton's law*, the total pressure exerted by the mixture is equal to the sum of the partial pressures of the individual gases (*see Problems 33, 86–89, 117*).

6. What are the various kinds of solids, and how do they differ? Solids are either crystalline or amorphous. *Crystalline solids* are those whose constituent particles have an ordered arrangement; *amorphous solids* lack internal order and do not have sharp melting points. There are several kinds of crystalline solids: *Ionic solids* are those such as sodium chloride, whose constituent particles are ions. *Molecular solids* are those such as ice, whose constituent particles are molecules held together by intermolecular forces. *Covalent network solids* are those such as diamond, whose atoms are linked together by covalent bonds into a giant three-dimensional array. *Metallic solids*, such as silver or iron, also consist of large arrays of atoms, but their crystals have metallic properties such as electrical conductivity (*see Problems 96–99*).

7. What factors affect a change of state? When a solid is heated, particles begin to move around freely at the *melting point*, and the substance becomes liquid. The amount of heat necessary to melt a given amount of solid at its melting point is its *heat of fusion*. As a liquid is heated, molecules escape from the surface of a liquid until an equilibrium is reached between liquid and gas, resulting in a *vapor pressure* of the liquid. At a liquid's *boiling point*, its vapor pressure equals atmospheric pressure, and the entire liquid is converted into gas. The amount of heat necessary to vaporize a given amount of liquid at its boiling point is called its *heat of vaporization* (*see Problems 27, 28, 31, 90–95, 98, 99, 104*).

KEY WORDS

CONCEPT MAP: GASES, LIQUIDS, AND SOLIDS

Concept Map. The physical state of matter (solid, liquid, gas) depends on the strength of the intermolecular forces between molecules compared to the kinetic energy of the molecules. When the kinetic energy (i.e, temperature) is greater than the forces holding molecules in a given state, then a phase change occurs. Thus, the physical properties of matter (melting and boiling points, etc.) depend on the strength of the intermolecular forces between molecules, which depend on chemical structure and molecular shape. These relationships are reflected here in Figure 8.25.

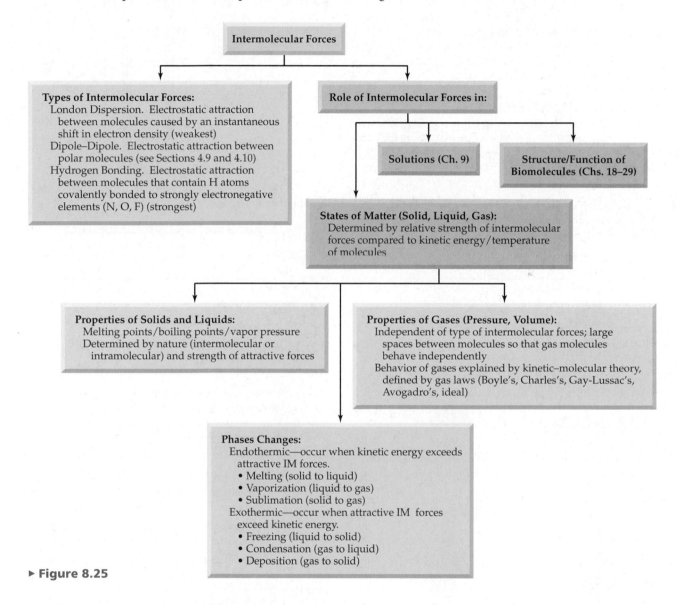

▶ **Figure 8.25**

UNDERSTANDING KEY CONCEPTS

8.26   Assume that you have a sample of gas in a cylinder with a movable piston, as shown in the following drawing:

Redraw the apparatus to show what the sample will look like after the following changes:

(a) The temperature is increased from 300 K to 450 K at constant pressure.

(b) The pressure is increased from 1 atm to 2 atm at constant temperature.

(c) The temperature is decreased from 300 K to 200 K and the pressure is decreased from 3 atm to 2 atm.

8.27   Assume that you have a sample of gas at 350 K in a sealed container, as represented in part (a). Which of the drawings (b)–(d) represents the gas after the temperature is lowered from 350 K to 150 K if the gas has a boiling point of 200 K? Which drawing represents the gas at 150 K if the gas has a boiling point of 100 K?

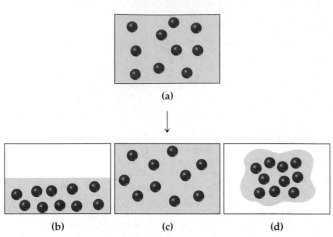

8.28   Assume that drawing (a) represents a sample of H_2O at 200 K. Which of the drawings (b)–(d) represents what the sample will look like when the temperature is raised to 300 K?

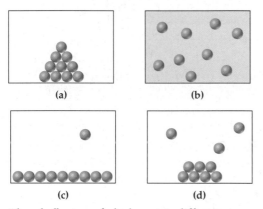

8.29   Three bulbs, two of which contain different gases and one of which is empty, are connected as shown in the following drawing:

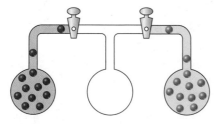

Redraw the apparatus to represent the gases after the stopcocks are opened and the system is allowed to come to equilibrium.

8.30   Redraw the following open-ended manometer to show what it would look like when stopcock A is opened.

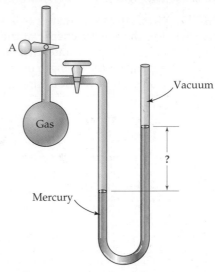

8.31   The following graph represents the heating curve of a hypothetical substance:

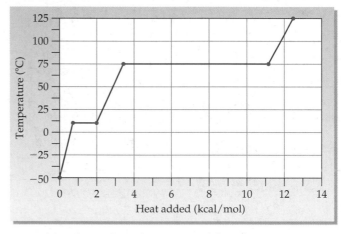

(a) What is the melting point of the substance?

(b) What is the boiling point of the substance?

(c) Approximately what is the heat of fusion for the substance in kcal/mol?

(d) Approximately what is the heat of vaporization for the substance in kcal/mol?

8.32   Show the approximate level of the movable piston in drawings (a)–(c) after the indicated changes have been made to the gas.

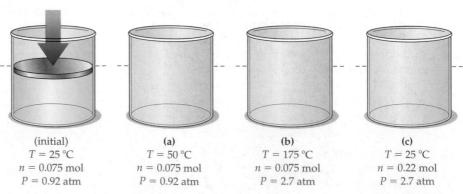

(initial)
$T = 25\,°C$
$n = 0.075$ mol
$P = 0.92$ atm

(a)
$T = 50\,°C$
$n = 0.075$ mol
$P = 0.92$ atm

(b)
$T = 175\,°C$
$n = 0.075$ mol
$P = 2.7$ atm

(c)
$T = 25\,°C$
$n = 0.22$ mol
$P = 2.7$ atm

8.33 The partial pressure of the blue gas in the container represented in the picture is 240 mmHg. What are the partial pressures of the yellow and red gases? What is the total pressure inside the container?

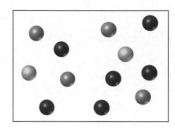

ADDITIONAL PROBLEMS

INTERMOLECULAR FORCES

8.34 What characteristic must a compound have to experience the following intermolecular forces?

(a) London dispersion forces (b) Dipole–dipole forces

(c) Hydrogen bonding

8.35 Identify the predominant intermolecular force in each of the following substances.

(a) N_2 (b) HCN (c) CCl_4

(d) NH_3 (e) CH_3Cl (f) CH_3COOH

8.36 Dimethyl ether (CH_3OCH_3) and ethanol (C_2H_5OH) have the same formula (C_2H_6O), but the boiling point of dimethyl ether is $-25\,°C$, while that of ethanol is $78\,°C$. Explain this difference in boiling points.

8.37 Iodine is a solid at room temperature $(mp = 113.5\,°C)$ while bromine is a liquid $(mp = -7\,°C)$. Explain this difference in terms of intermolecular forces.

GASES AND PRESSURE

8.38 How is 1 atm of pressure defined?

8.39 List four common units for measuring pressure.

8.40 What are the four assumptions of the kinetic–molecular theory of gases?

8.41 How does the kinetic–molecular theory of gases explain gas pressure?

8.42 Convert the following values into mmHg:

(a) Standard pressure (b) 25.3 psi (c) 7.5 atm

(d) 28.0 in. Hg (e) 41.8 Pa

8.43 Atmospheric pressure at the top of Mt. Whitney in California is 440 mmHg.

(a) How many atmospheres is this?

(b) How many pascals is this?

8.44 What is the pressure (in mmHg) inside a container of gas connected to a mercury-filled, open-ended manometer of the sort shown in Figure 8.10 when the level in the arm connected to the container is 17.6 cm lower than the level in the arm open to the atmosphere and the atmospheric pressure reading outside the apparatus is 754.3 mmHg? What is the pressure inside the container in atm?

8.45 What is the pressure (in atmospheres) inside a container of gas connected to a mercury-filled, open-ended manometer of the sort shown in Figure 8.10 when the level in the arm connected to the container is 28.3 cm higher than the level in the arm open to the atmosphere, and the atmospheric pressure reading outside the apparatus is 1.021 atm? What is the pressure in mmHg?

BOYLE'S LAW

8.46 What is Boyle's law, and what variables must be kept constant for the law to hold?

8.47 Which assumption(s) of the kinetic–molecular theory explain the behavior of gases described by Boyle's Law? Explain your answer.

8.48 The pressure of gas in a 600.0 mL cylinder is 65.0 mmHg. What is the new volume when the pressure is increased to 385 mmHg?

8.49 The volume of a balloon is 2.85 L at 1.00 atm. What pressure is required to compress the balloon to a volume of 1.70 L?

8.50 The use of chlorofluorocarbons (CFCs) as refrigerants and propellants in aerosol cans has been discontinued as a result of concerns about the ozone layer. If an aerosol can contained 350 mL of CFC gas at a pressure of 5.0 atm, what volume would this gas occupy at 1.0 atm?

8.51 A balloon occupies a volume of 1.25 L at sea level where the ambient pressure is 1 atm. What volume would the balloon occupy at an altitude of 35,000 ft, where the air pressure is only 220 mmHg?

CHARLES'S LAW

8.52 What is Charles's law, and what variables must be kept constant for the law to hold?

8.53 Which assumption(s) of the kinetic–molecular theory explain the behavior of gases described by Charles's Law? Explain your answer.

8.54 A hot-air balloon has a volume of 960 L at 291 K. To what temperature (in °C) must it be heated to raise its volume to 1200 L, assuming the pressure remains constant?

8.55 A hot-air balloon has a volume of 875 L. What is the original temperature of the balloon if its volume changes to 955 L when heated to $56\,°C$?

8.56 A gas sample has a volume of 185 mL at $38\,°C$. What is its volume at $97\,°C$?

8.57 A balloon has a volume of 43.0 L at $25\,°C$. What is its volume at $2.8\,°C$?

GAY-LUSSAC'S LAW

8.58   What is Gay-Lussac's law, and what variables must be kept constant for the law to hold?

8.59   Which assumption(s) of the kinetic–molecular theory explain the behavior of gases described by Gay-Lussac's Law? Explain your answer.

8.60   A glass laboratory flask is filled with gas at 25 °C and 0.95 atm pressure, sealed, and then heated to 117 °C. What is the pressure inside the flask?

8.61   An aerosol can has an internal pressure of 3.85 atm at 25 °C. What temperature is required to raise the pressure to 18.0 atm?

COMBINED GAS LAW

8.62   A gas has a volume of 2.84 L at 1.00 atm and 0 °C. At what temperature does it have a volume of 7.50 L at 520 mmHg?

8.63   A compressed-air tank carried by scuba divers has a volume of 6.80 L and a pressure of 120 atm at 20 °C. What is the volume of air in the tank at 0 °C and 1.00 atm pressure (STP)?

8.64   When H_2 gas was released by the reaction of HCl with Zn, the volume of H_2 collected was 75.4 mL at 23 °C and 748 mmHg. What is the volume of the H_2 at 0 °C and 1.00 atm pressure (STP)?

8.65   What is the effect on the volume of a gas if you simultaneously:

   (a) Halve its pressure and double its Kelvin temperature?

   (b) Double its pressure and double its Kelvin temperature?

8.66   What is the effect on the pressure of a gas if you simultaneously:

   (a) Halve its volume and double its Kelvin temperature?

   (b) Double its volume and halve its Kelvin temperature?

8.67   A small cylinder of helium gas used for filling balloons has a volume of 2.30 L and a pressure of 1850 atm at 25 °C. How many balloons can you fill if each one has a volume of 1.5 L and a pressure of 1.25 atm at 25 °C?

AVOGADRO'S LAW AND STANDARD MOLAR VOLUME

8.68   Explain Avogadro's law using the kinetic–molecular theory of gases.

8.69   What conditions are defined as standard temperature and pressure (STP)?

8.70   How many molecules are in 1.0 L of O_2 at STP or 1.0 L? How may grams of O_2?

8.71   How many moles of gas are in a volume of 48.6 L at STP?

8.72   What is the mass of CH_4 in a sample that occupies a volume of 16.5 L at STP?

8.73   Assume that you have 1.75 g of the deadly gas hydrogen cyanide, HCN. What is the volume of the gas at STP?

8.74   A typical room is 4.0 m long, 5.0 m wide, and 2.5 m high. What is the total mass of the oxygen in the room assum-ing that the gas in the room is at STP and that air contains 21% oxygen and 79% nitrogen?

8.75   What is the total volume and number of moles of nitrogen in the room described in Problem 8.74?

IDEAL GAS LAW

8.76   What is the ideal gas law?

8.77   How does the ideal gas law differ from the combined gas law?

8.78   Which sample contains more molecules: 2.0 L of Cl_2 at STP, or 3.0 L of CH_4 at 300 K and 1150 mmHg? Which sample weighs more?

8.79   Which sample contains more molecules: 2.0 L of CO_2 at 300 K and 500 mmHg, or 1.5 L of N_2 at 57 °C and 760 mmHg? Which sample weighs more?

8.80   If 2.3 mol of He has a volume of 0.15 L at 294 K, what is the pressure in atm? In psi?

8.81   If 3.5 mol of O_2 has a volume of 27.0 L at a pressure of 1.6 atm, what is its temperature in °C?

8.82   If 15.0 g of CO_2 gas has a volume of 0.30 L at 310 K, what is its pressure in mmHg?

8.83   If 20.0 g of N_2 gas has a volume of 4.00 L and a pressure of 6.0 atm, what is its temperature in degrees celsius?

8.84   If 18.0 g of O_2 gas has a temperature of 350 K and a pressure of 550 mmHg, what is its volume?

8.85   How many moles of a gas will occupy a volume of 0.55 L at a temperature of 347 K and a pressure of 2.5 atm?

DALTON'S LAW AND PARTIAL PRESSURE

8.86   What is meant by *partial pressure*?

8.87   What is Dalton's law?

8.88   If the partial pressure of oxygen in air at 1.0 atm is 160 mmHg, what is its partial pressure on the summit of Mt. Whitney, where atmospheric pressure is 440 mmHg? Assume that the percent oxygen is the same.

8.89   Scuba divers who suffer from decompression sickness are treated in hyperbaric chambers using heliox (21% oxygen, 79% helium), at pressures up to 120 psi. Calculate the par-tial pressure of O_2 (in mmHg) in a hyperbaric chamber under these conditions.

LIQUIDS

8.90   What is the vapor pressure of a liquid?

8.91   What is a liquid's heat of vaporization?

8.92   What is the effect of pressure on a liquid's boiling point?

8.93   Which of the following substances would you expect to have the higher vapor pressure: CH_3OH or CH_3Cl? Explain

8.94   The heat of vaporization of water is 9.72 kcal/mol.

   (a) How much heat (in kilocalories) is required to vapor-ize 3.00 mol of H_2O?

   (b) How much heat (in kilocalories) is released when 320 g of steam condenses?

8.95 Patients with a high body temperature are often given "alcohol baths." The heat of vaporization of isopropyl alcohol (rubbing alcohol) is 159 cal/g. How much heat is removed from the skin by the evaporation of 190 g (about 1/2 a cup) of isopropyl alcohol?

SOLIDS

8.96 What is the difference between an amorphous and a crystalline solid?

8.97 List three kinds of crystalline solids, and give an example of each.

8.98 The heat of fusion of acetic acid, the principal organic component of vinegar, is 45.9 cal/g. How much heat (in kilocalories) is required to melt 1.75 mol of solid acetic acid?

8.99 The heat of fusion of sodium metal is 630 cal/mol. How much heat (in kilocalories) is required to melt 262 g of sodium?

CHEMISTRY IN ACTION

8.100 What evidence is there that global warming is occurring? [*Greenhouse Gases and Global Warming, p. 224*]

8.101 What are the three most important greenhouse gases? [*Greenhouse Gases and Global Warming, p. 224*]

8.102 What is the difference between a systolic and a diastolic pressure reading? Is a blood pressure of 180/110 within the normal range? [*Blood Pressure, p. 228*]

8.103 Convert the blood pressure reading in Problem 8.102 to atm. [*Blood Pressure, p. 228*]

8.104 What is a supercritical fluid? [*CO_2 as an Environmentally Friendly Solvent, p. 245*]

8.105 What are the environmental advantages of using supercritical CO_2 in place of chlorinated organic solvents? [*CO_2 as an Environmentally Friendly Solvent, p. 245*]

GENERAL QUESTIONS AND PROBLEMS

8.106 Use the kinetic–molecular theory to explain why gas pressure increases if the temperature is raised and the volume is kept constant.

8.107 Hydrogen and oxygen react according to the equation $2 H_2(g) + O_2(g) \longrightarrow 2 H_2O(g)$. According to Avogadro's law, how many liters of hydrogen are required to react with 2.5 L of oxygen at STP?

8.108 If 3.0 L of hydrogen and 1.5 L of oxygen at STP react to yield water, how many moles of water are formed? What gas volume does the water have at a temperature of 100 °C and 1 atm pressure?

8.109 Approximately 240 mL/min of CO_2 is exhaled by an average adult at rest. Assuming a temperature of 37 °C and 1 atm pressure, how many moles of CO_2 is this?

8.110 How many grams of CO_2 are exhaled by an average resting adult in 24 hours? (See Problem 8.109.)

8.111 Imagine that you have two identical containers, one containing hydrogen at STP and the other containing oxygen at STP. How can you tell which is which without opening them?

8.112 When fully inflated, a hot-air balloon has a volume of 1.6×10^5 L at an average temperature of 375 K and 0.975 atm. Assuming that air has an average molar mass of 29 g/mol, what is the density of the air in the hot-air balloon? How does this compare with the density of air at STP?

8.113 A 10.0 g sample of an unknown gas occupies 14.7 L at a temperature of 25 °C and a pressure of 745 mmHg. How many moles of gas are in the sample? What is the molar mass of the gas?

8.114 One mole of any gas has a volume of 22.4 L at STP. What are the molecular weights of the following gases, and what are their densities in grams per liter at STP?

(a) CH_4 (b) CO_2 (c) O_2

8.115 Gas pressure outside the space shuttle is approximately 1×10^{-14} mm Hg at a temperature of approximately 1 K. If the gas is almost entirely hydrogen atoms (H, not H_2), what volume of space is occupied by 1 mol of atoms? What is the density of H gas in atoms per liter?

8.116 Ethylene glycol, $C_2H_6O_2$, has one OH bonded to each carbon.

(a) Draw the Lewis dot structure of ethylene glycol.

(b) Draw the Lewis dot structure of chloroethane, C_2H_5Cl.

(c) Chloroethane has a slightly higher molar mass than ethylene glycol, but a much lower boiling point (3 °C versus 198 °C). Explain.

8.117 A rule of thumb for scuba diving is that the external pressure increases by 1 atm for every 10 m of depth. A diver using a compressed air tank is planning to descend to a depth of 25 m.

(a) What is the external pressure at this depth? (Remember that the pressure at sea level is 1 atm.)

(b) Assuming that the tank contains 20% oxygen and 80% nitrogen, what is the partial pressure of each gas in the diver's lungs at this depth?

8.118 The *Rankine* temperature scale used in engineering is to the Fahrenheit scale as the Kelvin scale is to the Celsius scale. That is, 1 Rankine degree is the same size as 1 Fahrenheit degree, and 0 °R = absolute zero.

(a) What temperature corresponds to the freezing point of water on the Rankine scale?

(b) What is the value of the gas constant R on the Rankine scale in $(L \cdot atm)/(°R \cdot mol)$?

8.119 Isooctane, C_8H_{18}, is the component of gasoline from which the term *octane rating* derives.

(a) Write a balanced equation for the combustion of isooctane to yield CO_2 and H_2O.

(b) Assuming that gasoline is 100% isooctane and that the density of isooctane is 0.792 g/mL, what mass of CO_2 (in kilograms) is produced each year by the annual U.S. gasoline consumption of 4.6×10^{10} L?

(c) What is the volume (in liters) of this CO_2 at STP?

CHAPTER 9

Solutions

CONTENTS

◄ The giant sequoia relies on osmotic pressure—a colligative property of solutions—to transport water and nutrients from the roots to the treetops 300 ft up.

1. **What are solutions, and what factors affect solubility?**
   THE GOAL: Be able to define the different kinds of mixtures and explain the influence on solubility of solvent and solute structure, temperature, and pressure. (◄◄◄ B., E.)

2. **How is the concentration of a solution expressed?**
   THE GOAL: Be able to define, use, and convert between the most common ways of expressing solution concentrations.

3. **How are dilutions carried out?**
   THE GOAL: Be able to calculate the concentration of a solution prepared by dilution and explain how to make a desired dilution.

4. **What is an electrolyte?**
   THE GOAL: Be able to recognize strong and weak electrolytes and nonelectrolytes, and express electrolyte concentrations. (◄◄◄ A.)

5. **How do solutions differ from pure solvents in their behavior?**
   THE GOAL: Be able to explain vapor-pressure lowering, boiling-point elevation, and freezing-point depression for solutions. (◄◄◄ F., G.)

6. **What is osmosis?**
   THE GOAL: Be able to describe osmosis and some of its applications.

Up to this point, we have been concerned primarily with pure substances, both elements and compounds. In day-to-day life, however, most of the materials we come in contact with are mixtures. Air, for example, is a gaseous mixture of primarily oxygen and nitrogen; blood is a liquid mixture of many different components; and many rocks are solid mixtures of different minerals. In this chapter, we look closely at the characteristics and properties of mixtures, with particular attention to the uniform mixtures we call *solutions*.

9.1 Mixtures and Solutions

As we saw in Section 1.3, a *mixture* is an intimate combination of two or more substances, both of which retain their chemical identities. Mixtures can be classified as either *heterogeneous* or *homogeneous*, as indicated in Figure 9.1, depending on their appearance. **Heterogeneous mixtures** are those in which the mixing is not uniform and which therefore have regions of different composition. Rocky Road ice cream, for example, is a heterogeneous mixture, with something different in every spoonful. Granite and many other rocks are also heterogeneous, having a grainy character due to the heterogeneous mixing of different minerals. **Homogeneous mixtures** are those in which the mixing *is* uniform and that therefore have the same composition throughout. Seawater, a homogeneous mixture of soluble ionic compounds in water, is an example.

Homogeneous mixtures can be further classified as either *solutions* or *colloids*, according to the size of their particles. **Solutions**, the most important class of homogeneous mixtures, contain particles the size of a typical ion or small molecule—roughly 0.1–2 nm in diameter. **Colloids**, such as milk and fog, are also homogeneous in appearance but contain larger particles than solutions—in the range 2–500 nm diameter.

Liquid solutions, colloids, and heterogeneous mixtures can be distinguished in several ways. For example, liquid solutions are transparent (although they may be colored). Colloids may appear transparent if the particle size is small, but they have a murky or opaque appearance if the particle size is larger. Neither solutions nor small-particle colloids separate on standing, and the particles in both are too small to be removed by filtration. Heterogeneous mixtures and large-particle colloids, also known as "suspensions," are murky or opaque and their particles will slowly settle on prolonged standing. House paint is an example.

Heterogeneous mixture A nonuniform mixture that has regions of different composition.

Homogeneous mixture A uniform mixture that has the same composition throughout.

Solution A homogeneous mixture that contains particles the size of a typical ion or small molecule.

Colloid A homogeneous mixture that contains particles that range in diameter from 2 to 500 nm.

▶ **Figure 9.1**
Classification of mixtures.
The components in heterogeneous mixtures are not uniformly mixed, and the composition varies with location within the mixture. In homogeneous mixtures, the components are uniformly mixed at the molecular level.

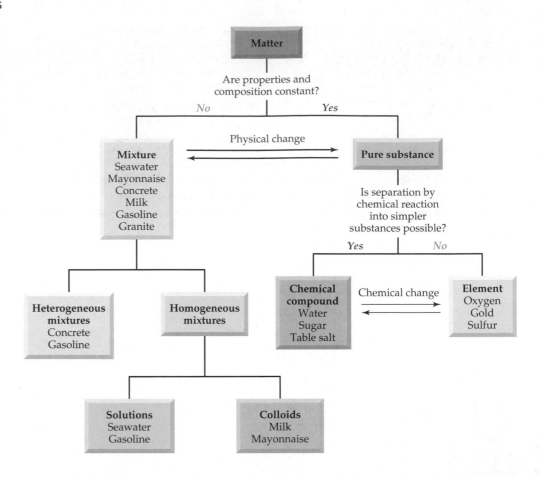

Table 9.1 gives some examples of solutions, colloids, and heterogeneous mixtures. It is interesting to note that blood has characteristics of all three. About 45% by volume of blood consists of suspended red and white cells, which settle slowly on standing; the remaining 55% is *plasma*, which contains ions in solution and colloidal protein molecules.

TABLE 9.1 Some Characteristics of Solutions, Colloids, and Heterogeneous Mixtures

Type of Mixture	Particle Size	Examples	Characteristics
Solution	<2.0 nm	Air, seawater, gasoline, wine	Transparent to light; does not separate on standing; nonfilterable
Colloid	2.0–500 nm	Butter, milk, fog, pearl	Often murky or opaque to light; does not separate on standing; nonfilterable
Heterogeneous	>500 nm	Blood, paint, aerosol sprays	Murky or opaque to light; separates on standing; filterable

Although we usually think of solids dissolved in liquids when we talk about solutions, solutions actually occur in all three phases of matter (Table 9.2). Metal alloys like 14-karat gold (58% gold with silver and copper) and brass (10–40% zinc with copper), for instance, are solutions of one solid with another. For solutions in which a gas or solid is dissolved in a liquid, the dissolved substance is called the **solute** and the liquid is called the **solvent**. In seawater, for example, the dissolved salts would be the solutes and water would be the solvent. When one liquid is dissolved in another, the minor component is usually considered the solute and the major component is the solvent.

Solute A substance that is dissolved in a solvent.

Solvent The substance in which another substance (the solute) is dissolved.

TABLE **9.2** Some Different Types of Solutions	
Type of Solution	**Example**
Gas in gas	Air (O_2, N_2, Ar, and other gases)
Gas in liquid	Seltzer water (CO_2 in water)
Gas in solid	H_2 in palladium metal
Liquid in liquid	Gasoline (mixture of hydrocarbons)
Liquid in solid	Dental amalgam (mercury in silver)
Solid in liquid	Seawater (NaCl and other salts in water)
Solid in solid	Metal alloys such as 14-karat gold (Au, Ag, and Cu)

PROBLEM 9.1

Classify the following liquid mixtures as heterogeneous or homogeneous. Further classify each homogeneous mixture as a solution or colloid.

(a) Orange juice   **(b)** Apple juice
(c) Hand lotion   **(d)** Tea

9.2 The Solution Process

What determines whether a substance is soluble in a given liquid? Solubility depends primarily on the strength of the attractions between solute and solvent particles relative to the strengths of the attractions within the pure substances. Ethyl alcohol is soluble in water, for example, because hydrogen bonding (Section 8.2) is nearly as strong between water and ethyl alcohol molecules as it is between water molecules alone or ethyl alcohol molecules alone.

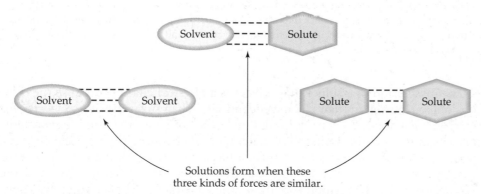

Solutions form when these
three kinds of forces are similar.

A good rule of thumb for predicting solubility is that "like dissolves like," meaning that substances with similar intermolecular forces form solutions with one another, whereas substances with different intermolecular forces do not (Section 8.2).

Polar solvents dissolve polar and ionic solutes; nonpolar solvents dissolve nonpolar solutes. Thus, a polar, hydrogen-bonding compound like water dissolves ethyl alcohol and sodium chloride, whereas a nonpolar organic compound like hexane (C_6H_{14}) dissolves other nonpolar organic compounds like fats and oils. Water and oil, however, do not dissolve one another, as summed up by the old saying, "Oil and water don't mix." The intermolecular forces between water molecules are so strong that after an oil–water mixture is shaken, the water layer re-forms, squeezing out the oil molecules.

Water solubility is not limited to ionic compounds and ethyl alcohol. Many polar organic substances, such as sugars, amino acids, and even some proteins, dissolve in water. In addition, small, moderately polar organic molecules such as chloroform ($CHCl_3$) are soluble in water to a limited extent. When mixed with water, a small amount of the organic compound dissolves, but the remainder forms a separate liquid layer. As the number of carbon atoms in organic molecules increases, though, water solubility decreases.

The process of dissolving an ionic solid in a polar liquid can be visualized as shown in Figure 9.2 for sodium chloride. When NaCl crystals are put in water, ions at the crystal surface come into contact with polar water molecules. Positively charged Na^+ ions are attracted to the negatively polarized oxygen of water, and negatively charged Cl^- ions are attracted to the positively polarized hydrogens. The combined forces of attraction between an ion and several water molecules pull the ion away from the crystal, exposing a fresh surface, until ultimately the crystal dissolves. Once in solution, Na^+ and Cl^- ions are completely surrounded by solvent molecules, a phenomenon called **solvation** (or, specifically for water, *hydration*). The water molecules form a loose shell around the ions, stabilizing them by electrical attraction.

Solvation The clustering of solvent molecules around a dissolved solute molecule or ion.

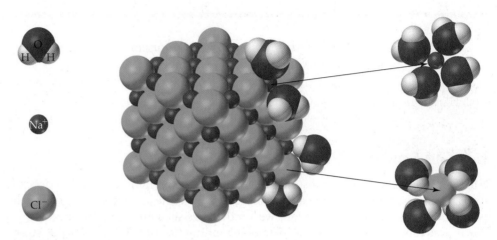

▲ **Figure 9.2**
Dissolution of an NaCl crystal in water.
Polar water molecules surround the individual Na^+ and Cl^- ions at an exposed edge or corner, pulling them from the crystal surface into solution and surrounding them. Note how the negatively polarized oxygens of water molecules cluster around Na^+ ions and the positively polarized hydrogens cluster around Cl^- ions.

The dissolution of a solute in a solvent is a physical change, because the solution components retain their chemical identities. When sugar dissolves in water, for example, the individual sugar and water molecules still have the same chemical formulas as in the pure or undissolved state. Like all chemical and physical changes, the dissolution of a substance in a solvent has associated with it a heat change, or *enthalpy* change (Section 7.2). Some substances dissolve exothermically, releasing heat and warming the resultant solution, whereas other substances dissolve endothermically, absorbing heat and cooling the resultant solution. Calcium chloride, for example, *releases* 19.4 kcal/mol (81.2 kJ/mol) of heat energy when it dissolves in water, but ammonium nitrate (NH_4NO_3) *absorbs* 6.1 kcal/mol (25.5 kJ/mol) of heat energy. Athletes and others take advantage of both situations when they use instant hot packs or cold packs to treat injuries. Both hot and cold packs consist of a pouch of water and a dry chemical, such as $CaCl_2$ or $MgSO_4$ for hot packs, and NH_4NO_3 for cold packs. Squeezing the pack breaks the pouch and the solid dissolves, either raising or lowering the temperature.

▲ Instant cold packs used to treat muscle strains and sprains often take advantage of the endothermic enthalpy of a solution of salts such as ammonium nitrate.

Worked Example 9.1 Formation of Solutions

Which of the following pairs of substances would you expect to form solutions?

(a) Carbon tetrachloride (CCl_4) and hexane (C_6H_{14}).

(b) Octane (C_8H_{18}) and methyl alcohol (CH_3OH).

ANALYSIS Identify the kinds of intermolecular forces in each substance (Section 8.2). Substances with similar intermolecular forces tend to form solutions.

SOLUTION

(a) Hexane contains only C—H and C—C bonds, which are nonpolar. Carbon tetrachloride contains polar C—Cl bonds, but they are distributed symmetrically in the tetrahedral molecule so that it too is nonpolar. The major intermolecular force for both compounds is London dispersion forces, so they will form a solution.

(b) Octane contains only C—H and C—C bonds and so is nonpolar; the major intermolecular force is dispersion. Methyl alcohol contains polar C—O and O—H bonds; it is polar and forms hydrogen bonds. The intermolecular forces for the two substances are so dissimilar that they do not form a solution.

PROBLEM 9.2

Which of the following pairs of substances would you expect to form solutions?

(a) CCl_4 and water

(b) Benzene (C_6H_6) and $MgSO_4$

(c) Hexane (C_6H_{14}) and heptane (C_7H_{16})

(d) Ethyl alcohol (C_2H_5OH) and heptanol $(C_7H_{15}OH)$

9.3 Solid Hydrates

Some ionic compounds attract water strongly enough to hold on to water molecules even when crystalline, forming what are called *solid hydrates*. For example, the plaster of Paris used to make decorative objects and casts for broken limbs is calcium sulfate hemihydrate, $CaSO_4 \cdot \frac{1}{2}H_2O$. The dot between $CaSO_4$ and $\frac{1}{2}H_2O$ in the formula indicates that for every two $CaSO_4$ formula units in the crystal there is also one water molecule present.

$$CaSO_4 \cdot \tfrac{1}{2}H_2O \quad \text{A solid hydrate}$$

After being ground up and mixed with water to make plaster, $CaSO_4 \cdot \frac{1}{2}H_2O$ gradually changes into the crystalline dihydrate $CaSO_4 \cdot 2\,H_2O$, known as *gypsum*. During the change, the plaster hardens and expands in volume, causing it to fill a mold or shape itself closely around a broken limb. Table 9.3 lists some other ionic compounds that are handled primarily as hydrates.

TABLE 9.3 Some Common Solid Hydrates

Formula	Name	Uses
$AlCl_3 \cdot 6\,H_2O$	Aluminum chloride hexahydrate	Antiperspirant
$CaSO_4 \cdot 2\,H_2O$	Calcium sulfate dihydrate (gypsum)	Cements, wallboard molds
$CaSO_4 \cdot \frac{1}{2}H_2O$	Calcium sulfate hemihydrate (plaster of Paris)	Casts, molds
$CuSO_4 \cdot 5\,H_2O$	Copper(II) sulfate pentahydrate (blue vitriol)	Pesticide, germicide, topical fungicide
$MgSO_4 \cdot 7\,H_2O$	Magnesium sulfate heptahydrate (epsom salts)	Laxative, anticonvulsant
$Na_2B_4O_7 \cdot 10\,H_2O$	Sodium tetraborate decahydrate (borax)	Cleaning compounds, fireproofing agent
$Na_2S_2O_3 \cdot 5\,H_2O$	Sodium thiosulfate pentahydrate (hypo)	Photographic fixer

Hygroscopic Having the ability to pull water molecules from the surrounding atmosphere.

Still other ionic compounds attract water so strongly that they pull water vapor from humid air to become hydrated. Compounds that show this behavior, such as calcium chloride ($CaCl_2$), are called **hygroscopic** and are often used as drying agents. You might have noticed a small bag of a hygroscopic compound (probably silica gel, SiO_2) included in the packing material of a new MP3 player, camera, or other electronic device to keep humidity low during shipping.

PROBLEM 9.3
Write the formula of sodium sulfate decahydrate, known as Glauber's salt and used as a laxative.

PROBLEM 9.4
What mass of Glauber's salt must be used to provide 1.00 mol of sodium sulfate?

9.4 Solubility

Miscible Mutually soluble in all proportions.

We saw in Section 9.2 that ethyl alcohol is soluble in water because hydrogen bonding is nearly as strong between water and ethyl alcohol molecules as it is between water molecules alone or ethyl alcohol molecules alone. So similar are the forces in this particular case, in fact, that the two liquids are **miscible**, or mutually soluble in all proportions. Ethyl alcohol will continue to dissolve in water no matter how much is added.

Most substances, however, reach a solubility limit beyond which no more will dissolve in solution. Imagine, for instance that you are asked to prepare a saline solution (aqueous NaCl). You might measure out some water, add solid NaCl, and stir the mixture. Dissolution occurs rapidly at first but then slows down as more and more NaCl is added. Eventually the dissolution stops because an equilibrium is reached when the numbers of Na^+ and Cl^- ions leaving a crystal and going into solution are equal to the numbers of ions returning from solution to the crystal. At this point, the solution is said to be **saturated**. A maximum of 35.8 g of NaCl will dissolve in 100 mL of water at 20 °C. Any amount above this limit simply sinks to the bottom of the container and sits there.

Saturated solution A solution that contains the maximum amount of dissolved solute at equilibrium.

The equilibrium reached by a saturated solution is like the equilibrium reached by a reversible reaction (Section 7.7). Both are dynamic situations in which no *apparent* change occurs because the rates of forward and backward processes are equal. Solute particles leave the solid surface and reenter the solid from solution at the same rate.

$$\text{Solid solute} \underset{\text{Crystallize}}{\overset{\text{Dissolve}}{\rightleftharpoons}} \text{Solution}$$

Solubility The maximum amount of a substance that will dissolve in a given amount of solvent at a specified temperature.

The maximum amount of a substance that will dissolve in a given amount of a solvent at a given temperature, usually expressed in grams per 100 mL (g/100 mL), is called the substance's **solubility**. Solubility is a characteristic property of a specific solute–solvent combination, and different substances have greatly differing solubilities. Only 9.6 g of sodium hydrogen carbonate will dissolve in 100 mL of water at 20 °C, for instance, but 204 g of sucrose will dissolve under the same conditions.

9.5 The Effect of Temperature on Solubility

As anyone who has ever made tea or coffee knows, temperature often has a dramatic effect on solubility. The compounds in tea leaves or coffee beans, for instance, dissolve easily in hot water but not in cold water. The effect of temperature is different for every substance, however, and is usually unpredictable. As shown in Figure 9.3(a), the solubilities of most molecular and ionic solids increase with increasing temperature, but the solubilities of others (NaCl) are almost unchanged, and the solubilities of still others [$Ce_2(SO_4)_3$] decrease with increasing temperature.

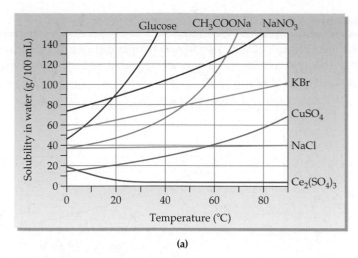

(a)

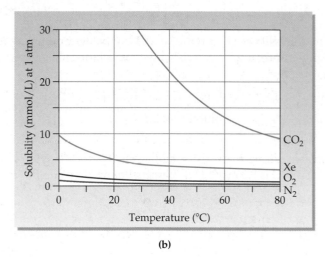

(b)

▲ Figure 9.3
Solubilities of some (a) solids and (b) gases, in water as a function of temperature.
Most solid substances become more soluble as temperature rises (although the exact relationship is usually complex), while the solubility of gases decreases.

Supersaturated solution A solution that contains more than the maximum amount of dissolved solute; a nonequilibrium situation.

Solids that are more soluble at high temperature than at low temperature can sometimes form what are called **supersaturated solutions**, which contain even more solute than a saturated solution. Suppose, for instance, that a large amount of a substance is dissolved at a high temperature. As the solution cools, the solubility decreases and the excess solute should precipitate to maintain equilibrium. But if the cooling is done very slowly, and if the container stands quietly, crystallization might not occur immediately and a supersaturated solution might result. Such a solution is unstable, however, and precipitation can occur dramatically when a tiny seed crystal is added or container disturbed to initiate crystallization (Figure 9.4).

Unlike solids, the influence of temperature on the solubility of gases *is* predictable: Addition of heat decreases the solubility of most gases, as seen in Figure 9.3(b) (helium is the only common exception). One result of this temperature-dependent decrease in gas solubility can sometimes be noted in a stream or lake near the outflow of warm water from an industrial operation. As water temperature increases, the concentration of dissolved oxygen in the water decreases, killing fish that cannot tolerate the lower oxygen levels.

▲ Figure 9.4
A supersaturated solution of sodium acetate in water.
When a tiny seed crystal is added, larger crystals rapidly grow and precipitate from the solution until equilibrium is reached.

Worked Example 9.2 Solubility of Gases: Effect of Temperature

From the following graph of solubility versus temperature for O_2, estimate the concentration of dissolved oxygen in water at 25 °C and at 35 °C. By what percentage does the concentration of O_2 change?

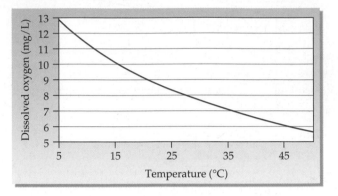

ANALYSIS The solubility of O_2 (on the y-axis) can be determined by finding the appropriate temperature (on the x-axis) and extrapolating. The percent change is calculated as

$$\frac{(\text{Solubility at } 25\,°C) - (\text{Solubility at } 35\,°C)}{(\text{Solubility at } 25\,°C)} \times 100$$

SOLUTION
From the graph we estimate that the solubility of O_2 at 25 °C is approximately 8.3 mg/L and at 35 °C is 7.0 mg/L. The percent change in solubility is

$$\frac{8.3 - 7.0}{8.3} \times 100 = 16\%$$

PROBLEM 9.5
A solution is prepared by dissolving 12.5 g of KBr in 20 mL of water at 60 °C (see Figure 9.3). Is this solution saturated, unsaturated, or supersaturated? What will happen if the solution is cooled to 10 °C?

9.6 The Effect of Pressure on Solubility: Henry's Law

Pressure has virtually no effect on the solubility of a solid or liquid, but it has a strong effect on the solubility of a gas. According to **Henry's law**, the solubility (or concentration) of a gas in a liquid is directly proportional to the partial pressure of the gas over the liquid. If the partial pressure of the gas doubles, solubility doubles; if the gas pressure is halved, solubility is halved (Figure 9.5).

▶▶▶ Recall from Section 8.11 that each gas in a mixture exerts a partial pressure independent of other gases present (Dalton's law of partial pressures).

▶ **Figure 9.5**
Henry's law.
The solubility of a gas is directly proportional to its partial pressure. An increase in pressure causes more gas molecules to enter solution until equilibrium is restored between the dissolved and undissolved gas.

(a) Equilibrium   **(b)** Pressure increase   **(c)** Equilibrium restored

Henry's law The solubility (or concentration) of a gas is directly proportional to the partial pressure of the gas if the temperature is constant. That is, concentration (C) divided by pressure (P) is constant when T is constant,

or $\dfrac{C}{P_{gas}} = k$ (At a constant temperature)

Henry's law can be explained using Le Châtelier's principle. In the case of a saturated solution of a gas in a liquid, an equilibrium exists whereby gas molecules enter and leave the solution at the same rate. When the system is stressed by increasing the pressure of the gas, more gas molecules go into solution to relieve that increase. Conversely, when the pressure of the gas is decreased, more gas molecules come out of solution to relieve the decrease.

▶▶▶ Le Châtelier's principle states that when a system at equilibrium is placed under stress, the equilibrium shifts to relieve that stress (Section 7.9).

$$\text{[Pressure increases} \longrightarrow]$$
$$\text{Gas + Solvent} \rightleftharpoons \text{Solution}$$

As an example of Henry's law in action, think about the fizzing that occurs when you open a bottle of soft drink or champagne. The bottle is sealed under greater than 1 atm of CO_2 pressure, causing some of the CO_2 to dissolve. When the bottle is opened, however, CO_2 pressure drops and gas comes fizzing out of solution.

Writing Henry's law in the form $P_{gas} = C/k$ shows that partial pressure can be used to express the concentration of a gas in a solution, a practice especially common in health-related sciences. Table 9.4 gives some typical values and illustrates the convenience of having the same unit for concentration of a gas in both air and blood. Compare the oxygen partial pressures in saturated alveolar air (air in the lungs) and in arterial blood, for instance. The values are almost the same because the gases dissolved in blood come to equilibrium with the same gases in the lungs.

TABLE 9.4 Partial Pressures and Normal Gas Concentrations in Body Fluids

Sample	Partial Pressure (mmHg)			
	P_{N_2}	P_{O_2}	P_{CO_2}	P_{H_2O}
Inspired air (dry)	597	159	0.3	3.7
Alveolar air (saturated)	573	100	40	47
Expired air (saturated)	569	116	28	47
Arterial blood	573	95	40	
Venous blood	573	40	45	
Peripheral tissues	573	40	45	

If the partial pressure of a gas over a solution changes while the temperature is constant, the new solubility of the gas can be found easily. Because C/P is a constant value at constant temperature, Henry's law can be restated to show how one variable changes if the other changes:

$$\frac{C_1}{P_1} = \frac{C_2}{P_2} = k \quad \text{(Where } k \text{ is constant at a fixed temperature)}$$

Worked Example 9.3 gives an illustration of how to use this equation.

Worked Example 9.3 Solubility of Gases: Henry's Law

At a partial pressure of oxygen in the atmosphere of 159 mmHg, the solubility of oxygen in blood is 0.44 g/100 mL. What is the solubility of oxygen in blood at 11,000 ft, where the partial pressure of O_2 is 56 mmHg?

ANALYSIS According to Henry's law, the solubility of the gas divided by its pressure is constant:

$$\frac{C_1}{P_1} = \frac{C_2}{P_2}$$

Of the four variables in this equation, we know P_1, C_1, and P_2, and we need to find C_2.

BALLPARK ESTIMATE The pressure drops by a factor of about 3 (from 159 mmHg to 56 mmHg). Since the ratio of solubility to pressure is constant, the solubility must also drop by a factor of 3 (from 0.44 g/100 mL to about 0.15 g/100 mL).

SOLUTION

STEP 1: **Identify known information.** We have values for P_1, C_1, and P_2.

P_1 = 159 mmHg
C_1 = 0.44 g/100 mL
P_2 = 56 mmHg

STEP 2: **Identify answer and units.** We are looking for the solubility of O_2 (C_2) at a partial pressure P_2.

Solubility of O_2, C_2 = ?? g/100 mL

STEP 3: **Identify conversion factors or equations.** In this case, we restate Henry's law to solve for C_2.

$$\frac{C_1}{P_1} = \frac{C_2}{P_2} \Rightarrow C_2 = \frac{C_1 P_2}{P_1}$$

STEP 4: **Solve.** Substitute the known values into the equation and calculate C_2.

$$C_2 = \frac{C_1 P_2}{P_1} = \frac{(0.44 \text{ g}/100 \text{ mL})(56 \text{ mmHg})}{159 \text{ mmHg}} = 0.15 \text{ g}/100 \text{ mL}$$

BALLPARK CHECK The calculated answer matches our estimate.

PROBLEM 9.6
At 20 °C and a partial pressure of 760 mmHg, the solubility of CO_2 in water is 0.169 g/100 mL at this temperature. What is the solubility of CO_2 at 2.5×10^4 mmHg?

PROBLEM 9.7
At a total atmospheric pressure of 1.00 atm, the partial pressure of CO_2 in air is approximately 4.0×10^{-4} atm. Using the data in Problem 9.6, what is the solubility of CO_2 in an open bottle of seltzer water at 20 °C?

PROBLEM 9.8
The atmospheric pressure at the top of Mt. Everest is only 265 mmHg. If the atmospheric composition is 21% oxygen, calculate the partial pressure of O_2 at this altitude and determine the percent saturation of hemoglobin under these conditions (see Chemistry in Action: Breathing and Oxygen Transport on p. 263).

9.7 Units of Concentration

Although we speak casually of a solution of, say, orange juice as either "dilute" or "concentrated," laboratory work usually requires an exact knowledge of a solution's concentration. As indicated in Table 9.5 on page 264, there are several common methods for expressing concentration. The units differ, but all the methods describe how much solute is present in a given quantity of solution.

CHEMISTRY IN ACTION

Breathing and Oxygen Transport

Like all other animals, humans need oxygen. When we breathe, the freshly inspired air travels through the bronchial passages and into the lungs. The oxygen then diffuses through the delicate walls of the approximately 150 million alveolar sacs of the lungs and into arterial blood, which transports it to all body tissues.

Only about 3% of the oxygen in blood is dissolved; the rest is chemically bound to *hemoglobin* molecules, large proteins with *heme* groups embedded in them. Each hemoglobin molecule contains four heme groups, and each heme group contains an iron atom that is able to bind 1 O_2 molecule. Thus, a single hemoglobin molecule can bind up to 4 molecules of oxygen. The entire system of oxygen transport and delivery in the body depends on the pickup and release of O_2 by hemoglobin (Hb) according to the following series of equilibria:

$$O_2(lungs) \rightleftharpoons O_2(blood) \quad (Henry's\ law)$$
$$Hb + 4\,O_2(blood) \rightleftharpoons Hb(O_2)_4$$
$$Hb(O_2)_4 \rightleftharpoons Hb + 4\,O_2\ (cell)$$

The delivery of oxygen depends on the concentration of O_2 in the various tissues, as measured by partial pressure (P_{O_2}, Table 9.4). The amount of oxygen carried by hemoglobin at any given value of P_{O_2} is usually expressed as a percent saturation and can be found from the curve shown in the accompanying figure. When $P_{O_2} = 100$ mmHg, the saturation in the lungs is 97.5%, meaning that each hemoglobin is carrying close to its maximum of 4 O_2 molecules. When $P_{O_2} = 26$ mmHg, however, the saturation drops to 50%.

So, how does the body ensure that enough oxygen is available to the various tissues? When large amounts of oxygen are needed—during a strenuous workout, for example—oxygen is released from hemoglobin to the hardworking, oxygen-starved muscle cells, where P_{O_2} is low. Increasing the supply of oxygen to the blood (by breathing harder and faster) shifts all the equilibria toward the right, according to Le Châtelier's principle (Section 7.9), to supply the additional O_2 needed by the muscles.

What about people living at high altitudes? In Leadville, CO, for example, where the altitude is 10,156 ft, the P_{O_2} in the lungs is only about 68 mmHg. Hemoglobin is only 90% saturated with O_2 at this pressure, meaning that less oxygen is available for delivery to the tissues. The body responds by producing erythropoietin (EPO), a hormone that stimulates the bone marrow to produce more red blood cells and hemoglobin molecules. The increase in Hb provides more capacity for O_2 transport and drives the Hb + O_2 equilibria to the right.

▲ At high altitudes, the partial pressure of oxygen in the air is too low to saturate hemoglobin sufficiently. Additional oxygen is therefore needed.

World-class athletes use the mechanisms of increased oxygen transport associated with higher levels of hemoglobin to enhance their performance. High-altitude training centers have sprung up, with living and training regimens designed to increase blood EPO levels. Unfortunately, some athletes have also tried to "cheat" by using injections of EPO and synthetic analogs, and "blood doping" to boost performance. This has led the governing bodies of many sports federations, including the Olympic Committee, to start testing for such abuse.

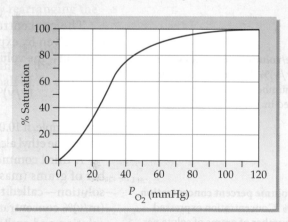

▲ An oxygen-carrying curve for hemoglobin. The percent saturation of the oxygen binding sites on hemoglobin depends on the partial pressure of oxygen P_{O_2}.

See Chemistry in Action Problem 9.90 at the end of the chapter.

If the ion has a charge of +1 or −1, 1 gram-equivalent of the ion is simply the molar mass of the ion in grams. Thus, 1 gram-equivalent of Na^+ is 23 g, and 1 gram-equivalent of Cl^- is 35.5 g. If the ion has a charge of +2 or −2, however, 1 gram-equivalent is equal to the ion's formula weight in grams divided by 2. Thus, 1 gram-equivalent of Mg^{2+} is $(24.3 \text{ g})/2 = 12.2$ g, and 1 gram-equivalent of CO_3^{2-} is $[12.0 \text{ g} + (3 \times 16.0 \text{ g})]/2 = 30.0$ g. The gram-equivalent is a useful conversion factor when converting from volume of solution to mass of ions, as seen in Worked Example 9.14.

The number of equivalents of a given ion per liter of solution can be found by multiplying the molarity of the ion (moles per liter) by the charge on the ion. Because ion concentrations in body fluids are often low, clinical chemists find it more convenient to talk about *milliequivalents* of ions rather than equivalents. One milliequivalent (mEq) of an ion is 1/1000 of an equivalent. For example, the normal concentration of Na^+ in blood is 0.14 Eq/L, or 140 mEq/L.

$$1 \text{ mEq} = 0.001 \text{ Eq} \qquad 1 \text{ Eq} = 1000 \text{ mEq}$$

Note that the gram-equivalent for an ion can now be expressed as grams per equivalent or as mg per mEq.

Average concentrations of the major electrolytes in blood plasma are given in Table 9.6. As you might expect, the total milliequivalents of positively and negatively charged electrolytes must be equal to maintain electrical neutrality. Adding the milliequivalents of positive and negative ions in Table 9.6, however, shows a higher concentration of positive ions than negative ions. The difference, called the *anion gap*, is made up by the presence of negatively charged proteins and the anions of organic acids.

TABLE **9.6** Concentrations of Major Electrolytes in Blood Plasma	
Cation	**Concentration (mEq/L)**
Na^+	136–145
Ca^{2+}	4.5–6.0
K^+	3.6–5.0
Mg^{2+}	3
Anion	**Concentration (mEq/L)**
Cl^-	98–106
HCO_3^-	25–29
SO_4^{2-} and HPO_4^{2-}	2

Worked Example **9.14** Equivalents as Conversion Factors: Volume to Mass

The normal concentration of Ca^{2+} in blood is 5.0 mEq/L. How many milligrams of Ca^{2+} are in 1.00 L of blood?

ANALYSIS We are given a volume and a concentration in milliequivalents per liter, and we need to find an amount in milligrams. Thus, we need to calculate the gram-equivalent for Ca^{2+} and then use concentration as a conversion factor between volume and mass, as indicated in the following flow diagram:

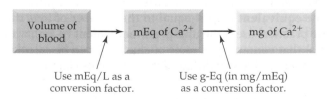

| Volume of blood | → | mEq of Ca^{2+} | → | mg of Ca^{2+} |

Use mEq/L as a conversion factor.   Use g-Eq (in mg/mEq) as a conversion factor.

BALLPARK ESTIMATE The molar mass of calcium is 40.08 g/mol, and the calcium ion carries a charge of 2+. Thus, 1 g-Eq of Ca^{2+} equals about 20 g/Eq or 20 mg/mEq. This means that the 5.0 mEq of Ca^{2+} ions in 1.00 L of blood corresponds to a mass of 5.0 mEq Ca^{2+} × 20 mg/mEq = 100 mg Ca^{2+}.

SOLUTION

$$(1.00 \text{ L blood})\left(\frac{5.0 \text{ mEq } Ca^{2+}}{1.0 \text{ L blood}}\right)\left(\frac{20.04 \text{ mg } Ca^{2+}}{1 \text{ mEq } Ca^{2+}}\right) = 100 \text{ mg } Ca^{2+}$$

BALLPARK CHECK The calculated answer (100 mg of Ca^{2+} in 1.00 L of blood) matches our estimate.

PROBLEM 9.21
How many grams are in 1 Eq of the following ions? How many grams in 1 mEq?
(a) K^+ **(b)** Br^- **(c)** Mg^{2+} **(d)** SO_4^{2-} **(e)** Al^{3+} **(f)** PO_4^{3-}

PROBLEM 9.22
Look at the data in Table 9.6, and calculate how many milligrams of Mg^{2+} are in 250 mL of blood.

PROBLEM 9.23
A typical sports drink for electrolyte replacement contains 20 mEq/L of Na^+ and 10 mEq/L of K^+ ions (see Chemistry in Action: Electrolytes, Fluid Replacement, and Sports Drinks on p. 276). Convert these concentrations to m/v%.

9.11 Properties of Solutions

The properties of solutions are similar in many respects to those of pure solvents, but there are also some interesting and important differences. One such difference is that solutions have higher boiling points than the pure solvents; another is that solutions have lower freezing points. Pure water boils at 100.0 °C and freezes at 0.0 °C, for example, but a 1.0 M solution of NaCl in water boils at 101.0 °C and freezes at −3.7 °C.

The elevation of boiling point and the lowering of freezing point for a solution as compared with a pure solvent are examples of **colligative properties**—properties that depend on the *concentration* of a dissolved solute but not on its chemical identity. Other colligative properties are a lower vapor pressure for a solution compared with the pure solvent and *osmosis*, the migration of solvent molecules through a semipermeable membrane.

Colligative property A property of a solution that depends only on the number of dissolved particles, not on their chemical identity.

Colligative Properties

- Vapor pressure is lower for a solution than for a pure solvent.
- Boiling point is higher for a solution than for a pure solvent.
- Freezing point is lower for a solution than for a pure solvent.
- Osmosis occurs when a solution is separated from a pure solvent by a semipermeable membrane.

Vapor-Pressure Lowering in Solutions

We said in Section 8.13 that the vapor pressure of a liquid depends on the equilibrium between molecules entering and leaving the liquid surface. Only those molecules at the surface of the liquid that are sufficiently energetic will evaporate. If, however, some of the liquid (solvent) molecules at the surface are replaced by other (solute) particles that do not evaporate, then the rate of evaporation of solvent molecules decreases and the

CHEMISTRY IN ACTION

Electrolytes, Fluid Replacement, and Sports Drinks

Electrolytes are essential in many physiological processes, and significant changes in electrolyte levels can be potentially life-threatening if not addressed quickly. Heavy and continuous diarrhea from conditions such as cholera can result in dehydration and very low sodium levels in the body (hyponatremia). Restoration of electrolytes can be accomplished by oral rehydration therapy (ORT). The introduction of ORT in developing countries decreased infant mortality from diarrhea, which had previously been the leading cause of death in children under 5 years of age. A typical ORT solution contains sodium (75 mEq/L), potassium (75b mEq/L), chloride (65 mEq/L), citrate (10 mEq/L), and glucose (75 mmol/L). Heavy sweating during strenuous exercise can also lead to dehydration and loss of electrolytes.

The composition of sweat is highly variable, but the typical concentration for the Na^+ ion is about 30–40 mEq/L, and that of K^+ ion is about 5–10 mEq/L. In addition, there are small amounts of other metal ions, such as Mg^{2+}, and there are sufficient Cl^- ions (35–50 mEq/L) to balance the positive charge of all these cations. If water and electrolytes are not replaced, dehydration, hyperthermia and heat stroke, dizziness, nausea, muscle cramps, impaired kidney function, and other difficulties ensue. As a rule of thumb, a sweat loss equal to 5% of body weight—about 3.5 L for a 150 lb person—is the maximum amount that can be safely allowed for a well-conditioned athlete.

Plain water works perfectly well to replace sweat lost during short bouts of activity up to a few hours in length, but a carbohydrate–electrolyte beverage, or "sports drink," is much superior for rehydrating during and after longer activity in which substantial amounts of electrolytes have been lost. Some of the better known sports drinks are little more than overpriced sugar–water solutions, but others are carefully formulated and highly effective for fluid replacement. Nutritional research has shown that a serious sports drink should meet the following criteria. There are several dry-powder mixes on the market to choose from.

- The drink should contain 6–8% of soluble complex carbohydrates (about 15 g per 8 oz serving) and only a small amount of simple sugar for taste. The complex carbohydrates, which usually go by the name "maltodextrin," provide a slow release of glucose into the bloodstream. Not only does the glucose provide a steady source of energy, it also enhances the absorption of water from the stomach.

▲ **Drinking water to replace fluids is adequate for short periods of activity, but extended exercise requires replacement of fluid and electrolytes, such as those found in sports drinks.**

- The drink should contain electrolytes to replenish those lost in sweat. Concentrations of approximately 20 mEq/L for Na^+ ions, 10 mEq/L for K^+ ion, and 4 mEq/L for Mg^{2+} ions are recommended. These amounts correspond to about 100 mg sodium, 100 mg potassium, and 25 mg magnesium per 8 oz serving.

- The drink should be noncarbonated because carbonation can cause gastrointestinal upset during exercise, and it should not contain caffeine, which acts as a diuretic.

- The drink should taste good so the athlete will want to drink it. Thirst is a poor indicator of fluid requirements, and most people will drink less than needed unless a beverage is flavored.

In addition to complex carbohydrates, electrolytes, and flavorings, some sports drinks also contain vitamin A (as beta-carotene), vitamin C (ascorbic acid), and selenium, which act as antioxidants to protect cells from damage. Some drinks also contain the amino acid glutamine, which appears to lessen lactic acid buildup in muscles and thus helps muscles bounce back more quickly after an intense workout.

See Chemistry in Actions Problems 9.91 and 9.92 at the end of the chapter.

vapor pressure of a solution is lower than that of the pure solvent (Figure 9.9). Note that the *identity* of the solute particles is irrelevant; only their concentration matters.

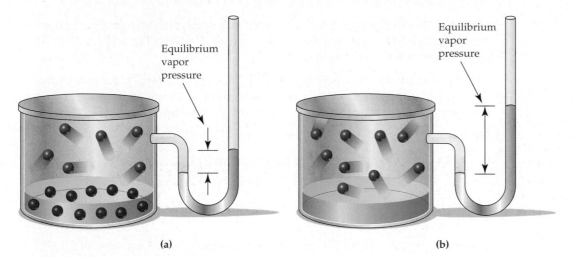

▲ Figure 9.9
Vapor-pressure lowering of solution.
(a) The vapor pressure of a solution is lower than (b) the vapor pressure of the pure solvent because fewer solvent molecules are able to escape from the surface of the solution.

Boiling Point Elevation of Solutions

One consequence of the vapor-pressure–lowering for a solution is that the boiling point of the solution is higher than that of the pure solvent. Recall from Section 8.13 that boiling occurs when the vapor pressure of a liquid reaches atmospheric pressure. But because the vapor pressure of a solution is lower than that of the pure solvent at a given temperature, the solution must be heated to a higher temperature for its vapor pressure to reach atmospheric pressure. Figure 9.10 shows a close-up plot of vapor pressure versus temperature for pure water and for a 1.0 M NaCl solution. The vapor pressure of pure water reaches atmospheric pressure (760 mmHg) at 100.0 °C, but the vapor pressure of the NaCl solution does not reach the same point until 101.0 °C.

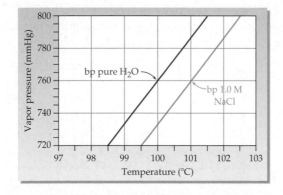

◄ Figure 9.10
Vapor pressure and temperature.
A close-up plot of vapor pressure versus temperature for pure water (red curve) and for a 1.0 M NaCl solution (blue curve). Pure water boils at 100.0 °C, but the solution does not boil until 101.0 °C.

For each mole of solute particles added, regardless of chemical identity, the boiling point of 1 kg of water is raised by 0.51 °C, or

$$\Delta T_{boiling} = \left(0.51\,°C \frac{\text{kg water}}{\text{mol particles}} \right)\left(\frac{\text{mol particles}}{\text{kg water}} \right)$$

The addition of 1 mol of a molecular substance like glucose to 1 kg of water therefore raises the boiling point from 100.0 °C to 100.51 °C. The addition of 1 mol of NaCl per kilogram of water, however, raises the boiling point by 2 × 0.51 °C = 1.02 °C because the solution contains 2 mol of solute particles—Na⁺ and Cl⁻ ions.

Worked Example **9.15** Properties of Solutions: Boiling Point Elevation

What is the boiling point of a solution of 0.75 mol of KBr in 1.0 kg of water?

ANALYSIS The boiling point increases 0.51 °C for each mole of solute per kilogram of water. Since KBr is a strong electrolyte, there are 2 moles of ions (K^+ and Br^-) for every 1 mole of KBr that dissolves.

BALLPARK ESTIMATE The boiling point will increase about 0.5 °C for every 1 mol of ions in 1 kg of water. Since 0.75 mol of KBr produce 1.5 mol of ions, the boiling point should increase by $(1.5 \text{ mol ions}) \times (0.5 \,°C/\text{mol ions}) = 0.75\,°C$.

SOLUTION

$$\Delta T_{\text{boiling}} = \left(0.51\,°C\frac{\text{kg water}}{\text{mol ions}}\right)\left(\frac{2\text{ mol ions}}{1\text{ mol KBr}}\right)\left(\frac{0.75\text{ mol KBr}}{1.0\text{ kg water}}\right) = 0.77\,°C$$

The normal boiling point of pure water is 100 °C, so the boiling point of the solution increases to 100.77 °C.

BALLPARK CHECK The 0.77 °C increase is consistent with our estimate of 0.75 °C.

PROBLEM 9.24

A solution is prepared by dissolving 0.67 mol of $MgCl_2$ in 0.50 kg of water.

(a) How many moles of ions are present in solution?

(b) What is the change in the boiling point of the aqueous solution?

PROBLEM 9.25

When 1.0 mol of HF is dissolved in 1.0 kg of water, the boiling point of the resulting solution is 100.5 °C. Is HF a strong or weak electrolyte? Explain.

🔑 **KEY CONCEPT PROBLEM 9.26**

The following diagram shows plots of vapor pressure versus temperature for a solvent and a solution.

(a) Which curve represents the pure solvent and which the solution?

(b) What is the approximate boiling point elevation for the solution?

(c) What is the approximate concentration of the solution in mol/kg, if 1 mol of solute particles raises the boiling point of 1 kg of solvent by 3.63 °C?

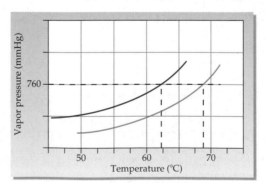

Freezing Point Depression of Solutions

Just as solutions have lower vapor pressure and consequently higher boiling points than pure solvents, they also have lower freezing points. Motorists in cold climates take advantage of this effect when they add "antifreeze" to the water in automobile cooling systems. Antifreeze is a nonvolatile solute, usually ethylene glycol ($HOCH_2CH_2OH$), that is added in sufficient concentration to lower the freezing point below the lowest expected outdoor temperature. In the same way, salt sprinkled on icy roads lowers the freezing point of ice below the road temperature and thus causes ice to melt.

Freezing point depression has much the same cause as vapor pressure lowering and boiling point elevation. Solute molecules are dispersed between solvent molecules throughout the solution, thereby making it more difficult for solvent molecules to come together and organize into ordered crystals.

For each mole of nonvolatile solute particles, the freezing point of 1 kg of water is lowered by 1.86 °C, or

$$\Delta T_{freezing} = \left(-1.86\ °C\ \frac{\text{kg water}}{\text{mol particles}}\right)\left(\frac{\text{mol particles}}{\text{kg water}}\right)$$

Thus, addition of 1 mol of antifreeze to 1 kg of water lowers the freezing point from 0.00 °C to −1.86 °C, and addition of 1 mol of NaCl (2 mol of particles) to 1 kg of water lowers the freezing point from 0.00 °C to −3.72 °C.

Worked Example 9.16 Properties of Solutions: Freezing Point Depression

The cells of a tomato contain mostly an aqueous solution of sugar and other substances. If a typical tomato freezes at −2.5 °C, what is the concentration of dissolved particles in the tomato cells (in moles of particles per kg of water)?

ANALYSIS The freezing point decreases by 1.86 °C for each mole of solute dissolved in 1 kg of water. We can use the decrease in freezing point (2.5 °C) to find the amount of solute per kg of water.

BALLPARK ESTIMATE The freezing point will decrease by about 1.9 °C for every 1 mol of solute particles in 1 kg of water. To lower the freezing point by 2.5 °C (about 30% more) will require about 30% more solute, or 1.3 mol.

SOLUTION

$$\Delta T_{freezing} = -2.5\ °C$$

$$= \left(-1.86\ °C\ \frac{\text{kg water}}{\text{mol solute particles}}\right)\left(\frac{??\ \text{mol solute particles}}{1.0\ \text{kg water}}\right)$$

We can rearrange this expression to

$$(-2.5\ °C)\left(\frac{1}{-1.86\ °C}\ \frac{\text{mol solute particles}}{\text{kg water}}\right) = 1.3\ \frac{\text{mol solute particles}}{\text{kg water}}$$

BALLPARK CHECK The calculated answer agrees with our estimate of 1.3 mol/kg.

PROBLEM 9.27
What is the freezing point of a solution of 1.0 mol of glucose in 1.0 kg of water?

PROBLEM 9.28
When 0.5 mol of a certain ionic substance is dissolved in 1.0 kg of water, the freezing point of the resulting solution is −2.8 °C. How many ions does the substance give when it dissolves?

9.12 Osmosis and Osmotic Pressure

Certain materials, including those that make up the membranes around living cells, are *semipermeable*. They allow water and other small molecules to pass through, but they block the passage of large solute molecules or ions. When a solution and a pure solvent, or two solutions of different concentration, are separated

Osmosis The passage of solvent through a semipermeable membrane separating two solutions of different concentration.

by a semipermeable membrane, solvent molecules pass through the membrane in a process called **osmosis**. Although the passage of solvent through the membrane takes place in both directions, passage from the pure solvent side to the solution side is favored and occurs more often. As a result, the amount of liquid on the pure solvent side decreases, the amount of liquid on the solution side increases, and the concentration of the solution decreases.

For the simplest explanation of osmosis, let us look at what happens on the molecular level. As shown in Figure 9.11, a solution inside a bulb is separated by a semipermeable membrane from pure solvent in the outer container. Solvent molecules in the outer container, because of their somewhat higher concentration, approach the membrane more frequently than do molecules in the bulb, thereby passing through more often and causing the liquid level in the attached tube to rise.

▶ **Figure 9.11**

The phenomenon of osmosis. A solution inside the bulb is separated from pure solvent in the outer container by a semipermeable membrane. Solvent molecules in the outer container have a higher concentration than molecules in the bulb and therefore pass through the membrane more frequently. The liquid in the tube therefore rises until an equilibrium is reached. At equilibrium, the osmotic pressure exerted by the column of liquid in the tube is sufficient to prevent further net passage of solvent.

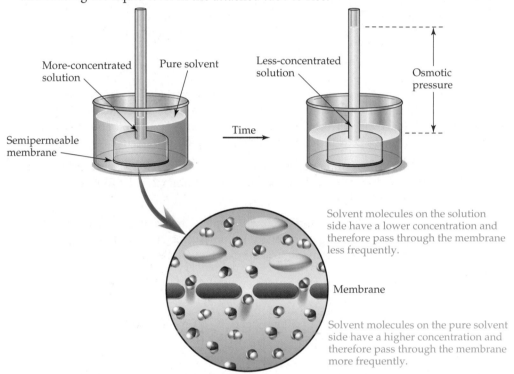

More-concentrated solution   Pure solvent   Less-concentrated solution   Osmotic pressure

Semipermeable membrane

Time

Solvent molecules on the solution side have a lower concentration and therefore pass through the membrane less frequently.

Membrane

Solvent molecules on the pure solvent side have a higher concentration and therefore pass through the membrane more frequently.

Osmotic pressure The amount of external pressure that must be applied to a solution to prevent the net movement of solvent molecules across a semipermeable membrane.

As the liquid in the tube rises, its increased weight creates an increased pressure that pushes solvent back through the membrane until the rates of forward and reverse passage become equal and the liquid level stops rising. The amount of pressure necessary to achieve this equilibrium is called the **osmotic pressure** (π) of the solution and can be determined from the expression

$$\pi = \left(\frac{n}{V}\right)RT$$

where n is the number of moles of particles in the solution, V is the solution volume, R is the gas constant (Section 8.10), and T is the absolute temperature of the solution. Note the similarity between this equation for the osmotic pressure of a solution and the equation for the pressure of an ideal gas, $P = (n/V)RT$. In both cases, the pressure has units of atmospheres.

Osmotic pressures can be extremely high, even for relatively dilute solutions. The osmotic pressure of a 0.15 M NaCl solution at 25 °C, for example, is 7.3 atm, a value that supports a difference in water level of approximately 250 ft!

Osmolarity (osmol) The sum of the molarities of all dissolved particles in a solution.

As with other colligative properties, the amount of osmotic pressure depends only on the concentration of solute particles, not on their identity. Thus, it is convenient to use a new unit, *osmolarity* (osmol), to describe the concentration of particles in solution. The **osmolarity** of a solution is equal to the number of moles of dissolved particles (ions or molecules) per liter of solution. A 0.2 M glucose solution, for instance, has an osmolarity of 0.2 osmol, but a 0.2 M solution of NaCl has an osmolarity of 0.4 osmol because it contains 0.2 mol of Na^+ ions and 0.2 mol of Cl^- ions.

Osmosis is particularly important in living organisms because the membranes around cells are semipermeable. The fluids both inside and outside cells must therefore have the same osmolarity to prevent buildup of osmotic pressure and consequent rupture of the cell membrane.

In blood, the plasma surrounding red blood cells has an osmolarity of approximately 0.30 osmol and is said to be **isotonic** with (that is, has the same osmolarity as) the cell contents. If the cells are removed from plasma and placed in 0.15 M NaCl (called *physiological saline solution*), they are unharmed because the osmolarity of the saline solution (0.30 osmol) is the same as that of plasma. If, however, red blood cells are placed in pure water or in any solution with an osmolarity much lower than 0.30 osmol (a **hypotonic** solution), water passes through the membrane into the cell, causing the cell to swell up and burst, a process called *hemolysis*.

Finally, if red blood cells are placed in a solution having an osmolarity greater than the cell contents (a **hypertonic** solution), water passes out of the cells into the surrounding solution, causing the cells to shrivel, a process called *crenation*. Figure 9.12 shows red blood cells under all three conditions: isotonic, hypotonic, and hypertonic. Therefore, it is critical that any solution used intravenously be isotonic to prevent red blood cells from being destroyed.

Isotonic Having the same osmolarity.

Hypotonic Having an osmolarity *less than* the surrounding blood plasma or cells.

Hypertonic Having an osmolarity *greater than* the surrounding blood plasma or cells.

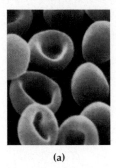  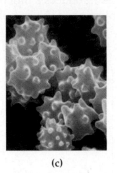

(a)   (b)   (c)

◄ **Figure 9.12**
Red blood cells.
In an isotonic solution the blood cells are normal in appearance (a), but the cells in a hypotonic solution (b) are swollen because of water gain, and those in a hypertonic solution (c) are shriveled because of water loss.

Worked Example **9.17** Properties of Solutions: Osmolarity

The solution of glucose commonly used intravenously has a concentration of 5.0% (m/v) glucose. What is the osmolarity of this solution? The molar mass of glucose is 180 g/mol.

ANALYSIS Since glucose is a molecular substance that does not give ions in solution, the osmolarity of the solution is the same as the molarity. Recall from Section 9.7 that a solution of 5.0% (m/v) glucose has a concentration of 5.0 g glucose per 100 mL of solution, which is equivalent to 50 g per liter of solution. Thus, finding the molar concentration of glucose requires a mass to mole conversion.

BALLPARK ESTIMATE One liter of solution contains 50 g of glucose (MW = 180 g/mol). Thus, 50 g of glucose is equal to a little more than 0.25 mol, so a solution concentration of 50 g/L is equal to about 0.25 osmol, or 0.25 M.

SOLUTION

STEP 1: Identify known information. We know the (m/v)% concentration of the glucose solution.

$$5.0\% \,(m/v) = \frac{5.0 \text{ g glucose}}{100 \text{ mL solution}} \times 100\%$$

STEP 2: Identify answer and units. We are looking for osmolarity, which in this case is equal to the molarity of the solution because glucose is a molecular substance and does not dissociate into ions.

$$\text{Osmolarity} = \text{Molarity} = ?? \text{ mol/liter}$$

STEP 3: **Identify conversion factors.** The (m/v)% concentration is defined as grams of solute per 100 mL of solution, and molarity is defined as moles of solute per liter of solution. We will need to convert from milliliters to liters and then use molar mass to convert grams of glucose to moles of glucose.

$$\frac{g \text{ glucose}}{100 \text{ mL}} \times \frac{1000 \text{ mL}}{L} \longrightarrow \frac{g \text{ glucose}}{L}$$

$$\frac{g \text{ glucose}}{L} \times \frac{1 \text{ mol glucose}}{180 \text{ g glucose}} \longrightarrow \frac{\text{moles glucose}}{L}$$

STEP 4: **Solve.** Starting with the (m/v)% glucose concentration, we first find the number of grams of glucose in 1 L of solution and then convert to moles of glucose per liter.

$$\left(\frac{5.0 \text{ g glucose}}{100 \text{ mL solution}}\right)\left(\frac{1000 \text{ mL}}{1 \text{ L}}\right) = \frac{50 \text{ g glucose}}{L \text{ solution}}$$

$$\left(\frac{50 \text{ g glucose}}{1 \text{ L}}\right)\left(\frac{1 \text{ mol}}{180 \text{ g}}\right) = 0.28 \text{ M glucose} = 0.28 \text{ osmol}$$

BALLPARK CHECK The calculated osmolarity is reasonably close to our estimate of 0.25 osmol.

Worked Example 9.18 Properties of Solutions: Osmolarity

What mass of NaCl is needed to make 1.50 L of a 0.300 osmol solution? The molar mass of NaCl is 58.44 g/mol.

ANALYSIS Since NaCl is an ionic substance that produces 2 mol of ions (Na^+, Cl^-) when it dissociates, the osmolarity of the solution is twice the molarity. From the volume and the osmolarity we can determine the moles of NaCl needed and then perform a mole to mass conversion.

SOLUTION

STEP 1: **Identify known information.** We know the volume and the osmolarity of the final NaCl solution.

$V = 1.50 \text{ L}$

$0.300 \text{ osmol} = \left(\dfrac{0.300 \text{ mol ions}}{L}\right)$

STEP 2: **Identify answer and units.** We are looking for the mass of NaCl.

Mass of NaCl = ?? g

STEP 3: **Identify conversion factors.** Starting with osmolarity in the form (moles NaCl/L), we can use volume to determine the number of moles of solute. We can then use molar mass for the mole to mass conversion.

$$\left(\frac{\text{moles NaCl}}{L}\right) \times (L) = \text{moles NaCl}$$

$$(\text{moles NaCl}) \times \left(\frac{g \text{ NaCl}}{\text{mole NaCl}}\right) = g \text{ NaCl}$$

STEP 4: **Solve.** Use the appropriate conversions, remembering that NaCl produces two ions per formula unit, to find the mass of NaCl.

$$\left(\frac{0.300 \text{ mol ions}}{L}\right)\left(\frac{1 \text{ mol NaCl}}{2 \text{ mol ions}}\right)(1.50 \text{ L}) = 0.225 \text{ mol NaCl}$$

$$(0.225 \text{ mol NaCl})\left(\frac{58.44 \text{ g NaCl}}{\text{mol NaCl}}\right) = 13.1 \text{ g NaCl}$$

PROBLEM 9.29

What is the osmolarity of the following solutions?

(a) 0.35 M KBr

(b) 0.15 M glucose + 0.05 M K_2SO_4

PROBLEM 9.30

A typical oral rehydration solution (ORS) for infants contains 90 mEq/L Na^+, 20 mEq/L K^+, 110 mEq/L Cl^-, and 2.0% (m/v) glucose (MW = 180 g/mol).

(a) Calculate the concentration of each ORS component in units of molarity.

(b) What is the osmolarity of the solution, and how does it compare with the osmolarity of blood plasma?

9.13 Dialysis

Dialysis is similar to osmosis, except that the pores in a dialysis membrane are larger than those in an osmotic membrane so that both solvent molecules and small solute particles can pass through, but large colloidal particles such as proteins cannot pass. (The exact dividing line between a "small" molecule and a "large" one is imprecise, and dialysis membranes with a variety of pore sizes are available.) Dialysis membranes include animal bladders, parchment, and cellophane.

Perhaps the most important medical use of dialysis is in artificial kidney machines, where *hemodialysis* is used to cleanse the blood of patients whose kidneys malfunction (Figure 9.13). Blood is diverted from the body and pumped through a long cellophane dialysis tube suspended in an isotonic solution formulated to contain many of the same components as blood plasma. These substances—glucose, NaCl, $NaHCO_3$, and KCl— have the same concentrations in the dialysis solution as they do in blood so that they have no net passage through the membrane.

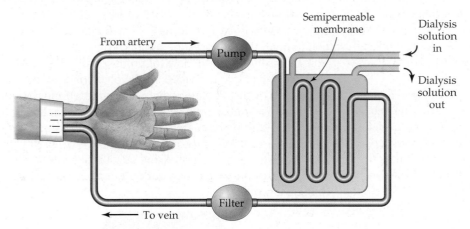

◄ **Figure 9.13**
Operation of a hemodialysis unit used for purifying blood.
Blood is pumped from an artery through a coiled semipermeable membrane of cellophane. Small waste products pass through the membrane and are washed away by an isotonic dialysis solution.

Small waste materials such as urea pass through the dialysis membrane from the blood to the solution side where they are washed away, but cells, proteins, and other important blood components are prevented from passing through the membrane because of their larger size. In addition, the dialysis fluid concentration can be controlled so that imbalances in electrolytes are corrected. The wash solution is changed every 2 h, and a typical hemodialysis procedure lasts for 4–7 h.

As noted above, colloidal particles are too large to pass through a semipermeable membreane. Protein molecules, in particular, do not cross semipermeable membranes and thus play an essential role in determining the osmolarity of body fluids. The distribution of water and solutes across the capillary walls that separate blood plasma from the fluid

◄ The delivery of oxygen and nutrients to the cells and the removal of waste products are regulated by osmosis.

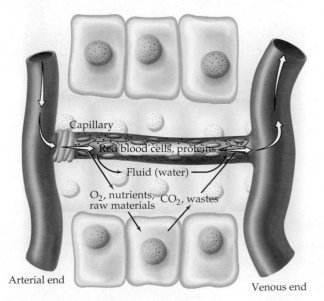

surrounding cells is controlled by the balance between blood pressure and osmotic pressure. The pressure of blood inside the capillary tends to push water out of the plasma (filtration), but the osmotic pressure of colloidal protein molecules tends to draw water into the plasma (reabsorption). The balance between the two processes varies with location in the body. At the arterial end of a capillary, where blood pumped from the heart has a higher pressure, filtration is favored, At the venous end, where blood pressure is lower, reabsorption is favored, causing waste products from metabolism to enter the bloodstream, to be removed by the kidneys.

CHEMISTRY IN ACTION

Timed-Release Medications

There is much more in most medications than medicine. Even something as simple as a generic aspirin tablet contains a binder to keep it from crumbling, a filler to bring it to the right size and help it disintegrate in the stomach, and a lubricant to keep it from sticking to the manufacturing equipment. Timed-release medications are more complex still.

The widespread use of timed-release medication dates from the introduction of Contac decongestant in 1961. The original idea was simple: tiny beads of medicine were encapsulated by coating them with varying thicknesses of a slow-dissolving polymer. Those beads with a thinner coat dissolve and release their medicine more rapidly; those with a thicker coat dissolve more slowly. Combining the right number of beads with the right thicknesses into a single capsule makes possible the gradual release of medication over a predictable time.

The technology of timed-release medications has become much more sophisticated in recent years, and the kinds of medications that can be delivered have become more numerous. Some medicines, for instance, either damage the stomach lining or are destroyed by the highly acidic environment in the stomach but can be delivered safely if given an *enteric coating*. The enteric coating is a polymeric material formulated so that it is stable in acid but reacts and is destroyed when it passes into the more basic environment of the intestines.

More recently, dermal patches have been developed to deliver drugs directly by diffusion through the skin. Patches are available to treat conditions from angina to motion sickness, as well as nicotine patches to help reduce cigarette cravings. One clever new device for timed release of medication through the skin uses the osmotic effect to force a drug from its reservoir. Useful only for drugs that do not dissolve in water, the device is divided into two compartments, one containing medication covered by a perforated membrane and the other containing a hygroscopic material (Section 9.3) covered by a semipermeable membrane. As moisture from the air diffuses through the membrane into the compartment with the hygroscopic material, the buildup of osmotic pressure squeezes the medication out of the other compartment through tiny holes.

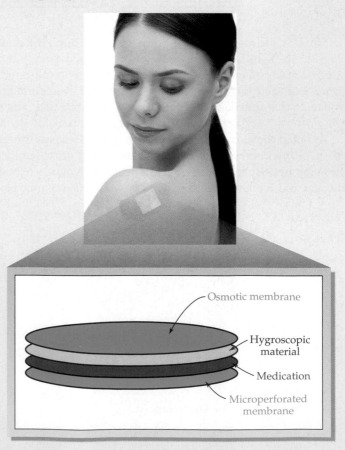

▲ The small beads of medicine are coated with different thicknesses of a slow-dissolving polymer so that they dissolve and release medicine at different times.

See Chemistry in Action Problem 9.93 at the end of the chapter.

SUMMARY: REVISITING THE CHAPTER GOALS

1. What are solutions, and what factors affect solubility? Mixtures are classified as either *heterogeneous*, if the mixing is nonuniform, or *homogeneous*, if the mixing is uniform. *Solutions* are homogeneous mixtures that contain particles the size of ions and molecules (<2.0 nm diameter), whereas larger particles (2.0–500 nm diameter) are present in *colloids*.

The maximum amount of one substance (the *solute*) that can be dissolved in another (the *solvent*) is called the substance's *solubility*. Substances tend to be mutually soluble when their intermolecular forces are similar. The solubility in water of a solid often increases with temperature, but the solubility of a gas always decreases with temperature. Pressure significantly affects gas solubilities, which are directly proportional to their partial pressure over the solution (*Henry's law*) (*see Problems 36–43, 94, 105*).

2. How is the concentration of a solution expressed? The concentration of a solution can be expressed in several ways, including molarity, weight/weight percent composition, weight/volume percent composition, and parts per million (or billion). Osmolarity is used to express the total concentration of dissolved particles (ions and molecules). Molarity, which expresses concentration as the number of moles of solute per liter of solution, is the most useful method when calculating quantities of reactants or products for reactions in aqueous solution (*see Problems 44–65, 86, 88, 89, 91, 94–105, 107, 108*).

3. How are dilutions carried out? A dilution is carried out by adding more solvent to an existing solution. Only the amount of solvent changes; the amount of solute remains the same. Thus,

the molarity times the volume of the dilute solution is equal to the molarity times the volume of the concentrated solution: $M_cV_c = M_dV_d$ (*see Problems 35, 66–71, 98*).

4. What is an electrolyte? Substances that form ions when dissolved in water and whose water solutions therefore conduct an electric current are called *electrolytes*. Substances that ionize completely in water are *strong electrolytes*, those that ionize partially are *weak electrolytes*, and those that do not ionize are *nonelectrolytes*. Body fluids contain small amounts of many different electrolytes, whose concentrations are expressed as moles of ionic charge, or equivalents, per liter (*see Problems 32,33, 72–79, 97, 108*).

5. How do solutions differ from pure solvents in their behavior? In comparing a solution to a pure solvent, the solution has a lower vapor pressure at a given temperature, a higher boiling point, and a lower melting point. Called *colligative properties*, these effects depend only on the number of dissolved particles, not on their chemical identity (*see Problems 32, 33, 43, 80–83, 108*).

6. What is osmosis? *Osmosis* occurs when solutions of different concentration are separated by a semipermeable membrane that allows solvent molecules to pass but blocks the passage of solute ions and molecules. Solvent flows from the more dilute side to the more concentrated side until sufficient *osmotic pressure* builds up and stops the flow. An effect similar to osmosis occurs when membranes of larger pore size are used. In *dialysis*, the membrane allows the passage of solvent and small dissolved molecules but prevents passage of proteins and larger particles (*see Problems 31, 84, 85, 87*).

KEY WORDS

Colligative property, *p. 275*

Colloid, *p. 253*

Dilution factor, *p. 271*

Electrolyte, *p. 273*

Equivalent (Eq), *p. 273*

Gram-equivalent (g-Eq), *p. 273*

Henry's law, *p. 261*

Heterogeneous mixture, *p. 253*

Homogeneous mixture, *p. 253*

Hygroscopic, *p. 258*

Hypertonic, *p. 281*

Hypotonic, *p. 281*

Isotonic, *p. 281*

Mass/mass percent concentration, (m/m)%, *p. 264*

mass/volume percent concentration, (m/v)%, *p. 264*

Miscible, *p. 258*

Molarity (M), *p. 268*

Nonelectrolyte, *p. 273*

Osmolarity (osmol), *p. 280*

Osmosis, *p. 280*

Osmotic pressure, *p. 280*

Parts per billion (ppb), *p. 267*

Parts per million (ppm), *p. 267*

Saturated solution, *p. 258*

Solubility, *p. 258*

Solute, *p. 254*

Solution, *p. 253*

Solvation, *p. 256*

Solvent, *p. 254*

Strong electrolyte, *p. 273*

Supersaturated solution, *p. 259*

Volume/volume percent concentration, (v/v)%, *p. 264*

Weak electrolyte, *p. 273*

CONCEPT MAP: SOLUTIONS

Formation of a solution depends on many factors, including the attractive forces between solute and solvent particles, temperature, and pressure (gases). The extent to which a solute dissolves in solution can be expressed either qualitatively or using quantitative concentration units. The most common concentration unit in chemical applications is molarity (moles of solute/L solution), which is also useful in quantitative relationships involving reactions that take place in solution. Colligative properties of solution, including boiling and freezing points, will vary with the amount of solute dissolved in solution. These relationships are illustrated in the concept map in Figure 9.14.

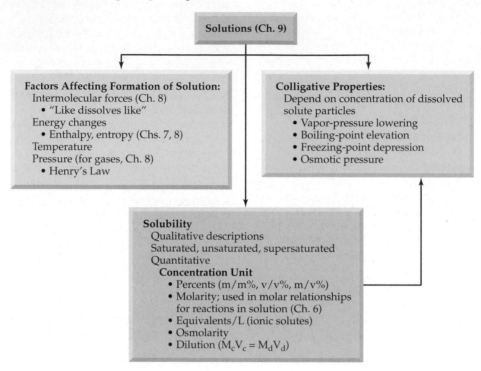

▲ **Figure 9.14**

UNDERSTANDING KEY CONCEPTS

9.31 Assume that two liquids are separated by a semipermeable membrane, with pure solvent on the right side, and a solution of a solute on the left side. Make a drawing that shows the situation after equilibrium is reached.

Before equilibrium

9.32 When 1 mol of HCl is added to 1 kg of water, the boiling point increases by 1.0 °C, but when 1 mol of acetic acid, CH_3CO_2H, is added to 1 kg of water, the boiling point increases by only 0.5 °C. Explain.

9.33 HF is a weak electrolyte and HBr is a strong electrolyte. Which of the curves in the figure represents the change in the boiling point of an aqueous solution when 1 mole of HF is added to 1 kg of water, and which represents the change when 1 mol of HBr is added?

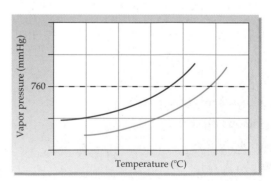

9.34 Assume that you have two full beakers, one containing pure water (blue) and the other containing an equal volume of a 10% (w/v) solution of glucose (green). Which of the drawings (a)–(c) best represents the two beakers after they have stood uncovered for several days and partial evaporation has occurred? Explain.

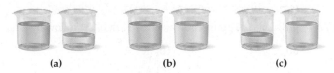

(a)   (b)   (c)

9.35   A beaker containing 150.0 mL of 0.1 M glucose is represented by (a). Which of the drawings (b)–(d) represents the

solution that results when 50.0 mL is withdrawn from (a) and then diluted by a factor of 4?

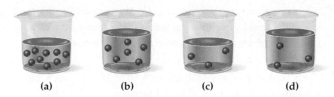

(a)   (b)   (c)   (d)

ADDITIONAL PROBLEMS

SOLUTIONS AND SOLUBILITY

9.36   What is the difference between a homogeneous mixture and a heterogeneous one?

9.37   How can you tell a solution from a colloid?

9.38   What characteristic of water allows it to dissolve ionic solids?

9.39   Why does water not dissolve motor oil?

9.40   Which of the following are solutions?

    (a) Italian salad dressing   **(b)** Rubbing alcohol

    (c) Algae in pond water   **(d)** Black coffee

9.41   Based on the predominant intermolecular forces, which of the following pairs of liquids are likely to be miscible?

    (a) H_2SO_4 and H_2O **(b)** C_8H_{18} and C_6H_6

    (c) CH_2Cl_2, and H_2O **(d)** CS_2 and CCl_4

9.42   The solubility of NH_3 gas in water at an NH_3 pressure of 760.0 mmHg is 51.8 g/100 mL. What is the solubility of NH_3 if its partial pressure is reduced to 225.0 mmHg?

9.43   The solubility of CO_2 gas in water is 0.15 g/100 mL at a CO_2 pressure of 760 mmHg. What is the solubility of CO_2 in a soft drink (which is mainly water) that was bottled under a CO_2 pressure of 4.5 atm?

CONCENTRATION AND DILUTION OF SOLUTIONS

9.44   Is a solution highly concentrated if it is saturated? Is a solution saturated if it is highly concentrated?

9.45   How is mass/volume percent concentration defined and for what types of solutions is it typically used?

9.46   How is molarity defined?

9.47   How is volume/volume percent concentration defined and for what types of solutions is it typically used?

9.48   How would you prepare 750.0 mL of a 6.0% (v/v) ethyl alcohol solution?

9.49   A dilute aqueous solution of boric acid, H_3BO_3 is often used as an eyewash. How would you prepare 500.0 mL of a 0.50% (m/v) boric acid solution?

9.50   Describe how you would prepare 250 mL of a 0.10 M NaCl solution.

9.51   Describe how you would prepare 1.50 L of a 7.50% (m/v) $Mg(NO_3)_2$ solution.

9.52   What is the mass/volume percent concentration of the following solutions?

    (a) 0.078 mol KCl in 75 mL of solution

    (b) 0.044 mol sucrose $(C_{12}H_{22}O_{11})$ in 380 mL of solution

9.53   The concentration of glucose in blood is approximately 90 mg/100 mL. What is the mass/volume percent concentration of glucose? What is the molarity of glucose?

9.54   How many moles of each substance are needed to prepare the following solutions?

    (a) 50.0 mL of 8.0% (m/v) KCl $(MW = 74.55 \text{ g/mol})$

    (b) 200.0 mL of 7.5% (m/v) acetic acid $(MW = 60.05 \text{ g/mol})$

9.55   Which of the following solutions is more concentrated?

    (a) 0.50 M KCl or 5.0% (m/v) KCl

    (b) 2.5% (m/v) $NaHSO_4$ or 0.025 M $NaHSO_4$

9.56   If you had only 23 g of KOH remaining in a bottle, how many milliliters of 10.0% (m/v) solution could you prepare? How many milliliters of 0.25 M solution?

9.57   Over-the-counter hydrogen peroxide (H_2O_2) solutions are 3% (m/v). What is this concentration in moles per liter?

9.58   The lethal dosage of potassium cyanide (KCN) in rats is 10 mg KCN per kilogram of body weight. What is this concentration in parts per million?

9.59   The maximum concentration set by the U.S. Environmental Protection Agency for lead in drinking water is 15 ppb. (*Hint*: 1 ppb = $1\,\mu g/L$)

    (a) What is this concentration in milligrams per liter?

    (b) How many liters of water contaminated at this maximum level must you drink to consume 1.0 μg of lead?

9.60   What is the molarity of the following solutions?

    (a) 12.5 g $NaHCO_3$ in 350.0 mL solution

    (b) 45.0 g H_2SO_4 in 300.0 mL solution

    (c) 30.0 g NaCl dissolved to make 500.0 mL solution

9.61   How many grams of solute are in the following solutions?

    (a) 200 mL of 0.30 M acetic acid, CH_3CO_2H

    (b) 1.50 L of 0.25 M NaOH

    (c) 750 mL of 2.5 M nitric acid, HNO_3

9.62 How many milliliters of a 0.75 M HCl solution do you need to obtain 0.0040 mol of HCl?

9.63 Nalorphine, a relative of morphine, is used to combat withdrawal symptoms in heroin users. How many milliliters of a 0.40% (m/v) solution of nalorphine must be injected to obtain a dose of 1.5 mg?

9.64 A flask containing 450 mL of 0.50 M H_2SO_4 was accidentally knocked to the floor. How many grams of $NaHCO_3$ do you need to put on the spill to neutralize the acid according to the following equation?

$$H_2SO_4(aq) + 2\,NaHCO_3(aq) \longrightarrow$$
$$Na_2SO_4(aq) + 2\,H_2O(l) + 2\,CO_2(g)$$

9.65 Sodium thiosulfate $(Na_2S_2O_3)$, the major component in photographic fixer solution, reacts with silver bromide to dissolve it according to the following reaction:

$$AgBr(s) + 2\,Na_2S_2O_3(aq) \longrightarrow$$
$$Na_3Ag(S_2O_3)_2(aq) + NaBr(aq)$$

(a) How many moles of $Na_2S_2O_3$ would be required to react completely with 0.450 g of AgBr?

(b) How many mL of 0.02 M $Na_2S_2O_3$ contain this number of moles?

9.66 What is the final volume of an orange juice prepared from 100.0 mL of orange juice concentrate if the final juice is to be 20.0% of the strength of the original?

9.67 What is the final volume of NaOH solution prepared from 100.0 mL of 0.500 M NaOH if you wanted the final concentration to be 0.150 M?

9.68 An aqueous solution that contains 285 ppm of potassium nitrate (KNO_3) is being used to feed plants in a garden. What volume of this solution is needed to prepare 2.0 L of a solution that is 75 ppm in KNO_3?

9.69 What is the concentration of a NaCl solution, in (m/v)%, prepared by diluting 65 mL of a saturated solution, which has a concentration of 37 (m/v)%, to 480 mL?

9.70 Concentrated (12.0 M) hydrochloric acid is sold for household and industrial purposes under the name "muriatic acid." How many milliliters of 0.500 M HCl solution can be made from 25.0 mL of 12.0 M HCl solution?

9.71 Dilute solutions of $NaHCO_3$ are sometimes used in treating acid burns. How many milliliters of 0.100 M $NaHCO_3$ solution are needed to prepare 750.0 mL of 0.0500 M $NaHCO_3$ solution?

ELECTROLYTES

9.72 What is an electrolyte?

9.73 Give an example of a strong electrolyte and a nonelectrolyte.

9.74 What does it mean when we say that the concentration of Ca^{2+} in blood is 3.0 mEq/L?

9.75 What is the total anion concentration (in mEq/L) of a solution that contains 5.0 mEq/L Na^+, 12.0 mEq/L Ca^{2+}, and 2.0 mEq/L Li^+?

9.76 Kaochlor, a 10% (m/v) KCl solution, is an oral electrolyte supplement administered for potassium deficiency. How many milliequivalents of K^+ are in a 30 mL dose?

9.77 Calculate the gram-equivalent for each of the following ions:

(a) Ca^{2+} (b) K^+

(c) SO_4^{2-} (d) PO_4^{3-}

9.78 Look up the concentration of Cl^- ion in blood in Table 9.6. How many milliliters of blood would be needed to obtain 1.0 g of Cl^- ions?

9.79 Normal blood contains 3 mEq/L of Mg^{2+}. How many milligrams of Mg^{2+} are present in 150.0 mL of blood?

PROPERTIES OF SOLUTIONS

9.80 Which lowers the freezing point of 2.0 kg of water more, 0.20 mol NaOH or 0.20 mol $Ba(OH)_2$? Both compounds are strong electrolytes. Explain.

9.81 Which solution has the higher boiling point, 0.500 M glucose or 0.300 M KCl? Explain.

9.82 Methanol, CH_3OH, is sometimes used as an antifreeze for the water in automobile windshield washer fluids. How many moles of methanol must be added to 5.00 kg of water to lower its freezing point to $-10.0\,°C$? (For each mole of solute, the freezing point of 1 kg of water is lowered $1.86\,°C$.)

9.83 Hard candy is prepared by dissolving pure sugar and flavoring in water and heating the solution to boiling. What is the boiling point of a solution produced by adding 650 g of cane sugar (molar mass 342.3 g/mol) to 1.5 kg of water? (For each mole of nonvolatile solute, the boiling point of 1 kg of water is raised $0.51\,°C$.)

OSMOSIS

9.84 Why do red blood cells swell up and burst when placed in pure water?

9.85 What does it mean when we say that a 0.15 M NaCl solution is isotonic with blood, whereas distilled water is hypotonic?

9.86 Which of the following solutions has the higher osmolarity?

(a) 0.25 M KBr or 0.20 M Na_2SO_4

(b) 0.30 M NaOH or 3.0% (m/v) NaOH

9.87 Which of the following solutions will give rise to a greater osmotic pressure at equilibrium: 5.00 g of NaCl in 350.0 mL water or 35.0 g of glucose in 400.0 mL water? For NaCl, MW = 58.5 amu; for glucose, MW = 180 amu.

9.88 A pickling solution for preserving food is prepared by dissolving 270 g of NaCl in 3.8 L of water. Calculate the osmolarity of the solution.

9.89 An isotonic solution must be approximately 0.30 osmol. How much KCl is needed to prepare 175 mL of an isotonic solution?

CHEMISTRY IN ACTION

9.90 How does the body increase oxygen availability at high altitude? [*Breathing and Oxygen Transport, p. 263*]

9.91 What are the major electrolytes in sweat, and what are their approximate concentrations in mEq/L? [*Electrolytes, Fluid Replacement, and Sports Drinks, p. 276*]

9.92 Why is a sports drink more effective than plain water for rehydration after extended exercise? [*Electrolytes, Fluid Replacement, and Sports Drinks, p. 276*]

9.93 How does an enteric coating on a medication work? [*Timed-Release Medications, p. 284*]

GENERAL QUESTIONS AND PROBLEMS

9.94 Hyperbaric chambers, which provide high pressures (up to 6 atm) of either air or pure oxygen, are used to treat a variety of conditions, ranging from decompression sickness in deep-sea divers to carbon monoxide poisoning.

  (a) What is the partial pressure of O_2 (in millimeters of Hg) in a hyperbaric chamber pressurized to 5 atm with air that is 18% in O_2?

  (b) What is the solubility of O_2 (in grams per 100 mL) in the blood at this partial pressure? The solubility of O_2 is 2.1 g/100 mL for $P_{O_2} = 1$ atm.

9.95 Express the solubility of O_2 in Problem 9.94(b) in units of molarity.

9.96 Uric acid, the principal constituent of some kidney stones, has the formula $C_5H_4N_4O_3$. In aqueous solution, the solubility of uric acid is only 0.067 g/L. Express this concentration in (m/v)%, in parts per million, and in molarity.

9.97 Emergency treatment of cardiac arrest victims sometimes involves injection of a calcium chloride solution directly into the heart muscle. How many grams of $CaCl_2$ are administered in an injection of 5.0 mL of a 5.0% (m/v) solution? How many milliequivalents of Ca^{2+}?

9.98 Nitric acid, HNO_3, is available commercially at a concentration of 16 M.

  (a) What volume would you need to obtain 0.150 mol HNO_3?

  (b) To what volume must you dilute this volume of HNO_3 from part (a) to prepare a 0.20 M solution?

9.99 One test for vitamin C (ascorbic acid, $C_6H_8O_6$) is based on the reaction of the vitamin with iodine:

$$C_6H_8O_6(aq) + I_2(aq) \longrightarrow C_6H_6O_6(aq) + 2\,HI(aq)$$

  (a) A 25.0 mL sample of a fruit juice requires 13.0 mL of 0.0100 M I_2 solution for reaction. How many moles of ascorbic acid are in the sample?

  (b) What is the molarity of ascorbic acid in the fruit juice?

  (c) The Food and Drug Administration recommends that 60 mg of ascorbic acid be consumed per day. How many milliliters of the fruit juice in part (a) must a person drink to obtain the recommended dosage?

9.100 *Ringer's solution*, used in the treatment of burns and wounds, is prepared by dissolving 8.6 g of NaCl, 0.30 g of KCl, and 0.33 g of $CaCl_2$ in water and diluting to a volume of 1.00 L. What is the molarity of each component?

9.101 What is the osmolarity of Ringer's solution (see Problem 9.100)? Is it hypotonic, isotonic, or hypertonic with blood plasma (0.30 osmol)?

9.102 The typical dosage of statin drugs for the treatment of high cholesterol is 10 mg. Assuming a total blood volume of 5.0 L, calculate the (m/v)% concentration of drug in the blood in units of g/100 mL.

9.103 Assuming the density of blood in healthy individuals is approximately 1.05 g/mL, report the concentration of drug in Problem 9.102 in units of ppm.

9.104 In all 50 states, a person with a blood alcohol concentration of 0.080% (v/v) is considered legally drunk. What volume of total alcohol does this concentration represent, assuming a blood volume of 5.0 L?

9.105 Ammonia, NH_3, is very soluble in water (51.8 g/L at 20 °C and 760 mmHg).

  (a) Show how NH_3 can hydrogen bond to water.

  (b) What is the solubility of ammonia in water in moles per liter?

9.106 Cobalt(II) chloride, a blue solid, can absorb water from the air to form cobalt(II) chloride hexahydrate, a pink solid. The equilibrium is so sensitive to moisture in the air that $CoCl_2$ is used as a humidity indicator.

  (a) Write a balanced equation for the equilibrium. Be sure to include water as a reactant to produce the hexahydrate.

  (b) How many grams of water are released by the decomposition of 2.50 g of cobalt(II) chloride hexahydrate?

9.107 How many milliliters of 0.150 M $BaCl_2$ are needed to react completely with 35.0 mL of 0.200 M Na_2SO_4? How many grams of $BaSO_4$ will be formed?

9.108 Many compounds are only partially dissociated into ions in aqueous solution. Trichloroacetic acid (CCl_3CO_2H), for instance, is partially dissociated in water according to the equation

$$CCl_3CO_2H(aq) \rightleftharpoons H^+(aq) + CCl_3CO_2^-(aq)$$

For a solution prepared by dissolving 1.00 mol of trichloroacetic acid in 1.00 kg of water, 36.0% of the trichloroacetic acid dissociates to form H^+ and $CCl_3CO_2^-$ ions.

  (a) What is the total concentration of dissolved ions and molecules in 1 kg of water?

  (b) What is the freezing point of this solution? (The freezing point of 1 kg of water is lowered 1.86 °C for each mole of solute particles.)

Acids and Bases

CONTENTS

◀ Acids are found in many of the foods we eat, including tomatoes, peppers, and these citrus fruits.

A cids! The word evokes images of dangerous, corrosive liquids that eat away everything they touch. Although a few well-known substances such as sulfuric acid (H_2SO_4) do indeed fit this description, most acids are relatively harmless. In fact, many acids, such as ascorbic acid (vitamin C), are necessary for life. We have already touched on the subject of acids and bases on several occasions, but the time has come for a more detailed study.

10.1 Acids and Bases in Aqueous Solution

Let us take a moment to review what we said about acids and bases in Sections 3.11 and 5.10 before going on to a more systematic study:

- An acid is a substance that produces hydrogen ions, H^+, when dissolved in water.
- A base is a substance that produces hydroxide ions, OH^-, when dissolved in water.
- The neutralization reaction of an acid with a base yields water plus a *salt*, an ionic compound composed of the cation from the base and the anion from the acid.

The above definitions of acids and bases were proposed in 1887 by the Swedish chemist Svante Arrhenius and are useful for many purposes. The definitions are limited, however, because they refer only to reactions that take place in aqueous solutions. (We will see shortly how the definitions can be broadened.) Another issue is that the H^+ ion is so reactive it does not exist in water. Instead, H^+ reacts with H_2O to give the **hydronium ion**, H_3O^+, as mentioned in Section 3.11. When gaseous HCl dissolves in water, for instance, H_3O^+ and Cl^- are formed. As described in Section 4.9, electrostatic potential maps show that the hydrogen of HCl is positively polarized and electron-poor (blue), whereas the oxygen of water is negatively polarized and electron-rich (red):

Hydronium ion The H_3O^+ ion, formed when an acid reacts with water.

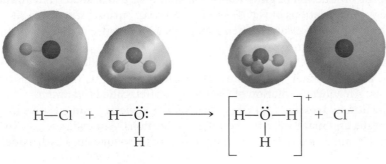

Thus, the Arrhenius definition is updated to acknowledge that an acid yields H_3O^+ in water rather than H^+. In practice, however, the notations H_3O^+ and $H^+(aq)$ are often used interchangeably.

The Arrhenius definition of a base is correct as far as it goes, but it is important to realize that the OH^- ions "produced" by the base can come from either of two sources. Metal hydroxides, such as NaOH, KOH, and $Ba(OH)_2$, are ionic compounds that already contain OH^- ions and merely release those ions when they dissolve in water. Some molecular compounds such as ammonia, however, are not ionic and contain no OH^- ions in their structure. Nonetheless, they can act as bases to produce OH^- ions in reactions with water, as will be seen in Section 10.3.

10.2 Some Common Acids and Bases

Acids and bases are present in a variety of foods and consumer products. Acids generally have a sour taste, and nearly every sour food contains an acid: Lemons, oranges, and grapefruit contain citric acid, for instance, and sour milk contains lactic acid. Bases are not so obvious in foods, but most of us have them stored under the kitchen or bathroom sink. Bases are present in many household cleaning agents, from perfumed bar soap, to ammonia-based window cleaners, to the substance you put down the drain to dissolve hair, grease, and other materials that clog it.

Some of the most common acids and bases are listed below. It is a good idea at this point to learn their names and formulas, because we will refer to them often.

- **Sulfuric acid, H_2SO_4,** is probably the most important raw material in the chemical and pharmaceutical industries, and it is manufactured in greater quantity worldwide than any other industrial chemical. Over 45 million tons are prepared in the United States annually for use in many hundreds of industrial processes, including the preparation of phosphate fertilizers. Its most common consumer use is as the acid found in automobile batteries. As anyone who has splashed battery acid on his or her skin or clothing knows, sulfuric acid is highly corrosive and can cause painful burns.
- **Hydrochloric acid, HCl,** or *muriatic acid*, as it was historically known, has many industrial applications, including its use in metal cleaning and in the manufacture of high-fructose corn syrup. Aqueous HCl is also present as "stomach acid" in the digestive systems of most mammals.
- **Phosphoric acid, H_3PO_4,** is used in vast quantities in the manufacture of phosphate fertilizers. In addition, it is also used as an additive in foods and toothpastes. The tart taste of many soft drinks is due to the presence of phosphoric acid.
- **Nitric acid, HNO_3,** is a strong oxidizing agent that is used for many purposes, including the manufacture of ammonium nitrate fertilizer and military explosives. When spilled on the skin, it leaves a characteristic yellow coloration because of its reaction with skin proteins.
- **Acetic acid, CH_3CO_2H,** is the primary organic constituent of vinegar. It also occurs in all living cells and is used in many industrial processes such as the preparation of solvents, lacquers, and coatings.
- **Sodium hydroxide, NaOH,** also called *caustic soda* or *lye*, is the most commonly used of all bases. Industrially, it is used in the production of aluminum from its ore, in the production of glass, and in the manufacture of soap from animal fat. Concentrated solutions of NaOH can cause severe burns if allowed to sit on the skin for long. Drain cleaners often contain NaOH because it reacts with the fats and proteins found in grease and hair.
- **Calcium hydroxide, $Ca(OH)_2$,** or *slaked lime*, is made industrially by treating lime (CaO) with water. It has many applications, including its use in mortars and cements. An aqueous solution of $Ca(OH)_2$ is often called *limewater*.
- **Magnesium hydroxide, $Mg(OH)_2$,** or *milk of magnesia*, is an additive in foods, toothpaste, and many over-the-counter medications. Antacids such as Rolaids™, Mylanta™, and Maalox™, for instance, all contain magnesium hydroxide.

▲ Common household cleaners typically contain bases (NaOH, NH_3). Soap is manufactured by the reaction of vegetable oils and animal fats with the bases NaOH and KOH.

- **Ammonia, NH₃,** is used primarily as a fertilizer, but it also has many other industrial applications, including the manufacture of pharmaceuticals and explosives. A dilute solution of ammonia is frequently used around the house as a glass cleaner.

10.3 The Brønsted–Lowry Definition of Acids and Bases

The Arrhenius definition of acids and bases discussed in Section 10.1 applies only to processes that take place in an aqueous solution. A far more general definition was proposed in 1923 by the Danish chemist Johannes Brønsted and the English chemist Thomas Lowry. A **Brønsted–Lowry acid** is any substance that is able to give a hydrogen ion, H^+, to another molecule or ion. A hydrogen *atom* consists of a proton and an electron, so a hydrogen *ion*, H^+, is simply a proton. Thus, we often refer to acids as *proton donors*. The reaction need not occur in water, and a Brønsted–Lowry acid need not give appreciable concentrations of H_3O^+ ions in water.

Brønsted–Lowry acid A substance that can donate a hydrogen ion, H^+, to another molecule or ion.

Different acids can supply different numbers of H^+ ions, as we saw in Section 3.11. Acids with one proton to donate, such as HCl or HNO_3, are called *monoprotic acids*; H_2SO_4 is a *diprotic acid* because it has two protons to donate, and H_3PO_4 is a *triprotic acid* because it has three protons to donate. Notice that the acidic H atoms (that is, the H atoms that are donated as protons) are bonded to electronegative atoms, such as chlorine or oxygen.

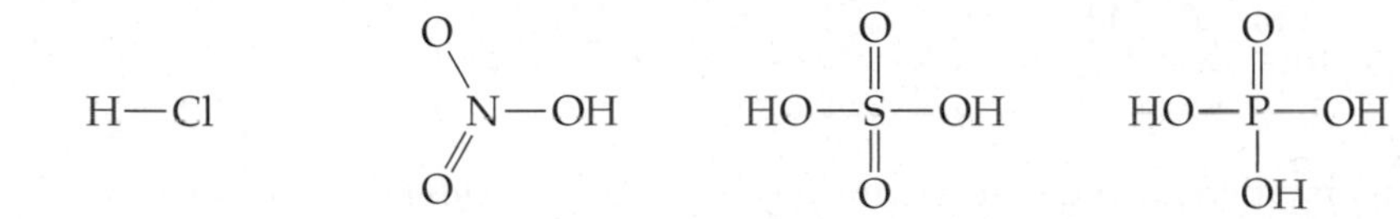

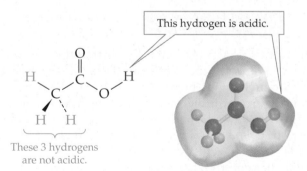

Acetic acid (CH_3CO_2H), an example of an organic acid, actually has a total of 4 hydrogens, but only the one bonded to the electronegative oxygen is positively polarized and therefore acidic. The 3 hydrogens bonded to carbon are not acidic. Most organic acids are similar in that they contain many hydrogen atoms, but only the one in the $-CO_2H$ group (blue in the electrostatic potential map) is acidic:

This hydrogen is acidic.

These 3 hydrogens are not acidic.

Acetic acid will react with water to produce H_3O^+ ions (Arrhenius acid definition) by donating a proton (Brønsted–Lowry acid definition) to water, as shown:

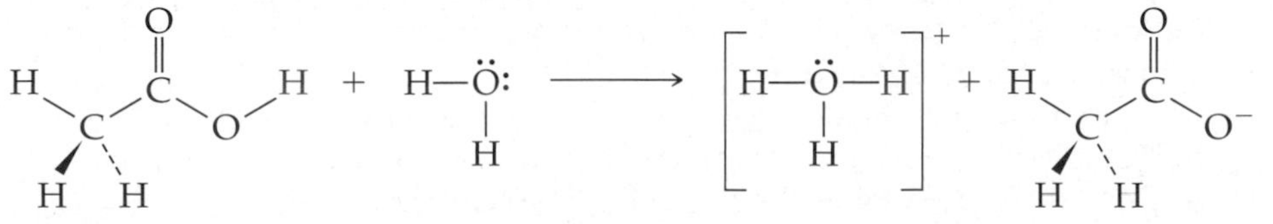

Whereas a Brønsted–Lowry acid is a substance that *donates* H^+ ions, a **Brønsted–Lowry base** is a substance that *accepts* H^+ ions from an acid. Ammonia will react

Brønsted–Lowry base A substance that can accept H^+ ions from an acid.

with water to produce OH^- ions (Arrhenius base definition) by accepting a proton (Brønsted–Lowry base definition), as shown:

> This OH^- ion comes from H_2O.

$$H-\overset{\cdot\cdot}{\underset{H}{N}}-H(g) \ + \ H_2O(l) \ \rightleftarrows \ H-\overset{+}{\underset{H}{N}}-H(aq) \ + \ OH^-(aq)$$

As with the acids, reactions involving Brønsted–Lowry bases need not occur in water, and the Brønsted–Lowry base need not give appreciable concentrations of OH^- ions in water. Gaseous NH_3, for example, acts as a base to accept H^+ from gaseous HCl and yield the ionic solid $NH_4^+ \ Cl^-$:

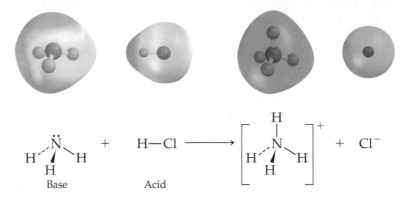

$$\underset{\text{Base}}{H\overset{\overset{\displaystyle \cdot\cdot}{N}}{\underset{H}{\diagdown}}H} \ + \ \underset{\text{Acid}}{H-Cl} \ \longrightarrow \ \left[H\overset{\overset{\displaystyle H}{|}}{\underset{H}{\diagdown}}{\underset{}{N}}H \right]^+ \ + \ Cl^-$$

Putting the acid and base definitions together, *an acid–base reaction is one in which a proton is transferred.* The general reaction between proton-donor acids and proton-acceptor bases can be represented as

> Electrons on base form bond with H^+ from acid.

$$B\colon \ + \ H-A \ \rightleftarrows \ B\overset{+}{-}H \ + \ A^-$$

$$B\colon^- \ + \ H-A \ \rightleftarrows \ B-H \ + \ A^-$$

where the abbreviation HA represents a Brønsted–Lowry acid and B: or B:$^-$ represents a Brønsted–Lowry base. Notice in these acid–base reactions that both electrons in the product B—H bond come from the base, as indicated by the curved arrow flowing from the electron pair of the base to the hydrogen atom of the acid. Thus, the B—H bond that forms is a coordinate covalent bond. In fact, a Brønsted–Lowry base *must* have such a lone pair of electrons; without them, it could not accept H^+ from an acid.

▶▶▶ Recall from Section 4.4 that a coordinate covalent bond is one where both electrons are donated by the same atom.

A base can either be neutral (B:) or negatively charged (B:$^-$). If the base is neutral, then the product has a positive charge (BH^+) after H^+ has been added. Ammonia is an example:

> Adding an H^+ creates positive charge.

$$\underset{\substack{\text{Ammonia} \\ \text{(a neutral base, B\colon)}}}{H-\overset{\overset{\displaystyle H}{|}}{\underset{\underset{\displaystyle H}{|}}{N}}\colon} \ + \ H-A \ \rightleftarrows \ \underset{\text{Ammonium ion}}{H-\overset{\overset{\displaystyle H}{|}}{\underset{\underset{\displaystyle H}{|}}{\overset{+}{N}}}-H} \ + \ \colon A^-$$

If the base is negatively charged, then the product is neutral (BH). Hydroxide ion is an example:

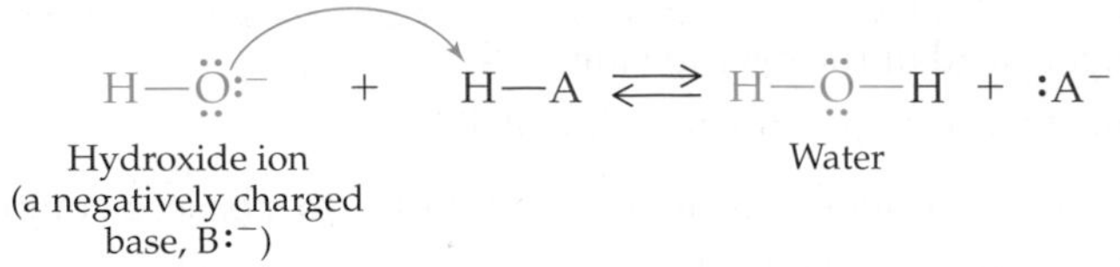

$$H-\ddot{O}:^- \quad + \quad H-A \rightleftharpoons H-\ddot{O}-H + :A^-$$

Hydroxide ion
(a negatively charged
base, $B:^-$)

Water

An important consequence of the Brønsted–Lowry definitions is that the *products* of an acid–base reaction can also behave as acids and bases. Many acid–base reactions are reversible, although in some cases the equilibrium constant for the reaction is quite large. For example, suppose we have as a forward reaction an acid HA donating a proton to a base B to produce A^-. This product A^- is a base because it can act as a proton acceptor in the reverse reaction. At the same time, the product BH^+ acts as an acid because it may donate a proton in the reverse reaction:

▶▶▶ When the equilibrium constant for a reaction is greater than 1, the forward reaction is favored. When the equilibrium constant is less than 1, the reverse reaction is favored (Section 7.8).

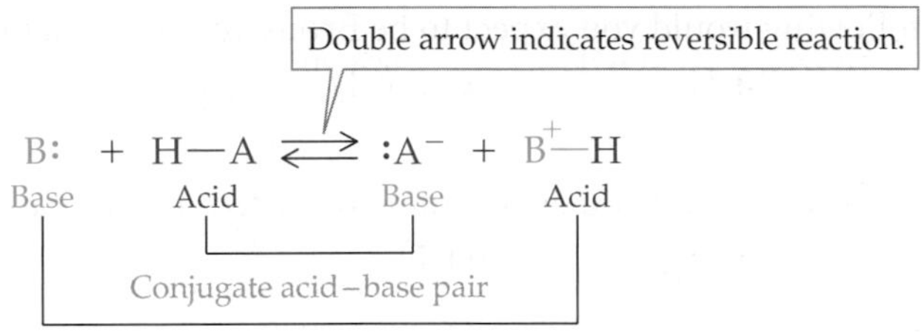

Double arrow indicates reversible reaction.

$$B: \; + \; H-A \; \rightleftharpoons \; :A^- \; + \; B\overset{+}{-}H$$

Base   Acid   Base   Acid

Conjugate acid–base pair

Pairs of chemical species such as B, BH^+ and HA, A^- are called **conjugate acid–base pairs**. They are species that are found on opposite sides of a chemical reaction whose formulas differ by only one H^+. Thus, the product anion A^- is the **conjugate base** of the reactant acid HA, and HA is the **conjugate acid** of the base A^-. Similarly, the reactant B is the conjugate base of the product acid BH^+, and BH^+ is the conjugate acid of the base B. The number of protons in a conjugate acid–base pair is always one greater than the number of protons in the base of the pair. To give some examples, acetic acid and acetate ion, the hydronium ion and water, and the ammonium ion and ammonia all make conjugate acid–base pairs:

Conjugate acid–base pair Two substances whose formulas differ by only a hydrogen ion, H^+.

Conjugate base The substance formed by loss of H^+ from an acid.

Conjugate acid The substance formed by addition of H^+ to a base.

Conjugate
acids
$$\begin{cases} CH_3\overset{O}{\overset{\|}{C}}OH \rightleftharpoons H^+ + CH_3\overset{O}{\overset{\|}{C}}O^- \\ H_3O^+ \rightleftharpoons H^+ + H_2O \\ NH_4^+ \rightleftharpoons H^+ + NH_3 \end{cases}$$
Conjugate
bases

Worked Example 10.1 Acids and Bases: Identifying Brønsted–Lowry Acids and Bases

Identify each of the following as a Brønsted–Lowry acid or base:

(a) PO_4^{3-} **(b)** $HClO_4$ **(c)** CN^-

ANALYSIS A Brønsted–Lowry acid must have a hydrogen that it can donate as H^+, and a Brønsted–Lowry base must have an atom with a lone pair of electrons that can bond to H^+. Typically, a Brønsted–Lowry base is an anion derived by loss of H^+ from an acid.

SOLUTION

(a) The phosphate anion (PO_4^{3-}) has no proton to donate, so it must be a Brønsted–Lowry base. It is derived by loss of 3 H^+ ions from phosphoric acid, H_3PO_4.

(b) Perchloric acid $(HClO_4)$ is a Brønsted–Lowry acid because it can donate an H^+ ion.

(c) The cyanide ion (CN^-) has no proton to donate, so it must be a Brønsted-Lowry base. It is derived by loss removal of an H^+ ion from hydrogen cyanide, HCN.

reaction occurs to a lesser extent, as indicated by the size of the forward and reverse arrows in the reaction:

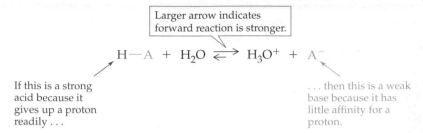

In the same way, a weak acid is one that gives up a proton with difficulty, meaning that its conjugate base has a high affinity for the proton. But this is just the definition of a strong base—a substance that has a high affinity for the proton. The reverse reaction now occurs more readily.

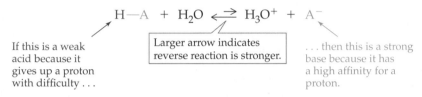

Knowing the relative strengths of different acids as shown in Table 10.1 makes it possible to predict the direction of proton-transfer reactions. *An acid–base proton-transfer equilibrium always favors reaction of the stronger acid with the stronger base and formation of the weaker acid and base.* That is, the proton always leaves the stronger acid (whose weaker conjugate base cannot hold the proton) and always ends up in the weaker acid (whose stronger conjugate base holds the proton tightly). Put another way, in a contest for the proton, the stronger base always wins.

$$\text{Stronger acid} + \text{Stronger base} \rightleftharpoons \text{Weaker base} + \text{Weaker acid}$$

To try out this rule, compare the reactions of acetic acid with water and with hydroxide ion. The idea is to write the equation, identify the acid on each side of the arrow, and then decide which acid is stronger and which is weaker. For example, the reaction of acetic acid with water to give acetate ion and hydronium ion is favored in the reverse direction, because acetic acid is a weaker acid than H_3O^+:

$$\underset{\text{Weaker acid}}{CH_3\overset{O}{\overset{\|}{C}}OH} + H_2O \rightleftharpoons CH_3\overset{O}{\overset{\|}{C}}O^- + \underset{\text{Stronger acid}}{H_3O^+} \qquad \text{Reverse reaction is favored.}$$

This base holds the proton less tightly . . . than this base does.

On the other hand, the reaction of acetic acid with hydroxide ion to give acetate ion and water is favored in the forward direction, because acetic acid is a stronger acid than H_2O:

$$\underset{\text{Stronger acid}}{CH_3\overset{O}{\overset{\|}{C}}OH} + OH^- \rightleftharpoons CH_3\overset{O}{\overset{\|}{C}}O^- + \underset{\text{Weaker acid}}{H_2O} \qquad \text{Forward reaction is favored.}$$

This base holds the proton more tightly . . . than this base does.

CHEMISTRY IN ACTION

GERD—Too Much Acid or Not Enough?

Strong acids are very caustic substances that can dissolve even metals, and no one would think of ingesting them. However, the major component of the gastric juices secreted in the stomach is hydrochloric acid—a strong acid—and the acidic environment in the stomach is vital to good health and nutrition.

Stomach acid is essential for the digestion of proteins and for the absorption of certain micronutrients, such as calcium, magnesium, iron, and vitamin B_{12}. It also creates a sterile environment in the gut by killing yeast and bacteria that may be ingested. If these gastric juices leak up into the esophagus, the tube through which food and drink enter the stomach, they can cause the burning sensation in the chest or throat known as either heartburn or acid indigestion. Persistent irritation of the esophagus is known as gastro-esophageal reflux disease (GERD) and, if untreated, can lead to more serious health problems.

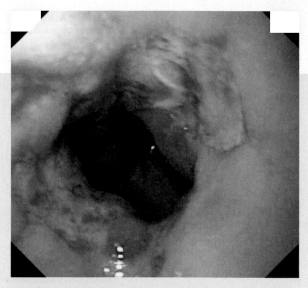

▲ If not treated, GERD can cause ulcers and scarring of esophageal tissue.

Hydrogen ions and chloride ions are secreted separately from the cytoplasm of parietal cells lining the stomach and then combine to form HCl that is usually close to 0.10 M. The HCl is then released into the stomach cavity, where the concentration is diluted to about 0.01–0.001 M. Unlike the esophagus, the stomach is coated by a thick mucus layer that protects the stomach wall from damage by this caustic solution.

Those who suffer from acid indigestion can obtain relief by using over-the-counter antacids, such as TUMS™ or Rolaids™ (see Section 10.12, p. 316). Chronic conditions such as GERD, however, are often treated with prescription medications. GERD can be treated by two classes of drugs. Proton-pump inhibitors (PPI), such as Prevacid™ and Prilosec™, prevent the production of the H^+ ions in the parietal cells, while H_2-receptor blockers (Tagamet™, Zantac™, and Pepcid™) prevent the release of stomach acid into the lumen. Both drugs effectively decrease the production of stomach acid to ease the symptoms of GERD.

Ironically, GERD can also be caused by not having enough stomach acid—a condition known as *hypochlorhydria*. The valve that controls the release of stomach contents to the small intestine is triggered by acidity. If this valve fails to open because the stomach is not acidic enough, the contents of the stomach can be churned back up into the esophagus.

See Chemistry in Action Problems 10.94 and 10.95 at the end of the chapter.

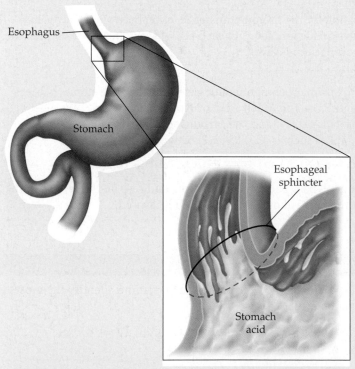

Esophagus

Stomach

Esophageal sphincter

Stomach acid

▲ **The burning sensation and other symptoms associated with GERD are caused by the reflux of the acidic contents of the stomach into the esophagus.**

Worked Example 10.3 Acid/Base Strength: Predicting Direction of H-transfer Reactions

Write a balanced equation for the proton-transfer reaction between phosphate ion (PO_4^{3-}) and water, and determine in which direction the equilibrium is favored.

ANALYSIS Look in Table 10.1 to see the relative acid and base strengths of the species involved in the reaction. The acid–base proton-transfer equilibrium will favor reaction of the stronger acid and formation of the weaker acid.

SOLUTION
Phosphate ion is the conjugate base of a weak acid (HPO_4^{2-}) and is therefore a relatively strong base. Table 10.1 shows that HPO_4^{2-} is a stronger acid than H_2O, and OH^- is a stronger base than PO_4^{3-}, so the reaction is favored in the reverse direction:

$$PO_4^{3-}(aq) \quad + \quad H_2O(l) \quad \rightleftharpoons \quad HPO_4^{3-}(aq) \quad + \quad OH^-(aq)$$

Weaker base   Weaker acid   Stronger acid   Stronger base

PROBLEM 10.5
Use Table 10.1 to identify the stronger acid in the following pairs:
(a) H_2O or NH_4^+ (b) H_2SO_4 or CH_3CO_2H (c) HCN or H_2CO_3

PROBLEM 10.6
Use Table 10.1 to identify the stronger base in the following pairs:
(a) F^- or Br^- (b) OH^- or HCO_3^-

PROBLEM 10.7
Write a balanced equation for the proton-transfer reaction between a hydrogen phosphate ion and a hydroxide ion. Identify each acid–base pair, and determine in which direction the equilibrium is favored.

PROBLEM 10.8
Hydrochloric acid is the primary component of gastric juice in the stomach (see Chemistry in Action: GERD—Too Much Acid or Not Enough? on p. 299). The reaction between hydrochloric acid and the carbonate ion, the primary active ingredient in antacid tablets such as TUMS®, can be written as

$$HCl(aq) + CO_3^{2-}(aq) \rightleftharpoons HCO_3^-(aq) + Cl^-(aq)$$

Identify the conjugate acid–base pairs in the reaction, and rewrite the arrows in the reaction to indicate if the forward or reverse reaction is favored.

🔑 **KEY CONCEPT PROBLEM 10.9**

From this electrostatic potential map of the amino acid alanine, identify the most acidic hydrogens in the molecule:

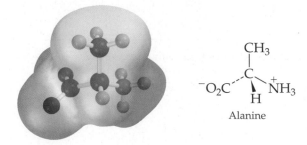

Alanine

10.5 Acid Dissociation Constants

The reaction of a weak acid with water, like any chemical equilibrium, can be described by an equilibrium equation (Section 7.8), where square brackets indicate the concentrations of the enclosed species in molarity (moles per liter).

For the reaction $HA(aq) + H_2O(l) \rightleftharpoons H_3O^+(aq) + A^-(aq)$

We have $K = \dfrac{[H_3O^+][A^-]}{[HA][H_2O]}$

Because water is a solvent as well as a participant for the reaction, its concentration is essentially constant and has no effect on the equilibrium. Therefore, we usually put the equilibrium constant K and the water concentration $[H_2O]$ together to make a new constant called the **acid dissociation constant, (K_a)**. The acid dissociation constant is simply the hydronium ion concentration $[H_3O^+]$ times the conjugate base concentration $[A^-]$ divided by the undissociated acid concentration $[HA]$:

Acid dissociation constant $\quad K_a = K[H_2O] = \dfrac{[H_3O^+][A^-]}{[HA]}$

Acid dissociation constant, (K_a)
The equilibrium constant for the dissociation of an acid (HA), equal to $[H^+][A^-]/[HA]$.

For a strong acid, the H_3O^+ and A^- concentrations are much larger than the HA concentration, so K_a is very large. In fact, the K_a values for strong acids such as HCl are so large that it is difficult and not very useful to measure them. For a weak acid, however, the H_3O^+ and A^- concentrations are smaller than the HA concentration, so K_a is small. Table 10.2 gives K_a values for some common acids and illustrates several important points:

- Strong acids have K_a values much greater than 1 because dissociation is favored.
- Weak acids have K_a values much less than 1 because dissociation is not favored.
- Donation of each successive H^+ from a polyprotic acid is more difficult than the one before it, so K_a values become successively lower.
- Most organic acids, which contain the $-CO_2H$ group, have K_a values near 10^{-5}.

TABLE 10.2 Some Acid Dissociation Constants, K_a, at 25 °C

Acid	K_a	Acid	K_a
Hydrofluoric acid (HF)	3.5×10^{-4}	*Polyprotic acids*	
Hydrocyanic acid (HCN)	4.9×10^{-10}	Sulfuric acid	
Ammonium ion (NH_4^+)	5.6×10^{-10}	H_2SO_4	Large
		HSO_4^-	1.2×10^{-2}
Organic acids		Phosphoric acid	
Formic acid (HCOOH)	1.8×10^{-4}	H_3PO_4	7.5×10^{-3}
Acetic acid (CH_3COOH)	1.8×10^{-5}	$H_2PO_4^-$	6.2×10^{-8}
Propanoic acid (CH_3CH_2COOH)	1.3×10^{-5}	HPO_4^{2-}	2.2×10^{-13}
		Carbonic acid	
Ascorbic acid (vitamin C)	7.9×10^{-5}	H_2CO_3	4.3×10^{-7}
		HCO_3^-	5.6×10^{-11}

PROBLEM 10.10
Benzoic acid ($C_7H_5CO_2H$) has $K_a = 6.5 \times 10^{-5}$ and citric acid ($C_6H_8O_7$) has $K_a = 7.2 \times 10^{-4}$. Which is the stronger conjugate base, benzoate ($C_7H_5CO_2^-$) or citrate ($C_6H_7O_7^-$)?

10.6 Water as Both an Acid and a Base

Water is neither an acid nor a base in the Arrhenius sense because it does not contain appreciable concentrations of either H_3O^+ or OH^-. In the Brønsted–Lowry sense, however, water can act as *both* an acid and a base. When in contact with a base, water reacts as a Brønsted–Lowry acid and *donates* a proton to the base. In its reaction with ammonia, for example, water donates H^+ to ammonia to form the ammonium ion:

$$NH_3 \ + \ H_2O \ \longrightarrow \ NH_4^+ \ + \ OH^-$$

Ammonia	Water	Ammonium ion	Hydroxide ion
(base)	(acid)	(acid)	(base)

When in contact with an acid, water reacts as a Brønsted–Lowry base and *accepts* H^+ from the acid. This, of course, is exactly what happens when an acid such as HCl dissolves in water, as discussed in Section 10.1.

Water uses two electrons to form a bond to H^+.

$$H\!-\!\ddot{O}\!: \ + \ H\!-\!Cl \ \longrightarrow \ H\!-\!\overset{+}{\underset{|}{\ddot{O}}}\!-\!H \ + \ Cl^-$$

Water	(An acid)	Hydronium ion
(A base)		

Amphoteric A substance that can react as either an acid or a base.

Substances like water, which can react as either an acid or a base depending on the circumstances, are said to be **amphoteric** (am-pho-**tare**-ic). When water acts as an acid, it donates H^+ and becomes OH^-; when it acts as a base, it accepts H^+ and becomes H_3O^+. (*Note*: HCO^{3-}, H_2PO^{4-} and HPO_4^{2-} are also amphoteric.)

Dissociation of Water

We have seen how water can act as an acid when a base is present and as a base when an acid is present. But what about when no other acids or bases are present? In this case, one water molecule acts as an acid while another water molecule acts as a base, reacting to form the hydronium and hydroxide ions:

$$H_2O(l) \ + \ H_2O(l) \ \rightleftharpoons \ H_3O^+(aq) \ + \ OH^-(aq)$$

Because each dissociation reaction yields 1 H_3O^+ ion and 1 OH^- ion, the concentrations of the 2 ions are identical. Also, the equilibrium arrows indicate that this reaction favors reactants, so that not many H_3O^+ and OH^- ions are present at equilibrium. At 25 °C, the concentration of each is 1.00×10^{-7} M. We can write the equilibrium constant expression for the dissociation of water as

$$K = \frac{[H_3O^+][OH^-]}{[H_2O][H_2O]}$$

where $[H_3O^+] = [OH^-] = 1.00 \times 10^{-7}\,M$ (at 25 °C)

▶▶▶ Refer to discussion of equilibria involving pure liquids and solids in Section 7.8.

As a pure substance the concentration of water is essentially constant. We can therefore put the water concentrations $[H_2O]$ together to make a new constant called the **ion-product constant for water** (K_w), which is simply the H_3O^+ concentration times the OH^- concentration. At 25 °C, $K_w = 1.00 \times 10^{-14}$.

Ion-product constant for water (K_w) The product of the H_3O^+ and OH^- molar concentrations in water or any aqueous solution ($K_w = [H_3O^+][OH^-] = 1.00 \times 10^{-14}$).

$$\text{Ion-product constant for water} \quad K_w = K[H_2O][H_2O]$$
$$= [H_3O^+][OH^-]$$
$$= 1.0 \times 10^{-14} \quad \text{(at 25 °C)}$$

The importance of the equation $K_w = [H_3O^+][OH^-]$ is that it applies to all aqueous solutions, not just to pure water. Since the product of $[H_3O^+]$ times $[OH^-]$ is always constant for any solution, we can determine the concentration of one species if we know the concentration of the other. If an acid is present in solution, for instance, so that $[H_3O^+]$ is large, then $[OH^-]$ must be small. If a base is present in solution so that $[OH^-]$ is large, then $[H_3O^+]$ must be small. For example, for a 0.10 M HCl solution, we know that $[H_3O^+] = 0.10$ M because HCl is 100% dissociated. Thus, we can calculate that $[OH^-] = 1.0 \times 10^{-13}$ M:

$$\text{Since } K_w \times [H_3O^+][OH^-] = 1.00 \times 10^{-14}$$

$$\text{we have } [OH^-] = \frac{K_w}{[H_3O^+]} = \frac{1.00 \times 10^{-14}}{0.10} = 1.0 \times 10^{-13} \text{ M}$$

Similarly, for a 0.10 M NaOH solution, we know that $[OH^-] = 0.10$ M, so $[H_3O^+] = 1.0 \times 10^{-13}$ M:

$$[H_3O^+] = \frac{K_w}{[OH^-]} = \frac{1.00 \times 10^{-14}}{0.10} = 1.0 \times 10^{-13} \text{ M}$$

Solutions are identified as acidic, neutral, or basic (*alkaline*) according to the value of their H_3O^+ and OH^- concentrations:

Acidic solution: $[H_3O^+] > 10^{-7}$ M   and $[OH^-] < 10^{-7}$ M
Neutral solution: $[H_3O^+] = 10^{-7}$ M   and $[OH^-] = 10^{-7}$ M
Basic solution: $[H_3O^+] < 10^{-7}$ M   and $[OH^-] > 10^{-7}$ M

Worked Example 10.4 Water Dissociation Constant: Using K_w to Calculate $[OH^-]$

Milk has an H_3O^+ concentration of 4.5×10^{-7} M. What is the value of $[OH^-]$? Is milk acidic, neutral, or basic?

ANALYSIS The OH^- concentration can be found by dividing K_w by $[H_3O^+]$. An acidic solution has $[H_3O^+] > 10^{-7}$ M, a neutral solution has $[H_3O^+] = 10^{-7}$ M, and a basic solution has $[H_3O^+] < 10^{-7}$ M.

BALLPARK ESTIMATE Since the H_3O^+ concentration is slightly *greater* than 10^{-7} M, the OH^- concentration must be slightly *less* than 10^{-7} M, on the order of 10^{-8}.

SOLUTION

$$[OH^-] = \frac{K_w}{[H_3O^+]} = \frac{1.00 \times 10^{-14}}{4.5 \times 10^{-7}} = 2.2 \times 10^{-8} \text{ M}$$

Milk is slightly acidic because its H_3O^+ concentration is slightly larger than 1×10^{-7} M.

BALLPARK CHECK The OH^- concentration is of the same order of magnitude as our estimate.

PROBLEM 10.11
Identify the following solutions as either acidic or basic. What is the value of $[OH^-]$ in each?
(a) Household ammonia, $[H_3O^+] = 3.1 \times 10^{-12}$ M
(b) Vinegar, $[H_3O^+] = 4.0 \times 10^{-3}$ M

10.7 Measuring Acidity in Aqueous Solution: pH

In many fields, from medicine to chemistry to winemaking, it is necessary to know the exact concentration of H_3O^+ or OH^- in a solution. If, for example, the H_3O^+ concentration in blood varies only slightly from a value of 4.0×10^{-8} M, death can result.

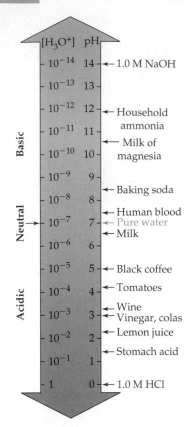

▲ Figure 10.1

The pH scale and the pH values of some common substances.
A low pH corresponds to a strongly acidic solution, a high pH corresponds to a strongly basic solution, and a pH of 7 corresponds to a neutral solution.

p function The negative common logarithm of some variable, $pX = -\log(X)$.

pH A measure of the acid strength of a solution; the negative common logarithm of the H_3O^+ concentration.

Although correct, it is nevertheless awkward or, in some instances inconvenient, to refer to low concentrations of H_3O^+ using molarity. Fortunately, there is an easier way to express and compare H_3O^+ concentrations—the *pH scale*.

The pH of an aqueous solution is a number, usually between 0 and 14, that indicates the H_3O^+ concentration of the solution. A pH smaller than 7 corresponds to an acidic solution, a pH larger than 7 corresponds to a basic solution, and a pH of exactly 7 corresponds to a neutral solution. The pH scale and pH values of some common substances are shown in Figure 10.1.

Mathematically, a **p function** is defined as the negative common logarithm of some variable. The **pH** of a solution, therefore, is the negative common logarithm of the H_3O^+ concentration:

$$pH = -\log[H^+] \ (or [H_3O^+])$$

If you have studied logarithms, you may remember that the common logarithm of a number is the power to which 10 must be raised to equal the number. The pH definition can therefore be restated as

$$[H_3O^+] = 10^{-pH}$$

For example, in neutral water at 25 °C, where $[H_3O^+] = 1 \times 10^{-7}$ M, the pH is 7; in a strong acid solution where $[H_3O^+] = 1 \times 10^{-1}$ M, the pH is 1; and in a strong base solution where $[H_3O^+] = 1 \times 10^{-14}$ M, the pH is 14:

Acidic solution: pH < 7, $[H_3O^+] > 1 \times 10^{-7}$ M
Neutral solution: pH = 7, $[H_3O^+] = 1 \times 10^{-7}$ M
Basic solution: pH > 7, $[H_3O^+] < 1 \times 10^{-7}$ M

Keep in mind that the pH scale covers an enormous range of acidities because it is a *logarithmic* scale, which involves powers of 10 (Figure 10.2). A change of only 1 pH unit means a 10-fold change in $[H_3O^+]$, a change of 2 pH units means a 100-fold change in $[H_3O^+]$, and a change of 12 pH units means a change of 10^{12} (a trillion) in $[H_3O^+]$.

To get a feel for the size of the quantities involved, think of a typical backyard swimming pool, which contains about 100,000 L of water. You would have to add only 0.10 mol of HCl (3.7 g) to lower the pH of the pool from 7.0 (neutral) to 6.0, but you would have to add 10,000 mol of HCl (370 kg!) to lower the pH of the pool from 7.0 to 1.0.

The logarithmic pH scale is a convenient way of reporting the relative acidity of solutions, but using logarithms can also be useful when calculating H_3O^+ and OH^- concentrations. Remember that the equilibrium between H_3O^+ and OH^- in aqueous solutions is expressed by K_w, where

$$K_w = [H_3O^+][OH^-] = 1 \times 10^{-14} \quad (at\ 25\ °C)$$

If we convert this equation to its negative logarithmic form, we obtain

$$-\log(K_w) = -\log[H_3O^+] - \log[OH^-]$$
$$-\log(1 \times 10^{-14}) = -\log[H_3O^+] - \log[OH^-]$$
$$or \quad 14.00 = pH + pOH$$

The logarithmic form of the K_w equation can simplify the calculation of solution pH from OH^- concentration, as demonstrated in Worked Example 10.7.

Worked Example 10.5 Measuring Acidity: Calculating pH from $[H_3O^+]$

The H_3O^+ concentration in coffee is about 1×10^{-5} M. What pH is this?

ANALYSIS The pH is the negative common logarithm of the H_3O^+ concentration: $pH = -\log[H_3O^+]$.

SOLUTION
Since the common logarithm of 1×10^{-5} M is -5.0, the pH is 5.0.

Worked Example 10.6 Measuring Acidity: Calculating $[H_3O^+]$ from pH

Lemon juice has a pH of about 2. What $[H_3O^+]$ is this?

ANALYSIS In this case, we are looking for the $[H_3O^+]$, where $[H_3O^+] = 10^{-pH}$.

SOLUTION
Since pH = 2.0, $[H_3O^+] = 10^{-2} = 1 \times 10^{-2}$ M.

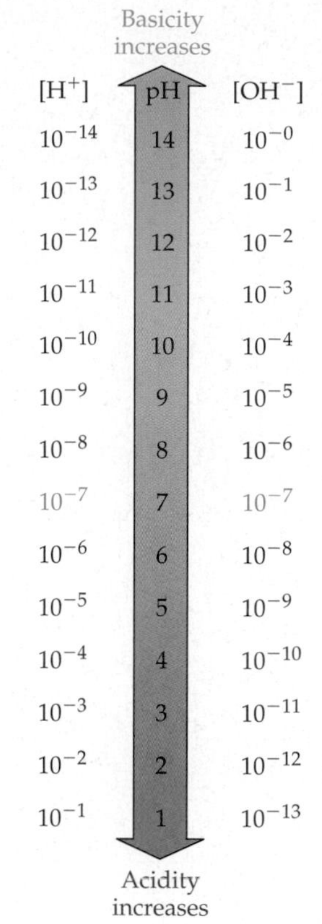

Worked Example 10.7 Measuring Acidity: Using K_w to Calculate $[H_3O^+]$ and pH

A cleaning solution is found to have $[OH^-] = 1 \times 10^{-3}$ M. What is the pH?

ANALYSIS To find pH, we must first find the value of $[H_3O^+]$ by using the equation $[H_3O^+] = K_w/[OH^-]$. Alternatively, we can calculate the pOH of the solution and then use the logarithmic form of the K_w equation: pH = 14.00 − pOH.

SOLUTION
Rearranging the K_w equation, we have

$$[H_3O^+] = \frac{K_w}{[OH^-]} = \frac{1.00 \times 10^{-14}}{1 \times 10^{-3}} = 1 \times 10^{-11}\ M$$
$$pH = -\log(1 \times 10^{-11}) = 11.0$$

Using the logarithmic form of the K_w equation, we have

$$pH = 14.0 - pOH = 14.0 - (-\log[OH^-])$$
$$pH = 14.0 - (-\log(1 \times 10^{-3}))$$
$$pH = 14.0 - 3.0 = 11.0$$

▲ **Figure 10.2**
The relationship of the pH scale to H^+ and OH^- concentrations.

Worked Example 10.8 Measuring Acidity: Calculating pH of Strong Acid Solutions

What is the pH of a 0.01 M solution of HCl?

ANALYSIS To find pH, we must first find the value of $[H_3O^+]$.

SOLUTION
Since HCl is a strong acid (Table 10.1), it is 100% dissociated, and the H_3O^+ concentration is the same as the HCl concentration: $[H_3O^+] = 0.01$ M, or 1×10^{-2} M, and pH = 2.0.

PROBLEM 10.12
Calculate the pH of the solutions in Problem 10.11.

PROBLEM 10.13
Give the hydronium ion and hydroxide ion concentrations of solutions with the following values of pH. Which of the solutions is most acidic? Which is most basic?
(a) pH 13.0   **(b)** pH 3.0   **(c)** pH 8.0

PROBLEM 10.14
Which solution would have the higher pH: 0.010 M HNO_2 or 0.010 M HNO_3? Explain.

10.8 Working with pH

Converting between pH and H_3O^+ concentration is easy when the pH is a whole number, but how do you find the H_3O^+ concentration of blood, which has a pH of 7.4, or the pH of a solution with $[H_3O^+] = 4.6 \times 10^{-3}$ M? Sometimes it is sufficient to make an estimate. The pH of blood (7.4) is between 7 and 8, so the H_3O^+ concentration of blood must be between 1×10^{-7} and 1×10^{-8} M. To be exact about finding pH values, though, requires a calculator.

Converting from pH to $[H_3O^+]$ requires finding the *antilogarithm* of the negative pH, which is done on many calculators with an "INV" key and a "log" key. Converting from $[H_3O^+]$ to pH requires finding the logarithm, which is commonly done with a "log" key and an "expo" or "EE" key for entering exponents of 10. Consult your calculator instructions if you are not sure how to use these keys. Remember that the sign of the number given by the calculator must be changed from minus to plus to get the pH.

The H_3O^+ concentration in blood with pH = 7.4 is

$$[H_3O^+] = \text{antilog}(-7.4) = 4 \times 10^{-8} \text{ M}$$

The pH of a solution with $[H_3O^+] = 4.6 \times 10^{-3}$ M is

$$\text{pH} = -\log(4.6 \times 10^{-3}) = -(-2.34) = 2.34$$

A note about significant figures: an antilogarithm contains the same number of significant figures as the original number has to the right of the decimal point. A logarithm contains the same number of digits to the right of the decimal point as the number of significant figures in the original number.

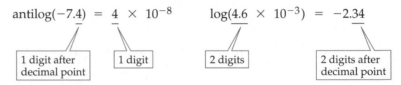

antilog(-7.4) = 4 × 10^{-8} log(4.6 × 10^{-3}) = -2.34

| 1 digit after decimal point | 1 digit | 2 digits | 2 digits after decimal point |

Worked Example 10.9 Working with pH: Converting a pH to $[H_3O^+]$

Soft drinks usually have a pH of approximately 3.1. What is the $[H_3O^+]$ concentration in a soft drink?

ANALYSIS To convert from a pH value to an $[H_3O^+]$ concentration requires using the equation $[H_3O^+] = 10^{-pH}$, which requires finding an antilogarithm on a calculator.

BALLPARK ESTIMATE Because the pH is between 3.0 and 4.0, the $[H_3O^+]$ must be between 1×10^{-3} and 1×10^{-4}. A pH of 3.1 is very close to 3.0, so the $[H_3O^+]$ must be just slightly below 1×10^{-3} M.

SOLUTION
Entering the negative pH on a calculator (-3.1) and pressing the "INV" and "log" keys gives the answer 7.943×10^{-4}, which must be rounded off to 8×10^{-4} because the pH has only one digit to the right of the decimal point.

BALLPARK CHECK The calculated $[H_3O^+]$ of 8×10^{-4} M is between 1×10^{-3} M and 1×10^{-4} M and, as we estimated, just slightly below 1×10^{-3} M. (Remember, 8×10^{-4} is 0.8×10^{-3}.)

Worked Example 10.10 Working with pH: Calculating pH for Strong Acid Solutions

What is the pH of a 0.0045 M solution of $HClO_4$?

ANALYSIS Finding pH requires first finding $[H_3O^+]$ and then using the equation $\text{pH} = -\log[H_3O^+]$. Since $HClO_4$ is a strong acid (see Table 10.1), it is 100% dissociated, and so the H_3O^+ concentration is the same as the $HClO_4$ concentration.

BALLPARK ESTIMATE Because $[H_3O^+] = 4.5 \times 10^{-3}$ M is close to midway between 1×10^{-2} M and 1×10^{-3} M, the pH must be close to the midway point between 2.0 and 3.0. (Unfortunately, because the logarithm scale is not linear, trying to estimate the midway point is not a simple process.)

SOLUTION
$[H_3O^+] = 0.0045$ M $= 4.5 \times 10^{-3}$ M. Taking the negative logarithm gives pH $= 2.35$.

BALLPARK CHECK The calculated pH is consistent with our estimate.

Worked Example 10.11 Working with pH: Calculating pH for Strong Base Solutions

What is the pH of a 0.0032 M solution of NaOH?

ANALYSIS Since NaOH is a strong base, the OH^- concentration is the same as the NaOH concentration. Starting with the OH^- concentration, finding pH requires either using the K_w equation to find $[H_3O^+]$ or calculating pOH and then using the logarithmic form of the K_w equation.

BALLPARK ESTIMATE Because $[OH^-] = 3.2 \times 10^{-3}$ M is close to midway between 1×10^{-2} M and 1×10^{-3} M, the pOH must be close to the midway point between 2.0 and 3.0. Subtracting the pOH from 14 would therefore yield a pH between 11 and 12.

SOLUTION

$$[OH^-] = 0.0032 \text{ M} = 3.2 \times 10^{-3} \text{ M}$$

$$[H_3O^+] = \frac{K_w}{(3.2 \times 10^{-3})} = 3.1 \times 10^{-12} \text{ M}$$

Taking the negative logarithm gives pH $= -\log(3.1 \times 10^{-12}) = 11.51$. Alternatively, we can calculate pOH and subtract from 14.00 using the logarithmic form of the K_w equation. For $[OH^-] = 0.0032$ M,

$$pOH = -\log(3.2 \times 10^{-3}) = 2.49$$

$$pH = 14.00 - 2.49 = 11.51$$

Since the given OH^- concentration included two significant figures, the final pH includes two significant figures beyond the decimal point.

BALLPARK CHECK The calculated pH is consistent with our estimate.

PROBLEM 10.15
Identify the following solutions as acidic or basic, estimate $[H_3O^+]$ and $[OH^-]$ values for each, and rank them in order of increasing acidity:
(a) Saliva, pH $= 6.5$
(b) Pancreatic juice, pH $= 7.9$
(c) Orange juice, pH $= 3.7$
(d) Wine, pH $= 3.5$

PROBLEM 10.16
Calculate the pH of the following solutions and report it to the correct number of significant figures:
(a) Seawater with $[H_3O^+] = 5.3 \times 10^{-9}$ M
(b) A urine sample with $[H_3O^+] = 8.9 \times 10^{-6}$ M

PROBLEM 10.17
What is the pH of a 0.0025 M solution of HCl?

10.9 Laboratory Determination of Acidity

The pH of water is an important indicator of water quality in applications ranging from swimming pool and spa maintenance to municipal water treatment. There are several ways to measure the pH of a solution. The simplest but least accurate method is to use an **acid–base indicator**, a dye that changes color depending on the pH of the solution. For example, the well-known dye *litmus* is red below pH 4.8 but blue above pH 7.8 and the indicator *phenolphthalein* (fee-nol-**thay**-lean) is colorless below pH 8.2 but red above pH 10. To make pH determination particularly easy, test kits are available that contain a mixture of indicators known as *universal indicator* to give approximate pH measurements in the range 2–10 (Figure 10.3a). Also available are rolls of "pH paper," which make it possible to determine pH simply by putting a drop of solution on the paper and comparing the color that appears to the color on a calibration chart (Figure 10.3b).

▶ **Figure 10.3**
Finding pH.
(a) The color of universal indicator in solutions of known pH from 1 to 12. (b) Testing pH with a paper strip. Comparing the color of the strip with the code on the package gives the approximate pH.

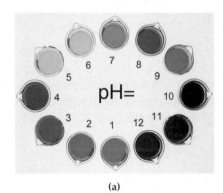
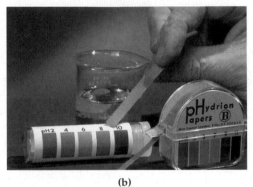

(a)　　　(b)

A much more accurate way to determine pH uses an electronic pH meter like the one shown in Figure 10.4. Electrodes are dipped into the solution, and the pH is read from the meter.

▲ **Figure 10.4**
Using a pH meter to obtain an accurate reading of pH.
Is milk of magnesia acidic or basic?

10.10 Buffer Solutions

Much of the body's chemistry depends on maintaining the pH of blood and other fluids within narrow limits. This is accomplished through the use of **buffers**—combinations of substances that act together to prevent a drastic change in pH.

Most buffers are mixtures of a weak acid and a roughly equal concentration of its conjugate base—for example, a solution that contains 0.10 M acetic acid and 0.10 M acetate ion. If a small amount of OH^- is added to a buffer solution, the pH increases, but not by much because the acid component of the buffer neutralizes the added OH^-. If a small amount of H_3O^+ is added to a buffer solution, the pH decreases, but again not by much because the base component of the buffer neutralizes the added H_3O^+.

To see why buffer solutions work, look at the equation for the acid dissociation constant of an acid HA.

For the reaction: $HA(aq) + H_2O(l) \rightleftharpoons A^-(aq) + H_3O^+(aq)$

we have $K_a = \dfrac{[H_3O^+][A^-]}{[HA]}$

Rearranging this equation shows that the value of $[H_3O^+]$, and thus the pH, depends on the ratio of the undissociated acid concentration to the conjugate base concentration, $[HA]/[A^-]$:

$$[H_3O^+] = K_a\dfrac{[HA]}{[A^-]}$$

In the case of the acetic acid–acetate ion buffer, for instance, we have

$$CH_3CO_2H(aq) + H_2O(l) \rightleftharpoons H_3O^+(aq) + CH_3CO_2^-(aq)$$
$$(0.10\ M) \qquad\qquad\qquad\qquad (0.10\ M)$$

$$\text{and} \quad [H_3O^+] = K_a \frac{[CH_3CO_2H]}{[CH_3CO_2^-]}$$

Initially, the pH of the 0.10 M acetic acid–0.10 M acetate ion buffer solution is 4.74. When acid is added, most will be removed by reaction with $CH_3CO_2^-$. The equilibrium reaction shifts to the left, and as a result the concentration of CH_3CO_2H increases and the concentration of $CH_3CO_2^-$ decreases. As long as the changes in $[CH_3CO_2H]$ and $[CH_3CO_2^-]$ are relatively small, however, the ratio of $[CH_3CO_2H]$ to $[CH_3CO_2^-]$ changes only slightly, and there is little change in the pH.

When base is added to the buffer, most will be removed by reaction with CH_3CO_2H. The equilibrium shifts to the right, and so the concentration of CH_3CO_2H decreases and the concentration of $CH_3CO_2^-$ increases. Here too, though, as long as the concentration changes are relatively small, there is little change in the pH.

The ability of a buffer solution to resist changes in pH when acid or base is added is illustrated in Figure 10.5. Addition of 0.010 mol of H_3O^+ to 1.0 L of pure water changes the pH from 7 to 2, and addition of 0.010 mol of OH^- changes the pH from 7 to 12. A similar addition of acid to 1.0 L of a 0.10 M acetic acid–0.10 M acetate ion buffer, however, changes the pH from only 4.74 to 4.68, and addition of base changes the pH from only 4.74 to 4.85.

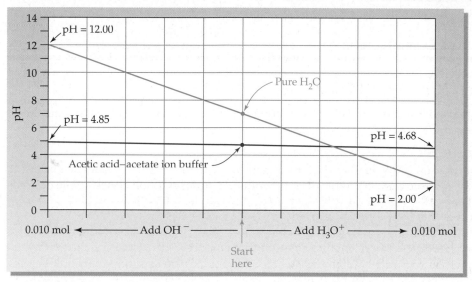

▲ **Figure 10.5**
A comparison of the change in pH.
When 0.010 mol of acid or 0.010 mol of base are added to 1.0 L of pure water and to 1.0 L of a 0.10 M acetic acid–0.10 M acetate ion buffer, the pH of the water varies between 12 and 2, while the pH of the buffer varies only between 4.85 and 4.68.

As we did with K_w, we can convert the rearranged K_a equation to its logarithmic form to obtain

$$pH = pK_a - \log\left(\frac{[HA]}{[A^-]}\right)$$

$$\text{or} \quad pH = pK_a + \log\left(\frac{[A^-]}{[HA]}\right)$$

This expression is known as the **Henderson–Hasselbalch equation** and is very useful in buffer applications, particularly in biology and biochemistry. Examination of the Henderson–Hasselbalch equation provides useful insights into how to prepare a buffer and into the factors that affect the pH of a buffer solution.

Henderson–Hasselbalch equation
The logarithmic form of the K_a equation for a weak acid, used in applications involving buffer solutions.

The effective pH range of a buffer will depend on the pK_a of the acid HA and on the relative concentrations of HA and conjugate base A^-. In general, the most effective buffers meet the following conditions:

- The pK_a for the weak acid should be close to the desired pH of the buffer solution.
- The ratio of $[HA]$ to $[A^-]$ should be close to 1, so that neither additional acid nor additional base changes the pH of the solution dramatically.
- The molar amounts of HA and A^- in the buffer should be approximately 10 times greater than the molar amounts of either acid or base you expect to add so that the ratio $[A^-]/[HA]$ does not undergo a large change.

The pH of body fluids is maintained by three major buffer systems. Two of these buffers, the carbonic acid–bicarbonate $(H_2CO_3 - HCO_3^-)$ system and the dihydrogen phosphate–hydrogen phosphate $(H_2PO_4 - HPO_4^{2-})$ system, depend on weak acid–conjugate base interactions exactly like those of the acetate buffer system described previously:

$$H_2CO_3(aq) + H_2O(l) \rightleftharpoons HCO_3^-(aq) + H_3O^+(aq) \qquad pK_a = 6.37$$
$$H_2PO_4^-(aq) + H_2O(l) \rightleftharpoons HPO_4^{2-}(aq) + H_3O^+(aq) \qquad pK_a = 7.21$$

The third buffer system depends on the ability of proteins to act as either proton acceptors or proton donors at different pH values.

LOOKING AHEAD ▶▶▶ In Chapter 29, we will see how the regulation of blood pH by the bicarbonate buffer system is particularly important in preventing *acidosis* and *alkalosis*.

Worked Example 10.12 Buffers: Selecting a Weak Acid for a Buffer Solution

Which of the organic acids in Table 10.2 would be the most appropriate for preparing a pH 4.15 buffer solution?

ANALYSIS The pH of the buffer solution depends on the pK_a of the weak acid. Remember that $pK_a = -\log(K_a)$.

SOLUTION

The K_a and pK_a values for the four organic acids in Table 10.2 are tabulated below. The ascorbic acid $(pK_a = 4.10)$ will produce a buffer solution closest to the desired pH of 4.15.

Organic Acid	K_a	pK_a
Formic acid (HCOOH)	1.8×10^{-4}	3.74
Acetic acid (CH_3COOH)	1.8×10^{-5}	4.74
Propanoic acid (CH_3CH_2COOH)	1.3×10^{-5}	4.89
Ascorbic acid (vitamin C)	7.9×10^{-5}	4.10

Worked Example 10.13 Buffers: Calculating the pH of a Buffer Solution

What is the pH of a buffer solution that contains 0.100 M HF and 0.120 M NaF? The K_a of HF is 3.5×10^{-4}, and so $pK_a = 3.46$.

ANALYSIS The Henderson–Hasselbalch equation can be used to calculate the pH of a buffer solution: $pH = pK_a + \log\left(\dfrac{[F^-]}{[HF]}\right)$.

BALLPARK ESTIMATE If the concentrations of F^- and HF were equal, the log term in our equation would be zero, and the pH of the solution would be equal to the pK_a for HF, which means pH = 3.46. However, since the concentration of the conjugate base $([F^-] = 0.120\text{ M})$ is slightly higher than the concentration of the conjugate acid $([HF] = 0.100\text{ M})$, then the pH of the buffer solution will be slightly higher (more basic) than the pK_a.

SOLUTION

$$pH = pK_a + \log\left(\frac{[F^-]}{[HF]}\right)$$

$$pH = 3.46 + \log\left(\frac{0.120}{0.100}\right) = 3.46 + 0.08 = 3.54$$

BALLPARK CHECK The calculated pH of 3.54 is consistent with the prediction that the final pH will be slightly higher than the pK_a of 3.46.

Worked Example 10.14 Buffers: Measuring the Effect of Added Base on pH

What is the pH of 1.00 L of the 0.100 M hydrofluoric acid–0.120 M fluoride ion buffer system described in Worked Example 10.13 after 0.020 mol of NaOH is added?

ANALYSIS Initially, the 0.100 M HF–0.120 M NaF buffer has pH $= 3.54$, as calculated in Worked Example 10.13. The added base will react with the acid as indicated in the neutralization reaction,

$$HF(aq) + OH^-(aq) \longrightarrow H_2O(l) + F^-(aq)$$

which means $[HF]$ decreases and $[F^-]$ increases. With the pK_a and the concentrations of HF and F^- known, pH can be calculated using the Henderson–Hasselbalch equation.

BALLPARK ESTIMATE After the neutralization reaction, there is more conjugate base (F^-) and less conjugate acid (HF), and so we expect the pH to increase slightly from the initial value of 3.54.

SOLUTION

When 0.020 mol of NaOH is added to 1.00 L of the buffer, the HF concentration *decreases* from 0.100 M to 0.080 M as a result of an acid–base reaction. At the same time, the F^- concentration *increases* from 0.120 M to 0.140 M because additional F^- is produced by the neutralization. Using these new values gives

$$pH = 3.46 + \log\left(\frac{0.140}{0.080}\right) = 3.46 + 0.24 = 3.70$$

The addition of 0.020 mol of base causes the pH of the buffer to rise only from 3.54 to 3.70.

BALLPARK CHECK The final pH, 3.70, is slightly more basic than the initial pH of 3.54, consistent with our prediction.

PROBLEM 10.18

What is the pH of 1.00 L of the 0.100 M hydrofluoric acid–0.120 M fluoride ion buffer system described in Worked Example 10.13 after 0.020 mol of HNO_3 is added?

PROBLEM 10.19

The ammonia/ammonium buffer system is sometimes used to optimize polymerase chain reactions (PCR) used in DNA studies. The equilibrium for this buffer can be written as

$$NH_4^+(aq) + H_2O(l) \rightleftharpoons H_3O^+(aq) + NH_3(aq)$$

Calculate the pH of a buffer that contains 0.050 M ammonium chloride and 0.080 M ammonia. The K_a of ammonium is 5.6×10^{-10}.

PROBLEM 10.20

What is the ratio of bicarbonate ion to carbonic acid $([HCO_3^-]/[H_2CO_3])$ in blood serum that has a pH of 7.40? (see Chemistry in Action: Buffers in the Body: Acidosis and Alkalosis on p. 312).

CHEMISTRY IN ACTION

Buffers in the Body: Acidosis and Alkalosis

A group of teenagers at a rock concert experience a collective fainting spell. A person taking high doses of aspirin for chronic pain appears disoriented and is having trouble breathing. A person with type 1 diabetes complains of tiredness and stomach pains. An athlete who recently completed a highly strenuous workout suffers from muscle cramps and nausea. A patient on an HIV drug regimen experiences increasing weakness and numbness in the hands and feet. What do all these individuals have in common? They are all suffering from abnormal fluctuations in blood pH, resulting in conditions known as *acidosis* (pH < 7.35) or *alkalosis* (pH > 7.45).

Each of the fluids in our bodies has a pH range suited to its function, as shown in the accompanying table. The stability of cell membranes, the shapes of huge protein molecules that must be folded in certain ways to function, and the activities of enzymes are all dependent on appropriate H_3O^+ concentrations. Blood plasma and the interstitial fluid surrounding cells, which together compose one-third of body fluids, have a slightly basic pH with a normal range of 7.35–7.45. The highly complex series of reactions and equilibria that take place throughout the body are very sensitive to pH—variations of even a few tenths of a pH unit can produce severe physiological symptoms.

pH of Body Fluids

Fluid	pH
Blood plasma	7.4
Interstitial fluid	7.4
Cytosol	7.0
Saliva	5.8–7.1
Gastric juice	1.6–1.8
Pancreatic juice	7.5–8.8
Intestinal juice	6.3–8.0
Urine	4.6–8.0
Sweat	4.0–6.8

Maintaining the pH of blood serum in its optimal range is accomplished by the carbonic acid–bicarbonate buffer system (Section 10.10), which depends on the relative amounts of CO_2 and bicarbonate dissolved in the blood. Because carbonic acid is unstable and therefore in equilibrium with CO_2 and water, there is an extra step in the bicarbonate buffer mechanism:

$$CO_2(aq) + H_2O(l) \rightleftharpoons$$
$$H_2CO_3(aq) \rightleftharpoons HCO_3^-(aq) + H_3O^+(aq)$$

As a result, the bicarbonate buffer system is intimately related to the elimination of CO_2, which is continuously produced in cells and transported to the lungs to be exhaled. Anything that significantly shifts the balance between dissolved CO_2 and HCO_3^- can upset these equilibria and raise or lower the pH. How does this happen, and how does the body compensate?

▲ Hyperventilation, the rapid breathing due to excitement or stress, removes CO_2 and increases blood pH resulting in respiratory alkalosis.

The relationships between the bicarbonate buffer system, the lungs, and the kidneys are shown in the figure on the next page. Under normal circumstances, the reactions shown in the figure are in equilibrium. Addition of excess acid (red arrows) causes formation of H_2CO_3 and results in lowering of H_3O^+ concentration. Removal of acid (blue arrows) causes formation of more H_3O^+ by dissociation of H_2CO_3. The maintenance of pH by this mechanism is supported by a reserve of bicarbonate ions in body fluids. Such a buffer can accommodate large additions of H_3O^+ before there is a significant change in the pH.

Additional backup to the bicarbonate buffer system is provided by the kidneys. Each day a quantity of acid equal to that produced in the body is excreted in the urine. In the process, the kidney returns HCO_3^- to the extracellular fluids, where it becomes part of the bicarbonate reserve.

Respiratory acidosis can be caused by a decrease in respiration, which leads to a buildup of excess CO_2 in the blood and a corresponding decrease in pH. This could be caused by a blocked air passage due to inhaled food—removal of the blockage restores normal breathing and a return to the optimal pH. *Metabolic acidosis* results from an excess of other acids in the blood that reduce the bicarbonate concentration. High doses of aspirin (acetylsalicylic acid, Section 17.5), for example, increase the hydronium ion concentration and decrease the pH. Strenuous exercise generates excess lactate in the muscles, which is released into the bloodstream (Section 23.11). The liver converts lactate into glucose, which is the body's major source of energy; this process consumes bicarbonate ions, which decreases the pH. Some HIV drug therapies can damage cellular mitochondria (Section 21.3), resulting in a buildup of lactic acid in the cells and bloodstream. In the case of a person with diabetes, lack of insulin causes the body to start burning fat, which generates ketones and keto acids (Chapter 16), organic compounds that lower the blood pH.

The body attempts to correct acidosis by increasing the rate and depth of respiration—breathing faster "blows off" CO_2, shifting the CO_2–bicarbonate equilibrium to the left and raising the pH. The net effect is rapid reversal of the acidosis.

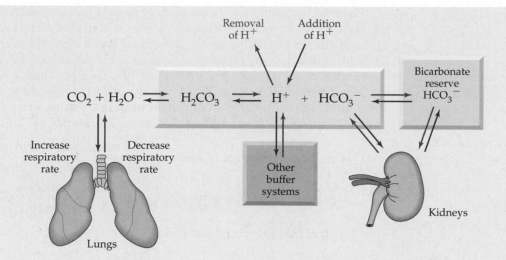

Although this may be sufficient for cases of respiratory acidosis, it provides only temporary relief for metabolic acidosis. A long-term solution depends on removal of excess acid by the kidneys, which can take several hours.

What about our teenage fans? In their excitement they have hyperventilated—their increased breathing rate has removed too much CO_2 from their blood and they are suffer-

ing from *respiratory alkalosis*. The body responds by "fainting" to decrease respiration and restore the CO_2 levels in the blood. When they regain consciousness, they will be ready to rock once again.

See Chemistry in Action Problems 10.96 and 10.97 at the end of the chapter.

🔑 KEY CONCEPT PROBLEM 10.21

A buffer solution is prepared using CN^- (from NaCN salt) and HCN in the amounts indicated. The K_a for HCN is 4.9×10^{-10}. Calculate the pH of the buffer solution.

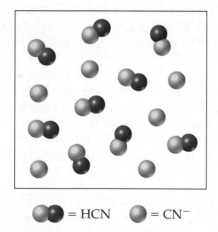

= HCN   = CN^-

10.11 Acid and Base Equivalents

We said in Section 9.10 that it is sometimes useful to think in terms of ion *equivalents* (Eq) and *gram-equivalents* (g Eq) when we are primarily interested in an ion itself rather than the compound that produced the ion. For similar reasons, it can also be useful to consider acid or base equivalents and gram-equivalents.

Equivalent of acid Amount of an acid that contains 1 mole of H^+ ions.

Equivalent of base Amount of base that contains 1 mole of OH^- ions.

When dealing with ions, the property of interest was the charge on the ion. Therefore, 1 Eq of an ion was defined as the number of ions that carry 1 mol of charge, and 1 g-Eq of any ion was defined as the molar mass of the ion divided by the ionic charge. For acids and bases, the property of interest is the number of H^+ ions (for an acid) or the number of OH^- ions (for a base) per formula unit. Thus, 1 **equivalent of acid** contains 1 mol of H^+ ions, and 1 g-Eq of an acid is the mass in grams that contains 1 mol of H^+ ions. Similarly, 1 **equivalent of base** contains 1 mol of OH^- ions, and 1 g-Eq of a base is the mass in grams that contains 1 mol of OH^- ions:

$$\text{One gram-equivalent of acid} = \frac{\text{Molar mass of acid (g)}}{\text{Number of } H^+ \text{ ions per formula unit}}$$

$$\text{One gram-equivalent of base} = \frac{\text{Molar mass of base (g)}}{\text{Number of } OH^- \text{ ions per formula unit}}$$

Thus 1 g-Eq of the monoprotic acid HCl is

$$1 \text{ g-Eq HCl} = \frac{36.5 \text{ g}}{1 \text{ } H^+ \text{ per HCl}} = 36.5 \text{ g}$$

which is equal to molar mass of the acid, but one gram-equivalent of the diprotic acid H_2SO_4 is

$$1 \text{ g-Eq } H_2SO_4 = \frac{98.0 \text{ g}}{2 \text{ } H^+ \text{ per } H_2SO_4} = 49.0 \text{ g}$$

which is the molar mass divided by 2, because 1 mol of H_2SO_4 contains 2 mol of H^+.

$$\text{One equivalent of } H_2SO_4 = \frac{\text{Molar mass of } H_2SO_4}{2} = \frac{98.0 \text{ g}}{2} = 49.0 \text{ g}$$

Divide by 2 because H_2SO_4 is diprotic.

Using acid–base equivalents has two practical advantages: First, they are convenient when only the acidity or basicity of a solution is of interest rather than the identity of the acid or base. Second, they show quantities that are chemically equivalent in their properties; 36.5 g of HCl and 49.0 g of H_2SO_4 are chemically equivalent quantities because each reacts with 1 Eq of base. *One equivalent of any acid neutralizes one equivalent of any base.*

Because acid–base equivalents are so useful, clinical chemists sometimes express acid and base concentrations in *normality* rather than molarity. The **normality (N)** of an acid or base solution is defined as the number of equivalents (or milliequivalents) of acid or base per liter of solution. For example, a solution made by dissolving 1.0 g-Eq (49.0 g) of H_2SO_4 in water to give 1.0 L of solution has a concentration of 1.0 Eq/L, which is 1.0 N. Similarly, a solution that contains 0.010 Eq/L of acid is 0.010 N and has an acid concentration of 10 mEq/L:

Normality (N) A measure of acid (or base) concentration expressed as the number of acid (or base) equivalents per liter of solution.

$$\text{Normality (N)} = \frac{\text{Equivalents of acid or base}}{\text{Liters of solution}}$$

The values of molarity (M) and normality (N) are the same for monoprotic acids, such as HCl, but are not the same for diprotic or triprotic acids. A solution made by diluting 1.0 g-Eq (49.0 g = 0.50 mol) of the diprotic acid H_2SO_4 to a volume of 1.0 L has a *normality* of 1.0 N but a *molarity* of 0.50 M. For any acid or base, normality is always equal to molarity times the number of H^+ or OH^- ions produced per formula unit:

Normality of acid = (Molarity of acid) × (Number of H^+ ions produced per formula unit)

Normality of base = (Molarity of base) × (Number of OH^- ions produced per formula unit)

Worked Example 10.15 Equivalents: Mass to Equivalent Conversion for Diprotic Acid

How many equivalents are in 3.1 g of the diprotic acid H_2S? The molar mass of H_2S is 34.0 g.

ANALYSIS The number of acid or base equivalents is calculated by doing a gram to mole conversion using molar mass as the conversion factor and then multiplying by the number of H^+ ions produced.

BALLPARK ESTIMATE The 3.1 g is a little less than 0.10 mol of H_2S. Since it is a diprotic acid, (two H^+ per mole), this represents a little less than 0.2 Eq of H_2S.

SOLUTION

$$(3.1 \text{ g } H_2S)\left(\frac{1 \text{ mol } H_2S}{34.0 \text{ g } H_2S}\right)\left(\frac{2 \text{ Eq } H_2S}{1 \text{ mol } H_2S}\right) = 0.18 \text{ Eq } H_2S$$

BALLPARK CHECK The calculated value of 0.18 is consistent with our prediction of a little less than 0.2 Eq of H_2S.

Worked Example 10.16 Equivalents: Calculating Equivalent Concentrations

What is the normality of a solution made by diluting 6.5 g of H_2SO_4 to a volume of 200 mL? What is the concentration of this solution in milliequivalents per liter? The molar mass of H_2SO_4 is 98.0 g.

ANALYSIS Calculate how many equivalents of H_2SO_4 are in 6.5 g by using the molar mass of the acid as a conversion factor and then determine the normality of the acid.

SOLUTION

STEP 1: Identify known information. We know the molar mass of H_2SO_4, the mass of H_2SO_4 to be dissolved, and the final volume of solution.

MW of H_2SO_4 = 98.0 g/mol
Mass of H_2SO_4 = 6.5 g
Volume of solution = 200 mL

STEP 2: Identify answer including units. We need to calculate the normality of the final solution.

Normality = ?? (equiv./L)

STEP 3: Identify conversion factors. We will need to convert the mass of H_2SO_4 to moles, and then to equivalents of H_2SO_4. We will then need to convert volume from mL to L.

$$(6.5 \text{ g } H_2SO_4)\left(\frac{1 \text{ mol } H_2SO_4}{98.0 \text{ g } H_2SO_4}\right)\left(\frac{2 \text{ Eq } H_2SO_4}{1 \text{ mol } H_2SO_4}\right)$$
$$= 0.132 \text{ Eq } H_2SO_4 \text{ (don't round yet!)}$$
$$(200 \text{ mL})\left(\frac{1 \text{ L}}{1000 \text{ mL}}\right) = 0.200 \text{ L}$$

STEP 4: Solve. Dividing the number of equivalents by the volume yields the Normality.

$$\frac{0.132 \text{ Eq } H_2SO_4}{0.200 \text{ L}} = 0.66 \text{ N}$$

The concentration of the sulfuric acid solution is 0.66 N, or 660 mEq/L.

PROBLEM 10.22

How many equivalents are in the following?

(a) 5.0 g HNO_3

(b) 12.5 g $Ca(OH)_2$

(c) 4.5 g H_3PO_4

PROBLEM 10.23

What are the normalities of the solutions if each sample in Problem 10.22 is dissolved in water and diluted to a volume of 300.0 mL?

10.12 Some Common Acid–Base Reactions

Among the most common of the many kinds of Brønsted–Lowry acid–base reactions are those of an acid with hydroxide ion, an acid with bicarbonate or carbonate ion, and an acid with ammonia or a related nitrogen-containing compound. Let us look briefly at each of the three types.

Reaction of Acids with Hydroxide Ion

One equivalent of an acid reacts with 1 Eq of a metal hydroxide to yield water and a salt in a neutralization reaction:

$$HCl(aq) + KOH(aq) \longrightarrow H_2O(l) + KCl(aq)$$

$$(\text{An acid}) \quad (\text{A base}) \quad\quad (\text{Water}) \quad (\text{A salt})$$

Such reactions are usually written with a single arrow because their equilibria lie far to the right and they have very large equilibrium constants ($K = 5 \times 10^{15}$; Section 7.8). The net ionic equation (Section 5.8) for all such reactions makes clear why acid–base equivalents are useful and why the properties of the acid and base disappear in neutralization reactions: The equivalent ions for the acid (H^+) and the base (OH^-) are used up in the formation of water.

$$H^+(aq) + OH^-(aq) \longrightarrow H_2O(l)$$

PROBLEM 10.24

Maalox, an over-the-counter antacid, contains aluminum hydroxide, $Al(OH)_3$, and magnesium hydroxide, $Mg(OH)_2$. Write balanced equations for the reaction of both with stomach acid (HCl).

Reaction of Acids with Bicarbonate and Carbonate Ion

Bicarbonate ion reacts with acid by accepting H^+ to yield carbonic acid, H_2CO_3. Similarly, carbonate ion accepts 2 protons in its reaction with acid. Carbonic acid is unstable, however, rapidly decomposing to carbon dioxide gas and water:

$$H^+(aq) + HCO_3^-(aq) \longrightarrow [H_2CO_3(aq)] \longrightarrow H_2O(l) + CO_2(g)$$
$$2\,H^+(aq) + CO_3^{2-}(aq) \longrightarrow [H_2CO_3(aq)] \longrightarrow H_2O(l) + CO_2(g)$$

Most metal carbonates are insoluble in water—marble, for example, is almost pure calcium carbonate, $CaCO_3$—but they nevertheless react easily with aqueous acid. In fact, geologists often test for carbonate-bearing rocks by putting a few drops of aqueous HCl on the rock and watching to see if bubbles of CO_2 form (Figure 10.6). This reaction is also responsible for the damage to marble and limestone artwork caused by acid rain (See Chemistry in Action: Acid Rain on p. 320). The most common application involving carbonates and acid, however, is the use of antacids that contain carbonates, such as TUMS™ or Rolaids™, to neutralize excess stomach acid.

▲ **Figure 10.6**
Marble.
Marble, which is primarily $CaCO_3$, releases bubbles of CO_2 when treated with hydrochloric acid.

PROBLEM 10.25
Write a balanced equation for each of the following reactions:
(a) $HCO_3^-(aq) + H_2SO_4(aq) \longrightarrow$?
(b) $CO_3^{2-}(aq) + HNO_3(aq) \longrightarrow$?

Reaction of Acids with Ammonia

Acids react with ammonia to yield ammonium salts, such as ammonium chloride, NH_4Cl, most of which are water-soluble:

$$NH_3(aq) + HCl(aq) \rightarrow NH_4Cl(aq)$$

Living organisms contain a group of compounds called *amines*, which contain nitrogen atoms bonded to carbon. Amines react with acids just as ammonia does, yielding water-soluble salts. Methylamine, for example, an organic compound found in rotting fish, reacts with HCl:

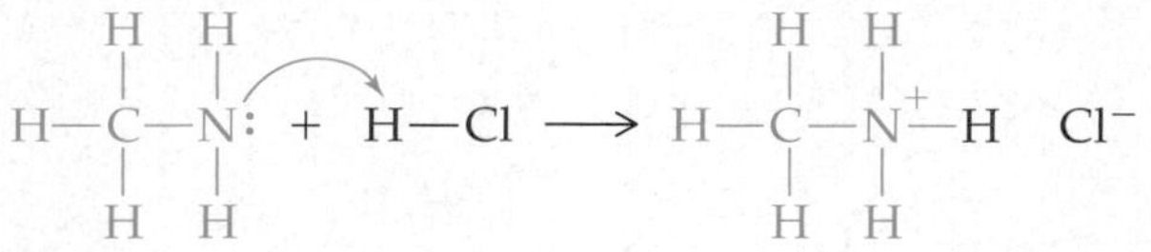

Methylamine   Methylammonium chloride

LOOKING AHEAD ▶▶▶ In Chapter 15, we will see that amines occur in all living organisms, both plant and animal, as well as in many pharmaceutical agents. Amines called amino acids form the building blocks from which proteins are made, as we will see in Chapter 18.

PROBLEM 10.26
What products would you expect from the reaction of ammonia and sulfuric acid in aqueous solution?

$$2\,NH_3(aq) + H_2SO_4(aq) \longrightarrow ?$$

PROBLEM 10.27
Show how ethylamine $(C_2H_5NH_2)$ reacts with hydrochloric acid to form an ethylammonium salt.

10.13 Titration

Determining the pH of a solution gives the solution's H_3O^+ concentration but not necessarily its total acid concentration. That is because the two are not the same thing. The H_3O^+ concentration gives only the amount of acid that has dissociated into ions, whereas total acid concentration gives the sum of dissociated plus undissociated acid. In a 0.10 M solution of acetic acid, for instance, the total acid concentration is 0.10 M, yet the H_3O^+ concentration is only 0.0013 M (pH $=$ 2.89) because acetic acid is a weak acid that is only about 1% dissociated.

The total acid or base concentration of a solution can be found by carrying out a **titration** procedure, as shown in Figure 10.7. Let us assume, for instance, that we want to find the acid concentration of an HCl solution. (Likewise, we might need to find the base concentration of an NaOH solution.) We begin by measuring out a known volume of the HCl solution and adding an acid–base indicator. Next, we fill a calibrated glass tube called a *buret* with an NaOH solution of known concentration, and we slowly add the NaOH to the HCl until neutralization is complete (the *end point*), identified by a color change in the indicator.

Reading from the buret gives the volume of the NaOH solution that has reacted with the known volume of HCl. Knowing both the concentration and volume of the NaOH solution then allows us to calculate the molar amount of NaOH, and the coefficients in the balanced equation allow us to find the molar amount of HCl that has been neutralized. Dividing the molar amount of HCl by the volume of the HCl solution

Titration A procedure for determining the total acid or base concentration of a solution.

▶ **Figure 10.7**
Titration of an acid solution of unknown concentration with a base solution of known concentration.
(a) A measured volume of the acid solution is placed in the flask along with an indicator. (b) The base of known concentration is then added from a buret until the color change of the indicator shows that neutralization is complete (the *end point*).

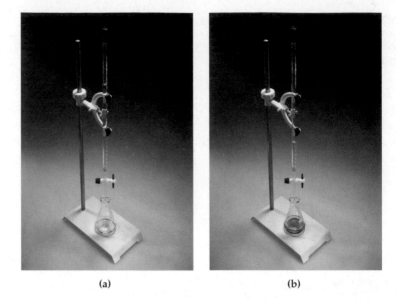

(a)   (b)

gives the concentration. The calculation thus involves mole–volume conversions just like those done in Section 9.7. Figure 10.8 shows a flow diagram of the strategy, and Worked Example 10.17 shows how to calculate total acid concentration.

When the titration involves a neutralization reaction in which one mole of acid reacts with one mole of base, such as that shown in Figure 10.8, then the moles of acid and base needed for complete reaction can be represented as

$$M_{acid} \times V_{acid} = M_{base} \times V_{base}$$

When the coefficients for the acid and base in the balanced neutralization reaction are not the same, such as in the reaction of a diprotic acid (H_2SO_4) with a monoprotic base (NaOH), then we can use equivalents of acid and base instead of moles, and Normality instead of Molarity:

$$(Eq)_{acid} = (Eq)_{base}$$
$$N_{acid} \times V_{acid} = N_{base} \times V_{base}.$$

We can convert between Normality and Molarity as described in Section 10.11.

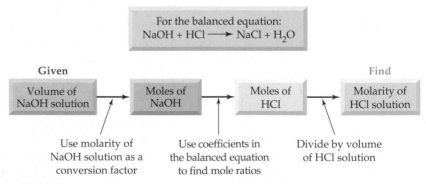

▲ **Figure 10.8**
A flow diagram for an acid–base titration.
This diagram summarizes the calculations needed to determine the concentration of an HCl solution by titration with an NaOH solution of known concentration. The steps are similar to those shown in Figure 9.7.

Worked Example 10.17 Titrations: Calculating Total Acid Concentration

When a 5.00 mL sample of household vinegar (dilute aqueous acetic acid) is titrated, 44.5 mL of 0.100 M NaOH solution is required to reach the end point. What is the acid concentration of the vinegar in moles per liter, equivalents per liter, and milliequivalents per liter? The neutralization reaction is

$$CH_3CO_2H(aq) + NaOH(aq) \longrightarrow CH_3CO_2{}^-Na^+(aq) + H_2O(l)$$

ANALYSIS To find the molarity of the vinegar, we need to know the number of moles of acetic acid dissolved in the 5.00 mL sample. Following a flow diagram similar to Figure 10.8, we use the volume and molarity of NaOH to find the number of moles. From the chemical equation, we use the mole ratio to find the number of moles of acid, and then divide by the volume of the acid solution. Because acetic acid is a monoprotic acid, the normality of the solution is numerically the same as its molarity.

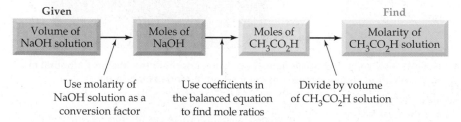

BALLPARK ESTIMATE The 5.00 mL of vinegar required nearly nine times as much NaOH solution (44.5 mL) for complete reaction. Since the neutralization stoichiometry is 1:1, the molarity of the acetic acid in the vinegar must be nine times greater than the molarity of NaOH, or approximately 0.90 M.

SOLUTION
Substitute the known information and appropriate conversion factors into the flow diagram, and solve for the molarity of the acetic acid:

$$(44.5 \text{ mL NaOH})\left(\frac{0.100 \text{ mol NaOH}}{1000 \text{ mL}}\right)\left(\frac{1 \text{ mol } CH_3CO_2H}{1 \text{ mol NaOH}}\right)$$

$$\times \left(\frac{1}{0.005\ 00 \text{ L}}\right) = 0.890 \text{ M } CH_3CO_2H$$

$$= 0.890 \text{ N } CH_3CO_2H$$

Expressed in milliequivalents, this concentration is

$$\frac{0.890 \text{ Eq}}{\text{L}} \times \frac{1000 \text{ mEq}}{1 \text{ Eq}} = 890 \text{ mEq/L}$$

BALLPARK CHECK The calculated result (0.890 M) is very close to our estimate of 0.90 M.

PROBLEM 10.28
A titration is carried out to determine the concentration of the acid in an old bottle of aqueous HCl whose label has become unreadable. What is the HCl concentration if 58.4 mL of 0.250 M NaOH is required to titrate a 20.0 mL sample of the acid?

CHEMISTRY IN ACTION

Acid Rain

As the water that evaporates from oceans and lakes condenses into raindrops, it dissolves small quantities of gases from the atmosphere. Under normal conditions, rain is slightly acidic, with a pH close to 5.6, because of atmospheric CO_2 that dissolves to form carbonic acid:

$$CO_2(aq) + H_2O(l) \rightleftharpoons$$
$$H_2CO_3(aq) \rightleftharpoons HCO_3^-(aq) + H_3O^+(aq)$$

In recent decades, however, the acidity of rainwater in many industrialized areas of the world has increased by a factor of over 100, to a pH between 3 and 3.5.

The primary cause of this so-called *acid rain* is industrial and automotive pollution. Each year, large power plants and smelters pour millions of tons of sulfur dioxide (SO_2) gas into the atmosphere, where some is oxidized by air to produce sulfur trioxide (SO_3). Sulfur oxides then dissolve in rain to form dilute sulfurous acid (H_2SO_3) and sulfuric acid (H_2SO_4):

$$SO_2(g) + H_2O(l) \longrightarrow H_2SO_3(aq)$$
$$SO_3(g) + H_2O(l) \longrightarrow H_2SO_4(aq)$$

Nitrogen oxides produced by the high-temperature reaction of N_2 with O_2 in coal-burning plants and in automobile engines further contribute to the problem. Nitrogen dioxide (NO_2) dissolves in water to form dilute nitric acid (HNO_3) and nitric oxide (NO):

$$3 NO_2(g) + H_2O(l) \longrightarrow 2 HNO_3(aq) + NO(g)$$

Oxides of both sulfur and nitrogen have always been present in the atmosphere, produced by such natural sources as volcanoes and lightning bolts, but their amounts have increased dramatically over the last century because of industrialization. The result is a notable decrease in the pH of rainwater in more densely populated regions, including Europe and the eastern United States.

Many processes in nature require such a fine pH balance that they are dramatically upset by the shift that has occurred in the pH of rain. Some watersheds contain soils that have high "buffering capacity" and so are able to neutralize acidic compounds in acid rain. Other areas, such as the northeastern United States and eastern Canada, where soil-buffering capacity is poor, have experienced negative ecological effects. Acid rain releases aluminum salts from soil, and the ions then wash into streams. The low pH and increased aluminum levels are so toxic to fish and other organisms that many lakes and streams in these areas are devoid of aquatic life. Massive tree die-offs have occurred throughout central and eastern Europe as acid rain has lowered the pH of the soil and has leached nutrients from leaves.

Fortunately, acidic emissions in the United States have been greatly reduced in recent years as a result of the Clean Air Act

▲ This limestone statue adorning the Rheims Cathedral in France has been severely eroded by acid rain.

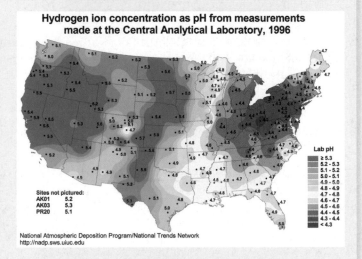

Hydrogen ion concentration as pH from measurements made at the Central Analytical Laboratory, 1996

Sites not pictured:
AK01 5.2
AK03 5.3
PR20 5.1

Lab pH
≥ 5.3
5.2 - 5.3
5.1 - 5.2
5.0 - 5.1
4.9 - 5.0
4.8 - 4.9
4.7 - 4.8
4.6 - 4.7
4.5 - 4.6
4.4 - 4.5
4.3 - 4.4
< 4.3

National Atmospheric Deposition Program/National Trends Network
http://nadp.sws.uiuc.edu

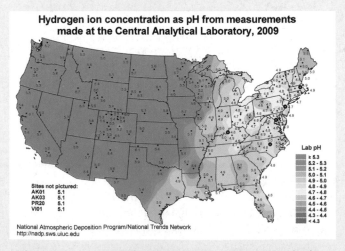

Hydrogen ion concentration as pH from measurements made at the Central Analytical Laboratory, 2009

Sites not pictured:
AK01 5.1
AK03 5.1
PR20 5.1
VI01 5.1

Lab pH
≥ 5.3
5.2 - 5.3
5.1 - 5.2
5.0 - 5.1
4.9 - 5.0
4.8 - 4.9
4.7 - 4.8
4.6 - 4.7
4.5 - 4.6
4.4 - 4.5
4.3 - 4.4
< 4.3

National Atmospheric Deposition Program/National Trends Network
http://nadp.sws.uiuc.edu

▲ These maps compare the average pH of precipitation in the United States in 1996 and in 2009. During this period, total acid deposition in much of the eastern United States decreased substantially.

Amendments of 1990. Industrial emissions of SO_2 and nitrogen oxides decreased by over 40% from 1990 to 2007, resulting in a decrease in acid rain depositions, particularly in the eastern United States and Canada (see accompanying figure). While significant reductions have been realized, most environmental scientists agree that additional reductions in these pollutant emissions are necessary to ensure the recovery of affected lakes and streams.

See Chemistry in Action Problems 10.98 and 10.99 at the end of the chapter.

PROBLEM 10.29
How many milliliters of 0.150 M NaOH are required to neutralize 50.0 mL of 0.200 M H_2SO_4? The balanced neutralization reaction is:

$$H_2SO_4(aq) + 2\,NaOH(aq) \longrightarrow Na_2SO_4(aq) + 2\,H_2O(l).$$

PROBLEM 10.30
A 21.5 mL sample of a KOH solution of unknown concentration requires 16.1 mL of 0.150 M H_2SO_4 solution to reach the end point in a titration.

(a) How many moles of H_2SO_4 were necessary to reach the end point? How many equivalents?

(b) What is the molarity of the KOH solution?

PROBLEM 10.31
Titration of a 50.00 ml sample of acid rain required 9.30 mL of 0.0012 M NaOH to reach the end point. What was the total $[H_3O^+]$ in the rain sample? What was the pH? (see Chemistry in Action: Acid Rain on p. 320).

10.14 Acidity and Basicity of Salt Solutions

It is tempting to think of all salt solutions as neutral; after all, they come from the neutralization reaction between an acid and a base. In fact, salt solutions can be neutral, acidic, or basic, depending on the ions present, because some ions react with water to produce H_3O^+ and some ions react with water to produce OH^-. To predict the acidity of a salt solution, it is convenient to classify salts according to the acid and base from which they are formed in a neutralization reaction. The classification and some examples are given in Table 10.3.

TABLE 10.3 Acidity and Basicity of Salt Solutions

Anion Derived from Acid That Is:	Cation Derived from Base That Is:	Solution	Example
Strong	Weak	Acidic	NH_4Cl, NH_4NO_3
Weak	Strong	Basic	$NaHCO_3$, KCH_3CO_2
Strong	Strong	Neutral	$NaCl$, KBr, $Ca(NO_3)_2$
Weak	Weak	More information needed	

The general rule for predicting the acidity or basicity of a salt solution is that the stronger partner from which the salt is formed dominates. That is, a salt formed from a strong acid and a weak base yields an acidic solution because the strong acid dominates; a salt formed from a weak acid and a strong base yields a basic solution because the base dominates; and a salt formed from a strong acid and a strong base yields a neutral solution because neither acid nor base dominates. Here are some examples.

Salt of Strong Acid + Weak Base ⟶ Acidic Solution

A salt such as NH_4Cl, which can be formed by reaction of a strong acid (HCl) with a weak base (NH_3), yields an acidic solution. The Cl^- ion does not react with water, but the NH_4^+ ion is a weak acid that gives H_3O^+ ions:

$$NH_4^+(aq) + H_2O(l) \rightleftharpoons NH_3(aq) + H_3O^+(aq)$$

Salt of Weak Acid + Strong Base ⟶ Basic Solution

A salt such as sodium bicarbonate, which can be formed by reaction of a weak acid (H_2CO_3) with a strong base (NaOH), yields a basic solution. The Na^+ ion does not react with water, but the HCO_3^- ion is a weak base that gives OH^- ions:

$$HCO_3^-(aq) + H_2O(l) \rightleftharpoons H_2CO_3(aq) + OH^-(aq)$$

Salt of Strong Acid + Strong Base ⟶ Neutral Solution

A salt such as NaCl, which can be formed by reaction of a strong acid (HCl) with a strong base (NaOH), yields a neutral solution. Neither the Cl^- ion nor the Na^+ ion reacts with water.

Salt of Weak Acid + Weak Base

Both cation and anion in this type of salt react with water, so we cannot predict whether the resulting solution will be acidic or basic without quantitative information. The ion that reacts to the greater extent with water will govern the pH—it may be either the cation or the anion.

Worked Example **10.18** Acidity and Basicity of Salt Solutions

Predict whether the following salts produce an acidic, basic, or neutral solution:

(a) $BaCl_2$ (b) NaCN   (c) NH_4NO_3

ANALYSIS Look in Table 10.1 to see the classification of acids and bases as strong or weak.

SOLUTION

(a) $BaCl_2$ gives a neutral solution because it is formed from a strong acid (HCl) and a strong base $[Ba(OH)_2]$.

(b) NaCN gives a basic solution because it is formed from a weak acid (HCN) and a strong base (NaOH).

(c) NH_4NO_3 gives an acidic solution because it is formed from a strong acid (HNO_3) and a weak base (NH_3).

PROBLEM 10.32
Predict whether the following salts produce an acidic, basic, or neutral solution:

(a) K_2SO_4 (b) Na_2HPO_4 (c) MgF_2 (d) NH_4Br

SUMMARY: REVISITING THE CHAPTER GOALS

1. What are acids and bases? According to the *Brønsted–Lowry definition*, an acid is a substance that donates a hydrogen ion (a proton, H^+) and a base is a substance that accepts a hydrogen ion. Thus, the generalized reaction of an acid with a base involves the reversible transfer of a proton:

$$B: + H\!-\!A \rightleftharpoons A:^- + H\!-\!B^+$$

In aqueous solution, water acts as a base and accepts a proton from an acid to yield a *hydronium ion*, H_3O^+. Reaction of an acid with a metal hydroxide, such as KOH, yields water and a salt; reaction with bicarbonate ion (HCO_3^-) or carbonate ion (CO_3^{2-}) yields water, a salt, and CO_2 gas; and reaction with ammonia yields an ammonium salt (*see Problems 33, 37, 38, 42, 43, 60, 94, 100, 102*).

2. What effect does the strength of acids and bases have on their reactions? Different acids and bases differ in their ability to give up or accept a proton. A *strong acid* gives up a proton easily and is 100% *dissociated* in aqueous solution; a *weak acid* gives up a proton with difficulty, is only slightly dissociated in water, and establishes an equilibrium between dissociated and undissociated forms. Similarly, a *strong base* accepts and holds a proton readily, whereas a *weak base* has a low affinity for a proton and establishes an equilibrium in aqueous solution. The two substances that are related by the gain or loss of a proton are called a *conjugate acid–base pair*. The exact strength of an acid is defined by an *acid dissociation constant*, K_a:

For the reaction $HA + H_2O \rightleftharpoons H_3O^+ + A^-$

we have $$K_a = \frac{[H_3O^+][A^-]}{[HA]}$$

A proton-transfer reaction always takes place in the direction that favors formation of the weaker acid (*see Problems 34–36, 38–41, 44–55, 58–65, 99, 104, 108*).

3. What is the ion-product constant for water? Water is *amphoteric*; that is, it can act as either an acid or a base. Water also dissociates slightly into H_3O^+ ions and OH^- ions; the product of whose concentrations in any aqueous solution is the *ion-product constant for water*, $K_w = [H_3O^+][OH^-] = 1.00 \times 10^{-14}$ at 25 °C (*see Problems 56, 69–71, 101*).

4. What is the pH scale for measuring acidity? The acidity or basicity of an aqueous solution is given by its *pH*, defined as the negative logarithm of the hydronium ion concentration, $[H_3O^+]$. A pH below 7 means an acidic solution; a pH equal to 7 means a neutral solution; and a pH above 7 means a basic solution (*see Problems 57, 61–71, 76, 78, 94, 96–101, 104, 110*).

5. What is a buffer? The pH of a solution can be controlled through the use of a *buffer* that acts to remove either added H_3O^+ ions or added OH^- ions. Most buffer solutions consist of roughly equal amounts of a weak acid and its conjugate base. The bicarbonate buffer present in blood and the hydrogen phosphate buffer present in cells are particularly important examples (*see Problems 72–79, 105, 107*).

6. How is the acid or base concentration of a solution determined? Acid (or base) concentrations are determined in the laboratory by *titration* of a solution of unknown concentration with a base (or acid) solution of known strength until an indicator signals that neutralization is complete (*see Problems 80–93, 103, 106, 109, 110*).

CONCEPT MAP: ACIDS AND BASES

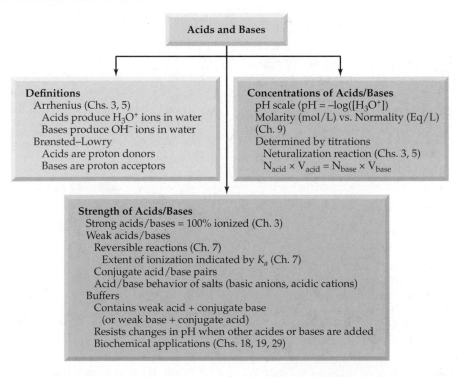

▲ **Figure 10.9**

Acids and bases play important roles in many chemical and biochemical processes, and many common substances are classified as acids or bases. Acid and base behavior is related to the ability to exchange protons, or to form H_3O^+ or OH^- ions, respectively, in water. Strong acids and bases ionize completely in aqueous solution, while weak acids/bases ionize only partially and establish an equilibrium with their conjugates. The relationship between these concepts and some of their practical and/or quantitative applications are illustrated in Figure 10.9.

KEY WORDS

Acid dissociation constant (K_a), *p. 301*

Acid–base indicator, *p. 308*

Amphoteric, *p. 302*

Brønsted–Lowry acid, *p. 293*

Brønsted–Lowry base, *p. 293*

Buffer, *p. 308*

Conjugate acid, *p. 295*

Conjugate acid–base pair, *p. 295*

Conjugate base, *p. 295*

Dissociation, *p. 296*

Equivalent of acid, *p. 314*

Equivalent of base, *p. 314*

Gram-equivalent of acid, *p. 314*

Gram-equivalent of base, *p. 314*

Henderson–Hasselbalch equation, *p. 309*

Hydronium ion, *p. 291*

Ion-product constant
   for water (K_w), *p. 302*

Normality (N), *p. 314*

p function, *p. 304*

pH, *p. 304*

Strong acid, *p. 296*

Strong base, *p. 297*

Titration, *p. 317*

Weak acid, *p. 296*

Weak base, *p. 297*

UNDERSTANDING KEY CONCEPTS

10.33   An aqueous solution of OH^-, represented as a blue sphere, is allowed to mix with a solution of an acid H_nA, represented as a red sphere. Three possible outcomes are depicted by boxes (1)–(3), where the green spheres represent A^{n-}, the anion of the acid:

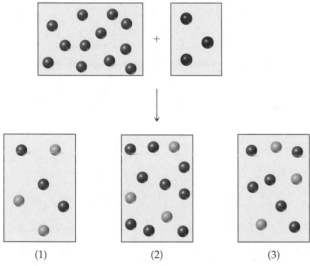

Which outcome corresponds to the following reactions?

    (a) $HF + OH^- \longrightarrow H_2O + F^-$

    (b) $H_2SO_3 + 2\,OH^- \longrightarrow 2\,H_2O + SO_3{}^{2-}$

    (c) $H_3PO_4 + 3\,OH^- \longrightarrow 3\,H_2O + PO_4{}^{3-}$

10.34   Electrostatic potential maps of acetic acid (CH_3CO_2H) and ethyl alcohol (CH_3CH_2OH) are shown. Identify the most acidic hydrogen in each, and tell which of the two is likely to be the stronger acid.

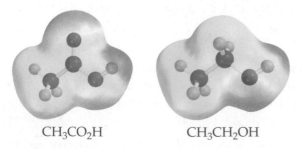

CH_3CO_2H CH_3CH_2OH

10.35   The following pictures represent aqueous acid solutions. Water molecules are not shown.

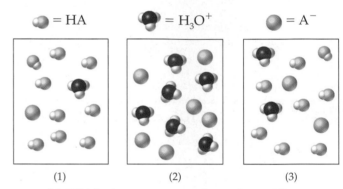

$= HA$ $= H_3O^+$ $= A^-$

   (1)   (2)   (3)

  (a) Which picture represents the weakest acid?

  (b) Which picture represents the strongest acid?

  (c) Which picture represents the acid with the smallest value of K_a?

10.36   The following pictures represent aqueous solutions of a diprotic acid H_2A. Water molecules are not shown.

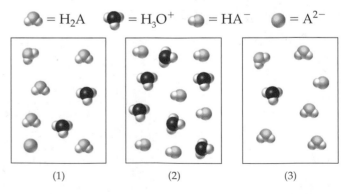

$= H_2A$ $= H_3O^+$ $= HA^-$ $= A^{2-}$

   (1)   (2)   (3)

  (a) Which picture represents a solution of a weak diprotic acid?

  (b) Which picture represents an impossible situation?

10.37   Assume that the red spheres in the buret represent H_3O^+ ions, the blue spheres in the flask represent OH^- ions, and you are carrying out a titration of the base with the acid. If the volumes in the buret and the flask are identical and the concentration of the acid in the buret is 1.00 M, what is the concentration of the base in the flask?

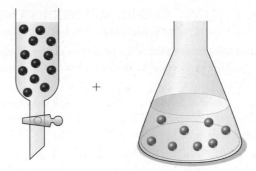

ADDITIONAL PROBLEMS

ACIDS AND BASES

10.38 What happens when a strong acid such as HBr is dissolved in water?

10.39 What happens when a weak acid such as CH_3CO_2H is dissolved in water?

10.40 What happens when a strong base such as KOH is dissolved in water?

10.41 What happens when a weak base such as NH_3 is dissolved in water?

10.42 What is the difference between a monoprotic acid and a diprotic acid? Give an example of each.

10.43 What is the difference between H^+ and H_3O^+?

10.44 Which of the following are strong acids? Look at Table 10.1 if necessary.

(a) $HClO_4$ (b) H_2CO_3 (c) H_3PO_4
(d) NH_4^+ (e) HI (f) $H_2PO_4^-$

10.45 Which of the following are weak bases? Look at Table 10.1 if necessary.

(a) NH_3 (b) $Ca(OH)_2$ (c) HPO_4^{2-}
(d) $LiOH$ (e) CN^- (f) NH_2^-

BRØNSTED–LOWRY ACIDS AND BASES

10.46 Identify the following substances as a Brønsted–Lowry base, a Brønsted–Lowry acid, or neither:

(a) HCN (b) $CH_3CO_2^-$ (c) $AlCl_3$
(d) H_2CO_3 (e) Mg^{2+} (f) $CH_3NH_3^+$

10.47 Label the Brønsted–Lowry acids and bases in the following equations, and tell which substances are conjugate acid–base pairs.

(a) $CO_3^{2-}(aq) + HCl(aq) \longrightarrow$
    $HCO_3^-(aq) + Cl^-(aq)$

(b) $H_3PO_4(aq) + NH_3(aq) \longrightarrow$
    $H_2PO_4^-(aq) + NH_4^+(aq)$

(c) $NH_4^+(aq) + CN^-(aq) \rightleftharpoons NH_3(aq) + HCN(aq)$

(d) $HBr(aq) + OH^-(aq) \longrightarrow H_2O(l) + Br^-(aq)$

(e) $H_2PO_4^-(aq) + N_2H_4(aq) \rightleftharpoons$
    $HPO_4^{2-}(aq) + N_2H_5^+(aq)$

10.48 Write the formulas of the conjugate acids of the following Brønsted–Lowry bases:

(a) $ClCH_2CO_2^-$ (b) C_5H_5N
(c) SeO_4^{2-} (d) $(CH_3)_3N$

10.49 Write the formulas of the conjugate bases of the following Brønsted–Lowry acids:

(a) HCN (b) $(CH_3)_2NH_2^+$
(c) H_3PO_4 (d) $HSeO_3^-$

10.50 The hydrogen-containing anions of many polyprotic acids are amphoteric. Write equations for HCO_3^- and $H_2PO_4^-$ acting as bases with the strong acid HCl and as acids with the strong base NaOH.

10.51 Write balanced equations for proton-transfer reactions between the listed pairs. Indicate the conjugate pairs, and determine the favored direction for each equilibrium.

(a) HCl and PO_4^{3-} (b) HCN and SO_4^{2-}
(c) $HClO_4$ and NO_2^- (d) CH_3O^- and HF

10.52 Sodium bicarbonate $(NaHCO_3)$, also known as baking soda, is a common home remedy for acid indigestion and is also used to neutralize acid spills in the laboratory. Write a balanced chemical equation for the reaction of sodium bicarbonate with

(a) Gastric juice (HCl) (b) Sulfuric acid (H_2SO_4)

10.53 Refer to Section 10.12 to write balanced equations for the following acid–base reactions:

(a) $LiOH + HNO_3 \longrightarrow$ (b) $BaCO_3 + HI \longrightarrow$
(c) $H_3PO_4 + KOH \longrightarrow$ (d) $Ca(HCO_3)_2 + HCl \longrightarrow$
(e) $Ba(OH)_2 + H_2SO_4 \longrightarrow$

ACID AND BASE STRENGTH: K_a AND pH

10.54 How is K_a defined? Write the equation for K_a for the generalized acid HA.

10.55 Rearrange the equation you wrote in Problem 10.54 to solve for $[H_3O^+]$ in terms of K_a.

10.56 How is K_w defined, and what is its numerical value at 25 °C?

10.57 How is pH defined?

10.58 A solution of 0.10 M HCl has a pH = 1.00, whereas a solution of 0.10 M CH_3COOH has a pH = 2.88. Explain.

10.59 Calculate $[H_3O^+]$ for the 0.10 M CH_3COOH solution in Problem 10.58. What percent of the weak acid is dissociated?

10.60 Write the expressions for the acid dissociation constants for the three successive dissociations of phosphoric acid, H_3PO_4, in water.

10.61 Based on the K_a values in Table 10.1, rank the following solutions in order of increasing pH: 0.10 M HCOOH, 0.10 M HF, 0.10 M H_2CO_3, 0.10 M HSO_4^-, 0.10 M NH_4^+.

10.62 The electrode of a pH meter is placed in a sample of urine, and a reading of 7.9 is obtained. Is the sample acidic, basic, or neutral? What is the concentration of H_3O^+ in the urine sample?

10.63 A 0.10 M solution of the deadly poison hydrogen cyanide, HCN, has a pH of 5.2. Calculate the $[H_3O^+]$ of the solution. Is HCN a strong or a weak acid?

10.64 Human sweat can have a pH ranging from 4.0–6.8. Calculate the range of $[H_3O^+]$ in normal human sweat. How many orders of magnitude does this range represent?

10.65 Saliva has a pH range of 5.8–7.1. Approximately what is the H_3O^+ concentration range of saliva?

10.66 What is the approximate pH of a 0.02 M solution of a strong monoprotic acid? Of a 0.02 M solution of a strong base, such as KOH?

10.67 Calculate the pOH of each solution in Problems 10.62–10.65.

10.68 Without using a calculator, match the H_3O^+ concentrations of the following solutions, (a)–(d), to the corresponding pH, i–iv:

(a) Fresh egg white: $[H_3O^+] = 2.5 \times 10^{-8}$ M
(b) Apple cider: $[H_3O^+] = 5.0 \times 10^{-4}$ M
(c) Household ammonia: $[H_3O^+] = 2.3 \times 10^{-12}$ M
(d) Vinegar (acetic acid): $[H_3O^+] = 4.0 \times 10^{-3}$ M

i. pH = 3.30   ii. pH = 2.40   iii. pH = 11.64   iv. pH = 7.60

10.69 What are the OH^- concentration and pOH for each solution in Problem 10.68? Rank the solutions according to increasing acidity.

10.70 What are the H_3O^+ and OH^- concentrations of solutions that have the following pH values?

(a) pH 4   (b) pH 11   (c) pH 0
(d) pH 1.38   (e) pH 7.96

10.71 About 12% of the acid in a 0.10 M solution of a weak acid dissociates to form ions. What are the H_3O^+ and OH^- concentrations? What is the pH of the solution?

BUFFERS

10.72 What are the two components of a buffer system? How does a buffer work to hold pH nearly constant?

10.73 Which system would you expect to be a better buffer: $HNO_3 + Na^+NO_3^-$, or $CH_3CO_2H + CH_3CO_2^-Na^+$? Explain.

10.74 The pH of a buffer solution containing 0.10 M acetic acid and 0.10 M sodium acetate is 4.74.

(a) Write the Henderson–Hasselbalch equation for this buffer.
(b) Write the equations for reaction of this buffer with a small amount of HNO_3 and with a small amount of NaOH.

10.75 Which of the following buffer systems would you use if you wanted to prepare a solution having a pH of approximately 9.5?

(a) 0.08 M $H_2PO_4^-$ / 0.12 M HPO_4^{2-}
(b) 0.08 M NH_4^+ / 0.12 M NH_3

10.76 What is the pH of a buffer system that contains 0.200 M hydrocyanic acid (HCN) and 0.150 M sodium cyanide (NaCN)? The pK_a of hydrocyanic acid is 9.31.

10.77 Consider 1.00 L of the buffer system described in Problem 10.76.

(a) What are the $[HCN]$ and $[CN^-]$ after 0.020 mol of HCl is added? What is the pH?
(b) What are the $[HCN]$ and $[CN^-]$ after 0.020 mol of NaOH is added? What is the pH?

10.78 What is the pH of a buffer system that contains 0.15 M NH_4^+ and 0.10 M NH_3? The pK_a of NH_4^+ is 9.25.

10.79 How many moles of NaOH must be added to 1.00 L of the solution described in Problem 10.78 to increase the pH to 9.25? (Hint: What is the $[NH_3]/[NH_4^+]$ when the pH = pK_a?)

CONCENTRATIONS OF ACID AND BASE SOLUTIONS

10.80 What does it mean when we talk about acid *equivalents* and base *equivalents*?

10.81 How does normality compare to molarity for monoprotic and polyprotic acids??

10.82 Calculate the gram-equivalent for each of the following acids and bases.

(a) HNO_3 (b) H_3PO_4 (c) KOH   (d) $Mg(OH)_2$

10.83 What mass of each of the acids and bases in Problem 10.82 is needed to prepare 500 mL of 0.15 N solution?

10.84 How many milliliters of 0.0050 N KOH are required to neutralize 25 mL of 0.0050 N H_2SO_4? To neutralize 25 mL of 0.0050 M H_2SO_4?

10.85 How many equivalents are in 75.0 mL of 0.12 M H_2SO_4 solution? In 75.0 mL of a 0.12 M H_3PO_4 solution?

10.86 How many equivalents of an acid or base are in the following?

(a) 0.25 mol $Mg(OH)_2$
(b) 2.5 g $Mg(OH)_2$
(c) 15 g CH_3CO_2H

10.87 What mass of citric acid (triprotic, $C_6H_5O_7H_3$) contains 152 mEq of citric acid?

10.88 What are the molarity and the normality of a solution made by dissolving 5.0 g of $Ca(OH)_2$ in enough water to make 500.0 mL of solution?

10.89 What are the molarity and the normality of a solution made by dissolving 25 g of citric acid (triprotic, $C_6H_5O_7H_3$) in enough water to make 800 mL of solution?

10.90 Titration of a 12.0 mL solution of HCl requires 22.4 mL of 0.12 M NaOH. What is the molarity of the HCl solution?

10.91 How many equivalents are in 15.0 mL of 0.12 M $Ba(OH)_2$ solution? What volume of 0.085 M HNO_3 is required to reach the end point when titrating 15.0 mL of this solution?

10.92 Titration of a 10.0 mL solution of KOH requires 15.0 mL of 0.0250 M H_2SO_4 solution. What is the molarity of the KOH solution?

10.93 If 35.0 mL of a 0.100 N acid solution is needed to reach the end point in titration of 21.5 mL of a base solution, what is the normality of the base solution?

CHEMISTRY IN ACTION

10.94 The concentration of HCl when released to the stomach cavity is diluted to between 0.01 and 0.001 M [*GERD—Too Much Acid or Not Enough? p. 299*]

(a) What is the pH range in the stomach cavity?

(b) Write a balanced equation for the neutralization of stomach acid by $NaHCO_3$.

(c) How many grams of $NaHCO_3$ are required to neutralize 15.0 mL of a solution having a pH of 1.8?

10.95 What are the functions of the acidic gastric juices in the stomach? [*GERD—Too Much Acid or Not Enough? p. 299*]

10.96 Metabolic acidosis is often treated by administering bicarbonate intravenously. Explain how this treatment can increase blood serum pH. [*Buffers in the Body: Acidosis and Alkalosis, p. 312*]

10.97 Which body fluid is most acidic? Which is most basic? [*Buffers in the Body: Acidosis and Alkalosis, p. 312*]

10.98 Rain typically has a pH of about 5.6. What is the H_3O^+ concentration in rain? [*Acid Rain, p. 320*]

10.99 Acid rain with a pH as low as 1.5 has been recorded in West Virginia. [*Acid Rain, p. 320*]

(a) What is the H_3O^+ concentration in this acid rain?

(b) How many grams of HNO_3 must be dissolved to make 25 L of solution that has a pH of 1.5?

GENERAL QUESTIONS AND PROBLEMS

10.100 A solution is prepared by bubbling 15.0 L of $HCl(g)$ at 25 °C and 1 atm into 250.0 mL of water.

(a) Assuming all the HCl dissolves in the water, how many moles of HCl are in solution?

(b) What is the pH of the solution?

10.101 The dissociation of water into H_3O^+ and OH^- ions depends on temperature. At 0 °C the $[H_3O^+] = 3.38 \times 10^{-8}$ M, at 25 °C the $[H_3O^+] = 1.00 \times 10^{-7}$ M, and at 50 °C the $[H_3O^+] = 2.34 \times 10^{-7}$ M.

(a) Calculate the pH of water at 0 °C and 50 °C.

(b) What is the value of K_w at 0 °C and 50 °C?

(c) Is the dissociation of water endothermic or exothermic?

10.102 Alka-Seltzer™, a drugstore antacid, contains a mixture of $NaHCO_3$, aspirin, and citric acid, $C_6H_5O_7H_3$. Why does Alka-Seltzer™ foam and bubble when dissolved in water? Which ingredient is the antacid?

10.103 How many milliliters of 0.50 M NaOH solution are required to titrate 40.0 mL of a 0.10 M H_2SO_4 solution to an end point?

10.104 Which solution contains more acid, 50 mL of a 0.20 N HCl solution or 50 mL of a 0.20 N acetic acid solution? Which has a higher hydronium ion concentration? Which has a lower pH?

10.105 One of the buffer systems used to control the pH of blood involves the equilibrium between $H_2PO_4^-$ and HPO_4^{2-}. The pK_a for $H_2PO_4^-$ is 7.21.

(a) Write the Henderson–Hasselbalch equation for this buffer system.

(b) What HPO_4^{2-} to $H_2PO_4^-$ ratio is needed to maintain the optimum blood pH of 7.40?

10.106 A 0.15 N solution of HCl is used to titrate 30.0 mL of a $Ca(OH)_2$ solution of unknown concentration. If 140.0 mL of HCl is required, what is the normality of the $Ca(OH)_2$ solution? What is the molarity?

10.107 Which of the following combinations produces an effective buffer solution? Assuming equal concentrations of each acid and its conjugate base, calculate the pH of each buffer solution.

(a) NaF and HF   (b) $HClO_4$ and $NaClO_4$

(c) NH_4Cl and NH_3 (d) KBr and HBr

10.108 One method of analyzing ammonium salts is to treat them with NaOH and then heat the solution to remove the NH_3 gas formed.

$$NH_4^+(aq) + OH^-(aq) \longrightarrow NH_3(g) + H_2O(l)$$

(a) Label the Brønsted–Lowry acid–base pairs.

(b) If 2.86 L of NH_3 at 60 °C and 755 mmHg is produced by the reaction of NH_4Cl, how many grams of NH_4Cl were in the original sample?

10.109 One method of reducing acid rain is "scrubbing" the combustion products before they are emitted from power plant smoke stacks. The process involves addition of an aqueous suspension of lime (CaO) to the combustion chamber and stack, where the lime reacts with SO_2 to give calcium sulfite $(CaSO_3)$:

$$CaO(aq) + SO_2(g) \longrightarrow CaSO_3(aq)$$

(a) How much lime (in g) is needed to remove 1 mol of SO_2?

(b) How much lime (in kg) is needed to remove 1 kg of SO_2?

10.110 Sodium oxide, Na_2O, reacts with water to give NaOH.

(a) Write a balanced equation for the reaction.

(b) What is the pH of the solution prepared by allowing 1.55 g of Na_2O to react with 500.0 mL of water? Assume that there is no volume change.

(c) How many milliliters of 0.0100 M HCl are needed to neutralize the NaOH solution prepared in (b)?

CHAPTER 11

Nuclear Chemistry

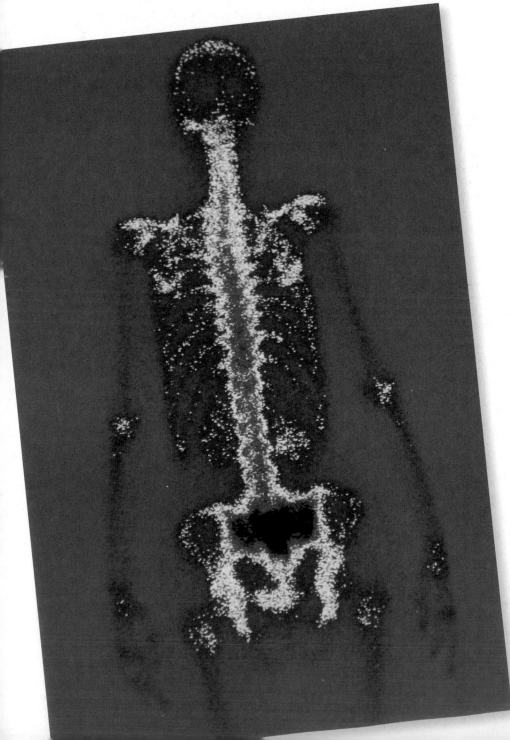

◄ Many medical diagnostic techniques, including this total body bone scan, take advantage of the properties of radioactive isotopes.

CONCEPTS
TO REVIEW

A. Atomic Theory
(Section 2.1)

B. Elements and Atomic
Number
(Section 2.2)

C. Isotopes
(Section 2.3)

CHAPTER GOALS

1. **What is a nuclear reaction, and how are equations for nuclear reactions balanced?**
   THE GOAL: Be able to write and balance equations for nuclear reactions. (◀◀ A, B, C.)

2. **What are the different kinds of radioactivity?**
   THE GOAL: Be able to list the characteristics of three common kinds of radiation—α, β, and γ (alpha, beta, and gamma).

3. **How are the rates of nuclear reactions expressed?**
   THE GOAL: Be able to explain half-life and calculate the quantity of a radioisotope remaining after a given number of half-lives.

4. **What is ionizing radiation?**
   THE GOAL: Be able to describe the properties of the different types of ionizing radiation and their potential for harm to living tissue.

5. **How is radioactivity measured?**
   THE GOAL: Be able to describe the common units for measuring radiation.

6. **What is transmutation?**
   THE GOAL: Be able to explain nuclear bombardment and balance equations for nuclear bombardment reactions. (◀◀ A, B, and C.)

7. **What are nuclear fission and nuclear fusion?**
   THE GOAL: Be able to explain nuclear fission and nuclear fusion.

I n all of the reactions we have discussed thus far, only the *bonds* between atoms have changed; the chemical identities of atoms themselves have remained unchanged. Anyone who reads the paper or watches television knows, however, that atoms *can* change, often resulting in the conversion of one element into another. Atomic weapons, nuclear energy, and radioactive radon gas in our homes are all topics of societal importance, and all involve *nuclear chemistry*—the study of the properties and reactions of atomic nuclei.

11.1 Nuclear Reactions

Recall from Section 2.2 that an atom is characterized by its *atomic number, Z,* and its *mass number, A.* The atomic number, written below and to the left of the element symbol, gives the number of protons in the nucleus and identifies the element. The mass number, written above and to the left of the element symbol, gives the total number of **nucleons**, a general term for both protons (p) and neutrons (n). The most common isotope of carbon, for example, has 12 nucleons: 6 protons and 6 neutrons: $^{12}_{6}C$.

Nucleon A general term for both protons and neutrons.

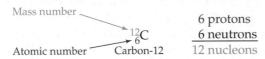

Mass number
$^{12}_{6}C$
Atomic number   Carbon-12

6 protons
6 neutrons
12 nucleons

Atoms with identical atomic numbers but different mass numbers are called *isotopes,* and the nucleus of a specific isotope is called a **nuclide**. Thirteen isotopes of carbon are known—two occur commonly (^{12}C and ^{13}C) and one (^{14}C) is produced in small amounts in the upper atmosphere by the action of neutrons from cosmic rays on ^{14}N. The remaining 10 carbon isotopes have been produced artificially. Only the two commonly occurring isotopes are stable indefinitely; the others undergo spontaneous **nuclear reactions**, which change their nuclei. Carbon-14, for example, is an unstable isotope that slowly decomposes and is converted to nitrogen-14 plus an electron, a process we can write as

$$^{14}_{6}C \longrightarrow \, ^{14}_{7}N + \, ^{0}_{-1}e$$

▶▶ The different isotopes of an atom each have the same number of protons and only differ in their number of neutrons (Section 2.3).

Nuclide The nucleus of a specific isotope of an element.

Nuclear reaction A reaction that changes an atomic nucleus, usually causing the change of one element into another.

The electron is often written as $^{0}_{-1}e$, where the superscript 0 indicates that the mass of an electron is essentially zero when compared with that of a proton or neutron, and the subscript -1 indicates that the charge is -1. (The subscript in this instance is not a true atomic number; in Section 11.4 the purpose of representing the electron this way will become clear.)

Nuclear reactions, such as the spontaneous decay of ^{14}C, are distinguished from chemical reactions in several ways:

- A *nuclear* reaction involves a change in an atom's nucleus, usually producing a different element. A *chemical* reaction, by contrast, involves only a change in distribution of the outer-shell electrons around the atom and never changes the nucleus itself or produces a different element.
- Different isotopes of an element have essentially the same behavior in chemical reactions but often have completely different behavior in nuclear reactions.
- The rate of a nuclear reaction is unaffected by a change in temperature or pressure or by the addition of a catalyst.
- The nuclear reaction of an atom is essentially the same whether it is in a chemical compound or in an uncombined, elemental form.
- The energy change accompanying a nuclear reaction can be up to several million times greater than that accompanying a chemical reaction. The nuclear transformation of 1.0 g of uranium-235 releases 3.4×10^8 kcal (1.4×10^9 kJ), for example, whereas the chemical combustion of 1.0 g of methane releases only 12 kcal (50 kJ).

11.2 The Discovery and Nature of Radioactivity

The discovery of *radioactivity* dates to the year 1896 when the French physicist Henri Becquerel made a remarkable observation. While investigating the nature of phosphorescence—the luminous glow of some minerals and other substances that remains when the light is suddenly turned off—Becquerel happened to place a sample of a uranium-containing mineral on top of a photographic plate that had been wrapped in black paper and put in a drawer to protect it from sunlight. On developing the plate, Becquerel was surprised to find a silhouette of the mineral. He concluded that the mineral was producing some kind of unknown radiation, which passed through the paper and exposed the photographic plate.

Marie Sklodowska Curie and her husband, Pierre, took up the challenge and began a series of investigations into this new phenomenon, which they termed **radioactivity**. They found that the source of the radioactivity was the element uranium (U) and that two previously unknown elements, which they named polonium (Po) and radium (Ra), were also radioactive. For these achievements, Becquerel and the Curies shared the 1903 Nobel Prize in physics.

Further work on radioactivity by the English scientist Ernest Rutherford established that there were at least two types of radiation, which he named *alpha* (α) and *beta* (β) after the first two letters of the Greek alphabet. Shortly thereafter, a third type of radiation was found and named for the third Greek letter, *gamma* (γ).

Subsequent studies showed that when the three kinds of radiation are passed between two plates with opposite electrical charges, each is affected differently. Alpha radiation bends toward the negative plate and must therefore have a positive charge. Beta radiation, by contrast, bends toward the positive plate and must have a negative charge, whereas gamma radiation does not bend toward either plate and has no charge (Figure 11.1).

Radioactivity The spontaneous emission of radiation from a nucleus.

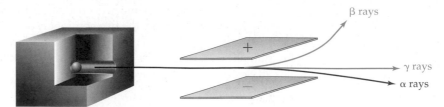

▲ **Figure 11.1**
The effect of an electric field on α, β, and γ, radiation.
The radioactive source in the shielded box emits radiation, which passes between the two electrically charged plates. Alpha radiation is deflected toward the negative plate, β radiation is deflected toward the positive plate, and γ radiation is not deflected.

Another difference among the three kinds of radiation soon became apparent when it was discovered that alpha and beta radiations are composed of small particles with a measurable mass, whereas **gamma (γ) radiation** consists of high-energy electromagnetic waves and has no mass. Rutherford was able to show that a **beta (β) particle** is an electron (e^-) and that an **alpha (α) particle** is actually a helium nucleus, He^{2+}. (Recall that a helium *atom* consists of two protons, two neutrons, and two electrons. When the two electrons are removed, the remaining helium nucleus, or α particle, has only the two protons and two neutrons.)

Yet a third difference among the three kinds of radiation is their penetrating power. Because of their relatively large mass, α particles move slowly (up to about $1/10$ the speed of light) and can be stopped by a few sheets of paper or by the top layer of skin. Beta particles, because they are much lighter, move at up to $9/10$ the speed of light and have about 100 times the penetrating power of α particles. A block of wood or heavy protective clothing is necessary to stop β radiation, which can otherwise penetrate the skin and cause burns and other damage. Gamma rays move at the speed of light (3.00×10^8 m/s) and have about 1000 times the penetrating power of α particles. A lead block several inches thick is needed to stop γ radiation, which can otherwise penetrate and damage the body's internal organs.

The characteristics of the three kinds of radiation are summarized in Table 11.1. Note that an α particle, even though it is an ion with a $+2$ charge, is usually written using the symbol $_2^4He$ without the charge. A β particle is usually written $_{-1}^0e$, as noted previously.

Gamma (γ) radiation Radioactivity consisting of high-energy light waves.

▶▶▶ See Chemistry in Action: Atoms and Light on p. 66 in Chapter 2 for a discussion of gamma rays and the rest of the electromagnetic spectrum.

Beta (β) particle An electron (e^-), emitted as radiation.

Alpha (α) particle A helium nucleus (He^{2+}), emitted as α radiation.

TABLE 11.1 Characteristics of α, β, and γ Radiation

Type of Radiation	Symbol	Charge	Composition	Mass (AMU)	Velocity	Relative Penetrating Power
Alpha	α, $_2^4He$	$+2$	Helium nucleus	4	Up to 10% speed of light	Low (1)
Beta	β, $_{-1}^0e$	-1	Electron	1/1823	Up to 90% speed of light	Medium (100)
Gamma	γ, $_0^0\gamma$	0	High-energy radiation	0	Speed of light (3.00×10^8 m/s)	High (1000)

11.3 Stable and Unstable Isotopes

Every element in the periodic table has at least one radioactive isotope, or **radioisotope**, and more than 3300 radioisotopes are known. Their radioactivity is the result of having unstable nuclei, although the exact causes of this instability are not fully understood. Radiation is emitted when an unstable radioactive nucleus, or **radionuclide**, spontaneously changes into a more stable one.

For elements in the first few rows of the periodic table, stability is associated with a roughly equal number of neutrons and protons (Figure 11.2). Hydrogen, for example, has stable $_1^1H$ (protium) and $_1^2H$ (deuterium) isotopes, but its $_1^3H$ isotope (tritium) is radioactive. As elements get heavier, the number of neutrons relative to protons in stable nuclei increases. Lead-208 ($_{82}^{208}Pb$), for example, the most abundant stable isotope of lead, has 126 neutrons and 82 protons in its nuclei. Nevertheless, of the 35 known isotopes of lead, only 3 are stable whereas 32 are radioactive. In fact, there are only 264 stable isotopes among all the elements. All isotopes of elements with atomic numbers higher than that of bismuth (83) are radioactive.

Most of the more than 3300 known radioisotopes have been made in high-energy particle accelerators by reactions that will be described in Section 11.10. Such isotopes are called *artificial radioisotopes* because they are not found in nature. All isotopes of the transuranium elements (those heavier than uranium) are artificial. The much smaller number of radioactive isotopes found in Earth's crust, such as $_{92}^{238}U$, are called *natural radioisotopes*.

Radioisotope A radioactive isotope.

Radionuclide The nucleus of a radioactive isotope.

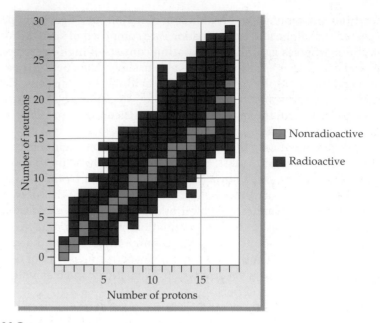

▲ **Figure 11.2**
A plot of the numbers of neutrons and protons for known isotopes of the first 18 elements.
Stable (nonradioactive) isotopes of these elements have equal or nearly equal numbers of neutrons and protons.

Aside from their radioactivity, different radioisotopes of the same element have the same chemical properties as stable isotopes, which accounts for their great usefulness as *tracers*. A chemical compound tagged with a radioactive atom undergoes exactly the same reactions as its nonradioactive counterpart. The difference is that the tagged compound can be located with a radiation detector and its location determined, as discussed in Chemistry in Action: Body Imaging on page 348.

11.4 Nuclear Decay

Think for a minute about the consequences of α and β radiation. If radioactivity involves the spontaneous emission of a small particle from an unstable atomic nucleus, then the nucleus itself must undergo a change. With that understanding of radioactivity came the startling discovery that atoms of one element can change into atoms of another element, something that had previously been thought impossible. The spontaneous emission of a particle from an unstable nucleus is called **nuclear decay**, or *radioactive decay*, and the resulting change of one element into another is called **transmutation**.

Nuclear decay: Radioactive element $\longrightarrow$ New element $+$ Emitted particle

We now look at what happens to a nucleus when nuclear decay occurs.

Alpha Emission

When an atom of uranium-238 $\left(^{238}_{92}\text{U}\right)$ emits an α particle, the nucleus loses 2 protons and 2 neutrons. Because the number of protons in the nucleus has now changed from 92 to 90, the *identity* of the atom has changed from uranium to thorium. Furthermore, since the total number of nucleons has decreased by 4, uranium-238 has become thorium-234 $\left(^{234}_{90}\text{Th}\right)$ (Figure 11.3).

Note that the equation for a nuclear reaction is not balanced in the usual chemical sense because the kinds of atoms are not the same on both sides of the arrow. Instead, we say that a nuclear equation is balanced when the number of nucleons on both sides of the equation is the same and when the sums of the charges on the nuclei plus any ejected subatomic particles (protons or electrons) are the same on both sides of the

Nuclear decay The spontaneous emission of a particle from an unstable nucleus.

Transmutation The change of one element into another.

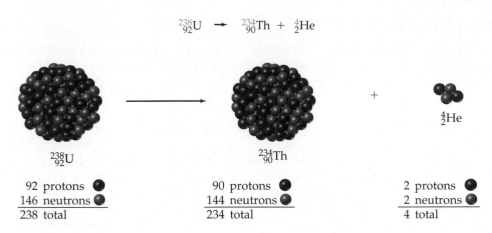

$$^{238}_{92}\text{U} \longrightarrow {}^{234}_{90}\text{Th} + {}^{4}_{2}\text{He}$$

$+$

$^{4}_{2}\text{He}$

$^{238}_{92}\text{U}$

$^{234}_{90}\text{Th}$

92 protons	90 protons	2 protons
146 neutrons	144 neutrons	2 neutrons
238 total	234 total	4 total

◄ **Figure 11.3**
Alpha emission.
Emission of an α particle from an atom of uranium-238 produces an atom of thorium-234.

equation. In the decay of $^{238}_{92}\text{U}$ to give $^{4}_{2}\text{He}$ and $^{234}_{90}\text{Th}$, for example, there are 238 nucleons and 92 nuclear charges on both sides of the nuclear equation.

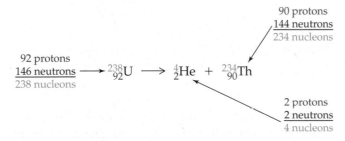

90 protons
144 neutrons
234 nucleons

92 protons
146 neutrons $^{238}_{92}\text{U} \longrightarrow {}^{4}_{2}\text{He} + {}^{234}_{90}\text{Th}$
238 nucleons

2 protons
2 neutrons
4 nucleons

Worked Example 11.1 Balancing Nuclear Reactions: Alpha Emission

Polonium-208 is one of the α emitters studied by Marie Curie. Write the equation for the α decay of polonium-208, and identify the element formed.

ANALYSIS Look up the atomic number of polonium (84) in the periodic table, and write the known part of the nuclear equation, using the standard symbol for polonium-208:

$$^{208}_{84}\text{Po} \longrightarrow {}^{4}_{2}\text{He} + \text{?}$$

Then, calculate the mass number and atomic number of the product element, and write the final equation.

SOLUTION
The mass number of the product is $208 - 4 = 204$, and the atomic number is $84 - 2 = 82$. A look at the periodic table identifies the element with atomic number 82 as lead (Pb).

$$^{208}_{84}\text{Po} \longrightarrow {}^{4}_{2}\text{He} + {}^{204}_{82}\text{Pb}$$

Check your answer by making sure that the mass numbers and atomic numbers on the two sides of the equation are balanced:

Mass numbers: $208 = 4 + 204$ Atomic numbers: $84 = 2 + 82$

PROBLEM 11.1
High levels of radioactive radon-222 $\left(^{222}_{86}\text{Rn}\right)$ have been found in many homes built on radium-containing rock, leading to the possibility of health hazards. What product results from α emission by radon-222?

PROBLEM 11.2
What isotope of radium (Ra) is converted into radon-222 by α emission?

Beta Emission

Whereas α emission leads to the loss of two protons and two neutrons from the nucleus, β emission involves the *decomposition* of a neutron to yield an electron and a proton. This process can be represented as

$$\,^{1}_{0}n \longrightarrow \,^{1}_{1}p + \,^{0}_{-1}e$$

where the electron ($\,^{0}_{-1}e$) is ejected as a β particle, and the proton is retained by the nucleus. Note that the electrons emitted during β radiation come from the *nucleus* and not from the occupied orbitals surrounding the nucleus. The decomposition of carbon-14 to form nitrogen-14 in Section 11.1 is an example of beta decay.

The net result of β emission is that the atomic number of the atom *increases* by 1 because there is a new proton. The mass number of the atom remains the same, however, because a neutron has changed into a proton, leaving the total number of nucleons unchanged. For example, iodine-131 ($\,^{131}_{53}I$), a radioisotope used in detecting thyroid problems, undergoes nuclear decay by β emission to yield xenon-131 ($\,^{131}_{54}Xe$):

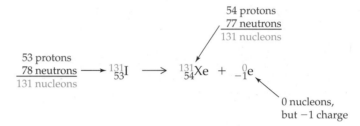

Note that the superscripts (mass numbers) are balanced in this equation because a β particle has a mass near zero, and the subscripts are balanced because a β particle has a charge of -1.

Worked Example 11.2 Balancing Nuclear Reactions: Beta Emission

Write a balanced nuclear equation for the β decay of chromium-55.

ANALYSIS Write the known part of the nuclear equation:

$$\,^{55}_{24}Cr \longrightarrow \,^{0}_{-1}e + ?$$

Then calculate the mass number and atomic number of the product element, and write the final equation.

SOLUTION
The mass number of the product stays at 55, and the atomic number increases by 1, $24 + 1 = 25$, so the product is manganese-55.

$$\,^{55}_{24}Cr \longrightarrow \,^{0}_{-1}e + \,^{55}_{25}Mn$$

Check your answer by making sure that the mass numbers and atomic numbers on the two sides of the equation are balanced:

Mass numbers: $55 = 0 + 55$ Atomic numbers: $24 = -1 + 25$

PROBLEM 11.3
Strontium-89 is a short-lived β emitter often used in the treatment of bone tumors. Write a nuclear equation for the decay of strontium-89.

PROBLEM 11.4
Write nuclear equations for the formation of each of the following nuclides by β emission.
(a) $\,^{3}_{2}He$ **(b)** $\,^{210}_{83}Bi$ **(c)** $\,^{20}_{10}Ne$

Gamma Emission

Emission of γ rays, unlike the emission of α and β particles, causes no change in mass or atomic number because γ rays are simply high-energy electromagnetic waves. Although γ emission can occur alone, it usually accompanies α or β emission as a mechanism for the new nucleus that results from a transmutation to release some extra energy.

Since γ emission affects neither mass number nor atomic number, it is often omitted from nuclear equations. Nevertheless, γ rays are of great importance. Their penetrating power makes them by far the most dangerous kind of external radiation for humans and also makes them useful in numerous medical applications. Cobalt-60, for example, is used in cancer therapy as a source of penetrating γ rays that kill cancerous tissue.

$$^{60}_{27}\text{Co} \longrightarrow {}^{60}_{28}\text{Ni} + {}^{0}_{-1}\text{e} + {}^{0}_{0}\gamma$$

Positron Emission

In addition to $\alpha, \beta,$ and γ radiation, there is another common type of radioactive decay process called *positron emission*, which involves the conversion of a proton in the nucleus into a neutron plus an ejected **positron**, ${}^{0}_{1}\text{e}$ or β^{+}. A positron, which can be thought of as a "positive electron," has the same mass as an electron but a positive charge. This process can be represented as

Positron A "positive electron," which has the same mass as an electron but a positive charge.

$$^{1}_{1}\text{p} \longrightarrow {}^{1}_{0}\text{n} + {}^{0}_{1}\text{e}$$

The result of positron emission is a decrease in the atomic number of the product nucleus because a proton has changed into a neutron, but no change in the mass number. Potassium-40, for example, undergoes positron emission to yield argon-40, a nuclear reaction important in geology for dating rocks. Note once again that the sum of the two subscripts on the right of the nuclear equation $(18 + 1 = 19)$ is equal to the subscript in the $^{40}_{19}\text{K}$ nucleus on the left.

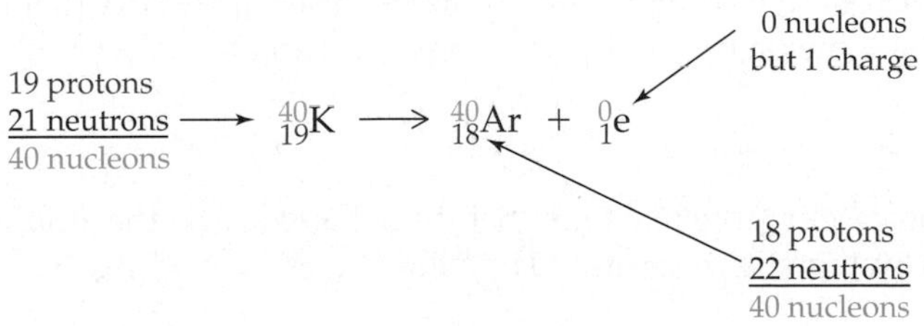

Electron Capture

Electron capture, symbolized E.C., is a process in which the nucleus captures an inner-shell electron from the surrounding electron cloud, thereby converting a proton into a neutron, and energy is released in the form of gamma rays. The mass number of the product nucleus is unchanged, but the atomic number decreases by 1, just as in positron emission. The conversion of mercury-197 into gold-197 is an example:

Electron capture (E.C.) A process in which the nucleus captures an inner-shell electron from the surrounding electron cloud, thereby converting a proton into a neutron.

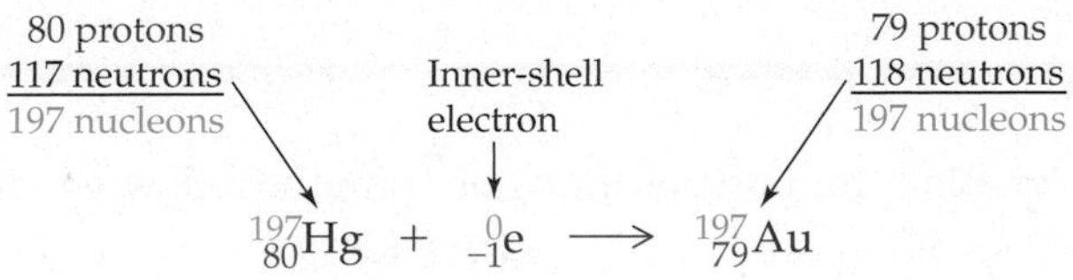

Do not plan on using this reaction to get rich, however. Mercury-197 is not one of the naturally occurring isotopes of Hg and is typically produced by transmutation reactions as discussed in Section 11.10.

In Figure 11.2 we see that most of the stable isotopes of the lighter elements have nearly the same number of neutrons and protons. With this fact in mind, we can often predict the most likely decay mode: unstable isotopes that have more protons than neutrons are more likely to undergo β decay to convert a proton to a neutron, while unstable isotopes having more neutrons than protons are more likely to undergo either positron emission or electron capture to convert a neutron to a proton. Also, the very heavy isotopes ($Z > 83$) will most likely undergo α-decay to lose both neutrons and protons to decrease the atomic number. Characteristics of the five kinds of radioactive decay processes are summarized in Table 11.2.

TABLE 11.2 A Summary of Radioactive Decay Processes

Process	Symbol	Change in Atomic Number	Change in Mass Number	Change in Number of Neutrons
α emission	$^4_2$He or α	-2	-4	-2
β emission	$^0_{-1}$e or β^{-*}	$+1$	0	-1
γ emission	$^0_0\gamma$ or γ	0	0	0
Positron emission	$^0_1$e or β^{+*}	-1	0	$+1$
Electron capture	E.C.	-1	0	$+1$

*Superscripts are used to indicate the charge associated with the two forms of beta decay; β^-, or a beta particle, carries a -1 charge, while β^+, or a positron, carries a $+1$ charge.

Worked Example 11.3 Balancing Nuclear Reactions: Electron Capture, Positron Emission

Write balanced nuclear equations for the following processes:

(a) Electron capture by polonium-204: $^{204}_{84}$Po $+\ ^0_{-1}$e $\longrightarrow$?
(b) Positron emission from xenon-118: $^{118}_{54}$Xe $\longrightarrow\ ^0_1$e $+$?

ANALYSIS The key to writing nuclear equations is to make sure that the number of nucleons is the same on both sides of the equation and that the number of charges is the same.

SOLUTION

(a) In electron capture, the mass number is unchanged and the atomic number decreases by 1, giving bismuth-204: $^{204}_{84}$Po $+\ ^0_{-1}$e $\longrightarrow\ ^{204}_{83}$Bi.

Check your answer by making sure that the number of nucleons and the number of charges are the same on both sides of the equation:

Mass number: $204 + 0 = 204$ Atomic number: $84 + (-1) = 83$

(b) In positron emission, the mass number is unchanged and the atomic number decreases by 1, giving iodine-118: $^{118}_{54}$Xe $\longrightarrow\ ^0_1$e $+\ ^{118}_{53}$I.

CHECK! Mass number: $118 = 0 + 118$ Atomic number: $54 = 1 + 53$

PROBLEM 11.5

Write nuclear equations for positron emission from the following radioisotopes:

(a) $^{38}_{20}$Ca   (b) $^{118}_{54}$Xe   (c) $^{79}_{37}$Rb

PROBLEM 11.6

Write nuclear equations for the formation of the following radioisotopes by electron capture:

(a) $^{62}_{29}$Cu   (b) $^{110}_{49}$In   (c) $^{81}_{35}$Br

The red arrow in this graph indicates the changes that occur in the nucleus of an atom during a nuclear reaction. Identify the isotopes involved as product and reactant, and name the type of decay process.

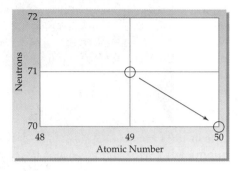

11.5 Radioactive Half-Life

The rate of radioactive decay varies greatly from one radioisotope to another. Some radioisotopes, such as uranium-238, decay at a barely perceptible rate over billions of years, but others, such as carbon-17, decay within thousandths of a second.

Rates of nuclear decay are measured in units of **half-life** $(t_{1/2})$, defined as the amount of time required for one-half of a radioactive sample to decay. For example, the half-life of iodine-131 is 8.021 days. If today you have 1.000 g of $^{131}_{53}I$, then 8.021 days from now you will have only 50% of that amount (0.500 g) because one-half of the sample will have decayed into $^{131}_{54}Xe$. After 8.021 more days (16.063 days total), you will have only 25% (0.250 g) of your original $^{131}_{53}I$ sample; after another 8.021 days (24.084 days total), you will have only 12.5% (0.125 g); and so on. Each passage of a half-life causes the decay of one-half of whatever sample remains. The half-life of any particular isotope is the same no matter what the size of the sample, the temperature, or any other external conditions. There is no known way to slow down, speed up, or otherwise change the characteristics of radioactive decay.

Half-life $(t_{1/2})$ The amount of time required for one-half of a radioactive sample to decay.

$$1.000 \text{ g } ^{131}_{53}I \xrightarrow[\text{days}]{8} 0.500 \text{ g } ^{131}_{53}I \xrightarrow[\text{days}]{8} 0.250 \text{ g } ^{131}_{53}I \xrightarrow[\text{days}]{8} 0.125 \text{ g } ^{131}_{53}I \longrightarrow$$

	One half-life	Two half-lives (16 days total)	Three half-lives (24 days total)
100%	50% remaining	25% remaining	12.5% remaining

The fraction of radioisotope remaining after the passage of each half-life is represented by the curve in Figure 11.4 and can be calculated as

$$\text{fraction remaining} = (0.5)^n$$

where n is the number of half-lives that have elapsed.

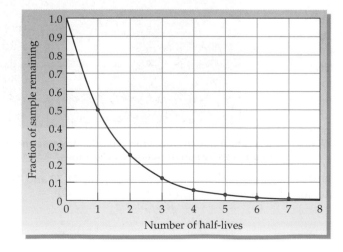

◄ **Figure 11.4**
The decay of a radioactive nucleus over time.
All nuclear decays follow this curve, whether the half-lives are measured in years, days, minutes, or seconds. That is, the fraction of sample remaining after one half-life is 0.50, the fraction remaining after two half-lives is 0.25, the fraction remaining after three half-lives is 0.125, and so on.

- **Rad** The *rad* (radiation absorbed dose) is a unit for measuring the energy absorbed per gram of material exposed to a radiation source and is defined as the absorption of 1×10^{-5} J of energy per gram. The energy absorbed varies with the type of material irradiated and the type of radiation. For most purposes, though, the roentgen and the rad are so close that they can be considered identical when used for X rays and γ rays: 1 R = 1 rad.

- **Rem** The *rem* (roentgen equivalent for man) measures the amount of tissue damage caused by radiation. One rem is the amount of radiation that produces the same effect as 1 R of X rays. Rems are the preferred units for medical purposes because they measure equivalent doses of different kinds of radiation. The rem is calculated as

$$\text{Rems} = \text{rads} \times \text{RBE}$$

  where RBE is a *relative biological effectiveness* factor, which takes into account the differences in energy and of the different types of radiation. Although the actual biological effects of radiation depend greatly on both the source and the energy of the radiation, the RBE of X rays, γ rays, and β particles are essentially equivalent (RBE = 1), while the accepted RBE for α particles is 20. For example, 1 rad of α radiation causes 20 times more tissue damage than 1 rad of γ rays, but 1 rem of α radiation and 1 rem of γ rays cause the same amount of damage. Thus, the rem takes both ionizing intensity and biological effect into account, whereas the rad deals only with intensity.

- **SI Units** In the SI system, the *becquerel* (Bq) is defined as one disintegration per second. The SI unit for energy absorbed is the *gray* (Gy; 1 Gy = 100 rad). For radiation dose, the SI unit is the *sievert* (Sv), which is equal to 100 rem.

The biological consequences of different radiation doses are given in Table 11.6. Although the effects seem frightening, the average radiation dose received annually by most people is only about 0.27 rem. About 80% of this *background radiation* comes from natural sources (rocks and cosmic rays); the remaining 20% comes from consumer products and from medical procedures such as X rays. The amount due to emissions from nuclear power plants and to fallout from testing of nuclear weapons in the 1950s is barely detectable.

TABLE 11.6 Biological Effects of Short-Term Radiation on Humans

Dose (rem)	Biological Effects
0–25	No detectable effects
25–100	Temporary decrease in white blood cell count
100–200	Nausea, vomiting, longer-term decrease in white blood cells
200–300	Vomiting, diarrhea, loss of appetite, listlessness
300–600	Vomiting, diarrhea, hemorrhaging, eventual death in some cases
Above 600	Eventual death in nearly all cases

PROBLEM 11.12

Radiation released during the 1986 Chernobyl nuclear power plant disaster is expected to increase the background radiation level worldwide by about 5 mrem. By how much will this increase the annual dose of the average person? Express your answer as a percentage.

PROBLEM 11.13

A solution of selenium-75, a radioisotope used in the diagnosis of pancreatic disease, is found just prior to administration to have an activity of 44 μCi/mL. If 3.98 mL were delivered intravenously to the patient, what dose of Se-75 (in μCi) did the patient receive?

PROBLEM 11.14
A typical food irradiation application for the inhibition of sprout formation in potatoes applies a dose of 0.20 kGy. What is this dose in units of rad if the radiation is predominantly γ rays? If it is predominantly α particles? (See Chemistry in Action: Irradiated Food on p. 345.)

11.10 Artificial Transmutation

Very few of the approximately 3300 known radioisotopes occur naturally. Most are made from stable isotopes by **artificial transmutation**, the change of one atom into another brought about by nuclear bombardment reactions.

When an atom is bombarded with a high-energy particle, such as a proton, a neutron, an α particle, or even the nucleus of another element, an unstable nucleus is created in the collision. A nuclear change then occurs, and a different element is produced. For example, transmutation of ^{14}N to ^{14}C occurs in the upper atmosphere when neutrons produced by cosmic rays collide with atmospheric nitrogen. In the collision, a neutron dislodges a proton (^{1}H) from the nitrogen nucleus as the neutron and nucleus fuse together:

$$^{14}_{7}N + ^{1}_{0}n \longrightarrow ^{14}_{6}C + ^{1}_{1}H$$

Artificial transmutation can lead to the synthesis of entirely new elements never before seen on Earth. In fact, all the *transuranium elements*—those elements with atomic numbers greater than 92—have been produced by bombardment reactions. For example, plutonium-241 (^{241}Pu) can be made by bombardment of uranium-238 with α particles:

$$^{238}_{92}U + ^{4}_{2}He \longrightarrow ^{241}_{94}Pu + ^{1}_{0}n$$

Plutonium-241 is itself radioactive, with a half-life of 14.35 years, decaying by β emission to yield americium-241, which in turn decays by α emission with a half-life of 432.2 years. (If the name *americium* sounds vaguely familiar, it is because this radioisotope is used in smoke detectors.)

$$^{241}_{94}Pu \longrightarrow ^{241}_{95}Am + ^{0}_{-1}e$$

Note that all the equations just given for artificial transmutations are balanced. The sum of the mass numbers and the sum of the charges are the same on both sides of each equation.

Artificial transmutation The change of one atom into another brought about by a nuclear bombardment reaction.

▲ Smoke detectors contain a small amount of americium-241. The α particles emitted by this radioisotope ionize the air within the detector, causing it to conduct a tiny electric current. When smoke enters the chamber, conductivity drops and an alarm is triggered.

Worked Example 11.7 Balancing Nuclear Reactions: Transmutation

Californium-246 is formed by bombardment of uranium-238 atoms. If 4 neutrons are also formed, what particle is used for the bombardment?

ANALYSIS First write an incomplete nuclear equation incorporating the known information:

$$^{238}_{92}U + ? \longrightarrow ^{246}_{98}Cf + 4^{1}_{0}n$$

Then find the numbers of nucleons and charges necessary to balance the equation. In this instance, there are 238 nucleons on the left and $246 + 4 = 250$ nucleons on the right, so the bombarding particle must have $250 - 238 = 12$ nucleons. Furthermore, there are 92 nuclear charges on the left and 98 on the right, so the bombarding particle must have $98 - 92 = 6$ protons.

SOLUTION
The missing particle is $^{12}_{6}C$.

$$^{238}_{92}U + ^{12}_{6}C \longrightarrow ^{246}_{98}Cf + 4^{1}_{0}n$$

CHAPTER 12

Introduction to Organic Chemistry: Alkanes

CONTENTS

◄ The gasoline, kerosene, and other products of this petroleum refinery are primarily mixtures of simple organic compounds called alkanes.

The study of chemistry progressed in the 1700s as scientists isolated substances from the world around them and examined their properties. Researchers began to notice differences between the properties of compounds obtained from living sources and those obtained from minerals. As a result, the term *organic chemistry* was introduced to describe the study of compounds derived from living organisms, while *inorganic chemistry* was used to refer to the study of compounds from minerals.

It was long believed that organic compounds could only be obtained from a living source; this concept, known as *vitalism*, hindered the study of these types of molecules because vitalist chemists believed that organic materials could not be synthesized from inorganic components. It wasn't until 1828 that Friedrich Wöhler first prepared an organic compound, urea, from an inorganic salt, ammonium cyanate, disproving the theory of vitalism and truly pioneering the field of organic chemistry.

Today, we know that there are no fundamental differences between organic and inorganic compounds: The same scientific principles are applicable to both. The only common characteristic of compounds from living sources is that they contain the element carbon as their primary component. Thus, organic chemistry is now defined as the study of carbon-based compounds.

Why is carbon special? The answer derives from its position in the periodic table. As a group 4A nonmetal, carbon atoms have the unique ability to form four strong covalent bonds. Also, unlike atoms of other elements, carbon atoms can readily form strong bonds with other carbon atoms to produce long chains and rings. As a result, only carbon is able to form such a diverse and immense array of compounds, from methane with 1 carbon atom to DNA with billions of carbons.

12.1 The Nature of Organic Molecules

Let us begin a study of **organic chemistry**—the chemistry of carbon compounds—by reviewing what we have seen in earlier chapters about the structures of organic molecules:

Organic chemistry The study of carbon compounds.

- **Carbon is tetravalent; it always forms four bonds** (Section 4.2). In methane, for example, carbon is connected to 4 hydrogen atoms:

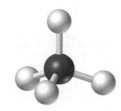

Methane, CH_4

- **Organic molecules have covalent bonds** (Section 4.2). In ethane, for example, the bonds result from the sharing of 2 electrons, either between 2 C atoms or a C and an H atom:

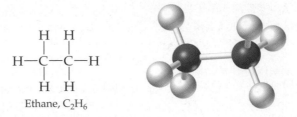

Ethane, C_2H_6

- **When carbon bonds to a more electronegative element, polar covalent bonds result** (Section 4.9). In chloromethane, for example, the electronegative chlorine atom attracts electrons more strongly than carbon, resulting in polarization of the C—Cl bond so that carbon and hydrogens have a partial positive charge, $\delta+$, and chlorine has a partial negative charge, $\delta-$. It is useful to think of polar covalent bonds in this manner, as it will later help to explain their reactivity. In electrostatic potential maps (Section 4.9), the chlorine atom is therefore in the red region of the map and the carbon atom in the blue region:

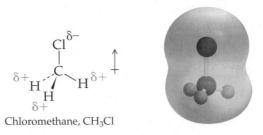

Chloromethane, CH_3Cl

- **Carbon forms multiple covalent bonds by sharing more than 2 electrons with a neighboring atom** (Section 4.3). In ethylene, for example, the 2 carbon atoms share 4 electrons in a double bond; in acetylene (also called ethyne), the 2 carbons share 6 electrons in a triple bond:

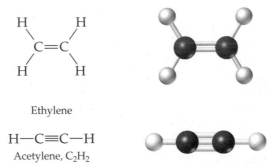

Ethylene

H—C≡C—H
Acetylene, C_2H_2

- **Organic molecules have specific three-dimensional shapes** (Section 4.8). When carbon is bonded to 4 atoms, as in methane, CH_4, the bonds are oriented toward the four corners of a regular tetrahedron with carbon in the center. Such three-dimensionality is commonly shown using normal lines for bonds in the plane of the page, dashed lines for bonds receding behind the page, and wedged lines for bonds coming out of the page:

- **Organic molecules often contain nitrogen and oxygen in addition to carbon and hydrogen** (Section 4.7). Nitrogen can form single, double, and triple bonds to carbon, while oxygen can form single and double bonds. Hydrogen can only form single bonds to carbon:

$$C-N \quad C-O \quad C-H$$
$$C=N \quad C=O$$
$$C\equiv N$$

Covalent bonding makes organic compounds quite different from the inorganic compounds we have been concentrating on up to this point. For example, inorganic compounds such as NaCl have high melting points and high boiling points because they consist of large numbers of oppositely charged ions held together by strong electrical attractions. By contrast, organic compounds consist of atoms joined by covalent bonds, forming individual molecules. Because the organic molecules are attracted to one another only by weak non-ionic intermolecular forces, organic compounds generally have lower melting and boiling points than inorganic salts. As a result, many simple organic compounds are liquids or low melting solids at room temperature, and a few are gases.

Other important differences between organic and inorganic compounds include solubility and electrical conductivity. Whereas many inorganic compounds dissolve in water to yield solutions of ions that conduct electricity, most organic compounds are insoluble in water, and almost all of those that are soluble do not conduct electricity. Only small polar organic molecules, such as glucose and ethyl alcohol, or large molecules with many polar groups, such as some proteins, interact with water molecules through both dipole–dipole interactions and/or hydrogen bonding and thus dissolve in water. This lack of water solubility for organic compounds has important practical consequences, varying from the difficulty in removing greasy dirt and cleaning up environmental oil spills to drug delivery.

▶▶▶ Other unique properties of ionic compounds are discussed in Section 3.4.

▶▶▶ Recall from Section 8.11 the various intermolecular forces: dipole–dipole forces, London dispersion forces, and hydrogen bonds.

▶▶▶ Section 9.9 explores how anions and cations in solution conduct electric current.

▶▶▶ Recall from Section 9.2 that a compound is only soluble when the intermolecular forces between solvent and solute are comparable in strength to the intermolecular forces of the pure solvent or solute.

◀ Oil spills can be a serious environmental problem because oil is insoluble in water.

LOOKING AHEAD ▶▶▶ The interior of a living cell is largely a water solution that contains many hundreds of different compounds. In later chapters, we will see how cells use membranes composed of water-insoluble organic molecules to enclose their watery interiors and to regulate the flow of substances across the cell boundary.

12.2 Families of Organic Molecules: Functional Groups

More than 18 *million* organic compounds are described in the scientific literature. Each of these 18 million compounds has unique chemical and physical properties, and many of them also have unique biological properties (both desired and undesired). How can we ever understand them all?

Chemists have learned through experience that organic compounds can be classified into families according to their structural features, and that the chemical behavior of family members is often predictable based on their specific grouping of atoms. Instead of 18 million compounds with seemingly random chemical reactivity, there are just a few general families of organic compounds whose chemistry falls into simple patterns.

The structural features that allow us to classify organic compounds into distinct chemical families are called **functional groups**. A functional group is an atom or group of atoms that has a characteristic physical and chemical behavior. Each functional group is always part of a larger molecule, and a molecule may have more than one class of functional group present, as we shall soon see. An important property of functional groups is that a given functional group *tends to undergo the same reactions in every molecule that contains it*. For example, the carbon–carbon double bond is a common functional group. Ethylene (C_2H_4), the simplest compound with a double bond, undergoes many chemical reactions similar to those of oleic acid ($C_{18}H_{34}O_2$), a much larger and more complex compound that also contains a double bond. Both, for example, react with hydrogen gas in the same manner, as shown in Figure 12.1. These identical reactions with hydrogen are typical: *The chemistry of an organic molecule is primarily determined by the functional groups it contains, not by its size or complexity.*

Functional group An atom or group of atoms within a molecule that has a characteristic physical and chemical behavior.

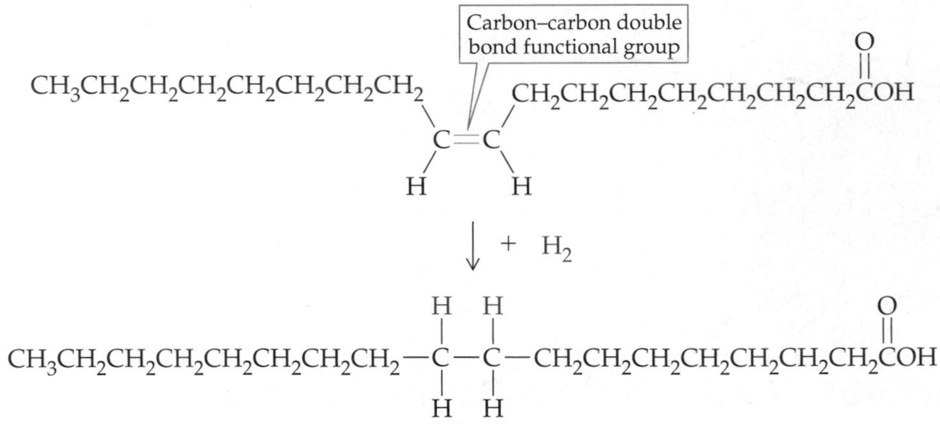

▶ **Figure 12.1**

The reactions of (a) ethylene and (b) oleic acid with hydrogen. The carbon–carbon double-bond functional group adds 2 hydrogen atoms in both cases, regardless of the complexity of the rest of the molecule.

(a) Reaction of ethylene with hydrogen

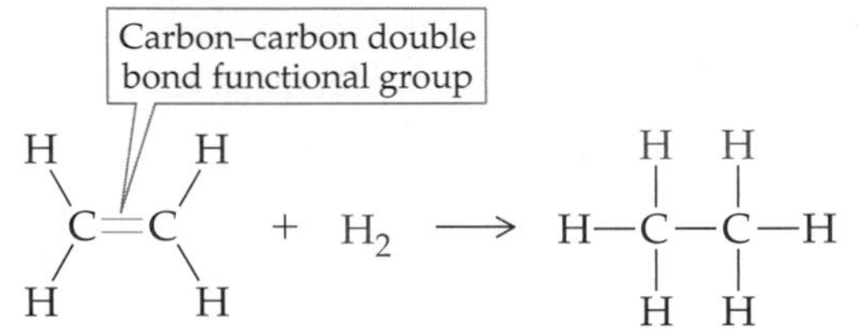

(b) Reaction of oleic acid with hydrogen

Table 12.1 lists some of the most important families of organic molecules and their distinctive functional groups. Compounds that contain a C=C double bond, for instance, are in the *alkene* family; compounds that have an —OH group bound to a tetravalent carbon are in the *alcohol* family; and so on. To aid in identifying the organic functional groups you will encounter, we have included an Organic Functional Group Flow Scheme (Figure 12.5) at the end of the chapter; it should be used in conjunction with Table 12.1. You will find it helpful as you proceed through the remainder of this text.

Much of the chemistry discussed in this and the next five chapters is the chemistry of the families listed in Table 12.1, so it is best to learn the names and become familiar with their structures now. Note that they fall into four groups:

Hydrocarbon An organic compound that contains only carbon and hydrogen.

- The first four families in Table 12.1 are **hydrocarbons**, organic compounds that contain only carbon and hydrogen. *Alkanes* have only single bonds and contain

TABLE 12.1 Some Important Families of Organic Molecules

FAMILY NAME	FUNCTIONAL GROUP STRUCTURE*	SIMPLE EXAMPLE	LINE STRUCTURE	NAME ENDING
Alkane	Contains only C—H and C—C single bonds	$CH_3CH_2CH_3$ Propane		-ane
Alkene	$\diagdown C=C \diagup$	$H_2C=CH_2$ Ethylene	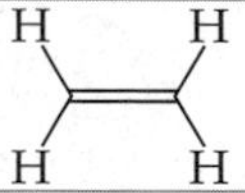	-ene
Alkyne	—C≡C—	H—C≡C—H Acetylene (Ethyne)	 H———H	-yne
Aromatic	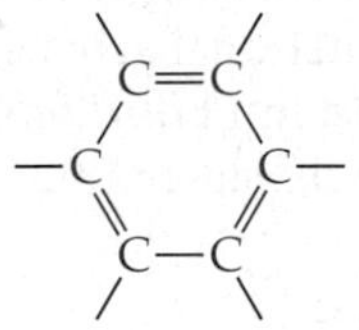	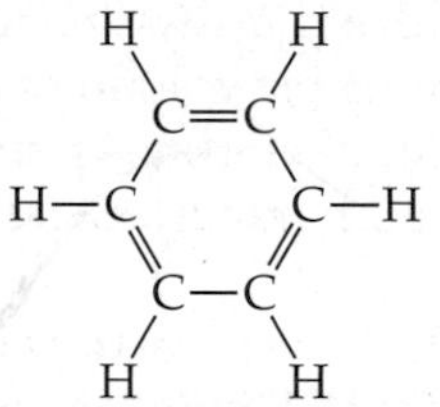 Benzene		None
Alkyl halide	—C—X (X=F, Cl, Br, I)	CH_3CH_2Cl Ethyl chloride		None
Alcohol	—C—O—H	CH_3CH_2OH Ethyl alcohol (Ethanol)	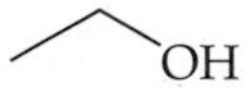	-ol
Ether	—C—O—C—	$CH_3CH_2—O—CH_2CH_3$ Diethyl ether	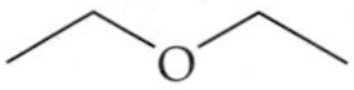	None
Amine	—C—N$\diagup$	$CH_3CH_2NH_2$ Ethylamine	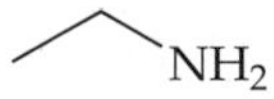	-amine
Aldehyde	—C—C—H (C=O)	$CH_3—C—H$ Acetaldehyde (Ethanal)	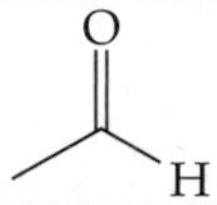	-al
Ketone	—C—C—C— (C=O)	$CH_3—C—CH_3$ Acetone	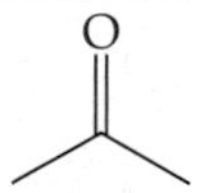	-one
Carboxylic acid	—C—C—OH (C=O)	$CH_3—C—OH$ Acetic acid	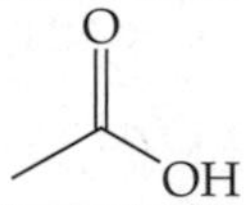	-ic acid
Anhydride	—C—C—O—C—C— (two C=O)	$CH_3—C—O—C—CH_3$ Acetic anhydride	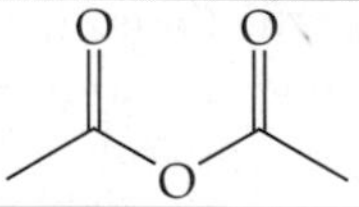	None
Ester	—C—C—O—C— (C=O)	$CH_3—C—O—CH_3$ Methyl acetate	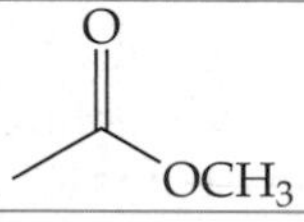	-ate
Amide	—C—C—NH₂, —C—C—N—H, —C—C—N—	$CH_3—C—NH_2$ Acetamide	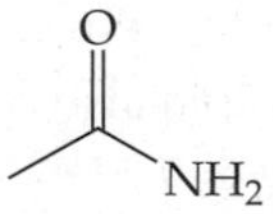	-amide
Thiol	—C—SH	CH_3CH_2SH Ethyl thiol		None
Disulfide	C—S—S—C	CH_3SSCH_3 Dimethyl disulfide	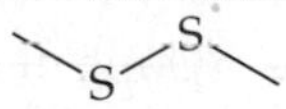	None
Sulfide	C—S—C	$CH_3CH_2SCH_3$ Ethyl methyl sulfide	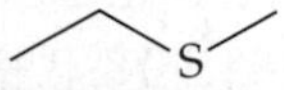	None

*The bonds whose connections are not specified are assumed to be attached to carbon or hydrogen atoms in the rest of the molecule.

no functional groups. As we will see, the absence of functional groups makes alkanes relatively unreactive. *Alkenes* contain a carbon–carbon double-bond functional group; *alkynes* contain a carbon–carbon triple-bond functional group; and *aromatic* compounds contain a six-membered ring of carbon atoms with three alternating double bonds.

- The next four families in Table 12.1 have functional groups that contain only single bonds and have a carbon atom bonded to an electronegative atom. *Alkyl halides* have a carbon–halogen bond; *alcohols* have a carbon–oxygen bond; *ethers* have two carbons bonded to the same oxygen; and *amines* have a carbon–nitrogen bond.
- The next six families in Table 12.1 have functional groups that contain a carbon–oxygen double bond: *aldehydes, ketones, carboxylic acids, anhydrides, esters,* and *amides*.
- The remaining three families in Table 12.1 have functional groups that contain sulfur: *thioalcohols* (known simply as *thiols*), *sulfides,* and *disulfides*. These three families play an important role in protein function (Chapter 18).

Worked Example 12.1 Molecular Structures: Identifying Functional Groups

To which family of organic compounds do the following compounds belong? Explain.

(a) 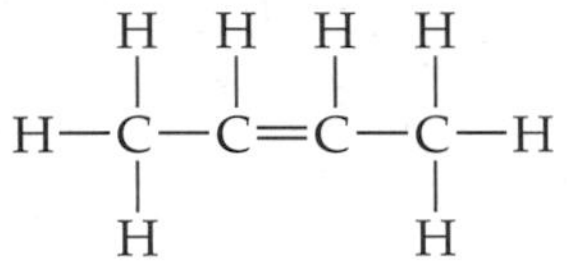
(b) 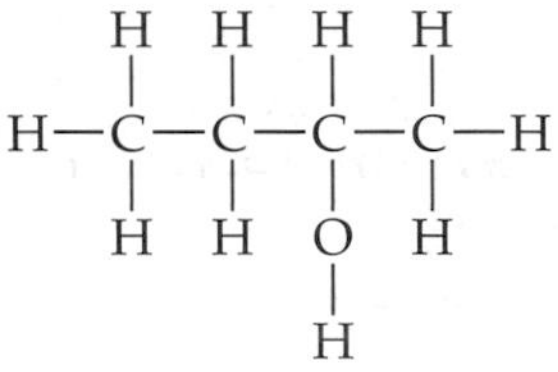
(c) 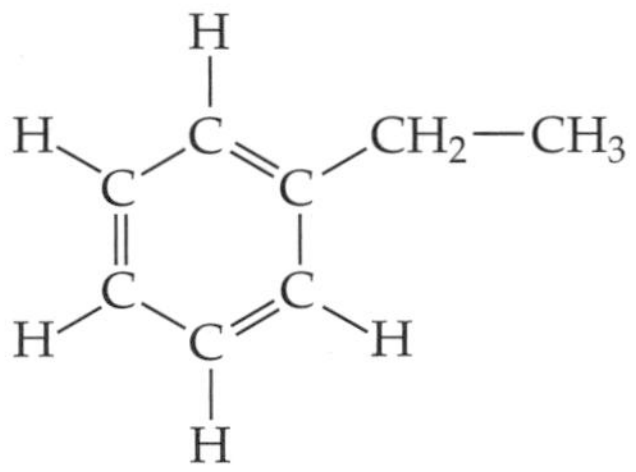
(d) 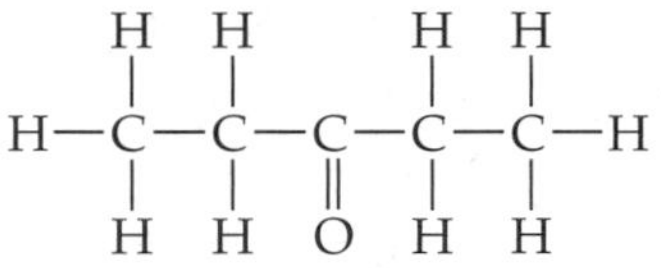
(e) 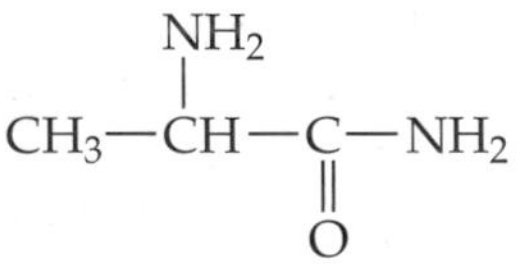
(f)

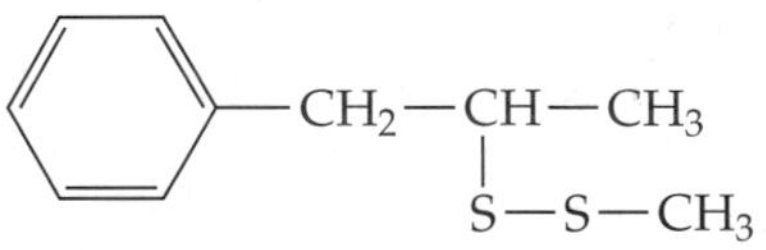

ANALYSIS Use the Organic Functional Group Flow Scheme (Figure 12.5, see end of chapter) and Table 12.1 to identify each functional group, and name the corresponding family to which the compound belongs. Begin by determining what elements are present and whether multiple bonds are present.

SOLUTION

(a) This compound contains only carbon and hydrogen atoms, so it is a *hydrocarbon*. There is only one carbon–carbon double bond, so it is an *alkene*.

(b) This compound contains an oxygen and has only single bonds. The presence of the O—H group bonded to tetravalent carbon identifies this compound as an *alcohol*.

(c) This compound also contains only carbon and hydrogen atoms, which identifies it as a *hydrocarbon*. It has three double bonds in a ring. The six-membered carbon ring with alternating double bonds also identifies this compound as an *aromatic* hydrocarbon compound.

(d) This molecule contains an oxygen that is double bonded to a carbon (a *carbonyl group*, discussed in Chapter 16), and there is no singly bound oxygen or nitrogen also connected to the carbon. The carbon–oxygen double bond is connected to two other carbons (as opposed to a hydrogen); that identifies this compound as a *ketone*.

(e) Many of the organic molecules we will come across have more than one functional group present in the same molecule; in these cases we will classify the molecule as belonging to multiple functional group families. This molecule contains oxygen and nitrogen in addition to carbon and hydrogen, so it is not a hydrocarbon. The presence of the carbonyl group further classifies this molecule, but here we run into a problem: one —NH₂ is attached to the carbonyl but the other —NH_2 is not. This leads us to conclude that there are two functional groups present: an *amide* **and** an *amine*:

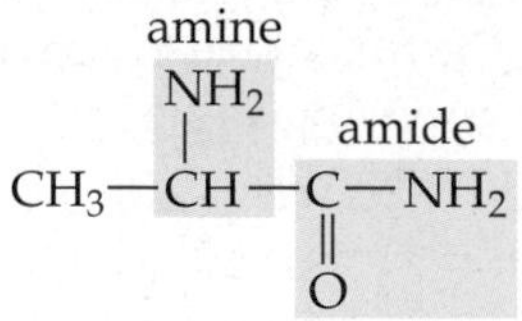

amine

NH$_2$

amide

$$CH_3-CH-C-NH_2$$

O

(f) This molecule also contains two functional groups: a ring containing alternating carbon–carbon single and double bonds as well as an S—S group. From our flow scheme, we trace the double bond to indicate we have an aromatic hydrocarbon, while the sulfurs indicate the presence of a disulfide:

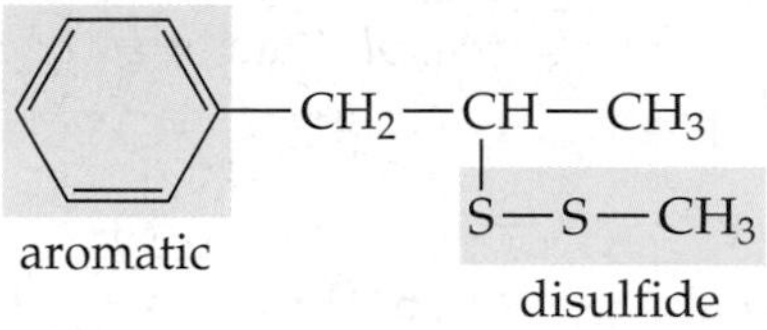

$$-CH_2-CH-CH_3$$

S—S—CH$_3$

aromatic

disulfide

Worked Example 12.2 Molecular Structures: Drawing Functional Groups

Given the family of organic compounds to which the compound belongs, propose structures for compounds having the following chemical formulas.

(a) An amine having the formula C_2H_7N
(b) An alkyne having the formula C_3H_4
(c) An ether having the formula $C_4H_{10}O$

ANALYSIS Identify the functional group for each compound from Table 12.1. Once the atoms in this functional group are eliminated from the chemical formula, the remaining structure can be determined. (Remember that each carbon atom forms four bonds, nitrogen forms three bonds, oxygen forms two bonds, and hydrogen forms only one bond.)

SOLUTION

(a) Amines have a C—NH_2 group. Eliminating these atoms from the formula leaves 1 C atom and 5 H atoms. Since only the carbons are capable of forming more than one bond, the 2 C atoms must be bonded together. The remaining H atoms are then bonded to the carbons until each C has 4 bonds.

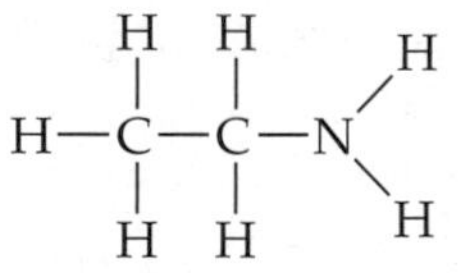

$$H-C-C-N$$

(b) The alkynes contain a C≡C bond. This leaves 1 C atom and 4 H atoms. Attach this C to one of the carbons in the triple bond, and then distribute the H atoms until each carbon has a full complement of four bonds.

$$H-C-C≡C-H$$

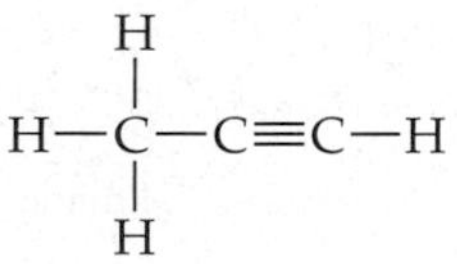

(c) The ethers contain a C—O—C group. Eliminating these atoms leaves 2 C atoms and 10 H atoms. The C atoms can be distributed on either end of the ether group, and the H atoms are then distributed until each carbon atom has a full complement of four bonds.

$$H-C-C-O-C-C-H \quad \text{or} \quad H-C-C-C-O-C-H$$

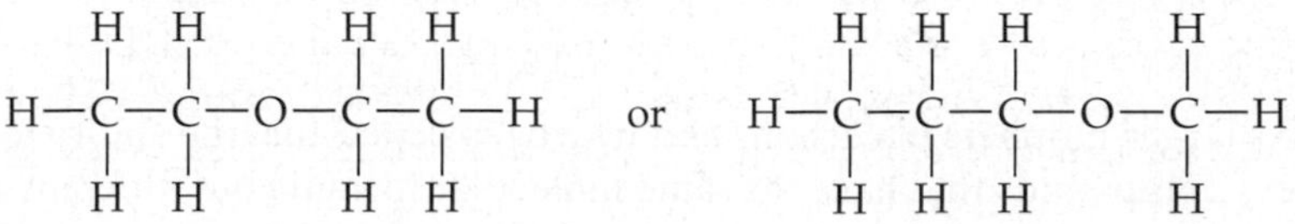

PROBLEM 12.1

Many organic compounds contain more than one functional group. Locate and identify the functional groups in (a) lactic acid, from sour milk; (b) methyl methacrylate, used in making Lucite and Plexiglas; and (c) phenylalanine, an amino acid found in proteins.

(a) 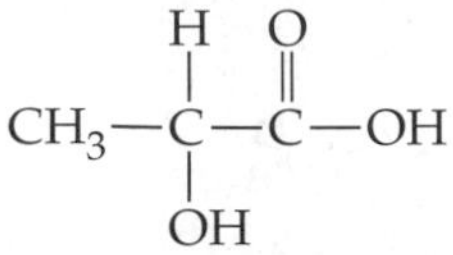
$$CH_3-\overset{\overset{\displaystyle H}{|}}{\underset{\underset{\displaystyle OH}{|}}{C}}-\overset{\overset{\displaystyle O}{\|}}{C}-OH$$

(b)
$$CH_2{=}\overset{\overset{\displaystyle }{|}}{\underset{\underset{\displaystyle CH_3}{|}}{C}}-\overset{\overset{\displaystyle O}{\|}}{C}-O-CH_3$$

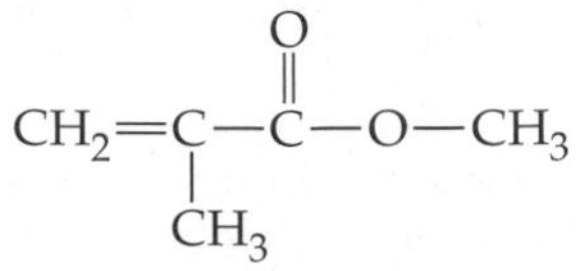

(c)
$$H-\underset{\underset{\displaystyle C}{\|}}{\overset{\overset{\displaystyle C}{\|}}{C}}\overset{\displaystyle H\quad H}{\underset{}{C{=}C}}\;C-CH_2-\overset{\overset{\displaystyle H}{|}}{\underset{\underset{\displaystyle NH_2}{|}}{C}}-\overset{\overset{\displaystyle O}{\|}}{C}-OH$$

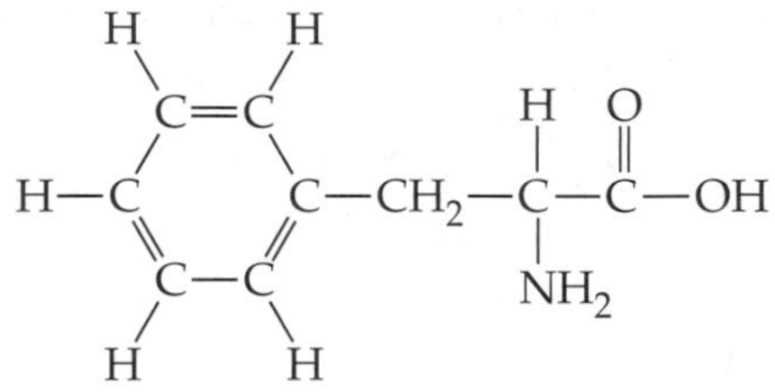

PROBLEM 12.2

Propose structures for molecules that fit the following descriptions:

(a) C_3H_6O containing an aldehyde functional group

(b) C_3H_6O containing a ketone functional group

(c) $C_3H_6O_2$ containing a carboxylic acid functional group

12.3 The Structure of Organic Molecules: Alkanes and Their Isomers

Alkane A hydrocarbon that has only single bonds.

Hydrocarbons that contain only single bonds belong to the family of organic molecules called **alkanes**. Imagine how 1 carbon and 4 hydrogens can combine, and you will realize there is only one possibility: methane, CH_4. Now, imagine how 2 carbons and 6 hydrogens can combine—only ethane, CH_3CH_3, is possible. Likewise, with the combination of 3 carbons with 8 hydrogens—only propane, $CH_3CH_2CH_3$, is possible. The general rule for *all* hydrocarbons except methane is that each carbon *must* be bonded to at least one other carbon. The carbon atoms bond together to form the "backbone" of the compound, with the hydrogens on the periphery. The general formula for alkanes is C_nH_{2n+2}, where n is the number of carbons in the compound.

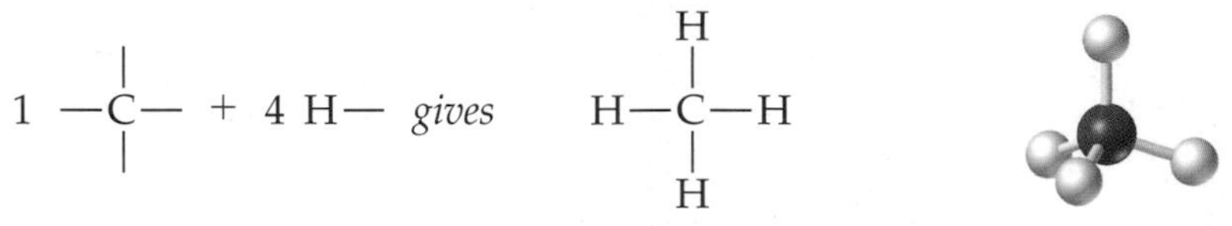

$$1\;-\overset{|}{\underset{|}{C}}-\;+\;4\;H-\;gives\qquad H-\overset{\overset{\displaystyle H}{|}}{\underset{\underset{\displaystyle H}{|}}{C}}-H$$

Methane

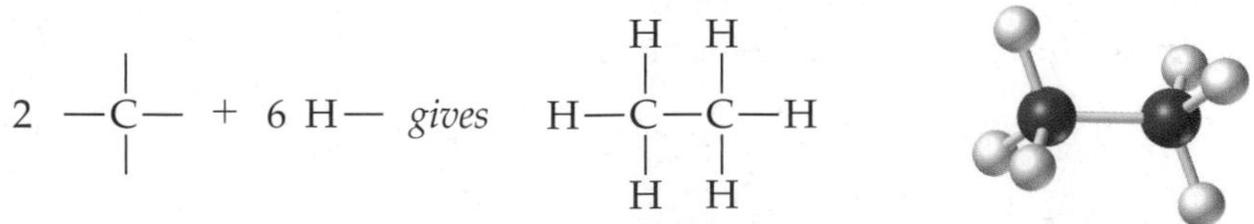

$$2\;-\overset{|}{\underset{|}{C}}-\;+\;6\;H-\;gives\qquad H-\overset{\overset{\displaystyle H}{|}}{\underset{\underset{\displaystyle H}{|}}{C}}-\overset{\overset{\displaystyle H}{|}}{\underset{\underset{\displaystyle H}{|}}{C}}-H$$

Ethane

$$3\;-\overset{|}{\underset{|}{C}}-\;+\;8\;H-\;gives\;\;H-\overset{\overset{\displaystyle H}{|}}{\underset{\underset{\displaystyle H}{|}}{C}}-\overset{\overset{\displaystyle H}{|}}{\underset{\underset{\displaystyle H}{|}}{C}}-\overset{\overset{\displaystyle H}{|}}{\underset{\underset{\displaystyle H}{|}}{C}}-H$$

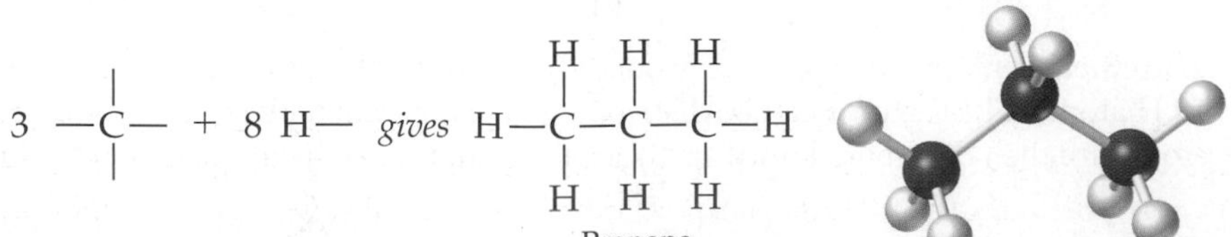

Propane

As larger numbers of carbons and hydrogens combine, the ability to form *isomers* arises. Compounds that have the same molecular formula but different structural formulas are called **isomers** of one another. For example, there are two ways in which molecules that have the formula C_4H_{10} can be formed. The 4 carbons can either be joined in a contiguous row or have a branched arrangement:

Isomers Compounds with the same molecular formula but different structures.

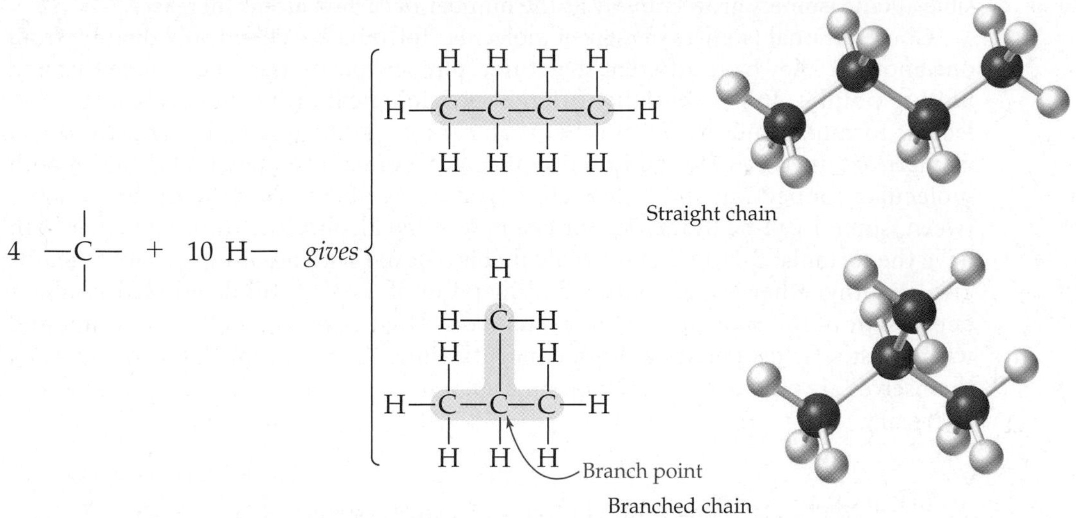

Straight chain

$$4 \; -\overset{|}{\underset{|}{C}}- \; + \; 10 \; H- \; gives$$

Branch point

Branched chain

The same is seen with the molecules that have the formula C_5H_{12}, for which three isomers are possible:

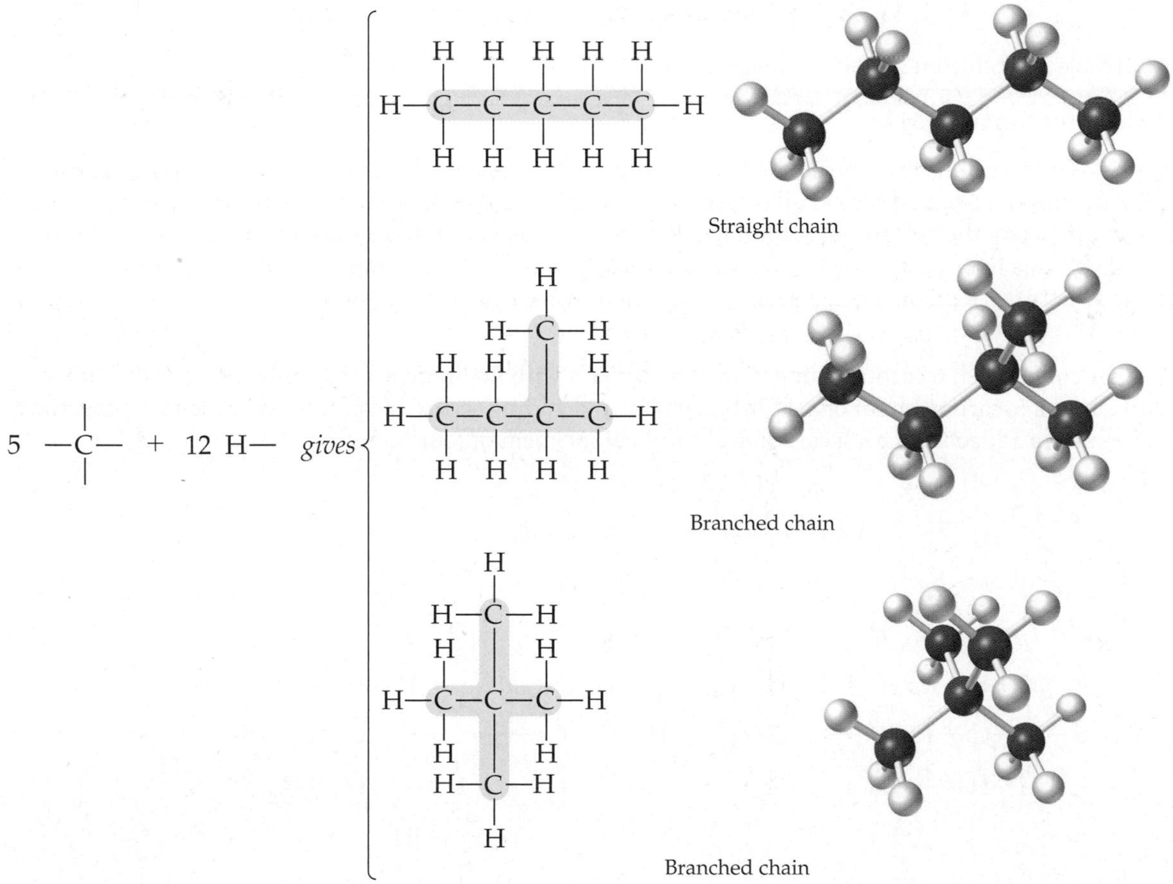

Straight chain

$$5 \; -\overset{|}{\underset{|}{C}}- \; + \; 12 \; H- \; gives$$

Branched chain

Branched chain

Compounds with all their carbons connected in a continuous chain are called **straight-chain alkanes**; those with a branching connection of carbons are called **branched-chain alkanes**. Note that in a straight-chain alkane, you can draw a line through all the carbon atoms without lifting your pencil from the paper. In a branched-chain alkane, however, you must either lift your pencil from the paper or retrace your steps to draw a line through all the carbons.

Straight-chain alkane An alkane that has all its carbons connected in a row.

Branched-chain alkane An alkane that has a branching connection of carbons.

Constitutional isomers Compounds with the same molecular formula but different connections among their atoms.

The two isomers of C_4H_{10} and the three isomers of C_5H_{12} shown above are **constitutional isomers**—compounds with the same molecular formula but with different connections among their constituent atoms. Needless to say, the number of possible alkane isomers grows rapidly as the number of carbon atoms increases.

Constitutional isomers of a given molecular formula are chemically distinct from one another. They have different structures, physical properties (such as melting and boiling points), and potentially different physiological properties. When the molecular formula contains atoms other than carbon and hydrogen, the constitutional isomers obtained can also be **functional group isomers**: isomers that differ in both molecular connection and family classification. In these cases the differences between isomers can be dramatic. For example, ethyl alcohol and dimethyl ether both have the formula C_2H_6O, but ethyl alcohol is a liquid with a boiling point of 78.5 °C and dimethyl ether is a gas with a boiling point of +23 °C. While ethyl alcohol is a depressant of the central nervous system, dimethyl ether is a nontoxic compound with anesthetic properties at high concentrations. Clearly, molecular formulas by themselves are not very useful in organic chemistry; a knowledge of structure is also necessary.

Functional group isomer Isomers having the same chemical formula but belonging to different chemical families due to differences in bonding; ethyl alcohol and dimethyl ether are examples of functional group isomers.

Ethyl alcohol
C_2H_6O

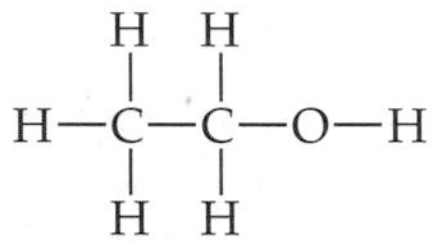

Dimethyl ether
C_2H_6O

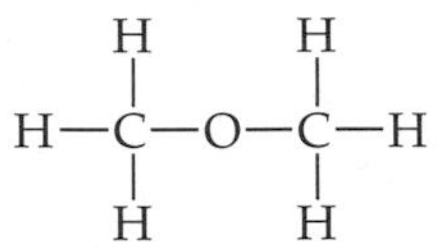

Worked Example 12.3 Molecular Structures: Drawing Isomers

Draw all isomers that have the formula C_6H_{14}.

ANALYSIS Knowing that all the carbons must be bonded together to form the molecule, find all possible arrangements of the 6 carbon atoms. Begin with the isomer that has all 6 carbons in a straight chain, then draw the isomer that has 5 carbons in a straight chain, using the remaining carbon to form a branch, then repeat for the isomer having 4 carbons in a straight chain and 2 carbons in branches. Once each carbon backbone is drawn, arrange the hydrogens around the carbons to complete the structure. (Remember that each carbon can only have *four* bonds total.)

SOLUTION
The straight-chain isomer contains all 6 carbons bonded to form a chain with no branches. The branched isomers are drawn by starting with either a 5-carbon chain or a 4-carbon chain, and adding the extra carbons as branches in the middle of the chain. Hydrogens are added until each carbon has a full complement of four bonds.

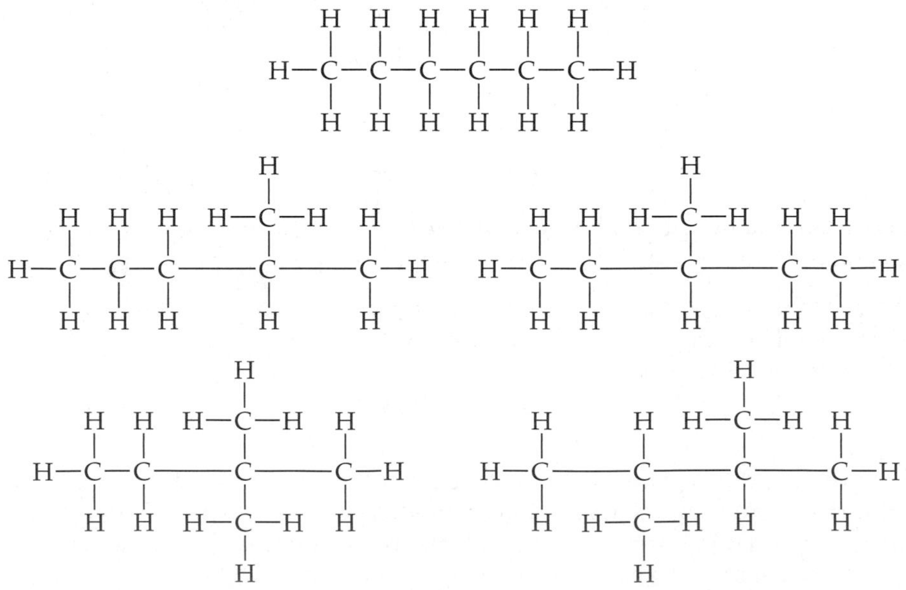

PROBLEM 12.3

Draw the straight-chain isomer with the formula (a) C_7H_{16}; (b) C_9H_{20}.

PROBLEM 12.4

Draw the two branched-chain isomers with the formula C_7H_{16}, where the longest chain in the molecule is 6 carbons long.

12.4 Drawing Organic Structures

Drawing structural formulas that show every atom and every bond in a molecule is both time-consuming and awkward, even for relatively small molecules. Much easier is the use of **condensed structures**, which are simpler but still show the essential information about which functional groups are present and how atoms are connected. In condensed structures, C—C and C—H single bonds are not necessarily shown; rather, they are "understood." If a carbon atom has 3 hydrogens bonded to it, we write CH_3; if the carbon has 2 hydrogens bonded to it, we write CH_2; and so on. For example, the 4-carbon, straight-chain alkane called butane and its branched-chain isomer (2-methylpropane) can be written as the following condensed structures:

Condensed structure A shorthand way of drawing structures in which C—C and C—H bonds are understood rather than shown.

▶▶▶ Condensed structures were explored in Section 4.7.

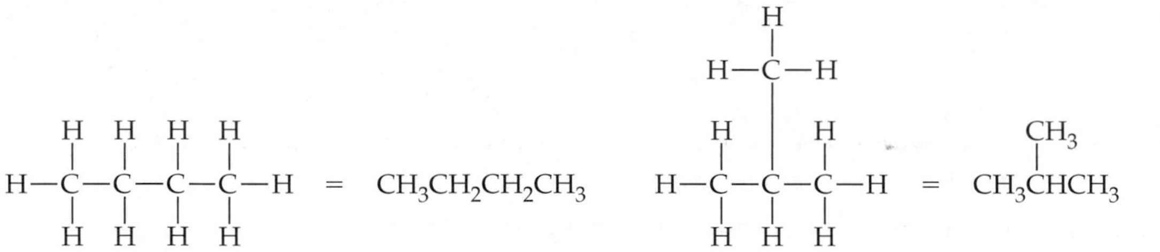

Butane	2-Methylpropane
Structural formula Condensed formula	Structural formula Condensed formula

Note in these condensed structures for butane and 2-methylpropane that the horizontal bonds between carbons are not usually shown—the CH_3 and CH_2 units are simply placed next to one another—but that the vertical bond in 2-methylpropane *is* shown for clarity.

Occasionally, as a further simplification, not all the CH_2 groups (called **methylenes**) are shown. Instead, CH_2 is shown once in parentheses, with a subscript indicating the number of methylene units strung together. For example, the 6-carbon straight-chain alkane (hexane) can be written as

Methylene Another name for a CH_2 unit.

$$CH_3CH_2CH_2CH_2CH_2CH_3 = CH_3(CH_2)_4CH_3$$

Worked Example 12.4 Molecular Structures: Writing Condensed Structures

Write condensed structures for the isomers from Worked Example 12.3.

ANALYSIS Eliminate all horizontal bonds, substituting reduced formula components (CH_3, CH_2, and so on) for each carbon in the compound. Show vertical bonds to branching carbons for clarity.

SOLUTION

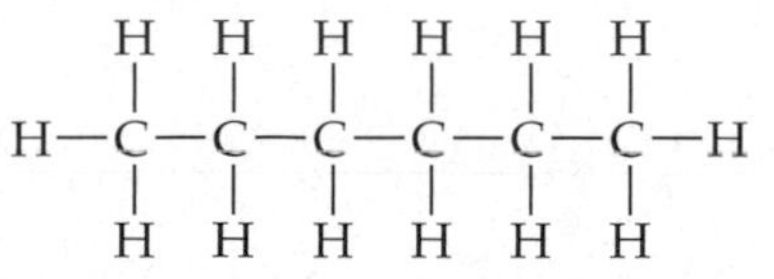

$$CH_3CH_2CH_2CH_2CH_2CH_3 \text{ or}$$
$$CH_3(CH_2)_4CH_3$$

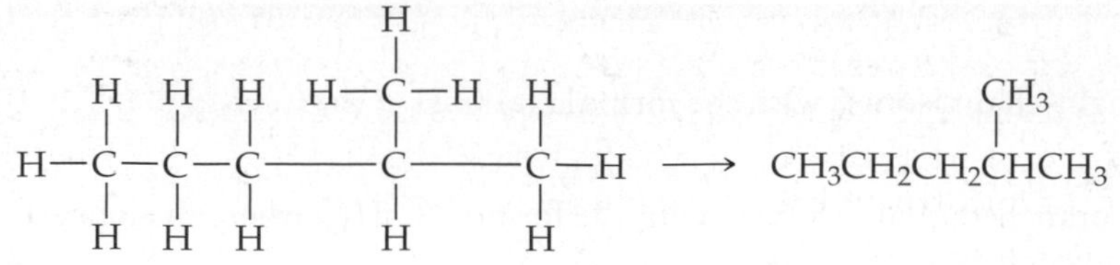

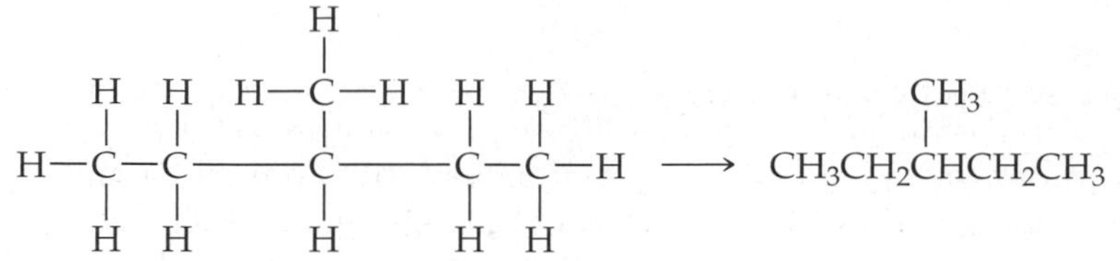

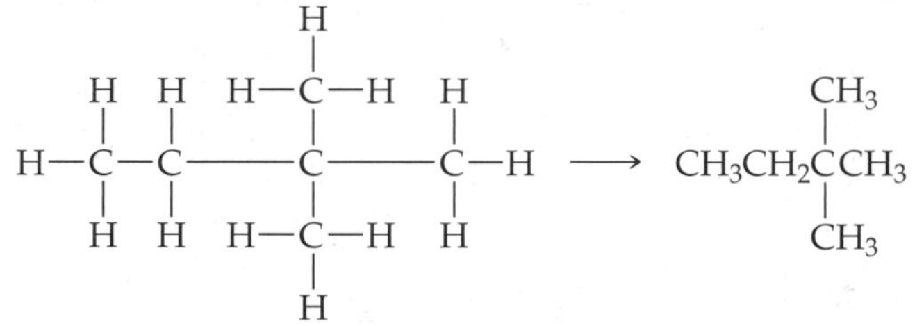

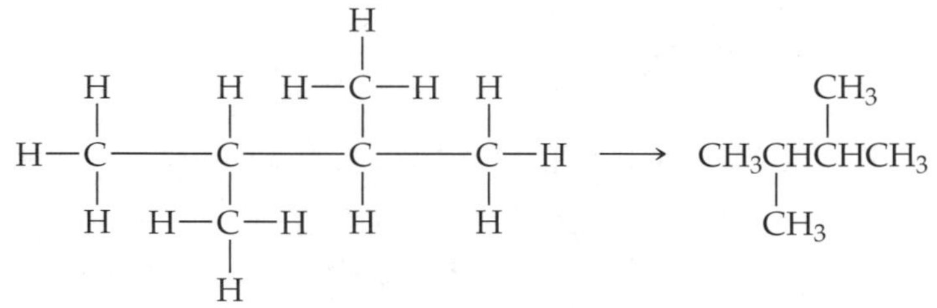

$$CH_3CH_2CH_2CHCH_3 \quad (CH_3)$$

$$CH_3CH_2CHCH_2CH_3 \quad (CH_3)$$

$$CH_3CH_2CCH_3 \quad (CH_3)(CH_3)$$

$$CH_3CHCHCH_3 \quad (CH_3)(CH_3)$$

PROBLEM 12.5

Draw the following three isomers of C_5H_{12} as condensed structures:

(a) 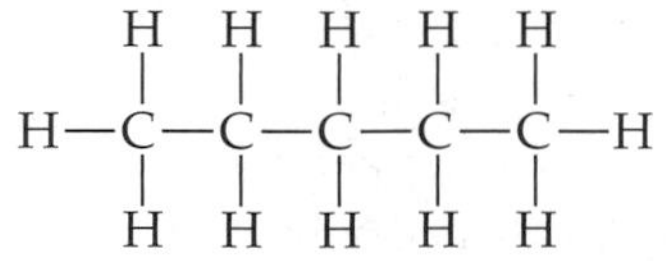 Pentane

(b) 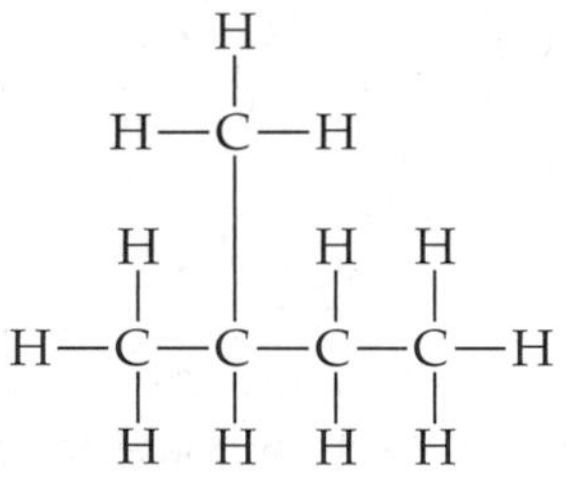 2-Methylbutane

(c) 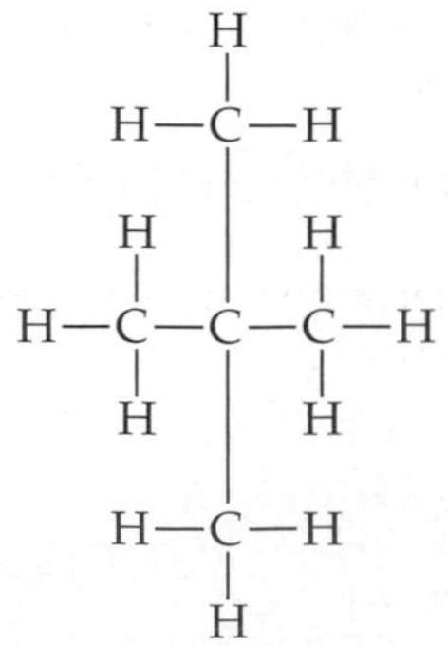 2,2-Dimethylpropane

Another way of representing organic molecules is to use **line (or line-angle) structures**, which are structures in which the symbols C and H do not appear. Instead, a chain of carbon atoms and their associated hydrogens are represented by a zigzag arrangement of short lines, with any branches off the main chain represented by additional lines. The line structure for 2-methylbutane, for instance, is

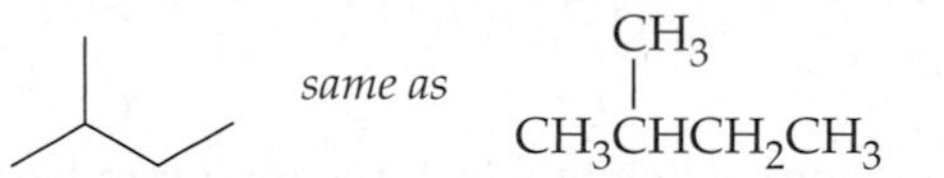
same as
CH_3
$CH_3CHCH_2CH_3$

Line structures are a simple and quick way to represent organic molecules without the clutter arising from showing all carbons and hydrogens present. Chemists, biologists, pharmacists, doctors, and nurses all use line structures to conveniently convey to one another very complex organic structures. Another advantage is that a line structure gives a more realistic depiction of the angles seen in a carbon chain.

Line structure Also known as line-angle structure; a shorthand way of drawing structures in which carbon and hydrogen atoms are not explicitly shown. Instead, a carbon atom is understood to be wherever a line begins or ends and at every intersection of two lines, and hydrogens are understood to be wherever they are needed to have each carbon form four bonds.

Drawing a molecule in this way is simple, provided one follows these guidelines:

1. Each carbon–carbon bond is represented by a line.
2. Anywhere a line ends or begins, as well as any vertex where two lines meet, represents a carbon atom.
3. Any atom other than another carbon or a hydrogen attached to a carbon must be shown.
4. Since a neutral carbon atom forms four bonds, all bonds not shown for any carbon are understood to be the number of carbon–hydrogen bonds needed to have the carbon form four bonds.

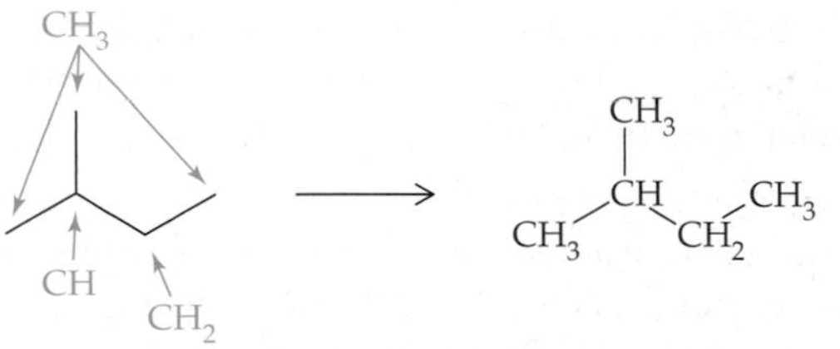
CH_3
CH
CH_2
CH_3
CH
CH_3
CH_3
CH_2

Converting line structures to structural formulas or to condensed structures is simply a matter of correctly interpreting each line ending and each intersection in a line structure. For example, the common pain reliever ibuprofen has the condensed and line structures

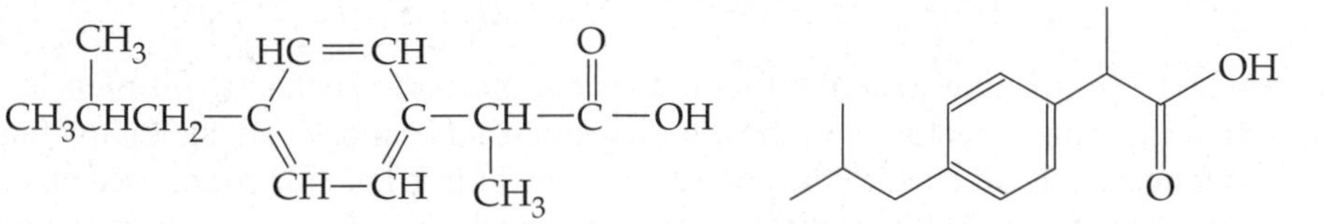
CH_3
HC=CH
O
CH_3CHCH_2—C
C—CH—C—OH
CH—CH
CH_3
OH
O

Finally, it is important to note that chemists and biochemists often use a mixture of structural formulas, condensed structures, and line structures to represent the molecules they study. As you progress through this textbook, you will see many complicated molecules represented in this way, so it is a good idea to get used to thinking interchangeably in all three formats.

Worked Example 12.5 Molecular Structures: Converting Condensed Structures to Line Structures

Convert the following condensed structures to line structures:

CH_3
(a) $CH_3CH_2CHCHCH_2CH_3$
CH_3
OH Cl
(b) CH_3CHCH—C CH_2CH_3
CH_3 CH_3

ANALYSIS Find the longest continuous chain of carbon atoms in the condensed structure. Begin the line structure by drawing a zigzag line in which the number of vertices plus line ends equals the number of carbon atoms in the chain. Show branches coming off the main chain by drawing vertical lines at the vertices as needed. Show all atoms that are not carbons or are not hydrogens attached to carbons.

SOLUTION

(a) Begin by drawing a zigzag line in which the total number of ends + vertices equals the number of carbons in the longest chain (here 6, with the carbons numbered for clarity):

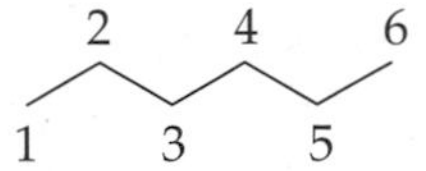

Looking at the condensed structure, you see CH_3 groups on carbons 3 and 4; these two methyl groups are represented by lines coming off those carbons in the line structure:

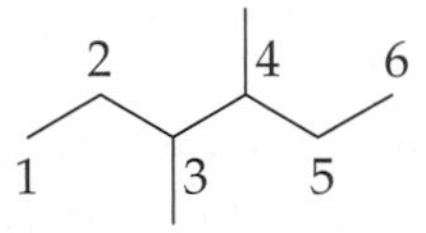

This is the complete line structure. Notice that the hydrogens are not shown, but understood. For example, carbon 4 has three bonds shown: one to carbon 3, one to carbon 5, and one to the branch methyl group; the fourth bond this carbon must have is understood to be to a hydrogen.

(b) Proceed as in (a), drawing a zigzag line for the longest chain of carbon atoms, which again contains 6 carbons. Next draw a line coming off each carbon bonded to a CH_3 group (carbons 3 and 4). Both the OH and the Cl groups must be shown to give the final structure:

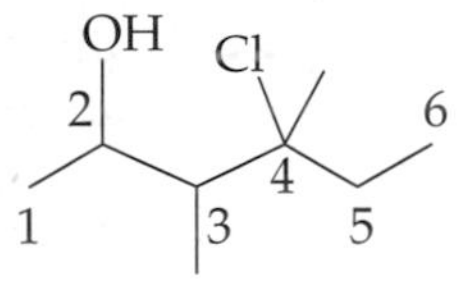

Note from this line structure that it does not matter in such a two-dimensional drawing what direction you show for a group that branches off the main chain, as long as it is attached to the correct carbon. This is true for condensed structures as well. Quite often, the direction that a group is shown coming off a main chain of carbon atoms is chosen simply for aesthetic reasons.

Worked Example 12.6 Molecular Structures: Converting Line Structures to Condensed Structures

Convert the following line structures to condensed structures:

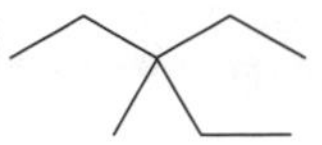

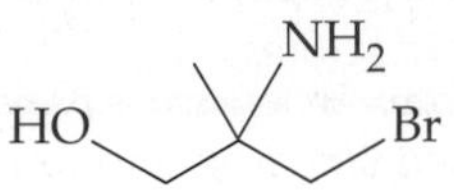

ANALYSIS Convert all vertices and line ends to carbons. Write in any noncarbon atoms and any hydrogens bonded to a noncarbon atom. Add hydrogens as needed so that each carbon has four groups attached. Remove lines connecting carbons except for branches.

SOLUTION

(a) Anywhere a line ends and anywhere two lines meet, write a C:

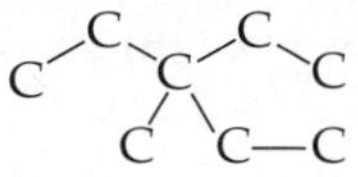

$$\text{C} \diagup \overset{\text{C}}{\underset{\text{C}}{|}} \diagup \overset{\text{C}}{\underset{\text{C}-\text{C}}{|}} \diagdown \text{C}$$

Because there are no atoms other than carbons and hydrogens in this molecule, the next step is to add hydrogens as needed to have four bonds for each carbon:

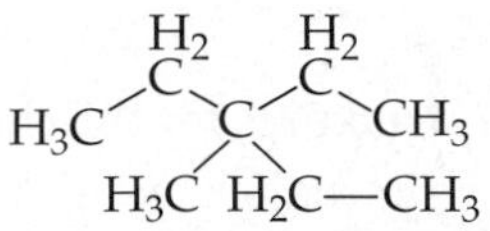

$$\text{H}_3\text{C} \diagup \overset{\overset{\text{H}_2}{\text{C}}}{\underset{\text{H}_3\text{C}}{|}} \diagup \overset{\overset{\text{H}_2}{\text{C}}}{\underset{\text{H}_2\text{C}-\text{CH}_3}{}} \diagdown \text{CH}_3$$

Finally, eliminate all lines except for branches to get the condensed structure:

$$\overset{\text{CH}_3}{\underset{\text{CH}_2\text{CH}_3}{\text{CH}_3\text{CH}_2\ \overset{|}{\underset{|}{\text{C}}}\ \text{CH}_2\text{CH}_3}}$$

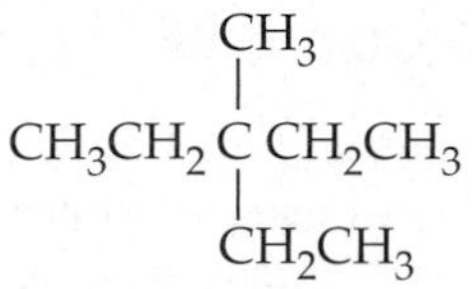

(b) Begin the condensed structure with a drawing showing a carbon at each line end and at each intersection of two lines:

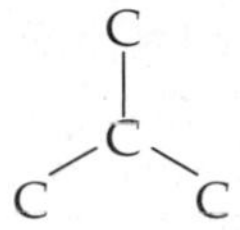

$$\overset{\text{C}}{\underset{\text{C}\quad\quad\text{C}}{\overset{|}{\text{C}}}}$$

Next, write in all the noncarbon atoms and the hydrogen bonded to the oxygen. Then, add hydrogens so that each carbon forms four bonds:

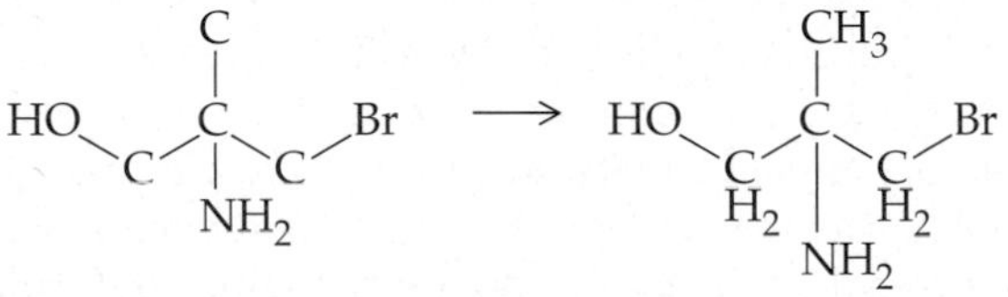

$$\text{HO} \diagdown \overset{\overset{\text{C}}{|}}{\underset{\text{NH}_2}{\underset{\text{C}}{|}}} \diagup \text{Br} \quad \longrightarrow \quad \text{HO} \diagdown \overset{\overset{\text{CH}_3}{|}}{\underset{\text{H}_2\ \underset{\text{NH}_2}{|}\ \text{H}_2}{\underset{\text{C}}{|}}} \diagup \text{Br}$$

Eliminate all lines except for branches for the completed condensed structure:

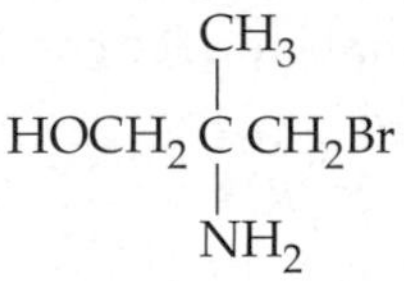

$$\overset{\text{CH}_3}{\underset{\text{NH}_2}{\text{HOCH}_2\ \overset{|}{\underset{|}{\text{C}}}\ \text{CH}_2\text{Br}}}$$

PROBLEM 12.6

Convert the following condensed structures to line structures:

(a)
$$\overset{\text{CH}_2\text{CH}_3}{\underset{\text{CH}_2\text{OH}}{\text{CH}_3\text{CH}_2\overset{|}{\underset{|}{\text{C}}}-\text{CH}_2\text{CH}_2\text{CH}_3}}$$

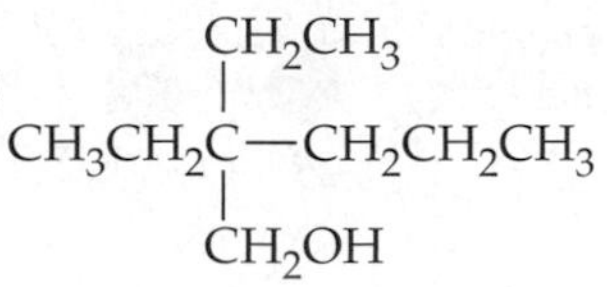

(b)
$$\overset{\text{CH}_2\text{CH}_3\quad\ \text{CH}_3}{\underset{\text{CH}_3\overset{|}{\text{CH}}\text{CH}_2\text{CH}_3}{\text{CH}_3\text{CH}\ \overset{|}{\text{CH}}\ \text{CH}_2\overset{|}{\text{CH}}\text{CH}_3}}$$

(c)
$$\overset{\text{Br}\qquad\qquad\ \text{Cl}}{\underset{\text{CH}_3\quad \text{CHCH}_2\text{CH}_3}{\text{CH}_3\overset{|}{\text{C}}-\overset{}{\underset{|}{\text{CH}}}\text{CH}_2\text{CH}_2\overset{|}{\text{CH}}\text{CH}_2\text{CH}_3}}$$

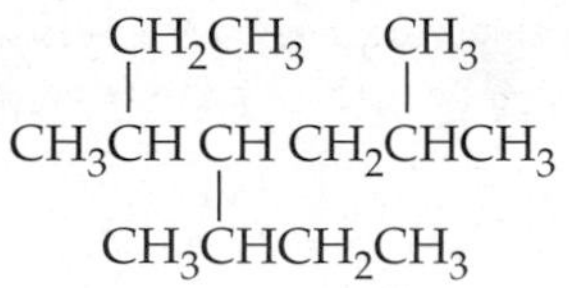

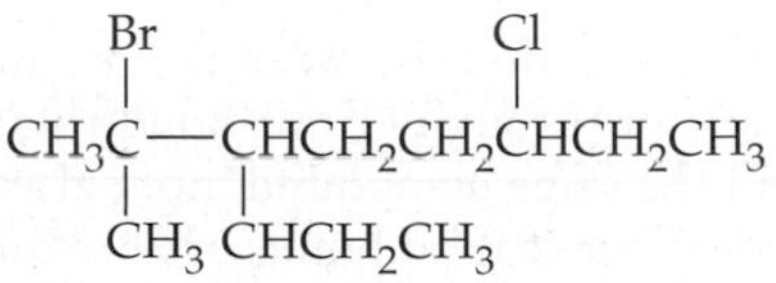

PROBLEM 12.7

Convert the following line structures to condensed structures:

(a)

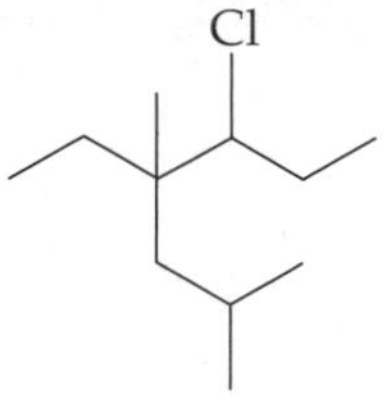

(b)

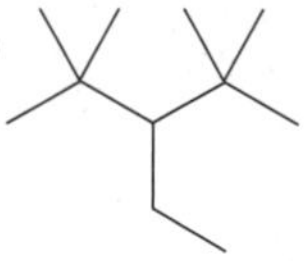

PROBLEM 12.8

Draw both condensed and line structures for the chemicals listed in Problem 12.2.

12.5 The Shapes of Organic Molecules

Every carbon atom in an alkane has its four bonds pointing toward the four corners of a tetrahedron, but chemists do not usually worry about three-dimensional shapes when writing condensed structures. Condensed structures do not imply any particular three-dimensional shape; they only indicate the connections between atoms without specifying geometry. Line structures do try to give some limited feeling for the shape of a molecule, but even here, the ability to show three-dimensional shape is limited unless dashed and wedged lines are used for the bonds (Section 4.8).

Butane, for example, has no one single shape because *rotation* takes place around carbon–carbon single bonds. The two parts of a molecule joined by a carbon–carbon single bond in a noncyclic structure are free to spin around the bond, giving rise to an infinite number of possible three-dimensional geometries, or **conformations**. The various conformations of a molecule such as butane are called **conformers** of one another. Conformers differ from one another as a result of rotation around carbon–carbon single bonds. Although the conformers of a given molecule have different three-dimensional shapes and different energies, the conformers cannot be separated from one another. A given butane molecule might be in its fully extended conformation at one instant but in a twisted conformation an instant later (Figure 12.2). An actual sample of butane contains a great many molecules that are constantly changing conformation. At any given instant, however, most of the molecules have the least crowded, lowest-energy extended conformation shown in Figure 12.2a. The same is true for all other alkanes: At any given instant, most molecules are in the least crowded conformation.

Conformation The specific three-dimensional arrangement of atoms in a molecule achieved specifically through rotations around carbon–carbon single bonds.

Conformer Molecular structures having identical connections between atoms and directly interconvertible through C—C bond rotations; that is, they represent identical compounds.

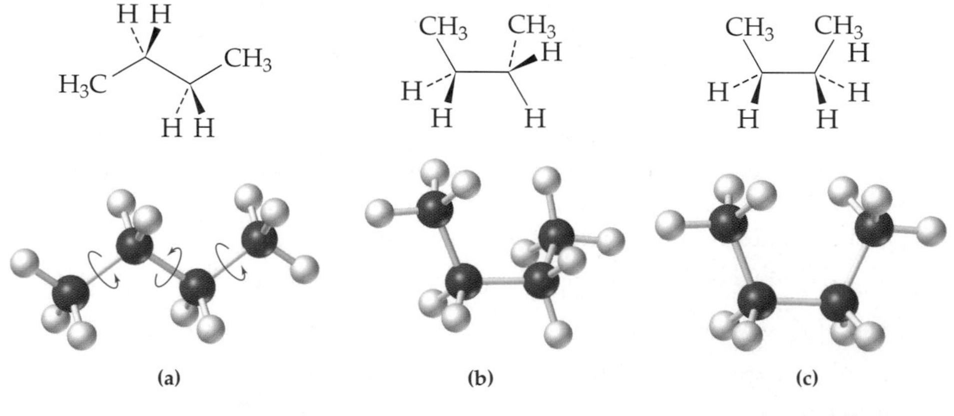

▶ **Figure 12.2**

Some conformations of butane (there are many others as well). The least crowded, extended conformation in (a) is the lowest-energy one, while the eclipsed conformation shown in (c) is the highest-energy one.

(a)   (b)   (c)

As long as any two structures have identical connections between atoms, and are interconvertible either by "flipping" the molecule or through C—C bond rotations, they are conformers of each other and represent the same compound, no matter how the structures are drawn. It is important to remember that no bonds are broken and reformed when interconverting conformers. Sometimes, you have to mentally rotate structures to see whether they are conformers or actually different molecules. To see that the following two structures represent conformers of the same compound rather than two isomers, picture one of them flipped right to left so that the red CH_3 groups are on the same side:

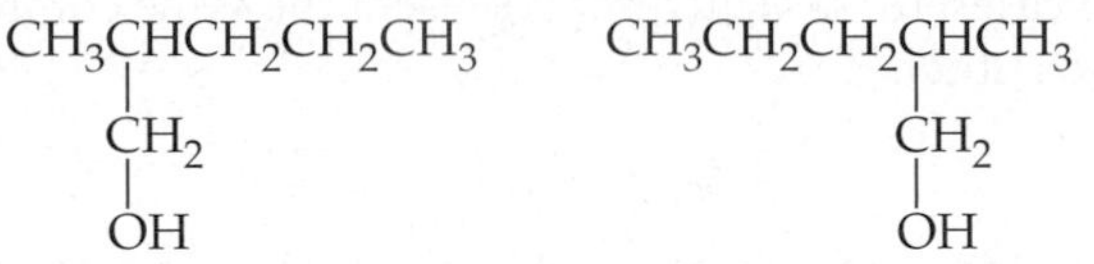

$$CH_3CHCH_2CH_2CH_3 \qquad CH_3CH_2CH_2CHCH_3$$
$$\qquad | \qquad\qquad\qquad\qquad\qquad |$$
$$\qquad CH_2 \qquad\qquad\qquad\qquad\qquad CH_2$$
$$\qquad | \qquad\qquad\qquad\qquad\qquad |$$
$$\qquad OH \qquad\qquad\qquad\qquad\qquad OH$$

Another way to determine whether two structures are conformers is to name each one using the IUPAC nomenclature rules (Section 12.6). If two structures have the same name, they are conformers of the same compound.

Worked Example 12.7 Molecular Structures: Identifying Conformers

The following structures all have the formula C_7H_{16}. Which of them represent the same molecule?

$$\qquad CH_3 \qquad\qquad\qquad\qquad\qquad\qquad CH_3$$
$$\qquad | \qquad\qquad\qquad\qquad\qquad\qquad |$$
(a) 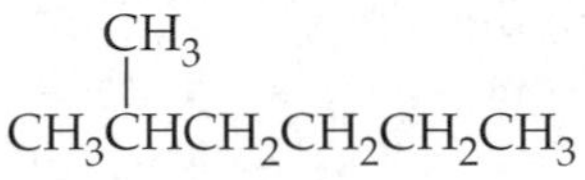 $CH_3CHCH_2CH_2CH_2CH_3$ (b)  $CH_3CH_2CH_2CH_2CHCH_3$

$$\qquad\qquad CH_3$$
$$\qquad\qquad |$$
(c) 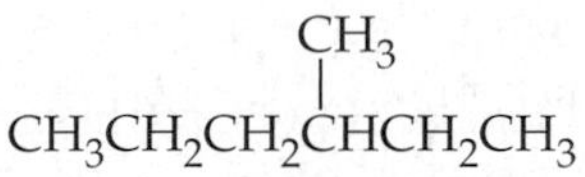 $CH_3CH_2CH_2CHCH_2CH_3$

ANALYSIS Pay attention to the *connections* between atoms. Do not get confused by the apparent differences caused by writing a structure right to left versus left to right. Begin by identifying the longest chain of carbon atoms in the molecule.

SOLUTION
Molecule (a) has a straight chain of 6 carbons with a $—CH_3$ branch on the second carbon from the end. Molecule (b) also has a straight chain of 6 carbons with a $—CH_3$ branch on the second carbon from the end and is therefore identical to (a). That is, (a) and (b) are conformers of the same molecule. The only difference between (a) and (b) is that one is written "forward" and one is written "backward." Molecule (c), by contrast, has a straight chain of 6 carbons with a $—CH_3$ branch on the *third* carbon from the end and is therefore an isomer of (a) and (b).

Worked Example 12.8 Molecular Structures: Identifying Conformers and Isomers

Are the following pairs of compounds the same (conformers), isomers, or unrelated?

$$\qquad CH_3 \qquad\qquad CH_3$$
$$\qquad | \qquad\qquad\quad |$$
(a) 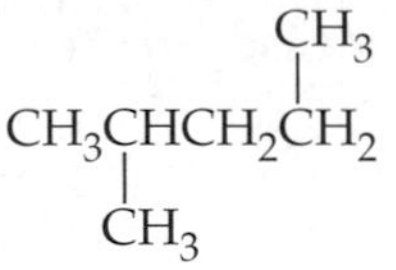 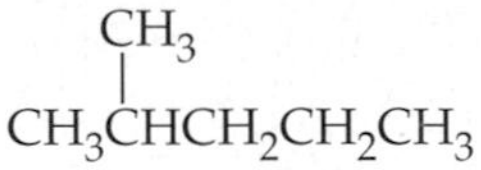 $CH_3CHCH_2CH_2 \qquad CH_3CHCH_2CH_2CH_3$
$$\qquad |$$
$$\qquad CH_3$$

$$\qquad\qquad\qquad\qquad\qquad CH_2CH_3$$
$$\qquad\qquad\qquad\qquad\qquad |$$
(b) 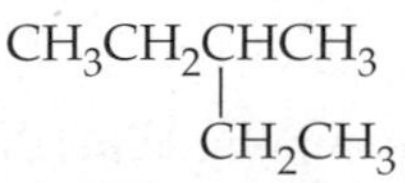 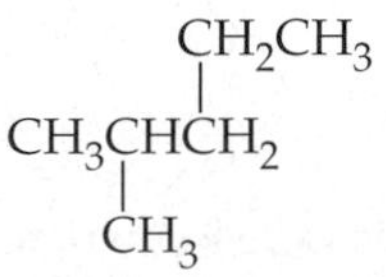 $CH_3CH_2CHCH_3 \qquad CH_3CHCH_2$
$$\qquad\quad | \qquad\qquad\qquad |$$
$$\qquad\quad CH_2CH_3 \qquad\qquad CH_3$$

$$\qquad\qquad\qquad\qquad\qquad\qquad O$$
$$\qquad\qquad\qquad\qquad\qquad\qquad ||$$
(c) $CH_3CH_2OCH_3 \qquad CH_3CH_2CH$

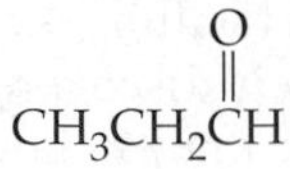

ANALYSIS First compare molecular formulas to see if the compounds are related, and then look at the structures to see if they are the same compound or isomers. Find the longest continuous carbon chain in each, and then compare the locations of the substituents connected to the longest chain.

SOLUTION

(a) Both compounds have the same molecular formula (C_6H_{14}), so they are related. Since the $—CH_3$ group is on the second carbon from the end of a 5-carbon chain in both cases, these structures represent the same compound and are conformers of each other.

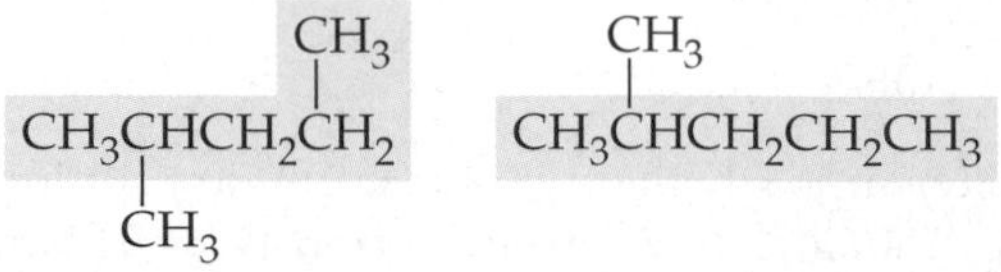

$$CH_3CHCH_2\overset{\overset{\displaystyle CH_3}{\displaystyle |}}{CH_2} \qquad CH_3\overset{\overset{\displaystyle CH_3}{\displaystyle |}}{CH}CH_2CH_2CH_3$$
$$\underset{\displaystyle CH_3}{|}$$

(b) Both compounds have the same molecular formula (C_6H_{14}), and the longest chain in each is 5 carbon atoms. A comparison shows, however, that the $—CH_3$ group is on the middle carbon atom in one structure and on the second carbon atom in the other. These compounds are isomers of each other.

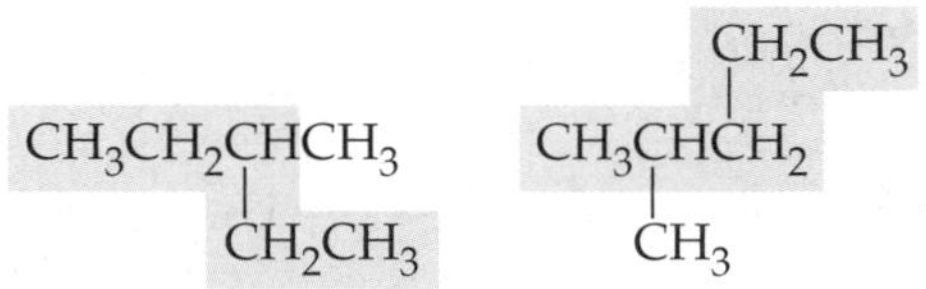

$$CH_3CH_2\overset{\overset{\displaystyle }{\displaystyle }}{CH}CH_3 \qquad CH_3\overset{\overset{\displaystyle CH_2CH_3}{\displaystyle |}}{CH}CH_2$$
$$\underset{\displaystyle CH_2CH_3}{|} \qquad \underset{\displaystyle CH_3}{|}$$

(c) These compounds have different formulas $(C_3H_8O$ and $C_3H_6O)$, so they are unrelated; they are neither conformers nor isomers of each other.

PROBLEM 12.9

Which of the following structures are conformers?

(a) 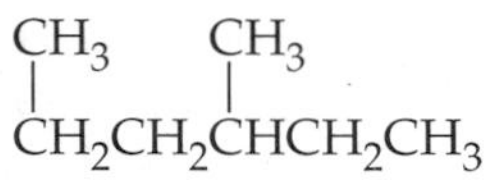 $CH_2CH_2\overset{\overset{\displaystyle CH_3}{\displaystyle |}}{CH}\overset{}{}CH_2CH_3$ where first substituent is CH_3

(a) $\overset{\overset{\displaystyle CH_3}{\displaystyle |}}{CH_2}CH_2\overset{\overset{\displaystyle CH_3}{\displaystyle |}}{CH}CH_2CH_3$

(b) 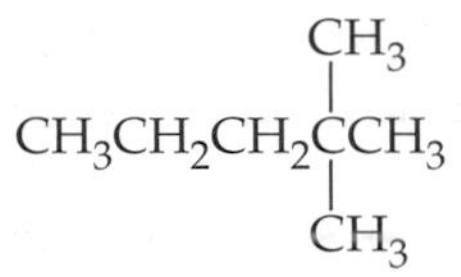 $CH_3CH_2CH_2\overset{\overset{\displaystyle CH_3}{\displaystyle |}}{\underset{\underset{\displaystyle CH_3}{\displaystyle |}}{C}}CH_3$

(c) $CH_3CH_2\overset{\overset{\displaystyle CH_3}{\displaystyle |}}{CH}CH_2CH_2CH_3$

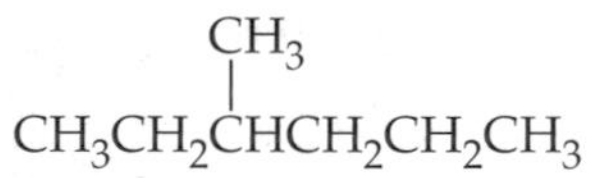

PROBLEM 12.10

In total, there are 18 isomers with the formula C_8H_{18}. Draw condensed structures for as many as you can that have only one or two $—CH_3$ groups as branch points (there are 9 isomers that fit these conditions). Convert the condensed structures you drew to line structures.

12.6 Naming Alkanes

When relatively few pure organic chemicals were known, new compounds were named at the whim of their discoverer. Thus, urea is a crystalline substance first isolated from urine, and the barbiturates were named by their discoverer in honor of his friend Barbara. As more and more compounds became known, however, the need for a systematic method of naming compounds became apparent.

The system of naming (*nomenclature*) now used is one devised by the International Union of Pure and Applied Chemistry, IUPAC (pronounced **eye**-you-pack). In the IUPAC system for organic compounds, a chemical name has three parts: *prefix, parent,* and *suffix.* The prefix specifies the location of functional groups and other **substituents** in the molecule; the parent tells how many carbon atoms are present

Substituent An atom or group of atoms attached to a parent compound.

in the longest continuous chain; and the suffix identifies what family the molecule belongs to:

Prefix—Parent—Suffix

Where are substituents located?   How many carbons?   What family does the molecule belong to?

Straight-chain alkanes are named by counting the number of carbon atoms and adding the family suffix -*ane*. With the exception of the first four compounds—*meth*ane, *eth*ane, *prop*ane, and *but*ane—whose parent names have historical origins, the alkanes are named from Greek numbers according to the number of carbons present (Table 12.2). Thus, *pentane* is the 5-carbon alkane, *hexane* is the 6-carbon alkane, and so on. Straight-chain alkanes have no substituents, so prefixes are not needed. The first ten alkane names are so common that they should be memorized.

TABLE 12.2 Names of Straight-Chain Alkanes

Number of Carbons	Structure	Name
1	CH_4	Methane
2	CH_3CH_3	Ethane
3	$CH_3CH_2CH_3$	Propane
4	$CH_3CH_2CH_2CH_3$	Butane
5	$CH_3CH_2CH_2CH_2CH_3$	Pentane
6	$CH_3CH_2CH_2CH_2CH_2CH_3$	Hexane
7	$CH_3CH_2CH_2CH_2CH_2CH_2CH_3$	Heptane
8	$CH_3CH_2CH_2CH_2CH_2CH_2CH_2CH_3$	Octane
9	$CH_3CH_2CH_2CH_2CH_2CH_2CH_2CH_2CH_3$	Nonane
10	$CH_3CH_2CH_2CH_2CH_2CH_2CH_2CH_2CH_2CH_3$	Decane

Substituents, such as $—CH_3$ and $—CH_2CH_3$, that branch off the main chain are called **alkyl groups**. An alkyl group can be thought of as the part of an alkane that remains when 1 hydrogen atom is removed to create an available bonding site. For example, removal of a hydrogen from methane gives the **methyl group,** $—CH_3$, and removal of a hydrogen from ethane gives the **ethyl group,** $—CH_2CH_3$. Notice that these alkyl groups are named simply by replacing the -*ane* ending of the parent alkane with an -*yl* ending:

Alkyl group The part of an alkane that remains when a hydrogen atom is removed.

Methyl group The $—CH_3$ alkyl group.

Ethyl group The $—CH_2CH_3$ alkyl group.

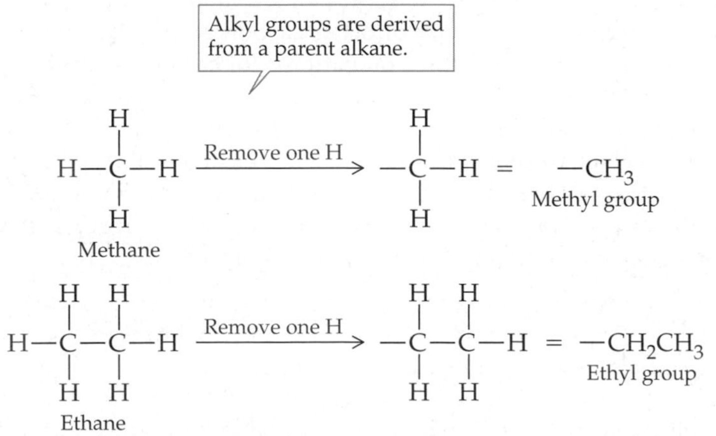

Alkyl groups are derived from a parent alkane.

Both methane and ethane have only one "kind" of hydrogen. It does not matter which of the 4 methane hydrogens is removed, so there is only one possible methyl group. Similarly, it does not matter which of the 6 equivalent ethane hydrogens is removed, so only one ethyl group is possible.

Propyl group The straight-chain alkyl group —$CH_2CH_2CH_3$.

Isopropyl group The branched-chain alkyl group —$CH(CH_3)_2$.

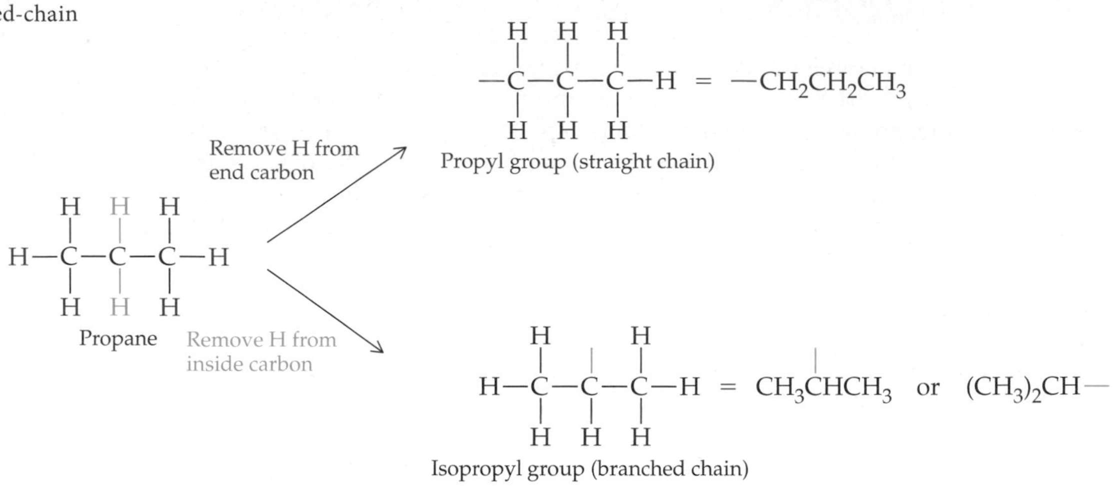

The situation is more complex for larger alkanes, which contain more than one kind of hydrogen. Propane, for example, has two different kinds of hydrogens. Removal of any one of the 6 hydrogens attached to an end carbon yields a straight-chain alkyl group called **propyl**, whereas removal of either one of the 2 hydrogens attached to the central carbon yields a branched-chain alkyl group called **isopropyl**:

Remove H from end carbon → Propyl group (straight chain)

$$-CH_2CH_2CH_3$$

Propane

Remove H from inside carbon →

$$CH_3CHCH_3 \quad \text{or} \quad (CH_3)_2CH-$$

Isopropyl group (branched chain)

It is important to realize that alkyl groups are not compounds but rather are simply partial structures that help us name compounds. The names of some common alkyl groups are listed in Figure 12.3; you will want to commit them to memory.

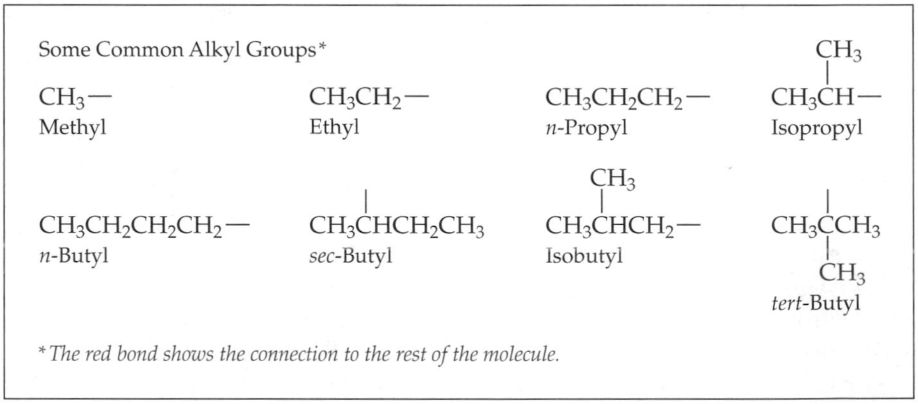

▶ **Figure 12.3**
The most common alkyl groups found in organic molecules are shown here; the red bond shows the attachment the group has to the rest of the molecule.*

Some Common Alkyl Groups*

CH_3—
Methyl

CH_3CH_2—
Ethyl

$CH_3CH_2CH_2$—
n-Propyl

$CH_3\overset{\displaystyle CH_3}{\underset{}{CH}}$—
Isopropyl

$CH_3CH_2CH_2CH_2$—
n-Butyl

$CH_3CHCH_2CH_3$
sec-Butyl

$CH_3\overset{\displaystyle CH_3}{\underset{}{CH}}CH_2$—
Isobutyl

$CH_3\overset{\displaystyle CH_3}{\underset{\displaystyle CH_3}{C}}CH_3$
tert-Butyl

*The red bond shows the connection to the rest of the molecule.

Notice that four butyl (4-carbon) groups are listed in Figure 12.3: butyl, sec-butyl, isobutyl, and tert-butyl. The prefix sec- stands for secondary, and the prefix tert- stands for tertiary, referring to the number of other carbon atoms attached to the branch point. There are four possible substitution patterns for carbons attached to four atoms and these are designated *primary, secondary, tertiary,* and *quaternary. It is important to note that these designations strictly apply to carbons having only single bonds.* A **primary (1°) carbon atom** has 1 other carbon attached to it (typically indicated as an —R group in the molecular structure), a **secondary (2°) carbon atom** has 2 other carbons attached, a **tertiary (3°) carbon atom** has 3 other carbons attached, and a **quaternary (4°) carbon atom** has 4 other carbons attached:

Primary (1°) carbon atom A carbon atom with 1 other carbon attached to it.

Secondary (2°) carbon atom A carbon atom with 2 other carbons attached to it.

Tertiary (3°) carbon atom A carbon atom with 3 other carbons attached to it.

Quaternary (4°) carbon atom A carbon atom with 4 other carbons attached to it.

$$R-\overset{\displaystyle H}{\underset{\displaystyle H}{C}}-H$$

Primary carbon (1°) has one other carbon attached.

$$R-\overset{\displaystyle R}{\underset{\displaystyle H}{C}}-H$$

Secondary carbon (2°) has two other carbons attached.

$$R-\overset{\displaystyle R}{\underset{\displaystyle R}{C}}-H$$

Tertiary carbon (3°) has three other carbons attached.

$$R-\overset{\displaystyle R}{\underset{\displaystyle R}{C}}-R$$

Quaternary carbon (4°) has four other carbons attached.

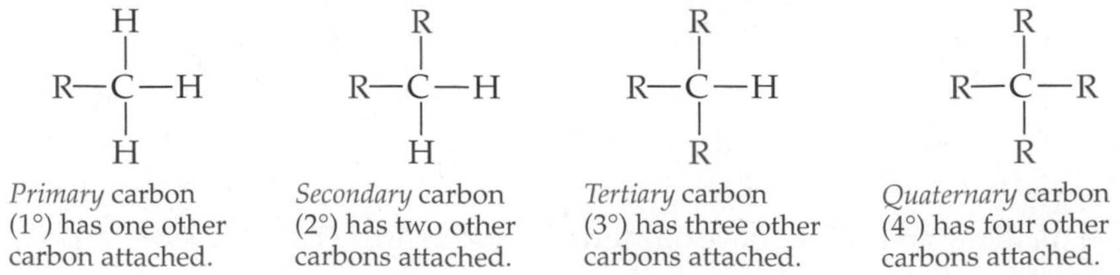

*The symbol **R** is used here and in later chapters as a general abbreviation for any organic substituent.* You should think of it as representing the **R**est of the molecule, which we are not bothering to specify. The R is used to allow you to focus on a particular structural feature of a molecule without the "clutter" of the other atoms in the molecule detracting from it. The R might represent a methyl, ethyl, or propyl group, or any of a vast number of other possibilities. For example, the generalized formula R—OH for an alcohol might refer to an alcohol as simple as CH_3OH or CH_3CH_2OH or one as complicated as cholesterol, shown here:

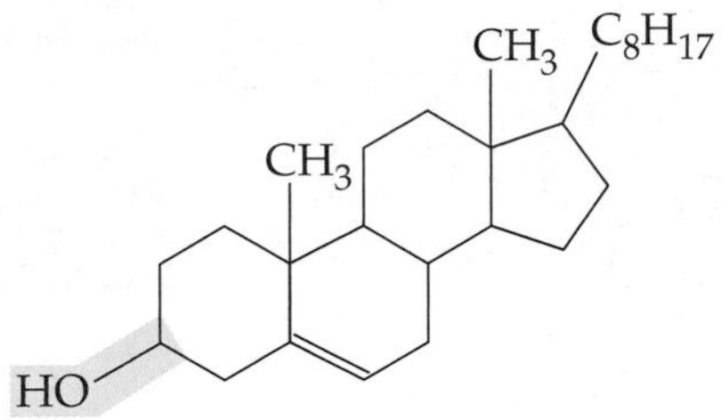

Branched-chain alkanes can be named by following four steps:

STEP 1: **Name the main chain.** Find the longest continuous chain of carbons, and name the chain according to the number of carbon atoms it contains. The longest chain may not be immediately obvious because it is not always written on one line; you may have to "turn corners" to find it.

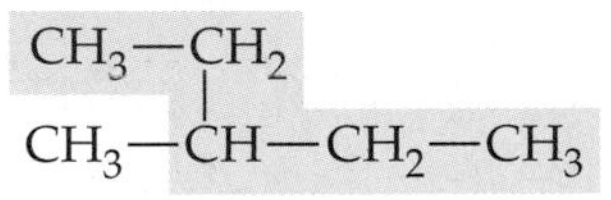

Name as a substituted pentane, not as a substituted butane, because the *longest* chain has five carbons.

STEP 2: **Number the carbon atoms in the main chain,** beginning at the end nearer the first branch point:

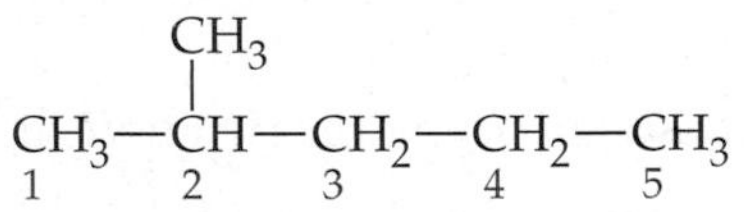

The first (and only) branch occurs at C2 if we start numbering from the left, but would occur at C4 if we started from the right by mistake.

STEP 3: **Identify the branching substituents, and number each** according to its point of attachment to the main chain:

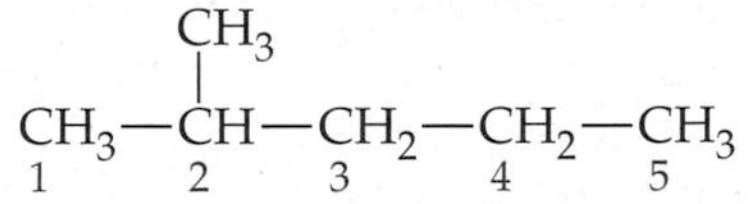

The main chain is a pentane. There is one —CH_3 substituent group connected to C2 of the chain.

If there are two substituents on the same carbon, assign the same number to both. There must always be as many numbers in the name as there are substituents.

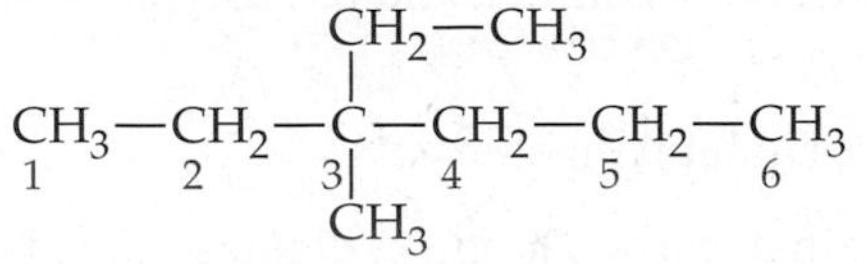

The main chain is a hexane. There are two substituents, a —CH_3 and a —CH_2CH_3, both connected to C3 of the chain.

STEP 4: **Write the name as a single word,** using hyphens to separate the numbers from the different prefixes and commas to separate numbers, if necessary. If two or more different substituent groups are present, cite them in alphabetical order. If two or more identical substituents are present, use one of the prefixes *di-*, *tri-*, *tetra-*, and so forth, but do not use these prefixes for alphabetizing purposes.

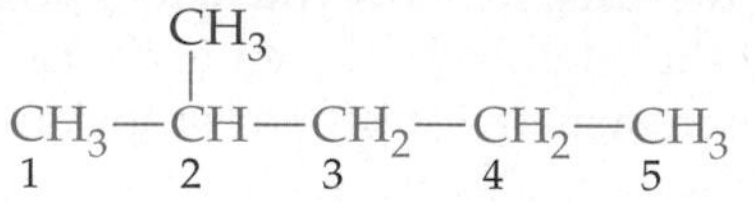

$$\underset{1}{CH_3}-\underset{2}{\overset{\overset{\displaystyle CH_3}{|}}{CH}}-\underset{3}{CH_2}-\underset{4}{CH_2}-\underset{5}{CH_3}$$

2-Methylpentane (a 5-carbon main chain with a 2-methyl substituent)

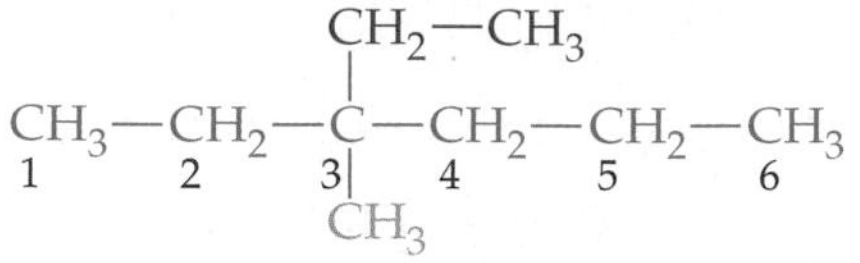

$$\underset{1}{CH_3}-\underset{2}{CH_2}-\underset{3}{\overset{\overset{\displaystyle CH_2-CH_3}{|}}{\underset{\underset{\displaystyle CH_3}{|}}{C}}}-\underset{4}{CH_2}-\underset{5}{CH_2}-\underset{6}{CH_3}$$

3-Ethyl-3-methylhexane (a 6-carbon main chain with 3-ethyl and 3-methyl substituents cited alphabetically)

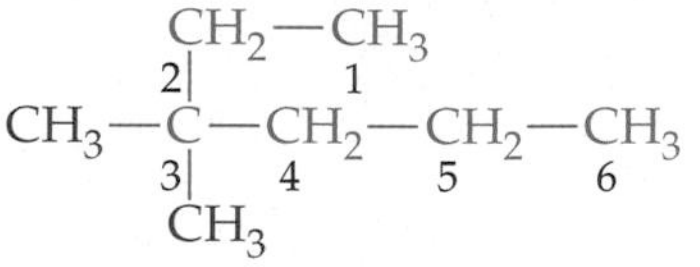

$$\underset{}{CH_3}-\underset{3}{\overset{\overset{\displaystyle \overset{2}{CH_2}-\overset{1}{CH_3}}{|}}{\underset{\underset{\displaystyle CH_3}{|}}{C}}}-\underset{4}{CH_2}-\underset{5}{CH_2}-\underset{6}{CH_3}$$

3,3-Dimethylhexane (a 6-carbon main chain with two 3-methyl substitutents)

Worked Example 12.9 Naming Organic Compounds: Alkanes

What is the IUPAC name of the following alkanes?

(a) 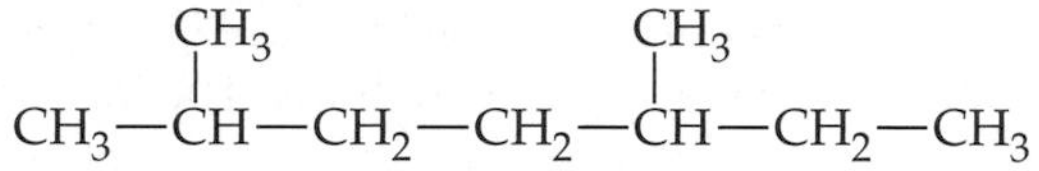 $$\underset{}{CH_3}-\overset{\overset{\displaystyle CH_3}{|}}{CH}-CH_2-CH_2-\overset{\overset{\displaystyle CH_3}{|}}{CH}-CH_2-CH_3$$

(b)

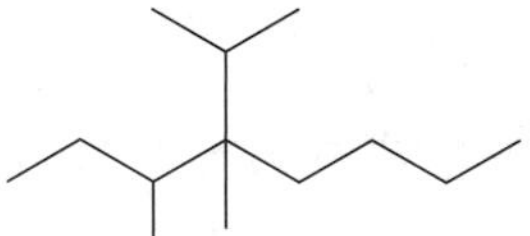

ANALYSIS Follow the four steps outlined in the text.

SOLUTION

(a) STEP 1: The longest continuous chain of carbon atoms is seven, so the main chain is a *hept*ane.

STEP 2: Number the main chain beginning at the end nearer the first branch:

$$\underset{1}{CH_3}-\underset{2}{\overset{\overset{\displaystyle CH_3}{|}}{CH}}-\underset{3}{CH_2}-\underset{4}{CH_2}-\underset{5}{\overset{\overset{\displaystyle CH_3}{|}}{CH}}-\underset{6}{CH_2}-\underset{7}{CH_3}$$

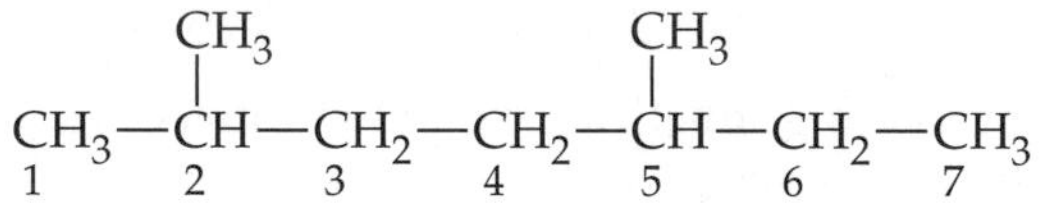

STEP 3: Identify and number the substituents (a 2-methyl and a 5-methyl in this case):

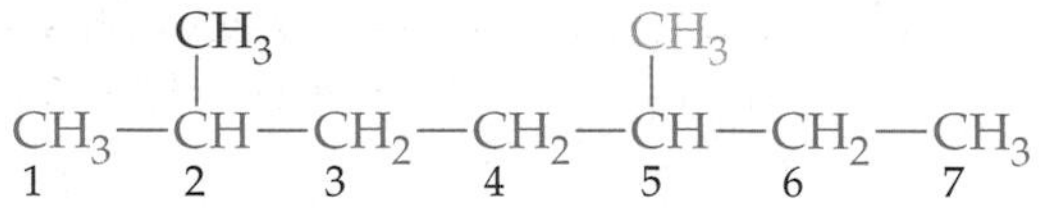

$$\underset{1}{CH_3}-\underset{2}{\overset{\overset{\displaystyle CH_3}{|}}{CH}}-\underset{3}{CH_2}-\underset{4}{CH_2}-\underset{5}{\overset{\overset{\displaystyle CH_3}{|}}{CH}}-\underset{6}{CH_2}-\underset{7}{CH_3}$$

Substituents: 2-methyl and 5-methyl

STEP 4: Write the name as one word, using the prefix *di-* because there are two methyl groups. Separate the two numbers by a comma, and use a hyphen between the numbers and the word.

Name: 2, 5-Dimethylheptane

(b) STEP 1: The longest continuous chain of carbon atoms is eight, so the main chain is an *oct*ane.

STEP 2: Number the main chain beginning at the end nearer the first branch:

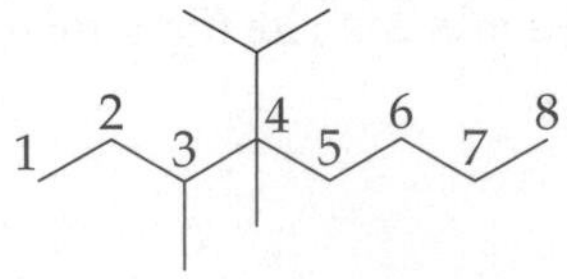

STEP 3: Identify and number the substituents:

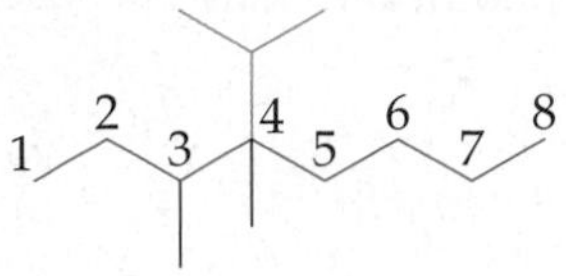

3-methyl, 4-methyl, 4-isopropyl

STEP 4: Write the name as one word, again using the prefix *di-* because there are two methyl groups.

Name: 3, 4-Dimethyl-4-isopropyloctane

Worked Example 12.10 Molecular Structure: Identifying 1°, 2°, 3°, and 4° Carbons

Identify each carbon atom in the following molecule as primary, secondary, tertiary, or quaternary.

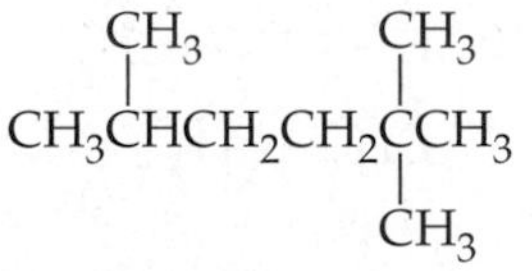

$$CH_3CHCH_2CH_2CCH_3$$

ANALYSIS Look at each carbon atom in the molecule, count the number of other carbon atoms attached, and make the assignment accordingly: primary (1 carbon attached); secondary (2 carbons attached); tertiary (3 carbons attached); quaternary (4 carbons attached).

SOLUTION

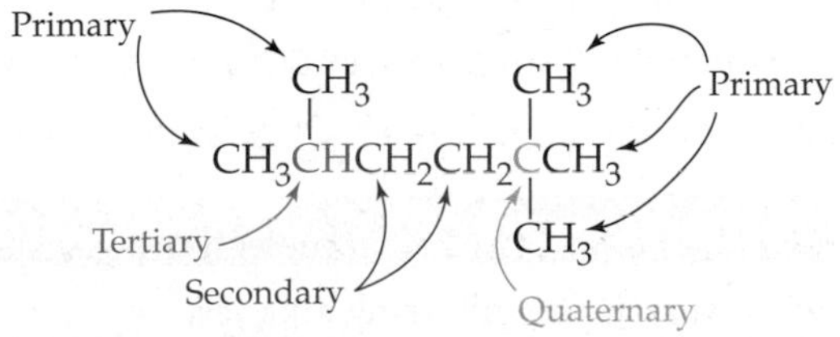

Worked Example 12.11 Molecular Structures: Drawing Condensed Structures
from Names

Draw condensed and line structures corresponding to the following IUPAC names:

(a) 2,3-Dimethylpentane
(b) 3-Ethylheptane

ANALYSIS Starting with the parent chain, add the named alkyl substituent groups to the appropriately numbered carbon atom(s).

SOLUTION

(a) The parent chain has 5 carbons (*pent*ane), with two methyl groups ($-CH_3$) attached to the second and third carbon in the chain:

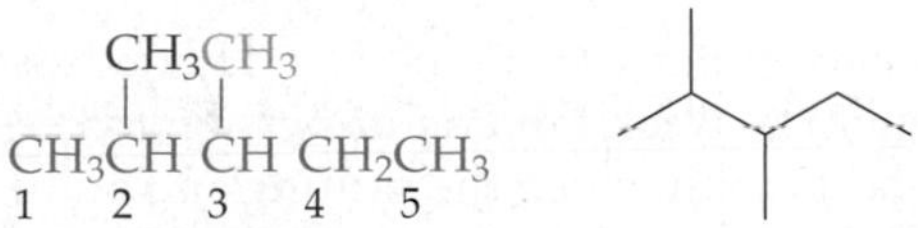

(b) The parent chain has 7 carbons (*hept*ane), with one ethyl group $(-CH_2CH_3)$ attached to the third carbon in the chain:

$$CH_2CH_3$$
$$CH_3CH_2CHCH_2CH_2CH_2CH_3$$
$$1 \quad 2 \quad 3 \quad 4 \quad 5 \quad 6 \quad 7$$

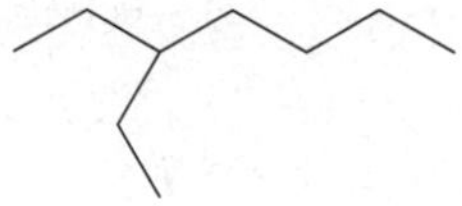

PROBLEM 12.11
Identify each carbon in the molecule shown in Worked Example 12.9b as primary, secondary, tertiary, or quaternary.

PROBLEM 12.12
What are the IUPAC names of the following alkanes?

$$CH_2-CH_3 \qquad\qquad CH_3$$
(a) $CH_3-CH-CH_2-CH_2-CH_2-CH-CH_3$

$$CH_2-CH_3$$
(b) $CH_3-CH_2-CH_2-CH_2-C-CH_2-CH_3$
$$CH_2-CH_3$$

PROBLEM 12.13
Draw both condensed and line structures corresponding to the following IUPAC names and label each carbon as primary, secondary, tertiary, or quaternary:
(a) 3-Methylhexane **(b)** 3,4-Dimethyloctane **(c)** 2,2,4-Trimethylpentane

PROBLEM 12.14
Draw and name alkanes that meet the following descriptions:
(a) A 5-carbon alkane with a tertiary carbon atom
(b) A 7-carbon alkane that has both a tertiary and a quaternary carbon atom

🔑 **KEY CONCEPT PROBLEM 12.15**

What are the IUPAC names of the following alkanes?

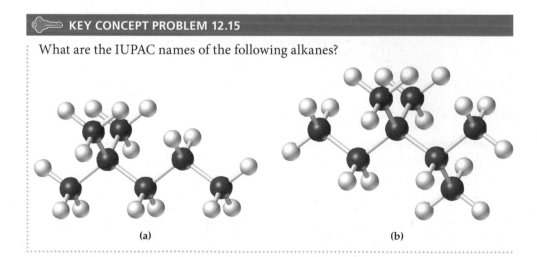

(a)   (b)

12.7 Properties of Alkanes

▶▶▶ Review the effects of London dispersion forces on molecules in Section 8.11.

Alkanes contain only nonpolar C—C and C—H bonds, so the only intermolecular forces influencing them are weak London dispersion forces. The effect of these forces is shown in the regularity with which the melting and boiling points of straight-chain alkanes increase with molecular size (Figure 12.4). The first four alkanes—methane, ethane, propane, and butane—are gases at room temperature and pressure. Alkanes

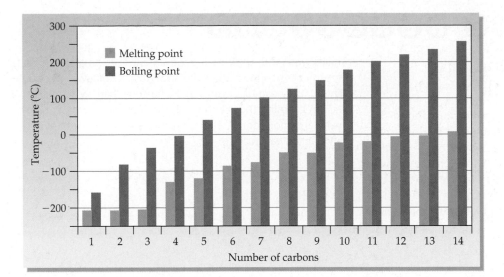

◄ **Figure 12.4**
The boiling and melting points for the C_1—C_{14} straight-chain alkanes increase with molecular size.

with 5–15 carbon atoms are liquids; those with 16 or more carbon atoms are generally low-melting, waxy solids.

In keeping with their low polarity, alkanes are insoluble in water but soluble in nonpolar organic solvents, including other alkanes. Because alkanes are generally less dense than water, they float on its surface. Low-molecular-weight alkanes are volatile and must be handled with care because their vapors are flammable. Mixtures of alkane vapors and air can explode when ignited by a single spark.

The physiological effects of alkanes are limited. Methane, ethane, and propane gases are nontoxic, but the danger of inhaling them lies in potential suffocation due to lack of oxygen. Breathing the vapor of larger alkanes in large concentrations can induce loss of consciousness. There is also a danger in breathing droplets of liquid alkanes because they dissolve nonpolar substances in lung tissue and cause pneumonia-like symptoms.

Mineral oil, petroleum jelly, and paraffin wax are mixtures of higher alkanes. All are harmless to body tissue and are used in numerous food and medical applications. Mineral oil passes through the body unchanged and is sometimes used as a laxative. Petroleum jelly (sold as Vaseline) softens, lubricates, and protects the skin. Paraffin wax is used in candle making, on surfboards, and in home canning. See Chemistry in Action box on page 385 for more surprising uses of alkanes.

Properties of Alkanes:

- Odorless or mild odor; colorless; tasteless; nontoxic
- Nonpolar; insoluble in water but soluble in nonpolar organic solvents; less dense than water
- Flammable; otherwise not very reactive

▶▶▶ Recall from Section 9.2 the rule of thumb when predicting solubility: "like dissolves like."

12.8 Reactions of Alkanes

Alkanes do not react with acids, bases, or most other common laboratory *reagents* (a substance that causes a reaction to occur). Their only major reactions are with oxygen (combustion) and with halogens (halogenation). Both of these reaction types have complicated mechanisms and occur through the intermediacy of free radicals (Section 13.8).

Combustion

Most of you probably get to school everyday using some sort of transportation that uses gasoline, which is a mixture of alkanes. To power a vehicle, that mixture of alkanes must be converted into energy. The reaction of an alkane with oxygen is called **combustion**, an oxidation reaction that commonly takes place in a controlled manner

Combustion A chemical reaction that produces a flame, usually because of burning with oxygen.

MASTERING REACTIONS

Organic Chemistry and the Curved Arrow Formalism

Starting with this chapter and continuing on through the remainder of this text, you will be exploring the world of organic chemistry and its close relative, biochemistry. Both of these areas of chemistry are much more "visual" than those you have been studying; organic chemists, for example, look at how and why reactions occur by examining the flow of electrons. For example, consider the following reaction of 2-iodopropane with sodium cyanide:

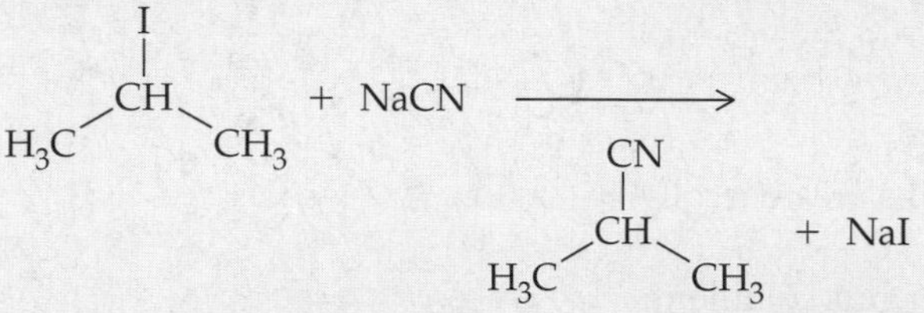

This seemingly simple process (known as a *substitution reaction*, discussed in Chapter 13) is not adequately described by the equation. To help to understand what may really be going on, organic chemists use what is loosely described as "electron pushing" and have adopted what is known as *curved arrow formalism* to represent it. The movement of electrons is depicted using curved arrows, where the number of electrons corresponds to the head of the arrow. Single-headed arrows represent movement of one electron, while a double-headed arrow indicates the movement of two:

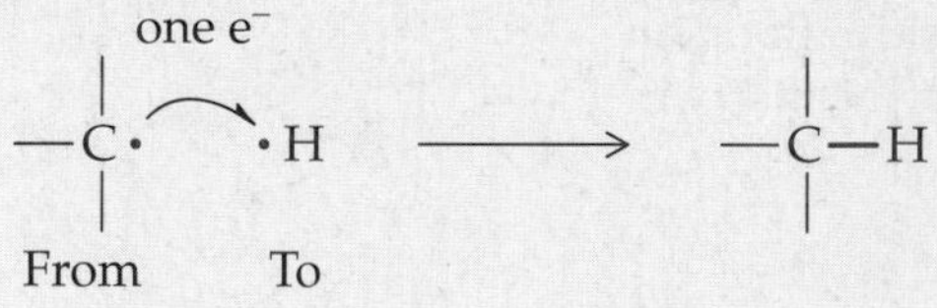

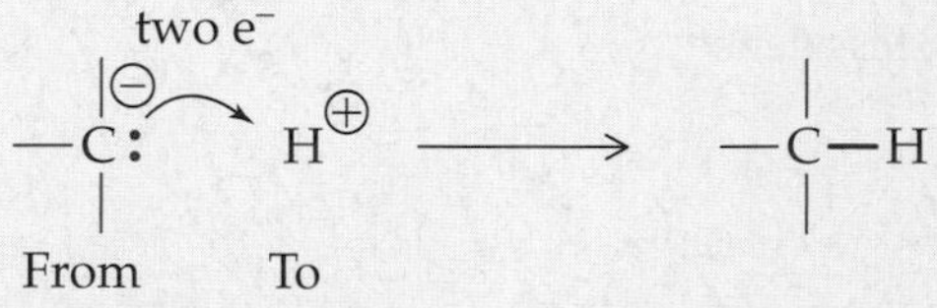

The convention is to show the movement *from* an area of high electron density (the start of the arrow) *to* one of lower electron density (the head of the arrow). Using curved arrow formalism, we can examine the reaction of 2-iodopropane with sodium cyanide in more detail. There are two distinct paths by which this reaction can occur:

Path 1

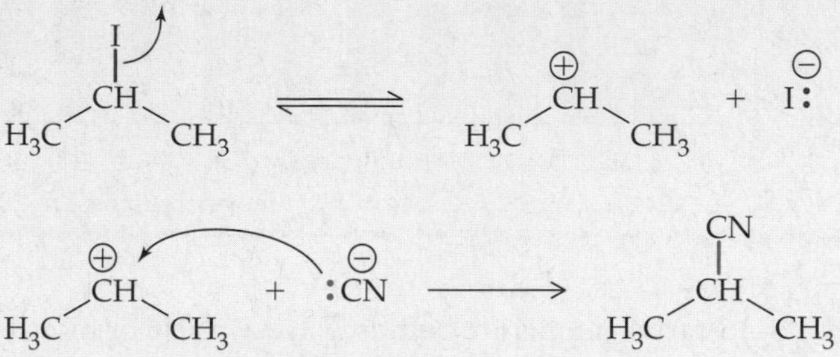

Path 2

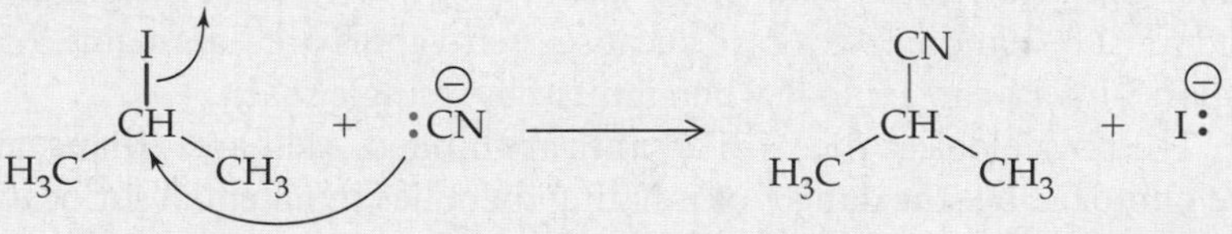

Notice that while both pathways lead ultimately to the same product, the curved arrow formalism shows us that they have significantly different ways of occurring. Although it is not important right now to understand which of the two paths is actually operative (it turns out to be a function of solvent), concentrations, catalysts, temperature, and other conditions) it is important that you get used to thinking of reactions as an "electron flow" of sorts. Throughout the next six chapters, you will see more of these "Mastering Reactions" boxes; they are intended to give you a little more insight into the otherwise seemingly random reactions that organic molecules undergo.

See Mastering Reactions Problems 12.76 and 12.77 at the end of the chapter.

▶▶▶ Combustion reactions are exothermic, as we learned in Section 7.3.

in an engine or furnace. Carbon dioxide and water are the products of complete combustion of any hydrocarbon, and a large amount of heat is released (ΔH is a negative number.) Some examples were given in Table 7.1.

$$CH_4(g) + 2 O_2(g) \longrightarrow CO_2(g) + 2 H_2O(g) \quad \Delta H = -213 \text{ kcal/mol} \ (-891 \text{ kJ/mol})$$

When hydrocarbon combustion is incomplete because of faulty engine or furnace performance, carbon monoxide and carbon-containing soot are among the products. Carbon monoxide is a highly toxic and dangerous substance, especially so because it has no odor and can easily go undetected (See the Chemistry in Action feature "CO and NO: Pollutants or Miracle Molecules?" in Chapter 4). Breathing air that contains as little as 2% CO for only one hour can cause respiratory and nervous system damage or death. The supply of oxygen to the brain is cut off by carbon monoxide because it binds strongly to blood hemoglobin at the site where oxygen is normally bound. By contrast with CO, CO_2 is nontoxic and causes no harm, except by suffocation when present in high concentration.

PROBLEM 12.16

Write a balanced equation for the complete combustion of ethane with oxygen.

The second notable reaction of alkanes is *halogenation*, the replacement of an alkane hydrogen by a chlorine or bromine in a process initiated by heat or light. Halogenation is important because it is used to prepare both a number of molecules that are key industrial solvents (such as dichloromethane, chloroform, and carbon tetrachloride) as well as others (such as bromoethane) that are used for the preparation of other larger organic molecules. In a halogenation reaction, only one H at a time is replaced; however, if allowed to react for a long enough time, all H's will be replaced with halogens. Complete chlorination of methane, for example, yields carbon tetrachloride:

$$CH_4 + 4\,Cl_2 \xrightarrow{\text{Heat or light}} CCl_4 + 4\,HCl$$

Although the above equation for the reaction of methane with chlorine is balanced, it does not fully represent what actually happens. In fact, this reaction, like many organic reactions, yields a mixture of products:

$$CH_4 + Cl_2 \longrightarrow CH_3Cl + HCl$$
$$\xrightarrow{Cl_2} CH_2Cl_2 + HCl$$
$$\xrightarrow{Cl_2} CHCl_3 + HCl$$
$$\xrightarrow{Cl_2} CCl_4 + HCl$$

CH_3Cl, chloromethane
CH_2Cl_2, dichloromethane
$CHCl_3$, chloroform
CCl_4, carbon tetrachloride

When we write the equation for an organic reaction, our attention is usually focused on converting a particular reactant into a desired product; any minor by-products and inorganic compounds (such as the HCl formed in the chlorination of methane) are often of little interest and are ignored. Thus, it is not always necessary to balance the equation for an organic reaction as long as the reactant, the major product, and any necessary reagents and conditions are shown. A chemist who plans to convert methane into bromomethane might therefore, write the equation as

$$CH_4 \xrightarrow[\text{Light, heat}]{Br_2} CH_3Br$$

Like many equations for organic reactions, this equation is not balanced.

In using this convention, it is customary to put reactants and reagents above the arrow and conditions, solvents, and catalysts below the arrow.

PROBLEM 12.17

Write the structures of all six possible products with either 1 or 2 chlorine atoms that form in the reaction of propane with Cl_2.

12.9 Cycloalkanes

The organic compounds described thus far have all been open-chain, or *acyclic*, alkanes. **Cycloalkanes**, which contain rings of carbon atoms, are also well known and are widespread throughout nature. To form a closed ring requires an additional

Cycloalkane An alkane that contains a ring of carbon atoms.

12.48 Which of the following pairs of structures are identical, which are isomers, and which are unrelated?

(a) 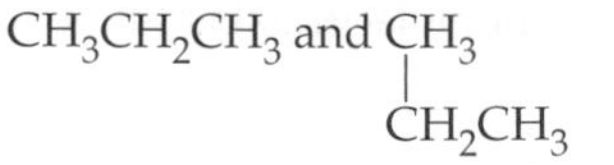 $CH_3CH_2CH_3$ and CH_3
$\qquad\qquad\qquad\qquad\quad CH_2CH_3$

(b) 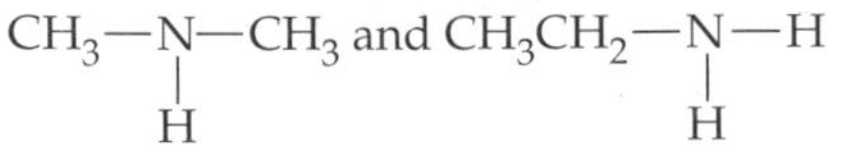 $CH_3-\underset{\underset{H}{|}}{N}-CH_3$ and $CH_3CH_2-\underset{\underset{H}{|}}{N}-H$

(c) 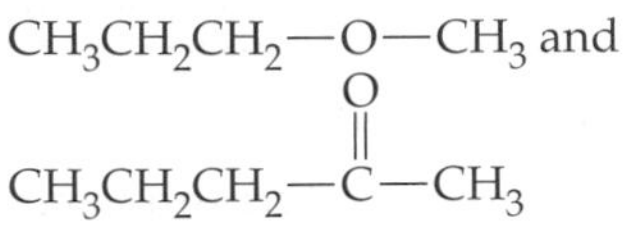 $CH_3CH_2CH_2-O-CH_3$ and
$CH_3CH_2CH_2-\overset{\overset{O}{\|}}{C}-CH_3$

(d) 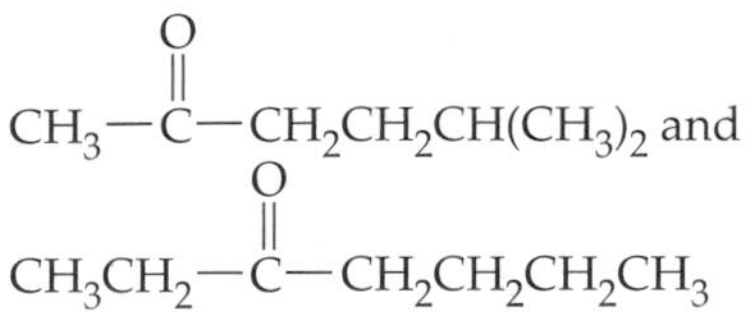 $CH_3-\overset{\overset{O}{\|}}{C}-CH_2CH_2CH(CH_3)_2$ and
$CH_3CH_2-\overset{\overset{O}{\|}}{C}-CH_2CH_2CH_2CH_3$

(e) 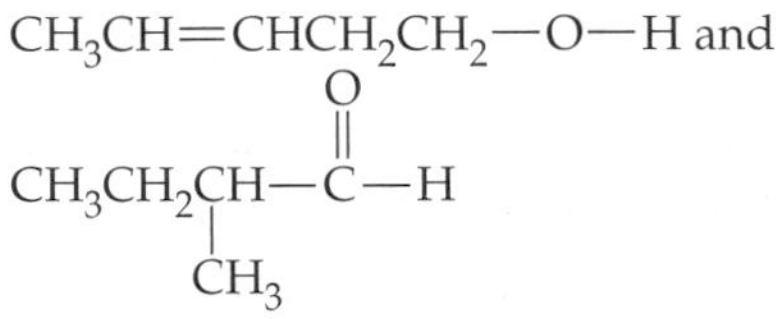 $CH_3CH=CHCH_2CH_2-O-H$ and
$CH_3CH_2\underset{\underset{CH_3}{|}}{CH}-\overset{\overset{O}{\|}}{C}-H$

12.49 Which structure(s) in each group represent the same compound, and which represent isomers?

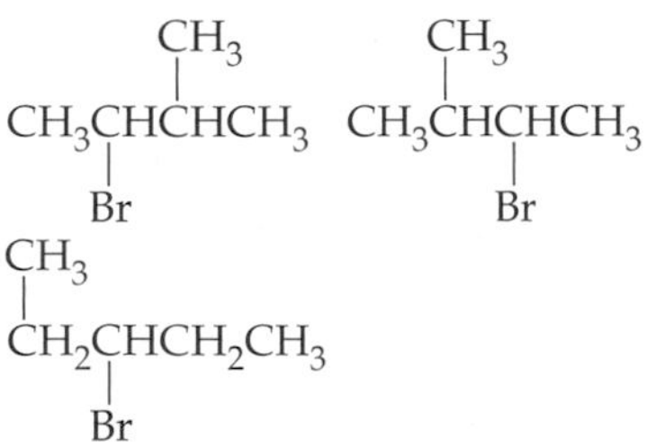

(a) 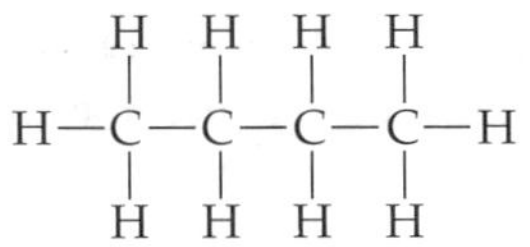 $H-\overset{\overset{H}{|}}{\underset{\underset{H}{|}}{C}}-\overset{\overset{H}{|}}{\underset{\underset{H}{|}}{C}}-\overset{\overset{H}{|}}{\underset{\underset{H}{|}}{C}}-\overset{\overset{H}{|}}{\underset{\underset{H}{|}}{C}}-H$

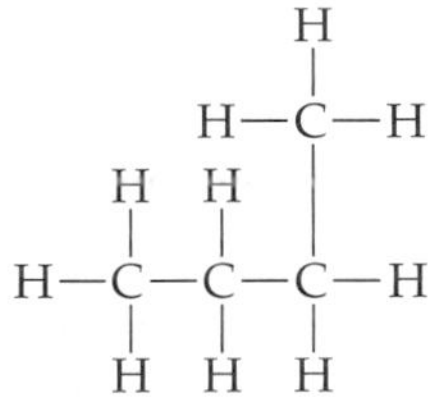

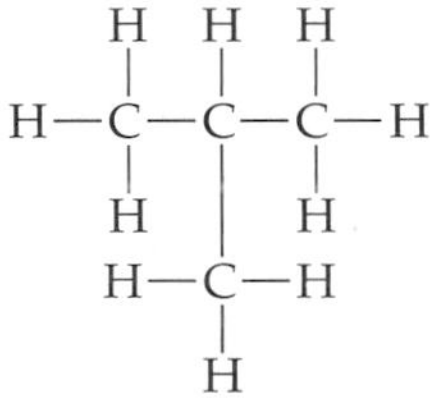

(b)

$H-\overset{\overset{H}{|}}{\underset{\underset{H}{|}}{C}}-H$

$H-\overset{\overset{H}{|}}{\underset{\underset{H}{|}}{C}}-\overset{\overset{H}{|}}{\underset{\underset{H}{|}}{C}}-\overset{}{\underset{}{C}}-H$

(c)

$H-\overset{\overset{H}{|}}{\underset{\underset{H}{|}}{C}}-\overset{\overset{H}{|}}{\underset{\underset{H}{|}}{C}}-\overset{\overset{H}{|}}{\underset{\underset{H}{|}}{C}}-H$

$H-\overset{\overset{H}{|}}{\underset{\underset{H}{|}}{C}}-H$

$CH_3\underset{\underset{Br}{|}}{CH}CHCH_3$ $CH_3\underset{\underset{Br}{|}}{CH}CHCH_3$
$\overset{\overset{CH_3}{|}}{}$ $\overset{\overset{CH_3}{|}}{}$

$\overset{\overset{CH_3}{|}}{CH_2}\underset{\underset{Br}{|}}{CH}CH_2CH_3$

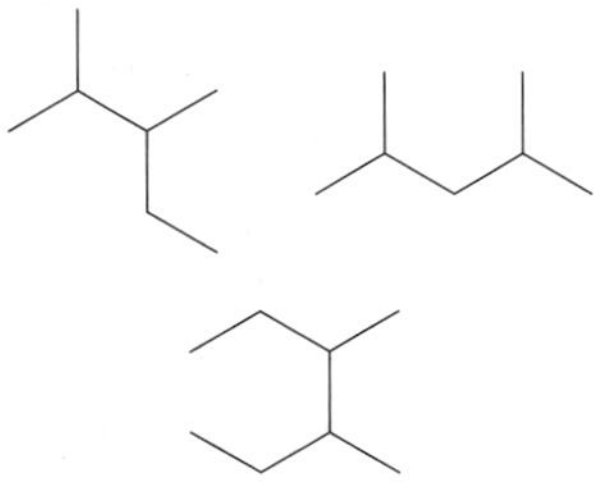

12.50 What is wrong with the following structures?

(a) $CH_3=CHCH_2CH_2OH$

(b) 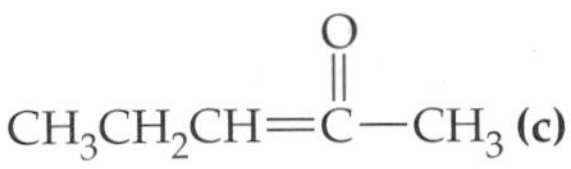 $CH_3CH_2CH=\overset{\overset{O}{\|}}{C}-CH_3$ (c) $CH_2CH_2CH_2C\equiv CCH_3$

12.51 There are two things wrong with the following structure. What are they?

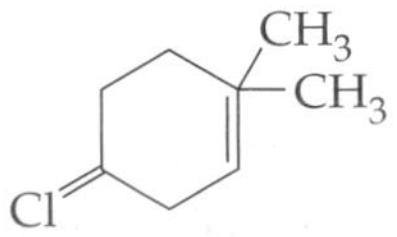

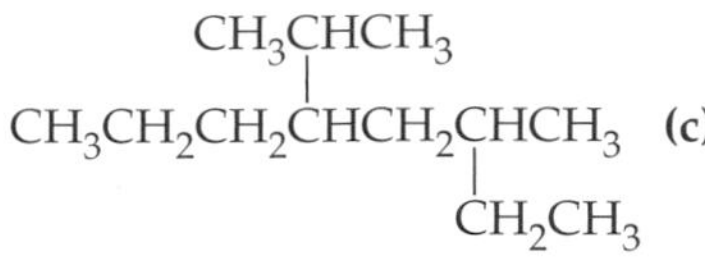

ALKANE NOMENCLATURE

12.52 What are the IUPAC names of the following alkanes?

(a) 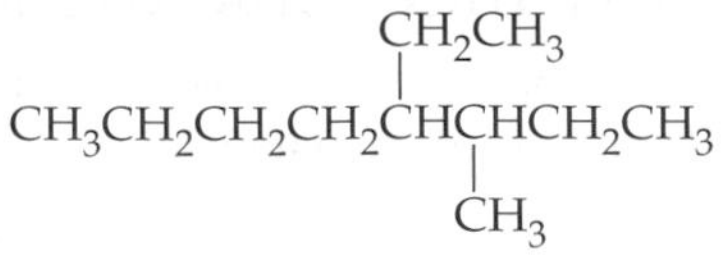 $CH_3CH_2CH_2CH_2\underset{\underset{CH_3}{|}}{\overset{\overset{CH_2CH_3}{|}}{C}}HCHCH_2CH_3$

(b) $CH_3CH_2CH_2\underset{\underset{CH_2CH_3}{|}}{\overset{\overset{CH_3CHCH_3}{|}}{C}}HCH_2CHCH_3$

(c) $CH_3\underset{\underset{CH_3}{|}}{\overset{\overset{CH_3}{|}}{C}}CH_2CH_2CH_2\underset{\underset{}{|}}{C}HCH_3$

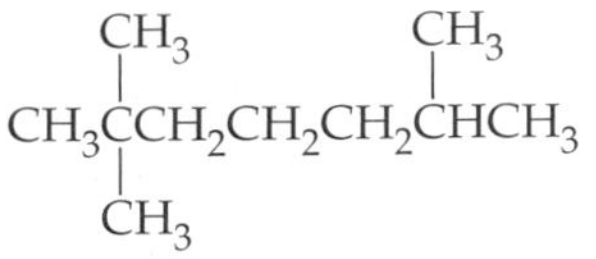

(d) 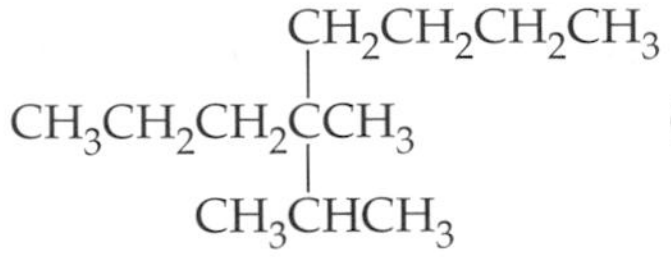 $CH_3CH_2CH_2\underset{\underset{CH_3CHCH_3}{|}}{\overset{\overset{CH_2CH_2CH_2CH_3}{|}}{C}}CH_3$

(e) 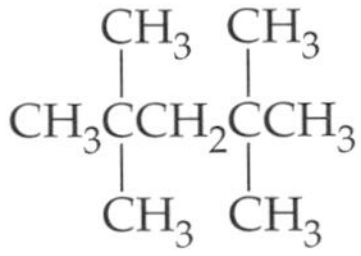 $CH_3\underset{\underset{CH_3}{|}}{\overset{\overset{CH_3}{|}}{C}}CH_2\underset{\underset{CH_3}{|}}{\overset{\overset{CH_3}{|}}{C}}CH_3$

(f) 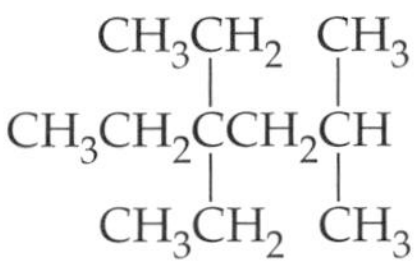 $CH_3CH_2\underset{\underset{CH_3CH_2}{|}}{\overset{\overset{CH_3CH_2}{|}}{C}}CH_2\underset{\underset{CH_3}{|}}{\overset{\overset{CH_3}{|}}{C}}H$

(g) 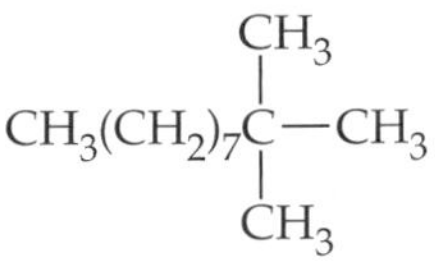 $CH_3(CH_2)_7\underset{\underset{CH_3}{|}}{\overset{\overset{CH_3}{|}}{C}}-CH_3$

12.53 Give IUPAC names for the five isomers with the formula C_6H_{14}.

12.54 Write condensed structures for the following compounds:

(a) 4-*tert*-Butyl-3,3,5-trimethylheptane

(b) 2,4-Dimethylpentane

(c) 4,4-Diethyl-3-methyloctane

(d) 3-Isopropyl-2,3,6,7-tetramethylnonane

(e) 3-Isobutyl-1-isopropyl-5-methylcycloheptane

(f) 1,1,3-Trimethylcyclopentane

12.55 Draw line structures for the following cycloalkanes:

(a) 1,1-Dimethylcyclopropane

(b) 1,2,3,4-Tetramethylcyclopentane

(c) Ethylhexane   (d) Cycloheptane

(e) 1-Methyl-3-propylcyclohexane

(f) 1-*sec*-Butyl-4-isopropylcyclooctane

12.56 Name the following cycloalkanes:

(a)

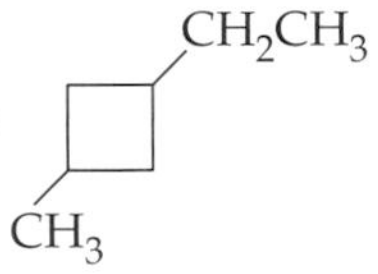

(b)

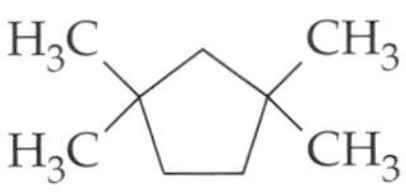

(c)

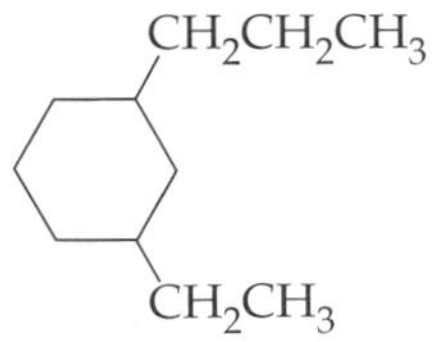

(d)

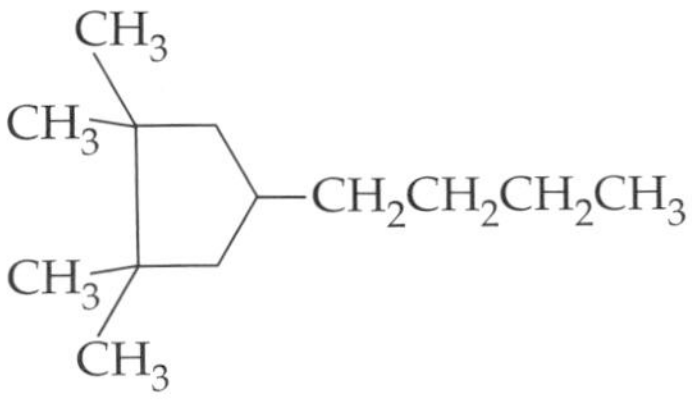

12.57 Name the following cycloalkanes:

(a)

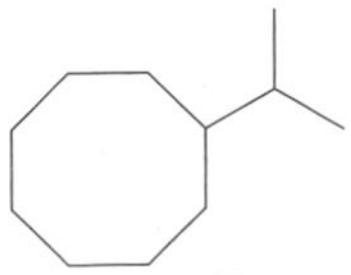

(b)

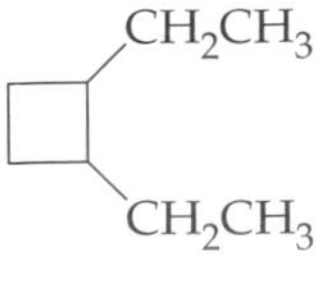

(c) 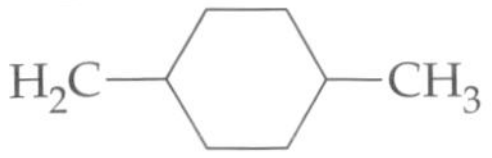 H_2C—⬡—CH_3

12.58 The following names are incorrect. Tell what is wrong with each, and provide the correct names.

(a)

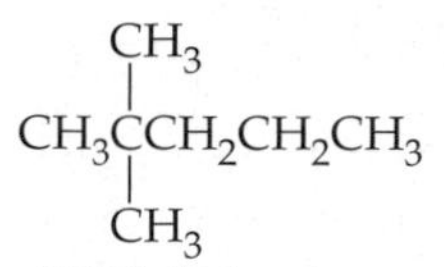

$$CH_3CCH_2CH_2CH_3$$

with CH_3 above and CH_3 below

2,2-Methylpentane

(b)

$$CH_3CH—CH_2—CHCH_3$$

with CH_3 groups

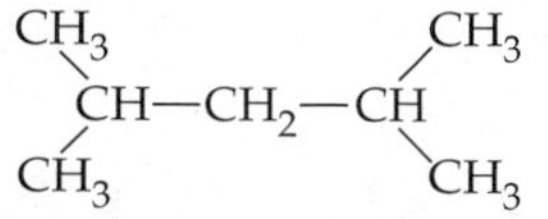

1,1-Diisopropylmethane

(c)

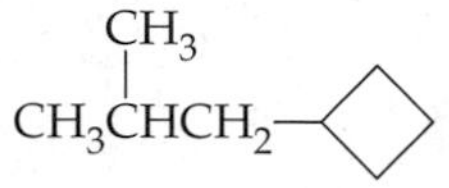

$$CH_3CHCH_2—\diamondsuit$$

with CH_3 above

1-Cyclobutyl-2-methylpropane

12.59 The following names are incorrect. Write the structural formula that agrees with the apparent name, and then write the correct name of the compound.

(a) 2-Ethylbutane

(b) 2-Isopropyl-2-methylpentane

(c) 5-Ethyl-1,1-methylcyclopentane

(d) 3-Ethyl-3,5,5-trimethylhexane

(e) 1,2-Dimethyl-4-ethylcyclohexane

(f) 2,4-Diethylpentane

(g) 5,5,6,6-Methyl-7,7-ethyldecane

12.60 Draw structures and give IUPAC names for the nine isomers of C_7H_{16}.

12.61 Draw the structural formulas and name all cyclic isomers with the formula C_5H_{10}.

REACTIONS OF ALKANES

12.62 Propane, commonly known as LP gas, burns in air to yield CO_2 and H_2O. Write a balanced equation for the reaction.

12.63 Write a balanced equation for the combustion of isooctane, C_8H_{16}, a component of gasoline.

12.64 Write the formulas of the three singly chlorinated isomers formed when 2,2-dimethylbutane reacts with Cl_2 in the presence of light.

12.65 Write the formulas of the seven doubly brominated isomers formed when 2,2-dimethylbutane reacts with Br_2 in the presence of light.

GENERAL QUESTIONS AND PROBLEMS

12.66 Identify the indicated functional groups in the following molecules:

(a) Testosterone, a male sex hormone

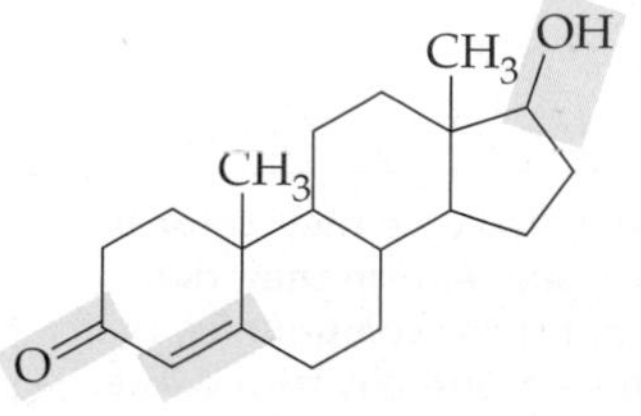

(b) Thienamycin, an antibiotic

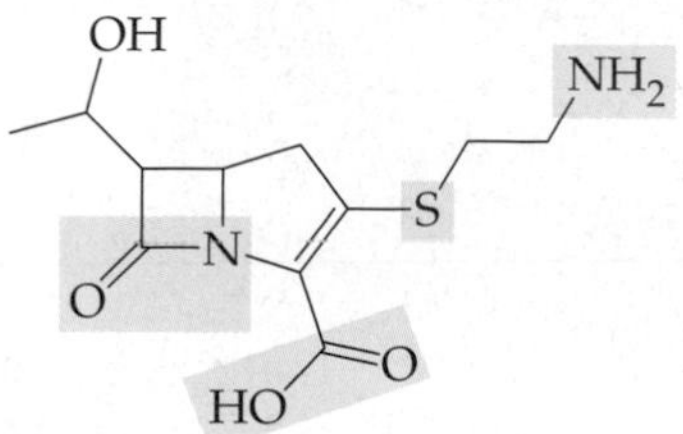

12.67 The line structure for aspartame is shown below:

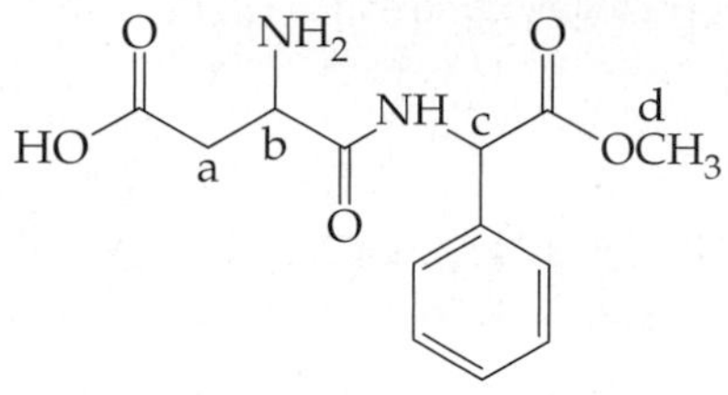

Identify carbons a–d as primary, secondary, tertiary, or quaternary.

12.68 Consider the compound shown in Problem 12.66a; how many tertiary carbons does it have?

12.69 If someone reported the preparation of a compound with the formula C_3H_9 most chemists would be skeptical. Why?

12.70 Most lipsticks are about 70% castor oil and wax. Why is lipstick more easily removed with petroleum jelly than with water?

12.71 When pentane is exposed to Br_2 in the presence of light, a halogenation reaction occurs. Write the formulas of:

(a) All possible products containing only one bromine.

(b) All possible products containing two bromines that are *not* on the same carbon.

12.72 Which do you think has a higher boiling point, pentane or neopentane (2,2-dimethylpropane)? Why?

12.73 Propose structures for the following:

(a) An aldehyde, C_4H_8O

(b) An iodo-substituted alkene, C_5H_9I

(c) A cycloalkane, C_7H_{14}

(d) A diene (dialkene), C_5H_8

CHEMISTRY IN ACTION

12.74 What is a chemical feedstock? [*Surprising Uses of Petroleum, p. 385*]

12.75 Why is the demand for synthetic rubber greater than that of natural rubber? [*Surprising Uses of Petroleum, p. 385*]

MASTERING REACTIONS

12.76 When ethyl alcohol is treated with acid, the initially formed intermediate is known as an oxonium ion:

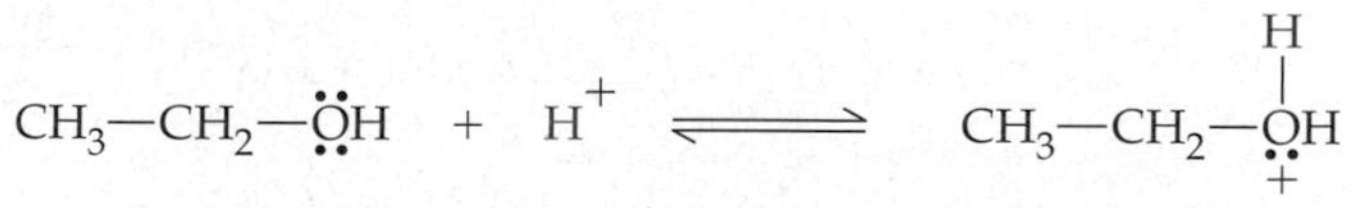

$$CH_3—CH_2—\overset{..}{O}H + H^+ \rightleftharpoons CH_3—CH_2—\overset{H}{\underset{+}{\overset{|}{O}}}H$$

Using the curved arrow formalism, show how this process most likely occurs.

12.77 Consider the following two-step process:

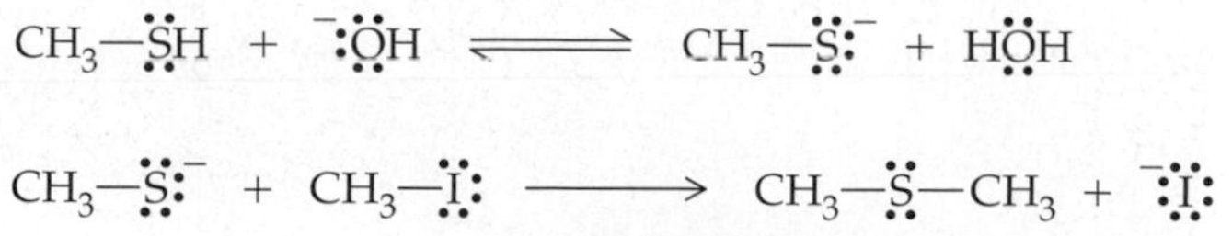

$$CH_3—\overset{..}{S}H + ^-\!\!:\overset{..}{O}H \rightleftharpoons CH_3—\overset{..}{\underset{..}{S}}\!:^- + H\overset{..}{O}H$$

$$CH_3—\overset{..}{\underset{..}{S}}\!:^- + CH_3—\overset{..}{I}\!: \longrightarrow CH_3—\overset{..}{S}—CH_3 + :\overset{..}{\underset{..}{I}}\!:^-$$

Using the curved arrow formalism, show how each step of this process is most likely to occur.

CHAPTER 13

Alkenes, Alkynes, and Aromatic Compounds

◄ Flamingos owe their color to alkene pigments in their diet. Without these compounds, their feathers eventually turn white.

1. **What are alkenes, alkynes, and aromatic compounds?**
   THE GOAL: Be able to recognize the functional groups in these three families of unsaturated organic compounds and give examples of each. (◀◀ B.)

2. **How are alkenes, alkynes, and aromatic compounds named?**
   THE GOAL: Be able to name an alkene, alkyne, or simple aromatic compound from its structure or write the structure, given the name. (◀◀ C., E.)

3. **What are cis–trans isomers?**
   THE GOAL: Be able to identify cis–trans isomers of alkenes and predict their occurrence. (◀◀ A., D.)

4. **What are the categories of organic reactions?**
   THE GOAL: Be able to recognize and describe addition, elimination, substitution, and rearrangement reactions.

5. **What are the typical reactions of alkenes, alkynes, and aromatic compounds?**
   THE GOAL: Be able to predict the products of reactions of alkenes, alkynes, and aromatic compounds.

6. **(Mastery Goal) How do organic reactions take place?**
   THE GOAL: Be able to show how addition reactions occur.

CONCEPTS TO REVIEW

A. VSEPR and Molecular Shapes
(Section 4.8)

B. Families of Organic Molecules: Functional Groups
(Section 12.2)

C. Drawing Organic Structures
(Section 12.4)

D. The Shapes of Organic Molecules
(Section 12.5)

E. Naming Alkanes
(Section 12.6)

In this and the remaining four chapters on organic chemistry, we examine some families of organic compounds whose functional groups give them characteristic properties. In this chapter, we will look at the chemistry of molecules that contain carbon–carbon multiple bonds. *Alkenes*, such as ethylene, contain a double-bond functional group; *alkynes*, such as acetylene, contain a triple-bond functional group; and *aromatic compounds*, such as benzene, contain a six-membered ring of carbon atoms usually pictured as having three alternating double bonds with properties different from those of a typical alkene. All three functional groups are widespread in nature and are found in many biologically important molecules.

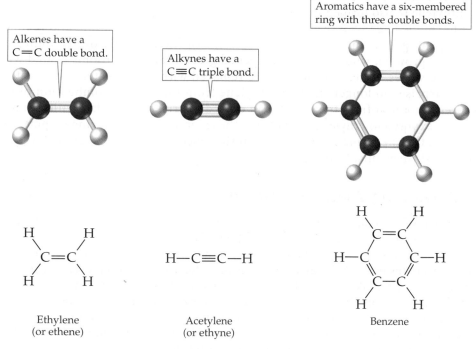

Ethylene
(or ethene)

Acetylene
(or ethyne)

Benzene

13.1 Alkenes and Alkynes

Alkanes, introduced in Chapter 12, are often referred to as **saturated** because each carbon atom has four single bonds. Because this is the maximum number of single bonds a carbon can have, no more atoms can be added to any of the carbons in an

Saturated A molecule in which each carbon atom has the maximum number of single bonds possible (four).

▶▶▶ Recall from Section 12.5 that rotation around C—C single bonds allows a molecule to exist in multiple conformations.

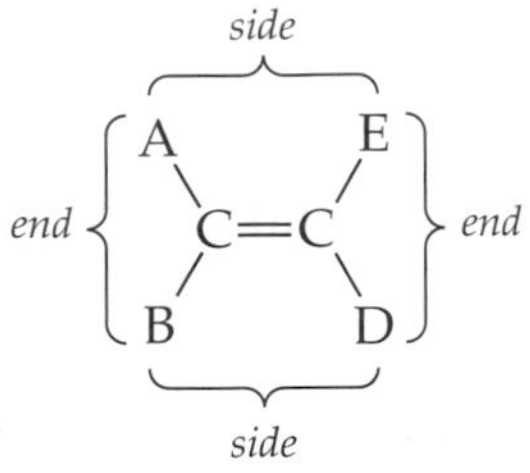

The two carbons and four attached atoms that make up the double-bond functional group lie in a plane. Unlike the situation in alkanes, where free rotation around the C—C single bond occurs, there is no rotation around a double bond, and the molecules are more rigid. However, their restricted freedom of rotation makes a new kind of isomerism possible for alkenes. As a consequence of their rigid nature, alkenes possess *ends* and *sides*:

side

$$end \left\{ \begin{matrix} A \\ \\ B \end{matrix} C=C \begin{matrix} E \\ \\ D \end{matrix} \right\} end$$

side

To see this new kind of isomerism, look at the four C_4H_8 compounds shown below. When written as condensed structures, there appear to be only three alkene isomers of formula C_4H_8: 1-butene ($CH_2=CHCH_2CH_3$), 2-butene ($CH_3CH=CHCH_3$), and 2-methylpropene ($(CH_3)_2C=CH_2$). The compounds 1-butene and 2-butene are constitutional isomers of each other because their double bonds occur at different positions along the chain, and 2-methylpropene is a constitutional isomer of both 1-butene and 2-butene because it has the same molecular formula but a different connection of carbon atoms (see Section 12.3). In fact, though, there are *four* isomers of C_4H_8. Because rotation cannot occur around carbon–carbon double bonds, *there are two different 2-butenes.* In one isomer, the two —CH_3 groups are on the same side of the double bond; in the other isomer, they are on opposite sides of the double bond.

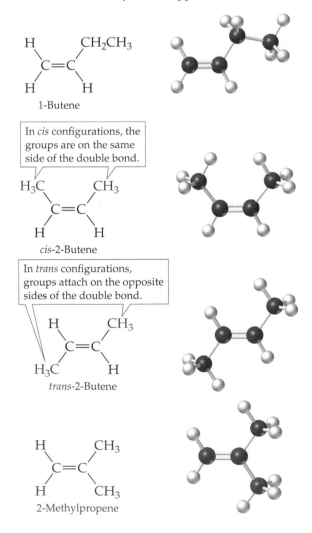

$$\begin{matrix} H \\ \\ H \end{matrix} C=C \begin{matrix} CH_2CH_3 \\ \\ H \end{matrix}$$

1-Butene

In *cis* configurations, the groups are on the same side of the double bond.

$$\begin{matrix} H_3C \\ \\ H \end{matrix} C=C \begin{matrix} CH_3 \\ \\ H \end{matrix}$$

cis-2-Butene

In *trans* configurations, groups attach on the opposite sides of the double bond.

$$\begin{matrix} H \\ \\ H_3C \end{matrix} C=C \begin{matrix} CH_3 \\ \\ H \end{matrix}$$

trans-2-Butene

$$\begin{matrix} H \\ \\ H \end{matrix} C=C \begin{matrix} CH_3 \\ \\ CH_3 \end{matrix}$$

2-Methylpropene

The two 2-butenes are called **cis–trans isomers**. They have the same formula and connections between atoms but have different three-dimensional structures because of the way that groups attach to different sides of the double bond. In this case, the isomer with its methyl groups on the same side of the double bond is named *cis*-2-butene, and the isomer with its methyl groups on opposite sides of the double bond is named *trans*-2-butene.

Cis–trans isomerism is possible whenever an alkene has two *different* substituent groups on each of its ends. (This means that in the earlier drawing illustrating the sides and ends of an alkene molecule, A ≠ B and D ≠ E.) If one of the carbons composing the double bond is attached to two identical groups, cis–trans isomerism cannot exist. In 2-methyl-1-butene, for example, cis–trans isomerism is not possible because C1 is bonded to two identical groups (hydrogen atoms). To convince yourself of this, mentally flip either one of these two structures top to bottom; note that it becomes identical to the other structure:

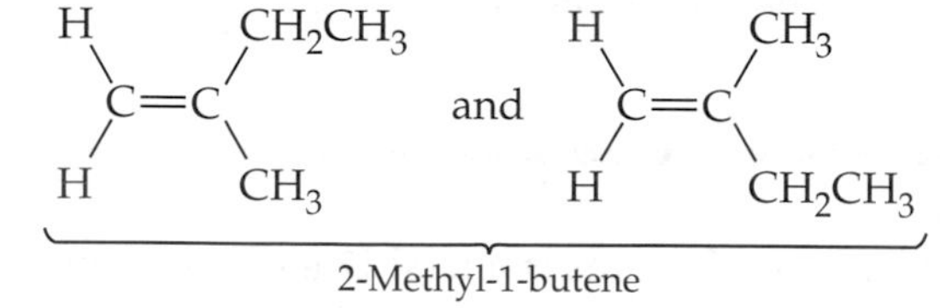

> **Cis–trans isomer** Alkenes that have the same connections between atoms but differ in their three-dimensional structures because of the way that groups attach to different sides of the double bond.

These compounds are identical. Because the carbon left of the double bond has two H atoms attached, cis–trans isomerism is impossible.

2-Methyl-1-butene

In 2-pentene, however, the structures do not become identical when one of them is flipped, so cis–trans isomerism does occur:

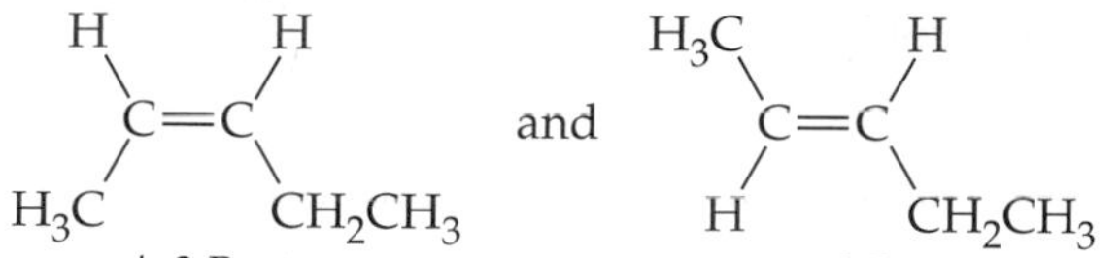

These compounds are not identical. Neither carbon of the double bond has two identical groups attached to it.

cis-2-Pentene   *trans*-2-Pentene

It is important to note that the molecule must remain intact when you perform this analysis; you cannot break and reform any bonds when flipping and comparing the two structures.

The two substituents that are on the same side of the double bond in an alkene are said to be cis to each other, and those on opposite sides of the double bond are said to be trans to each other. In our generic molecule on the previous page showing ends and sides, for example, A and E are cis to each other, B and D are cis to each other, B and E are trans to each other, and A and D are trans to each other. Thus, in alkenes, the terms cis and trans are used in two ways: (i) as a *relative* term to indicate how various groups are attached to the double-bond carbons (for example, "groups A and E are cis") and (ii) in nomenclature as a way to indicate how the longest chain in the molecule goes in, through, and out of the double bond (for example, *cis*-2-butene and *trans*-2-butene).

Worked Example 13.3 Molecular Structure: Cis and Trans Isomers

Draw structures for both the cis and trans isomers of 2-hexene.

ANALYSIS First, draw a condensed structure of 2-hexene to see which groups are attached to the double-bond carbons:

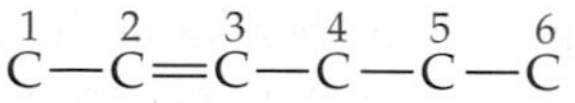

$$\overset{1}{C}-\overset{2}{C}=\overset{3}{C}-\overset{4}{C}-\overset{5}{C}-\overset{6}{C} \quad \text{2-Hexene}$$

Next, begin to draw the two isomers. Choose one end of the double bond, and attach its groups in the *same way* to generate two identical partial structures:

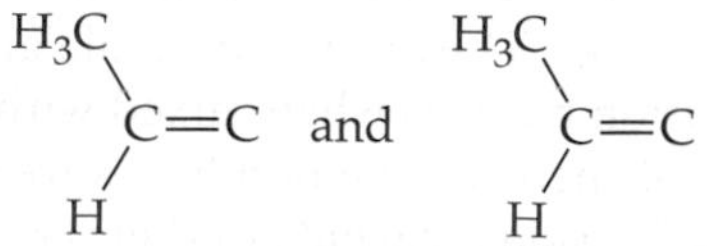

Finally, attach groups to the other end in the two possible *different ways*.

As an example of an elimination reaction, we will see in the next chapter that an alcohol, such as ethanol, splits apart into an alkene and water when treated with an acid catalyst. This specific process is known as a *dehydration reaction*: (Mastering Reactions: How Elimination Reactions Occur on p. 441)

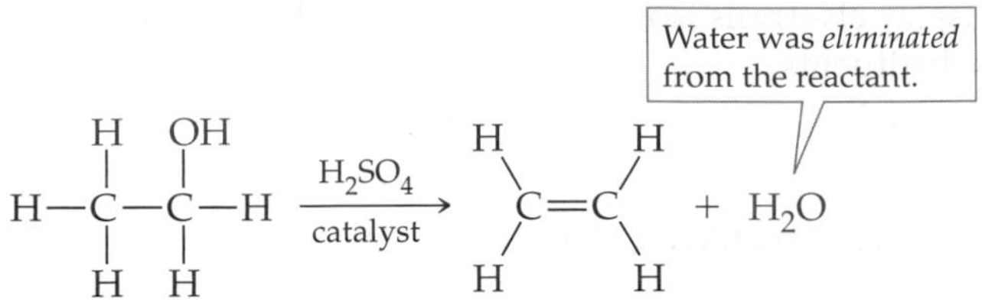

Water was *eliminated* from the reactant.

$$H-\underset{\underset{H}{|}}{\overset{\overset{H}{|}}{C}}-\underset{\underset{H}{|}}{\overset{\overset{OH}{|}}{C}}-H \xrightarrow[\text{catalyst}]{H_2SO_4} \underset{\underset{H}{}}{\overset{\overset{H}{}}{C}}=\underset{\underset{H}{}}{\overset{\overset{H}{}}{C}} + H_2O$$

Ethanol   Ethylene

Substitution reaction A general reaction type in which an atom or group of atoms in a molecule is replaced by another atom or group of atoms.

• **Substitution Reactions** Substitutions occur when two reactants exchange parts to give two new products, a process we can generalize as

These two reactants exchange parts ... $AB + C \longrightarrow AC + B$ ... to give these two products.

As an example of a substitution reaction, we saw in Section 12.8 that alkanes, such as methane, react with Cl_2 in the presence of ultraviolet light to yield alkyl chlorides. Here, a —Cl group substitutes for the —H group of the alkane, and two new products result:

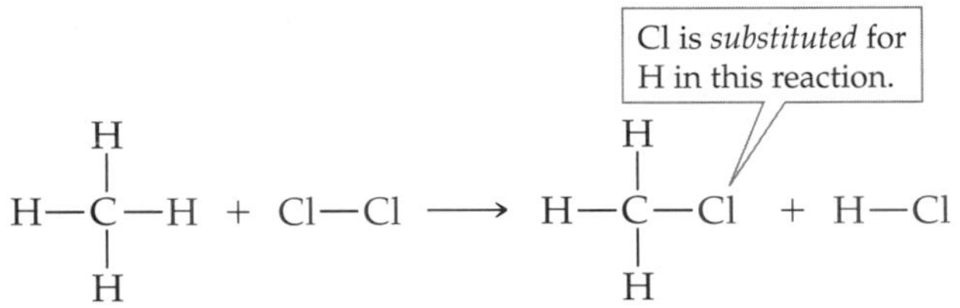

Cl is *substituted* for H in this reaction.

$$H-\underset{\underset{H}{|}}{\overset{\overset{H}{|}}{C}}-H + Cl-Cl \longrightarrow H-\underset{\underset{H}{|}}{\overset{\overset{H}{|}}{C}}-Cl + H-Cl$$

Methane   Chloromethane

A much more common type of substitution reaction is one that involves alkyl halides and Lewis bases, such as the reaction shown here:

$$CH_3CH_2CH_2Cl + CH_3O^- Na^+ \longrightarrow CH_3CH_2CH_2OCH_3 + Na^+Cl^-$$

We previously saw another example of this type of substitution reaction in Chapter 12 in Mastering Reactions: Organic Chemistry and the Curved Arrow Formalism on p. 382. We'll learn more about alkyl halides and Lewis bases in Chapters 14 and 15.

Rearrangement reaction A general reaction type in which a molecule undergoes bond reorganization to yield an isomer.

• **Rearrangement Reactions** Rearrangements are of bonds and atoms to yield a single product that is an isomer of the reactant. A generalized example of one type of rearrangement seen in organic chemistry is

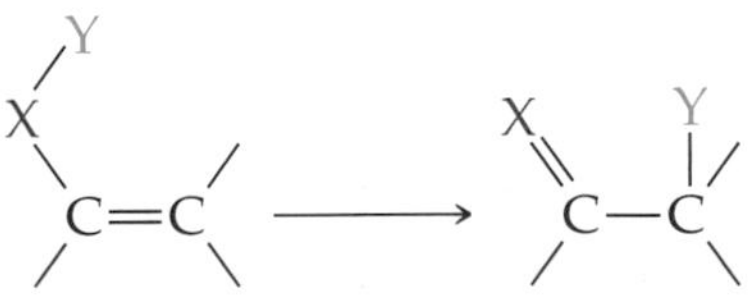

$$\underset{}{\overset{}{C}}=\underset{}{\overset{}{C}} \longrightarrow \underset{}{\overset{}{C}}-\underset{}{\overset{}{C}}$$

Rearrangement reactions are important in organic chemistry as well as biochemistry. Because of their complex nature, however, we will not discuss them in detail in this book. An example of a rearrangement is the conversion of *cis*-2-butene into its isomer *trans*-2-butene by treatment with an acid catalyst:

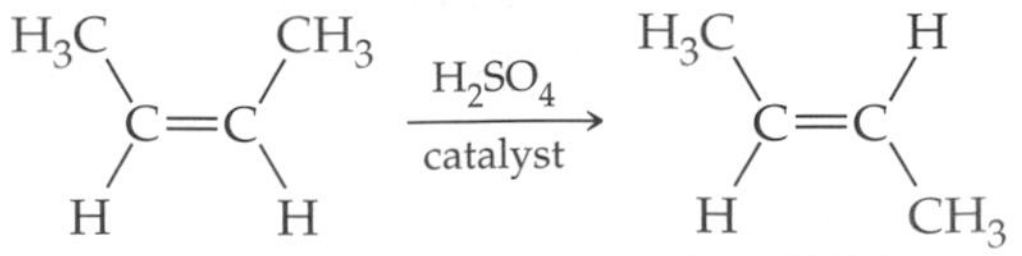

$$\underset{\underset{H}{}}{\overset{\overset{H_3C}{}}{C}}=\underset{\underset{H}{}}{\overset{\overset{CH_3}{}}{C}} \xrightarrow[\text{catalyst}]{H_2SO_4} \underset{\underset{H}{}}{\overset{\overset{H_3C}{}}{C}}=\underset{\underset{CH_3}{}}{\overset{\overset{H}{}}{C}}$$

cis-2-Butene   *trans*-2-Butene

This simple-looking interconversion involves the breaking of the C=C bond followed by rotation and reformation of the double bond. A more common rearrangement seen in organic chemistry is the keto-enol interconversion known as keto-enol tautomerization:

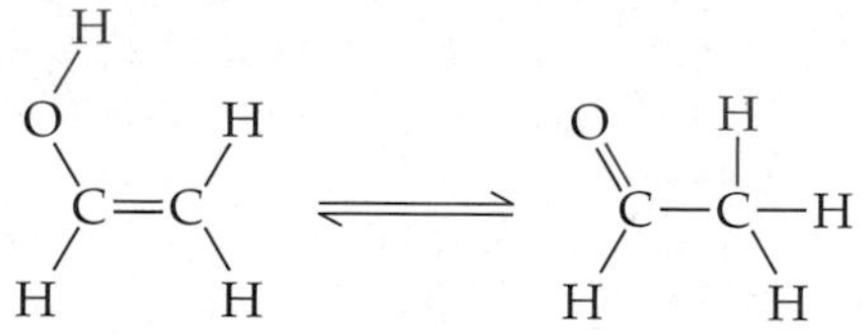

Worked Example 13.4 Identifying Reactions of Alkenes

Classify the following alkene reactions as addition, elimination, or substitution reactions:

(a) $CH_3CH{=}CH_2 + H_2 \longrightarrow CH_3CH_2CH_3$

(b) $CH_3CH_2CH_2OH \xrightarrow[\text{catalyst}]{H_2SO_4} CH_3CH{=}CH_2 + H_2O$

(c) $CH_3CH_2Cl + KOH \longrightarrow CH_3CH_2OH + KCl$

ANALYSIS Determine whether atoms have been added to the starting compound (addition), removed from the starting compound (elimination), or switched with another reactant (substitution).

SOLUTION

(a) Two H atoms have been *added* in place of the double bond, so this is an *addition* reaction.

(b) A water molecule (H_2O) has been formed by *removing* an H atom and an —OH group from adjacent C atoms, forming a double bond in the process, so this is an *elimination* reaction.

(c) The reactants $(CH_3CH_2Cl$ and KOH) have *traded* the —OH and the —Cl substituent groups, so this is a *substitution* reaction.

PROBLEM 13.7
Classify the following reactions as an addition, elimination, substitution, or rearrangement:

(a) $CH_3Br + NaOH \longrightarrow CH_3OH + NaBr$

(b) $H_2C{=}CH_2 + HCl \longrightarrow CH_3CH_2Cl$

(c) $CH_3CH_2Br \longrightarrow H_2C{=}CH_2 + HBr$

PROBLEM 13.8
In the box Chemistry in Action: The Chemistry of Vision and Color on p. 406, the role of the compound 11-*cis*-retinal in vision was discussed.

(a) After the reaction of 11-*cis*-retinal with opsin, classify the reaction rhodopsin undergoes in the presence of light to produce 11-*trans*-rhodopsin.

(b) How many hydrogens are present in 11-*cis*-retinal?

(c) What are the functional groups present in this molecule?

CHEMISTRY IN ACTION

The Chemistry of Vision and Color

One thing we often take for granted, until we lose it or some aspect of it, is our vision. The vibrant colors we see, the smooth flow of motion we observe, the ability of our eyes to adapt to both bright sunlight and pitch darkness—what is the role of chemistry in the diverse functions of this key sensory system? While the answer to that is somewhat complicated, a critical player in the ability to see is vitamin A, an important biological alkene.

A vitamin is an organic molecule required by the body in trace amounts and usually obtained through diet (Section 19.10). Carrots, peaches, sweet potatoes, and other yellow vegetables are rich in beta-carotene, a purple-orange alkene that provides our main dietary source of vitamin A (also known as *retinol*). The enzymatic conversion of beta-carotene to vitamin A takes place in the mucosal cells of the small intestine; vitamin A is then stored in the liver, from which it can be transported to the eye. In the eye, vitamin A is oxidized to *retinal*, which undergoes cis–trans isomerization of its C11–C12 double bond to produce 11-*cis*-retinal. Reaction with the protein *opsin* then produces the light-sensitive substance *rhodopsin*.

The human eye has two kinds of light-sensitive cells, *rod cells* and *cone cells*. The 3 million rod cells are primarily responsible for seeing in dim light, whereas the 100 million cone cells are responsible for seeing in bright light and for the perception of

bright colors. When light strikes the rod cells, cis–trans isomerization of the C11–C12 double bond occurs via a rearrangement reaction, and 11-*trans*-rhodopsin, also called *metarhodopsin II*, is produced. This cis–trans isomerization is accompanied by a change in molecular geometry, which in turn causes a nerve impulse to be sent to the brain, where it is perceived as vision. Metarhodopsin II is then changed back to 11-*cis*-retinal for use in another vision cycle.

While this sheds light on how we see, it does not tell us what causes the actual colors themselves. We have already seen that beta-carotene is a purple-orange color; other organic compounds such as the purple dye mauveine and the plant pigment cyanidin are also brightly colored. What do all these compounds have in common? If you look carefully at each structure, you will see that each has numerous alternating double and single bonds (known as *conjugation*).

In Section 13.8, we will discuss aromatic systems, the most famous of which is benzene. Benzene, as well as compounds like mauveine and beta-carotene, belong to a larger class of molecules known as *conjugated systems*. Conjugated systems are molecules that contain arrays of alternating double and single bonds, and the electrons within the double bonds are said to be spread out, or *delocalized*, over the whole molecule. Whenever there is conjugation in a molecule, a delocalized region of electron density is formed that is in turn capable of absorbing light. Organic compounds with small numbers of delocalized electrons, such as benzene (which has three conjugated double bonds), absorb in the ultraviolet region of the electromagnetic spectrum, which our eyes

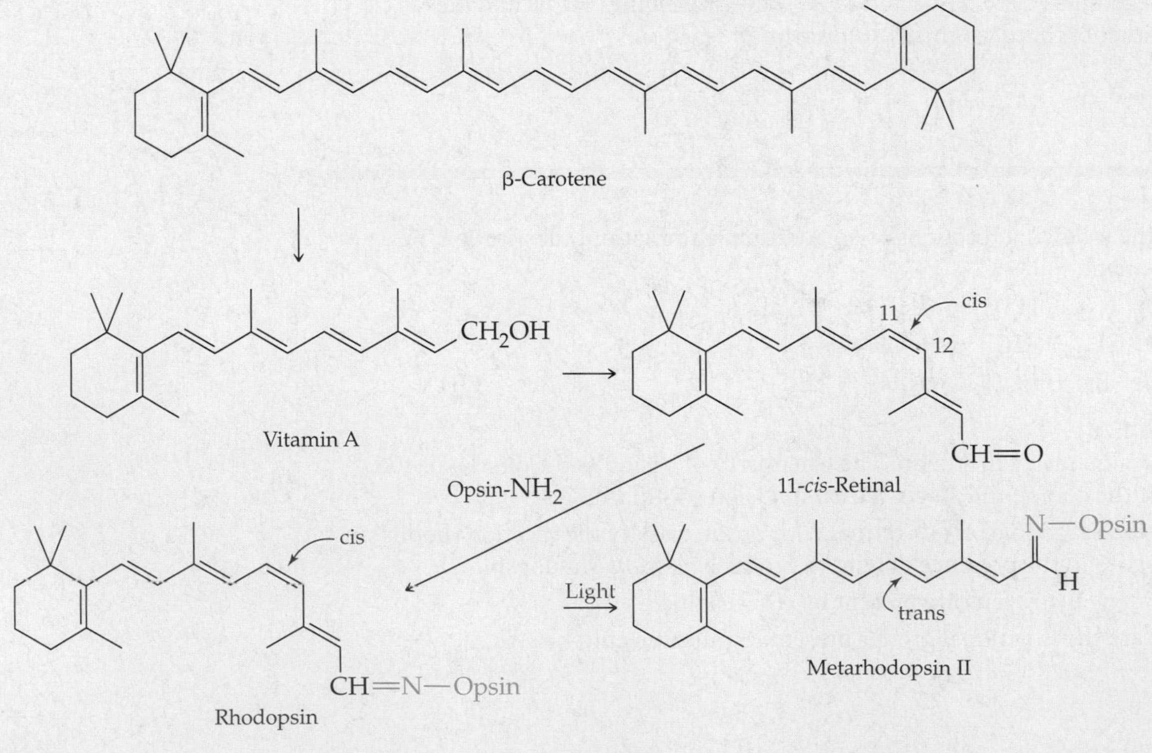

β-Carotene

Vitamin A

11-*cis*-Retinal

Rhodopsin

Metarhodopsin II

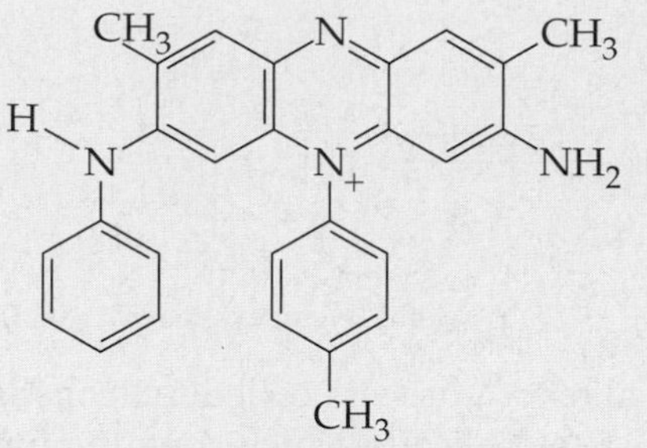

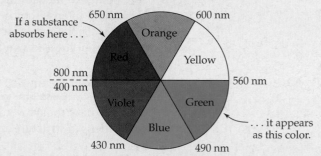

Mauverine
(the first synthetic dye)

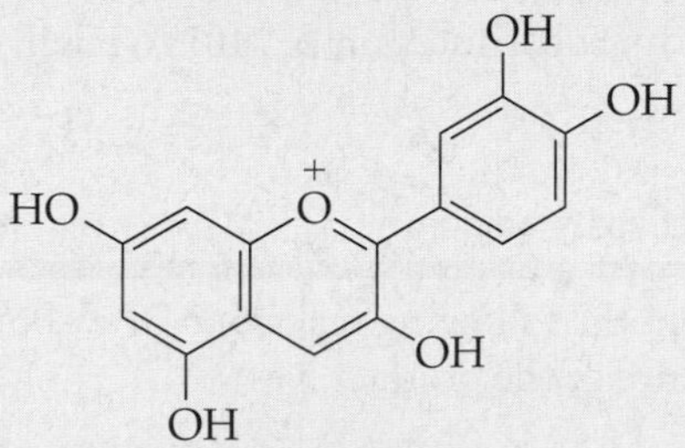

Cyanidin
(reddish-blue color in flowers
and cranberries)

cannot detect. Compounds with longer stretches of alternating double and single bonds (10 or more) absorb in the visible region. The presence of a charged atom in the conjugated system, such as the nitrogen in mauve or the oxygen in cyanidin, allow absorption in the visible range to occur with fewer conjugated double bonds.

The color that we see is complementary to the color that is absorbed; that is, we see what is left of the white light after certain colors have been absorbed. For example, the plant pigment cyanidin absorbs greenish-yellow light and thus appears reddish-blue. It is speculated that this is also the reason that red-colored mulch seems to promote plant growth: the reflected red color is absorbed by the green plant, creating the effect of additional incoming sunlight for photosynthesis.

If a substance absorbs here . . .
650 nm
600 nm
Orange
Red
800 nm
400 nm
Yellow
560 nm
Violet
Green
. . . it appears as this color.
Blue
430 nm
490 nm

▲ **Using an artist's color wheel, it is possible to determine the observed color of a substance by knowing the color of the light absorbed. Observed and absorbed colors are complementary. Thus, if a substance absorbs red light, it has a green color.**

See Chemistry in Action Problems 13.84–13.87 at the end of the chapter.

13.6 Reactions of Alkenes and Alkynes

Most of the reactions of carbon–carbon multiple bonds are *addition reactions*. A generalized reagent we might write as X—Y adds to the multiple bond in the unsaturated reactant to yield a saturated product that has only single bonds:

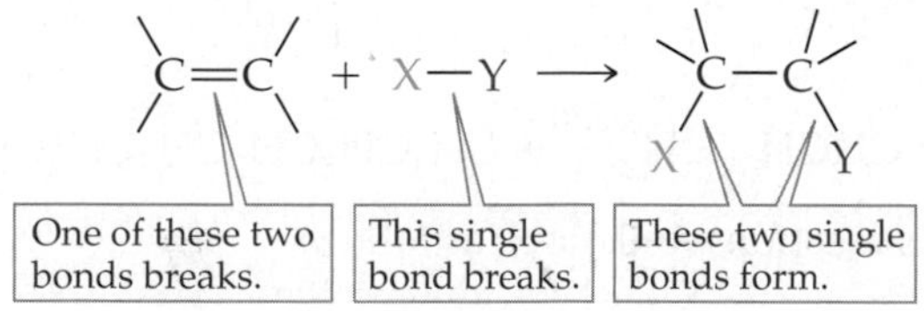

$$\text{C=C} + \text{X—Y} \longrightarrow \text{C—C}$$
$$\qquad\qquad\qquad\qquad X\ \ \ Y$$

An addition reaction

| One of these two bonds breaks. | This single bond breaks. | These two single bonds form. |

Alkenes and alkynes react similarly in many ways, but we will look mainly at alkenes in this chapter because they are more commonly found in nature and industrially are used as precursors to other organic molecules. Simple molecules that are prepared in large quantities for this purpose are known as *chemical feedstocks* (see Chemistry in Action: Surprising Uses of Petroleum on p. 385).

Addition of H₂ to Alkenes and Alkynes: Hydrogenation

Alkenes and alkynes react with hydrogen in the presence of a metal catalyst such as palladium to yield the corresponding alkane product:

(An alkene) $\text{C=C} + \text{H}_2 \xrightarrow{\text{Catalyst}}$ $-\overset{\text{H}\ \ \text{H}}{\underset{\text{H}\ \ \text{H}}{\text{C}-\text{C}}}-$ (An alkane)

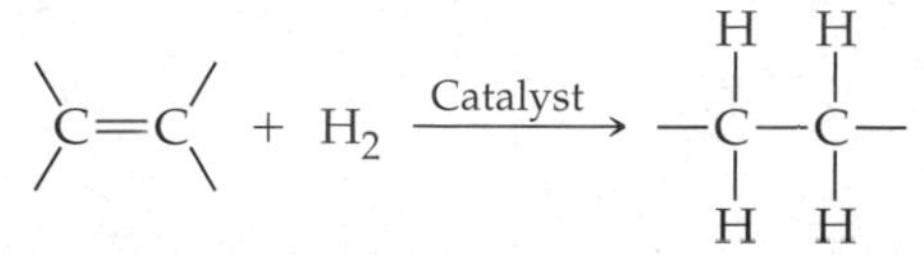

(An alkyne) $-\text{C}\equiv\text{C}- + 2\,\text{H}_2 \xrightarrow{\text{Catalyst}}$ $-\overset{\text{H}\ \ \text{H}}{\underset{\text{H}\ \ \text{H}}{\text{C}-\text{C}}}-$ (An alkane)

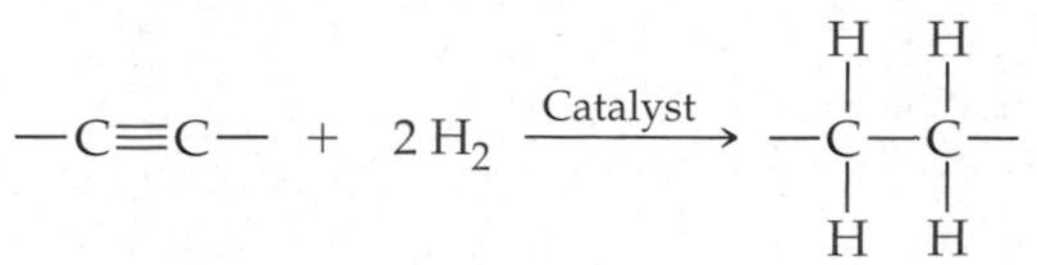

For example,

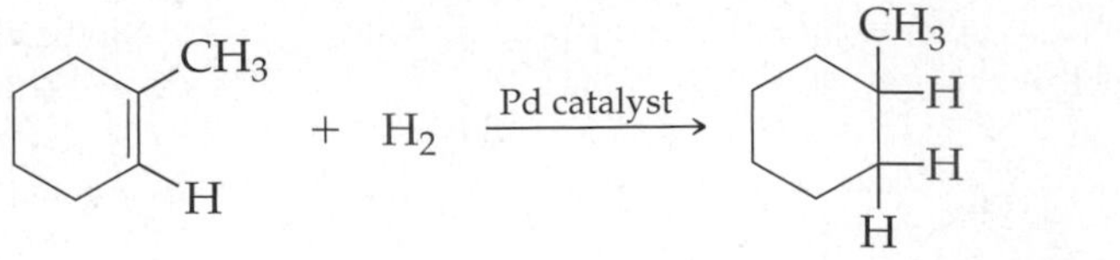

1-Methylcyclohexene   Methylcyclohexane (85% yield)

Hydrogenation The addition of H_2 to a multiple bond to give a saturated product.

The addition of hydrogen to an alkene, a process called **hydrogenation**, is used commercially to convert unsaturated vegetable oils, which contain numerous double bonds, to the saturated fats used in margarine and cooking fats. This process has come under intense scrutiny in recent years because it creates *trans*-fatty acids in the product (see Chemistry in Action: Butter and Its Substitutes on p. 740). We will see the structures of these fats and oils in Chapter 23.

Worked Example 13.5 Organic Reactions: Addition

What product would you obtain from the following reaction? Draw both the condensed structure and the line structure of the product.

$$CH_3CH_2CH_2CH{=}CHCH_3 + H_2 \xrightarrow{\text{Pd}} ?$$

ANALYSIS   Rewrite the reactant, showing a single bond and two partial bonds in place of the double bond:

$$CH_3CH_2CH_2CH{-}CHCH_3$$

Then, add a hydrogen to each carbon atom of the double bond, and rewrite the product in condensed form:

$$CH_3CH_2CH_2CH{-}CHCH_3 \quad \text{is the same as} \quad CH_3CH_2CH_2CH_2CH_2CH_3$$
$$\qquad\qquad\quad \underset{H}{|} \quad \underset{H}{|} \qquad\qquad\qquad\qquad\qquad\qquad \text{Hexane}$$

SOLUTION
The reaction is

$$CH_3CH_2CH_2CH{=}CHCH_3 + H_2 \xrightarrow{\text{Pd}} CH_3CH_2CH_2CH_2CH_2CH_3$$

In line structure format, this reaction would look as follows:

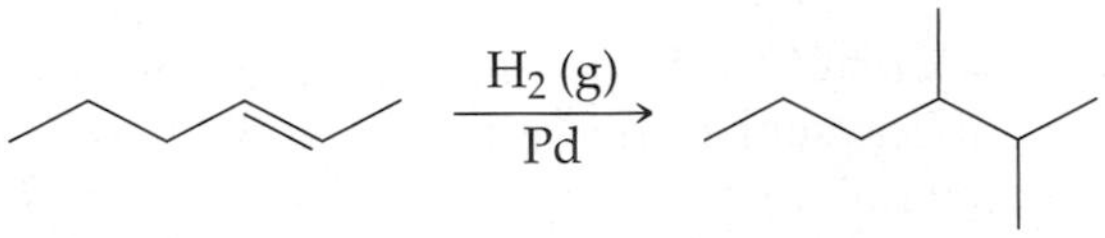

PROBLEM 13.9
Write the structures of the products from the following hydrogenation reactions:

(a) 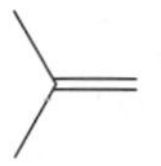 $+ H_2 \xrightarrow{\text{Pd}} ?$

(b) *cis*-2-Butene $+ H_2 \xrightarrow{\text{Pd}} ?$

(c) *trans*-3-Heptene $+ H_2 \xrightarrow{\text{Pd}} ?$

(d) 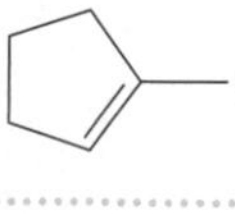 $-CH_3 + H_2 \xrightarrow{\text{Pd}} ?$

Addition of Cl_2 and Br_2 to Alkenes: Halogenation

Alkenes react with the halogens Br_2 and Cl_2 to give 1,2-dihaloalkane addition products in a **halogenation** reaction:

$$\underset{/}{\overset{\backslash}{C}}=\underset{\backslash}{\overset{/}{C}} + X_2 \longrightarrow -\underset{\underset{X}{|}}{C}-\underset{\underset{X}{|}}{C}-$$

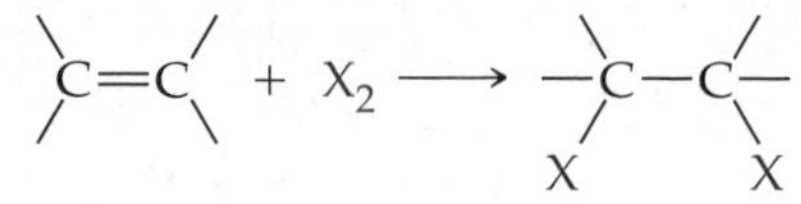

(A 1,2-dihaloalkane where X = Br or Cl)

Halogenation The addition of Cl_2 or Br_2 to a multiple bond to give a dihalide product.

For example,

$$\underset{H}{\overset{H}{\diagdown}}C=C\underset{H}{\overset{H}{\diagup}} + Cl_2 \longrightarrow H-\underset{\underset{Cl}{|}}{\overset{\overset{H}{|}}{C}}-\underset{\underset{Cl}{|}}{\overset{\overset{H}{|}}{C}}-H$$

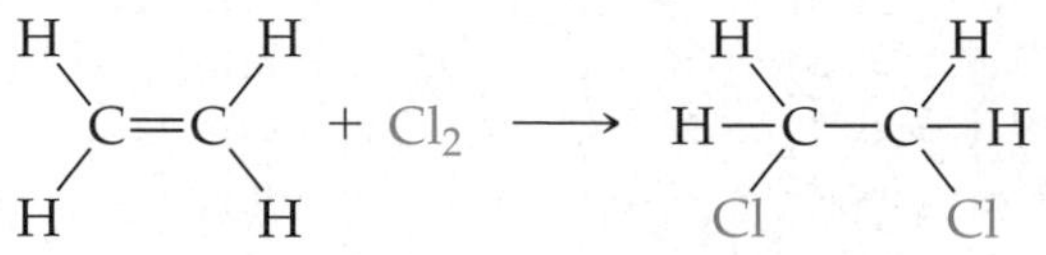

Ethylene   1, 2-Dichloroethane

This reaction is used to manufacture nearly eight million tons of 1,2-dichloroethane each year in the United States. It is the first step in making the widely used poly(vinyl chloride) plastics (PVC).

Another halogen, Br_2, provides a convenient test for the presence of a carbon–carbon double or triple bond in a molecule (Figure 13.1). A few drops of a reddish-brown solution of Br_2 are added to a sample of an unknown compound. Immediate disappearance of the color reveals the presence of the multiple bond, because the bromine reacts with the compound to form a colorless dibromide. This test can also be used to determine the level of unsaturation of fats (Chapter 23). Although chlorine also adds to double bonds, it is not used to test for their presence because it is a gas at room temperature and is harder to handle. Furthermore, its color in solution is a very light yellow, and thus, a color change is more difficult to detect.

(a)

(b)

◄ **Figure 13.1**
Testing for unsaturation with bromine.
(a) No color change results when the bromine solution is added to hexane (C_6H_{14}). (b) Disappearance of the bromine color when it is added to 1-hexene (C_6H_{12}) indicates the presence of a double bond.

PROBLEM 13.10

What products would you expect from the following halogenation reactions?

(a) 2-Methylpropene + Br_2 $\longrightarrow$?   (b) 1-Pentene + Cl_2 $\longrightarrow$?

(c) $CH_3CH_2CH=\overset{\overset{\displaystyle CH_3}{|}}{C}CH_2\underset{\underset{\displaystyle CH_3}{|}}{C}HCH_3 + Cl_2 \longrightarrow$?

(d) 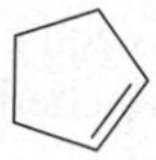 ⬠ + Br_2 $\longrightarrow$?

Addition of HBr and HCl to Alkenes

Alkenes react with hydrogen bromide (HBr) to yield *alkyl bromides* (R—Br) and with hydrogen chloride (HCl) to yield *alkyl chlorides* (R—Cl), in what are called **hydrohalogenation** reactions:

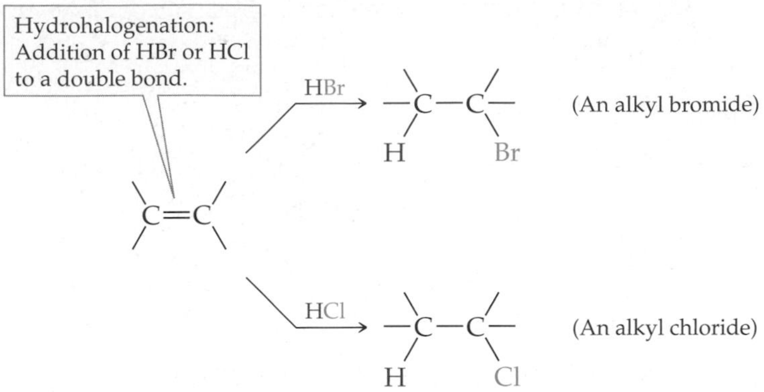

Hydrohalogenation The addition of HCl or HBr to a multiple bond to give an alkyl halide product.

Hydrohalogenation: Addition of HBr or HCl to a double bond.

$$\text{C}=\text{C} \xrightarrow{\text{HBr}} \underset{\text{H}}{\overset{}{-}}\text{C}-\underset{\text{Br}}{\overset{}{-}}\text{C}- \quad \text{(An alkyl bromide)}$$

$$\xrightarrow{\text{HCl}} \underset{\text{H}}{\overset{}{-}}\text{C}-\underset{\text{Cl}}{\overset{}{-}}\text{C}- \quad \text{(An alkyl chloride)}$$

The addition of HBr to 2-methylpropene is an example:

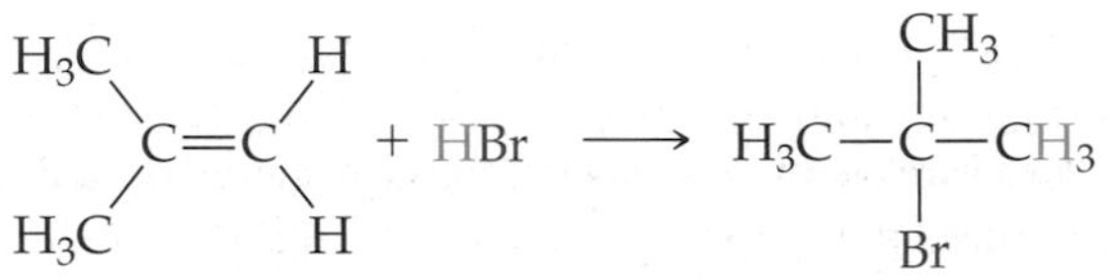

$$\underset{\text{H}_3\text{C}}{\overset{\text{H}_3\text{C}}{>}}\text{C}=\text{C}\underset{\text{H}}{\overset{\text{H}}{<}} + \text{HBr} \longrightarrow \text{H}_3\text{C}-\underset{\text{Br}}{\overset{\text{CH}_3}{\underset{|}{\overset{|}{\text{C}}}}}-\text{CH}_3$$

2-Methylpropene   2-Bromo-2-methylpropane

Look carefully at the above example. Only one of the two possible addition products is obtained. 2-Methylpropene *could* add HBr to give 1-bromo-2-methylpropane, but it does not; it gives only 2-bromo-2-methylpropane as the major product.

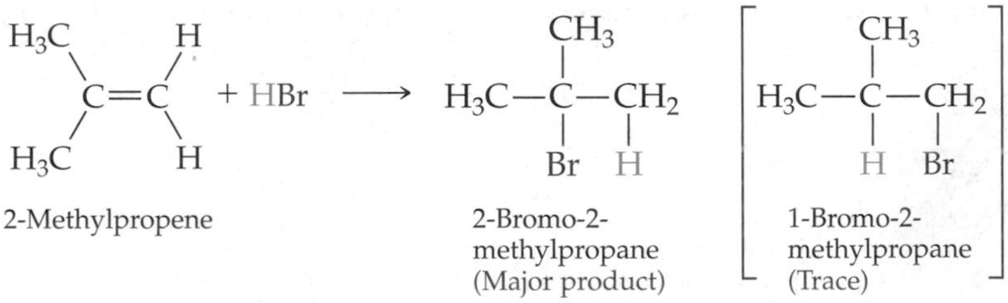

$$\underset{\text{H}_3\text{C}}{\overset{\text{H}_3\text{C}}{>}}\text{C}=\text{C}\underset{\text{H}}{\overset{\text{H}}{<}} + \text{HBr} \longrightarrow \text{H}_3\text{C}-\underset{\text{Br}\ \ \text{H}}{\overset{\text{CH}_3}{\underset{|\ \ \ |}{\overset{|}{\text{C}}}}}-\text{CH}_2 \qquad \left[\text{H}_3\text{C}-\underset{\text{H}\ \ \text{Br}}{\overset{\text{CH}_3}{\underset{|\ \ \ |}{\overset{|}{\text{C}}}}}-\text{CH}_2 \right]$$

2-Methylpropene   2-Bromo-2-   1-Bromo-2-
                     methylpropane   methylpropane
                     (Major product) (Trace)

This result is typical of what happens when HBr and HCl add to an alkene in which one of the double-bond carbons has more hydrogens than the other (an unsymmetrically substituted alkene). The results of such additions can be predicted by **Markovnikov's rule**, formulated in 1869 by the Russian chemist Vladimir Markovnikov:

Markovnikov's rule In the addition of HX to an alkene, the major product arises from the H attaching to the double-bond carbon that has the larger number of H atoms *directly* attached to it, and the X attaching to the carbon that has the smaller number of H atoms attached.

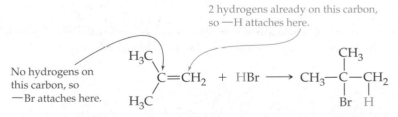

2 hydrogens already on this carbon, so —H attaches here.

No hydrogens on this carbon, so —Br attaches here.

Note that the terms "unsymmetrically substituted" and "symmetrically substituted" here refer only to the *number* of hydrogens and carbons attached to each carbon engaged in the double bond and not to the *identity* of the carbon groups attached.

The scientific reason behind Markovnikov's rule is a powerful and important principle in organic chemistry. An explanation for Markovnikov's rule, which has to do with the stability of intermediates known as *carbocations* that form during the reaction, is discussed in Mastering Reactions: How Addition Reactions Occur on p. 414.

If an alkene has equal numbers of H atoms attached to the double-bond carbons (a symmetrically substituted double bond), both possible products are formed in approximately equal amounts:

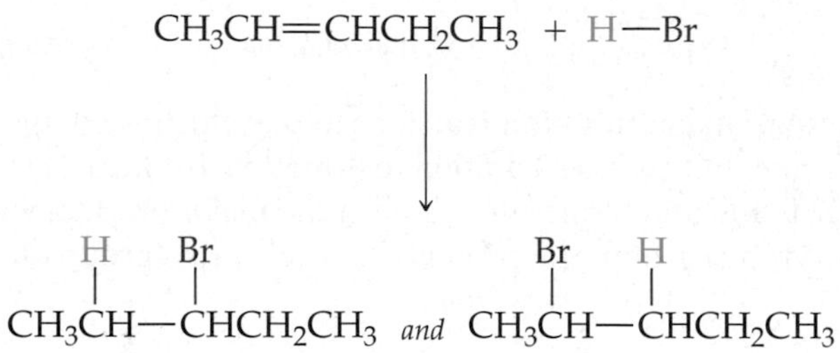

$$CH_3CH{=}CHCH_2CH_3 \ + \ H{-}Br$$

$$\downarrow$$

$$\underset{\text{3-Bromopentane}}{\overset{\overset{\displaystyle H \quad\ Br}{\mid\qquad\mid}}{CH_3CH{-}CHCH_2CH_3}} \quad and \quad \underset{\text{2-Bromopentane}}{\overset{\overset{\displaystyle Br \quad\ H}{\mid\qquad\mid}}{CH_3CH{-}CHCH_2CH_3}}$$

(1:1 ratio)

Worked Example 13.6 Organic Reactions: Markovnikov's Rule

What major product do you expect from the following reaction?

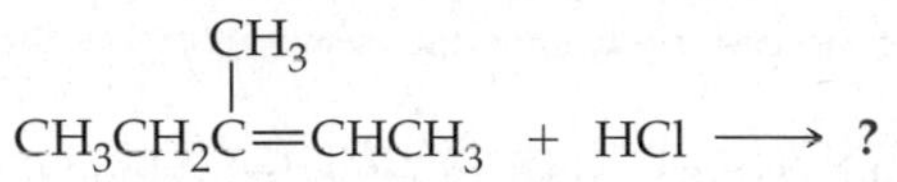

$$\overset{\overset{\displaystyle CH_3}{\mid}}{CH_3CH_2C{=}CHCH_3} \ + \ HCl \longrightarrow \ ?$$

ANALYSIS The reaction of an alkene with HCl leads to formation of an alkyl chloride addition product according to Markovnikov's rule. To make a prediction, look at the starting alkene and count the number of hydrogens attached to each double-bond carbon. Then write the product by attaching H to the carbon with more hydrogens and attaching Cl to the carbon with fewer hydrogens.

SOLUTION

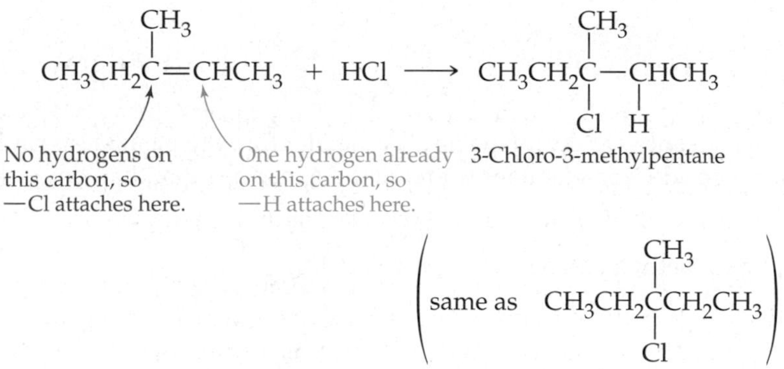

$$\overset{\overset{\displaystyle CH_3}{\mid}}{CH_3CH_2C{=}CHCH_3} \ + \ HCl \longrightarrow \ \underset{\underset{\displaystyle Cl \ \ H}{\mid\ \ \ \mid}}{\overset{\overset{\displaystyle CH_3}{\mid}}{CH_3CH_2C{-}CHCH_3}}$$

No hydrogens on this carbon, so —Cl attaches here.

One hydrogen already on this carbon, so —H attaches here.

3-Chloro-3-methylpentane

$$\left(\text{same as} \quad \underset{\underset{\displaystyle Cl}{\mid}}{\overset{\overset{\displaystyle CH_3}{\mid}}{CH_3CH_2CCH_2CH_3}} \right)$$

Worked Example 13.7 Organic Reactions: Markovnikov's Rule

From what alkene might 2-chloro-3-methylbutane be made?

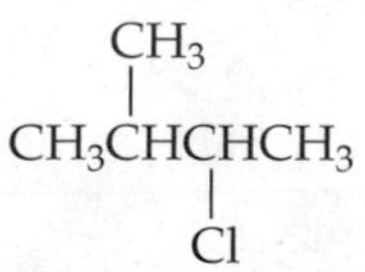

$$\underset{\underset{\displaystyle Cl}{\mid}}{\overset{\overset{\displaystyle CH_3}{\mid}}{CH_3CHCHCH_3}}$$

2-Chloro-3-methylbutane

ANALYSIS 2-Chloro-3-methylbutane is an alkyl chloride that might be made by addition of HCl to an alkene. To generate the possible alkene precursors, remove the —Cl group and an —H atom from adjacent carbons, and replace with a double bond:

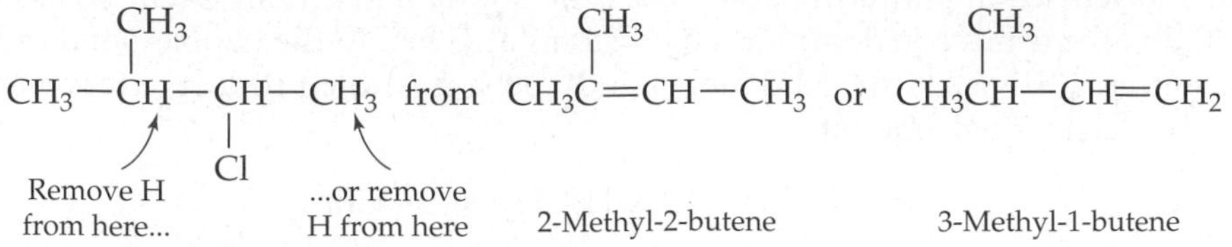

$$
\underset{\substack{\uparrow \\ \text{Remove H} \\ \text{from here...}}}{\overset{\displaystyle CH_3}{CH_3\!-\!CH\!-\!\underset{\substack{| \\ Cl \\ \uparrow \\ \text{...or remove} \\ \text{H from here}}}{CH}\!-\!CH_3}}
\quad \text{from} \quad
\underset{\text{2-Methyl-2-butene}}{\overset{\displaystyle CH_3}{CH_3C\!=\!CH\!-\!CH_3}}
\quad \text{or} \quad
\underset{\text{3-Methyl-1-butene}}{\overset{\displaystyle CH_3}{CH_3CH\!-\!CH\!=\!CH_2}}
$$

Look at the possible alkene addition reactions to see which is compatible with Markovnikov's rule. In this case, addition to 3-methyl-1-butene is compatible. Note that if HCl is added to 2-methyl-2-butene the major product will have the Cl attached to the wrong carbon (the carbon with the methyl group on it).

SOLUTION

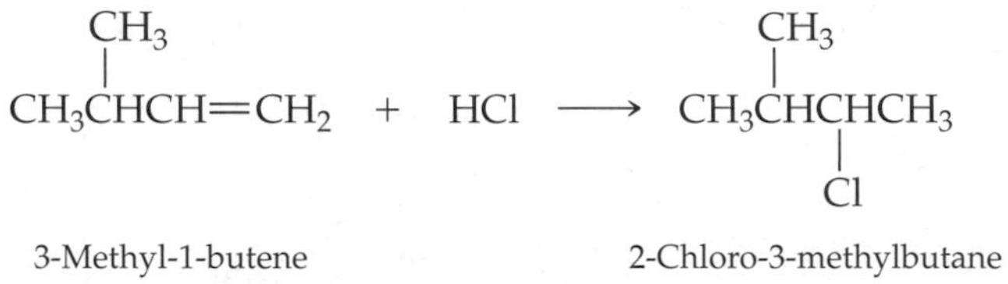

$$
\underset{\text{3-Methyl-1-butene}}{\overset{\displaystyle CH_3}{CH_3CHCH\!=\!CH_2}} \;+\; HCl \;\longrightarrow\; \underset{\text{2-Chloro-3-methylbutane}}{\overset{\displaystyle CH_3}{\underset{\underset{\displaystyle Cl}{|}}{CH_3CHCHCH_3}}}
$$

PROBLEM 13.11

Draw all possible products formed when 2-methyl-2-butene undergoes addition with HCl. Label them as being either the major or the minor product.

PROBLEM 13.12

What major products do you expect from the following reactions?

(a) 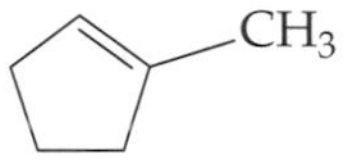 [cyclopentene with CH₃ group] + HCl ⟶ ?   (b) 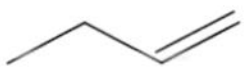 [alkene] + HBr ⟶ ?

(c) 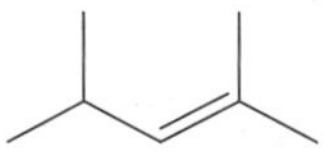 [alkene] + HCl ⟶ ?

PROBLEM 13.13

From what alkenes are the following alkyl halides likely to be made as the major product of an addition reaction? (Careful, there may be more than one answer.)

(a) 3-Chloro-3-ethylpentane   (b) 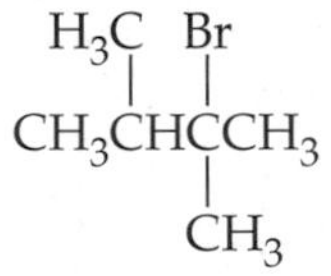 $\underset{\underset{\displaystyle CH_3}{|}}{\overset{\displaystyle \overset{H_3C}{|}\;\;\overset{Br}{|}}{CH_3CHCCH_3}}$

🔑 **KEY CONCEPT PROBLEM 13.14**

What product do you expect from the following reaction?

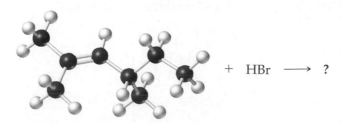

+ HBr ⟶ ?

Addition of Water to Alkenes: Hydration

Although a water molecule (H—OH) could be considered as another type of H—X, an alkene will not react with pure water alone. If, however, a small amount of a strong acid catalyst such as H_2SO_4 is added, an addition reaction takes place to yield an *alcohol* (R—OH). This reaction is known as a **hydration** reaction. In fact, nearly 100 million gallons of ethyl alcohol (ethanol) are produced each year in the United States by this method.

Hydration The addition of water to a multiple bond to give an alcohol product.

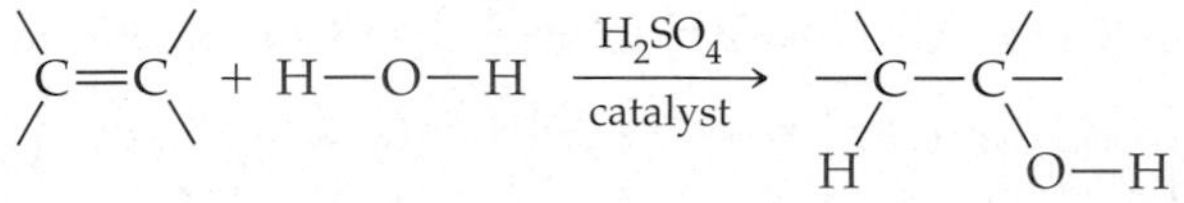

For example,

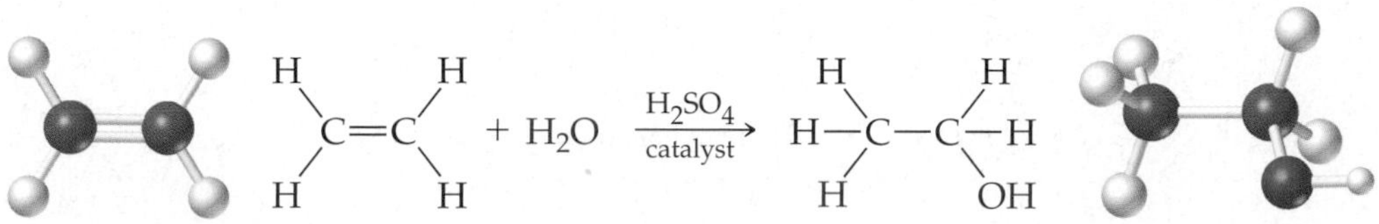

Ethylene

Ethyl alcohol

As with the addition of HBr and HCl, we can use Markovnikov's rule to predict the product when water adds to an unsymmetrically substituted alkene. Hydration of 2-methylpropene, for example, gives 2-methyl-2-propanol as the major product:

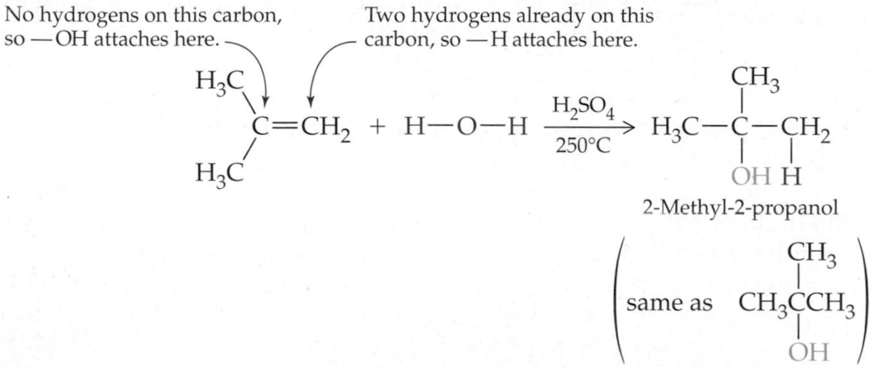

No hydrogens on this carbon, so —OH attaches here.

Two hydrogens already on this carbon, so —H attaches here.

2-Methyl-2-propanol

$$\left(\text{same as} \quad CH_3\overset{\overset{\displaystyle CH_3}{|}}{\underset{\underset{\displaystyle OH}{|}}{C}}CH_3 \right)$$

Worked Example 13.8 Reaction of Alkenes: Hydration

What product(s) do you expect from the following hydration reaction?

$$CH_3CH = CHCH_2CH_3 + H_2O \xrightarrow{H_2SO_4} ?$$

ANALYSIS Water is added to the double bond, with an H atom added to one carbon and an —OH group added to the other carbon of the double bond.

SOLUTION
Because this is *not* an unsymmetrically substituted alkene, we can add the —OH group to either carbon:

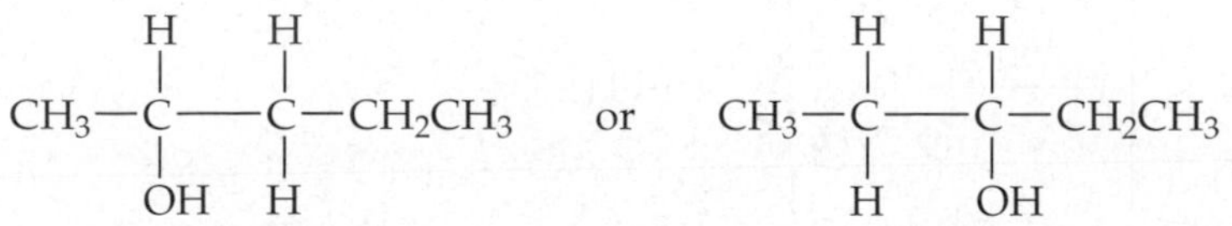

2-Pentanol   3-Pentanol

PROBLEM 13.15

What products do you expect from the following hydration reactions? Label them as major and minor if more than one is formed.

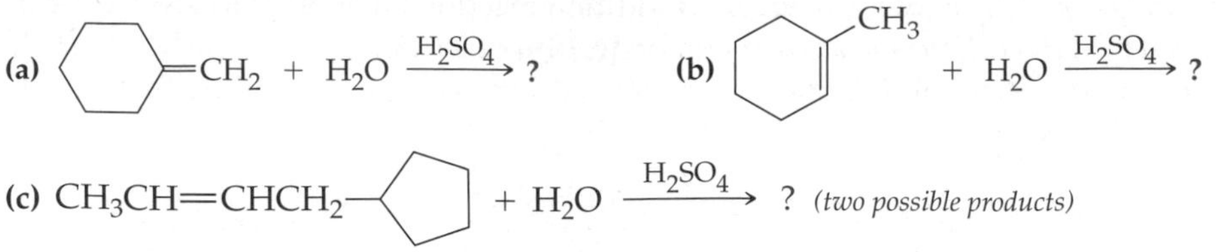

(a) $\langle\text{cyclohexane ring}\rangle=CH_2$ + H_2O $\xrightarrow{H_2SO_4}$?

(b) $\langle\text{cyclohexene ring with } CH_3\rangle$ + H_2O $\xrightarrow{H_2SO_4}$?

(c) $CH_3CH=CHCH_2-\langle\text{cyclopentane ring}\rangle$ + H_2O $\xrightarrow{H_2SO_4}$? *(two possible products)*

PROBLEM 13.16

From what alkene reactant might 3-methyl-3-pentanol be made?

$$\begin{array}{c} CH_3 \\ | \\ CH_3CH_2CCH_2CH_3 \\ | \\ OH \end{array}$$

3-Methyl-3-pentanol

MASTERING REACTIONS

How Addition Reactions Occur

How do alkene addition reactions take place? Do two molecules, say ethylene and HBr, simply collide and immediately form a product molecule of bromoethane, or is the process more complex? In Chapter 12, we presented a useful and convenient way for organic chemists to visualize reactions (see Mastering Reactions: Organic Chemistry and the Curved Arrow Formalism on p. 382). Here we apply this to the study of addition reactions, specifically those involving H⁺. Detailed studies show that alkene addition reactions take place in two distinct steps, as illustrated in this figure for the addition of HBr to ethylene.

It is instructive to begin by recognizing that almost all organic reactions can be visualized as occurring between an electron rich species and an electron poor species. In the first step, the electron-rich alkene reacts with the electron-poor H^+ from the acid HBr. The carbon–carbon double bond partially breaks, and two electrons move from the double bond to form a new single bond (indicated by the curved red arrow in the figure). The remaining double-bond carbon, having had electrons that were being shared removed from it, now has only 6 electrons in its outer shell and bears a positive charge. Carbons that possess a positive charge, or *carbocations*, are highly reactive. As soon as this carbocation is formed, it immediately reacts with Br^- to form a

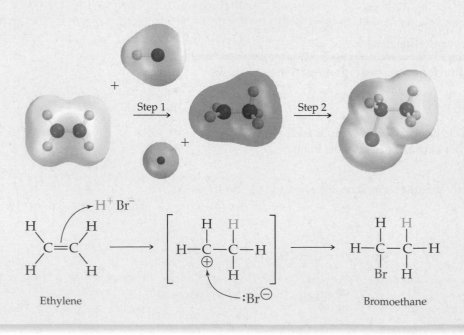

◄ **The mechanism of the addition of HBr to an alkene.** The reaction takes place in two steps and involves a carbocation intermediate. In the first step, 2 electrons move from the C=C double bond to form a C—H bond. In the second step, Br^- uses 2 electrons to form a bond to the positively charged carbon.

Ethylene

Bromoethane

neutral product. Note how electrostatic potential maps illustrate the electron-rich (red) nature of the ethylene double bond and the electron-poor (blue) nature of the H atom in HBr. (See Section 4.9). Also, note the extremely electron-poor (blue) nature of the carbocation, and you can readily see why it is so reactive!

For ethylene, the mechanism is without complication; both carbons have identical substitution. What about the case where the double bond is unsymmetrically substituted, say, with 2-methyl-2-butene? Here we perform the same analysis as the one we did for ethylene:

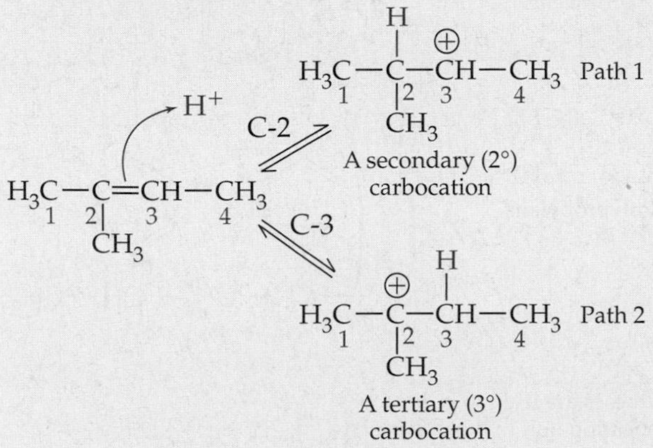

The double bond, being electron rich, attacks the electron-poor H⁺ and in doing so, causes a carbocation to form; however, here we have two possibilities. If the H⁺ attaches to C2, the carbocation will form on C3 (Path 1); if the H⁺ attaches to C3, the carbocation will form on C2 (Path 2). Since this is an equilibrium process (the H⁺ can just as easily be removed to regenerate the alkene) we should see both, but is one favored over the other? The answer to that can be arrived at by examining the two carbocations. Carbocations are electron-deficient species, so anything that can help stabilize one over another will cause a preference for that species to be seen. Carbons are known to donate electron density through the single bond; therefore, the more carbons attached to a carbocation, the less electron poor it feels and the more stable it will be, making it more favorable. The more favorable the carbocation, the more product will arise from it. Studies have shown that tertiary (3°) carbocations are more stable than secondary (2°) carbocations, which are much more stable than primary (1°) carbocations:

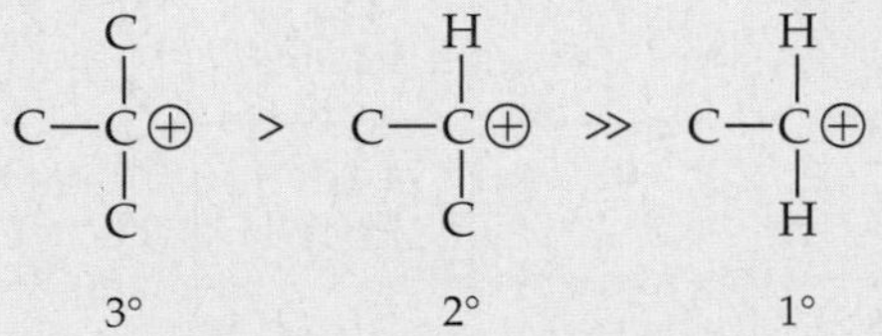

(Primary carbocations are so unfavorable as to almost never be formed.) Thus, when the bromide reacts, two possible products are formed, with the major product arising from the more stable carbocation:

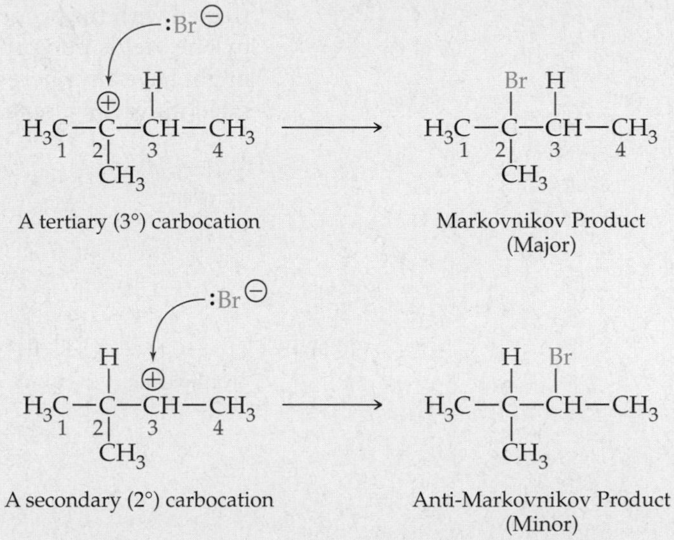

A tertiary (3°) carbocation   Markovnikov Product (Major)

A secondary (2°) carbocation   Anti-Markovnikov Product (Minor)

You should notice that the major product is that predicted by Markovnikov's rule. This now shows you the scientific basis for his observations: The major product arises because the intermediate it is derived from is more stable than any other intermediate (here, the 3° carbocation). This concept of the stability of intermediates lies at the very core of organic chemistry and is so powerful that it allows chemists to successfully predict the outcomes of diverse organic reactions.

A description of the individual steps by which old bonds are broken and new bonds are formed in a reaction is called a **reaction mechanism**. They are an important part of organic chemistry, and we will examine a few of them in future Mastering Reactions boxes. Mechanisms allow chemists to classify thousands of seemingly unrelated organic reactions into only a few categories and help us to understand what is occurring during a reaction. Their study is essential to our ever-expanding ability to understand biochemistry and the physiological effects of drugs.

Reaction mechanism A description of the individual steps by which old bonds are broken and new bonds are formed in a reaction.

See Mastering Reactions Problems 13.90–13.92 at the end of the chapter.

13.7 Alkene Polymers

A **polymer** is a large molecule formed by the repetitive bonding together of many smaller molecules called **monomers**. As we will see in later chapters, biological polymers occur throughout nature. Cellulose and starch are polymers built from sugars, proteins are polymers built from amino acids, and the DNA that makes up our genetic

Polymer A large molecule formed by the repetitive bonding together of many smaller molecules.

Monomer A small molecule that is used to prepare a polymer.

heritage is a polymer built from nucleic acids. Although the basic idea is the same, synthetic polymers are much simpler than biopolymers because the starting monomer units are usually small, simple organic molecules.

Many simple alkenes (often called *vinyl monomers* because the partial structure $H_2C=CH-$ is known as a *vinyl group*) undergo *polymerization* reactions when treated with the proper catalyst. Ethylene yields polyethylene on polymerization, propylene yields polypropylene, and styrene yields polystyrene. The polymer product might have anywhere from a few hundred to a few thousand monomer units incorporated into a long, repeating chain.

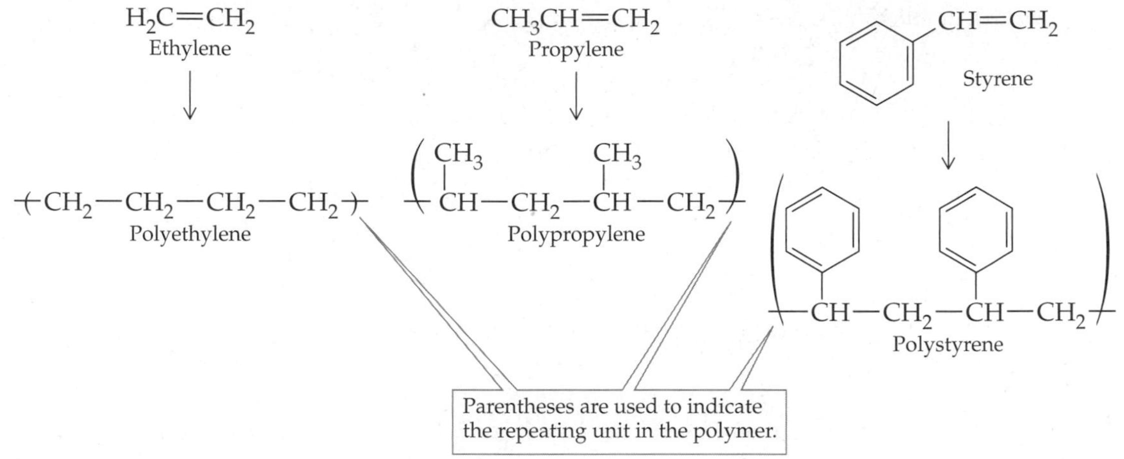

Parentheses are used to indicate the repeating unit in the polymer.

The fundamental reaction in the polymerization of an alkene monomer resembles the addition to a carbon–carbon double bond described in the preceding sections. The reaction begins by addition of a species called an *initiator* to an alkene; this results in the breaking of one of the bonds making up the double bond. A reactive intermediate that contains an unpaired electron (known as a *radical*) is formed in this step, and it is this reactive intermediate that adds to a second alkene molecule. This produces another reactive intermediate, which adds to a third alkene molecule, and so on. Because the result is continuous addition of one monomer after another to the end of the growing polymer chain, polymers formed in this way are called *chain-growth polymers*. The basic repeating unit is enclosed in parentheses, and the subscript n indicates how many repeating units are in the polymer:

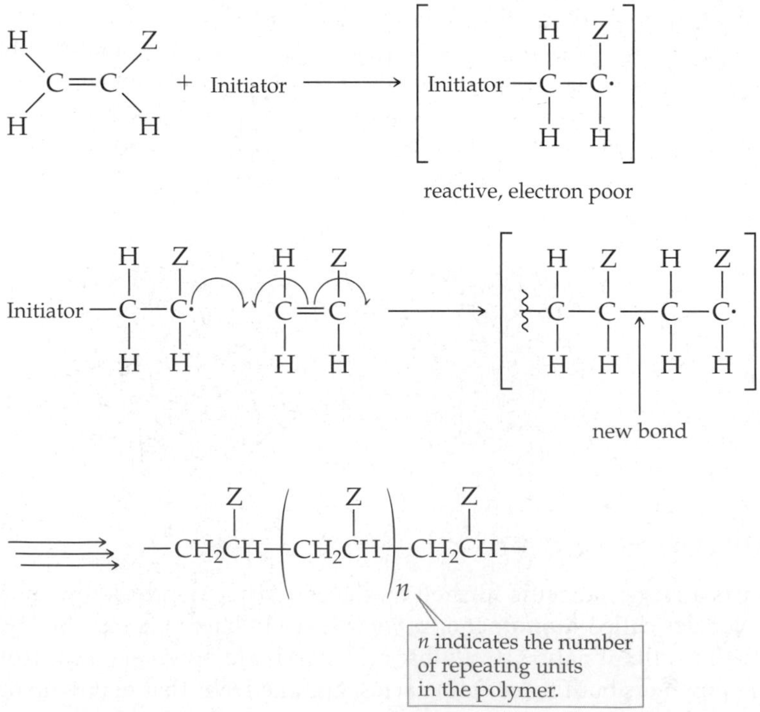

reactive, electron poor

new bond

n indicates the number of repeating units in the polymer.

TABLE 13.1 Some Alkene Polymers and Their Uses

MONOMER NAME	MONOMER STRUCTURE	POLYMER NAME	USES
Ethylene	$H_2C{=}CH_2$	Polyethylene	Packaging, bottles
Propylene	$H_2C{=}CH{-}CH_3$	Polypropylene	Bottles, rope, pails, medical tubing
Vinyl chloride	$H_2C{=}CH{-}Cl$	Poly(vinyl chloride)	Insulation, plastic pipe
Styrene	$H_2C{=}CH{-}\bigcirc$	Polystyrene	Foams and molded plastics
Styrene and 1, 3–butadiene	$H_2C{=}CH{-}\bigcirc$ and $H_2C{=}CHCH{=}CH_2$	Styrene-butadiene rubber (SBR)	Synthetic rubber for tires
Acrylonitrile	$H_2C{=}CH{-}C{\equiv}N$	Orlon, Acrilan	Fibers, outdoor carpeting
Methyl methacrylate	$H_2C{=}\overset{\displaystyle \overset{O}{\|}}{\underset{\underset{\displaystyle CH_3}{\|}}{C}}COCH_3$	Plexiglas, Lucite	Windows, contact lenses, fiber optics
Tetrafluoroethylene	$F_2C{=}CF_2$	Teflon	Nonstick coatings, bearings, replacement heart valves and blood vessels

Variations in the substituent group Z attached to the double bond impart different properties to the product, as illustrated by the alkene polymers listed in Table 13.1. Polymer rigidity is controlled by addition of a small amount of a cross-linking agent, typically 1–2% of a dialkene (an alkene containing two double bonds), whose role is to covalently link two chains of monomer units together.

The properties of a polymer depend not only on the monomer but also on the average size of the huge molecules in a particular sample and on how extensively they cross-link and branch. The long molecules in straight-chain polyethylene pack closely together, giving a rigid material called *high-density polyethylene*, which is mainly used in bottles for products such as milk and motor oil. When polyethylene molecules contain many branches (due to the Z groups present), they cannot pack together as tightly and instead form a flexible material called *low-density polyethylene*, which is used mainly in packaging materials.

◀ (a) High-density polyethylene is strong and rigid enough to be used in many kinds of bottles. (b) These disposable polypropylene medical supplies are used once and then discarded.

(a)   (b)

Polymer technology has come a long way since the development of synthetic rubber, nylon, Plexiglas, and Teflon. The use of polymers has changed the nature of activities from plumbing and carpentry to clothing and auto manufacturing. In the healthcare fields, the use of inexpensive, disposable equipment is now common.

Worked Example 13.9 Reactions of Alkenes: Polymerization

Write the structure of a segment of polystyrene, used in foams and molded plastics. The monomer is

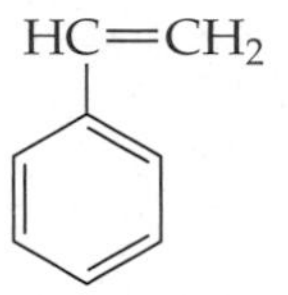

$$HC = CH_2$$

ANALYSIS The polymerization reaction resembles the addition of two monomer units to either end of the double bond.

SOLUTION
Draw three molecules of styrene with the double bonds aligned next to each other; then add the monomer units together with single bonds, eliminating the double bonds in the process:

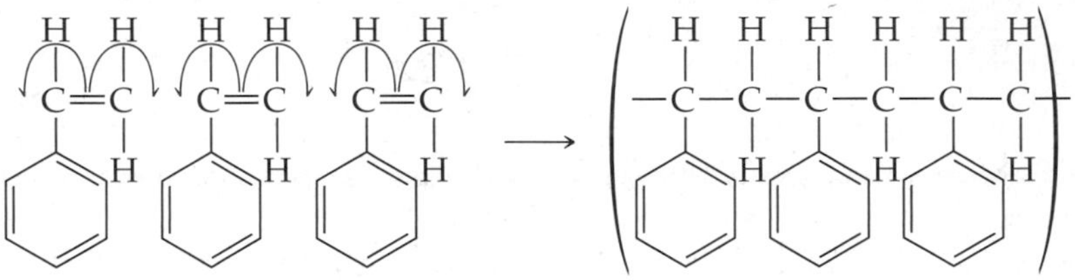

PROBLEM 13.17
Write the structure of a segment of poly(vinyl acetate), a polymer used for the springy soles in running shoes. The structure of the monomer is

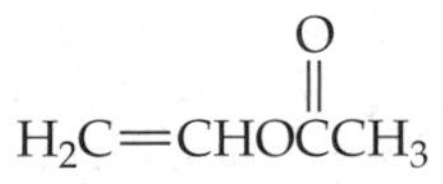

$$H_2C=CHOCCH_3 \quad \text{Vinyl acetate}$$

PROBLEM 13.18
Write the structures of the monomers used to make the following polymers.

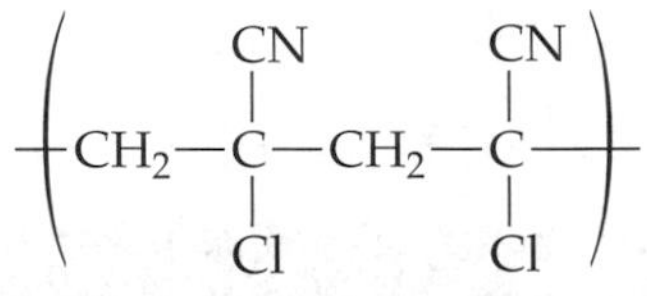

(a) 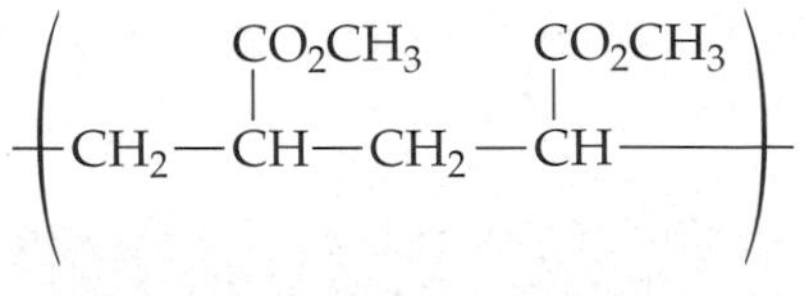   (b)

13.8 Aromatic Compounds and the Structure of Benzene

In the early days of organic chemistry, the word *aromatic* was used to describe many fragrant substances from fruits, trees, and other natural sources. It was soon realized, however, that substances grouped as aromatic behave differently from most other organic compounds. Today, chemists use the term **aromatic** to refer to the class of compounds that contain benzene-like rings.

Aromatic The class of compounds containing benzene-like rings.

Benzene, the simplest aromatic compound, is a flat, symmetrical molecule with the molecular formula C_6H_6. It is often represented as cyclohexatriene, a 6-membered carbon ring with three double bonds. Though useful, the problem with this representation is that it gives the wrong impression about benzene's chemical reactivity and bonding. Because benzene appears to have three double bonds, you might expect it to react with H_2, Br_2, HCl, and H_2O to give the same kinds of addition products that alkenes do. But this expectation would be wrong. Benzene and other aromatic compounds are much less reactive than alkenes and do not normally undergo addition reactions.

▲ **The odor of cherries is due to benzaldehyde, an aromatic compound.**

Benzene's relative lack of chemical reactivity is a consequence of its structure. If you were to draw a six-membered ring with alternating single and double bonds, where would you place the double bonds? There are two equivalent possibilities (Figure 13.2b), neither of which is fully correct by itself. Experimental evidence shows that all six carbon–carbon bonds in benzene are identical, so a picture with three double bonds and three single bonds cannot be correct.

The properties of benzene are best explained by assuming that its true structure is an *average* of the two equivalent conventional Lewis structures. Rather than being held between specific pairs of atoms, the double-bond electrons are instead free to move over the entire ring. Each carbon–carbon bond is thus intermediate between a single bond and a double bond. The name **resonance** is given to this phenomenon where the true structure of a molecule is an average among two or more possible conventional structures, and a special double-headed arrow ($\longleftrightarrow$) is used to show the resonance relationship. It is important to note that *no atoms move between resonance structures, only pairs of electrons* (in this case, double bonds).

Resonance The phenomenon where the true structure of a molecule is an average among two or more conventional Lewis structures that differ only in the placement of double bonds.

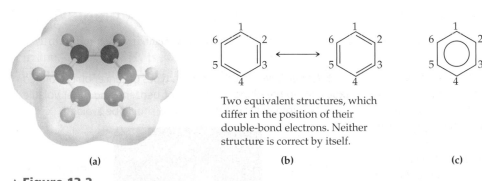

Two equivalent structures, which differ in the position of their double-bond electrons. Neither structure is correct by itself.

(a)   (b)   (c)

▲ **Figure 13.2**
Some representations of benzene.
(a) An electrostatic potential map shows the equivalency of the carbon–carbon bonds. Benzene is usually represented by the two equivalent structures in (b) or by the single structure in (c).

Because the real structure of benzene is intermediate between the two forms shown in Figure 13.2b, it is difficult to represent benzene with the standard conventions using lines for covalent bonds. Thus, we sometimes represent the double bonds as a circle inside the six-membered ring, as shown in Figure 13.2c. It is more common, though, to draw the ring with three double bonds, with the understanding that it is an aromatic ring with equivalent bonding all around. It is this convention that we use in this book.

Many substituted aromatic compounds have common names in addition to their systematic names. For example, methylbenzene is familiarly known as *toluene*, hydroxybenzene as *phenol*, aminobenzene as *aniline*, and so on, as shown in Table 13.2. Frequently, these common names are also used together with *o-* (*ortho*), *m-* (*meta*), or *p-* (*para*) prefixes. For example:

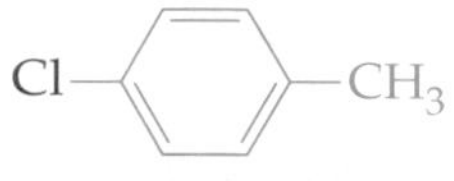

p-Chlorotoluene 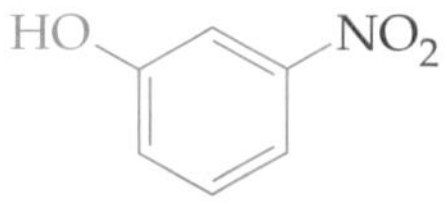   *m*-Nitrophenol 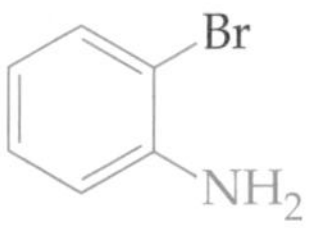   *o*-Bromoaniline

TABLE **13.2** **Common Names of Some Aromatic Compounds**

STRUCTURE	NAME	STRUCTURE	NAME
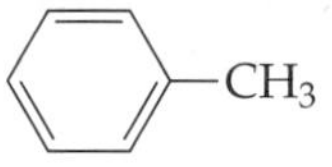 ⬡—CH₃	Toluene	 H₃C—⬡—CH₃	*para*-Xylene
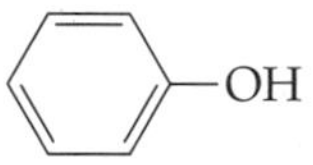 ⬡—OH	Phenol	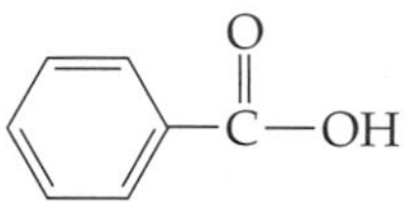 ⬡—C(=O)—OH	Benzoic acid
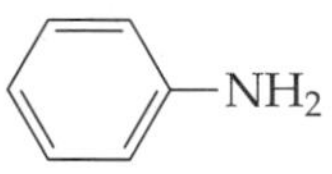 ⬡—NH₂	Aniline	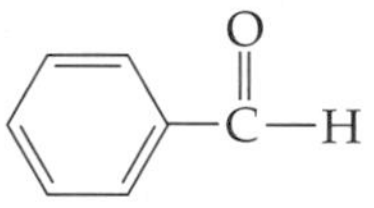 ⬡—C(=O)—H	Benzaldehyde

Phenyl The C_6H_5— group.

Occasionally, the benzene ring itself may be considered a substituent group attached to another parent compound. When this happens, the name **phenyl** (pronounced **fen**-nil and commonly abbreviated Ph—) is used for the C_6H_5— unit:

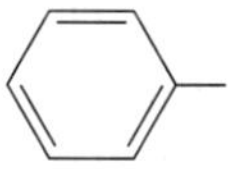

A phenyl group
C_6H_5—

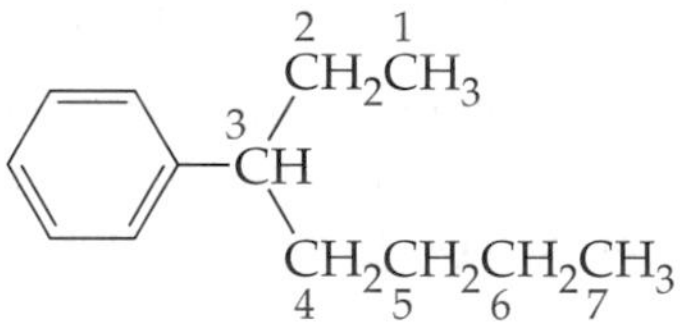

3-Phenylheptane

Worked Example 13.10 Naming Organic Compounds: Aromatic Compounds

Name the following aromatic compound:

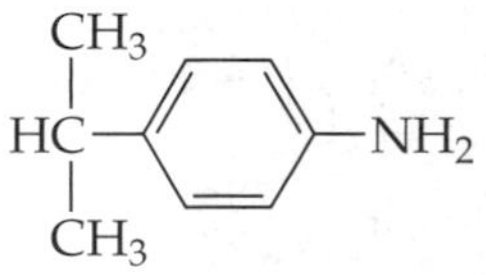

ANALYSIS First identify the parent organic compound, then identify the location of substituent groups on the benzene ring either by number, or by *ortho, meta,* or *para*.

SOLUTION
The parent compound is a benzene ring with an amine group (*aminobenzene*, which is commonly known as *aniline*). The substituent group is attached at the C4, or para,

position relative to the amino group. The propyl group is attached to the benzene ring by the middle carbon, so it is *isopropyl*.

The substituent group is at the para position.

$$CH_3 \quad 3 \qquad 2$$
$$HC \quad 4 \qquad 1 - NH_2$$
$$CH_3 \quad 5 \qquad 6$$

The propyl group is attached to the middle carbon, so it is isopropyl.

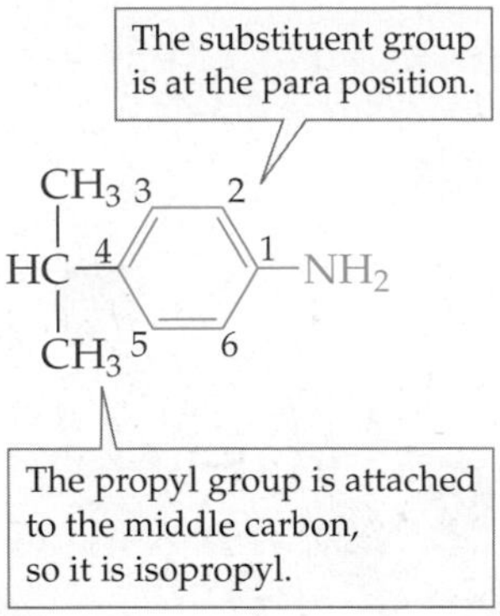

Name: *para*-isopropylaniline, or 4-isopropylaminobenzene

Worked Example 13.11 Molecular Structures: Aromatic Compounds

Draw the structure of *m*-chloroethylbenzene.

ANALYSIS *m*-Chloroethylbenzene has a benzene ring with two substituents, chloro and ethyl, in a meta relationship (that is, on C1 and C3).

SOLUTION
Since all carbons in the benzene ring are equivalent, draw a benzene ring and attach one of the substituents—for example, chloro—to any position:

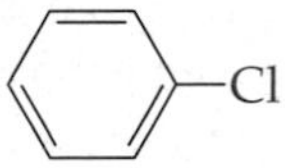

—Cl

Now go to a meta position two carbons away from the chloro-substituted carbon, and attach the second (ethyl) substituent:

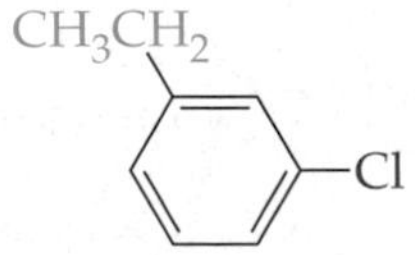

$$CH_3CH_2$$

—Cl   *m*-Chloroethylbenzene

PROBLEM 13.19

What are the IUPAC names for the following compounds?

(a) HO
   —CH$_2$CH$_3$

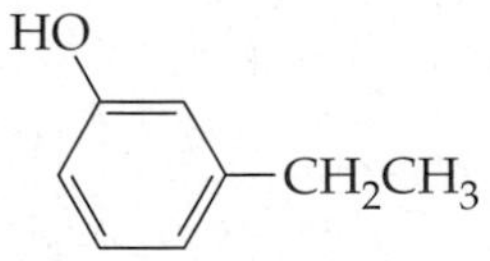

(b) Cl
   CH$_3$

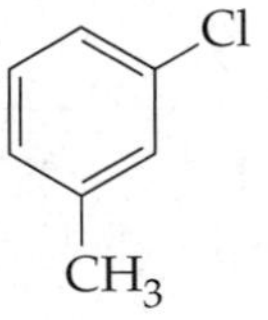

(c)

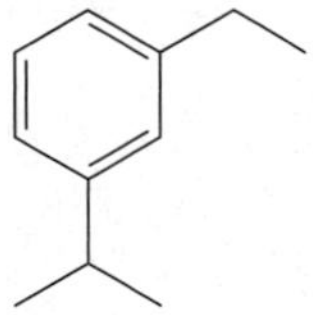

PROBLEM 13.20

Draw structures corresponding to the following names:

(a) *p*-Diiodobenzene

(b) *o*-Nitrotoluene

(c) *m*-Xylene

(d) *p*-Nitrophenol

Name the following compounds (red = O, blue = N, brown = Br):

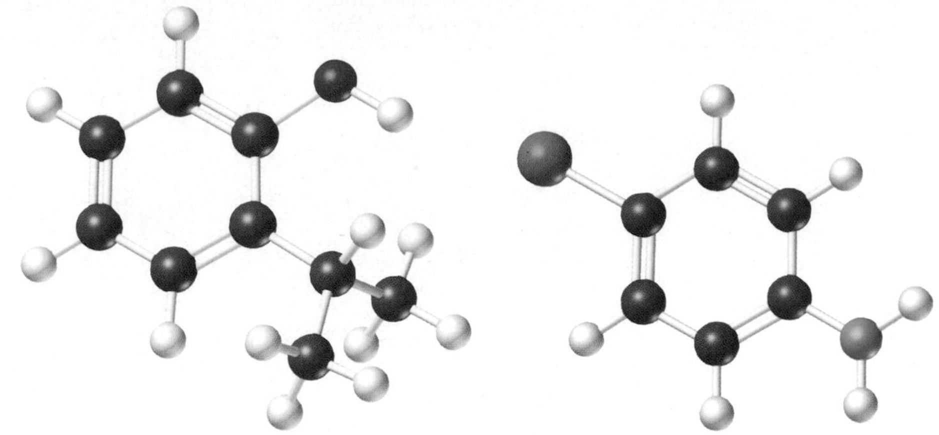

(a)

(b)

13.10 Reactions of Aromatic Compounds

Unlike alkenes, which undergo addition reactions, aromatic compounds usually undergo a special type of substitution reaction known as an *electrophilic aromatic substitution* reaction. That is, a group Y substitutes for 1 hydrogen atom on the aromatic ring without changing the ring itself. It does not matter which of the 6 ring hydrogens in benzene is replaced because all 6 are equivalent.

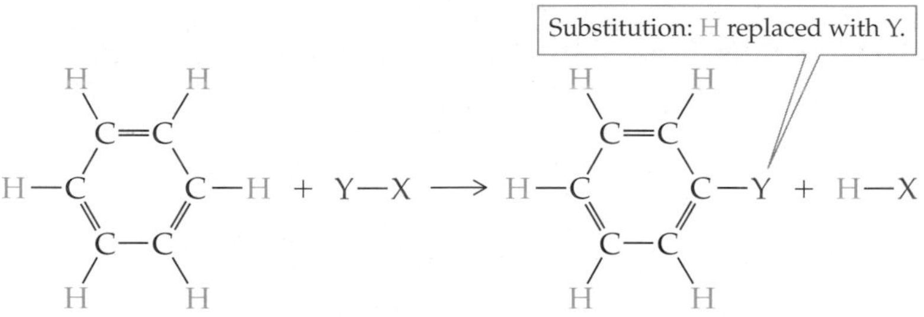

Substitution: H replaced with Y.

The mechanism responsible for this type of reaction is similar to that seen for alkenes, with the key difference being regeneration of the aromatic ring:

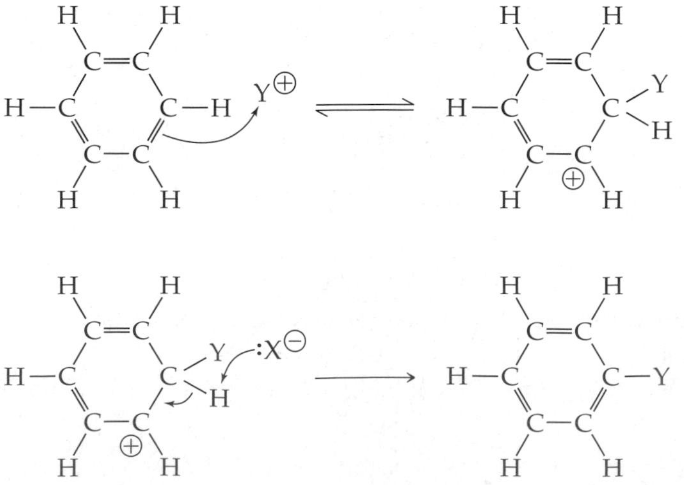

Nitration is the substitution of a *nitro group* ($-NO_2$) for one of the ring hydrogens. The reaction occurs when benzene reacts with nitric acid in the presence of sulfuric acid as catalyst:

Nitration The substitution of a nitro group ($-NO_2$) for a hydrogen on an aromatic ring.

Nitration: Substitution of H with nitro group.

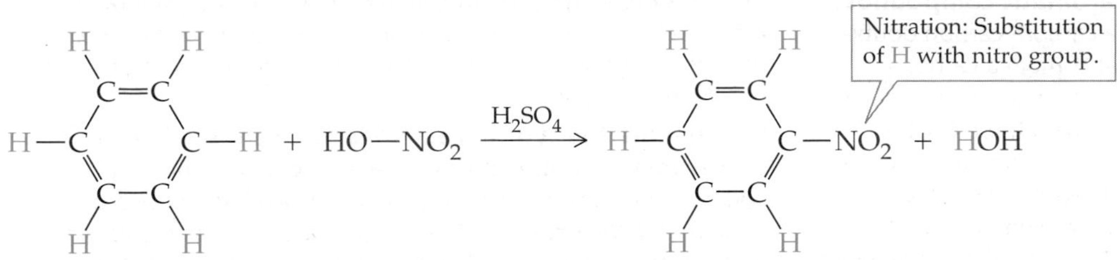

Benzene   Nitric acid   Nitrobenzene

Nitration of aromatic rings is a key step in the synthesis both of explosives like TNT (trinitrotoluene) and of many important pharmaceutical agents. Nitrobenzene itself is the industrial starting material for the preparation of aniline, which is used to make many of the brightly colored dyes in clothing.

Halogenation is the substitution of a halogen atom, usually bromine or chlorine, for one of the ring hydrogens. The reaction occurs when benzene reacts with Br_2 or Cl_2 in the presence of $FeBr_3$ or $FeCl_3$ as catalyst:

Halogenation The substitution of a halogen group ($-X$) for a hydrogen on an aromatic ring.

Halogenation: Substitution of H with a halogen

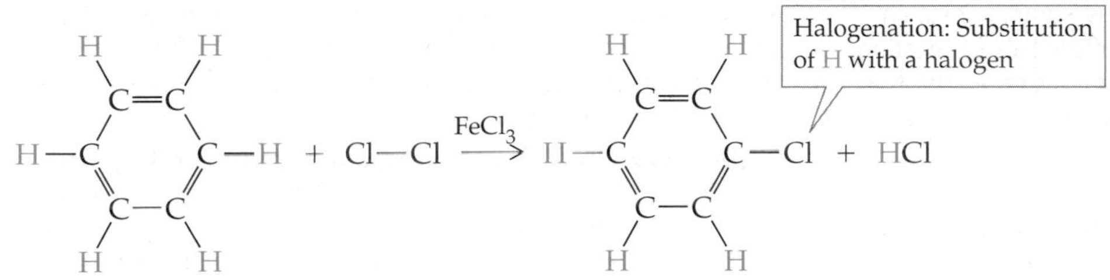

Benzene   Chlorine   Chlorobenzene

Sulfonation is the substitution of a sulfonic acid group ($-SO_3H$) for one of the ring hydrogens. The reaction occurs when benzene reacts with concentrated sulfuric acid and SO_3:

Sulfonation The substitution of a sulfonic acid group ($-SO_3H$) for a hydrogen on an aromatic ring.

Sulfonation: Substitution of H with sulfonic acid group

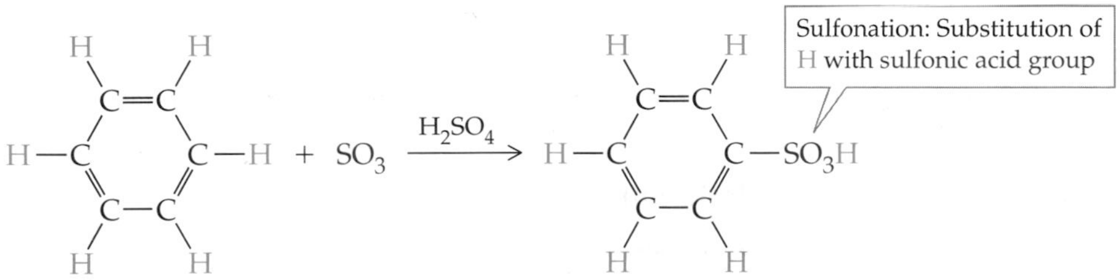

Benzene   Benzenesulfonic acid

Aromatic-ring sulfonation is a key step in the synthesis of such compounds as the sulfa-drug family of antibiotics:

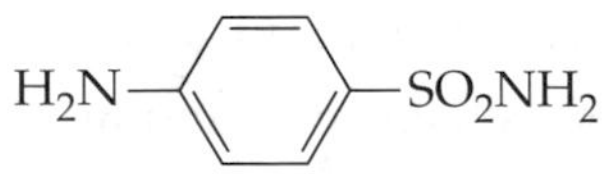

Sulfanilamide—a sulfa antibiotic

PROBLEM 13.22

Write the products from the reaction of the following reagents with *p*-xylene (*p*-dimethylbenzene).

(a) Br_2 and $FeBr_3$ **(b)** HNO_3 and H_2SO_4 catalyst **(c)** SO_3 in H_2SO_4

PROBLEM 13.23

Reaction of Br_2 and an $FeBr_3$ with phenol can lead to *three* possible substitution products. Show the structure of each and name them.

ANALYSIS First, identify the longest carbon chain, and number the carbon atoms beginning at the end nearer the —OH group. The longest chain attached to the —OH has 5 carbon atoms:

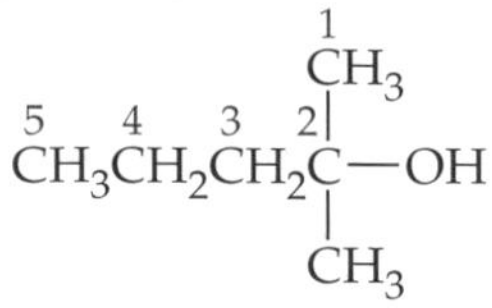

$$\underset{5}{CH_3}\underset{4}{CH_2}\underset{3}{CH_2}\underset{2}{\overset{\overset{1}{CH_3}}{\underset{CH_3}{C}}}-OH \qquad \text{Name as a pentanol.}$$

Next, identify and number the hydroxyl group and the substituents. Finally, write the name of the compound.

SOLUTION

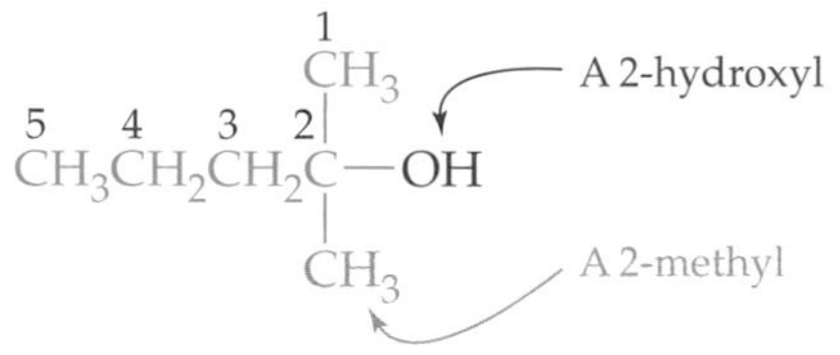

$$\underset{5}{CH_3}\underset{4}{CH_2}\underset{3}{CH_2}\underset{2}{\overset{\overset{1}{CH_3}}{\underset{CH_3}{C}}}-OH$$

A 2-hydroxyl

A 2-methyl

2-Methyl-2-pentanol

Since the —OH group is bonded to a carbon atom that has three alkyl substituents, this is a tertiary alcohol.

PROBLEM 14.3
Draw structures corresponding to the following names:
(a) 4-Methyl-1-pentanol
(b) 1-Methyl-1,3-cyclopentanediol
(c) 2-Methyl-3-hexanol
(d) 3-Heptanol
(e) 2,3-Diethylcyclohexanol

PROBLEM 14.4
Give systematic names for the following compounds:

(a) 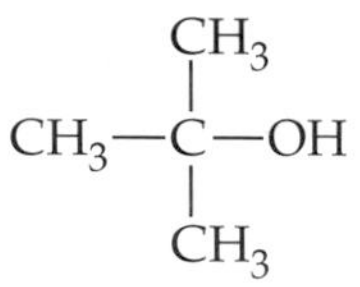 $CH_3-\overset{\overset{CH_3}{|}}{\underset{\underset{CH_3}{|}}{C}}-OH$

(b)

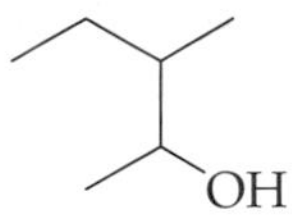

(c) 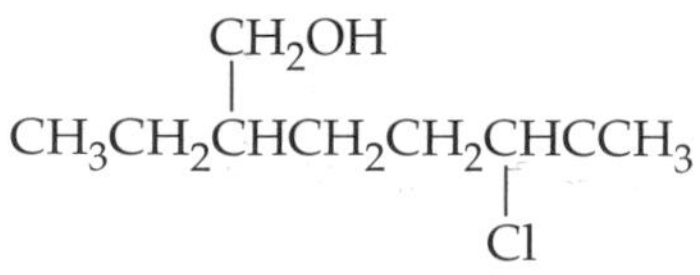 $CH_3CH_2\overset{\overset{CH_2OH}{|}}{C}HCH_2CH_2\overset{}{C}HCCH_3$ with Cl below

(d)

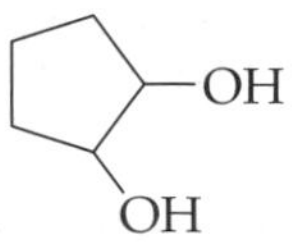

PROBLEM 14.5
Identify each alcohol in Problems 14.3 and 14.4 as primary, secondary, or tertiary.

14.4 Properties of Alcohols

Alcohols are much more polar than hydrocarbons because of the electronegative oxygen atom that withdraws electrons from the neighboring atoms. Because of this polarity, hydrogen bonding occurs and has a strong influence on alcohol properties.

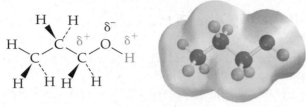

1-Propanol

Straight-chain alcohols with up to 12 carbon atoms are liquids, and each boils at a considerably higher temperature than the related alkane. Alcohols with a small organic part, such as methanol and ethanol, resemble water in their solubility behavior. Methanol and ethanol are miscible with water, with which they can form hydrogen bonds, and these two alcohols can dissolve small amounts of many ionic compounds. Nevertheless, both are also miscible with many organic solvents.

All alcohols can be thought of as composed of two distinct parts: a "water-loving," or *hydrophilic*, part and a "water-fearing," or *hydrophobic*, part. Alcohols with a larger hydrophobic organic part, such as 1-heptanol, are much more like alkanes and less like water. 1-Heptanol is nearly insoluble in water, for example, and cannot dissolve ionic compounds but does dissolve alkanes. The reason is that in order for water and another liquid to be miscible, water molecules must be able to entirely surround a molecule of the other liquid; the larger the hydrophobic (or "oily") portion of an alcohol molecule, the harder this is to accomplish:

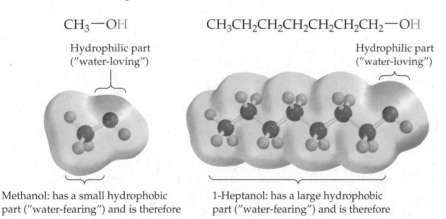

$CH_3—OH$

Hydrophilic part
("water-loving")

$CH_3CH_2CH_2CH_2CH_2CH_2CH_2—OH$

Hydrophilic part
("water-loving")

Methanol: has a small hydrophobic part ("water-fearing") and is therefore

1-Heptanol: has a large hydrophobic part ("water-fearing") and is therefore

Alcohols with two or more —OH groups can form more than one hydrogen bond. Therefore, they are higher boiling and more water-soluble than similar alcohols with one —OH group. Compare 1-butanol and 1,4-butanediol, for example:

$CH_3CH_2CH_2CH_2OH$ { bp 117 °C, water solubility of 7 g/100 ml.
1-Butanol

$HOCH_2CH_2CH_2CH_2OH$ { Added –OH raises bp to 230 °C and gives miscibility with water
1,4-Butanediol

PROBLEM 14.6

Rank the following according to boiling point, highest to lowest:

(a) $CH_3CH_2CH_2OH$

(b) $CH_3CH_2(OH)CH_2OH$

(c) $CH_3CH_2CH_3$

(d) $CH_2(OH)CH(OH)CH_2OH$

PROBLEM 14.7

Rank the following compounds according to their water solubility, most soluble first. Explain your ranking.

(a) $CH_3(CH_2)_{10}CH_2OH$ (b) $CH_3CH_2CHCH_3$ (c) $CH_3CH_2OCH_3$
                                              |
                                              OH

14.5 Reactions of Alcohols

Alcohols are perhaps one of the most important classes of organic molecules because of their versatility in the preparation of other organic molecules. We will examine two of the more important reactions of alcohols here: *dehydration* (an elimination reaction; see Section 13.5) and *oxidation*.

Dehydration

Dehydration The loss of water from an alcohol to yield an alkene.

Alcohols undergo loss of water (**dehydration**) on treatment with a strong acid catalyst; the reaction is driven to completion, typically, by heating. The —OH group is lost from one carbon, and an —H is lost from an adjacent carbon to yield an alkene product:

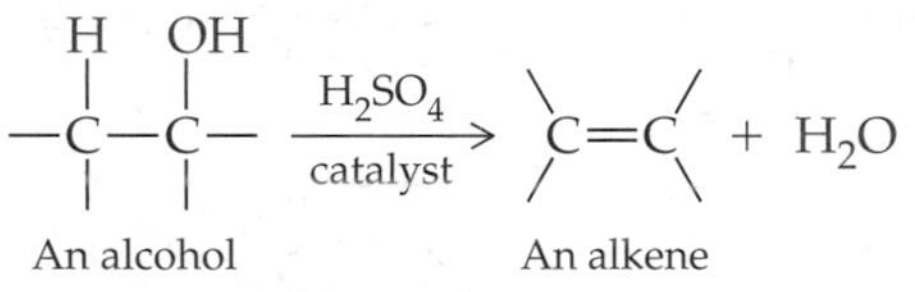

$$\underset{\text{An alcohol}}{\overset{\overset{\displaystyle H \quad OH}{\displaystyle |\quad\;\; |}}{-\underset{|}{C}-\underset{|}{C}-}} \;\xrightarrow[\text{catalyst}]{H_2SO_4}\; \underset{\text{An alkene}}{\overset{\displaystyle \diagdown\;\;\diagup}{\underset{\displaystyle \diagup\;\;\diagdown}{C=C}}} \; + \; H_2O$$

For example,

tert-Butyl alcohol   2-Methylpropene

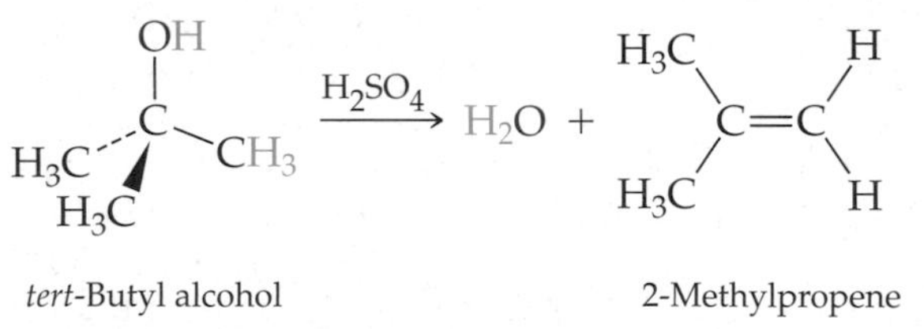

When more than one alkene can result from dehydration of an alcohol, a mixture of products is usually formed. A good rule of thumb is that the major product has the greater number of alkyl groups directly attached to the double-bond carbons. For example, dehydration of 2-butanol leads to a mixture containing 80% 2-butene and only 20% 1-butene:

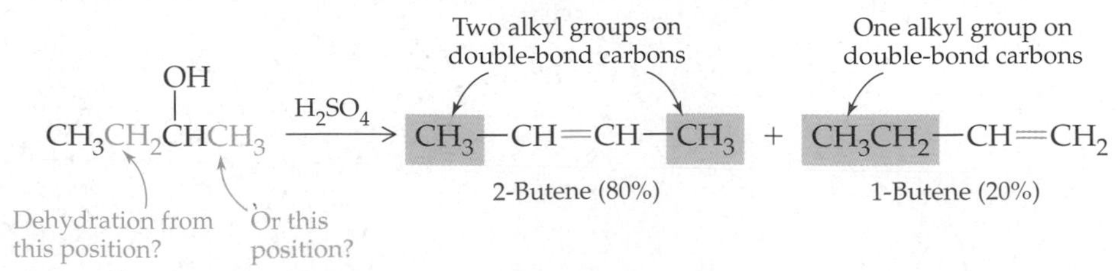

MASTERING REACTIONS

How Eliminations Occur

We have previously discussed the mechanism by which addition reactions occur (p. 414); let us now examine what is essentially the reverse of this reaction, an *elimination*. Eliminations can occur in one of two ways: as a one-step process (known as an *E2 reaction*) or as a two-step process (known as an *E1 reaction*). We will concentrate our efforts here on the latter, the E1 process.

When an alcohol is treated with a strong mineral acid (such as H_2SO_4), the first thing that happens is that the oxygen atom of the alcohol protonates in an equilibrium process:

$$\text{:}\overset{\curvearrowright \text{H}^+}{\underset{H_3C-CH-CH_3}{\overset{|}{O}H}} \quad \rightleftharpoons \quad \overset{H}{\underset{H_3C-CH-CH_3}{\overset{|}{\overset{\oplus}{\text{:}O}-H}}}$$

Notice that the —OH has been converted into what is essentially a water molecule. This portion can then leave, and what remains is a carbocation:

$$\overset{\oplus}{\underset{H_3C-CH-CH_3}{\overset{|}{\overset{\curvearrowleft}{O}H_2}}} \quad \rightleftharpoons \quad H_3C-\overset{\oplus}{C}H-CH_3 + H_2\overset{..}{O}\text{:}$$

The favorability of this process is a direct function of the stability of the carbocation formed (see Mastering Reactions: How Additions Occur, p. 414). As a result, 3° alcohols will undergo this process more readily than 2° alcohols, and 1° alcohols undergo the process slowly at best.

The carbocation can then readily undergo loss of H^+ to form the alkene:

$$H_2\overset{..}{O}\text{:} \quad \overset{\oplus}{\underset{H}{\underset{|}{H_2C-CH-CH_3}}} \quad \rightleftharpoons \quad H_2C=CH-CH_3 + H_3O^+$$

Here, water acting as a Lewis base can remove a hydrogen directly adjacent to the carbocation, forming the alkene. This sets up an equilibrium between the protonated alcohol, the carbocation, and the alkene. Recall that the reaction is typically heated; since the alkene formed has a lower boiling point than the alcohol, it simply escapes from the heated mixture, causing the reaction to proceed to the right (Le Châtelier's principle, Section 7.9).

This back and forth process may occur many times before the alkene is able to escape from the reaction, which helps to explain another observation: if it is possible to form more than one alkene isomer, the one having the more substituted double bond will be favored. This observation is known as *Zaitsev's Rule*. Consider the dehydration of 2-butanol; after the initial formation of the carbocation, there are two possible eliminations that can then occur (see below).

Each alkene is in equilibrium with the carbocation, but the more substituted alkene (here, 2-butene) is thermodynamically more stable than the less substituted alkene. Once formed, it will be less likely to re-form the carbocation than the less substituted alkene will. Thus, the more substituted alkene accumulates, becoming the major product of the reaction, while the less substituted alkene is the minor product.

$$\underset{CH_3-CH_2-\overset{|}{C}H-CH_3}{\overset{OH}{\overset{|}{}}}$$

$$\Big\downarrow \begin{array}{l} + H^+ \\ (-H_2O) \end{array}$$

$$CH_3-CH-\overset{\oplus}{C}H-CH_2$$

loss of H_a / add H_a $H_a \curvearrowleft$ *or* $\curvearrowright H_b$ loss of H_b / add H_b

$$\underset{\overset{|}{H_b}}{CH_3-CH=CH-CH_2} \qquad \overset{..}{\underset{H \quad H}{O}} \qquad \underset{\overset{|}{H_a}}{CH_3-CH-CH=CH_2}$$

Major
(Zeitsev product)   Minor

See Mastering Reactions Problems 14.75–14.77 at the end of the chapter.

Worked Example 14.2 Organic Reactions: Dehydration

What products would you expect from the following dehydration reaction? Which product will be major and which will be minor?

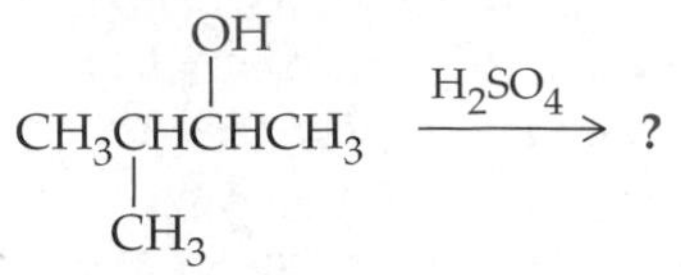

$$\underset{\overset{|}{CH_3}}{CH_3CHCHCH_3} \overset{OH}{\underset{}{}} \xrightarrow{H_2SO_4} \ ?$$

ANALYSIS Find the hydrogens on carbons next to the OH-bearing carbon, and rewrite the structure to emphasize these hydrogens:

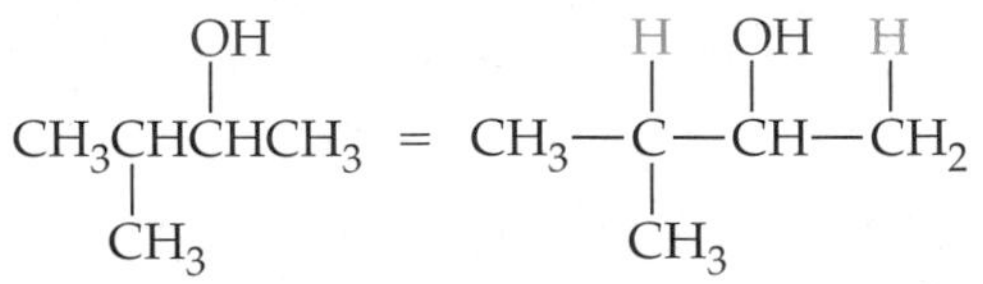

$$\underset{\overset{|}{CH_3}}{\overset{OH}{CH_3CHCHCH_3}} = \ CH_3-\underset{\overset{|}{CH_3}}{\overset{H\ \ OH\ \ H}{C-CH-CH_2}}$$

Then, remove the possible combinations of —H and —OH, drawing a double bond each —H and —OH could be removed:

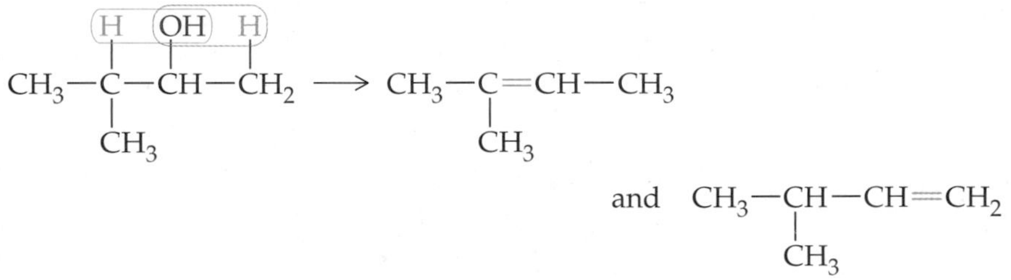

$$CH_3-\underset{\overset{|}{CH_3}}{\overset{\boxed{H\ \ \boxed{OH}\ \ H}}{C-CH-CH_2}} \longrightarrow CH_3-\underset{\overset{|}{CH_3}}{\overset{}{C}}=CH-CH_3$$

$$\text{and}\quad CH_3-\underset{\overset{|}{CH_3}}{\overset{}{CH}}-CH=CH_2$$

Finally, determine which alkene has the larger number of alkyl substituents on its double-bond carbons and is therefore the major product.

SOLUTION

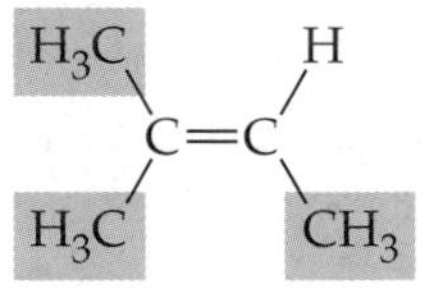

| 2-Methyl-2-butene | and | 3-Methyl-1-butene |
| major product (three alkyl groups) | | minor product (one alkyl group) |

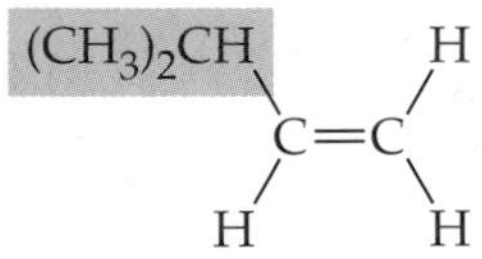

Worked Example 14.3 Organic Reactions: Dehydration

Which alcohol(s) yield 4-methyl-2-hexene on dehydration? Are there any other alkenes that arise from dehydration of these alcohols?

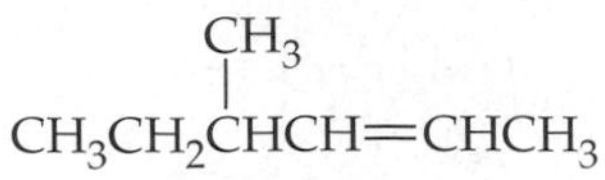

$$\underset{}{CH_3CH_2CHCH=CHCH_3}\overset{\overset{CH_3}{|}}{}$$

4-Methyl-2-hexene

ANALYSIS The double bond in the alkene is formed by removing —H and —OH from adjacent carbons of the starting alcohol. This removal occurs in two possible ways, depending on which carbon is bonded to the —OH and to the —H.

SOLUTION

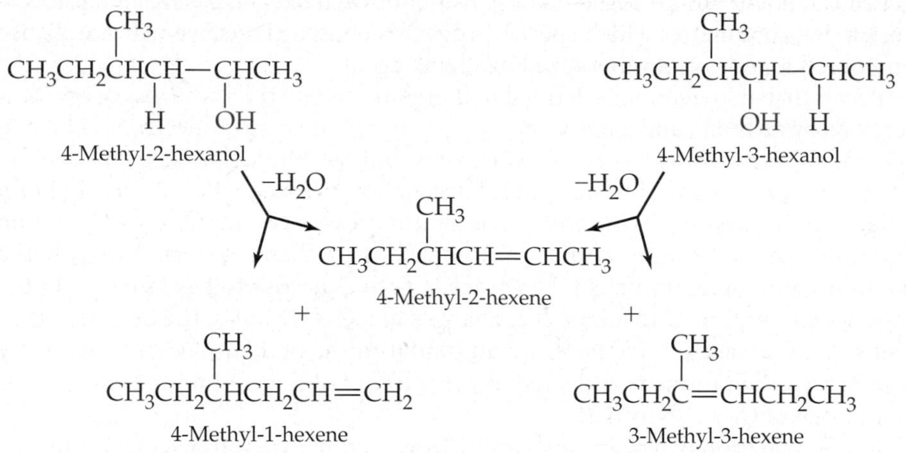

$$CH_3CH_2CHCH-CHCH_3$$
with substituents CH_3 (top), H and OH (bottom)

4-Methyl-2-hexanol

$$CH_3CH_2CHCH-CHCH_3$$
with substituents CH_3 (top), OH and H (bottom)

4-Methyl-3-hexanol

$-H_2O$

$-H_2O$

$$CH_3CH_2CHCH=CHCH_3$$
with CH_3 substituent

4-Methyl-2-hexene

$+$

$+$

$$CH_3CH_2CHCH_2CH=CH_2$$
with CH_3 substituent

4-Methyl-1-hexene

$$CH_3CH_2C=CHCH_2CH_3$$
with CH_3 substituent

3-Methyl-3-hexene

Dehydration of 4-methyl-2-hexanol yields 4-methyl-2-hexene as the major product, along with 4-methyl-1-hexene. Dehydration of 4-methyl-3-hexanol also gives 4-methyl-2-hexene but as the minor product, along with 3-methyl-3-hexene as the major product.

PROBLEM 14.8

What alkenes might be formed by dehydration of the following alcohols? If more than one product is possible in a given case, indicate which is major.

(a) $CH_3CH_2CH_2OH$

(b) 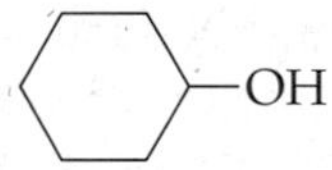 cyclohexyl—OH

(c) 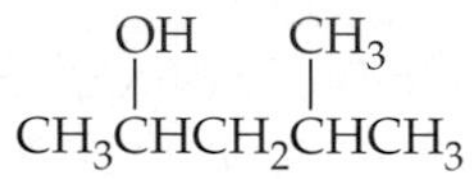 $CH_3CHCH_2CHCH_3$ with OH and CH_3 substituents

PROBLEM 14.9

What alcohols yield the following alkenes as the major product on dehydration?

(a) $CH_3-CH=C-CH_3$ with CH_3 substituent

(b) 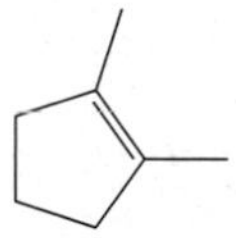 cyclopentene with two methyl substituents

(c) 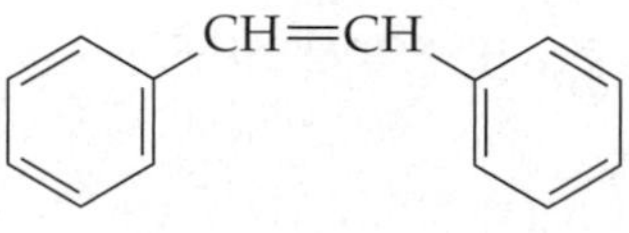 Ph—$CH=CH$—Ph (stilbene structure)

🔑 **KEY CONCEPT PROBLEM 14.10**

What alkene(s) might be formed by dehydration of the following alcohol?

cycloheptane ring with a $C-CH_2CH_3$ and OH and CH_2 substituents

---

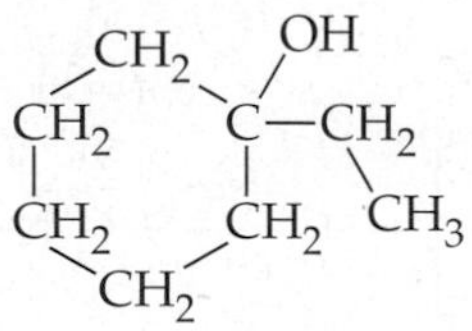

Oxidation

Primary and secondary alcohols are converted into *carbonyl*-containing compounds on treatment with an oxidizing agent. A **carbonyl group** (pronounced car-bo-**neel**) is a functional group that has a carbon atom joined to an oxygen atom by a double

Carbonyl group The C=O functional group.

bond, C=O. Many different oxidizing agents can be used—potassium permanganate ($KMnO_4$), potassium dichromate ($K_2Cr_2O_7$), or even oxygen gas in some cases—and it often does not matter which specific reagent is chosen. Thus, we will simply use the symbol [O] to indicate a generalized oxidizing agent.

▶▶▶ Review redox reactions in Section 5.6.

Recall that an *oxidation* is defined in inorganic chemistry as the loss of one or more electrons by an atom, and a *reduction* as the gain of one or more electrons. These terms have the same meaning in organic chemistry, but because of the size and complexity of organic compounds, a more general distinction is made when discussing organic molecules. An *organic oxidation* is one that increases the number of C—O bonds and/or decreases the number of C—H bonds. (Note that in determining whether or not an organic oxidation has taken place, a C=O is counted as *two* C—O bonds. Thus, whenever C—O in a molecule changes to a C=O bond, the number of C—O bonds has increased, and therefore an oxidation has taken place.) Conversely, an *organic reduction* is one that decreases the number of C—O bonds and/or increases the number of C—H bonds.

In the oxidation of an alcohol, two hydrogen atoms are removed from the alcohol and converted into water during the reaction by the oxidizing agent [O]. One hydrogen comes from the —OH group, and the other hydrogen from the carbon atom bonded to the —OH group. In the process, a new C—O bond is formed and a C—H bond is broken:

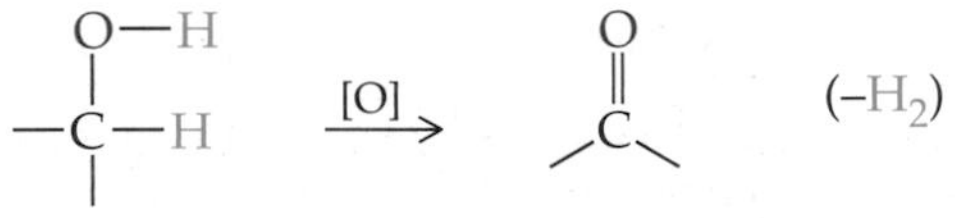

$$
\underset{\text{An alcohol}}{\overset{\overset{\displaystyle O-H}{\mid}}{-\overset{\mid}{\underset{\mid}{C}}-H}} \quad \xrightarrow{[O]} \quad \underset{\text{A carbonyl compound}}{\overset{\overset{\displaystyle O}{\parallel}}{\diagdown C \diagup}} \quad (-H_2)
$$

Different kinds of carbonyl-containing products are formed, depending on the structure of the starting alcohol and on the reaction conditions. Primary alcohols (RCH_2OH) are converted either into *aldehydes* ($RCH=O$) if carefully controlled conditions are used, or into *carboxylic acids* (pronounced car-box-**ill**-ic) (RCO_2H) if an excess of oxidant is used:

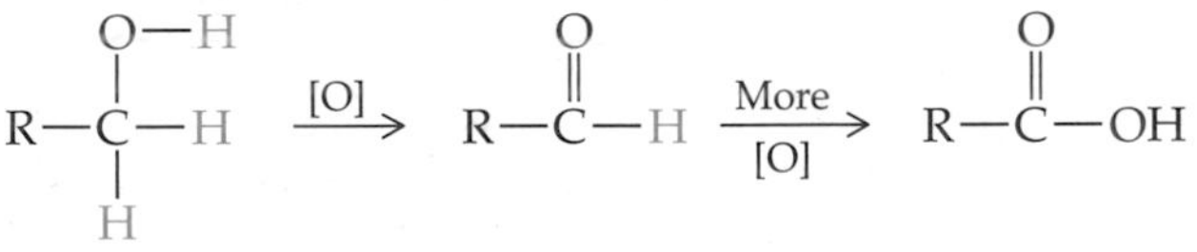

$$
\underset{\text{A primary alcohol}}{\overset{\overset{\displaystyle O-H}{\mid}}{R-\overset{\mid}{\underset{\underset{\displaystyle H}{\mid}}{C}}-H}} \xrightarrow{[O]} \underset{\text{An aldehyde}}{\overset{\overset{\displaystyle O}{\parallel}}{R-C-H}} \xrightarrow[\text{[O]}]{\text{More}} \underset{\text{A carboxylic acid}}{\overset{\overset{\displaystyle O}{\parallel}}{R-C-OH}}
$$

For example,

$$
\underset{\text{1-Butanol}}{CH_3CH_2CH_2CH_2OH} \xrightarrow{[O]} \underset{\text{Butanal}}{CH_3CH_2CH_2\overset{\overset{\displaystyle O}{\parallel}}{C}H} \xrightarrow[\text{[O]}]{\text{More}} \underset{\text{Butanoic acid}}{CH_3CH_2CH_2\overset{\overset{\displaystyle O}{\parallel}}{C}-OH}
$$

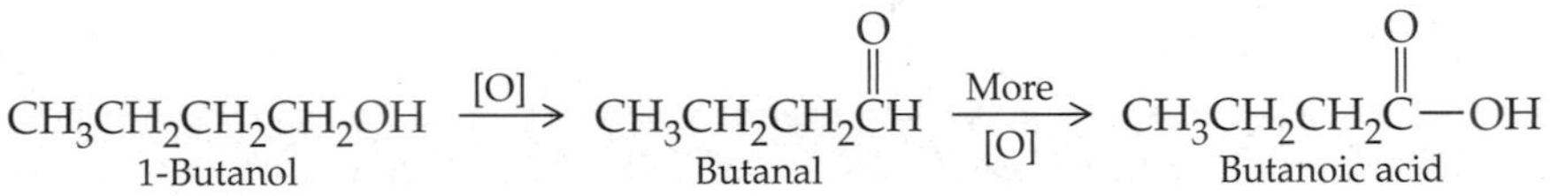

Secondary alcohols (R_2CHOH) are converted into *ketones* ($R_2C=O$) on treatment with oxidizing agents:

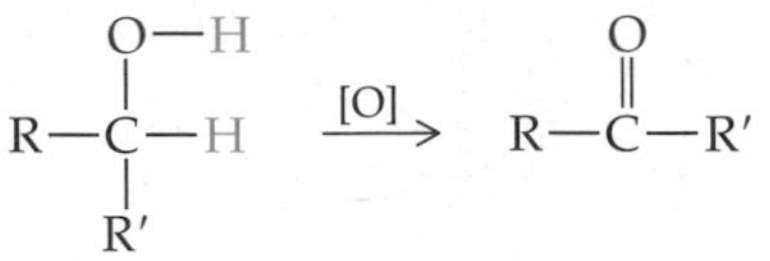

$$
\underset{\text{A secondary alcohol}}{\overset{\overset{\displaystyle O-H}{\mid}}{R-\overset{\mid}{\underset{\underset{\displaystyle R'}{\mid}}{C}}-H}} \xrightarrow{[O]} \underset{\text{A ketone}}{\overset{\overset{\displaystyle O}{\parallel}}{R-C-R'}}
$$

For example,

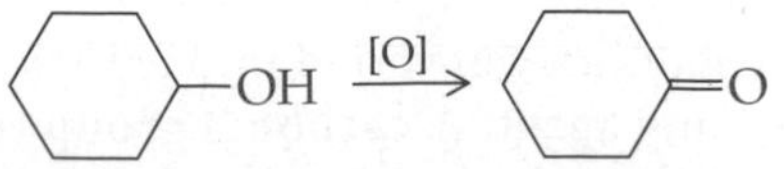

Cyclohexanol   [O]   Cyclohexanone

Tertiary alcohols do not normally react with oxidizing agents because they do not have a hydrogen on the carbon atom to which the —OH group is bonded:

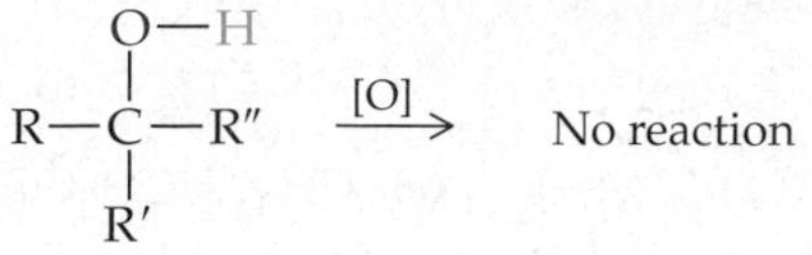

$$R-\underset{\underset{R'}{|}}{\overset{\overset{O-H}{|}}{C}}-R'' \xrightarrow{[O]} \text{No reaction}$$

A tertiary alcohol

LOOKING AHEAD ▶▶▶ In Chapter 22, we will see that alcohol oxidations are critically important steps in many key biological processes. When lactic acid builds up in tired, overworked muscles, for example, the liver removes it by oxidizing it to pyruvic acid. Our bodies, of course, do not use $K_2Cr_2O_7$ or $KMnO_4$ for the oxidation; instead, they use specialized, highly selective enzymes to carry out this chemistry. Regardless of the details, though, the net chemical transformation is the same whether carried out in a laboratory flask or in a living cell.

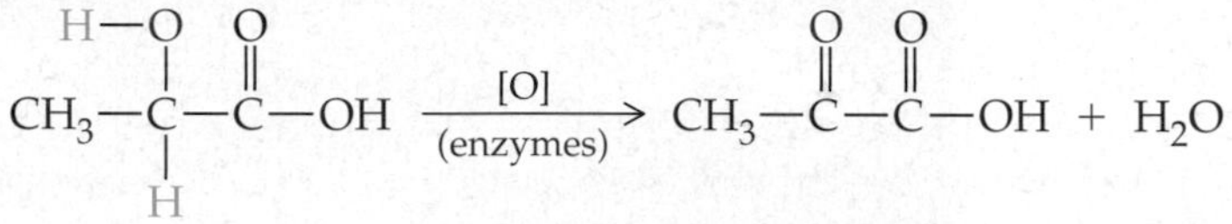

$$CH_3-\underset{\underset{H}{|}}{\overset{\overset{H-O}{|}}{C}}-\overset{\overset{O}{||}}{C}-OH \xrightarrow[\text{(enzymes)}]{[O]} CH_3-\overset{\overset{O}{||}}{C}-\overset{\overset{O}{||}}{C}-OH + H_2O$$

Lactic acid   Pyruvic acid

Worked Example 14.4 Organic Reactions: Oxidation

What is the product of the following oxidation reaction?

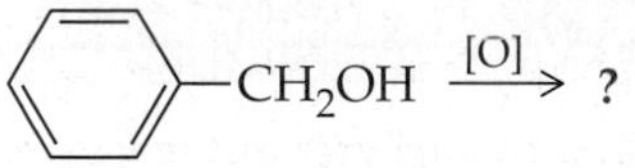

$$\langle\text{benzene}\rangle-CH_2OH \xrightarrow{[O]} ?$$

Benzyl alcohol

ANALYSIS The starting material is a primary alcohol, so it will be converted first to an aldehyde and then to a carboxylic acid. To find the structures of these products, first redraw the structure of the starting alcohol to identify the hydrogen atoms on the hydroxyl-bearing carbon:

$$\langle\text{benzene}\rangle-CH_2OH \quad \text{same as} \quad \langle\text{benzene}\rangle-\underset{\underset{H}{|}}{\overset{\overset{O-H}{|}}{C}}-H$$

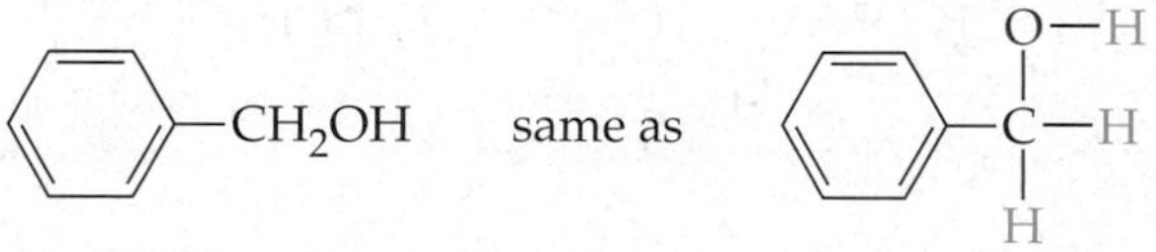

Next, remove 2 hydrogens, one from the —OH group and one from the hydroxyl-bearing carbon. In their place, make a C=O double bond. This is the aldehyde product that forms initially. Finally, convert the aldehyde to a carboxylic acid by replacing the hydrogen in the —CH=O group with an —OH group.

SOLUTION

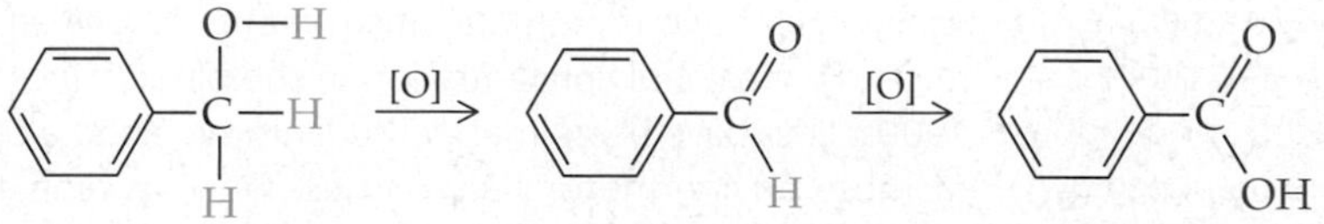

$$\langle\text{benzene}\rangle-\underset{\underset{H}{|}}{\overset{\overset{O-H}{|}}{C}}-H \xrightarrow{[O]} \langle\text{benzene}\rangle-\overset{\overset{O}{\diagup}}{C}-H \xrightarrow{[O]} \langle\text{benzene}\rangle-\overset{\overset{O}{||}}{C}-OH$$

Aldehyde   Carboxylic acid

PROBLEM 14.11

What products would you expect from oxidation of the following alcohols?

(a) $CH_3CH_2CH_2OH$ (b) $CH_3\overset{\overset{OH}{|}}{C}HCH_2CH_2CH_3$ (c) 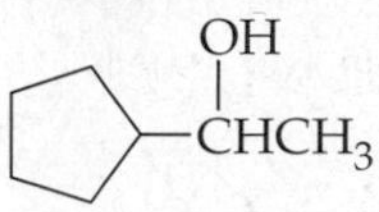 $\langle\text{cyclopentane}\rangle-\overset{\overset{OH}{|}}{C}HCH_3$

PROBLEM 14.12

From what alcohols might the following carbonyl-containing products have been made?

(a) CH_3CCH_3 (with =O above central C)

(b) (cycloheptanone ring) =O

(c) CH_3CHCH_2COH (with CH_3 above second C and =O above last C)

CHEMISTRY IN ACTION

Ethyl Alcohol as a Drug and a Poison

Ethyl alcohol is classified for medical purposes as a central nervous system (CNS) depressant. Its direct effects (being "drunk") resemble the response to anesthetics and are quite predictable. At a blood alcohol concentration of 80–300 mg/dL, motor coordination and pain perception are affected, accompanied by loss of balance, slurred speech, and amnesia. At a concentration of 300–400 mg/dL, there may be nausea and loss of consciousness. Further increases in blood alcohol levels cause progressive loss of protective reflexes in stages like those of surgical anesthesia. Above 600 mg/dL of blood alcohol, spontaneous respiration and cardiovascular regulation are affected, ultimately resulting in death.

The passage of ethyl alcohol through the body begins with its absorption in the stomach and small intestine, followed by rapid distribution to all body fluids and organs. In the pituitary gland, alcohol inhibits the production of a hormone that regulates urine flow, causing increased urine production and leading to dehydration. In the stomach, ethyl alcohol stimulates production of acid. Throughout the body, it causes blood vessels to dilate, resulting in flushing of the skin and a sensation of warmth as blood moves into capillaries beneath the surface. The result, though, is not a warming of the body but an increased loss of heat at the surface, making drinking alcoholic beverages a poor method of "warming up" in cold weather.

Ethyl alcohol metabolism in the liver is a two-step process: oxidation of the alcohol to acetaldehyde, followed by oxidation of the aldehyde to acetic acid. These oxidations are mediated by the liver enzyme alcohol dehydrogenase. One of the hydrogen atoms lost in the oxidation at each stage binds to the biochemical oxidizing agent NAD$^+$ (nicotinamide adenine dinucleotide, a coenzyme, Chapter 19), and the other leaves as a hydrogen ion, H$^+$. When continuously present in the bodies of chronic alcoholics, alcohol and acetaldehyde are toxic, leading to devastating physical and metabolic deterioration. The liver usually

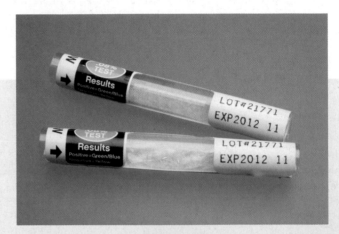

▲ **The Breathalyzer test measures blood alcohol concentration.**

suffers the worst damage because it is the major site of alcohol metabolism.

$$CH_3CH_2OH \xrightarrow[\substack{\text{Alcohol} \\ \text{dehydrogenase} \\ \text{enzyme}}]{NAD^+} CH_3CH \xrightarrow[\substack{\text{Aldehyde} \\ \text{dehydrogenase} \\ \text{enzyme}}]{NAD^+} CH_3COH$$

The quick and uniform distribution of ethyl alcohol in body fluids, the ease with which it crosses lung membranes, and its ready oxidizability provide the basis for tests of blood alcohol concentration. The Breathalyzer test measures alcohol concentration in expired air by the color change that occurs when the bright yellow-orange oxidizing agent potassium dichromate ($K_2Cr_2O_7$) is reduced to blue-green chromium(III). The color change can be interpreted by instruments to give an accurate measure of alcohol concentration in the blood. Since the early 1900s, laws have been in effect to limit the blood alcohol level of those driving motorized vehicles. Once as high as 0.15% (150 mg/dL), legal limits have been steadily lowered over the years. As of 2011, driving with a blood alcohol level above 0.08% (80 mg/dL) is illegal in all 50 states.

See Chemistry in Action Problems 14.67–14.70 at the end of the chapter.

From what alcohols might the following carbonyl-containing products have been made (red = O, reddish-brown = Br)?

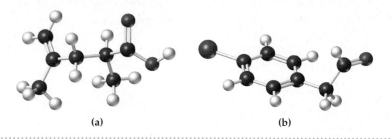

(a)　　　　　　　　　　　(b)

14.6 Phenols

The word *phenol* is the name both of a specific compound (hydroxybenzene, C_6H_5OH) as well as a family of compounds. Phenol itself, formerly called carbolic acid, is a medical antiseptic that was first used by Joseph Lister in 1867. Lister showed that the occurrence of postoperative infection dramatically decreased when phenol was used to cleanse the operating room and the patient's skin. Because phenol numbs the skin, it also became popular in topical drugs for pain and itching and in treating sore throats.

The medical use of phenol is now restricted because it can cause severe skin burns and has been found to be toxic, both by ingestion and by absorption through the skin. The once common use of phenol for treating diaper rash is especially hazardous because phenol is more readily absorbed through a rash. Only solutions containing less than 1.5% phenol or lozenges containing a maximum of 50 mg of phenol are now allowed in nonprescription drugs. Many mouthwashes and throat lozenges contain alkyl-substituted phenols such as thymol as active ingredients for pain relief. The presence of an alkyl group lowers the absorption of the compound through skin (among other things), rendering alkyl-substituted phenols less toxic than straight phenol.

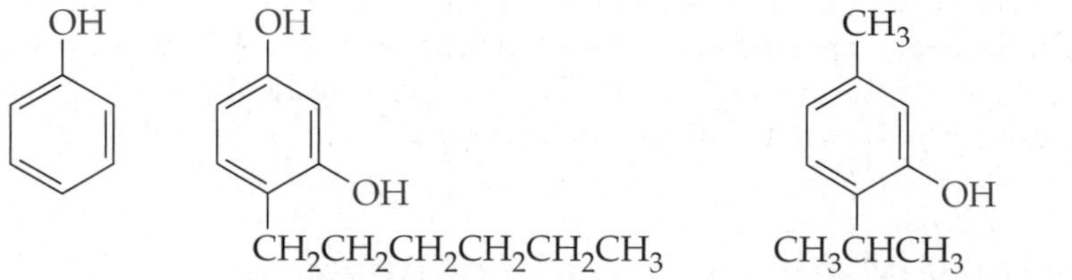

Phenol

4-Hexylresorcinol
(a topical anesthetic)

Thymol
(a topical anesthetic; occurs naturally in the herb thyme)

Some other alkyl-substituted phenols such as the cresols (methylphenols) are common as *disinfectants* in hospitals and elsewhere. In contrast to an *antiseptic*, which safely kills microorganisms on living tissue, a disinfectant should be used only on inanimate objects. The germicidal properties of phenols can be partially explained by their ability to disrupt the permeability of cell walls of microorganisms.

Phenols are usually named with the ending *-phenol* rather than *-benzene* even though their structures include a benzene ring. For example,

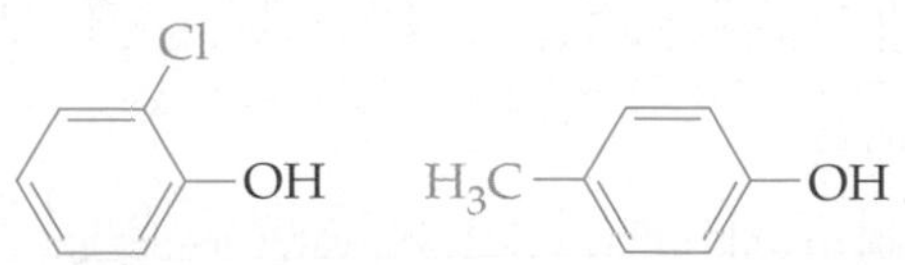

o-Chlorophenol　　　*p*-Methylphenol

The properties of phenols, like those of alcohols, are influenced by the presence of the electronegative oxygen atom and by hydrogen bonding. Most phenols are water-soluble to some degree and have higher melting and boiling points than similarly substituted alkylbenzenes. They are in general less soluble in water than alcohols are.

Biomolecules that contain a hydroxyl-substituted benzene ring include the amino acid tyrosine, as well as many other compounds.

▲ **Careful! The urushiol in this poison ivy plant causes severe skin rash.**

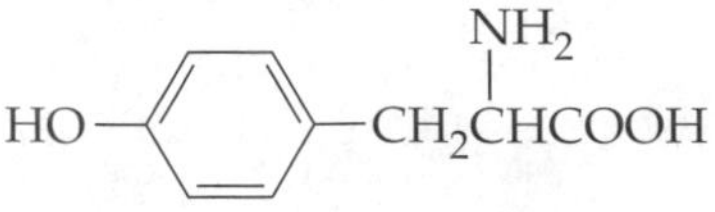

Tyrosine
(an *amino* acid)

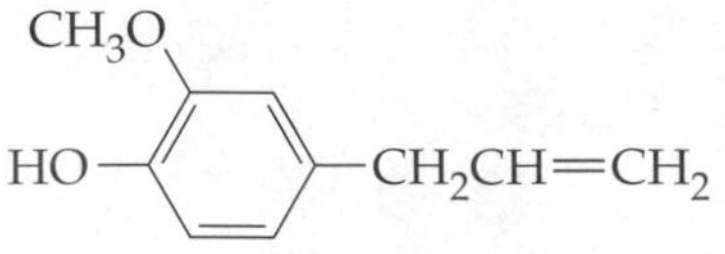

Eugenol
(in cloves, bananas, and other fruits; used for toothache pain)

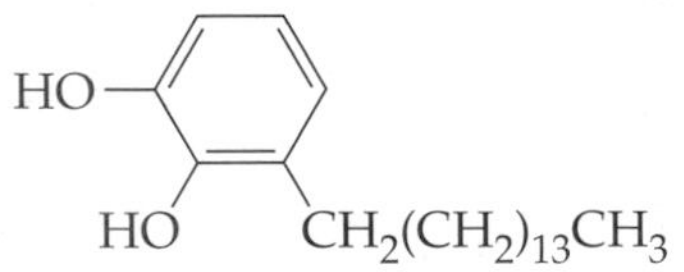

A urushiol
(skin irritant in poison ivy)

PROBLEM 14.14

Draw structures for the following:

(a) 2,4-Dinitrophenol   **(b)** *m*-Ethylphenol

PROBLEM 14.15

Name the following compounds:

(a) 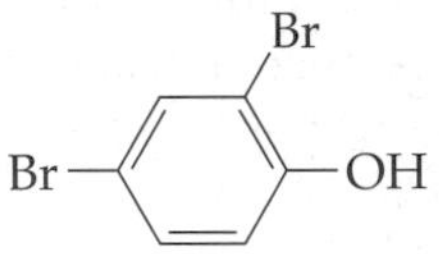 Br—⬡(Br)—OH   **(b)** 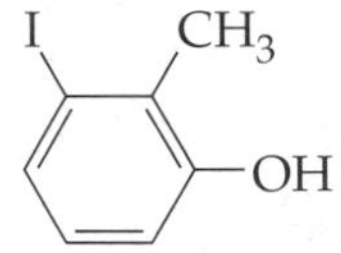 ⬡(I)(CH$_3$)—OH

PROBLEM 14.16

In Chemistry in Action: Ethyl Alcohol as a Drug and Poison p. 446, metabolism of alcohol in the liver was said to be a two-step process. Write a chemical reaction for each of the two steps, showing structures, if the starting alcohol was 1-propanol (do not concern yourself with balancing the reaction).

14.7 Acidity of Alcohols and Phenols

Alcohols and phenols are very weakly acidic because of the positively polarized OH hydrogen. They dissociate slightly in aqueous solution and establish equilibria between neutral and anionic forms:

$$CH_3CH_2OH \underset{\text{water}}{\overset{\text{Dissolve in}}{\rightleftharpoons}} CH_3CH_2O^- + H_3O^+$$

An alcohol

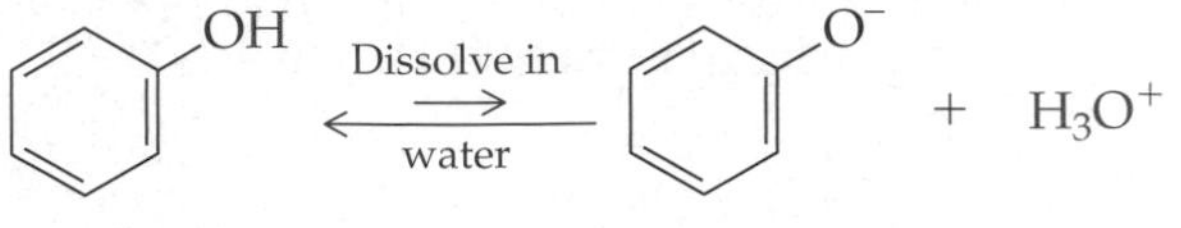

A phenol OH $\underset{\text{water}}{\overset{\text{Dissolve in}}{\rightleftharpoons}}$ O$^-$ + H$_3$O$^+$

A phenol

Methanol and ethanol are about as acidic as water itself (Section 10.7), with K_a values near 10^{-15}. By comparison, acetic acid has a K_a of 10^{-5}. In fact, both dissociate so little in water that their aqueous solutions are neutral (pH 7). Thus, an **alkoxide ion** (RO^-), or the anion of an alcohol, is as strong a base as a hydroxide ion, OH^-. An alkoxide ion

Alkoxide ion The anion resulting from deprotonation of an alcohol, RO^-.

CHEMISTRY IN ACTION

Phenols as Antioxidants

If you read the labels on food packages, the names butylated hydroxytoluene and butylated hydroxyanisole, or their abbreviations BHT and BHA, are probably familiar to you. You can find them on most cereal, cookie, and cracker boxes. Both compounds are substituted phenols.

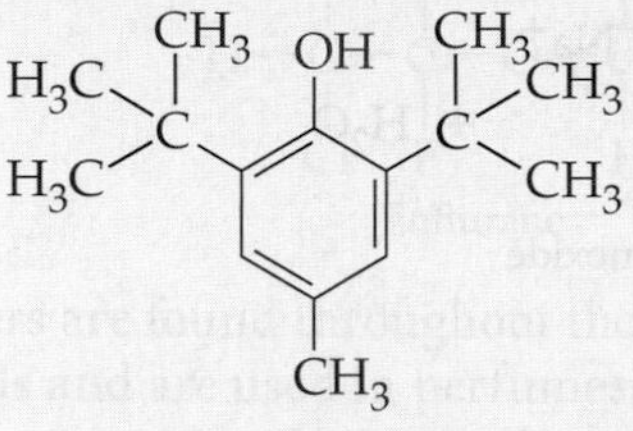

▲ **Most processed foods contain the antioxidants BHT and BHA to preserve freshness and increase shelf life.**

Butylated hydroxytoluene
(BHT)

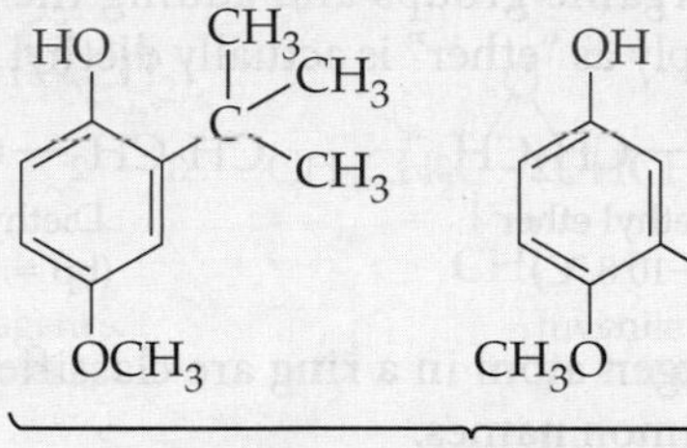

Butylated hydroxyanisole
(BHA)

Foods that contain unsaturated fats—those having carbon–carbon double bonds—become rancid when oxygen from the air reacts with their double bonds, producing ketones and other oxygen-containing substances with bad smells and tastes. The chemistry of oxidative rancidity is complex but involves the formation of reactive substances that contain unpaired electrons and are known as *free radicals*. Each free radical reacts further with O_2 in a *chain reaction* that ultimately leads to the destruction of a great many fat molecules:

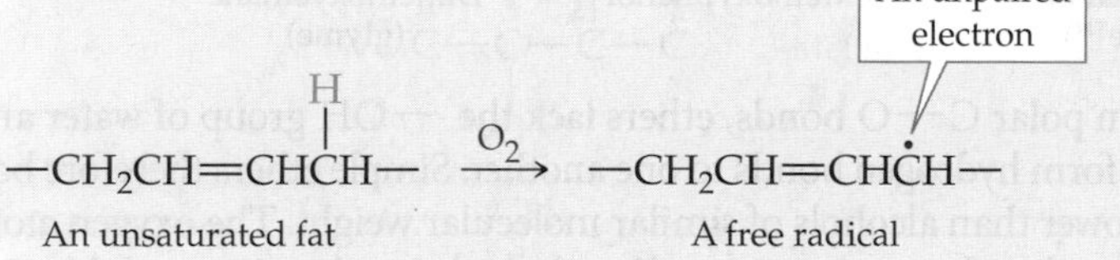

An unsaturated fat   A free radical

BHT and BHA prevent oxidation by donating a hydrogen atom from their —OH group to the free radical as soon as it

forms, thereby converting the radical back to the starting fat and interrupting the destructive chain reaction. In the process, the BHA or BHT is converted into a stable and unreactive free radical, which causes no damage. Vitamin E, a natural antioxidant within the body, acts similarly.

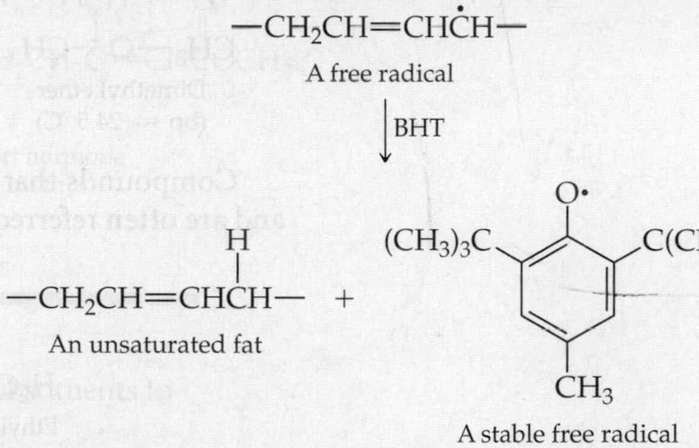

$$-CH_2CH{=}CHCH-$$

A free radical

↓ BHT

An unsaturated fat

A stable free radical

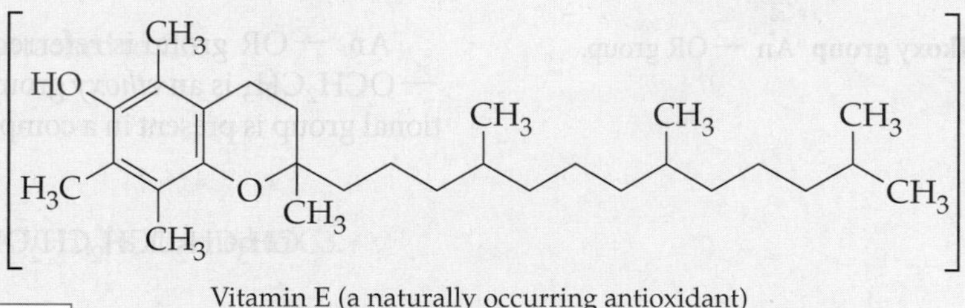

Vitamin E (a naturally occurring antioxidant)

The formation of free radicals is suspected of playing a role in both cancer and the normal aging of living tissue. Although there is no conclusive evidence, antioxidants may well be effective in slowing the progress of both conditions.

See Chemistry in Action Problems 14.71 and 14.72 at the end of the chapter.

PROBLEM 14.17

Name the following compounds:

(a) CH₂—CH—CH₃   (b) 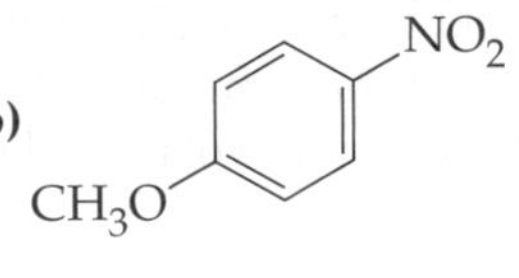   (c)

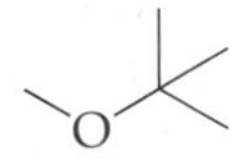

PROBLEM 14.18

In Chemistry in Action: Phenols as Antioxidants on p. 449, the compounds BHA and BHT were discussed. What process do they inhibit, and how do they do it?

14.9 Thiols and Disulfides

Sulfur is just below oxygen in group 6A of the periodic table, and many oxygen-containing compounds have sulfur analogs. For example, **thiols** (R—SH), also called *mercaptans*, are sulfur analogs of alcohols. The systematic name of a thiol is formed by adding *-thiol* to the parent hydrocarbon name. Otherwise, thiols are named in the same way as alcohols.

$$CH_3CH_2SH \qquad CH_3CHCH_2CH_2SH \qquad CH_3CH=CHCH_2SH$$

Ethanethiol   3-Methyl-1-butanethiol   2-Butene-1-thiol

The most outstanding characteristic of thiols is their appalling odor. Skunk scent is caused by two of the simple thiols shown above, 3-methyl-1-butanethiol and 2-butene-1-thiol. Thiols are also in the air whenever garlic and onions are being sliced, or when there is a natural gas leak. Natural gas itself is odorless, but a low concentration of methanethiol (CH_3SH) is added as a safety measure to make leak detection easy.

Thiols react with mild oxidizing agents, such as Br_2 in water or even O_2, to yield **disulfides**, RS—SR. Two thiols join together in this reaction, the hydrogen from each is lost, and a bond forms between the 2 sulfurs:

$$RSH + HSR \xrightarrow{[O]} RSSR$$

Two thiol molecules   A disulfide

For example,

$$H_3C-S-H + H-S-CH_3 \xrightarrow{[O]} CH_3-S-S-CH_3 + H_2O$$

Methanethiol   Dimethyl disulfide

The reverse reaction occurs when a disulfide is treated with a reducing agent, represented by [H]:

$$RSSR \xrightarrow{[H]} RSH + RSH$$

Thiols are important biologically because they occur as a functional group in the amino acid cysteine, which is part of many proteins:

Thiol A compound that contains an —SH group, R—SH.

▲ Skunks repel predators by releasing several thiols with appalling odors.

Disulfide A compound that contains a sulfur–sulfur bond, RS—SR.

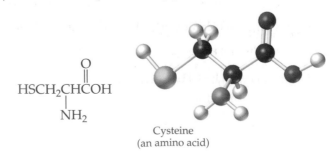

HSCH₂CHCOH
|
NH₂

Cysteine
(an amino acid)

CHEMISTRY IN ACTION

Inhaled Anesthetics

William Morton's demonstration in 1846 of ether-induced anesthesia during dental surgery represents one of the most important medical breakthroughs of all time. Before that date, all surgery had been carried out with the patient fully conscious. Use of chloroform ($CHCl_3$) as an anesthetic quickly followed Morton's work, popularized by Queen Victoria of England, who in 1853 gave birth to a child while anesthetized by chloroform.

Hundreds of substances have subsequently been shown to act as inhaled anesthetics. Halothane, enflurane, isoflurane, and methoxyflurane are at present the most commonly used agents in hospital operating rooms. All four are potent at relatively low doses, are nontoxic, and are nonflammable, an important safety feature.

Despite their importance, surprisingly little is known about how inhaled anesthetics work in the body. Remarkably, the potency of different inhaled anesthetics correlates well with their solubility in olive oil, leading many scientists to believe that anesthetics act by dissolving in the fatty membranes surrounding nerve cells. The resultant changes in the fluidity and shape of the membranes apparently decrease the ability of sodium ions to pass into the nerve cells, thereby blocking the firing of nerve impulses.

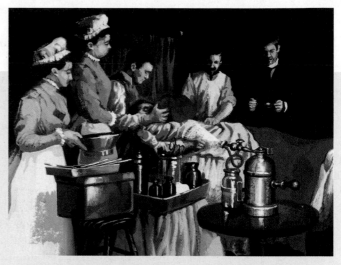

▲ **William Morton performed the first public demonstration of ether as an anesthetic on October 16, 1846, at Massachusetts General Hospital.**

Depth of anesthesia is determined by the concentration of anesthetic agent that reaches the brain. Brain concentration, in turn, depends on the solubility and transport of the anesthetic agent in the bloodstream and on its partial pressure in inhaled air. Anesthetic potency is usually expressed as a *minimum alveolar concentration* (MAC), defined as the concentration of anesthetic in inhaled air that results in anesthesia in 50% of patients. As shown in the following table, nitrous oxide, N_2O, is the least potent of the common anesthetics and methoxyflurane is the most potent; a partial pressure of only 1.2 mm Hg is sufficient to anesthetize 50% of patients.

Relative Potency of Inhaled Anesthetics

Anesthetic	MAC (%)	MAC (Partial pressure, mm Hg)
Nitrous oxide		>760
Enflurane	1.7	13
Isoflurane	1.4	11
Halothane	0.75	5.7
Methoxyflurane	0.16	1.2

See Chemistry in Action Problems 14.73 and 14.74 at the end of the chapter.

Structures:

Halothane

Enflurane

Isoflurane

Methoxyflurane

The easy formation of S—S bonds between two cysteines helps pull large protein molecules into the shapes they need to function. The proteins in hair, for example, are unusually rich in —S—S— and —SH groups. When hair is "permed," some disulfide bonds are broken and others are then formed. As a result, the hair proteins are held in a different shape (Figure 14.2). The hair straightening procedure known as "rebonding" works in a similar way. The importance of the disulfide linkage will be discussed further in Section 18.8.

$$\xrightarrow{[O]}$$

SH   SH   S—S

◄ **Figure 14.2**
Chemistry can curl your hair. A permanent wave results when disulfide bridges are formed between —SH groups in hair protein molecules.

PROBLEM 14.19

What disulfides would you obtain from oxidation of the following thiols?

(a) $CH_3CH_2CH_2SH$

(b) 3-Methyl-1-butanethiol (skunk scent)

14.10 Halogen-Containing Compounds

Alkyl halide A compound that has an alkyl group bonded to a halogen atom, R—X.

The simplest halogen-containing compounds are the **alkyl halides**, RX, where R is an alkyl group and X is a halogen. Their common names consist of the name of the alkyl group followed by the halogen name with an *-ide* ending. The compound CH_3Br, for example, is commonly called *methyl bromide*.

Systematic names (IUPAC) consider the halogen atom as a substituent on a parent alkane. The parent alkane is named in the usual way by selecting the longest continuous chain and numbering from the end nearer the first substituent, either alkyl or halogen. The *halo*-substituent name is then given as a prefix, just as if it were an alkyl group. A few common halogenated compounds, such as chloroform ($CHCl_3$), are also known by nonsystematic names.

$$\underset{3\quad 2\quad 1}{CH_3CH_2CH_2Cl} \qquad \underset{6\quad 5\quad 4\quad 3\quad 2\quad 1}{CH_3\overset{\overset{\displaystyle CH_3}{|}}{C}HCH_2CH_2\overset{\overset{\displaystyle Br}{|}}{C}HCH_3} \qquad CHCl_3$$

1-Chloropropane   2-Bromo-5-methylhexane   Trichloromethane
                                                                                      (Chloroform)

Halogenated organic compounds have a variety of medical and industrial uses. Ethyl chloride is used as a topical anesthetic because it cools the skin through rapid evaporation; halothane is an important anesthetic. Chloroform was once employed as an anesthetic and as a solvent for cough syrups and other medicines but is now considered too toxic for such uses. Bromotrifluoromethane, CF_3Br, is useful for extinguishing fires in aircraft and electronic equipment because it is nonflammable and nontoxic, and it evaporates without a trace.

Although a large number of halogen-containing organic compounds are found in nature, especially in marine organisms, few are significant in human biochemistry. One exception is thyroxine, an iodine-containing hormone secreted by the thyroid gland. A deficiency of iodine in the human diet leads to a low thyroxine level, which causes a swelling of the thyroid gland called a *goiter*. To ensure adequate iodine in the diet of people who live far from an ocean, potassium iodide is sometimes added to table salt (to create the product we know as *iodized salt*).

Thyroid gland hormone; deficiency causes goiter

Thyroxine

Halogenated compounds are also used widely in industry and agriculture. Dichloromethane (CH_2Cl_2, methylene chloride), trichloromethane ($CHCl_3$, chloroform), and trichloroethylene ($Cl_2C=CHCl$) are used as solvents and degreasing agents, although their use is diminishing as less-polluting alternatives become available. Because these substances are excellent solvents for the oils in skin, continued exposure often causes dermatitis.

The use of halogenated herbicides such as 2,4-D and fungicides such as Captan has resulted in vastly increased crop yields in recent decades, and the widespread application of chlorinated insecticides such as DDT is largely responsible for the progress made toward worldwide control of malaria and typhus. Despite their enormous benefits, however, chlorinated pesticides present problems because they persist in the environment and are not broken down rapidly. They remain in the fatty tissues of organisms and accumulate up the food chain as larger organisms consume smaller ones. Eventually, the concentration in some animals becomes high enough to cause harm. In an effort to maintain a balance between the value of halogenated pesticides and the harm they can do, the use of many has been restricted, and others have been banned altogether.

2,4-D   Captan   DDT

PROBLEM 14.20
Give systematic names for the following alkyl halides:

(a) [cyclopentane structure with Cl and CH$_2$CH$_3$]

(b) $CH_3CH_2CHCH_2CHCH_2CH_3$ (with CH$_3$ and Br substituents)

SUMMARY: REVISITING THE CHAPTER GOALS

1. What are the distinguishing features of alcohols, phenols, ethers, thiols, and alkyl halides? An *alcohol* has an —OH group (a *hydroxyl* group) bonded to a saturated, alkane-like carbon atom; a *phenol* has an —OH group bonded directly to an aromatic ring; and an *ether* has an oxygen atom bonded to two organic groups. *Thiols* are sulfur analogs of alcohols, R—SH. *Alkyl halides* contain a halogen atom bonded to an alkyl group, R—X.

The —OH group is present in many biochemically active molecules. Phenols are notable for their use as disinfectants and antiseptics; ethers are used primarily as solvents. Thiols are found in proteins. Halogenated compounds are rare in human biochemistry but are widely used in industry as solvents and in agriculture as herbicides, fungicides, and insecticides (*see Problems 26–27, 50, 51*).

2. How are alcohols, phenols, ethers, thiols, and alkyl halides named? Alcohols are named using the *-ol* ending, and phenols are named using the *-phenol* ending. Ethers are named by identifying the two organic groups attached to oxygen, followed by the word *ether*. Thiols use the name ending *-thiol*, and alkyl halides are named as halo-substituted alkanes (*see Problems 21–22, 36, 56, 61–64*).

3. What are the general properties of alcohols, phenols, and ethers? Both alcohols and phenols are like water in their

ability to form hydrogen bonds. As the size of the organic part increases, alcohols become less soluble in water. Ethers do not hydrogen-bond and are more alkane-like in their properties (*see Problems 28, 36–39, 54–55, 58*).

4. Why are alcohols and phenols weak acids? Like water, alcohols and phenols are weak acids that can donate H$^+$ from their —OH group to a strong base. Alcohols are similar to water in acidity; phenols are more acidic than water and will react with aqueous NaOH (*see Problems 29, 60, 65*).

5. What are the main chemical reactions of alcohols and thiols? Alcohols undergo loss of water (*dehydration*) to yield alkenes when treated with a strong acid, and they undergo *oxidation* to yield compounds that contain a *carbonyl group* (C=O). Primary alcohols (RCH$_2$OH) are oxidized to yield either aldehydes (RCHO) or carboxylic acids (RCO$_2$H), secondary alcohols (R$_2$CHOH) are oxidized to yield ketones (R$_2$C=O), and tertiary alcohols are not oxidized. Thiols react with mild oxidizing agents to yield *disulfides* (RSSR), a reaction of importance in protein chemistry. Disulfides can be reduced back to thiols (*see Problems 22–25, 40, 59, 53, 57, 59, 62–63, 66*).

KEY WORDS

Alcohol, *p. 433*

Alkoxide ion, *p. 448*

Alkoxy group, *p. 450*

Alkyl halide, *p. 454*

Carbonyl group, *p. 443*

Dehydration, *p. 440*

Disulfide, *p. 452*

Ether, *p. 433*

Glycol, *p. 437*

Phenol, *p. 433*

Thiol, *p. 452*

SUMMARY OF REACTIONS

1 **Reactions of alcohols** (Section 14.5)

(a) Loss of H₂O to yield an alkene (dehydration):

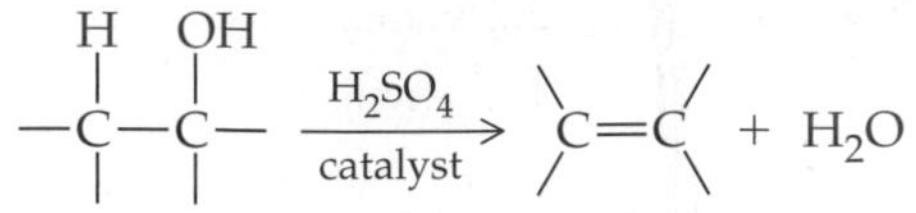

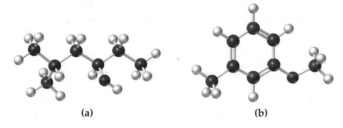

(b) Oxidation to yield a carbonyl compound:

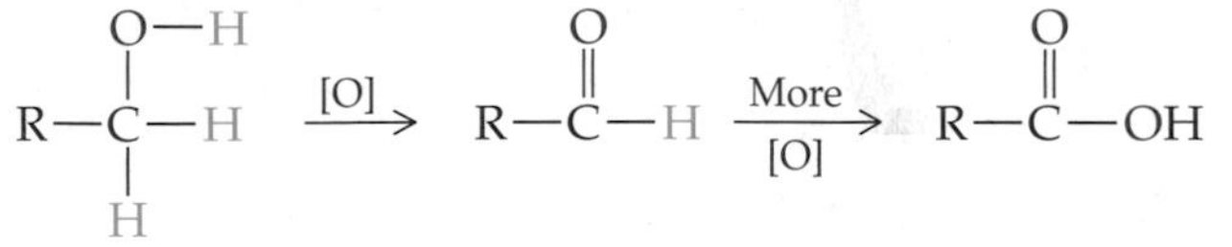

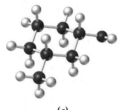

2 **Reactions of thiols** (Section 14.9); oxidation to yield a disulfide:

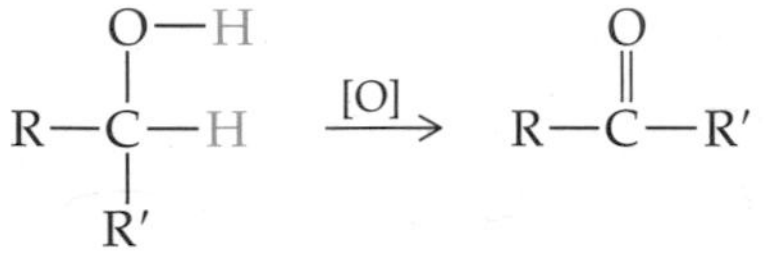

$$RSH + HSR \xrightarrow{[O]} RSSR$$

Two thiol molecules   A disulfide

UNDERSTANDING KEY CONCEPTS

14.21 Give IUPAC names for the following compounds (black = C, red = O, white = H):

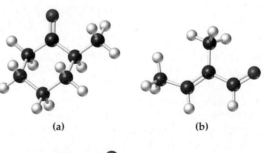

(a)   (b)

(c)

14.22 Predict the product of the following reaction:

H₂SO₄

14.23 Predict the products of the following reaction:

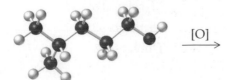

[O]

14.24 Predict the product of the following reaction (yellow = S):

[O]

14.25 From what alcohols might the following carbonyl compounds have been made from (reddish-brown = Br)?

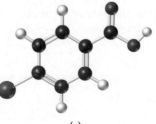

(a)   (b)

(c)

ADDITIONAL PROBLEMS

ALCOHOLS, ETHERS, AND PHENOLS

14.26 How do alcohols, ethers, and phenols differ structurally?

14.27 What is the structural difference between primary, secondary, and tertiary alcohols?

14.28 Why do alcohols have higher boiling points than ethers of the same molecular weight?

14.29 Which is the stronger acid, ethanol or phenol?

14.30 The steroidal compound prednisone is often used to treat poison ivy and poison oak inflammations. Identify the functional groups present in prednisone.

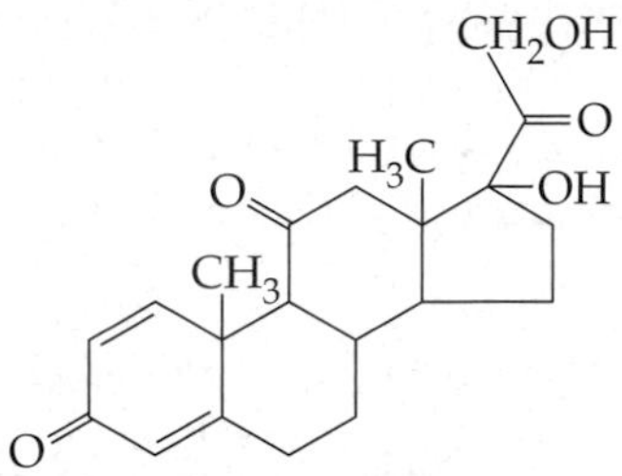

Prednisone

14.31 Vitamin E has the structure shown on page 449. Identify the functional group to which each oxygen belongs.

14.32 Give systematic names for the following alcohols:

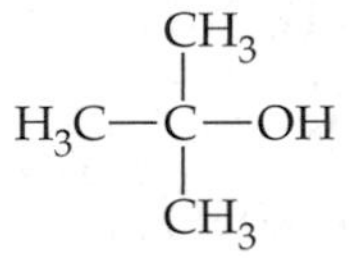

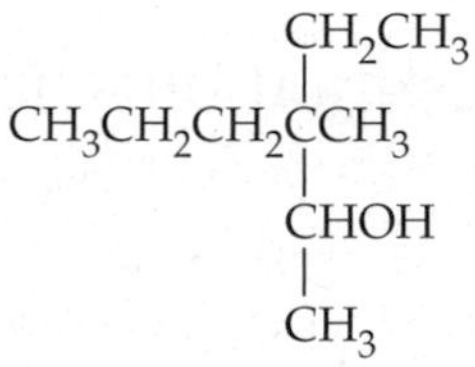

14.33 Give systematic names for the following compounds:

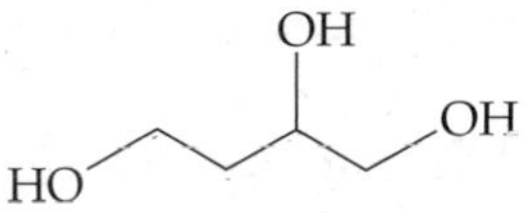

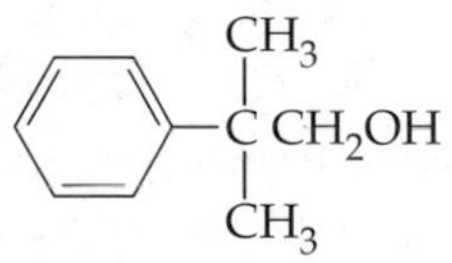

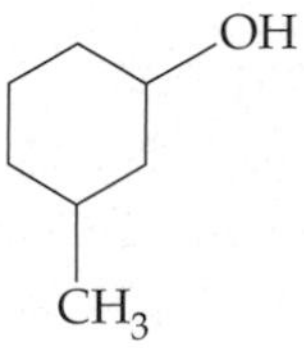

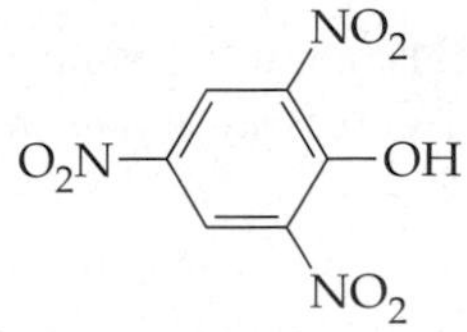

(Also known as picric acid)

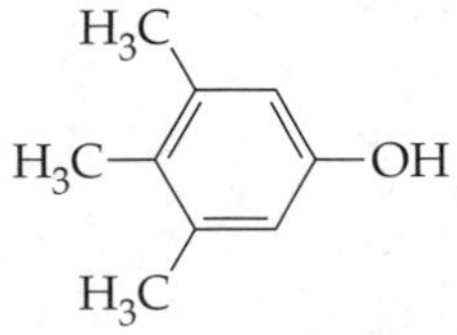

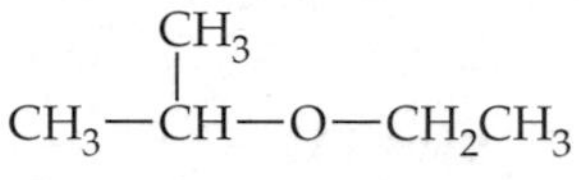

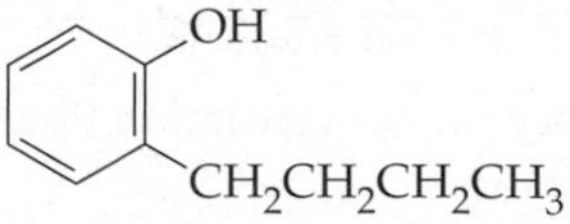

(f) $CH_3CH_2CH_2OCH_2CH_2CH_3$

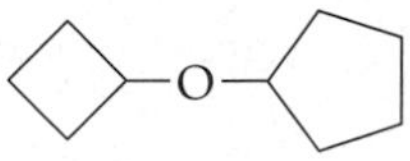

14.34 Draw structures corresponding to the following names:

(a) 2,4-Dimethyl-2-heptanol

(b) 2,2-Dimethoxycyclohexanol

(c) 5-Ethyl-5-methyl-1-heptanol

(d) 3,4-Diethyl-2-hexanol

(e) 2,3-Dimethyl-5-phenylcyclooctanol

(f) 3,3-Diethyl-1,6-heptanediol

14.35 Draw structures corresponding to the following names:

(a) Isopropyl methyl ether

(b) o-Dihydroxybenzene (catechol)

(c) Phenyl tert-butyl ether

(d) m-Iodophenol

(e) 2,4-Dimethoxy-3-methylpentane

(f) 3-Methoxy-4-methyl-1-pentene

14.36 Identify each alcohol named in Problem 14.32 as primary, secondary, or tertiary.

14.37 Locate the alcohol functional groups in prednisone (Problem 30), and identify each as primary, secondary, or tertiary.

14.38 Arrange the following 6-carbon compounds in order of their expected boiling points, and explain your ranking:

(a) Hexane   **(b)** 1-Hexanol

(c) Dipropyl ether

14.39 Glucose is much more soluble in water than 1-hexanol, even though both contain 6 carbons. Explain.

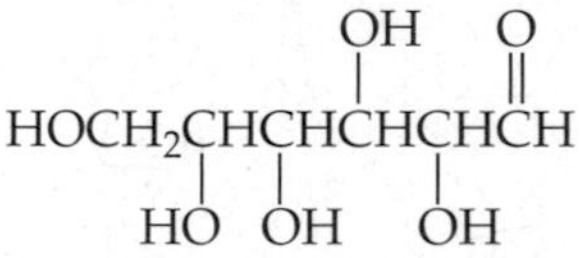

Glucose

REACTIONS OF ALCOHOLS

14.40 What functional group is formed on oxidation of a secondary alcohol? Demonstrate your answer using isopropyl alcohol.

14.41 What structural feature is necessary for an alcohol to undergo oxidation reactions?

14.42 What product can form on oxidation of a primary alcohol with an excess of oxidizing agent?

14.43 What type of product is formed on reaction of an alcohol with Na metal?

14.44 Assume that you have samples of the following two compounds, both with formula C_7H_8O. Both compounds dissolve in ether, but only one of the two dissolves in aqueous NaOH. How could you use this information to distinguish between them?

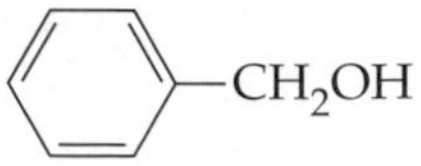

14.45 Assume that you have samples of the following two compounds, both with formula $C_7H_{14}O$. What simple chemical reaction will allow you to distinguish between them? Explain.

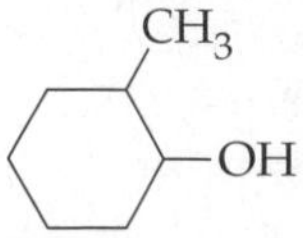

and

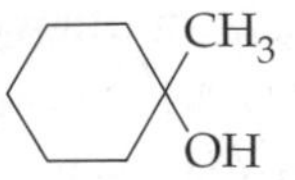

14.46 The following alkenes can be prepared by dehydration of either an appropriate alcohol or an appropriate diol. Show the structure of the alcohol in each case. If the alkene can arise from dehydration of more than one alcohol, show all possibilities.

(a)

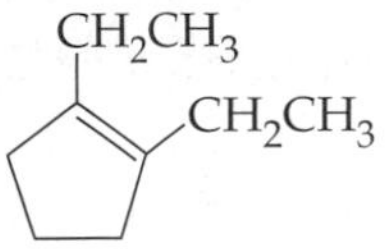

(b)

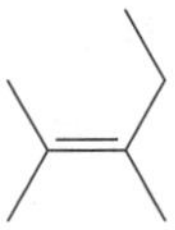

(c) 2-Phenyl-2-hexene

(d)

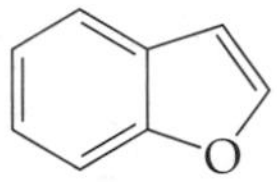

(Hint: ignore benzene ring)

(e) 1,4-Pentadiene

(f)

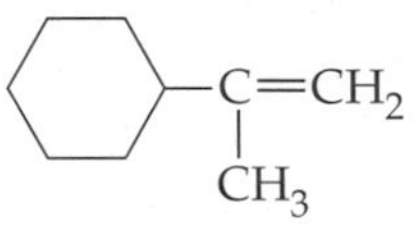

14.47 What alkenes might be formed by dehydration of the following alcohols? If more than one product is possible, indicate which you expect to be major.

(a)

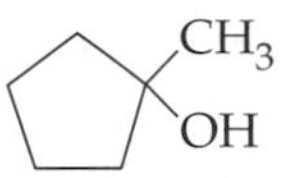

(b)
$$\begin{array}{c} CH_3 \\ | \\ CH_3CH_2CH_2CCH_3 \\ | \\ OH \end{array}$$

(c)

(d)

(e)
$$\begin{array}{c} OH \\ | \\ CH_3CH_2CCH_2CH_3 \\ | \\ CH_2CH_3 \end{array}$$

14.48 What carbonyl-containing products would you obtain from oxidation of the following alcohols? If no reaction occurs, write "NR."

(a)

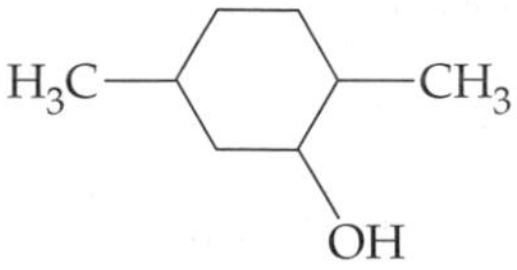

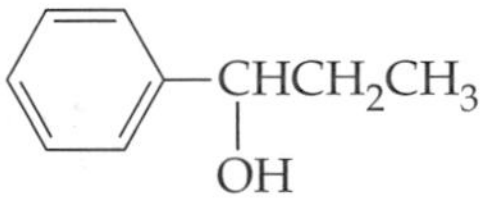

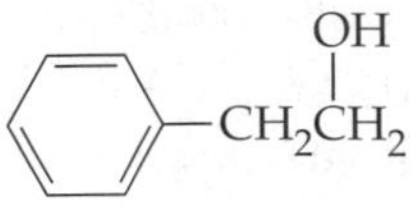

(b)
$$\begin{array}{c} CH_3CH_2CHOH \\ | \\ CH_3 \end{array}$$

(c) 2,3-Pentanediol

(d)

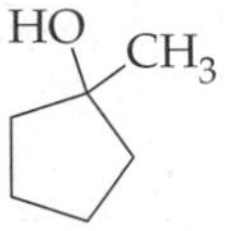

(e)

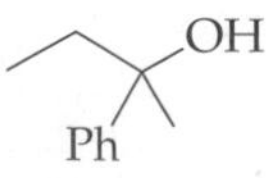

(f)

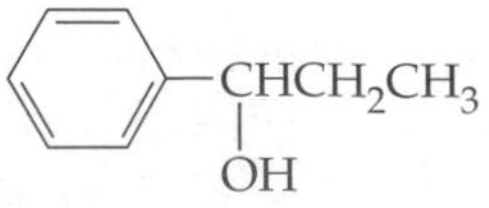

14.49 What alcohols would you oxidize to obtain the following carbonyl compounds?

(a)

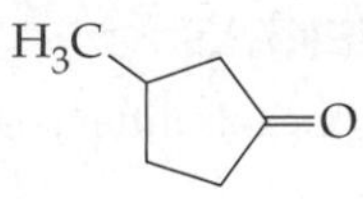

(b)

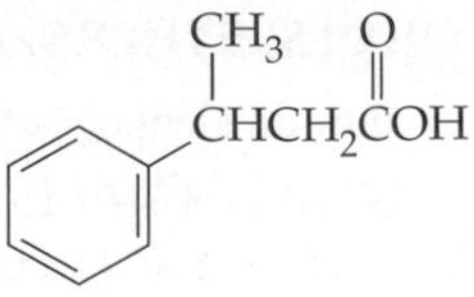

(c)
$$\begin{array}{c} CH_3 \quad O \\ | \quad\ \ \| \\ CH_3CH_2CHCH_2CCH_2CH_3 \end{array}$$

THIOLS AND DISULFIDES

14.50 What is the most noticeable characteristic of thiols?

14.51 What is the structural relationship between a thiol and an alcohol?

14.52 The amino acid cysteine forms a disulfide when oxidized. What is the structure of the disulfide?

$$\begin{array}{c} O \\ \| \\ HSCH_2CHCOH \\ | \\ NH_2 \end{array} \quad \text{Cysteine}$$

14.53 Oxidation of a dithiol such as 2,5-hexanedithiol forms a cyclic disulfide. Draw the structure of the cyclic disulfide.

$$\begin{array}{c} CH_3CHCH_2CH_2CHCH_3 \\ |\qquad\qquad | \\ SH \qquad\quad SH \end{array}$$

2,5-Hexanedithiol

14.54 The boiling point of propanol is 97 °C, much higher than that of either ethanethiol (37 °C) or chloroethane (13 °C), even though all three compounds have similar molecular weights. Explain.

14.55 Propanol is very soluble in water, but ethanethiol and chloroethane are only slightly soluble. Explain.

GENERAL QUESTIONS AND PROBLEMS

14.56 Name all unbranched ether and alcohol isomers with formula $C_5H_{12}O$, and write their structural formulas.

14.57 Thyroxine (Section 14.10) is synthesized in the body by reaction of thyronine with iodine. Write the reaction, and tell what kind of process is occurring.

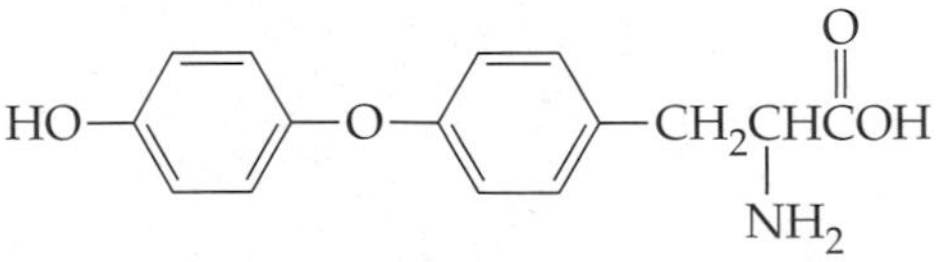

Thyronine

14.58 1-Propanol is freely soluble in water, 1-butanol is marginally soluble, and 1-hexanol is essentially insoluble. Explain.

14.59 Phenols undergo the same kind of substitution reactions that other aromatic compounds do (Section 13.10). Formulate the reaction of *p*-methylphenol with Br_2 to give a mixture of two substitution products.

14.60 What is the difference between an antiseptic and a disinfectant?

14.61 Write the formulas and IUPAC names for the following common alcohols:

(a) Rubbing alcohol

(b) Wood alcohol

(c) Grain alcohol

(d) Diol used as antifreeze (two answers)

14.62 Name the following compounds:

(a) Br—⟨benzene ring⟩—Br

(b) $BrCH=CCH_2CH_3$ with Br below

(c) ⟨benzene ring with OCH$_3$ and CH$_2$CH$_2$CH$_3$⟩

(d) ⟨cyclopentane with two Br⟩

(e) $CH_3CCH_2CCH_3$ with OH, OH above and CH_3, CH_3 below

(f) $CH_3CH_2CH-CCH_2CHCH_3$ with OH OH OH above and CH_3 below

(g) $CH_3C\equiv CCHCH_2CCH_3$ with Br, CH_3 above and CH_3 below

(h) ⟨cyclobutane with Cl and I⟩

14.63 Complete the following reactions:

(a) $CH_3C=CHCH_3 + HBr \longrightarrow$ with CH_3 below

(b) $CH_3CH_2CH_2C-CHCH_3 \xrightarrow{[O]}$ with H_3C, OH above and H_3C below

(c) $CH_3CH_2CH_2C-CHCH_3 \xrightarrow{H_2SO_4}$ with H_3C, OH above and H_3C below

(d) $CH_3-C-C=C-CH_3 + Br_2 \longrightarrow$ with OH above and H_3C, CH_3, CH_3 below

(e) $2(CH_3)_3C-SH \xrightarrow{[O]}$

(f) $CH_3CH_2C=CCH_3 \xrightarrow[H_2SO_4]{H_2O}$ with CH_3, CH_3 above

(g) ⟨benzene⟩$-CH_2CHCH_3 \xrightarrow{[O]}$ with OH below

14.64 The aroma of roses is due to geraniol.

$CH_3C=CHCH_2CH_2C=CHCH_2OH$ with CH_3 and CH_3 below
Geraniol

(a) What is the systematic name of geraniol?

(b) When geraniol is oxidized, the aldehyde citral, one of the compounds responsible for lemon scent, is formed. Write the structure of citral.

14.65 Concentrated ethanol solutions can be used to kill microorganisms. At low concentrations, however, such as in some wines, the microorganisms can survive and cause oxidation of the alcohol. What is the structure of the acid formed?

14.66 "Flaming" desserts, such as cherries jubilee, use the ethanol in brandy or other distilled spirits as the flame carrier. Write the equation for the combustion of ethanol.

CHEMISTRY IN ACTION

14.67 Is ethanol a stimulant or a depressant? [*Ethyl Alcohol as a Drug and a Poison, p. 446*]

14.68 At what blood alcohol concentration does speech begin to be slurred? What is the approximate lethal concentration of ethyl alcohol in the blood? [*Ethyl Alcohol as a Drug and a Poison, p. 446*]

14.69 Cirrhosis of the liver is a common disease of alcoholics. Why is the liver particularly affected by alcohol consumption? [*Ethyl Alcohol as a Drug and a Poison, p. 446*]

14.70 Describe the basis of the Breathalyzer test for alcohol concentration. [*Ethyl Alcohol as a Drug and a Poison, p. 446*]

14.71 What is a free radical? [*Phenols as Antioxidants, p. 449*]

14.72 What vitamin appears to be a phenolic antioxidant? [*Phenols as Antioxidants, p. 449*]

14.73 What substance was used as the first general anesthetic? [*Inhaled Anesthetics, p. 453*]

14.74 How is "minimum alveolar concentration" for an anesthetic defined? [*Inhaled Anesthetics, p. 453*]

MASTERING REACTIONS

14.75 We said in Chapter 13 that H_2SO_4 catalyzes the addition of water to alkenes to form alcohols. In this chapter, however, we saw that H_2SO_4 is also used to dehydrate alcohols to make alkenes. Looking at the two mechanisms, explain with drawings what role sulfuric acid plays in both and why its role in both makes sense.

14.76 Referring back to Problem 14.47, provide the mechanism for the dehydration of:

(a) 14.47(b);   (b) 14.47(e)

14.77 When 4-methyl-2-pentanol is heated in H_2SO_4, two alkenes are formed in significant amounts: 4-methyl-2-pentene, the expected product and 2-methyl-2-pentene, the unexpected product. Using just the mechanism you learned here, suggest a reasonable explanation for the formation of this unexpected alkene (Hint: think about the equilibria discussed in the Mastering Reactions box).

⟨structure⟩ OH $\xrightarrow[\text{heat}]{H_2SO_4}$ ⟨structure⟩ + ⟨structure⟩

4-Methyl-2-pentanol   4-Methyl-2-pentene   2-Methyl-2-pentene

Amines

◄ The blooming of the titan arum plant, also known as the "corpse flower," is an extremely rare event, occurring to date only 12 times in the United States (as far as we know). The nickname derives from the plant's strong odor, which resembles the odor given off by rotting flesh. The odor is caused by the many amine compounds that exude from the blossoming plant.

W̲e now turn our attention to amines, which have single bonds between carbon and nitrogen. The amine functional group is present in so many essential biomolecules and important pharmaceutical agents that they are worthy of a chapter to themselves.

From a biochemical standpoint, many of the molecules that carry chemical messages (such as the neurotransmitters, Chapter 28) are relatively simple amines with extraordinary powers. Histamine, the compound that initiates hay fever and other allergic reactions, is an amine; you have experienced its power first-hand if you have ever had an insect bite. In addition, many of the drugs that have been developed to mimic or to control the activity of histamine—the antihistamines present in cold and allergy medications—are amines. The amino group ($-NH_2$) is important in the formation and stability of proteins, and heterocyclic amines play a crucial part in the function of DNA and RNA. These are but a few examples of the roles played by amines.

▶▶▶ We will explore the function of amines in proteins and DNA in Chapters 18 and 25, respectively.

15.1 Amines

Amines contain one or more organic groups bonded to nitrogen; they have the general formulas RNH_2, R_2NH, and R_3N. In the same way that alcohols and ethers can be thought of as organic derivatives of water, amines are organic derivatives of ammonia (NH_3). In general, they are classified as *primary* (1°), *secondary* (2°), or *tertiary* (3°), according to how many organic groups are individually bound *directly* to the nitrogen atom. The organic groups (represented below by colored rectangles) may be large or small, they may be the same or different, or they may be connected to one another through a ring.

Amine A compound that has one or more organic groups bonded to nitrogen: primary, RNH_2; secondary, R_2NH; or tertiary, R_3N.

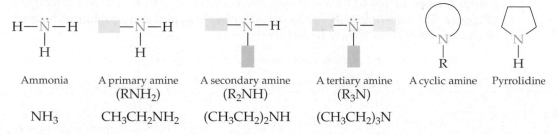

Quaternary ammonium ion A positive ion with four organic groups bonded to the nitrogen atom (R_4N^+).

Note that each amine nitrogen atom has a lone pair of electrons. The lone pair, although not always shown, is always there and is responsible in large part for the chemistry of amines. When a fourth group bonds to the nitrogen through this lone pair, the product is a **quaternary ammonium ion**, which has a permanent positive charge and forms ionic compounds with anions [for example, $(CH_3CH_2)_4N^+ Cl^-$]:

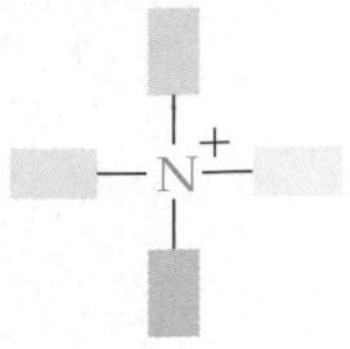

A quaternary
ammonium ion
(R_4N^+)

The groups bonded to the amine nitrogen atom may be alkyl or aryl (aromatic) groups and may or may not contain other functional groups. For example:

CH_3NH_2

Methylamine
(a primary alkyl amine)

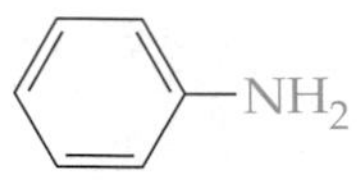

Aniline
(a primary
aromatic amine)

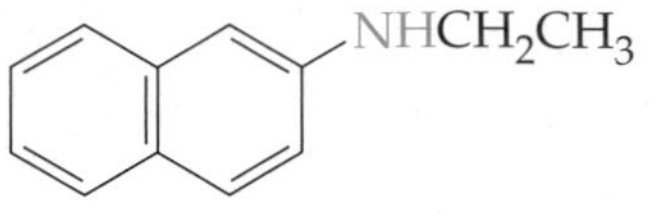

N-Ethylnaphthylamine
(a secondary aromatic amine)

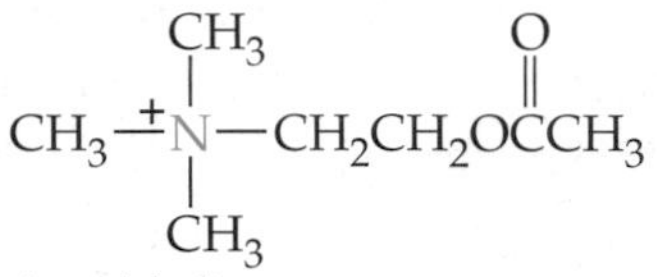

Acetylcholine, a neurotransmitter
(a quaternary ammonium ion)

Primary alkyl amines (RNH_2) are named by identifying the alkyl group attached to nitrogen and adding the suffix -*amine* to the alkyl group name.

Some examples of naming primary amines

$CH_3CH_2{-}NH_2$

$CH_3CH{-}NH_2$

${-}NH_2$

Ethylamine

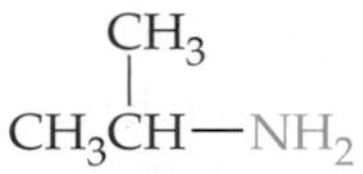

Isopropylamine

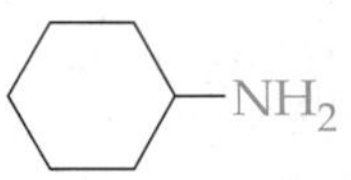

Cyclohexylamine

Simple, non-heterocyclic secondary (R_2NH) and tertiary (R_3N) amines (those possessing two or three identical groups on the nitrogen, respectively) are named by adding the appropriate prefix, *di*- or *tri*-, to the alkyl group name along with the suffix -*amine*.

Some examples of naming simple 2° and 3° amines

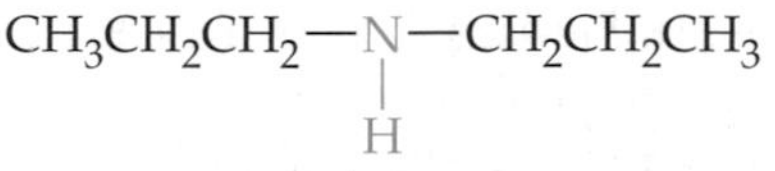

$CH_3CH_2CH_2{-}N{-}CH_2CH_2CH_3$
H

$CH_3CH_2{-}N{-}CH_2CH_3$
CH_2CH_3

Dipropylamine

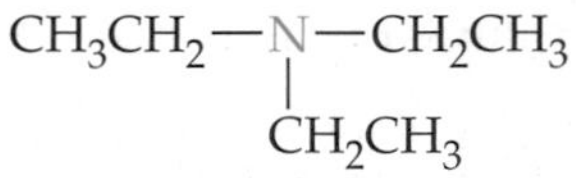

Triethylamine

When the R groups in secondary or tertiary amines are different, the compounds are named as N-substituted derivatives of a primary amine. The parent compound chosen as the primary amine is the one that contains the largest of the R groups; all other groups are considered to be N-substituents (N because they are attached directly to nitrogen). The following compounds, for example, are named as propylamines because the propyl group in each is the largest alkyl group:

Some examples of naming more complex 2° and 3° amines

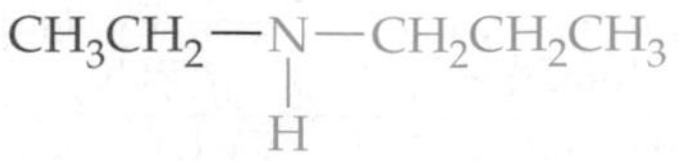

$CH_3CH_2{-}N{-}CH_2CH_2CH_3$
H

$CH_3{-}N{-}CH_2CH_2CH_3$
CH_3

N-Ethylpropylamine

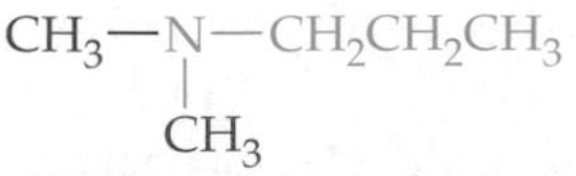

N,N-Dimethylpropylamine

Heteroyclic amines (Section 15.3) are an important family of amines in which the nitrogen is part of the ring structure; the nomenclature of these compounds is too complicated to discuss here and will be addressed as needed.

The —NH$_2$ functional group is an **amino group**, and when this group is a substituent, *amino-* is used as a prefix in the name of the compound (for example, when the compound has a C=O present, Chapters 16 and 17). Aromatic amines are an exception to this rule and are primarily known by their historical, or common, names. The simplest aromatic amine is known by its common name aniline, and derivatives of it are named as anilines:

Amino group The —NH$_2$ functional group.

H$_2$NCH$_2$CH$_2$COOH   CH$_3$—CH—CH=CH$_2$ (NH$_2$)

3-Aminopropanoic acid   3-Amino-1-butene   Aniline—NH$_2$ —NHCH$_3$ N-Methylaniline

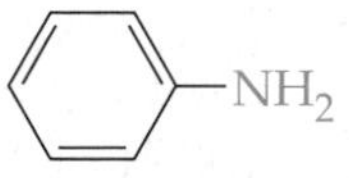

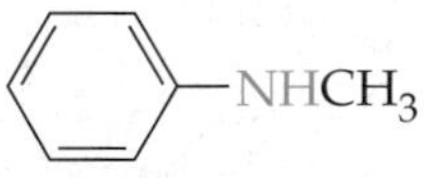

Proteins are polymers of *amino acids*; these have the general structure shown here—a primary amino group bonded to the carbon atom next to a *carboxylic acid group* (—COOH), with a characteristic side chain for any given amino acid on the same carbon:

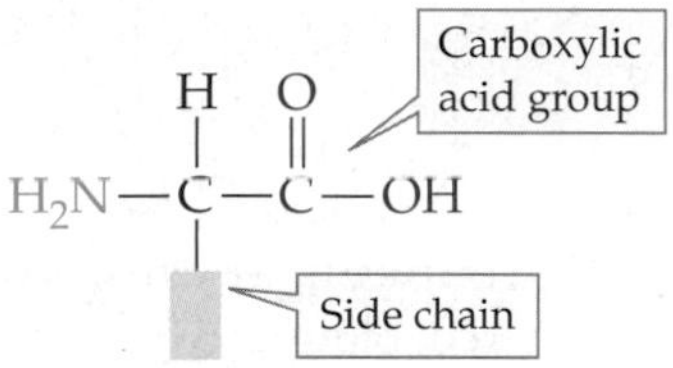

H$_2$N—C—C—OH (Carboxylic acid group, Side chain)

An amino acid

LOOKING AHEAD ▶▶▶ All amino acids contain both the amino functional group, —NH$_2$, and the carboxylic acid functional group, —COOH (in addition to whatever functional groups are part of the side chain). The chemistry of the carboxylic acid group is discussed in Chapter 17. The amino acids and their combination to form proteins are covered in Chapter 18.

Worked Example 15.1 Drawing and Classifying Amines from Their Names

Write the structure of N,N-diethylbutylamine and identify it as a primary, secondary, or tertiary amine.

ANALYSIS Look for terms within the name that provide clues about the parent compound and its substituents. For example, the word "butyl" immediately preceding the -amine suffix indicates that butylamine, the 4-carbon alkyl amine, is the parent compound. The N,N indicates that two other groups are bonded to the amino nitrogen, and the *diethyl* indicates they are both ethyl groups.

SOLUTION
The structure shows that three alkyl groups are bonded to the N atom, so this must be a tertiary amine.

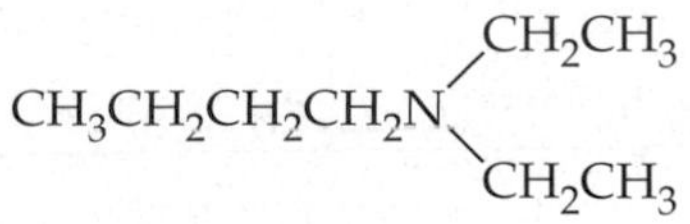

CH$_3$CH$_2$CH$_2$CH$_2$N(CH$_2$CH$_3$)(CH$_2$CH$_3$)

Worked Example 15.2 Naming and Classifying an Amine from Its Structure

Name the following compound. Is it a primary, secondary, or tertiary amine?

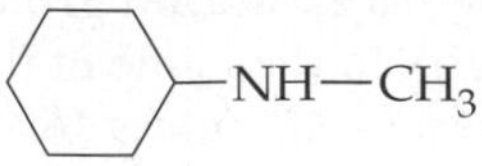

ANALYSIS Determine how many organic groups are attached to the nitrogen. We can see that two carbon groups are bonded to the nitrogen. Since the cyclohexyl group is the largest alkyl group bonded to N, the compound is named as a cyclohexylamine. One methyl group is bonded to the nitrogen; we indicate this with the prefix N.

SOLUTION
The name is N-methylcyclohexylamine. Because the compound has two groups bonded to N, it is a secondary amine.

Worked Example 15.3 Classifying a Cyclic Amine from Its Structure

The following heterocyclic amine is named octahydroindolizine. Is it a primary, secondary, or tertiary amine?

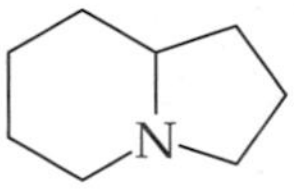

ANALYSIS Start by looking at the nitrogen; we can see that it is attached to three different carbons (as indicated by red, blue, and black bond lines). Even when the nitrogen is part of a ring, an amine will be classified by the number of organic groups that are bonded to it.

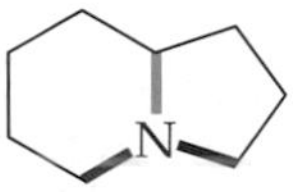

SOLUTION
In this molecule, three individual carbon groups are bound to N; it therefore is a tertiary amine.

PROBLEM 15.1
Identify the following compounds as primary, secondary, or tertiary amines.

(a) $CH_3(CH_2)_4CH_2NH_2$ (b) $CH_3CH_2CH_2NHCH(CH_3)_2$

(c) 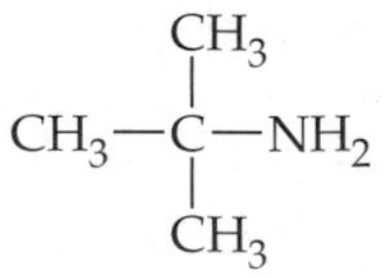 $CH_3 - \overset{\overset{\displaystyle CH_3}{|}}{\underset{\underset{\displaystyle CH_3}{|}}{C}} - NH_2$ (d) 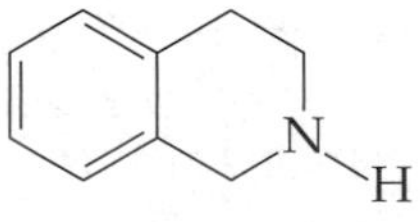   (e)

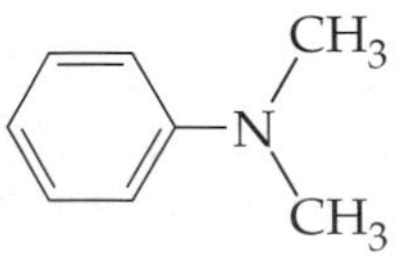

PROBLEM 15.2
What are the names of these amines?

(a) $(CH_3CH_2CH_2)_2NH$

(b) 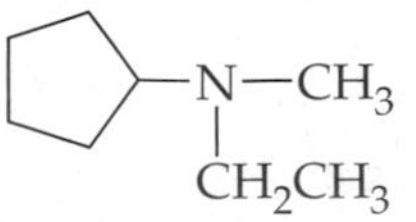   (c)

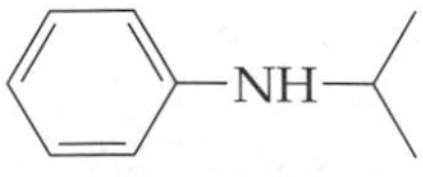

CHEMISTRY IN ACTION

Knowing What You Work With: Material Safety Data Sheets

As you have no doubt realized, there are millions of different chemical compounds; how does a chemist or, for that matter, an average citizen know what hazards might be associated with each one? If a compound is spilled, inhaled, or ingested, what kind of clean up or first aid is required? Chemists are asked these kind of questions with the regularity of an alarm clock, but how can one individual keep all of this information at his or her fingertips? The answer is that they do not: all of the information is readily available through what are known as Material Safety Data Sheets (MSDSs).

Material safety data sheets (hereafter known as MSDSs) are a commonly used system for cataloging information on chemicals. The U.S. Government's Occupational Health and Safety Administration (OSHA) began requiring MSDSs for hazardous materials effective May 26, 1986. These documents contain basic information needed to ensure the safety and health of the user of a given chemical material at all stages of its preparation, usage, storage, and ultimate disposal. It is important to note that MSDSs are not meant for consumers, but rather for occupational use; this is primarily to limit confusion arising from the MSDSs themselves. These data sheets can be found anywhere where chemicals are being used; all college laboratories

Material Safety Data Sheet
Ethyl Alcohol, 70%

ACC# 91791

Section 1 - Chemical Product and Company Identification

MSDS Name: Ethyl Alcohol, 70%
Catalog Numbers:S75119, S75120, S556CA4
Synonyms: Ethyl Alcohol; Ethyl Hydrate; Ethyl Hydroxide; Fermentation Alcohol; Grain Alcohol; Methylcarbinol; Molasses Alcohol; Spirits of Wine.
Company Identification:
    Fisher Scientific
    1 Reagent Lane
    Fair Lawn, NJ 07410
For information, call: 201-796-7100
Emergency Number:201-796-7100
For CHEMTREC assistance, call:800-424-9300
For International CHEMTREC assistance, call:703-527-3887

Section 2 - Composition, Information on Ingredients

CAS#	Chemical Name	Percent	EINECS/ELINCS
64-17-5	Ethyl alcohol	70	200-578-6
7732-18-5	Water	30	231-791-2

Hazard Symbols:F
Risk Phrases: 11

Section 3 - Hazards Identification

EMERGENCY OVERVIEW

Appearance: colorless clear liquid. Flash Point: 16.6 deg C.   **Flammable liquid and vapor.**May cause central nervous system depression. Causes severe eye irritation. Causes respiratory tract irritation. Causes moderate skin irritation. This substance has caused adverse reproductive and fetal effects in humans.   **Warning!** May cause liver, kidney and heart damage.
Target Organs: Kidneys, heart, central nervous system, liver.

Potential Health Effects

Eye: Causes severe eye irritation. May cause painful sensitization to light. May cause chemical conjunctivitis and corneal damage.
Skin: Causes moderate skin irritation. May cause cyanosis of the extremities.
Ingestion: May cause gastrointestinal irritation with nausea, vomiting and diarrhea. May cause systemic toxicity with acidosis. May cause central nervous system depression, characterized by excitement, followed by headache, dizziness, drowsiness, and nausea. Advanced stages may cause collapse, unconsciousness, coma and possible death due to respiratory failure.
Inhalation: Inhalation of high concentrations may cause central nervous system effects characterized by nausea, headache, dizziness, unconsciousness and coma. Causes respiratory tract irritation. May cause narcotic effects in high concentration. Vapors may cause dizziness or suffocation.
Chronic: May cause reproductive and fetal effects. Laboratory experiments have resulted in mutagenic effects. Animal studies have reported the development of tumors. Prolonged exposure may cause liver, kidney, and heart damage.

Section 4 - First Aid Measures

Eyes: Immediately flush eyes with plenty of water for at least 15 minutes, occasionally lifting the upper and lower eyelids. Get medical aid. Gently lift eyelids and flush continuously with water.
Skin: Get medical aid. Flush skin with plenty of water for at least 15 minutes while removing contaminated clothing and shoes. Wash clothing before reuse. Flush skin with plenty of soap and water.
Ingestion: Do NOT induce vomiting. If victim is conscious and alert, give 2-4 cupfuls of milk or water. Never give anything by mouth to an unconscious person. Get medical aid.
Inhalation: Remove from exposure and move to fresh air immediately. If not breathing, give artificial respiration. If

maintain binders full of them for the chemicals they have on site. OSHA requires MSDSs *only* for materials that a) meet OSHA's definition of hazardous and b) are "known to be present in the workplace in such a manner that employees may be exposed under normal conditions of use or in a foreseeable emergency." For example, if you used a chemical spray to clean your computer keyboard and monitor once a month or so, no MSDS would be necessary; however if your job was to clean keyboards and monitors every day with that spray, you probably might need one!

How did MSDSs arise? You might be surprised to learn that their history is part of antiquity. Early healers and alchemists would verbally exchange information regarding preparation, sources, uses, storage, and hazards about two of the most important chemical families to early civilization: medicines and dyes. Some of the earliest written material has been found in the tombs of the Egyptians, dating back over 3500 years; the prescriptions of the Egyptian physician Imhotep were first discovered in the mid-nineteenth century. These medical documents showed that ancient Egyptian physicians treated wounds with honey, resins, and metals now known to have an antimicrobial action. Also discovered were prescriptions for treating colic with hyoscyamus plants (the henbanes) and relieving flatulence with cumin and coriander, all of which are still used today. From this early history, the idea of keeping data regarding chemical compounds was born. It was not until the advent of movable type and finally the development of standard units of measurement that the widespread use of chemical data sheets came to be. Today, MSDSs (or their equivalents) can be found worldwide.

What does a typical MSDS contain? A modern MSDS has 15 specific categories of information that need to be present, the most important being

1. Composition and Information on Ingredients: what is present and in what percentages?
2. Hazards Identification: what kinds of hazards does the material present to humans, including potential health effects?

3. First Aid Measures: how to treat someone exposed to the material, including notes for physicians and antidotes if applicable
4. Fire Fighting Measures: how to extinguish fires involving the material, as well as explosion hazards it may present
5. Accidental Release Measures: how to deal with spills and leaks
6. Handling and Storage: what precautions need to be used when handling the material; also, where and how to store it
7. Exposure Controls and Personal Protection: permissible exposure limits (PEL) for the material as well as a time-weighted average (TWA) for exposure over an 8-hour work shift. This section also lists personal protective equipment required for handling the material.
8. Physical and Chemical Properties: important properties such as chemical formula, melting point, boiling point, molecular weight, and solubility
9. Stability and Reactivity: conditions to avoid and incompatibilities with other materials
10. Toxicological Information: information related to testing for carcinogenicity, human and animal toxicity, etc.
11. Ecological Information: effects that the material has on the environment
12. Disposal Considerations: how to safely and legally dispose of the material.

Interestingly, MSDSs for pharmaceuticals are the most difficult to find on the Internet; given the likelihood of patient confusion, most drug companies do not make their MSDSs freely available to the general public. It is not hard to find MSDS information for almost anything else; if you simply type the name of a chemical followed by "MSDS" into your favorite search engine you will see for yourself how easy it is.

See Chemistry in Action Problems 15.62 and 15.63 at the end of the chapter.

PROBLEM 15.3

Draw structures corresponding to the following names:

(a) Octylamine

(b) *N*-Methylpentylamine

(c) *N*-Ethylaniline

(d) 4-Amino-2-butanol

PROBLEM 15.4

In Chemistry in Action: Knowing What You Work With: Material Safety Data Sheets, what class of compounds is the hardest for the average person to find MSDSs for? Why?

KEY CONCEPT PROBLEM 15.5

Draw the structure of the tetramethylammonium ion, count its valence electrons, and explain why the ion has a positive charge.

KEY CONCEPT PROBLEM 15.6

Draw the condensed formula of the following molecule and name it.

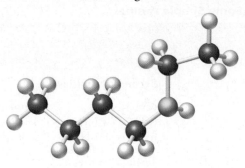

15.2 Properties of Amines

The lone electron pair on the nitrogen in amines, like the lone electron pair in ammonia, causes amines to act as either weak Brønsted–Lowry bases or as **Lewis bases**, by forming a bond with an H^+ ion from an acid or water (Section 15.4).

> The lone pair on the nitrogen makes it a Lewis base.

$$H-\overset{\underset{|}{H}}{\underset{\underset{H}{|}}{N}}:(aq) + H_2O\ (l) \rightleftharpoons H-\overset{\underset{|}{H}}{\underset{\underset{H}{|}}{\overset{+}{N}}}-H\ (aq) + OH^-(aq)$$

$$CH_3-\overset{\underset{|}{H}}{\underset{\underset{H}{|}}{N}}:(aq) + HCl\ (aq) \rightleftharpoons CH_3-\overset{\underset{|}{H}}{\underset{\underset{H}{|}}{\overset{+}{N}}}-H(aq) + Cl^-(aq)$$

Lewis base A compound containing an unshared pair of electrons (an amine, for example).

In primary and secondary amines, hydrogen bonds can form between the lone pair on the very electronegative nitrogen atom and the slightly positive hydrogen atom on another primary or secondary amine. All amines (primary, secondary, and tertiary) can form hydrogen bonds with water (Figure 15.1).

(a)   **(b)**

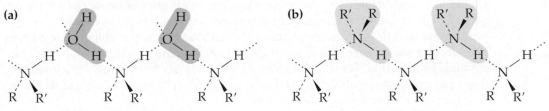

2° amine–H_2O hydrogen bonds   2° amine–2° amine hydrogen bonds

▲ **Figure 15.1**

Hydrogen bonding of a secondary amine.

Hydrogen bonding (shown by red dots) between (a) a secondary amine and water; and (b) two secondary amines.

▶▶▶ Remember that, in the absence of hydrogen bonding, boiling points of molecules increase with increasing molecular mass; see Figure 12.4.

Because of their ability to engage in hydrogen bonding, primary and secondary amines have higher boiling points than alkanes of similar size. Amines are, in general, lower boiling than alcohols of similar size due to the fact that oxygen, with its two lone pairs, can form more hydrogen bonds per molecule than nitrogen, with its single lone pair. In fact, mono-, di-, and trimethylamine, as well as ethylamine, are all gases at room temperature. The boiling points of some simple amines can be found in Table 15.1.

TABLE 15.1 Boiling Points of Some Simple Amines

Structure	Name	Boiling Point (C)	Structure	Name	Boiling Point (C)
NH_3	Ammonia	−33.3	**Secondary amines**		
Primary amines			$(CH_3)_2NH$	Dimethylamine	7.4
			$(CH_3CH_2)_2NH$	Diethylamine	56.3
CH_3NH_2	Methylamine	−6.3	$((CH_3)_2CH)_2NH$	Diisopropylamine	84
$CH_3CH_2NH_2$	Ethylamine	16.6	**Tertiary amines**		
$(CH_3)_3CNH_2$	*tert*-Butylamine	44.4	$(CH_3)_3N$	Trimethylamine	3
			$(CH_3CH_2)_3N$	Triethylamine	89.3
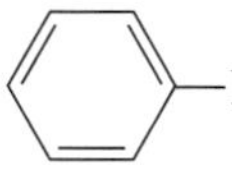 ⬡—NH_2	Aniline	184.1	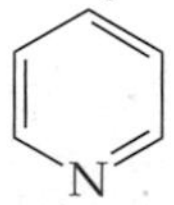 ⬡N (pyridine)	Pyridine	115

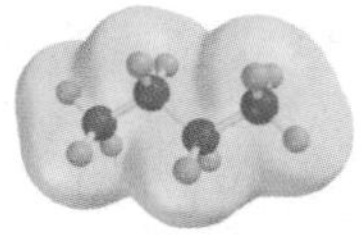

$CH_3CH_2CH_2CH_3$

Butane, bp 0 °C
MW = 58

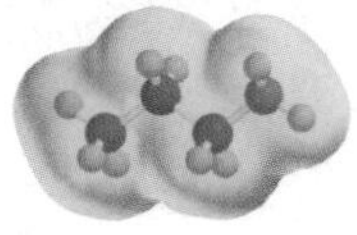

$CH_3CH_2CH_2NH_2$

Propylamine, bp 48 °C
MW = 59

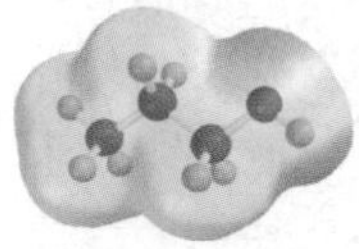

$CH_3CH_2CH_2OH$

Propanol, bp 97 °C
MW = 60

Tertiary amine molecules have no hydrogen atoms attached to nitrogen and therefore cannot hydrogen-bond with each other. As a result they are much lower boiling than alcohols or primary or secondary amines of similar molecular weight. Compare the boiling point of trimethylamine (3 °C) with those of propylamine (48 °C) and the other compounds shown in Table 15.1.

All amines, however, can hydrogen-bond to water molecules through the lone electron pair on their nitrogen atoms. As a result, amines with up to about 6 carbon atoms have appreciable solubility in water.

Many volatile amines have strong odors. Some smell like ammonia and others like stale fish or decaying meat. The protein in flesh contains amine groups, and the smaller, volatile amines produced during decay and protein breakdown are responsible for the odor of rotten meat. One such amine, 1,5-diaminopentane, is commonly known as cadaverine.

Another significant property of amines is that many cause physiological responses. The simpler amines are irritating to the skin, eyes, and mucous membranes and are toxic by ingestion. Some of the more complex amines from plants (alkaloids, Section 15.6) can be very poisonous. All living things nevertheless contain a wide variety of amines, and many useful drugs are amines.

Properties of Amines

- Primary and secondary amines can hydrogen-bond with each other and thus are higher boiling than alkanes but lower boiling than alcohols.
- Tertiary amines are lower boiling than secondary or primary amines because hydrogen bonding between tertiary amines is not possible.
- The simplest amines are gases; other common amines are liquids.

- Volatile amines can have unpleasant odors.
- Simple amines are water-soluble because of hydrogen bonding with water.
- Amines are weak Brønsted–Lowry/Lewis bases (Section 15.4).
- Many amines are physiologically active, and many are toxic (see Chemistry in Action: Toxicology on p. 478).

PROBLEM 15.7

Arrange the following compounds in order of increasing boiling point. Explain why you placed them in that order.

(a) $CH_3-\underset{\underset{CH_3}{|}}{N}-CH_2CH_3$ (b) $CH_3CH_2CH_2CH_2OH$ (c) $CH_3CH_2CH_2CH_2NH_2$

PROBLEM 15.8

Draw the structures of (a) ethylamine and (b) trimethylamine. Use dashed lines to show how they would form hydrogen bonds to water molecules.

15.3 Heterocyclic Nitrogen Compounds

In many nitrogen-containing compounds, the nitrogen atom is in a ring with carbon atoms. Compounds that contain atoms other than carbon in the ring are known as **heterocycles**. Heterocyclic nitrogen compounds may be nonaromatic or aromatic. Piperidine, for example, is a saturated heterocyclic amine with a six-membered ring, and pyridine is an aromatic heterocyclic amine that, like other aromatic compounds, is often represented on paper as a ring with alternating double and single bonds.

Heterocycle A ring that contains nitrogen or some other atom in addition to carbon.

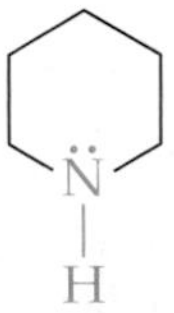

Piperidine
(a saturated cyclic amine)

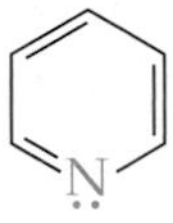

Pyridine
(an aromatic amine)

The names and structures of several heterocyclic nitrogen compounds are given in Table 15.2; note how seemingly random the names are. You need not memorize

TABLE 15.2 Some Heterocyclic Nitrogen Compounds

| 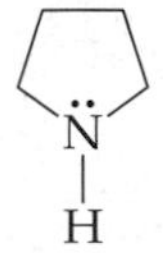 Pyrrolidine (in nicotine and other alkaloids) | 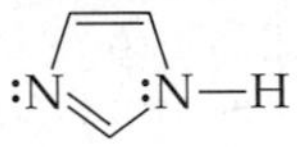 Imidazole (in histamine) | 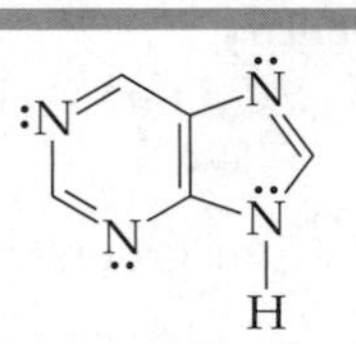 Purine (nitrogen ring system in DNA; present in anticancer drugs) | 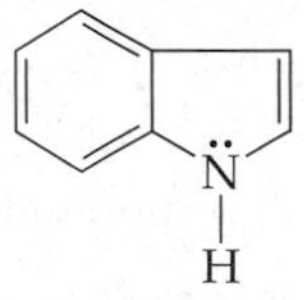 Indole (in many alkaloids and drugs) |
| 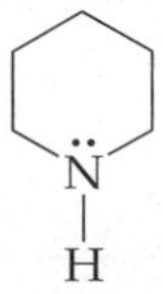 Piperidine (in many drugs) | 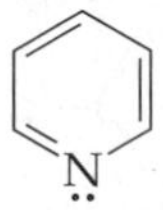 Pyridine (in several B vitamins) | 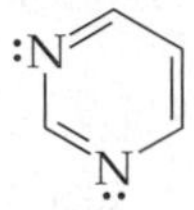 Pyrimidine (nitrogen ring present in DNA and in some B vitamins) | 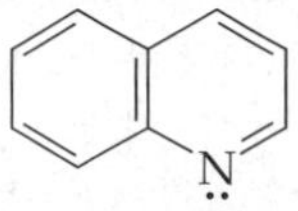 Quinoline (in antibacterial agents) |

these names and structures, but you should take note that such rings are very common in many natural compounds found in plants and animals. For example, nicotine, from tobacco leaves, contains one pyridine ring and one pyrrolidine ring; quinine, an antimalarial drug isolated from the bark of the South American *Cinchona* tree, contains a quinoline ring system plus a nitrogen ring with a 2-carbon bridge across it. The amino acid tryptophan contains an indole ring system in addition to its amino group.

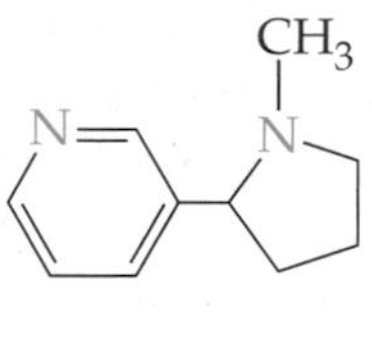

Nicotine
from tobacco
(an insecticide; an
active ingredient
in cigarette smoke)

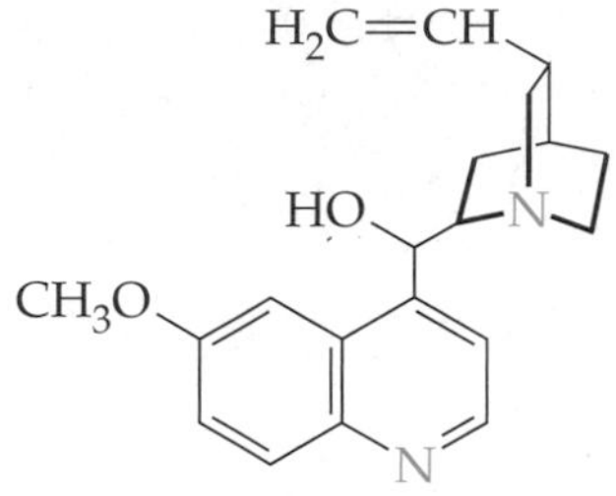

Quinine
from the *Cinchona* tree
(an antimalarial drug)

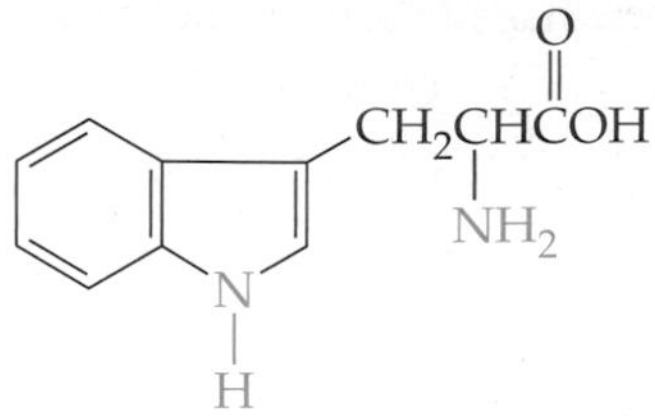

Tryptophan
(an amino acid)

Adenine, a nitrogen-containing cyclic compound, is one of the four amines that compose the "bases" in DNA that code for genetic traits.

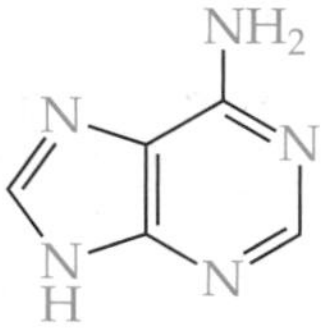

Adenine

LOOKING AHEAD ▶▶▶ Hydrogen bonding that occurs between hydrogen atoms on nitrogens and oxygens and the oxygen or nitrogen atoms of other groups within a molecule helps to determine the shape of many biomolecules. Such attractions contribute to the complex shapes into which large protein molecules are folded (Section 18.8). Hydrogen bonding of amine groups also plays a crucial role in the helical structure of the molecule that carries hereditary information—deoxyribonucleic acid, DNA (Section 25.4).

PROBLEM 15.9
Consult Table 15.1 and identify:
(a) Two amines that are gases at room temperature
(b) A heterocyclic amine
(c) A compound with an amine group on an aromatic ring

PROBLEM 15.10
Consult Table 15.2 and write the molecular formulas for pyrimidine and purine.

PROBLEM 15.11
Which of the following compounds are heterocyclic nitrogen compounds?

(a) 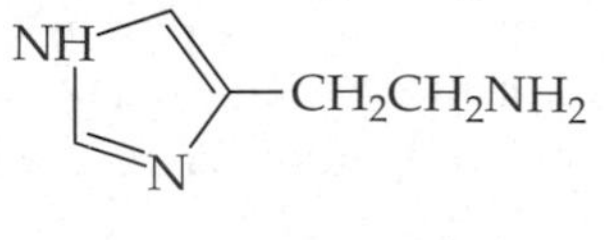 $-CH_2CH_2NH_2$ (b) 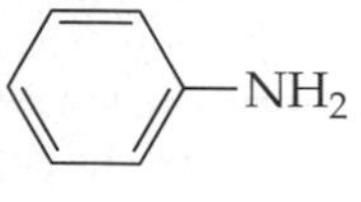 $-NH_2$

(c) 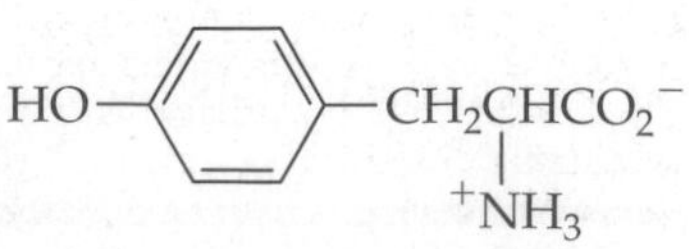 $HO-$ $-CH_2CHCO_2^-$ $^+NH_3$ (d) 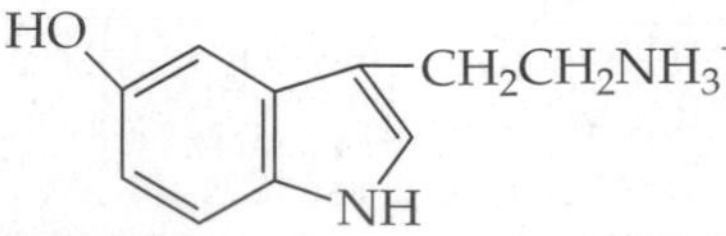 $HO-$ $-CH_2CH_2NH_3^+$

15.4 Basicity of Amines

Just like ammonia, aqueous solutions of amines are weakly basic because of the formation of OH^- and R_3NH^+ ions in water. Consider the following equilibria of the neutral amines and their **ammonium ions**:

$$CH_3CH_2NH_2 + H_2O \rightleftharpoons CH_3CH_2NH_3^+ + OH^-$$

$$(CH_3CH_2)_2NH + H_2O \rightleftharpoons (CH_3CH_2)_2NH_2^+ + OH^-$$

$$(CH_3CH_2)_3N + H_2O \rightleftharpoons (CH_3CH_2)_3NH^+ + OH^-$$

Notice that these are reversible reactions; ammonium ions can react as acids in the presence of bases to regenerate the amines. This equilibrium is found to exist in solutions with pH values as high as 8.

Ammonium ions are also formed when amines react with the hydronium ion in acidic solutions:

$$CH_3CH_2NH_2 + H_3O^+ \rightleftharpoons CH_3CH_2NH_3^+ + H_2O$$

$$(CH_3CH_2)_2NH + H_3O^+ \rightleftharpoons (CH_3CH_2)_2NH_2^+ + H_2O$$

$$(CH_3CH_2)_3N + H_3O^+ \rightleftharpoons (CH_3CH_2)_3NH^+ + H_2O$$

The positive ions formed by addition of H^+ to alkylamines are named by replacing the ending -*amine* with -*ammonium*. To name the ions of heterocyclic amines, the amine name is modified by replacing the -*e* with -*ium*. For example:

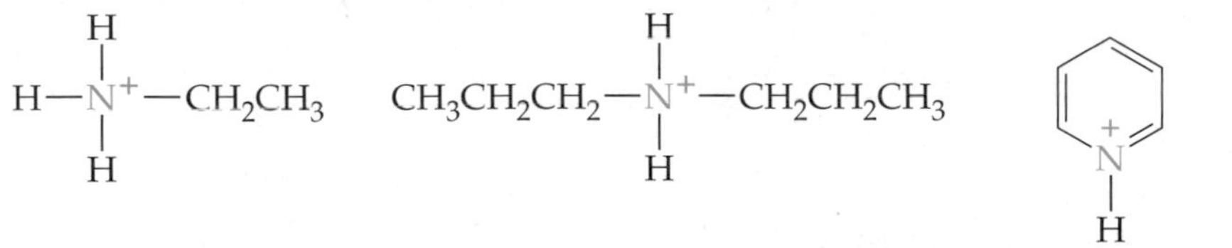

Ethylammonium ion
(from ethylamine)

Dipropylammonium ion
(from dipropylamine)

Pyridinium ion
(from pyridine)

As a result of the equilibria just shown, amines exist as ammonium ions in the aqueous environment of blood and other body fluids, which have a typical pH value of 7.4; for this reason, they are written as ions in the context of biochemistry. For example, histamine and serotonin (both neurotransmitters, Sections 28.8, 28.9) are represented as follows:

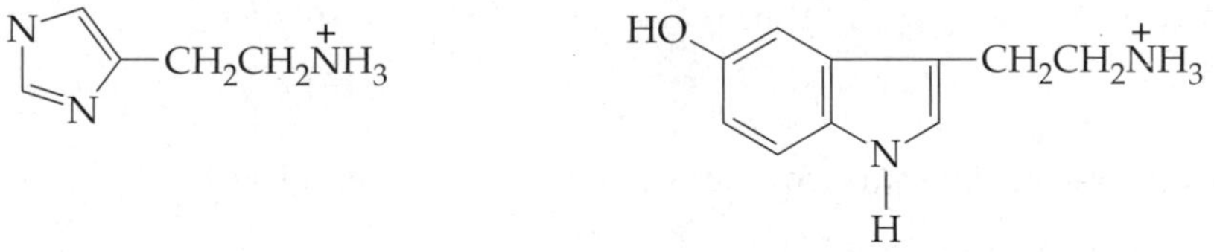

Histamine
(causes allergic reaction)

Serotonin
(a neurotransmitter active in the brain)

In general, nonaromatic amines (such as $CH_3CH_2NH_2$ or piperidine, Table 15.2) are slightly stronger bases than ammonia, and aromatic amines (such as aniline or pyridine, Table 15.2) are weaker bases than ammonia:

Basicity: Nonaromatic amines > Ammonia > Aromatic amines

Ammonium ion A positive ion formed by addition of hydrogen to ammonia or an amine (may be primary, secondary, or tertiary).

Worked Example 15.4 Amines as Bases in Water

Write balanced equations for the reaction of ammonia with water and for the reaction of ethylamine with water. Label each species in your equations as either an acid or a base.

ANALYSIS Determine which species is the base and which is the acid. Remember that the base will accept a hydrogen ion from the acid. Review the definitions for a Brønsted–Lowry base (Section 10.3) and a Lewis base (Section 15.2).

SOLUTION

Like ammonia, amines have a lone pair of electrons on the nitrogen atom. Because ammonia is a base that reacts with water to accept a hydrogen ion (which bonds to the lone pair), it is reasonable to expect that amines are bases that react in a similar manner.

$$\underset{Base}{NH_3} + \underset{Acid}{H_2O} \rightleftharpoons \underset{Acid}{NH_4^+} + \underset{Base}{OH^-}$$

$$\underset{Base}{CH_3CH_2NH_2} + \underset{Acid}{H_2O} \rightleftharpoons \underset{Acid}{CH_3CH_2NH_3^+} + \underset{Base}{OH^-}$$

Notice that in both cases water acts as an acid because it donates a hydrogen ion to the nitrogen.

PROBLEM 15.12

Write an equation for the acid–base equilibrium of:

(a) Pyrrolidine and water   **(b)** Pyridine and water

Label each species in the equilibrium as either an acid or a base.

PROBLEM 15.13

Complete the following equations:

(a) 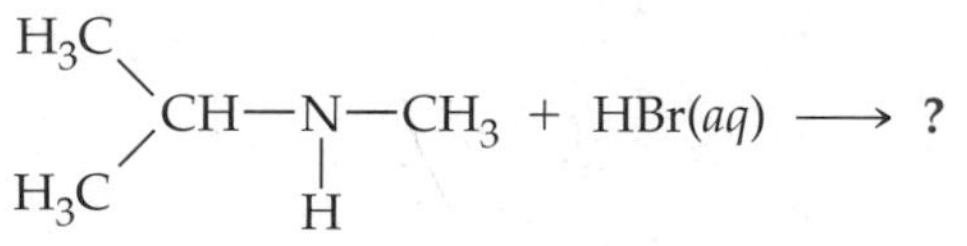
$$\underset{H_3C}{\overset{H_3C}{>}}CH-\underset{\underset{H}{|}}{N}-CH_3 + HBr(aq) \longrightarrow ?$$

(b) 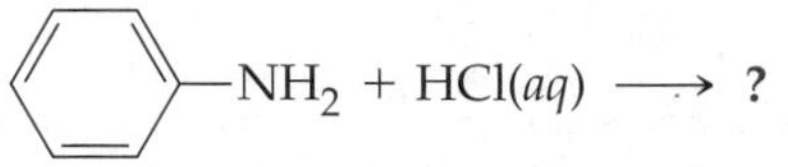
$$\bigcirc\!\!-NH_2 + HCl(aq) \longrightarrow ?$$

(c) 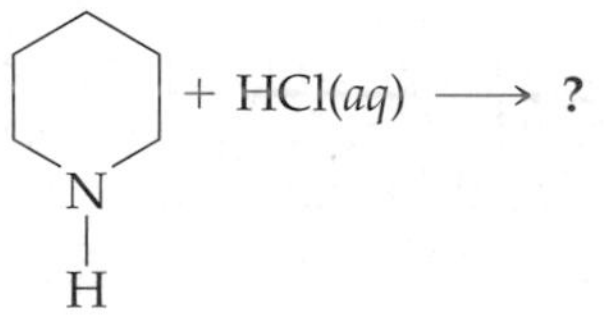
$$\bigcirc\!\!\!\!\underset{\underset{H}{|}}{\underset{N}{}} + HCl(aq) \longrightarrow ?$$

(d) 
$$\overset{+}{-\!\!-}NH_3 + NaOH(aq) \longrightarrow ?$$

PROBLEM 15.14

Name the organic ions produced in reactions (a)–(c) in Problem 15.13.

PROBLEM 15.15

Which is the stronger base in each pair?

(a) Ammonia or ethylamine   **(b)** Triethylamine or pyridine

PROBLEM 15.16

When each of the following biologically active amines is placed into the body, they immediately pick up an H^+ to form an ammonium ion. Draw the structures of the ammonium ions formed by the following amines:

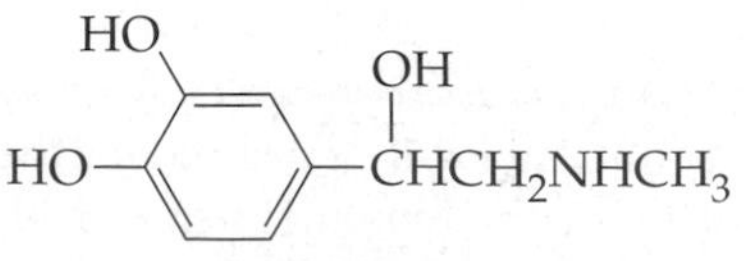

$$HO\!\!-\!\!\bigcirc\!\!\overset{HO}{\underset{}{}}\!\!-CHCH_2NHCH_3$$
$$\overset{OH}{|}$$

Epinephrine
(a biochemical messenger)

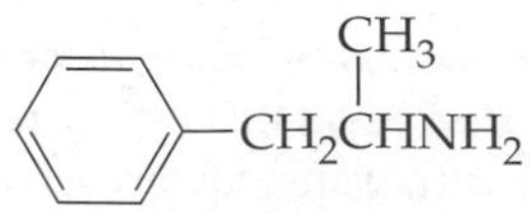

$$\bigcirc\!\!-CH_2CHNH_2$$
$$\overset{CH_3}{|}$$

Amphetamine
(a CNS stimulant and drug of abuse

CHEMISTRY IN ACTION

Organic Compounds in Body Fluids and the "Solubility Switch"

The chemical reactions that keep us alive and functioning occur in the aqueous solutions known as *body fluids*—blood, digestive juices, and the fluid inside cells. Waste products from these metabolic reactions are excreted in urine. For organic compounds of all classes, water solubility decreases as the hydrocarbon-like portions of the molecules become larger and molecular weight increases. How does the body manage to carry out reactions in water, especially when large and complex biomolecules are involved?

Many biomolecules contain acidic and basic functional groups. At the pH of body fluids (for example, approximately 7.4 for blood), many of these groups are ionized and thus water-soluble, providing what is often called a *solubility switch*. The most frequently seen ionized functional groups present in biomolecules are carboxylate (pronounced car-**box-ill**-late) groups (from carboxylic acids, —COOH, discussed in Section 17.3), phosphate groups (as well as diphosphates and triphosphates, discussed in Section 17.8), and ammonium groups.

Ionic solubility switches

Carboxylate ($-COO^-$)   Phosphate ($-OPO_3^{2-}$)   Ammonium ($-NR_3^+$)

For example, nicotinamide adenine dinucleotide (NAD$^+$, an important biochemical oxidizing agent, Section 20.7) has three charges as it exists in body fluids: two negative charges from a diphosphate and one positive charge from a quaternary amine.

Nicotinamide adenine dinucleotide; NAD$^+$
(a coenzyme and biochemical oxidizing agent)

In the biochemistry that lies ahead, you will see that most of the major biochemical pathways occur inside cells in the aqueous medium of the cytosol. It would be disastrous if these pathways could be shut down by diffusion of reactants out of the cells. Such diffusion would require passage of intermediates through the cell wall, which is a nonpolar medium. Diffusion does not occur because the intermediates are ionized within the cytosol and are therefore charged and polar; as a result, they cannot pass through the nonpolar cell wall.

Medications must be soluble in body fluids in order to be transported from their entry point in the body to their site of action. Many drugs are weak acids or bases and therefore are present as their ions in body fluids. Aspirin and amphetamine are two examples:

Aspirin
(an acid)

Amphetamine
(a base)

The extent of ionization of a drug helps determine how it is distributed in the body. Weak acids, such as aspirin, are essentially un-ionized in the acidic environment in the stomach and are therefore readily absorbed there. Weak bases, however, are completely ionized in the stomach, and therefore no significant absorption occurs there. It is not until they reach the more basic environment of the small intestine that these weak bases revert to their neutral form and are absorbed.

Phenylephrine hydrochloride
(a decongestant)

Many pharmaceutical agents must be delivered to the body in their more water-soluble forms as salts. Converting amines such as phenylephrine (the decongestant in Neo-Synephrine) to ammonium hydrochlorides increases their solubility to the point where delivery in solution is possible.

See Chemistry in Action Problems 15.64–15.65 at the end of the chapter.

15.5 Amine Salts

Ammonium salt An ionic compound composed of an ammonium cation and an anion; an amine salt.

An **ammonium salt** (also known as an *amine salt*) is composed of a cation and an anion and is named by combining the ion names. For example, in methylammonium chloride ($CH_3NH_3{}^+Cl^-$), the methylammonium ion, $CH_3NH_3{}^+$, is the cation and the chloride ion is the anion.

Ammonium salts are generally odorless, white, crystalline solids that are much more water-soluble than neutral amines because they are ionic (see Chemistry in Action: Organic Compounds in Body Fluids and the "Solubility Switch" on p. 473). For example:

$$CH_3CH_2CH_2CH_2-\underset{\underset{\displaystyle CH_2CH_2CH_2CH_3}{|}}{N}-CH_2CH_2CH_2CH_3 \ + \ HCl(aq) \ \rightleftharpoons \ CH_3CH_2CH_2CH_2-\underset{\underset{\displaystyle CH_2CH_2CH_2CH_3}{|}}{\overset{\overset{\displaystyle H}{|}}{N^+}}-CH_2CH_2CH_2CH_3 \ Cl^-(aq)$$

Tributylamine (water-insoluble) Hydrochloric acid Tributylammonium chloride (water-soluble)

In medicinal chemistry, amine salt formulas are quite often written and named by combining the structures and names of the amine and the acid used to form its salt. By this system, methylammonium chloride is written $CH_3NH_2 \cdot HCl$ and named methylamine hydrochloride (this will be a convention you will see more as you study the biochemistry sections of this book). You will often see this system used with drugs that are amine salts. For example, diphenhydramine is one of a family of antihistamines available in over-the-counter medications. Antihistamines of this type are oily liquids and difficult to formulate as such, so they are converted to amine salts for formulation into medications.

$$(C_6H_5)_2CHOCH_2CH_2N(CH_3)_2 \cdot HCl$$

or

$$(C_6H_5)_2CHOCH_2CH_2CH_2NH(CH_3)_2{}^+Cl^-$$

Diphenhydramine hydrochloride
(Benadryl), an antihistamine

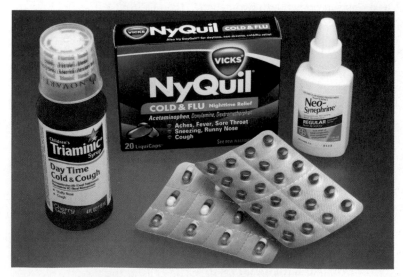

▲ Over-the-counter ammonium salts. The active ingredient in each of these over-the-counter medications is an ammonium salt.

If a free amine is needed, it is easily regenerated from an amine salt by treatment with a base:

$$CH_3NH_3{}^+Cl^-(aq) + NaOH(aq) \longrightarrow CH_3NH_2(aq) + NaCl(aq) + H_2O(l)$$

Quaternary ammonium ions have four organic groups bonded to the nitrogen atom, and this bonding gives the nitrogen a positive charge. With no H atom that can be removed by a base and no lone pair on the nitrogen that can bond to H^+, ammonium ions are neither acidic nor basic, and their structures in solution are unaffected by changes in pH. Their salts are known as **quaternary ammonium salts**. One commonly encountered quaternary ammonium salt has the following structure, where R represents a range of C_8 to C_{18} alkyl groups:

Quaternary ammonium salt An ionic compound composed of a quaternary ammonium ion and an anion.

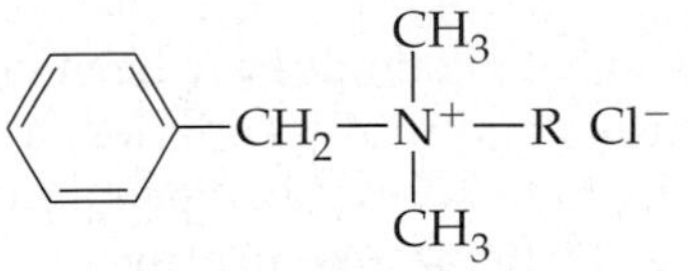

$$R = -C_8H_{17} \text{ to } -C_{18}H_{37}$$

Benzalkonium chloride
(an antiseptic and disinfectant)

These benzalkonium chlorides have both antimicrobial and detergent properties. As dilute solutions, they are used in surgical scrubs and for sterile storage of instruments; concentrated solutions, however, are harmful to body tissues.

PROBLEM 15.17

Write the structures of the following compounds:

(a) Butyldiethylammonium bromide

(b) Tetrabutylammonium hydroxide

(c) Propylammonium iodide

(d) Isopropylmethylammonium chloride

PROBLEM 15.18

Identify each compound in Problem 15.17 as the salt of a primary, secondary, tertiary, or quaternary amine.

PROBLEM 15.19

Write an equation for the formation of the free amine from butylammonium chloride by reaction with aqueous OH^-.

PROBLEM 15.20

Compare the structure of Benadryl (p. 474) with the general antihistamine structure:

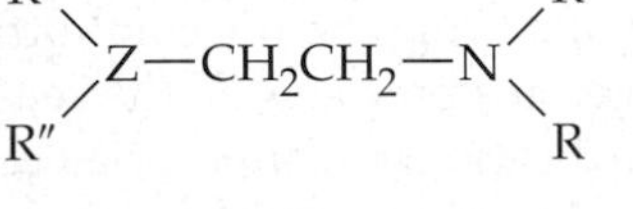

$$Z = N, C, C-O$$

Does Benadryl have that general structure? Write your comparison of the structures.

PROBLEM 15.21

Write the structure of benzylamine hydrochloride in two different ways, and name the hydrochloride as an ammonium salt.

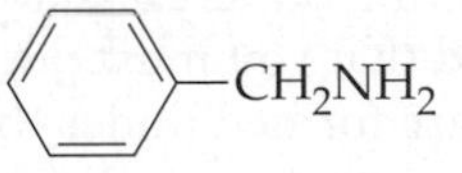

Benzylamine

PROBLEM 15.22

In Chemistry in Action: Organic Compounds in Body Fluids and the "Solubility Switch," on page 473, what are the most frequently found solubility switches present in biomolecules?

15.6 Amines in Plants: Alkaloids

Alkaloid A naturally occurring, nitrogen-containing compound isolated from a plant; usually basic, bitter, and poisonous.

The roots, leaves, and fruits of flowering plants are a rich source of nitrogen compounds. These compounds, once called "vegetable alkali" because their water solutions are basic, are now referred to as **alkaloids**.

The molecular structures of many thousands of alkaloids have been determined. Most are bitter-tasting, physiologically active, structurally complex, and toxic to human beings and other animals in sufficiently high doses. Most people are familiar with the physiological activity of two alkaloids—caffeine and nicotine (p. 470), which are stimulants. Quinine (p. 470) is used as a standard for bitterness: Even a 1×10^{-6} M solution tastes bitter. For a long time, quinine was the only drug available for treating malaria (caused by a parasitic protozoan).

The bitterness and poisonous nature of alkaloids probably evolved to protect plants from being devoured by animals. The three poisonous compounds described here— coniine, atropine, and solanine—illustrate some of the many types of alkaloid structures.

Examples of toxic alkaloids

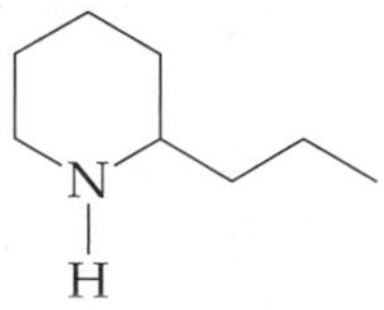

Coniine

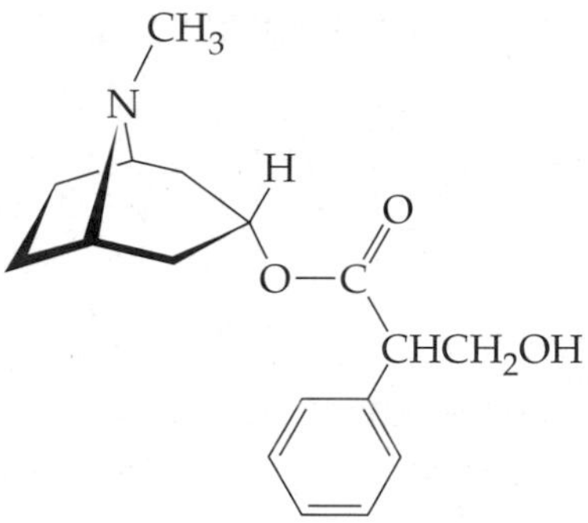

Atropine

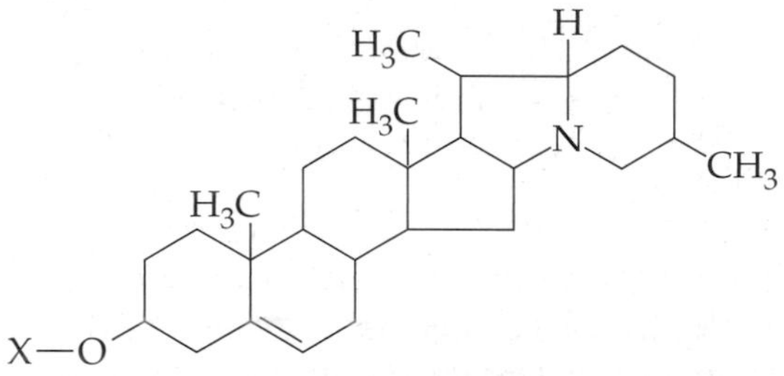

Solanine
(X = a group of three sugar molecules)

- **Coniine** is extracted from poison hemlock (*Conium maculatum*). Socrates used this poison to end his life after being convicted of corrupting Greek youth with his philosophical discussions.
- **Atropine** is the toxic substance in the herb known as *deadly nightshade* or *belladonna (Atropa belladonna)*. In Meyerbeer's opera, *L'Africaine*, the heroine sings of the peaceful death this plant brings before committing suicide over her lost love. Like many other alkaloids, atropine acts on the central nervous system, a property sometimes applied in medications (in appropriately low dosage!) to reduce cramping of the digestive tract. Atropine is also used as an antidote against nerve gases, such as Sarin.
- **Solanine,** an even more potent poison than atropine, is found in potatoes and tomatoes, both of which belong to the same botanical family as the deadly nightshade (*Solanaceae*). The tiny amount of solanine in properly stored potatoes actually contributes to their characteristic flavor, but when potatoes are exposed to sunlight or stored under very cold or very warm conditions, the production of solanine is increased to levels that can be dangerous. The reason you are warned that you must peel green potatoes deeply is that alkaloids such as solanine are formed under the peel. Alkaloids are not

▲ A potato that has turned green because of exposure to sunlight. Before it is eaten, this potato must be peeled to remove all of the green chlorophyll so that the poisonous alkaloid solanine is also removed.

destroyed during cooking but can be removed by peeling. Fortunately, sunlight also stimulates the formation of chlorophyll under the skin of the potato, and the green color of the chlorophyll provides a warning. By peeling away all of the green color, you most likely remove the excess solanine. Potato sprouts (the "eyes") also contain solanine and should be cut out before the potatoes are cooked.

Not all alkaloids are known for their poisonous nature; some are notable as pain relievers (*analgesics*), as sleep inducers, and for the euphoric states they can create. Raw opium, a paste derived from the opium poppy (*Papaver somniferum*), has been known for these properties since ancient times. About 20 alkaloids are present in the poppy, including morphine and codeine. The free alkaloids are oily liquids, and not very soluble in water. The medicinal use of morphine for pain was expanded in the sixteenth century when the German physician Paracelsus extracted opium into brandy to produce *laudanum*, essentially a solution of morphine in alcohol. A similar extract (10% opium by weight in alcohol) is still sometimes prescribed for diarrhea, as is *paregoric*, a more dilute solution of opium combined with anise oil, glycerin, benzoic acid, and camphor. Heroin does not occur naturally but is easily synthesized from its parent compound morphine. Within the body, removal of the $CH_3C{=}O$ groups (highlighted in orange) converts heroin back to morphine.

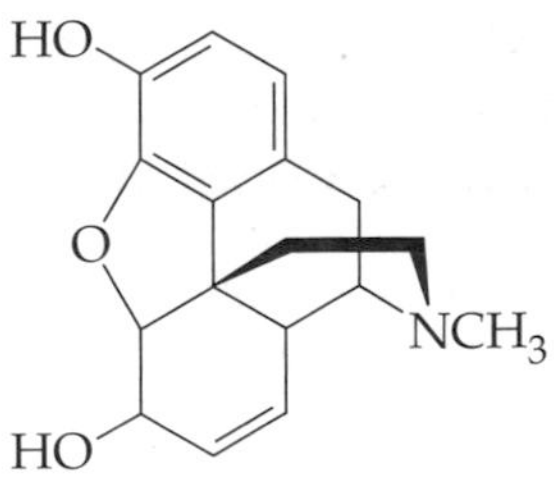

▲ All parts of the poppy, including poppy seeds, contain morphine. Eating poppy seeds can introduce enough morphine into your body fluids to show up in a laboratory drug screen.

Morphine

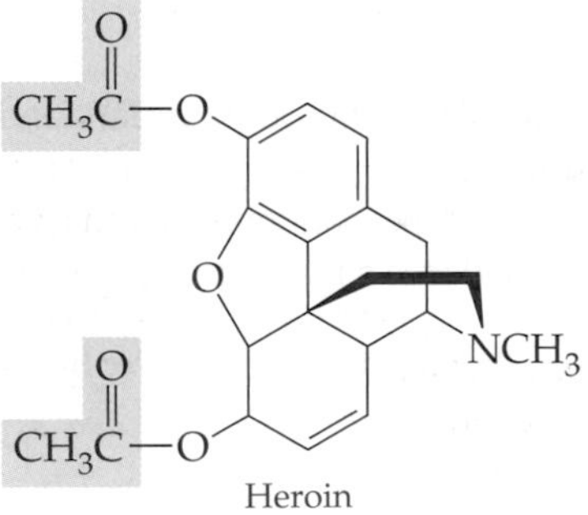

Heroin

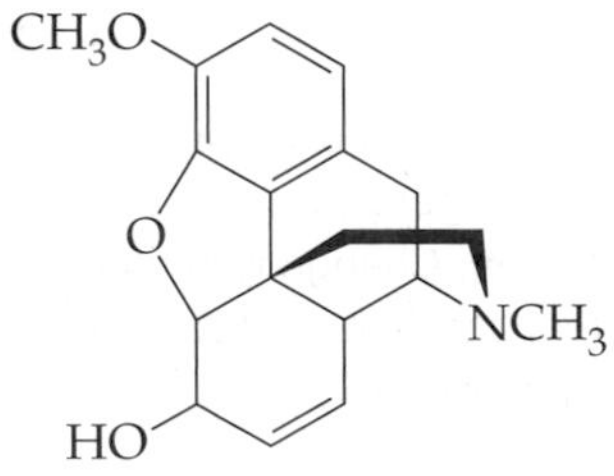

Codeine

UNDERSTANDING KEY CONCEPTS

15.23

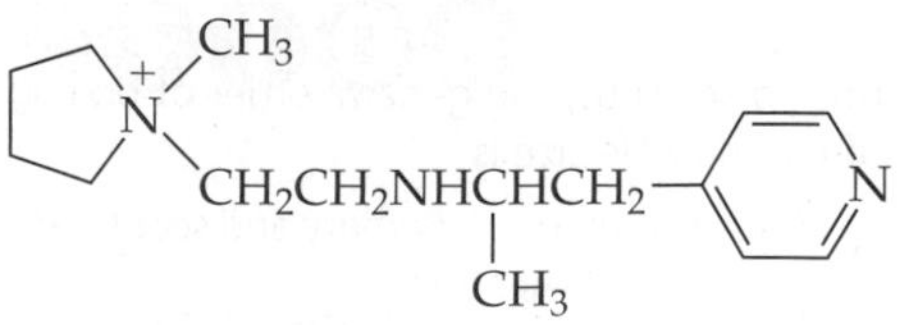

(a) For the compound above, identify each nitrogen as either a primary, secondary, tertiary, quaternary, or aromatic amine.

(b) Which amine group(s) would be able to provide a hydrogen bond? Which could accept a hydrogen bond?

15.24 The structure of the amino acid lysine (in its uncharged form) is shown below.

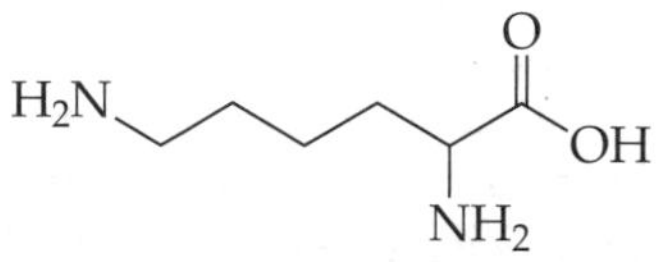

(a) Which amine groups would be able to participate in hydrogen bonding?

(b) Is lysine likely to be water-soluble? Explain.

15.25 Draw structures to illustrate hydrogen bonding (similar to those on p. 467) between the following compounds.

(a) Four ⟨phenyl⟩—NH$_2$ molecules

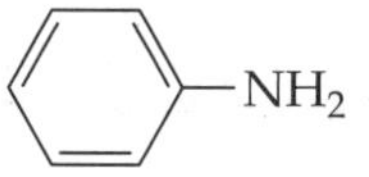

(b) Two ⟨isopropyl⟩—NH$_2$ and two H$_2$O

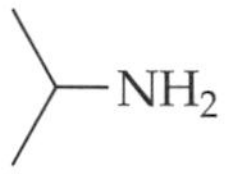

(c) Two CH$_3$NH$_2$ and two ⟨pyrrolidine⟩ N—H

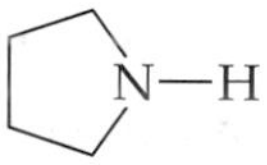

15.26 Explain what bonds must be made or broken and where the electrons go when the hydrogen-bonded water between the two amines shown at the bottom of page 472 reacts to form an amine, ammonium ion, and OH$^-$.

15.27 Which of these amines is the strongest base? The weakest? (See Section 15.4).

NH$_3$ ⟨phenyl⟩—NH$_2$ (CH$_3$)$_2$NH

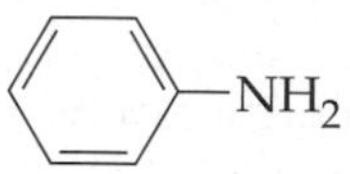

15.28 Complete the following equations:

(a) 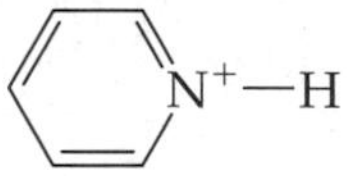 ⟨pyridinium⟩ N$^+$—H + OH$^-$ ⟶

(b) 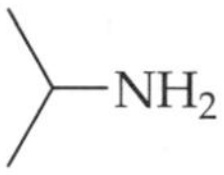 ⟨isopropyl⟩—NH$_2$ + H$_2$O ⇌

(c) (CH$_3$CH$_2$)$_3$N + HBr ⟶

(d)  ⟨pyrrolidine⟩ NH + HCl ⟶

ADDITIONAL PROBLEMS

AMINES AND AMMONIUM SALTS

15.29 Draw the structures corresponding to the following names:

(a) *N*-Methylcyclohexylamine

(b) Dipropylamine

(c) Pentylamine

15.30 Draw the structures corresponding to the following names:

(a) *N*-Methylpentylamine

(b) *N*-Ethylcyclobutylamine

(c) *p*-Propylaniline

15.31 Name the following amines, and identify them as primary, secondary, or tertiary:

(a) 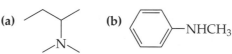   (b) ⟨phenyl⟩—NHCH$_3$

15.32 Name the following amines, and identify them as primary, secondary, or tertiary:

(a) 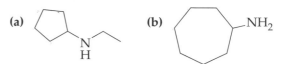   (b) ⟨cycloheptyl⟩—NH$_2$

15.33 Is water a weaker or stronger base than ammonia?

15.34 Which is a stronger base, diethyl ether or diethylamine?

15.35 Give names or structures for the following ammonium salts. Indicate whether each is the ammonium salt of a primary, secondary, or tertiary amine.

(a) $CH_3CH_2CH_2 \overset{+}{\underset{\underset{CH_3}{|}}{N}}H_2 \ Br^-$ (b) $\overset{\overset{CH_3}{|}}{\underset{\underset{CH_3}{|}}{N}H}^+ \ Cl^-$

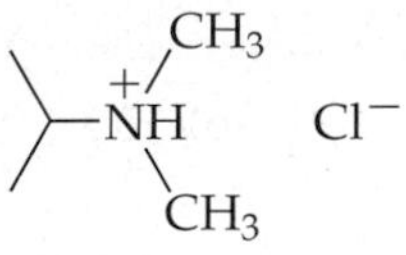

(c) N-Propylbutylammonium bromide

(d) Cyclobutylammonium bromide

15.36 Give names or structures for the following ammonium salts. Indicate whether each is the ammonium salt of a primary, secondary, or tertiary amine.

(a) $CH_3CH_2\overset{\overset{CH_3}{|}}{\underset{\underset{NH_2CH_3}{+}}{CH}} \ NO_3^-$

(b) Pyridinium chloride

(c) N-Butyl-N-isopropylhexylammonium chloride

15.37 The compound lidocaine is used medically as a local anesthetic. Identify the functional groups present in lidocaine (refer to Section 12.2).

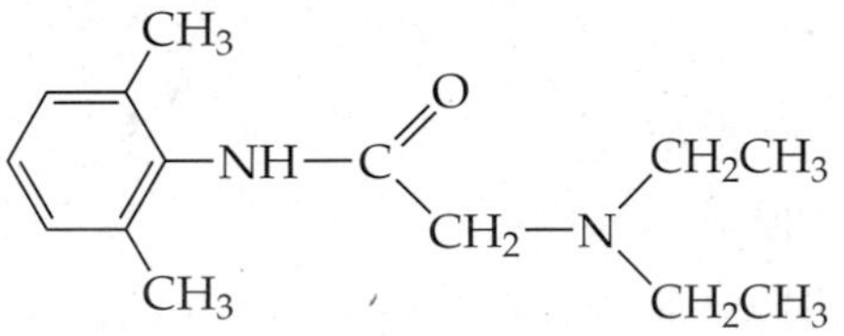

Lidocaine

15.38 Identify the functional groups in cocaine (refer to Section 12.2).

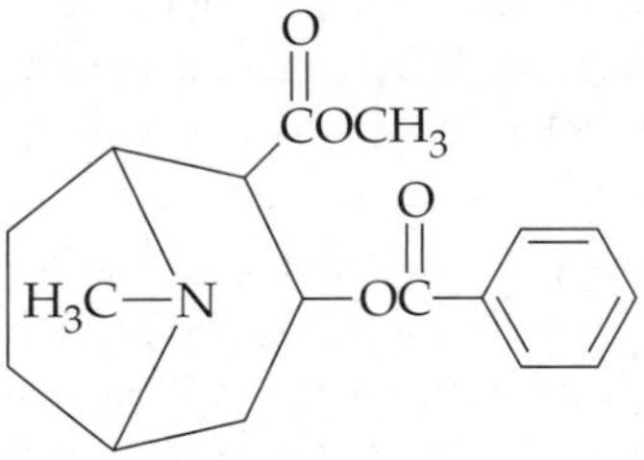

Cocaine

15.39 Most illicit cocaine is actually cocaine hydrochloride—the product of the reaction of cocaine (Problem 15.38) with HCl. Show the structure of cocaine hydrochloride.

15.40 When quinine (an antimalarial drug, p. 470) reacts with HCl, which nitrogen is first to form the ammonium salt? Show the structure of quinine hydrochloride.

REACTIONS OF AMINES

15.41 Complete the following equations:

(a) $\text{(cyclohexyl)}-NHCH_2CH_3 \ + \ HBr \longrightarrow \ ?$

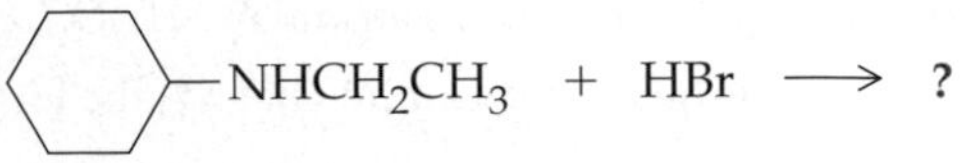

(b) $\text{(phenyl)}-NH_3^+Br^- \ + \ OH^- \longrightarrow \ ?$

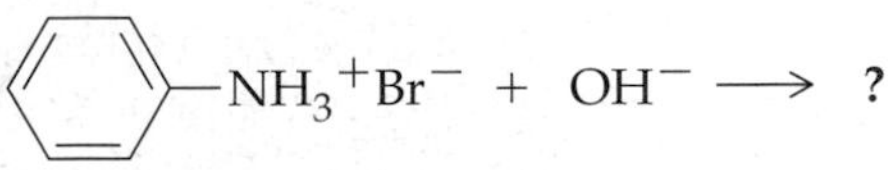

(c) $CH_3CH_2\underset{\underset{CH_3}{|}}{N}H \ + \ H_3O^+ \longrightarrow \ ?$

15.42 Complete the following equations:

(a) $\text{(cyclobutyl)}-NH_2 \ + \ HCl \longrightarrow \ ?$

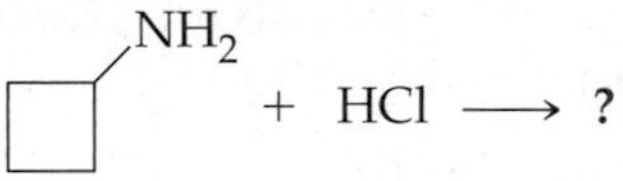

(b) $CH_3CH_2CH_2 \overset{\overset{H}{|}}{N} CH_3 \ + \ H_2O \rightleftharpoons \ ?$

(c) $\text{(phenyl)}-\overset{\overset{H}{|}}{\underset{\underset{H}{|}}{N}}^+-\text{(phenyl)} \ Br^- \ + \ NaOH \longrightarrow \ ?$

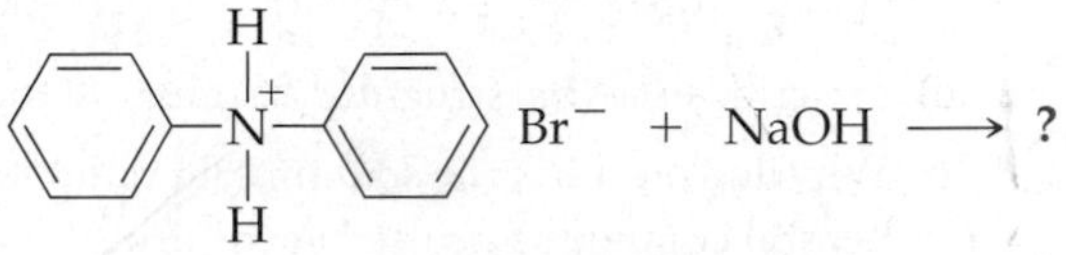

15.43 Many hair conditioners contain an ammonium salt such as the following to help prevent "fly-away" hair. Will this salt react with acids or bases? Why or why not?

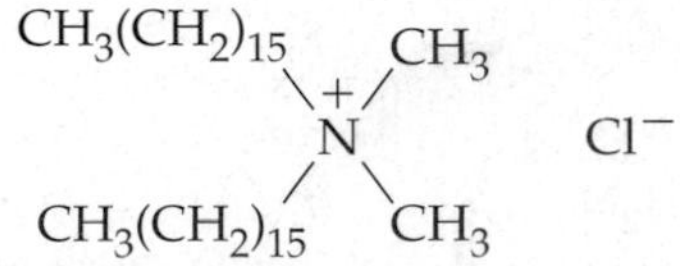

$$\underset{CH_3(CH_2)_{15}}{\overset{CH_3(CH_2)_{15}}{\diagdown}}\overset{\overset{CH_3}{+}}{\underset{\underset{CH_3}{\diagup}}{N}} \ Cl^-$$

15.44 Choline has the following structure. Do you think that this substance reacts with aqueous hydrochloric acid? If so, what is the product? If not, why not?

$$HO\overset{CH_2}{\diagup}\underset{CH_2}{\diagdown}\overset{+}{N}(CH_3)_3$$

GENERAL QUESTIONS AND PROBLEMS

15.45 1-Propylamine, 1-propanol, acetic acid, and butane have about the same molar masses. Which would you expect to have the (a) highest boiling point, (b) lowest boiling point, (c) least solubility in water, and (d) least chemical reactivity? Explain.

15.46 Explain why decylamine is much less soluble in water than ethylamine.

15.47 Propose structures for amines that fit these descriptions:

(a) A secondary amine with formula $C_5H_{13}N$

(b) A tertiary amine with formula $C_6H_{13}N$

(c) A cyclic quaternary amine that has the formula $C_6H_{14}N^+$

15.48 *para*-Aminobenzoic acid (PABA) is a common ingredient in sunscreens. Draw the structure of PABA (refer to Table 13.2).

15.49 PABA (Problem 15.48) is used by certain bacteria as a starting material from which folic acid (a necessary vitamin, Table 19.3) is made. Sulfa drugs such as sodium sulfanilamide work because they resemble PABA. The bacteria try to metabolize the sulfa drug, fail to do so, and die due to lack of folic acid.

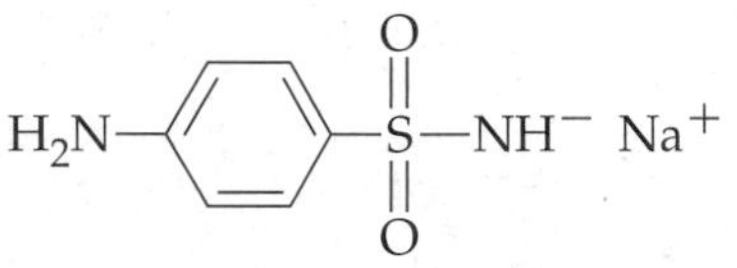

Sodium sulfanilamide

(a) Describe how this structure is similar to that of PABA.

(b) Why do you think the sodium salt, rather than the neutral compound, is used as the drug?

15.50 Acyclovir is an antiviral drug used to treat herpes infections. It has the following structure:

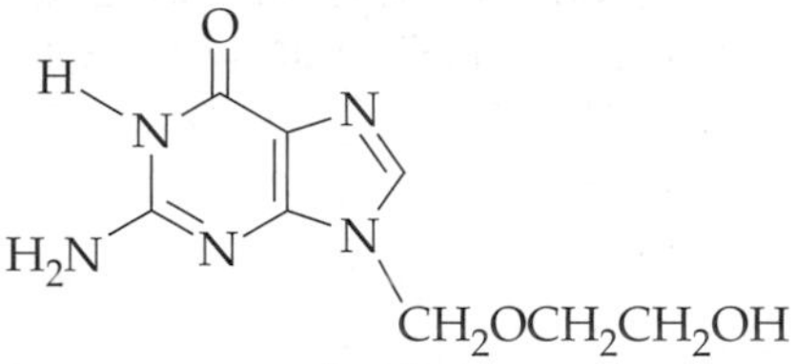

Acyclovir

(a) What heterocyclic base (Table 15.2) is the parent of this compound?

(b) Label the other functional groups present.

15.51 Which is the stronger base, trimethylamine or ammonia? In which direction will the following reaction proceed?

15.52 How do amines differ from analogous alcohols in (a) odor, (b) basicity, and (c) boiling point?

15.53 What two undesirable characteristics are often associated with alkaloids?

15.54 Name the following compounds:

(a) $CH_3\overset{\underset{|}{CH_3}}{CH}CH_2CH_2CH{=}CHCH_3$

(b)

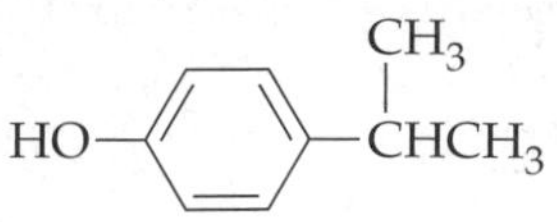

(c) $(CH_3CH_2CH_2CH_2)_2NH$

15.55 Complete the following equations:

(a) $CH_3CH_2\overset{\underset{|}{CH_3}}{\underset{|}{C}}CH_2CH{=}\overset{\underset{|}{CH_2CH_3}}{C}CH_3 + HCl \longrightarrow$?

(b) $CH_3CH_2\overset{\underset{|}{OH}}{CH}CH(CH_3)_2 + H_2SO_4 \longrightarrow$?

(c) $2\ CH_3CH_2SH \xrightarrow{[O]}$?

(d)

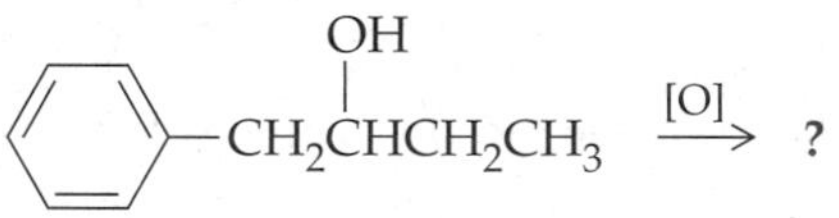

(e) $(CH_3)_3N + H_2O \rightleftharpoons$?

(f) $(CH_3)_3N + HCl \longrightarrow$?

(g) $(CH_3)_3NH^+ + OH^- \longrightarrow$?

15.56 Hexylamine and triethylamine have the same molar mass. The boiling point of hexylamine is 129 °C, whereas that of triethylamine is only 89 °C. Explain these observations.

15.57 Lemon juice, which contains citric acid, is traditionally recommended for removing the odor associated with cleaning fish. What functional group is responsible for a "fishy" odor, and why does lemon juice work to remove the odor?

15.58 Baeocystin is a hallucinogenic compound that is isolated from the mushroom *Psilocybe baeocystis* and has the structure shown below. What heterocyclic base (Table 15.2) is the parent of this compound?

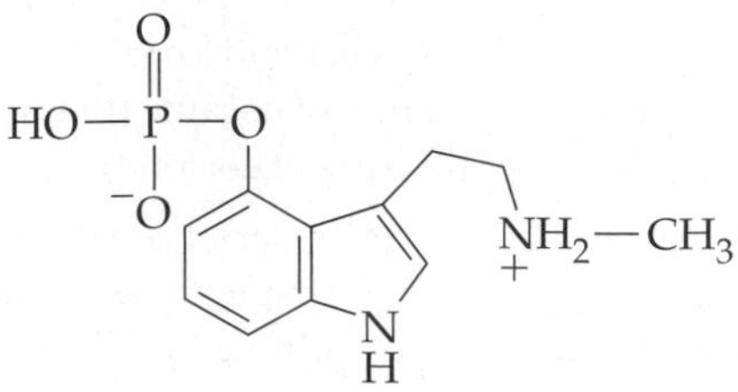

Baeocystin

15.59 Why is cyclohexylamine not considered to be a heterocyclic nitrogen compound?

15.60 Benzene and pyridine are both single-ring, aromatic compounds. Benzene is a neutral compound that is insoluble in water. Pyridine, with a similar molar mass, is basic and completely miscible with water. Explain these phenomena.

15.61 Name the organic reactants in Problem 15.41.

CHEMISTRY IN ACTION

15.62 OSHA requires material safety data sheets for only what types of materials? Under what circumstances might you need an MSDS for sodium chloride? Why? [*Knowing What You Work With: Material Safety Data Sheets,* p. 465]

15.63 Using your favorite internet search engine, type in the search term "sodium chloride msds" and examine the MSDS for required categories of information. What is sodium chloride's toxicity in man? Repeat this exercise for triethylamine. [*Knowing What You Work With: Material Safety Data Sheets,* p. 465]

15.64 Promazine, a potent antipsychotic tranquilizer, is administered as the hydrochloride salt. Write the formula of the salt (there is only one HCl in the salt). [*Organic Compounds in Body Fluids and the "Solubility Switch,"* p. 473]

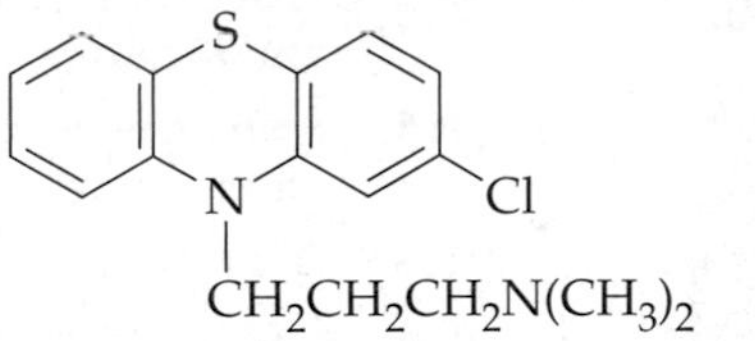

Promazine

15.65 Both morphine (a powerful analgesic) and thorazine (a powerful antipsychotic) cannot be effectively administered in their neutral form. Why? [*Organic Compounds in Body Fluids and the "Solubility Switch,"* p. 473]

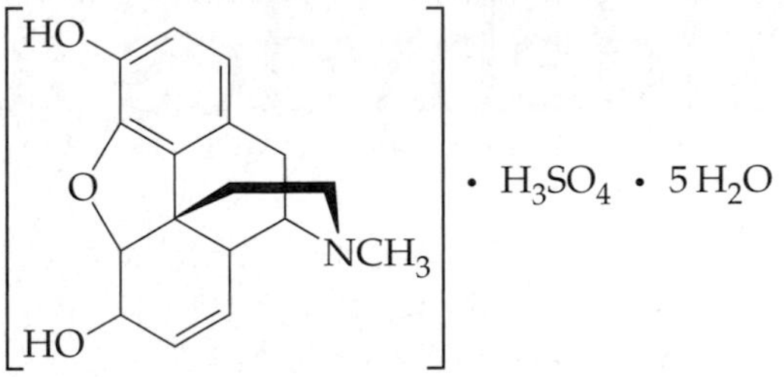

Morphine sulphate

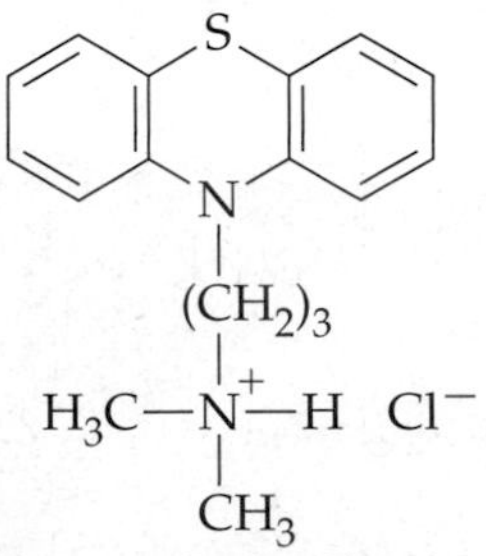

Thorazine hydrochloride

15.66 (a) What kind of work might a forensic toxicologist be called upon to do?
(b) As you study a new toxin, what three questions need to be answered so that you can better understand it and, hopefully, develop an antidote for the toxin? [*Toxicology,* p. 478]

Aldehydes and Ketones

CONTENTS

◀ Vanillin is the molecule responsible for the flavor of vanilla ice cream; it is an aldehyde.

CHAPTER GOALS

1. **What is the carbonyl group?**
   THE GOAL: Be able to recognize the carbonyl group and describe its polarity and shape. (◀◀ A., F.)

2. **How are ketones and aldehydes named?**
   THE GOAL: Be able to name the simple members of these families and write their structures, given the names. (◀◀ D., E.)

3. **What are the general properties of aldehydes and ketones?**
   THE GOAL: Be able to describe such properties as polarity, hydrogen bonding, and water solubility. (◀◀ A., C.)

4. **What are some of the significant occurrences and applications of aldehydes and ketones?**
   THE GOAL: Be able to specify where aldehydes and ketones are found, list

their major applications, and discuss some important members of each family. (◀◀ D.)

5. **What are the results of the oxidation and reduction of aldehydes and ketones?**
   THE GOAL: Be able to describe and predict the products of the oxidation and reduction of aldehydes and ketones. (◀◀ B., F.)

6. **What are hemiacetals and acetals, how are they formed, and how do they react?**
   THE GOAL: Be able to recognize hemiacetals and acetals, describe the conditions under which they are formed, and predict the products of hemiacetal and acetal formation and acetal hydrolysis. (◀◀ A., D., F.)

CONCEPTS TO REVIEW

◀◀

A. Electronegativity and Molecular Polarity
(Sections 4.9, 4.10)

B. Oxidation and Reduction
(Section 5.6)

C. Hydrogen Bonds
(Section 8.2)

D. Functional Groups
(Section 12.2)

E. Naming Alkanes
(Section 12.6)

F. Types of Organic Reactions
(Section 13.5)

I n this and the next chapter, we will study the families of compounds that contain what is known as a *carbonyl group*. The carbonyl group has a carbon atom and an oxygen atom connected by a double bond, C=O. The two simplest families of carbonyl compounds are the subject of this chapter, the *aldehydes* and *ketones*. In aldehydes, the carbonyl group is bonded to at least one hydrogen atom, so that the —CHO group falls at one end of a molecule (—CHO is the common abbreviation for the aldehyde functional group; don't confuse it with an alcohol, which you may see written as —COH). In ketones, the carbonyl group is bonded to 2 carbon atoms and thus is never on the end of a molecule.

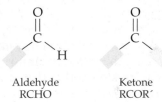

Aldehyde
RCHO

Ketone
RCOR′

Where might you encounter aldehydes or ketones? The aromas of many flowers and plants derive largely from natural aldehydes. Cookies baking in the oven fill the air with the smell of cinnamon, vanilla, or almond—all natural flavors and aromas due to aldehydes. Have you ever burned a citronella candle to repel mosquitoes? Or enjoyed the smell of cherries? These too are the aromas of aldehydes. Among ketones, jasmone from the jasmine flower and muscone from the male musk deer are vital to the complex formulations of expensive perfumes. Aldehyde and ketone functional groups also play essential roles in the carbohydrates, biomolecules that will be our focus in Chapter 21.

16.1 The Carbonyl Group

Carbonyl compounds are distinguished by the presence of a **carbonyl group** (C=O) and are classified according to what is bonded to the carbonyl carbon, as illustrated in Table 16.1.

Since oxygen is more electronegative than carbon, carbonyl groups are strongly polarized, with a partial positive charge on the carbon atom and a partial negative

Carbonyl compound Any compound that contains a carbonyl group (C=O).

Carbonyl group A functional group that has a carbon atom joined to an oxygen atom by a double bond.

485

TABLE **16.1** Some Kinds of Carbonyl Compounds

FAMILY NAME	STRUCTURE	EXAMPLE	
Aldehyde	$$R-\overset{\overset{\textstyle O}{\|\|}}{C}-H$$	$$H_3C-\overset{\overset{\textstyle O}{\|\|}}{C}-H$$	Acetaldehyde
Ketone	$$R-\overset{\overset{\textstyle O}{\|\|}}{C}-R'$$	$$H_3C-\overset{\overset{\textstyle O}{\|\|}}{C}-CH_3$$	Acetone
Carboxylic acid	$$R-\overset{\overset{\textstyle O}{\|\|}}{C}-O-H$$	$$H_3C-\overset{\overset{\textstyle O}{\|\|}}{C}-O-H$$	Acetic acid
Ester	$$R-\overset{\overset{\textstyle O}{\|\|}}{C}-O-R'$$	$$H_3C-\overset{\overset{\textstyle O}{\|\|}}{C}-O-CH_3$$	Methyl acetate
Amide	$$R-\overset{\overset{\textstyle O}{\|\|}}{C}-N\big\langle$$	$$H_3C-\overset{\overset{\textstyle O}{\|\|}}{C}-NH_2$$	Acetamide

▶▶▶ Remember that electronegativity is the ability of an atom to attract electrons to itself; see Figure 4.6.

charge on the oxygen atom. The polarity of the carbonyl group gives rise to its reactivity. Another property common to all carbonyl groups is planarity. The bond angles between the three substituents on the carbonyl carbon atom are 120°, or close to it.

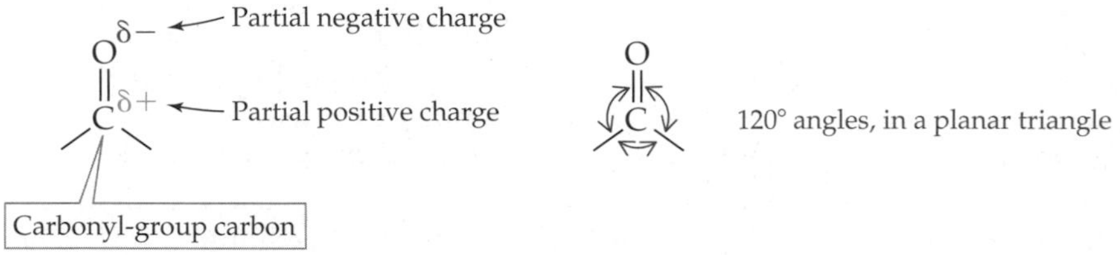

O$^{\delta-}$ ← Partial negative charge

C$^{\delta+}$ ← Partial positive charge

Carbonyl-group carbon

120° angles, in a planar triangle

Aldehyde A compound that has a carbonyl group bonded to at least one hydrogen, RCHO.

Ketone A compound that has a carbonyl group bonded to two carbons in organic groups that can be the same or different, $R_2C{=}O$, RCOR′.

Chemists find it useful to divide carbonyl compounds into two major classes based on their chemical properties. In one group are the **aldehydes** and **ketones**, which have similar properties because their carbonyl groups are bonded to atoms that do not attract electrons strongly—carbon and hydrogen. In the second group are *carboxylic acids, esters,* and *amides* (the *carboxyl* family). The carbonyl-group carbon in these compounds is bonded to an atom (other than carbon or hydrogen) that *does* attract electrons strongly, typically an oxygen or nitrogen atom. This second group of carbonyl-containing compounds is discussed in Chapter 17.

There are various ways of representing carbonyl compound structures on paper. Because of the trigonal planar arrangement of atoms around the carbonyl group, the bonds of the carbonyl carbon are often drawn at 120° angles to remind us that such angles are present in the molecules. Structures like those in Table 16.1, on the other hand, which emphasize the location of the double bond, do not fit well on a single line of type, so the simplified formulas shown below are often used for aldehydes and ketones:

Aldehydes   *Ketones*

$$R-\overset{\overset{\textstyle O}{\|\|}}{C}-H \quad RCHO \qquad\qquad R-\overset{\overset{\textstyle O}{\|\|}}{C}-R' \quad RCOR' \ \text{ or } \ R_2C{=}O$$

For example,

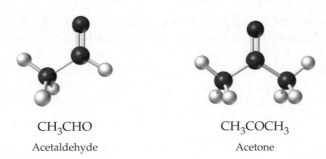

CH₃CHO

Acetaldehyde

CH₃COCH₃

Acetone

The aldehyde group, you will notice, can only be connected to one carbon atom and therefore is always at the end of a carbon chain. The ketone group, by contrast, must be connected to two carbon groups, and thus always occurs within a carbon chain.

PROBLEM 16.1

Which of the following molecules contain aldehyde or ketone functional groups? You may want to refer to Figures 12.1 and 12.5 to help in your identification. Copy the formulas and circle these functional groups.

(a)

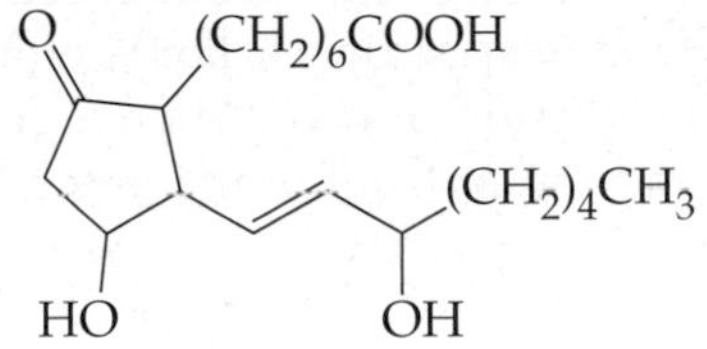

$(CH_2)_6COOH$

$(CH_2)_4CH_3$

HO   OH

Prostaglandin E_1

(b)

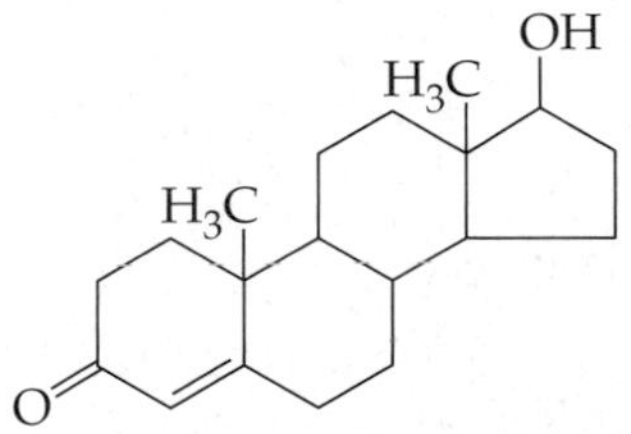

OH

H₃C

H₃C

O

Testosterone
(a male hormone)

(c)   CH₃O

HO—   —CHO

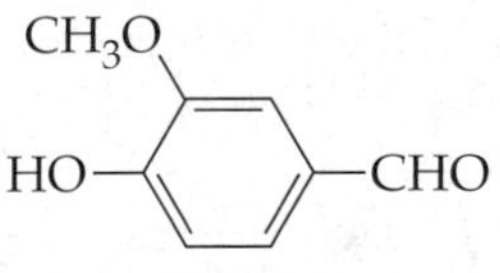

Vanillin
(a flavoring agent)

(d) $C_4H_9COCH_3$ **(e)** C_4H_9CHO

PROBLEM 16.2

Draw the structures of compounds (d) and (e) in Problem 16.1 to show all individual atoms and all covalent bonds. Assume that all carbons are connected in a continuous chain.

LOOKING AHEAD ▶▶▶ Aldehyde or ketone groups are present in biomolecules with a wide range of functions, from the steroid hormones that regulate sexual function (Section 28.5), to the bases that are essential to nucleic acids and the genetic code (Section 25.2). Most distinctively, the structure and reactions of aldehydes and ketones are fundamental to the chemistry of carbohydrates, those in our diet and those that provide energy and structure to our bodies (Chapters 21 and 22).

16.2 Naming Aldehydes and Ketones

The simplest aldehydes are known by their common names, which end in *aldehyde*, for example, formaldehyde, acetaldehyde, and benzaldehyde. To name aldehydes systematically in the IUPAC system, the final *-e* of the name of the alkane with the same number of carbons is replaced by *-al*. The 3-carbon aldehyde derived from propane is named systematically as propanal, the 4-carbon aldehyde as butanal, and so on. When substituents are present, the chain is numbered beginning with 1 for the carbonyl carbon, as illustrated below for 3-methylbutanal.

Aldehydes

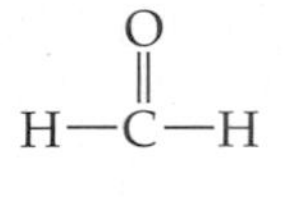

Formaldehyde	Acetaldehyde	Benzaldehyde	3-Methylbutanal

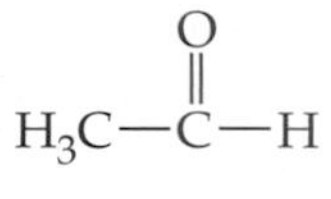

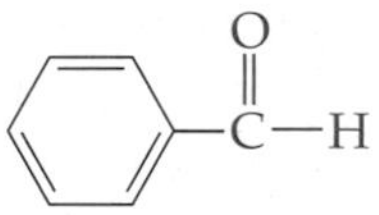

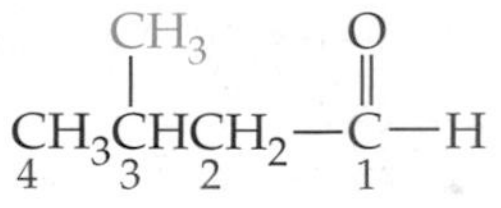

Most simple ketones are best known by common names that give the names of the two alkyl groups bonded to the carbonyl carbon followed by the word *ketone*—for example, methyl ethyl ketone, shown below. An exception to this common-name scheme is seen for the simplest ketone, acetone. Ketones are named systematically by replacing the final *-e* of the corresponding alkane name with *-one* (pronounced **own**). The numbering of the alkane chain begins at the end nearest the carbonyl group. As shown here for 2-butanone and 2-pentanone, the location of the carbonyl group is indicated by placing the number of the carbonyl carbon in front of the name. Using this nomenclature scheme, acetone would be named 2-propanone.

Ketones

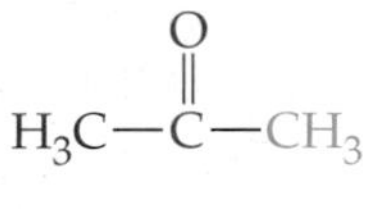

Acetone (2-Propanone)	Methyl ethyl ketone (2-Butanone)	Methyl propyl ketone (2-Pentanone)	Cyclohexanone

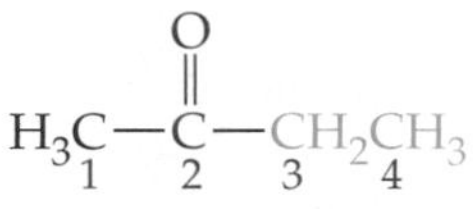

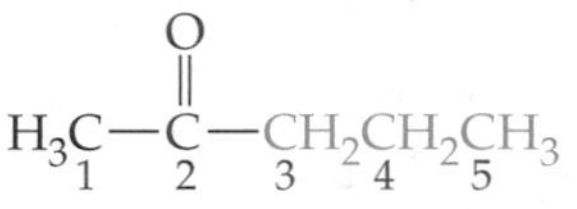

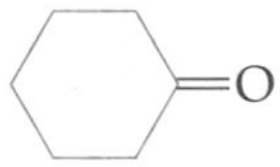

Worked Example 16.1 Naming a Ketone Given Its Structure

Give both the systematic (IUPAC) name and the common name for the following compound:

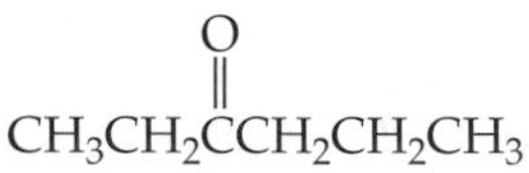

$$\underset{\text{CH}_3\text{CH}_2\overset{\displaystyle \text{O}}{\overset{\displaystyle \|}{\text{C}}}\text{CH}_2\text{CH}_2\text{CH}_3}{}$$

ANALYSIS The compound is a ketone, as shown by the single carbonyl group bonded to two alkyl groups: an ethyl group on the left (CH_3CH_2—) and a propyl group on the right (—$CH_2CH_2CH_3$). The IUPAC system identifies and numbers carbon chains to indicate where the carbonyl group is located, counting in the direction that gives the carbonyl carbon the lowest number possible.

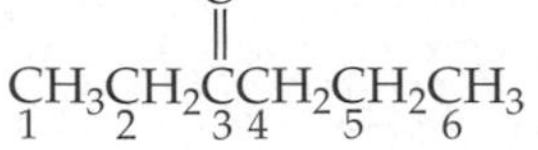

$$\underset{\text{1}\quad\text{2}\quad\text{3 4}\quad\text{5}\quad\text{6}}{\text{CH}_3\text{CH}_2\overset{\displaystyle \text{O}}{\overset{\displaystyle \|}{\text{C}}}\text{CH}_2\text{CH}_2\text{CH}_3}$$

The common name uses the names of the two alkyl groups.

SOLUTION
The IUPAC name is 3-hexanone. The common name is ethyl propyl ketone.

PROBLEM 16.3
Draw structures corresponding to the following names:
(a) Octanal
(b) Methyl phenyl ketone
(c) 4-Methylhexanal
(d) Methyl *tert*-butyl ketone

CHEMISTRY IN ACTION

Chemical Warfare among the Insects

Life in the insect world is a jungle. Predators abound, just waiting to make a meal of any insect that happens along. To survive, insects have evolved extraordinarily effective means of chemical protection. Take the humble millipede *Apheloria corrugata*, for example. When attacked by ants, the millipede protects itself by discharging benzaldehyde cyanohydrin.

In the laboratory, cyanohydrins [RCH(OH)C≡N] are formed by addition of the toxic gas HCN (hydrogen cyanide) to ketones or aldehydes, not unlike the addition of HCl or H_2O to alkenes (Section 13.6, and Mastering Reactions: Carbonyl Addition Reactions on p. 506). The reaction with HCN to yield a cyanohydrin is reversible, just like the reaction of a ketone or aldehyde with an alcohol to yield a hemiacetal, as we'll see in Section 16.7. Thus, the benzaldehyde cyanohydrin secreted by the millipede decomposes to yield benzaldehyde and HCN. This action protects the millipede because while the cyanohydrin itself is safe, the decomposition reaction releases deadly hydrogen cyanide gas, a remarkably clever and very effective kind of chemical warfare.

The potent chemical weapon of the bombardier beetle is benzoquinone, the simplest member of a class of compounds that are cyclohexadienediones (cyclohexene rings with two double bonds and two carbonyl groups; see illustration). When threatened, the bombardier beetle initiates the enzyme-catalyzed oxidation of dihydroxybenzene by hydrogen peroxide. A hot cloud (up to 100 °C) of irritating benzoquinone vapor

▲ The beautifully colored millipede *Apheloria corrugata* can produce as much as 0.6 mg of HCN to defend itself against attacks.

shoots out of the beetle's defensive organ with such force that it sounds like a pistol shot.

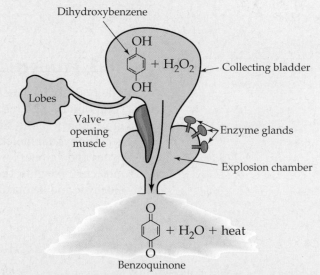

▲ Defensive organ of the bombardier beetle and the chemical warfare factory it contains.

See Chemistry in Action Problems 16.63 and 16.64 at the end of the chapter.

PROBLEM 16.4

Give systematic, IUPAC names for the following compounds:

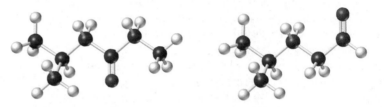

(a) CH₃CH₂CH₂CH₂CH (with O double bonded)

(b) CH₃CH₂CCH₂CH₃ (with O double bonded)

(c) CH₃CH₂CHCH₂CH₂CH (with CH₃ branch and O double bonded)

(d) Dipropyl ketone

PROBLEM 16.5

In Chemistry in Action: Chemical Warfare among the Insects on p. 489, we saw how benzaldehyde cyanohydrin was used by the millipede. Cyanohydrins can be made from any ketone or aldehyde. Draw the structures of the cyanohydrins expected to be formed when HCN is added to compounds (a) and (b) in Problem 16.4.

🔑 **KEY CONCEPT PROBLEM 16.6**

Which of these two molecules is a ketone and which is an aldehyde? Write the condensed formulas for both of them.

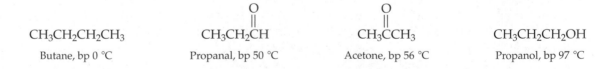

16.3 Properties of Aldehydes and Ketones

The polarity of the carbonyl group makes aldehydes and ketones moderately polar compounds. As a result, they boil at a higher temperature than alkanes with similar molecular weights. Since they have no hydrogen atoms bonded to oxygen or nitrogen, individual molecules do not hydrogen-bond with each other, which makes aldehydes and ketones lower boiling than alcohols. In a series of compounds with similar molecular weights, the alkane is lowest boiling, the alcohol is highest boiling, and the aldehyde and ketone fall in between.

CH₃CH₂CH₂CH₃   CH₃CH₂CH (with O double bonded)   CH₃CCH₃ (with O double bonded)   CH₃CH₂CH₂OH

Butane, bp 0 °C   Propanal, bp 50 °C   Acetone, bp 56 °C   Propanol, bp 97 °C

Formaldehyde (HCHO), the simplest aldehyde, is a gas; acetaldehyde (CH₃CHO) boils close to room temperature. The other simple aldehydes and ketones are liquids (Table 16.2), and those with more than 12 carbon atoms are solids.

Aldehydes and ketones are soluble in common organic solvents, and those with fewer than 5 or 6 carbon atoms are also soluble in water because they are able to accept hydrogen-bonds from water molecules (Figure 16.1).

Simple ketones are excellent solvents because they dissolve both polar and nonpolar compounds. With increasing numbers of carbon atoms, aldehydes and ketones become more alkane-like and less water-soluble.

TABLE **16.2 Physical Properties of Some Simple Aldehydes and Ketones**

STRUCTURE	NAME	BOILING POINT (°C)	WATER SOLUBILITY (g/100 mL H_2O)
HCHO	Formaldehyde	−21	55
CH_3CHO	Acetaldehyde	21	Soluble
CH_3CH_2CHO	Propanal	49	16
$CH_3CH_2CH_2CHO$	Butanal	76	7
$CH_3CH_2CH_2CH_2CHO$	Pentanal	103	1
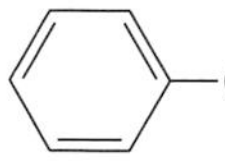 ⬡—CHO	Benzaldehyde	178	0.3
CH_3COCH_3	Acetone	56	Soluble
$CH_3CH_2COCH_3$	2-Butanone	80	26
$CH_3CH_2CH_2COCH_3$	2-Pentanone	102	6
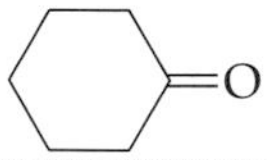 ⬡=O	Cyclohexanone	156	2

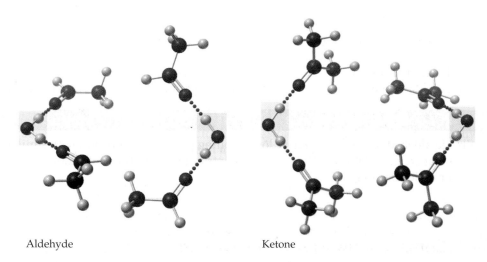

Aldehyde   Ketone

◄ **Figure 16.1**
Hydrogen bonding with water (highlighted in blue) of an aldehyde (CH_3CHO) and a ketone (CH_3COCH_3).

The structures of a few naturally occurring aldehydes and ketones with distinctive odors are shown below. Citronellal (used in citronella candles) is one of about a dozen compounds with similar structures that contribute to the aroma of oils extracted from geraniums, roses, citronella (a tropical plant), and lemon grass. All are used in soaps, cosmetics, and perfumes.

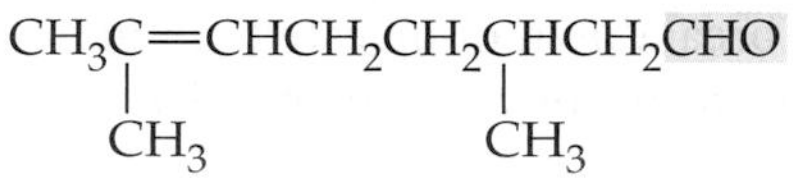

CH_3C=$CHCH_2CH_2CHCH_2CHO$
　　|　　　　　|
　　CH_3　　　　CH_3

Citronellal
(insect repellant, also used in perfumes; from citronella and lemon grass oils)

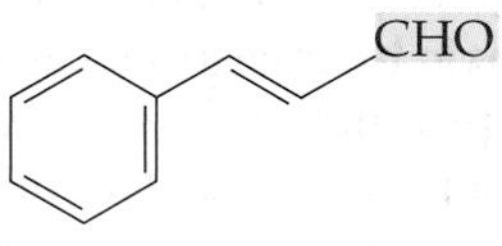

CHO

Cinnamaldehyde
(cinnamon flavor in foods, drugs; from cinnamon bark)

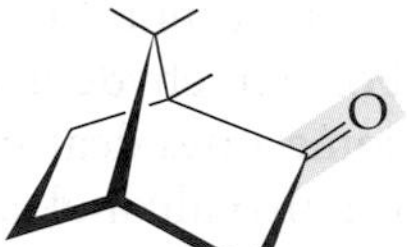

Camphor
(moth repellant from camphor tree)

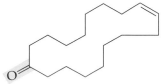

Civetone
(musky odor in perfumes; from the scent gland of the civet cat)

Worked Example 16.3 Predicting the Products of Hemiacetal and Acetal Formation

Write the structure of the intermediate hemiacetal and the acetal final product formed in the following reaction:

$$CH_3CH_2\overset{\displaystyle O}{\overset{\displaystyle \|}{C}}H + 2\,CH_3OH \xrightarrow{\text{Acid catalyst}} ?$$

ANALYSIS First, rewrite the structure showing only a single bond between C and O, along with partial bonds to both C and O:

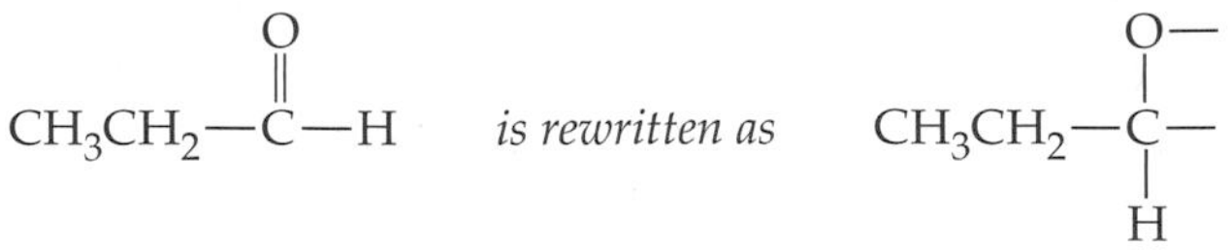

$$CH_3CH_2-\overset{\displaystyle O}{\overset{\displaystyle \|}{C}}-H \quad \text{is rewritten as} \quad CH_3CH_2-\overset{\displaystyle O-}{\underset{\displaystyle H}{C}}-$$

Next, add 1 molecule of the alcohol (CH_3OH in this case) by attaching —H to the oxygen partial bond and —OCH_3 to the carbon partial bond. This yields the hemiacetal intermediate:

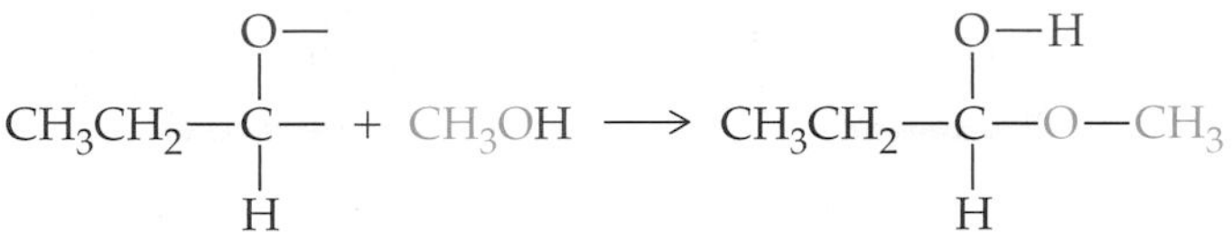

$$CH_3CH_2-\overset{\displaystyle O-}{\underset{\displaystyle H}{C}}- + CH_3OH \longrightarrow CH_3CH_2-\overset{\displaystyle O-H}{\underset{\displaystyle H}{C}}-O-CH_3$$

Hemiacetal

Finally, replace the —OH group of the hemiacetal with an —OCH_3 from a second molecule of alcohol.

SOLUTION
The reaction produces the acetal and water:

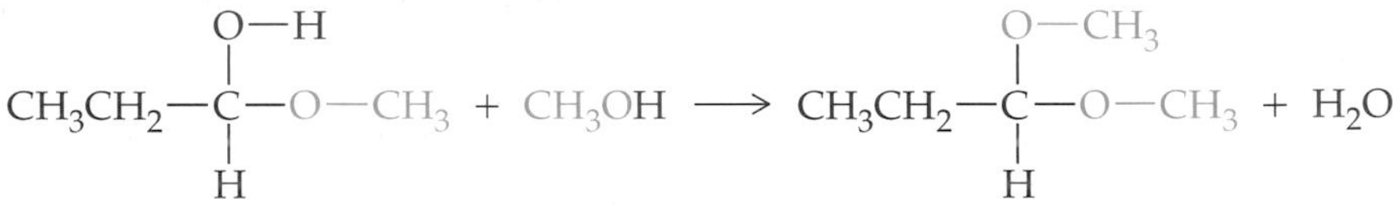

$$CH_3CH_2-\overset{\displaystyle O-H}{\underset{\displaystyle H}{C}}-O-CH_3 + CH_3OH \longrightarrow CH_3CH_2-\overset{\displaystyle O-CH_3}{\underset{\displaystyle H}{C}}-O-CH_3 + H_2O$$

Acetal

Worked Example 16.4 Identification of Hemiacetals

Which of the following compounds are hemiacetals?

(a) 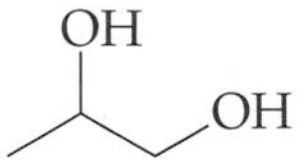   (b) 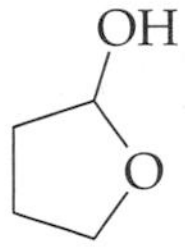   (c) 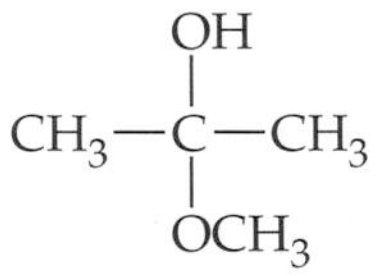 $CH_3-\overset{\displaystyle OH}{\underset{\displaystyle OCH_3}{C}}-CH_3$

ANALYSIS To identify a hemiacetal, look for a carbon atom with single bonds to 2 oxygen atoms, one an —OH group and one an —OR group. Note that the O of the —OR group can be part of a ring.

SOLUTION
Compound (a) contains 2 O atoms, but they are bonded to *different* C atoms; it is not a hemiacetal. Compound (b) has 1 ring C atom bonded to 2 oxygen atoms, one in the substituent —OH group and one bonded to the rest of the ring, which is the R group; it is a cyclic hemiacetal. Compound (c) also contains a C atom bonded to one —OH group and one —OR group, so it too is a hemiacetal.

Worked Example 16.5 Identification of Acetals

Which of the following compounds are acetals?

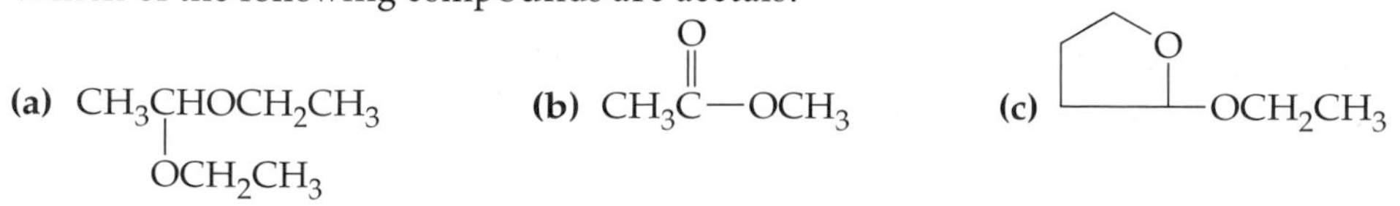

(a) $CH_3CHOCH_2CH_3$
$\quad\quad\quad$ |
$\quad\quad$ OCH_2CH_3

(b) $CH_3\overset{\displaystyle O}{\overset{\|}{C}}{-}OCH_3$

(c) $-OCH_2CH_3$

ANALYSIS As in identifying hemiacetals, look for a carbon atom that has single bonds to 2 oxygen atoms, but in this case both of them will be —OR groups. Note that the O of the —OR group can be part of a ring.

SOLUTION
In (a), the central carbon atom is bonded to one —CH₃, one —H, and *two* —OCH₂CH₃ groups, so the compound is an acetal. Compound (b) does have a carbon atom bonded to 2 oxygen atoms, but one of the bonds is a double bond rather than a single bond, so this is not an acetal. Compound (c) has an oxygen atom in a ring, making it also part of an —OR group, where R is the ring. Since one of the carbons connected to the O in the ring is also connected to an —OCH₂CH₃ group, compound (c) is an acetal.

It should be noted that cyclic hemiacetals and cyclic acetals are the most difficult to recognize, yet they will be the ones you will see most often as you progress through biochemistry, so the more practice you get at recognizing these, the better!

PROBLEM 16.13
Which of the following compounds are hemiacetals?

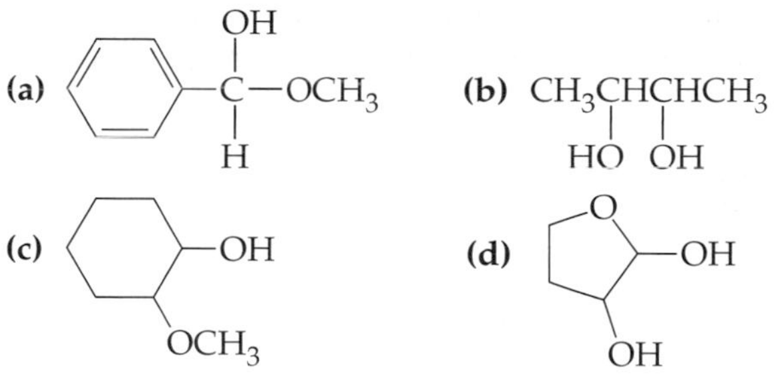

(a)

(b) $CH_3CHCHCH_3$
$\quad\quad\quad$ | |
$\quad\quad$ HO OH

(c)

(d)

PROBLEM 16.14
Draw the structure of the acetal formed from methanol and each of the hemiacetals you identified in Problem 16.13.

PROBLEM 16.15
Draw the structures of the hemiacetals formed in these reactions:

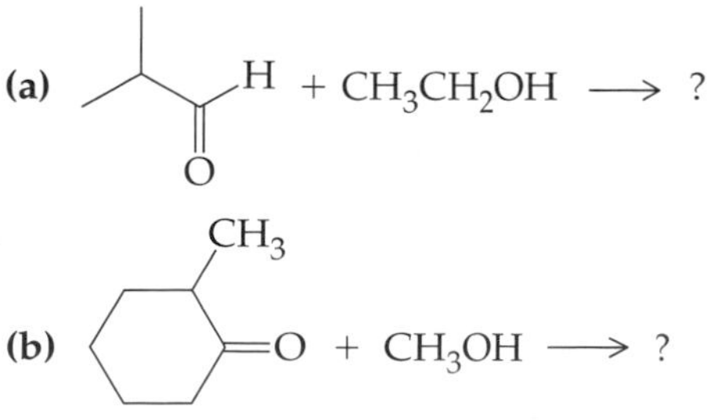

(a) $+ CH_3CH_2OH \longrightarrow$?

(b) $+ CH_3OH \longrightarrow$?

PROBLEM 16.16
Draw the structure of each acetal final product formed in the reactions shown in Problem 16.15.

TABLE 17.1 Physical Properties of Some Carboxylic Acids

STRUCTURE	COMMON NAME	MELTING POINT (°C)	BOILING POINT (°C)
Carboxylic Acids			
HCOOH	Formic	8	101
CH_3COOH	Acetic	17	118
CH_3CH_2COOH	Propionic	−22	141
$CH_3CH_2CH_2COOH$	Butyric	−4	163
$CH_3CH_2CH_2CH_2COOH$	Valeric	−34	185
$CH_3(CH_2)_{16}COOH$	Stearic	70	383
Dicarboxylic Acids			
HOOCCOOH	Oxalic	190	Decomposes
$HOOCCH_2COOH$	Malonic	135	Decomposes
$HOOCCH_2CH_2COOH$	Succinic	188	Decomposes
$HOOCCH_2CH_2CH_2COOH$	Glutaric	98	Decomposes
Unsaturated Acids			
$H_2C{=}CHCOOH$	Acrylic	13	141
$CH_3CH{=}CHCOOH$	Crotonic	72	185
Aromatic Acids			
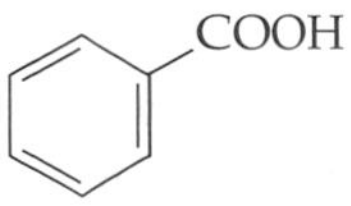 COOH (benzene ring)	Benzoic	122	249
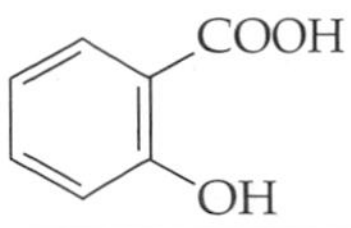 COOH, OH (benzene ring)	Salicylic	159	Decomposes

Acetyl group A $CH_3{-}\overset{\overset{O}{\|}}{C}{-}$ group.

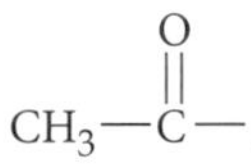

The acyl group that remains after a carboxylic acid loses its —OH is named by replacing the -*ic* at the end of the acid name with -*oyl*. One very important exception is the acyl group from acetic acid, which is traditionally called an **acetyl group**.

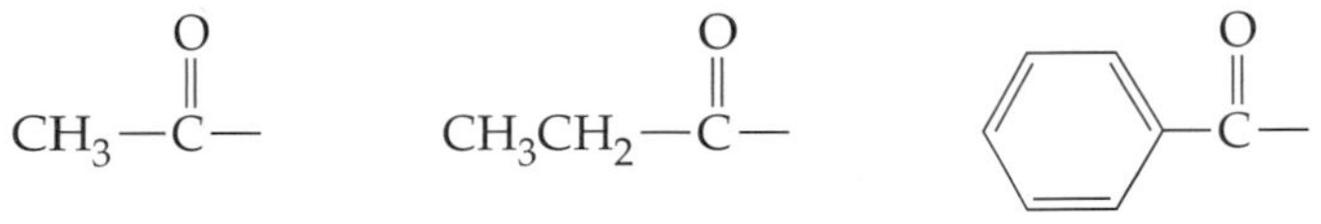

$$CH_3{-}\overset{\overset{O}{\|}}{C}{-} \qquad CH_3CH_2{-}\overset{\overset{O}{\|}}{C}{-} \qquad \text{(benzene ring)}{-}\overset{\overset{O}{\|}}{C}{-}$$

Acetyl group   Propanoyl group   Benzoyl group

Dicarboxylic acids, which contain two —COOH groups, are named systematically by adding the ending -*dioic acid* to the alkane name (the -*e* is retained). Here again the simple dicarboxylic acids are usually referred to by their common names. Oxalic acid (IUPAC name: ethanedioic acid) is found in plants of the genus *Oxalis*, which includes rhubarb and spinach. You will encounter succinic acid, glutaric acid, and several other dicarboxylic acids when we come to the generation of biochemical energy and the citric acid cycle (Section 20.8).

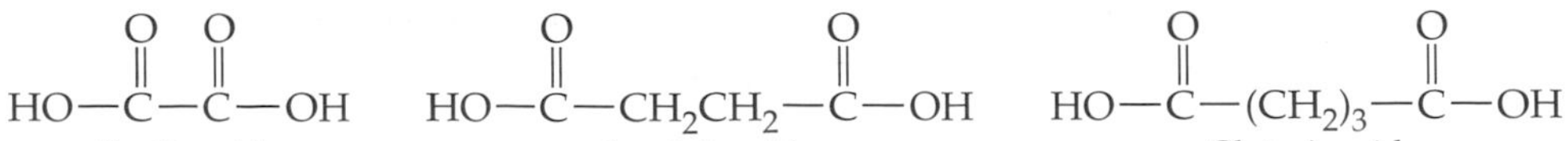

$$HO{-}\overset{\overset{O}{\|}}{C}{-}\overset{\overset{O}{\|}}{C}{-}OH \qquad HO{-}\overset{\overset{O}{\|}}{C}{-}CH_2CH_2{-}\overset{\overset{O}{\|}}{C}{-}OH \qquad HO{-}\overset{\overset{O}{\|}}{C}{-}(CH_2)_3{-}\overset{\overset{O}{\|}}{C}{-}OH$$

Oxalic acid   Succinic acid   Glutaric acid
(Ethanedioic acid)   (Butanedioic acid)   (Pentanedioic acid)

Unsaturated acids are named systematically in the IUPAC system with the ending -enoic. For example, the simplest unsaturated acid, H_2C=CHCOOH, is named propenoic acid. It is, however, best known as acrylic acid, which is a raw material for acrylic polymers.

LOOKING AHEAD ▶▶▶ Biochemistry is dependent on the continual breakdown of food molecules. Frequently this process requires transfer of acetyl groups from one molecule to another. Acetyl-group transfer occurs, for example, at the beginning of the citric acid cycle, which is central to the production of life-sustaining energy (Section 20.8).

Worked Example 17.1 Naming a Carboxylic Acid

Give the systematic and common names for this compound:

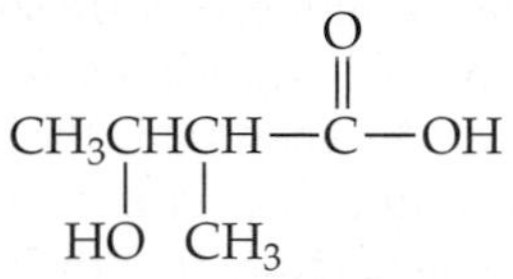

$$\underset{\underset{HO\ \ CH_3}{|\ \ \ |}}{CH_3CHCH}-\overset{\overset{O}{\|}}{C}-OH$$

ANALYSIS For the systematic name of a carboxylic acid, first identify the longest chain containing the —COOH group and number it starting with the carboxyl-group carbon:

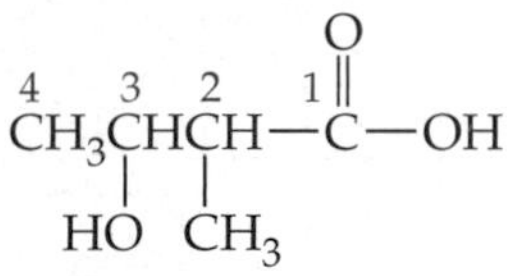

$$\underset{\underset{HO\ \ CH_3}{|\ \ \ |}}{\overset{4\quad 3\ \ 2}{CH_3CHCH}}-\overset{\overset{O}{1\|}}{C}-OH$$

The parent compound is the 4-carbon acid, butanoic acid. It has a methyl group on carbon 2 and a hydroxyl group on carbon 3. From Table 17.1 we see that the common name for the 4-carbon acid is butyric acid. In the common nomenclature scheme, substituents are located by Greek letters rather than numbers:

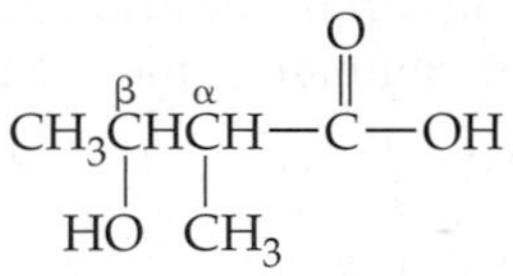

$$\underset{\underset{HO\ \ CH_3}{|\ \ \ |}}{\overset{\beta\quad \alpha}{CH_3CHCH}}-\overset{\overset{O}{\|}}{C}-OH$$

SOLUTION
The IUPAC name of this molecule is 3-hydroxy-2-methylbutanoic acid; the common name of this acid is β-hydroxy-α-methylbutyric acid.

PROBLEM 17.2
Draw the structures of the following acids:
(a) 2-Ethyl-3-hydroxyhexanoic acid
(b) *m*-Nitrobenzoic acid

PROBLEM 17.3
Write both the complete structural formula of succinic acid (refer to Table 17.1), showing all bonds, and the line-angle structural formula.

PROBLEM 17.4
Draw and name the acid that is formed by addition of Br_2 to the double bond in acrylic acid (refer to Table 17.1 and Section 13.6).

Esters

Ester

When the —OH of the carboxyl group is converted to the —OR' of an ester group (—COOR'), the ability of the molecules to hydrogen-bond with each other is lost (although esters can still hydrogen bond to water). Simple esters therefore have lower boiling than the acids from which they are derived.

$$CH_3\overset{O}{\underset{||}{C}}-OH \qquad CH_3\overset{O}{\underset{||}{C}}-O-CH_3 \qquad CH_3\overset{O}{\underset{||}{C}}-O-CH_2CH_3$$

Acetic acid, bp 118 °C   Methyl ester, bp 57 °C   Ethyl ester, bp 77 °C

The simple esters are colorless, volatile liquids with pleasant odors, and many of them contribute to the natural fragrance of flowers and ripe fruits. Prolonged exposure to high concentrations of the vapors of volatile esters can be irritating and have a narcotic effect. The lower-molecular-weight esters are somewhat soluble in water and are quite flammable. Esters are neither acids nor bases in aqueous solution.

Ester names consist of two words. The first is the name of the alkyl group R' in the ester group —COOR'. The second is the name of the parent acid, with the family-name ending *-ic acid* replaced by *-ate*. (Note that the order of the two parts of the name is the reverse of the order in which ester condensed formulas are usually written.)

Naming an ester

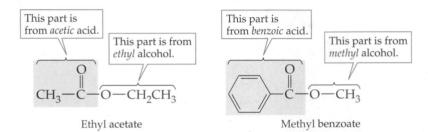

Ethyl acetate   Methyl benzoate

▲ Pineapples are among the many fruits with flavors derived from esters.

Both common and systematic names are derived in this manner. For example, an ester of a straight-chain, 4-carbon carboxylic acid is named systematically as a butanoate (from butanoic acid) or by its common name as a butyrate (from butyric acid):

$$CH_3CH_2CH_2\overset{O}{\underset{||}{C}}OCH_2CH_3$$

Ethyl butyrate
(Ethyl butanoate)

This ester is used as a food flavoring to give the taste and smell of pineapples.

Worked Example 17.2 Writing the Structure of an Ester from Its Name

What is the structure of butyl acetate?

ANALYSIS The two-word name consisting of an alkyl group name followed by an acid name with an *-ate* ending shows that the compound is an ester. The name "acetate" shows that the RCO— part of the molecule is from acetic acid (CH_3COOH). The "butyl" part of the name indicates that a butyl group has replaced H in the carboxyl group.

SOLUTION
The structure of butyl acetate is

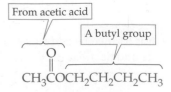

From acetic acid   A butyl group

$$CH_3\overset{O}{\underset{||}{C}}OCH_2CH_2CH_2CH_3$$

Worked Example 17.3 Naming an Ester from Its Structure

What is the name of this compound?

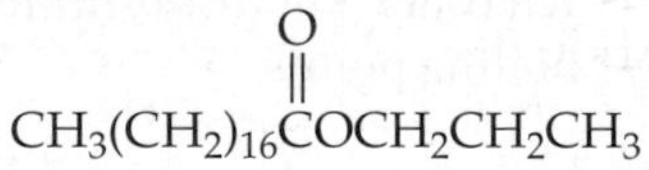

$$\underset{\displaystyle CH_3(CH_2)_{16}\overset{\textstyle O}{\overset{\|}{C}}OCH_2CH_2CH_3}{}$$

ANALYSIS The compound has the general formula RCOOR′, so it is an ester. The acyl part of the molecule (RCO—) is from stearic acid (see Table 17.1). The R′ group has 3 C atoms and is therefore a propyl group.

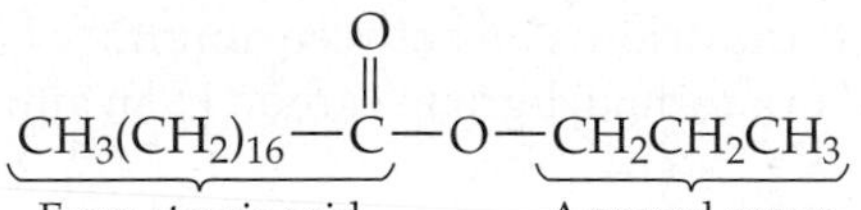

$$CH_3(CH_2)_{16}\!-\!\overset{\textstyle O}{\overset{\|}{C}}\!-\!O\!-\!CH_2CH_2CH_3$$

$$\underbrace{\text{From stearic acid}} \qquad \underbrace{\text{A propyl group}}$$

SOLUTION
The compound is propyl stearate.

PROBLEM 17.5
Draw the structures of
(a) Hexyl benzoate   **(b)** Methyl formate   **(c)** Ethyl acrylate (See Table 17.1.)

PROBLEM 17.6
Which of the following compounds has the highest boiling point and which has the lowest boiling point? Explain your answer.
(a) CH_3OCH_3 **(b)** CH_3COOH **(c)** $CH_3CH_2CH_3$

PROBLEM 17.7
In the following pairs of compounds, which would you expect to be more soluble in water? Why?
(a) $C_8H_{17}COOH$ or $CH_3CH_2CH_2COOH$

(b) $CH_3\underset{\displaystyle CH_3}{\underset{|}{CHCOOH}}$ or $CH_3CH_2COO\underset{\displaystyle CH_3}{\underset{|}{CHCH_3}}$

Amides

Compounds with a nitrogen directly attached to the carbonyl carbon atom are *amides*. The nitrogen of an amide may be an —NH$_2$ group or may have one or two R′ groups bonded to it. *Unsubstituted amides* (RCONH$_2$) can form multiple hydrogen bonds to other amide molecules and thus have higher melting points and higher boiling points than the acids from which they are derived.

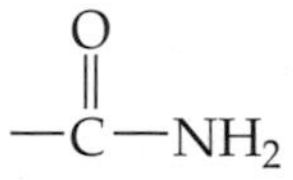

$$-\overset{\textstyle O}{\overset{\|}{C}}\!-\!NH_2$$

Amide

Hydrogen bonding in $R\overset{\textstyle O}{\overset{\|}{C}}NH_2$

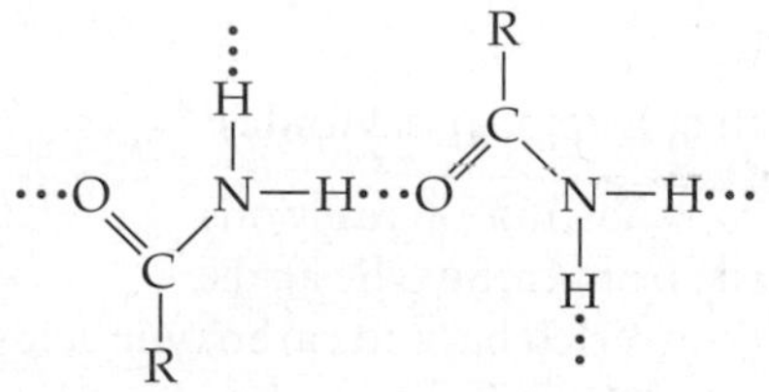

Low-molecular-weight unsubstituted amides are solids (except for the simplest amide (formamide, $HCONH_2$, a liquid)) that are soluble in both water (with which they form hydrogen bonds) and organic solvents. *Monosubstituted amides* ($RCONHR'$) can also form hydrogen bonds to each other, but *disubstituted amides* ($RCONR'_2$) cannot do so and therefore have lower boiling points.

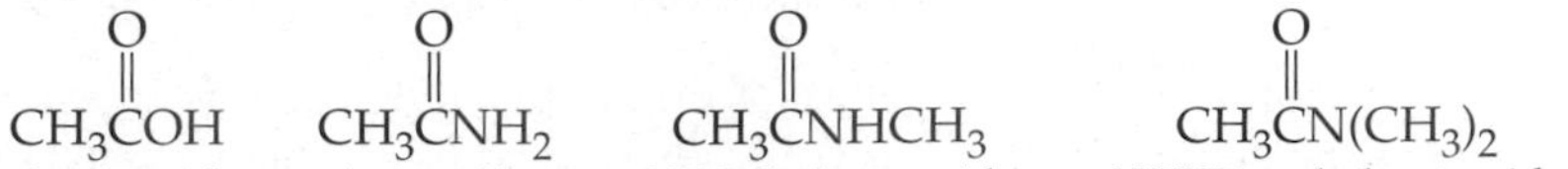

$$CH_3\overset{O}{\overset{\|}{C}}OH \qquad CH_3\overset{O}{\overset{\|}{C}}NH_2 \qquad CH_3\overset{O}{\overset{\|}{C}}NHCH_3 \qquad CH_3\overset{O}{\overset{\|}{C}}N(CH_3)_2$$

| Acetic acid | Acetamide | N-Methylacetamide | N,N-Dimethylacetamide |
| (bp 118 °C) | (bp 222 °C) | (bp 206 °C) | (bp 165 °C) |

It is important to note the distinction between amines (Chapter 15) and amides. The nitrogen atom is bonded to a carbonyl-group carbon in an amide, but *not* in an amine:

An amide
$(RCONH_2)$

An amine
(RNH_2)

The positive end of the carbonyl group attracts the unshared pair of electrons on nitrogen strongly enough to prevent it from acting as a base by accepting a hydrogen atom. As a result, *amides are NOT basic like amines are.*

Amides with an unsubstituted —NH_2 group are named by replacing the *-ic acid* or *-oic acid* of the corresponding carboxylic acid name with *-amide*. For example, the amide derived from acetic acid is called acetamide. If the nitrogen atom of the amide has alkyl substituents on it, the compound is named by first specifying the alkyl group and then identifying the amide name. The alkyl substituents are preceded by the letter *N* to identify them as being attached directly to nitrogen.

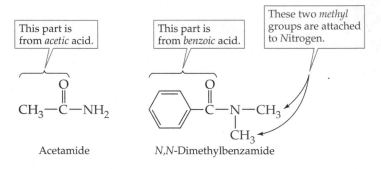

This part is from *acetic* acid.

This part is from *benzoic* acid.

These two *methyl* groups are attached to Nitrogen.

Acetamide

N,N-Dimethylbenzamide

To review, some derivatives of acetic acid are shown below:

Carbonyl derivatives of acetic acid

$$CH_3\overset{O}{\overset{\|}{C}}-OCH_3 \quad CH_3\overset{O}{\overset{\|}{C}}-NH_2 \quad CH_3\overset{O}{\overset{\|}{C}}-NHCH_3 \quad CH_3\overset{O}{\overset{\|}{C}}-N\overset{CH_3}{\underset{CH_3}{}} \quad CH_3\overset{O}{\overset{\|}{C}}-N\overset{CH_3}{\underset{CH_2CH_3}{}}$$

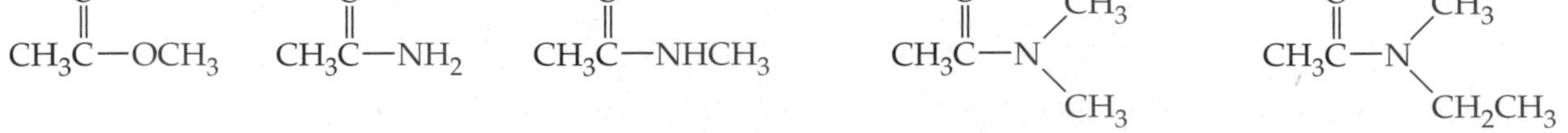

| Methyl acetate | Acetamide | N-Methylacetamide | N,N-Dimethylacetamide | N-Ethyl-N-Methylacetamide |

Properties of Carboxylic Acids, Esters, and Amides:

- All undergo carbonyl-group substitution reactions.
- Esters and amides are made from carboxylic acids.
- Esters and amides can be converted back to carboxylic acids.

- Carboxylic acids and unsubstituted or monosubstituted amides exhibit strong hydrogen bonding to one another; disubstituted amides and esters do not hydrogen-bond to one another. All these, however, can still hydrogen bond to water molecules.
- Simple acids and esters are liquids; all unsubstituted amides (except formamide) are solids.
- Carboxylic acids produce acidic aqueous solutions. Esters and amides are neither acids nor bases (pH neutral).
- Small (low-molecular-weight) amides are water-soluble, while small esters are somewhat water-soluble.
- Volatile acids have strong, sharp odors while volatile esters have pleasant, fruity odors. Amides generally are odorless.

LOOKING AHEAD ▶▶▶ In later chapters, you will see that the fundamental bonding connections in proteins are amide bonds (Section 18.2) and those in oils and fats are ester bonds (Section 24.2).

Worked Example 17.4 Formation of Acid Anhydrides

An important but often overlooked class of carboxylic acid derivatives is the *acid anhydrides*. (*Anhydride* means "without water.") Acid anhydrides are formed when pairs of acid molecules react (dimerize) via a carbonyl-group substitution reaction to lose water. Relate the reactants below to the substitution reaction pattern (on p. 516) and complete the equation.

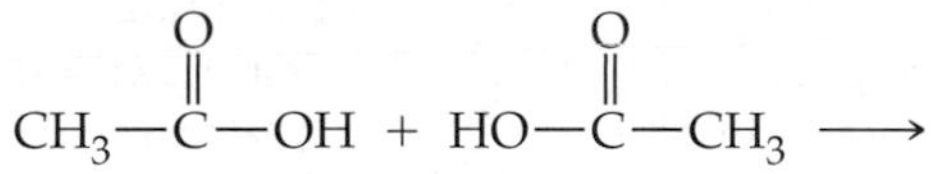

$$CH_3-\overset{\displaystyle O}{\overset{\|}{C}}-OH \ + \ HO-\overset{\displaystyle O}{\overset{\|}{C}}-CH_3 \ \longrightarrow$$

ANALYSIS The reaction here fits the substitution-reaction pattern as follows:

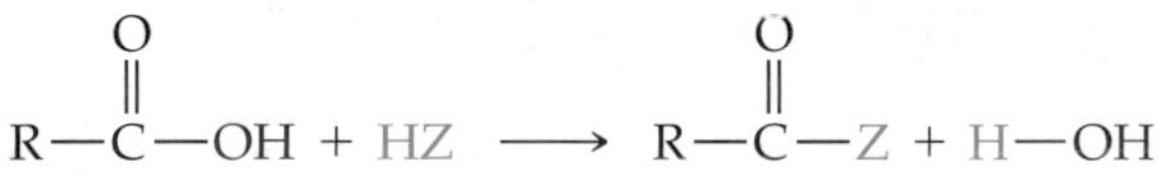

$$R-\overset{\displaystyle O}{\overset{\|}{C}}-OH \ + \ HZ \ \longrightarrow \ R-\overset{\displaystyle O}{\overset{\|}{C}}-Z \ + \ H-OH$$

with Z equal to

$$-O-\overset{\displaystyle O}{\overset{\|}{C}}-CH_3$$

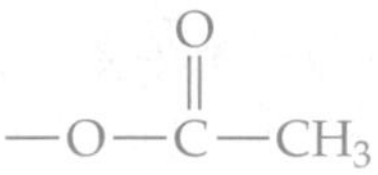

SOLUTION
The reaction is

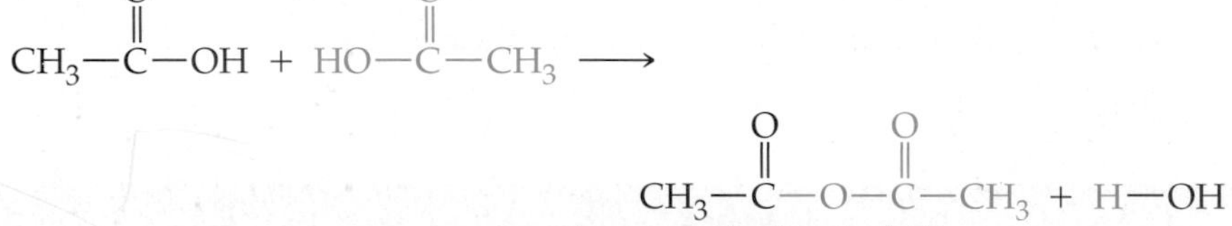

$$CH_3-\overset{\displaystyle O}{\overset{\|}{C}}-OH \ + \ HO-\overset{\displaystyle O}{\overset{\|}{C}}-CH_3 \ \longrightarrow$$

$$CH_3-\overset{\displaystyle O}{\overset{\|}{C}}-O-\overset{\displaystyle O}{\overset{\|}{C}}-CH_3 \ + \ H-OH$$
Acetic anhydride

Carboxylic acid anhydrides, although important in an organic chemistry lab, are of little importance in biochemistry. They easily react with water to give back the acids they came from (the reverse of the above reaction), so they are not found in biological systems. They are introduced here to prepare the way for the introduction of phosphoric acid anhydrides in Section 17.8, which *do* play a key role in biochemistry.

PROBLEM 17.8

Write both condensed and line structures for (a) the ester formed when butyric acid reacts with cyclopentanol, (b) the amide formed when isopropyl amine is reacted with butyric acid, and (c) the amide formed when diethylamine is reacted with butyric acid. (d) Name the derivatives you created in parts (a)–(c).

PROBLEM 17.9

What are the names of the following compounds?

(a)

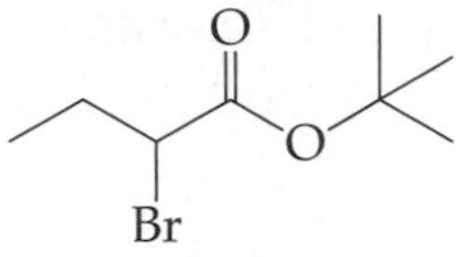

(b)

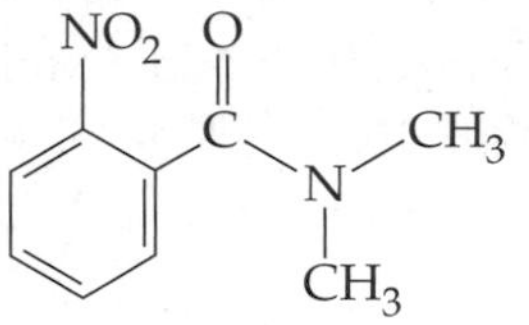

PROBLEM 17.10

Draw structures corresponding to these names:

(a) 4-Methylpentanamide   (b) *N*-Ethyl-*N*-methylpropanamide

PROBLEM 17.11

Many important biomolecules are multifunctional; given the molecule shown below, identify the following classes of compounds: (i) α-amino group, (ii) monosubstituted amide, (iii) methyl ester, (iv) carboxylic acid, and (v) disubstituted amide.

(c)

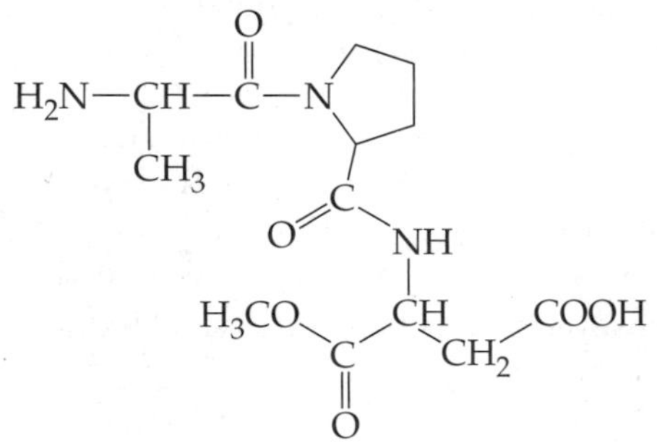

PROBLEM 17.12

Classify each compound (a)–(f) as one of the following: (i) amide, (ii) ester, (iii) carboxylic acid.

(a) CH_3COOCH_3 (b) RCONHR

(c) C_6H_5COOH (d) $CH_3CH_2C-N(CH_3)_2$ (with O double bonded to C)

(e) $CH_3CH_2CH_2CONH_2$ (f) $HOOCCH_2-CH-CH_3$ with CH_3

🔑 **KEY CONCEPT PROBLEM 17.13**

Identify the following molecules as an ester, a carboxylic acid, or an amide, and write the condensed molecular structural formula and the line-angle structural formula for each.

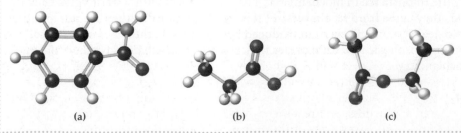

(a)   (b)   (c)

17.2 Some Common Carboxylic Acids

Carboxylic acids occur throughout the plant and animal kingdoms, and the common names of many come from the plants or animals in which they were first identified. Formic acid is known as the chemical that puts the sting in ant bites (from the Latin *formica,* "ant"). Acetic acid and lactic acid are named from the Latin *acetum,* meaning vinegar, and *lactis,* meaning milk. Butyric acid (from the Latin *butyrum,* "butter") is responsible for the terrible odor of rancid butter (formed by oxidation of butyralde-hyde). Caproic acid (from the Latin *caper,* "goat") was first isolated from the skin of goats (and causes their distinctive odor). The esters of long-chain carboxylic acids such as stearic acid and oleic acid are components of all animal fats and vegetable oils.

Some naturally occurring carboxylic acids

$$CH_3CH_2CH_2-\overset{\displaystyle O}{\overset{\|}{C}}-OH \qquad CH_3CH_2CH_2CH_2CH_2-\overset{\displaystyle O}{\overset{\|}{C}}-OH$$

Butyric acid
(rancid butter)

Caproic acid
(goats)

$$CH_3CH_2CH_2CH_2CH_2CH_2CH_2CH_2CH_2CH_2CH_2CH_2CH_2CH_2CH_2CH_2CH_2-\overset{\displaystyle O}{\overset{\|}{C}}-OH$$

Stearic acid ($C_{18}H_{36}O_2$, from animal fat)

Acetic Acid (CH₃COOH): In Vinegar

Everyone recognizes the sour taste of the best known of the carboxylic acids, acetic acid, since it is the primary organic component of vinegar. Vinegar is a solution of 4–8% acetic acid in water (with various flavoring agents). When fermentation of grapes, apples, and other fruits proceeds in the presence of ample oxygen, oxidation goes beyond the formation of ethanol to the formation of acetic acid (Section 14.5). The production of "boutique" vinegars from various wine varietals has become big business today; for example, it is common to find champagne vinegar in many cooking stores. Aqueous acetic acid solutions are also common laboratory reagents.

In concentrations over 50%, acetic acid is corrosive and can damage the skin, eyes, nose, and mouth. There is no pain when the concentrated acid is spilled on unbroken skin, but painful blisters form about 30 minutes later. Pure acetic acid is known as *glacial acetic acid* because, with just a slight amount of cooling below room temperature (to 17 °C), the liquid forms icy-looking crystals that resemble glaciers. Acetic acid is a reactant in many industrial processes and is sometimes used as a solvent. As a food additive, it is used to adjust acidity.

$$CH_3\overset{\displaystyle O}{\overset{\|}{C}}-OH$$

Acetic acid

Citric Acid: In Citrus Fruits and Blood

$$HO-\overset{\displaystyle O}{\overset{\|}{C}}-CH_2-\overset{\overset{\displaystyle OH}{|}}{\underset{\underset{\displaystyle OH}{|}}{\underset{C=O}{C}}}-CH_2-\overset{\displaystyle O}{\overset{\|}{C}}-OH$$

Citric acid

Citric acid is produced by almost all plants and animals during metabolism, and its normal concentration in human blood is about 2 mg/100 mL. Citrus fruits owe their tartness to citric acid; for example, lemon juice contains 4–8% and orange juice about 1% citric acid. Pure citric acid is a white, crystalline solid (mp 153 °C) that is very soluble in water. Citrates (a term used to describe mixtures of citric acid and its salts) are commonly used to buffer pH in shampoos and hair-setting lotions, add tartness to candies and soft drinks, and react with bicarbonate ion to produce the fizz in Alka-Seltzer; they are also used extensively in pharmaceuticals and cosmetics.

LOOKING AHEAD ▶▶▶ Citric acid lends its name to the *citric acid cycle*, part of the major biochemical pathway that leads directly to the generation of energy. Citric acid is the product of the first reaction of an eight-reaction cycle, which is presented in Section 20.8.

17.3 Acidity of Carboxylic Acids

Carboxylate anion The anion that results from ionization of a carboxylic acid, RCOO⁻.

Carboxylic acids are weak acids that establish equilibria in aqueous solution with **carboxylate anions**, RCOO⁻. The carboxylate anions are named by replacing the *-ic* ending in the carboxylic acid name with *-ate* (giving the same names and endings used in naming esters). At pH 7.4 in body fluids, carboxylic acids exist mainly as their carboxylate anions:

$$CH_3\overset{O}{\underset{\|}{C}}-OH + H_2O \rightleftharpoons CH_3\overset{O}{\underset{\|}{C}}-O^- + H_3O^+$$

Acetic acid ⟶ Acetate ion

$$CH_3\overset{O}{\underset{\|}{C}}-\overset{O}{\underset{\|}{C}}-OH + H_2O \rightleftharpoons CH_3\overset{O}{\underset{\|}{C}}-\overset{O}{\underset{\|}{C}}-O^- + H_3O^+$$

Pyruvic acid ⟶ Pyruvate ion

The comparative strength of an acid is measured by its acid dissociation constant (K_a); the smaller the value of K_a, the weaker the acid (Section 10.5). Many carboxylic acids have about the same acid strength as acetic acid, as shown by the acid dissociation constants in Table 17.2. There are some exceptions, though. Trichloroacetic acid, used to prepare microscope slides, for chemical skin peeling, and to precipitate proteins from body fluids, is a strong acid that must be handled with the same respect as sulfuric acid.

TABLE 17.2 Carboxylic Acid Dissociation Constants*

Name	Structure	Acid Dissociation Constant (K_a)
Trichloroacetic acid	Cl_3CCOOH	2.3×10^{-1}
Chloroacetic acid	$ClCH_2COOH$	1.4×10^{-3}
Formic acid	$HCOOH$	1.8×10^{-4}
Acetic acid	CH_3COOH	1.8×10^{-5}
Propanoic acid	CH_3CH_2COOH	1.3×10^{-5}
Hexanoic acid	$CH_3(CH_2)_4COOH$	1.3×10^{-5}
Benzoic acid	C_6H_5COOH	6.5×10^{-5}
Acrylic acid	$H_2C{=}CHCOOH$	5.6×10^{-5}
Oxalic acid	$HOOCCOOH$	5.4×10^{-2}
	$^-OOCCOOH$	5.2×10^{-5}
Glutaric acid	$HOOC(CH_2)_3COOH$	4.5×10^{-5}
	$^-OOC(CH_2)_3COOH$	3.8×10^{-6}

*The acid dissociation constant K_a is the equilibrium constant for the ionization of an acid; the smaller its value, the weaker the acid:

$$RCOOH + H_2O \rightleftharpoons RCOO^- + H_3O^+ \quad K_a = \frac{[RCOO^-][H_3O^+]}{[RCOOH]}$$

Carboxylic acid salt An ionic compound containing a cation and a carboxylate acid anion.

Carboxylic acids undergo neutralization reactions with bases in the same manner as other acids. With strong bases, such as sodium hydroxide, a carboxylic acid reacts to give water and a **carboxylic acid salt**, as shown below for the formation of sodium acetate. (Like all other such aqueous acid–strong base reactions, this reaction proceeds much more favorably in the forward direction than in the reverse direction and is thus written with a single arrow.) As for all salts, a carboxylic acid salt is named with cation and anion names.

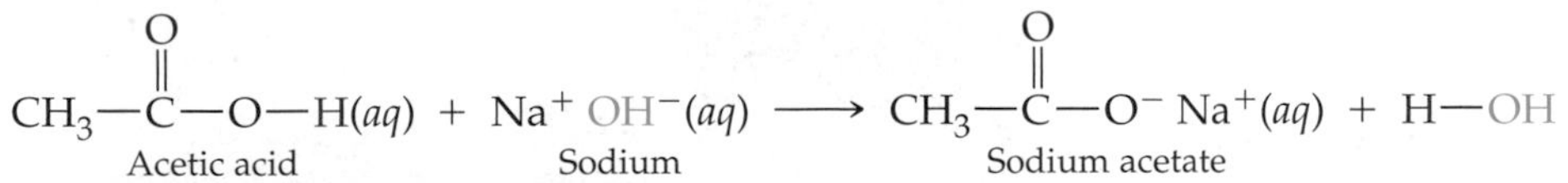

$$CH_3-\overset{\overset{\displaystyle O}{\|}}{C}-O-H(aq) \ + \ Na^+ \ OH^-(aq) \longrightarrow CH_3-\overset{\overset{\displaystyle O}{\|}}{C}-O^- \ Na^+(aq) \ + \ H-OH$$

Acetic acid	Sodium	Sodium acetate
(a weak acid)	hydroxide	

   The sodium and potassium salts of carboxylic acids are ionic solids that are usually far more soluble in water than the carboxylic acids themselves. For example, benzoic acid has a water solubility of only 3.4 g/L at 25 °C, whereas water solubility for sodium benzoate is 550 g/L. The formation of carboxylic acid salts, like the formation of amine salts, is useful in creating water-soluble derivatives of drugs. (See Chemistry in Action: Organic Compounds in Body Fluids and the "Solubility Switch" in Chapter 15, p. 473.)

Worked Example 17.5 Effect of Structure on Carboxylic Acid Strength

Write the structural formulas of trichloroacetic acid and acetic acid and explain why trichloroacetic acid is the much stronger acid of the two.

ANALYSIS

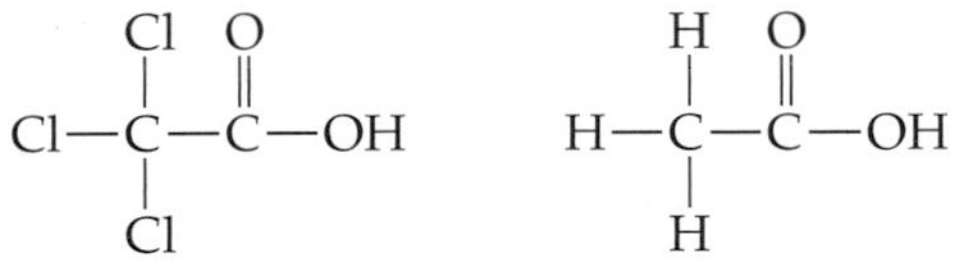

$$\overset{\overset{\displaystyle Cl}{|}}{\underset{\underset{\displaystyle Cl}{|}}{Cl-C}}-\overset{\overset{\displaystyle O}{\|}}{C}-OH \qquad\qquad \overset{\overset{\displaystyle H}{|}}{\underset{\underset{\displaystyle H}{|}}{H-C}}-\overset{\overset{\displaystyle O}{\|}}{C}-OH$$

Trichloroacetic acid	Acetic acid

The structural difference is the replacement of 3 hydrogen atoms on the alpha carbon by 3 chlorine atoms. The chlorines are much more electronegative than the hydrogen and therefore draw electrons away from the rest of the molecule in trichloroacetic acid. The result is that the hydrogen atom of the —COOH group in trichloroacetic acid is held less strongly and is much more easily removed than the corresponding hydrogen atom in acetic acid.

SOLUTION
Since the —COOH hydrogen atom in trichloroacetic acid is held less strongly, it is the stronger acid.

PROBLEM 17.14
Write the products of the following reactions:
(a) $CH_3CH(OH)COOH + NaOH \longrightarrow$?
(b) 2,2-Dimethylpentanoic acid + $Ca(OH)_2 \longrightarrow$?

PROBLEM 17.15
Write the formulas of potassium salicylate and disodium oxalate (refer to Table 17.1).

PROBLEM 17.16
Suppose that potassium acetate and disodium glutarate are dissolved in water. Write the formulas of each organic ion present in the solution (refer to Table 17.1).

ANALYSIS The name of an ester gives a good indication of the names of the two products. Thus, ethyl formate yields ethyl alcohol and formic acid. To find the product structures in a more systematic way, write the structure of the ester and locate the bond between the carbonyl-group carbon and the —OR′ group:

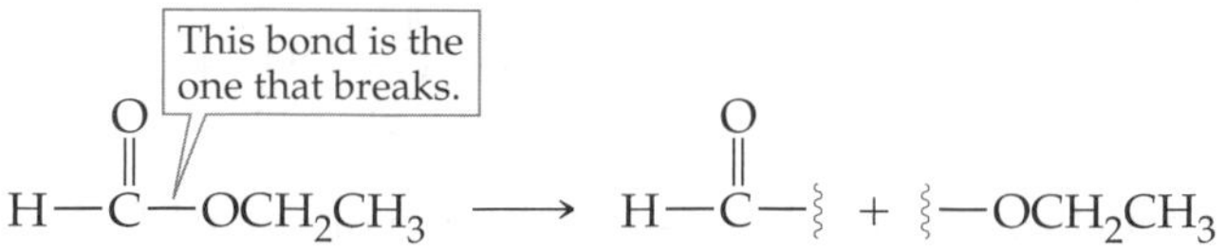

SOLUTION
Carry out a hydrolysis reaction on paper. First form the carboxylic acid product by connecting an —OH to the carbonyl-group carbon. Then add an —H to the —OCH$_2$CH$_3$ group to form the alcohol product.

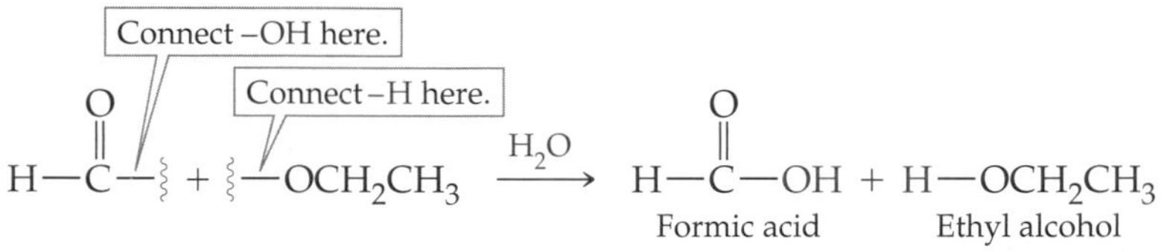

PROBLEM 17.24
If a bottle of aspirin tablets has the aroma of vinegar, it is time to discard those tablets. Explain why, and include a chemical equation in the explanation.

PROBLEM 17.25
What products would you obtain from acid-catalyzed hydrolysis of the following esters?
(a) Isopropyl *p*-nitrobenzoate

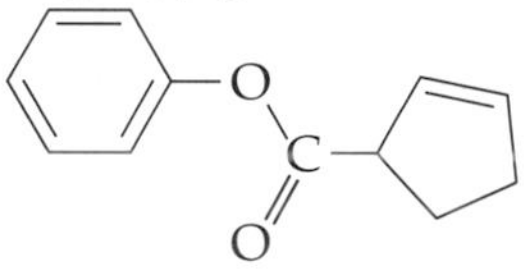

(c) $CH_3 - \overset{\overset{NH_2}{|}}{CH} - \overset{\overset{O}{\|}}{C} - O\,CH_2CH_3$

Amide Hydrolysis

Amides are extremely stable in water but undergo hydrolysis with prolonged heating in the presence of acids or bases. The products are the carboxylic acid and amine from which the amide was synthesized:

In practice, the products obtained depend on whether the hydrolysis is done using acid or base. Under acidic conditions, the carboxylic acid and amine salt are obtained. Doing this reaction using base produces the neutral amine and carboxylate anion. For example, in the hydrolysis of *N*-methylacetamide:

*Hydrolysis products of **N**-Methylacetamide*

$$CH_3\overset{\overset{O}{\|}}{C}-NHCH_3 + H_3O^+ \longrightarrow CH_3\overset{\overset{O}{\|}}{C}-OH + CH_3NH_3^+ \qquad \text{Acid hydrolysis}$$

$$CH_3\overset{\overset{O}{\|}}{C}-NHCH_3 + OH^- \longrightarrow CH_3\overset{\overset{O}{\|}}{C}-O^- + CH_3NH_2 \qquad \text{Base hydrolysis}$$

LOOKING AHEAD ▶▶▶ In Chapter 27 you will see that the cleavage of amide bonds by hydrolysis is the key process that occurs in the stomach during digestion of proteins.

Worked Example 17.9 Writing the Products of an Amide Hydrolysis

What carboxylic acid and amine are produced by the hydrolysis of
N-ethylbutanamide?

$$\underset{\text{N-Ethylbutanamide}}{CH_3CH_2CH_2\overset{\overset{\displaystyle O}{\|}}{C}-NHCH_2CH_3} + H_2O \longrightarrow ?$$

ANALYSIS First, look at the name of the starting amide. Often, the amide's name incorporates the names of the two products. Thus, N-ethylbutanamide yields ethylamine and butanoic acid. To find the product structures systematically, write the amide and locate the bond between the carbonyl-group carbon and the nitrogen. Then break this amide bond and write the two fragments:

This amide bond is the one that breaks.

$$CH_3CH_2CH_2\overset{\overset{\displaystyle O}{\|}}{C}-NHCH_2CH_3 \longrightarrow CH_3CH_2CH_2\overset{\overset{\displaystyle O}{\|}}{C}{-} + {-}NHCH_2CH_3$$

SOLUTION
Carry out a hydrolysis reaction on paper and form the products by connecting an —OH to the carbonyl-group carbon and an —H to the nitrogen:

Connect —OH here.

Connect —H here.

$$CH_3CH_2CH_2\overset{\overset{\displaystyle O}{\|}}{C}{-} + {-}NHCH_2CH_3 \xrightarrow{H_2O}$$

$$\underset{\text{Butanoic acid}}{CH_3CH_2CH_2\overset{\overset{\displaystyle O}{\|}}{C}-OH} + \underset{\text{Ethylamine}}{H-NHCH_2CH_3}$$

PROBLEM 17.26
What carboxylic acids and amines result from hydrolysis of the following amides?

(a) $CH_3CH{=}CH\overset{\overset{\displaystyle O}{\|}}{C}NHCH_3$ (b) N,N-Dimethyl-p-nitrobenzamide

17.7 Polyamides and Polyesters

Imagine what would happen if a molecule with *two* carboxylic acid groups reacted with a molecule having *two* amino groups. Amide formation could join the two molecules together, but further reactions could then link more and more molecules together until a giant chain resulted. This is exactly what happens when certain kinds of synthetic polymers are made.

Nylons are *polyamides* produced by reaction of diamines with diacids. One such nylon, nylon 6,6 (pronounced "six-six"), is so named because of the structures of the two compounds that are used to produce it. Nylon 6,6 is made by heating adipic acid (hexanedioic acid, a 6-carbon dicarboxylic acid) with hexamethylenediamine (1,6-hexanediamine, a 6-carbon diamine) at 280 °C:

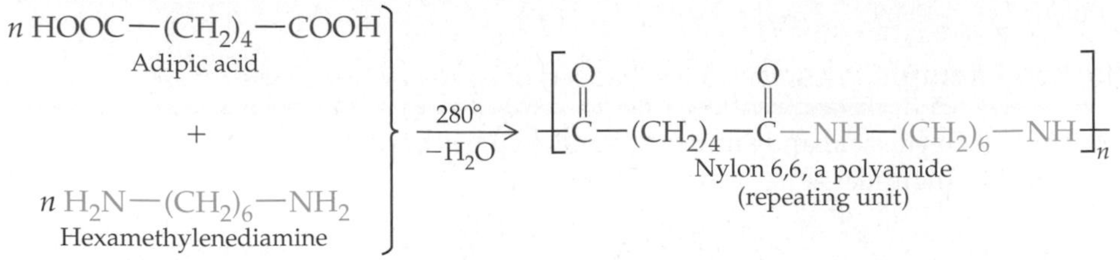

$$n \text{ HOOC}-(\text{CH}_2)_4-\text{COOH}$$
Adipic acid

$$+$$

$$n \text{ H}_2\text{N}-(\text{CH}_2)_6-\text{NH}_2$$
Hexamethylenediamine

$$\xrightarrow[-\text{H}_2\text{O}]{280°}$$

$$\begin{bmatrix} \overset{\displaystyle O}{\underset{\displaystyle \|}{C}}-(\text{CH}_2)_4-\overset{\displaystyle O}{\underset{\displaystyle \|}{C}}-\text{NH}-(\text{CH}_2)_6-\text{NH} \end{bmatrix}_n$$
Nylon 6,6, a polyamide
(repeating unit)

▲ Nylon being pulled from the interface between adipic acid and hexamethylenediamine.

The polymer molecules are composed of thousands of the repeating units, shown here enclosed in square brackets. (In the next chapter, you will see that proteins are also polyamides; unlike nylon, however, proteins do not normally have identical repeating units.)

The properties of nylon make it suitable for a wide range of applications. High-impact strength, abrasion resistance, and a naturally slippery surface make nylon an excellent material for bearings and gears. It can be formed into very strong fibers, making it valuable for a range of applications from nylon stockings, to clothing, to mountaineering ropes and carpets. Sutures and replacement arteries are also fabricated from nylon, which is resistant to deterioration in body fluids.

Just as diacids and diamines react to yield polyamides, diacids and dialcohols react to yield *polyesters*. The most widely used polyester is made by the reaction of terephthalic acid (1,4-benzenedicarboxylic acid) with ethylene glycol:

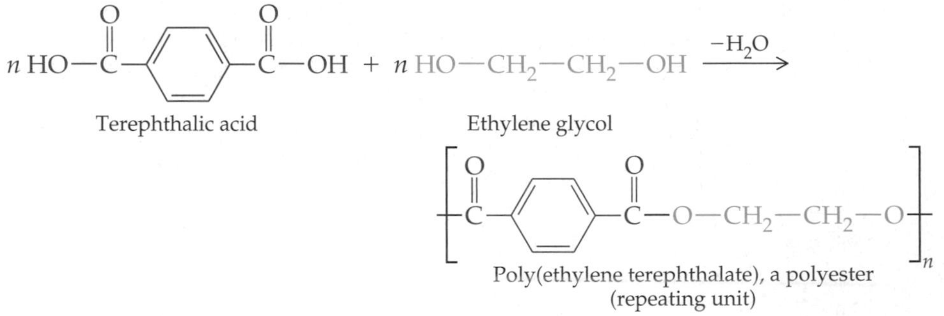

$$n \text{ HO}-\overset{\displaystyle O}{\underset{\displaystyle \|}{C}}-\overbrace{}-\overset{\displaystyle O}{\underset{\displaystyle \|}{C}}-\text{OH} \; + \; n \text{ HO}-\text{CH}_2-\text{CH}_2-\text{OH} \xrightarrow{-\text{H}_2\text{O}}$$
Terephthalic acid $\qquad\qquad\qquad\qquad\qquad$ Ethylene glycol

$$\begin{bmatrix} \overset{\displaystyle O}{\underset{\displaystyle \|}{C}}-\overbrace{}-\overset{\displaystyle O}{\underset{\displaystyle \|}{C}}-\text{O}-\text{CH}_2-\text{CH}_2-\text{O} \end{bmatrix}_n$$
Poly(ethylene terephthalate), a polyester
(repeating unit)

We know this polyester best in clothing fiber, where it has the trade name Dacron. Under the name Mylar it is used in plastic film and recording tape. Its chemical name, poly(ethylene terephthalate) or PET, is usually applied when it is used in clear, flexible, soft-drink bottles.

CHEMISTRY IN ACTION

Kevlar: A Life-Saving Polymer

Imagine you are a member of a bomb-disposal unit or a police officer about to take part in capturing a dangerous, well-armed criminal. You know your temperament and training will serve you well. But there is another protection you are very grateful for—your bulletproof vest. It is filled with fibers made of Kevlar, an amazing polymer that protects police officers, soldiers, firefighters, bicycle riders, lumberjacks, and others engaged in hazardous activities.

▲ "Cut-Proof" gloves are made with Kevlar.

Kevlar is a polyamide created in 1965 at DuPont by chemist Stephanie L. Kwloek, who, in anticipation of gasoline shortages, was searching for a new fiber to use in making light but strong tires. Kevlar was introduced to commercial applications in the 1970s as a replacement for steel in racing tires. Today there is an ever-expanding list of applications for Kevlar. In its various forms it is five times stronger than steel, almost half as dense as fiberglass, highly resistant to damage by chemicals, dimensionally stable, very difficult to cut or break, a poor electrical conductor, and flame-resistant (if ignited, it self-extinguishes). In fact, surgical gloves made partly of Kevlar are used by orthopedic surgeons to virtually eliminate the possibility of being cut by broken bone.

Like nylon, Kevlar is produced by the reaction of a dicarboxylic acid with a diamine, and because it contains aromatic rings, it is classified as a *polyaramide:*

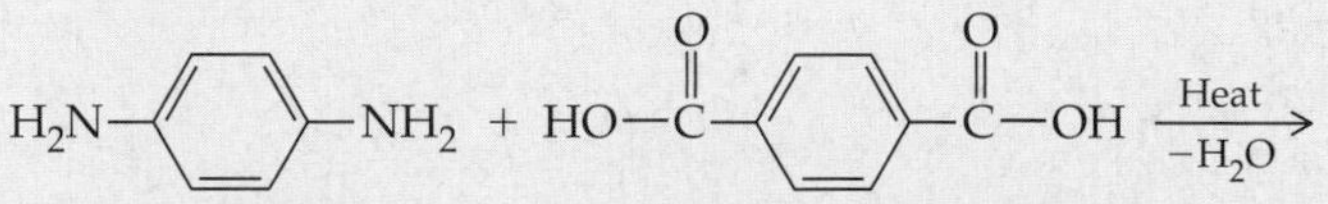

1,4-Diaminobenzene 1,4-Benzenedicarboxylic acid

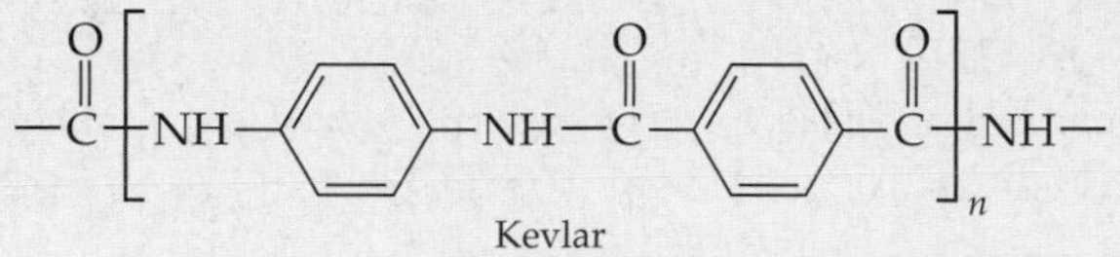

Kevlar
(an aramid)

Kevlar is an example of a *para-aramid*, since both the diamine and the dicarboxylic acid that make it are *para* substituted. The great strength of Kevlar results from the way that uniformly arranged hydrogen bonding holds the polymer chains together, as indicated by the red dots in the structural diagram shown here.

In 1995, Kwolek was inducted into the National Inventors Hall of Fame. Her achievements in designing a tough polymer are thus recognized alongside those of inventors such as Louis Pasteur, Alexander Graham Bell, Thomas Edison, and Henry Ford.

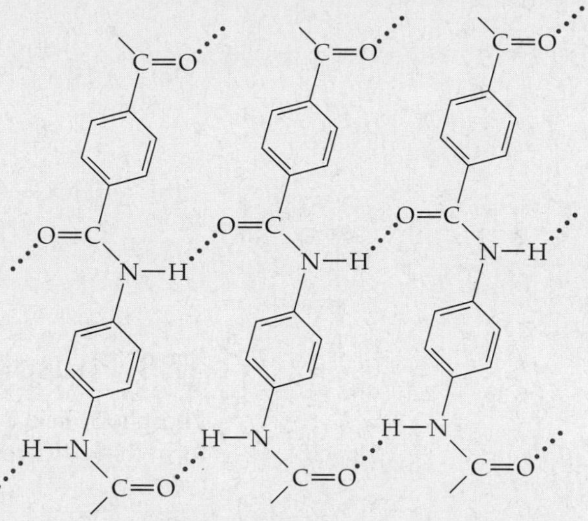

Hydrogen bonding in Kevlar

Some Uses of Kevlar

- Bulletproof vests
- Heat-protective apparel
- Cut-resistant gloves and other apparel
- Helmets for firefighters and bicycle riders
- Automotive and industrial hoses
- Structural composites for boats and aircraft
- Emergency tow lines for boats
- Brake linings and other friction-resistant applications

See Chemistry in Action Problem 17.86 at the end of the chapter.

PROBLEM 17.27

Kevlar belongs to a class of compounds known as the *para-aramids* (see Chemistry in Action: Kevlar: A Life-Saving Polymer, above). One of the first polyaramides discovered was Nomex, which is a *meta-aramid*; it is not as strong as Kevlar, but has excellent thermal, chemical, and radiation resistance. Provide the structure of the repeating unit in Nomex, given that it is made from the following compounds:

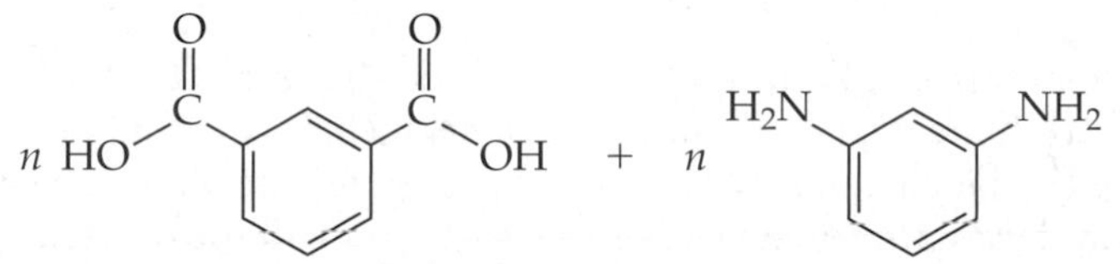

🔑 KEY CONCEPT PROBLEM 17.28

Give the structure of the repeating units in the polymers that are formed in the reactions of the following compounds.

(a) 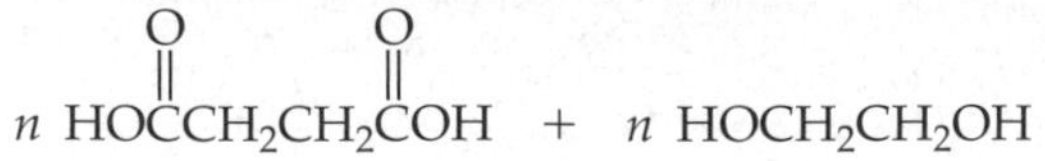 n HOCCH$_2$CH$_2$COH $\;+\;$ n HOCH$_2$CH$_2$OH

(b)  n HOC—⟨benzene ring⟩—COH $\;+\;$ n H$_2$NCH$_2$CH$_2$NH$_2$

17.8 Phosphoric Acid Derivatives

Phosphoric acid is an inorganic acid with 3 acidic hydrogen atoms (blue), allowing it to form three different anions:

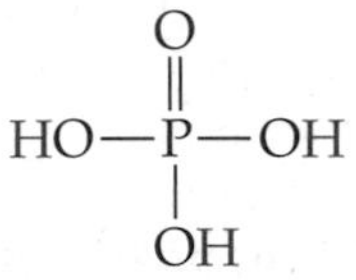

HO—P(=O)—OH with OH below	HO—P(=O)—O⁻ with OH below	HO—P(=O)—O⁻ with O⁻ below	⁻O—P(=O)—O⁻ with O⁻ below
Phosphoric acid (H_3PO_4)	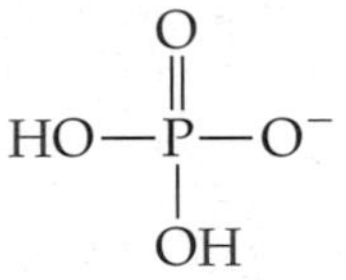 Dihydrogen phosphate ion $(H_2PO_4^-)$	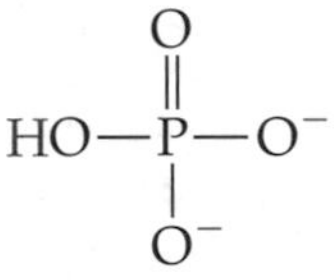 Hydrogen phosphate ion (HPO_4^{2-})	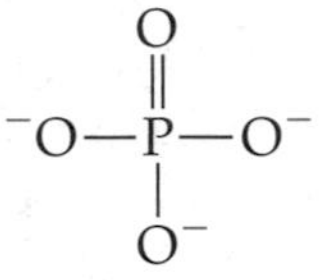 Phosphate ion (PO_4^{3-})

Notice the similarities between phosphoric acid and a carboxylic acid:

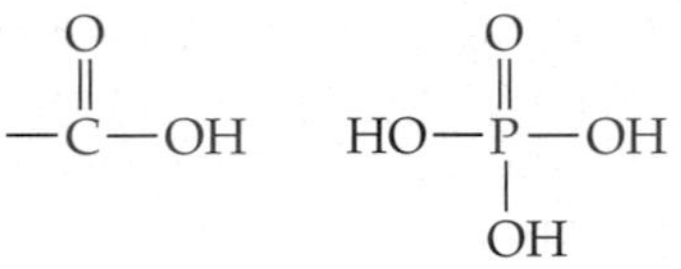

—C(=O)—OH   HO—P(=O)—OH with OH below

Phosphate ester A compound formed by reaction of an alcohol with phosphoric acid; may be a monoester, $ROPO_3H_2$; a diester, $(RO)_2PO_3H$; or a triester, $(RO)_3PO$; also may be a di- or triphosphate.

Just like a carboxylic acid, phosphoric acid reacts with alcohols to form **phosphate esters**. It may be esterified at one, two, or all three of its —OH groups by reaction with an alcohol. Reaction with 1 molecule of methanol gives the monoester:

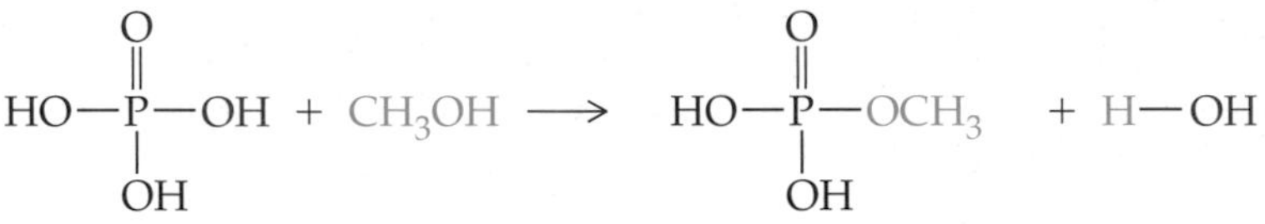

HO—P(=O)—OH with OH below $+$ CH$_3$OH $\longrightarrow$ HO—P(=O)—OCH$_3$ with OH below $+$ H—OH

Methyl phosphate
(a phosphate monoester)

The corresponding diester and triester are

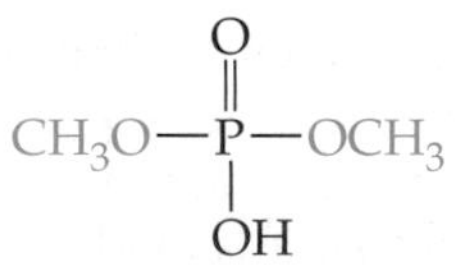

CH$_3$O—P(=O)—OCH$_3$ with OH below   CH$_3$O—P(=O)—OCH$_3$ with OCH$_3$ below

Dimethyl phosphate
(a phosphate diester)

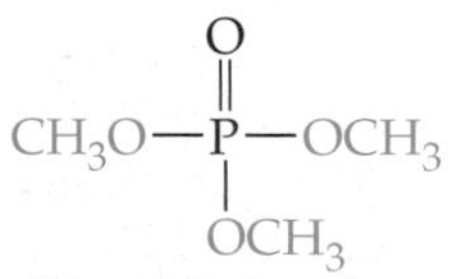

Trimethyl phosphate
(a phosphate triester)

Phosphate monoesters and diesters are acidic because they still contain acidic hydrogen atoms. In neutral or alkaline solutions, including most body fluids, they are present as ions. In biochemical formulas and equations, the phosphate groups are usually written in their ionized forms. For example, you will most often see the formula for glyceraldehyde monophosphate, a key intermediate in the metabolism of glucose (Section 22.2), written as an ion in one of these two ways:

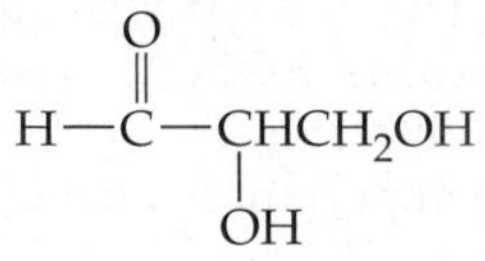

Glyceraldehyde 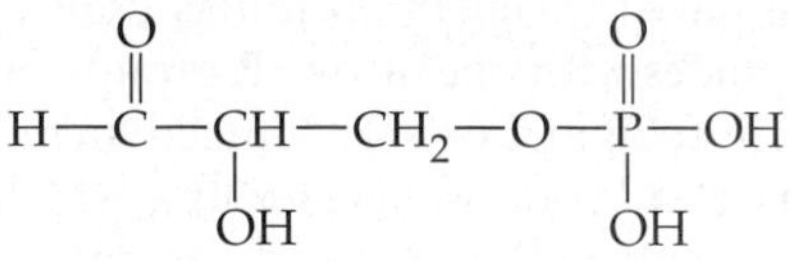   Glyceraldehyde monophosphate

Phosphoryl group

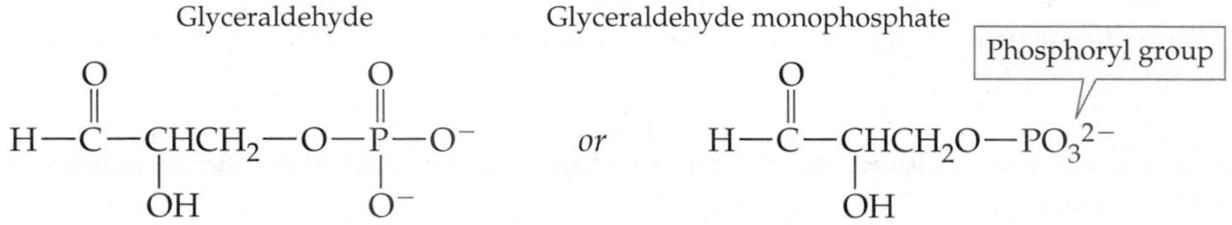

Ionized glyceraldehyde monophosphate

The $-PO_3^{2-}$ group as part of a larger molecule is referred to as a **phosphoryl group** (pronounced fos-for-**eel**).

If 2 molecules of phosphoric acid combine to lose water, they form a phosphoric acid anhydride. (See Worked Example 17.4 for the analogous reaction involving carboxylic acids.) The resulting acid (*pyrophosphoric acid*, or *diphosphoric acid*) reacts with yet another phosphoric acid molecule to give *triphosphoric acid*.

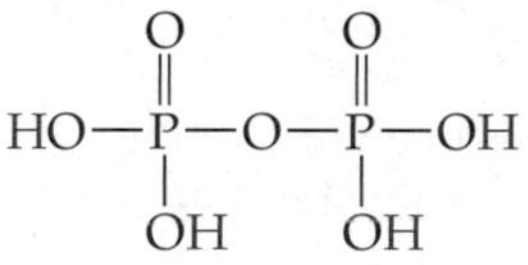

Phosphoryl group The $-PO_3^{2-}$ group in organic phosphates.

Pyrophosphoric acid 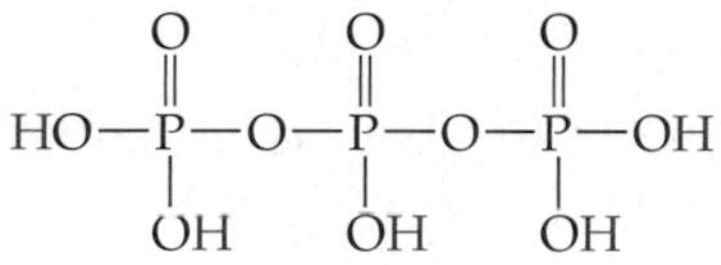   Triphosphoric acid

These acids can also form esters, which are known as diphosphates and triphosphates. In the following two methyl phosphate esters, written in their ionized forms, note the difference between the $C-O-P$ ester linkage and the $P-O-P$ phosphoric anhydride linkages:

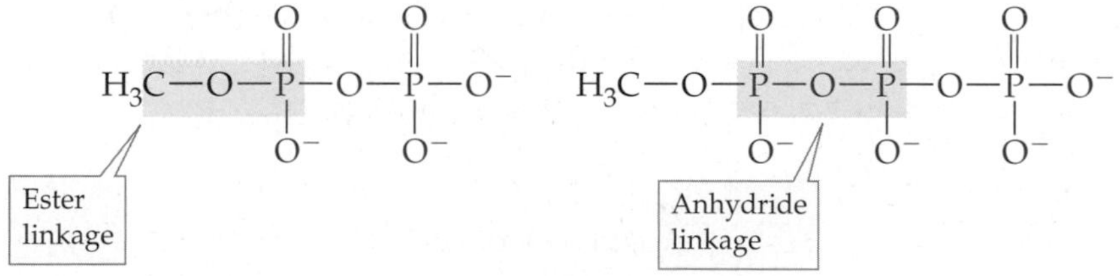

Ester linkage

Anhydride linkage

Transfer of a phosphoryl group from one molecule to another is known as **phosphorylation**. In biochemical reactions, the phosphoryl groups are often provided by a triphosphate (adenosine triphosphate, ATP), which is converted to a diphosphate (adenosine diphosphate, ADP) in a reaction accompanied by the release of energy. The addition and removal of phosphoryl groups is a common mechanism for regulating the activity of biomolecules (Section 19.9).

Phosphorylation Transfer of a phosphoryl group, $-PO_3^{2-}$, between organic molecules.

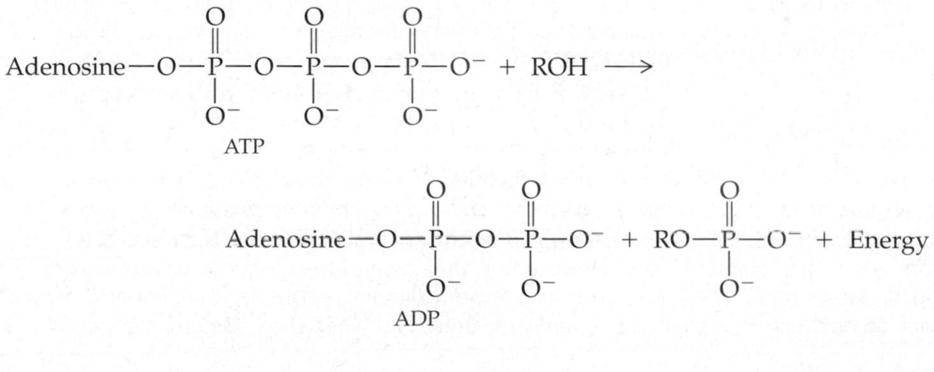

ATP

ADP

Organic Phosphates:

- Organic phosphates contain —C—O—P— linkages; those with one, two, or three R groups have the general formulas $ROPO_3H_2$, $(RO)_2PO_2H$, and $(RO)_3PO$.
- Organic phosphates with one or two R groups (monoesters, $ROPO_3^{2-}$, or diesters, $(RO)_2PO_2^-$) are acids and exist in ionized form in body fluids.
- The diphosphate and triphosphate groups, which are important in biomolecules, contain one or two P—O—P anhydride linkages, respectively.
- Phosphorylation is the transfer of a phosphoryl group $(-PO_3^{2-})$ from one molecule to another.

PROBLEM 17.29

Write the formula for the phosphate monoester formed from isopropyl alcohol in both its nonionized and ionized forms.

PROBLEM 17.30

Identify the functional group in the following compounds and give the structures of the products of hydrolysis for these compounds.

(a) $CH_3\overset{O}{\overset{\|}{C}}NH_2$ (b) $CH_3CH_2OPO_3^{2-}$ (c) $CH_3CH_2\overset{O}{\overset{\|}{C}}OCH_3$

PROBLEM 17.31

In the structure of acetyl coenzyme A drawn below, identify a phosphate monoester group, a phosphorus anhydride linkage, two amide groups, and the acetyl group.

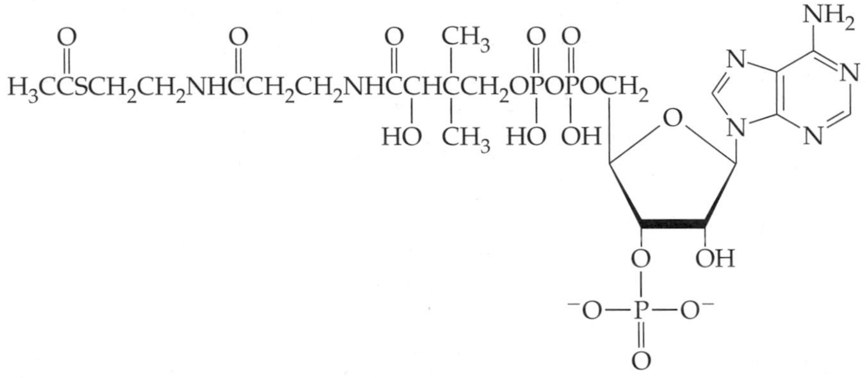

Acetyl coenzyme A
(AcCoA)

SUMMARY: REVISITING THE CHAPTER GOALS

1. What are the general structures and properties of carboxylic acids and their derivatives? *Carboxylic acids, amides,* and *esters* have the general structures

$$R-\overset{O}{\overset{\|}{C}}-OH \qquad R-\overset{O}{\overset{\|}{C}}-NH_2 \qquad R-\overset{O}{\overset{\|}{C}}-OR'$$

Carboxylic acid   Amide   Ester

They undergo *carbonyl-group substitution reactions*. Most carboxylic acids are weak acids (a few are strong acids), but esters and amides are neither acids nor bases. Acids and unsubstituted or monosubstituted amides hydrogen-bond with each other, but esters and disubstituted amide molecules do not. Simple

acids and esters are liquids; all amides (except formamide) are solids. The simpler compounds of all three classes are water-soluble or partially water-soluble (*see Problems 32, 34, 40–41, 78, 80–81*).

2. How are carboxylic acids, esters, and amides named? Many carboxylic acids are best known by their common names (Table 17.1), and these names are the basis for the common names of esters and amides. Esters are named with two words: the first is the name of the alkyl group from the alcohol that has replaced the —H in —COOH, and the second is the name of the parent acid with *-ic acid* replaced by *-ate* (for example, methyl acetate). For amides, the ending *-amide* is used, and when there are organic groups on the N, these are named first, preceded by *N* (as in *N*-methyl-acetamide) (see *Problems 35, 37, 39, 42–61, 79, 83*).

3. What are some occurrences and applications of significant carboxylic acids, esters, and amides? Natural carboxylic acids and esters are common; the acids have bad odors, whereas esters contribute to the pleasant odors of fruits and flowers. Acetic acid and citric acid occur in vinegar and citrus fruits, respectively. Aspirin and other salicylates are esters; acetaminophen (Tylenol) is an amide; ibuprofen (Advil, Motrin) is a carboxylic acid; benzocaine is representative of a family of amides that are local anesthetics. Proteins and nylon are polymers containing amide bonds. Fats and oils are esters, as are polyesters such as Dacron (see *Problems 64–69*).

4. How are esters and amides synthesized from carboxylic acids and converted back to carboxylic acids? In ester formation, the —OH of a carboxylic acid group is replaced by the —OR′ group of an alcohol. In amide formation, the —OH group of a carboxylic acid is replaced by —NH_2 from ammonia, or by —NHR′ or —NR′$_2$ from an amine. Hydrolysis with acids or bases adds —H and —OH to the atoms from the broken bond to restore the carboxylic acid and the alcohol, ammonia, or amine. (see *Problems 33, 36, 38, 40, 62–63, 65–68, 70–71, 82*).

5. What are the organic phosphoric acid derivatives? Phosphoric acid forms mono-, di-, and triesters: $ROPO_3H_2$, $(RO)_2PO_2H$, and $(RO)_3PO$. There are also esters that contain the diphosphate and triphosphate groups from pyrophosphoric acid and triphosphoric acid (p. 540). Esters that retain hydrogen atoms are ionized in body fluids—for example, $ROPO_3^{2-}$, $(RO)_2PO_2^-$. *Phosphorylation* is the transfer of a *phosphoryl group*, —PO_3^{2-}, from one molecule to another. In biochemical reactions, the phosphoryl group is often donated by a triphosphate (such as ATP) with release of energy (see *Problems 72–77*).

KEY WORDS

Acetyl group, *p. 518*

Acyl group, *p. 516*

Amide, *p. 515*

Carbonyl-group substitution reaction, *p. 516*

Carboxyl group, *p. 517*

Carboxylate anion, *p. 526*

Carboxylic acid, *p. 515*

Carboxylic acid salt, *p. 526*

Ester, *p. 515*

Esterification, *p. 529*

Phosphate ester, *p. 540*

Phosphoryl group, *p. 541*

Phosphorylation, *p. 541*

Saponification, *p. 535*

SUMMARY OF REACTIONS

1.   Reactions of carboxylic acids

(a) Acid–base reaction with water (Section 17.3):

$$CH_3\overset{O}{\overset{\|}{C}}OH + H_2O \rightleftharpoons CH_3\overset{O}{\overset{\|}{C}}O^- + H_3O^+$$

(b) Acid–base reaction with a strong base to yield a carboxylic acid salt (Section 17.3):

$$CH_3\overset{O}{\overset{\|}{C}}OH(aq) + NaOH(aq) \longrightarrow CH_3\overset{O}{\overset{\|}{C}}O^-\,Na^+(aq) + H_2O$$

(c) Substitution with an alcohol to yield an ester (Section 17.4):

$$CH_3\overset{O}{\overset{\|}{C}}OH + CH_3OH \xrightarrow{H^+} CH_3\overset{O}{\overset{\|}{C}}OCH_3 + H_2O$$

(d) Substitution with an amine to yield an amide (Section 17.4):

$$CH_3\overset{O}{\overset{\|}{C}}OH + CH_3NH_2 \xrightarrow{heat} CH_3\overset{O}{\overset{\|}{C}}NHCH_3 + H_2O$$

2.   Reactions of esters (Section 17.6)

(a) Hydrolysis to yield an acid and an alcohol:

$$CH_3\overset{O}{\overset{\|}{C}}OCH_3 \xrightarrow[H_2O]{H^+} CH_3\overset{O}{\overset{\|}{C}}OH + CH_3OH$$

(b) Hydrolysis with a strong base to yield a carboxylate anion and an alcohol (saponification):

$$CH_3CH_2CH_2CH_2CH_2\overset{O}{\overset{\|}{C}}OCH_3 + NaOH(aq) \xrightarrow{H_2O}$$

$$CH_3CH_2CH_2CH_2CH_2\overset{O}{\overset{\|}{C}}O^-\,Na^+ + CH_3OH$$

3.   Reactions of amides (Section 17.6)

(a) Hydrolysis to yield an acid and an amine:

$$CH_3\overset{O}{\overset{\|}{C}}NHCH_3 \xrightarrow[H_2O]{H^+\ or\ OH^-} CH_3\overset{O}{\overset{\|}{C}}OH + CH_3NH_2$$

4. **Phosphate reactions (Section 17.8)**

(a) Phosphate ester formation

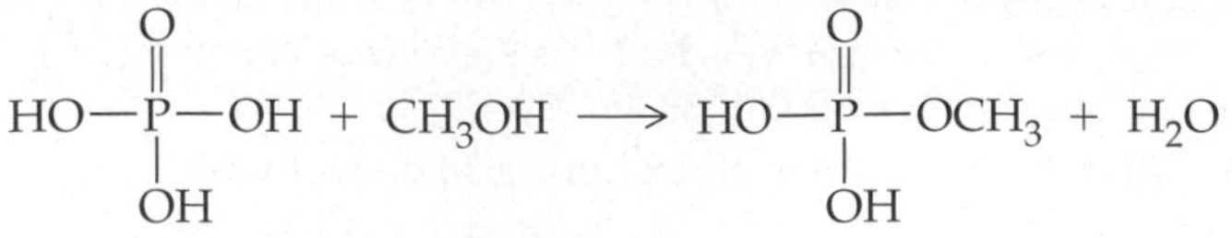

$$HO-\overset{\displaystyle O}{\underset{\displaystyle OH}{\overset{\|}{P}}}-OH \; + \; CH_3OH \; \longrightarrow \; HO-\overset{\displaystyle O}{\underset{\displaystyle OH}{\overset{\|}{P}}}-OCH_3 \; + \; H_2O$$

(b) Phosphorylation

$$Adenosine-O-\overset{\displaystyle O}{\underset{\displaystyle O^-}{\overset{\|}{P}}}-O-\overset{\displaystyle O}{\underset{\displaystyle O^-}{\overset{\|}{P}}}-O-\overset{\displaystyle O}{\underset{\displaystyle O^-}{\overset{\|}{P}}}-O^- \; + \; ROH \; \longrightarrow$$

$$Adenosine-O-\overset{\displaystyle O}{\underset{\displaystyle O^-}{\overset{\|}{P}}}-O-\overset{\displaystyle O}{\underset{\displaystyle O^-}{\overset{\|}{P}}}-O^- \; + \; RO-\overset{\displaystyle O}{\underset{\displaystyle O^-}{\overset{\|}{P}}}-O^- \; + \; Energy$$

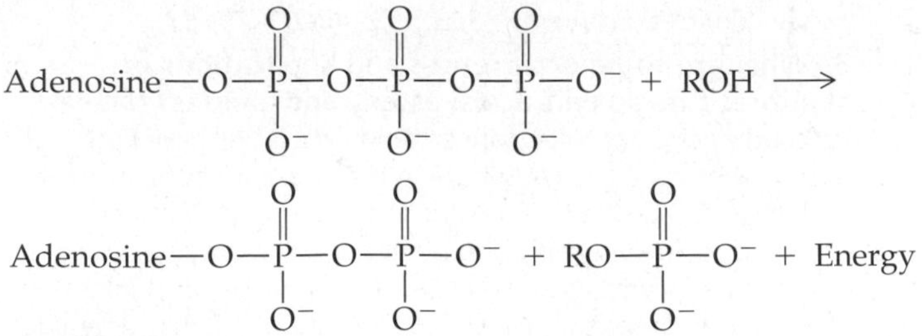

UNDERSTANDING KEY CONCEPTS

17.32 Muscle cells deficient in oxygen reduce pyruvate (an intermediate in metabolism) to lactate at a cellular pH of approximately 7.4:

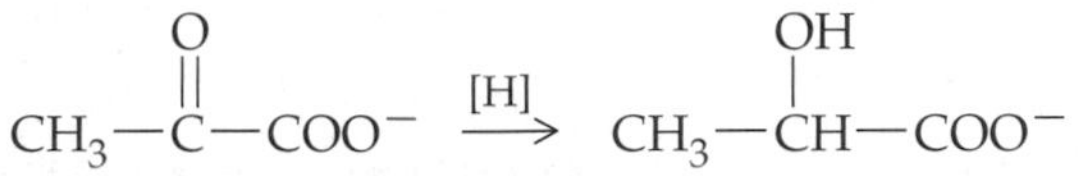

$$CH_3-\overset{\displaystyle O}{\overset{\|}{C}}-COO^- \; \xrightarrow{[H]} \; CH_3-\overset{\displaystyle OH}{\overset{|}{CH}}-COO^-$$

$$\text{Pyruvate} \qquad\qquad \text{Lactate}$$

(a) Why do we say pyruvate and lactate, rather than pyruvic acid and lactic acid?

(b) Alter the above structures to create pyruvic acid and lactic acid.

(c) Show hydrogen bonding of water to both pyruvate and lactate. Would you expect a difference in water solubility of lactate and pyruvate? Explain.

17.33 *N*-Acetylglucosamine (also known as NAG) is an important component on the surfaces of cells.

(a) Under what chemical conditions might the acetyl group be removed, changing the nature of the cell-surface components?

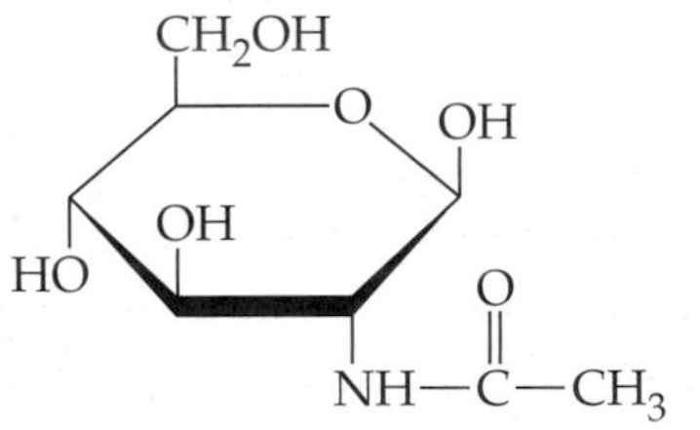

N-Acetylglucosamine

(b) Draw the structures of the products of acid hydrolysis.

17.34 One phosphorylated form of glycerate is 3-phosphoglycerate (a metabolic intermediate found in the glycolytic cycle, Section 22.3):

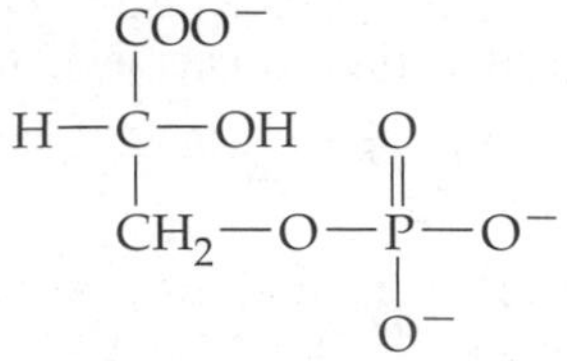

(a) Identify the type of linkage between glycerate and phosphate.

(b) 1,3-Bisphosphoglycerate (two phosphates on glycerate) has an anhydride linkage between the carbonyl

at C1 of glycerate and phosphate. Draw the structure of 1,3-bisphosphoglycerate (another metabolic intermediate).

17.35 The names of the first nine dicarboxylic acids can be remembered by using the first letter of each word of the saying "*Oh My, Such Good Apple Pie! Sweet As Sugar!*" to remind us of *o*xalate, *m*alonate, *s*uccinate, *g*lutarate, *a*dipate, *p*imelate, *s*uberate, *a*zelate, and *s*ebacate (the dianionic form in which these acids occur at physiological pH). Write the structures of the first six dicarboxylate anions.

17.36 Consider the following unnatural amino acid:

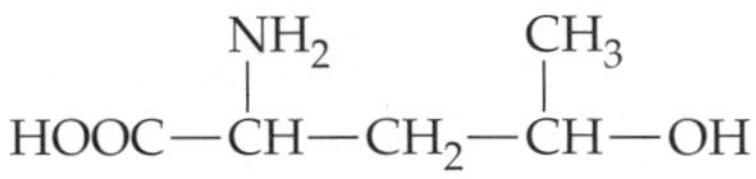

$$HOOC-\overset{\displaystyle NH_2}{\overset{|}{CH}}-CH_2-\overset{\displaystyle CH_3}{\overset{|}{CH}}-OH$$

(a) If 2 molecules react to form an ester, what is the structure of the ester product?

(b) If 2 molecules react to form an amide, what is the structure of the amide product?

(c) Draw the cyclic ester resulting from the intramolecular reaction of the hydroxyl group this amino acid with its carboxyl group (cyclic esters are called *lactones*).

17.37 (a) Draw the structures of the following compounds and use dashed lines to indicate where they form hydrogen bonds to other molecules of the same kind: (i) formic acid, (ii) methyl formate, (iii) formamide.

(b) Arrange these compounds in order of increasing boiling points and explain your rationale for the order.

17.38 Volicitin, in the "spit" from beet armyworms, causes corn plants to produce volatile compounds that act as signaling compounds for parasitoid wasps. Draw the three hydrolysis products that form from volicitin that match the common names given below.

(a) Glutamic acid (α-aminoglutaric acid)

(b) Ammonia

(c) 17-Hydroxylinolenic acid

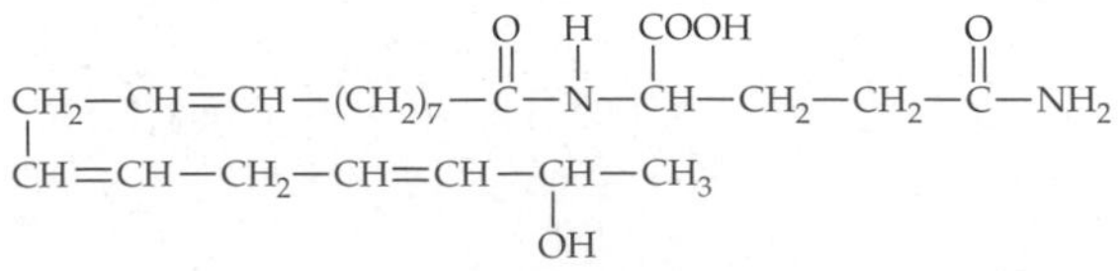

Volicitin

17.39 For the following compounds, give the systematic name.

(a) 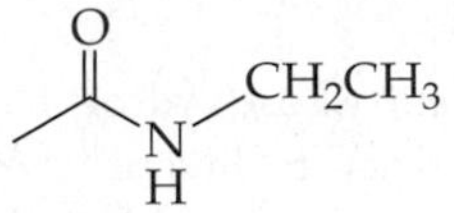 [structure: CH₃C(=O)−N(H)−CH₂CH₃]

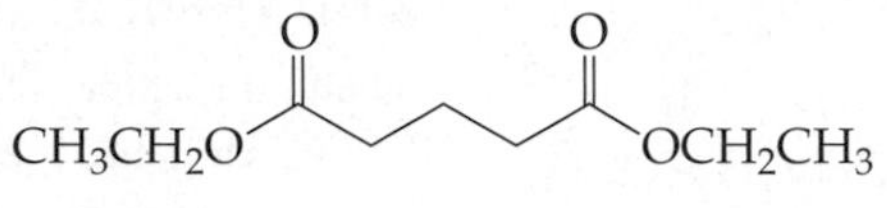

(b) 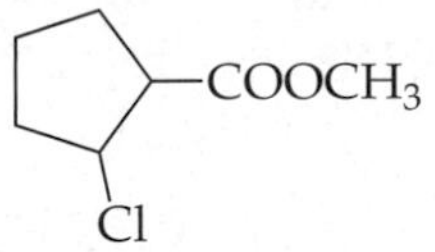 [structure: cyclopentane ring with −COOCH₃ and Cl substituents]

(c) [structure: CH₃CH₂O−C(=O)−CH₂CH₂CH₂−C(=O)−OCH₂CH₃]

(d) 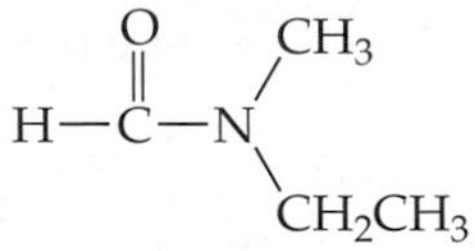 H−C(=O)−N(CH₃)(CH₂CH₃)

ADDITIONAL PROBLEMS

CARBOXYLIC ACIDS

17.40 Write the equation for the ionization of hexanoic acid in water.

17.41 Suppose you have a sample of benzoic acid dissolved in water at pH 7.

    (a) Draw the structure of the major species present in the water solution.

    (b) Now assume that aqueous HCl is added to the benzoic acid solution until pH 2 is reached. Draw the structure of the major species present.

    (c) Finally, assume that aqueous NaOH is added to the benzoic acid solution until pH 12 is reached. Draw the structure of the major species present.

17.42 Draw and name all carboxylic acids with the formula $C_4H_8O_2$.

17.43 Draw and name any three different carboxylic acids with the formula $C_5H_{10}O_2$.

17.44 Give systematic names for the following carboxylic acids:

    (a) 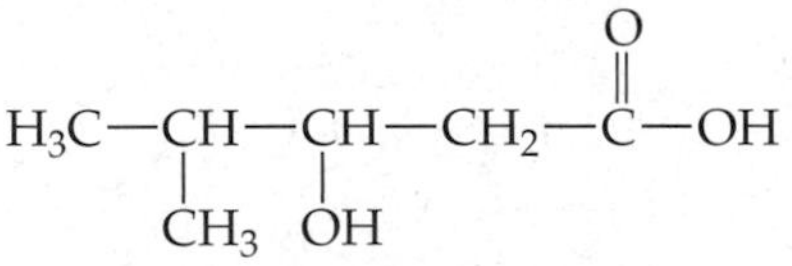 $H_3C-CH-CH-CH_2-C(=O)-OH$ with CH₃ and OH substituents

    (b) $HOOC-(CH_2)_7-COOH$

    (c) 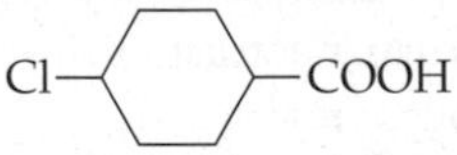 Cl—⟨cyclohexane⟩—COOH (d)  H_2N—⟨benzene⟩—COOH

17.45 Give systematic names for the following carboxylic acids:

    (a) 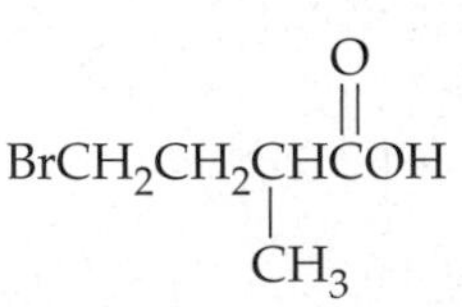 $BrCH_2CH_2CHCOH$ with CH₃ substituent (carboxyl C=O)

    (b) 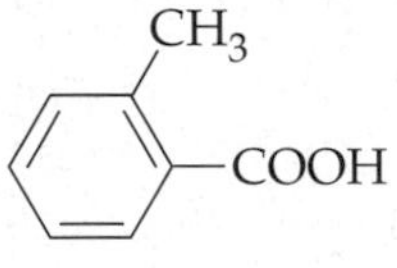 ⟨benzene with CH₃⟩—COOH

    (c) $(CH_3CH_2)_3CCOOH$ (d) $CH_3(CH_2)_5COOH$

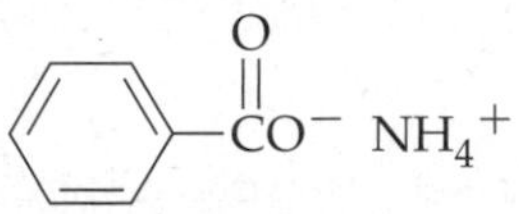

17.46 Give systematic names for the following carboxylic acid salts:

    (a) 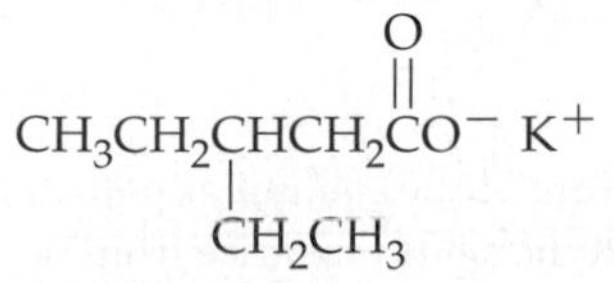 $CH_3CH_2CHCH_2CO^- \; K^+$ with CH₂CH₃ substituent (C=O)

    (b) ⟨benzene⟩—$CO^- \; NH_4^+$ (C=O)

    (c) $[CH_3CH_2CO^-]_2 \; Ca^{2+}$ (C=O)

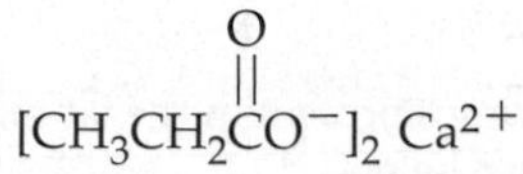

17.47 Give systematic names and common names for the following carboxylic acid salts:

    (a) 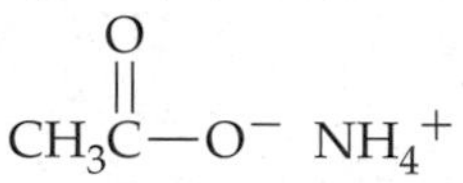 $CH_3C(=O)-O^- \; NH_4^+$

    (b) 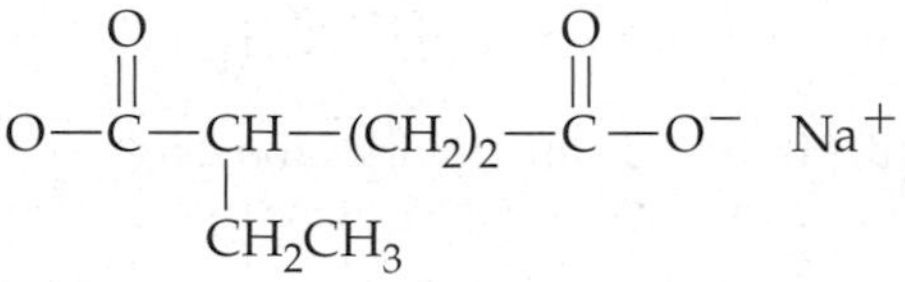 $^-O-C(=O)-CH-(CH_2)_2-C(=O)-O^- \; Na^+$ with CH₂CH₃ substituent

    (c) $\begin{array}{c} C(=O)-O^- \\ | \\ C(=O)-O^- \end{array} \; Ca^{2+}$

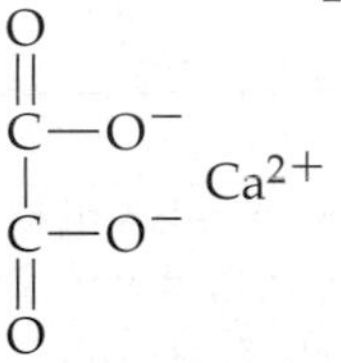

17.48 Draw structures corresponding to these names:

    (a) 3,4-Dimethylhexanoic acid

    (b) Phenylacetic acid

    (c) 3,4-Dinitrobenzoic acid

    (d) Triethylammonium butanoate

17.49 Draw structures corresponding to these names:

    (a) 2,2,3-Trifluorobutanoic acid

    (b) 3-Hydroxybutanoic acid

    (c) 3,3-Dimethyl-4-phenylpentanoic acid

17.50 Malic acid, a dicarboxylic acid found in apples, has the systematic name hydroxybutanedioic acid. Draw its structure.

17.51 Fumaric acid is a metabolic intermediate that has the systematic name *trans*-2-butenedioic acid. Draw its structure.

17.52 What is the formula for the diammonium salt of fumaric acid? (See Problem 17.51)

17.53 Aluminum acetate is used as an antiseptic ingredient in some skin-rash ointments. Draw its structure.

ESTERS AND AMIDES

17.54 Draw and name compounds that meet these descriptions:

    (a) Three different amides with the formula $C_5H_{11}NO$

    (b) Three different esters with the formula $C_6H_{12}O_2$

17.55 Draw and name compounds that meet these descriptions:

    (a) Three different amides with the formula $C_6H_{13}NO$

    (b) Three different esters with the formula $C_5H_{10}O_2$

17.56 Give systematic names for the following structures, and structures for the names:

(a) $CH_3COCH_2CH_2CHCH_3$ (with C=O and CH_3 substituent)

(b) $CH_3CHCH_2CH_2COCH_3$ (with CH_3 substituent and C=O)

(c) Cyclohexyl acetate

(d) Phenyl *o*-hydroxybenzoate

17.57 Give systematic names for the following structures, and structures for the names:

(a) 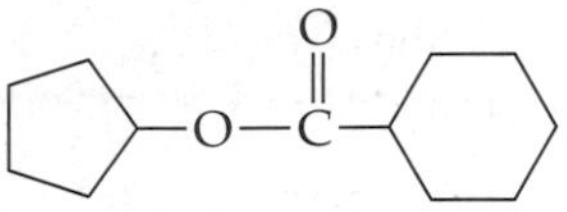 cyclopentyl—O—C(=O)—cyclohexyl

(b) Ethyl 2-hydroxypropanoate

(c) 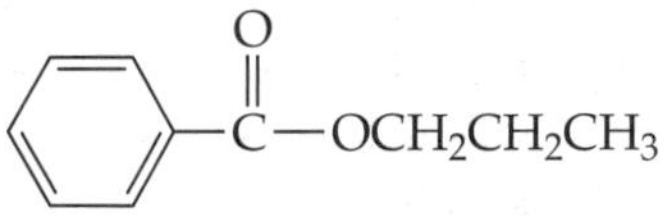 phenyl—C(=O)—OCH_2CH_2CH_3

(d) Butyl 3,3-dimethylhexanoate

(e) $(CH_3)_2CHCOC(CH_3)_3$

17.58 Draw structures of the carboxylic acids and alcohols you would use to prepare each ester in Problem 17.56.

17.59 Draw structures of the carboxylic acids and alcohols you would use to prepare each ester in Problem 17.57.

17.60 Give systematic names for the following structures, and give structures for the names:

(a) $CH_3CH_2CH-C-NH_2$ with CH_2CH_3 substituent and C=O

(b) 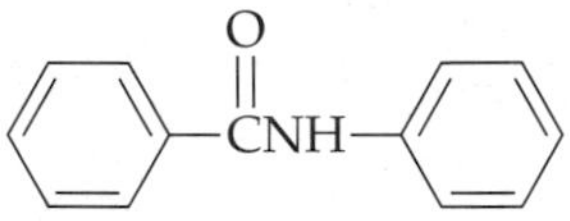 phenyl—C(=O)NH—phenyl

(c) *N*-Ethyl-*N*-methylbenzamide

(d) 2,3-Dibromohexanamide

17.61 Give systematic names for the following structures, and give structures for the names:

(a) 3-Methylpentanamide

(b) *N*-Phenylacetamide

(c) $HCN(CH_3)_2$ (with C=O)

(d) $CH_3CH_2CNHCHCH_3$ (with C=O and CH_3 substituent)

17.62 Show how you would prepare each amide in Problem 17.60 from the appropriate carboxylic acid and amine.

17.63 What compounds are produced from hydrolysis of each amide in Problem 17.61?

REACTIONS OF CARBOXYLIC ACIDS AND THEIR DERIVATIVES

17.64 Procaine, a local anesthetic whose hydrochloride is Novocain, has the following structure. Identify the functional groups present, and show the structures of the alcohol and carboxylic acids you would use to prepare procaine.

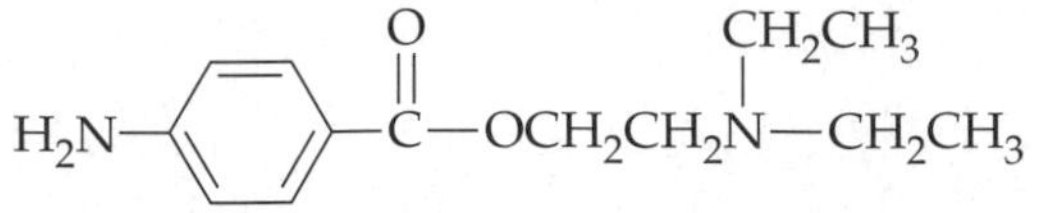

H_2N—phenyl—$C(=O)$—OCH_2CH_2N—CH_2CH_3 with CH_2CH_3 substituent   Procaine

17.65 Lidocaine (Xylocaine) is a local anesthetic closely related to procaine. Identify the functional groups present in lidocaine, and show how you might prepare it from a carboxylic acid and an amine.

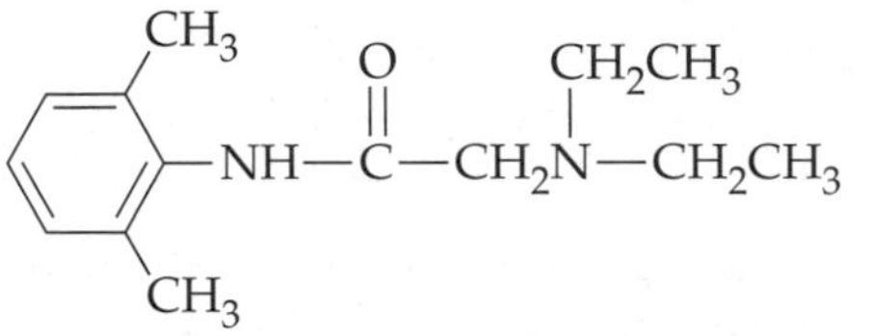

(structure with CH_3 groups on ring) —NH—$C(=O)$—CH_2N—CH_2CH_3 with CH_2CH_3 substituent   Lidocaine

17.66 Lactones are cyclic esters in which the carboxylic acid part and the alcohol part are connected to form a ring. One of the most notorious lactones is gamma-butyrolactone (GBL), whose hydrolysis product is the "date-rape" drug GHB. Draw the structure of GHB.

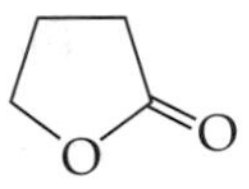

GBL (cyclic ester structure)

17.67 When both the carboxylic acid and the amine are in the same molecule, amide formation produces lactams. A *lactam* is a cyclic amide, where the amide group is part of the ring. Draw the structure of the product(s) obtained from acid hydrolysis of these lactams:

(a) 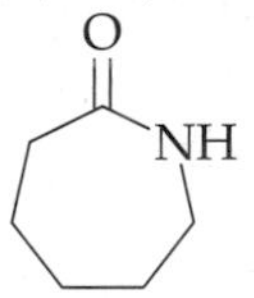 epsilon-lactam (seven-membered ring with NH and C=O)

(b) 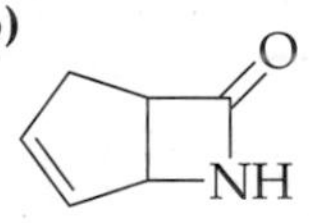 beta-lactam (fused bicyclic ring with NH and C=O)

17.68 LSD (lysergic acid diethylamide), a semisynthetic psychedelic drug of the ergoline family, has the structure shown here. Identify the functional groups present, and give the structures of the products you would obtain from hydrolysis of LSD.

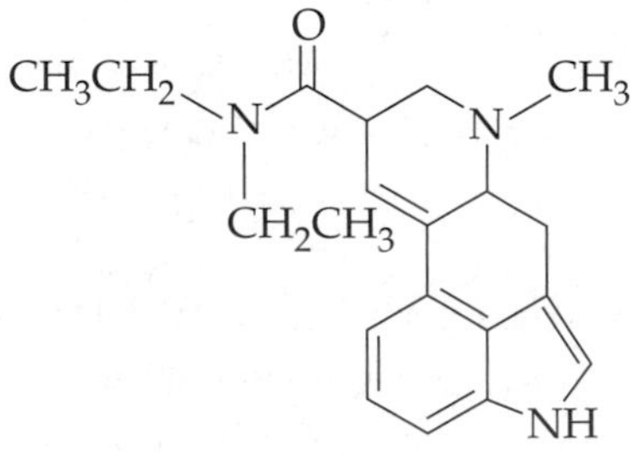

LSD (structure)

17.69 Household soap is a mixture of the sodium or potassium salts of long-chain carboxylic acids that arise from saponification of animal fat.

(a) Identify the functional groups present in the fat molecule shown in the reaction below.

(b) Draw the structures of the soap molecules produced in the following reaction:

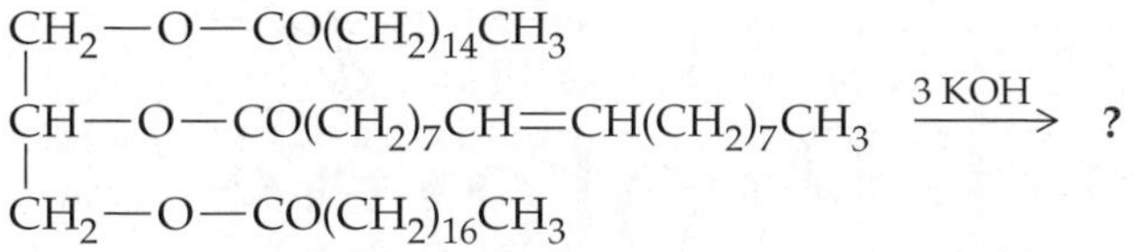

$$CH_2—O—CO(CH_2)_{14}CH_3$$
$$CH—O—CO(CH_2)_7CH=CH(CH_2)_7CH_3 \xrightarrow{\text{3 KOH}} ?$$
$$CH_2—O—CO(CH_2)_{16}CH_3$$

A fat

POLYESTERS AND POLYAMIDES

17.70 Baked-on paints used for automobiles and many appliances are often based on *alkyds*, such as can be made from terephthalic acid (*p.* 538) and glycerol (at right). Sketch a section of the resultant polyester polymer. Note that the glycerol can be esterified at any of the three alcohol groups, providing *cross-linking* to form a very strong surface.

$$CH_2OH$$
$$CHOH$$
$$CH_2OH$$
Glycerol

17.71 A simple polyamide can be made from ethylenediamine and oxalic acid (*p.* 518). Draw the polymer formed when three units of ethylenediamine reacts with three units of oxalic acid.

$$H_2N—CH_2—CH_2—NH_2$$
Ethylenediamine

PHOSPHATE ESTERS AND ANHYDRIDES

17.72 The following phosphate ester is an important intermediate in carbohydrate metabolism. What products result from hydrolysis of this ester?

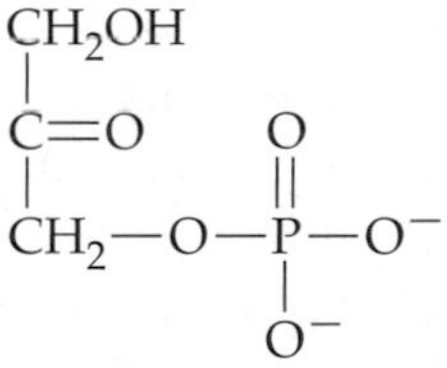

$$CH_2OH$$
$$C=O$$
$$CH_2—O—P—O^-$$
$$O^-$$

17.73 In the compound

(structure: HO—P(=O)(OH)—O—P(=O)(OH)—O—CH₂—phenyl)

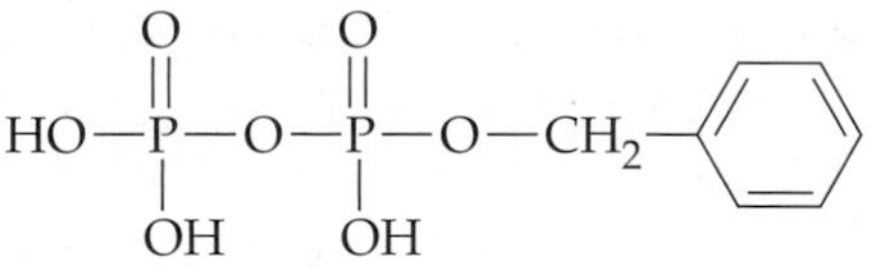

(a) Identify the ester linkage.
(b) Identify the anhydride linkage.
(c) Show the complete acid hydrolysis products.

17.74 The metabolic intermediate *acetyl phosphate* is an anhydride formed from acetic acid and phosphoric acid. What is the structure of acetyl phosphate?

17.75 Acetyl phosphate (see Problem 17.74) has what is called "high phosphoryl-group transfer potential." Write a reaction in which there is phosphoryl-group transfer from acetyl phosphate to ethanol to make a phosphate ester.

17.76 Cyclic ribose nucleotide phosphates, which are important signaling agents in living cells, all have the general structure shown here. What kind of linkage holds the phosphate to the ribose (see arrows; ribose is highlighted in blue)?

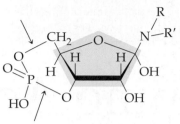

Cyclic Ribose Phosphate

17.77 Differentiate between a phosphate diester and a diphosphate. Give an example of each.

GENERAL QUESTIONS AND PROBLEMS

17.78 Three amide isomers, *N,N*-dimethylformamide, *N*-methylacetamide, and propanamide, have respective boiling points of 153 °C, 202 °C, and 213 °C. Explain these boiling points in light of their structural formulas.

17.79 Salol, the phenyl ester of salicylic acid, is used as an intestinal antiseptic. Draw the structure of phenyl salicylate.

17.80 Propanamide and methyl acetate have about the same molar mass, both are quite soluble in water, and yet the boiling point of propanamide is 213 °C whereas that of methyl acetate is 57 °C. Explain.

17.81 Mention at least two simple chemical tests by which you can distinguish between benzaldehyde and benzoic acid.

17.82 Write the formula of the triester formed from glycerol and stearic acid (Table 17.1).

17.83 Name the following compounds.

(a) 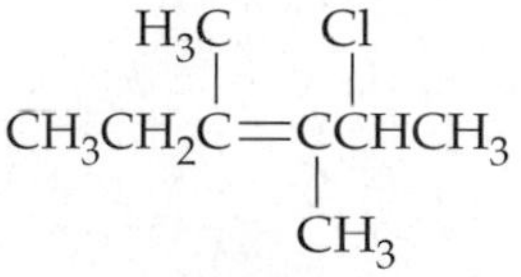 $CH_3CH_2C{=}CCHCH_3$ (with H₃C and Cl on the double-bond carbons, CH₃ below)

(b) 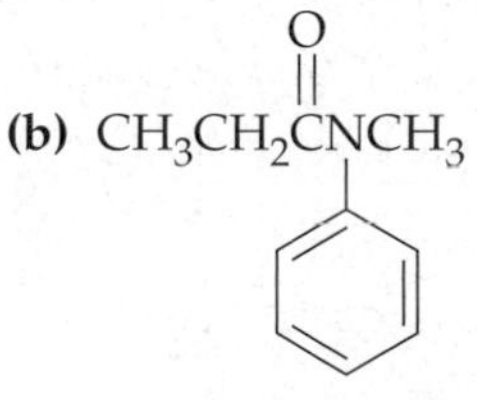 $CH_3CH_2CNCH_3$ (C=O, with phenyl on N)

(c) $(CH_3CH_2)_3CCO{-}$phenyl (C=O)

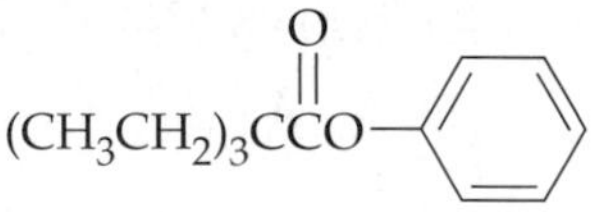

(d) 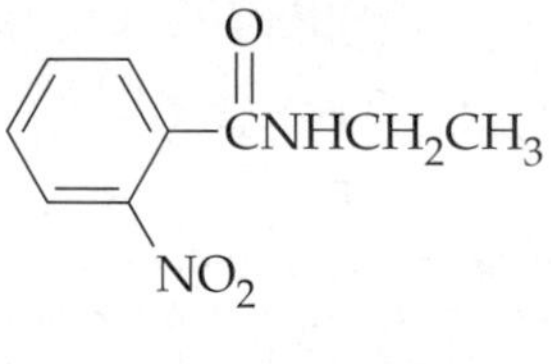 phenyl (with NO₂)$-CNHCH_2CH_3$ (C=O)

CHEMISTRY IN ACTION

17.84 Name these two compounds, and explain what chemical properties account for how they are used in skin treatment. [*Acids for the Skin*, p. 528]

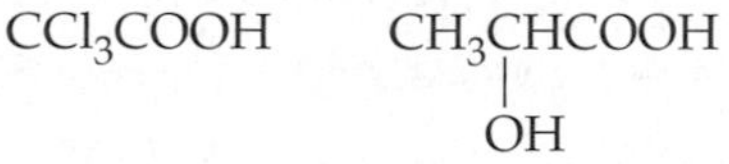

$$CCl_3COOH \qquad CH_3CHCOOH$$
$$OH$$

17.85 If you were working as a health care professional, what should you warn your clients about as far as using α-hydroxy acids during the summer beach season? [*Acids for the Skin*, p. 528]

17.86 Kevlar appears to be nearly indestructible; however, there are still groups of chemicals to which it is not resistant. Based on the structure of Kevlar, name one group of chemicals that Kevlar is susceptible to, and explain why this is the case. [*Kevlar: A Life-Saving Polymer*, p. 538]

CHAPTER 18

Amino Acids and Proteins

▲ Meat, fish, dairy products, beans, and nuts are all high in protein content.

CONTENTS

1. **What are the structural features of amino acids?**
   THE GOAL: Be able to describe and recognize amino acid structures and illustrate how they are connected in proteins. (◀◀◀ C.)

2. **What are the properties of amino acids?**
   THE GOAL: Be able to describe how the properties of amino acids depend on their side chains and how their ionic charges vary with pH. (◀◀◀ A.)

3. **Why do amino acids have "handedness"?**
   THE GOAL: Be able to explain what is responsible for handedness and recognize simple molecules that display this property.

4. **What is the primary structure of a protein, and what conventions are used for drawing and naming primary structures?**
   THE GOAL: Be able to define protein primary structure, explain how primary structures are represented, and draw and name a simple protein structure, given its amino acid sequence. (◀◀◀ D.)

5. **What types of interactions determine the overall shapes of proteins?**
   THE GOAL: Be able to describe and recognize disulfide bonds, hydrogen bonding along the protein backbone, and noncovalent interactions between amino acid side chains in proteins. (◀◀◀ C.)

6. **What are the secondary and tertiary structures of proteins?**
   THE GOAL: Be able to define these structures and the attractive forces that determine their nature, describe the α-helix and β-sheet, and distinguish between fibrous and globular proteins. (◀◀◀ C.)

7. **What is quaternary protein structure?**
   THE GOAL: Be able to define quaternary structure, identify the forces responsible for quaternary structure, and give examples of proteins with quaternary structure. (◀◀◀ C.)

8. **What chemical properties do proteins have?**
   THE GOAL: Be able to describe protein hydrolysis and denaturation, and give some examples of agents that cause denaturation. (◀◀◀ B, C.)

A. Acid–base Properties
(Sections 5.5, 10.9, 17.3)

B. Hydrolysis Reactions
(Section 17.6)

C. Intermolecular Forces
(Section 8.11)

D. Polymers
(Sections 13.7, 17.7)

The word *protein* is a familiar one. Taken from the Greek *proteios*, meaning "primary," "protein" is an apt description for the biological molecules that are of primary importance to all living organisms. Approximately 50% of your body's dry weight is protein. Some proteins, such as the collagen in connective tissue, serve a structural purpose. Other proteins direct responses to internal and external conditions. And still other proteins defend the body against foreign invaders. Most importantly, as enzymes, proteins catalyze almost every chemical reaction that occurs in your body. Because of their importance and the role they play in all biochemical functions, we have chosen to discuss proteins, which are polymers of amino acids, in this first chapter devoted to biochemistry.

18.1 An Introduction to Biochemistry

Biochemistry, the study of molecules and their reactions in living organisms, is based on the inorganic and organic chemical principles outlined in the first chapters of this book. Now we are ready to investigate the chemical basis of life. Physicians are faced with biochemistry every day because all diseases are associated with abnormalities in biochemistry. Nutritionists evaluate our dietary needs based on our biochemistry. And the pharmaceutical industry designs molecules that mimic or alter the action of biomolecules. The ultimate goal of biochemistry is to understand the structures of biomolecules and the relationships between their structures and functions.

Biochemistry is the common ground for the life sciences. Microbiology, botany, zoology, immunology, pathology, physiology, toxicology, neuroscience, cell biology—in all these fields, answers to fundamental questions are being found at the molecular level.

The principal classes of biomolecules are *proteins, carbohydrates, lipids*, and *nucleic acids*. Some biomolecules are small and have only a few functional groups. Others are huge and their biochemistry is governed by the interactions of large numbers of functional groups. Proteins, the subject of this chapter; nucleic acids (Chapters 25 and 26); and large carbohydrates (Section 21.9) are all polymers, some containing hundreds, thousands, or even millions of repeating units.

Biochemical reactions must continuously break down food molecules, generate and store energy, build up new biomolecules, and eliminate waste. Each biomolecule has its own role to play in these processes. But despite the huge size of some biomolecules and the complexity of their interactions, their functional groups and chemical reactions are no different from those of simpler organic molecules. ***All the principles of chemistry introduced thus far apply to biochemistry.*** Of the functional groups introduced in previous chapters, those listed in Table 18.1 are of greatest importance in biomolecules.

TABLE 18.1 Functional Groups of Importance in Biochemical Molecules

FUNCTIONAL GROUP	STRUCTURE	TYPE OF BIOMOLECULE
Amino group	$-NH_3^+$, $-NH_2$	Amino acids and proteins (Sections 18.3, 18.7)
Hydroxyl group	$-OH$	Monosaccharides (carbohydrates) and glycerol: a component of triacylglycerols (lipids) (Sections 21.4, 23.2)
Carbonyl group	$\overset{\displaystyle O}{\overset{\|}{-C-}}$	Monosaccharides (carbohydrates); in acetyl group (CH_3CO) used to transfer carbon atoms during catabolism (Sections 21.4, 20.4, 20.8)
Carboxyl group	$\overset{\displaystyle O}{\overset{\|}{-C-OH}}$, $\overset{\displaystyle O}{\overset{\|}{-C-O^-}}$	Amino acids, proteins, and fatty acids (lipids) (Sections 18.3, 18.7, 23.2)
Amide group	$\overset{\displaystyle O}{\overset{\|}{-C-N-}}$	Links amino acids in proteins; formed by reaction of amino group and carboxyl group (Section 18.7)
Carboxylic acid ester	$\overset{\displaystyle O}{\overset{\|}{-C-O-R}}$	Triacylglycerols (and other lipids); formed by reaction of carboxyl group and hydroxyl group (Section 23.2)
Phosphates, mono-, di-, tri-	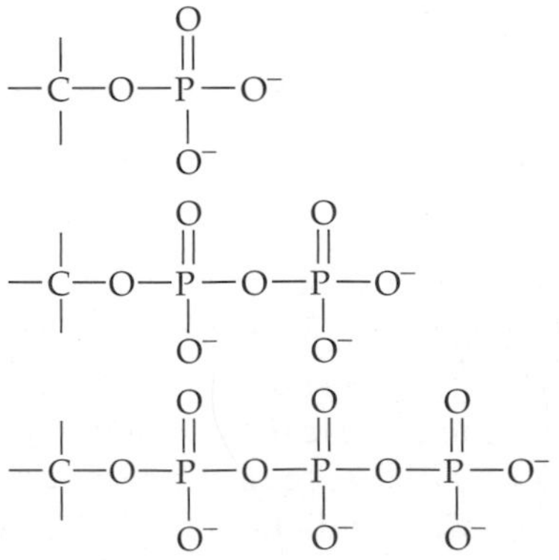 $-C-O-P-O^-$	ATP and many metabolism intermediates (Sections 17.8, 20.5, and throughout metabolism sections)
Hemiacetal group	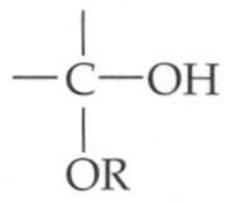 $-C-OH$ over OR	Cyclic forms of monosaccharides; formed by a reaction of carbonyl group with hydroxyl group (Sections 16.7, 21.4)
Acetal group	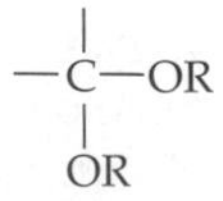 $-C-OR$ over OR	Connects monosaccharides in disaccharides and larger carbohydrates; formed by reaction of carbonyl group with hydroxyl group (Sections 16.7, 21.7, 21.9)

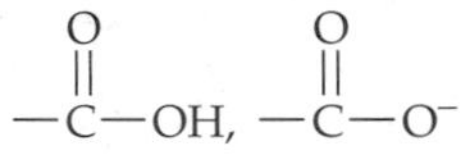

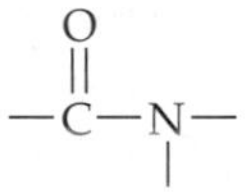

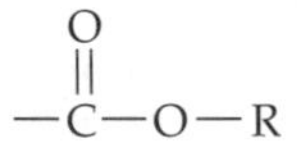

LOOKING AHEAD ▶▶▶ The focus in the rest of this book is on human biochemistry and the essential structure–function relationships of biomolecules. In this and the next chapter, we examine the structure of proteins and the roles of proteins and other molecules in controlling biochemical reactions. Next, we present an overview of metabolism and the production of energy (Chapter 20). Then, we discuss the structure and function of carbohydrates (Chapters 21 and 22), the structure and function of lipids (Chapters 23 and 24), the role of nucleic acids in protein synthesis and heredity (Chapters 25 and 26), the metabolism of proteins (Chapter 27), the role of small molecules in neurochemistry (Chapter 28), and the chemistry of body fluids (Chapter 29).

18.2 Protein Structure and Function: An Overview

Proteins are polymers of small molecules called **amino acids**. Every amino acid contains an amine group (NH_2), a carboxyl group (COOH), and an R group called a **side chain**, all bonded to the same carbon atom. This central carbon is known as the alpha (α)-carbon, named so because it is the carbon atom directly adjacent to a carboxylic acid group. Thus, the amino acids in proteins are **alpha-amino (α-amino) acids** because the amine group in each is connected to the alpha-carbon atom. Each α-amino acid has a different R group, and this is what distinguishes amino acids from one another. The R groups may be hydrocarbons, or they may contain a functional group.

Protein A large biological molecule made of many amino acids linked together through amide (peptide) bonds.

Amino acid A molecule that contains both an amino group and a carboxylic acid functional group.

Side chain (amino acid) The variable group bonded to the central carbon atom in an amino acid; different in different amino acids.

Alpha- $(\alpha -)$ amino acid An amino acid in which the amino group is bonded to the carbon atom next to the —COOH group.

An α-amino acid

> The alpha carbon is the central carbon in an amino acid to which the amine, carboxyl, and side-chain R groups attach.

$$H_2N-\underset{\underset{R}{|}}{\overset{\overset{H}{|}}{C}}_{\alpha}-\overset{\overset{O}{||}}{C}-OH$$

Side-chain R group, different for each amino acid

Two or more amino acids can link together by forming amide bonds, which are known as **peptide bonds** when they occur in proteins. A *dipeptide* results from the formation of a peptide bond between the —NH_2 group of one amino acid and the —COOH group of a second amino acid. For example, valine and cysteine are connected in a dipeptide as follows:

Peptide bond An amide bond that links two amino acids together.

▶▶▶ Review amide bonds in Section 17.4.

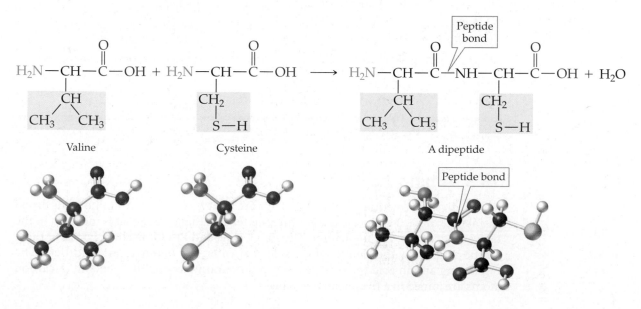

Valine   Cysteine   A dipeptide

A *tripeptide* results from the linkage of three amino acids via two peptide bonds. Any number of amino acids can link together to form a linear chainlike polymer—a *polypeptide*.

Proteins have four levels of structure, each of which is explored later in this chapter.

- *Primary structure* is the sequence of amino acids in a protein chain.
- *Secondary structure* is the regular and repeating spatial organization of neighboring segments of single protein chains.
- *Tertiary structure* is the overall shape of a protein molecule produced by regions of secondary structure combined with the overall bending and folding of the protein chain.
- *Quaternary structure* refers to the overall structure of proteins composed of more than one polypeptide chain.

What roles do proteins play in living things? No doubt you are aware that a hamburger is produced from animal muscle protein and that we depend on our own muscle proteins for every move we make. But this is only one of many essential roles of proteins. They provide *structure* and *support* to tissues and organs throughout our bodies. As *hormones* and *enzymes*, they control all aspects of metabolism. In body fluids, water-soluble proteins pick up other molecules for *storage* or *transport*. And the proteins of the immune system provide *protection* against invaders such as bacteria and viruses. To accomplish their biological functions, which are summarized in Table 18.2, some proteins must be tough and fibrous, whereas others must be globular and soluble in body fluids. The overall shape of a protein molecule, as you will see often in the following chapters, is essential to the role of that protein in our metabolism.

TABLE 18.2 Classification of Proteins by Function

Type	Function	Example
Enzymes	Catalyze biochemical reactions	*Amylase*—begins digestion of carbohydrates by hydrolysis
Hormones	Regulate body functions by carrying messages to receptors	*Insulin*—facilitates use of glucose for energy generation
Storage proteins	Make essential substances available when needed	*Myoglobin*—stores oxygen in muscles
Transport proteins	Carry substances through body fluids	*Serum albumin*—carries fatty acids in blood
Structural proteins	Provide mechanical shape and support	*Collagen*—provides structure to tendons and cartilage
Protective proteins	Defend the body against foreign matter	*Immunoglobulin*—aids in destruction of invading bacteria
Contractile proteins	Do mechanical work	*Myosin and actin*—govern muscle movement

18.3 Amino Acids

All the diverse proteins in living organisms are built from just 20 α-amino acids, listed in Table 18.3. Each amino acid has a three-letter shorthand code that is included in the table; for example, Ala for alanine, Gly for glycine, and Pro for proline. For 19 of these amino acids, only the identity of the side chain attached to the α-carbon differs. The remaining amino acid (proline) is a secondary amine whose nitrogen and α-carbon atoms are joined in a five-membered ring.

TABLE 18.3 The 20 α-amino acids found in proteins, with their abbreviations and isoelectric points. The structures are written here in their fully ionized forms. These ions and the isoelectric points given in parentheses are explained in Section 18.4.

Nonpolar, Neutral Side Chains

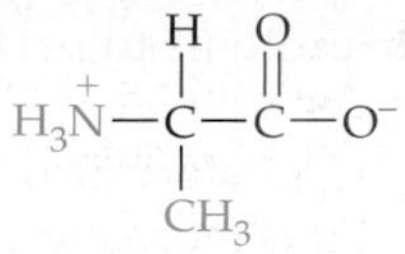

Alanine, Ala (6.0)

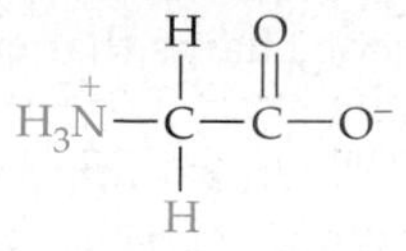

Glycine, Gly (6.0)

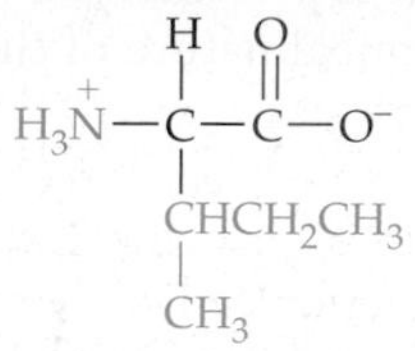

Isoleucine, Ile (6.0)

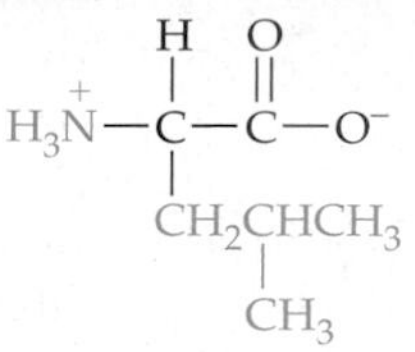

Leucine, Leu (6.0)

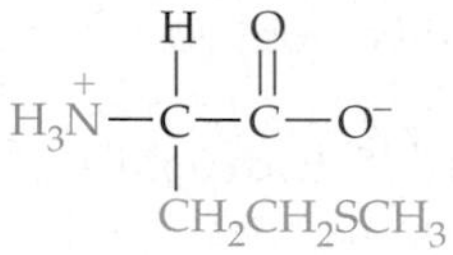

Methionine, Met (5.7)

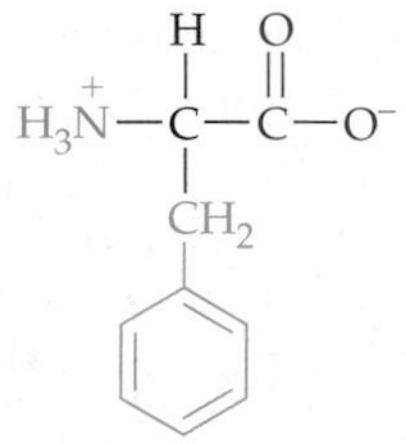

Phenylalanine, Phe (5.5)

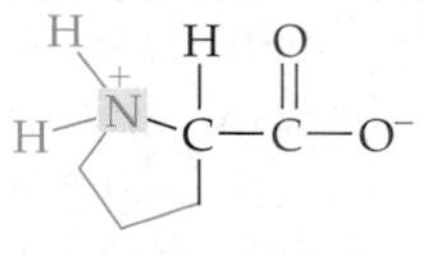

Proline, Pro (6.3)

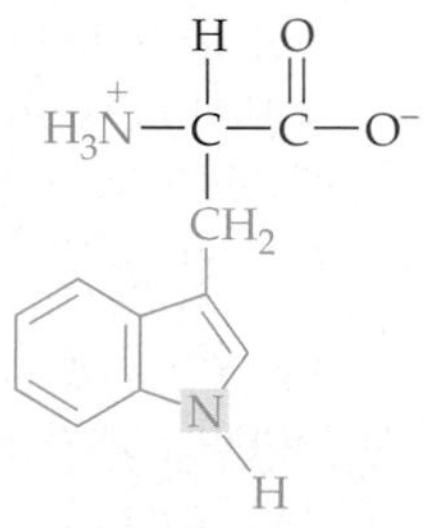

Tryptophan, Trp (5.9)

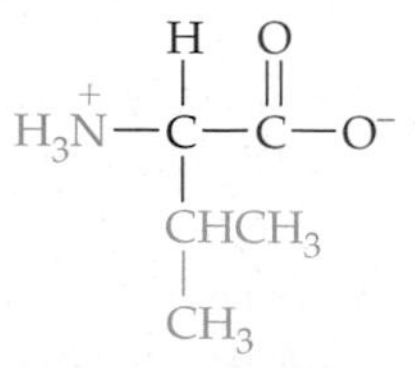

Valine, Val (6.0)

Polar, Neutral Side Chains

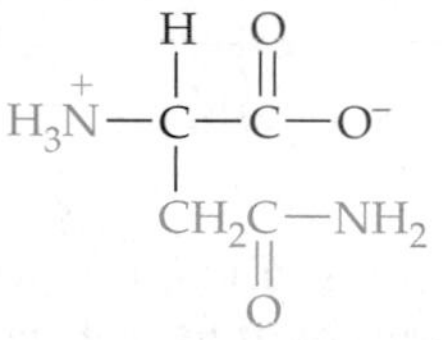

Asparagine, Asn (5.4)

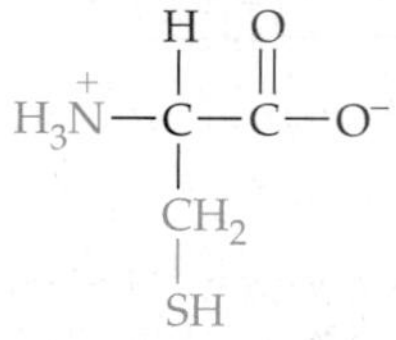

Cysteine, Cys (5.0)

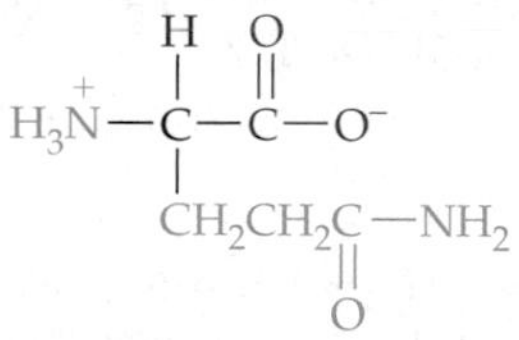

Glutamine, Gln (5.7)

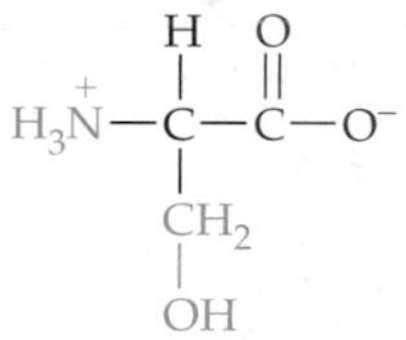

Serine, Ser (5.7)

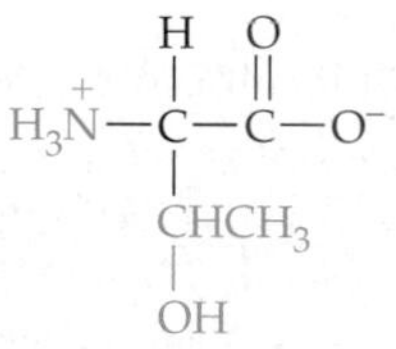

Threonine, Thr (5.6)

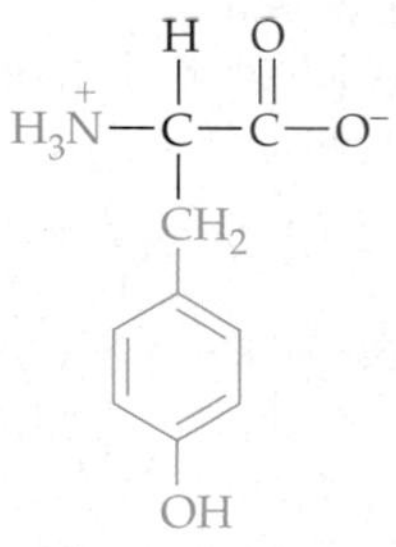

Tyrosine, Tyr (5.7)

Acidic Side Chains

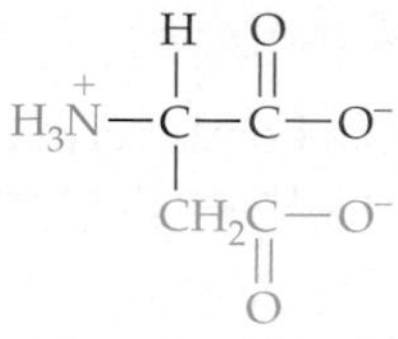

Aspartic acid, Asp (3.0)
(Aspartate)

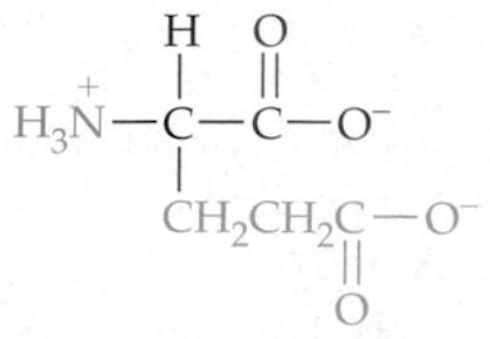

Glutamic acid, Glu (3.2)
(Glutamate)

Basic Side Chains

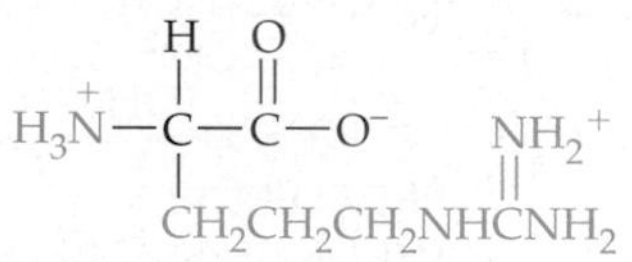

Arginine, Arg (10.8)

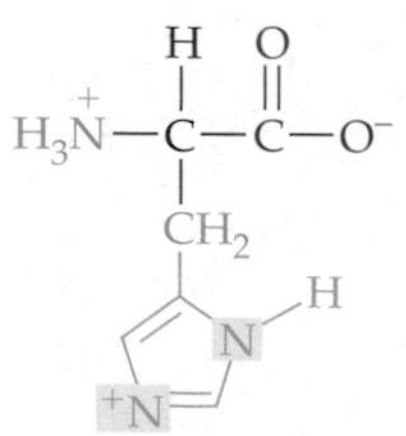

Histidine, His (7.6)

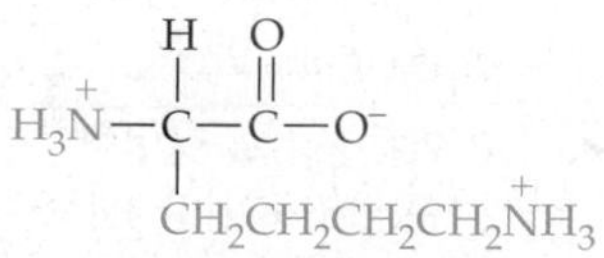

Lysine, Lys (9.7)

The 20 α-amino acids that make up proteins are classified as neutral, acidic, or basic, depending on the nature of their side chains. The 15 neutral amino acids are further divided into those with nonpolar side chains and those with polar functional groups such as amide or hydroxyl groups in their side chains. As we explore the structure and function of proteins, you will see that it is the sequence of amino acids in a protein and the chemical nature of their side chains that enable proteins to perform their varied functions.

Intermolecular forces are of central importance in determining the shapes and functions of proteins. In the context of biochemistry, it is more meaningful to refer to all interactions other than covalent bonding as **noncovalent forces**. Noncovalent forces act between different molecules or between different parts of the same large molecule, which, as we will see shortly, is often the case in proteins.

The nonpolar side chains are described as **hydrophobic** ("water-fearing")—they are *not* attracted to water molecules. To avoid aqueous body fluids, nonpolar side chains gather into clusters to create a water-free environment, often forming a pocket within a large protein molecule. The polar, acidic, and basic side chains are **hydrophilic** ("water-loving") polar side chains that *are* attracted to polar water molecules. They interact with water molecules much as water molecules interact with one another. Attractions between water molecules and hydrophilic groups on the surface of folded proteins impart water solubility to the proteins.

▶▶▶ The various types of intermolecular forces were introduced in Section 8.11.

Noncovalent forces Forces of attraction other than covalent bonds that can act between molecules or within molecules.

Hydrophobic "Water-fearing"; a hydrophobic substance does not dissolve in water.

Hydrophilic "Water-loving"; a hydrophilic substance dissolves in water.

▶▶▶ Review water interactions with other molecules in Section 9.2.

PROBLEM 18.1
Using Table 18.3, name the α-amino acids that contain an aromatic ring, contain sulfur, are alcohols, and have alkyl-group side chains.

PROBLEM 18.2
Draw alanine, showing the tetrahedral geometry of its α-carbon.

PROBLEM 18.3
Valine is an amino acid with a nonpolar side chain and serine is one with a polar side chain. Draw the two amino acids. Why is the side chain for valine nonpolar and the side chain for serine polar?

PROBLEM 18.4
Indicate whether each of the molecules shown below is an α-amino acid or not, and explain why.

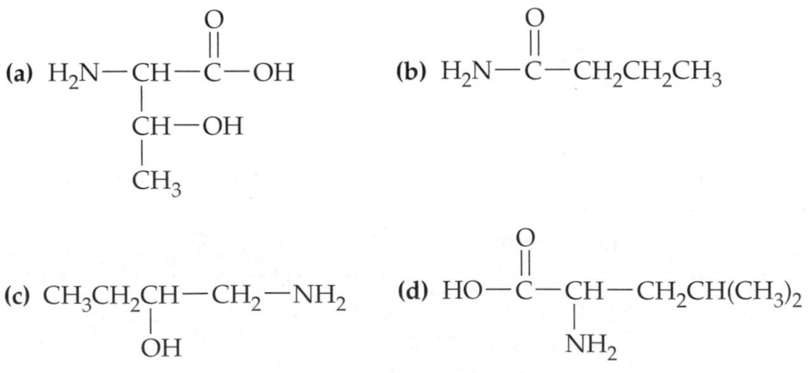

(a) $H_2N-CH-\overset{\overset{\textstyle O}{\|}}{C}-OH$
       $|$
       $CH-OH$
       $|$
       CH_3

(b) $H_2N-\overset{\overset{\textstyle O}{\|}}{C}-CH_2CH_2CH_3$

(c) $CH_3CH_2CH-CH_2-NH_2$
              $|$
              OH

(d) $HO-\overset{\overset{\textstyle O}{\|}}{C}-CH-CH_2CH(CH_3)_2$
                    $|$
                    NH_2

PROBLEM 18.5
Which of the following pairs of amino acids can form hydrogen bonds between their side-chain groups? Draw the pairs that can hydrogen bond through their side chains and indicate the hydrogen bonds.
(a) Phe, Thr   (b) Asn, Ser   (c) Thr, Tyr   (d) Gly, Trp

PROBLEM 18.6
Examine the ball-and-stick model of valine near the beginning of Section 18.2. Identify the carboxyl group, the amino group, and the R group.

18.4 Acid–Base Properties of Amino Acids

Amino acids contain both an acidic group, $-COOH$, and a basic group, $-NH_2$. As you might expect, these two groups can undergo an intramolecular acid–base reaction. The result is transfer of the hydrogen from the $-COOH$ group to the $-NH_2$ group to form a *dipolar* ion, an ion that has one positive charge and one negative charge and is thus electrically neutral. Dipolar ions are known as **zwitterions** (from the German *zwitter*, "hybrid"). The zwitterion form of threonine is shown here, and the α-amino acids in Table 18.3 are also shown in their zwitterion forms.

Zwitterion A neutral dipolar ion that has one + charge and one − charge.

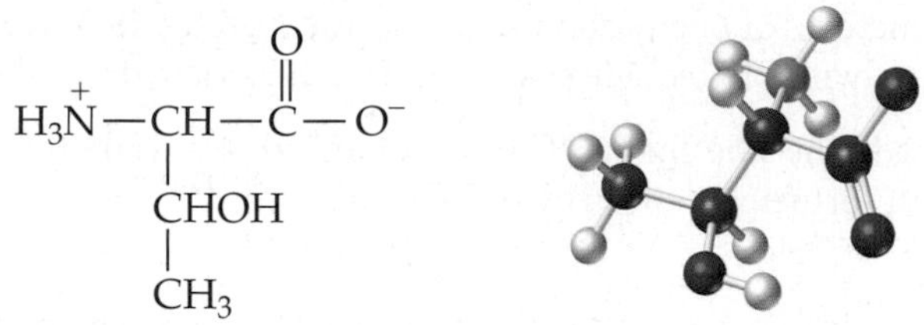

Threonine—zwitterion

Because they are zwitterions, amino acids have many of the physical properties we associate with salts. Pure amino acids can form crystals, have high melting points, and are soluble in water but not in hydrocarbon solvents.

▶▶▶ Review the properties of ionic compounds introduced in Section 3.4.

In acidic solution (low pH), amino acid zwitterions accept protons on their basic $-COO^-$ groups, to leave only the positively charged $-NH_3{}^+$ groups. In basic solution (high pH), amino acid zwitterions *lose* protons from their acidic $-NH_3{}^+$ groups, to leave only the negatively charged $-COO^-$ groups:

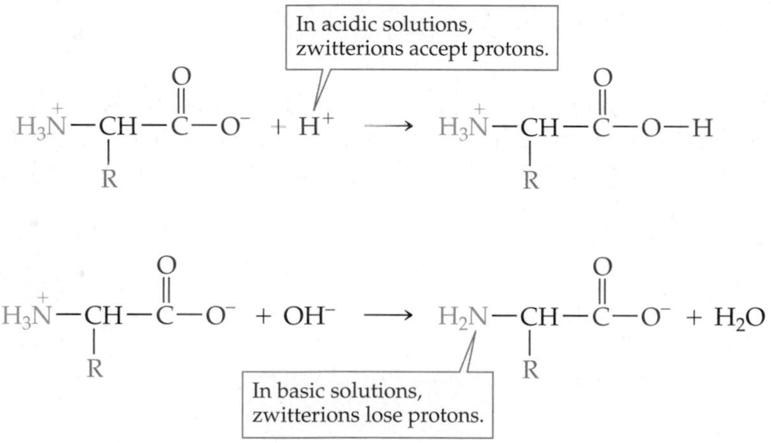

In acidic solutions, zwitterions accept protons.

In basic solutions, zwitterions lose protons.

Amino acids are never present in the completely un-ionized form in either the solid state or in aqueous solution. The charge of an amino acid molecule at any given moment depends on the particular amino acid and the pH of the solution. The pH at which the net positive and negative charges are evenly balanced is the **isoelectric point (pI)** for that particular amino acid. At this point, the net charge of all the molecules of that amino acid in a pure sample is zero. The pI for each different amino acid is different, due to the influence of the side chain.

Isoelectric point (pI) The pH at which a sample of an amino acid has equal numbers of + and − charges.

A few amino acids have isoelectric points that are not near neutrality (pH 7). For example, the two amino acids with acidic side chains, aspartic acid and glutamic acid, have isoelectric points at more acidic (lower) pH values than those with neutral side chains. Since the side-chain $-COOH$ groups of these compounds are substantially ionized at physiological pH of 7.4, these amino acids are usually referred to as *aspartate* and *glutamate*, the names of the anions formed when the $-COOH$ groups in the side chains are ionized. (Recall that the same convention is used, for example, for sulfate ion from sulfuric acid or nitrate ion from nitric acid; see Table 3.3.)

Side-chain interactions are important in stabilizing protein structure; thus it is important to be aware of their charges at physiological pH. Furthermore, pI influences protein solubility and determines which amino acids in an enzyme participate directly in enzymatic reactions. The acidic and basic side chains are particularly important because at physiological pH these groups are fully charged and can participate not only in ionic bonds within a protein chain but can also transfer H^+ from one molecule to another during reactions, as we will see in Chapter 19.

Worked Example **18.1** Determining Side-Chain Hydrophobicity/Hydrophilicity

Consider the structures of phenylalanine and serine in Table 18.3. Which of these two amino acids has a hydrophobic side chain and which has a hydrophilic side chain?

ANALYSIS Identify the side chains. The side chain in phenylalanine is an alkane. The side chain in serine contains a hydroxyl group.

SOLUTION
The hydrocarbon side chain in phenylalanine is an alkane, which is nonpolar and hydrophobic. The hydroxyl group in the side chain of serine is polar and is therefore hydrophilic.

Worked Example **18.2** Drawing Zwitterion Forms

Look up the zwitterionic structure of valine in Table 18.3. Draw valine as it would be found (a) at low pH and (b) at high pH.

ANALYSIS At low pH, which is acidic, basic groups may gain H^+. At high pH, which is basic, acidic groups may lose H^+. In the zwitterion form of an amino acid, the $-COO^-$ group is basic and the $-NH_3^+$ is acidic.

SOLUTION
Valine has an alkyl-group side chain that is unaffected by pH. At low pH, valine adds a hydrogen ion to its carboxyl group to give the structure on the left. At high pH, valine loses a hydrogen ion from its acidic $-NH_3^+$ group to give the structure on the right.

$$\overset{+}{H_3N}-CH-\overset{\overset{O}{\|}}{C}-OH \qquad H_2N-CH-\overset{\overset{O}{\|}}{C}-O^-$$
$$\hspace{1.5em}\underset{|}{CHCH_3} \hspace{6em} \underset{|}{CHCH_3}$$
$$\hspace{1.5em}CH_3 \hspace{7em} CH_3$$
$$\hspace{1.5em}\text{Low pH} \hspace{6em} \text{High pH}$$

PROBLEM 18.7
Draw the structure of glutamic acid at low pH and at high pH.

PROBLEM 18.8
Use the definitions of acids and bases as proton donors and proton acceptors to explain which functional group in the zwitterion form of an amino acid is an acid and which is a base. (See Section 10.3.)

18.5 Handedness

Are you right-handed or left-handed? Although you may not think about it very often, handedness affects almost everything you do. It also affects the biochemical activity of molecules.

Anyone who plays softball knows that the last available glove always fits the wrong hand. This happens because your hands are not identical. Rather, they are mirror images. When you hold your left hand up to a mirror, the image you see looks like your right hand (Figure 18.1). Try it.

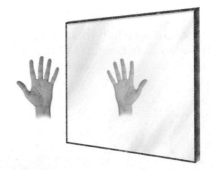

▲ **Figure 18.1**
The meaning of *mirror image*. If you hold your left hand up to a mirror, the image you see looks like your right hand.

Additionally, note that the mirror images of your hand cannot be superimposed on each other; one does not completely fit on top of the other. Objects that have handedness in this manner are said to be **chiral** (pronounced **ky**-ral, from the Greek *cheir*, meaning "hand").

Not all objects are chiral, of course. There is no such thing as a right-handed tennis ball or a left-handed coffee mug. When a tennis ball or a coffee mug is held up to a mirror, the image reflected is identical to the ball or mug itself. Objects like the coffee mug that lack handedness are said to be nonchiral, or **achiral**. Their mirror images are superimposable because they have a plane of symmetry. Take a minute to convince yourself of this by studying the chair in Figure 18.2.

Chiral Having right- or left-handedness with two *different* mirror-image forms.

Achiral The opposite of chiral; having superimposable mirror images and thus no right- or left-handedness.

PROBLEM 18.9
Which of the following objects are chiral?

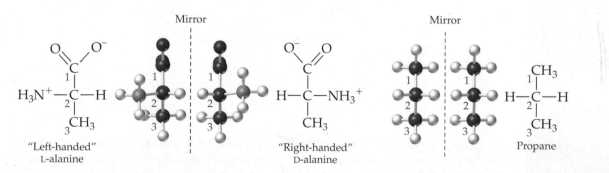

(a)   (b)   (c)   (d)

PROBLEM 18.10
List three common objects that are chiral and three that are not.

▲ **Figure 18.2**
The meaning of *superimposable*. It is easy to visualize the chair on top of its mirror image.

18.6 Molecular Handedness and Amino Acids

Just as certain objects are chiral, certain molecules are also chiral. Alanine and propane provide a visual comparison between chiral and achiral molecules:

Alanine, a chiral molecule

Propane, an achiral molecule

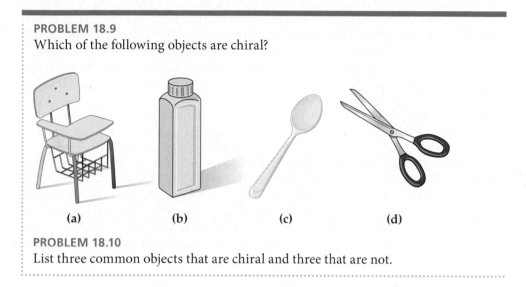

"Left-handed"   "Right-handed"   Propane
L-alanine   D-alanine

Alanine is a chiral molecule. Its mirror images cannot be superimposed. As a result, alanine exists in two forms that are mirror images of each other: a "right-handed" form known as D-alanine and a "left-handed" form known as L-alanine. Propane, by contrast, is an achiral molecule. The molecule and its mirror image are identical, and it has no left- and right-handed isomers.

Why are some molecules chiral but others are not? Can we predict chirality from structural formulas? Recall that carbon forms four bonds oriented to the four corners of an imaginary tetrahedron. The formulas for alanine and propane are drawn next in a manner that emphasizes the four groups bonded to the central carbon atom. In

▶▶▶ The D- and L-designations are derived from the relationship of the structures of the amino acids to the structure of glyceraldehyde, as we will see in Section 21.2.

▶▶▶ Review the tetrahedral structure of carbon in Section 4.8.

Mirror

▲ **Figure 18.3**
A chiral molecule.
The central atom is bonded to four different groups; the molecule is therefore chiral.

Chiral carbon atom A carbon atom bonded to four different groups.

Enantiomers (optical isomers) The two mirror-image forms of a chiral molecule.

▶▶▶ We will explore polarized light and how it is affected by enantiomers in Section 21.2.

Stereoisomers Isomers that have the same molecular and structural formulas but different spatial arrangements of their atoms.

▲ **Spearmint leaves and caraway seeds. The very different flavors of these food seasonings are imparted by a pair of enantiomers, which interact in different ways with our taste buds.**

alanine, this carbon is connected to *four different groups*: a —COO⁻ group, an —H atom, an —NH₃⁺ group, and a —CH₃ group:

$$H_3\overset{+}{N}-\underset{CH_3}{\overset{COO^-}{\underset{|}{\overset{|}{C}}}}-H \qquad \begin{matrix} 1.-COO^- \\ 2.-H \\ 3.-NH_3^+ \\ 4.-CH_3 \end{matrix} \Big\} Different \qquad H-\underset{CH_3}{\overset{CH_3}{\underset{|}{\overset{|}{C}}}}-H \qquad \begin{matrix} 1.-CH_3 \\ 2.-CH_3 \end{matrix} \Big\} Identical \\ \begin{matrix} 3.-H \\ 4.-H \end{matrix} \Big\} Identical$$

Alanine (chiral) · Propane (achiral)

Such a carbon atom is referred to as a **chiral carbon atom**, or a chiral center. The presence of one chiral carbon atom always produces a chiral molecule that exists in two mirror-image forms. Thus, alanine is chiral. In propane, the central carbon atom is bonded to two pairs of identical groups, and the two other carbon atoms are each bonded to three hydrogen atoms. The propane molecule has no chiral carbon atoms and is therefore achiral. (If a molecule has two or more chiral carbon atoms, it may or may not be chiral, depending on its overall shape.)

The two mirror-image forms of a chiral molecule like alanine are called either **enantiomers** (pronounced en-*a*n-ti-o-mers) or **optical isomers** ("optical" because of their effect on polarized light). The mirror-image relationship of the enantiomers of a compound with four different groups on one carbon atom is illustrated in Figure 18.3.

Like other isomers, enantiomers have the same formula but different arrangements of their atoms. More specifically, enantiomers are one kind of **stereoisomer**, compounds that have the same formula and atoms with the same connections but different spatial arrangements. (Cis–trans isomers discussed in Section 13.3 are stereoisomers, too.) Pairs of enantiomers have many of the same physical properties. Both enantiomers of alanine, for example, have the same melting point, the same solubility in water, the same isoelectric point, and the same density. But pairs of enantiomers always differ in their effects on polarized light and in how they react with other molecules that are also chiral. Most importantly, pairs of enantiomers often differ in their biological activity, odors, tastes, or activity as drugs. For example, the very different natural flavors of spearmint and caraway seeds are attributed to these two enantiomers:

L-carvone (in spearmint) · D-carvone (in caraway)

What about the amino acids listed in Table 18.3; are any of them chiral? Of the 20 common amino acids, 19 are chiral because they have four different groups bonded to their α-carbons, —H, —NH₂, —COOH, and —R (the side chain). Only glycine, H₂NCH₂COOH, is achiral; its side chain is a hydrogen atom and thus its α-carbon is bonded to two hydrogen atoms. Even though the 19 chiral α-amino acids can exist either as D- or L-enantiomers, nature selectively uses only L-amino acids for making proteins.

The artificial sweetener aspartame (sold as Equal™ or NutraSweet™) provides another excellent illustration of the delicate nature of the structure–function relationship and its role in biochemistry. Aspartame is the methyl ester of a dipeptide made from aspartate and phenylalanine in which both amino acids have the naturally occurring "left-handed," or L, chirality. In contrast, if either of the two amino acids in this molecular structure were the D rather than the L isomer, the compound would taste bitter.

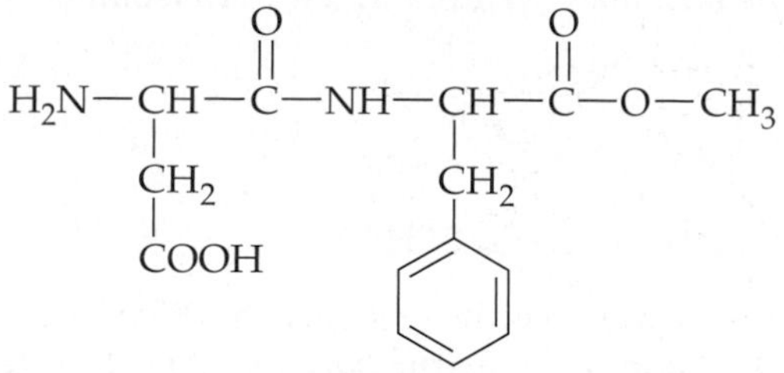

$$H_2N-CH-\overset{\overset{\displaystyle O}{\|}}{C}-NH-CH-\overset{\overset{\displaystyle O}{\|}}{C}-O-CH_3$$

Aspartame
(methyl ester of aspartylphenylalanine)

LOOKING AHEAD ▶▶▶ Amino acids, as you have seen, are chiral. Chirality is an important property of another major class of biomolecules. The individual sugar units in all carbohydrates are chiral, a topic addressed in Sections 21.2 and 21.3.

Worked Example 18.3 Determining Chirality

Lactic acid can be isolated from sour milk. Is lactic acid chiral?

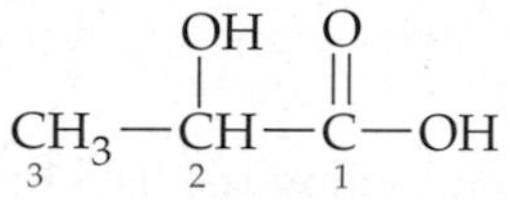

$$\underset{3}{CH_3}-\underset{2}{\overset{\overset{\displaystyle OH}{|}}{CH}}-\underset{1}{\overset{\overset{\displaystyle O}{\|}}{C}}-OH$$

Lactic acid

ANALYSIS A molecule is chiral if it contains one C atom bonded to four different groups. Identify any C atoms that meet this condition.

SOLUTION
To find out if lactic acid is chiral, list the groups attached to each carbon atom:

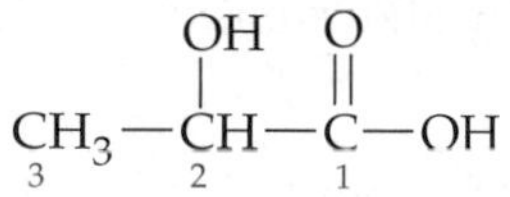

$$\underset{3}{CH_3}-\underset{2}{\overset{\overset{\displaystyle OH}{|}}{CH}}-\underset{1}{\overset{\overset{\displaystyle O}{\|}}{C}}-OH$$

Lactic acid

Groups on carbon 1	Groups on carbon 2	Groups on carbon 3
1. —OH	1. —COOH	1. —CH(OH)COOH
2. =O	2. —OH	2. —H
3. —CH(OH)CH₃	3. —H	3. —H
	4. —CH₃	4. —H

Next, look at the lists to see if any carbon atom is attached to four different groups. Of the three carbons, carbon 2 has four different groups, and lactic acid is therefore chiral.

PROBLEM 18.11
2-Aminopropane is an achiral molecule, but 2-aminobutane is chiral. Explain.

PROBLEM 18.12
Which of the following molecules are chiral? (Hint: Draw each molecule and analyze it as illustrated in Worked Example 18.3.)

(a) 3-Chloropentane   (b) 2-Chloropentane   (c) $CH_3CHCH_2CHCH_2CH_3$
$$\underset{\overset{|}{CH_3}\quad\overset{|}{CH_3}}{}$$

PROBLEM 18.13
Two of the 20 common amino acids have two chiral carbon atoms in their structures. Identify these amino acids and their chiral carbon atoms.

🔑 **KEY CONCEPT PROBLEM 18.14**

Two isomers have the formula C_2H_4BrCl. Draw both isomers and identify any chiral carbon atoms.

18.7 Primary Protein Structure

Primary protein structure The sequence in which amino acids are linked by peptide bonds in a protein.

The **primary structure** of a protein is the sequence in which its amino acids are lined up and connected by peptide bonds. Along the *backbone* of the protein is a chain of alternating peptide bonds and α-carbon atoms. The amino acid side chains (R_1, R_2, . . .) are substituents along the backbone, where they are bonded to the α-carbon atoms:

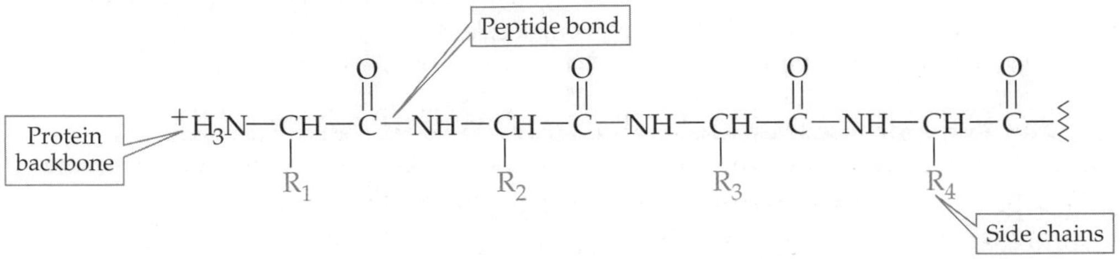

The carbon and nitrogen atoms along the backbone lie in a zigzag arrangement, with tetrahedral bonding around the α-carbon atoms. The electrons of each carbonyl-group double bond are shared to a considerable extent with the adjacent C—N bond. This sharing makes the C—N bond sufficiently like a double bond that there is no rotation around it. The result is that the carbonyl group, the —NH group bonded to it, and the two adjacent α-carbons form a rigid, planar unit. The side-chain groups on the two α-carbons extend out to opposite sides of the plane. A long polymer chain forms a connected series of these planar peptide units:

▶▶▶ Review the properties of carbon—carbon double bonds in Section 13.3.

Planar units along a protein chain

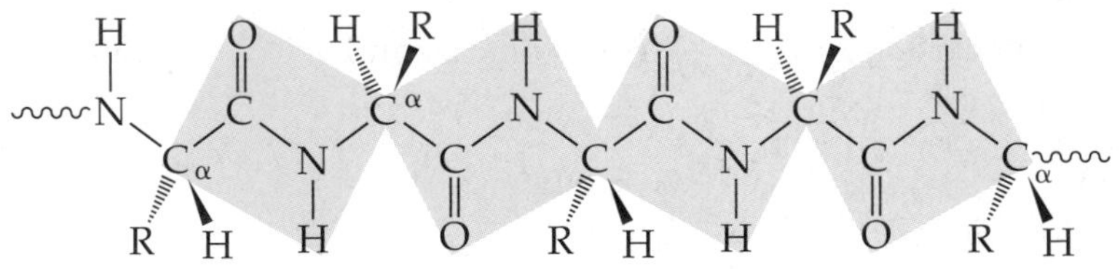

One planar unit

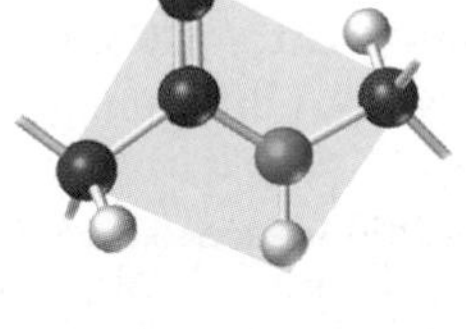

A pair of amino acids—for example, alanine and serine—can be combined to form two different dipeptides. The alanine —COO^- can react with the serine —NH_3^+:

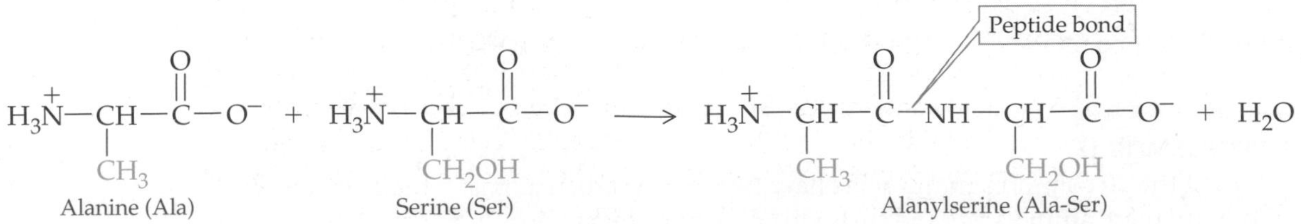

Alanine (Ala)   Serine (Ser)   Alanylserine (Ala-Ser)

Or the serine —COO⁻ can react with the alanine —NH₃⁺:

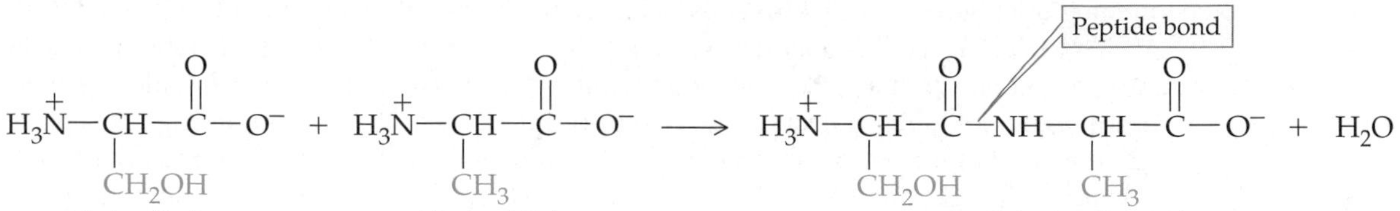

Serine (Ser) + Alanine (Ala) → Serylalanine (Ser-Ala) + H_2O

By convention, peptides and proteins are always written with the **amino-terminal amino acid** (also called N-terminal amino acid, the one with the free —NH₃⁺) on the left and the **carboxyl-terminal amino acid** (also called the C-terminal amino acid, the one with the free —COO⁻ group) on the right. The individual amino acids joined in the chain are referred to as **residues**.

A peptide is named by citing the amino acid residues in order, starting at the N-terminal amino acid and ending with the C-terminal amino acid. All residue names except the C-terminal one have the -*yl* ending instead of -*ine*, as in alanylserine (abbreviated Ala-Ser) or serylalanine (Ser-Ala).

The primary structure of a protein is the result of the amino acids being lined up one by one to form peptide bonds in precisely the correct order. Consider that there are six ways in which three different amino acids can be joined, more than 40,000 ways in which eight amino acids can be joined, and more than 360,000 ways in which 10 amino acids can be joined. Despite the rapid increase in possible combinations as the number of amino acid residues present increases, the function of a protein depends on the precise order of amino acids, and only the one correct isomer can do the job. For example, human *angiotensin II* must have its eight amino acids arranged in exactly the correct order:

Amino-terminal (N-terminal) amino acid The amino acid with the free —NH₃⁺ group at the end of a protein.

Carboxyl-terminal (C-terminal) amino acid The amino acid with the free —COO⁻ group at the end of a protein.

Residue An amino acid unit in a polypeptide.

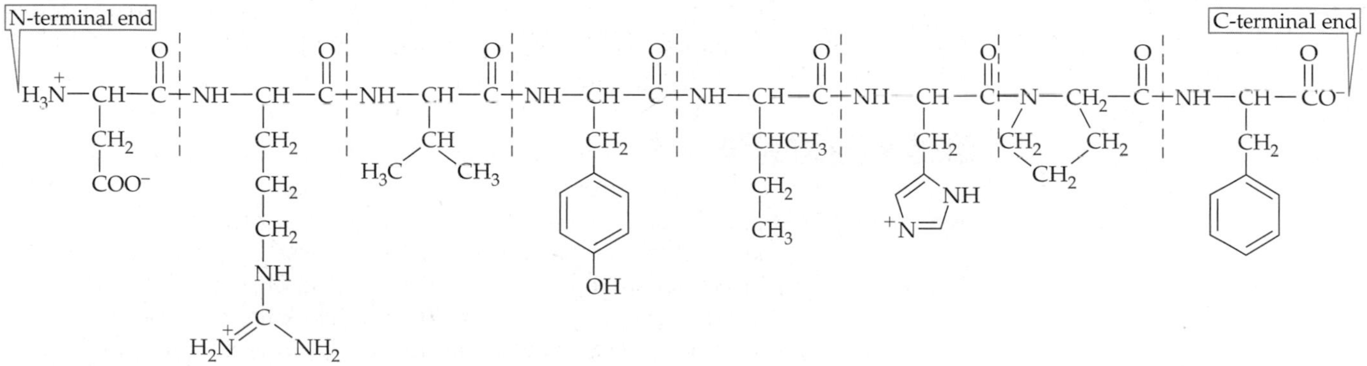

If its amino acids are not arranged properly, this hormone will not participate as it should in regulating blood pressure.

So crucial is primary structure to function—no matter how big the protein—that the change of only one amino acid can sometimes drastically alter a protein's biological properties. Sickle-cell anemia is the best-known example of the potentially devastating result of a single amino acid substitution. It is a hereditary disease caused by a genetic difference that replaces one amino acid (glutamate, Glu) with another (valine, Val) in each of two polypeptide chains of the hemoglobin molecule.

Sickle-cell anemia is named for the "sickle" shape of affected red blood cells. (A sickle is a tool with a curved blade and short handle that is used to cut tall grass.) The sickling of the cells and the resultant painful, debilitating, and potentially fatal disease are entirely the result of this one single amino acid substitution. The change replaces a hydrophilic, carboxylic acid–containing side chain (Glu) on hemoglobin with a hydrophobic, neutral hydrocarbon side chain (Val) and thus alters the shape of the hemoglobin molecule. (The effect of this change on the charge of hemoglobin is illustrated in the Chemistry in Action box, "Protein Analysis by Electrophoresis," p. 568.)

Hemoglobin, found solely inside red blood cells, is the molecule that carries oxygen in the blood and releases it where it is needed. Each red blood cell contains millions of hemoglobin molecules. Sickling takes place in red blood cells carrying the sickle-cell form of hemoglobin that has released oxygen. Without bound oxygen, a hydrophobic pocket is exposed on the surface of the hemoglobin and the hydrophobic valine side chain on another hemoglobin molecule is drawn into this pocket. As this combining takes place in more and more hemoglobin molecules in a red blood cell, insoluble fibrous chains are formed. The stiff fibers force the cell into the sickled shape. Normal hemoglobin molecules that have released oxygen do not form such fibers because the $—COO^-$ side chain in glutamate is too hydrophilic to enter the hydrophobic pocket on another hemoglobin molecule. Thus, each individual molecule of normal hemoglobin does not form part of a fibrous chain and no deformation of a normal red blood cell occurs. Furthermore, the hydrophobic pocket is not available in any oxygen-carrying hemoglobin molecule because of a change in shape that occurs when the molecule picks up oxygen.

Sickled red blood cells are fragile, and because they are inflexible, they tend to collect and block capillaries, causing inflammation and pain, and possibly blocking blood flow in a manner that damages major organs. Also, they have a shorter lifespan than normal red blood cells causing afflicted individuals to become severely anemic.

Sickle-cell anemia arises when a person inherits two defective copies of the hemoglobin gene, one from each parent. If a person has one functional gene and one defective gene, he or she is said to carry the sickle-cell trait but does not have sickle-cell anemia. The percentage of individuals carrying the genetic trait for sickle-cell anemia is highest among people in ethnic groups with origins in tropical regions where malaria is prevalent. The ancestors of these individuals survived because if they were infected with malaria, it was not fatal. Malaria-causing parasites enter red blood cells and reproduce there. In a person with the sickle-cell trait, the cells respond by sickling and the parasites cannot multiply. As a result, the genetic trait for sickle-cell anemia is carried forward in the surviving population. Those who carry sickle-cell trait are generally healthy and lead normal lives; those who have sickle-cell anemia have multiple health problems due to this disease throughout their lives. Carrying one gene for sickle-cell anemia (conferring sickle-cell trait) is an advantage only in an environment where malaria is prevalent.

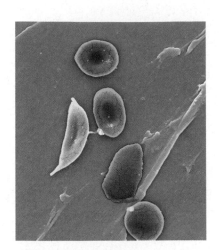

▲ **Four normal (convex) red blood cells and one sickled red blood cell. Because of their shape, sickled cells tend to clog vessels.**

LOOKING AHEAD ▶▶▶ More than any other kind of biomolecule, proteins are in control of our biochemistry. Are you wondering how each of our thousands of proteins is produced with all their amino acids lined up in the correct order? The information necessary to do this is stored in DNA, and the remarkable machinery that does the job resides in the nuclei of our cells. Chapter 25 provides the details of how protein synthesis is accomplished. In order to synthesize proteins, our cells need a constant supply of amino acid building blocks from the diet because human cells can synthesize only some of the 20 amino acids used to make proteins. Read more about diet and protein requirements in the Chemistry in Action box "Proteins in the Diet," p. 564.

Worked Example 18.4 Drawing Dipeptides

Draw the structure of the dipeptide Ala-Gly.

ANALYSIS You need the names and structures of the two amino acids. Since alanine is named first, it is the amino-terminal and glycine is the carboxyl-terminal. Ala-Gly must have a peptide bond between the $—COO^-$ on alanine and the $—NH_3^+$ on glycine.

SOLUTION

The structures of alanine and glycine, and the structure of the Ala-Gly dipeptide are

$$\overset{+}{H_3N}—\underset{\underset{CH_3}{|}}{CH}—\overset{\overset{O}{||}}{C}—O^- \qquad \overset{+}{H_3N}—CH_2—\overset{\overset{O}{||}}{C}—O^-$$

Alanine (Ala) Glycine (Gly)

and

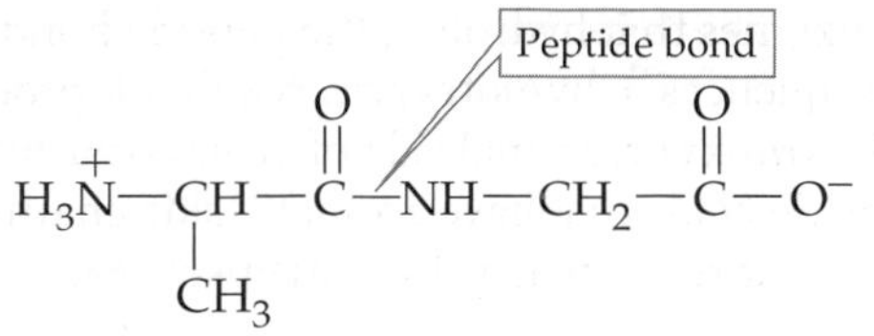

Peptide bond

$$H_3\overset{+}{N}-CH-\overset{O}{\overset{||}{C}}-NH-CH_2-\overset{O}{\overset{||}{C}}-O^-$$
$$\quad\quad\quad |$$
$$\quad\quad CH_3$$

Ala-Gly

PROBLEM 18.15
Valine is an amino acid with a nonpolar side chain and serine is an amino acid with a polar side chain. Draw the two dipeptides that can be formed by these two amino acids.

PROBLEM 18.16
Tripeptides are composed of three amino acids linked by peptide bonds. Given a set of amino acids, you can make several different tripeptides.
(a) Use the three-letter shorthand notations to name all the isomeric tripeptides that can be made from serine, tyrosine, and glycine. Each amino acid will be used once in each tripeptide.
(b) Draw the complete structure of the tripeptides that have glycine as the amino-terminal amino acid.

PROBLEM 18.17
Using three-letter abbreviations, show the six tripeptides that contain isoleucine, arginine, and valine.

PROBLEM 18.18
Identify the amino acids in the following dipeptide and tripeptide, and write the abbreviated forms of the peptide names. Copy the dipeptides; draw a box around the peptide bonds and use an arrow to identify the α-carbon atoms. Draw a circle around the R groups and indicate if the R groups are neutral, polar, acidic, or basic.

(a) $H_3\overset{+}{N}-CH-\overset{O}{\overset{||}{C}}-NH-CH-\overset{O}{\overset{||}{C}}-O^-$
with CH_2, CH_3CHCH_3, and CH_2COO^-

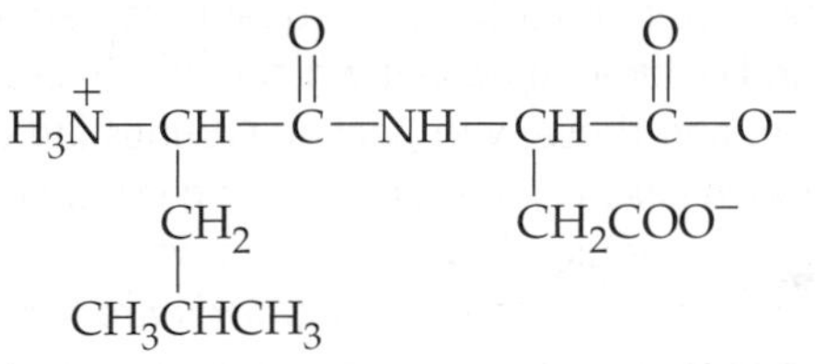

(b) $H_3\overset{+}{N}-CH-\overset{O}{\overset{||}{C}}-NH-CH-\overset{O}{\overset{||}{C}}-NH-CH-\overset{O}{\overset{||}{C}}-O^-$
with CH_2 (phenol ring, OH), CH_2OH, $CH_2(CH_2)_3\overset{+}{N}H_3$

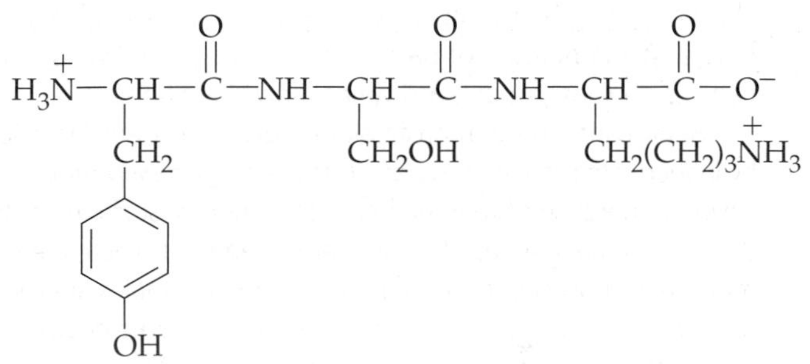

PROBLEM 18.19
Copy the structure of the tripeptide in Problem 18.18b, and circle the two planar regions along the backbone.

This type of hydrogen bonding creates pleated sheet and helical secondary structures, as described in Section 18.9 and as illustrated in the imaginary protein in Figure 18.4.

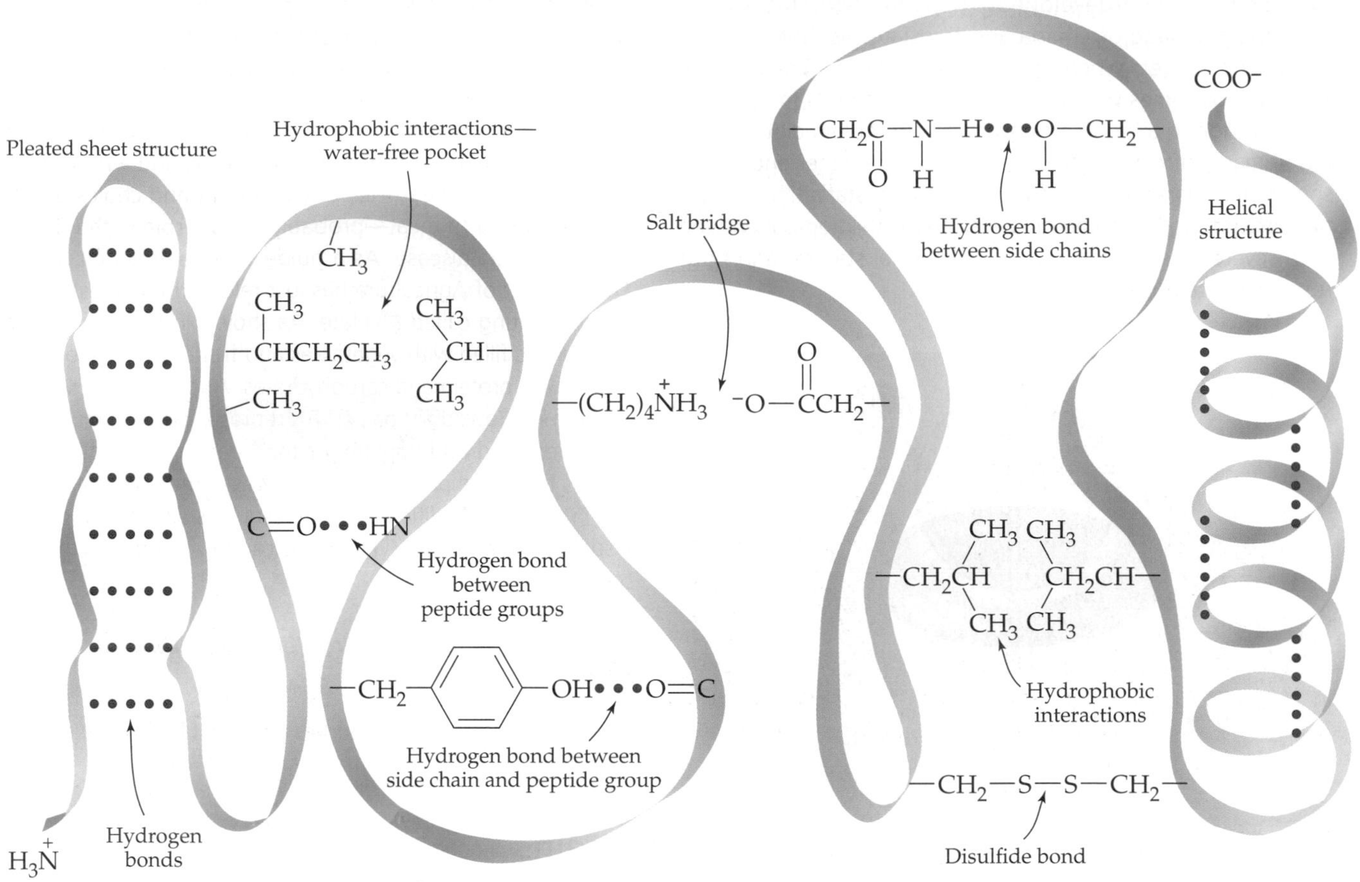

▲ **Figure 18.4**
Interactions that determine protein shape.
The regular pleated sheet (*left*) and helical structure (*right*) are created by hydrogen bonding between neighboring backbone atoms; the other interactions involve side-chain groups that can be nearby or quite far apart in the protein chain.

Hydrogen Bonds of R Groups with Each Other or with Backbone Atoms

Some amino acid side chains contain atoms that can form hydrogen bonds. Side-chain hydrogen bonds can connect different parts of a protein molecule, whether they are in close proximity or far apart along the polypeptide chain. In the protein in Figure 18.4, hydrogen bonds between side chains have created folds in two places. Often, hydrogen-bonding side chains are present on the surface of a folded protein, where they can form hydrogen bonds with surrounding water molecules.

Ionic Attractions between R Groups (Salt Bridges)

Where there are ionized acidic and basic side chains, the attraction between their positive and negative charges creates *salt bridges*. A basic lysine side chain and an acidic aspartate side chain have formed a salt bridge in the middle of the protein shown in Figure 18.4.

Hydrophobic Interactions between R Groups

Hydrocarbon side chains are attracted to each other by the dispersion forces caused by the momentary uneven distribution of electrons. The result is that these groups cluster together in the same way that oil molecules cluster on the surface of water, so that these interactions are often referred to as *hydrophobic*. By clustering in this manner, the hydrophobic groups shown in Figure 18.4 create a water-free pocket in the protein chain. Although the individual attractions are weak, their large number in proteins plays a major role in stabilizing the folded structures.

▶▶▶ Review dispersion forces in Section 8.11 and van der Waals forces in Section 9.2.

Covalent Sulfur–Sulfur Bonds

In addition to the noncovalent interactions, one type of covalent bond plays a role in determining protein shape. Cysteine amino acid residues have side chains containing thiol functional groups (—SH) that can react to form sulfur–sulfur bonds (—S—S—):

▶▶▶ Disulfide bond formation was explored in Section 14.9.

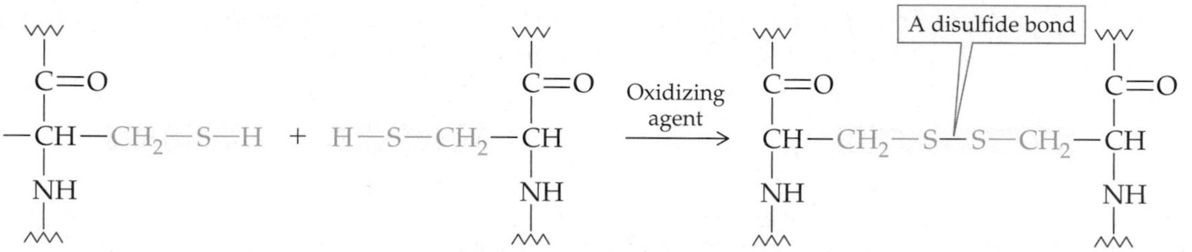

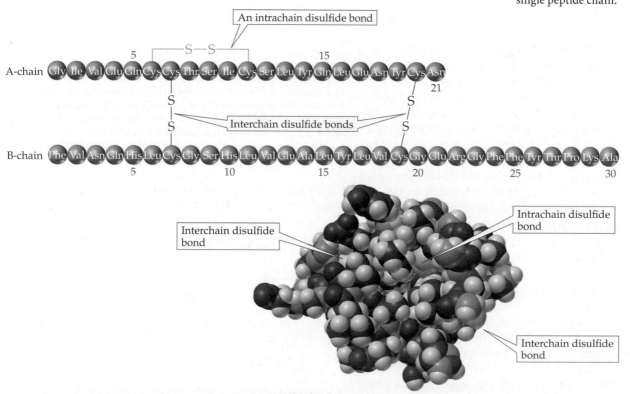

Cysteine (Cys)   Cysteine (Cys)

A disulfide bond

If the two cysteine residues are in different protein chains, the two separate chains become linked together by the disulfide bond. If the two cysteine residues are in the same chain, a loop is formed in the chain. Insulin provides a good example. It consists of two polypeptide chains connected by **disulfide bonds** in two places. One of the chains also has a loop caused by a third disulfide bond.

Disulfide bond An S—S bond formed between two cysteine side chains; can join two separate peptide chains together or cause a loop in a single peptide chain.

Structure of insulin

An intrachain disulfide bond

A-chain Gly Ile Val Glu Gln Cys Cys Thr Ser Ile Cys Ser Leu Tyr Gln Leu Glu Asn Tyr Cys Asn

Interchain disulfide bonds

B-chain Phe Val Asn Gln His Leu Cys Gly Ser His Leu Val Glu Ala Leu Tyr Leu Val Cys Gly Glu Arg Gly Phe Phe Tyr Thr Pro Lys Ala

Interchain disulfide bond

Intrachain disulfide bond

Interchain disulfide bond

Insulin is representative of a class of small polypeptides that function as hormones, which are released when a chemical message must be carried from one place to another (angiotensin II on p. 561 is another example of a polypeptide hormone).

▶▶▶ We will learn more about polypeptide hormones in Chapter 28, and diabetes in Section 22.9.

The structure and function of insulin are of intense interest because of its role in glucose metabolism and the need for supplementary insulin by individuals with diabetes. Undoubtedly because of this need, studies of insulin have led the way in our still-developing ability to determine the structure of a biomolecule and prepare it synthetically.

In a historically important accomplishment, the amino acid sequence of insulin was determined in 1951—it was the *first* protein for which this was done. It took 15 years before the cross-linking and complete structure of the molecule were determined and a successful laboratory synthesis was carried out. With the advent of biotechnology in the 1980s, once again insulin was first. Until then, individuals with diabetes relied on insulin extracted from the pancreases of cows, and because of differences in three amino acids between bovine and human insulin, allergic reactions occasionally resulted. In 1982, human insulin became the first commercial product of genetic engineering to be licensed by the U.S. government for clinical use.

CHEMISTRY IN ACTION

Protein Analysis by Electrophoresis

Protein molecules in solution can be separated from each other by taking advantage of their net charges. In the electric field between two electrodes, a positively charged particle moves toward the negative electrode and a negatively charged particle moves toward the positive electrode. This movement, known as *electrophoresis*, varies with the strength of the electric field, the charge of the particle, the size and shape of the particle, and the buffer/polymer gel combination through which the protein is moving.

The net charge on a protein is determined by how many of the acidic or basic side-chain functional groups in the protein are ionized, and this, like the charge of an amino acid, depends on the pH. Thus, the mobility of a protein during electrophoresis depends on the pH of the buffer. If the buffer is at a pH equal to the isoelectric point of the protein, the protein does not move.

By varying the nature of the buffer between the electrodes and other conditions, proteins can be separated in a variety of ways, including by their molecular weight. Once the separation is complete, the various proteins are made visible by the addition of a dye.

Electrophoresis is routinely used in the clinical laboratory for determining which proteins are present, and in what amounts, in a blood sample. One commonly used test is for the diagnosis of sickle-cell anemia (p. 561). Normal adult hemoglobin (HbA) and hemoglobin showing the inherited sickle-cell trait (HbS) differ in their net charges. Therefore, HbA and HbS move different distances during electrophoresis. The accompanying diagram compares the results of electrophoresis of the hemoglobin extracted from red blood cells for a normal individual, one with sickle-cell anemia (two inherited sickle-cell genes), and one with sickle-cell trait (one normal and one inherited sickle-cell gene). With sickle-cell trait, an individual is likely to suffer symptoms of the disease only under conditions of severe oxygen deprivation.

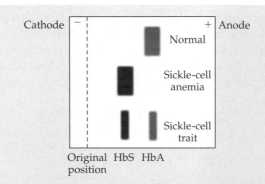

▲ **Gel electrophoresis of hemoglobin. Hemoglobin in samples placed at the original position in a porous polymer gel immersed in a constant pH buffer have moved left to right during electrophoresis. The normal individual has only HbA. The individual with sickle-cell anemia has no HbA, and the individual with sickle-cell trait has roughly equal amounts of HbA and HbS. HbA and HbS have negative charges of different magnitudes because HbS has two fewer Glu residues than HbA.**

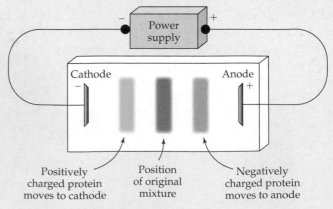

▲ Movement of charged molecules in electrophoresis.

See Chemistry in Action Problems 18.78 and 18.79 at the end of the chapter.

Worked Example 18.5 Drawing Side-Chain Interactions

What type of noncovalent interaction occurs between the threonine and glutamine side chains? Draw the structures of these amino acids to show the interaction.

ANALYSIS The side chains of threonine and glutamine contain an amide group and a hydroxyl group, respectively. These groups do not form salt bridges because they do not ionize. They are polar and therefore not hydrophobic. They form a hydrogen bond between the oxygen of the amide carbonyl group and the hydrogen of the hydroxyl group.

SOLUTION
The noncovalent, hydrogen bond interaction between threonine and glutamine is as follows:

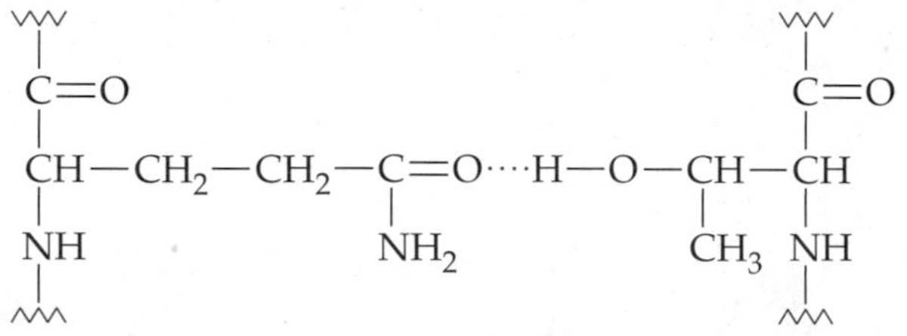

PROBLEM 18.21
Look at Table 18.3 and identify the type of noncovalent interaction expected between the side chains of the following pairs of amino acids:

(a) Glutamine and serine

(b) Isoleucine and proline

(c) Aspartate and lysine

(d) Alanine and phenylalanine

PROBLEM 18.22
In Figure 18.4, identify the amino acids that have formed (a) hydrogen bonds from their side chains and (b) hydrophobic side-chain interactions.

18.9 Secondary Protein Structure

The spatial arrangement of the polypeptide backbones of proteins constitutes **secondary protein structure**. The secondary structure includes two kinds of repeating patterns known as the **alpha-helix** (α-helix) and the **beta-sheet** (β-sheet). In both, hydrogen bonding between *backbone* atoms holds the polypeptide chain in place. The hydrogen bonding connects the carbonyl oxygen atom of one peptide unit with the amide hydrogen atom of another peptide unit ($-C=O \cdots H-N-$). In large protein molecules, regions of α-helix and β-sheet structure are connected by randomly arranged loops or coils that are a third type of secondary structure.

Secondary protein structure Regular and repeating structural patterns (for example, α-helix, β-sheet) created by hydrogen bonding between backbone atoms in neighboring segments of protein chains.

α-Helix

A single protein chain coiled in a spiral with a right-handed (clockwise) twist is known as an **alpha-helix (α-helix)** (Figure 18.5a). The helix, which resembles a coiled telephone cord, is stabilized by hydrogen bonds between each backbone carbonyl oxygen atom and an amide hydrogen atom four amino acid residues farther along the backbone. The hydrogen bonds lie vertically along the helix, and the amino acid R groups extend to the outside of the coil. Although the strength of each individual hydrogen bond is small, the large number of bonds in the helix results in an extremely stable secondary structure. A view of the helix from the top (Figure 18.5b) clearly shows the side chains on the amino acids oriented to the exterior of the helix.

Alpha- (α-) helix Secondary protein structure in which a protein chain forms a right-handed coil stabilized by hydrogen bonds between peptide groups along its backbone.

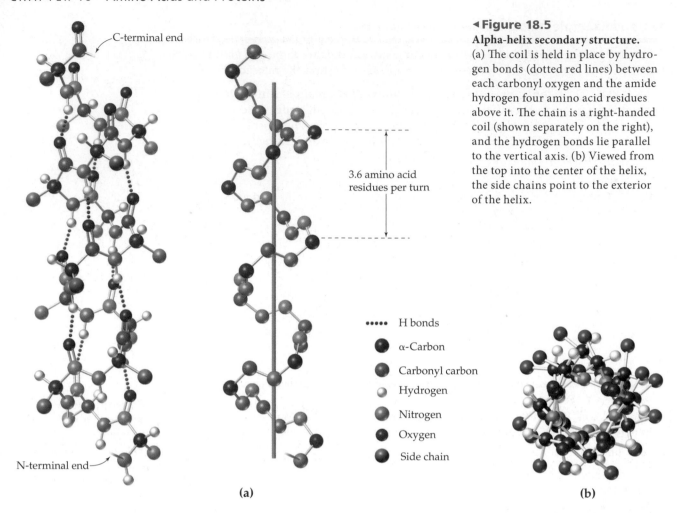

C-terminal end

N-terminal end

3.6 amino acid
residues per turn

•••• H bonds

● α-Carbon

● Carbonyl carbon

○ Hydrogen

● Nitrogen

● Oxygen

● Side chain

(a)

(b)

◄ **Figure 18.5**
Alpha-helix secondary structure.
(a) The coil is held in place by hydrogen bonds (dotted red lines) between each carbonyl oxygen and the amide hydrogen four amino acid residues above it. The chain is a right-handed coil (shown separately on the right), and the hydrogen bonds lie parallel to the vertical axis. (b) Viewed from the top into the center of the helix, the side chains point to the exterior of the helix.

β-Sheet

Beta- (β-) sheet Secondary protein structure in which adjacent protein chains either in the same molecule or in different molecules are held together by hydrogen bonds along the backbones, forming a flat sheet-like structure.

In the **beta-sheet (β-sheet)** structure, the polypeptide chains are held in place by hydrogen bonds between pairs of peptide units along neighboring backbone segments. The protein chains, which are extended to their full length, bend at each α-carbon so that the sheet has a pleated contour, with the R groups extending above and below the sheet (Figure 18.6).

PROBLEM 18.23
Examine the α-helix in Figure 18.5 and determine how many backbone C and N atoms are included in the loop between an amide hydrogen atom and the carbonyl oxygen to which it is hydrogen bonded.

PROBLEM 18.24
Consult the β-sheet in Figure 18.6 and (a) name the bonding responsible for the sheet formation and (b) identify the specific atoms responsible for this bonding.

Secondary Structure in Fibrous and Globular Proteins

Proteins are classified in several ways, one of which is to identify them as either *fibrous proteins* or *globular proteins*. In an example of the integration of molecular structure and function that is central to biochemistry, fibrous and globular proteins each have functions made possible by their distinctive structures.

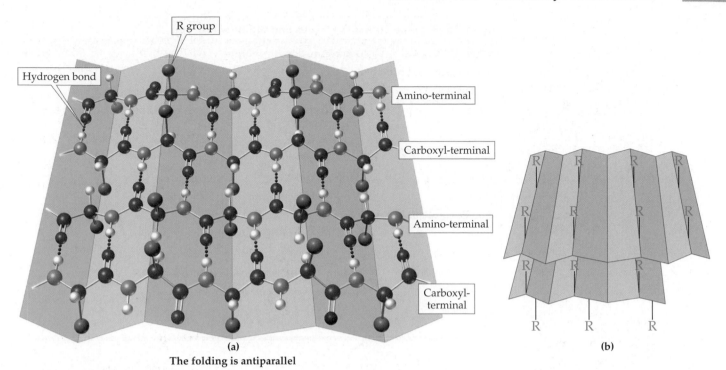

(a)
The folding is antiparallel

(b)

▲ **Figure 18.6**

Beta-sheet secondary structure.

(a) The hydrogen bonds between neighboring protein chains. The protein chains usually lie side-by-side so that alternating chains run from the N-terminal end to the C-terminal end and from the C-terminal end to the N-terminal end (known as the *antiparallel* arrangement). (b) A pair of stacked pleated sheets illustrate how the R groups point above and below the sheets.

Fibrous protein A tough, insoluble protein whose protein chains form fibers or sheets.

Globular protein A water-soluble protein whose chain is folded in a compact shape with hydrophilic groups on the outside.

Secondary structure is primarily responsible for the nature of **fibrous proteins**—tough, insoluble proteins in which the chains form long fibers, or sheets. Wool, hair, and fingernails are made of fibrous proteins known as *α-keratins*, which are composed almost completely of α-helices. In α-keratins, pairs of α-helixes are twisted together into small fibrils that are in turn twisted into larger and larger bundles. The hardness, flexibility, and stretchiness of the material varies with the number of disulfide bonds. In fingernails, for example, large numbers of disulfide bonds hold the bundles in place.

Natural silk and spider webs are made of *fibroin*, a fibrous protein almost entirely composed of stacks of β-sheets. For such close stacking, the R groups must be relatively small (see Figure 18.6b). Fibroin contains regions of alternating glycine (— H on the α carbon) and alanine (— CH_3 on the α carbon). The sheets stack so that sides with the smaller glycine hydrogens face each other and sides with the larger alanine methyl groups face each other.

Globular proteins are water-soluble proteins whose chains are folded into compact, globe-like shapes. Their structures, which vary widely with their functions, are not regular like those of fibrous proteins. Where the protein chain folds back on itself, sections of α-helix and β-sheet are usually present, as illustrated in Figure 18.4. The presence of hydrophilic side chains on the outer surfaces of globular proteins accounts for their water solubility, allowing them to travel through the blood and other body fluids to sites where their activity is needed. Furthermore, many globular proteins are enzymes that are dissolved in the intercellular fluids inside cells. The overall shapes of globular proteins represent another level of structure, tertiary structure, discussed in the next section.

Table 18.4 compares the occurrences and functions of some fibrous and globular proteins.

▲ **The proteins found in eggs, milk, and cheese are examples of globular proteins. A spider web is made from fibrous protein.**

TABLE **18.4** Some Common Fibrous and Globular Proteins	
Name	**Occurrence and Function**
Fibrous proteins (insoluble)	
Keratins	Found in skin, wool, feathers, hooves, silk, fingernails
Collagens	Found in animal hide, tendons, bone, eye cornea, and other connective tissue
Elastins	Found in blood vessels and ligaments, where ability of the tissue to stretch is important
Myosins	Found in muscle tissue
Fibrin	Found in blood clots
Globular proteins (soluble)	
Insulin	Regulatory hormone for controlling glucose metabolism
Ribonuclease	Enzyme that catalyzes RNA hydrolysis
Immunoglobulins	Proteins involved in immune response
Hemoglobin	Protein involved in oxygen transport
Albumins	Proteins that perform many transport functions in blood; protein in egg white

18.10 Tertiary Protein Structure

Tertiary protein structure The way in which an entire protein chain is coiled and folded into its specific three-dimensional shape.

The overall three-dimensional shape that results from the folding of a protein chain is the protein's **tertiary structure**. In contrast to secondary structure, which depends mainly on attraction between backbone atoms, tertiary structure depends mainly on interactions of amino acid side chains that are far apart along the same backbone.

Although the bends and twists of the protein chain in a globular protein may appear irregular and the three-dimensional structure may appear random, this is not the case. Each protein molecule folds in a distinctive manner that is determined by its primary structure and results in its maximum stability. A protein with the shape in which it functions in living systems is known as a **native protein**.

Native protein A protein with the shape (secondary, tertiary, and quaternary structure) in which it exists naturally in living organisms.

The noncovalent interactions and disulfide covalent bonds described earlier govern tertiary structure. The enzyme *ribonuclease*, shown here as an example, is drawn in a style that shows the combination of α-helix and β-sheet regions, the loops connecting them, and four disulfide bonds:

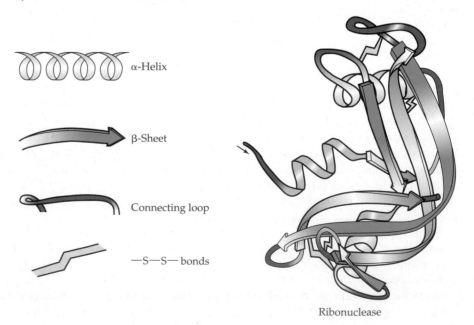

α-Helix

β-Sheet

Connecting loop

—S—S— bonds

Ribonuclease

The structure of ribonuclease is representative of the tertiary structure of globular, water-soluble proteins. The hydrophobic, nonpolar side chains congregate in a hydrocarbon-like interior, and the hydrophilic side chains, which provide water solubility, congregate on the outside. Ribonuclease is classified as a **simple protein** because it is composed only of amino acid residues (124 of them). The drawing shows ribonuclease in a style that clearly represents the combination of secondary structures in the overall tertiary structure of a globular protein.

Myoglobin is another example of a small globular protein. A relative of hemoglobin, myoglobin stores oxygen in skeletal muscles for use when there is an immediate need for energy. Structurally, the 153 amino acid residues of myoglobin are arranged in eight α-helical segments connected by short segments looped so that hydrophilic amino acid residues are on the exterior of the compact, spherical tertiary structure. Like many proteins, myoglobin is not a simple protein, but is a **conjugated protein**—a protein that is aided in its function by an associated non–amino acid unit. The oxygen-carrying portion of myoglobin has a heme group embedded within the polypeptide chain. In Figure 18.7 the myoglobin molecule is shown in two different ways; both types of molecular representation are routinely used to illustrate the shapes of protein molecules. Some examples of other kinds of conjugated proteins are listed in Table 18.5.

Simple protein A protein composed of only amino acid residues.

Conjugated protein A protein that incorporates one or more non–amino acid units in its structure.

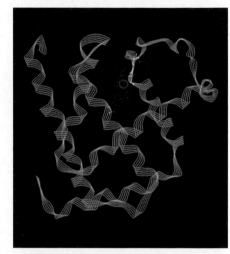

(a)

TABLE **18.5** Some Examples of Conjugated Proteins

Class of Protein	Nonprotein Part	Examples
Glycoproteins	Carbohydrates	Glycoproteins in cell membranes (Section 21.9)
Lipoproteins	Lipids	High- and low-density lipoproteins that transport cholesterol and other lipids through the body (Section 24.2)
Metalloproteins	Metal ions	The enzyme cytochrome oxidase, necessary for biological energy production, and many other enzymes
Phosphoproteins	Phosphate groups	Milk casein, which provides essential nutrients to infants
Hemoproteins	Heme	Hemoglobin (transports oxygen) and myoglobin (stores oxygen)
Nucleoproteins	RNA (ribonucleic acid)	Found in cell ribosomes, where they take part in protein synthesis

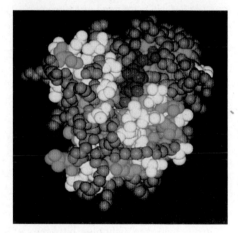

(b)

▲ Figure 18.7
Myoglobin, drawn in two styles.
In each panel, the red structure embedded in the protein is a molecule of heme, to which O_2 binds. (a) A protein *ribbon model* shows the helical portions as a ribbon. This type of representation clearly shows protein secondary structure. (b) A computer-generated *space-filling* model of myoglobin shows the hydrophobic residues in blue and the hydrophilic residues in purple. This type of representation better conveys the overall shape and dimensions of the protein.

🔑 **KEY CONCEPT PROBLEM 18.25**

Hydrogen bonds are important in stabilizing both the secondary and tertiary structures of proteins. How do the groups that form hydrogen bonds in the secondary and tertiary structures differ?

18.11 Quaternary Protein Structure

The fourth and final level of protein structure, and the most complex, is **quaternary protein structure**—the way in which two or more polypeptide subunits associate to form a single three-dimensional protein unit. The individual polypeptides are held together by the same noncovalent forces responsible for tertiary structure. In some cases, there are also covalent bonds and the protein may incorporate a non–amino acid portion. *Hemoglobin* and *collagen* are both well-understood examples of proteins with quaternary structure essential to their function.

Hemoglobin

Hemoglobin (Figure 18.8a) is a conjugated quaternary protein composed of four polypeptide chains (two each of two different polypeptides called the α-chain and the β-chain) held together primarily by the interaction of hydrophobic groups and four heme

Quaternary protein structure The way in which two or more protein chains aggregate to form large, ordered structures.

▶ **Figure 18.8**

Heme and hemoglobin, a protein with quaternary structure.

(a) The polypeptides are shown in purple, green, blue, and yellow, with their heme units in red. Each polypeptide resembles myoglobin in structure.

(b) A heme unit is present in each of the four polypeptides in hemoglobin.

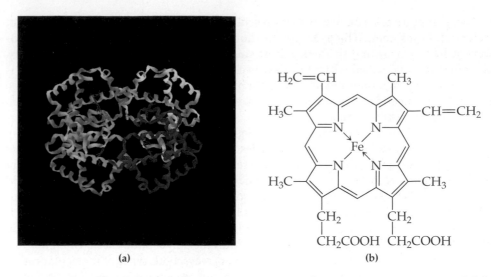

(a) (b)

groups. Each polypeptide is similar in composition and tertiary structure to myoglobin (Figure 18.7). The α-chains have 141 amino acids, and the β-chains have 146 amino acids.

The hemes (Figure 18.8b), one in each of the four polypeptides, each contain an iron atom that is essential to their function. Hemoglobin is the oxygen carrier in red blood cells. In the lungs, O_2 binds to Fe^{2+}, so that each hemoglobin can carry a maximum of four O_2 molecules. In tissues in need of oxygen, the O_2 is released, and CO_2 (the product of respiration) is picked up and carried back to the lungs.

 We will learn more about oxygen transport in Chapter 29.

Collagen

Collagen is the most abundant of all proteins in mammals, making up 30% or more of the total. A fibrous protein, collagen is the major constituent of skin, tendons, bones, blood vessels, and other connective tissues. The basic structural unit of collagen (*tropocollagen*) consists of three intertwined chains of about 1000 amino acids each. Each chain is loosely coiled in a left-handed (counter-clockwise) direction (Figure 18.9a). Three of these coiled chains wrap around one another (in a clockwise direction) to form a stiff, rod-like tropocollagen triple helix (Figure 18.9b) in which the chains are held together by hydrogen bonds.

▶ **Figure 18.9**

Collagen.

(a) A single collagen helix (carbon, green; hydrogen, light blue; nitrogen, dark blue; oxygen, red). (b) The triple helix of tropocollagen. (c) The quaternary structure of a cross-linked collagen, showing the assemblage of tropocollagen molecules.

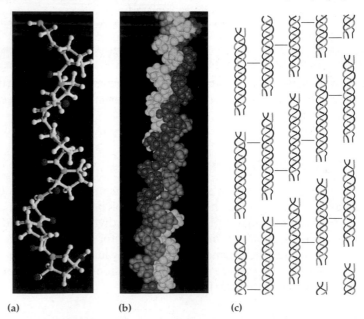

(a) (b) (c)

There are several different types of collagen found throughout the body that vary slightly in their primary sequence of amino acids. However, all the various kinds of collagen have in common a glycine residue at every third position. Only glycine residues (with —H as the side chain on the α-carbon) can fit in the center of the tightly coiled tropocollagen triple helix. The larger side chains face the exterior of the helix. After the collagen protein is synthesized, hydroxyl groups are added to some of its proline residues in a reaction that requires vitamin C. This hydroxylation of proline residues is important for strong collagen fiber formation. Herein lies the explanation for the symptoms of scurvy, the disease that results from vitamin C deficiency. When vitamin C is in short supply, collagen is deficient in hydroxylated proline residues and, as a result, forms fibers poorly. The results are the skin lesions and fragile blood vessels that accompany scurvy (see Chemistry in Action: Collagen—A Tale of Two Diseases on p. 576).

▶▶▶ For more on the role of vitamin C in collagen synthesis, see Section 19.10.

The tropocollagen triple helices are assembled into collagen in a quaternary structure formed by a great many strands overlapping lengthwise (Figure 18.9c). Depending on the exact purpose collagen serves in the body, further structural modifications occur. In connective tissue like tendons, covalent bonds between strands give collagen fibers a rigid, cross-linked structure. In teeth and bones, calcium hydroxyapatite $\left[Ca_5(PO_4)_3OH \right]$ deposits in the gaps between chains to further harden the overall assembly.

Protein Structure Summary

- **Primary structure**—the sequence of amino acids connected by peptide bonds in the polypeptide chain; for example, Asp-Arg-Val-Tyr.
- **Secondary structure**—the arrangement in space of the polypeptide chain, which includes the regular patterns of the α-helix and the β-sheet motifs (held together by hydrogen bonds between backbone carbonyl and amino groups in amino acid residues) plus the loops and coils that connect these segments.

α-Helix

β-Sheet

- **Tertiary structure**—the folding of a protein molecule into a specific three-dimensional shape held together by noncovalent interactions primarily between amino acid side chains that can be quite far apart along the backbone and, in some cases, by disulfide bonds between side-chain thiol groups.

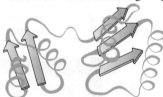

- **Quaternary structure**—two or more protein chains assembled in a larger three-dimensional structure held together by noncovalent interactions.

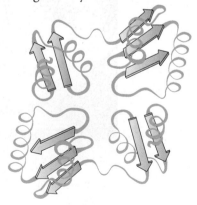

Classes of Proteins Summary

- *Fibrous proteins* are tough, insoluble, and composed of fibers and sheets.
- *Globular proteins* are water-soluble and have chains folded into compact shapes.
- *Simple proteins* contain only amino acid residues.
- *Conjugated proteins* include one or more non–amino acid units.

animals were slaughtered as a public health measure. Changes in the production procedures for feed supplements have greatly decreased the possibility of another episode of BSE. It is unlikely that humans will develop CJD from eating beef in the United States because all nerve and brain tissue as well as intestinal tissue are excluded from the food chain—both human and animal.

See Chemistry in Action Problems 18.82 and 18.83 at the end of the chapter.

SUMMARY: REVISITING THE CHAPTER GOALS

1. What are the structural features of amino acids?
Amino acids in body fluids have an ionized carboxylic acid group ($-COO^-$), an ionized amino group ($-NH_3^+$), and a side-chain R group bonded to a central carbon atom (the α-carbon). Twenty different amino acids occur in *proteins* (Table 18.3), connected by *peptide bonds* (amide bonds) formed between the carboxyl group of one amino acid and the amino group of the next (*see Problems 1–4, 6, 34–37, 86, 88, 89, 92, 94*).

2. What are the properties of amino acids? Amino acid side chains have acidic or basic functional groups or neutral groups that are either polar or nonpolar. In glycine, the "side chain" is a hydrogen atom. The dipolar ion in which the amino and carboxylic acid groups are both ionized is known as a *zwitterion*. For each amino acid, there is a distinctive *isoelectric point*—the pH at which the numbers of positive and negative charges in a solution are equal. At more acidic pH, some carboxylic acid groups are not ionized; at more basic pH, some amino groups are not ionized (*see Problems 2, 3, 5, 7, 8, 28, 38–41, 72, 73, 78, 79, 95*).

3. Why do amino acids have "handedness"? An object, including a molecule, has "handedness" —is *chiral*—when it has no plane of symmetry and thus has mirror images that cannot be superimposed on each other. A simple molecule can be identified as chiral if it contains a carbon atom bonded to four different groups. All α-amino acids except glycine meet this condition by having four different groups bonded to the α-carbon (*see Problems 9–14, 33, 42–49*).

4. What is the primary structure of a protein and what conventions are used for drawing and naming primary structures? Proteins are polymers of amino acids (*polypeptides*). Their *primary structure* is the linear sequence in which the amino acids are connected by peptide bonds. Using formulas or amino acid abbreviations, the primary structures are written with the amino-terminal end on the left ($^+H_3N-$) and the carboxyl-terminal end on the right ($-COO^-$). To name a peptide, the names of the amino acids are combined, starting at the amino-terminal end, with the endings of all but the carboxyl-terminal amino acid changed to *-yl*. Primary structures are often represented by combining three-letter abbreviations for the amino acids (*see Problems 15–19, 50–53, 63, 66, 67, 74–78*).

5. What types of interactions determine the overall shapes of proteins? Protein chains are drawn into their distinctive and biochemically active shapes by attractions between atoms along their backbones and between atoms in side-chain groups. Hydrogen bonding can occur between the backbone carbonyl groups and amide hydrogens of adjacent protein chains. *Noncovalent interactions* between side chains include ionic bonding between acidic and basic groups (*salt bridges*), and *hydrophobic interactions* among nonpolar groups. Covalent sulfur–sulfur bonds (*disulfide bonds*) can form bridges between the side chains in cysteine (*see Problems 21, 22, 29, 55–58, 90, 91*).

6. What are the secondary and tertiary structures of proteins? *Secondary structures* include the regular, repeating three-dimensional structures held in place by hydrogen bonding between backbone atoms within a chain or in adjacent chains. The α-helix is a coil with hydrogen bonding between carbonyl oxygen atoms and amide hydrogen atoms four amino acid residues farther along the same chain. The β-sheet is a pleated sheet with adjacent protein-chain segments connected by hydrogen bonding between peptide groups. The adjacent chains in the β-sheet may be parts of the same protein chain or different protein chains. Secondary structure mainly determines the properties of *fibrous proteins*, which are tough and insoluble. *Tertiary structure* is the overall three-dimensional shape of a folded protein chain. Tertiary structure determines the properties of *globular proteins*, which are water-soluble, with hydrophilic groups on the outside and hydrophobic groups on the inside. Globular proteins often contain regions of α-helix and/or β-sheet secondary structures (*see Problems 23–25, 30–32, 54, 57, 64, 65, 80, 81, 85–88*).

7. What is quaternary protein structure? Proteins that incorporate more than one peptide chain are said to have *quaternary structure*. In a quaternary structure, two or more folded protein subunits are united in a single structure by noncovalent interactions. Hemoglobin, for example, consists of two pairs of subunits, with a nonprotein heme molecule in each of the four subunits. Collagen is a fibrous protein composed of protein chains twisted together in triple helixes (*see Problems 26, 27, 80, 81*).

8. What chemical properties do proteins have? The peptide bonds are broken by *hydrolysis*, which may occur in acidic solution or during enzyme-catalyzed digestion of proteins in food. The end result of hydrolysis is production of the individual amino acids from the protein. *Denaturation* is the loss of overall structure by a protein while retaining its primary structure. Among the agents that cause denaturation are heat, mechanical agitation, pH change, and exposure to a variety of chemical agents, including detergents (*see Problems 20, 60, 61, 68–71, 82–85, 96–99*).

CONCEPT MAP: AMINO ACIDS AND PROTEINS

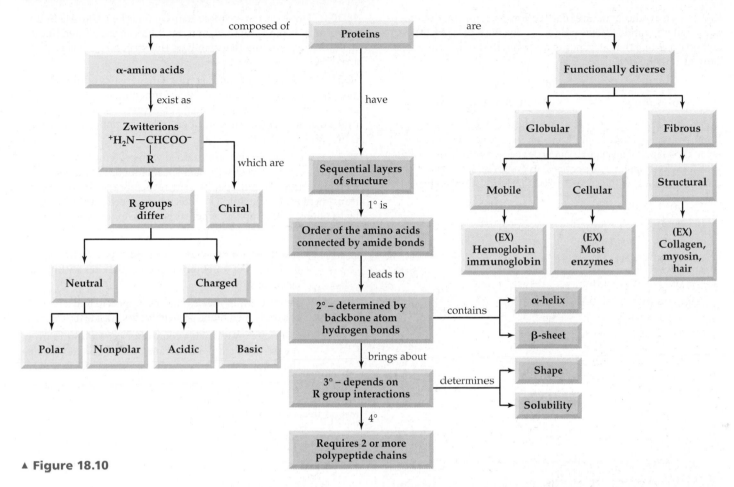

▲ **Figure 18.10**

Concept Map. Although the wide variety of structures that various proteins assume can seem complex, examination of the concept map in Figure 18.10 illustrates the connection between proteins, their building blocks (amino acids), and the fundamental principles underlying protein structure. The levels of structure are organized from simplest to most complex, and interrelated concepts are shown. The functional groups can be found in the Functional Group Flow Scheme (Figure 12.5) if you need to review those. Earlier concept maps (Figs. 4.7, 8.25) will aid in review of molecular interactions and bonding. All of these concepts are integrated in biological molecules.

KEY WORDS

Achiral, *p. 557*

Alpha- (α-) amino acid, *p. 551*

Alpha- (α-) helix, *p. 569*

Amino acid, *p. 551*

Amino-terminal amino acid (N-terminal amino acid), *p. 561*

Beta- (β-) sheet, *p. 570*

Carboxyl-terminal amino acid (C-terminal amino acid), *p. 561*

Chiral, *p. 557*

Chiral carbon atom, *p. 558*

Conjugated protein, *p. 573*

Denaturation, *p. 578*

Disulfide bond (in protein), *p. 567*

Enantiomers (optical isomers), *p. 558*

Fibrous protein, *p. 571*

Globular protein, *p. 571*

Hydrophilic, *p. 554*

Hydrophobic, *p. 554*

Isoelectric point (pI), *p. 555*

Native protein, *p. 572*

Noncovalent forces, *p. 554*

Peptide bond, *p. 551*

Primary protein structure, *p. 560*

Protein, *p. 551*

Quaternary protein structure, *p. 573*

Residue (amino acid), *p. 561*

Secondary protein structure, *p. 569*

Side chain (amino acid), *p. 551*

Simple protein, *p. 573*

Stereoisomers, *p. 558*

Tertiary protein structure, *p. 572*

Zwitterion, *p. 555*

UNDERSTANDING KEY CONCEPTS

18.28 Draw the structure of the following amino acids, dipeptides, and tripeptides at low pH (pH 1) and high pH (pH 14). At each pH, assume that all functional groups that might do so are ionized. (Hint: See Worked Example 18.2)

(a) Val   (d) Glu-Asp

(b) Arg   (e) Gln-Ala-Asn

(c) Tyr- Ser   (f) Met-Trp-Cys

18.29 Interactions of amino acids on the interior of proteins are key to the shapes of proteins. In group (a) below, which pairs of amino acids form hydrophobic interactions? In group (b), which pairs form ionic interactions? Which pairs in group (c) form hydrogen bonds?

(a) 1 Pro ... Phe

  2 Lys ... Ser

  3 Thr ... Leu

  4 Ala ... Gly

(b) 1 Val ... Leu

  2 Glu ... Lys

  3 Met ... Cys

  4 Asp ... His

(c) 1 Cys ... Cys

  2 Asp ... Ser

  3 Val ... Gly

  4 Met ... Cys

18.30 Draw the hexapeptide Asp-Gly-Phe-Leu-Glu-Ala in linear form showing all of the atoms, and show (using dotted lines) the hydrogen bonding that stabilizes this structure if it is part of an α-helix.

18.31 Compare and contrast the characteristics of fibrous and globular proteins. Consider biological function, water solubility, amino acid composition, secondary structure, and tertiary structure. Give examples of three fibrous and three globular proteins. (Hint: Make a table.)

18.32 Cell membranes are studded with proteins. Some of these proteins, involved in the transport of molecules across the membrane into the cell, span the entire membrane and are called trans-membrane proteins. The interior of the cell membrane is hydrophobic and nonpolar, whereas both the extracellular and intracellular fluids are water-based.

(a) List three amino acids you would expect to find in the part of a trans-membrane protein that lies within the cell membrane.

(b) List three amino acids you would expect to find in the part of a trans-membrane protein that lies outside the cell.

(c) List three amino acids you would expect to find in the part of a trans-membrane protein that lies inside the cell.

18.33 Threonine has two chiral centers. Draw L-threonine and indicate which carbon atoms are chiral. Which carbon atom is responsible for D and L configuration?

ADDITIONAL PROBLEMS

AMINO ACIDS

18.34 What amino acids do the following abbreviations stand for? Draw the structure of each.

(a) Val   (b) Ser   (c) Glu

18.35 What amino acids do the following abbreviations stand for? Draw the structure of each.

(a) Ile   (b) Thr   (c) Gln

18.36 Name and draw the structures of the amino acids that fit these descriptions:

(a) Contains a thiol group

(b) Contains a phenol group

18.37 Name and draw the structures of the amino acids that fit these descriptions:

(a) Contains an isopropyl group

(b) Contains a secondary alcohol group

18.38 At neutral pH, which of the following amino acids has a net positive charge, which has a net negative charge, and which is neutral? (Hint: Draw the various charged forms of each amino acid before deciding.)

(a) Asparagine   (b) Lysine   (c) Proline

18.39 At neutral pH, which of the following amino acids has a net positive charge, which has a net negative charge, and which is neutral? (Hint: Draw the various charged forms of each amino acid before deciding.)

(a) Aspartic acid

(b) Histidine

(c) Valine

18.40 Which of the following forms of aspartic acid would you expect to predominate at low pH, neutral pH, and high pH?

(a) $HOC(=O)-CH_2CH(^+NH_3)-CO^-(=O)$

(b) $^-OC(=O)-CH_2CH(NH_2)-CO^-(=O)$

(c) $HOC(=O)-CH_2CH(^+NH_3)-COH(=O)$

18.41 Which of the following forms of lysine would you expect to predominate at low pH, neutral pH, and high pH?

(a)
$$\overset{+}{NH_3}-\overset{\overset{\displaystyle H}{|}}{C}-\overset{\overset{\displaystyle O}{||}}{C}-O^-$$
$$\underset{\underset{\displaystyle NH_3^+}{|}}{\underset{(CH_2)_4}{|}}$$

(b)
$$\overset{+}{NH_3}-\overset{\overset{\displaystyle H}{|}}{C}-\overset{\overset{\displaystyle O}{||}}{C}-OH$$
$$\underset{\underset{\displaystyle NH_3^+}{|}}{\underset{(CH_2)_4}{|}}$$

(c)
$$\overset{+}{NH_3}-\overset{\overset{\displaystyle H}{|}}{C}-\overset{\overset{\displaystyle O}{||}}{C}-O^-$$
$$\underset{\underset{\displaystyle NH_2}{|}}{\underset{(CH_2)_4}{|}}$$

HANDEDNESS IN MOLECULES

18.42 What does the term *chiral* mean? Give two examples.

18.43 What does the term *achiral* mean? Give two examples.

18.44 Which of the following objects is chiral?

(a) A mayonnaise jar   (b) A screw   (c) A brick

18.45 Which of the following objects is achiral?

(a) A pair of scissors   (b) A comb

(c) A drinking glass

18.46 Draw the structures of the following compounds. Which of them is chiral? Mark each chiral carbon with an asterisk.

(a) 2-Bromo-2-chloropropane

(b) 2-Bromo-2-chlorobutane

(c) 2-Bromo-2-chloro-3-methylbutane

18.47 Draw the structures of the following compounds. Which of them is chiral? Mark each chiral carbon with an asterisk.

(a) 2-Chloropentane   (b) Cyclopentane

(c) Methylpropanol

18.48 Draw leucine and identify any chiral carbon atoms with arrows.

18.49 Draw isoleucine and identify any chiral carbon atoms with arrows.

PEPTIDES AND PROTEINS

18.50 What is the difference between a simple protein and a conjugated protein?

18.51 What kinds of molecules are found in the following classes of conjugated proteins in addition to the protein part?

(a) Metalloproteins   (b) Hemoproteins

(c) Lipoproteins   (d) Nucleoproteins

18.52 Name four biological functions of proteins in the human body, and give an example of a protein for each function.

18.53 What kind of biological function would each of the following proteins perform?

(a) human growth hormone   (b) myosin

(c) protease   (d) myoglobin

18.54 What is meant by the following terms as they apply to protein structure, and what bonds or molecular interactions stabilize that level of structure?

(a) Primary structure   (b) Secondary structure

(c) Tertiary structure   (d) Quaternary structure

18.55 What level of protein structure is determined by

(a) Peptide bonds between amino acids?

(b) Hydrogen bonds between backbone carbonyl oxygen atoms and hydrogen atoms attached to backbone nitrogen atoms?

(c) R group interactions that may involve van der Waals forces, ionic interactions, or hydrogen bonds?

18.56 Why is cysteine such an important amino acid for defining the tertiary structure of some proteins?

18.57 What conditions are required for disulfide bonds to form between cysteine residues in a protein?

18.58 How do the following noncovalent interactions help to stabilize the tertiary and quaternary structure of a protein? Give an example of a pair of amino acids that could give rise to each interaction.

(a) Hydrophobic interactions

(b) Salt bridges (ionic interactions)

18.59 How do the following interactions help to stabilize the tertiary and quaternary structure of a protein? Give an example of a pair of amino acids that could give rise to each interaction.

(a) Side-chain hydrogen bonding

(b) Disulfide bonds

18.60 What kinds of changes take place in a protein when it is denatured?

18.61 Explain how a protein is denatured by the following:

(a) Heat   (b) Strong acids

(c) Organic solvents

18.62 Use the three-letter abbreviations to name all tripeptides that contain valine, methionine, and leucine.

18.63 Write structural formulas for the two dipeptides that contain leucine and aspartate.

18.64 Which of the following amino acids is most likely to be found on the outside of a globular protein, and which of them is more likely to be found on the inside? Explain each answer. (Hint: Consider the effect of the amino acid side chain in each case.)

(a) Valine   (b) Aspartate

(c) Histidine   (d) Alanine

18.65 Which of the following amino acids is most likely to be found on the outside of a globular protein? Which is more likely to be found on the inside? Explain each answer. (Hint: Consider the effect of the amino acid side chain in each case.)

(a) Leucine

(b) Glutamate

(c) Phenylalanine

(d) Glutamine

18.66 The *endorphins* are a group of naturally occurring neurotransmitters that act in a manner similar to morphine to control pain. Research has shown that the biologically active parts of the endorphin molecules are simple pentapeptides called *enkephalins*. Draw the structure of the methionine enkephalin with the sequence Tyr-Gly-Gly-Phe-Met. Identify the N-terminal and C-terminal amino acids.

18.67 Refer to Problem 18.66. Draw the structure of the leucine enkephalin with the sequence Tyr-Gly-Gly-Phe-Leu. Identify the N-terminal and C-terminal amino acids.

PROPERTIES AND REACTIONS OF AMINO ACIDS AND PROTEINS

18.68 Much of the chemistry of amino acids is the familiar chemistry of carboxylic acids and amine functional groups. What products would you expect to obtain from the following reactions of glycine?

(a) $\overset{+}{H_3N}-CH_2-\overset{\overset{\displaystyle O}{\|}}{C}O^- + HCl \longrightarrow ?$

(b) $\overset{+}{H_3N}-CH_2-\overset{\overset{\displaystyle O}{\|}}{C}OH + CH_3OH \xrightarrow{H^+ \text{ catalyst}} ?$

18.69 A scientist tried to prepare the simple dipeptide glycylglycine by the following reaction:

$$2\ \overset{+}{H_3N}CH_2\overset{\overset{\displaystyle O}{\|}}{C}O^- \longrightarrow \overset{+}{H_3N}CH_2\overset{\overset{\displaystyle O}{\|}}{C}NHCH_2\overset{\overset{\displaystyle O}{\|}}{C}O^-$$

An unexpected product formed during the reaction. This product is found to have the molecular formula $C_4H_6N_2O_2$ and to contain two peptide bonds. What happened?

18.70 (a) Identify the amino acids present in the peptide shown below.

(b) Identify the N-terminal and C-terminal amino acids of the peptide.

(c) Show the structures of the products that are obtained on digestion of the peptide at physiological pH (pH 7.4).

$$\overset{+}{H_3N}-CH-\overset{\overset{\displaystyle O}{\|}}{C}-N-CH-\overset{\overset{\displaystyle O}{\|}}{C}-N-CH-\overset{\overset{\displaystyle O}{\|}}{C}-N-CH-\overset{\overset{\displaystyle O}{\|}}{C}-N-CHCO^-$$

with side chains CH_3CHCH_3, H (on N), H (on N), CH_2OH, H (on N), CH_3, H (on N), CH_2COO^-

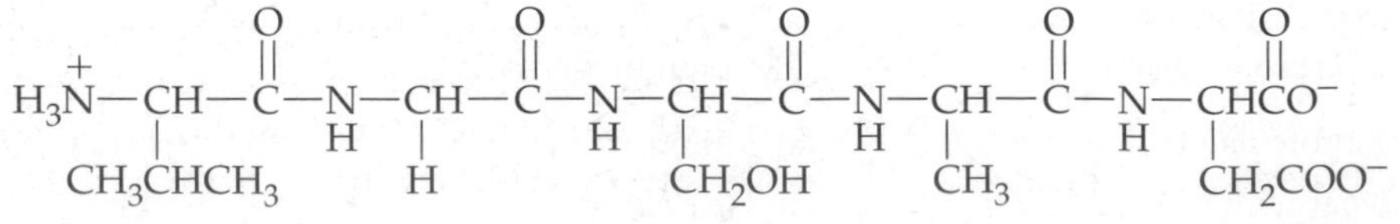

18.71 (a) Identify the amino acids present in the peptide shown below.

(b) Identify the N-terminal and C-terminal amino acids of the peptide.

(c) Show the structures of the products that are obtained on digestion of the peptide at physiological pH (pH 7.4).

$$\overset{+}{H_3N}-CH-\overset{\overset{\displaystyle O}{\|}}{C}-N-CH-\overset{\overset{\displaystyle O}{\|}}{C}-N-CH-\overset{\overset{\displaystyle O}{\|}}{C}-N-CH-COO^-$$

with side chains CH_2–SH; $(CH_2)_4$–$\overset{+}{N}H_3$; $(CH_2)_2$–C–O^- (with $\|O$); and CH_2 CH_2 CH_2 (ring)

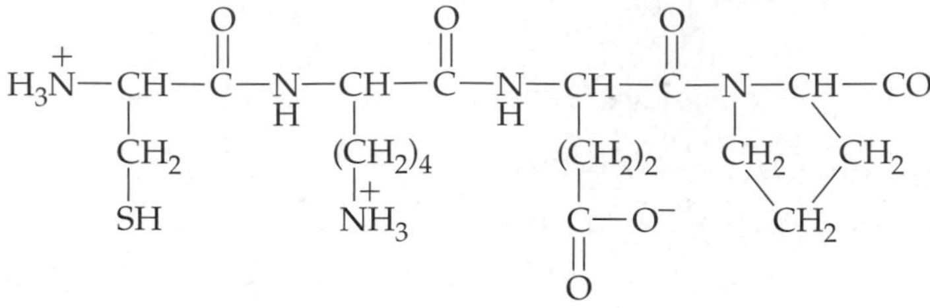

18.72 Which would you expect to be more soluble in water, a peptide containing mostly alanine and leucine or a peptide containing mostly lysine and aspartate? Explain. (Hint: Consider side-chain interactions with water.)

18.73 Proteins are usually least soluble in water at their isoelectric points. Explain.

CHEMISTRY IN ACTION

18.74 Why is it more important to have a daily source of protein than a daily source of fat or carbohydrates? [*Proteins in the Diet, p. 564*]

18.75 What is an incomplete protein? [*Proteins in the Diet, p. 564*]

18.76 In general, which is more likely to contain a complete (balanced) protein for human use—food from plant sources or food from animal sources? Explain. [*Proteins in the Diet, p. 564*]

18.77 Two of the most complete (balanced) proteins (that is, proteins that have the best ratio of the amino acids for humans) are cow's milk protein (casein) and egg-white protein. Explain why (not surprisingly) these are very balanced proteins for human growth and development. [*Proteins in the Diet, p. 564*]

18.78 The proteins collagen, bovine insulin, and human hemoglobin have isoelectric points of 6.6, 5.4, and 7.1, respectively. Suppose a sample containing these proteins is subjected to electrophoresis in a buffer at pH 6.6. Describe the motion of each with respect to the positive and negative electrodes in the electrophoresis apparatus. [*Protein Analysis by Electrophoresis, p. 568*]

18.79 Three dipeptides are separated by electrophoresis at pH 5.8. If the dipeptides are Arg-Trp, Asp-Thr, and Val-Met, describe the motion of each with respect to the positive and negative electrodes in the electrophoresis apparatus. [*Protein Analysis by Electrophoresis, p. 568*]

18.80 In the middle ages, both citizens of besieged cities and members of the armies laying siege would die of scurvy, a non-contagious disease, during long sieges. Explain why this would occur. [*Collagen—A Tale of Two Diseases, p. 576*]

18.81 Describe the cause of the biochemical defect and the defect itself that results in osteogenesis imperfecta. [*Collagen—A Tale of Two Diseases, p. 576*]

18.82 The change from a normal to a disease-causing prion results in a change from α-helices to β-sheets. How might this change alter the overall structure and intermolecular forces in the prion? [*Prions: Proteins That Cause Disease, p. 579*]

18.83 List the properties of disease-causing prions that made their existence difficult to accept. [*Prions: Proteins That Cause Disease, p. 579*]

GENERAL QUESTIONS AND PROBLEMS

18.84 What is the difference between protein digestion and protein denaturation? Both occur after a meal.

18.85 Why is hydrolysis of a protein not considered to be denaturation?

18.86 Bradykinin, a peptide that helps to regulate blood pressure, has the primary structure Arg-Pro-Pro-Gly-Phe-Ser-Pro-Phe-Arg.

   (a) Draw the complete structural formula of bradykinin.

   (b) Bradykinin has a very kinked secondary structure. Why?

18.87 For each amino acid listed, tell whether its influence on tertiary structure is largely through hydrophobic interactions, hydrogen bonding, formation of salt bridges, covalent bonding, or some combination of these effects.

   (a) Tyrosine   **(b)** Cysteine   **(c)** Asparagine

   (d) Lysine   **(e)** Tryptophan   **(f)** Alanine

   (g) Leucine   **(h)** Methionine

18.88 Oxytocin is a small peptide that is used to induce labor by causing contractions in uterine walls. It has the primary structure Cys-Tyr-Ile-Gln-Asn-Cys-Pro-Leu-Gln. This peptide is held in a cyclic configuration by a disulfide bridge. Draw a diagram of oxytocin, showing the disulfide bridge.

18.89 Methionine has a sulfur atom in its formula. Explain why methionine does not form disulfide bridges.

18.90 List the amino acids that are capable of hydrogen bonding if included in a peptide chain. Draw an example of two of these amino acids hydrogen bonding to one another. For each one, draw a hydrogen bond to water in a separate sketch. Refer to Section 8.11 for help with drawing hydrogen bonds.

18.91 Four of the most abundant amino acids in proteins are leucine, alanine, glycine, and valine. What do these amino acids have in common? Would you expect these amino acids to be found on the interior or on the exterior of the protein?

18.92 Globular proteins are water-soluble, whereas fibrous proteins are insoluble in water. Indicate whether you expect the following amino acids to be on the surface of a globular protein or on the surface of a fibrous protein.

   (a) Ala   **(b)** Glu   **(c)** Leu

   (d) Phe   **(e)** Ser   **(f)** Val

18.93 Figure 18.7 shows sharp directional changes in the path of the peptide-chain. This can be seen in both the ribbon model and the space-filling rendering. These sharp directional changes connecting adjacent regions of secondary structure are often referred to either as "reverse turns" or as "bends." The two most common amino acids in reverse turns are glycine and proline. Use your knowledge of the structures of these two amino acids to speculate on why they might be found in reverse turns.

18.94 During sickle-cell anemia research to determine the modification involved in sickling, sequencing of the affected person's hemoglobin β-subunit reveals that the sixth amino acid is valine rather than glutamate; thus, the replacement of glutamate by valine severely alters the three-dimensional structure of hemoglobin. Which amino acid, if it replaced the Glu, would cause the least disruption in hemoglobin structure? Why?

18.95 A family visits their physician with their sick child. The four-month-old baby is pale, has obvious episodes of pain, and is not thriving. The doctor orders a series of blood tests, including a test for hemoglobin types. The results show that the infant is not only anemic but that the anemia is due to sickle-cell anemia. The family wants to know if their other two children have sickle-cell anemia, sickle-cell trait, or no sickle-cell gene at all.

   (a) What test will be used?

   (b) Sketch the expected results if samples for each child are tested at the same time.

   (c) What is the difference between sickle-cell anemia and sickle-cell trait?

18.96 Fresh pineapple cannot be used in gelatin desserts because it contains an enzyme that hydrolyzes the proteins in gelatin, destroying the gelling action. Canned pineapple can be added to gelatin with no problem. Why?

18.97 As a chef, you prepare a wide variety of foods daily. The following dishes all contain protein. What method (if any) has been used to denature the protein present in each food?

   (a) Charcoal grilled steak

   (b) Pickled pigs' feet

   (c) Meringue

   (d) Steak tartare (raw chopped beef)

   (e) Salt pork

18.98 Why do you suppose individuals with diabetes must receive insulin subcutaneously by injection rather than orally?

18.99 Individuals with phenylketonuria (PKU) are sensitive to phenylalanine in their diet. Why is a warning on foods containing aspartame (L-aspartyL-L-phenylalanine methyl ester) of concern to individuals with PKU?

18.100 What could you prepare for dinner for a strict vegan that provides all of the essential amino acids in appropriate amounts? (Remember, strict vegans do not eat meat, eggs, milk, or products that contain those animal products.)

CHAPTER 19

Enzymes and Vitamins

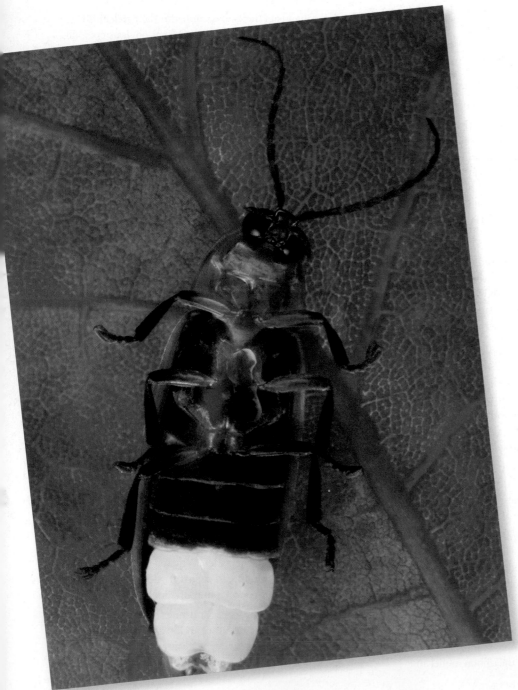

◄ Luciferinase, an enzyme found in firefly tails, yields light as a reaction product.

CONTENTS

1. **What are enzymes?**
   THE GOAL: Be able to describe the chemical nature of enzymes and their function in biochemical reactions. (◀◀◀ E.)

2. **How do enzymes work, and why are they so specific?**
   THE GOAL: Be able to provide an overview of what happens as one or more substrates and an enzyme come together so that the catalyzed reaction can occur, and be able to list the properties of enzymes that make their specificity possible. (◀◀◀ A, E.)

3. **What effects do temperature, pH, enzyme concentration, and substrate concentration have on enzyme activity?**
   THE GOAL: Be able to describe the changes in enzyme activity that result when temperature, pH, enzyme concentration, or substrate concentration change. (◀◀◀ B, C, D.)

4. **How is enzyme activity regulated?**
   THE GOAL: Be able to define and identify feedback control, allosteric control, reversible and irreversible inhibition, inhibition by covalent modification, and genetic control of enzymes. (◀◀◀ B.)

5. **What are vitamins and minerals?**
   THE GOAL: Be able to describe the two major classes of vitamins, the reasons vitamins are necessary in our diets, and the general results of excesses or deficiencies. Be able to identify essential minerals, explain why minerals are necessary in the diet, and explain the results of deficiencies. (◀◀◀ A, B.)

Think of your body as a living chemical laboratory. Although the analogy is not perfect, there is a good deal of relevance to it. In your body, as in the laboratory, chemical reactions are the major activity. In a laboratory, however, chemical reactions are carried out singly by mixing pure chemicals in individual containers. In your body, many thousands of reactions take place simultaneously in the same cells or body fluids.

An important difference between chemistry in a laboratory and chemistry in a living organism is control. In a laboratory, the speed of a reaction is controlled by adjusting experimental conditions such as temperature, solvent, and pH. In an organism, these conditions cannot be adjusted. The human body must maintain a temperature of 37 °C, the solvent must be water, and the pH must be close to 7.4 in most body fluids.

Animals and plants are composed of millions of cells organized into different functional types. Among the many thousands of protein molecules in each cell, there are more than 2000 different specialized proteins, called enzymes, each one used in a different reaction. Although enzymes—powerful and highly selective biological catalysts—carry out the chemical reactions in cells, how do cells organize so many different reactions so that all occur to the proper extent? The answer is that all enzyme reactions in living organisms are under tight regulation by a variety of mechanisms.

In this chapter, the focus will be on enzymes and the regulation of enzymatic reactions. We will also look at *vitamins* and *minerals*, because they are essential to the function of certain enzymes. Chapter 28 is devoted to the role of *hormones* and *neurotransmitters* in keeping our biochemistry under control, which they do primarily by regulating the activity of enzymes.

19.1 Catalysis by Enzymes

Catalysts accelerate the rates of chemical reactions but at the end of the reaction have undergone no change themselves. **Enzymes**, the catalysts of biochemical reactions, fit this definition. Like all catalysts, an enzyme does not affect the equilibrium point of a reaction and cannot bring about a reaction that is energetically unfavorable. Rather, an enzyme decreases the time it takes for the reaction to reach equilibrium by lowering its activation energy.

Enzymes, with few exceptions, are water-soluble globular proteins (Section 18.9). As proteins, they are far larger and more complex molecules than simple inorganic catalysts.

Enzyme A protein or other molecule that acts as a catalyst for a biological reaction.

▶▶▶ See Figure 7.4 for a visual representation of the effect of a catalyst on a reaction's activation energy.

Active site A pocket in an enzyme with the specific shape and chemical makeup necessary to bind a substrate.

Substrate A reactant in an enzyme-catalyzed reaction.

Specificity (enzyme) The limitation of the activity of an enzyme to a specific substrate, specific reaction, or specific type of reaction.

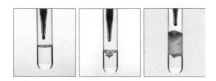

▲ **Figure 19.1**
In the experiment shown, a drop of blood is added to a solution of hydrogen peroxide, the colorless liquid in the test tube. Catalase in red blood cells reacts rapidly with hydrogen peroxide, releasing oxygen gas, which causes the foam observed in the third panel.

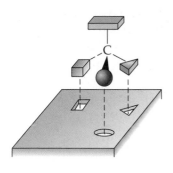

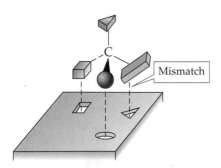

▲ **Figure 19.2**
A chiral reactant and a chiral reaction site.
The enantiomer at the top fits the reaction site like a hand in a glove, but the enantiomer at the bottom does not fit and therefore cannot be a substrate for this enzyme.

Turnover number The maximum number of substrate molecules acted upon by one molecule of enzyme per unit time.

Because of their size and complexity, enzymes have more ways available in which to connect with reactants, speed up reactions, and be controlled by other molecules.

Within the folds of an enzyme's protein chain is the **active site**—the region where the reaction takes place. The active site has the specific shape and chemical reactivity needed to catalyze the reaction. One or more **substrates**, the reactants in an enzyme-catalyzed reaction, are held in place by attractions to groups that line the active site.

The extent to which an enzyme's activity is limited to a certain substrate and a certain type of reaction is referred to as the **specificity** of the enzyme. Enzymes differ greatly in their specificity. *Catalase*, for example, is almost completely specific for one reaction—the decomposition of hydrogen peroxide (Figure 19.1). This reaction is needed to destroy the peroxide before it oxidizes essential biomolecules, thereby damaging them:

$$2 \, H_2O_2 \xrightleftharpoons[\text{Catalase}]{} 2 \, H_2O + O_2 \, (g)$$

Thrombin is specific for catalyzing hydrolysis of a peptide bond following an arginine, and primarily acts on fibrinogen, a protein essential to blood clotting. When this bond breaks, the product (fibrin) proceeds to polymerize into a blood clot (Section 29.5). *Carboxypeptidase A* is less limited—it removes many different C-terminal amino acid residues from protein chains during digestion. And the enzyme *papain* from papaya fruit catalyzes the hydrolysis of peptide bonds in many locations. It is this ability to break down proteins that accounts for the use of papain in meat tenderizers, in contact-lens cleaners, and in cleansing dead or infected tissue from wounds (*debridement*).

Since the amino acids in enzymes are all L-amino acids, it should come as no surprise that enzymes are also specific with respect to stereochemistry. If a substrate is chiral, an enzyme usually catalyzes the reaction of only one of the pair of enantiomers because only one fits the active site in such a way that the reaction can occur. The enzyme lactate dehydrogenase, for example, catalyzes the removal of hydrogen from L-lactate but not from D-lactate:

$$\underset{\text{L-Lactate}}{\underset{\displaystyle \begin{array}{c} O=C-O^- \\ | \\ HO-C-H \\ | \\ CH_3 \end{array}}{}} + NAD^+ \xrightleftharpoons[\text{dehydrogenase}]{\text{Lactate}} \underset{\text{Pyruvate}}{\underset{\displaystyle \begin{array}{c} O=C-O^- \\ | \\ C=O \\ | \\ CH_3 \end{array}}{}} + NADH + H^+$$

This is another example of the importance of molecular shape in biochemistry. The specificity of an enzyme for one of two enantiomers is a matter of fit. A left-handed enzyme cannot fit with a right-handed substrate any more than a left-handed glove fits on a right hand (Figure 19.2).

The catalytic activity of an enzyme is measured by its **turnover number**, the maximum number of substrate molecules acted upon by one molecule of enzyme per unit time (Table 19.1). Most enzymes turn over 10–1000 molecules per second, but some are much faster. Catalase, with its essential role in protecting against molecular damage, is one of the fastest—it can turn over 10 million molecules per second. This is the fastest reaction rate attainable in the body because it is the rate at which molecules collide.

PROBLEM 19.1
Which of the enzymes listed in Table 19.1 catalyzes a maximum of 100 reactions per second?

PROBLEM 19.2
Why is it essential to rinse contact lenses in saline solution after they have been cleaned by an enzyme solution and before they are placed in the eyes?

TABLE **19.1** Turnover Numbers for Some Enzymes		
Enzyme	**Reaction Catalyzed**	**Turnover Number (Maximum Number of Catalytic Events Per Second)**
Papain	Hydrolysis of peptide bonds	10
Ribonuclease	Hydrolysis of phosphate ester link in RNA	10^2
Kinase	Transfer of phosphoryl group between substrates	10^3
Acetylcholinesterase	Deactivation of the neurotransmitter acetylcholine	10^4
Carbonic anhydrase	Converts CO_2 to HCO_3^-	10^6
Catalase	Decomposition of H_2O_2 to $H_2O + O_2$	10^7

19.2 Enzyme Cofactors

Many enzymes are conjugated proteins that require nonprotein portions known as **cofactors** as part of their functional structure. Some cofactors are metal ions, and others are nonprotein organic molecules called **coenzymes**. To be active, an enzyme may require a metal ion, a coenzyme, or both. Some enzyme cofactors are tightly held by noncovalent attractions or are covalently bound to their enzymes; others are more loosely bound so that they can enter and leave the active site as needed.

Why are cofactors necessary? The functional groups in enzyme proteins are limited to those of the amino acid side chains in the protein. By combining with cofactors, enzymes acquire chemically reactive groups not available in side chains. For example, the NAD^+ reactant in the equation for the dehydrogenation of L-lactate shown in Section 19.1 is a coenzyme and is the oxidizing agent that makes the reaction possible. (Vitamins that function as cofactors are discussed in Section 19.10.)

The requirement that many enzymes have for metal ion cofactors explains our dietary need for trace minerals. The ions of iron, zinc, copper, manganese, molybdenum, cobalt, nickel, vanadium, and selenium all function as enzyme cofactors. These ions are able to form coordinate covalent bonds by accepting lone-pair electrons present on nitrogen or oxygen atoms in enzymes or substrates.

This bonding may anchor a substrate in the active site and may also allow the metal ion to participate in the catalyzed reaction. For example, every molecule of the digestive enzyme carboxypeptidase A contains one Zn^{2+} ion that is essential for its catalytic action. We say that the zinc ion is "coordinated" to two nitrogens in histidine side chains and one oxygen in a glutamate side chain. In this way, the ion is held in place in the active site of the enzyme.

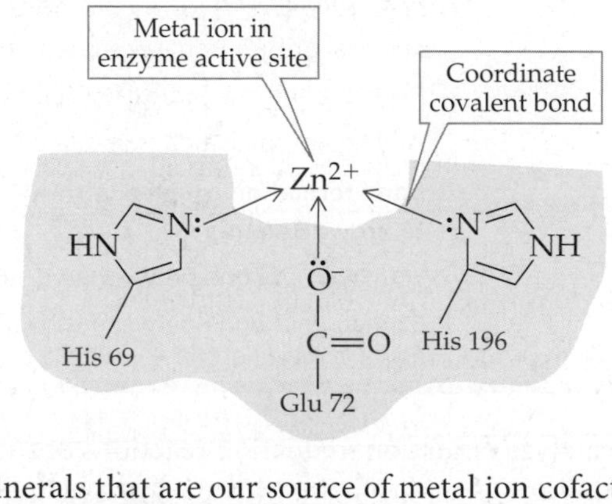

Cofactor A nonprotein part of an enzyme that is essential to the enzyme's catalytic activity; a metal ion or a coenzyme.

Coenzyme An organic molecule that acts as an enzyme cofactor.

▶▶▶ Recall from Section 4.4 that a coordinate covalent bond is one that is formed when both electrons are donated by the same atom.

Like the trace minerals that are our source of metal ion cofactors, certain vitamins are also a dietary necessity for humans because we cannot synthesize them, yet they are critical building blocks for coenzymes.

PROBLEM 19.3

Check the label on a bottle of multivitamin/multimineral tablets and identify the metal ion cofactors listed on the preceding page that are included in the supplement.

 KEY CONCEPT PROBLEM 19.4

The cofactors NAD^+, Cu^{2+}, Zn^{2+}, coenzyme A, FAD, and Ni^{2+} are all needed by your body for enzymatic reactions.

(a) Which coenzymes have vitamins as part of their structure? (Hint: Look ahead in this chapter to the structures of the vitamins.)

(b) What is the primary difference between the coenzymes and the remaining cofactors in the list?

19.3 Enzyme Classification

Enzymes are divided into six main classes according to the general kind of reaction catalyzed, and each main class is further subdivided based on substrate specificity (Table 19.2). Most of the names of the main classes are self-explanatory; they are listed below with examples:

TABLE 19.2 Classification of Enzymes

Main Class and Subclass	Examples of Reaction Types Catalyzed
Oxidoreductases	**Oxidation–reduction reactions**
Oxidases	Addition of O_2 to a substrate
Reductases	Reduction of a substrate
Dehydrogenases	Removal of two atoms to form a double bond
Transferases	**Transfer of functional groups**
Transaminases	Transfer of amino group between substrates
Kinases	Transfer of a phosphoryl group between substrates
Hydrolases	**Hydrolysis reactions**
Lipases	Hydrolysis of ester groups in lipids
Proteases	Hydrolysis of peptide bonds in proteins
Nucleases	Hydrolysis of phosphate ester bonds in nucleic acids
Isomerases	**Isomerization of a substrate**
Lyases	**Group elimination to form double bond or addition to a double bond**
Dehydrases	Removal of H_2O from substrate to give double bond
Decarboxylases	Replacement of a carboxyl group by a hydrogen
Synthases	Addition of small molecule to a double bond
Ligases	**Bond formation coupled with ATP hydrolysis to provide energy**
Synthetases	Formation of bond between two substrates
Carboxylases	Formation of bond between substrate and CO_2 to add a carboxyl group ($-COO^-$)

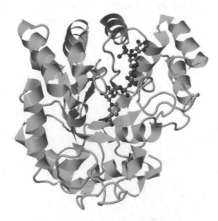

▲ The ribbon structure for aldose reductase, an oxidoreductase enzyme that reduces a C═O group in a sugar molecule to a ─C─OH group with the aid of the coenzyme NADH. The sugar glucose (orange) and NADH (gray) are shown in the active site of the enzyme.

- *Oxidoreductases* catalyze oxidation–reduction reactions of substrate molecules, most commonly addition or removal of oxygen or hydrogen. Because oxidation and reduction must occur together, these enzymes require coenzymes that are reduced or oxidized as the substrate is oxidized or reduced. Alcohol dehydrogenase is typical of this enzyme class. Found in liver cells, it oxidizes naturally occurring alcohols found in foods to aldehydes and ketones, providing the first step in metabolizing ethanol, a component of beer, wine, and distilled spirits.

$$A(\text{Reduced}) + B(\text{Oxidized}) \longrightarrow A'(\text{Oxidized}) + B'(\text{Reduced})$$

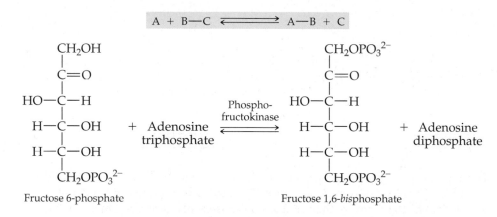

$$CH_3-CH_2-OH + NAD^+ \underset{\text{Alcohol dehydrogenase}}{\overset{}{\rightleftharpoons}} CH_3-\overset{\overset{\displaystyle O}{\|}}{C}-H + NADH + H^+$$

Reduced substrate | Oxidized coenzyme | Oxidized product | Reduced coenzyme

- **Transferases** catalyze transfer of a group from one molecule to another. Subclasses of transferases include transaminases, which transfer an amino group between substrates, and kinases, which transfer a phosphate group from adenosine triphosphate (ATP) to produce adenosine diphosphate (ADP) and a phosphorylated product. For example, phosphofructokinase transfers a phosphate group from ATP to fructose-6-phosphate to complete the energy priming process in the catabolism of glucose. Glucose catabolism is an important energy source for our bodies and is examined in depth in Chapter 22.

$$A + B-C \rightleftharpoons A-B + C$$

▲ The ribbon structure for adenylate kinase, a small transferase enzyme (194 amino acid residues), that adds a phosphate group to adenosine monophosphate.

- **Hydrolases** catalyze the hydrolysis of substrates—the breaking of bonds with addition of water. These enzymes are particularly important during digestion. Proteins are hydrolyzed into amino acids by various proteases, and carbohydrates such as starch, lactose, and sucrose are hydrolyzed to glucose, fructose, and galactose by specific enzymes. Hydrolases are essential to provide amino acids for protein synthesis and glucose for use in energy generating pathways.

$$A-B + H_2O \longrightarrow A-OH + B-H$$

- **Isomerases** catalyze the isomerization (rearrangement of atoms) of a substrate in reactions that have but one substrate and one product. In some metabolic pathways a molecule must be rearranged—isomerized—for the next step of the pathway to occur. During glycolysis (the catabolism of glucose for energy) the enzyme triose phosphate isomerase ensures that both of the products of the previous step can be fully metabolized. It does so by converting dihydroxyacetone phosphate, which otherwise cannot be further metabolized, to D-glyceraldehyde 3-phosphate, which is a substrate for the next enzyme in the glycolysis pathway. Because of isomerases, maximum energy can be obtained from glucose metabolism. Other metabolic pathways employ the same strategy.

$$A \longrightarrow B$$

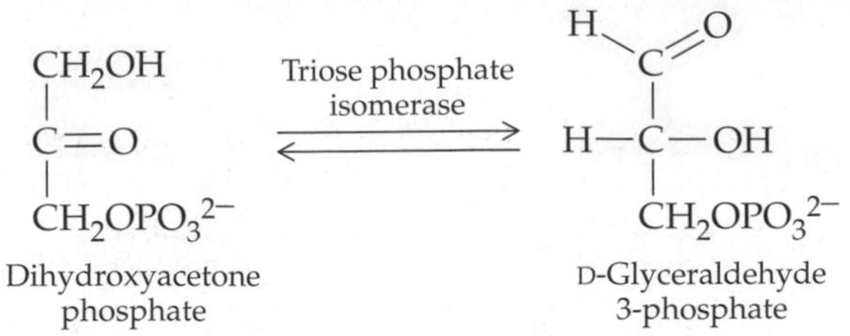

$$
\begin{array}{c}
CH_2OH \\
| \\
C=O \\
| \\
CH_2OPO_3^{2-}
\end{array}
\quad
\underset{\text{isomerase}}{\overset{\text{Triose phosphate}}{\rightleftarrows}}
\quad
\begin{array}{c}
H\text{—}C=O \\
| \\
H\text{—}C\text{—}OH \\
| \\
CH_2OPO_3^{2-}
\end{array}
$$

Dihydroxyacetone phosphate   D-Glyceraldehyde 3-phosphate

- *Lyases* (from the Greek *lein*, meaning "to break") catalyze the addition of a molecule such as H_2O, CO_2, or NH_3 to a double bond or the reverse reaction in which a molecule is eliminated to leave a double bond. Fumarase, an enzyme found in the citric acid cycle, is an example of a lyase. Other lyases are involved in the degradation of some amino acids such as histidine and tyrosine. Plant lyases are responsible for fruit softening and ripening by degrading pectin, a structural component of plant cell walls.

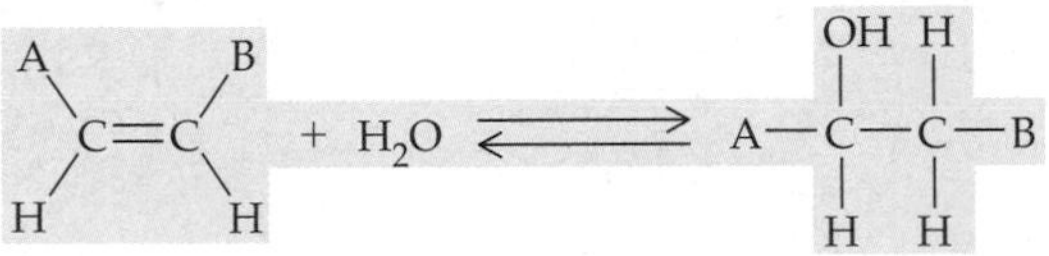

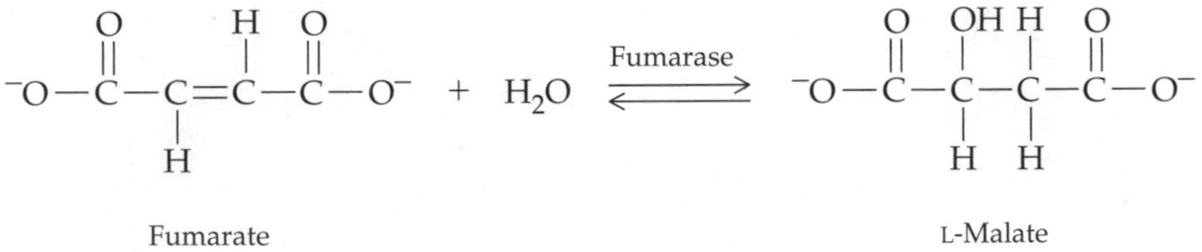

Fumarate   L-Malate

- *Ligases* (from the Latin *ligare*, meaning "to tie together") catalyze the bonding together of two substrate molecules. Because such reactions are generally not favorable, they require the simultaneous release of energy by a hydrolysis reaction, usually by the conversion of ATP to ADP (such energy release is discussed in Section 20.5). Ligases are involved in synthesis of biological polymers such as proteins and DNA. DNA ligase is a very important molecule used in DNA repair (in response to environmental damage such as UV rays from the sun or exposure to chemical carcinogens) and DNA replication (which occurs in cell division during development and tissue regeneration). The action of the ligase pyruvate carboxylase generates oxaloacetate, an important substrate of the energy-generating citric acid cycle, discussed in Chapter 20.

$$A + B + \text{Adenosine triphosphate (ATP)} \longrightarrow A\text{–}B + \text{Adenosine diphosphate (ADP)} + HOPO_3^{2-} + H^+$$

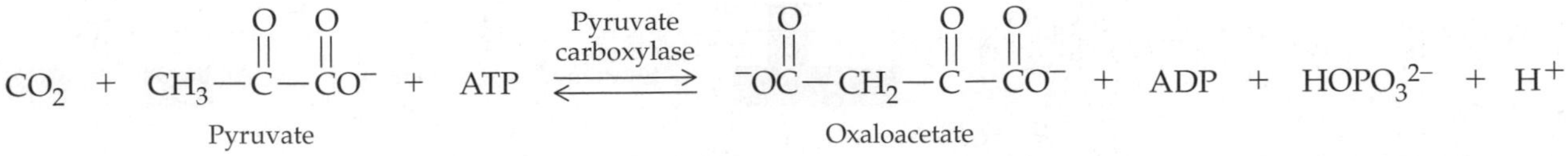

Note in the preceding examples that the enzymes have the family-name ending *-ase*. Exceptions to this rule occur for enzymes such as papain and trypsin, which are still referred to by older common names. The more informative modern systematic names typically have two parts: the first identifies the substrate on which the enzyme operates, and the second part is an enzyme subclass name like those shown in Table 19.2. For example, *pyruvate carboxylase* is a ligase that acts on the substrate *pyruvate* to add a *carboxyl group*. Sometimes enzymes are named by adding –ase to the substrate name, often dropping the terminal syllable. Fumarase, an enzyme that converts fumarate to succinate in the citric acid cycle, is one. The enzymes that act on a few other long-studied substrates such as urea and sucrose are named in the same way, i.e., urease and sucrase. Note also that some enzymes are capable of catalyzing both forward and reverse reactions, and where both directions are of significance, the equations are often written with double arrows.

Worked Example 19.1 Classifying Enzymes

To what class does the enzyme that catalyzes the following reaction belong?

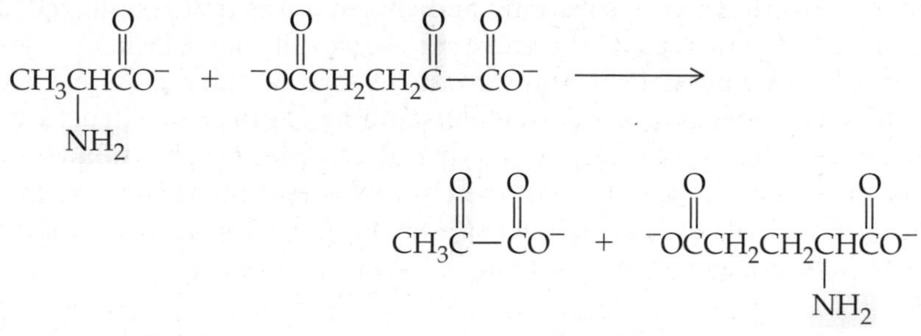

$$CH_3\underset{\underset{NH_2}{|}}{CH}CO^- \ + \ ^-OCCH_2CH_2\overset{O}{\overset{||}{C}}-CO^- \ \longrightarrow$$

$$CH_3\overset{O}{\overset{||}{C}}-CO^- \ + \ ^-OCCH_2CH_2\underset{\underset{NH_2}{|}}{CH}CO^-$$

ANALYSIS First, identify the type of reaction that has occurred. An amino group and a carbonyl group have changed places. Then, determine what class of enzyme catalyzes this type of reaction.

SOLUTION
The reaction is a transfer of an amino functional group; therefore, the enzyme is a transferase.

PROBLEM 19.5
Describe the reactions that you would expect these enzymes to catalyze.
(a) Alcohol dehydrogenase   (b) Aspartate transaminase
(c) Tyrosine-tRNA synthetase   (d) Phosphohexose isomerase

PROBLEM 19.6
Name the enzyme whose substrate is
(a) Urea   (b) Cellulose

PROBLEM 19.7
To what class of enzymes does hexokinase belong? Describe in general the reaction it catalyzes.

PROBLEM 19.8
Identify and describe the chemical change in the lyase-catalyzed reaction on p. 592. Identify the substrate(s) and product(s).

PROBLEM 19.9
Which of the following reactions can be catalyzed by a decarboxylase?
(a)

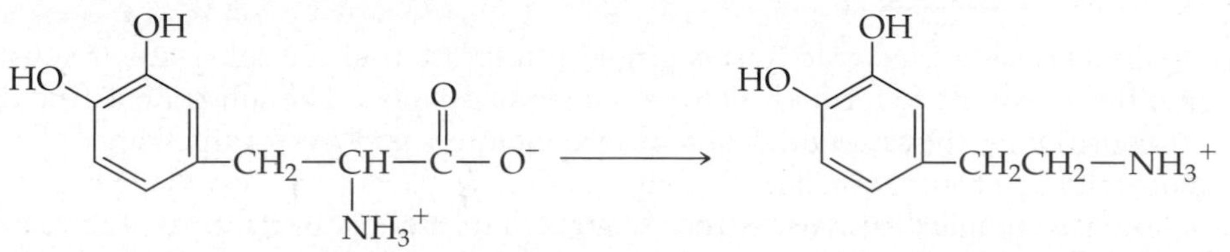

$$HO-\text{C}_6\text{H}_2(OH)-CH_2-\underset{\underset{NH_3^+}{|}}{CH}-\overset{O}{\overset{||}{C}}-O^- \longrightarrow HO-\text{C}_6\text{H}_2(OH)-CH_2CH_2-NH_3^+$$

(b)

$$^+H_3NCH_2CH_2CH_2-\overset{O}{\overset{||}{C}}-O^- \longrightarrow H-\overset{O}{\overset{||}{C}}-CH_2CH_2\overset{O}{\overset{||}{C}}-O^-$$

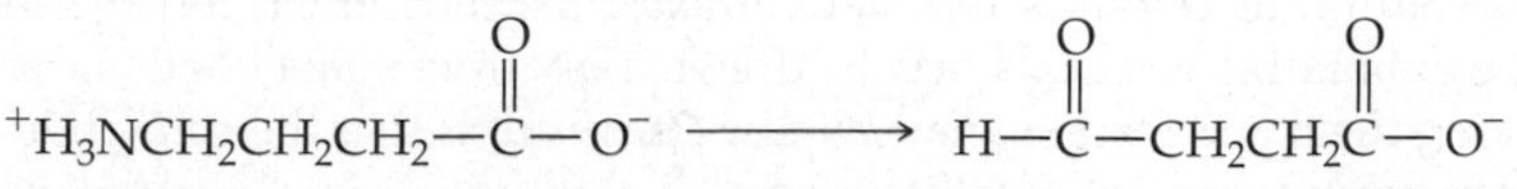

19.4 How Enzymes Work

Any theory of how enzymes work must explain why they are so specific and how they lower activation energies. The explanation for enzyme *specificity* is found in the active site. Exactly the right environment for the reaction is provided within the active site. There, amino acid side-chain groups from the enzyme attract and hold the substrate or substrates in position by noncovalent interactions and sometimes by temporary covalent bonding. The active site also has the groups needed for catalysis of the reaction.

Two models are invoked to represent the interaction between substrates and enzymes. Historically, the *lock-and-key model* came first; it was proposed when the need for a spatial fit between substrates and enzymes was first recognized. The substrate is described as fitting into the active site as a key fits into a lock.

When it became possible to study enzyme–substrate interaction more closely, a new model was needed. Our modern understanding of molecular structure makes it clear that enzyme molecules are not totally rigid, like locks. The **induced-fit model** accounts for changes in the shape of the enzyme active site that accommodate the substrate and facilitate the reaction. As an enzyme and substrate come together, their interaction *induces* exactly the right fit for catalysis of the reaction.

Induced-fit model A model of enzyme action in which the enzyme has a flexible active site that changes shape to best fit the substrate and catalyze the reaction.

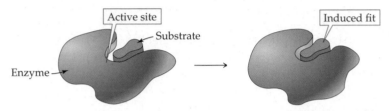

A well-studied example of induced fit, the interaction between glucose (a hexose) and hexokinase, is illustrated in Figure 19.3. The reaction, a common one, is a phosphorylation—the addition of a phosphoryl group to a —OH group, catalyzed by a kinase. The reaction is the first step in glucose metabolism (Section 22.2). Notice in Figure 19.3 how the enzyme closes in once the glucose molecule has entered the active site—this is the induced fit.

▶ **Figure 19.3**
The induced fit of hexokinase (blue) and its substrate, glucose (red).
(a) The active site is a groove in the hexokinase molecule. (b) When glucose enters the active site, the enzyme changes shape, wrapping itself more snugly around the substrate.

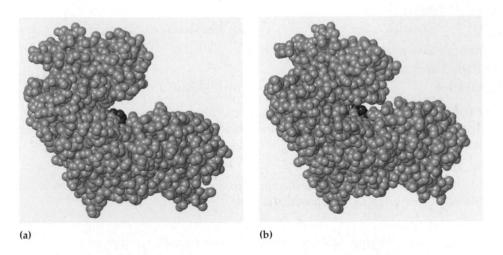

(a)　　　　　　　　　　(b)

Enzyme-catalyzed reactions begin with migration of the substrate or substrates into the active site to form an *enzyme–substrate complex*. The substrate is first drawn into position by the same kinds of noncovalent forces that govern the shapes of protein molecules (see Figure 18.4).

Before complex formation, the substrate molecule is in its most stable, lowest-energy shape. Within the enzyme-substrate complex, the substrate is forced into a less stable shape, and bonding electrons may be drawn away from some bonds in preparation for breaking them and forming new bonds. The result is that the *activation energy barrier between substrate and product is lowered.*

CHEMISTRY IN ACTION

Extremozymes—Enzymes from the Edge

What do your laundry detergent, dishwasher detergent, oil drilling slurry, and the production of "stone washed" fabric have in common? One thing—the presence of enzymes that are active under unusual conditions. Most mammalian enzymes display optimum activity around 40 °C near pH 7.0 at 1 atmosphere of pressure; these are the predominant physiological conditions in most mammalian tissues and cell compartments. *Extremozymes* are enzymes from extremophiles, organisms that live in conditions hostile to mammalian cells. The conditions under which extremophiles live would inactivate mammalian enzymes as well as those of many other organisms. Of greatest interest are bacteria that live under conditions of extreme heat or cold, in highly acid or alkaline environments, or in very salty environments. Commercially useful enzymes have been developed from bacteria that have optimum growth temperatures as high as 106 °C and from those with an optimum as low as 4 °C. Other enzymes have been isolated from various bacteria species that grow in pH as low as 0.7 and as high as 10.

Enzymes from thermophiles ("heat lovers") include ones that break down starch and cellulose. These enzymes find wide use in the food, feed, textile ("stone washing"), and paper industries. One of the widest uses in the food industry is the hydrolysis of corn starch to glucose. Use of thermophilic enzymes for glucose production allows the reaction to occur at a higher temperature, increasing the reaction rate, and thus the amount of product yield per hour, without denaturing the enzymes involved. Biobleaching of paper pulp using heat-stable xylanases lowers the use of halogen-containing bleaching products, decreasing halogen release into the environment. Forensic science and basic molecular biology research both take advantage of the thermostable enzyme Taq polymerase, first identified in the microorganism *Thermus aquaticus* isolated from a hot spring in Yellowstone National Park. For a description of its use, see Chemistry in Action: Serendipity and the Polymerase Chain Reaction in Chapter 26.

Enzymes from cold-environment microorganisms (psychrophiles) are used in products such as cold-water-wash laundry detergents. Typical enzymes used in these products are lipases to break down greasy deposits and proteases to hydrolyze proteins deposited on clothing. Other applications for these enzymes exist in the cold-food industry where meat is tenderized and fruit juice is clarified using pectinases prior to sale. If

▲ **Extremophiles such as the bacteria that inhabit hot springs in Yellowstone National Park live in conditions that would denature most mammalian enzymes.**

you wear contact lenses, your cleaning solution contains room-temperature-stable, active proteases.

How do extremozymes withstand conditions that denature most enzymes? The strategy appears to vary depending on the type of extreme condition under which the organism lives. Thermophiles synthesize special proteins called *chaperonins*. Chaperonins recognize and bind to heat-denatured proteins, refolding them into their active forms. Also, proteins from thermophiles have tightly folded, highly nonpolar cores that resist denaturing forces. This "sticky" core is reinforced by the absence of amino acids that provide flexibility and by the presence of numerous ionic bonds on the surface of the protein. The result is a rigid protein that resists heat denaturation. In contrast, psychrophiles have more polar, flexible proteins than thermophiles. This structure is necessary to maintain activity at low temperatures.

So why do oil drillers use enzymes? Often, oil and gas are trapped in rock. A thick, gooey mixture of thermophilic enzymes, guar gum, sand, and water is forced into the well hole. The drillers then set off an explosion, simultaneously cracking the rock and forcing the enzyme-laced mixture into the cracks. The enzymes hydrolyze the guar gum, turning the viscous mixture into a thin solution that allows the oil and gas to flow out of the rock and up the well. Because of the tremendous heat in the drill hole, only heat-stable thermophilic enzymes will work. Also, the use of enzymes with optimum activity at high temperatures ensures the guar gum will not be hydrolyzed prematurely.

See Chemistry in Action Problems 19.78 and 19.79 at the end of the chapter.

Within the enzyme–substrate complex, atoms that will form new bonds must connect with each other. The new bonds might be with a second substrate or temporary bonds with atoms in the enzyme. Also, groups needed for catalysis must be close to the necessary locations in the substrate. Many organic reactions, for example, require acidic, basic, or metal ion catalysts. An enzyme's active site can provide acidic and basic groups without disrupting the constant-pH environment in body fluids, while the necessary metal ions are present as cofactors. Once the chemical reaction is completed, enzyme and product molecules separate from each other and the enzyme, restored to its original condition, becomes available for another substrate.

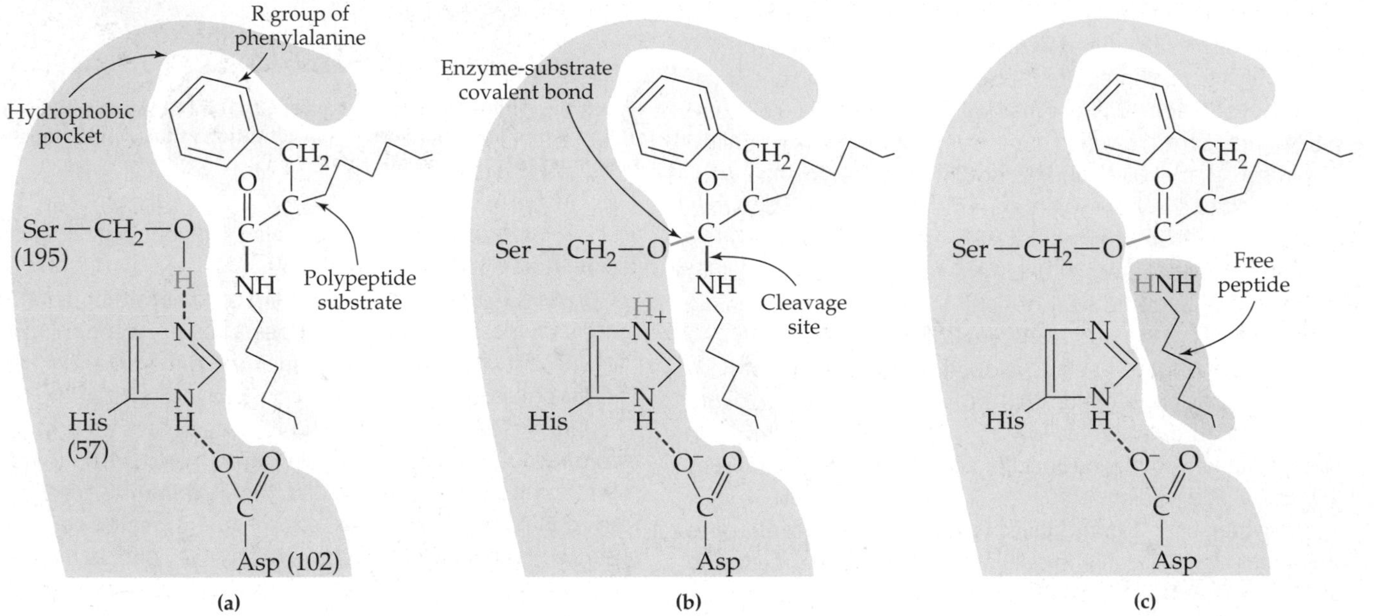

(a)   (b)   (c)

▲ **Figure 19.4**

Hydrolysis of a peptide bond by chymotrypsin.

(a) The polypeptide enters the enzyme active site with its hydrophobic side chain (the aromatic ring) in the hydrophobic pocket and the peptide bond to be broken (red) opposite serine and histidine residues. (b) Hydrogen ion transfer from serine to histidine allows formation of a strained intermediate in which the serine side chain bonds to the peptide bond carbon (green). (c) The peptide bond is broken and the segment with the new terminal —NH$_2$ group leaves the active site. In subsequent steps (not shown), a water molecule enters the active site; its H atom restores the serine side chain and its —OH bonds to the other piece of the substrate protein to give a new terminal —COOH group so that this piece can leave the active site.

The hydrolysis of a peptide bond by chymotrypsin, shown in Figure 19.4, illustrates how an enzyme functions. Chymotrypsin is one of the enzymes that participates in the digestion of proteins by breaking them down to smaller molecules. It cleaves polypeptide chains by breaking the peptide bond on the carbonyl side of amino acid residues that include an aromatic ring:

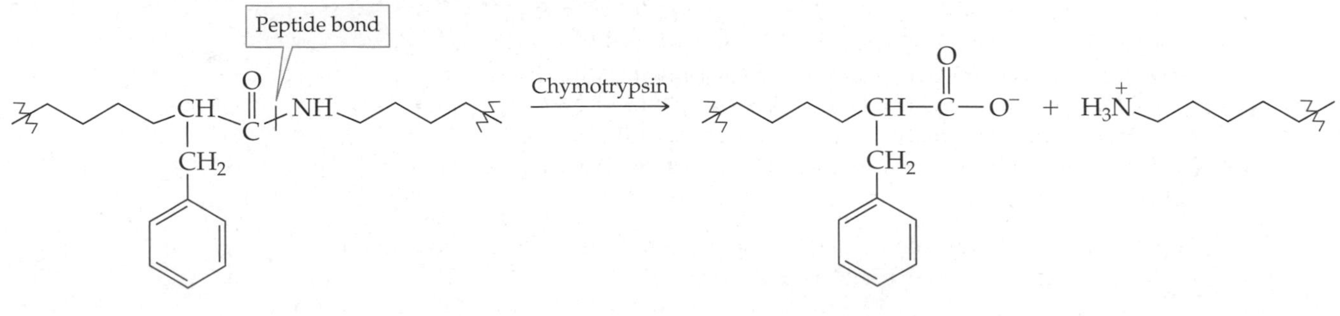

The enzyme–substrate complex forms (Figure 19.4a and b) by attraction of a hydrophobic side chain of the substrate (here, the aromatic ring) into a hydrophobic pocket in the enzyme active site and the subsequent formation of a covalent bond (green) to the substrate. The result is to position the substrate with the peptide bond to be broken (red) next to the amino acid side chains that function as catalysts. The enzyme has not only bound to the substrate (the *proximity effect*), but has done so in such a way as to bring the groups that must connect close to each other (the *orientation effect*). Aspartate, histidine, and serine provide functional groups needed for catalysis within the active site (the *catalytic effect*). As an illustration of the critical nature of protein folding, note that in the 241-amino-acid primary structure of chymotrypsin, aspartate is number 102, histidine is number 57, and serine is number 195. These amino acids are distant from each other along the linear backbone but are brought close together by backbone folding so that their side chains are in exactly the positions needed in the active site.

With the peptide bond carbon atom temporarily bonded to serine in the active site, it is easier for the peptide bond to break because the activation energy barrier has been lowered (the *energy effect*). As the bond breaks, the nitrogen picks up a hydrogen (blue) from histidine to form the new terminal amino group and this portion of the substrate is set free (Figure 19.4c). Reaction with a water molecule then restores the hydrogen to serine and supplies an OH group to form the new terminal carboxyl group of the shortened peptide. This part of the substrate is set free and the enzyme is restored to its original state.

In summary, enzymes act as catalysts because of their ability to

- Bring substrate(s) and catalytic sites together (*proximity effect*)
- Hold substrate(s) at the exact distance and in the exact orientation necessary for reaction (*orientation effect*)
- Provide acidic, basic, or other types of groups required for catalysis (*catalytic effect*)
- Lower the energy barrier by inducing strain in bonds in the substrate molecule (*energy effect*)

Worked Example 19.2 Identifying active site side-chain functions

Look at the hydrolysis of a peptide bond by chymotrypsin in Figure 19.4. **(a)** Which amino acids have side chains that could provide stabilization to the aromatic ring shown in the substrate? **(b)** What does the serine side chain do in the reaction and why can it do this? **(c)** What does the histidine side chain do in the reaction and why can it do this?

ANALYSIS Look critically at the diagrams of the reaction in Figure 19.4. Consider each part of the question separately, using the diagrams as an aid. **(a)** Note that the aromatic ring of phenylalanine fits into a "hydrophobic pocket." Therefore, the side chains of the amino acids surrounding this pocket in chymotrypsin must be nonpolar. **(b)** In the second diagram, note that serine has donated a hydrogen ion to histidine. Remember that acids are proton donors. **(c)** Also in the second diagram, note that histidine has accepted a proton from serine. Remember that bases are proton acceptors.

SOLUTION
(a) Any of the following nonpolar amino acids could be part of the hydrophobic pocket in chymotrypsin: alanine, leucine, isoleucine, methionine, proline, valine, phenylalanine, or tryptophan (see Table 18.3). **(b)** Serine is a polar amino acid and can donate a proton from the —OH group on the side chain, functioning as an acid. The RO⁻ remaining can interact with the substrate, initiating cleavage of the substrate. **(c)** Histidine is a basic amino acid and can accept a proton until needed to complete the cleavage reaction.

In this example, nonpolar amino acids held the substrate in place while amino acids that could act as acids or bases carried out the reaction.

🔑 **KEY CONCEPT PROBLEM 19.10**

The active sites of enzymes usually contain amino acids with acidic, basic, and polar side chains. Some enzymes also have amino acids with nonpolar side chains in their active sites. Which types of side chains would you expect to participate in holding the substrate in the active site? Which types would you expect to be involved in the catalytic activity of the enzyme?

19.5 Effect of Concentration on Enzyme Activity

For a reaction to occur, the enzyme and substrate molecules must come together and form the enzyme–substrate complex. You might predict that variation in the reaction rate can be expected if the enzyme or substrate concentration changes.

Substrate Concentration

Consider the common situation in which the substrate concentration varies while the enzyme concentration remains unchanged. If the substrate concentration is low relative to that of the enzyme, not all the enzyme molecules are in use. The rate therefore increases with the concentration of substrate because more of the enzyme molecules are put to work. In this situation, shown at the far left of the curve in Figure 19.5, the rate increases as the available substrate increases. If the substrate concentration doubles, the rate doubles (a directly proportional relationship).

As the substrate concentration continues to increase, however, the increase in the rate begins to level off as more and more of the active sites are occupied. (Think of people waiting in line to take their seats in a theater. The line moves more slowly as more seats fill and it becomes more difficult to find an empty one.) Eventually, the substrate concentration reaches a point at which none of the available active sites are free. Since the reaction rate is now determined by how fast the enzyme–substrate complex is converted to product, the reaction rate becomes constant—the enzyme is saturated.

Once the enzyme is saturated, increasing substrate concentration has no effect on the rate. In the absence of a change in the concentration of the enzyme, the rate when the enzyme is saturated is determined by the efficiency of the enzyme, the pH, and the temperature.

Under most conditions, an enzyme is not likely to be saturated. Therefore, at a given pH and temperature, the reaction rate is controlled by the amount of substrate and the overall efficiency of the enzyme. If the enzyme–substrate complex is rapidly converted to product, the rate at which enzyme and substrate combine to form the complex becomes the limiting factor. Calculations show an upper limit to this rate: enzyme and substrate molecules moving at random in solution can collide with each other no more often than about 10^8 collisions per mole per liter per second. Remarkably, a few enzymes actually operate with close to this efficiency—every one of the collisions results in the formation of product! We saw an example of such an efficient enzyme earlier in catalase, the enzyme that breaks down hydrogen peroxide at the rate of 10^7 catalytic events per second (see Table 19.1).

Enzyme Concentration

It is possible for the concentration of an active enzyme to vary according to our metabolic needs. So long as the concentration of substrate does not become a limitation, the reaction rate varies directly with the enzyme concentration (Figure 19.6). If the enzyme concentration doubles, the rate doubles; if the enzyme concentration triples, the rate triples; and so on.

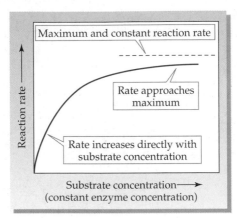

▲ **Figure 19.5**

Change of reaction rate with substrate concentration when enzyme concentration is constant.

At low substrate concentration, the reaction rate is directly proportional to the substrate concentration (at constant pH and temperature). With increasing substrate concentration, the increase in rate slows as more of the active sites are occupied. Eventually, with all active sites occupied, the rate reaches a maximum and constant rate.

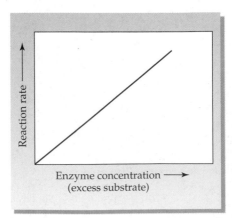

▲ **Figure 19.6**

Change of reaction rate with enzyme concentration in the presence of excess substrate.

🔑 **KEY CONCEPT PROBLEM 19.11**

What do we mean when we say an enzyme is saturated with substrate? When an enzyme is saturated with substrate, how does adding more (a) substrate and (b) enzyme affect the rate of the reaction?

19.6 Effect of Temperature and pH on Enzyme Activity

Enzymes have been finely tuned through evolution so that their maximum catalytic activity is highly dependent on pH and temperature. As you might expect, optimum conditions vary slightly for each enzyme but are generally near normal body temperature and the pH of the body fluid in which the enzyme functions.

Effect of Temperature on Enzyme Activity

An increase in temperature increases the rate of most chemical reactions, and enzyme-catalyzed reactions are no exception. Unlike many simple reactions, however, the rates of enzyme-catalyzed reactions do not increase continuously with rising temperature. Instead, the rates reach a maximum and then begin to decrease, as shown in Figure 19.7a. This falloff in rate occurs because enzymes begin to denature when heated too strongly. The noncovalent attractions between protein side chains are disrupted, the delicately maintained three-dimensional shape of the enzyme begins to come apart, and as a result the active site needed for catalytic activity is destroyed.

▶▶▶ Review the chemical properties of proteins in Section 18.12.

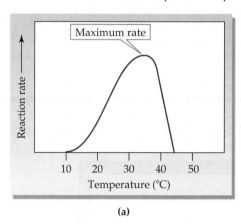

(a)

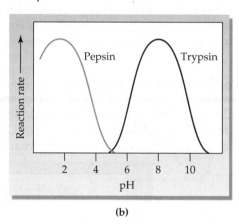

(b)

▶ **Figure 19.7**
Effect of temperature (a) and pH (b) on reaction rate.
(a) The reaction rate increases with increasing temperature until a temperature is reached at which the enzyme begins to denature; then the rate decreases rapidly. (b) The optimum activity for an enzyme occurs at the pH where it acts, as illustrated for two protein hydrolysis enzymes—pepsin, which acts in the highly acidic environment of the stomach, and trypsin, which acts in the small intestine, an alkaline environment.

Most enzymes denature and lose their catalytic activity above 50–60 °C, a fact that explains why medical instruments and laboratory glassware can be sterilized by heating with steam in an autoclave. The high temperature of the steam permanently denatures the enzymes of any bacteria present, thereby killing them.

A severe drop in body temperature creates the potentially fatal condition of hypothermia, which is accompanied by a slowdown in metabolic reactions. This effect is used to advantage by cooling the body during cardiac surgery. Upon gentle warming, enzymatic reaction rates return to normal because cooling does not denature proteins.

Effect of pH on Enzyme Activity

The catalytic activity of many enzymes depends on pH and usually has a well-defined optimum point at the normal, buffered pH of the enzyme's environment. For example, pepsin, which initiates protein digestion in the highly acidic environment of the stomach, has its optimum activity at pH 2 (Figure 19.7b). By contrast, trypsin—like chymotrypsin, an enzyme that aids digestion of proteins in the small intestine—has optimum activity at pH 8. Most enzymes have their maximum activity between the pH values of 5 to 9. Eventually, both extremes of pH will denature a protein.

▶ **Figure 19.8**

An allosteric enzyme.
(a) One of the four identical subunits in phosphofructokinase, an enzyme that catalyzes transfer of a phosphoryl group from ATP to fructose 6-phosphate (see transferase reaction in Section 19.3). The subunit is shown after the reaction has occurred, with the diphosphate portion of the phosphorylated substrate (yellow) and ADP (green) in the active site and the allosteric activator (red, also ADP) in the regulatory site. (b) The four subunits of the complete enzyme are shown in blue. ADP (green), the cofactor, is shown in the active site and ADP (red) that acts as the allosteric activator is shown in the regulatory site. Note that there is one cofactor and one regulator molecule per protein chain.

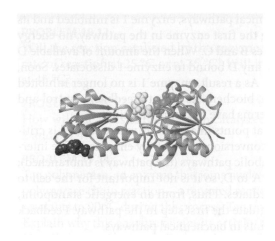
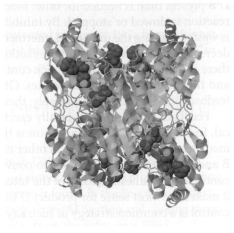

(a) (b)

Allosteric control can be either positive or negative. Binding a positive regulator changes the active sites so that the enzyme becomes a better catalyst and the rate accelerates. Binding a negative regulator changes the active sites so that the enzyme is a less effective catalyst and the rate slows down. Because allosteric enzymes can have several substrate binding sites and several regulator binding sites and because there may be interaction among them, very fine control is achieved.

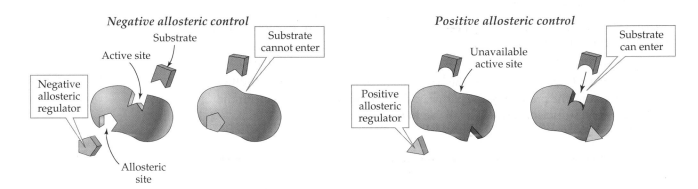

19.8 Enzyme Regulation: Inhibition

The inhibition of an enzyme can be *reversible* or *irreversible*. In reversible inhibition, the inhibitor can leave, restoring the enzyme to its uninhibited level of activity. In irreversible inhibition, the inhibitor remains permanently bound and the enzyme is permanently inhibited. The inhibition can also be *competitive, unncompetitive* or *mixed*, depending on whether the inhibitor binds to the active site, the substrate, or some combination of enzyme and substrate.

Reversible Uncompetitive Inhibition

Uncompetitive (enzyme) inhibition
Enzyme regulation in which an inhibitor binds reversibly to the enzyme-substrate complex, blocking the binding of the second substrate to the active site.

In **uncompetitive inhibition**, the inhibitor does not compete with the substrate for the active site and cannot bind to enzyme alone. An uncompetitive inhibitor exerts control by binding to the enzyme-substrate complex so that the reaction occurs less efficiently or not at all. This type of inhibition is reversible and occurs in reactions where two substrates are involved.

In Figure 19.9, reaction rates with and without an uncompetitive inhibitor are compared in the bottom and top curves. With the inhibitor, the reaction rate increases with increasing substrate concentration more gradually than when no inhibitor is present. The maximum rate is lowered, and once that rate is reached, no amount of substrate can increase it further. As long as the inhibitor is present at constant concentration, this upper limit does not change.

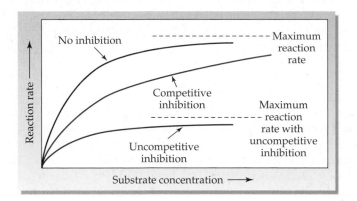

◄ **Figure 19.9**
Enzyme inhibition.
The top curve and dashed line show the reaction rate and maximum rate with no inhibitor. With a competitive inhibitor (middle curve), the maximum rate is unchanged, but a higher substrate concentration is required to reach it. With an uncompetitive inhibitor (bottom curve), the maximum rate (bottom dashed line) is lowered.

Reversible Competitive Inhibition

What happens if an enzyme encounters a molecule very much like its normal substrate in shape, size, and functional groups? The impostor molecule enters the enzyme's active site, binds to it, and thereby prevents the usual substrate molecule from binding to the same site. Consequently, the enzyme is tied up, making it unavailable as a catalyst. This situation is called **competitive inhibition**—the inhibitor *competes* with substrate for binding to the active site. A competitive inhibitor binds reversibly to an active site through noncovalent interactions, but undergoes no reaction. While it is there, it prevents the substrate from entering the active site.

Competitive (enzyme) inhibition Enzyme regulation in which an inhibitor competes with a substrate for binding to the enzyme active site.

$$\text{Substrate} + \text{Enzyme} \rightleftharpoons \text{Substrate–enzyme complex}$$
$$\text{Inhibitor} + \text{Enzyme} \rightleftharpoons \text{Inhibitor–enzyme complex}$$

Whether the substrate or the inhibitor occupies the active site depends on their relative concentrations. A substrate in relatively high concentration occupies more of the active sites, so the reaction is less inhibited. An inhibitor in relatively high concentration occupies more of the active sites, so the reaction is more inhibited.

The middle curve in Figure 19.9 shows that in the presence of a competitive inhibitor at constant concentration, the reaction rate increases more gradually with increasing substrate concentration than when there is no inhibitor present. Unlike uncompetitive inhibition, however, the maximum reaction rate is unchanged. Eventually all of an enzyme's active sites can be occupied by substrate, but a higher substrate concentration is required to reach that condition.

The product of a reaction may be a competitive inhibitor for the enzyme that catalyzes that reaction. For example, glucose 6-phosphate is a competitive inhibitor for hexokinase, which catalyzes formation of this phosphorylated form of glucose. Thus, when supplies of glucose 6-phosphate are ample, glucose is available for other reactions.

A competitive inhibitor is sometimes put to use in treating an unhealthy condition because the inhibitor mimics the structure of the substrate and fits into the enzyme's active site. For example, competitive inhibition is used to good advantage in the treatment of methanol poisoning. Although not harmful itself, methanol (wood alcohol) is oxidized in the body to formaldehyde, which is highly toxic $(CH_3OH \longrightarrow H_2C{=}O)$. Because of its molecular similarity to methanol, ethanol acts as a competitive inhibitor of the methanol dehydrogenase enzyme. With the oxidation of methanol blocked by ethanol, the methanol is excreted without causing harm. Thus, the medical treatment of methanol poisoning includes administering ethanol, to avoid blindness or death of the patient.

Another example of reversible inhibition involves lead poisoning. Lead can poison animals, including humans, in two ways. One way is by displacing an essential metal cofactor from the active site of an enzyme. When lead displaces zinc in an enzyme essential to the synthesis of heme, which is the oxygen-carrying part of hemoglobin,

Competitive inhibition

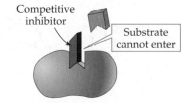

the enzyme becomes inactive and anemia can result. Physicians can treat this sort of lead poisoning with chelation therapy. Ethylenediaminetetraacetic acid (EDTA) forms coordinate covalent bonds preferentially with lead in the body, and the lead is then excreted in the urine as a chelated compound.

The second way lead can poison involves the process known as irreversible inhibition, the topic we look at next.

Irreversible Inhibition

Irreversible (enzyme) inhibition
Enzyme deactivation in which an inhibitor forms covalent bonds to the active site, permanently blocking it.

If an inhibitor forms a bond that is not easily broken with a group in an active site, the result is **irreversible inhibition**. The enzyme's reaction cannot occur because the substrate cannot connect appropriately with the active site. Many irreversible inhibitors are poisons as a result of their ability to completely shut down the active site. Heavy metal ions, such as mercury (Hg^{2+}) and lead (Pb^{2+}), are irreversible inhibitors that form covalent bonds to the sulfur atoms in the —SH groups of cysteine residues.

Often, heavy metal ions like lead and mercury affect enzymes that function in the nervous system. At low levels, lead can cause decreased attention span and mental difficulties. These symptoms are noticed in children who develop the habit of ingesting flakes of lead-containing paint, which have a sweet taste. Primarily for this reason, lead-containing paint has not been used since the 1950s. It is, however, still present in older homes. Small amounts of mercury in the diet cause similar problems. For this reason, children and pregnant women are advised to severely limit their intake of fish, particularly large deep-sea fish such as tuna. Tuna accumulate mercury in their tissues; the mercury is absorbed from our digestive system and remains in our bodies.

Organophosphorus insecticides, such as parathion and malathion, and nerve gases, such as Sarin, are irreversible inhibitors of the enzyme acetylcholinesterase, which breaks down a chemical messenger (*acetylcholine*) that transmits nerve impulses (Section 28.7). The acetylcholinesterase inhibitors bond covalently to a serine residue in the enzyme's active site:

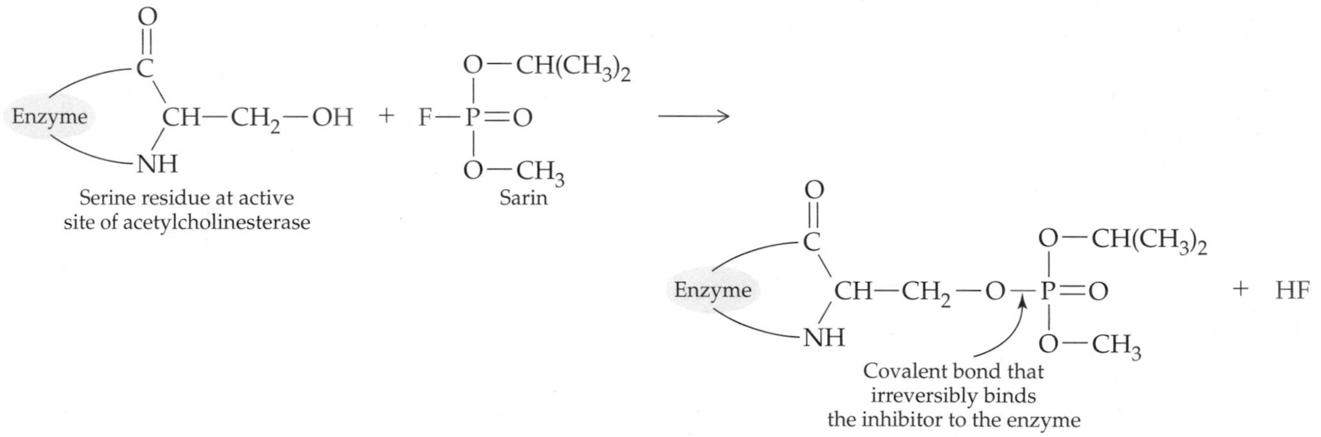

Serine residue at active site of acetylcholinesterase

Sarin

Covalent bond that irreversibly binds the inhibitor to the enzyme

Normally, acetylcholinesterase breaks down acetylcholine immediately after that molecule transmits a nerve impulse. Removal of acetylcholine "resets" the receiving cells, getting them ready to receive further signals. Without acetylcholinesterase activity, accumulating acetylcholine blocks transmission of further nerve impulses, resulting in paralysis of muscle fibers and death from respiratory failure. Sarin was the poison released by terrorists in the Tokyo subway system in 1995. The attack resulted in 12 deaths and varying degrees of injury to more than 5000 people. There is no effective treatment to counteract this irreversible inhibitor of acetylcholinesterase.

CHEMISTRY IN ACTION

Enzyme Inhibitors as Drugs

Consider a situation in which the chemical structures of a substrate and the active site to which it binds are known. A drug designer can than create a molecule sufficiently similar to the substrate that it binds to the active site and acts as an inhibitor. Inhibiting a particular enzyme can be desirable for many reasons.

The family of drugs known as ACE inhibitors is a good example of enzyme inhibitors as drugs. Angiotensin II, the octapeptide illustrated in Section 18.7, is a potent *pressor*—it elevates blood pressure, in part by causing contraction of blood vessels. Angiotensin I, a decapeptide, is an inactive precursor of angiotensin II. To become active, two amino acid residues—His and Leu—must be cut off the end of angiotensin I, a reaction catalyzed by angiotensin-converting enzyme (ACE).

$$\text{Asp-Arg-Val-Tyr-Ile-His-Pro-Phe-His-Leu} \xrightarrow[\text{(ACE)}]{\substack{\text{Angiotensin-} \\ \text{converting} \\ \text{enzyme}}}$$

Angiotensin I

$$\text{Asp-Arg-Val-Tyr-Ile-His-Pro-Phe} + \text{His-Leu}$$

Angiotensin II

This reaction is part of a normal pathway for blood pressure control and is accelerated when blood pressure drops because of bleeding or dehydration.

The development of inhibitors for ACE was aided by knowing that a zinc(II) ion is present in the ACE active site. Knowing that the extract of venom from a South American pit viper is a mild ACE inhibitor and that this extract contains a pentapeptide with a proline residue at the carboxyl-terminal end was also helpful. This information led to a search for a proline-containing molecule that would bind to the zinc(II) ion.

The first ACE inhibitor on the market, *captopril*, was developed by experimenting with modifications of the proline structure. Success was achieved by introducing an —SH group that binds to the zinc ion in the active site:

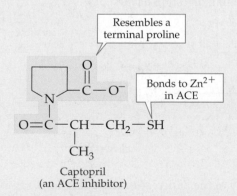

Captopril
(an ACE inhibitor)

Several other ACE inhibitors have subsequently been developed, and they are now common medications for patients with high blood pressure.

The development of enzyme inhibitors also plays a continuing, major role in the battle against *acquired immunodeficiency syndrome*, AIDS. The battle is far from won, but two important AIDS-fighting drugs are enzyme inhibitors. The first, known as AZT (*azidothymidine*, also called *zidovudine*), resembles in structure a molecule essential to reproduction of the AIDS-causing *human immunodeficiency virus (HIV)*. Because AZT is accepted by an HIV enzyme as a substrate, it prevents the virus from producing duplicate copies of itself.

The most successful AIDS drug thus far inhibits a *protease*, an enzyme that cuts a long protein chain into smaller pieces needed by the HIV. *Protease inhibitors*, such as ritonavir, cause dramatic decreases in the virus population and AIDS symptoms. The success is only achieved, however, by taking a "cocktail" of several drugs, including AZT. The cocktail is expensive and requires precise adherence to a schedule of taking 20 pills a day. These conditions make it unavailable or too difficult for many individuals to use.

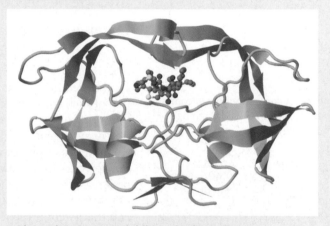

▲ **Ritonavir, an enzyme inhibitor, in the active site of HIV protease.**

See Chemistry in Action Problems 19.82 and 19.83 at the end of the chapter.

PROBLEM 19.17

Could either of the molecules shown below be a competitive inhibitor for the enzyme that has *p*-aminobenzoate as its substrate? If so, why?

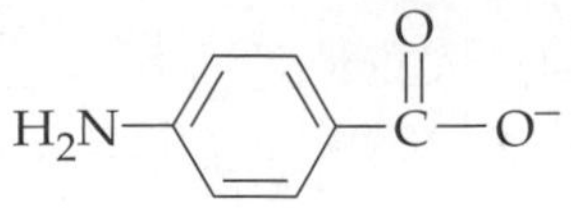

$$H_2N-\text{\textcircled{}}-\overset{\overset{O}{\|}}{C}-O^-$$

p-Aminobenzoate, the substrate

(a) $H_2NCH_2CH_3$ (b) 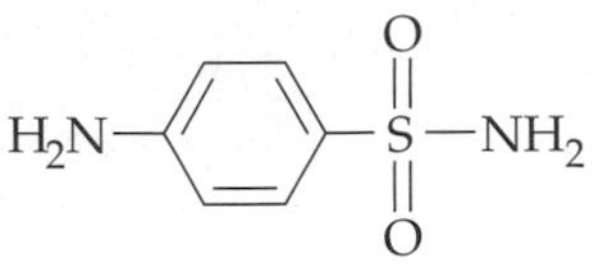 $H_2N-\text{\textcircled{}}-\overset{\overset{O}{\|}}{\underset{\underset{O}{\|}}{S}}-NH_2$

PROBLEM 19.18

What kind of reaction product might be a competitive inhibitor for the enzyme that catalyzes its formation?

PROBLEM 19.19

Ritonavir inhibits the action of HIV protease (see the illustration of ritonovir bound to HIV protease in Chemistry in Action: Enzyme Inhibitors as Drugs on p. 607). What kind of inhibition is imposed on HIV protease by ritonavir?

19.9 Enzyme Regulation: Covalent Modification and Genetic Control

Covalent Modification

There are two general modes of enzyme regulation by covalent modification—removal of a covalently bonded portion of an enzyme or addition of a group. Some enzymes are synthesized in inactive forms that differ from the active forms in composition. Activation of such enzymes, known as **zymogens** or *proenzymes*, requires a chemical reaction that splits off part of the molecule. Blood clotting, for example, is initiated by activation of zymogens.

Other examples of zymogens include *trypsinogen, chymotrypsinogen*, and *proelastase*, precursors of enzymes that digest proteins in the small intestine. Produced in the pancreas, these enzymes must be inactive when they are synthesized so that they do not immediately digest the pancreas. Each zymogen has a polypeptide segment at one end that is not present in the active enzymes. The extra segments are snipped off to produce trypsin, chymotrypsin, and elastase, the active enzymes, when the zymogens reach the small intestine, where protein digestion occurs.

Zymogen A compound that becomes an active enzyme after undergoing a chemical change.

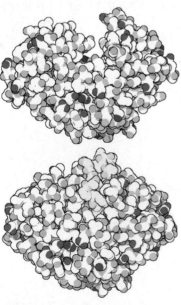

▲ Pepsinogen (a zymogen) at bottom, and the active enzyme pepsin at top.

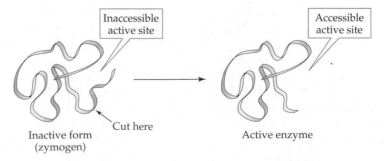

One danger of traumatic injury to the pancreas or the duct that leads to the small intestine is premature activation of these zymogens, resulting in acute pancreatitis, a painful and potentially fatal condition in which the activated enzymes attack the pancreas.

Another mode of covalent modification is the reversible addition of phosphoryl groups ($-PO_3^{2-}$) to a serine, tyrosine, or threonine residue. *Kinase* enzymes catalyze the addition of a phosphoryl group supplied by ATP (*phosphorylation*). *Phosphatase enzymes* catalyze the removal of the phosphoryl group (*dephosphorylation*). This control strategy swings into action, for example, when glycogen stored in muscles must be hydrolyzed to glucose that is needed for quick energy. Two serine residues in glycogen phosphorylase, the enzyme that initiates glycogen breakdown, are phosphorylated. Only with these phosphoryl groups in place is glycogen phosphorylase active. The groups are removed, changing both the shape and charge on the enzyme, once the need to break down glycogen for quick energy has passed.

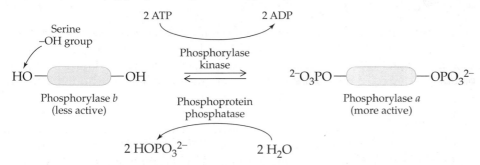

The curved arrows shown above are used frequently in biochemical equations in later chapters. While the focus of the main reaction arrow is on changes in the major biomolecule reactant, the participation of other reactants needed to accomplish the chemical change is shown by the curved arrows adjacent to the main reaction arrow. Coenzymes and energy-providing molecules like ATP are often included in this manner. Here, the top curved arrow shows that the reaction in the forward direction requires ATP to supply the phosphoryl groups and produces ADP. The bottom curved arrow shows that water is needed for the reverse reaction, the hydrolysis that removes the phosphoryl groups as hydrogen phosphate anions.

Genetic Control

Yet another enzyme control strategy affects the supply of the enzyme itself. The synthesis of enzymes, like that of all proteins, is regulated by genes (Chapter 25). The **genetic control** strategy is especially useful for enzymes needed only at certain stages of development. Mechanisms controlled by hormones (Section 28.2) can accelerate or decelerate enzyme synthesis.

> **Genetic (enzyme) control** Regulation of enzyme activity by control of the synthesis of enzymes.

In summary, we have described the most important strategies that control the activity of enzymes. In any given biochemical pathway in a healthy individual, several of these strategies are likely in use at once.

Mechanisms of Enzyme Control

- *Feedback control* is exerted on an earlier reactant by a later product in a reaction pathway and is made possible by *allosteric control*. The feedback molecule binds to a specific enzyme early in the pathway in a way that alters the shape and therefore the efficiency of the enzyme.
- *Inhibition*, which is either *reversible* or *irreversible*. *Reversible inhibition* can involve both the substrate and the active site (*uncompetitive inhibition*) or only the active site (*competitive inhibition*) by molecules that often mimic substrate structure. *Irreversible inhibition* occurs because of covalent bonding of the inhibitor to the enzyme. Competitive inhibition is a strategy often utilized in medications, and irreversible inhibition is a mode of action of many poisons.
- *Production of inactive enzymes (zymogens)*, which must be activated by cleaving a portion of the molecule.
- *Covalent modification of an enzyme by addition and removal of a phosphoryl group*, with the phosphoryl group supplied by ATP.
- *Genetic control*, whereby the amount of enzyme available is regulated by limiting its synthesis.

PROBLEM 19.20

Which type of enzyme regulation is best for the following situations?

(a) An enzyme that becomes overactive during a disease

(b) An enzyme needed only when there is low blood glucose

(c) An enzyme that springs into action when a traumatic injury occurs

(d) An enzyme needed only during adolescence

19.10 Vitamins and Minerals

Vitamin An organic molecule, essential in trace amounts that must be obtained in the diet because it is not synthesized in the body.

Long before the reasons were understood, it was known that lime and other citrus juices cure scurvy, meat and milk cure pellagra, and cod-liver oil prevents rickets. Eventually, it was discovered that these diseases are caused by deficiencies of **vitamins**—organic molecules required in only trace amounts that must be obtained through the diet. Vitamins are a dietary necessity for humans because our bodies do not have the ability to synthesize them.

The symptoms of scurvy—muscle weakness; swollen, bleeding gums; and the easy bruising that result from defective collagen synthesis—are cured by consuming foods that contain vitamin C, the coenzyme necessary for collagen synthesis. Pellagra, with such varied symptoms as weight loss, dermatitis, depression, and dementia, results from a deficiency of niacin. And rickets, the occurrence of soft bones in children because of inadequate availability of calcium and phosphate, is due to a deficiency of vitamin D, which is essential to the incorporation of calcium in bones.

▶▶ The role of vitamin C in collagen synthesis was examined in Section 18.11 and also in Chemistry in Action: Collagen—A Tale of Two Diseases on p. 576.

Water-Soluble Vitamins

Vitamins are grouped by solubility into two classes: water-soluble and fat-soluble. The water-soluble vitamins, listed in Table 19.3, are found in the aqueous environment inside cells, where most of them are needed as components of coenzymes. Over time, an assortment of names, letters, and numbers for designating vitamins have accumulated. (One reason is that what was originally known as vitamin B turned out to be several different vitamins.) Structurally, the water-soluble vitamins have in common the presence of —OH, —COOH, or other polar groups that impart their water solubility, but otherwise they range from simple molecules like vitamin C to quite large and complex structures like vitamin B_{12}.

Most vitamins are components of larger coenzymes, but some function as coenzymes themselves. *Vitamin C is biologically active without any change in structure* from the molecules present in foods. It is increasingly shown to be a valuable *antioxidant*, as described later in this section. Similarly, *biotin* is connected to enzymes by an amide bond at its carboxyl group but otherwise undergoes no structural change from dietary biotin.

▲ **A myriad of vitamin pills in capsule and tablet form.**

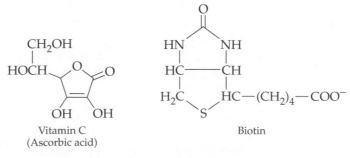

Vitamin C
(Ascorbic acid)

Biotin

The other water-soluble vitamins are incorporated into coenzymes. The vitamin-derived portions of two of the most important coenzymes, NAD^+ and coenzyme A, are illustrated in Figure 19.10. The functions, deficiency symptoms, and major dietary sources of the water-soluble vitamins are included in Table 19.3.

TABLE 19.3 The Water-Soluble Vitamins*

Vitamin	Significance	Sources	Reference Daily Intake**	Effects of Deficiency	Effects of Excess
Thiamine (B$_1$)	In coenzyme for decarboxylation reactions	Milk, meat, bread, legumes	1.5 mg	Muscle weakness, and cardiovascular problems including heart disease; causes beriberi	Low blood pressure
Riboflavin (B$_2$)	In coenzymes FMN and FAD	Milk, meat	1.7 mg	Skin and mucous membrane deterioration	Itching, tingling sensations
Niacin (nicotinic acid, nicotinamide, B$_3$)	In coenzyme NAD$^+$	Meat, bread, potatoes	2.0 mg	Nervous system, gastrointestinal, skin, and mucous membrane deterioration; causes pellagra	Itching, burning sensations, blood vessel dilation, death after large dose
B$_6$ (pyridoxine)	In coenzyme for amino acid and lipid metabolism	Meat, legumes	2.0 mg	Retarded growth, anemia, convulsions, epithelial changes	Central nervous system alterations, perhaps fatal
Folic acid	In coenzyme for amino acid and nucleic acid metabolism	Vegetables, cereal, bread	0.4 mg	Retarded growth, anemia, gastrointestinal disorders; neural tube defects	Few noted except at massive doses
B$_{12}$ (cobalamin)	In coenzyme for nucleic acid metabolism	Milk, meat	6 μg	Pernicious anemia	Excess red blood cells
Biotin	Coenzyme for carboxylation reactions	Eggs, meat, vegetables	0.3 mg	Fatigue, muscular pain, nausea, dermatitis	None reported
Pantothenic acid (B$_5$)	In coenzyme A	Milk, meat	10 mg	Retarded growth, central nervous system disturbances	None reported
C (ascorbic acid)	Coenzyme; delivers hydride ions; antioxidant	Citrus fruits, broccoli; greens	60 mg	Epithelial and mucosal deterioration, causing scurvy	Kidney stones

*Adapted in part from Frederic H. Martini, Fundamentals of Anatomy and Physiology, 4th edition (Prentice Hall, 1998).
**RDI values are the basis for information on the Nutrition Facts Label included on most packaged foods. The values are based on the Recommended Dietary Allowances of 1968.

Worked Example 19.6 Identifying Coenzymes

Identify the substrate, product, and coenzyme in the reaction shown below. The reaction is catalyzed by the enzyme alcohol dehydrogenase.

$$\text{Ethanol} + \text{NAD}^+ \longrightarrow \text{Acetaldehyde} + \text{NADH} + \text{H}^+$$

ANALYSIS Identify which molecules have been changed and how, starting from the left side of the arrow (the beginning of the reaction) to the right side of the arrow (the end of the reaction). In this case, ethanol is oxidized to acetaldehyde and NAD$^+$ is reduced to NADH/H$^+$. Recognize that nicotinamide adenine dinucleotide (NAD$^+$) is a coenzyme involved in oxidation/reduction reactions.

SOLUTION Since NAD$^+$ is a coenzyme involved in oxidation/reduction reactions, ethanol (the other molecule on the left side of the equation) is the substrate and acetaldehyde (on the right side of the arrow) is the product of the reaction. NADH + H$^+$ is the reduced form of nicotinamide adenine dinucleotide and is considered to be reduced coenzyme only—not a product of the reaction.

▶ **Figure 19.10**
The vitamin-derived portions of NAD⁺ and coenzyme A.

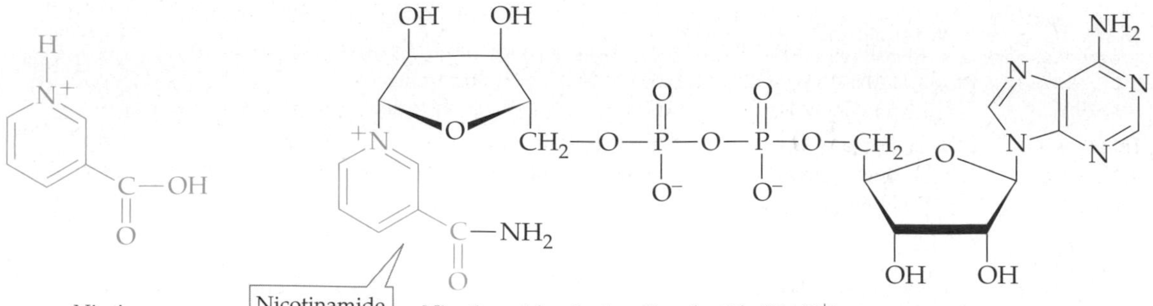

Niacin
(Nicotinic acid)

Nicotinamide

Nicotinamide adenine dinucleotide (NAD⁺), a coenzyme

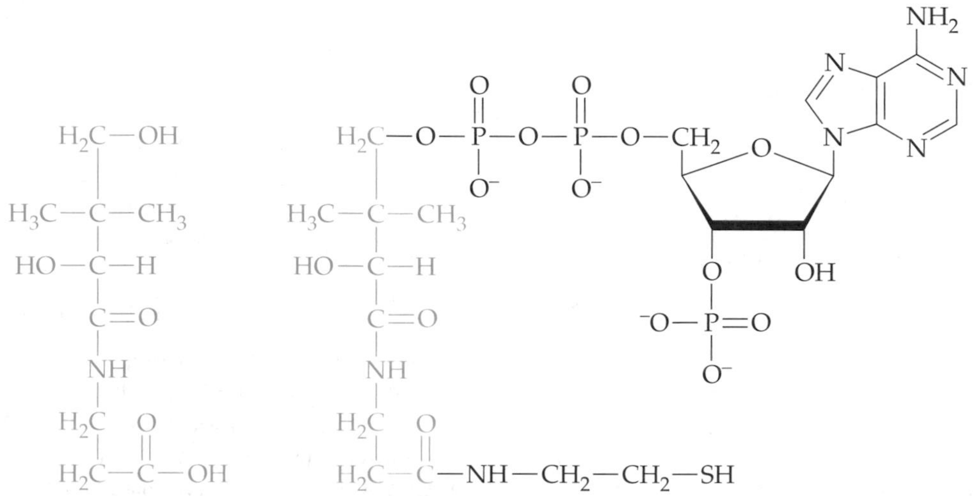

Pantothenic acid

Coenzyme A

Fat-Soluble Vitamins

The fat-soluble vitamins A, D, E, and K are stored in the body's fat deposits. Although the clinical effects of deficiencies of these vitamins are well documented, the molecular mechanisms by which they act are not nearly as well understood as those of the water-soluble vitamins. None has been identified as a coenzyme. Their functions, sources, and deficiency symptoms are summarized in Table 19.4. The hazards of overdosing

TABLE 19.4 The Fat-Soluble Vitamins*

Vitamin	Significance	Sources	Reference Daily Intake**	Effects of Deficiency	Effects of Excess
A	Maintains epithelia; required for synthesis of visual pigments; antioxidant	Leafy green and yellow vegetables	1000 μg	Retarded growth, night blindness, deterioration of epithelial membranes	Liver damage, skin peeling, central nervous system effects (nausea, anorexia)
D	Required for normal bone growth, calcium and phosphorus absorption at gut, and retention in kidneys	Synthesized in skin exposed to sunlight	10 μg	Rickets, skeletal deterioration	Calcium deposits in many tissues, disrupting functions
E	Prevents breakdown of vitamin A and fatty acids; antioxidant	Meat, milk, vegetables	10 mg	Anemia; other problems suspected	None reported
K	Essential for liver synthesis of prothrombin and other clotting factors	Vegetables; production by intestinal bacteria	80 μg	Bleeding disorders	Liver dysfunction, jaundice

*Adapted in part from Frederic H. Martini, Fundamentals of Anatomy and Physiology, 4th edition (Prentice Hall, 1998).
**RDI values are the basis for information on the Nutrition Facts Label included on most packaged foods. The values are based on the Recommended Dietary Allowances of 1968. RDIs for fat-soluble vitamins are often reported in International Units (IU), which are defined differently for each vitamin. The values given here are approximate equivalents in mass units.

on fat-soluble vitamins are greater than the hazards of overdosing on water-soluble vitamins because the fat-soluble vitamins accumulate in body fats. Excesses of the water-soluble vitamins are more likely to be excreted in the urine.

Vitamin A, which is essential for night vision, healthy eyes, and normal development of epithelial tissue, has three active forms: retinol, retinal, and retinoic acid. It is produced in the body by cleavage of β-carotene, the molecule that gives an orange color to carrots and other vegetables.

▲ **Deeply pigmented vegetables and fruits contain vitamins.**

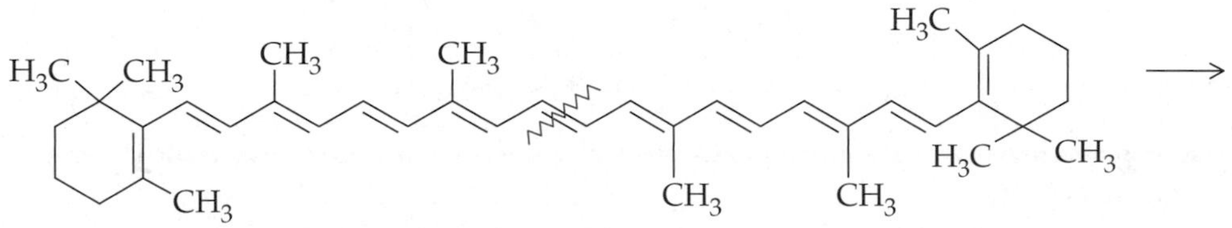

β-Carotene

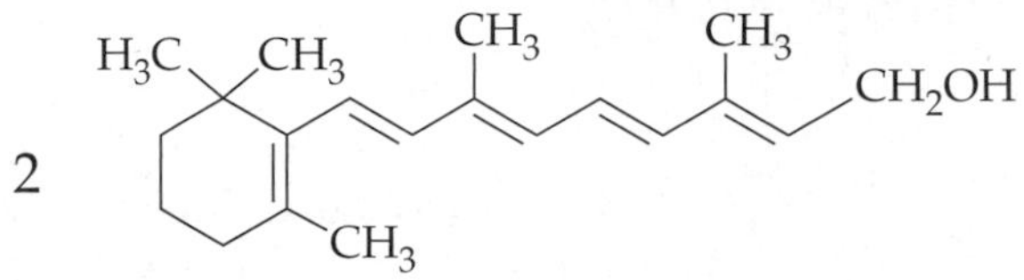

2

Vitamin A
(Retinol)

▶▶▶ The role of vitamin A in vision was explored in Chemistry in Action: The Chemistry of Vision and Color in Chapter 13.

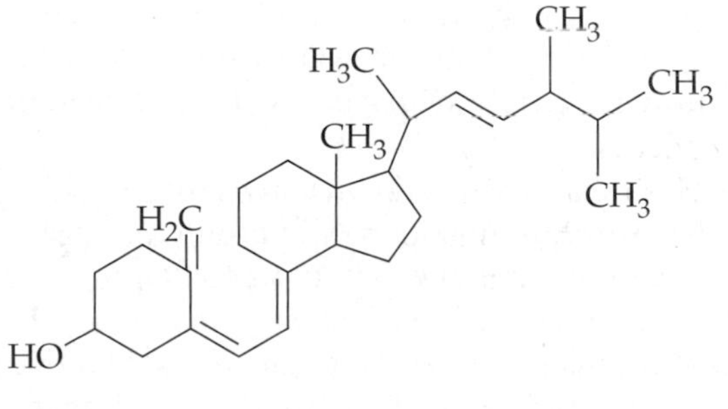

Vitamin D, which is related in structure to cholesterol, is synthesized when ultraviolet light from the sun strikes a cholesterol derivative in the skin. In the kidney, vitamin D is converted to a hormone that regulates calcium absorption and bone formation. Vitamin D deficiencies are most likely to occur in malnourished individuals living where there is little sunlight. (It is interesting to note that a sunscreen of SPF factor 6–8 completely blocks vitamin D synthesis.) For many people, as little as 15 minutes of sunshine daily without sunscreen is sufficient for maintenance of adequate vitamin D levels.

Vitamin D

Vitamin E comprises a group of structurally similar compounds called tocopherols, the most active of which is α-tocopherol. Like vitamin C, it is an antioxidant: it prevents the breakdown of vitamin A and polyunsaturated fats by oxidation. Although vitamin E apparently is not toxic in overdosage as are the other fat-soluble vitamins, it is best to avoid excessively large doses of vitamin E.

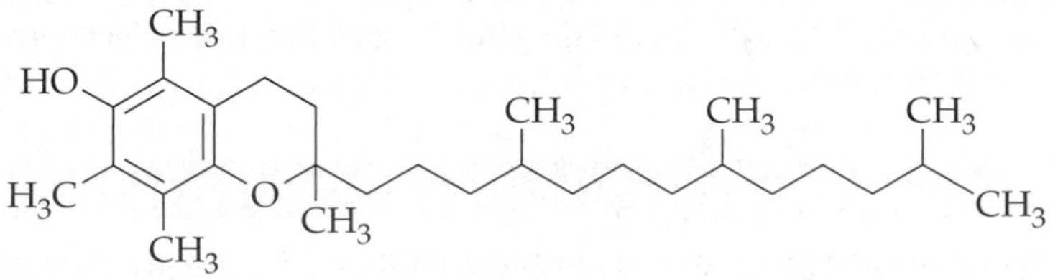

Vitamin E

Vitamin K is a family of structurally related compounds distinguished from each other by hydrocarbon side chains of varying length. This vitamin is essential to the synthesis of several blood-clotting factors. It is produced by intestinal bacteria, so deficiencies are rare.

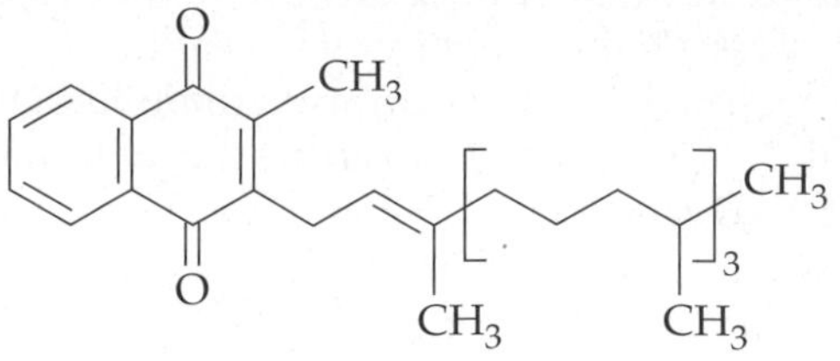

Vitamin K

PROBLEM 19.21
Compare the structures of vitamin A and vitamin C. What structural features does each have that make one water-soluble and the other fat-soluble?

PROBLEM 19.22
Based on the structure shown for retinol (vitamin A) and the names of the two related forms of vitamin A, retinal and retinoic acid, what do you expect to be the structural differences among these three compounds?

Antioxidants

Antioxidant A substance that prevents oxidation by reacting with an oxidizing agent.

An **antioxidant** is a substance that prevents oxidation. The food industry uses antioxidants to combat oxidation of unsaturated fats by air, which causes deterioration of baked goods (see Chemistry in Action: Phenols as Antioxidants in Chapter 14). In the body, we need similar protection against active oxidizing agents that are by-products of normal metabolism.

Our principal dietary antioxidants are vitamin C, vitamin E, β-carotene, and the mineral selenium. They work together to defuse the potentially harmful action of **free radicals**, highly reactive molecular fragments with unpaired electrons (for example, superoxide ion, $\cdot O_2^-$). Free radicals quickly gain stability by picking up electrons from nearby molecules, which are thereby damaged. (We will have more to say about this in Section 20.10.)

Free radical An atom or molecule with an unpaired electron.

Vitamin E is unique in having antioxidant activity as its principal biochemical role. It acts by giving up the hydrogen from its —OH group to oxygen-containing free radicals. The hydrogen is then restored by reaction with vitamin C. Selenium joins the list of important antioxidants because it is a cofactor in an enzyme that converts hydrogen peroxide (H_2O_2) to water before the peroxide can go on to produce free radicals.

Evidence for the benefits of antioxidants in disease prevention, especially in the prevention of cancer and heart disease, is accumulating. Laboratory experiments have demonstrated anticancer activity for vitamin C, vitamin E, β-carotene, and selenium, and the results are supported by a variety of studies in defined human populations. For example, vitamin E appears to reduce the risk of cancer among smokers, though not among nonsmokers. Low levels of serum selenium and vitamin E have been associated with a greater risk of breast cancer in a group of Finnish women.

In a study of over 100,000 people, those who took vitamin E supplements had fewer heart attacks. Vitamin C may slow the development of blocked arteries and may also prevent cancer by inhibiting the formation of carcinogens in the gastrointestinal tract.

KEY CONCEPT PROBLEM 19.23

Vitamins are a diverse group of compounds that must be present in the diet. List four functions of vitamins in the body.

CHEMISTRY IN ACTION

Vitamins, Minerals, and Food Labels

It is not uncommon to encounter incomplete or incorrect information about vitamins and minerals. We have been frightened by the possibility that aluminum causes Alzheimer's disease and tantalized by the possibility that vitamin C defeats the common cold. Sorting out fact from fiction or distinguishing preliminary research results from scientifically proven relationships is especially difficult in this area of nutrition. Much is yet to be learned about the functions of vitamins and minerals in the body, and new information is continuously being reported. It is tempting for health-conscious individuals to look for guaranteed routes to better health by taking vitamins or minerals, and taking advantage of this motivation is just as tempting to profit-making organizations.

One consistent source of information on nutrition is the Food and Nutrition Board of the National Academy of Sciences-National Research Council. They periodically survey the latest nutritional information and publish Recommended Dietary Allowances (RDAs) that are "designed for the maintenance of good nutrition of the majority of healthy persons in the United States." Another source is the U.S. Food and Drug Administration (FDA), which has among its many responsibilities setting the rules for food labeling.

Since 1994, as mandated by the FDA, most packaged food products carry standardized *Nutrition Facts* labels. The nutritional value of a food serving of a specified size is reported as *% Daily Value*. For vitamins and minerals, these percentages are calculated from *Reference Daily Intake* values (RDIs). The RDIs are mostly derived from the 1968 RDAs and were designed to avoid deficiencies. The RDIs are averages for adults and children over 4 years of age. The values for vitamins are included in Tables 19.3 and 19.4. For minerals, they are listed in the accompanying table.

All vitamins and minerals are important and essential, but in choosing which vitamins and minerals *must* be listed on the new labels, the government has focused on those currently of greatest importance in maintaining good health. The choices reflect a new emphasis on preventing disease rather than preventing deficiencies. The *mandatory* listings are for vitamin A, vitamin C, calcium, and iron. These recommendations are based on evidence for the benefits of high dietary levels of the antioxidants vitamin A (or the related compound, β-carotene) and vitamin C. Calcium deficiencies are related to osteoporosis, and iron deficiencies are a special concern for women because of their menstrual blood loss. Thiamin, riboflavin, and niacin listings are no longer mandatory because deficiencies of these vitamins are no longer a public health problem in the United States.

Reference Daily Intake Values* for Minerals

Mineral	RDI	Mineral	RDI
Calcium	1.0 g	Selenium	70 μg
Iron	18 mg	Manganese	2 mg
Phosphorus	1.0 g	Fluoride	2.5 mg
Iodine	150 μg	Chromium	120 μg
Magnesium	400 mg	Molybdenum	75 μg
Zinc	15 mg	Chloride	3.4 g
Copper	2 mg		

On Nutrition Facts labels, calcium and iron must be listed; phosphorus, iodine, magnesium, zinc, and copper listings are optional; by law the others cannot be listed.

Nutrition Facts

Serving Size 55 pieces (30g/1.1oz)
Servings Per Container About 6

Amount Per Serving

Calories 140   Calories from Fat 45

	% Daily Value*
Total Fat 5g	**8%**
Saturated Fat 1g	**5%**
Trans Fat 0g	
Polyunsaturated Fat 1.5g	
Monounsaturated Fat 2.5g	
Cholesterol Less than 5mg	**1%**
Sodium 250mg	**10%**
Total Carbohydrate 19g	**6%**
Dietary Fiber 2g	**7%**
Sugars Less than 1g	
Protein 4g	

Vitamin A	0%	•	Vitamin C	0%
Calcuim	4%	•	Iron	6%

*Percent Daily Values are based on a 2,000 calorie diet. Your daily values may be higher or lower depending on your caloric needs:

	Calories:	2,000	2,500
Total Fat	Less than	65g	80g
Sat. Fat	Less than	20g	25g
Cholesterol	Less than	300mg	300mg
Sodium	Less than	2,400mg	2,400mg
Total Carbohydrate		300g	375g
Dietary Fiber		25g	30g

See Chemistry in Action Problems 19.84–19.87 at the end of the chapter.

PROBLEM 19.24

See Chemistry in Action: Vitamins, Minerals, and Food Labels above. Which vitamins function as antioxidants in the body? Why is this important?

Minerals

The other important group of micronutrients is minerals, composed primarily, but not entirely, of transition group elements. The essential minerals, their sources and functions are listed in Table 19.5. A balanced diet supplies sufficient amounts of each of these micronutrients. Many of the transition elements are necessary for proper functioning of enzymes, since these elements are used as cofactors. Other minerals are used as building blocks for the body and some exist as ions, called electrolytes, in our body fluids. The Reference Daily Intake for most of these minerals is listed in Chemistry in Action: Vitamins, Minerals, and Food Labels.

Dietary minerals are divided into macrominerals, those with required daily amounts greater than 100 mg per day, and trace minerals, those needed in lesser quantities. The macrominerals include calcium, phosphorus, magnesium, potassium, sodium, chloride, and sulfur. (Sulfur is not included in the table because it is an integral part of the amino acids cysteine and methionine, generally taken in adequate amounts in the diet.) Adequate, regular intake of calcium and phosphorus is necessary for formation and maintenance of bone. Magnesium is also necessary for bone metabolism and is stored in bone tissue; it is also a cofactor in many different enzymes ranging from glucose and lipid metabolism to protein synthesis.

We generally do not think of the other three macrominerals as essential, since deficiencies are rare. Rather, we often consume too much sodium, chloride, and potassium by eating processed food. These macronutrients function as electrolytes, maintaining osmotic balance in both intra- and extracellular spaces. They also help in the production of electrical signals throughout the nervous system; potassium ions are important in regulating heart beat.

The transition elements, chromium, copper, magnesium, manganese, molybdenum, selenium, and zinc are classed as micronutrients. Our bodies need only minute amounts

TABLE 19.5 Macro and Trace Minerals

Mineral	Significance	Sources	Effects of Deficiency	Effects of Excess
Calcium	Bone formation, muscle contraction	Dairy, eggs, beans	Osteoporosis, muscle cramps	Kidney stones, heart arrhythmias
Phosphorus	Bone formation, component of DNA and energy molecules	Any protein	Muscle weakness	Impaired calcium metabolism
Potassium	Osmotic balance inside cells	Fruit, vegetables, meat	Loss of appetite, muscle cramps	Inhibited heart function
Chloride	Primary negative ion in extracellular fluid	All foods, especially processed	Convulsions (rare)	Hypertension
Sodium	Nerve impulse conduction; electrolyte (osmotic balance)	All foods, especially processed	Muscle cramps, nausea	Hypertension
Magnesium	Protein synthesis, glucose metabolism	Dairy, whole grain, plants	Muscle weakness	Nausea
Iron	Hemoglobin and cytochrome component	Meat, whole grains, legumes	Fatigue, anemia	Hemochromatosis
Fluoride	Part of vitamin B_{12}	Milk, eggs, seafood	Dental cavities	Discolored teeth
Zinc	Enzyme cofactor; smell and taste functions	Meat, dairy, whole grains	Poor immune function; slow wound healing	Poor immune system; increased LDL cholesterol
Copper	Enzymes for oxidations and connective tissue formation	Meat, nuts, eggs, bran cereal	Anemia	Nausea
Selenium	Cofactor for glutathione peroxidase	Meat, whole grains	Cardiac muscle damage	Nausea, hair loss
Manganese	Coenzyme for many enzymes in energy metabolism	Whole grains, legumes	Poor growth	Weakness, mental confusion
Iodine	Production of thyroid hormones	Iodized salt, seafood	Goiter	Depressed thyroid activity
Molybdenum	Coenzyme	Meat, whole grains, legumes	Not found	Not found
Chromium	Enhances insulin function	Meat, whole grain	Glucose intolerance	Rare from diet

of these elements to supply enough cations to function as cofactors for enzymes. Some of these elements, such as copper and selenium, are highly toxic if ingested in high amounts. Each of these transition elements exists as a cation that can form covalent-coordinated bonds with specific, charged residues in the protein structure of their respective enzymes. Because these are transition element cations, with variable oxidation states, they can also serve as transient holders of electrons during enzymatic reactions.

Two of the essential micronutrients have special roles in the body. Iron is a necessary component of the heme ring present in both myoglobin and hemoglobin, as well as in the cytochromes found in the electron transport system. In hemoglobin, iron is responsible for picking up oxygen so red blood cells can transport oxygen through the body. Iodine is essential for synthesis of thyroid hormones, which regulate many functions in the body.

Vitamins and micronutrient minerals serve complementary functions. Both serve as cofactors for enzymatic reactions. Minerals serve directly, while vitamins may be modified into other organic molecules in order to participate in a reaction. The other essential minerals are used as building material or to maintain electrolyte balance.

PROBLEM 19.25
Which micronutrient mineral do you think is the most toxic in excess? Why is it necessary if it is toxic?

SUMMARY: REVISITING THE CHAPTER GOALS

1. What are enzymes? *Enzymes* are the catalysts for biochemical reactions. They are mostly water-soluble, globular proteins, and many incorporate *cofactors*, which are either metal ions or the nonprotein organic molecules known as *coenzymes*. One or more *substrate* molecules (the reactants) enter an *active site* lined by those protein side chains and cofactors necessary for catalyzing the reaction. Six major classes and many subclasses of reactions are catalyzed by enzymes (Table 19.2) *(see Problems 1–9, 26, 29, 34–37, 40, 41)*.

2. How do enzymes work, and why are they so specific? A substrate is drawn into the active site by noncovalent interactions. As the substrate enters the active site, the enzyme shape adjusts to best accommodate the substrate and catalyze the reaction (the *induced fit*). Within the *enzyme–substrate complex*, the substrate is held in the best orientation for reaction and in a strained condition that allows the activation energy to be lowered. When the reaction is complete, the product is released and the enzyme returns to its original condition. The *specificity* of each enzyme is determined by the presence within the active site of catalytically active groups, hydrophobic pockets, and ionic or polar groups that exactly fit the chemical makeup of the substrate *(see Problems 26, 28, 33, 38, 39, 42–45, 48–53, 93, 94)*.

3. What effects do temperature, pH, enzyme concentration, and substrate concentration have on enzyme activity? With increasing temperature, reaction rate increases to a maximum and then decreases as the enzyme protein denatures. Reaction rate is maximal at a pH that reflects the pH of the enzyme's site of action in the body. In the presence of excess substrate, reaction rate is directly proportional to enzyme concentration. With fixed enzyme concentration, reaction rate first increases with increasing substrate concentration and then approaches a fixed maximum at which all active sites are occupied (see Figures 19.5, 19.6, and 19.7) *(see Problems 12, 13, 30, 56, 57, 78–81, 91)*.

4. How is enzyme activity regulated? The effectiveness of enzymes is controlled by a variety of *activation* and *inhibition* strategies. A product of a later reaction can exercise *feedback control* over an enzyme for an earlier reaction in a pathway. Feedback control acts through *allosteric control* of enzymes that have regulatory sites separate from their active sites. Binding a regulator induces a change of shape in the active site, increasing or decreasing the efficiency of the enzyme. *Uncompetitive inhibitors* act on the enzyme–substrate complex, blocking a second substrate from entering the active site; they lower the maximum reaction rate. *Competitive inhibitors* typically resemble the substrate and reversibly block the active site; they slow the reaction rate but do not change the maximum rate. *Irreversible inhibitors* form covalent bonds to an enzyme that permanently inactivate it; most are poisons. Enzyme activity is also regulated by *reversible* phosphorylation and dephosphorylation and by synthesis of inactive *zymogens* that are later activated by removal of part of the molecule. *Genetic control* is exercised by regulation of the synthesis of enzymes *(see Problems 16–19, 31, 32, 58–71, 82, 83, 92)*.

5. What are vitamins and minerals? *Vitamins* are organic molecules required in small amounts in the body that must be obtained from the diet because our bodies cannot synthesize them. The water-soluble vitamins (Table 19.3) are coenzymes or parts of coenzymes. The fat-soluble vitamins (Table 19.4) have diverse and less well-understood functions. In general, excesses of water-soluble vitamins are excreted and excesses of fat-soluble vitamins are stored in body fat, making excesses of the fat-soluble vitamins potentially more harmful. Vitamin C, β-carotene (a precursor of vitamin A), vitamin E, and selenium work together as *antioxidants* to protect biomolecules from damage by free radicals. Minerals are chemical elements needed in small amounts in the diet. Minerals function as macronutrients (calcium and phosphorus for bone), electrolytes, and micronutrients used primarily as enzyme cofactors *(see Problems 21, 22, 46, 47, 72–77, 84–90)*.

KEY WORDS

Activation (of an enzyme), *p. 602*

Active site, *p. 588*

Allosteric control, *p. 603*

Allosteric enzyme, *p. 603*

Antioxidant, *p. 614*

Coenzyme, *p. 589*

Cofactor, *p. 589*

Competitive (enzyme) inhibition, *p. 604*

Enzyme, *p. 587*

Feedback control, *p. 602*

Free radical, *p. 614*

Genetic (enzyme) control, *p. 609*

Induced-fit model, *p. 594*

Inhibition (of an enzyme), *p. 602*

Irreversible (enzyme) inhibition, *p. 606*

Specificity (enzyme), *p. 588*

Substrate, *p. 588*

Turnover number, *p. 588*

Uncompetitive (enzyme) inhibition, *p. 604*

Vitamin, *p. 610*

Zymogen, *p. 608*

UNDERSTANDING KEY CONCEPTS

19.26 On the diagram shown below, indicate with dotted lines the bonding between the enzyme (a dipeptidase; several amino acid residues in black) and the substrate (in blue) that might occur to form the enzyme–substrate complex. What are the two types of bonding likely to occur?

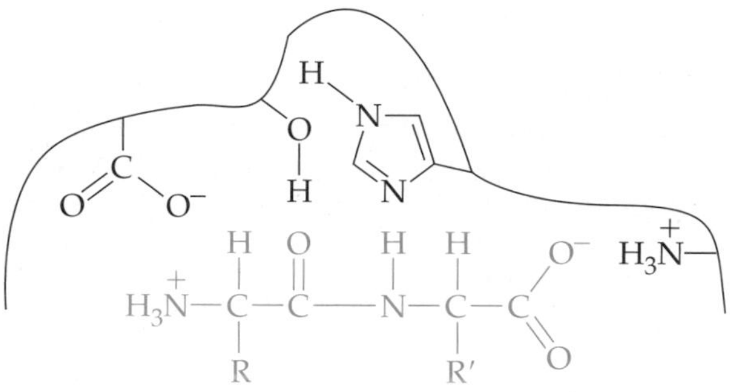

19.27 Answer questions (a)–(e) concerning the following reaction:

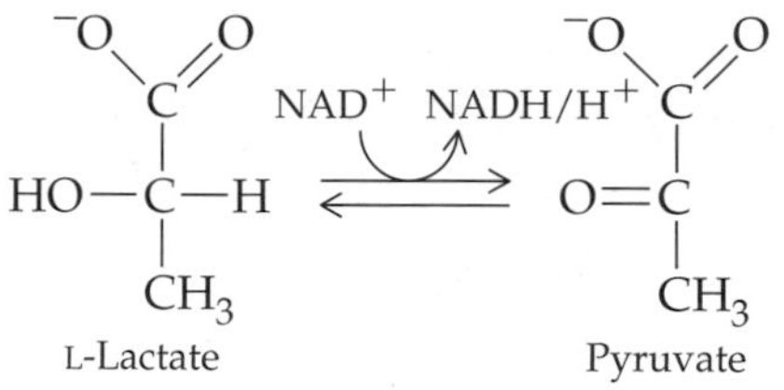

L-Lactate   Pyruvate

(a) The enzyme involved in this reaction belongs to what class of enzymes?

(b) Since hydrogens are removed, the enzyme belongs to what subclass of the enzyme class from part (a)?

(c) What is the substrate for the reaction as written?

(d) What is the product for the reaction as written?

(e) The enzyme name is derived from the substrate name and the subclass of the enzyme and ends in the family-name ending for an enzyme. Name the enzyme.

19.28 In the reaction shown in Problem 19.27, will the enzyme likely also use D-lactate as a substrate? Explain your answer. If D-lactate binds to the enzyme, how is it likely to affect the enzyme?

19.29 In the reaction shown in Problem 19.27, identify the coenzyme required for catalytic activity. Is the coenzyme an oxidizing agent or a reducing agent? What vitamin is a part of the coenzyme for this reaction?

19.30 Explain how the following changes affect the rate of an enzyme-catalyzed reaction in the presence of an uncompetitive inhibitor: (a) increasing the substrate concentration at a constant inhibitor concentration, (b) decreasing the inhibitor concentration at a constant substrate concentration.

19.31 Explain how the following mechanisms regulate enzyme activity.

(a) Covalent modification   (b) Genetic control

(c) Allosteric regulation   (d) Feedback inhibition

19.32 What type of enzyme inhibition occurs in the following situations?

(a) Buildup of the product of the pathway that converts glucose to pyruvate stops at the first enzyme in the multistep process.

(b) Sarin, a nerve gas, covalently binds to acetylcholinesterase, stopping nerve signal transmission.

(c) Lactase is not produced in the adult.

(d) Conversion of isocitrate to α-ketoglutarate is inhibited by high levels of ATP. (Hint: ATP is neither a product nor a substrate in this reaction.)

19.33 Acidic and basic groups are often found in the active sites of enzymes. Identify the acidic and basic amino acids in the active site in the diagram below. (Hint: Consult Table 18.3 and Chapter 10 for the definition of acids and bases.)

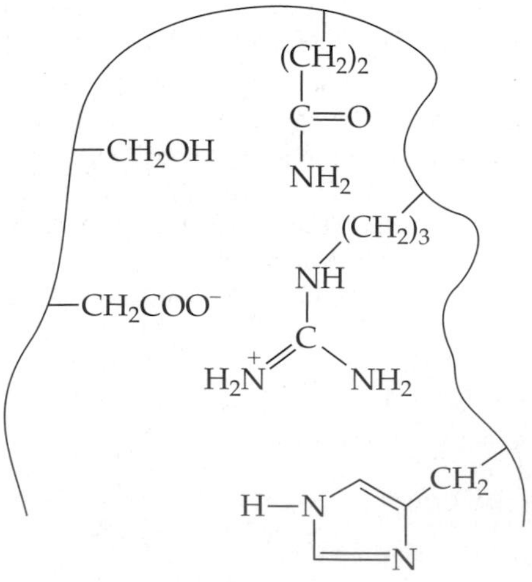

ADDITIONAL PROBLEMS

STRUCTURE AND CLASSIFICATION OF ENZYMES

19.34 What general kinds of reactions do the following types of enzymes catalyze?

    (a) Dehydrogenases   **(b)** Decarboxylases   **(c)** Lipases

19.35 What general kinds of reactions do the following types of enzymes catalyze?

    (a) Kinases   **(b)** Isomerases   **(c)** Synthetases

19.36 Name an enzyme that acts on each molecule.

    (a) Amylose   **(b)** Peroxide   **(c)** DNA

19.37 Name an enzyme that acts on each molecule.

    (a) Lactose   **(b)** Protein   **(c)** RNA

19.38 What features of enzymes make them so specific in their action?

19.39 Describe in general terms how enzymes act as catalysts.

19.40 What classes of enzymes would you expect to catalyze the following reactions?

(a)
$$\underset{\underset{R}{|}}{H_2NCHCNHCHCOH} + H_2O \longrightarrow$$
(with two C=O groups shown)

$$\underset{\underset{R}{|}}{H_2NCHCOH} + \underset{\underset{R'}{|}}{H_2NCHCOH}$$

(b)
$$HOOC-CH_2-\overset{O}{\overset{\|}{C}}-COOH \longrightarrow$$

$$CH_3-\overset{O}{\overset{\|}{C}}-COOH + CO_2$$

(c) $HO\overset{O}{\overset{\|}{C}}CH_2CH_2\overset{O}{\overset{\|}{C}}OH \longrightarrow HO\overset{O}{\overset{\|}{C}}CH=CH\overset{O}{\overset{\|}{C}}OH$

19.41 What classes of enzymes would you expect to catalyze the following reactions?

(a)

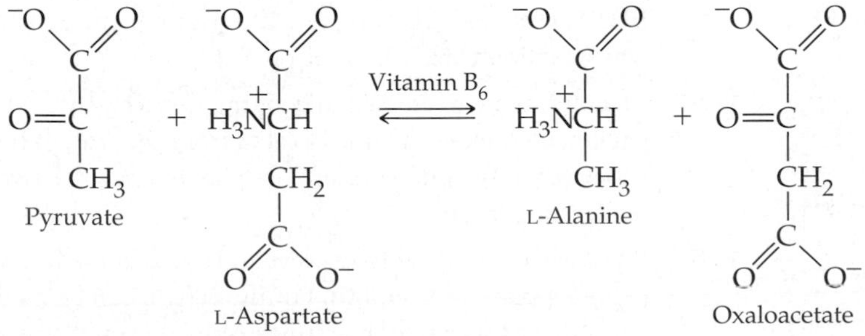

Pyruvate + H_3NCH $\underset{Vitamin\ B_6}{\rightleftharpoons}$ L-Alanine + Oxaloacetate

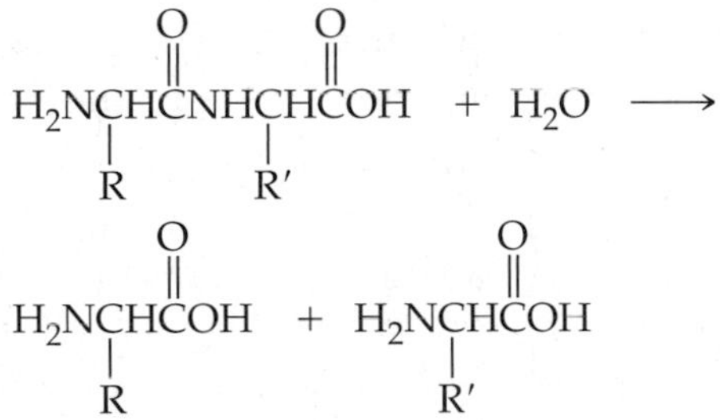

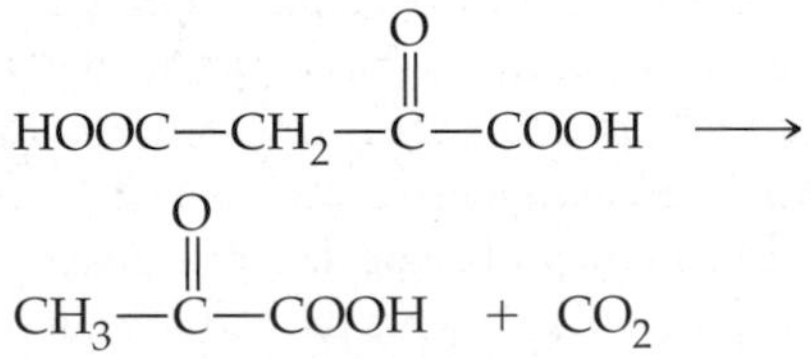

(structures shown: Pyruvate, L-Aspartate, L-Alanine, Oxaloacetate)

(b)

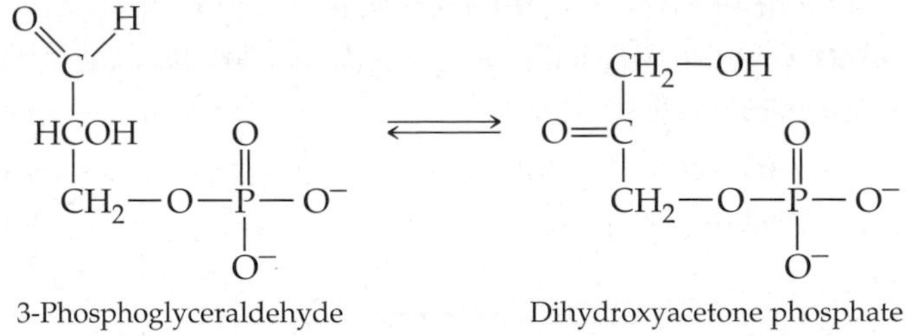

3-Phosphoglyceraldehyde $\rightleftharpoons$ Dihydroxyacetone phosphate

(c)

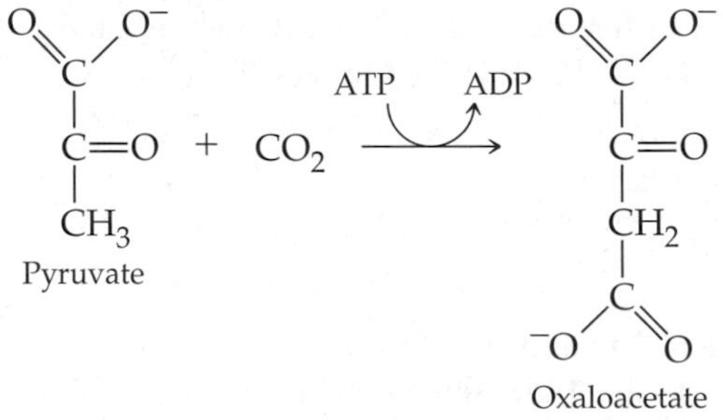

Pyruvate + CO_2 $\xrightarrow{ATP \quad ADP}$ Oxaloacetate

19.42 What kind of reaction does each of these enzymes catalyze?

    (a) A dehydrase

    (b) A transmethylase

    (c) A reductase

19.43 What kind of reaction does each of these enzymes catalyze?

    (a) A dehydrase

    (b) A carboxylase

    (c) A protease

19.44 The following reaction is catalyzed by the enzyme urease. To what class of enzymes does urease belong?

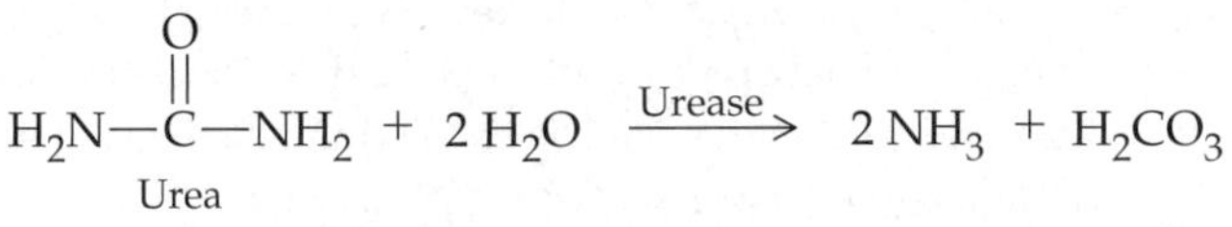

$$H_2N-\overset{O}{\overset{\|}{C}}-NH_2 + 2\,H_2O \xrightarrow{Urease} 2\,NH_3 + H_2CO_3$$
Urea

19.45 Alcohol dehydrogenase (ADH) catalyzes the following reaction. To what class of enzymes does ADH belong?

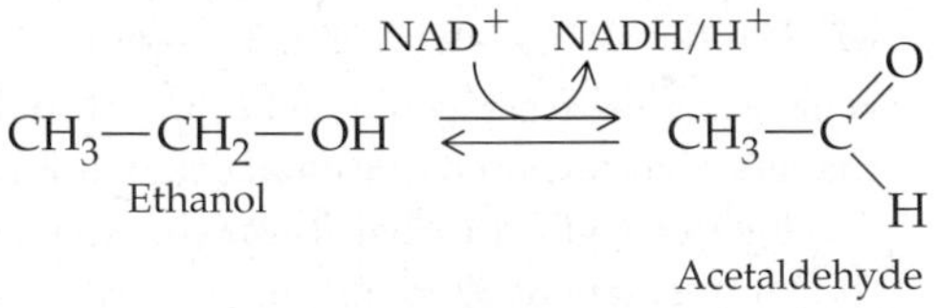

$$CH_3-CH_2-OH \underset{\xrightarrow{NAD^+ \quad NADH/H^+}}{\rightleftharpoons} CH_3-\overset{O}{\overset{\|}{C}}{\diagdown}_H$$
Ethanol   Acetaldehyde

19.46 Name the vitamin to which each of these coenzymes is related.

    (a) FAD   **(b)** Coenzyme A   **(c)** NAD$^+$

19.47 Which of the following is a cofactor and which is a coenzyme?

    (a) Cu^{2+} **(b)** Tetrahydrofolate

    (c) NAD$^+$ **(d)** Mg^{2+}

ENZYME FUNCTION AND REGULATION

19.48 What is the difference between the lock-and-key model of enzyme action and the induced-fit model?

19.49 Why is the induced-fit model a more likely model than the lock-and-key model?

19.50 Must the amino acid residues in the active site be near each other along the polypeptide chain? Explain.

19.51 The active site of an enzyme is a small portion of the enzyme molecule. What is the function of the rest of the huge molecule?

19.52 How do you explain the observation that pepsin, a digestive enzyme found in the stomach, has a high catalytic activity at pH 1.5, while trypsin, an enzyme of the small intestine, has no activity at pH 1.5?

19.53 Amino acid side chains in the active sites of enzymes can act as acids or bases during catalysis. List the amino acid side chains that can accept H$^+$ and those that can donate H$^+$ during enzyme-catalyzed reactions.

19.54 If the rate of an enzymatic reaction doubles when the amount of enzyme is doubled, what do you expect the rate of reaction to be if the amount of enzyme is tripled? Why?

19.55 What happens to the rate of an enzymatic reaction if the amount of substrate is doubled? Why?

19.56 What general effects would you expect the following changes to have on the rate of an enzyme-catalyzed reaction for an enzyme that has its maximum activity at body temperature (about 37 °C)?

    (a) Raising the temperature from 37 °C to 70 °C

    (b) Lowering the pH from 7 to 3

    (c) Adding an organic solvent, such as methanol

19.57 What general effects would you expect the following changes to have on the rate of an enzyme-catalyzed reaction for an enzyme that has its maximum activity at body temperature (about 37 °C)?

    (a) Lowering the reaction temperature from 40 °C to 10 °C

    (b) Adding a drop of a dilute HgCl$_2$ solution

    (c) Adding an oxidizing agent, such as hydrogen peroxide

19.58 The text discusses three forms of enzyme inhibition: uncompetitive inhibition, competitive inhibition, and irreversible inhibition.

    (a) Describe how an enzyme inhibitor of each type works.

    (b) What kinds of bonds are formed between an enzyme and each of these three kinds of inhibitors?

19.59 What kind of inhibition (uncompetitive, competitive, or irreversible) is present in each of the following:

    (a) Penicillin is used to treat certain bacterial infections. Penicillin is effective because it binds to the enzyme glycopeptide transpeptidase and does not dissociate.

    (b) Accidental methanol consumption is fairly common. The treatment includes the ingestion of ethanol. Both molecules can be converted to aldehydes by alcohol dehydrogenase. Ethanol is the true substrate.

    (c) The antibiotic deoxycycline inhibits the bacterial enzyme collagenase, slowing bacterial growth. Deoxycycline does not fit into the active site of collagenase and binds elsewhere on the enzyme.

19.60 EcoRI, an enzyme that hydrolyzes DNA strands, requires Mg^{2+} as a cofactor for activity. Ethylenediaminetetraacetic acid (EDTA) chelates divalent metal ions in solution. In the graphs shown here, the arrow indicates the point at which EDTA is added to a reaction mediated by EcoRI. Which graph represents the activity curve you would expect to see? (Activity is shown as total product from the reaction as time increases.)

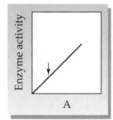 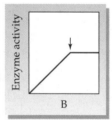 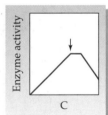

19.61 The enzyme lactic dehydrogenase converts lactic acid to pyruvate with the aid of the coenzyme NAD$^+$. In the graphs of Problem 19.60, the arrow indicates the point at which ethylenediaminetetraacetic acid (EDTA) is added to a reaction mixture of lactic dehydrogenase and lactic acid. Which graph represents the activity curve you would you expect to see? (Activity is shown as total product from the reaction as time increases.)

19.62 Lead exerts its poisonous effect on enzymes by two mechanisms. Which mechanism is irreversible and why?

19.63 One mechanism by which lead exerts its poisonous effect on enzymes can be stopped by chelation therapy with EDTA. Describe this type of lead poisoning and explain why it is reversible.

19.64 The meat tenderizer used in cooking is primarily papain, a protease enzyme isolated from the fruit of the papaya tree. Why do you suppose papain is so effective at tenderizing meat?

19.65 Bumblebee venom contains several related heptadeca-peptides from the bomditin family. Papain can be used to help relieve the pain of bee stings. Why do you suppose it works?

19.66 Why do allosteric enzymes have two types of binding sites?

19.67 Discuss the purpose of positive and negative regulation.

19.68 What is feedback inhibition?

19.69 What are the cellular advantages to feedback inhibition?

19.70 What is a zymogen? Why must some enzymes be secreted as zymogens?

19.71 Activation of a zymogen is by covalent modification. How might phosphorylation or dephosphorylation (also covalent modification) modify an enzyme to make it more active (or more inactive)?

VITAMINS AND MINERALS

19.72 What criteria make a compound a vitamin?

19.73 What is the relationship between vitamins and enzymes?

19.74 Why is daily ingestion of vitamin C more critical than daily ingestion of vitamin A?

19.75 List the four fat-soluble vitamins. Why is excess consumption of three of these vitamins of concern?

19.76 Why is it important that the macronutrients calcium and phosphorus be ingested in approximately equal amounts?

19.77 Most of the micronutrients are transition elements. What property of the transition elements makes them especially suitable for their roles in the body?

CHEMISTRY IN ACTION

19.78 Enzymes that hydrolyze starch to glucose can be isolated from many different microorganisms for use by food chemists. Why would the food industry prefer to use these enzymes from thermophiles? [*Extremozymes: Enzymes from the Edge, p. 595*]

19.79 When energy companies drill for oil, are enzymes from thermophiles or psychrophiles used? Why? [*Extremozymes: Enzymes from the Edge, p. 595*]

19.80 Enzyme levels in blood are often elevated in various disease states. Which enzyme gives the earliest indication of a heart attack? Which enzyme is used to confirm a heart attack, after several tests over several days? [*Enzymes in Medical Diagnosis, p. 601*]

19.81 Why must enzyme activity be monitored under standard conditions? [*Enzymes in Medical Diagnosis, p. 601*]

19.82 The primary structure of angiotensin II has … Pro-Phe at the C-terminal end of the octapeptide. The angiotensin-converting enzyme (ACE) inhibitor from the South American pit viper is a pentapeptide with a C-terminal proline and is a mild ACE inhibitor. Captopril has a modified proline structure and is also a mild ACE inhibitor. Why do you suppose that a mild ACE inhibitor is more valuable for the treatment of high blood pressure than a very potent ACE inhibitor? What structural modifications to the pit viper peptide might make it a more powerful ACE inhibitor? [*Enzyme Inhibitors as Drugs, p. 607*]

19.83 AZT (zivovudine) inhibits the synthesis of the HIV virus RNA because AZT resembles substrate molecules. Which kind of inhibition is most likely taking place in this reaction? [*Enzyme Inhibitors as Drugs, p. 607*]

19.84 Which vitamins and minerals are listed on the food label and in what amount? Is this a good nutritional choice for vitamins and minerals? [*Vitamins, Minerals, and Food Labels, p. 615*]

19.85 Read the labels on foods that you eat for a day, or look up the foods in a nutrition table and determine what percent of your daily dosage of vitamins and minerals you get from each. Are you getting the recommended amounts from the food you eat, or should you be taking a vitamin or mineral supplement? [*Vitamins, Minerals, and Food Labels, p. 615*]

19.86 For what reasons are listings for vitamin A, vitamin C, iron, and calcium mandatory on food labels? [*Vitamins, Minerals, and Food Labels, p. 615*]

19.87 In addition to the four nutrients named in Problem 19.86, what other nutrients may be listed on food labels? (Hint: Look at all the ingredients that have amounts listed on the label shown in the Chemistry in Action box.) [*Vitamins, Minerals, and Food Labels, p. 615*]

GENERAL QUESTIONS AND PROBLEMS

19.88 Look up the structures of vitamin C and vitamin E in Section 19.10, and identify the functional groups in these vitamins.

19.89 What is the relationship between vitamin A and β-carotene? (Hint: Look at the structures in Section 19.10.)

19.90 The adult recommended daily allowance (RDA) of riboflavin is 1.6 mg. If one glass (100 mL) of apple juice contains 0.014 mg of riboflavin, how much apple juice would an adult have to consume to obtain the RDA?

19.91 Many vegetables are "blanched" (dropped into boiling water) for a few minutes before being frozen. Why is blanching necessary?

19.92 How can you distinguish between a competitive inhibitor and an uncompetitive inhibitor experimentally?

19.93 Trypsin is an enzyme that cleaves on the C-terminal side (that is, to the right of) all basic amino acids in a protein or peptide. (Consult Table 18.3 to identify basic amino acids.) Consider the peptide shown below. Predict the fragments that would be formed by treatment of this peptide with trypsin:

N-terminal end-Leu-Gly-Arg-Ile-Met-His-Tyr-Trp-Ala-C-terminal end

19.94 The ability to change a selected amino acid residue to another amino acid is referred to as "point mutation" by biochemists. Referring to the reaction for peptide bond hydrolysis in Figure 19.4, speculate on the effects that the following point mutations might have on the chymotrypsin mechanism shown in Figure 19.4: serine to valine; aspartate to glutamate.

Living systems make constant use of this principle in the series of chemical reactions we know as the biochemical *pathways*. Energy is stored in the products of an overall endergonic reaction pathway. This stored energy is released as needed in an overall exergonic reaction pathway that regenerates the original reactants. It is not necessary that every reaction in the pathways between the reactants and products be the same, so long as the pathways connect the same reactants and products.

Worked Example 20.1 Determining Reaction Energy

Are the following reactions exergonic or endergonic?

(a) Glucose 6-phosphate $\rightarrow$ Fructose 6-phosphate
$\Delta G = +0.5 \, \text{kcal/mol} \, (+2.09 \, \text{kJ/mol})$

(b) Fructose 6-phosphate + ATP $\rightarrow$ Fructose 1,6-bisphosphate + ADP
$\Delta G = -3.4 \, \text{kcal/mol} \, (-14.2 \, \text{kJ/mol})$

ANALYSIS Exergonic reactions release free energy, and ΔG is negative. Endergonic reactions gain free energy, and so ΔG is positive.

SOLUTION
Reaction (a), the conversion of glucose 6-phosphate to fructose 6-phosphate has a positive ΔG; therefore it is endergonic. Reaction (b), the conversion of fructose 6-phosphate to fructose 1,6-bisphosphate has a negative ΔG; therefore it is exergonic.

Worked Example 20.2 Determining Reaction Energy for Reverse Reactions

Write the reverse reaction for each reaction in Worked Example 20.1. For each reverse reaction, determine ΔG and characterize the reaction as either exergonic or endergonic.

ANALYSIS First, remember that reactions are written left to right, with the reaction arrow pointing to the right. Second, remember that the compounds that are products in the original reaction are reactants in the reverse reaction and the compounds that are reactants in the original reaction are products in the reverse reaction. (We are assuming the reaction is directly reversible; this is not always true inside cells.) Third, remember that if ΔG for the forward reaction is positive, ΔG for the reverse reaction has the same numeric value but is negative. If ΔG for the forward reaction is negative, ΔG for the reverse reaction has the same number value but is positive. Negative ΔG values indicate exergonic reactions, and positive ΔG values indicate endergonic reactions.

SOLUTION

(a) Fructose 6-phosphate $\rightarrow$ Glucose 6-phosphate
$\Delta G = -0.5 \, \text{kcal/mol} \, (-2.09 \, \text{kJ/mol})$
This reaction is exergonic.

(b) Fructose 1,6-bisphosphate + ADP $\rightarrow$ Fructose 6-phosphate + ATP
$\Delta G = +3.4 \, \text{kcal/mol} \, (+14.2 \, \text{kJ/mol})$
This reaction is endergonic.

PROBLEM 20.1
The following reactions occur in the citric acid cycle, an energy-producing sequence of reactions that we will discuss later in this chapter. Which of the reactions listed is (are) exergonic? Which is (are) endergonic? Which will release the most energy? Write the complete equation for the reverse of reaction (c). (Recall that organic acids are usually referred to in biochemistry with the -*ate* ending because they exist as anions in body fluids.)

(a) Acetyl coenzyme A + Oxaloacetate + $H_2O \longrightarrow$ Citrate + Coenzyme A
$\Delta G = -9 \, \text{kcal/mol} \, (-37.7 \, \text{kJ/mol})$

(b) Citrate $\longrightarrow$ Isocitrate $\Delta G = +3 \, \text{kcal/mol} \, (+12.6 \, \text{kJ/mol})$

(c) Fumarate + $H_2O \longrightarrow$ L-Malate $\Delta G = -0.9 \, \text{kcal/mol} \, (-3.77 \, \text{kJ/mol})$

CHEMISTRY IN ACTION

Life without Sunlight

Before we had the equipment to descend deep into the ocean, no one imagined that life existed there. What could provide the food and energy? Textbooks firmly stated that all life depends on sunlight.

Not true! In 1977, hydrothermal vents—openings spewing water heated to 400 °C deep within the earth—were found on the ocean floor. The hydrothermal vents were dubbed "black smokers" because the water was black with mineral sulfides precipitating from the hot, acidic water as it exited the vents. At 2200 m below the ocean surface, there is no chance for the penetration of energy from sunlight. Therefore, the discovery of thriving clusters of tube worms, giant clams, mussels, and other creatures surrounding the black smokers was a great surprise.

Distinctive types of bacteria form the basis for the web of life in these locations. What replaces sunlight as their source of energy? The hot water is rich in dissolved inorganic substances that are reducing agents and therefore electron donors. Life-supporting energy is set free by their oxidation. Hydrogen sulfide, for example, is abundant in the hot seawater, which has passed through sulfur-bearing mineral deposits on its way to the surface. This is the same gas produced during anaerobic decomposition of organic matter in a swamp; it is also the gas that gives the awful odor to rotten eggs. As the hydrogen sulfide is converted to sulfate ions in sulfate-reducing bacteria, the electrons set free in the oxidation move through an electron-transport chain that makes ATP formation possible for these bacteria.

Carbon dioxide dissolved in the seawater is the raw material used by the bacteria to make their own essential carbon-containing biomolecules. Experiments have shown that the tube worms, giant clams, and other creatures surrounding the black

▲ **Sea life near a hydrothermal vent at the ocean's floor.**

smokers do not eat the bacteria. Rather, the bacteria colonize their digestive organs, where bacterial waste products and cell remnants are the carbon source for biosynthesis by their hosts.

An opportunity to observe the colonization of a hot deep-ocean environment came in 1991 when scientists discovered a volcano erupting underneath the ocean. Initially, all life in the vicinity was wiped out, yet soon afterward, the area was thriving with bacteria. This discovery and others have raised some intriguing questions. The same black smoker bacteria have been found in the vicinity of the Mount St. Helens volcanic eruption, and hydrothermal vents with their communities of living things have been found in the fresh waters of the deepest lake on earth, Lake Baikal in Russia. Could it be that a thriving population of bacteria has been living in the hot interior of the earth ever since it formed? Were these anaerobic bacteria earth's first inhabitants, and could they exist beneath the surface of other planets? Research will eventually answer these questions.

See Chemistry in Actions Problems 20.79 and 20.80 at the end of the chapter.

 KEY CONCEPT PROBLEM 20.2

In a cell, glucose can be oxidized via metabolic pathways. Alternatively, you could burn glucose in the laboratory. Which of these methods consumes or produces more energy? (Hint: all of the energy comes from converting the energy stored in the reduced bonds in glucose into the most oxidized form, carbon dioxide.)

KEY CONCEPT PROBLEM 20.3

The overall equation in this section,

$$6\,CO_2 + 6\,H_2O \underset{\text{oxidation}}{\overset{\text{photosynthesis}}{\rightleftarrows}} C_6H_{12}O_6 + 6\,O_2,$$

shows the cycle between photosynthesis and oxidation. Pathways operating in opposite directions cannot be exergonic in both directions.

(a) Which of the two pathways in this cycle is exergonic and which is endergonic?

(b) Where does the energy for the endergonic pathway come from?

20.3 Cells and Their Structure

Before we proceed with our overview of metabolism, it is important to see where the energy-generating reactions take place within the cells of living organisms. There are two main categories of cells: *prokaryotic cells*, usually found in single-celled organisms including bacteria and blue-green algae, and *eukaryotic cells*, found in some single-celled organisms such as yeast and all plants and animals.

Eukaryotic cells are about 1000 times larger than bacterial cells, have a membrane-enclosed nucleus that contains their DNA, and include several other kinds of internal structures known as *organelles*—small, functional units that perform specialized tasks. A generalized eukaryotic cell is shown in Figure 20.3; the accompanying table describes the functions of some of its major parts. Everything between the cell membrane and the nuclear membrane in a eukaryotic cell, including the various organelles, is referred to as the **cytoplasm**. The organelles are surrounded by the fluid part of the cytoplasm, the **cytosol**, which contains electrolytes, nutrients, and many enzymes, all in aqueous solution.

Cytoplasm The region between the cell membrane and the nuclear membrane in a eukaryotic cell.

Cytosol The fluid part of the cytoplasm surrounding the organelles within a cell.

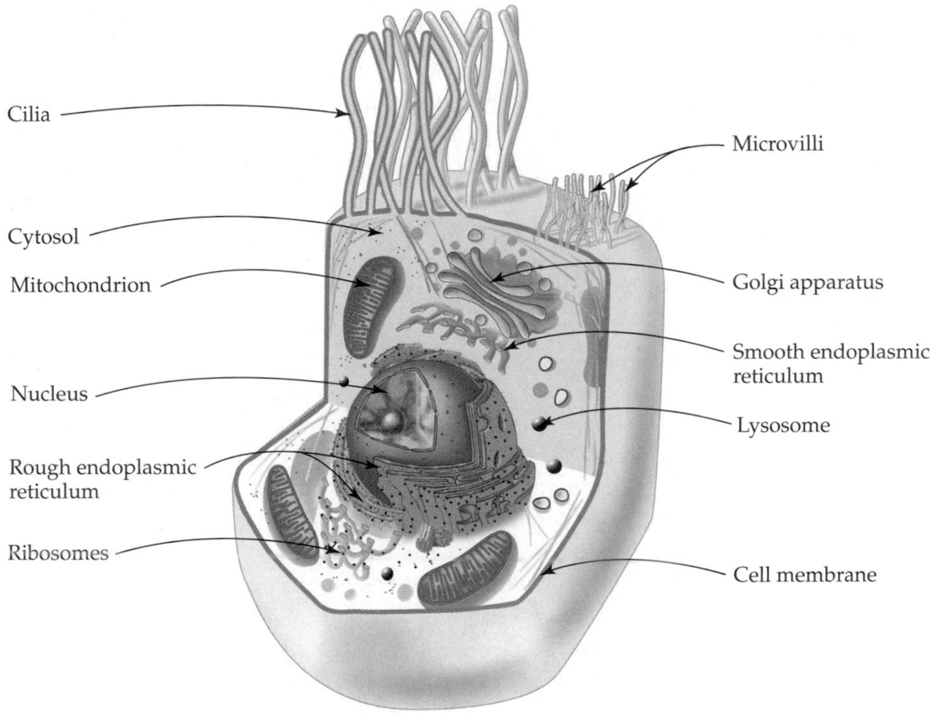

▶ **Figure 20.3**
A generalized eukaryotic cell.
The table below lists the functions of the cell components most important for metabolism.

Cell Component	Principal Function
Cilia	Movement of materials; for example, mucus in lungs (not present in all cells)
Golgi apparatus	Synthesis and packaging of macromolecules for secretion or use within the cell
Mitochondrion	Synthesis of ATP from ADP
Rough endoplasmic reticulum	Protein synthesis and transport
Nucleus	Replication of DNA, which carries genetic information and governs protein synthesis
Ribosome	Protein synthesis
Microvilli	Absorption of extracellular substances; for example, in the digestive tract (not present in all cells)
Cytosol	Intracellular fluid; contains dissolved proteins and nutrients
Lysosome	Removal of pathogens or damaged organelles
Smooth endoplasmic reticulum	Lipid and carbohydrate synthesis
Cell membrane	Composed of lipids plus proteins that govern entry and exit from the cell and deliver signals to the interior of the cell

The **mitochondria** (singular, **mitochondrion**), often called the cell's "power plants," are the most important of the organelles for energy production. In the mitochondria, about 90% of the body's energy-carrying molecule, ATP, is produced.

A mitochondrion is a roughly egg-shaped structure composed of a smooth outer membrane and a folded inner membrane (Figure 20.4). The space enclosed by the inner membrane is the **mitochondrial matrix**. It is within the matrix that the citric acid cycle (Section 20.8) and the production of most of the body's **adenosine triphosphate (ATP)** take place. The coenzymes and proteins that manage the transfer of energy to the chemical bonds of ATP (Section 20.9) are embedded in the inner membrane of the mitochondrion.

Mitochondrion (plural, **mitochondria**) An egg-shaped organelle where small molecules are broken down to provide the energy for an organism.

Mitochondrial matrix The space surrounded by the inner membrane of a mitochondrion.

Adenosine triphosphate (ATP) The principal energy-carrying molecule; removal of a phosphoryl group to give ADP releases free energy.

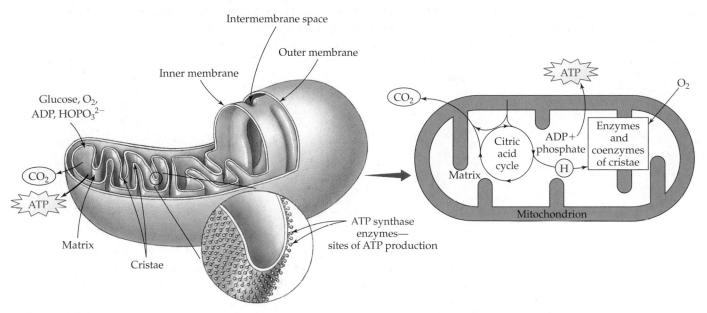

▲ **Figure 20.4**
The mitochondrion.
Cells have many mitochondria. The citric acid cycle takes place in the matrix. Electron transport and ATP production, the final stage in biochemical energy generation (described in Section 20.9), takes place at the inner surface of the inner membrane. The numerous folds in the inner membrane—known as *cristae*—increase the surface area over which these pathways can take place.

It is believed that millions of years ago, mitochondria were free-living bacteria that became trapped within single-celled plants and animals. As evidence for this, consider that mitochondria still contain their own DNA, can synthesize some of their own proteins, and can multiply without outside assistance. The relationship of mitochondria to their host cells became a symbiotic one—the mitochondria produced energy needed by the eukaryotic cells, and the cells provided the mitochondria with nutrients. (This kind of relationship is known as endosymbiosis.) Thus, mitochondria remained within the host cells throughout evolution. The number of mitochondria is greatest in eye, brain, heart, and muscle cells, where the need for energy is greatest. The ability of mitochondria to reproduce is called upon in athletes who put heavy energy demands on their bodies—they develop an increased number of mitochondria to aid in energy production.

20.4 An Overview of Metabolism and Energy Production

Together, all of the chemical reactions that take place in an organism constitute its metabolism. Most of these reactions occur in the reaction sequences of *metabolic pathways*. Such pathways may be linear (that is, the product of one reaction serves as the starting material for the next); cyclic (a series of reactions regenerates one of the first reactants); or spiral (the same set of enzymes progressively builds up or breaks down a molecule):

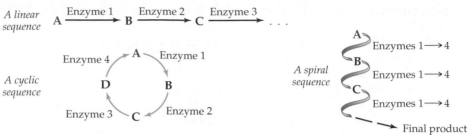

As we study metabolism we will encounter each of these types of pathways. Those pathways that break molecules apart are known collectively as **catabolism**, whereas those that put building blocks back together to assemble larger molecules are known collectively as **anabolism**. The purpose of catabolism is to release energy from food, and the purpose of anabolism is to synthesize new biomolecules, including those that store energy.

> **Catabolism** Metabolic reaction pathways that break down food molecules and release biochemical energy.

> **Anabolism** Metabolic reactions that build larger biological molecules from smaller pieces.

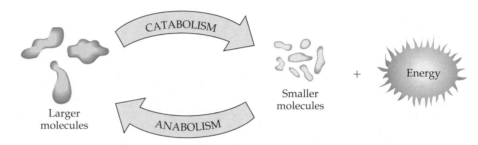

The overall picture of digestion, catabolism, and energy production is simple: eating provides fuel, breathing provides oxygen, and our bodies oxidize the fuel to extract energy. The process can be roughly divided into the four stages described below and shown in Figure 20.5.

Stage 1: Digestion Enzymes in saliva, the stomach, and the small intestine convert the large molecules of carbohydrates, proteins, and lipids to smaller molecules. Carbohydrates are broken down to glucose and other sugars; proteins are broken down to amino acids; and triacylglycerols, the lipids commonly known as fats and oils, are broken down to glycerol plus long-chain carboxylic acids, termed fatty acids. These smaller molecules are transferred into the blood for transport to cells throughout the body.

Stage 2: Acetyl-coenzyme A production The small molecules from digestion follow separate pathways that separate their carbon atoms into two-carbon acetyl groups. The acetyl groups are attached to coenzyme A by a bond between the sulfur atom of the thiol (—SH) group at the end of the coenzyme A molecule and the carbonyl carbon atom of the acetyl group:

> **Acetyl-coenzyme A (acetyl-CoA)** Acetyl-substituted coenzyme A—the common intermediate that carries acetyl groups into the citric acid cycle.

> ▶▶▶ See the chemical structure of coenzyme A in Figure 19.10.

Attachment of acetyl group to coenzyme A

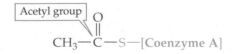

The resultant compound, **acetyl-coenzyme A**, which we abbreviate **acetyl-CoA**, is an intermediate in the breakdown of *all* classes of food molecules. It carries the acetyl groups into the common pathways of catabolism—Stage 3, the citric acid cycle and Stage 4, electron transport and ATP production.

Stage 3: Citric acid cycle Within mitochondria, the acetyl-group carbon atoms are oxidized to the carbon dioxide that we exhale. Most of the energy released in the oxidation leaves the citric acid cycle in the chemical bonds of reduced coenzymes (NADH,

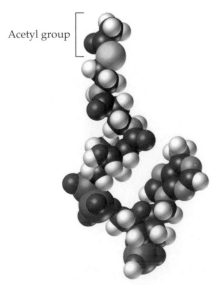

Acetyl group

Acetyl-coenzyme A

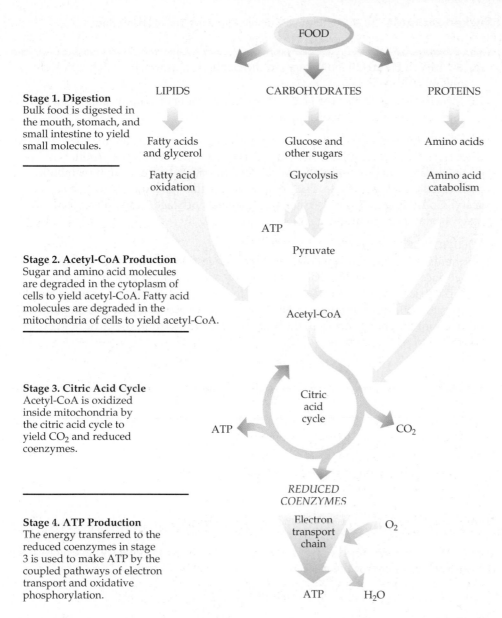

Stage 1. Digestion
Bulk food is digested in the mouth, stomach, and small intestine to yield small molecules.

Stage 2. Acetyl-CoA Production
Sugar and amino acid molecules are degraded in the cytoplasm of cells to yield acetyl-CoA. Fatty acid molecules are degraded in the mitochondria of cells to yield acetyl-CoA.

Stage 3. Citric Acid Cycle
Acetyl-CoA is oxidized inside mitochondria by the citric acid cycle to yield CO_2 and reduced coenzymes.

Stage 4. ATP Production
The energy transferred to the reduced coenzymes in stage 3 is used to make ATP by the coupled pathways of electron transport and oxidative phosphorylation.

◄ **Figure 20.5**
Pathways for the digestion of food and the production of biochemical energy.
This diagram summarizes pathways covered in this chapter (the citric acid cycle and electron transport), and also the pathways discussed in Chapter 22 for carbohydrate metabolism, in Chapter 24 for lipid metabolism, and in Chapter 27 for protein metabolism.

$FADH_2$). Some energy also leaves the cycle stored in the chemical bonds of adenosine triphosphate (ATP) or a related triphosphate.

Stage 4: ATP production Electrons from the reduced coenzymes are passed from molecule to molecule down an electron-transport chain. Along the way, their energy is harnessed to produce more ATP. At the end of the process, these electrons—along with hydrogen ions from the reduced coenzymes—combine with oxygen we breathe to produce water. Thus, the reduced coenzymes are in effect oxidized by atmospheric oxygen, and the energy that they carried is stored in the chemical bonds of ATP molecules.

LOOKING AHEAD ▶▶▶ Digestion and conversion of food molecules to acetyl-CoA, Stages 1 and 2 in Figure 20.5, occur by different metabolic pathways for carbohydrates, lipids, and proteins. Each of these pathways is discussed separately in later chapters: carbohydrate metabolism in Chapter 22, lipid metabolism in Chapter 24, and protein metabolism in Chapter 27.

Worked Example 20.3 Identifying Metabolic Pathways That Convert Basic
Molecules to Energy

(a) Identify in Figure 20.5 the stages in the catabolic pathway in which lipids ultimately yield ATP.

(b) Identify in Figure 20.5 the place at which the products of lipid catabolism can
join the common metabolism pathway.

ANALYSIS Look at Figure 20.5 and find the pathway for lipids. Follow the arrows to
trace the flow of energy. Note that Stage 3 is the point at which the products of lipid,
carbohydrate, and protein catabolism all feed into a central, common metabolic
pathway, the citric acid cycle. The lipid molecules that feed into Stage 3 do so via
acetyl-CoA (Stage 2). Note also that most products of Stage 3 catabolism feed into
Stage 4 catabolism to produce ATP.

SOLUTION
The lipids in food are broken down in Stage 1 (digestion) to fatty acids and glycerol.
Stage 2 (acetyl-CoA production) results in fatty acid oxidation to acetyl-CoA. In
Stage 3 (citric acid cycle) acetyl-CoA enters the citric acid cycle (the common metabolism pathway), which produces ATP, reduced coenzymes, and CO_2. In Stage 4 (ATP
production) the energy stored in the reduced coenzymes (from the citric acid cycle) is
converted to ATP energy.

PROBLEM 20.4

(a) Identify in Figure 20.5 the stages in the pathway for the conversion of the energy
from carbohydrates to energy stored in ATP molecules.

(b) Identify in Figure 20.5 the three places at which the products of amino acid
catabolism can join the central metabolism pathway.

20.5 Strategies of Metabolism: ATP and Energy Transfer

We have described ATP as the body's energy-transporting molecule. What exactly does
that mean? Consider that the molecule has three $-PO_3^-$ groups:

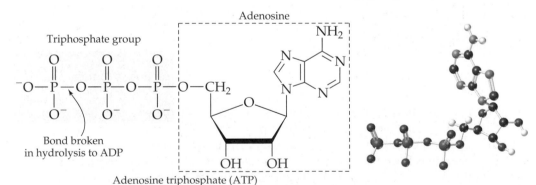

Adenosine triphosphate (ATP)

Removal of one of the $-PO_3^{2-}$ groups from ATP by hydrolysis gives adenosine
diphosphate (ADP). The ATP → ADP reaction is exergonic; it releases chemical energy
that was held in the bond to the $-PO_3^{2-}$ group:

$$ATP + H_2O \longrightarrow ADP + HOPO_3^{2-} + H^+ \quad \Delta G = -7.3\,\text{kcal/mol}\,(-30.5\,\text{kJ/mol})$$

The reverse of ATP hydrolysis—a phosphorylation reaction—is, of course, endergonic:

$$ADP + HOPO_3^{2-} + H^+ \longrightarrow ATP + H_2O \quad \Delta G = +7.3\,\text{kcal/mol}\,(+30.5\,\text{kJ/mol})$$

(In equations for biochemical reactions, we represent ATP and other energy-carrying
molecules in red and their lower-energy equivalent molecules in blue.)

ATP is an energy transporter because its production from ADP requires an input of energy that is then released wherever the reverse reaction occurs. Biochemical energy is gathered from exergonic reactions and stored in the bonds of the ATP molecule. The ATP then travels to where energy is needed inside the cell, and ATP hydrolysis releases the energy for whatever energy-requiring work must take place. *Biochemical energy production, transport, and use all depend upon the ATP $\rightleftharpoons$ ADP interconversion.*

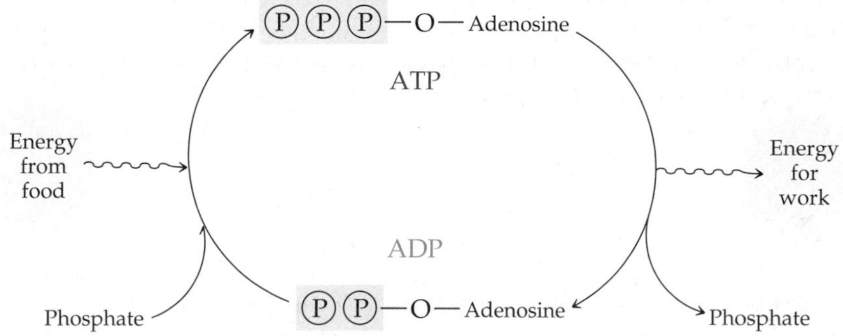

The hydrolysis of ATP to give ADP and its reverse, the phosphorylation of ADP, are reactions perfectly suited to their role in metabolism for two major reasons. One reason is the slow rate of ATP hydrolysis in the absence of a catalyst, so that the stored energy is released only in the presence of the appropriate enzymes.

The second reason is the intermediate value of the free energy of hydrolysis of ATP, as illustrated in Table 20.1. Since the primary metabolic function of ATP is to transport energy, it is often referred to as a "high-energy" molecule or as containing "high-energy" phosphorus–oxygen bonds. These terms are misleading because they promote the idea that ATP is somehow different from other compounds. The terms mean only that ATP is reactive and that a useful amount of energy is released when a phosphoryl group is removed from it by hydrolysis.

TABLE 20.1   Free Energies of Hydrolysis of Some Phosphates

Compound Name	Function	ΔG (kcal/mol)	ΔG (kJ/mol)
Phosphoenol pyruvate	Final intermediate in conversion of glucose to pyruvate (glycolysis)— Stage 2, Figure 20.5	−14.8	−61.9
1, 3-Bisphosphoglycerate	Another intermediate in glycolysis	−11.8	−49.4
Creatine phosphate	Energy storage in muscle cells	−10.3	−43.1
ATP ($\longrightarrow$ ADP)	Principal energy carrier	−7.3	−30.5
Glucose 1-phosphate	First intermediate in breakdown of carbohydrates stored as starch or glycogen	−5.0	−20.9
Glucose 6-phosphate	First intermediate in glycolysis	−3.3	−13.8
Fructose 6-phosphate	Second intermediate in glycolysis	−3.3	−13.8

In fact, if removal of a phosphoryl group from ATP released *unusually* large amounts of energy, other reactions would not be able to provide enough energy to convert ADP back to ATP. ATP is a convenient energy carrier in metabolism because its free energy of hydrolysis has an *intermediate value* (among high energy carriers). For this reason, the phosphorylation of ADP can be driven by coupling this reaction with a more exergonic reaction, as illustrated in the next section.

PROBLEM 20.5

Acetyl phosphate, whose structure is given here, is another compound with a relatively high free energy of hydrolysis.

$$CH_3-\overset{\overset{\displaystyle O}{\|}}{C}-O-\overset{\overset{\displaystyle O}{\|}}{\underset{\underset{\displaystyle O^-}{|}}{P}}-O^-$$

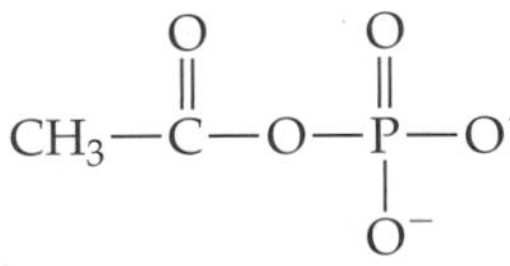

Using structural formulas, write the equation for the hydrolysis of this phosphate.

PROBLEM 20.6

A common metabolic strategy is the lack of reactivity—that is, the slowness to react—of compounds whose breakdown is exergonic. For example, hydrolysis of ATP to ADP or AMP is exergonic but does not take place without an appropriate enzyme present. Why would the cell use this metabolic strategy?

20.6 Strategies of Metabolism: Metabolic Pathways and Coupled Reactions

Now that you are acquainted with ATP, we will explore how stored chemical energy is gradually released and how it can be used to drive endergonic (uphill) reactions. We have noted before that our bodies cannot burn up the energy obtained from consuming a steak all at once. As shown in Figure 20.2a, however, the energy difference between a reactant (the steak) and the ultimate products of its catabolism (mainly carbon dioxide and water) is a fixed quantity. The same amount of energy is released no matter what pathway is taken between reactants and products. The metabolic pathways of catabolism take advantage of this fact by releasing energy bit by bit in a series of reactions, somewhat like the stepwise release of potential energy as water flows down an elaborate waterfall.

The overall reaction and the overall free-energy change for any series of reactions can be found by summing up the equations and the free-energy changes for the individual steps. For example, glucose is converted to pyruvate via the 10 reactions of the glycolysis pathway (part of Stage 2, Figure 20.5). The overall free-energy change for glycolysis is about -8 kcal/mol (-33.5 kJ/mol), showing that the pathway is exergonic—that is, downhill and favorable. The reactions of all metabolic pathways *add up* to favorable processes with negative free-energy changes.

Unlike the waterfall, however, not every individual step in every metabolic pathway is downhill. The metabolic strategy for dealing with what would be an energetically unfavorable reaction is to *couple* it with an energetically favorable reaction so that the overall energy change for the two reactions is favorable. For example, consider the reaction of glucose with hydrogen phosphate ion ($HOPO_3^{2-}$) to yield glucose 6-phosphate plus water, for which $\Delta G = +3.3$ kcal/mol ($+13.8$ kJ/mol). The reaction is unfavorable because the two products are 3.3 kcal/mol (13.8 kJ/mol) higher in energy than the starting materials. This phosphorylation of glucose is, however, the essential first

▲ **This waterfall illustrates a step-wise release of potential energy. No matter what the pathway from the top to the bottom, the amount of potential energy released as the water falls from the top to the very bottom is the same.**

step toward all metabolic use of glucose. To accomplish this reaction, it is coupled with the exergonic hydrolysis of ATP to give ADP:

(*Unfavorable*) $Glucose + HOPO_3^{2-} \longrightarrow Glucose\ 6\text{-phosphate} + H_2O$ $\Delta G = +3.3\ kcal/mol\ (+13.8\ kJ/mol)$

(*Favorable*) $ATP + H_2O \longrightarrow ADP + HOPO_3^{2-} + H^+$ $\Delta G = -7.3\ kcal/mol\ (-30.5\ kJ/mol)$

(*Favorable*) $Glucose + ATP \longrightarrow Glucose\ 6\text{-phosphate} + ADP$ $\Delta G = -4.0\ kcal/mol\ (-16.7\ kJ/mol)$

The net energy change for these two coupled reactions is favorable: 4.0 kcal (16.7 kJ) of free energy is released for each mole of glucose that is phosphorylated. Only by such coupling can the energy stored in one chemical compound be transferred to other compounds. Any excess energy is released as heat and contributes to maintaining body temperature (Figure 20.6).

Although we have written these reactions separately to show how their energies combine, coupled reactions do not take place separately. The net change occurs all at once as represented by the overall equation. The phosphoryl group is transferred directly from ATP to glucose without the intermediate formation of $HOPO_3^{2-}$. (Also, under physiological conditions, a reaction may be more or less exergonic than in the examples given here. We have stated the free-energy values for standard conditions.)

What about the endergonic synthesis of ATP from ADP, which has $\Delta G = +7.3\ kcal/mol\ (+30.5\ kJ/mol)$? The same principle of coupling is put to use. For this endergonic reaction to occur, it must be coupled with a reaction that releases *more* than 7.3 kcal/mol (30.5 kJ/mol). In a different step of glycolysis, for example, the formation of ATP is coupled with the hydrolysis of phosphoenolpyruvate, a phosphate of higher energy than ATP (Table 20.1). Here, the overall reaction is transfer of a phosphoryl group from phosphoenolpyruvate to ADP:

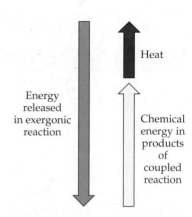

▲ **Figure 20.6**
Energy exchange in coupled reactions. The energy provided by an exergonic reaction is either released as heat or stored as chemical potential energy in the bonds of products of the coupled endergonic reaction.

$$H_2C\!\!=\!\!\underset{\underset{\text{Phosphoenolpyruvate}}{\overset{|}{O\!-\!PO_3^{2-}}}}{C}\!\!-\!\!COO^- + H_2O \longrightarrow CH_3\!\!-\!\!\underset{\underset{\text{Pyruvate}}{\overset{\displaystyle O}{\|}}}{C}\!\!-\!\!COO^- + HOPO_3^{2-}$$

$\Delta G = -14.8\ kcal/mol$
$\Delta G = (-61.9\ kJ/mol)$

$$ADP + HOPO_3^{2-} + H^+ \longrightarrow ATP + H_2O$$

$\Delta G = +7.3\ kcal/mol$
$\Delta G = (+30.5\ kJ/mol)$

$$H_2C\!\!=\!\!\underset{\overset{|}{O\!-\!PO_3^{2-}}}{C}\!\!-\!\!COO^- + ADP \longrightarrow CH_3\overset{\displaystyle O}{\overset{\|}{C}}\!\!-\!\!COO^- + ATP$$

$\Delta G = -7.5\ kcal/mol$
$\Delta G = (-31.4\ kJ/mol)$

Remember that in equations representing coupled reactions, a curved arrow often connects the reactants and products in one of the two chemical changes. For example, the reaction of phosphoenolpyruvate illustrated above can be written

$$H_2C\!\!=\!\!\underset{\overset{|}{O\!-\!PO_3^{2-}}}{C}\!\!-\!\!COO^- \quad\overset{\displaystyle ADP\quad ATP}{\underset{\quad}{\curvearrowright}}\quad CH_3\!\!-\!\!\overset{\displaystyle O}{\overset{\|}{C}}\!\!-\!\!COO^-$$

PROBLEM 20.7
One of the steps in lipid metabolism is the reaction of glycerol (1,2,3-propanetriol, $HOCH_2CH(OH)CH_2OH$), with ATP to yield glycerol 1-phosphate. Write the equation for this reaction using the curved arrow symbolism.

PROBLEM 20.8
Why must a metabolic pathway that synthesizes a given molecule occur by a different series of reactions than a pathway that breaks down the same molecule?

PROBLEM 20.9

An average 12 oz. can of soda pop contains 160 Calories and a typical hamburger contains 500 Calories. Using the table in Chemistry in Action: Basal Metabolism, calculate how long would you need to jog at 5 miles per hour to burn off these calories.

CHEMISTRY IN ACTION

Basal Metabolism

The minimum amount of energy expenditure required per unit of time to stay alive—to breathe, maintain body temperature, circulate blood, and keep all body systems functioning—is referred to as the *basal metabolic rate*. Ideally, it is measured in a person who is awake, is lying down at a comfortable temperature, has fasted and avoided strenuous exercise for 12 hours, and is not under the influence of any medications. The basal metabolic rate can be measured by monitoring respiration and finding the rate of oxygen consumption, which is proportional to the energy used.

An *average* basal metabolic rate is 70 kcal/hr (293 kJ/hr), or about 1700 kcal/day (7100 kJ/day). The rate varies with many factors, including sex, age, weight, and physical condition. A rule of thumb used by nutritionists to estimate basal energy needs per day is the requirement for 1 kcal/hr (4.2 kJ/hr) per kilogram of body weight by a male and 0.95 kcal/hr (4 kJ/hr) per kilogram of body weight by a female. For example, a 50 kg (110 lb) female has an estimated basal metabolic rate of (50 kg)(0.95 kcal/kg hr) = (48 kcal/hr) giving a daily requirement of approximately 1200 kcal. Calculated in joules this would be (50 kg)(4 kJ/kg hr) = 200 kJ/hr, resulting in a daily requirement of 4800 kJ.

The total calories a person needs each day is determined by his or her basal requirements plus the energy used in additional physical activities. The caloric consumption rates associated with some activities are listed in the accompanying table. A relatively inactive person requires about 30% above basal requirements per day, a lightly active person requires about 50% above basal, and a very active person such as an athlete or construction worker can use 100% above basal requirements in a day. Each day that you consume food with more calories than you use, the excess calories are stored as potential energy in the chemi-

▲ The cola drink contains 160 Cal (kcal) (680 kJ) and the hamburger contains 500 Cal (2100 kJ). How long would you have to jog at 5 mph to burn off these calories?

cal bonds of fats in your body and your weight rises. Each day that you consume food with fewer calories than you burn, some chemical energy in your body is taken out of storage to make up the deficit. Fat is metabolized to CO_2 and H_2O, which the body gets rid of, and your weight drops.

Calories Used in Various Activities

Activity	Kilocalories (Nutrition Calories) or Kilojoules Used per Minute
Sleeping	1.2 (5 kJ)
Reading	1.3 (5.4 kJ)
Listening to lecture	1.7 (7.1 kJ)
Weeding garden	5.6 (23 kJ)
Walking, 3.5 mph	5.6 (23 kJ)
Pick-and-shovel work	6.7 (25 kJ)
Recreational tennis	7.0 (29 kJ)
Soccer, basketball	9.0 (38 kJ)
Walking up stairs	10.0–18.0 (42–75 kJ)
Running, 12 min/mi (5 mph)	10.0 (42 kJ)
Running, 5 min/mi (12 mph)	25.0 (105 kJ)

See Chemistry in Actions Problems 20.81 through 20.84 at the end of the chapter.

Worked Example **20.4** Determining if a Coupled Reaction Is Favorable

The hydrolysis of succinyl-CoA is coupled with the production of GTP (guanosine triphosphate—closely related to ATP). The equations for the reactions are given below. Combine the equations appropriately and determine if the coupled reaction is favorable.

Succinyl-CoA $\longrightarrow$ Succinate + CoA	$\Delta G = -9.4 \, \text{kcal/mol} \, (-39.3 \, \text{kJ/mol})$
$GDP + HOPO_3^{2-} + H^+ \longrightarrow GTP + H_2O$	$\Delta G = +7.3 \, \text{kcal/mol} \, (+30.5 \, \text{kJ/mol})$

ANALYSIS Add the two equations together to produce the equation for the coupled reaction. Also add the ΔG values together, paying close attention to the signs. If the ΔG is positive, the reaction is not favorable and will not occur; if the ΔG is negative, the reaction is favorable and will occur.

SOLUTION

$$\text{Succinyl-CoA} + \text{GDP} + \text{HOPO}_3^{2-} + \text{H}^+ \longrightarrow \text{Succinate} + \text{GTP} + \text{H}_2\text{O}$$

$$\Delta G = -2.1 \, \text{kcal/mol} \, (-8.8 \, \text{kJ/mol})$$

Since ΔG is negative, the coupled reaction will occur as written.

PROBLEM 20.10

The hydrolysis of acetyl phosphate to give acetate and hydrogen phosphate ion has $\Delta G = -10.3 \, \text{kcal/mol} \, (-43.1 \, \text{kJ/mol})$. Combine the equations and ΔG values to determine whether coupling of this reaction with phosphorylation of ADP to produce ATP is favorable. (You need give only compound names or abbreviations in the equations.)

20.7 Strategies of Metabolism: Oxidized and Reduced Coenzymes

The net result of catabolism is the oxidation of food molecules to release energy. Many metabolic reactions are therefore oxidation–reduction reactions, which means that a steady supply of oxidizing and reducing agents must be available. To deal with this requirement, a few coenzymes cycle continuously between their oxidized and reduced forms, just as adenosine cycles continuously between its triphosphate and diphosphate forms:

$$
\begin{array}{ccc}
\text{AH}_2 & \text{Coenzyme} & \text{BH}_2 \\
 & \text{(oxidized)} & \\
\text{A} & \text{Coenzyme-H}_2 & \text{B} \\
 & \text{(reduced)} &
\end{array}
$$

Table 20.2 lists some important cycling coenzymes in their oxidized and reduced forms.

TABLE 20.2 Oxidized and Reduced Forms of Important Coenzymes

COENZYME	AS OXIDIZING AGENT	AS REDUCING AGENT
Nicotinamide adenine dinucleotide	NAD$^+$	NADH/H$^+$
Nicotinamide adenine dinucleotide phosphate	NADP$^+$	NADPH/H$^+$
Flavin adenine dinucleotide	FAD	FADH$_2$
Flavin mononucleotide	FMN	FMNH$_2$

To review briefly, keep in mind these important points about oxidation and reduction:

- Oxidation can be loss of electrons, loss of hydrogen, or addition of oxygen.
- Reduction can be gain of electrons, gain of hydrogen, or loss of oxygen.
- Oxidation and reduction always occur together.

Each increase in the number of carbon–oxygen bonds is an oxidation, and each decrease in the number of carbon–hydrogen bonds is a reduction, as shown in Figure 20.7. Oxidation of carbon increases by increased bonding to oxygen.

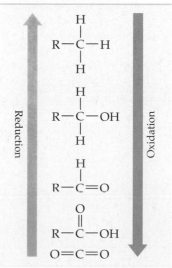

FIGURE 20.7 Oxidation of Carbon by Increased Bonding to Oxygen

Nicotinamide adenine dinucleotide and its phosphate are widespread, independent coenzymes that enter and leave enzyme active sites in which they are required for redox reactions. As oxidizing agents (NAD^+ and $NADP^+$) they remove hydrogen from a substrate, and as reducing agents (NADH and NADPH) they provide hydrogen that adds to a substrate. The complete structure of NAD^+ is shown below with the change that converts it to NADH. The only difference between the structures of NAD^+/NADH and $NADP^+$/NADPH is that the color-shaded —OH group in NAD^+/NADH is instead a —OPO_3^{2-} group in $NADP^+$ and NADPH:

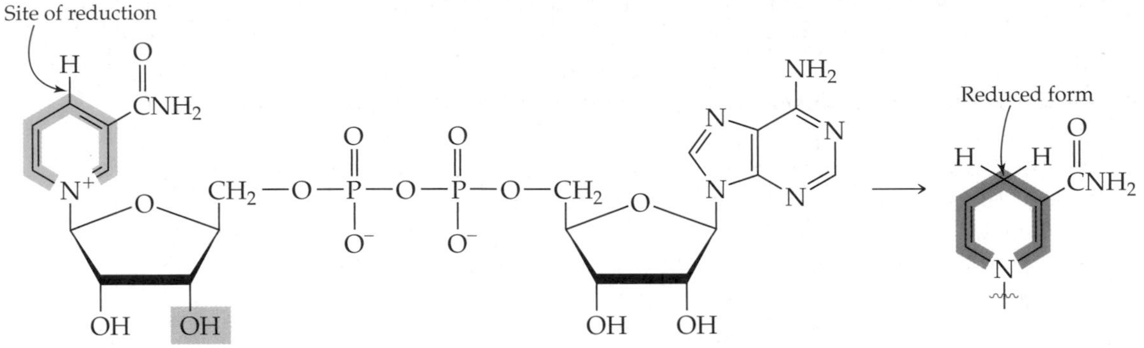

As an example, consider a reaction in the citric acid cycle (Step 8 in Figure 20.9, Section 20.8) from the oxidation–reduction, or redox, point of view:

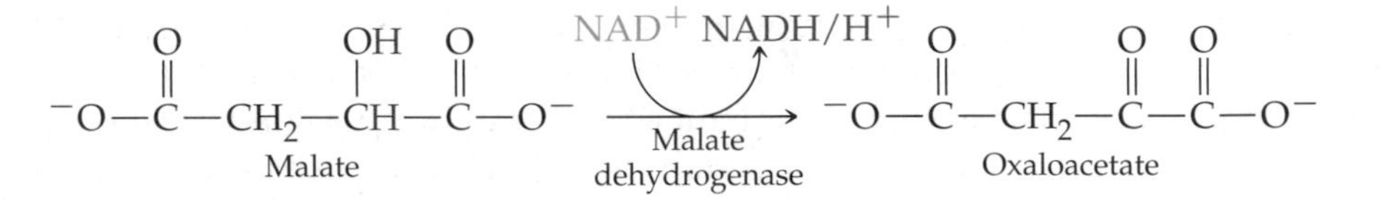

Recall from Section 14.5 that a ketone is $R_2C=O$.

The oxidation of malate to oxaloacetate requires the removal of two hydrogen atoms to convert a secondary alcohol to a ketone. The oxidizing agent, which will be reduced during the reaction, is NAD^+, functioning as a *coenzyme* for the enzyme malate dehydrogenase. (Sometimes NAD^+ is written as a reactant or product to emphasize its role in a reaction. Keep in mind that although it is free to enter and leave the active site, it always functions as a coenzyme with the appropriate enzyme for the reaction.)

When considering enzyme-catalyzed redox reactions, it is important to recognize that a hydrogen atom is equivalent to a hydrogen *ion*, H^+, plus an electron, e^-. Thus, for the two hydrogen atoms removed in the oxidation of malate,

$$2 \text{ H atoms} = 2 \text{ H}^+ + 2 \text{ e}^-$$

When NAD^+ is reduced, both electrons accompany one of the hydrogens to give a hydride ion,

$$\text{H}^+ + 2 \text{ e}^- = :\text{H}^-$$

The reduction of NAD occurs by addition of H^- to the ring in the nicotinamide part of the structure, where the two electrons of H^- form a covalent bond:

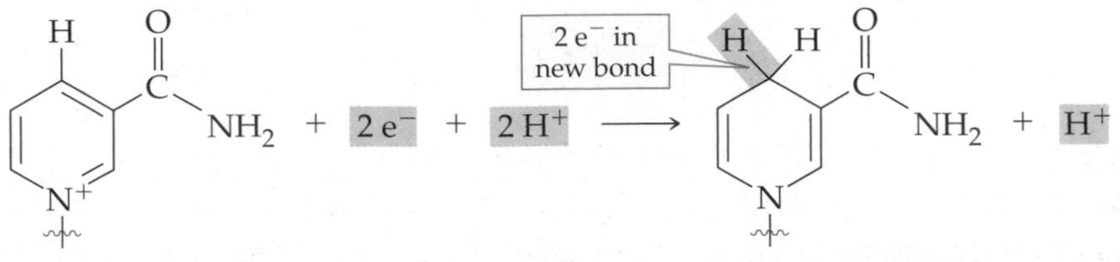

The second hydrogen removed from the oxidized substrate enters the surrounding aqueous solution as a hydrogen ion, H^+. The product of NAD^+ reduction is therefore often represented as $NADH/H^+$ to show that two hydrogen atoms have been removed from the reactant, one of which has bonded to NAD^+ and the other of which is a hydrogen ion in solution. ($NADP^+$ is reduced in the same way to form $NADPH/H^+$.)

Flavin adenine dinucleotide (FAD), another common oxidizing agent in catabolic reactions, is reduced by the formation of covalent bonds to two hydrogen atoms to give $FADH_2$. It participates in several reactions of the citric acid cycle, which is described in the next section.

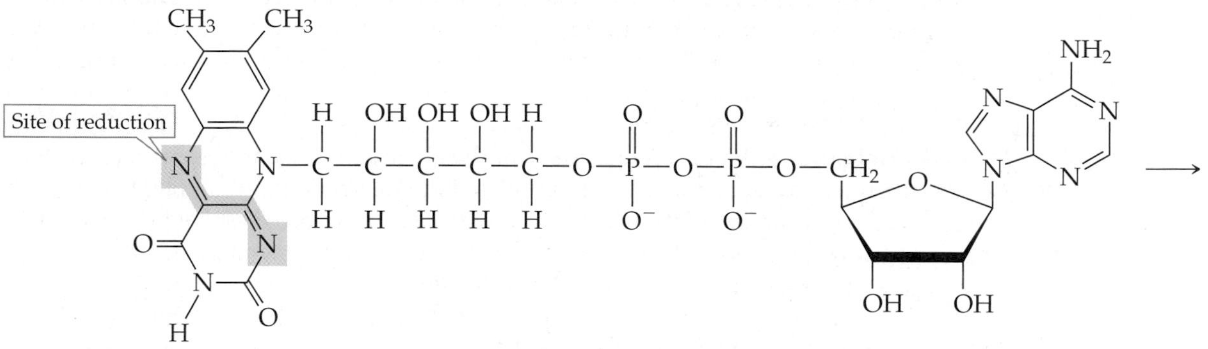

FAD

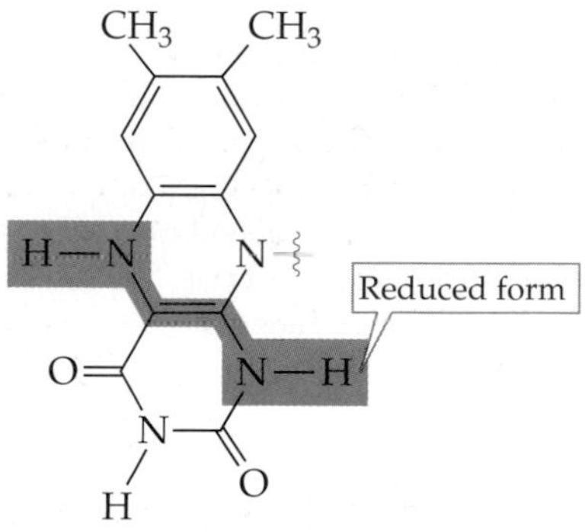

$FADH_2$

Because the reduced coenzymes, NADH and $FADH_2$, have picked up electrons (in their bonds to hydrogen) that are passed along in subsequent reactions, they are often referred to as *electron carriers*. As these coenzymes cycle through their oxidized and reduced forms, they also carry energy along from reaction to reaction. Ultimately, this energy is passed on to the bonds in ATP, as described in Section 20.9.

PROBLEM 20.11

Which of the following is found in the coenzyme FAD?

(a) two heterocyclic rings (b) ADP (c) a substituted benzene ring (d) a phosphate anhydride bond

PROBLEM 20.12

Look ahead to Figure 20.9 for the citric acid cycle. (a) Draw the structures of the reactants in Steps 3, 6, and 8, and indicate which hydrogen atoms are removed in these reactions. (b) What class of enzymes carry out these reactions?

20.8 The Citric Acid Cycle

The carbon atoms from the first two stages of catabolism are carried into the third stage as acetyl groups bonded to coenzyme A. Like the phosphoryl groups in ATP molecules, the acetyl groups in acetyl-SCoA molecules are readily removed in an energy-releasing hydrolysis reaction:

$$\underset{\text{Acetyl-CoA}}{CH_3-\overset{\overset{\displaystyle O}{\|}}{C}-SCoA} + H_2O \longrightarrow CH_3-\overset{\overset{\displaystyle O}{\|}}{C}-O^- + \underset{\text{Coenzyme A}}{H-SCoA} + H^+ \qquad \begin{array}{l}\Delta G = -7.5\ \text{kcal/mol}\\ (\Delta G = -31.4\ \text{kJ/mol})\end{array}$$

Citric acid cycle The series of biochemical reactions that breaks down acetyl groups to produce energy carried by reduced coenzymes and carbon dioxide.

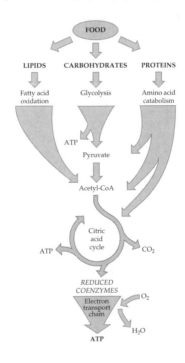

▲ **Figure 20.8**

Significant outcomes of the citric acid cycle.

The eight steps of the cycle produce two molecules of carbon dioxide, four molecules of reduced coenzymes, and one energy-rich phosphate (GTP). The final step regenerates the reactant for Step 1 of the next turn of the cycle. (Step 1 occurs where C_2 enters the cycle to form C_6 by adding to C_4.

Guanosine diphosphate (GDP) An energy-carrying molecule that can gain or lose a phosphoryl group to transfer energy.

Guanosine triphosphate (GTP) An energy-carrying molecule similar to ATP; removal of a phosphoryl group to give GDP releases free energy.

Oxidation of two carbons to give two CO_2 and transfer of energy to reduced coenzymes occurs in the **citric acid cycle**, also known as the *tricarboxylic acid cycle (TCA)* or *Krebs cycle* (after Sir Hans Krebs, who unraveled its complexities in 1937). As its name implies, the citric acid *cycle* is a closed loop of reactions in which the product of the final step, oxaloacetate, a 4-carbon molecule, is the reactant in the first step. The pathway of carbon atoms through the cycle and the significant products formed are summarized in Figure 20.8 and shown in greater detail in Figure 20.9. The two carbon atoms of the acetyl group add to the four carbon atoms of oxaloacetate in Step 1, and two carbon atoms are set free as carbon dioxide in Steps 3 and 4. The cycle continues as 4-carbon intermediates progress toward regeneration of oxaloacetate and production of additional reduced coenzymes.

A brief description of the eight steps of the citric acid cycle is given in Figure 20.9. The enzymes involved in each step are listed in the accompanying table. The cycle takes place in mitochondria, where seven of the enzymes are dissolved in the matrix and one (for Step 6) is embedded in the inner mitochondrial membrane.

The cycle operates as long as (1) acetyl groups are available from acetyl-CoA and (2) the oxidizing agent coenzymes NAD^+ and FAD are available. To meet condition 2, the reduced coenzymes NADH and $FADH_2$ must be reoxidized via the electron-transport chain in Stage 4 of catabolism (described in the next section). Because Stage 4 relies on oxygen as the final electron acceptor, the cycle is also dependent upon (3) the availability of oxygen.

The steps of the citric acid cycle are summarized below, with an emphasis on what each step accomplishes.

STEPS 1 and 2: The first two steps set the stage for oxidation. Acetyl groups enter the cycle at Step 1 by addition to 4-carbon oxaloacetate to give citrate, a 6-carbon intermediate. Citrate is a tertiary alcohol and cannot be oxidized; it must be converted in Step 2 to its isomer, isocitrate, a secondary alcohol that can be oxidized to a ketone in Step 3. The two steps of the isomerization are catalyzed by the same enzyme, aconitase. Water is first removed and then added back to the intermediate, which remains in the active site, so that the —OH is on a different carbon atom. For Step 1 $\Delta G = -7.7 \text{ kcal/mol} (-32.2 \text{ kJ/mol})$ and $\Delta G = +3.2 \text{ kcal/mol} (+13.3 \text{ kJ/mol})$ for Step 2.

$$
\begin{array}{ccccc}
\text{COO}^- & & \text{COO}^- & & \text{COO}^- \\
| & & | & & | \\
\text{CH}_2 & & \text{CH}_2 & & \text{CH}_2 \\
| & \xrightarrow[\text{Aconitase}]{+\text{H}_2\text{O}} & | & \xrightarrow[\text{Aconitase}]{+\text{H}_2\text{O}} & | \\
\text{HO}-\text{C}-\text{COO}^- & & \text{C}-\text{COO}^- & & \text{H}-\text{C}-\text{COO}^- \\
| & & \| & & | \\
\text{CH}_2 & & \text{CH} & & \text{HO}-\text{CH} \\
| & & | & & | \\
\text{COO}^- & & \text{COO}^- & & \text{COO}^- \\
\text{Citrate} & & \text{Aconitate} & & \text{Isocitrate}
\end{array}
$$

STEPS 3 and 4: Both steps are oxidations that rely on NAD^+ as the oxidizing agent. One CO_2 leaves at Step 3 as the —OH group of isocitrate and is simultaneously oxidized to a keto group. A second CO_2 leaves at Step 4, and the resulting succinyl group is added to coenzyme A. In both steps, electrons and energy are transferred in the reduction of NAD^+. Succinyl-CoA carries four carbon atoms along to the next step. $\Delta G = -2.0 \text{ kcal/mol} (-8.4 \text{ kJ/mol})$ for Step 3 and $\Delta G = -8.0 \text{ kcal/mol} (-33.5 \text{ kJ/mol})$ for Step 4.

STEP 5: With two carbon atoms now removed as carbon dioxide (though not the original two from the acetyl group), the 4-carbon molecule oxaloacetate must be restored for Step 1 of the next cycle. In Step 5, the exergonic conversion of succinyl-CoA to succinate is coupled with phosphorylation of **guanosine diphosphate (GDP)** to give **guanosine triphosphate (GTP)**. GTP is similar in structure to ATP and, like ATP, carries energy that can be released during transfer of one of its phosphoryl groups. In many cells, GTP is directly converted to ATP. Step 5 is the only step in the cycle that generates an energy-rich triphosphate. $\Delta G = -0.7 \text{ kcal/mol} (-2.9 \text{ kJ/mol})$ for this step.

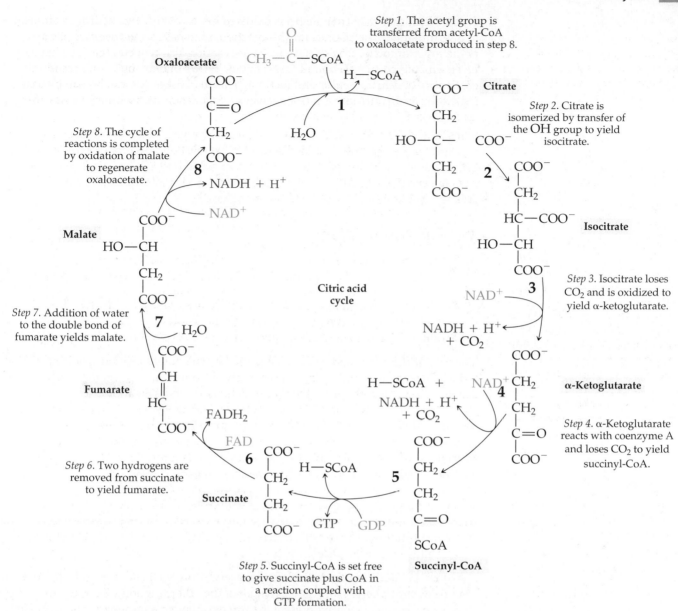

Enzymes of the Citric Acid Cycle

STEP NO.	ENZYME NAME	REACTION PRODUCT
1	Citrate synthase	Citrate
2	Aconitase	Isocitrate
3	Isocitrate dehydrogenase complex	α-Ketoglutarate
4	α-Ketoglutarate dehydrogenase complex	Succinyl-CoA
5	Succinyl CoA synthetase	Succinate
6	Succinate dehydrogenase	Fumarate
7	Fumarase	Malate
8	Malate dehydrogenase	Oxaloacetate

▲ **Figure 20.9**

The citric acid cycle.

The net effect of this eight-step cycle of reactions is the metabolic breakdown of acetyl groups (from acetyl-CoA) into two molecules of carbon dioxide and energy carried by reduced coenzymes. Here and throughout this and the following chapters, energy-rich reactants or products (ATP, reduced coenzymes) are shown in red and their lower-energy counterparts (ADP, oxidized coenzymes) are shown in blue.

STEP 6: Next, succinate from Step 5 is oxidized by removal of two hydrogen atoms to give fumarate. The enzyme for this reaction, succinate dehydrogenase, is part of the inner mitochondrial membrane. The reaction also requires the coenzyme FAD, which is covalently bound to its enzyme rather than being free to come and go. Succinate dehydrogenase and FAD participate in Stage 4 of catabolism by passing electrons directly into electron transport. Step 6 neither uses nor releases energy; $\Delta G = 0$ kcal/mol (0 kJ/mol) for this step.

STEPS 7 and 8: The citric acid cycle is completed by regeneration of oxaloacetate, a reactant for Step 1. Water is added across the double bond of fumarate to give malate (Step 7) and oxidation of malate, a secondary alcohol, gives oxaloacetate (Step 8). $\Delta G = -0.9$ kcal/mol (-3.8 kJ/mol) for Step 7 and $\Delta G = +7.1$ kcal/mol ($+29.7$ kJ/mol) for Step 8.

Net result of citric acid cycle

$$\text{Acetyl-CoA} + 3\,\text{NAD}^+ + \text{FAD} + \text{GDP} + \text{HOPO}_3^{2-} + \text{H}_2\text{O} \longrightarrow$$
$$\text{HSCoA} + 3\,\text{NADH} + 3\,\text{H}^+ + \text{FADH}_2 + \text{GTP} + 2\,\text{CO}_2$$

- Production of four reduced coenzyme molecules (3 NADH, 1 $FADH_2$)
- Conversion of an acetyl group to two CO_2 molecules
- Production of one energy-rich molecule (GTP, converted immediately to ATP)

The rate of the citric acid cycle is controlled by the body's cellular need for ATP and reduced coenzymes, and for the energy derived from them. For example, when energy is being used at a high rate, ADP accumulates and acts as an allosteric activator (positive regulator, see Section 19.7) for isocitrate dehydrogenase, the enzyme for Step 3. When the body's supply of energy is abundant, NADH is present in excess and acts as an inhibitor of isocitrate dehydrogenase. By such feedback mechanisms, as well as by variations in the concentrations of necessary reactants, the cycle is activated when energy is needed and inhibited when energy is in good supply.

Worked Example 20.5 Identifying Reactants and Products in the Citric Acid Cycle

What substance(s) are the substrate(s) for the citric acid cycle? What are the products of the citric acid cycle?

ANALYSIS Study Figure 20.9. Note that acetyl-CoA feeds into the cycle, but does not come out anywhere. Can you see that all of the other reaction substrates are integral to the cycle and are always present, being continuously synthesized and degraded? Note also that the coenzymes NAD^+ and FAD are reduced and the reduced versions are considered energy-carrying products of the cycle. Also, CO_2 is produced at two different steps in the cycle. Finally, GDP is converted to GTP in Step 5 of the cycle.

SOLUTION
Acetyl-CoA is the substrate for the cycle. Along with GDP and CoA, the oxidized coenzymes NAD^+ and FAD might also be considered substrates, despite their status as coenzymes, because these substances cycle between the reduced and oxidized states. The products of the cycle are CO_2 and the energy-rich reduced coenzymes NADH/H^+ and $FADH_2$ as well as GTP.

PROBLEM 20.13
Which substances in the citric acid cycle are tricarboxylic acids (thus giving the cycle its alternative name)?

PROBLEM 20.14
In Figure 20.9, identify the steps at which reduced coenzymes are produced.

PROBLEM 20.15

Why, do you suppose, the coenzyme for the reaction in the citric acid cycle that is catalyzed by succinate dehydrogenase is FAD and not NAD$^+$?

PROBLEM 20.16

Identify the participants in the citric acid cycle that contain alcohol groups. Identify these groups as primary, secondary, or tertiary alcohols.

PROBLEM 20.17

Which of the reactants in the citric acid cycle have two chiral carbon atoms?

🔑 KEY CONCEPT PROBLEM 20.18

The citric acid cycle can be divided into two stages. In one stage, carbon atoms are added and removed, and in the second stage, oxaloacetate is regenerated. Which steps of the citric acid cycle correspond to each stage?

20.9 The Electron-Transport Chain and ATP Production

Keep in mind that in some ways catabolism is just like burning petroleum or natural gas. In both cases, the goal is to produce useful energy and the reaction products are water and carbon dioxide. The difference is that in catabolism the products are not released all at once and not all of the energy is released as heat.

At the conclusion of the citric acid cycle, the reduced coenzymes formed during the cycle are ready to donate their energy to making additional ATP. The energy is released in a series of oxidation–reduction reactions that move electrons from one electron carrier to the next as each carrier is reduced (gains an electron from the preceding carrier) and then oxidized (loses an electron by passing it along to the next carrier). Each reaction in the series is favorable; that is, it is exergonic. You can think of each reaction as a step along the way down our waterfall. The sequence of reactions that move the electrons along is known as the **electron-transport chain** (also called the *respiratory chain*). The enzymes and coenzymes of the chain and ATP synthesis are embedded in the inner membrane of the mitochondrion (Figure 20.10).

In the last step of the chain, the electrons combine with the oxygen that we breathe and with hydrogen ions from their surroundings to produce water:

$$O_2 + 4\,e^- + 4\,H^+ \longrightarrow 2H_2O$$

This reaction is fundamentally the combination of hydrogen and oxygen gases. Carried out all at once with the gases themselves, the reaction is explosive. What happens to all that energy during electron transport?

As electrons move down the electron-transport pathway, the energy released is used to move hydrogen ions out of the mitochondrial matrix (across the inner membrane) and into the intermembrane space. Because the inner membrane is otherwise impermeable to the H$^+$ ion, the result is a higher H$^+$ concentration in the intermembrane space than in the mitochondrial matrix. Moving ions from a region of lower concentration to one of higher concentration opposes the natural tendency for random motion to equalize concentrations throughout a mixture and therefore requires energy to make it happen. This energy is recaptured for use in ATP synthesis.

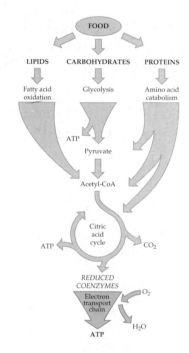

Electron-transport chain The series of biochemical reactions that passes electrons from reduced coenzymes to oxygen and is coupled to ATP formation.

Electron Transport

Electron transport proceeds via four enzyme complexes held in fixed positions within the inner membrane of mitochondria, along with two electron carriers that move through the membrane from one complex to another. The complexes and mobile electron carriers are organized in the sequence of their ability to pick up electrons, as illustrated in Figure 20.10. The four fixed complexes are very large assemblages of

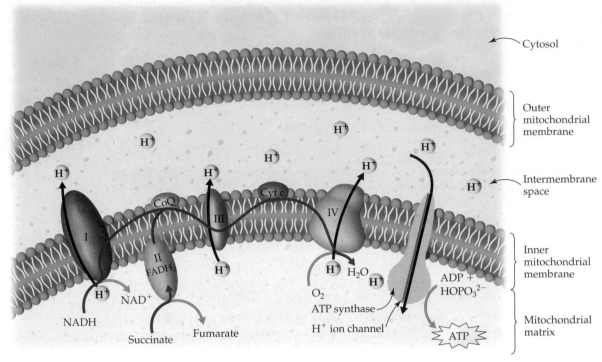

▲ Figure 20.10

The mitochondrial electron-transport chain and ATP synthase.
The red line shows the path of electrons, and the black lines show the paths of hydrogen ions. The movement of hydrogen ions across the inner membrane at complexes I, III, and IV creates a higher concentration on the intermembrane side of the inner membrane than on the matrix side. The energy released by hydrogen ions returning to the matrix through ATP synthase provides the energy needed for ATP synthesis.

polypeptides and electron acceptors. The most important electron acceptors are of three types: (1) various cytochromes, which are proteins that contain heme groups (Figure 20.11 a) in which the iron cycles between Fe^{2+} and Fe^{3+}; (2) proteins containing iron–sulfur groups in which the iron also cycles between Fe^{2+} and Fe^{3+}; and (3) coenzyme Q (CoQ), often known as *ubiquinone* because of its ubiquitous (widespread) occurrence and because its ring structure with the two ketone groups is a *quinone*:

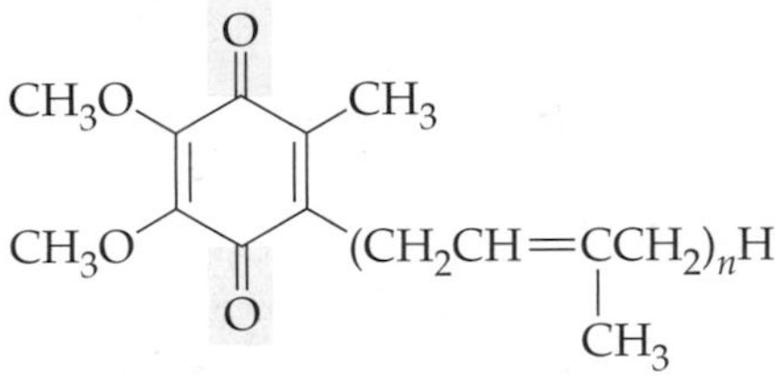

Oxidized coenzyme Q

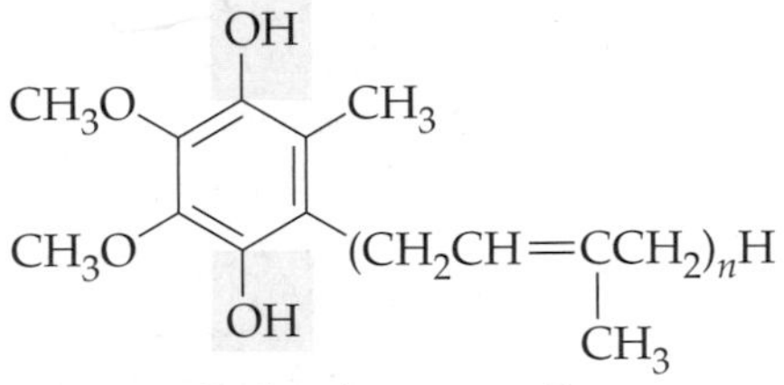

Reduced coenzyme Q

► Figure 20.11

A heme group and a cytochrome
(a) Heme groups, in which the substituents at the bonds marked in red vary, are iron-containing coenzymes in the cytochromes of the electron-transport chain. They are also the oxygen carriers in hemoglobin in red blood cells. (b) In the cytochrome shown here, the coiled blue ribbon is the amino acid chain and the heme group is in red.

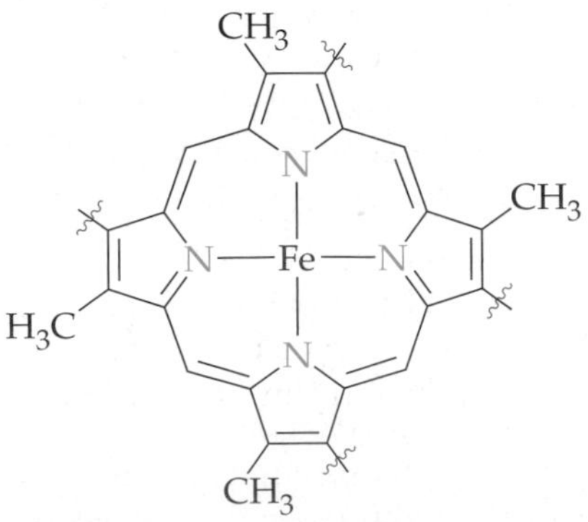

(a) A heme group

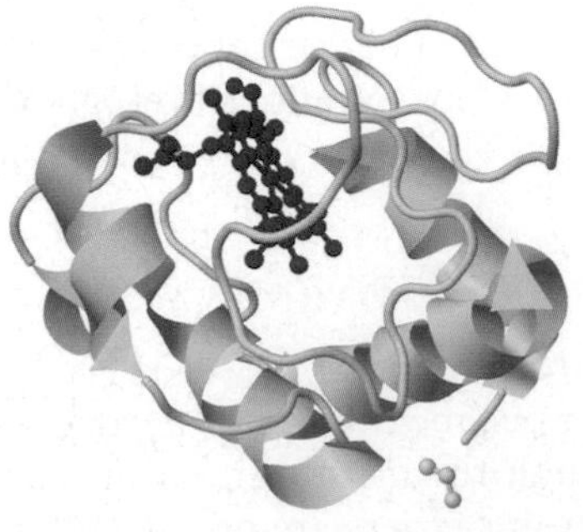

(b) A representative cytochrome protein

The details of the reactions that move electrons in the electron-transport chain are not important to us here. We need only focus on the following essential features of the pathway (Figure 20.12; refer also to Figure 20.10).

- Hydrogen ions and electrons from NADH and $FADH_2$ enter the electron-transport chain at enzyme complexes I and II, respectively. (In this case, the complexes function independently and not necessarily in numerical order.) The enzyme for Step 6 of the citric acid cycle is part of complex II, where $FADH_2$ is produced when that step of the cycle occurs. $FADH_2$ does not leave complex II. It is immediately oxidized there by reaction with mobile coenzyme Q, forming QH_2. Following formation of reduced mobile coenzyme QH_2, hydrogen ions no longer participate directly in the reductions of electron carriers. Instead, electrons are transferred directly, one by one from carrier to carrier.
- Electrons are passed from weaker to increasingly stronger oxidizing agents, with energy released at each transfer. Much of this energy is conserved during the transfer; however, some energy is used to pump protons across the inner mitochondrial membrane, and some is lost as heat at each electron transfer.
- Hydrogen ions are released for transport through the inner mitochondrial membrane to the intermembrane space at complexes I, III, and IV, creating an H^+ gradient, with the intermembrane space becoming acidic and the matrix alkaline due to changes in H^+ concentration. Some of these ions come from the reduced coenzymes and some from the matrix—exactly how the hydrogen ions are transported to the intermembrane space is not yet fully understood, although the process appears to be via an energy-requiring pump.
- The H^+ concentration difference creates a potential energy difference across the two sides of the inner membrane (like the energy difference between water at the top and bottom of a waterfall). The maintenance of this concentration gradient across the membrane is *crucial*—it is the mechanism by which energy for ATP formation is made available.

Plant cells, like animal cells, contain mitochondria and carry out oxidative phosphorylation. In addition, plant cells also contain chloroplasts, organelles that are similar to mitochondria but instead carry out photosynthesis, a series of reactions that also involve electron and hydrogen ion transfer through a series of enzyme complexes arranged in an electron transport chain. See Chemistry in Action: Plants and Photosynthesis on p. 649 for more information.

ATP Synthesis

The reactions of the electron-transport chain are tightly coupled to **oxidative phosphorylation**, the conversion of ADP to ATP, by a reaction that is both an oxidation and a phosphorylation. Hydrogen ions can return to the matrix only by passing through a channel that is part of the **ATP synthase** enzyme complex (black pathway at the right in Figure 20.10). In doing so, they release the potential energy gained as they were moved against the concentration gradient at the enzyme complexes of the electron-transport chain. This energy release drives the phosphorylation of ADP by reaction with hydrogen phosphate ion $(HOPO_3^{2-})$:

$$ADP + HOPO_3^{2-} \longrightarrow ATP + H_2O$$

ATP synthase has knob-tipped stalks that protrude into the matrix and are clearly visible in electron micrographs, as seen in the accompanying drawing based on structural studies. ADP and $HOPO_3^{2-}$ are attracted into the knob portion. As hydrogen ions flow through the complex, ATP is produced and released back into the matrix. The reaction is facilitated by changes in the shape of the enzyme complex that are induced by the flow of hydrogen ions.

How much ATP energy is produced from a molecule of NADH or a molecule of $FADH_2$ by oxidative phosphorylation? The electrons from molecules of NADH enter

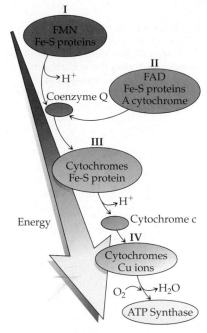

▲ **Figure 20.12**

Pathway of electrons in electron transport.
Each of the enzyme complexes I–IV contains several electron carriers. (FMN in complex I is similar in structure to FAD.) Hydrogen ions and electrons move through the components of the electron-transport pathway in the direction of the arrow. Energy is transferred, with some loss, at each complex; each succeeding complex is at a lower energy level than the preceding, as indicated by the color change.

Oxidative phosphorylation The synthesis of ATP from ADP using energy released in the electron-transport chain.

ATP synthase The enzyme complex in the inner mitochondrial membrane at which hydrogen ions cross the membrane and ATP is synthesized from ADP.

▲ A color enhanced model of ATP synthase. The blue portion is embedded in the inner mitochondrial membrane facing the mitochondrial matrix. H$^+$ travels through the blue stalk and into the red knob, as oxidative phosphorylation occurs.

the electron-transport chain at complex I, while those from FADH$_2$ enter at complex II. These different entry points into the electron-transport chain result in different yields of ATP molecules. Recent research suggests that each NADH molecule yields about 2.5 molecules of ATP and that each FADH$_2$ molecule yields approximately 1.5 molecules of ATP. In this book, we round these numbers up and use the older yields of 3 ATP molecules generated for every NADH molecule and 2 ATP molecules generated from every FADH$_2$ molecule during oxidative phosphorylation.

PROBLEM 20.19
Within the mitochondrion, is the pH higher in the intermembrane space or in the mitochondrial matrix? Why?

PROBLEM 20.20
Plants carry out both photosynthesis and oxidative phosphorylation (see Chemistry in Action: Plants and Photosynthesis on p. 649). Photosynthesis occurs in chloroplasts, while oxidative phosphorylation occurs in mitochondria. Name some similarities and some differences between photosynthesis and oxidative phosphorylation.

🗝 **KEY CONCEPT PROBLEM 20.21**

The reduced coenzymes NADH and FADH$_2$ are oxidized in the electron-transport system. What is the final electron acceptor of the electron-transport system? What is the function of the H$^+$ ion in ATP synthesis?

Blockers and Uncouplers of Oxidative Phosphorylation

The order of the components of the electron-transport chain was elucidated through the use of compounds that block the passage of electrons at different points in the chain. Subsequent research showed that there are also compounds that uncouple—disconnect—oxidative phosphorylation from the generation of ATP.

Cyanide and barbiturates such as amytal have long been known to be so dangerous—even fatal—that mystery writers often use these substances in their books as murder weapons. What makes them so dangerous? They are among a group of substances that block respiration (oxidative phosphorylation) at one of the electron transfer stages, resulting in blockage of electron flow through the electron-transport system and cessation of ATP production. Continuous production of ATP at tightly regulated levels is crucial to an organism's survival. ATP is the energy link between the oxidation of fuels and energy-requiring processes. Without continuous ATP production, the organism will die.

The blockers act at the cytochromes in the electron-transport chain, with different blockers acting on different cytochromes. Rotenone, derived from plants and used to kill both fish and insects, and barbiturates like amytal inhibit complex I proteins in the electron-transport system, so that electrons are not transferred to coenzyme Q from complex I. (See Figure 20.12.) The antibiotic antimycin A inhibits some of the cytochromes and proteins of complex III from transferring electrons to cytochrome c. The third blockage point in the electron-transport system occurs between complex IV and oxygen. Here cyanide and hydrogen sulfide bind tightly to the iron and copper in the enzymes involved, preventing the conversion of oxygen to water. Cyanide is released from bitter almonds, cassava, and the seeds of apples, peaches, and apricots (used to make amygdalin, an alternative cancer drug) and is used in various industrial processes. Cyanide is no longer available as a pest-control agent due to its toxicity. The mode of action of each inhibitor is similar—binding tightly to the complex in the chain, interrupting the flow of electrons. For example, cyanide binds nearly irreversibly to the iron center in the heme group that is part of complex IV. No matter what the inhibitor is, once electron movement has ceased, no ATP can be produced and the cell soon runs out of energy from its best source.

Just as the production of ATP can be blocked, some substances, such as dicumarol, an anticoagulant, allow electron transport to occur but prevent the conversion of ADP to ATP by ATP synthase. If this happens, the rate of oxygen use increases as the proton gradient between the mitochondrial matrix and the intermembrane space dissipates, with the simultaneous formation of water. When ATP production is thus severed from energy use, it is said that ATP production is *uncoupled* from the energy of the proton gradient. One chemical that has this effect, once used as a weight-reducing agent, is 2,4-dinitrophenol. Uncoupling electron transport does result in weight loss; however, the toxic dose is too close to the therapeutic dose, so 2,4-dinitrophenol is no longer used as a reducing agent.

The body does have a tissue with the capacity to uncouple oxidative phosphorylation intentionally. It comes into play when the environment is cold. Brown fat, rich in mitochondria, can uncouple oxidative phosphorylation in order to generate heat through dissipation of the proton gradient. This is accomplished by the presence of a special uncoupling protein, thermogenin, in the inner membrane of the mitochondrion in these cells. Human infants and other newborn mammals have deposits of brown fat in order to keep warm. This type of fat disappears in most humans unless they have an occupation that routinely puts them in a cold environment for an extended period. Pearl divers, who spend several hours daily diving in the ocean, tend to have deposits of brown fat as do mammals that hibernate.

Worked Example 20.6 Determining Phosphorylation Type

(a) Succinyl-SCoA + P_i + GDP $\rightleftharpoons$ Succinate + GTP + CoA

(b) ADP + $HOPO_3^{2-}$ $\xrightarrow{\text{ATP synthase}}$ ATP + H_2O

ANALYSIS Both substrate-level phosphorylation and oxidative phosphorylation involve the transfer of a phosphate group and its energy to another molecule. Both may result in the production of ATP. The key difference is that substrate-level phosphorylation involves the transfer of a phosphate group from one molecule to another, whereas oxidative phosphorlyation adds a phosphate ion directly to ADP with the aid of ATP synthase.

SOLUTION
Reaction (a), involving the formation of GTP coupled with the conversion of succinyl-CoA to succinate, is an example of substrate-level phosphorylation. Reaction (b), involving the direct addition of phosphate to ADP by ATP synthase, is oxidative phosphorylation.

20.10 Harmful Oxygen By-Products and Antioxidant Vitamins

More than 90% of the oxygen we breathe is used in the coupled electron-transport–ATP synthesis reactions. In these and other oxygen-consuming redox reactions, the product may not be water, but one or more of three highly reactive species. Two are free radicals, which contain unpaired electrons (represented by single dots in the following formulas). Like all free radicals, these two oxygen-containing species, the superoxide ion ($\cdot O_2^-$) and the hydroxyl free radical ($\cdot OH^-$), react as soon as possible to get rid of the unpaired electron. Often, they do this by grabbing an electron from a bond in another molecule, which results in breaking that bond. The third oxygen by-product is hydrogen peroxide, H_2O_2, which is a relatively strong oxidizing agent. The conditions that can enhance production of these three reactive oxygen species are represented in the drawing below. Some causes are environmental, such as exposure to smog

20.58 How many NADH and how many $FADH_2$ molecules are formed in the citric acid cycle?

20.59 Which reaction(s) of the citric acid cycle store energy as $FADH_2$?

20.60 Which reaction(s) of the citric acid cycle store energy as NADH?

THE ELECTRON-TRANSPORT CHAIN; OXIDATIVE PHOSPHORYLATION

20.61 What are the two primary functions of the electron-transport chain?

20.62 How are the processes of the citric acid cycle and the electron-transport chain interrelated?

20.63 What two coenzymes are involved with initial events of the electron-transport chain?

20.64 What are the ultimate products of the electron-transport chain?

20.65 Where are the following found in the cell?

(a) FAD

(b) CoQ

(c) NADH/H$^+$

(d) Cytochrome *c*

20.66 What do the following abbreviations stand for?

(a) FAD

(b) CoQ

(c) NADH/H$^+$

(d) Cytochrome *c*

20.67 What atom in the cytochromes undergoes oxidation and reduction in the electron-transport chain? What atoms in coenzyme Q undergo oxidation and reduction in the electron-transport chain?

20.68 Put the following substances in the correct order of their action in the electron-transport chain: cytochrome *c*, coenzyme Q, NADH.

20.69 Fill in the missing substances in these coupled reactions:

$$FAD \longleftarrow \quad \longrightarrow CoQH_2 \quad \longrightarrow ?$$
$$? \longrightarrow \quad ? \longleftarrow \quad \longrightarrow 2\ Fe^{2+}$$

20.70 What would happen to the citric acid cycle if NADH and $FADH_2$ were not reoxidized?

20.71 What does the term "oxidative phosphorylation" mean? What is substrate-level phosphorylation? Are these processes the same? Explain.

20.72 In oxidative phosphorylation, what is oxidized and what is phosphorylated?

20.73 Oxidative phosphorylation has three reaction products.

(a) What is the energy-carrying product?

(b) What are the other two products?

20.74 What supplies the energy to drive oxidative phosphorylation?

20.75 The antibiotic piericidin, a nonpolar molecule, is structurally similar to ubiquinone (coenzyme Q) and can cross the mitochondrial membrane. What effect might the presence of piericidin have on oxidative phosphorylation?

20.76 When oxidative phosphorylation is uncoupled, does oxygen consumption decrease, increase, or stay the same? Explain.

20.77 Why is 2,4-dinitrophenol no longer used as a weight-loss aid?

20.78 Which animal would you expect to have more brown fat, a seal or a domestic cat? Explain.

CHEMISTRY IN ACTION

20.79 Photosynthetic plants use a sunlight-driven electron-transport system to remove electrons from H_2O to produce O_2 and generate ATP and NADPH. In the bacteria found in deep-sea hydrothermal vents, H_2S is the electron donor and corresponds to what component of the electron-transport system in photosynthetic plants? [*Life without Sunlight, p. 627*]

20.80 Why do you suppose bacteria found around deep-sea hydrothermal vents and near the Mount St. Helens volcanic eruption use H_2S as a source of electrons in energy-generating reactions? [*Life without Sunlight, p. 627*]

20.81 How is basal metabolic rate defined? [*Basal Metabolism, p. 636*]

20.82 Estimate your basal metabolic rate using the guidelines in the application. Calculate the answer in kcal. [*Basal Metabolism, p. 636*]

20.83 Calculate the total calories needed in a day for an 80 kg lightly active male. Use the "Kilocalories used per minutes" values given in the table in the application. [*Basal Metabolism, p. 636*]

20.84 Why do activities such as walking raise a body's needs above the basal metabolic rate? [*Basal Metabolism, p. 636*]

20.85 Chlorophyll is similar in structure to heme in red blood cells but does not have an iron atom. What metal ion is present in chlorophyll? [*Plants and Photosynthesis, p. 649*]

20.86 Photosynthesis consists of both light-dependent and light-independent reactions. What is the purpose of each type of reaction? [*Plants and Photosynthesis, p. 649*]

20.87 One step of the cycle that incorporates CO_2 into glyceraldehyde in plants is the production of two 3-phosphoglycerates. This reaction has $\Delta G = -0.84$ kcal/mol (-3.5 kJ/mol). Is this process endergonic or exergonic? [*Plants and Photosynthesis, p. 649*]

20.88 What general process does refrigeration of harvested fruits and vegetables slow? What cellular processes are slowed by refrigeration? [*Plants and Photosynthesis, p. 649*]

GENERAL QUESTIONS AND PROBLEMS

20.89 Why must the breakdown of molecules for energy in the body occur in several steps, rather than in one step?

20.90 The first step in the citric acid cycle involves the reaction of acetyl-CoA and oxaloacetate. Show the product of this reaction before hydrolysis to yield citrate.

20.91 Fumarate produced in Step 6 of the citric acid cycle must have a trans double bond to continue on in the cycle. Suggest a reason why the corresponding cis double-bond isomer cannot continue in the cycle.

20.92 With what class of enzymes are the coenzymes NAD^+ and FAD associated?

20.93 We talk of burning food in a combustion process, producing CO_2 and H_2O from food and O_2. Explain how O_2 is involved in the process although no O_2 is directly involved in the citric acid cycle.

20.94 One of the steps that occurs when lipids are metabolized is shown below. Does this process require FAD or NAD^+ as the coenzyme? What is the general class of enzyme that catalyzes this process?

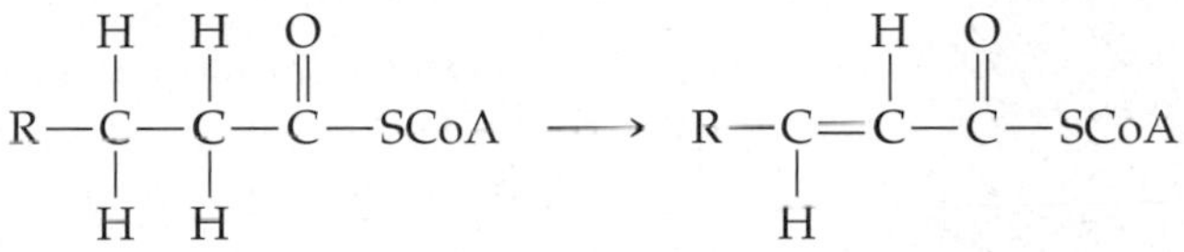

$$\underset{\substack{|\\H}}{\overset{\substack{H\\|}}{R-C}}-\underset{\substack{|\\H}}{\overset{\substack{H\\|}}{C}}-\overset{\substack{O\\\|}}{C}-SCoA \longrightarrow \underset{\substack{|\\H}}{\overset{\substack{H\\|}}{R-C}}=\overset{H}{C}-\overset{\substack{O\\\|}}{C}-SCoA$$

20.95 Solutions of hydrogen peroxide can be kept for months in a brown closed bottle with only moderate decomposition. When used on a cut as an antiseptic, hydrogen peroxide begins to bubble rapidly. Give a possible explanation for this observation.

20.96 If you use a flame to burn a pile of glucose completely to give carbon dioxide and water, the overall reaction is identical to the metabolic oxidation of glucose. Explain the differences in the fate of the energy released in each case.

20.97 Which of the following are reactive oxygen species?

(a) H_2O **(b)** H_2O_2 **(c)** $ROO\cdot$ **(d)** $\cdot OH^-$

20.98 How does a cell disarm each of the reactive oxygen species in Problem 20.97? What enzymes and vitamins are involved?

20.99 After running a mile, you stop and breathe heavily for a short period due to oxygen debt. Why do you need to breathe so heavily? (Hint: think about the metabolic pathway that uses oxygen.)

20.100 Put in order, from lowest to highest number of mitochondria per cell, the following tissues: adipose tissue (regular), heart muscle, skin cells, skeletal muscle.

20.101 Sodium fluoroacetate $\left(FH_2CCOO^-Na^+\right)$ is highly toxic. Patients with fluoroacetate poisoning accumulate citrate and fluorocitrate in their cells. Which enzyme is inhibited by fluoroacetate for this to occur? Explain.

20.102 The mitochondrion pumps H^+ from the matrix into the intermembrane space. Which region is more acidic, the matrix or the intermembrane space? Why?

20.103 Does any step of the citric acid cycle directly produce ATP? Explain.

20.104 The citric acid cycle contains four four-carbon dicarboxylic acids.

(a) Name them

(b) Arrange them in order from least oxidized to most oxidized

20.105 Sometimes ATP is referred to as the "energy-storage molecule." The cell does not actually store energy as a lot of extra ATP but as glycogen or triacylglycerides. Why do you suppose this is the case?

Carbohydrates

CONTENTS

◄ Corn stores glucose in the polysaccharides starch and cellulose.

The word *carbohydrate* originally described glucose, the simplest and most readily available sugar. Because glucose has the formula $C_6H_{12}O_6$, it was once thought to be a "hydrate of carbon," $C_6(H_2O)_6$. Although this view has been abandoned, the name "carbohydrate" persisted, and we now use it to refer to a large class of biomolecules with similar structures. Carbohydrates have in common many hydroxyl groups on adjacent carbons together with either an aldehyde or ketone group. Glucose, for example, has five hydroxyl ($-OH$) groups and one aldehyde ($-CHO$) group:

$$HO-\overset{\overset{\displaystyle H}{|}}{\underset{\underset{\displaystyle H}{|}}{C}}-\overset{\overset{\displaystyle H}{|}}{\underset{\underset{\displaystyle OH}{|}}{C}}-\overset{\overset{\displaystyle H}{|}}{\underset{\underset{\displaystyle OH}{|}}{C}}-\overset{\overset{\displaystyle OH}{|}}{\underset{\underset{\displaystyle H}{|}}{C}}-\overset{\overset{\displaystyle H}{|}}{\underset{\underset{\displaystyle OH}{|}}{C}}-\overset{\overset{\displaystyle O}{||}}{C}-H$$

Glucose

Carbohydrates are synthesized by plants and stored as starch, a polymer of glucose. When starch is eaten and digested, the freed glucose becomes a major source of the energy required by living organisms. Thus, carbohydrates are intermediaries by which energy from the sun is made available to animals.

21.1 An Introduction to Carbohydrates

Carbohydrates are a large class of naturally occurring polyhydroxy aldehydes and ketones. **Monosaccharides**, sometimes known as **simple sugars**, are the simplest carbohydrates. They have from three to seven carbon atoms, and each contains one

Carbohydrate A member of a large class of naturally occurring polyhydroxy aldehydes and ketones.

Monosaccharide (simple sugar) A carbohydrate with three to seven carbon atoms.

Aldose A monosaccharide that contains an aldehyde carbonyl group.

Ketose A monosaccharide that contains a ketone carbonyl group.

aldehyde or one ketone functional group. If the sugar has an aldehyde group, it is classified as an **aldose**. If it has a ketone group, the sugar is classified as a **ketose**. The aldehyde group is always at the end of the carbon chain, and the ketone group is always on the second carbon of the chain. In either case, there is a —CH$_2$OH group at the other end of the chain.

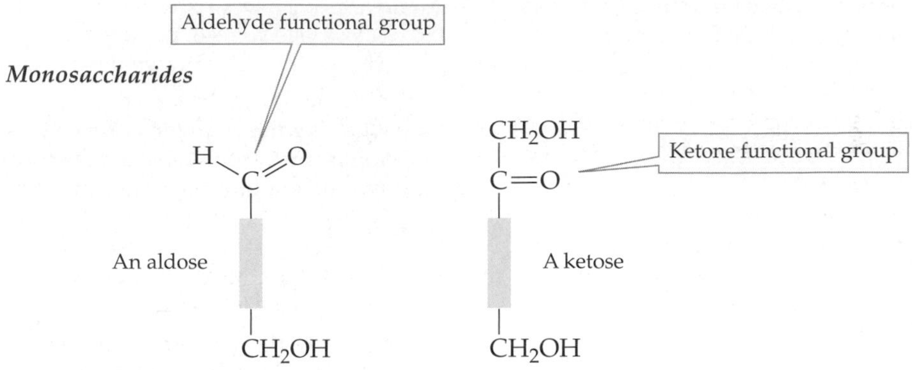

Monosaccharides

An aldose

A ketose

There are hydroxyl groups on all the carbon atoms between the carbonyl carbon atom and the —CH$_2$OH at the other end and also on the end carbon next to a ketone group, as illustrated in the following three structures. The family-name ending *-ose* indicates a carbohydrate, and simple sugars are known by common names like *glucose*, *ribose*, and *fructose* rather than systematic names.

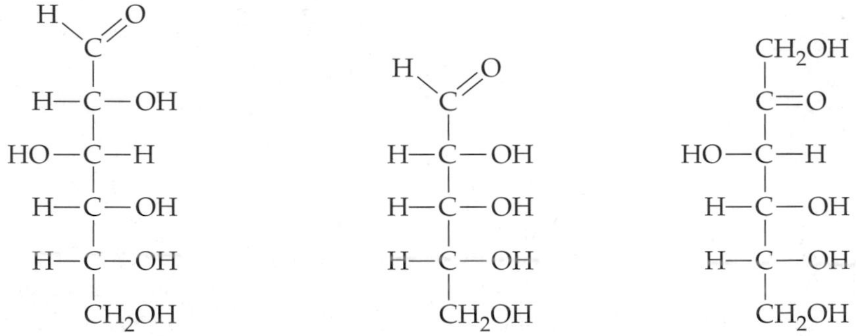

Glucose, an aldohexose
(monomer for starch and cellulose;
major source of energy)

Ribose, an aldopentose
(a component of ATP,
coenzymes, and RNA)

Fructose, a ketohexose
(present in corn syrup
and fruit)

The number of carbon atoms in an aldose or ketose is specified by the prefixes *tri-*, *tetr-*, *pent-*, *hex-*, or *hept-*. Thus, glucose is an aldo*hex*ose (*aldo* = aldehyde; *-hex* = 6 carbons; *-ose* = sugar); fructose is a keto*hex*ose (a 6-carbon ketone sugar); and ribose is an aldo*pent*ose (a five-carbon aldehyde sugar). Most naturally occurring simple sugars are aldehydes with either five or six carbons.

Because of their many functional groups, monosaccharides undergo a variety of structural changes and chemical reactions. They react with each other to form **disaccharides** and **polysaccharides** (also known as **complex carbohydrates**), which are polymers of monosaccharides. Their functional groups are involved in reactions with alcohols, lipids, or proteins to form biomolecules with specialized functions. These and other carbohydrates are introduced in later sections of this chapter. First, we are going to discuss two important aspects of carbohydrate structure:

Disaccharide A carbohydrate composed of two monosaccharides.

Polysaccharide (complex carbohydrate) A carbohydrate that is a polymer of monosaccharides.

- Monosaccharides are chiral molecules (Sections 21.2, 21.3).
- Monosaccharides exist mainly in cyclic forms rather than the straight-chain forms shown above (Section 21.4).

Worked Example 21.1 Classifying Monosaccharides

Classify the monosaccharide shown as an aldose or a ketose, and name it according to its number of carbon atoms.

$$\begin{array}{ccccccc} & H & H & OH & H & OH & O \\ & | & | & | & | & | & \| \\ HO-C&-C&-C&-C&-C&-C&-H \\ & | & | & | & | & | \\ & H & OH & H & OH & H \end{array}$$

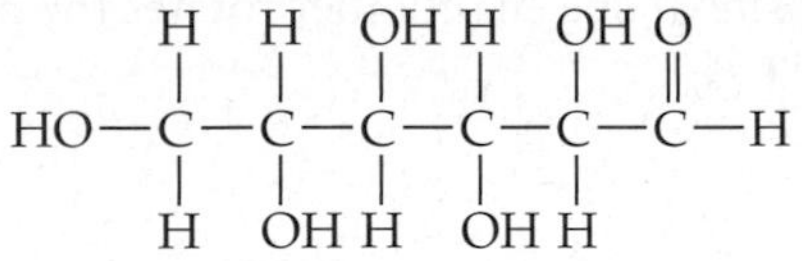

ANALYSIS First determine if the monosaccharide is an aldose or a ketose. Then determine the number of carbon atoms present. This monosaccharide is an aldose because an aldehyde group is present. It contains 6 carbon atoms.

SOLUTION
The monosaccharide is a 6-carbon aldose, so we refer to it as an aldohexose.

PROBLEM 21.1
Classify the following monosaccharides as an aldose or a ketose, and name each according its number of carbon atoms.

(a) 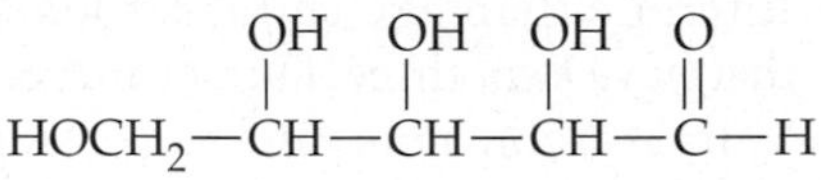 $\begin{array}{cccc} OH & OH & OH & O \\ | & | & | & \| \\ HOCH_2-CH&-CH&-CH&-C&-H \end{array}$

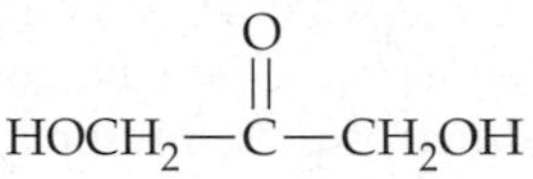

(b) $\begin{array}{c} O \\ \| \\ HOCH_2-C-CH_2OH \end{array}$

(c) $\begin{array}{ccc} OH & OH & O \\ | & | & \| \\ HOCH_2-CH&-CH&-C&-H \end{array}$

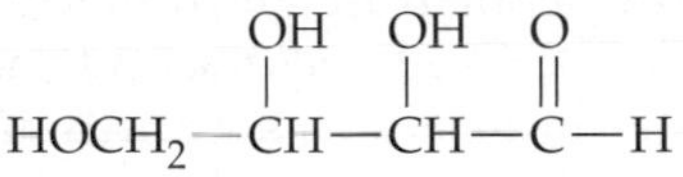

PROBLEM 21.2
Draw the structures of an aldopentose and a ketohexose.

21.2 Handedness of Carbohydrates

You have seen that amino acids are chiral because they contain carbon atoms bonded to four different groups. Glyceraldehyde, an aldotriose and the simplest naturally occurring carbohydrate, has the structure shown below. Because four different groups are bonded to the number 2 carbon atom ($-CHO$, $-H$, $-OH$, and $-CH_2OH$), glyceraldehyde is also chiral.

▶▶▶ Chiral molecules are not superimposable on their mirror images (see Sections 18.5 and 18.6).

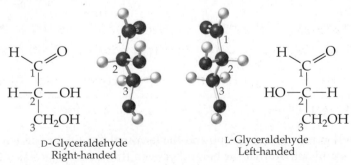

D-Glyceraldehyde
Right-handed

L-Glyceraldehyde
Left-handed

Chiral compounds lack a plane of symmetry and exist as a pair of enantiomers in either a "right-handed" D form or a "left-handed" L form. Like all enantiomers, the two forms of glyceraldehyde have the same physical properties except for the way in which they affect polarized light.

Light as we usually see it consists of electromagnetic waves oscillating in all planes at right angles to the direction of travel of the light beam. When ordinary light is transmitted through a polarizer, only waves in one plane pass through, producing what is known as *plane-polarized light*. (Polarized sunglasses work on a similar principle.)

Solutions of *optically active* chemical compounds change the plane in which the light is polarized. The angle by which the plane is rotated can be measured in an instrument known as a *polarimeter*, which works on the principle diagrammed in Figure 21.1. Each enantiomer of a pair rotates the plane of the light by the same amount, but the directions of rotation are *opposite*. If one enantiomer rotates the plane of the light to the left, the other rotates it to the right.

▶ **Figure 21.1**
Principle of a polarimeter, used to determine optical activity.
A solution of an optically active isomer rotates the plane of the polarized light by a characteristic amount.

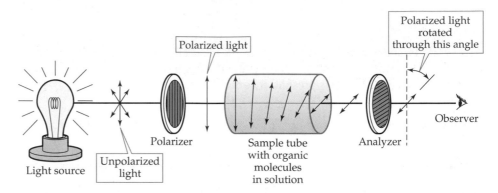

Compounds like glyceraldehyde that have *one* chiral carbon atom can exist as two enantiomers. But what about compounds with more than one chiral carbon atom? How many isomers are there for compounds that have two, three, four, or more chiral carbons? Aldotetroses, for example, have two chiral carbon atoms and can exist in the four isomeric forms shown in Figure 21.2. These four aldotetrose stereoisomers consist of two mirror-image pairs of enantiomers, one pair named *erythrose* and one pair named *threose*. Because erythrose and threose are stereoisomers but not mirror images of each other, they are described as **diastereomers**.

Diastereomers Stereoisomers that are not mirror images of each other.

▶ **Figure 21.2**
Two pairs of enantiomers: The four isomeric aldotetroses (2,3,4-trihydroxybutanals).
Carbon atoms 2 and 3 are chiral. Their —H atoms and —OH groups are written here to show their mirror-image relationship. Erythrose and threose exist as enantiomeric pairs.

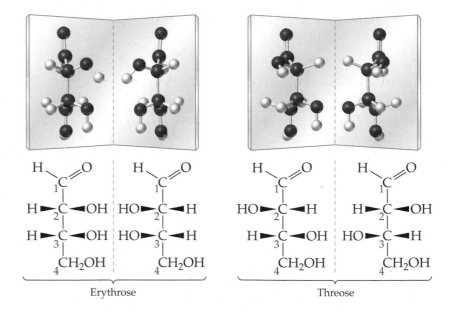

By convention the carbonyl group and the terminal CH_2OH are drawn pointing to the right. It is understood that the bonds between those carbon atoms and the other carbon atoms freely rotate and do not affect the symmetry of the molecule.

In general, a compound with n chiral carbon atoms has a maximum of 2^n possible stereoisomers and half that many pairs of enantiomers. The aldotetroses, for example, have $n = 2$ so that $2^n = 2^2 = 4$, meaning that four stereoisomers are possible. Glucose, an aldohexose, has four chiral carbon atoms and a total of $2^4 = 16$ possible stereoisomers (eight pairs of enantiomers). All 16 stereoisomers of glucose are known. (In some cases, fewer than the maximum predicted number of stereoisomers exist because some of the molecules have symmetry planes that make them identical to their mirror images.)

PROBLEM 21.3

Aldoheptoses have five chiral carbon atoms. What is the maximum possible number of aldoheptose stereoisomers?

PROBLEM 21.4

From monosaccharides (a)–(d) in Problem 21.5, choose the one that is the enantiomer of the unlabeled monosaccharide shown.

PROBLEM 21.5

Notice in structures (a)–(d) below that the bottom carbon and its substituents are written as CH$_2$OH in every case. How does the C in this group differ in each case from the C atoms above it? Why must the locations of the H atoms and —OH groups attached to the carbons between this one and the carbonyl group be shown?

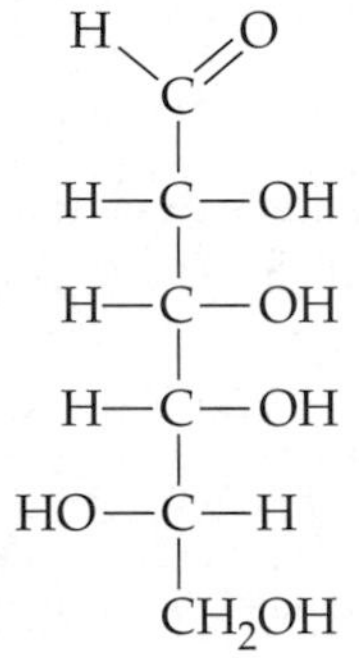

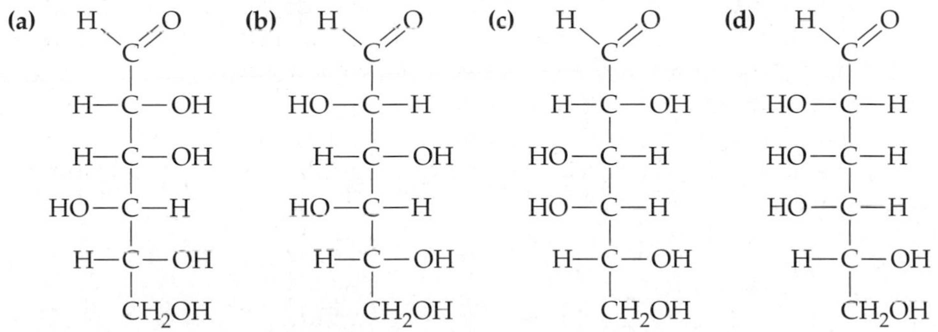

21.3 The D and L Families of Sugars: Drawing Sugar Molecules

A standard method of representation called a **Fischer projection** has been adopted for drawing stereoisomers on a flat page so that we can tell one from another. A chiral carbon atom is represented in a Fischer projection as the intersection of two crossed lines, and this carbon atom is considered to be on the printed page. Bonds that point up and out of the page are shown as horizontal lines, and bonds that point behind the page are shown as vertical lines. Until now, we have used solid wedges and dashed lines to represent bonds above and behind the printed page, respectively, with ordinary solid lines for bonds in the plane of the page. The relationship between such a structure and a Fischer projection is as follows:

Fischer projection Structure that represents chiral carbon atoms as the intersections of two lines, with the horizontal lines representing bonds pointing out of the page and the vertical lines representing bonds pointing behind the page. For sugars, the aldehyde or ketone is at the top.

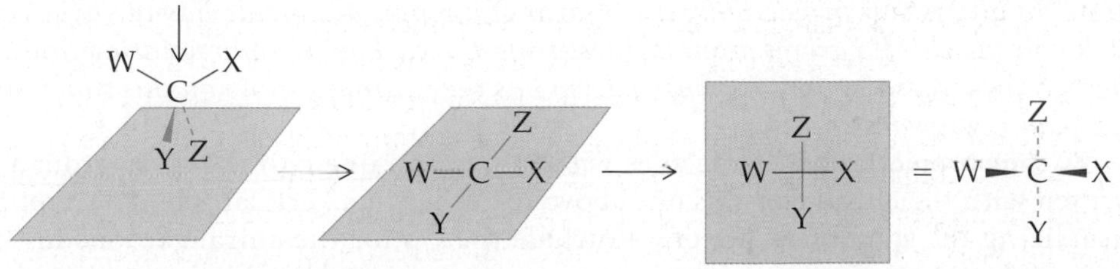

In a Fischer projection, the aldehyde or ketone carbonyl group of a monosaccharide is always placed at the top. The result is that —H and —OH groups projecting above the page are on the left and right of the chiral carbons, and groups projecting behind the page are above and below the chiral carbons. The Fischer projection of one of the enantiomers of glyceraldehyde is therefore interpreted as follows:

Fischer projection of a glyceraldehyde enantiomer

$$
\underset{\text{Fischer projection}}{\overset{\displaystyle\text{CHO}}{\underset{\displaystyle\text{CH}_2\text{OH}}{\text{HO} \!-\!\!\!\mid\!\!\!-\!\text{H}}}}
\quad = \quad
\overset{\displaystyle\text{CHO}}{\underset{\displaystyle\text{CH}_2\text{OH}}{\text{HO} - \text{C} - \text{H}}}
\quad = \quad
$$

Bonds out of page / Bonds into page

For comparison, the same glyceraldehyde enantiomer is represented below in the conventional manner, showing the tetrahedral arrangement of bonds to the chiral carbon.

$$
\overset{\displaystyle\text{CHO}}{\underset{\displaystyle\text{H}}{\text{HO} \diagdown \overset{\displaystyle\text{C}}{\diagup} \text{CH}_2\text{OH}}}
\quad = \quad
$$

Monosaccharides are divided into two families—the **D sugars** and the **L sugars**—based on their structural relationships to glyceraldehyde. Consistently writing monosaccharide formulas as Fischer projections allows us to identify the D and L forms at a glance. Look again at the structural formulas of the D and L forms of glyceraldehyde.

Mirror

$$
\underset{\text{D-Glyceraldehyde}}{\overset{\displaystyle\text{H}\diagdown \text{C}\!=\!\text{O}}{\underset{\displaystyle\text{CH}_2\text{OH}}{\text{H}\!-\!\!\!\mid\!\!\!-\!\text{OH}}}}
\qquad \vert \qquad
\underset{\text{L-Glyceraldehyde}}{\overset{\displaystyle\text{H}\diagdown \text{C}\!=\!\text{O}}{\underset{\displaystyle\text{CH}_2\text{OH}}{\text{HO}\!-\!\!\!\mid\!\!\!-\!\text{H}}}}
$$

In the D form, the —OH group on carbon 2 comes out of the plane of the paper and points to the *right*; in the L form, the —OH group at carbon 2 comes out of the plane of the paper and points to the *left*. If you mentally place a mirror plane between these Fischer projections, you can see that they are mirror images.

Nature has a strong preference for one type of handedness in carbohydrates, just as it does in amino acids and in snail shells. It happens, however, that carbohydrates and amino acids have opposite handedness. Most naturally occurring α-amino acids belong to the L family, but most carbohydrates belong to the D family.

The designations D and L derive from the Latin *dextro* for "right" and *levo* for "left." *In all Fischer projections, the D form of a monosaccharide has the hydroxyl group on the chiral carbon atom farthest from the carbonyl group pointing toward the right, whereas the mirror-image L form has the hydroxyl group on this same carbon pointing toward the left.*

Fischer projections of molecules with more than one chiral carbon atom are written with the chiral carbons one above the other in a vertical line. To simplify visualizing the structures, we often include the C's for the chiral carbons in the plane of the page. Otherwise, the structures are interpreted like Fischer projections.

D Sugar Monosaccharide with the —OH group on the chiral carbon atom farthest from the carbonyl group pointing to the right in a Fischer projection.

L Sugar Monosaccharide with the —OH group on the chiral carbon atom farthest from the carbonyl group pointing to the left in a Fischer projection.

▲ **Nature's preference. Snail shells have a preferred handedness, as do many molecules.**

CHEMISTRY IN ACTION

Chirality and Drugs

Nature is better at synthesizing single optical isomers than chemists are. Laboratory synthesis schemes that yield a mixture of optical isomers (a *racemic mixture*) are easy to develop. It is more difficult to devise synthetic schemes that yield a single isomer, but a goal of modern drug development is creation of a drug molecule that binds with a specific hormone, enzyme, or cellular receptor. Because most biomolecules are chiral, a chiral drug molecule (single isomer) is likely to meet the need most effectively by fitting with the target best. Whether a pharmaceutical company decides to produce a racemic mixture of a particular drug molecule or a single isomer of the molecule is an issue of scientific, medical, and commercial importance in the drug industry.

The route to a chiral drug molecule begins with chiral reactants and an enzyme, or with chemical synthesis of a pair of enantiomers that are then separated from each other. It is often important to have the separate enantiomers available during the elaborate testing needed to prove a drug effective. Sometimes, marketing the mixture of isomers is the wrong thing to do. Naproxen, for example, the active ingredient in the pain killer and anti-inflammatory Aleve, is sold as a single enantiomer. The other enantiomer causes liver damage.

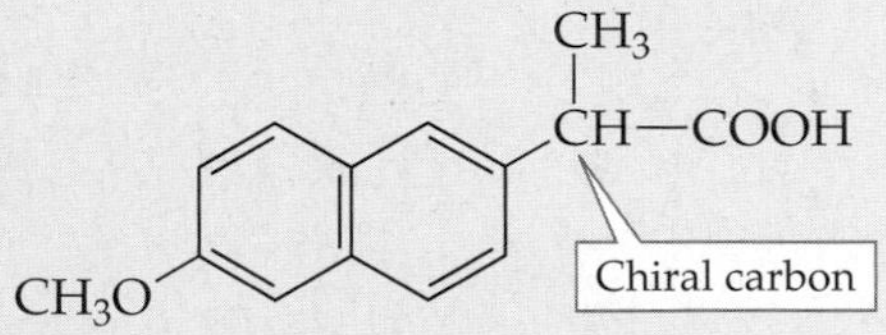

The size of the single-enantiomer drug market has increased every year since its inception. With expanding research efforts, the ability to produce such drugs is growing easier. The top five classes of single-enantiomer drugs are cardiovascular drugs, antibiotics, hormones, cancer drugs, and those for central-nervous-system disorders.

See Chemistry in Action Problems 21.77 and 21.78 at the end of the chapter.

Two pairs of aldohexose enantiomers are represented below in this manner. Given the Fischer projection of one enantiomer, you can draw the other by reversing the substituents on the left and right of each chiral atom. Note that each pair of enantiomers has a different name.

Two pairs of aldohexose enantiomers

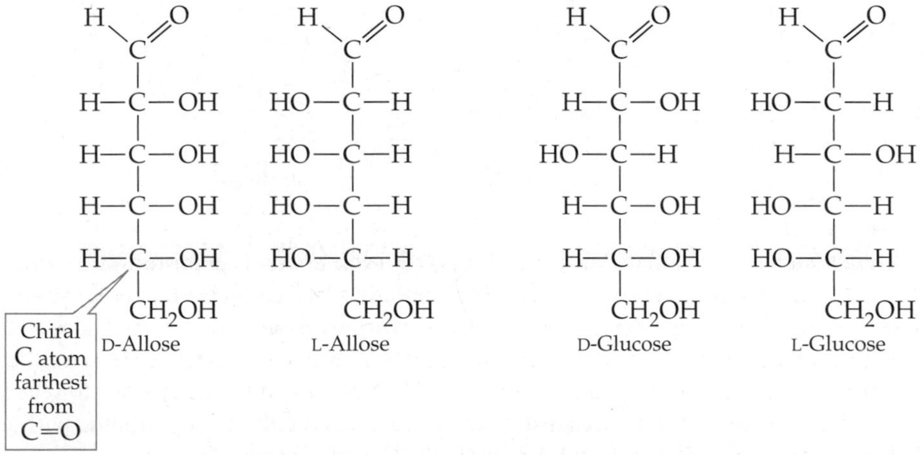

It would be easy to assume that the use of D and L, because they stand for *dextro* and *levo*, carries some meaning about the direction of rotation of plane-polarized light. Logical as it seems, this is not the case. The D and L relate directly only to the position of that —OH group on the chiral carbon farthest from the carbonyl carbon in a Fischer projection. And the D and L isomers do indeed rotate plane-polarized light in opposite directions. But—and here is the point to remember—*the direction of rotation cannot be predicted.* There are D isomers that rotate polarized light to the left and L isomers that rotate it to the right.

Worked Example **21.2** Identifying D and L Isomers

Identify the following monosaccharides as (a) D-ribose or L-ribose, (b) D-mannose or L-mannose.

(a) 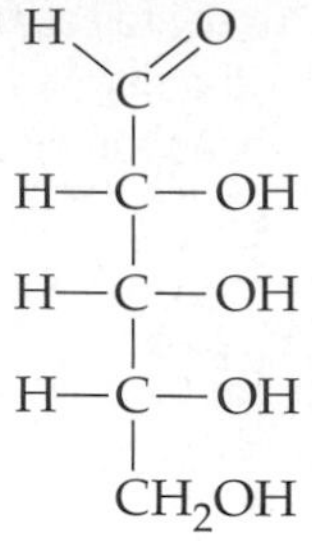
```
      H    O
       \  /
        C
        |
   H—C—OH
        |
   H—C—OH
        |
   H—C—OH
        |
      CH₂OH
```

(b) 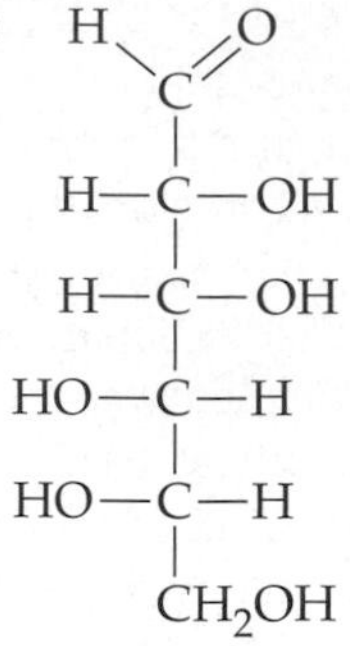
```
      H    O
       \  /
        C
        |
   H—C—OH
        |
   H—C—OH
        |
  HO—C—H
        |
  HO—C—H
        |
      CH₂OH
```

ANALYSIS To identify D or L isomers, you must check the location of the —OH group on the chiral carbon atom farthest from the carbonyl group. In a Fischer projection, this is the carbon atom above the bottom one. The —OH group points left in an L enantiomer and right in a D enantiomer.

SOLUTION
In (a) the —OH group on the chiral carbon above the bottom of the structure points to the right, so this is D-ribose. In (b) this —OH group points to the left, so this is L-mannose.

PROBLEM 21.6
Draw the enantiomer of the following monosaccharides, and in each pair identify the D sugar and the L sugar.

(a) 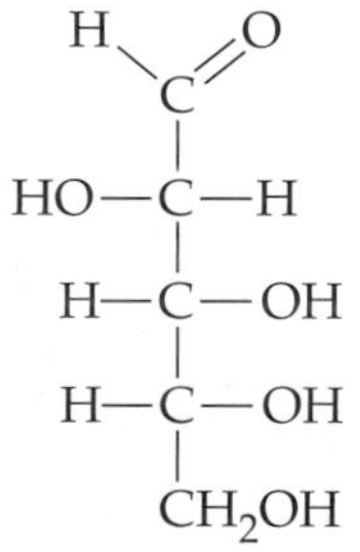
```
      H    O
       \  /
        C
        |
  HO—C—H
        |
   H—C—OH
        |
   H—C—OH
        |
      CH₂OH
```

(b) 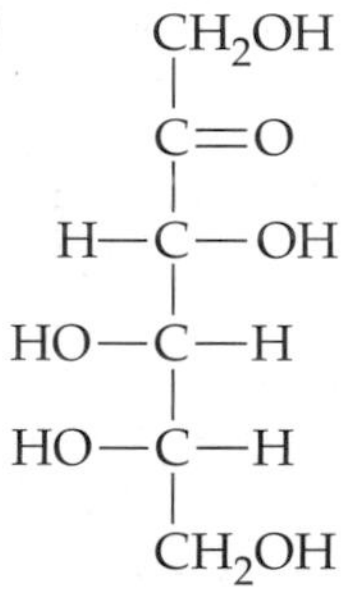
```
      CH₂OH
        |
        C=O
        |
   H—C—OH
        |
  HO—C—H
        |
  HO—C—H
        |
      CH₂OH
```

PROBLEM 21.7
Drugs such as topiramate (an anticonvulsant), esomeprazole (a proton-pump inhibitor used to treat gastric reflux), and estradiol (a steroid hormone) are currently synthesized entirely by chemical means. Chemical synthesis nearly always produces a mixture of enantiomers that are difficult to separate. Drug companies are required to test both enantiomers separately to determine effectiveness and toxicity prior to release of the drug. What would be the advantage of devising an enzymatic synthetic path for these drugs? [See Chemistry in Action: Chirality and Drugs, p. 663.]

21.4 Structure of Glucose and Other Monosaccharides

D-Glucose, also called *dextrose* or *blood sugar*, is the most abundant of all monosaccharides and has the most important function. In nearly all living organisms, D-glucose serves as a source of energy to fuel biochemical reactions. It is stored as starch in plants and glycogen in animals (Section 21.9). Our discussion here of the structure of D-glucose illustrates a major point about the structure of monosaccharides: Although they can be written with the carbon atoms in a straight chain, monosaccharides with five or six carbon atoms exist primarily in their cyclic forms when in solution, as they are found in living organisms.

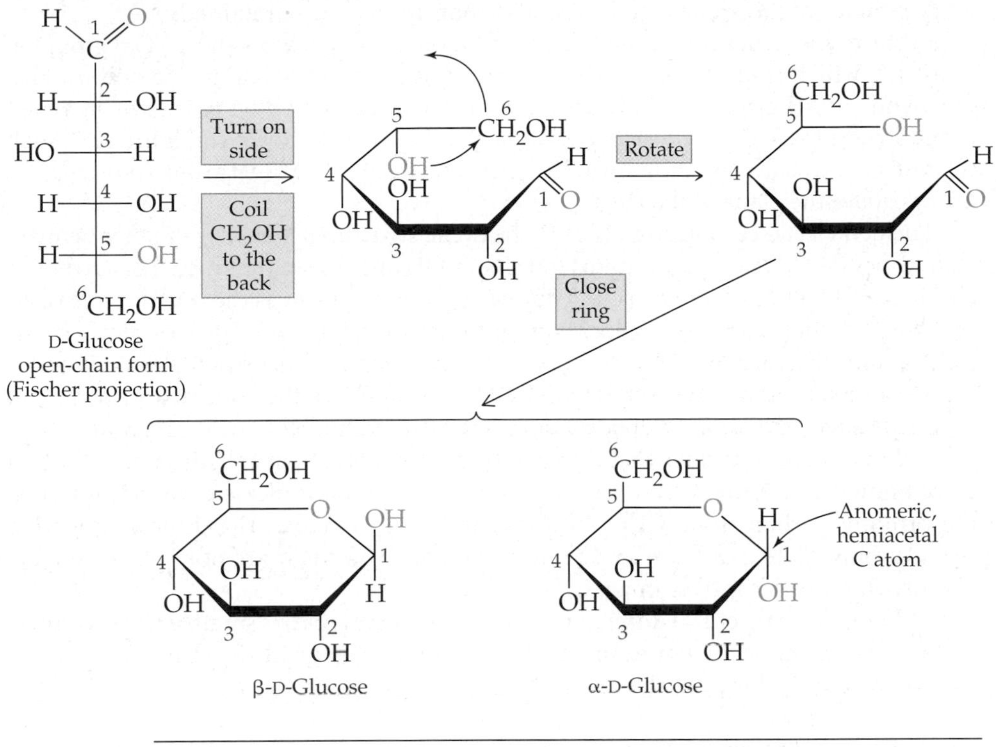

▲ **Figure 21.3**

The structure of D-glucose.

D-Glucose can exist as an open-chain polyhydroxy aldehyde or as a pair of cyclic hemiacetals. The cyclic forms differ only at C1, where the —OH group is either on the opposite side of the six membered ring from the CH_2OH (α) or on the same side (β). To convert the Fischer projection into the six-membered ring formula, the Fischer projection is laid down with C1 to the right and the other end curled around at the back. Then the single bond between C4 and C5 is rotated so that the —CH_2OH group is vertical. Finally, the hemiacetal O—R bond is formed by connecting oxygen from the —OH group on C5 to C1, and the hemiacetal O—H group is placed on C1. (H's on carbons 2–5 are omitted here for clarity.)

Look at the Fischer projection of D-glucose at the top left-hand corner of Figure 21.3, and notice the locations of the aldehyde group and the hydroxyl groups. You have seen that aldehydes and ketones react reversibly with alcohols to yield hemiacetals as shown below.

▶▶▶ Recall from Section 16.7 that the key to recognizing the hemiacetal is a carbon atom bonded to both an —OH group and an —OR group.

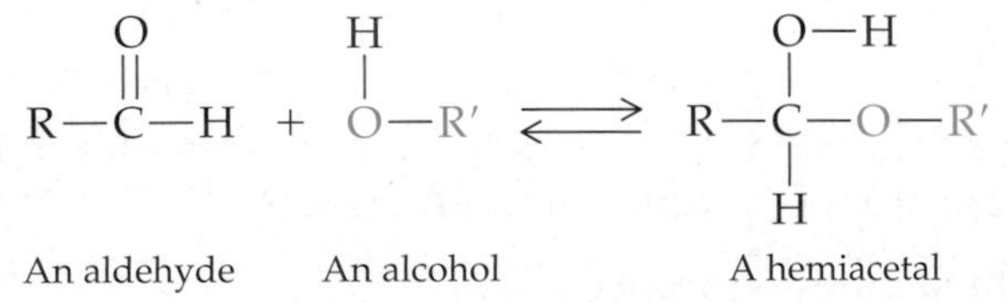

Since glucose has alcohol hydroxyl groups and an aldehyde carbonyl group in the same molecule, *internal* hemiacetal formation is possible. The aldehyde carbonyl group at carbon 1 (C1) and the hydroxyl group at carbon 5 (C5) in glucose react to form a six-membered ring that is a hemiacetal. Ketones undergo internal hemiacetal formation as well; in ketones, the reacting carbonyl group is on C2. Monosaccharides with five or six carbon atoms form rings in this manner.

The three structures at the top in Figure 21.3 show how to picture the C5-hydroxyl and the C1-aldehyde group approaching each other for hemiacetal formation. When visualized in this manner, Fischer projections are converted to cyclic structures that (like the Fischer projections) can be interpreted consistently because the same relative arrangements of the groups on the chiral carbon atoms are maintained.

In the cyclic structures at the bottom of Figure 21.3, note how the —OH group on carbon 3, which is on the left in the Fischer projection, points *up* in the cyclic structure, and —OH groups that are on the right on carbons 2 and 4 point *down*. When cyclic structures (called *Haworth projections*) are drawn as shown in Figure 21.3, such relationships are always maintained. Note also that the —CH$_2$OH group in D sugars is always *above* the plane of the ring.

The hemiacetal carbon atom (C1) in the cyclic structures, like that in other hemiacetals, is bonded to two oxygen atoms (one in —OH and one in the ring). This carbon is chiral. As a result, there are two cyclic forms of glucose, known as the α and β forms. To see the difference, compare the locations of the hemiacetal —OH groups on C1 in the two bottom structures in Figure 21.3. In the β form, the hydroxyl at C1 points *up* and is on the same side of the ring as the —CH$_2$OH group at C5. In the α form, the hydroxyl at C1 points *down* and is on the opposite side of the ring from the —CH$_2$OH group.

Cyclic monosaccharides that differ only in the positions of substituents at carbon 1 are known as **anomers**, and carbon 1 is said to be an **anomeric carbon atom**. It is the carbonyl carbon atom (C1 in an aldose and C2 in a ketose) that is now bonded to two O atoms. Note that the α and β anomers of a given sugar are not optical isomers because they are not mirror images.

Although the structural difference between anomers appears small, it has enormous biological consequences. For example, this one small change in structure accounts for the vast difference between the digestibility of starch, which we can digest, and that of cellulose, which we cannot digest (Section 21.9).

Ordinary crystalline glucose is entirely in the cyclic α form. Once dissolved in water, however, equilibrium is established among the open-chain form and the two anomers. The optical rotation of a freshly made solution of α-D-glucose gradually changes from its original value until it reaches a constant value that represents the optical activity of the equilibrium mixture. A solution of β-D-glucose or a mixture of the α and β forms also undergoes this gradual change in rotation, known as **mutarotation**, until the ring opening and closing reactions come to the following equilibrium:

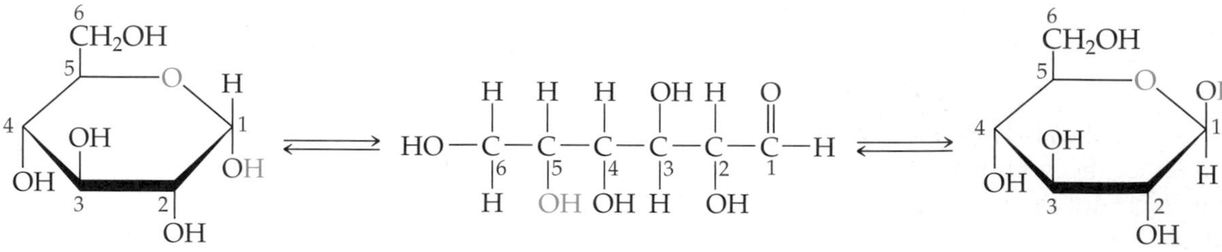

Anomers Cyclic sugars that differ only in positions of substituents at the hemiacetal carbon (the anomeric carbon); α the form has the —OH on the opposite side from the —CH$_2$OH; the β form has the —OH on the same side as the —CH$_2$OH.

Anomeric carbon atom The hemiacetal C atom in a cyclic sugar; the C atom bonded to an —OH group and an O in the ring.

Mutarotation Change in rotation of plane-polarized light resulting from the equilibrium between cyclic anomers and the open-chain form of a sugar.

α-D-Glucose (36%)	Open-chain D-Glucose (0.02%)	β-D-Glucose (64%)

All monosaccharides with five or six carbon atoms establish similar equilibria, but with different percentages of the different forms present.

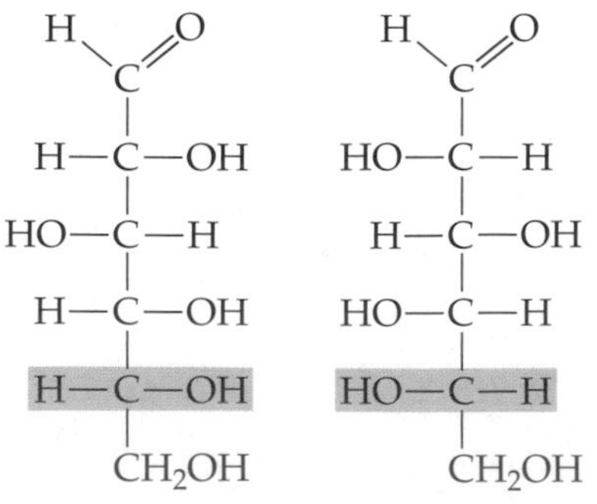

Monosaccharide Structures—Summary

Enantiomers

D-Glucose   L-Glucose

- Monosaccharides are polyhydroxy aldehydes or ketones.
- Monosaccharides have three to seven carbon atoms, and a maximum of 2^n possible stereoisomers, where *n* is the number of chiral carbon atoms.
- D and L *enantiomers* differ in the orientation of the —OH group on the chiral carbon atom farthest from the carbonyl. In Fischer projections, D sugars have this —OH on the right and L sugars have this —OH on the left.
- D-Glucose (and other 6-carbon aldoses) forms cyclic hemiacetals conventionally represented (as in Figure 21.3) so that —OH groups on chiral carbons on the left in Fischer projections point up and those on the right in Fischer projections point down.

- In glucose, the hemiacetal carbon (*the anomeric carbon*) is chiral, and α and β anomers differ in the orientation of the —OH groups on this carbon. The α anomer has the —OH on the opposite side from the —CH$_2$OH, and the β anomer has the —OH on the same side as the —CH$_2$OH.

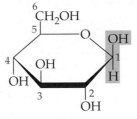

Anomers

α-D-Glucose

β-D-Glucose

Worked Example 21.3 Converting Fisher Projections to Cyclic Hemiacetals

The open-chain form of D-altrose, an aldohexose isomer of glucose, has the following structure. Draw D-altrose in its cyclic hemiacetal form:

$$
\underset{\text{D-Altrose}}{
\text{HO}-\underset{\underset{\text{H}}{|}}{\overset{\overset{\text{H}}{|}}{\text{C}}}-\underset{\underset{\text{OH}}{|}}{\overset{\overset{\text{H}}{|}}{\text{C}}}-\underset{\underset{\text{OH}}{|}}{\overset{\overset{\text{H}}{|}}{\text{C}}}-\underset{\underset{\text{OH}}{|}}{\overset{\overset{\text{H}}{|}}{\text{C}}}-\underset{\underset{\text{H}}{|}}{\overset{\overset{\text{OH}}{|}}{\text{C}}}-\overset{\overset{\text{O}}{||}}{\text{C}}-\text{H}
}
$$

SOLUTION

First, coil D-altrose into a circular shape by mentally grasping the end farthest from the carbonyl group and bending it backward into the plane of the paper:

Coil up

Next, rotate the bottom of the structure around the single bond between C4 and C5 so that the —CH$_2$OH group at the end of the chain points up and the —OH group on C5 points toward the aldehyde carbonyl group on the right:

Rotate

Finally, add the —OH group at C5 to the carbonyl C=O to form a hemiacetal ring. The new —OH group formed on C1 can be either up (β) or down (α):

β + α

PROBLEM 21.8

D-Talose, a constituent of certain antibiotics, has the open-chain structure shown below. Draw D-talose in its cyclic hemiacetal form.

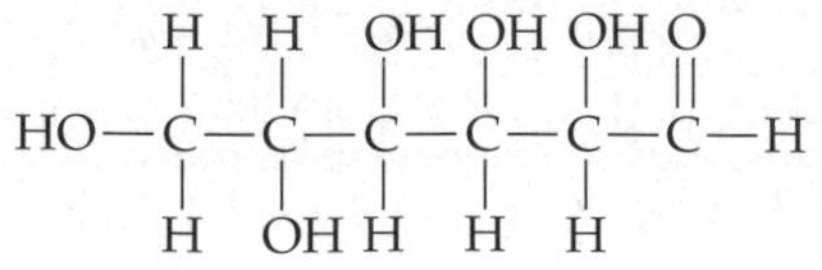

D-Talose

PROBLEM 21.9

The cyclic structure of D-idose, an aldohexose, is shown below. Convert this to the straight-chain Fischer projection structure.

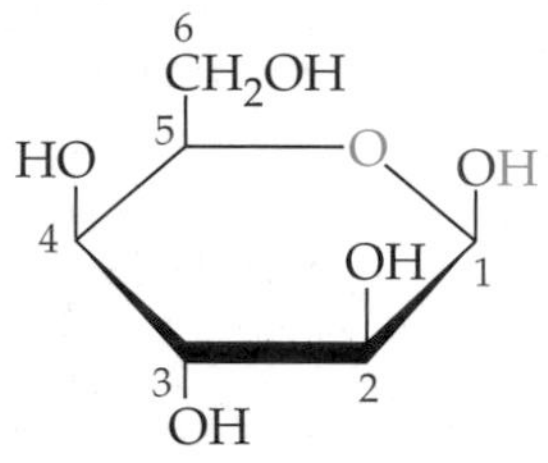

D-Idose

Worked Example 21.4 Identifying Sugars and Sugar Derivatives in Polysaccharides

Framycetin, a topical antibiotic, is a four-ring molecule consisting of several amino-glycosides—sugars that have some of the —OH groups on the sugars replaced by —NH₂ groups—and another ring, with oxygen links between the rings. What sugar or other molecule is each ring derived from?

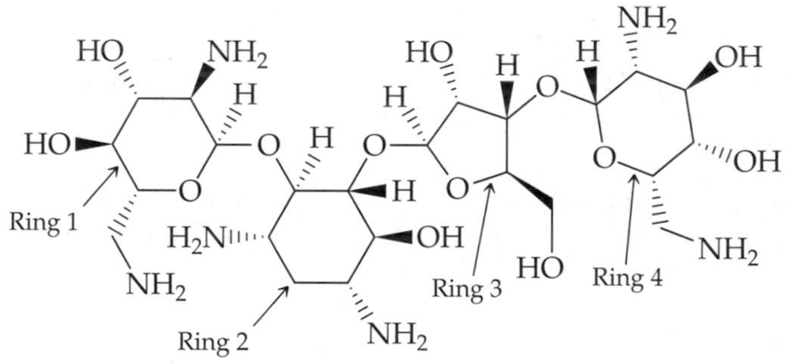

ANALYSIS Look at each ring carefully. Ring 2 does not include an O. It cannot be a sugar. Rings 1, 3, and 4 all contain O as a ring member. Imagine the rings as underivatized sugars, that is with —OH groups instead of —NH₂ groups; count the number of carbon atoms in each sugar and draw the sugar form to help identify the sugar.

SOLUTION

Ring 2 has six carbon atoms and no oxygen atoms as part of the ring; it is not a sugar, but is a cyclohexane derivative. Rings 1 and 4 are derived from the aldohexose, glucose, while ring 3 is derived from the aldopentose, ribose.

Neomycin is an antibiotic used in topical applications to inhibit the growth of bacteria. It is an aminoglycoside, that is, some of the —OH groups on the sugars have been replaced by —NH$_2$ or R groups. The four rings that constitute neomycin are joined by glycosidic bonds and two of the rings are amino sugars. In the structure shown, identify (a) the amino sugar rings by number, (b) the unmodified sugar ring structure, and (c) the non-sugar ring structure. List how many carbon atoms are in each ring.

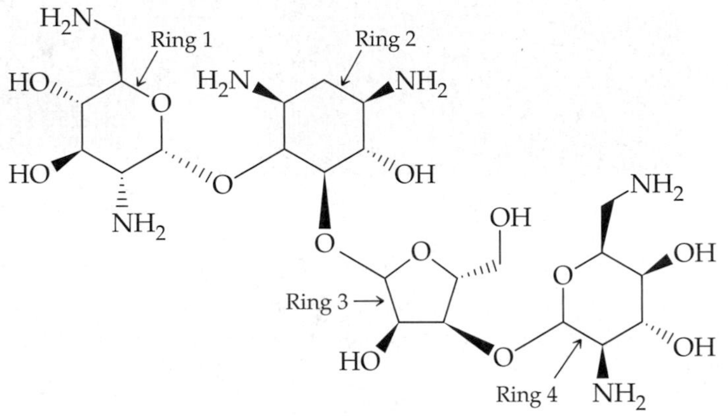

21.5 Some Important Monosaccharides

The monosaccharides can form multiple hydrogen bonds through their hydroxyl groups and are generally high-melting, white, crystalline solids that are soluble in water and insoluble in nonpolar solvents. Most monosaccharides and disaccharides are sweet-tasting (Table 21.1), digestible, and nontoxic (Figure 21.4). Except for glyceraldehyde (an aldotriose) and fructose (a ketohexose), the carbohydrates of interest in human biochemistry are all aldohexoses or aldopentoses. Most are in the D family.

TABLE 21.1 Relative Sweetness of Some Sugars and Sugar Substitutes

Name	Type	Sweetness
Lactose	Disaccharide	16
Galactose	Monosaccharide	30
Maltose	Disaccharide	33
Glucose	Monosaccharide	75
Sucrose	Disaccharide	100
Fructose	Monosaccharide	175
Cyclamate	Artificial	3000
Aspartame	Artificial	15,000
Saccharin	Artificial	35,000
Sucralose	Artificial	60,000

(a)

(b)

(c)

▲ **Figure 21.4**
Common sugars.
(a) The disaccharide sucrose (glucose + fructose) is found in sugar cane and sugar beets. (b) Jam contains the monosaccharide galactose in the pectin that stiffens it. (c) Honey is high in the monosaccharide fructose.

Glucose

Glucose is the most important simple carbohydrate in human metabolism. It is the final product of complex carbohydrate digestion and provides acetyl groups for entry into the citric acid cycle as acetyl-CoA (Section 20.8). Maintenance of an appropriate blood glucose level is essential to human health. The hormones insulin and glucagon regulate blood glucose concentration. Because glucose is metabolized without further digestion, glucose solutions can be supplied intravenously to restore blood glucose levels.

LOOKING AHEAD ▶▶▶ In Chapter 22 we will describe the metabolic pathway (glycolysis) by which glucose is converted to pyruvate and then to acetyl-CoA for entry into the citric acid cycle. The role of insulin in controlling blood glucose concentrations and the way in which those concentrations are affected by diabetes mellitus are also examined there.

Galactose

D-Galactose is widely distributed in plant gums and pectins, the sticky polysaccharides present in plant cells. It is also a component of the disaccharide lactose (milk sugar) and is produced from lactose hydrolysis during digestion. Like glucose, galactose is an aldohexose; it differs from glucose only in the spatial orientation of the —OH group at carbon 4. In the body, galactose is converted to glucose to provide energy and is synthesized from glucose to produce lactose for milk and compounds needed in brain tissue.

α-D-Galactose ⇌ Open-chain galactose ⇌ β-D-Galactose

A group of genetic disorders known as *galactosemias* result from an inherited deficiency of any of several enzymes needed to metabolize galactose. The result is a buildup of galactose or galactose 1-phosphate in blood and tissues. Early symptoms in infants include vomiting, an enlarged liver, and general failure to thrive. Other possible outcomes are liver failure, mental retardation, and development of cataracts when galactose in the eye is reduced to galactitol, a polyhydroxy alcohol that accumulates. Treatment of galactosemia consists of a galactose-free diet for life.

Fructose

D-Fructose, often called *levulose* or *fruit sugar*, occurs in honey and many fruits. It is one of the two monosaccharides combined in the disaccharide sucrose. Fructose is produced commercially in large quantities by hydrolysis of cornstarch to make high-fructose corn syrup. Like glucose and galactose, fructose is a 6-carbon sugar. However, it is a ketohexose rather than an aldohexose. In solution, fructose forms five-membered rings:

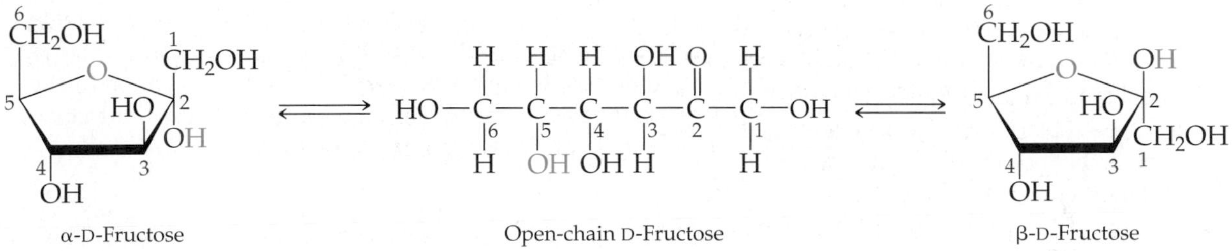

α-D-Fructose   Open-chain D-Fructose   β-D-Fructose

Fructose is sweeter than sucrose and is an ingredient in many sweetened beverages and prepared foods. As a phosphate, it is an intermediate in glucose metabolism.

Ribose and 2-Deoxyribose

Ribose and its relative 2-deoxyribose are both 5-carbon aldehyde sugars. These two sugars are most important as parts of larger biomolecules. You have already seen ribose as a constituent of coenzyme A (Figure 19.10), in ATP (p. 612), and in oxidizing and reducing agent coenzymes (p. 612). Ribose is also a part of the second messenger cyclic AMP, which we will discuss in Chapter 28.

As its name indicates, *2-deoxy*ribose differs from ribose by the absence of one oxygen atom, that in the —OH group at C2. Both ribose and 2-deoxyribose exist in the usual mixture of open-chain and cyclic hemiacetal forms.

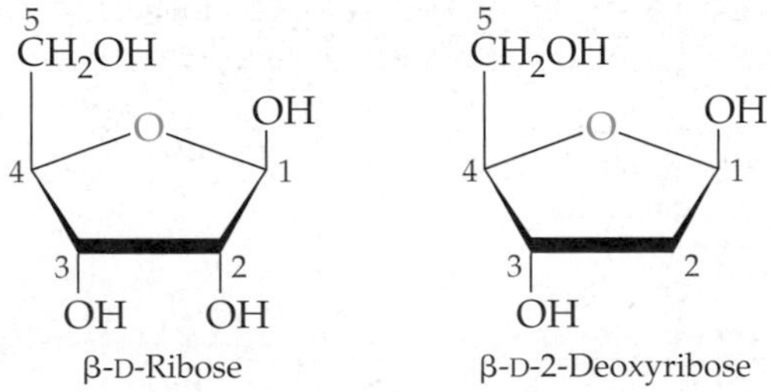

β-D-Ribose   β-D-2-Deoxyribose

LOOKING AHEAD ▶▶▶   Ribose is part of RNA, ribonucleic acid, and deoxyribose is part of DNA, deoxyribonucleic acid. Chapter 25 is devoted to the roles of DNA in protein synthesis and heredity.

CHEMISTRY IN ACTION

Cell-Surface Carbohydrates and Blood Type

Nearly 100 years ago, scientists discovered that human blood can be classified into four blood group types, called A, B, AB, and O. This classification indirectly results from the presence on red blood cell surfaces of three different oligosaccharide units, designated A, B, and O (see the diagram). Individuals with type AB blood have both A and B oligosaccharides displayed on the same cells.

Selecting a matching blood type is vitally important in choosing blood for transfusions because a major component of the body's immune system (Chapter 29) is a collection of proteins called *antibodies* that recognize and attack foreign substances, such as viruses, bacteria, potentially harmful macromolecules, and foreign blood cells. Among the targets of these antibodies are cell-surface molecules that are not present on the individual's own cells and are thus "foreign blood cells." For example, if you have type A blood, your plasma (the liquid portion of the blood) contains antibodies to the type B oligosaccharide. Thus, if type B blood enters your body, its red blood cells will be recognized as foreign and your immune system will launch an attack on them. The result is clumping of the cells (agglutination), blockage of capillaries, and possibly death.

Because of the danger of such interactions, both the blood types that individuals can receive and the blood types of recipients to whom they can donate blood are limited, as indicated in the accompanying table. A few features of the table deserve special mention:

- Note in the diagram that type O cell-surface oligosaccharides are similar in composition to those of types A and B.

Consequently, people with blood types A, B, and AB all lack antibodies to type O cells. Individuals with type O blood are therefore known as "universal donors"—in an emergency, their blood can safely be given to individuals of all blood types.

- Similarly, type AB individuals are known as "universal recipients." Because people with type AB blood have both A and B molecules on their red cells, their blood contains no antibodies to A, B, or O, and they can, if necessary, receive blood cells of all types.

- In theory, antibodies in the plasma of donated blood could also attack the red cells of the recipient. In practice, such reactions are unlikely to cause significant harm. Unless very large quantities of whole blood or plasma (the fluid portion of the blood) are transfused, the donor's blood is quickly diluted by mixing with the much larger volume of the recipient's blood. Moreover, many transfusions today consist of packed red cells, with a minimum of the antibody-containing plasma. Nevertheless, exact matching of blood types is preferred whenever possible.

Individuals with blood type...	... have antibodies to type...,	... can receive from type...,	... and can donate to type
O	A and B	O	O, A, and B*
A	B	O and A	A and AB
B	A	O and B	B and AB
AB	None	O, A and B*	AB

*Red blood cells only

See *Chemistry in Action* Problems 21.79 and 21.80 at the end of the chapter.

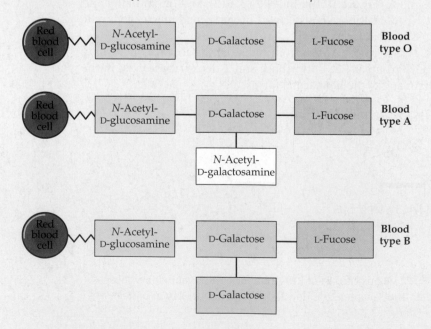

PROBLEM 21.11

In the following monosaccharide hemiacetal, number all the carbon atoms, identify the anomeric carbon atom, and identify it as the α or β anomer.

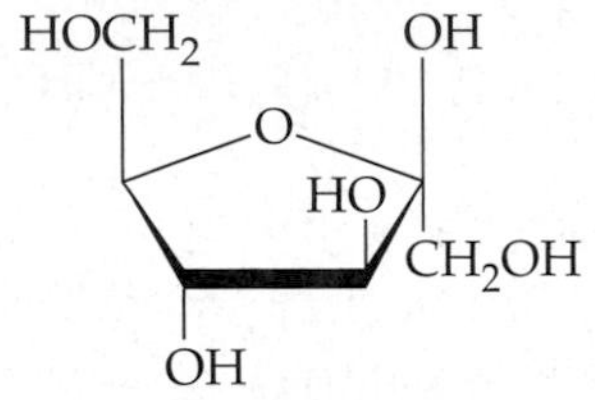

PROBLEM 21.12

Identify the chiral carbons in α-D-fructose, α-D-ribose, and β-D-2-deoxyribose.

PROBLEM 21.13

L-Fucose is one of the naturally occurring L monosaccharides. It is present in the short chains of monosaccharides by which blood groups are classified (see Chemistry in Action: Cell-Surface Carbohydrates and Blood Type on p. 672). Compare the structure of L-fucose given below with the structures of α- and β-D-galactose and answer the following questions.

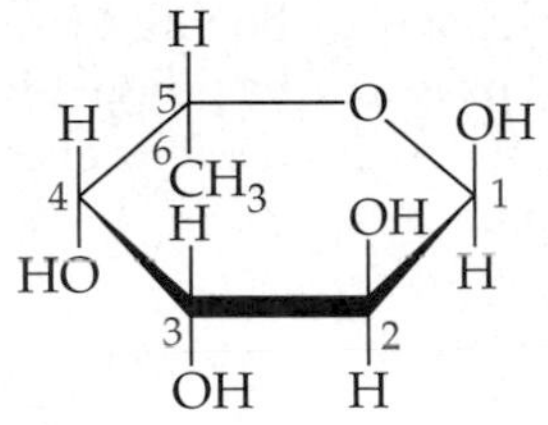

L-Fucose

(a) Is L-fucose an α or β anomer?

(b) Compared with galactose, on which carbon is L-fucose missing an oxygen?

(c) How do the positions of the —OH groups above and below the plane of the ring on carbons 2, 3, and 4 compare in D-galactose and L-fucose?

(d) "Fucose" is a common name. Is 6-deoxy-L-galactose a correct name for fucose? Why or why not?

PROBLEM 21.14

All cells in your body contain glycoproteins (proteins with short oligosaccharide chains attached) as part of the cell membrane. The carbohydrate part of a glyco-protein extends out of the membrane into the intercellular fluid and is the sig-naling part of the molecule. Red blood cells have specific glycoproteins that we use to specify the different blood types (see Chemistry in Action: Cell Surface Carbohydrates and Blood Type on p. 672). Which sugars and sugar derivatives are found in all blood types?

21.6 Reactions of Monosaccharides

Reaction with Oxidizing Agents: Reducing Sugars

Aldehydes can be oxidized to carboxylic acids ($RCHO \longrightarrow RCOOH$), a reaction that applies only to the open-chain form of aldose monosaccharides (Section 16.5). As the open-chain aldehyde is oxidized, its equilibrium with the cyclic form is displaced, and, in accordance with Le Châtelier's principle, the open-chain form continues to be

▶▶▶ Le Châtelier's principle states that when a stress is applied to a system at equilibrium, the equilibrium shifts to relieve the stress (Section 7.9).

produced. As a result, the aldehyde group of the monosaccharide is ultimately oxidized to a carboxylic acid group. For glucose, the reaction is

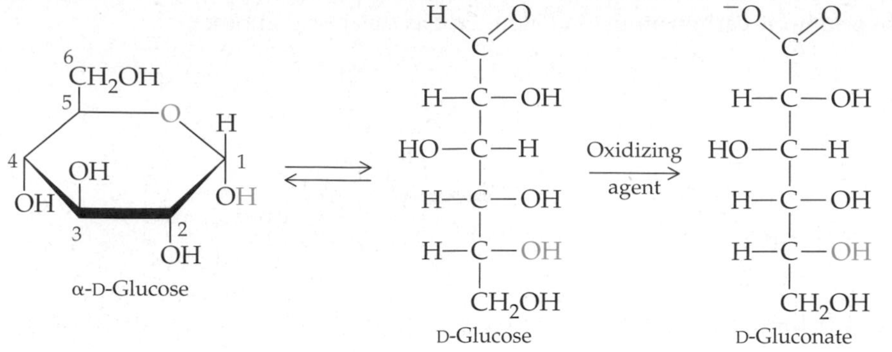

α-D-Glucose   D-Glucose   D-Gluconate

Reducing sugar A carbohydrate that reacts in basic solution with a mild oxidizing agent.

Carbohydrates that react with mild oxidizing agents are classified as **reducing sugars** (they reduce the oxidizing agent).

    Recall from Section 16.5 that ketones do not generally undergo oxidation, because they lack the hydrogen attached to the carbonyl carbon that aldehydes have. But although you probably would not predict it, in basic solution ketoses are reducing sugars. The explanation is that, under these conditions, a ketone that has a hydrogen atom on the carbon adjacent to the carbonyl carbon undergoes a rearrangement. This hydrogen moves over to the carbonyl oxygen. The product is an *enediol,* "ene" for the double bond and "diol" for the two hydroxyl groups. The enediol rearranges to give an aldose, which is susceptible to oxidation.

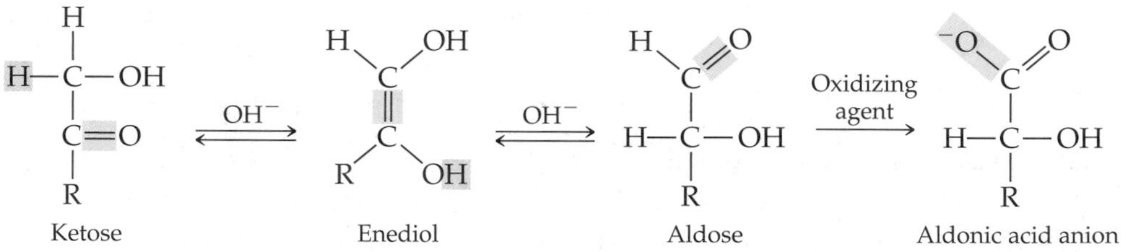

Ketose   Enediol   Aldose   Aldonic acid anion

Here also, oxidation of the aldehyde to an acid drives the equilibria toward the right, and complete oxidation of the ketose occurs. Thus, *in basic solution, all monosaccharides, whether aldoses or ketoses, are reducing sugars.* This ability to act as reducing agents is the basis for most laboratory tests for the presence of monosaccharides.

    The first equilibrium above—between the ketose and the enediol—is an example of *keto–enol tautomerism,* an equilibrium that results from a shift in position of a hydrogen atom and a double bond. Keto–enol tautomerism is possible whenever there is a hydrogen atom on a carbon adjacent to a carbonyl carbon.

Reaction with Alcohols: Glycoside and Disaccharide Formation

Hemiacetals react with alcohols with the loss of water to yield acetals, compounds with two — OR groups bonded to the same carbon (Section 16.7).

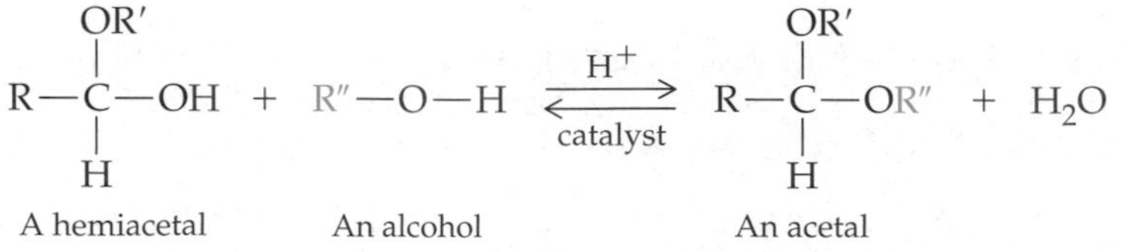

A hemiacetal   An alcohol   An acetal

Glycoside A cyclic acetal formed by reaction of a monosaccharide with an alcohol, accompanied by loss of H_2O.

Because glucose and other monosaccharides are cyclic hemiacetals, they also react with alcohols to form acetals, which are called **glycosides**. In a glycoside, the — OH group on the anomeric carbon atom is replaced by an — OR group. For example, glucose reacts with methanol to produce methyl glucoside. (Note that a *gluc*oside is a cyclic acetal formed by glucose. A cyclic acetal derived from *any* sugar is a *glyc*oside.)

Formation of a glycoside

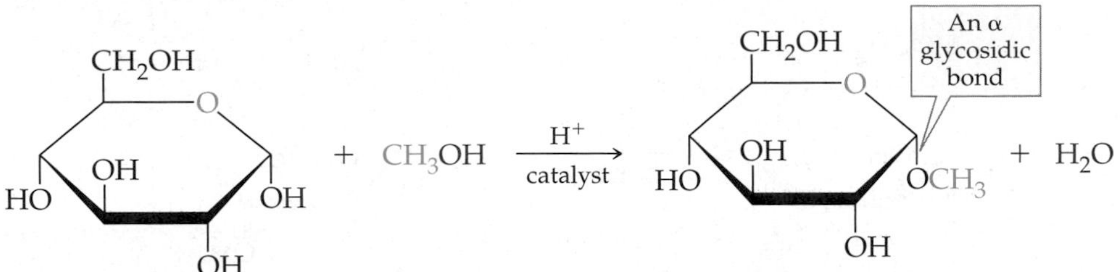

Methyl α-D-glucoside, an acetal

α-D-Glucose

The bond between the anomeric carbon atom of the monosaccharide and the oxygen atom of the —OR group is called a **glycosidic bond**. Since glycosides like the one shown above do not contain hemiacetal groups that establish equilibria with open-chain forms, they are *not* reducing sugars.

In larger molecules, including disaccharides and polysaccharides, monosaccharides are connected to each other by glycosidic bonds. For example, a disaccharide forms by reaction of the anomeric carbon of one monosaccharide with an —OH group of a second monosaccharide.

Glycosidic bond Bond between the anomeric carbon atom of a monosaccharide and an —OR group.

Formation of a glycosidic bond between two monosaccharides

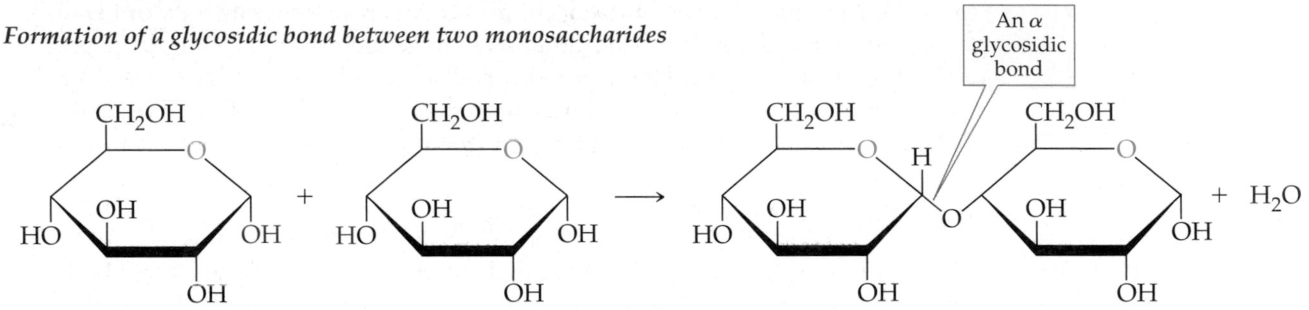

The reverse of this reaction is a *hydrolysis* and is the reaction that takes place during digestion of all carbohydrates.

Hydrolysis of a disaccharide

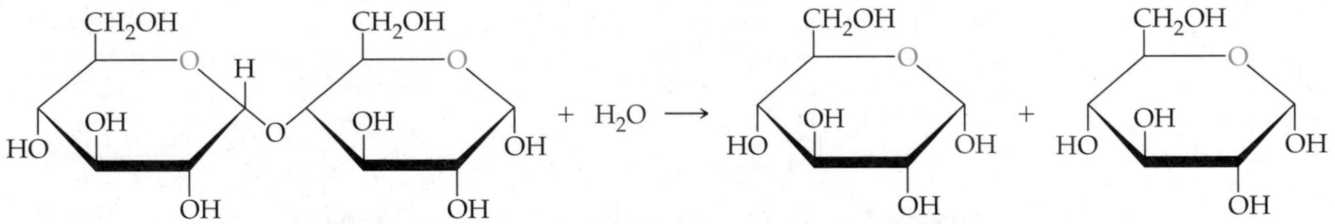

PROBLEM 21.15

Draw the structure of the α and β anomers that result from the reaction of methanol and ribose. Are these compounds acetals or hemiacetals?

Formation of Phosphate Esters of Alcohols

Phosphate esters of alcohols contain a —PO_3^{2-} group bonded to the oxygen atom of an —OH group. The —OH groups of sugars can add —PO_3^{2-} groups to form phosphate esters in the same manner. The resulting phosphate esters of monosaccharides appear as reactants and products throughout the metabolism of carbohydrates. Glucose phosphate is the first to be formed and sets the stage for subsequent reactions. It is produced by the transfer of a $-PO_3^{2-}$ group from ATP to glucose in the first step of glycolysis, the multi-step metabolic pathway followed by glucose and other sugars, which is described in Chapter 22. Glycolysis converts glucose to the acetyl groups that are carried into the citric acid cycle.

Glucose   →   Glucose
6-phosphate

(ATP ADP, hexokinase)

21.7 Disaccharides

Every day, you eat a disaccharide—sucrose, common table sugar. Sucrose is made of two monosaccharides, one glucose and one fructose, covalently bonded to each other. Sucrose is present in modest amounts, along with other mono- and disaccharides, in most fresh fruits and many fresh vegetables. But most sucrose in our diets has been added to something. Perhaps you add it to your coffee or tea. Or it is there in a ready-to-eat food product that you buy—maybe breakfast cereal, ice cream, or a "super-sized" soda, or even bread. Excessive consumption of high-sucrose foods has been blamed for everything from criminal behavior to heart disease to hyperactivity in children, but without any widely accepted scientific proof. A proven connection with heart disease does exist, of course, but by way of the contribution of excess sugar calories to obesity.

Disaccharide Structure

The two monosaccharides in a disaccharide are connected by a glycosidic bond. The bond may be α or β, as in cyclic monosaccharides: α points below the ring and β points above the ring (see Figure 21.3). The structures include glycosidic bonds that create a **1,4 link**, that is, a link between C1 of one monosaccharide and C4 of the second monosaccharide:

1,4 Link A glycosidic link between the hemiacetal hydroxyl group at C1 of one sugar and the hydroxyl group at C4 of another sugar.

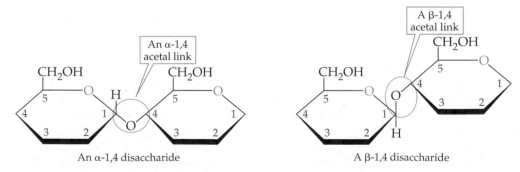

An α-1,4 disaccharide   A β-1,4 disaccharide

The three naturally occurring disaccharides discussed in the following sections are the most common ones. They illustrate the three different ways monosaccharides are linked: by a glycosidic bond in the α orientation (maltose), a glycosidic bond in the β orientation (lactose), or a bond that connects two anomeric carbon atoms (sucrose).

Maltose

Maltose, often called malt sugar, is present in fermenting grains and can be prepared by enzyme-catalyzed degradation of starch. It is used in prepared foods as a sweetener. In the body, it is produced during starch digestion by α-amylase in the small intestine and then hydrolyzed to glucose by a second enzyme, maltase.

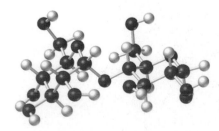

Two α-D-glucose molecules are joined in maltose by an α-1,4 link. A careful look at maltose shows that it is both an acetal (at C1 in the glucose on the left) and a hemiacetal (at C1 in the glucose on the right). Since the acetal ring on the left does not open and close spontaneously, it cannot react with an oxidizing agent. The hemiacetal group on the right, however, establishes equilibrium with the aldehyde, making maltose a reducing sugar.

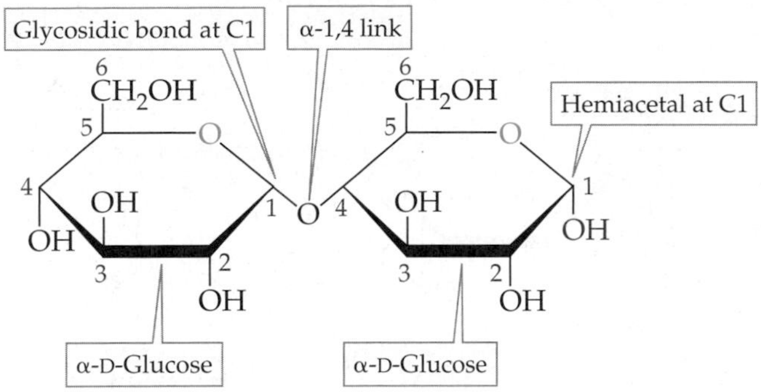

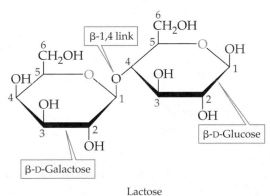

Maltose

Lactose

Lactose, or milk sugar, is the major carbohydrate in mammalian milk. Human milk, for example, is about 7% lactose. Structurally, lactose is a disaccharide composed of β-D-galactose and β-D-glucose. The two monosaccharides are connected by a β-1,4 link. Like maltose, lactose is a reducing sugar because the glucose ring (on the right in the following structure) is a hemiacetal at C1.

Lactose

Lactose intolerance in adults is an unpleasant, though not life-threatening, condition that is prevalent in all populations. In fact, it has been suggested that the *absence* of this condition in adults, rather than its presence, is the deviation from the norm. The activity of lactase, the enzyme that allows lactose digestion by infants, apparently gradually diminishes over the years. In lactose-intolerant individuals, lactose remains in the intestines rather than being absorbed, raising the osmolarity there, which draws in excess water (Section 9.12). At the same time, bacteria in the intestine ferment the lactose to produce lactate, carbon dioxide, hydrogen, and methane. The result is bloating, cramps, flatulence, and diarrhea. The condition is treated by a lactose-free diet, which extends to limitations on taking the many medications and artificial sweeteners in which lactose is an inactive ingredient. Alternatives include the use of commercial enzyme preparations taken before milk products are consumed and consuming foods like Lactaid®, milk that has been treated with lactase to reduce its lactose content.

▲ Milk for lactose-intolerant individuals. The lactose content of the milk has been decreased by treating it with lactase.

Sucrose

Sucrose—plain table sugar—is probably the most common highly purified organic chemical used in the world. Sugar beets and sugarcane are the most common sources of sucrose. Hydrolysis of sucrose yields one molecule of D-glucose and one

molecule of D-fructose. The 50:50 mixture of glucose and fructose that results, often referred to as *invert sugar*, is commonly used as a food additive because it is sweeter than sucrose.

Sucrose differs from maltose and lactose in that it has no hemiacetal group because a 1,2 link joins *both* anomeric carbon atoms (C1 on glucose, C2 on fructose). The absence of a hemiacetal group means that sucrose is not a reducing sugar. Sucrose is the only common disaccharide that is not a reducing sugar.

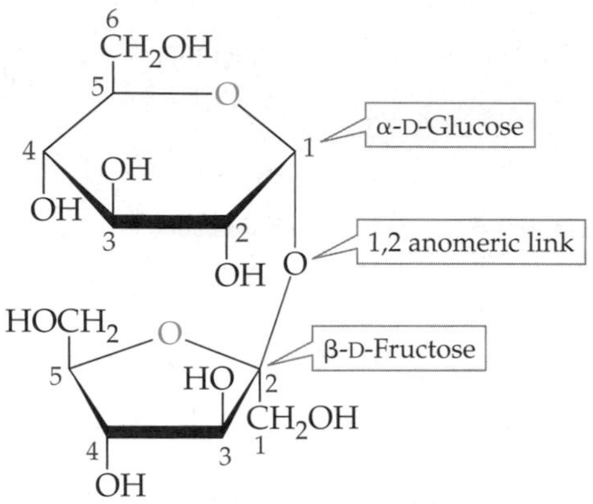

Sucrose

Worked Example 21.5 Identifying Reducing Sugars

The disaccharide cellobiose can be obtained by enzyme-catalyzed hydrolysis of cellulose. Do you expect cellobiose to be a reducing or a nonreducing sugar?

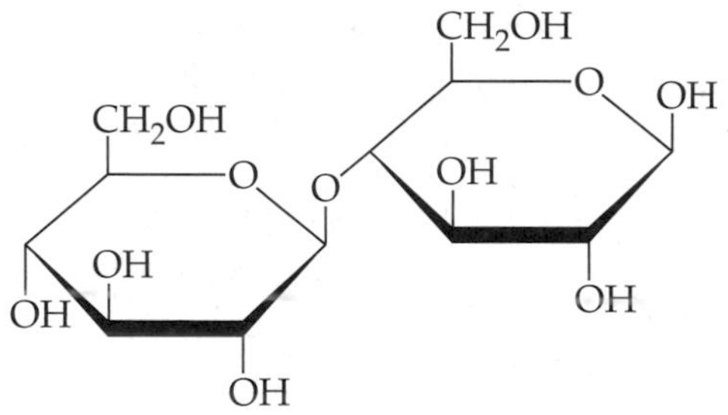

Cellobiose

ANALYSIS To be a reducing sugar, a disaccharide must contain a hemiacetal group, that is, a carbon bonded to one —OH group and one —OR group. The ring at the right in the structure above has such a group.

SOLUTION
Cellobiose is a reducing sugar.

PROBLEM 21.16
Refer to the cellobiose structure in Worked Example 21.5. How would you classify the link between the monosaccharides in cellobiose?

PROBLEM 21.17
Refer to the cellobiose structure in Worked Example 21.5. Show the structures of the two monosaccharides that are formed on hydrolysis of cellobiose. What are their names?

CHEMISTRY IN ACTION

Carbohydrates and Fiber in the Diet

The major monosaccharides in our diets are fructose and glucose from fruits and honey. The major disaccharides are sucrose, commonly called table sugar and refined from both sugar cane and sugar beets, and lactose from milk. In addition, our diets contain large amounts of the digestible polysaccharide starch, present in grains such as wheat and rice, root vegetables such as potatoes, and legumes such as beans and peas. Nutritionists often refer to these digestible polysaccharides as *complex carbohydrates*. Some polysaccharides, such as cellulose, are not digested by humans. Cellulose and all other indigestible carbohydrates are collectively known as *dietary fiber*.

How easily and how rapidly complex carbohydrates are digested and absorbed affects blood sugar levels. Consumption of the more-easily-digested carbohydrates, found in potatoes and in refined foods such as white bread and white rice, results in rapid elevation of blood glucose levels followed by lower-than-desired levels a few hours later. Carbohydrates that are digested and absorbed more slowly, such as those found in pasta, whole grain cereals and breads, and beans are associated with healthier blood sugar responses. The *glycemic index* is a scale that compares the blood sugar response from eating a complex carbohydrate with the response evoked by glucose. Foods with a low glycemic index release glucose slowly; foods with a high glycemic index release glucose rapidly during digestion and should be limited in the diet.

The body's major use of digestible carbohydrates is to provide energy, 4 kcal (16.7 kJ) per gram of carbohydrate. A small amount of any excess carbohydrate is converted to glycogen for storage in the liver and muscles, but most dietary carbohydrate in excess of our immediate needs for energy is converted into fat.

The MyPlate meal-planning tool (p. 565) reflects the emphasis on decreasing the amounts of meat and increasing the amounts of other foods in our diet, especially complex carbohydrates and fiber through the consumption of whole grains, vegetables, and fruit.

In terms of *total* carbohydrate, which includes both digestible carbohydrates and fiber, the *Nutrition Facts* labels on packaged foods (p. 615) give percentages based on a recommended 300 g per day of total carbohydrate and 25 g per day of dietary fiber. This quantity of total carbohydrate represents 60% of the calories in a 2000 Cal/day (8400 kJ/day) diet. The *Nutrition Facts* label also gives the total grams of sugars in the food without a percentage because there is no recommended daily quantity of sugars. For purposes of the label, "sugars" are defined as all monosaccharides and disaccharides, whether naturally present or added.

▲ Part of a healthy diet includes a variety of complex carbohydrates that can be supplied by whole grains, beans, and peas.

As an option, the label may also include grams of *soluble fiber* and *insoluble fiber*. Taken together, these are the types of polysaccharides that are neither hydrolyzed to monosaccharides nor absorbed into the bloodstream. These polysaccharides include cellulose and all other indigestible polysaccharides in vegetables, both soluble and insoluble. The major categories of noncellulose fiber are hemicellulose, pectins and gums, and lignins.

Hemicellulose is a collective term for insoluble plant polysaccharides other than cellulose. These polysaccharides are composed of xylose, mannose, galactose, and modifications of these monosaccharides.

Pectins and vegetable gums, which contain galactose modified by the addition of carboxylic acid and *N*-acetyl groups, comprise the "soluble" portion of dietary fiber. Their outstanding characteristic is solubility in water, or the formation of sticky or gelatinous dispersions with water. Pectins, which are present in fruits, are responsible for the "gel" in jelly. Because this texture of their dispersions in water is a desirable characteristic, pectins are often added to prepared foods to retain moisture, thicken sauces, or give a creamier texture.

Lignin, which like cellulose provides rigid structure in plants and especially in trees, is an insoluble dietary fiber. It is not a polysaccharide, however, but a polymer of complex structure that contains phenyl groups connected by carbon–carbon and carbon–oxygen bonds.

Foods high in insoluble fiber include wheat, bran cereals, and brown rice. Beans, peas, and other legumes contain both soluble and insoluble fiber and are high in small polysaccharides that contain galactose bonded to glucose residues. These small polysaccharides are digested by bacteria in the gut, with the production of lactate, short-chain fatty acids, and gaseous by-products including hydrogen, carbon dioxide, and methane.

Fiber functions in the body to soften and add bulk to solid waste. Studies have shown that increased fiber in the diet may reduce the risk of colon and rectal cancer, hemorrhoids, diverticulosis, and cardiovascular disease. A reduction in the risk of developing colon and rectal cancer may also occur because potentially carcinogenic substances are absorbed on fiber surfaces and eliminated before doing any harm. Pectin may also absorb and carry away bile acids, causing an increase in their synthesis from cholesterol in the liver and a resulting decrease in blood cholesterol levels.

The U.S. Food and Drug Administration is responsible for reviewing the scientific basis for health claims for foods. Two allowed claims relate to carbohydrates. The first states that a diet high in fiber may lower the risk of cancer and heart disease if the diet is also low in saturated fats and cholesterol. The second states that foods high in the soluble fiber from whole oats (oat bran) may also reduce the risk of heart disease, again when the diet is also low in saturated fats and cholesterol.

See Chemistry in Action Problems 21.81 and 21.82 at the end of the chapter.

🔑 KEY CONCEPT PROBLEM 21.18

Identify the following disaccharides. Give a natural source for each of these disaccharides. (a) The disaccharide that contains two glucose units joined by an α-glycosidic linkage. (b) The disaccharide that contains fructose and glucose. (c) The disaccharide that contains galactose and glucose.

PROBLEM 21.19

Give an example of a complex carbohydrate in the diet and a simple carbohydrate in the diet. Are soluble fiber and insoluble fiber complex or simple carbohydrates? (See Chemistry in Action: Carbohydrates and Fiber in the Diet p. 679.)

21.8 Variations on the Carbohydrate Theme

Monosaccharides with modified functional groups are components of a wide variety of biomolecules. Also, short chains of monosaccharides (known as *oligosaccharides*) enhance the functions of proteins and lipids to which they are bonded.

In this section we mention a few of the more interesting and important variations on the carbohydrate theme, several of which incorporate the modified glucose molecules shown here. Their distinctive functional groups are highlighted in yellow:

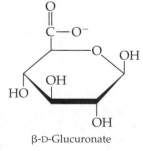

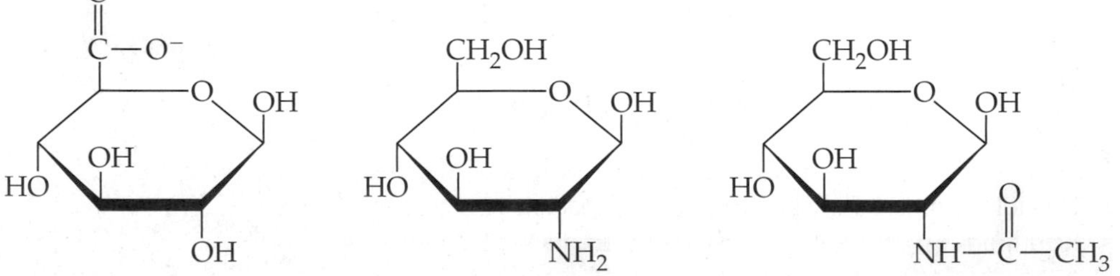

β-D-Glucuronate

β-D-Glucosamine

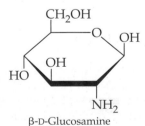

N-Acetyl-β-D-Glucosamine

Chitin

▲ **This horned beetle's exoskeleton is made of chitin.**

The shells of lobsters, beetles, and spiders are made of chitin, the second most abundant polysaccharide in the natural world. (Cellulose is the most abundant.) Chitin is a hard, structural polymer. It is composed of N-acetyl-D-glucosamine subunits rather than glucose subunits, but is otherwise identical in form to cellulose, discussed in the next section.

Connective Tissue and Polysaccharides

Connective tissues such as blood vessels, cartilage, and tendons are composed of protein fibers embedded in a syrupy matrix that contains unbranched polysaccharides (*mucopolysaccharides*). The gel-like mixtures of these polysaccharides with water serve as lubricants and shock absorbers around joints and in extracellular spaces. Note the repeating disaccharide units in two of these polysaccharides, hyaluronate and chondroitin:

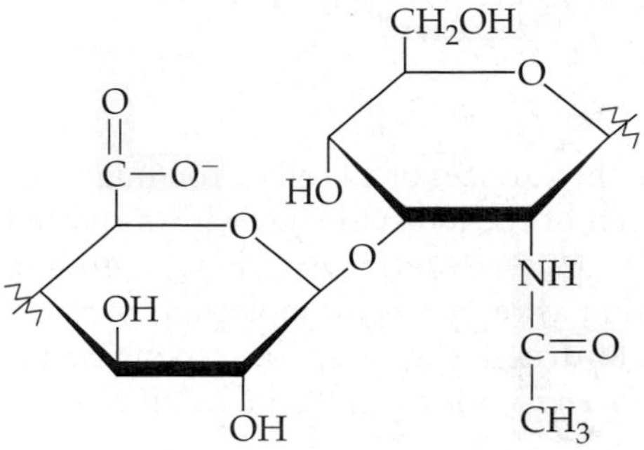

Hyaluronate repeating unit 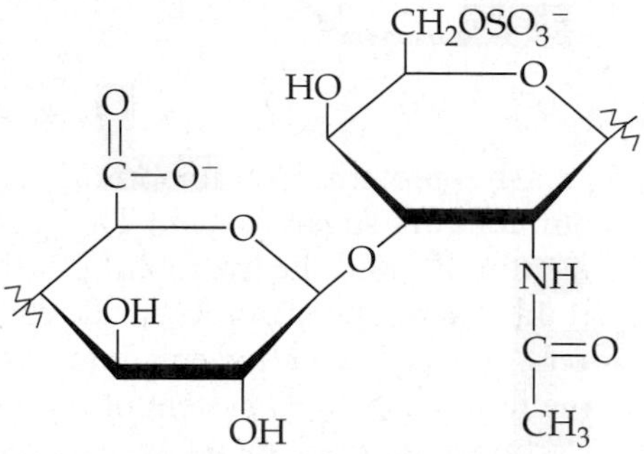   Chondroitin 6-sulfate repeating unit

Hyaluronate molecules contain up to 25,000 disaccharide units and form a quite rigid, very viscous mixture with water molecules attracted to its negative charges. This mixture is the *synovial fluid* that lubricates joints. It is also present within the eye. *Chondroitin 6-sulfate* (also the 4-sulfate) is present in tendons and cartilage, where it is linked to proteins. It has been used in artificial skin. Chondroitin sulfates and glucosamine sulfate are available as dietary supplements in health food stores and are promoted as cures for osteoarthritis, a disease characterized by joint cartilage deterioration. They are prescribed by veterinarians for arthritic dogs, and there is anecdotal evidence for benefits in humans.

Heparin

Another of the polysaccharides associated with connective tissue, heparin is valuable medically as an *anticoagulant* (an agent that prevents or retards the clotting of blood). Heparin is composed of a variety of different monosaccharides, many of them containing sulfate groups.

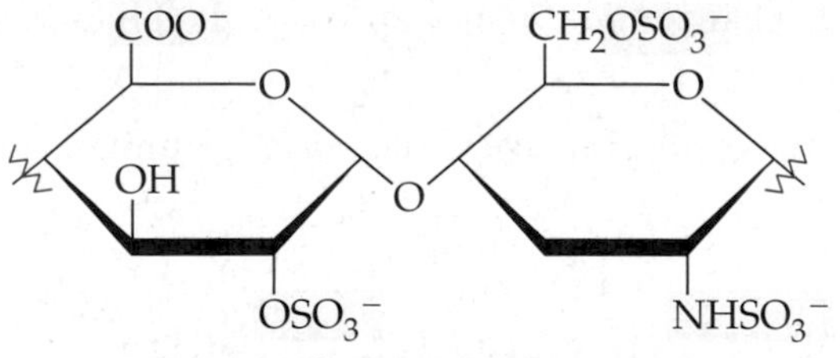

Example of repeating unit in heparin

Notice the large number of negative charges in this heparin repeating unit. Heparin binds strongly to a blood-clotting factor and in this way prevents clot formation. It is used clinically to prevent clotting after surgery or serious injury. Also, a coating of heparin is applied to any surfaces that will come into contact with blood that must not clot, such as the interiors of test tubes used for blood samples collected for analysis or materials in prosthetic implants for the body.

Glycoproteins

Proteins that contain short carbohydrate chains (*oligosaccharide* chains) are known as **glycoproteins**. (The prefix *glyco-* always refers to carbohydrates.) The carbohydrate is connected to the protein by a glycosidic bond between an anomeric carbon and a side

Glycoprotein A protein that contains a short carbohydrate chain.

chain of the protein. The bond is either a C—N glycosidic bond or a C—O glycosidic bond:

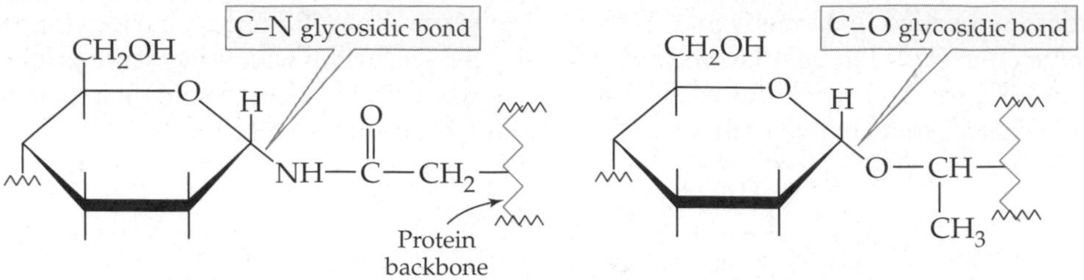

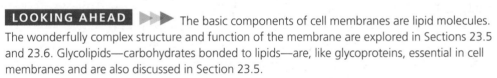

Glycoproteins have important functions on the surfaces of all cells. (You might say our cells are sugar-coated.) The protein portion of the molecule lies within the cell membrane, and the hydrophilic carbohydrate portion extends into the surrounding fluid. There, the oligosaccharide chains function as receptors for molecular messengers, other cells, pathogenic microorganisms, or drugs. They are also responsible for the familiar A, B, O system of typing blood. (See Chemistry in Action: Cell-Surface Carbohydrates and Blood Type on p. 672.)

One unusual glycoprotein, found in the bloodstream and other body fluids of some Antarctic fish species, functions as an antifreeze. This glycoprotein is a polymer with a repeating tripeptide (alanine-alanine-threonine) unit that has a disaccharide (galactosyl-N-acetylgalactosamine) bonded to every threonine. The polymer varies in length from 17 to 50 units. It does not protect against freezing by lowering the freezing point, as does the antifreeze used in car radiators; instead the polar groups on the glycoprotein bind with water molecules at the surface of tiny ice crystals, slowing the growth of the crystals. As the blood circulates through the liver, it warms enough for the ice crystals to melt before they harm the organism.

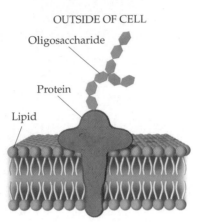

OUTSIDE OF CELL

Oligosaccharide

Protein

Lipid

INSIDE OF CELL

LOOKING AHEAD ▶▶▶ The basic components of cell membranes are lipid molecules. The wonderfully complex structure and function of the membrane are explored in Sections 23.5 and 23.6. Glycolipids—carbohydrates bonded to lipids—are, like glycoproteins, essential in cell membranes and are also discussed in Section 23.5.

PROBLEM 21.20
In *N*-linked glycoproteins, the sugar is usually attached to the protein by a bond to the N atom in a side-chain amide. Which amino acids can form such a bond?

PROBLEM 21.21
Identify the type of glycosidic linkage in the repeating unit of heparin illustrated in this section.

21.9 Some Important Polysaccharides

Polysaccharides are polymers of tens, hundreds, or even many thousands of monosaccharides linked together through glycosidic bonds of the same type as in maltose and lactose. Three of the most important polysaccharides are *cellulose, starch*, and *glycogen*. The repeating units making up cellulose and starch are compared in the following structures:

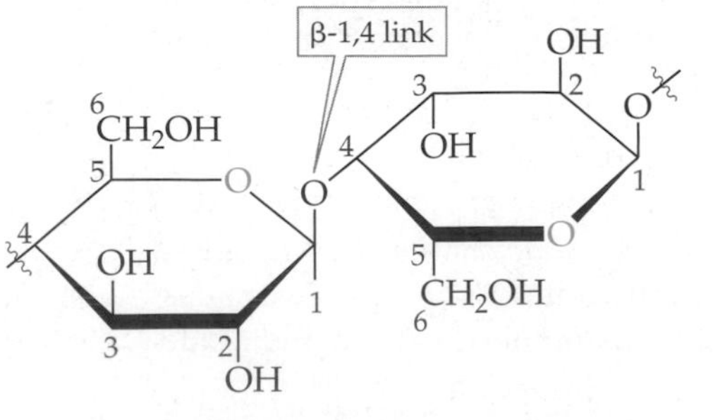

Cellulose repeating unit

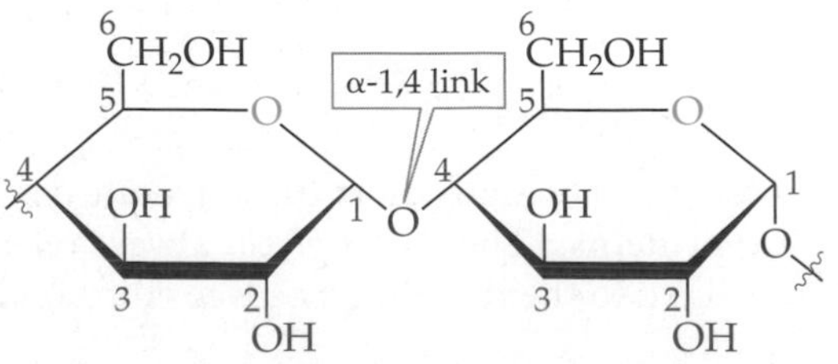

Starch and glycogen repeating unit

Cellulose

Cellulose is the fibrous substance that provides structure in plants. Each huge cellulose molecule consists of several thousand β-D-glucose units joined in a long, straight chain by β-1,4 links. The bonding in cellulose is illustrated above by the flat hexagons we have used so far for monosaccharides. In reality, because of the tetrahedral bonding at each carbon atom, the carbohydrate rings are not flat but are bent up at one end and down at the other in what is known as the *chair conformation*:

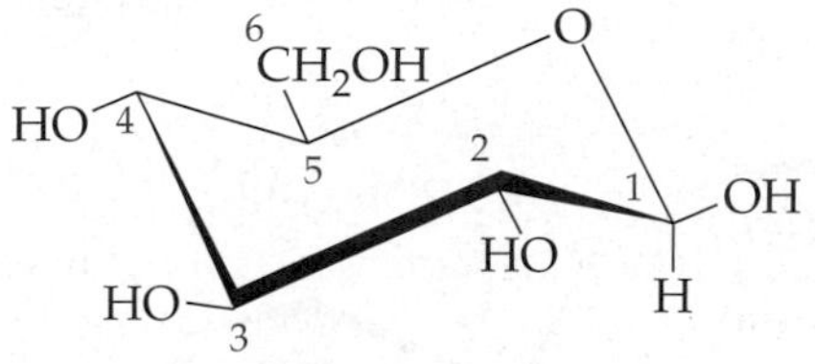

Chair conformation of β-D-glucose

Inspection of the chair conformation shows that the bulkier hydroxyl groups point toward the sides of the ring, as does the —CH₂OH. This *equatorial* position minimizes interactions between these bulky substituents on the ring. The smaller substituents on the ring (the H atoms) extend either above or below the ring in the *axial* position. This axial/equatorial arrangement resulting from the chair conformation is the most energetically stable form of a six-membered carbohydrate ring.

When the cellulose structure is drawn with all the rings in the chair conformation it is much easier to see how each glucose ring is reversed relative to the next by comparing the locations of the ring O atoms:

Cellulose

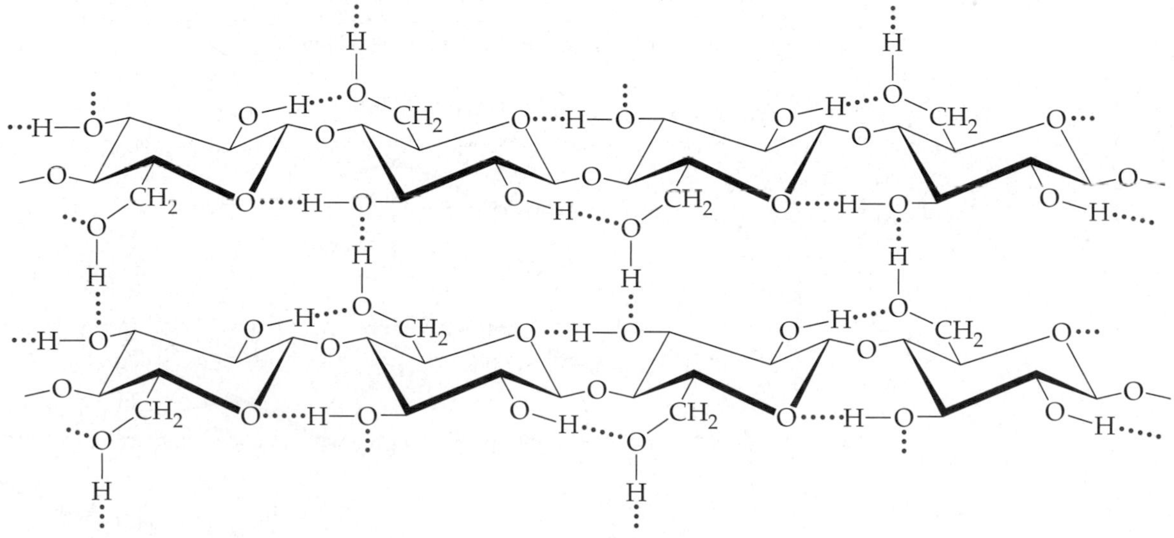

Note in this drawing how the ring O in the top left ring is at the bottom of the ring, the ring O in the ring to the right is at the top of the ring, and so on. The hydrogen bonds within chains and between chains (shown in red) contribute to the rigidity and toughness of cellulose fibers.

Earlier we noted that the seemingly minor distinction between the α and β forms of cyclic sugars accounts for a vast difference between cellulose and starch. Cows and other grazing animals, termites, and moths are able to digest cellulose because microorganisms colonizing their digestive tracts produce enzymes that hydrolyze its β glycosidic bonds. Humans neither produce such enzymes nor harbor such organisms and therefore cannot hydrolyze cellulose, although some is broken down by bacteria in the large intestine. Cellulose is what Grandma used to call "roughage," and we need it in our diets in addition to starch.

Starch

Starch, like cellulose, is a polymer of glucose. In starch, individual glucose units are joined by α-1,4 links rather than by the β-1,4 links of cellulose. Starch is fully digestible

▲ **Figure 21.5**
Helical structure of amylose.

and is an essential part of the human diet. It is present only in plant material; our major sources are beans, the grains wheat and rice, and potatoes.

Unlike cellulose, which has only one form, there are two kinds of starch—amylose and amylopectin. *Amylose*, which accounts for about 20% of starch, is somewhat soluble in hot water and consists of several hundred to a thousand α-D-glucose units linked in long chains by the α-1,4 glycosidic bonds. Instead of lying side by side and flat as in cellulose, amylose tends to coil into helices (Figure 21.5). Dissolved amylose makes the cooking water cloudy when you boil potatoes.

Amylose

Amylopectin, which accounts for about 80% of starch, is similar to amylose but has much larger molecules (up to 100,000 glucose units per molecule) and has α-1,6 branches approximately every 25 units along its chain. A glucose molecule at one of these branch points (shaded below) is linked to three other sugars. Amylopectin is not water-soluble due to its large molecular weight (up to 200 million) and highly branched structure. These properties make amylopectin an ideal glucose storage compound.

Branch point in amylopectin (also glycogen)

Starch molecules are digested mainly in the small intestine by α-amylase, which catalyzes hydrolysis of the α-1,4 links. As is usually the case in enzyme-catalyzed reactions, α-amylase is highly specific in its action. It hydrolyzes only α acetal links between glucose units (found in starch) and leaves β acetal links (found in cellulose) untouched.

PROBLEM 21.22
An individual starch molecule contains thousands of glucose units but has only a single hemiacetal group at the end of the long polymer chain. Would you expect starch to be a reducing carbohydrate? Explain.

Glycogen

Glycogen, sometimes called *animal starch*, serves the same energy storage role in animals that starch serves in plants. Some of the glucose from starches in our diet is used immediately as fuel, and some is stored as glycogen for later use. The largest amounts of glycogen are stored in the liver and muscles. In the liver, glycogen is a source of glucose, which is formed there when hormones signal a need for glucose in the blood. In muscles, glycogen is converted to glucose 6-phosphate for the synthesis of ATP.

Structurally, glycogen is similar to amylopectin in being a long polymer of α-D-glucose with the same type of branch points in its chain. Glycogen has many more branches than amylopectin, however, and is much larger—up to one million glucose units per molecule.

Comparison of branching in amylopectin and glycogen

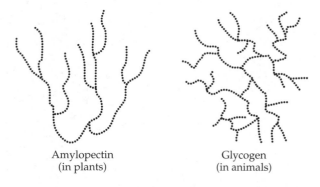

Amylopectin
(in plants)

Glycogen
(in animals)

PROBLEM 21.23

Glycogen is stored as compact granules in liver and muscle cells. Explain why each of these storage modes is a biological advantage to the organism.

PROBLEM 21.24

Some antibiotics function as "suicide inhibitors" of bacterial protein synthesis. Based on what you learned about enzyme regulation in Chapter 19, what kind of inhibition must this be? Why is this type of inhibition so effective? Why is this a problem in cell-wall formation for bacteria? What is the composition of bacterial cell walls? (See Chemistry in Action: Cell Walls: Rigid Defense Systems.)

CHEMISTRY IN ACTION

Cell Walls: Rigid Defense Systems

All cells are defined by the presence of a plasma membrane, which confines the cell's contents inside a lipid bilayer studded with proteins (Section 20.3). Bacteria and higher plants surround the plasma membrane with a rigid cell wall. Cell walls differ markedly in composition, but not in primary function, between higher plants and bacteria. The primary function of a cell wall is to make the cell rigid. The rigidity of the wall prevents the cell from bursting due to osmotic pressure, because the dissolved metabolites and ions inside the cell are at a greater concentration than outside. In addition to its rigidity, the cell wall also gives shape to the cell and protects it from pathogens.

Plant cell walls are composed of fibrils of cellulose (a polysaccharide, see Section 21.9) in a polymer matrix of pectins, lignin, and hemicellulose. Although you might think each cell is isolated from the others, plant cell walls contain small perforations that permit contact between adjacent cells. This allows for the transfer of nutrients and signals. Cellulose chains range from about 6000 to 16,000 glucose units in length. Neighboring chains of cellulose form hydrogen bonds between them, thereby strengthening the cell wall.

Bacterial cell walls, in addition to providing strength and shape, provide a rigid platform for the attachment of flagella and pilli. The composition of the cell wall also provides attachment sites for bacteriophages (viruses that infect bacteria). Although bacterial cell walls do contain modified sugar polymers, they do not contain cellulose. Cell-wall composition varies among bacterial species and is an important factor in distinguishing between some groups of bacteria. A majority of bacterial cell walls are composed of a polymer of *peptidoglycan*, an alternating sequence of the modified sugars *N*-acetylglucosamine (NAG) and *N*-acetylmuraminic acid (NAMA). Peptidoglycan strands are cross-linked to one another by short peptide bridges; these bridges are unique in that both D-alanine and L-alanine are present. The interlocked strands form a porous, multilayered grid over the bacterial plasma membrane.

Fortunately, animals have developed natural defenses that can control many bacteria. For example, lysozyme—an enzyme found naturally in tears, saliva, and egg white—hydrolyzes the peptidoglycan cell wall of pathogenic bacteria, thereby killing them. In the middle of the twentieth century the antibiotic penicillin was developed. The penicillin family members all contain a beta-lactam ring that allows these compounds to act as "suicide inhibitors" of the enzymes that synthesize the peptidoglycan cross-linking peptide chain. Penicillin and its relatives target only reproducing bacteria. Mammals do not contain the enzyme pathway that synthesizes peptidoglycans, and this is what allows us to kill the bacteria without harming ourselves.

Today we take the availability and effectiveness of antibiotics for granted. When penicillin was discovered, it was hailed as a "magic bullet" because it could cure bacterial infections that were often fatal. Unfortunately, many bacteria have developed resistance to penicillin and its relatives; resistant bacteria have developed enzymes that destroy the beta-lactam ring, thereby destroying the effectiveness of penicillin. Other antibiotics have since been developed, but the spread of antibiotic-resistant bacterial strains is a public health concern due to the "bullet-proof vest" nature of the bacterial cell wall in resistant strains.

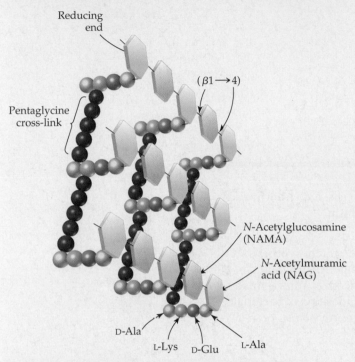

▲ **Peptidoglycan structure: Strands of alternating NAG and NAMA connected by peptides form a mesh covering the bacterial cell membrane.**

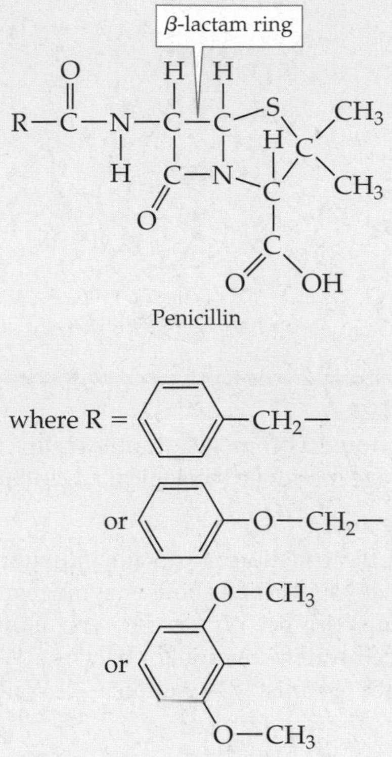

See Chemistry in Action Problems 21.83 through 21.85 at the end of the chapter.

SUMMARY: REVISITING THE CHAPTER GOALS

1. What are the different kinds of carbohydrates? *Monosaccharides* are compounds with three to seven carbons, an aldehyde group on carbon 1 (an *aldose*) or a ketone group on carbon 2 (a *ketose*), and hydroxyl groups on all other carbons. *Disaccharides* consist of two monosaccharides; *polysaccharides* are polymers composed of up to thousands of monosaccharides *(see Problems 1, 2, 25, 33–36, 97, 98)*.

2. What makes monosaccharides chiral, and how does this influence the numbers and types of their isomers? Monosaccharides can contain several chiral carbon atoms, each bonded to one —H, one —OH, and two other carbon atoms in the carbon chain. A monosaccharide with n chiral carbon atoms may have 2^n stereoisomers and half that number of pairs of enantiomers. The members of different enantiomeric pairs are *diastereomers*—they are *not* mirror images of each other *(see Problems 3–7, 26, 27, 37–41)*.

3. What are the structures of monosaccharides, and how are they represented in written formulas? *Fischer projection formulas* represent the open-chain structures of monosaccharides. They are interpreted as shown below, with the D and L enantiomers in a pair identified by having the —OH group on the chiral carbon farthest from the carbonyl group on the right (the D isomer) or the left (the L isomer).

C=O at top

C at each intersection

Vertical line = Bond pointing behind page

Horizontal line = Bond pointing above page

A D isomer   A D isomer   An L isomer

Mirror-image pair

In solution, open-chain monosaccharides with five or six carbons establish equilibria with cyclic forms that are hemiacetals. The hemiacetal carbon (bonded to two O atoms) is referred to as the *anomeric carbon*, and this carbon is chiral. Two isomers of the cyclic form of a D or L monosaccharide, known as *anomers*, are possible because the —OH on the anomeric carbon may lie above or below the plane of the ring (see Problems 8–14, 28, 43–50, 87–92).

Anomeric (hemiacetal) carbon

β anomer
−OH on C1 on same side as −CH₂OH on C5

α anomer
−OH on C1 on opposite side from −CH₂OH on C5

4. How do monosaccharides react with oxidizing agents and alcohols? Oxidation of a monosaccharide can result in a carboxyl group on the first carbon atom (C1 in the Fischer projection). Ketoses, as well as aldoses, are *reducing sugars* because the ketose is in equilibrium with an aldose form (via an enediol) that can be oxidized.

Reaction of a hemiacetal with an alcohol produces an acetal. For a cyclic monosaccharide, reaction with an alcohol converts the —OH group on the anomeric carbon to an —OR group. The bond to the —OR group, known as a *glycosidic bond*, is α or β to the ring as was the —OH group. Disaccharides result from glycosidic bond formation between two monosaccharides (see Problems 15, 27, 32, 60–66).

5. What are the structures of some important disaccharides? In *maltose*, two D-glucose molecules are joined by an α-glycosidic bond that connects C1 (the anomeric carbon) of one molecule to C4 of the other—an α-1,4 *link*. In *lactose*, D-galactose and D-glucose are joined by a β-1,4 link. In *sucrose*, D-fructose and D-glucose are joined by a glycosidic bond between the two anomeric carbons, a 1,2 link. Unlike maltose and lactose, sucrose is not a *reducing sugar* because it has no hemiacetal that can establish equilibrium with an aldehyde (see Problems 16–18, 30, 67, 68, 71–74, 93–96, 100, 101).

6. What are the functions of some important carbohydrates that contain modified monosaccharide structures? *Chitin* is a hard structural polysaccharide found in the shells of lobsters and insects. Joints and intracellular spaces are lubricated by polysaccharides like *hyaluronate* and *chondroitin 6-sulfate*, which have ionic functional groups and form gel-like mixtures with water. *Heparin*, a polysaccharide with many ionized sulfate groups, binds to a clotting factor in the blood and thus acts as an anticoagulant. *Glycoproteins* have short carbohydrate chains bonded to proteins; the carbohydrate segments (*oligosaccharides*) function as receptors at cell surfaces (see Problems 20, 21, 24, 31, 79, 80, 83–86).

7. What are the structures and functions of cellulose, starch, and glycogen? *Cellulose* is a straight-chain polymer of β-D-glucose with β-1,4 links; it provides structure in plants. Cellulose is not digestible by humans, but is digestible by animals whose digestive tract contains bacteria that provide enzymes which hydrolyze the β-glycosidic bonds. *Starch* is a polymer of α-D-glucose connected by α-1,4 links in straight-chain (*amylose*) and branched-chain (*amylopectin*) forms. Starch is a storage form of glucose for plants and is digestible by humans. *Glycogen* is a storage form of glucose for animals, including humans. It is structurally similar to amylopectin, but is more highly branched. Glycogen from meat in the diet is also digestible (see Problems 19, 22–24, 69, 70, 75, 76, 81, 82, 100–102).

KEY WORDS

1,4 Link, *p. 676*

Aldose, *p. 658*

Anomeric carbon atom, *p. 666*

Anomers, *p. 666*

Carbohydrate, *p. 657*

D Sugar, *p. 662*

Diastereomers, *p. 660*

Disaccharide, *p. 658*

Fischer projection, *p. 661*

Glycoprotein, *p. 681*

Glycoside, *p. 674*

Glycosidic bond, *p. 675*

Ketose, *p. 658*

L Sugar, *p. 662*

Monosaccharide (simple sugar), *p. 657*

Mutarotation, *p. 666*

Polysaccharide (complex carbohydrate), *p. 658*

Reducing sugar, *p. 674*

UNDERSTANDING KEY CONCEPTS

21.25 During the digestion of starch from potatoes, the enzyme α-amylase catalyzes the hydrolysis of starch into maltose. Subsequently, the enzyme maltase catalyzes the hydrolysis of maltose into two glucose units. Write an equation (in words) for the enzymatic conversion of starch to glucose. Classify each of the carbohydrates in the equation as a disaccharide, monosaccharide, or polysaccharide.

21.26 Identify the following as diastereomers, enantiomers, and/or anomers. (a) α-D-fructose and β-D-fructose (b) D-galactose and L-galactose (c) L-allose and D-glucose (both aldohexoses)

21.27 Consider the trisaccharide A, B, C shown in problem 21.28.

   (a) Identify the hemiacetal and acetal linkages.

   (b) Identify the anomeric carbon atoms, and indicate whether each is α or β.

   (c) State the numbers of the carbon atoms that form glycosidic linkages between monosaccharide A and monosaccharide B.

   (d) State the numbers of the carbon atoms that form glycosidic linkages between monosaccharide B and monosaccharide C.

21.28 Hydrolysis of both glycosidic bonds in the following trisaccharide A, B, C yields three monosaccharides.

   (a) Are any two of these monosaccharides the same?

   (b) Are any two of these monosaccharides enantiomers?

   (c) Draw the Fischer projections for the three monosaccharides.

   (d) Assign a name to each monosaccharide.

21.29 The trisaccharide shown with Problem 21.28 has a specific sequence of monosaccharides. To determine this sequence, we could react the trisaccharide with an oxidizing agent. Since one of the monosaccharides in the trisaccharide is a reducing sugar, it would be oxidized from an aldehyde to a carboxylate. Which of the monosaccharides (A, B, or C) is oxidized? Write the structure of the oxidized monosaccharide that results after hydrolysis of the trisaccharide. How does this reaction assist in identifying the sequence of the trisaccharide?

21.30 Are one or more of the disaccharides maltose, lactose, cellobiose, and sucrose part of the trisaccharide in Problem 21.28? If so, identify which disaccharide and its location. (Hint: look for an α-1,4 link, β-1,4 link, or 1,2 link, and then determine if the correct monosaccharides are present.)

21.31 Cellulose, amylose, amylopectin, and glycogen are the polysaccharides of glucose that we examined in this chapter. The major criteria that distinguish these four polysaccharides include α-glycosidic links or β-glycosidic links, 1,4 links or both 1,4 and 1,6 links, and the degree of branching. Create a table evaluating each polysaccharide using these five criteria.

21.32 In solution, glucose exists predominantly in the cyclic hemiacetal form, which does not contain an aldehyde group. How is it possible for mild oxidizing agents to oxidize glucose?

A   B   C

ADDITIONAL PROBLEMS

CLASSIFICATION AND STRUCTURE OF CARBOHYDRATES

21.33 What is a carbohydrate?

21.34 What is the family-name ending for a sugar?

21.35 What is the structural difference between an aldose and a ketose?

21.36 Classify the following carbohydrates by indicating the nature of the carbonyl group and the number of carbon atoms present. For example, glucose is an aldohexose.

(a) Threose   (b) Ribulose

(c)

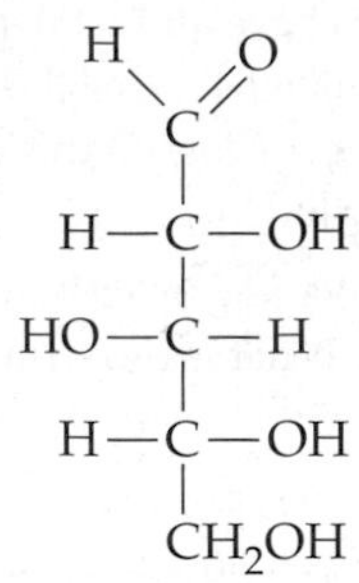

H O
\\ //
C
|
H—C—OH
|
HO—C—H
|
H—C—OH
|
CH₂OH

Xylose

(d)

CH₂OH
|
C=O
|
HO—C—H
|
HO—C—H
|
H—C—OH
|
CH₂OH

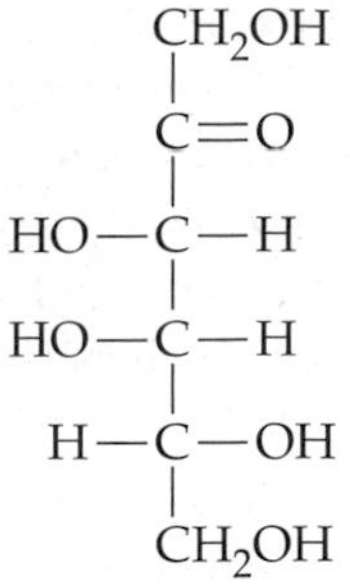

Tagatose

21.37 How many chiral carbon atoms are present in each of the molecules shown in Problem 21.36?

21.38 How many chiral carbon atoms are there in each of the two parts of the repeating unit in heparin (p. 681)? What is the total number of chiral carbon atoms in the repeating unit?

21.39 Draw the open-chain structure of a ketoheptose.

21.40 Draw the open-chain structure of a 4-carbon deoxy sugar.

21.41 Name four important monosaccharides and tell where each occurs in nature.

21.42 Name a common use for each monosaccharide listed in Problem 21.41.

HANDEDNESS IN CARBOHYDRATES

21.43 How are enantiomers related to each other?

21.44 What is the structural relationship between L-glucose and D-glucose?

21.45 Only three stereoisomers are possible for 2,3-dibromo-2,3-dichlorobutane. Draw them, indicating which pair are enantiomers (optical isomers). Why does the other isomer not have an enantiomer?

21.46 In Section 16.6 you saw that aldehydes react with reducing agents to yield primary alcohols (RCH=O → RCH₂OH). The structures of two D-aldotetroses are shown. One of them can be reduced to yield a chiral product, but the other yields an achiral product. Explain.

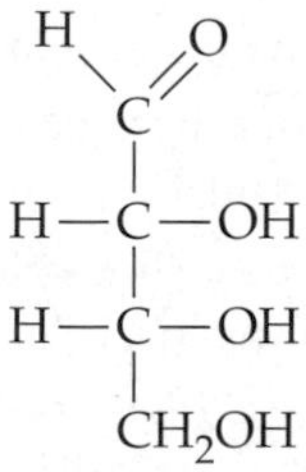

H O
\\ //
C
|
H—C—OH
|
H—C—OH
|
CH₂OH

D-Erythrose

H O
\\ //
C
|
HO—C—H
|
H—C—OH
|
CH₂OH

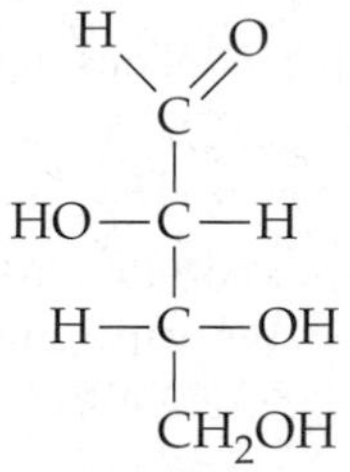

D-Threose

21.47 What is the definition of an optically active compound?

21.48 What does a polarimeter measure?

21.49 Sucrose and D-glucose rotate plane-polarized light to the right; D-fructose rotates light to the left. When sucrose is hydrolyzed, the glucose–fructose mixture rotates light to the left.

(a) What does this indicate about the relative degrees of rotation of light of glucose and fructose?

(b) Why do you think the mixture is called "invert sugar"?

21.50 What generalization can you make about the direction and degree of rotation of light by enantiomers?

REACTIONS OF CARBOHYDRATES

21.51 What does the term *reducing sugar* mean?

21.52 What structural property makes a sugar a reducing sugar?

21.53 What is mutarotation? Do all chiral molecules do this?

21.54 What are anomers, and how do the anomers of a given sugar differ from each other?

21.55 What is the structural difference between the α hemiacetal form of a carbohydrate and the β form?

21.56 D-Gulose, an aldohexose isomer of glucose, has the cyclic structure shown here. Which is shown, the α form or the β form?

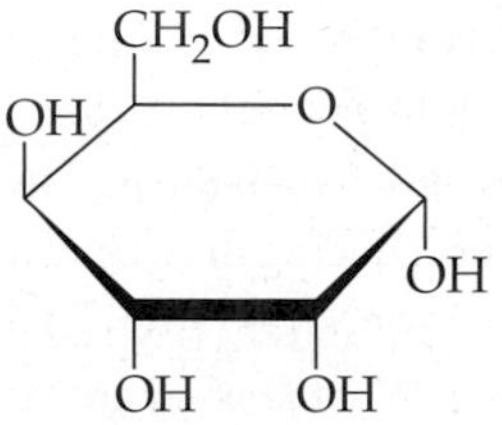

CH₂OH
OH O
OH
OH OH

D-Gulose

21.57 In its open-chain form, D-mannose, an aldohexose found in orange peels, has the structure shown here. Coil mannose around and draw it in the cyclic hemiacetal α and β forms.

H H H OH OH O
| | | | | ||
HO—C—C—C—C—C—C—H
| | | | |
H OH OH H H

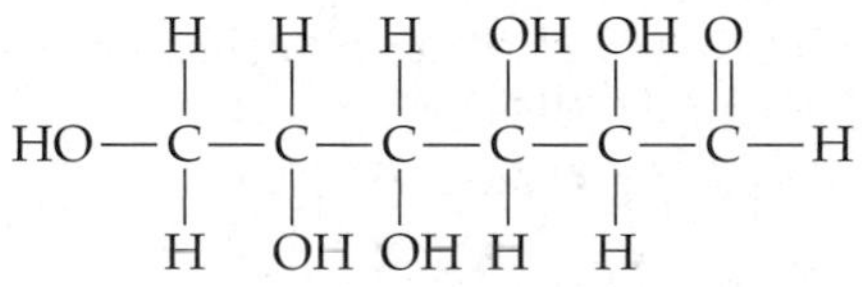

D-Mannose

21.58 In its open-chain form, D-altrose has the structure shown here. Coil altrose around and draw it in the cyclic hemiacetal α and β forms.

H H H H OH O
| | | | | ||
HO—C—C—C—C—C—C—H
| | | | |
H OH OH OH H

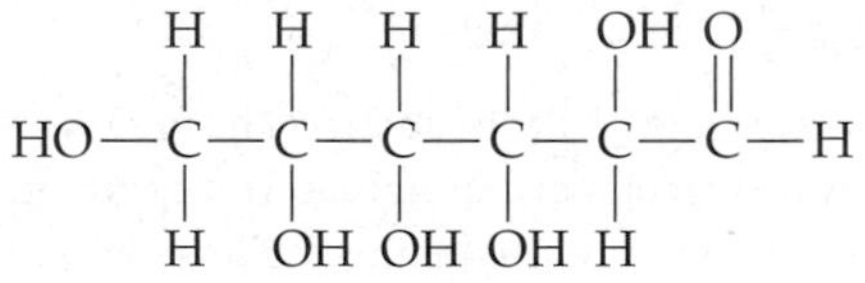

D-Altrose

21.59 Treatment of D-glucose with a reducing agent yields sorbitol, a substance used as a sugar substitute by people with diabetes. Draw the structure of sorbitol.

21.60 Reduction of D-fructose with a reducing agent yields a mixture of D-sorbitol along with a second, isomeric product. What is the structure of the second product?

21.61 Treatment of an aldose with an oxidizing agent such as Tollens' reagent (Section 16.5) yields a carboxylic acid. Gluconic acid, the product of glucose oxidation, is used as its magnesium salt for the treatment of magnesium deficiency. Draw the structure of gluconic acid.

21.62 Oxidation of the aldehyde group of ribose yields a carboxylic acid. Draw the structure of ribonic acid.

21.63 What is the structural difference between a hemiacetal and an acetal?

21.64 What are glycosides, and how can they be formed?

21.65 Look at the open-chain form of D-mannose (Problem 21.57) and draw the two glycosidic products that you expect to obtain by reacting D-mannose with methanol.

21.66 Draw a disaccharide of two cyclic mannose molecules attached by an α-1,4 glycosidic linkage. Explain why the glycosidic products in Problem 21.65 are *not* reducing sugars, but the product in this problem *is* a reducing sugar.

DISACCHARIDES AND POLYSACCHARIDES

21.67 Give the names of three important disaccharides. Tell where each occurs in nature. From which two monosaccharides is each made?

21.68 Lactose and maltose are reducing disaccharides, but sucrose is a nonreducing disaccharide. Explain.

21.69 Amylose (a form of starch) and cellulose are both polymers of glucose. What is the main structural difference between them? What roles do these two polymers have in nature?

21.70 How are amylose and amylopectin similar to each other, and how are they different from each other?

21.71 *Gentiobiose*, a rare disaccharide found in saffron, has the following structure. What simple sugars do you obtain on hydrolysis of gentiobiose?

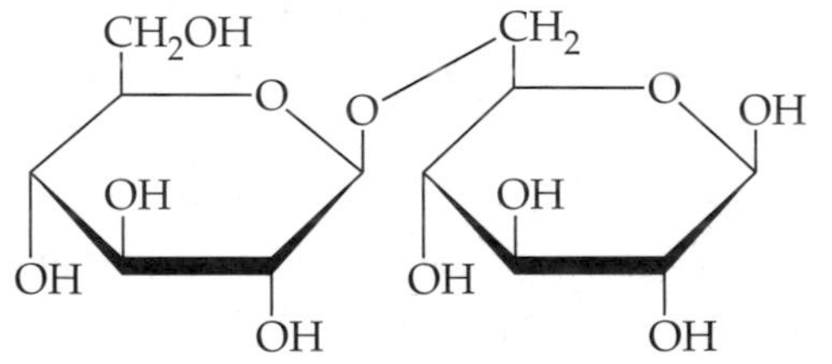

Gentiobiose

21.72 Does gentiobiose (Problem 21.71) have an acetal grouping? A hemiacetal grouping? Do you expect gentiobiose to be a reducing or nonreducing sugar? How would you classify the linkage (α or β and carbon numbers) between the two monosaccharides?

21.73 *Trehalose*, a disaccharide found in the blood of insects, has the following structure. What simple sugars would you obtain on hydrolysis of trehalose? (Hint: rotate one of the rings in your head or redraw it rotated.)

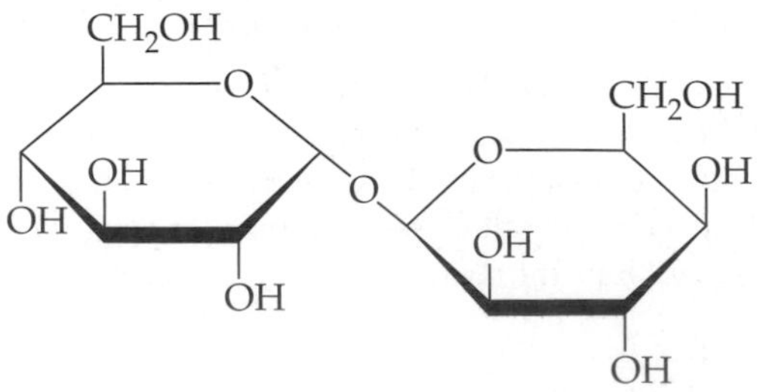

Trehalose

21.74 Does trehalose (Problem 21.73) have an acetal grouping? A hemiacetal grouping? Do you expect trehalose to be a reducing or nonreducing sugar? Classify the linkage between the two monosaccharides.

21.75 Amylopectin (a form of starch) and glycogen are both α-linked polymers of glucose. What is the structural difference between them?

21.76 What is the physiological purpose of starch in a seed or other plant tissue? What is the physiological purpose of glycogen in a mammal?

CHEMISTRY IN ACTION

21.77 Give some advantages and disadvantages of synthesizing and marketing a single-enantiomer drug. [*Chirality and Drugs, p. 663*]

21.78 What is the advantage of using enzymes in the synthesis of single-enantiomer drugs? [*Chirality and Drugs, p. 663*]

21.79 Look at the structures of the blood group determinants. What makes the blood types different? [*Cell-Surface Carbohydrates and Blood Type, p. 672*]

21.80 People with type O blood can donate blood to anyone, but they cannot receive blood from everyone. From whom can they not receive blood? People with type AB blood can receive blood from anyone, but they cannot give blood to everyone. To whom can they give blood? Why? [*Cell-Surface Carbohydrates and Blood Type, p. 672*]

21.81 Our bodies do not have the enzymes required to digest cellulose, yet it is a necessary addition to a healthy diet. Why? [*Carbohydrates and Fiber in the Diet, p. 679*]

21.82 Name two types of soluble fiber and their sources. [*Carbohydrates and Fiber in the Diet, p. 679*]

21.83 List three functions of all cell walls. [*Cell Walls: Rigid Defense Systems, p. 685*]

21.84 Name the monomeric unit and the polymer that makes up most of a plant cell wall. [*Cell Walls: Rigid Defense Systems, p. 685*]

21.85 Name the individual units and the crosslink for the polymer that makes up most of a bacterial cell wall. [*Cell Walls: Rigid Defense Systems, p. 685*]

21.86 When you take the antibiotic penicillin when you are ill, why does the penicillin kill a bacterial cell but not your liver cells? [*Cell Walls: Rigid Defense Systems, p. 685*]

GENERAL QUESTIONS AND PROBLEMS

21.87 Are the α and β forms of monosaccharides enantiomers of each other? Why or why not?

21.88 Are the α and β forms of the disaccharide lactose enantiomers of each other? Why or why not?

21.89 D-Fructose can form a six-membered cyclic hemiacetal as well as the more prevalent five-membered cyclic form. Draw the α isomer of D-fructose in the six-membered ring.

21.90 *Raffinose*, found in sugar beets, is the most prevalent trisaccharide. It is formed by an α-1,6 linkage of D-galactose to the glucose portion of sucrose. Draw the structure of raffinose.

21.91 Write the open-chain structure of the only ketotriose. Name this compound and explain why it has no optical isomers.

21.92 Write the open-chain structure of the only ketotetrose. Name this compound. Does it have an optical isomer?

21.93 What is lactose intolerance, and what are its symptoms?

21.94 Many people who are lactose intolerant can eat yogurt, which is prepared from milk curdled by bacteria, without any digestive problems. Give a reason why this is possible.

21.95 What is the group of disorders that result when the body lacks an enzyme necessary to digest galactose? What are the symptoms?

21.96 When a person cannot digest galactose, its reduced form, called dulcitol, often accumulates in the blood and tissues. Write the structure of the open-chain form of dulcitol. Does dulcitol have an enantiomer? Why or why not?

21.97 Carbohydrates provide 4 kcal per gram. If a person eats 200 g per day of digestible carbohydrates, what percentage of a 2000 kcal daily diet would be digestible carbohydrate?

21.98 A 12 oz can of cherry-flavored cola contains 42 grams of sugar. If sugar provides 4 kcal per gram (16.7 kJ/g), how many kilocalories are in one can of cola? How many kilojoules?

21.99 Describe the differences between mono-, di-, and polysaccharides.

21.100 Name a naturally occurring carbohydrate and its source for each type of carbohydrate listed in Problem 21.99.

21.101 Compare and contrast lactose intolerance with galactosemia. (Hint: make a table.)

21.102 Explain why cotton fibers, which are nearly pure cellulose, are insoluble in water, while glycogen, another polymer of glucose, will dissolve in water.

Carbohydrate Metabolism

CONTENTS

◄ The simple and complex carbohydrates in this meal provide fuel for metabolism.

1. **What happens during digestion of carbohydrates?**
THE GOAL: Be able to describe carbohydrate digestion, its location, the enzymes involved, and name the major products of this process. (◀◀ D, E.)

2. **What are the major pathways in the metabolism of glucose?**
THE GOAL: Be able to identify the pathways by which glucose is (1) synthesized and (2) broken down, and describe their interrelationships. (◀◀ C, D, E.)

3. **What is glycolysis?**
THE GOAL: Be able to give an overview of the glycolysis pathway and its products and identify where the major monosaccharides enter the pathway. (◀◀ A, B, C, D, E.)

4. **What happens to pyruvate once it is formed?**
THE GOAL: Be able to describe the pathways involving pyruvate and their respective outcomes. (◀◀ C, D.)

5. **How is glucose metabolism regulated, and what are the influences of starvation and diabetes mellitus?**
THE GOAL: Be able to identify the hormones that influence glucose metabolism and describe the changes in metabolism during starvation and diabetes mellitus. (◀◀ B, C.)

6. **What are glycogenesis and glycogenolysis?**
THE GOAL: Be able to define these pathways and their purpose. (◀◀ B, C, D.)

7. **What is the role of gluconeogenesis in metabolism?**
THE GOAL: Be able to identify the functions, substrates, and products of this pathway. (◀◀ C, D.)

CONCEPTS TO REVIEW

A. Phosphorylation
(Section 17.8)

B. Function of ATP
(Sections 20.5, 20.9)

C. Oxidized and Reduced Coenzymes
(Section 20.7)

D. Carbohydrate Structure
(Chapter 21)

E. Enzymes
(Chapter 19)

The story of carbohydrate metabolism is essentially the story of glucose: how it is converted to acetyl-coenzyme A (acetyl-CoA) for entrance into the citric acid cycle, how it is stored and then released for use, and how it is synthesized when carbohydrates are in short supply. Because of the importance of glucose, the body has several alternative strategies for regulating the glucose concentration in blood and providing glucose to cells that depend on it.

22.1 Digestion of Carbohydrates

The first stage in catabolism is **digestion**, the breakdown of food into small molecules. Digestion entails the physical grinding, softening, and mixing of food, as well as the enzyme-catalyzed hydrolysis of carbohydrates, proteins, and fats. Digestion begins in the mouth, continues in the stomach, and concludes in the small intestine.

The products of digestion are mostly small molecules that are absorbed from the intestinal tract. Nutrient absorption happens through millions of tiny projections (the *villi*) that provide a total surface area as big as a football field. Once in the bloodstream, the small molecules are transported into target cells, where many are further broken down for the purpose of releasing energy as their carbon atoms are converted to carbon dioxide. Others are excreted, and some are used as building blocks to synthesize new biomolecules.

The digestion of carbohydrates is summarized in Figure 22.1. α-Amylase present in saliva catalyzes the hydrolysis of the α glycosidic bonds in the carbohydrates amylose and amylopectin—plant starches. Starches from plants and glycogen from meat are hydrolyzed to give smaller polysaccharides and the disaccharide maltose. Plant cellulose, with its β glycosidic bonds linking glucose molecules together, is not digested. Salivary α-amylase continues to act upon dietary polysaccharides in the stomach until it is inactivated by stomach acid. No further carbohydrate digestion takes place in the stomach.

α-Amylase is also secreted by the pancreas and enters the small intestine, where conversion of polysaccharides to maltose continues. Other enzymes secreted from the mucous lining of the small intestine hydrolyze maltose and the dietary disaccharides sucrose and lactose to the monosaccharides glucose, fructose, and galactose, which are then transported across the intestinal wall into the bloodstream. The focus in this

Digestion A general term for the breakdown of food into small molecules.

▶▶ Recall from Section 21.9 that the plant starches amylose and amylopectin, plant cellulose, and glycogen (animal starch) are all large polymers of glucose. Plant starches and glycogen are digestible, while cellulose is not.

▲ A micrograph showing *villi*, the projections that line the small intestine. Each villus is covered with microvilli, where the digested food molecules are absorbed into the bloodstream.

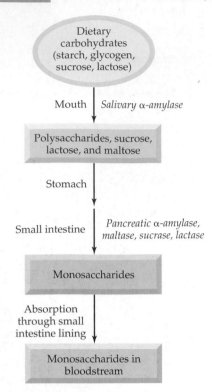

▲ Figure 22.1
The digestion of carbohydrates.

chapter is on the metabolism of glucose; both fructose and galactose can be converted to intermediates that enter the same metabolic pathway followed by glucose.

22.2 Glucose Metabolism: An Overview

Glucose is the major fuel for your body. It is the preferred fuel for the brain, working muscle cells, and red blood cells. The energy it yields through a series of metabolic oxidations is carried by ATP to power other reactions within the cell. The initial metabolic fate of glucose is conversion into pyruvate and then usually to acetyl-CoA, the common intermediate in the catabolism of all foods. Acetyl-CoA proceeds down the central pathway of metabolism, through the citric acid cycle, with the energy captured transferred through the electron transport system, resulting ultimately in the formation of ATP. We discussed the citric acid cycle and the electron transport chain in Chapter 20.

In this chapter, we examine the central position of glucose in metabolism, as summarized in Figure 22.2. Glycolysis is the major catabolic pathway leading to ATP synthesis. The reverse of glycolysis (gluconeogenesis) and the pathways leading to and from glycogen are discussed in the sections of this chapter noted in the figure. As you read this chapter, you will find it helpful to refer to Figure 22.2 and its accompanying table to sort out these pathways that have highly similar names.

When glucose enters a cell from the bloodstream, it is immediately converted to glucose 6-phosphate. Once this phosphate is formed, glucose is trapped within the cell because phosphorylated molecules cannot cross the cell membrane. Like the first step in many metabolic pathways, the formation of glucose-6-phosphate is highly exergonic and not reversible in the glycolytic pathway, thereby committing the initial substrate to subsequent reactions.

Several pathways are available to glucose 6-phosphate:

- When energy is needed, glucose 6-phosphate moves down the central catabolic pathway shown in light brown in Figure 22.2, proceeding via the reactions of *glycolysis* to pyruvate and then to acetyl-coenzyme A, which enters the citric acid cycle (discussed in Section 20.8).

$$\text{Glucose} \xrightarrow{\text{Phosphorylation}} \text{Glucose 6-phosphate} \xrightarrow{\text{Glycolysis}} 2\;CH_3-\underset{\underset{O}{\|}}{C}-\underset{\underset{O}{\|}}{C}-O^- \longrightarrow 2\;CH_3-\underset{\underset{O}{\|}}{C}-SCoA$$

Glucose   Glucose 6-phosphate   Pyruvate   Acetyl-CoA

- When cells are already well supplied with glucose, excess glucose is converted to other forms for storage: into glycogen, the glucose storage polymer, by the *glycogenesis* pathway, or into fatty acids by entrance of acetyl-CoA into the pathways of lipid metabolism (Chapter 24) rather than the citric acid cycle.
- Glucose-6-phosphate can also enter the **pentose phosphate pathway**. This multistep pathway yields two products important to our metabolism. One is a supply of the coenzyme NADPH, a reducing agent that is essential for various biochemical reactions. The other is ribose 5-phosphate, which is necessary for the synthesis of nucleic acids (DNA and RNA). Glucose-6-phosphate enters the pentose phosphate pathway when a cell's need for NADPH or ribose-5-phosphate exceeds its need for ATP.

Pentose phosphate pathway The biochemical pathway that produces ribose (a pentose), NADPH, and other sugar phosphates from glucose; an alternative to glycolysis.

PROBLEM 22.1
Name the following pathways:
(a) Pathway for synthesis of glycogen
(b) Pathway for release of glucose from glycogen
(c) Pathway for synthesis of glucose from lactate

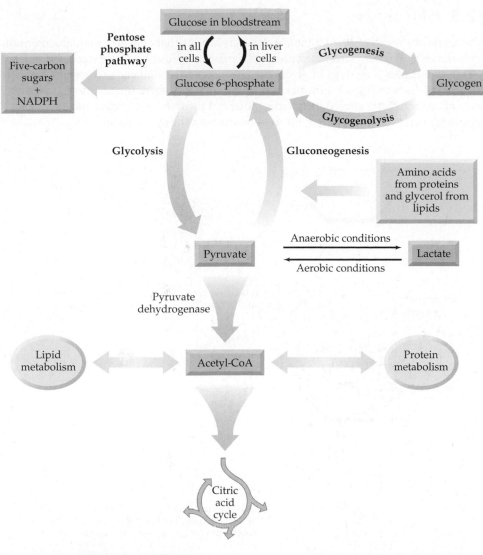

◄ Figure 22.2
Glucose metabolism.
Synthetic pathways (anabolism) are shown in blue, pathways that break down biomolecules (catabolism) are shown in light brown, and connections to lipid and protein metabolism are shown in green.

Metabolic Pathways of Glucose

NAME	DERIVATION OF NAME	FUNCTION
Glycolysis (Section 22.3)	*glyco-*, glucose (from Greek, meaning "sweet") *-lysis*, decomposition	Conversion of glucose to pyruvate
Gluconeogenesis (Section 22.11)	*gluco-*, glucose *-neo-*, new *-genesis*, creation	Synthesis of glucose from amino acids, pyruvate, and other noncarbohydrates
Glycogenesis (Section 22.10)	*glyco(gen)-*, glycogen *-genesis*, creation	Synthesis of glycogen from glucose
Glycogenolysis (Section 22.10)	*glycogen-*, glycogen *-lysis*, decomposition	Breakdown of glycogen to glucose
Pentose phosphate pathway (Section 22.2)	*pentose-*, a five-carbon sugar	Conversion of glucose to five-carbon sugar phosphates

PROBLEM 22.2
Name the synthetic pathways that have glucose 6-phosphate as their first reactant.

22.3 Glycolysis

Glycolysis The biochemical pathway that breaks down a molecule of glucose into two molecules of pyruvate plus energy.

Glycolysis is a series of 10 enzyme-catalyzed reactions that converts each glucose molecule into two pyruvate molecules, and in the process yields two ATP molecules and two NADH molecules. The steps of glycolysis (also called the *Embden–Meyerhoff pathway* after its co-discoverers) are summarized in Figure 22.3, where the reactions and structures of intermediates should be noted as you read the following paragraphs. Almost all organisms carry out glycolysis; in humans it occurs in the cytosol of all cells.

▶ **Figure 22.3**
The glycolysis pathway for converting glucose to pyruvate.

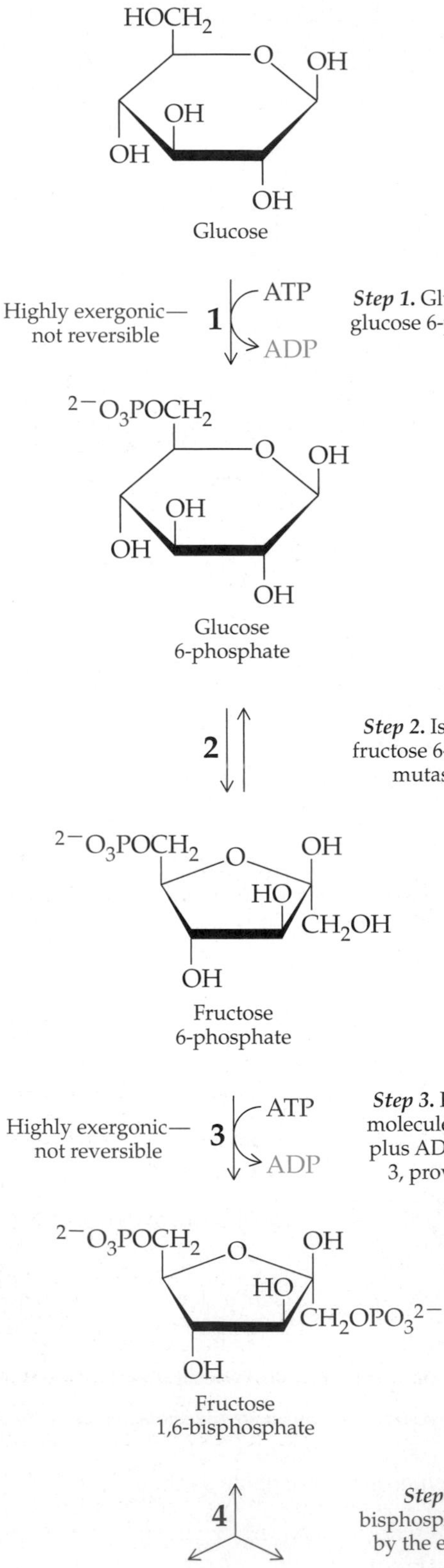

HOCH₂

Glucose

Highly exergonic—not reversible **1** ⟨ ATP → ADP

Step 1. Glucose undergoes reaction with ATP to yield glucose 6-phosphate plus ADP in a reaction catalyzed by *hexokinase*.

²⁻O₃POCH₂

Glucose 6-phosphate

2

Step 2. Isomerization of glucose 6-phosphate yields fructose 6-phosphate. The reaction is catalyzed by the mutase enzyme, *glucose 6-phosphate isomerase*.

²⁻O₃POCH₂

Fructose 6-phosphate

Highly exergonic—not reversible **3** ⟨ ATP → ADP

Step 3. Fructose 6-phosphate reacts with a second molecule of ATP to yield fructose 1,6-bisphosphate plus ADP. *Phosphofructokinase*, the enzyme for step 3, provides a major control point in glycolysis.

²⁻O₃POCH₂

Fructose 1,6-bisphosphate

Step 4. The six-carbon chain of fructose 1,6-bisphosphate is cleaved into two three-carbon pieces by the enzyme *aldolase*. (Continued on next page.)

$$2^-O_3POCH_2-\overset{\overset{\textstyle O}{\|}}{C}-CH_2OH \quad \overset{5}{\rightleftharpoons} \quad 2^-O_3POCH_2-\overset{\overset{\textstyle OH}{|}}{CH}-\overset{\overset{\textstyle O}{\|}}{C}-H$$

Dihydroxyacetone phosphate D-Glyceraldehyde 3-phosphate

Step 5. The two products of step 4 are both three-carbon sugars, but only glyceraldehyde 3-phosphate can continue in the glycolysis pathway. Dihydroxyacetone phosphate must first be isomerized by the enzyme *triose phosphate isomerase*.

$$6 \quad \begin{array}{c} NAD^+ + HOPO_3{}^{2-} \\ \downarrow \\ NADH/H^+ \end{array}$$

Step 6. Two reactions occur as glyceraldehyde 3-phosphate is first oxidized to a carboxylic acid and then phosphorylated by the enzyme *glyceraldehyde 3-phosphate dehydrogenase*. The coenzyme nicotinamide adenine dinucleotide (NAD^+) and inorganic phosphate ion ($HOPO_3{}^{2-}$) are required.

$$2^-O_3POCH_2-\overset{\overset{\textstyle OH}{|}}{CH}-\overset{\overset{\textstyle O}{\|}}{C}-OPO_3{}^{2-}$$

1,3-Bisphosphoglycerate

$$7 \quad \begin{array}{c} ADP \\ \downarrow \\ ATP \end{array}$$

Step 7. A phosphate group from 1,3-bisphosphoglycerate is transferred to ADP, resulting in synthesis of ATP, and catalyzed by *phosphoglycerate kinase*.

$$2^-O_3POCH_2-\overset{\overset{\textstyle OH}{|}}{CH}-\overset{\overset{\textstyle O}{\|}}{C}-O^-$$

3-Phosphoglycerate

$$8 \quad \updownarrow$$

Step 8. A phosphate group is next transferred from carbon 3 to carbon 2 of phosphoglycerate in a step catalyzed by the enzyme *phosphoglycerate mutase*.

$$HO-CH_2-\overset{\overset{\textstyle 2^-O_3PO}{|}}{CH}-\overset{\overset{\textstyle O}{\|}}{C}-O^-$$

2-Phosphoglycerate

$$9 \quad \begin{array}{c} \\ \downarrow \\ H_2O \end{array}$$

Step 9. Loss of water from 2-phosphoglycerate produces phosphoenolpyruvate (PEP). The dehydration is catalyzed by the enzyme *enolase*.

$$H_2C=\overset{\overset{\textstyle 2^-O_3PO}{|}}{C}-\overset{\overset{\textstyle O}{\|}}{C}-O^-$$

Phosphoenolpyruvate

Highly exergonic— not reversible $$10 \quad \begin{array}{c} ADP \\ \downarrow \\ ATP \end{array}$$

Step 10. Transfer of the phosphate group from phosphoenolpyruvate to ADP yields pyruvate and generates ATP, catalyzed by *pyruvate kinase*.

$$CH_3-\overset{\overset{\textstyle O}{\|}}{C}-\overset{\overset{\textstyle O}{\|}}{C}-O^-$$

Pyruvate

STEP 1 of Glycolysis: Phosphorylation Glucose is carried in the bloodstream to cells, where it is transported across the cell membrane into the cytosol. As soon as it enters the cell, glucose is phosphorylated in Step 1 of glycolysis, which requires an energy investment from ATP. This is the first of three highly exergonic, irreversible steps in glycolysis. From here on, all pathway intermediates are sugar phosphates, and they are trapped within the cells because, as charged moieties, phosphates cannot cross cell membranes unaided.

The product of Step 1, glucose 6-phosphate, is an allosteric inhibitor for the enzyme for this step (*hexokinase*), and therefore plays an important role in the elaborate and delicate control of glucose metabolism.

▶▶▶ Phosphorylation is the transfer of a phosphoryl group ($-PO_3{}^{2-}$) from one molecule to another (see Section 17.8).

▶▶▶ Review enzyme regulation by allosteric control in Section 19.7.

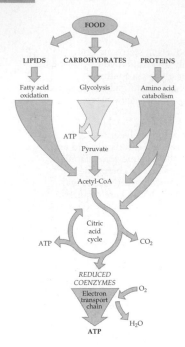

STEP 2 is the isomerization of glucose 6-phosphate to fructose 6-phosphate. The enzyme (*glucose 6-phosphate isomerase*) acts by converting glucose 6-phosphate (an aldohexose) to fructose 6-phosphate (a ketohexose). The result is conversion of the six-membered glucose ring to a five-membered ring with a $-CH_2OH$ group, which prepares the molecule for addition of another phosphoryl group in the next step.

STEP 3 makes a second energy investment as fructose 6-phosphate is converted to fructose 1,6-bisphosphate by reaction with ATP in another exergonic reaction. (*Bis-* means "two"—that is, fructose with two phosphate groups. The "bis" prefix is used to distinguish between a molecule containing two phosphate groups in different locations and a "diphosphate"—a compound that contains a single diphosphate group, $-OP_2O_6^{4-}$; see Section 17.8.) Step 3 is another major control point for glycolysis. When the cell is short of energy, ADP and AMP (adenosine monophosphate) concentrations build up and activate the Step 3 enzyme, *phosphofructokinase*. When energy is in good supply, ATP and citrate build up and allosterically inhibit this enzyme. The outcome of Steps 1–3 is the formation of a molecule ready to be split into the two 3-carbon intermediates that will ultimately become two molecules of pyruvate.

STEPS 4 and 5 of Glycolysis: Cleavage and Isomerization Step 4 converts the 6-carbon bisphosphate from Step 3 into two 3-carbon monophosphates, one an aldose phosphate and one a ketose phosphate. *Aldolase* catalyzes the breakage of the bond between carbons 3 and 4 in fructose 1,6-bisphosphate, and a $C=O$ group is formed.

$$
\underset{\text{Fructose 1,6-bisphosphate}}{
\begin{array}{c}
\overset{1}{C}H_2OPO_3^{2-} \\
|\\
\overset{2}{C}=O \\
|\\
HO-\overset{3}{C}-H \\
|\\
H-\overset{4}{C}-OH \\
|\\
H-\overset{5}{C}-OH \\
|\\
\overset{6}{C}H_2OPO_3^{2-}
\end{array}
}
\quad
\xrightleftharpoons{\text{Aldolase}}
\quad
\underset{\text{Dihydroxyacetone phosphate}}{
\begin{array}{c}
CH_2OPO_3^{2-} \\
|\\
C=O \\
|\\
CH_2OH
\end{array}
}
\;+\;
\underset{\text{D-Glyceraldehyde 3-phosphate}}{
\begin{array}{c}
H\;\;\;O \\
\;\;C \\
|\\
H-C-OH \\
|\\
CH_2OPO_3^{2-}
\end{array}
}
$$

The two 3-carbon sugar phosphates produced in Step 4 are isomers that are interconvertible in an aldose–ketose equilibrium (Step 5 in Figure 22.3) catalyzed by *triose phosphate isomerase*. However, only glyceraldehyde 3-phosphate can continue on the glycolysis pathway. As glyceraldehyde 3-phosphate reacts in Step 6, the equilibrium of Step 5 shifts to the right. The overall result of Steps 4 and 5 is therefore the production of *two* molecules of glyceraldehyde 3-phosphate.

Steps 1–5 are referred to as the *energy investment* part of glycolysis. So far, two ATP molecules have been invested and no income earned, but the stage is now set for a small energy profit. Note that since one glucose molecule yields two glyceraldehyde 3-phosphate molecules that pass separately down the rest of the pathway; Steps 6–10 of glycolysis each take place twice for every glucose molecule that enters at Step 1.

STEPS 6–10 of Glycolysis: Energy Generation The second half of glycolysis is devoted to generating molecules with phosphate groups that can be transferred to ATP.

Step 6 is the oxidation of glyceraldehyde 3-phosphate to 1,3-bisphosphoglycerate by *glyceraldehyde 3-phosphate dehydrogenase*. The enzyme cofactor NAD^+ is the oxidizing agent for this reaction. Some of the energy from the exergonic oxidation is captured in NADH, and some is devoted to forming the phosphate. This is the first energy-generating step of glycolysis.

Step 7 generates the first ATP of glycolysis by transferring a phosphate group from 1,3-bisphosphoglycerate to ADP; the enzyme *phosphoglycerate kinase* accomplishes this. The other product of the reaction is 3-phosphoglycerate. Because this step occurs twice for each glucose molecule, the ATP-energy balance sheet in glycolysis is even after Step 7. Two ATP molecules were spent in Steps 1–5, and now they have been replaced.

Steps 8 and 9—an isomerization of 3-phosphoglycerate to 2-phosphoglycerate, catalyzed by *phosphoglycerate mutase* followed by dehydration of 2-phosphoglycerate by *enolase*—generate phosphoenolpyruvate, the second energy-providing phosphate of glycolysis. Step 8 sets the stage for Step 9 by rearranging the position of the phosphate group in the molecule. Then, Step 9 generates a double bond by way of water loss.

Step 10 is a highly exergonic, irreversible transfer of a phosphate group to ADP catalyzed by *pyruvate kinase*. The production of ATP by transfer of a phosphate group to ADP from another molecule is called *substrate-level phosphorylation*. Once the phosphate group leaves phosphoenolpyruvate, the less-stable enol form of pyruvate spontaneously rearranges into the more-stable keto form of pyruvate. The large amount of free energy released is accounted for by this rearrangement (see Section 21.6).

The two ATP molecules formed by the reactions in Step 10 are pure profit, and the overall results of glycolysis are as follows:

Net result of glycolysis

$$C_6H_{12}O_6 + 2\,NAD^+ + 2\,HOPO_3{}^{2-} + 2\,ADP \longrightarrow 2\,CH_3-\overset{\overset{O}{\|}}{C}-\overset{\overset{O}{\|}}{C}-O^- + 2\,NADH + 2\,ATP + 2\,H_2O + 2\,H^+$$

Glucose   Pyruvate

- Conversion of glucose to two pyruvate molecules
- Net production of two ATP molecules
- Production of two molecules of reduced coenzyme NADH from NAD^+

Worked Example 22.1 Relating Enzyme Names with Reaction Steps of Glycolysis

How do the names of the enzymes involved in the first two steps of glycolysis relate to the reactions involved?

ANALYSIS Look at the names of the enzymes and the reactions. Also recall the enzyme classification scheme from Chapter 19 (see p. 590).

SOLUTION
In the first reaction, a phosphoryl group is added to glucose. The enzyme name is hexokinase; *kinase* because kinases transfer phosphoryl groups, and *hexo-* for a hexose sugar as the substrate. In the second reaction glucose 6-phosphate is rearranged to fructose 6-phosphate by phosphoglucose isomerase. This enzyme belongs to the enzyme class of isomerases, enzymes that rearrange molecules to an isomer of the original molecule. The phosphoglucose part of the name tells us that a phosphorylated glucose molecule will be rearranged; inspection of the reaction shows that this is true.

PROBLEM 22.3
Identify the two pairs of steps in glycolysis in which phosphate intermediates are synthesized and their energy harvested as ATP.

PROBLEM 22.4
Identify each step in glycolysis that is an isomerization.

PROBLEM 22.5
Verify the isomerization that occurs in Step 2 of glycolysis by drawing the open-chain forms of glucose 6-phosphate and fructose 6-phosphate.

KEY CONCEPT PROBLEM 22.6

In Figure 22.3 compare the starting compound (glucose) and the final product (pyruvate).
(a) Which is oxidized to a greater extent?
(b) Are there any steps in the glycolytic pathway in which an oxidation or reduction occurs? Identify the oxidizing or reducing agents that are involved in these steps.

22.4 Entry of Other Sugars into Glycolysis

Glucose is not the only monosaccharide that our bodies metabolize. The other major monosaccharides from digestion—fructose, galactose, and mannose—eventually join the glycolysis pathway. Like glucose, these sugars are also metabolized by the bacteria that populate our mouths and digestive systems. The effect of dietary sugars on dental health is explored in Chemistry in Action: Tooth Decay.

Fructose, from fruits or hydrolysis of the disaccharide sucrose, is converted to glycolysis intermediates in two ways: in muscle, it is phosphorylated to fructose 6-phosphate, and in the liver, it is converted to glyceraldehyde 3-phosphate. Fructose 6-phosphate is the substrate for Step 3 of glycolysis; glyceraldehyde 3-phosphate is the substrate for Step 6.

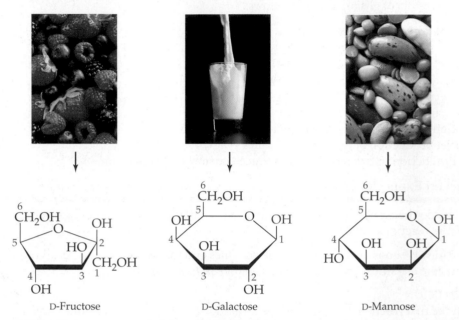

▲ **Major dietary monosaccharides other than glucose.**

Galactose from hydrolysis of the disaccharide lactose is converted to glucose 6-phosphate, the substrate for Step 2 of glycolysis, by a five-step pathway. A hereditary defect affecting any enzyme in this pathway can cause galactosemia (see p. 671 of Section 21.5).

Mannose is a product of the hydrolysis of plant polysaccharides other than starch. It is converted (by hexokinase) to mannose 6-phosphate, which then undergoes a multistep, enzyme-catalyzed rearrangement in order to enter glycolysis as the substrate for Step 3 (as fructose 6-phosphate).

PROBLEM 22.7

Why is table sugar bad for your teeth? Would using honey instead be a better choice for tooth health? (See Chemistry in Action: Tooth Decay, p. 701.)

PROBLEM 22.8

Use curved arrows (like those in Figure 22.3) to write an equation for the conversion of fructose to fructose 6-phosphate by ATP. At what step does fructose 6-phosphate enter glycolysis?

PROBLEM 22.9

Compare glucose and galactose (see Section 21.5), and explain how their structures differ.

CHEMISTRY IN ACTION

Tooth Decay

Tooth decay is a complex interaction between food, bacteria, and a host organism. The clinical term for tooth decay is *dental caries*. It is recognized as an infectious microbial disease that results in the destruction of the calcified structures of the teeth.

The mouth is home to many different species of bacteria. A variety of habitats are provided by the diverse surfaces of the teeth, tongue, gums, and cheeks, and there are nutrients specific to each. Two permanent bacterial residents of the oral cavity, *Streptococcus sanguis* and *Streptococcus mutans*, compete for the same habitat on the biting surfaces of the teeth.

Dental plaque is defined as bacterial aggregations on the teeth that cannot be removed by the mechanical action of a strong water spray. Immediately after plaque has been removed by scrubbing with an abrasive paste, a coating of organic material composed of glycoproteins from the saliva begins to form. It completely covers the teeth within two hours after a visit to the dentist's office.

Bacteria then quickly colonize this newly formed film. They secrete a sticky matrix of an insoluble polysaccharide known as *dextran*, a branched polymer of the glucose that the bacteria have produced by hydrolysis of sucrose from food. The dextran allows the bacteria to stick firmly to the teeth so that the bacteria cannot be washed away by the saliva and swallowed. Bacteria that live comfortably in the mouth do not take well to the acidic environment of the stomach, so staying on the teeth is essential for their survival. The mass of bacteria, their sticky matrix, and the glycoprotein film together comprise dental plaque. Plaque is therefore not simply adherent food debris, but rather a community of microorganisms (known as a *biofilm*) that forms through an orderly sequence of events.

The bacteria resident in plaque release products consisting of proteins and carbohydrates. Some polysaccharides form intracellular granules that serve as energy storage depots for periods of low nutrient availability (between meals for the host). Other products are toxic to the gums and can promote periodontal

disease. Carbohydrates, including structural components of the bacteria themselves, the storage granules, and the sticky matrix, constitute 20% of the dry weight of plaque.

What our dentists and parents told us—that eating candy would create cavities—is true! A diet high in sucrose favors the growth of *S. mutans* over that of *S. sanguis*. Although both bacteria can cause tooth decay, *S. mutans* attacks teeth much more vigorously. It has an enzyme (a glucosyltransferase) that transfers glucose units from sucrose to the dextran polymer. The enzyme is specific to sucrose, and does not act on free glucose or the glucose from other carbohydrates. The mature plaque community then metabolizes fructose from the sucrose to lactate, and this acid causes the local pH in the area of the tooth to drop dramatically. If the pH stays low enough for a long enough time, the minerals in the teeth are dissolved away and the tooth begins to decay.

Cleaning teeth by brushing and flossing disrupts the bacterial plaque, removing many of the bacteria. However, enough bacteria always remain so that the colonization process can begin anew almost immediately. The disruption of plaque via oral hygiene and a diet low in sucrose, however, favors the growth of *S. sanguis* over *S. mutans*. To control the decay process, it is necessary to limit both the amount of sucrose in the diet and the frequency with which it is ingested.

The third factor in tooth decay is the host—ourselves. Many variables prevent or promote tooth decay, including the composition of saliva, the shape of the teeth, and exposure to fluoride. As individuals, however, we have little control over these elements, leaving us reliant on proper oral hygiene habits, low sucrose diets, and preventive maintenance by dental professionals. Modern preventative maintenance includes the use of sealants on the chewing surfaces of both deciduous and permanent teeth as they develop in children. The result is many more young adults with healthy, unblemished teeth.

See Chemistry in Action Problems 22.69 through 22.72 at the end of the chapter.

22.5 The Fate of Pyruvate

The conversion of glucose to pyruvate is a central metabolic pathway in most living systems. The further reactions of pyruvate, however, depend on metabolic conditions and on the nature of the organism. Under normal oxygen-rich (**aerobic**) conditions, pyruvate is converted to acetyl-CoA. This pathway, however, is short-circuited in some tissues, especially when there is not enough oxygen present (**anaerobic** conditions). Under anaerobic conditions, pyruvate is instead reduced to lactate. When sufficient oxygen again becomes available, lactate is recycled back to pyruvate in muscle cells or to glucose via the Cori cycle in liver cells. A third pathway for pyruvate is conversion back to glucose by *gluconeogenesis*, which also occurs only in liver cells (we will discuss gluconeogenesis and the Cori cycle in Section 22.11). This pathway is essential when the body is starved for glucose. The pyruvate necessary for gluconeogenesis may come not only from glycolysis but also from amino acids or glycerol from lipids. Use

Aerobic In the presence of oxygen.

Anaerobic In the absence of oxygen.

of protein and lipid for glucose synthesis occurs when calories needed exceed calorie intake as in starvation, certain diseases, and some carbohydrate-restricted diets.

Yeast is an organism with a different pathway for pyruvate; it converts pyruvate to ethanol under anaerobic conditions. Humans exploit this property of yeast in leavening bread and brewing beer (see Chemistry in Action: Microbial Fermentations: Ancient and Modern on p. 703).

$$CH_3CH_2OH \xleftarrow{\text{Anaerobic yeast}} CH_3-\overset{\overset{O}{\|}}{C}-\overset{\overset{O}{\|}}{C}-O^- \xrightarrow{\text{Anaerobic muscle}} CH_3-\overset{\overset{OH}{|}}{C}H-\overset{\overset{O}{\|}}{C}-O^-$$

| Ethyl alcohol | ← | Pyruvate | → | Lactate |

$$\downarrow \boxed{\text{Aerobic cells}}$$

Acetyl-CoA

$$CH_3-\overset{\overset{O}{\|}}{C}-SCoA$$

▲ **The biochemical transformations of pyruvate.**

Aerobic Oxidation of Pyruvate to Acetyl-CoA

For aerobic oxidation to proceed, pyruvate first moves across the outer mitochondrial membrane from the cytosol where it was produced. Then pyruvate must be carried by a transporter protein across the otherwise impenetrable inner mitochondrial membrane. Once within the mitochondrial matrix, pyruvate encounters the *pyruvate dehydrogenase complex* (Figure 22.4), a large multienzyme complex that catalyzes the conversion of pyruvate to acetyl-CoA.

$$CH_3-\overset{\overset{O}{\|}}{C}-\overset{\overset{O}{\|}}{C}-O^- + HS-CoA \xrightarrow[\substack{\text{Pyruvate} \\ \text{dehydrogenase} \\ \text{complex}}]{NAD^+ \quad NADH/H^+} CH_3\overset{\overset{O}{\|}}{C}-SCoA + CO_2$$

Pyruvate · · · · · · · · · · · · · Acetyl-CoA

Anaerobic Reduction to Lactate

Why does pyruvate take an alternative pathway when oxygen is in short supply? Since oxygen has not been needed in glucose catabolism thus far, what is the connection? The problem lies with the NADH formed in Step 6 of glycolysis (Figure 22.3). Under aerobic conditions, NADH is continually reoxidized to NAD^+ during electron transport (see Section 20.9), so NAD^+ is in constant supply. If electron transport slows down because of insufficient oxygen, however, NADH concentration increases, decreasing the supply of NAD^+, and glycolysis cannot continue. An alternative way to reoxidize NADH is therefore essential because glycolysis *must* continue—it is the only available source of fresh ATP.

The reduction of pyruvate to lactate solves the problem. NADH serves as the reducing agent and is reoxidized to NAD^+, which is then available in the cytosol for glycolysis. Lactate formation serves no purpose other than NAD^+ production, and the lactate is reoxidized to pyruvate when oxygen is available.

$$CH_3-\overset{\overset{O}{\|}}{C}-\overset{\overset{O}{\|}}{C}-O^- \underset{\substack{\text{Aerobic} \\ \text{conditions}}}{\overset{\substack{NADH/H^+ \quad NAD^+ \\ \text{Anaerobic} \\ \text{conditions}}}{\rightleftharpoons}} CH_3-\overset{\overset{OH}{|}}{C}H-\overset{\overset{O}{\|}}{C}-O^-$$

Pyruvate · · · · · · · · · · · · · Lactate

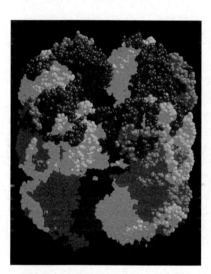

▲ **Figure 22.4**
The central core of the pyruvate dehydrogenase complex.
The core is composed of 24 proteins arranged in three kinds of subunits shown in three different colors. The entire huge complex contains 60 subunits of three different enzymes. It requires NAD^+, CoA, FAD, and two other coenzymes. The enzyme subunits, which are adjacent to each other, swing into position one after the other as pyruvate loses CO_2 and is converted to an acetyl group that is then transferred to coenzyme A.

CHEMISTRY IN ACTION

Microbial Fermentations: Ancient and Modern

Archaeological evidence shows that several ancient civilizations used fermentation in the preparation of food and drink. Residues found in pottery in both China and Egypt point to wine making as long as 9000 years ago. Analysis of lees (yeast residue) from jars dating to the sixth century B.C. found ribosomal DNA sequences from *Saccharomyces cerevisiae*, the same organism used today in wine making, brewing beer, and leavening bread. Other microorganisms can also perform fermentations and are important in producing cheese, sauerkraut, soy sauce, and other foods.

The fermentations most widely exploited by humans involve converting grain and other vegetable matter into ethanol through "alcohol fermentation," as described by Louis Pasteur, who studied wine making and developed the pasteurization process. Under anaerobic conditions in yeast and some other microorganisms, pyruvate, the product of glycolysis, is converted first to acetaldehyde and carbon dioxide by pyruvate decarboxylase and then to ethanol by alcohol dehydrogenase:

$$CH_3COCOOH \xrightleftharpoons{\text{pyruvate decarboxylase}} CH_3CHO +$$
$$CO_2 \xrightleftharpoons{\text{alcohol dehydrogenase}} CH_3CH_2OH$$

Any fruit can be fermented but many societies have focused on fermenting grapes. Fermentation of fruit is a way to preserve some of the food value without spoilage. Grapes take up little space when grown with other crops and are high in fermentable sugars. An added bonus is the natural coating of several varieties of yeast on the grapes, although during fermentation *Saccharomyces cerevisiae* rapidly replaces the others. Many wines contain about 12% ethanol; when ethanol in the fermenting mixture reaches that level, the yeast die and fermentation ceases. It was known for many years that if the fermentation vessel was tightly sealed, the gas (CO_2) produced made the wine "bubbly" if the seal held against the increased pressure inside the container; unfortunately, most containers were not strong enough to yield a reliably fizzy product. In the seventeenth century, glass bottles and corks were introduced for wine storage, replacing wooden barrels, and the production of champagne became possible.

Similarly, beer making from the fermentation of grain is nearly as old as wine production. In South America beer was fermented from boiled maize or manioc root with some of the cooked starch chewed and added, along with salivary enzymes, to the mix. The presence of salivary enzymes hydrolyzed the starch to maltose for fermentation. In much of Asia, millet, sorghum, and rice were made into beer; in Europe and Africa, malted (sprouted) grains like millet, wheat, rye, and barley were used. The enzymes present in malted grains hydrolyze the starch in the grain to maltose. The maltose is fermented to produce ethanol and carbon dioxide by *Saccharomyces cerevisiae* and related yeasts.

When curdled milk is fermented, cheese is produced. Humans have been making cheese for over 5000 years. The characteristic flavors and aromas of the different varieties of cheeses depend partly on the bacteria used in the fermentation and the molecules that are changed. For example, the characteristic flavor and appearance of Swiss cheese are due to the conversion of lactic acid to propionic acid, acetic acid, and carbon dioxide gas, which produces the holes in the cheese. Fresh milk can also be fermented; we know these products as yogurt, sour cream, and buttermilk.

Not all bacterial fermentations are friendly. *Clostridium* species are responsible for gas gangrene, a condition that causes the death of living tissue and can cause the death of the infected person. The bacteria invade the body, generally through a puncture wound, and multiply in an anaerobic area. Fermentation products of these bacteria are butyric acid, butanol, acetone, ethanol, and carbon dioxide. CO_2 infiltrates surrounding tissues, maintains an anaerobic environment by excluding O_2 from the cells, and causes necrosis (tissue death). The presence of the organic acids, CO_2, and toxins secreted by the bacteria leads to the spread of gangrene and makes it difficult to treat. Treatment usually involves surgical removal of necrotic tissue and sometimes hyperbaric (at a pressure above atmospheric pressure) oxygen treatment, because O_2 is toxic to these bacteria.

See Chemistry in Action Problems 22.73 and 22.74 at the end of the chapter.

Red blood cells have no mitochondria and therefore always form lactate as the end product of glycolysis. Tissues where oxygen is in short supply also rely on the anaerobic production of ATP by glycolysis. Examples are the cornea of the eye, where there is little blood circulation, and muscles during intense activity. The resulting buildup of lactate in working muscles causes fatigue and discomfort (see Chemistry in Action: The Biochemistry of Running on p. 712).

Alcoholic Fermentation

Microorganisms often must survive in the absence of oxygen and have evolved numerous anaerobic strategies for energy production, generally known as

Fermentation The production of energy under anaerobic conditions.

Alcoholic fermentation The anaerobic breakdown of glucose to ethanol plus carbon dioxide by the action of yeast enzymes.

fermentation. When pyruvate undergoes fermentation by yeast, it is converted into ethanol plus carbon dioxide. This process, known as **alcoholic fermentation**, is used to produce beer, wine, and other alcoholic beverages and also to make bread. The carbon dioxide causes the bread to rise, and the alcohol evaporates during baking. The first leavened, or raised, bread was probably made by accident when airborne yeasts got into the dough. The tempting aroma of baking bread includes the aroma of alcohol vapors. Beer can also be made by exposing the mash to outside air, where airborne yeasts drift in from the surroundings.

Worked Example 22.2 Identifying Catabolic Stages

Complete oxidation of glucose produces six molecules of carbon dioxide. Describe the stage of catabolism at which each one is formed.

ANALYSIS   Look at each stage of catabolism for the complete oxidation of glucose to carbon dioxide. Notice how many molecules of carbon dioxide are produced and by which step. Pathways to consider (in order) are glycolysis, conversion of pyruvate to acetyl-CoA, and the citric acid cycle. (There is no need to consider oxidative phosporylation because glucose is completely oxidized at the end of the citric acid cycle.)

SOLUTION

No molecules of carbon dioxide are produced during glycolysis. Conversion of one molecule of pyruvate to one molecule of acetyl-CoA yields one molecule of carbon dioxide. In the citric acid cycle, two molecules of carbon dioxide are released for each molecule of acetyl-CoA oxidized. One is released in Step 3 when isocitrate is converted to α-ketoglutarate and the other when α-ketoglutarate is converted to succinyl-CoA in Step 4. Since each glucose molecule produces two pyruvate molecules, the total is three molecules twice, or six molecules of carbon dioxide.

KEY CONCEPT PROBLEM 22.10

In alcoholic fermentation, each mole of pyruvate is converted to one mole of carbon dioxide and one mole of ethanol. In the process, about (50 kcal/mol) (209 kJ/mol) of energy is produced. Under the most favorable conditions, more than half of this energy is stored as ATP.

(a) What happens to the remaining energy produced in alcoholic fermentation?

(b) Give two reasons why it would be nearly impossible to reverse the reaction that converts pyruvate to ethanol and carbon dioxide.

22.6 Energy Output in Complete Catabolism of Glucose

The total energy output from oxidation of glucose is the combined result of (a) glycolysis, (b) conversion of pyruvate to acetyl-CoA, (c) conversion of two acetyl groups to four molecules of CO_2 in the citric acid cycle, and, finally, (d) the passage of reduced coenzymes from each of these pathways through electron transport and the production of ATP by oxidative phosphorylation.

To determine the total number of ATP molecules generated from one glucose molecule, we first sum the net equations for each pathway that precedes oxidative phosphorylation. Since each glucose yields two pyruvate molecules and two acetyl-CoA

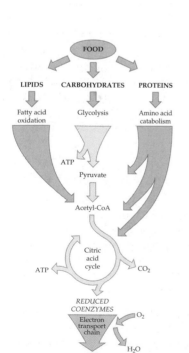

molecules, the net equations for pyruvate oxidation and the citric acid cycle are multiplied by 2:

Net result of catabolism of one glucose molecule

Glycolysis (Section 22.3)

Glucose + 2 NAD$^+$ +2 HOPO$_3^{2-}$ + 2 ADP $\longrightarrow$ 2 Pyruvate + 2 NADH + 2 ATP + 2 H$_2$O + 2 H$^+$

Pyruvate oxidation (Section 22.5)

2 Pyruvate + 2 NAD$^+$ + 2 HSCoA $\longrightarrow$ 2 Acetyl-CoA + 2 CO$_2$ + 2 NADH + 2 H$^+$

Citric acid cycle (Section 20.8)

2 Acetyl-CoA + 6 NAD$^+$ + 2 FAD + 2 ADP + 2 HOPO$_3^{2-}$ + 4 H$_2$O $\longrightarrow$

2 HSCoA + 6 NADH + 6 H$^+$ + 2 FADH$_2$ + 2 ATP + 4 CO$_2$

Glucose + 10 NAD$^+$ + 2 FAD + 2 H$_2$O + 4 ADP + 4 HOPO$_3^{2-}$ $\longrightarrow$

10 NADH + 10 H$^+$ + 2 FADH$_2$ + 4 ATP + 6 CO$_2$

The summation above shows a total of 4 ATP molecules produced per glucose molecule. The remainder of our ATP is generated via electron transport and oxidative phosphorylation. Thus, the total number of ATP molecules produced per glucose molecule is the 4 ATP molecules from glucose catabolism plus the number of ATP molecules produced for each reduced coenzyme that enters electron transport.

Based on an energy-yield assumption of 3 ATP molecules per NADH and 2 ATP molecules per FADH$_2$ (see Section 20.9, p. 643), the maximum yield for the complete catabolism of one molecule of glucose is 38 ATP molecules, as calculated below:

$$10\ \text{NADH}\left(\frac{3\ \text{ATP}}{\text{NADH}}\right) + 2\ \text{FADH}_2\left(\frac{2\ \text{ATP}}{\text{FADH}_2}\right) + 4\ \text{ATP} = 38\ \text{ATP}$$

Our ever-expanding understanding of biochemical pathways has led to a revision in the potential number of ATP molecules per reduced coenzyme. The 38 ATP molecules per glucose molecule is viewed as a maximum yield of ATP possible, most likely in bacteria and other prokaryotes. In humans and other mammals the yield is probably lower; the maximum is most likely 30–32 ATP molecules per glucose molecule.

PROBLEM 22.11

Name three ways humans have exploited the ability of microorganisms to ferment carbohydrates (see Chemistry in Action: Microbial Fermentations: Ancient and Modern, p. 703).

22.7 Regulation of Glucose Metabolism and Energy Production

Normal blood glucose concentration a few hours after a meal ranges roughly from 65 to 100 mg/dL. When departures from normal occur, we are in trouble (Figure 22.5). Low blood glucose (**hypoglycemia**) causes weakness, sweating, and rapid heartbeat, and in severe cases, low glucose in brain cells causes mental confusion, convulsions, coma, and eventually death. Glucose is the primary energy source for the brain; alternate fuels are not normally available for brain cells. At a blood glucose level of 30 mg/dL, consciousness is impaired or lost, and prolonged hypoglycemia can cause permanent dementia. High blood glucose (**hyperglycemia**) causes increased urine flow as the normal osmolarity balance of fluids within the kidney is disturbed. Prolonged hyperglycemia can cause low blood pressure, coma, and death.

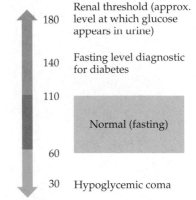

Glucose concentration (mg/dL)

Hyperglycemia

180 — Renal threshold (approx. level at which glucose appears in urine)

140 — Fasting level diagnostic for diabetes

110

Normal (fasting)

60

30 — Hypoglycemic coma

Hypoglycemia

▲ **Figure 22.5**
Blood glucose.
The ranges for low blood glucose (in green; hypoglycemia), normal blood glucose (in purple), and high blood glucose (in orange; hyperglycemia) are indicated.

Hypoglycemia Lower-than-normal blood glucose concentration.

Hyperglycemia Higher-than-normal blood glucose concentration.

Two hormones from the pancreas have the major responsibility for blood glucose regulation. The first, insulin, is released when blood glucose concentration rises (Figure 22.6). Its role is to decrease blood glucose concentrations by accelerating the uptake of glucose by cells, where it is used for energy production, and by stimulating synthesis of glycogen, proteins, and lipids.

Rising blood glucose concentration   *Falling blood glucose concentration*

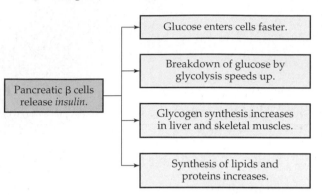

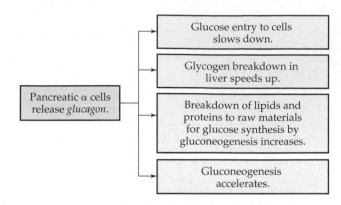

▲ **Figure 22.6**
Regulation of glucose concentration by insulin and glucagon from the pancreas.

The second hormone, glucagon, is released when blood glucose concentration drops. In a reversal of insulin's effects, glucagon stimulates the breakdown of glycogen in the liver and release of glucose. Proteins and lipids are also broken down so that amino acids from proteins and glycerol from lipids can be converted to glucose in the liver by the gluconeogenesis pathways (see Section 22.11). Epinephrine (the "fight-or-flight" hormone) also accelerates the breakdown of glycogen, but primarily in muscle tissue, where glucose is used to generate energy needed for quick action (discussed in Section 28.3).

22.8 Metabolism in Fasting and Starvation

Imagine that you are lost in the woods. You have had no carbohydrates and very little else to eat for hours, and you are exhausted. The glycogen stored in your liver and muscles will soon be used up, but your brain relies on glucose to keep functioning. What happens next? Fortunately, your body is not ready to give up yet. It has mechanisms to ensure that the limited glucose supplies will be delivered preferentially to your brain. In the liver, the gluconeogenesis pathway (Section 22.11) can make glucose from proteins. And if you are lost for a long time, there is a further backup system that extracts energy from compounds other than glucose.

The metabolic changes in the absence of food begin with a gradual decline in blood glucose concentration accompanied by an increased release of glucose from glycogen (Figure 22.7 and glycogenolysis, Section 22.10). All cells contain glycogen, but most is stored in liver cells (about 90 g in a 70 kg man) and muscle cells (about 350 g in a 70 kg man). Circulating free glucose and stored glycogen represent less than 1% of our energy reserves and are used up in 15–20 hours of normal activity (three hours in a marathon race).

Fats are our largest energy reserve, but adjusting to dependence on them for energy takes time because there is no direct pathway for generating glucose from the fatty acids in fats (as shown in Figure 22.2). Energy from fatty tissue must be generated by catabolism of fatty acids to acetyl-CoA, oxidation of acetyl-CoA via the citric acid cycle, and production of ATP energy from electron transport.

As glucose and glycogen reserves are exhausted, metabolism turns first to breakdown of proteins and glucose production from amino acids via gluconeogenesis in the liver. During the first few days of starvation, protein is used up at a rate as high

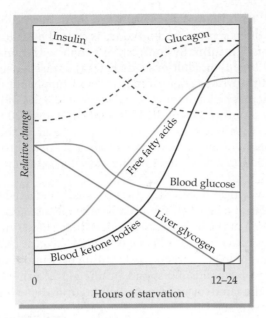

as 75 g/day. Meanwhile, lipid catabolism is mobilized, and acetyl-CoA molecules derived from breakdown of lipids accumulate. Eventually, the citric acid cycle is overloaded and cannot degrade acetyl-CoA as rapidly as it is produced. Acetyl-CoA therefore builds up inside cells and begins to be removed by a new series of metabolic reactions that transform it into a group of compounds known as *ketone bodies.*

Ketone bodies

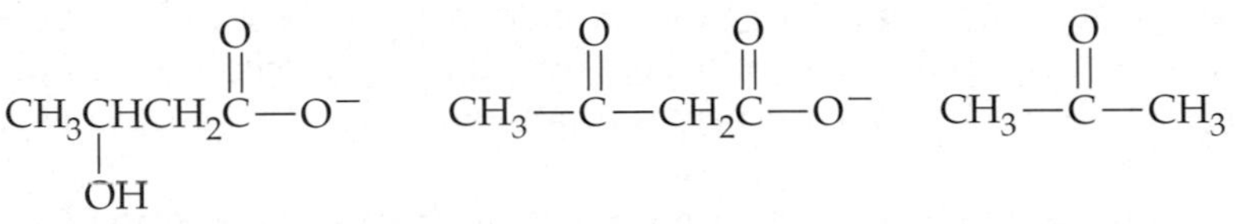

$$\underset{\text{3-Hydroxybutyrate}}{CH_3CHCH_2\overset{\displaystyle O}{\overset{\|}{C}}-O^-} \qquad \underset{\text{Acetoacetate}}{CH_3-\overset{\displaystyle O}{\overset{\|}{C}}-CH_2\overset{\displaystyle O}{\overset{\|}{C}}-O^-} \qquad \underset{\text{Acetone}}{CH_3-\overset{\displaystyle O}{\overset{\|}{C}}-CH_3}$$

These ketone bodies enter the bloodstream and, as starvation continues, the brain and other tissues are able to switch over to producing up to 50% of their ATP from catabolism of ketone bodies instead of glucose. By the fortieth day of starvation, metabolism has stabilized at the use of about 25 g of protein and 180 g of fat each day, a condition that conserves glucose and protein as much as possible. So long as adequate water is available, an average person can survive in this state for several months; those with more fat can survive longer.

LOOKING AHEAD ▶▶▶ The breakdown of triacylglycerols from fatty tissue produces not only ketone bodies but also glycerol, one of the compounds that can be converted to glucose by gluconeogenesis. The production of glycerol and ketone bodies from triacylglycerols is described in Chapter 24, which is devoted to lipid metabolism.

PROBLEM 22.12
Refer to Figure 22.7 and summarize the changes in liver glycogen and blood glucose during the starvation period represented in the figure.

22.9 Metabolism in Diabetes Mellitus

Diabetes mellitus is one of the most common metabolic diseases. It is not a single disease but is classified into two major types, insulin-dependent, or Type I, and non-insulin-dependent, or Type II, recently identified as a pre-diabetic condition called

Diabetes mellitus A chronic condition due to either insufficient insulin or failure of insulin to promote the passage of glucose across cell membranes.

metabolic syndrome. The insulin-dependent disease, also called Type I or juvenile-onset diabetes (because it often appears in childhood) is caused by failure of the pancreatic cells to produce enough insulin. By contrast, in people with non-insulin-dependent diabetes, also called Type II or adult-onset diabetes (because it usually occurs in individuals over about 40 years of age), insulin is in good supply but fails to promote the passage of glucose across cell membranes. An estimated 8.3% of the U.S. population has Type II diabetes. Another 35% of the U.S. population over 20 is estimated to have metabolic syndrome, with an estimated 50% of those over 65 in this pre-diabetic state. Although often thought of only as a disease of glucose metabolism, diabetes affects protein and fat metabolism as well, and in some ways the metabolic response resembles starvation.

The symptoms by which diabetes (Type I) is usually detected are excessive thirst accompanied by frequent urination, abnormally high glucose concentrations in urine and blood, and wasting of the body despite a good diet. These symptoms result when available glucose does not enter cells where it is needed. Glucose builds up in the blood, causing the symptoms of hyperglycemia and spilling over into the urine (glucosuria). In untreated diabetes, metabolism responds to the glucose shortage within cells by proceeding through the same stages as in starvation, from depletion of glycogen stores to breakdown of proteins and fats.

Type II diabetes is thought to result when cell membrane receptors fail to recognize insulin. This state is sometimes referred to as insulin resistance. Drugs that increase either insulin or insulin receptor levels are an effective treatment because more of the undamaged receptors are put to work. Treatment also includes diet modification and exercise.

Metabolic syndrome resembles a pre-diabetic state with slightly elevated fasting blood glucose levels and an impaired glucose response. Long-term population studies show that metabolic syndrome is a strong predictor for the development of Type II diabetes as the population ages, as well as coronary heart disease and stroke. Metabolic syndrome is characterized by abdominal obesity, elevated blood pressure and impaired glucose metabolism. Current treatment recommends lifestyle changes involving diet and exercise.

Type I diabetes is classified as an autoimmune disease, a condition in which the body misidentifies some part of itself as an invader (Section 29.4). Gradually, the immune system wrongly identifies pancreatic beta cells as foreign matter, develops antibodies to them, and destroys them. To treat Type I diabetes, the missing insulin must be supplied by injection. Commercially available human insulin is now produced by yeast modified by recombinant DNA techniques (Section 26.4) and was the first product of genetic engineering approved for use in humans.

Individuals with diabetes are subject to several serious conditions that result from elevated blood glucose levels. One reasonably well-understood outcome is blindness due to cataracts. Increased glucose levels within the eye increase the quantity of glucose converted to sorbitol (in which the $-$CHO group of glucose is converted to $-$CH$_2$OH). Because sorbitol is not transported out of the cell, as is glucose, its rising concentration increases the osmolarity of fluid in the eye, causing increased pressure and cataracts. Elevated sorbitol is also associated with blood vessel lesions and gangrene in the legs, conditions that can accompany long-term diabetes.

A person with Type I diabetes is at risk for two types of medical emergencies: ketoacidosis and hypoglycemia. Ketoacidosis results from the buildup of acidic ketones if blood sugar is high. This condition can lead to coma and diminished brain function but can also be reversed by timely insulin administration. Hypoglycemia, or "insulin shock," by contrast, may be due to an overdose of insulin or failure to eat. If untreated, diabetic hypoglycemia can cause nerve damage or death.

The arrival at the emergency room of a diabetic patient in a coma requires quick determination of whether the condition is due to ketoacidosis or excess insulin. One indication of ketoacidosis is the aroma of acetone on the breath. Another is rapid

CHEMISTRY IN ACTION

Diagnosis and Monitoring of Diabetes

Glucose measurements are essential in the diagnosis of diabetes mellitus and in the management of diabetic patients, both in a clinical setting and on a day-to-day basis by patients themselves. The glucose-tolerance test is among the clinical laboratory tests usually done to pin down a diagnosis of diabetes mellitus. The patient must fast for 10–16 hours, avoid a diet high in carbohydrates prior to the fast, and refrain from taking any of a long list of drugs that can interfere with the test.

First, a blood sample is drawn to determine the fasting glucose concentration. The average normal fasting glucose level is 65–100 mg/dL. Then, the patient drinks a solution containing 75 g of glucose, and additional blood samples are taken at regular intervals thereafter. The accompanying figure compares the changes in blood sugar levels in individuals who are either diabetic, prediabetic, or not diabetic. The diabetic patient has a higher fasting blood glucose level than the nondiabetic individual. In both, blood glucose concentration rises in the first hour. A difference becomes apparent after two hours, when the concentration in a normal individual has dropped to close to the fasting level but that in a diabetic individual remains high. The metabolic syndrome, pre-diabetic patient has an intermediate response; the fasting glucose level is greater than 100 mg/dL and the challenge response is intermediate between that of the diabetic and nondiabetic patient.

A fasting blood glucose concentration of 140 mg/dL or higher and/or a glucose tolerance test concentration that remains above 200 mg/dL beyond one hour are considered diagnostic criteria for diabetes. For a firm diagnosis, the glucose tolerance test is usually given more than once.

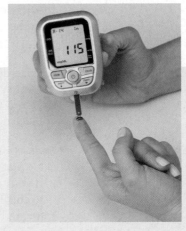

▲ **Glucose blood test. A tiny drop of blood is absorbed on the test strip in the blood glucose monitor. The results of the test are read in less than 10 seconds by most modern monitors and displayed on an LCD screen.**

Key Diagnostic Features of Diabetes Mellitus

- Classic symptoms such as frequent urination, excessive thirst, rapid weight loss (Type I only)
- Random blood glucose concentration (without fasting) greater than 200 mg/dL
- Fasting blood glucose greater than 140 mg/dL
- Sustained blood glucose concentration greater than 200 mg/dL after glucose challenge in glucose tolerance test

Individuals with diabetes must monitor their blood glucose levels at home daily, often several times a day. Most tests for glucose in urine or blood rely on detecting a color change that accompanies the oxidation of glucose. Because glucose and its oxidation product, gluconate, are colorless, the oxidation must be tied chemically to the color change of a suitable indicator. Modern methods for glucose detection rely on the action of an enzyme specific for glucose. The most commonly used enzyme is glucose oxidase, and the products of the oxidation are gluconate and hydrogen peroxide (H_2O_2). A second enzyme in the reaction mixture, a peroxidase, catalyzes the reaction of hydrogen peroxide with a dye that gives a detectable color change.

$$Glucose + O_2 \xrightarrow{\text{Glucose oxidase}} Gluconate + H_2O_2$$

$$H_2O_2 + \text{Reduced dye} \xrightarrow{\text{Peroxidase}} H_2O_2 + \text{Oxidized dye}$$
$$\text{(Colorless)} \qquad\qquad \text{(Colored)}$$

The glucose oxidase test is available for urine and blood. Many diabetic individuals monitor their glucose levels in blood rather than urine, using an instrument that reads the color change electronically and can store several weeks' data at a time. The enzymes needed for the reactions are embedded in the test strip itself and only a miniscule drop of blood is needed. The blood test is desirable because it is more specific and it detects rising glucose levels earlier than the urine test. It is used to achieve tighter control of blood glucose levels to help those with diabetes live longer, healthier lives.

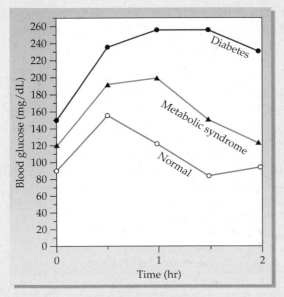

▲ **Blood glucose concentration in glucose tolerance test for normal and diabetic individuals.**

See Chemistry in Action Problems 22.75 through 22.78 at the end of the chapter.

respiration driven by the need to diminish acid concentration by eliminating carbon dioxide:

$$H^+ + HCO_3^- \longrightarrow H_2CO_3 \longrightarrow H_2O + CO_2 \text{ (Exhaled)}$$

An overdose of insulin does not cause rapid respiration.

Observations are backed up by bedside tests for glucose and ketones in blood and urine. A patient in insulin shock will, for example, have a very low blood glucose concentration.

PROBLEM 22.13

If your doctor suspects that you have diabetes, what tests would your doctor order to confirm the presence of diabetes? (See Chemistry in Action: Diagnosis and Monitoring Diabetes, p. 709.)

PROBLEM 22.14

Sorbitol is the alcohol that accumulates in the eye and can cause cataracts. Draw the open-chain structure of sorbitol, which is identical to that of D-glucose except that the aldehyde group has been reduced to an alcohol group. Can sorbitol form a five- or six-membered cyclic hemiacetal? Explain why or why not.

🔑 KEY CONCEPT PROBLEM 22.15

Ketoacidosis is relieved by rapid breathing, which converts bicarbonate ions and hydrogen ions in the blood to gaseous carbon dioxide and water, as shown in the equation above.

(a) Assuming that these reactions can go in either direction, how does a state of acidosis help to increase the generation of carbon dioxide?

(b) What principle describes the effect of added reactants and products on an equilibrium?

22.10 Glycogen Metabolism: Glycogenesis and Glycogenolysis

Glycogenesis The biochemical pathway for synthesis of glycogen, a branched polymer of glucose.

Glycogen, the storage form of glucose in animals, is a branched polymer of glucose. Glycogen synthesis, known as **glycogenesis**, occurs when glucose concentrations are high. It begins with glucose 6-phosphate and occurs via the three steps shown on the right in Figure 22.8.

Glucose 6-phosphate is first isomerized to glucose 1-phosphate by *phosphoglucomutase*. The glucose residue is then attached to uridine diphosphate (UDP) in a reaction catalyzed by *UDP-glucose pyrophosphorylase* and driven by the release of inorganic pyrophosphate. The pyrophosphate (diphosphate) is then hydrolyzed, yielding two hydrogen phosphate ions (see Worked Example 22.3).

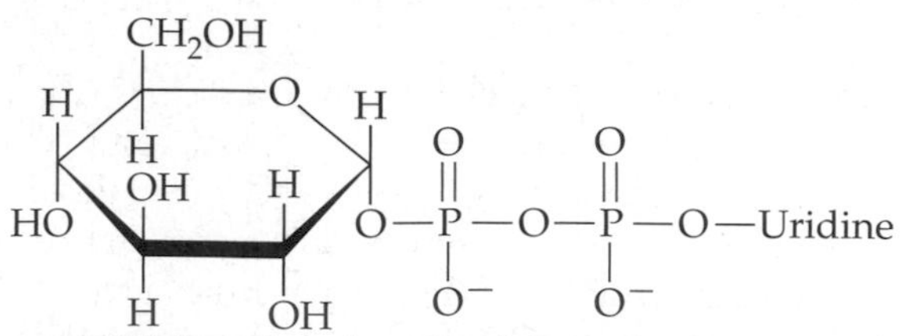

Glucose-UDP, the activated carrier of glucose in glycogen synthesis

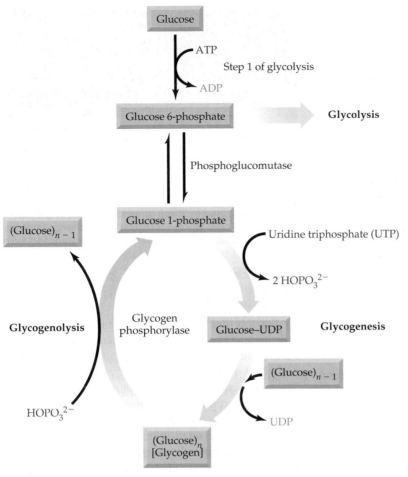

▲ **Figure 22.8**
Glycogenolysis and glycogenesis.
Reading from the top down shows the pathway for glycogen synthesis from glucose
(glycogenesis). Reading from the bottom up shows the pathway for release of glucose from
glycogen (glycogenolysis).

The resulting glucose-UDP transfers glucose to a growing glycogen chain in an
exergonic reaction catalyzed by *glycogen synthase.*

As is usually true in metabolism, synthesis and breakdown are not accomplished by exactly reverse pathways. **Glycogenolysis** occurs in the two steps on
the left in Figure 22.8. The first step is formation of glucose 1-phosphate by the
action of *glycogen phosphorylase* on a terminal glucose residue in glycogen. Glucose
1-phosphate is then converted to glucose 6-phosphate by *phosphoglucomutase* in
the reverse of the reaction by which it is formed. These reactions occur inside
liver and muscle cells and are different from the reactions involved in the hydrolysis of glycogen during the digestion of muscle that you have eaten, perhaps in a
hamburger.

In muscle cells, glycogenolysis occurs when there is an immediate need for energy.
The glucose 6-phosphate produced from glycogen breakdown never leaves the cell,
instead going directly into glycolysis to generate energy. In the liver, glycogenolysis
occurs when blood glucose is low (for example, during starvation; see Section 22.8).
Because glucose 6-phosphate cannot cross cell membranes, liver cells contain glucose
6-phosphatase, an enzyme that hydrolyzes glucose 6-phosphate to free glucose,
which can then be released into the bloodstream to raise blood sugar levels.

Glycogenolysis The biochemical pathway for breakdown of glycogen to free
glucose.

23.2 Fatty Acids and Their Esters

Naturally occurring fats and oils are triesters formed between glycerol and fatty acids. Fatty acids are long, unbranched hydrocarbon chains with a carboxylic acid group at one end. Most have even numbers of carbon atoms. Fatty acids may or may not contain carbon–carbon double bonds. Those without double bonds are known as **saturated fatty acids**; those containing some double bonds are known as **unsaturated fatty acids**. If double bonds are present in naturally occurring fats and oils, the double bonds are usually *cis* rather than *trans*.

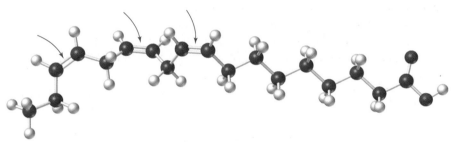

$$CH_3CH_2CH_2CH_2CH_2CH_2CH_2CH_2CH_2CH_2CH_2CH_2CH_2CH_2CH_2\overset{\displaystyle O}{\overset{\|}{C}}{-}OH$$

A saturated fatty acid
(palmitic acid)

$$CH_3CH_2CH{=}CHCH_2CH{=}CHCH_2CH{=}CHCH_2CH_2CH_2CH_2CH_2CH_2\overset{\displaystyle O}{\overset{\|}{C}}{-}OH$$

A cis unsaturated fatty acid
(linolenic acid)

Some of the common fatty acids are listed in Table 23.1. Chemists use a short-hand nomenclature for fatty acids that avoids using the common names. The notation uses C for carbon followed by the number of carbon atoms present in the fatty acid, a colon, and the number of unsaturated bonds present. Thus, lauric acid, which contains 12 carbon atoms and no double bonds, is represented by C12:0. Palmitic acid (C16:0) and stearic acid (C18:0) are the most common saturated acids; oleic (C18:1) and linoleic acids (C18:2) are the most common unsaturated ones. Oleic acid is *monounsaturated*, that is, it has only one carbon–carbon double bond. The **polyunsaturated fatty acids** have more than one carbon–carbon double bond.

Two of the polyunsaturated fatty acids, linoleic and linolenic, are essential in the human diet because the body does not synthesize them, even though they are needed for the synthesis of other lipids. Infants grow poorly and develop severe skin lesions if fed a diet lacking these acids. Adults usually have sufficient reserves in body fat to avoid such problems. A deficiency in adults can arise, however, after long-term intravenous feeding that contains inadequate essential fatty acids or among those surviving on limited and inadequate diets. Malnutrition in the developed world also results from many other causes; two common ones are unusual weight-loss diets and anorexia.

Waxes

The simplest fatty acid esters in nature are waxes. A **wax** is a mixture of fatty acid–long-chain alcohol esters. The acids usually have an even number of carbon atoms, generally from 16 to 36 carbons, whereas the alcohols have an even number of carbon atoms, ranging from 24 to 36 carbons. For example, a major component in beeswax

---

▶▶▶ Recall that an ester, RCOOR′, is formed from a carboxylic acid and an alcohol (Section 17.4).

▶▶▶ In the cis configuration, the groups attached to the double-bond carbons are on the same side of the double bond (Section 13.3).

Saturated fatty acid A long-chain carboxylic acid containing only carbon–carbon single bonds.

Unsaturated fatty acid A long-chain carboxylic acid containing one or more carbon–carbon double bonds.

Polyunsaturated fatty acid A long-chain carboxylic acid that has two or more carbon–carbon double bonds.

Wax A mixture of monoesters of long-chain carboxylic acids with long-chain alcohols.

TABLE 23.1 Structures of Some Common Fatty Acids

Name	Typical Source	Number of Carbons	Number of Double Bonds	Condensed Formula	Melting Point (°C)
Saturated					
Lauric	Coconut oil	12	0	$CH_3(CH_2)_{10}COOH$	44
Myristic	Butter fat	14	0	$CH_3(CH_2)_{12}COOH$	58
Palmitic	Most fats and oils	16	0	$CH_3(CH_2)_{14}COOH$	63
Stearic	Most fats and oils	18	0	$CH_3(CH_2)_{16}COOH$	70
Unsaturated					
Oleic	Olive oil	18	1	$CH_3(CH_2)_7CH{=}CH(CH_2)_7COOH(cis)$	4
Linoleic	Vegetable oils	18	2	$CH_3(CH_2)_4CH{=}CHCH_2CH{=}CH(CH_2)_7COOH(all\ cis)$	−5
Linolenic	Soybean and canola oils	18	3	$CH_3CH_2CH{=}CHCH_2CH{=}CHCH_2CH{=}CH(CH_2)_7COOH(all\ cis)$	−11
Arachidonic	Animal fat	20	4	$CH_3(CH_2)_4(CH{=}CHCH_2)_4CH_2CH_2COOH(all\ cis)$	−50

is the ester formed from a 30-carbon alcohol (triacontanol) and a 16-carbon acid (palmitic acid). The waxy protective coatings on most fruits, berries, leaves, and animal furs have similar structures. Aquatic birds have a water-repellent waxy coating on their feathers. When caught in an oil spill, the waxy coating dissolves in the oil and the birds lose their buoyancy.

Example of a wax

Long-chain alcohol	Long-chain acid

$$CH_3(CH_2)_{28}CH_2{-}O{-}\overset{\displaystyle O}{\overset{\displaystyle \|}{C}}(CH_2)_{14}CH_3$$

Triacontanyl hexadecanoate (from beeswax)

▲ This grebe is coated with oil spilled by a tanker that sank off Brittany on the northwest coast of France. If the oil is not removed from its feathers, the bird will perish.

Triacylglycerols

Animal fats and vegetable oils are the most plentiful lipids in nature. Although they appear different—animal fats like butter and lard are solid, whereas vegetable oils like corn, olive, soybean, and peanut oil are liquid—their structures are closely related. All fats and oils are composed of triesters of glycerol (1,2,3-propanetriol, also known as glycerine) with three fatty acids. They are named chemically as **triacylglycerols**, but are often called **triglycerides**.

Triacylglycerol (triglyceride)
A triester of glycerol with three fatty acids.

Triacylglycerols

CH_2OH	$R\overset{\displaystyle O}{\overset{\displaystyle \|}{C}}{-}OH$	$CH_2{-}O{-}\overset{\displaystyle O}{\overset{\displaystyle \|}{C}}{-}R$	
$CHOH$ +	$R'\overset{\displaystyle O}{\overset{\displaystyle \|}{C}}{-}OH$ →	$CH{-}O{-}\overset{\displaystyle O}{\overset{\displaystyle \|}{C}}{-}R'$	Glycerol
CH_2OH	$R''\overset{\displaystyle O}{\overset{\displaystyle \|}{C}}{-}OH$	$CH_2{-}O{-}\overset{\displaystyle O}{\overset{\displaystyle \|}{C}}{-}R''$	
Glycerol	Fatty acids		

Fatty acid

Fatty acid

Fatty acid

The three fatty acids of any specific triacylglycerol are not necessarily the same, as is the case in the molecule below.

Example of a triacylglycerol

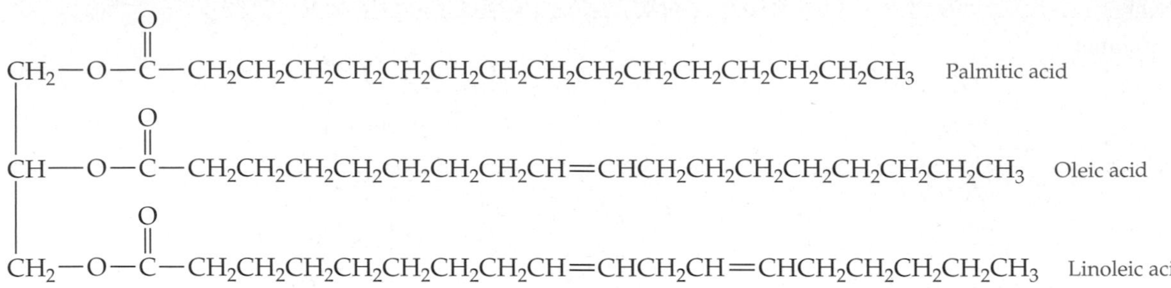

$$CH_2-O-\overset{\overset{\displaystyle O}{\|}}{C}-CH_2CH_2CH_2CH_2CH_2CH_2CH_2CH_2CH_2CH_2CH_2CH_2CH_2CH_3 \quad \text{Palmitic acid}$$

$$CH-O-\overset{\overset{\displaystyle O}{\|}}{C}-CH_2CH_2CH_2CH_2CH_2CH_2CH_2CH=CHCH_2CH_2CH_2CH_2CH_2CH_2CH_2CH_3 \quad \text{Oleic acid}$$

$$CH_2-O-\overset{\overset{\displaystyle O}{\|}}{C}-CH_2CH_2CH_2CH_2CH_2CH_2CH_2CH=CHCH_2CH=CHCH_2CH_2CH_2CH_3 \quad \text{Linoleic acid}$$

Furthermore, the fat or oil from a given natural source is a complex mixture of many different triacylglycerols. Table 23.2 lists the average composition of fats and oils from several different sources. Note particularly that vegetable oils consist almost entirely of unsaturated fatty acids, whereas animal fats contain a much larger percentage of saturated fatty acids. This difference in composition is the primary reason for the different melting points of fats and oils, as explained in the next section.

TABLE 23.2 Approximate Composition of Some Common Fats and Oils*

Source	Saturated Fatty Acids (%)				Unsaturated Fatty Acids (%)	
	C12:0 Lauric	C14:0 Myristic	C16:0 Palmitic	C18:0 Stearic	C18:1 Oleic	C18:2 Linoleic
Animal Fat						
Lard	—	1	25	15	50	6
Butter	2	10	25	10	25	5
Human fat	1	3	25	8	46	10
Whale blubber	—	8	12	3	35	10
Vegetable Oil						
Corn	—	1	8	4	46	42
Olive	—	1	5	5	83	7
Peanut	—	—	7	5	60	20
Soybean	—	—	7	4	34	53

Where totals are less than 100%, small quantities of several other acids are present, with cholesterol also present in animal fats.

PROBLEM 23.2

One of the constituents of the carnauba wax used in floor and furniture polish is an ester of a 32-carbon straight-chain alcohol with a C20:0 straight-chain carboxylic acid. Draw the structure of this ester. (Use subscripts to show the numbers of connected CH_2 groups.)

PROBLEM 23.3

Draw the structure of a triacylglycerol whose components are glycerol and three oleic acid acyl groups.

PROBLEM 23.4

Which one should you choose for a treat—a small dipped ice cream cone from kiosk A or two oatmeal cookies from kiosk B? Some of the nutrition facts for these choices are listed in the table below. To decide, consider which snack would best help you stay within the nutrition guidelines regarding daily intake of total fat and saturated fat in the diet. (See Chemistry in Action: Lipids in the Diet on page 728.)

Food	Total Calories	Total Fat (g)	Saturated Fat (g)	% Calories from Fat	Carbohydrates (g)	% Calories from Carbohydrates
Cone	340	17	9	45	42	49
2 Cookies	300	12	2	36	46	61

🔑 KEY CONCEPT PROBLEM 23.5

(a) Which animal fat has the largest percentage of saturated fatty acids?

(b) Which vegetable oil has the largest percentage of polyunsaturated fatty acids?

(c) Which fat or oil has the largest percentage of the essential fatty acid linoleic acid?

23.3 Properties of Fats and Oils

The melting points listed in Table 23.1 show that the more double bonds a fatty acid has, the lower its melting point. For example, the saturated 18-carbon acid (stearic) melts at 70 °C, the monounsaturated 18-carbon acid (oleic) melts at 4 °C, and the diunsaturated 18-carbon acid (linoleic) melts at −5 °C. The same trend also holds true for triacylglycerols: the more highly unsaturated the acyl groups in a triacylglycerol, the lower its melting point. The difference in melting points between fats and oils is a consequence of this difference. Vegetable **oils** are lower melting because oils generally have a higher proportion of unsaturated fatty acids than animal **fats**.

How do the double bonds make such a significant difference in the melting point? Compare the shapes of a saturated and an unsaturated fatty acid molecule:

Oil A mixture of triacylglycerols that is liquid because it contains a high proportion of unsaturated fatty acids.

Fat A mixture of triacylglycerols that is solid because it contains a high proportion of saturated fatty acids.

A saturated fat has only single C–C bonds and appears straight

Unsaturated fats bend due to cis double bonds

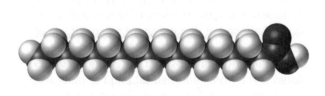

Stearic acid, an 18-carbon saturated fatty acid

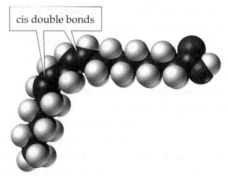

cis double bonds

Linoleic acid, an 18-carbon unsaturated fatty acid

The hydrocarbon chains in saturated acids are uniform in shape with identical angles at each carbon atom, and the chains are flexible, allowing them to nestle together. By contrast, the carbon chains in unsaturated acids have rigid kinks wherever they contain cis double bonds. The kinks make it difficult for such chains to fit next to each other in the orderly fashion necessary to form a solid. The more double bonds there are in a triacylglycerol, the harder it is for it to solidify. The shapes of the molecular models in Figure 23.2 further illustrate this concept.

Triacylglycerols are uncharged, nonpolar, hydrophobic molecules. When stored in fatty tissue they coalesce, and the interior of an adipocyte (fat cell) is occupied by one large fat droplet with the cell's nucleus pushed to one side. The primary function of triacylglycerols is long-term storage of energy for the organism. In addition, adipose tissue serves to provide thermal insulation and protective padding. Most fatty tissue is located under the skin or in the abdominal cavity, where it cushions the organs.

SOLUTION

Molecule (a) has 18 carbon atoms and two unsaturated bonds. Molecule (b) has 16 carbon atoms and one unsaturated bond. Although molecule (a) is slightly larger than molecule (b) and would be expected to have a higher melting point, molecule (a) has two double bonds, whereas molecule (b) has only one double bond. Since the degree of unsaturation is more important in these similarly sized molecules, molecule (b) has the higher melting point.

PROBLEM 23.7
Can there be any chiral carbon atoms in triacylglycerols? If so, which one(s) can be chiral and what determines their chirality?

🔑 KEY CONCEPT PROBLEM 23.8

What noncovalent interactions (covered in Section 8.2) hold lipid molecules together? Are these forces generally weak or strong? Why do lipids not mix readily with water?

23.4 Chemical Reactions of Triacylglycerols

Hydrogenation

The carbon–carbon double bonds in vegetable oils can be hydrogenated to yield saturated fats in the same way that any alkene can react with hydrogen to yield an alkane (see Section 13.6). Margarine and solid cooking fats (shortenings) are produced commercially by hydrogenation of vegetable oils to give a product chemically similar to that found in animal fats:

Partial structure of an unsaturated vegetable oil

$$-O-\overset{\overset{\displaystyle O}{\|}}{C}-CH_2CH_2CH_2CH_2CH_2CH_2CH_2CH=CHCH_2CH=CHCH_2CH_2CH_2CH_2CH_3$$

$$2\,H_2 \mid \text{Pd catalyst}$$

Partial structure of hydrogenated oil

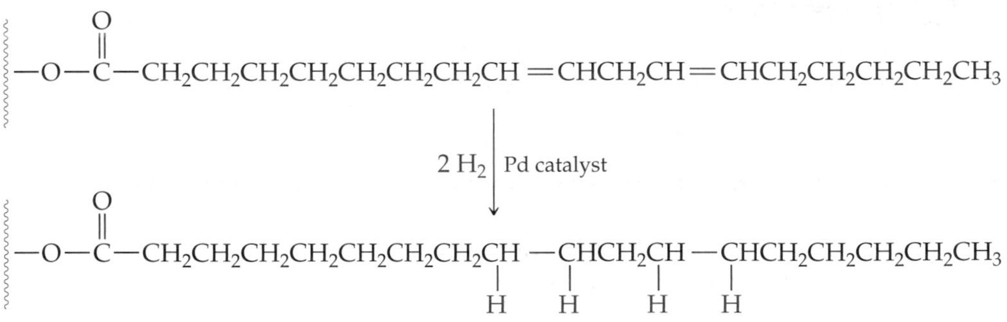

$$-O-\overset{\overset{\displaystyle O}{\|}}{C}-CH_2CH_2CH_2CH_2CH_2CH_2CH_2\underset{\overset{\displaystyle |}{H}}{C}H-\underset{\overset{\displaystyle |}{H}}{C}HCH_2\underset{\overset{\displaystyle |}{H}}{C}H-\underset{\overset{\displaystyle |}{H}}{C}HCH_2CH_2CH_2CH_2CH_3$$

The extent of hydrogenation varies with the number of double bonds in the unsaturated acids and their locations. In general, the number of double bonds is reduced in a stepwise fashion from three to two to one. By controlling the extent of hydrogenation and monitoring the composition of the product, it is possible to control consistency. In margarine, for example, only about two-thirds of the double bonds present in the starting vegetable oil are hydrogenated. The remaining double bonds, which vary in their locations, are left intact so that the margarine has exactly the right consistency to remain soft in the refrigerator and melt on warm toast. (See Chemistry in Action: Butter and Its Substitutes, p. 740.)

PROBLEM 23.9
Write an equation for the complete hydrogenation of triolein, the triacylglycerol with three oleic acid acyl groups for which you drew the structure in Problem 23.3. Name the fatty acid from which the resulting acyl groups are derived.

CHEMISTRY IN ACTION

Detergents

Strictly speaking, anything that washes away dirt is a *detergent*. The term is usually applied, however, to synthetic materials made from petroleum chemicals. In the 1950s, synthetic detergents began to replace natural soaps. The goal was to overcome the problems caused by soap used in hard water, which dissolved metal ions (mostly Ca^{2+} and Mg^{2+}). When the metal ions in solution encounter fatty acid anions, they form what we call soap scum—precipitates of salts (for example, $[CH_3(CH_2)_{14}COO^-]_2Ca^{2+}$). The results are that soap is wasted, residues are left in washed clothing, and the hard-to-remove scum is left behind in bathtubs and washing machines.

Like soaps, synthetic detergent molecules have hydrophobic hydrocarbon tails and hydrophilic heads, and they cleanse by the same mechanism as soap—forming micelles around greasy dirt. All substances that function in this manner are described as surface-active agents, or *surfactants*. The hydrophilic heads may be anionic, cationic, or nonionic. Anionic surfactants are commonly used in home laundry products; cationic surfactants are used in fabric softeners and in disinfectant soaps; and nonionic surfactants are low-sudsing and are effective at low temperatures.

Anionic detergents usually contain a sulfate group. These sulfate groups will interact with the metal cations in wash water, but because these sulfate salts are soluble, no soap scum precipitates. Other detergents are either cationic or neutral and consequently do not interact with dissolved metal cations.

Note that the hydrocarbon chains in the representative surfactants shown below are unbranched. Some of the first detergents contained branched-chain hydrocarbons, but this was soon discovered to be a mistake. The bacteria in natural waters and sewage treatment plants are slow to consume branched-chain hydrocarbons, so detergents containing them were not decomposed and produced suds in streams and lakes.

See Chemistry in Action Problems 23.86 and 23.87 at the end of the chapter.

$$Na^+ \ ^-O-\overset{\overset{O}{\|}}{\underset{\underset{O}{\|}}{S}}-\bigcirc-CH_2CH_2CH_2CH_2CH_2CH_2CH_2CH_2CH_2CH_2CH_2CH_3$$

Sodium dodecylbenzenesulfonate
(An ionic detergent)

$$CH_3(CH_2)_{10}CH_2OCH_2CH_2(OCH_2CH_2)_7OH$$

A polyether
(A nonionic detergent)

$$\bigcirc-CH_2-\overset{\overset{CH_3}{|}}{\underset{\underset{CH_3}{|}}{N^+}}-R \ Cl^-$$

A benzalkonium chloride; $R=C_8H_{17}$ to $C_{18}H_{37}$
(A cationic detergent)

Hydrolysis of Triacylglycerols; Soap

Triacylglycerols, like all esters, can be hydrolyzed—that is, they can react with water to form their carboxylic acids and alcohols. In the body, this hydrolysis is catalyzed by enzymes (hydrolases) and is the first reaction in the digestion of dietary fats and oils, as we will see in the next chapter (Section 24.1).

Soap-making is an ancient art involving the base-catalyzed hydrolysis of triacylglycerols. This process was probably discovered accidentally. Throughout the centuries, soap has been made both at home and in "factories" by much the same process; the principal variation was in the source of fat. Northern societies, like the English, used solid animal fats, but the most abundant fat in southern Italy was olive oil. Indeed, any mixture of triacylglycerols, whether from animal or plant sources, can be used. American colonials made soap at home, generally once a year when animal fat was abundant. The second ingredient needed was lye or a potash solution. This was obtained by soaking wood ashes in rainwater and slowly straining out the ashes. Saved and fresh fat was rendered and cleaned—freed from meat, skin, and any other material that was not fat. Then water, cleaned fat, and lye were mixed and boiled for several hours outdoors over an open fire. This dangerous process was complete when the soap foamed up well in the pot. After cooling, the soft soap was poured into storage barrels,

Soap The mixture of salts of fatty acids formed by saponification of animal fat.

to be dipped out for use. This process made soft soap because wood ashes contain KOH; potassium fatty acid salts dissolved readily in water and the soap retained some water. Hard soap was made by adding salt (NaCl) at the last step. Na^+ replaces K^+ in the fatty acid salt formed, and these salts are solids. The smooth soap that precipitated was then dried, perfumed, and pressed into bars for household use. When a new method of producing NaOH became available in the middle of the nineteenth century, factory soap production increased and home production became less important. Today's soaps contain less residual lye, more additives, and are kinder to our skin and clothes than the soap produced at home by the colonists. Although soap-making was a standard home process on the frontier and in small factories in towns, the chemistry was not understood until the twentieth century.

In the laboratory and in commercial production of soap, hydrolysis of fats and oils is usually carried out by strong aqueous bases (NaOH or KOH) and is called *saponification* (pronounced sae-**pon**-if-i-**ka**-tion, from the Latin *sapon*, soap [see Section 17.6]). The initial products of saponification of a fat or oil molecule are one molecule of glycerol and three molecules of fatty acid carboxylate salts:

▲ **Where are the lipids in this picture?**

Saponification

Strong aqueous base catalyzes fat hydrolysis

A fat or oil $\xrightarrow[\text{H}_2\text{O}]{\text{NaOH}}$ Glycerol + Fatty acid salts (soap)

How does soap do its job? Soaps work as cleaning agents because the two ends of a soap molecule are so different. The sodium salt end is ionic and therefore hydrophilic (water-loving); it tends to dissolve in water. The long hydrocarbon chain portion of the molecule, however, is nonpolar and therefore hydrophobic (water-fearing). Like an alkane, it tends to avoid water and to dissolve in nonpolar substances such as grease, fat, and oil. Because of these opposing tendencies, soap molecules are attracted to both grease and water.

When soap is dispersed in water, the big organic anions cluster together so that their long, hydrophobic hydrocarbon tails are in contact. By doing so, they avoid disrupting the strong hydrogen bond interactions of water and instead create a nonpolar microenvironment. At the same time, their hydrophilic ionic heads on the surface of the cluster stick out into the water. The resulting spherical clusters are called **micelles** (Figure 23.3). Grease and dirt become coated by the nonpolar tails of the soap molecules and trapped in the center of the micelles as they form. Once suspended within micelles, the grease and dirt can be rinsed away.

Micelle A spherical cluster formed by the aggregation of soap or detergent molecules so that their hydrophobic ends are in the center and their hydrophilic ends are on the surface.

PROBLEM 23.10
Detergents and soaps have similar properties and functions. Name one chemical similarity and one similar physical property. What advantage is there to using a detergent for cleaning, rather than soap?

PROBLEM 23.11
Write the complete equation for the hydrolysis of a triacylglycerol in which the fatty acids are two molecules of stearic acid and one of oleic acid (see Table 23.1).

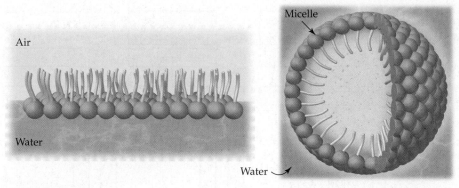

▲ **Figure 23.3**
Soap or detergent molecules in water.
The hydrophilic ionic ends remain in the water. At the surface of the water, a film forms with the hydrocarbon chains on the surface. Within the solution, the hydrocarbon chains cluster together at the centers of micelles. Greasy dirt is dissolved in the oily center and carried away. Lipids are transported in the bloodstream in similar micelles, as described in Section 24.2.

23.5 Phospholipids and Glycolipids

Cell membranes separate the aqueous interior of cells from the aqueous environment surrounding the cells. To accomplish this, the membranes establish a hydrophobic barrier between the two watery environments. Lipids are ideal for this function.

The three major kinds of cell membrane lipids in animals are phospholipids, glycolipids, and cholesterol. The **phospholipids** contain a phosphate ester link. They are built up from either glycerol (to give *glycerophospholipids*) or from the alcohol sphingosine (to give *sphingomyelins*).

Phospholipid A lipid that has an ester link between phosphoric acid and an alcohol (either glycerol or sphingosine).

$$\underset{\substack{\text{Glycerol 3-phosphate}\\ \text{(alcohol in glycerophospholipids)}}}{\overset{\overset{1}{HOCH_2}}{\underset{3}{\underset{|}{\overset{|}{HOCH}}}} \overset{2}{\underset{|}{\underset{CH_2O}{}}} \overset{O}{\underset{|}{\overset{||}{P}}} O^-}$$

Location of phosphate in sphingomyelins

$$\underset{\substack{\text{Sphingosine}\\ \text{(alcohol in sphingolipids)}}}{\overset{\overset{1}{CH_2OH}}{\underset{4}{\underset{|}{\overset{|}{CH_3(CH_2)_{12}CH}}}} \overset{2}{\underset{|}{\overset{|}{H_2NCH}}} \overset{3}{\underset{|}{\overset{|}{HOCH}}} CH}$$

The **glycolipids** are also derived from sphingosine, a diol with an amine group. Glycolipids do not contain a phosphate group, but have an attached carbohydrate that is a monosaccharide or a short chain of monosaccharides. The general structures of these lipids and the relationships of their classification are shown at the top in Figure 23.4. Note the overlapping classes of membrane lipids. **Glycolipids** and sphingomyelins both contain sphingosine and are therefore classified as **sphingolipids**, whereas glycerophospholipids and sphingomyelins both contain phosphate groups and are therefore classified as phospholipids.

Cholesterol is a sterol, a class of biomolecules that are characterized by a system of four fused rings. The presence of cholesterol in cell membranes is explored in Section 23.6. Sterols are discussed in the context of their other significant role as hormones in Chapter 28 (Section 28.5), and their connection to heart disease is discussed in Chemistry in Action: Lipids and Atherosclerosis, in Chapter 24 (p. 757). Cholesterol is modified in liver cells to produce bile acids, essential in the digestion of dietary fats.

Glycolipid A lipid with a fatty acid bonded to the $C2-NH_2$ group and a sugar bonded to the $C1-OH$ group of sphingosine.

Sphingolipid A lipid derived from the amino alcohol sphingosine.

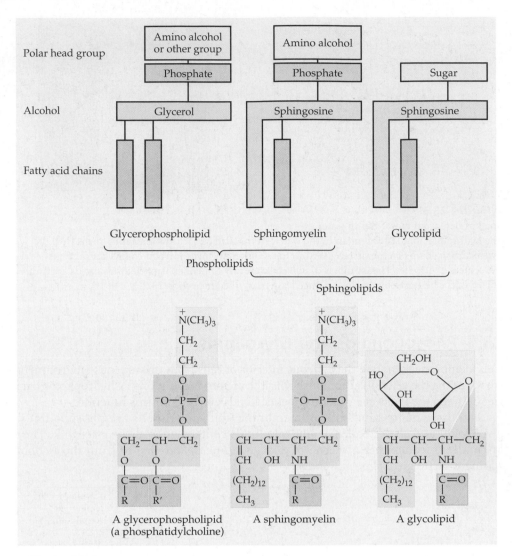

▲ **Figure 23.4**
Membrane lipids.
All have two hydrocarbon tails and polar, hydrophilic head groups. In the sphingolipids (sphingo-myelins and glycolipids), one of the two hydrocarbon tails is part of the alcohol sphingosine (blue).

▲ **Lecithin (phosphatidylcholine) is the emulsifying agent in most chocolates.**

Glycerophospholipid (phosphoglyceride) A lipid in which glycerol is linked by ester bonds to two fatty acids and one phosphate, which is in turn linked by another ester bond to an amino alcohol (or other alcohol).

Phospholipids

Because phospholipids have ionized phosphate groups at one end, they are similar to soap and detergent molecules in having ionic, hydrophilic heads and hydrophobic tails (see Figure 23.3). They differ, however, in having *two* tails instead of one.

Glycerophospholipids (also known as **phosphoglycerides**) are triesters of glycerol 3-phosphate and are the most abundant membrane lipids. Two of the ester bonds are with fatty acids, which provide the two hydrophobic tails (pink in the general glycero-phospholipid structure in Figure 23.4). The fatty acids may be any of the fatty acids normally present in fats or oils. The fatty acid acyl group ($R-C=O$) bonded to C1 of glycerol is usually saturated, whereas the fatty acyl group at C2 is usually unsatu-rated. At the third position in glycerophospholipids there is a phosphate ester group (orange in Figure 23.4). This phosphate has a second ester link to one of several dif-ferent OH-containing compounds, often ethanolamine, choline, or serine (green in Figure 23.4; see structures in Table 23.3).

TABLE 23.3 Some Glycerophospholipids

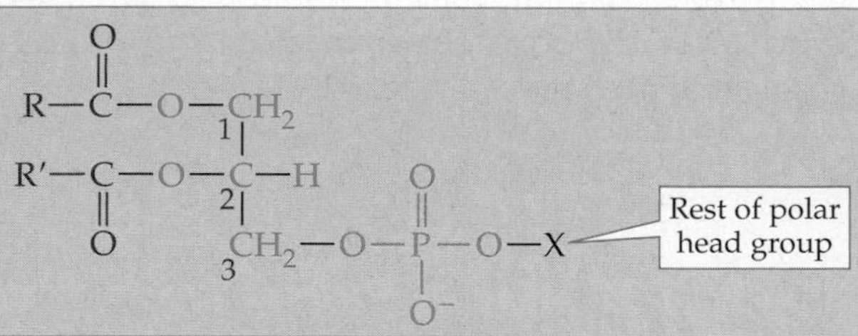

PRECURSOR OF X (HO–X)	FORMULA OF X	NAME OF RESULTING GLYCEROPHOSPHOLIPID FAMILY	FUNCTION
Water	$-H$	Phosphatidate	Basic structure of glycerophospholipids
Choline	$-CH_2CH_2\overset{+}{N}(CH_3)_3$	Phosphatidylcholine	Basic structure of lecithins; most abundant membrane phospholipids
Ethanolamine	$-CH_2CH_2\overset{+}{N}H_3$	Phosphatidylethanolamine	Membrane lipids
Serine	$-CH_2-\underset{\underset{COO^-}{}}{\overset{\overset{+}{N}H_3}{CH}}$	Phosphatidylserine	Present in most tissues; abundant in brain
myo-Inositol	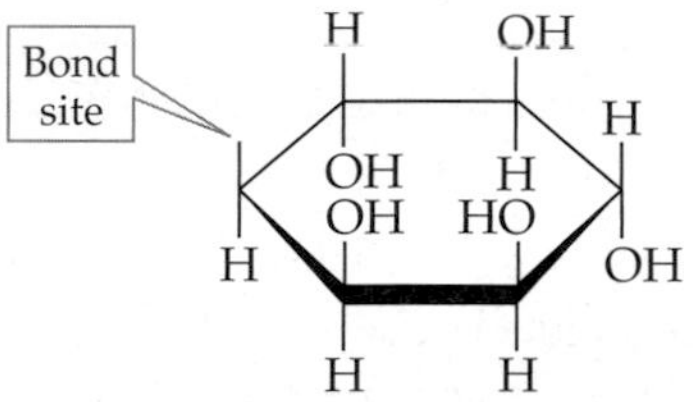 (ring structure, Bond site)	Phosphatidylinositol	Relays chemical signals across cell membranes

The glycerophospholipids are named as derivatives of phosphatidic acids. In the molecule below on the right, for example, the phosphate ester link to the right of the phosphorous atom is the amino alcohol choline, $HOCH_2CH_2N^+(CH_3)_3$. Lipids of this type are known as either *phosphatidylcholines*, or *lecithins*. (A substance referred to in the singular as either lecithin or phosphatidylserine, or any of the other classes of phospholipids, is usually a mixture of molecules with different R and R′ tails.) Examples of some other classes of glycerophospholipids are included in Table 23.3.

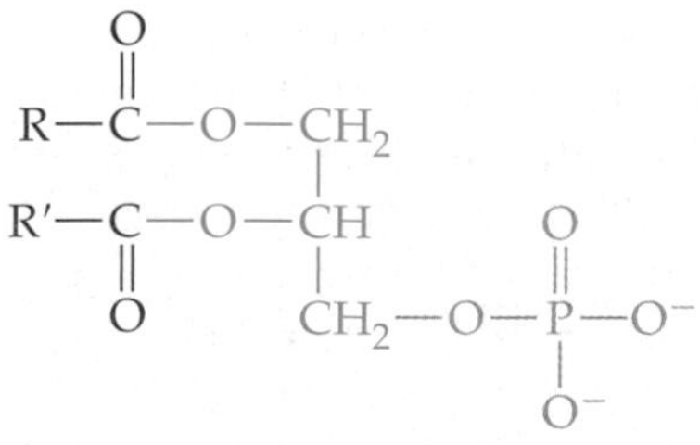

A phosphatidate

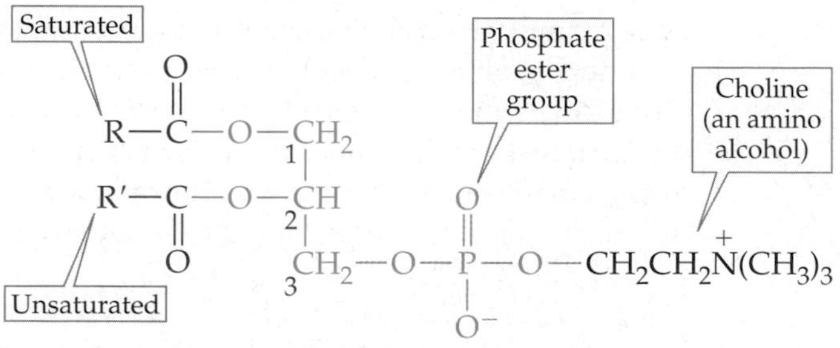

A phosphatidatidylcholine
(a glycerophospholipid that is a lecithin)

Because of their combination of hydrophobic tails and hydrophilic head groups, the glycerophospholipids are *emulsifying agents*—substances that surround droplets of nonpolar liquids and hold them in suspension in water (see the micelle diagram in Figure 23.3). You will find lecithin, usually obtained from soybean oil, listed as an ingredient in chocolate bars and other foods, where it is added to keep oils from separating out. It is the lecithin in egg yolk that emulsifies the oil droplets in mayonnaise.

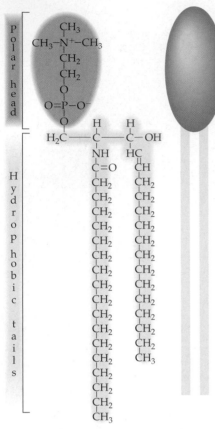

A sphingomyelin

▲ **Figure 23.5**
A sphingomyelin, showing its polar, hydrophilic head group and its two hydrophobic tails.
The drawing on the right is the representation of phospholipids used in picturing cell membranes. It shows the relative positions of the hydrophilic head and the hydrophobic tails.

A glycolipid

In sphingolipids, the amino alcohol sphingosine provides one of the two hydrophobic hydrocarbon tails (blue here and in Figure 23.4). The second hydrocarbon tail is from a fatty acid acyl group connected by an amide link to the —NH_2 group in sphingosine (red here; pink in Figure 23.4).

A sphingomyelin (a sphingolipid)

Sphingomyelins are sphingosine derivatives with a phosphate ester group at C1 of sphingosine. The sphingomyelins are major components of the coating around nerve fibers (the *myelin sheath*) and are present in large quantities in brain tissue. A diminished amount of sphingomyelins and phospholipids in brain myelin has been associated with multiple sclerosis. Whether this is a cause or a result of multiple sclerosis is unclear. The orientation of the hydrophilic and hydrophobic regions of a sphingomyelin is shown in Figure 23.5, together with a general representation of this and other types of cell membrane lipids used in drawing cell membranes.

PROBLEM 23.12
Lecithins are often used as food additives to provide emulsification. How do they accomplish this purpose?

PROBLEM 23.13
Identify the products formed by complete hydrolysis of all ester bonds in (a) the phosphatidylcholine on p. 735 and (b) the sphingomyelin in Figure 23.5.

Glycolipids

Glycolipids, like sphingomyelins, are derived from sphingosine. They differ in having a carbohydrate group at C1 (orange in the glycolipid in Figure 23.4) instead of a phosphate bonded to an amino alcohol.

Just like glycoproteins (see Section 22.8), glycolipids reside in cell membranes with their carbohydrate segments extending into the fluid surrounding the cells. In this location they function as receptors that, as you will see in Chapter 28, are essential for recognizing chemical messengers, other cells, pathogens, and drugs.

The glycolipid molecule is classified as a *cerebroside*. Cerebrosides, which contain a single monosaccharide, are particularly abundant in nerve cell membranes in the brain, where the monosaccharide is D-galactose. They are also found in other cell membranes, where the sugar unit is D-glucose.

A glycolipid
(A cerebroside)

Gangliosides are glycolipids in which the carbohydrate is a small polysaccharide (an oligosaccharide) rather than a monosaccharide. Over 60 different gangliosides are known. The oligosaccharides responsible for blood types are ganglioside molecules (see Chemistry in Action: Cell-Surface Carbohydrates and Blood Type in Chapter 21).

Tay-Sachs disease, a genetic disorder found mainly in persons of Eastern European descent, is the result of a deficiency in the enzyme β-hexosaminidase A, that causes a greatly elevated concentration of a particular ganglioside in the brain. An infant born with this defect suffers mental retardation and liver enlargement and usually dies by age three. Tay-Sachs is one of a group of sphingolipid storage diseases. Another well-known, fatal disease in this group is Niemann-Pick disease, in which sphingomyelin accumulates due to a deficiency in the enzyme sphingomyelinase. These metabolic diseases result from deficiencies in the supply of enzymes that break down sphingolipids.

Currently there is no known therapy for either Tay-Sachs disease or Niemann-Pick disease. The harmful consequences result from the *storage* of the excess sphingolipids. A more promising outcome may be available for those with Gaucher's disease, the most common lipid storage disease. In Gaucher's patients, fats accumulate in many organs (liver, lungs, and brain) due to a deficiency in the enzyme glucocerebrosidase. Enzyme replacement therapy allows many of these patients to avoid some of the non-neurological effects of Gaucher's disease, although the treatment is very expensive and must be given frequently.

Worked Example 23.3 Identifying Complex Lipid Components

A class of membrane lipids known as *plasmalogens* has the general structure shown here. Identify the component parts of this lipid and choose the terms that apply to it: phospholipid, glycerophospholipid, sphingolipid, glycolipid. Is it most similar to a phosphatidylethanolamine, a phosphatidylcholine, a cerebroside, or a ganglioside?

$$R-CH=CH-O-CH_2$$

$$R-\overset{\overset{\displaystyle O}{\|}}{C}-O-CH$$

$$CH_2-O-\overset{\overset{\displaystyle O}{\|}}{\underset{\underset{\displaystyle O^-}{|}}{P}}-O-CH_2CH_2\overset{+}{N}H_3$$

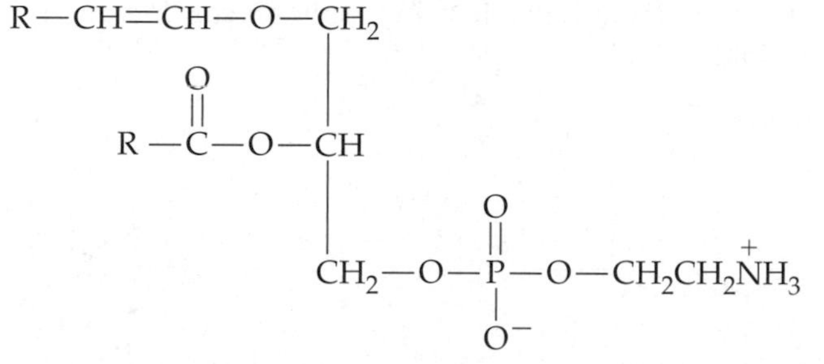

ANALYSIS Compare each part of the molecule with the basic components found in complex lipids and decide which lipid component the part resembles most. The molecule contains a phosphate group and thus is a phospholipid. The glycerol backbone of three carbon atoms bonded to three oxygen atoms is also present, so the compound is a glycerophospholipid, but one in which there is an ether linkage $(-CH_2-O-CH=CHR)$ in place of one of the ester linkages. The phosphate group is bonded to ethanolamine $(HOCH_2CH_2NH_2)$. This compound is not a sphingolipid or a glycolipid because it is not derived from sphingosine; for the same reason it is not a cerebroside or a ganglioside. Except for the ether group in place of an ester group, the compound has the same structure as a phosphatidylethanolamine.

SOLUTION
The terms that apply to this plasmalogen are *phospholipids* and *glycerophospholipid*. It has a structure nearly identical to phosphatidylethanolamine, so it is most similar to phosphatidylethanolamine.

PROBLEM 23.14
Draw the structure of the sphingomyelin that contains a myristic acid acyl group. Identify the hydrophilic-head group and the hydrophobic tails in this molecule.

PROBLEM 23.15
Draw the structure of the glycerophospholipid that contains a stearic acid acyl group, an oleic acid acyl group, and a phosphate bonded to ethanolamine.

PROBLEM 23.16
Which of the following terms apply to the compound shown below? (Hint: Look at the functional groups and the bonds involved to begin analyzing the compound part by part in comparison to the lipids discussed in this chapter.)

(a) A phospholipid   (b) A steroid

(c) A sphingolipid   (d) A glycerophospholipid

(e) A lipid   (f) A phosphate ester

(g) A ketone

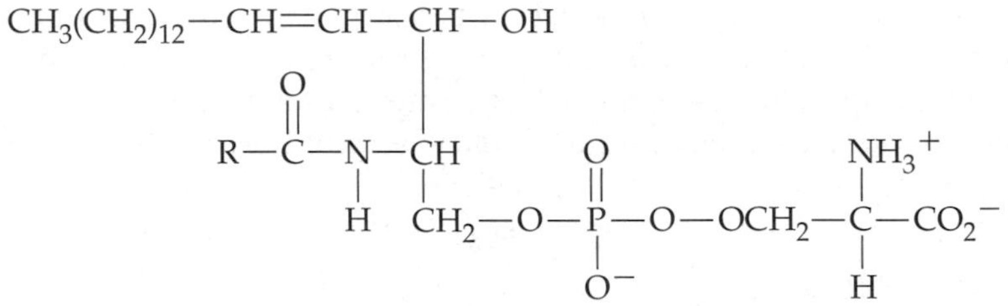

$$CH_3(CH_2)_{12}-CH{=}CH-CH-OH$$

$$R-\overset{\displaystyle O}{\overset{\|}{C}}-N-\underset{\displaystyle CH_2-O-\underset{\displaystyle O^-}{\overset{\displaystyle O}{\overset{\|}{P}}}-O-OCH_2-\underset{\displaystyle H}{\overset{\displaystyle NH_3^+}{C}}-CO_2^-}{\underset{\displaystyle H}{C}H}$$

23.6 Sterols

Sterol A lipid whose structure is based on a fused tetracyclic (four-ring) carbon skeleton.

All **sterols** have a common central structure composed of the four connected rings shown below. Because they are soluble in hydrophobic solvents and not in water, sterols are classified as lipids.

The steroid nucleus

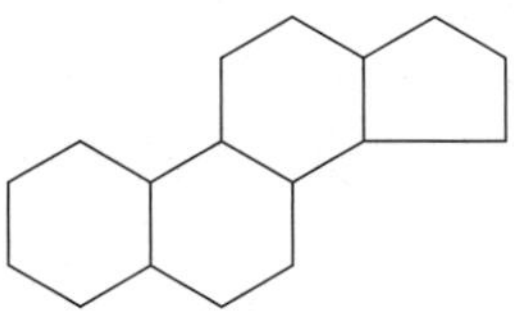

Sterols have many roles throughout both the plant and animal kingdoms. In human biochemistry, the main sterol is cholesterol, which is an important component of the cell membrane. The major functions of sterols other than cholesterol are as the bile acids that are essential for the digestion of fats and oils in the diet (Section 24.1) and as hormones.

Cholesterol

Cholesterol has the molecular structure and shape shown here:

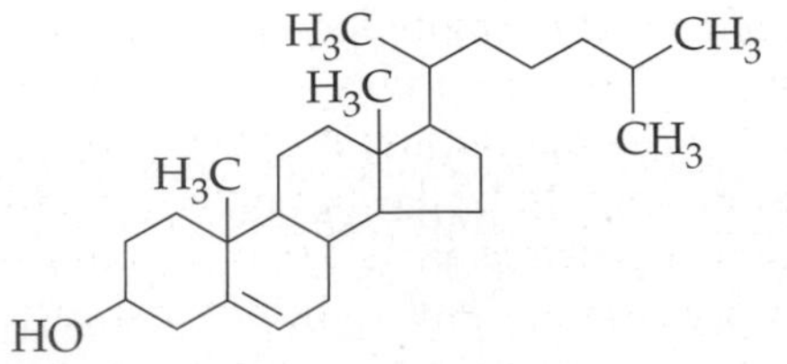

Cholesterol is the most abundant animal sterol. The body of a 60 kg person contains about 175 g of cholesterol, which serves two important functions: as a component of cell membranes and as the starting material for the synthesis of all other sterols. "Cholesterol" has become a household word because of its presence in the arterial plaque that contributes to heart disease (see Chemistry in Action: Lipids and Atherosclerosis, Chapter 24). Some cholesterol is obtained from the diet, but cholesterol is also synthesized in the liver. Even on a strict no-cholesterol diet, an adult's organs can manufacture approximately 800 mg of cholesterol per day.

The molecular model of cholesterol reveals the nearly flat shape of the molecule. Except for its —OH group, cholesterol is hydrophobic. Within a cell membrane, cholesterol molecules are distributed among the hydrophobic tails of the phospholipids. Because they are more rigid than the hydrophobic tails, the cholesterol molecules help to maintain the structural rigidity of the membrane. Approximately 25% of liver cell membrane lipid is cholesterol.

Bile Acids

Bile acids are essential for the emulsification of fats during digestion. Synthesized in liver cells from cholesterol and stored in the gall bladder until their release into the small intestine is stimulated by a meal, these molecules have a polar end and a nonpolar end. Solubility of bile acids is increased by conjugation with either taurine, a cysteine derivative, or glycine. This structural alteration increases solubility and enhances the formation of micelles of bile acids and fats in the digestive system, with the polar heads exposed to the aqueous medium of the small intestine and the nonpolar ends and fats on the interior of the micelle. Formation of micelles is essential for the digestion of dietary fat, as you will see in Chapter 24.

Note the acidic group added to cholesterol in each of the two most common bile acids, cholic acid and chenodeoxycholic acid. In the intestinal tract these acids are ionized to anions and referred to as *bile salts*.

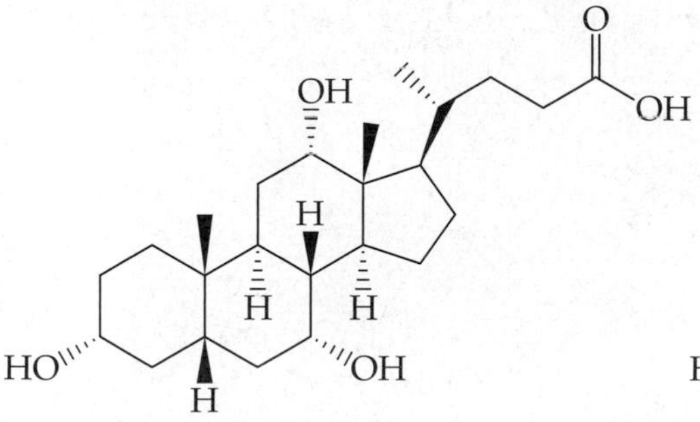

Cholic acid

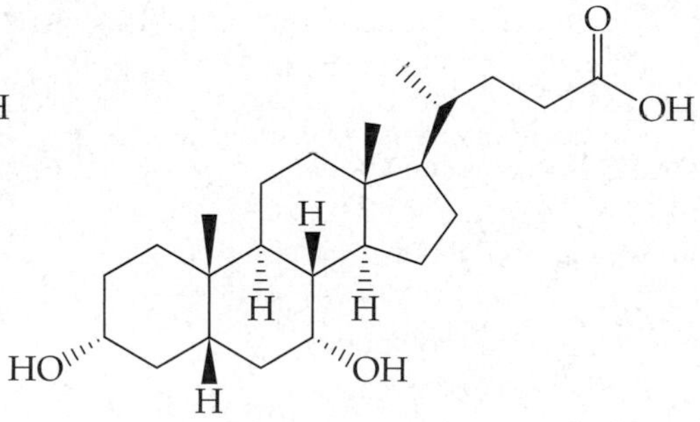

Chenodeoxycholic acid

Steroid Hormones

The steroid hormones are divided according to function into three types. *Mineralocorticoids*, such as *aldosterone*, regulate the delicate cellular fluid balance between Na^+ and K^+ ions (hence the "mineral" in their name). The second type, *glucocorticoids*, such as cortisol (also known as *hydrocortisone*) and its close relative cortisone, help to regulate glucose metabolism and inflammation. You have probably used an anti-inflammatory ointment containing hydrocortisone to reduce the swelling and itching of poison ivy or some other skin irritation. The third type of steroid hormones is the family of *sex hormones*. The two most important male sex hormones, or *androgens*, are *testosterone* and *androsterone*. They are responsible for the development of male secondary sex characteristics during puberty and for promoting tissue and muscle growth. *Estrone* and *estradiol*, the female hormones known as *estrogens*, are synthesized from testosterone, primarily in the ovaries but also to a small extent in the adrenal cortex. Estrogens govern development of female secondary sex characteristics and participate in regulation of the menstrual cycle. We will learn more about the signaling properties of the sex hormones in Chapter 28. The structures of testosterone and estrone are shown below. Note the steroid ring system common to these molecules.

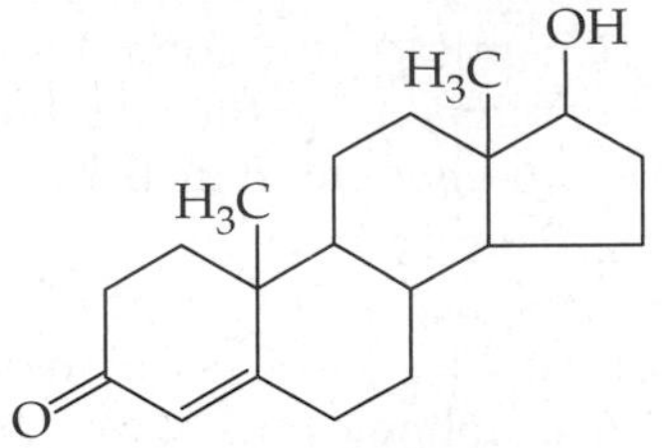

Testosterone
(an androgen)

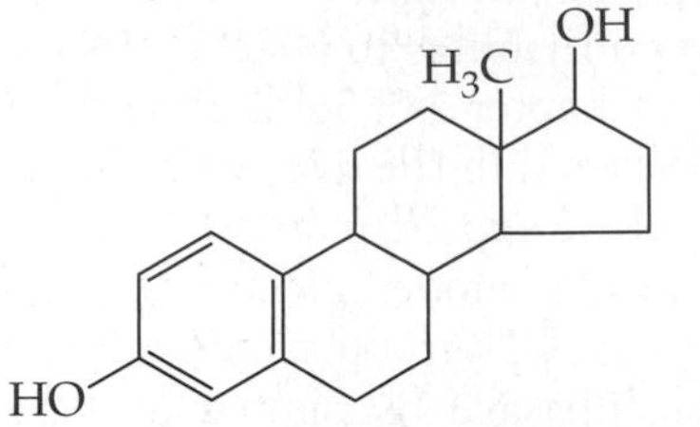

Estradiol
(an estrogen)

In addition to the several hundred known steroids isolated from plants and animals, a great many more have been synthesized in the laboratory in the search for new drugs. You will discover more about steroids as cellular signals in Chapter 28.

PROBLEM 23.17
Butter and an equally solid margarine both contain an abundance of saturated fatty acids (see Chemistry in Action: Butter and Its Substitutes). What lipid that has been identified as a health hazard is not present in margarine but is present in butter? Conversely, what other lipid that may cause health problems is present in large amounts in some margarines, but is present in small amounts in butter as a naturally occurring lipid?

CHEMISTRY IN ACTION

Butter and Its Substitutes

Sometimes the more scientific evidence we accumulate about the relationship between diet and health, the more difficult it is to choose what to eat. The choice between butter and margarine provides an excellent example.

It has become medically accepted that butter can contribute to elevated blood cholesterol, which is to be avoided because of cholesterol's role in heart disease. (We will have more to say about the cholesterol–heart disease connection in Chemistry in Action: Lipids and Atherosclerosis, Chapter 24.) In response to this information, many individuals switched from butter to margarine. Margarine, which is made from vegetable oils, contains no cholesterol and much less saturated fat than butter.

Gradually, however, information has accumulated that margarine contains what *might* be an even more unhealthy ingredient—*trans fatty acids*. Oils are catalytically hydrogenated to give them a firmer consistency and also to lessen their tendency to become rancid as oxidation breaks the double bonds. (see Section 13.6). During the partial hydrogenation, some of the cis double bonds are inevitably converted to trans double bonds.

Numerous studies have linked the quantity of trans fatty acids in a person's diet to a greater risk for heart disease and cancer. One such study, widely reported in 1997, came from following the diet and health of 80,000 nurses for 14 years. Those with higher quantities of hydrogenated oils in their diets had a

▲ **Is butter better?**

significantly higher risk of heart disease. One suggested explanation is that trans fats alter the metabolism of polyunsaturated fats, which are protective against heart disease.

Meat and dairy products contain a very small amount of trans fatty acids (about 0.2% in butter), but the quantities in foods containing hydrogenated oils are much higher—up to 40% in the stiffer margarines. If you choose to be serious about avoiding trans fats, much more is involved than choosing a softer margarine, however. By reading the lists of ingredients on food labels, you will discover that almost all commercial baked goods, cookies, and crackers, as well as many other packaged food products, contain partially hydrogenated oils. Food labels must now list the quantity of trans fats present per serving.

See Chemistry in Action Problems 23.88 and 23.89 at the end of the chapter.

23.7 Structure of Cell Membranes

Phospholipids provide the basic structure of cell membranes, where they aggregate in a closed, sheet-like, *double leaflet* structure—the **lipid bilayer** (Figure 23.6). The bilayer is formed by two parallel layers of lipids oriented so that the ionic head groups are exposed to the aqueous environments on either side of the bilayer. The nonpolar tails cluster together in the middle of the bilayer, where they interact and avoid water. Each half of the bilayer is termed a *leaflet*.

Lipid bilayer The basic structural unit of cell membranes; composed of two parallel sheets of membrane lipid molecules arranged tail to tail.

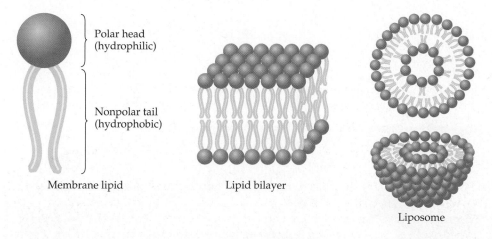

Polar head (hydrophilic)

Nonpolar tail (hydrophobic)

Membrane lipid

Lipid bilayer

Liposome

◀ **Figure 23.6**
Aggregation of membrane lipids.
The lipid bilayer provides the basic structure of a cell membrane.

The bilayer is a favorable arrangement for phospholipids—it is highly ordered and stable, but still flexible. When phospholipids are shaken vigorously with water, they spontaneously form **liposomes**—small spherical vesicles with a lipid bilayer surrounding an aqueous center, as shown in Figure 23.6. Water-soluble substances can be trapped in the center of liposomes, and lipid-soluble substances can be incorporated into the bilayer. Liposomes are potentially useful as carriers for drug delivery because they can fuse with cell membranes and empty their contents into the cell. One approved medical use of liposomes targets systemic fungal infections. Individuals with compromised immune systems due to AIDS are especially susceptible to this kind of infection. The liposomes carry amphotericin B, an antibiotic that attacks the fungal cell membrane. By delivering amphotericin to the fungal cells, the liposomal drug diminishes the serious side effects of attack by this antibiotic on kidney cells and cells in other healthy organs. Current medical research includes investigation of liposomes as delivery agents for other drugs.

Liposome A spherical structure in which a lipid bilayer surrounds a water droplet.

The overall structure of cell membranes is represented by the *fluid-mosaic model.* The membrane is described as *fluid* because it is not rigid and molecules can move around within it and as a *mosaic* because it contains many kinds of molecules. The components of the cell membrane are shown in Figure 23.7.

Glycolipids and cholesterol are present in cell membranes, and 20% or more of the weight of a membrane consists of protein molecules, many of them glycoproteins (p. 573). *Peripheral proteins* are associated with just one face of the bilayer (that is, with one leaflet) and are held within the membrane by noncovalent interactions with the hydrophobic lipid tails or the hydrophilic head groups. *Integral proteins* extend completely through the cell membrane and are anchored by hydrophobic regions that extend through the bilayer. In some cases, the hydrophobic amino acid chain may traverse the membrane many times before ending on the exterior of the membrane with a hydrophilic sugar group. The carbohydrate parts of glycoproteins and glycolipids mediate the interactions of the cell with outside agents. Some integral proteins form channels to allow specific molecules or ions to enter or leave the cell.

Because the bilayer membrane is fluid rather than rigid, it is not easily ruptured. The lipids in the bilayer simply flow back together to repair any small hole or puncture. The effect is similar to what is observed in cooking when a thin film of oil or melted butter floats on water in a cooking pot. The film can be punctured and broken, but it immediately flows together when left alone.

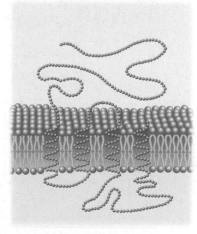

▲ **An example of an integral membrane protein.**
The green circles represent amino acids. Many membrane proteins pass in and out of the membrane numerous times.

EXTRACELLULAR FLUID

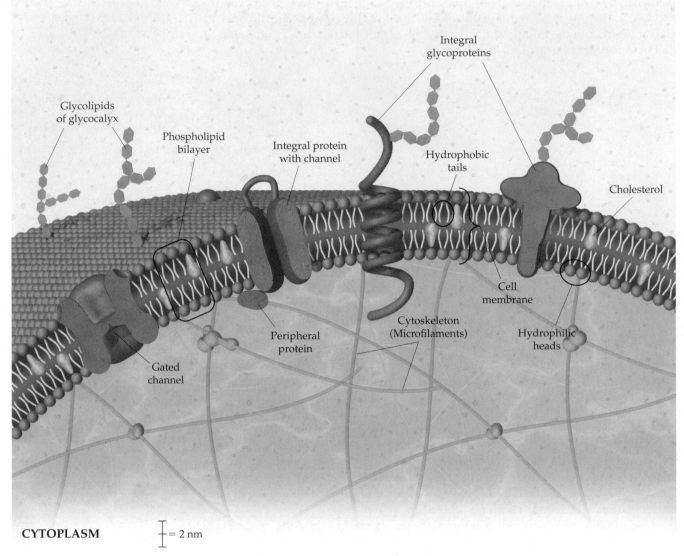

CYTOPLASM $\bar{\underline{}}$ = 2 nm

▲ **Figure 23.7**

The cell membrane.

Cholesterol forms part of the membrane, proteins are embedded in the lipid bilayer, and the carbo-hydrate chains of glycoproteins and glycolipids extend into the extracellular space, where they act as receptors. Integral proteins form channels to the outside of the cell and also participate in trans-porting large molecules across the membrane.

One consequence of membrane fluidity is the movement of proteins within the membrane. For example, low-density lipoprotein receptors, which are glycoproteins that interact with lipoproteins in the extracellular fluid (discussed in Section 24.2), move sideways within the membrane to form clusters of receptors on the cell surface. The glycoproteins move sideways in the membrane layers continuously, not unlike floating on a pond; this is an energetically neutral motion. However, phospholipids and other membrane components do not flip from the inside leaflet of the membrane to the outside leaflet, or vice versa. That is an energetically unfavored action because it would force polar and nonpolar interactions between membrane components.

Two other consequences of bilayer fluidity are that small *nonpolar* molecules can easily enter the cell through the membrane and that some individual lipid or protein molecules can diffuse rapidly from place to place within the membrane.

The fluidity of the membrane varies with the relative amounts of saturated and unsaturated fatty acids in the glycerophospholipids. Such variation is put to use in the adaptation of organisms to their environment. In reindeer, for example, the membranes of cells near the hooves contain a higher proportion of unsaturated fatty acid chains than in other cells. These chains do not pack tightly together. The result is a membrane that remains fluid while the animals stand in snow.

🔑 KEY CONCEPT PROBLEM 23.18

Integral membrane proteins are not water-soluble. Why? How must these proteins differ from globular proteins?

23.8 Transport Across Cell Membranes

The cell membrane must accommodate opposing needs in allowing the passage of molecules and ions into and out of a cell. On one hand, the membrane surrounding a living cell cannot be impermeable, because nutrients must enter and waste products must leave the cell. On the other hand, the membrane cannot be completely permeable, or substances would just move back and forth until their concentrations were equal on both sides—hardly what is required for the maintenance of a constant internal environment in the body, or *homeostasis* (see Chemistry in Action: Homeostasis, Chapter 28, p. 845).

The problem is solved by two modes of passage across the membrane (Figure 23.8). In **passive transport**, substances move across the membrane freely by diffusion from regions of higher concentration to regions of lower concentration. In **active transport**, substances can cross the membrane only when energy is supplied because they must go in the reverse direction—from lower to higher concentration regions.

Passive transport Movement of a substance across a cell membrane without the use of energy, from a region of higher concentration to a region of lower concentration.

Active transport Movement of substances across a cell membrane with the assistance of energy (for example, from ATP).

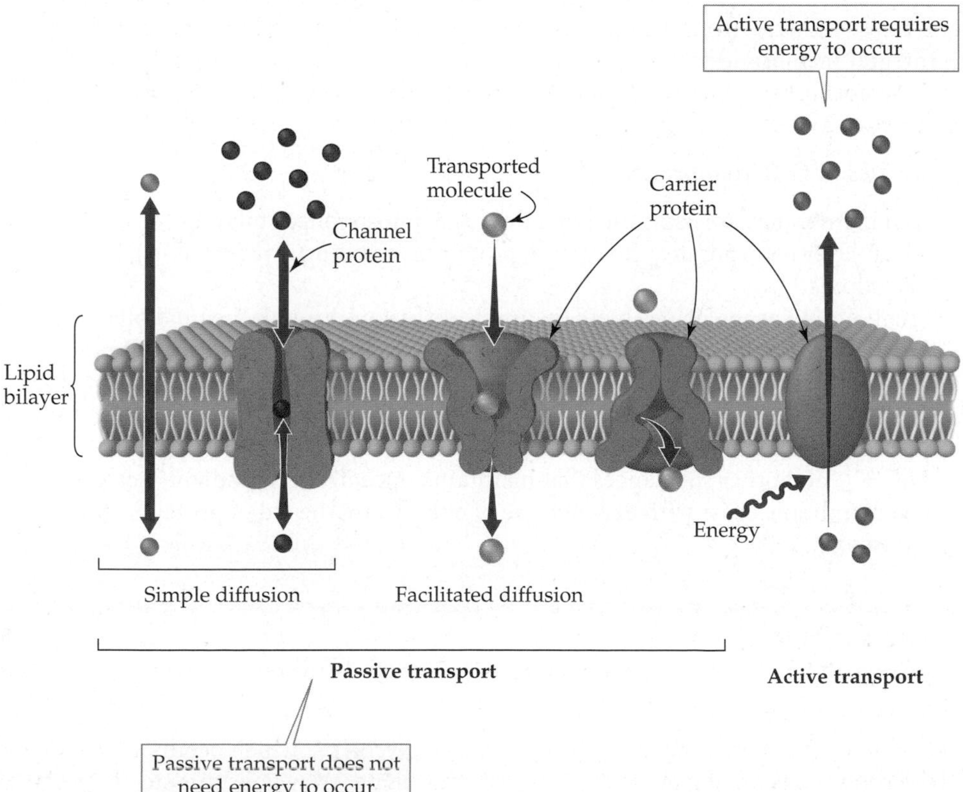

▲ **Figure 23.8**
Modes of transport across cell membranes.

Passive Transport by Simple Diffusion

Simple diffusion Passive transport by the random motion of diffusion through the cell membrane.

Some solutes enter and leave cells by **simple diffusion**—they simply wander by normal molecular motion into areas of lower concentration. Small, nonpolar molecules, such as CO_2 and O_2, and lipid-soluble substances, including steroid hormones, move through the hydrophobic lipid bilayer in this way. Hydrophilic substances similarly pass through the aqueous solutions inside channels formed by integral proteins. What can pass through the protein channels is limited by the size of the molecules relative to the size of the openings. The lipid bilayer is essentially impermeable to ions and larger polar molecules, which are not soluble in the nonpolar hydrocarbon region.

Passive Transport by Facilitated Diffusion

Facilitated diffusion Passive transport across a cell membrane with the assistance of a protein that changes shape.

Like simple diffusion, **facilitated diffusion** is passive transport and requires no energy input. The difference is that in facilitated diffusion solutes are helped across the membrane by proteins. The interaction is similar to that between enzymes and substrates. The molecule to be transported binds to a membrane protein, which changes shape so that the transported molecule is released on the other side of the membrane. Glucose is transported into many cells in this fashion.

Active Transport

Concentration gradient A difference in concentration within the same system.

It is essential to life that the concentrations of some solutes be different inside and outside cells. Such differences are contrary to the natural tendency of solutes to move about until the concentration equalizes. Therefore, maintaining **concentration gradients** (differences in concentration within the same system) requires the expenditure of energy. An important example of active transport is the continuous movement of sodium and potassium ions across cell membranes. Only by this means is it possible to maintain homeostasis, which requires low Na^+ concentrations within cells and higher Na^+ concentrations in extracellular fluids, with the opposite concentration ratio for K^+. Energy from the conversion of ATP to ADP is used to change the shape of an integral membrane protein (an ATPase referred to as the sodium/potassium pump), simultaneously bringing two K^+ ions into the cell and moving three Na^+ ions out of the cell (Figure 23.9).

Properties of Cell Membranes

- Cell membranes are composed of a fluid-like phospholipid bilayer.
- The bilayer incorporates cholesterol, proteins (including glycoproteins), and glycolipids.
- Small nonpolar molecules cross by simple diffusion through the lipid bilayer.
- Small ions and polar molecules diffuse across the membrane via protein pores (*simple diffusion*).
- Glucose and certain other substances (including amino acids) cross with the aid of proteins and without energy input (*facilitated diffusion*).
- Na^+, K^+, and other substances that maintain concentration gradients across the cell membrane cross with expenditure of energy and the aid of proteins (*active transport*).

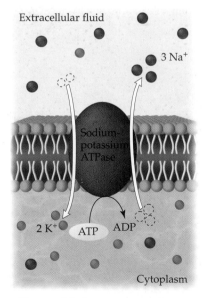

▲ **Figure 23.9**
An example of active transport.
A protein known as sodium–potassium ATPase uses energy from ATP to move Na^+ and K^+ ions across cell membranes against their concentration gradients.

PROBLEM 23.19
Does an NO molecule cross a lipid bilayer by simple diffusion? Explain.

PROBLEM 23.20
As noted earlier (Section 22.3), the first step in glycolysis, which occurs within cells, is phosphorylation of glucose to glucose 6-phosphate. Why does this step prevent passive diffusion of glucose back out of the cell?

🗝️ **KEY CONCEPT PROBLEM 23.21**

The compositions of the inner and outer surfaces of the lipid bilayer are different. Why do these differences exist and how might they be of use to a living cell?

23.9 Eicosanoids: Prostaglandins and Leukotrienes

The **eicosanoids** are a group of compounds derived from 20-carbon unsaturated fatty acids (*eicosanoic acids*) and synthesized throughout the body. They function as short-lived chemical messengers that act near their points of synthesis ("local hormones").

Eicosanoid A lipid derived from a 20-carbon unsaturated carboxylic acid.

The *prostaglandins* (named for their discovery in prostate cells) and the *leukotrienes* (named for their discovery in leukocytes) are two classes of eicosanoids that differ somewhat in their structure. The prostaglandins all contain a five-membered ring, which the leukotrienes lack.

Prostaglandins and leukotrienes are synthesized in the body from the 20-carbon unsaturated fatty acid arachidonic acid. Arachidonic acid, in turn, is synthesized from linolenic acid, helping to explain why linolenic is one of the two essential fatty acids. The relationships among arachidonic acid, the prostaglandins, and the leukotrienes are illustrated here; arachidonic acid and the leukotriene are drawn "bent" into a shape similar to the shape they take within the cell:

Arachidonic acid

Arachidonic acid (bent)

Multistep enzyme-catalyzed synthesis

PGE₁, a prostaglandin

Leukotriene D₄

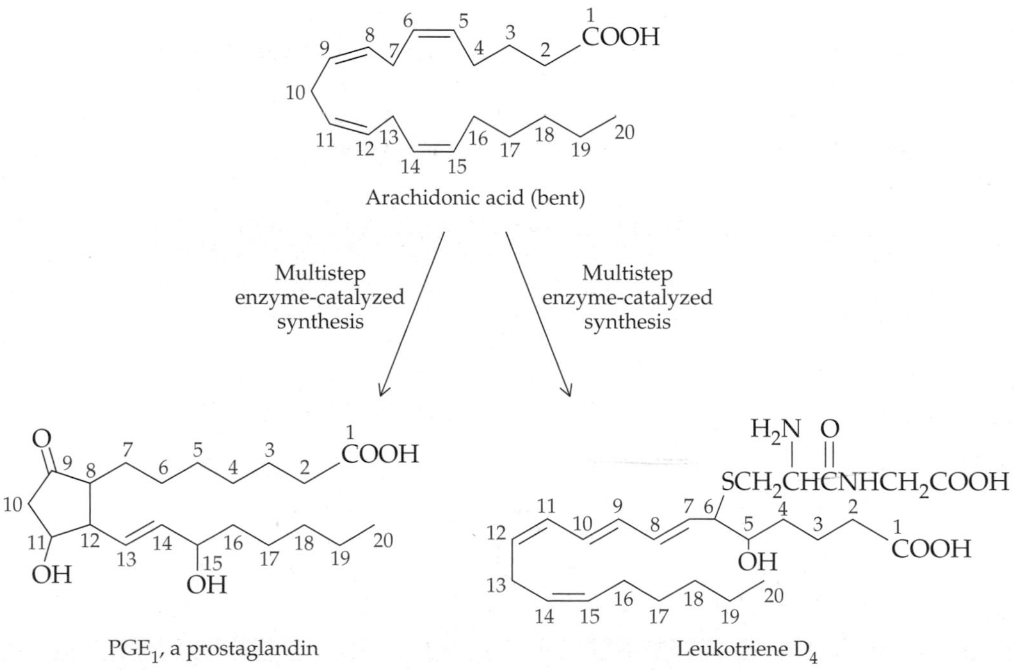

Research targets the myriad of potential therapeutic applications prostaglandins promise. The several dozen known prostaglandins have an extraordinary range of biological effects. They can lower blood pressure, influence platelet aggregation during blood clotting, stimulate uterine contractions, and lower the extent of gastric secretions. In addition, they are responsible for some of the pain and swelling that accompany inflammation. The first approved clinical uses of prostaglandins include stimulation of uterine contractions in therapeutic abortion (for example, of a dead fetus) and to halt persistent bleeding after delivery of a baby (postpartum bleeding).

In 1971, it was discovered that the anti-inflammatory and fever-reducing (*anti-pyretic*) action of aspirin results in part from its inhibition of prostaglandin synthesis. Aspirin transfers its acetyl group to a serine side chain in cyclooxygenase (COX), the enzyme that catalyzes the first step in conversion of arachidonic acid to prostaglandins, irreversibly inhibiting the enzyme. This inhibition is also thought to explain the effect of aspirin on combating heart attacks. Cyclooxygenase is present in two forms in cells, referred to as COX-1 and COX-2. Drugs have been designed to inhibit either one or the other of these enzymes. Of great interest are drugs that block the activity of COX-2, the enzyme responsible for prostaglandins that are involved in inflammation and pain responses in diseases such as arthritis. Celebrex™ and Vioxx™, two drugs introduced in the 1990s, both inhibit COX-2. Unfortunately, Vioxx™ is no longer available because of unexpected potentially lethal side effects, and Celebrex™ is prescribed with a strong warning of side effects on the label. While basic research seeking alternative COX-2 inhibitors continues, current medical practice prescribes these drugs sparingly and depends on older, better-understood analgesics such as aspirin and acetaminophen to lessen pain and fever.

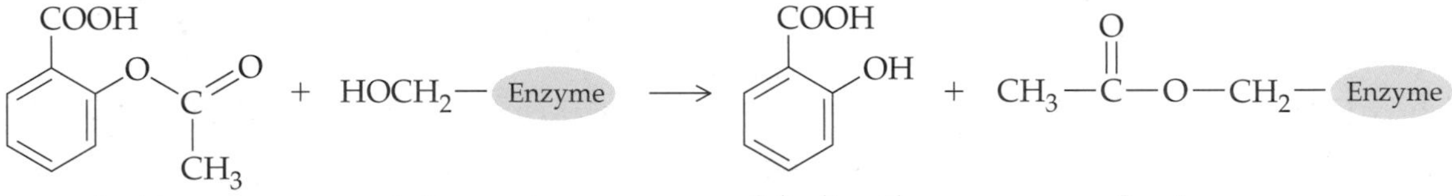

Aspirin (Acetylsalicylic acid) + Active enzyme (cyclooxygenase) → Salicylic acid + Inactive enzyme

There is also great interest in the leukotrienes. Leukotriene release has been found to trigger the asthmatic response, severe allergic reactions, and inflammation. Asthma treatment with drugs that inhibit leukotriene synthesis is being studied, although the available drugs are not yet as effective as the standard steroid treatments.

🔑 KEY CONCEPT PROBLEM 23.22

In the eicosanoid shown here, identify all the functional groups. Which groups are capable of hydrogen bonding? Which are most acidic? Is this molecule primarily nonpolar, polar, or something in between?

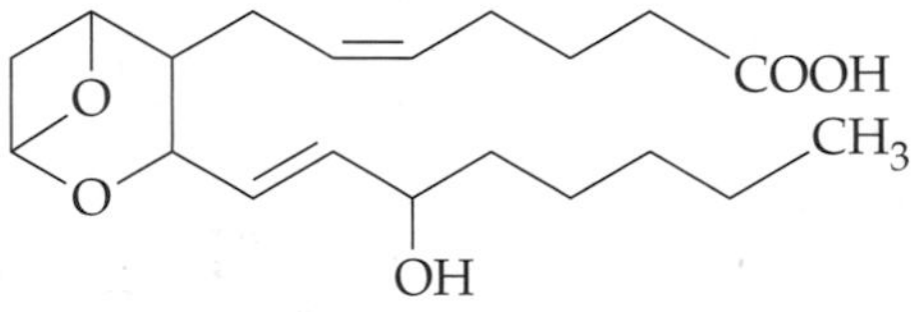

SUMMARY: REVISITING THE CHAPTER GOALS

1. What are the major classes of fatty acids and lipids? *Fatty acids* are carboxylic acids with long, straight (unbranched) hydrocarbon chains; they may be saturated or unsaturated. *Waxes* are esters of fatty acids and alcohols with long, straight hydrocarbon chains. *Fats* and *oils* are *triacylglycerols*—triesters of glycerol with fatty acids. In fats, the fatty acid chains are mostly saturated; in oils, the proportions of unsaturated fatty acid chains vary. Fats are solid because the saturated hydrocarbon chains pack together neatly; oils are liquids because the kinks at the cis double bonds prevent such packing (see *Problems 1–7, 17, 28–47, 84–89, 94, and 97*).

2. What reactions do triacylglycerols undergo? The principal reactions of triacylglycerols are catalytic *hydrogenation* and *hydrolysis*. Hydrogen adds to the double bonds of unsaturated hydrocarbon chains in oils, thereby thickening the consistency of the oils and raising their melting points. Treatment of a fat or oil with a strong base such as NaOH hydrolyzes the triacylglycerols to give glycerol and salts of fatty acids. Such *saponification* reactions produce soap, a mixture of fatty acid salts (see *Problems 9–10,12, 23, 24. 48–53, 90–93, and 103*).

3. What are sterols? The unifying feature of sterols is a fused four-ring system. Sterols include cholesterol, an important participant in membrane structure. Bile acids and salts, necessary for the emulsification of fats during digestion, are synthesized from cholesterol. The third major group of sterols includes steroid hormones, including the sex hormones, which function as signaling molecules (see *Problems 54–57, 95, 96, and 104*).

4. What are the membrane lipids? The membrane lipids include *phospholipids* and *glycolipids* (which have hydrophilic, polar head groups and two hydrophobic tails) and cholesterol (a steroid). *Phospholipids*, which are either *glycerophospholipids* (derived from glycerol) or *sphingomyelins* (derived from the amino alcohol sphingosine), have charged phosphate diester groups in their hydrophilic heads. *Sphingolipids*, which are either sphingomyelins or *glycolipids*, are sphingosine derivatives. The glycolipids have carbohydrate head groups (see *Problems 12–16, 25, 27, 58–63, 68–71, and 98–100*).

5. What is the nature of a cell membrane? The basic structure of cell membranes is a *bilayer of lipids*, with their hydrophilic heads in the aqueous environment outside and inside the cells, and their hydrophobic tails clustered together in the center of

the bilayer. *Cholesterol* molecules fit between the hydrophobic tails and help maintain membrane structure and rigidity. The membrane also contains *glycoproteins* and *glycolipids* (with their carbohydrate segments at the cell surface, where they serve as receptors), as well as *proteins*. Some of the proteins extend through the membrane (*integral proteins*), and others are only partially embedded at one surface (*peripheral proteins*) (see *Problems 8, 18, 21, 26, and 64–67*).

6. How do substances cross cell membranes? Small, nonpolar molecules and lipid-soluble substances can cross the lipid bilayer by simply diffusing through it. Ions and hydrophilic substances can move through aqueous fluid-filled channels in membrane proteins. Some substances cross the membrane by binding to an integral protein, which then releases them inside the cell. These modes of crossing are all *passive transport*—they do not require energy because the substances move from regions of higher concentration to regions of lower concentration. Passive transport takes the form of *simple diffusion*, crossing the membrane by passing through it unimpeded, or *facilitated diffusion*, crossing the membrane with the aid of a protein embedded in the membrane. *Active transport*, which requires energy and is carried out by certain integral membrane proteins, moves substances against their *concentration gradients* (see *Problems 19, 20, and 72–75*).

7. What are eicosanoids? The *eicosanoids* are a group of compounds derived from 20-carbon unsaturated fatty acids. They are *local hormones*—that is, they act near their point of origin and are short-lived. *Prostaglandins*, which contain a five-membered ring, have a wide range of actions (such as stimulating uterine contractions and causing inflammation). *Leukotrienes*, which do not contain a five-membered ring, trigger the asthmatic response, severe allergic reactions, and inflammation (see *Problems 22, 76–83, 101, and 102*).

KEY WORDS

Active transport, *p. 743*

Concentration gradient, *p. 744*

Degree of unsaturation, *p. 729*

Eicosanoid, *p. 745*

Facilitated diffusion, *p. 744*

Fat, *p. 727*

Fatty acid, *p. 722*

Glycerophospholipid (phosphoglyceride), *p. 734*

Glycolipid, *p. 733*

Lipid, *p. 721*

Lipid bilayer, *p. 741*

Liposome, *p. 741*

Micelle, *p. 732*

Oil, *p. 727*

Passive transport, *p. 743*

Phospholipid, *p. 733*

Polyunsaturated fatty acid, *p. 724*

Saturated fatty acid, *p. 724*

Simple diffusion, *p. 744*

Soap, *p. 731*

Sphingolipid, *p. 733*

Sterol, *p. 738*

Triacylglycerol (triglyceride), *p. 725*

Unsaturated fatty acid, *p. 724*

Wax, *p. 724*

UNDERSTANDING KEY CONCEPTS

23.23 The fatty acid composition of three triacylglycerols (A, B, and C) is reported below. Predict which one has the highest melting point. Which one do you expect to be liquid (oil) at room temperature? Explain.

	Palmitic Acid	Stearic Acid	Oleic Acid	Linoleic Acid
A	21.4%	27.8%	35.6%	11.9%
B	12.2%	16.7%	48.2%	22.6%
C	11.2%	8.3%	28.2%	48.6%

23.24 Complete hydrogenation of triacylglycerol C in Problem 23.23 yields a triacylglycerol of what fatty acid composition? Would the hydrogenation product of triacylglycerol C be more like the hydrogenation product of triacylglycerol A or B? Explain.

23.25 A membrane lipid was isolated and completely hydrolyzed. The following products were detected: ethanolamine, phosphate, glycerol, palmitic acid, and oleic acid. Propose a structure for this membrane lipid, and name the family (Table 23.3) to which it belongs.

23.26 According to the fluid-mosaic model (Figure 23.7), the cell membrane is held together mostly by hydrophobic interactions. Considering the forces applied, why does the cell membrane not rupture as you move, press against objects, etc.?

23.27 Dipalmitoyl phosphatidylcholine (DPPC) is a surfactant on the surface of the alveoli in the lungs. What is the nature of its fatty acid groups? In what arrangement is it likely to exist at the lung surfaces?

ADDITIONAL PROBLEMS

WAXES, FATS, AND OILS

23.28 What makes a molecule a lipid?

23.29 Name two classes of lipids found in your body.

23.30 Draw an 18-carbon saturated fatty acid. Is this a "straight chain" molecule or a "bent" molecule?

23.31 Draw an 18-carbon unsaturated fatty acid that contains two carbon–carbon double bonds, one on carbon 6 and one on carbon 9 (count starting with the carboxyl carbon). Is this a "straight chain" molecule or a "bent" molecule?

23.32 Differentiate between saturated, monounsaturated, and polyunsaturated fatty acids.

23.33 Are the carbon–carbon double bonds in naturally occurring fatty acids primarily cis or trans?

23.34 What is an essential fatty acid?

23.35 Name two essential fatty acids. What are good sources of these fatty acids?

23.36 Which of these fatty acids has the lower melting point? Explain why.

(a) linoleic acid

(b) stearic acid

23.37 Which of these fatty acids has the higher melting point? Explain why.

(a) linolenic acid

(b) stearic acid

23.38 What are the chemical and physical differences between fats and oils?

23.39 List typical food sources for oils and fats. Are there similarities or differences in the sources for each?

23.40 Draw the structure of glyceryl trilaurate, which is made from glycerol and three lauric acid molecules.

23.41 There are two isomeric triacylglycerol molecules whose components are glycerol, one palmitic acid unit, and two stearic acid units. Draw the structures of both, and explain how they differ.

23.42 What function does a wax serve in a plant or animal?

23.43 What functions do fats serve in an animal?

23.44 *Spermaceti*, a fragrant substance isolated from sperm whales, was commonly used in cosmetics until it was banned in 1976 to protect the whales from extinction. Chemically, spermaceti is cetyl palmitate, the ester of palmitic acid with cetyl alcohol (the straight-chain 16-carbon alcohol). Draw the structure of spermaceti.

23.45 What kind of lipid is spermaceti—a fat, a wax, or a sterol?

23.46 A major ingredient in peanut butter cup candy is soy lecithin. Draw the structure of lecithin.

23.47 Which kind of lipid is lecithin?

CHEMICAL REACTIONS OF LIPIDS

23.48 What is the name of the reaction that converts unsaturated fatty acids to saturated fatty acids?

23.49 When a vegetable oil is converted to a soft margarine, a non-natural product is synthesized. What is this product?

23.50 Is the reaction shown here esterification, hydrogenation, hydrolysis, saponification, or substitution?

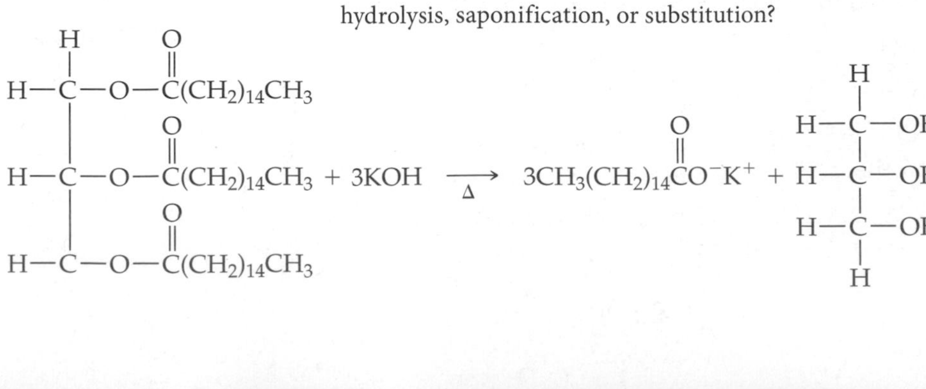

23.51 Draw the structures of all products you would obtain by saponification of the following lipid with aqueous KOH. What are the names of the products?

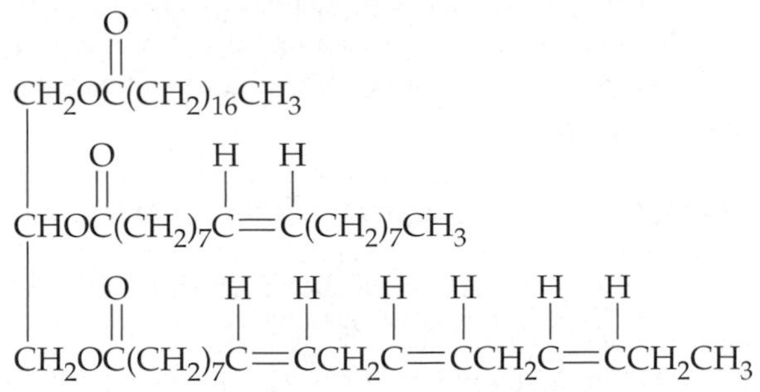

$$CH_2OC(CH_2)_{16}CH_3$$
(with O double-bonded to C above)

$$CHOC(CH_2)_7C=C(CH_2)_7CH_3$$
(with O double-bonded to C, and H H on the C=C)

$$CH_2OC(CH_2)_7C=CCH_2C=CCH_2C=CCH_2CH_3$$
(with O double-bonded to C, and H H / H H / H H on the three C=C bonds)

23.52 Draw the structure of the product you would obtain on complete hydrogenation of the triacylglycerol in Problem 23.51. What is its name? Does it have a higher or lower melting temperature than the original triacylglycerol?

23.53 Tell how many different products you would obtain on hydrogenation of the triacylglycerol in Problem 23.51 if

(a) one double bond was converted to a single bond

(b) two double bonds were converted to single bonds

(c) three double bonds were converted to single bonds

(d) all four double bonds were converted to single bonds

PHOSPHOLIPIDS, GLYCOLIPIDS, AND CELL MEMBRANES

23.54 Describe the difference between a triacylglycerol and a phospholipid.

23.55 Why are glycerophospholipids, rather than triacylglycerols, found in cell membranes?

23.56 How do sphingomyelins and cerebrosides differ structurally?

23.57 Name the two different kinds of sphingosine-based lipids.

23.58 Why are glycerophospholipids more soluble in water than triacylglycerols?

23.59 What are the functions of glycerophospholipids in the human body? Of triacylglycerides in the human body?

23.60 Explain how a soap micelle differs from a membrane bilayer.

23.61 Describe the similarities and differences between a liposome and a micelle.

23.62 What constituents besides phospholipids are present in a cell membrane?

23.63 What would happen if cell membranes were freely permeable to all molecules?

23.64 Show the structure of a cerebroside made up of D-galactose, sphingosine, and myristic acid.

23.65 Draw the structure of a sphingomyelin that contains a stearic acid unit.

23.66 Draw the structure of a glycerophospholipid that contains palmitic acid, oleic acid, and the phosphate bonded to propanolamine.

23.67 *Cardiolipin*, a compound found in heart muscle, has the following structure. What products are formed if all ester bonds in the molecule are saponified by treatment with aqueous NaOH?

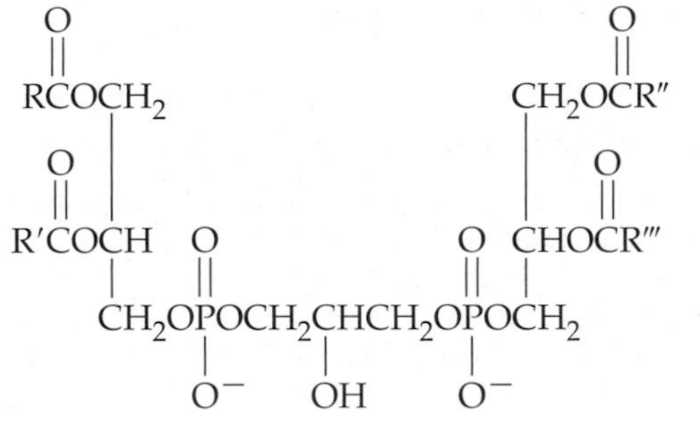

$$RCOCH_2 \qquad CH_2OCR''$$
$$R'COCH \qquad CHOCR'''$$
$$CH_2OPOCH_2CHCH_2OPOCH_2$$
$$O^- \quad OH \quad O^-$$
Cardiolipin

23.68 Which process requires energy—passive or active transport? Why is energy sometimes required to move solute across the cell membrane?

23.69 How does facilitated diffusion differ from simple diffusion?

23.70 Based on the information in Section 23.8, how would you expect each of these common metabolites to cross the cell membrane?

(a) NO (nitrous oxide)

(b) Fructose

(c) Ca^{2+}

23.71 Based on the information in Section 23.8, how would you expect each of these common metabolites to cross the cell membrane?

(a) Galactose

(b) CO

(c) Mg^{2+}

STEROLS

28.72 What is a major function of cholesterol in your body?

28.73 What is the function of the bile acids?

28.74 Name a male sex hormone and a female sex hormone.

28.75 Compare the structures of the sex hormones named in question 28.74. What portions of the structures are the same? Where do they differ?

EICOSANOIDS

23.76 Why are the eicosanoids often called "local hormones"?

23.77 Give an example of an eicosanoid serving as a local hormone.

23.78 Arachidonic acid is used to produce prostaglandins and leukotrienes. From what common fatty acid is arachidonic acid synthesized?

23.79 *Thromboxane A₂* is a lipid involved in the blood-clotting process. To what category of lipids does thromboxane A₂ belong?

Thromboxane A₂

What fatty acid do you think serves as a biological precursor of thromboxane A₂?

23.80 Under what circumstances is it desirable to inhibit the production of leukotrienes?

23.81 After a fall hike through fields of goldenrod and ragweed, you develop severe hay-fever followed by an asthmatic attack. What class of molecule is most likely responsible for the asthmatic attack?

23.82 How does aspirin function to inhibit the formation of prostaglandins from arachidonic acid?

23.83 Typically the pain and swelling from a scrape or cut is confined to the area around the injury. What class of molecules is responsible for this effect?

CHEMISTRY IN ACTION

23.84 Fats and oils are major sources of triacylglycerols. List some other foods that are associated with high lipid content. [*Lipids in the Diet, p. 728*]

23.85 According to the FDA, what is the maximum percentage of your daily calories that should come from fats and oils? [*Lipids in the Diet, p. 728*]

23.86 Describe the mechanism by which soaps and detergents provide cleaning action. [*Detergents, p. 731*]

23.87 Why are branched-chain hydrocarbons no longer used for detergents? [*Detergents, p. 731*]

23.88 Dietary guidelines suggest we limit our intake of butter due to the cholesterol content and substitute oils or margarine. The table below shows the major fatty acid distribution for a typical stick of margarine and also for butter. Values are percentages.

Sample	Myrstic Acid (C14:0)	Palmitic Acid (C16:0)	Stearic Acid (C 18:0)	Oleic Acid (C18:1)	Linoleic Acid (C18:2)
Margarine	0.7	14.1	7.0	60.7	17.0
Butter	12	31	11	24	3

(a) Which contains more monounsaturated fatty acids?

(b) Which contains more polyunsaturated fatty acids?

(c) Which is likely to contain fewer trans-fatty acids? [*Butter and Its Substitutes, p. 740*]

23.89 Recently it has been suggested that using oils with more monounsaturated fatty acids (for example, oleic acid) is better for our health than those with polyunsaturated fatty acids or saturated fatty acids. What are good sources of oils with predominantly monounsaturated fatty acids? (*Hint:* See Table 23.2.) [*Butter and Its Substitutes, p. 740*]

GENERAL QUESTIONS AND PROBLEMS

23.90 Which of the following are saponifiable lipids? (Recall that ester bonds are broken by base hydrolysis.)

(a) Progesterone

(b) Glyceryl trioleate

(c) A sphingomyelin

(d) Prostaglandin E₁

(e) A cerebroside

(f) A lecithin

23.91 Identify the component parts of each saponifiable lipid listed in Problem 23.90.

23.92 Draw the structure of a triacylglycerol made from two molecules of myristic acid and one molecule of linolenic acid.

23.93 Would the triacylglycerol described in Problem 23.92 have a higher or lower melting temperature than the triacylglycerol made from one molecule each of linolenic, myristic, and stearic acids? Why?

23.94 Common names for some triacylglycerols depend on their source. Identify the source. Choices are plant oils (soybean, canola, corn, sunflower, and so on), beef fat, pork fat.

(a) tallow

(b) cooking oil

(c) lard

23.95 Explain why cholesterol is not saponifiable.

23.96 Draw cholesterol acetate. Is this molecule saponifiable? Explain.

23.97 Jojoba wax, used in candles and cosmetics, is partially composed of the ester of stearic acid and a straight-chain 22-carbon atom alcohol. Draw the structure of this wax component. Compare this structure with the structure drawn for spermaceti in Problem 23.44. Do you think jojoba wax could replace spermaceti in the cosmetic industry?

23.98 Which three types of lipids are particularly abundant in brain tissue?

23.99 What is the function of sphingomyelin?

23.100 In what disease is a decrease in sphingomyelin observed?

23.101 List some of the functions prostaglandins serve in the body.

23.102 Which two of the following would involve a prostaglandin response?

(a) the itchy bump from a mosquito bite

(b) a sunburn after spending the day at the beach

(c) a strep throat caught from your sibling

(d) the sneezing, stuffy nose, and itchy eyes after working in the rose garden

23.103 If the average molar mass of a sample of soybean oil is 1500 g/mol, how many grams of NaOH are needed to saponify 5.0 g of the oil?

23.104 The concentration of cholesterol in the blood serum of a normal adult is approximately 200 mg/dL. How many grams of cholesterol does a person with a blood volume of 5.75 L have circulating in his or her blood? (You may need to review Chapter 1.)

CHAPTER 24

Lipid Metabolism

CONTENTS

◄ These Emperor penguins will survive for several months on the energy supplied by lipid metabolism.

CHAPTER GOALS

1. **What happens during the digestion of triacylglycerols?**
   THE GOAL: Be able to list the sequence of events in the digestion of dietary tri-acylglycerols and their transport into the bloodstream. (◄◄ A.)

2. **What are the various roles of lipopro-teins in lipid transport?**
   THE GOAL: Be able to name the major classes of lipoproteins, specify the nature and function of the lipids they transport, and identify their destinations. (◄◄ A.)

3. **What are the major pathways in the metabolism of triacylglycerols?**
   THE GOAL: Be able to name the major pathways for the synthesis and break-down of triacylglycerols and fatty acids, and identify their connections to other metabolic pathways. (◄◄ C.)

4. **How are triacylglycerols moved into and out of storage in adipose tissue?**

   THE GOAL: Be able to explain the reac-tions by which triacylglycerols are stored and mobilized, and how these reactions are regulated. (◄◄ B, C.)

5. **How are fatty acids oxidized, and how much energy is produced by their oxidation?**
   THE GOAL: Be able to explain what hap-pens to a fatty acid from its entry into a cell until its conversion to acetyl-CoA. (◄◄ C.)

6. **What is the function of ketogenesis?**
   THE GOAL: Be able to identify ketone bodies, describe their properties and syn-thesis, and explain their role in metabo-lism. (◄◄ C.)

7. **How are fatty acids synthesized?**
   THE GOAL: Be able to compare the pathways for fatty acid synthesis and oxi-dation, and describe the reactions of the synthesis pathway. (◄◄ C.)

CONCEPTS TO REVIEW

◄◄◄

A. Types of Lipids
(Sections 23.1, 23.2)

B. Cell Membranes
(Sections 23.5–23.7)

C. Metabolism and Energy Production
(Section 20.4)

Carbohydrate metabolism (discussed in Chapter 22) is one of our two major sources of energy. Lipid metabolism, the topic of this chapter, is the other. Of the various classes of lipids you saw in Chapter 23, the majority of the lipids in our diet are triacylglycerols. Therefore, our focus here is on the metabolism of triacyl-glycerols, which are stored in fatty tissue and constitute our chief energy reserve.

24.1 Digestion of Triacylglycerols

When food containing triacylglycerols is eaten, the triacylglycerols pass through the mouth unchanged and enter the stomach (Figure 24.1). (Recall that an *acyl* group is the R—C=O portion of an ester. The acyl groups from fatty acids have relatively long, R chain groups.) The heat and churning action of the stomach break the triacyl-glycerols into smaller droplets, a process that takes longer than the physical breakdown and digestion of other foods in the stomach. To ensure that there is time for this break-down, the presence of triacylglycerols in consumed food slows down the rate at which the mixture of partially digested foods leaves the stomach. (One reason foods contain-ing lipids are a pleasing part of the diet is that the stomach feels full for a longer time after a fatty meal.) No catabolism of triacylglyceols has taken place yet, only prepara-tion for this step by breaking fats into microscopic droplets.

The pathway of dietary triacylglycerols from the mouth to their ultimate biochemi-cal fate in the body is not as straightforward as that of carbohydrates. Complications arise because triacylglycerols are not water-soluble but nevertheless must enter an aqueous environment. To be moved around within the body by the blood and lymph systems, they must therefore be dispersed and surrounded by a water-soluble coat-ing, a process that must happen more than once as the triacylglycerols travel along their metabolic pathways. During these travels, they are packaged in various types of **lipoproteins**, which consist of droplets of hydrophobic lipids surrounded by phos-pholipids, proteins and other molecules with their hydrophilic ends to the outside (Figure 24.2). Lipoproteins are special forms of micelles.

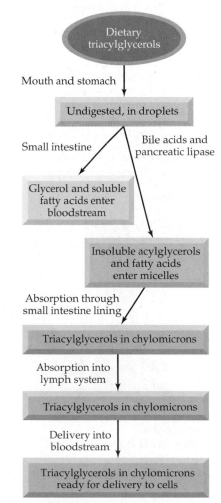

▲ **Figure 24.1**
Digestion of triacylglycerols.

Lipoprotein A lipid–protein complex that transports lipids.

▶▶▶ Recall from Section 23.5 that polar phospholipids are the major component of cell membranes.

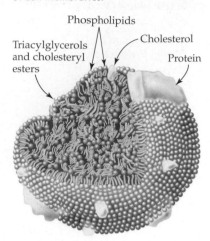

▲ **Figure 24.2**
A lipoprotein.
A lipoprotein contains a core of neutral lipids, including triacylglycerols and cholesteryl esters. Surrounding the core is a layer of phospholipids in which varying proportions of proteins and cholesterol are embedded.

Bile Fluid secreted by the liver and released into the small intestine from the gallbladder during digestion; contains bile acids, cholesterol, phospholipids, bicarbonate ions, and other electrolytes.

Bile acids Sterol acids derived from cholesterol that are secreted in bile.

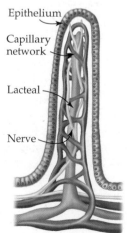

▲ **Figure 24.3**
A villus, site of absorption in the intestinal lining.
A huge number of villi provide the surface at which lipids and other nutrients are absorbed. Small molecules enter the capillary network, and larger lipids enter the lacteals, small vessels of the lymph system.

When partially digested food leaves the stomach, it enters the upper end of the small intestine (the *duodenum*), where its arrival triggers the release of *pancreatic lipases*—enzymes for the hydrolysis of lipids. The gallbladder simultaneously releases **bile**, a mixture that is manufactured in the liver and stored in the gallbladder until needed. Among other components, bile contains cholesterol and cholesterol-derived **bile acids**, both of which are sterols, and phospholipids.

By the time dietary triacylglycerols enter the small intestine, they are dispersed as small, greasy, insoluble droplets, and for this reason enzymes in the small intestine cannot attack them. It is the job of the bile acids and phospholipids to emulsify the triacylglycerols by forming micelles much like soap micelles (see Figure 23.3). The major bile acid is cholic acid, and you can see from the structure of its anion that it resembles soaps and detergents because it contains both hydrophilic and hydrophobic regions allowing it to act as an emulsifying agent:

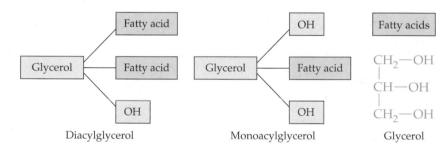

Pancreatic lipase partially hydrolyzes the emulsified triacylglycerols, producing mono- and diacylglycerols plus fatty acids and a small amount of glycerol.

Small fatty acids and glycerol are water-soluble and are absorbed directly, by diffusion through the surface of the villi that line the small intestine. Once they are in the villi (Figure 24.3), these molecules enter the bloodstream through capillaries and are carried by the blood to the liver (via the hepatic portal vein).

The water-insoluble acylglycerols and larger fatty acids are once again emulsified within the intestine. Then, at the intestinal lining they are released from the micelles and absorbed by the cells lining the intestine. Because these lipids, and also cholesterol and partially hydrolyzed phospholipids, must next enter the aqueous bloodstream for transport, they are once again packaged into water-soluble units—in this case, the lipoproteins known as *chylomicrons*. This elaborate process of hydrolysis, absorption, resynthesis, secretion, and transport is necessary for the triacylglycerol components to cross cell membranes and also for their travel through aqueous media. Remember, triacylglycerols and cholesterol must move from food particles in the intestinal system to the cytosol or mitochondria of liver cells and other cells for use in your body.

Chylomicrons are too large to enter the bloodstream through capillary walls. Instead, they are absorbed into the lymphatic system through lacteals, small vessels analogous to capillaries, within the villi (see Figure 24.3). Then, chylomicrons are carried to the thoracic duct (just below the collarbone), where the lymphatic system empties into the bloodstream. At this point, the lipids within these chylomicrons are ready to be used either for energy generation or to be put into storage; once leaving the thoracic duct the chylomicrons are carried directly to the liver, where hepatocytes use the lipid components depending on their own needs and the needs of other cells.

The pathways of lipids through the villi and into the transport systems of the bloodstream and the lymphatic system are summarized in Figure 24.4.

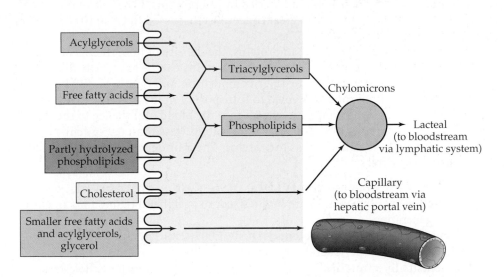

◄ **Figure 24.4**
Pathways of lipids through the villi.

🔑 **KEY CONCEPT PROBLEM 24.1**

Cholesterol (see structure in margin) and cholate (a bile acid anion, whose structure is shown on p. 754) are sterols with very similar structures. However, the roles they play in the body are different: Cholate is an emulsifier, whereas cholesterol plays an important role in membrane structure. Identify the small differences in their structures that make them well suited to their jobs in the body. Given their similar structures, can the roles of these molecules be reversed?

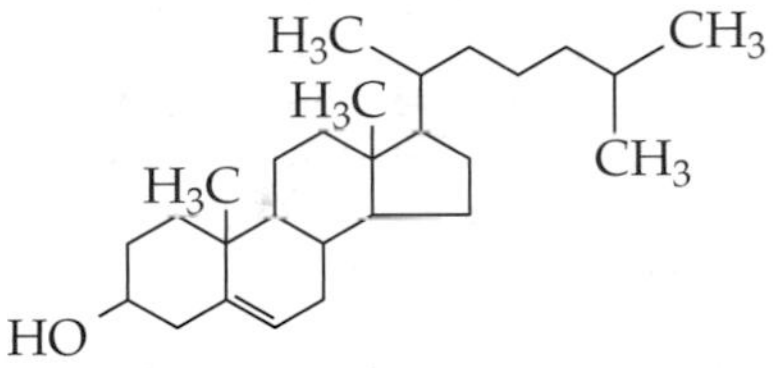

24.2 Lipoproteins for Lipid Transport

The lipids used in the body's metabolic pathways have three sources. They enter the pathways (1) from the digestive tract as food is broken down; (2) from adipose tissue, where excess lipids have been stored; and (3) from the liver, where lipids are synthesized. Whatever their source, these lipids must eventually be transported in blood, an aqueous medium, as summarized in Figure 24.5.

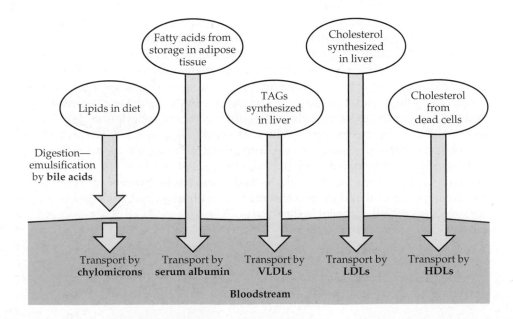

◄ **Figure 24.5**
Transport of lipids.
Fatty acids released from storage are carried by albumin, which is a large protein. All of the other lipids are carried packaged in various lipoproteins.

To become water-soluble, fatty acids released from adipose tissue associate with albumin, a protein found in blood plasma that binds up to 10 fatty acid molecules per protein molecule. All other lipids are carried by lipoproteins. (The role of lipoproteins in heart disease, where they are of great concern, is discussed in Chemistry in Action: Lipids and Atherosclerosis on p. 757.)

Because lipids are less dense than proteins, the density of lipoproteins depends on their ratio of lipids to proteins. Therefore, lipoproteins can be arbitrarily divided into five major types distinguishable by their composition and densities. Chylomicrons, which are the only lipoproteins devoted to transport of lipids from the diet, carry triacylglycerols through the lymphatic system into the blood and thence to the liver for processing. These are the lowest-density lipoproteins (less than 0.95 g/cm^3) because they carry the highest ratio of lipids to proteins. The four denser lipoprotein fractions have the following roles:

- **Very-low-density lipoproteins (VLDLs)** $(0.96–1.006 \text{ g/cm}^3)$ carry triacylglycerols from the liver (where they are synthesized) to peripheral tissues for storage or energy generation.
- **Intermediate-density lipoproteins (IDLs)** $(1.007–1.019 \text{ g/cm}^3)$ carry remnants of the VLDLs from peripheral tissues back to the liver for use in synthesis.
- **Low-density lipoproteins (LDLs)** $(1.020–1.062 \text{ g/cm}^3)$ transport cholesterol from the liver to peripheral tissues, where it is used in cell membranes or for steroid synthesis (and is also available for formation of arterial plaque).
- **High-density lipoproteins (HDLs)** $(1.063–1.210 \text{ g/cm}^3)$ transport cholesterol *from* dead or dying cells back to the liver, where it is converted to bile acids. The bile acids are then available for use in digestion or are excreted via the digestive tract when in excess.

Worked Example 24.1 Digesting and Transporting Fats

Describe how the fat in an ice cream cone gets from the ice cream to a liver cell.

ANALYSIS Dietary fat from animal sources (such as the whole milk often found in ice cream) is primarily triacylglycerols with a small amount of cholesterol present. Cholesterol is not degraded in the digestive system. Fat-digesting enzymes are secreted by the pancreas and delivered via the common duct to the small intestine, along with bile acids. As discussed above, only free fatty acids and mono- and diacylglycerols can cross the intestinal cell wall before being passed on to the blood stream. Smaller molecules such as some free fatty acids and glycerol diffuse across the cell membrane to enter the bloodstream; larger molecules must be delivered there in special packaging, called lipoproteins.

SOLUTION

As the ice cream cone is eaten, it passes through the mouth to the stomach, where mixing occurs. This mixing action promotes the formation of triacylglycerols into small droplets. No enzymatic digestion of lipids occurs in the stomach. When the stomach contents move to the small intestine, bile acids and pancreatic lipases are secreted into the mixture. The bile acids help to emulsify the fat droplets into micelles. Once micelles have formed, lipases hydrolyze the triacylglycerols to mono- and diacylglycerols; the hydrolysis also produces fatty acids. These three hydrolysis products cross into the cells lining the small intestine, are resynthesized into triacylglycerides, and are secreted into the bloodstream in the form of chylomicrons. Chylomicrons travel to the liver and enter cells for processing. The small amount of cholesterol in the ice cream will be directly absorbed, packaged into chylomicrons as well, and sent to the liver.

CHEMISTRY IN ACTION

Lipids and Atherosclerosis

According to the U.S. Food and Drug Administration (FDA), and in agreement with many other authorities, there is "strong, convincing, and consistent evidence" for the connection between heart disease and diets high in saturated fats and cholesterol. (Research has provided strong evidence that high dietary fat is one risk factor for certain types of cancer.)

Several points are clear:

- A diet rich in saturated animal fats leads to an increase in blood-serum cholesterol.
- A diet lower in saturated fat and higher in unsaturated fat can lower the serum cholesterol level.
- High levels of serum cholesterol are correlated with *atherosclerosis*, a condition in which yellowish deposits (*arterial plaque*) composed of cholesterol and other lipid-containing materials form within the larger arteries. The result of atherosclerosis is an increased risk of coronary artery disease and heart attack brought on by blockage of blood flow to heart muscles or an increased risk of stroke due to blockage of blood flow to the brain.

Factors considered in an overall evaluation of an individual's risk of heart disease are the following:

Risk factors for heart disease

High blood levels of cholesterol and low levels of high-density lipoproteins (HDLs)

Cigarette smoking

High blood pressure

Diabetes

Obesity

Low level of physical activity

Family history of early heart disease

As discussed in Section 24.2, lipoproteins are complex assemblages of lipids and proteins that transport lipids throughout the body. If LDL (the so-called "bad" cholesterol) delivers more cholesterol than is needed to peripheral tissues, and if not enough HDL (the so-called "good" cholesterol) is present to remove it, the excess cholesterol is deposited in cells and arteries. Thus, the higher the HDL level, the less the likelihood of deposits and the lower the risk of heart disease. There is some evidence that a low HDL level (less than 35 mg/dL) may be the single best predictor of heart attack potential. Also, LDL has

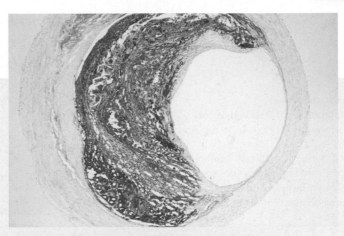

▲ **Plaque. Deposits of cholesterol and associated lipids (known collectively as plaque) have partially blocked the flow of blood in this artery.**

the harmful potential to trigger inflammation and the buildup of plaque in artery walls. (Remember it this way—**low L**DL is good; **high H**DL is good.)

Many groups recommend that individuals strive for the following cholesterol levels in blood:

Total cholesterol	200 mg/dL or lower
LDL	130 mg/dL or lower
HDL	40 mg/dL or higher

To further assess the risk level represented by an individual's cholesterol and HDL values, the total cholesterol/HDL ratio is calculated. The ideal ratio is considered to be 3.5. A ratio of 4.5 indicates an average risk, and a ratio of 5 or higher shows a high and potentially dangerous risk. The ratio overcomes the difficulty in evaluating the significance of, for example, a high cholesterol level of 290 mg/dL (negative) combined with a high HDL value of 75 mg/dL (positive). The resultant ratio of 3.9 indicates a low risk level.

Decreasing saturated fats and cholesterol in the diet, adopting an exercise program, and not smoking constitute the first line of defense for those at risk. For those at high risk or for whom the first-line defenses are inadequate, drugs are available that prevent or slow the progress of coronary artery disease by lowering serum cholesterol levels. Among the drugs are indigestible resins (*cholestyramine* and *colestipol*) that bind bile acids and accelerate their excretion, causing the liver to use up more cholesterol in bile acid synthesis. Another class of effective drugs is the statins (for example, lovastatin), which inhibit an enzyme crucial to the synthesis of cholesterol.

See Chemistry in Action Problems 24.60 through 24.63 at the end of the chapter.

PROBLEM 24.2

What is arterial plaque? Why is it desirable to have a high HDL value and a relatively low LDL value? (See Chemistry in Action: Lipids and Atherosclerosis above.)

24.3 Triacylglycerol Metabolism: An Overview

The metabolic pathways for triacylglycerols are summarized in Figure 24.6 and further explained in the following sections of this chapter.

▶ **Figure 24.6**
Metabolism of triacylglycerols.
Pathways that break down molecules (catabolism) are shown in light brown, and synthetic pathways (anabolism) are shown in blue. Connections to other pathways or intermediates of metabolism are shown in green.

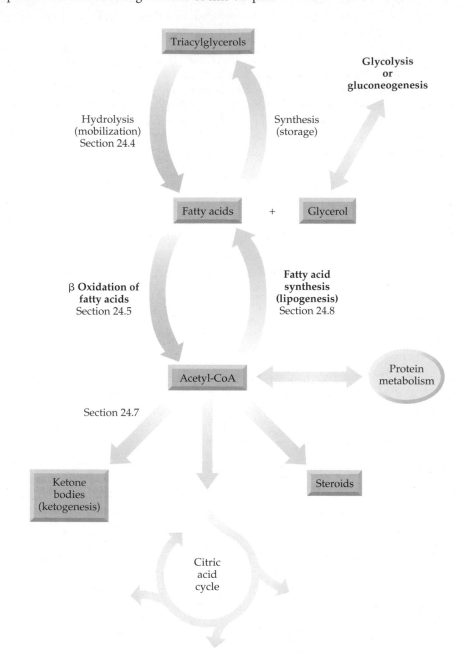

Dietary Triacylglycerols

For triacylglycerols from the diet, hydrolysis occurs when chylomicrons in the bloodstream encounter lipoprotein lipase anchored in capillary walls as chylomicrons are moving to hepatocytes for processing. The resulting fatty acids then have two possible fates: (1) When energy is in good supply, they are converted back to triacylglycerols for storage in adipose tissue. (2) When cells need energy, the fatty acid carbon atoms are activated by conversion to fatty acyl-CoA and then oxidized to acetyl-CoA, shortening the fatty acyl-CoA molecule by two carbon atoms for each oxidation.

The primary metabolic fate of acetyl-CoA is the generation of energy via the citric acid cycle and oxidative phosphorylation (see Figure 20.5). Acetyl-CoA has several important roles in lipid metabolism as well. Acetyl-CoA serves as the starting material for the biosynthesis of fatty acids (*lipogenesis*) in the liver (Section 24.8). In addition, it enters the *ketogenesis* pathway for production of ketone bodies, a source of energy called on when glucose is in short supply (Section 24.7). Acetyl-CoA is also the starting material for the synthesis of cholesterol, from which all other steroids are made.

Triacylglycerols from Adipocytes

When stored triacylglycerols are needed as an energy source, lipases within fat cells are activated by hormone level variation (low insulin and high glucagon, Section 22.7). The stored triacylglycerols are hydrolyzed to fatty acids, and the free fatty acids and glycerol are then released into the bloodstream. These fatty acids travel in association with *albumins* (blood-plasma proteins) to cells (primarily muscle and liver cells), where they are converted to acetyl-CoA for energy generation.

Glycerol from Triacylglycerols

The glycerol produced from triacylglycerol hydrolysis is carried in the bloodstream to the liver or kidneys, where it is converted in a series of reactions to glyceraldehyde 3-phosphate and dihydroxyacetone phosphate (DHAP):

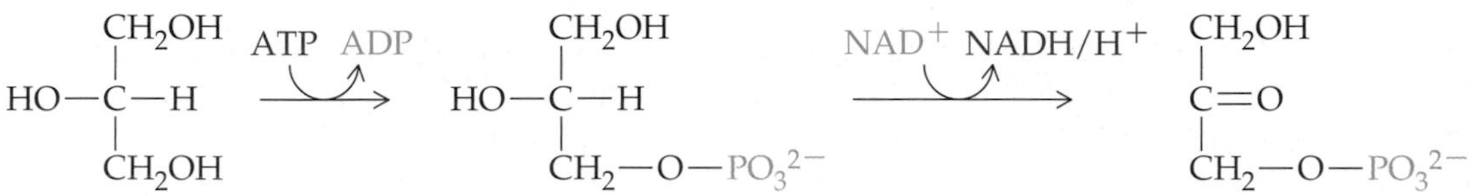

Glycerol → Glycerol 3-phosphate → Dihydroxyacetone phosphate (DHAP)

DHAP, which is a reactant in the synthesis of triacylglycerols (Section 24.4), enters the glycolysis/gluconeogenesis pathways (see Figure 22.3, Step 5 and Figure 22.10, Step 7) and thus is a link between carbohydrate metabolism and lipid metabolism.

The varied possible metabolic destinations of the fatty acids, glycerol, and acetyl-CoA from dietary triacylglycerols are summarized as follows:

Fate of Dietary Triacylglycerols

- *Triacylglycerols* undergo hydrolysis to fatty acids and glycerol.
- *Fatty acids* undergo
  - Resynthesis of triacylglycerols for storage
  - Conversion to acetyl-CoA
- *Glycerol* is converted to glyceraldehyde 3-phosphate and DHAP, which participate in
  - *Glycolysis*—energy generation (Section 22.3)
  - *Gluconeogenesis*—glucose formation (Section 22.11)
  - *Triacylglycerol synthesis*—energy storage (Section 24.4)
- *Acetyl-CoA* participates in
  - *Triacylglycerol synthesis* (Section 24.4)
  - Ketone body synthesis (*ketogenesis*, Section 24.7)
  - Synthesis of sterols and other lipids
  - *Citric acid cycle and oxidative phosphorylation* (Sections 20.8, 20.9)

PROBLEM 24.3
Examine Figure 22.3 (p. 696) and explain how dihydroxyacetone phosphate can enter the glycolysis pathway and be converted to pyruvate.

PROBLEM 24.4
Storage of excess calories as fat has been identified as unhealthy when carried to extreme. Why is this unhealthy? Give an example of a disease that an obese person is at higher risk of developing than a normal weight person (see Chemistry in Action: Fat Storage: A Good Thing or Not? on p. 760).

CHEMISTRY IN ACTION

Fat Storage: A Good Thing or Not?

Bears do it, ground hogs do it, even humans do it. Do what? Store fat. Mammals store excess dietary calories as triacylglycerols in adipocytes (fat cells, the cells that make up adipose tissue). Some mammals, like bears and ground hogs, eat to store energy for use during hibernation; others, humans among them, seem simply to eat more calories than necessary when given the opportunity. Your body can do several things with extra calories. It can burn fuel through exercise, use it to create heat, or store it for future use. Our bodies are very efficient at storing the extra calories against future need.

Excessive storage of triacylglycerols is a predictor of serious health problems, and has been associated with increased risk of developing Type II diabetes and colon cancer, as well as an increased risk of having a heart attack or stroke. Health professionals have developed charts based on body mass index (see Chemistry in Action: Obesity and Body Fat on p. 35) to estimate obesity. Although these charts do not allow for individual variation in percent body fat, the general trend is clear. For example, those with a body mass index (BMI) of 30 or greater (defined as obese) develop Type II diabetes at a higher rate than those with a normal BMI. The problem is even more acute in obese children. Not only do they risk developing serious health problems at an earlier age than those who become obese as adults, but they also have more fat cells than adults. Clinical research shows that adipocytes in an obese child can divide, making more fat cells and allowing for storage of even more triacylglycerols; this process does not appear to occur in adults.

Why do people eat too much? Nature or nurture? Many factors are intertwined; environmental factors (including availability of food and cultural attitudes toward food choices and exercise) are involved as are "natural" factors such as variations in metabolic rates and hormone levels. Some of the latter variations may be due to genetic differences. It has recently been discovered that a deficiency in *leptin* can lead to overeating. Leptin, a peptide hormone, is synthesized in adipocytes and acts on the brain to stop eating—it suppresses appetite. *Grehlin*, another peptide hormone, influences appetite in a different way. Made

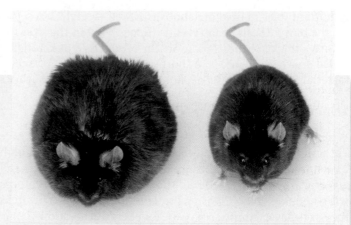

▲ **Both mice have a mutation that causes increased fat storage. The mouse on the right is normal-sized due to treatment with leptin, while the untreated mouse on the left is obese.**

in cells lining the stomach, grehlin stimulates intense sensations of hunger. Other hormones, including insulin, are also apparently involved in appetite and satiety regulation. Research shows that genetics may be involved in extreme cases of obesity. Mice with defective leptin genes apparently have little control over the amount of food eaten and can grow to three times the size of mice with normal leptin levels. Although this discovery initiated promising new treatments for obese individuals found to be leptin deficient (leptin treatment can help those individuals lose weight), the majority of obese people are not leptin deficient.

Weight control is a complex process. The bodies of mammals are seemingly "programmed" to conserve all extra calories as fat against a time when calories might be scarce. Remember that metabolic pathways exist to convert carbohydrate and protein into fat for storage; it is not only dietary fat that is stored. Scientists do not yet understand all the hormonal, metabolic connections in the storage process. It is known, however, that a sensible diet combined with regular exercise habits can sustain a stable weight without excess fat accumulation. Today's supersized meals, fatty snacks, and sedentary habits are undoubtedly tied to increasing rates of energy storage as fat. Remember, our basal metabolism rates have not changed, only our diets and activity levels (see Chemistry in Action: Basal Metabolism on p. 636).

See Chemistry in Action Problems 24.64 through 25.67 at the end of the chapter.

24.4 Storage and Mobilization of Triacylglycerols

We have noted that adipose tissue is the storage depot for triacylglycerols and that triacylglycerols are our primary energy-storage form. Triacylglycerols do not just sit unused until needed, however. The passage of fatty acids in and out of storage in adipose tissue is a continuous process essential to maintaining homeostasis (see Chemistry in Action: Homeostasis, p. 845).

Triacylglycerol Synthesis

Our bodies regulate the storage and **mobilization** of triacylglycerols through the same hormones that regulate blood glucose concentration, insulin and glucagon. After a meal, blood glucose levels increase rapidly levels rise, and glucagon levels drop. Glucose enters cells, and the rate of glycolysis increases. Under these conditions, insulin activates the synthesis of triacylglycerols for storage.

The reactants in triacylglycerol synthesis are glycerol 3-phosphate and fatty acid acyl groups carried by coenzyme A. Triacylglycerol synthesis proceeds by transfer of first one and then another fatty acid acyl group from coenzyme A to glycerol 3-phosphate. The reaction is catalyzed by acyl transferase, and the product is phosphatidic acid:

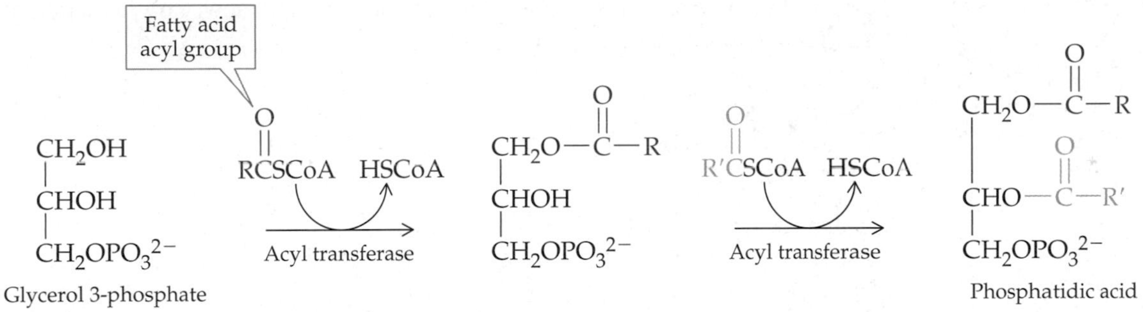

Mobilization (of triacylglycerols) Hydrolysis of triacylglycerols in adipose tissue and release of fatty acids into the bloodstream.

▶▶▶ Figure 22.6 shows the effects of insulin and glucagon hormones on metabolism.

Next, the phosphate group is removed from phosphatidic acid by phosphatidic acid phosphatase to produce 1,2-diacylglycerol. In the presence of acyl transferase, the third fatty acid group is then added to give a triacylglycerol:

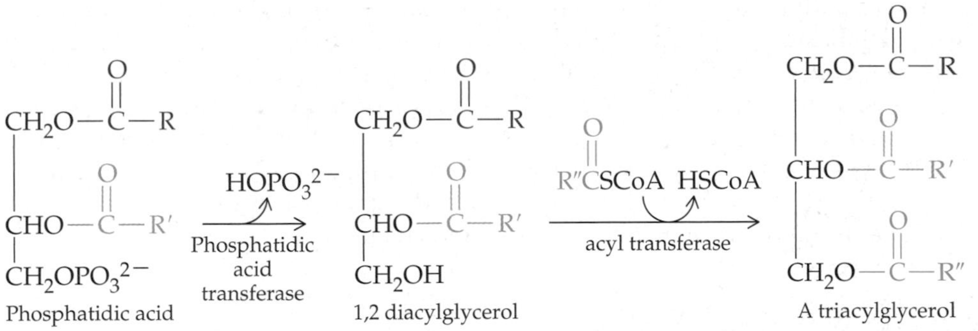

As the reaction on p. 759 shows, glycerol is one source of glycerol-3-phosphate. But adipocytes do not synthesize glycerol kinase, which is the enzyme needed to convert glycerol to glycerol 3-phosphate; thus they cannot synthesize glycerol 3-phosphate from glycerol. However, glycerol 3-phosphate can also be synthesized from dihydroxyacetone phosphate (DHAP) (by the reverse of the reaction on p. 715), and adipocytes can synthesize triacylglycerols as long as DHAP is available. In adipocytes, this pathway is called *glyceroneogenesis,* and it supplies the DHAP for conversion to glycerol 3-phosphate. Glyceroneogenesis is an abbreviated form of gluconeogenesis (see Figure 22.10), ending with the conversion of DHAP to glycerol 3-phosphate followed by triacylglycerol synthesis.

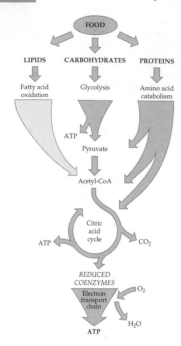

β-Oxidation pathway A repetitive series of biochemical reactions that degrades fatty acids to acetyl-CoA by removing carbon atoms two at a time.

TAG Mobilization

When digestion of a meal is finished, blood glucose levels return to normal; consequently, insulin levels drop and glucagon levels rise. The lower insulin level and higher glucagon level together activate *triacylglycerol lipase*, the enzyme within adipocytes that controls hydrolysis of stored triacylglycerols. When glycerol 3-phosphate is in short supply—an indication that glycolysis is not producing sufficient energy—the fatty acids and glycerol produced by hydrolysis of the stored triacylglycerols are released to the bloodstream for transport to energy-generating cells. Otherwise, the fatty acids and glycerol are cycled back into new TAGs for storage. Dieters on special low-carbohydrate diets are trying to produce this metabolic state in order to "burn fat." An undesirable side effect of these diets is ketosis and the production of ketone bodies (Section 24.7).

24.5 Oxidation of Fatty Acids

Once a fatty acid enters the cytosol of a cell that needs energy, three successive processes must occur.

1. **Activation** The fatty acid must be activated by conversion to fatty acyl-CoA. This activation, which occurs in the cytosol, serves the same purpose as the first few steps in oxidation of glucose by glycolysis. Initially, some energy from ATP must be invested in converting the fatty acid to fatty acyl-CoA, a form that breaks down more easily.

$$R-\overset{\overset{\text{O}}{\|}}{C}-O^- + HSCoA + ATP \longrightarrow R-\overset{\overset{\text{O}}{\|}}{C}-SCoA + AMP + P_2O_7^{4-}$$

Fatty acid   Fatty acyl-CoA

2. **Transport** The fatty acyl-CoA, which cannot cross the mitochondrial membrane by diffusion, must be transported from the cytosol into the mitochondrial matrix, where energy generation will occur. Carnitine, an amino-oxy acid, undergoes an ester-formation exchange reaction with the fatty acyl-CoA, resulting in a fatty acyl-carnitine ester that moves across the membrane into the mitochondria by facilitated diffusion. There, another ester-formation exchange reaction regenerates the fatty acyl-CoA and carnitine.

3. **Oxidation** The fatty acyl-CoA must be oxidized by enzymes in the mitochondrial matrix to produce acetyl-CoA plus the reduced coenzymes to be used in ATP generation. The oxidation occurs by repeating the series of four reactions shown in Figure 24.7, which make up the **β-oxidation pathway**. Each repetition of these reactions cleaves a 2-carbon acetyl group from the end of a fatty acid acyl group and produces one acetyl-CoA. This pathway is a *spiral* rather than a cycle because the long-chain fatty acyl group must continue to return to the pathway until each pair of carbon atoms is removed.

The β-Oxidation Pathway

The name β oxidation refers to the oxidation of the carbon atom β to the thioester linkage in two steps of the pathway.

$$R-CH_2CH_2-\overset{\overset{\text{H}}{|}}{CH}-\overset{\overset{\text{H}}{|}}{CH}-\overset{\overset{\text{O}}{\|}}{C}-SCoA$$

β carbon atom

A fatty acyl-CoA

STEP 1: The first β oxidation *Acyl-CoA dehydrogenase* and its coenzyme FAD remove hydrogen atoms from the carbon atoms α and β to the carbonyl group in the fatty acyl-CoA, forming a carbon–carbon double bond. These hydrogen atoms and their electrons are passed directly from $FADH_2$ to coenzyme Q so that the electrons can enter the electron transport chain (Section 20.9).

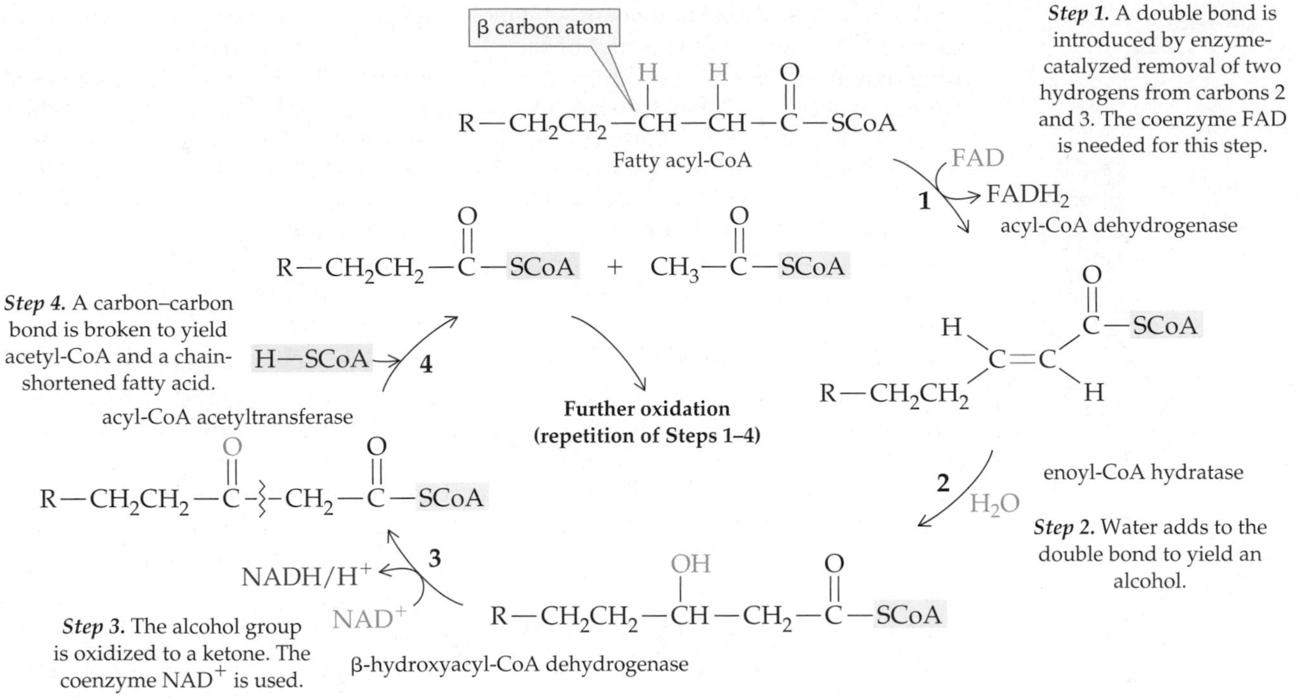

β carbon atom

$$R-CH_2CH_2-\overset{H}{\underset{|}{CH}}-\overset{H}{\underset{|}{CH}}-\overset{O}{\overset{||}{C}}-SCoA$$

Fatty acyl-CoA

Step 1. A double bond is introduced by enzyme-catalyzed removal of two hydrogens from carbons 2 and 3. The coenzyme FAD is needed for this step.

FAD

1 → FADH$_2$

acyl-CoA dehydrogenase

$$R-CH_2CH_2-\overset{O}{\overset{||}{C}}-SCoA \quad + \quad CH_3-\overset{O}{\overset{||}{C}}-SCoA$$

Step 4. A carbon–carbon bond is broken to yield acetyl-CoA and a chain-shortened fatty acid.

H—SCoA → **4**

acyl-CoA acetyltransferase

Further oxidation (repetition of Steps 1–4)

$$\overset{H}{\underset{R-CH_2CH_2}{\diagdown}}C=C\overset{\overset{O}{\overset{||}{C}}-SCoA}{\diagup}_{H}$$

2 H$_2$O

enoyl-CoA hydratase

Step 2. Water adds to the double bond to yield an alcohol.

$$R-CH_2CH_2-\overset{O}{\overset{||}{C}}-\{-CH_2-\overset{O}{\overset{||}{C}}-SCoA$$

NADH/H$^+$

3

NAD$^+$

Step 3. The alcohol group is oxidized to a ketone. The coenzyme NAD$^+$ is used.

β-hydroxyacyl-CoA dehydrogenase

$$R-CH_2CH_2-\overset{OH}{\underset{|}{CH}}-CH_2-\overset{O}{\overset{||}{C}}-SCoA$$

▲ **Figure 24.7**
β Oxidation of fatty acids.
Passage of an acyl-CoA through these four steps cleaves one acetyl group from the end of the fatty acid chain. In this manner, carbon atoms are removed from a fatty acid two at a time. This process takes place in the mitochondrial matrix.

STEP 2: **Hydration** *Enoyl-CoA hydratase* adds a water molecule across the newly created double bond to give an alcohol with the —OH group on the β carbon.

STEP 3: **The second β oxidation** The coenzyme NAD$^+$ is the oxidizing agent for conversion of the β—OH group to a carbonyl group by *β-hydroxyacyl-CoA dehydrogenase*.

STEP 4: **Cleavage to remove an acetyl group** An acetyl group is split off by *thiolase (acyl-CoA acetyltransferase)* and attached to a new coenzyme A molecule, leaving behind an acyl-CoA that is two carbon atoms shorter.

For a fatty acid with an even number of carbon atoms, all of the carbons are transferred to acetyl-CoA molecules by an appropriate number of trips through the β-oxidation spiral. Additional steps are required to oxidize fatty acids with odd numbers of carbon atoms and those with double bonds. Ultimately, all fatty acid carbons are released for further oxidation in the citric acid cycle.

🔑 **KEY CONCEPT PROBLEM 24.5**

In β oxidation, (a) identify the steps that are oxidations and describe the changes that occur; (b) identify the oxidizing agents; (c) identify the reaction that is an addition; (d) identify the reaction that is a substitution.

24.6 Energy from Fatty Acid Oxidation

The total energy output from fatty acid catabolism, like that from glucose catabolism, is measured by the total number of ATP molecules produced. In the case of fatty acids, this is the total number of ATP molecules from the passage of acetyl-CoA through the citric acid cycle, including those produced from the reduced coenzymes NADH and FADH$_2$ during oxidative phosphorylation, plus those produced by the reduced coenzymes (NADH and FADH$_2$) during fatty acid oxidation.

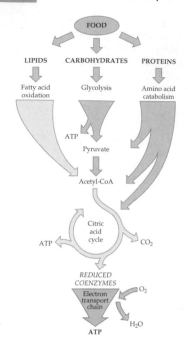

▲ **Fat as a source of water.**
A camel's hump is almost entirely fat, which serves as a source of energy and also water. As reduced coenzymes from fatty acid oxidation pass through electron transport to generate ATP, large amounts of water are formed (about one water molecule for each carbon atom in a fatty acid). This water sustains camels during long periods when no drinking water is available.

To compute the total number of ATP molecules gained in the process, we first need to know the number of molecules of acetyl-CoA obtained from the fatty acid undergoing oxidation. Two carbon atoms are removed with each acetyl-CoA, so the total number of acetyl-CoA molecules produced from a fatty acid is its number of carbon atoms divided by 2. These acetyl-CoA molecules proceed to the citric acid cycle, where each one yields 1 ATP and a total of 3 NADH molecules and 1 $FADH_2$ molecule. Using the estimates of 3 ATP molecules produced for each NADH and 2 ATP molecules produced for each $FADH_2$ (Section 22.6), each acetyl-CoA generates 11 ATP molecules from reduced coenzymes. Adding the single ATP molecule generated in the citric acid cycle to the 11 obtained from the reduced coenzymes, we get a total of 12 ATP molecules per acetyl-CoA.

In addition, we must take into account the number of ATP molecules derived from the two reduced coenzymes (1 $FADH_2$ and 1 NADH) from each repetition of β oxidation. With 2 ATP molecules produced per $FADH_2$ and 3 ATP molecules produced per NADH, the total is 5 ATP molecules produced for each β oxidation. Note that the number of repetitions is always one fewer than the number of acetyl-CoA molecules produced because the last β oxidation cleaves a 4-carbon chain to give 2 acetyl-CoA molecules. Also, we must subtract the equivalent of 2 ATP molecules spent in activation of a fatty acid, the step that precedes the β oxidations.

As an example, complete oxidation of the 12-carbon fatty acid, lauric acid $(CH_3(CH_2)_{10}COOH)$, yields 95 ATP molecules:

From the citric acid cycle:

$$12 \text{ C atoms}/2 = 6 \text{ acetyl-CoA molecules}$$

$$\frac{12 \text{ ATP molecules}}{\text{acetyl-CoA molecule}} \times 6 \text{ acetyl-CoA molecules} = 72 \text{ ATP molecules}$$

Activation of the fatty acid: $= -2$ ATP molecules

From the 5 β oxidations:

$$\frac{5 \text{ ATP molecules}}{\beta \text{ oxidation}} \times 5 \text{ } \beta \text{ oxidations} = 25 \text{ ATP molecules}$$

Summation of the ATP used and produced:

$$Total = (72 - 2 + 25) \text{ ATP molecules} = 95 \text{ ATP molecules}$$

Comparing the amount of ATP produced by fatty acid catabolism with the amount produced by glucose catabolism illustrates why our bodies use triacylglycerols rather than carbohydrates for long-term energy storage. We use lauric acid as our example because it has a molar mass close to that of glucose. Our best estimates show that 1 mol of glucose (180 g) generates 38 mol of ATP, whereas 1 mol of lauric acid (200 g) generates 95 mol of ATP. Thus, fatty acids yield nearly three times as much energy per gram as carbohydrates. In terms of nutritional Calories (that is, kilocalories), carbohydrates yield 4 Cal/g (16.7 kJ/g), whereas fats and oils yield 9 Cal/g (37.7 kJ/g).

In addition, stored fats have a greater "energy density" than stored carbohydrates. Because glycogen—the storage form of carbohydrates—is hydrophilic, about 2 g of water are held with each gram of glycogen. The hydrophobic fats do not hold water in this manner.

Worked Example 24.2 Spiraling through β Oxidation

How many times does stearic acid $(CH_3(CH_2)_{16}COOH)$ spiral through the β-oxidation pathway to produce acetyl-CoA?

ANALYSIS Each turn of the β-oxidation spiral pathway produces 1 acetyl-CoA. To determine the number of turns, divide the total number of carbon atoms in the fatty acid, 18 in this case, by 2 since an acetyl group contains two carbon atoms and they come from the fatty acid. Subtract one turn, since the last turn produces two acetyl-CoA molecules.

SOLUTION
Stearic acid contains 18 carbon atoms; the acetyl group contains two carbon atoms. Therefore eight β-oxidation turns occur, and nine molecules of acetyl-CoA are produced.

PROBLEM 24.6
How many molecules of acetyl-CoA are produced by catabolism of the following fatty acids, and how many β oxidations are needed?
(a) Palmitic acid, $CH_3(CH_2)_{14}COOH$
(b) Lignoceric acid, $CH_3(CH_2)_{22}COOH$

PROBLEM 24.7
Look back at the reactions of the citric acid cycle (Figure 20.9) and identify the three reactions in that cycle that are similar to the first three reactions of the β oxidation of a fatty acid.

We have now examined the metabolism of carbohydrates and lipids, which together provide most of our energy. Can proteins be used for energy production? Protein catabolism is utilized for energy production primarily when the carbohydrate and lipid supply is inadequate. Proteins are too important for their essential roles in providing structure and regulating function to be routinely used for energy production.

24.7 Ketone Bodies and Ketoacidosis

What happens if lipid catabolism (or any other condition) produces more acetyl-CoA than the citric acid cycle can handle? This happens when β oxidation of the fatty acids from triacylglcerols produces acetyl-CoA faster than the citric acid cycle can process it. Not only does β oxidation produce several molecules of acetyl-CoA from each molecule of fatty acid, but the enzymes in the β-oxidation pathway catalyze reactions more rapidly than the enzymes in the citric acid cycle do. Consequently, the energy is preserved by conversion of excess acetyl-CoA in liver mitochondria to 3-hydroxybutyrate and acetoacetate. Because it is a β-keto acid and therefore somewhat unstable, acetoacetate undergoes spontaneous, nonenzymatic decomposition to acetone:

Ketone bodies

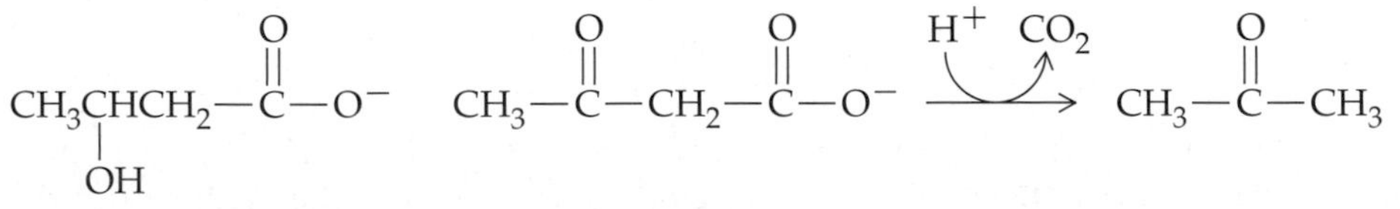

$$CH_3CHCH_2-\overset{\overset{O}{\|}}{C}-O^- \qquad CH_3-\overset{\overset{O}{\|}}{C}-CH_2-\overset{\overset{O}{\|}}{C}-O^- \xrightarrow[\quad]{H^+ \quad CO_2} CH_3-\overset{\overset{O}{\|}}{C}-CH_3$$
$$\underset{OH}{|}$$

3-Hydroxybutyrate　　　　　　　　　Acetoacetate　　　　　　　　　　　Acetone

These compounds are traditionally known as **ketone bodies**, although one of them, 3-hydroxybutyrate, contains no ketone functional group. Because they are water-soluble, ketone bodies do not need protein carriers to travel in the bloodstream. Once formed, they become available to all tissues in the body.

The formation of the three ketone bodies, a process known as **ketogenesis**, occurs in four enzyme-catalyzed steps plus the spontaneous decomposition of acetoacetate.

Ketone bodies Compounds produced in the liver that can be used as fuel by muscle and brain tissue; 3-hydroxybutyrate, acetoacetate, and acetone.

Ketogenesis The synthesis of ketone bodies from acetyl-CoA.

Ketogenesis

STEPS 1 and 2 of Ketogenesis: Assembly of 6-Carbon Intermediate

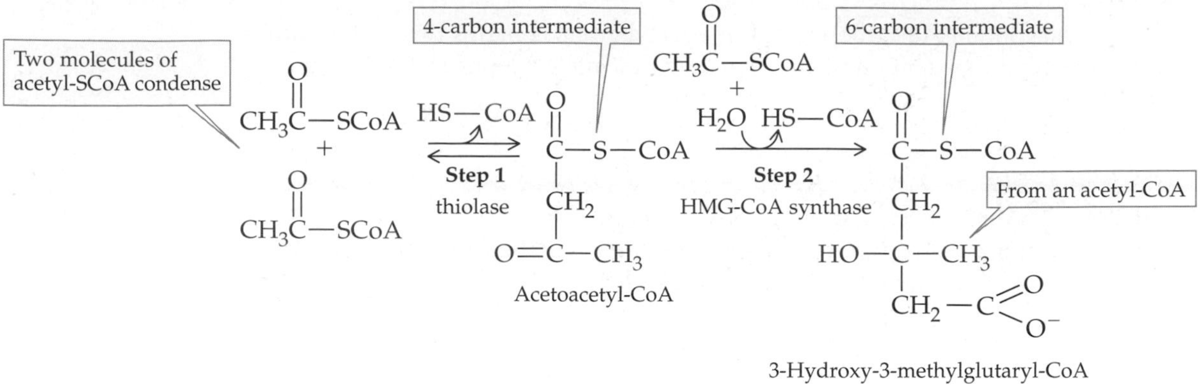

In Step 1, which is the reverse of the final step of β oxidation (Step 4 in Figure 24.7), two acetyl-CoA molecules combine in a reaction catalyzed by *thiolase* to produce acetoacetyl-CoA. Then, in Step 2, a third acetyl-CoA and a water molecule react with acetoacetyl-CoA to give 3-hydroxy-3-methylglutaryl-CoA (HMG-CoA). The enzyme for this step, *HMG-CoA synthase*, is found only in mitochondria and is specific only for the D isomer of the substrate. The enzyme for the β-oxidation pathway, also found in mitochondria, has the same name but is specific for the L form of 3-hydroxy-3-methylglutaryl-CoA. The pathways are separated by the specificity of the enzymes for their respective substrates.

STEPS 3 and 4 of Ketogenesis: Formation of the Ketone Bodies

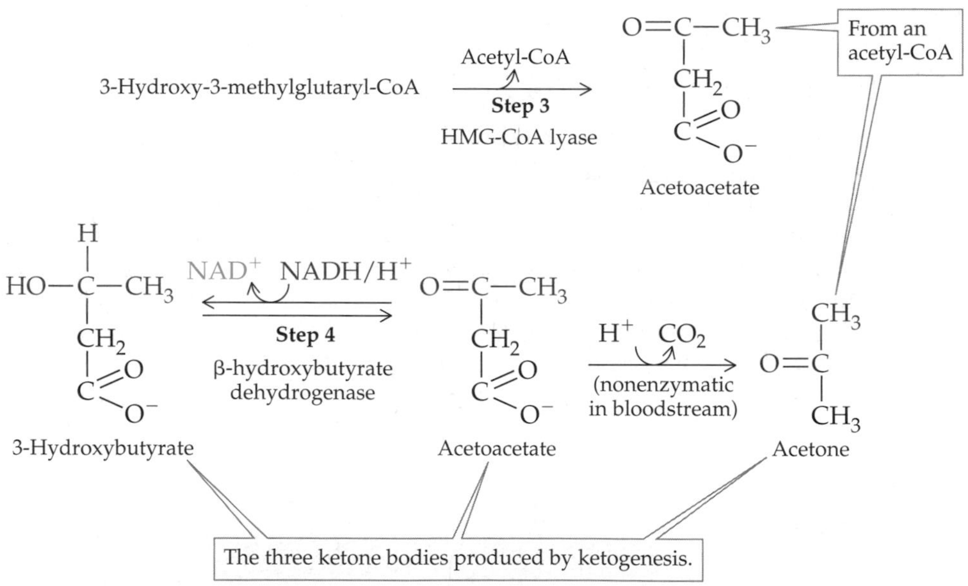

In Step 3, removal of acetyl-CoA from the product of Step 2 by *HMG-CoA lyase* produces the first of the ketone bodies, *acetoacetate*. Acetoacetate is the precursor of the other two ketone bodies produced by ketogenesis, 3-hydroxybutyrate and acetone. In Step 4, the acetoacetate produced in Step 3 is reduced to 3-hydroxybutyrate by *3-hydroxybutyrate dehydrogenase*. (Note in the equation for Step 4 that 3-hydroxybutyrate and acetoacetate are connected by a reversible reaction. In tissues that need energy, acetoacetate is produced by different enzymes than those used for ketogenesis. Acetyl-CoA can then be produced from the acetoacetate.) As acetoacetate and 3-hydroxybutyrate are synthesized by ketogenesis in liver mitochondria, they are released to the bloodstream. Acetone is then formed in the bloodstream by the decomposition of acetoacetate and is excreted primarily by exhalation.

CHEMISTRY IN ACTION

The Liver, Clearinghouse for Metabolism

The liver is the largest reservoir of blood in the body and also the largest internal organ, making up about 2.5% of the body's mass. Blood carrying the end products of digestion (glucose, other sugars, amino acids, and so forth) enters the liver through the hepatic portal vein before going into general circulation, so the liver is ideally situated to regulate the concentrations of nutrients and other substances in the blood. The liver is important as the gateway for entry of drugs into the circulation and also contains the enzymes needed to inactivate toxic substances as well.

Various functions of the liver have been described in scattered sections of this book, but it is only by taking an overview that the central role of the liver in metabolism can be appreciated. Among its many functions, the liver synthesizes glycogen from glucose, glucose from noncarbohydrate precursors, triacylglycerols from mono- and diacylglycerols, and fatty acids from acetyl-CoA. It is also the site of synthesis of cholesterol, bile acids, plasma proteins, and blood-clotting factors. In addition, liver cells can catabolize glucose, fatty acids, and amino acids to yield carbon dioxide and energy stored in ATP. The *urea cycle*, by which nitrogen from amino acids is converted to urea for excretion, takes place in the liver (Section 27.4).

The liver stores reserves of glycogen, certain lipids and amino acids, iron, and fat-soluble vitamins, in order to release them as needed to maintain homeostasis. In addition, only liver cells have the enzyme needed to convert glucose 6-phosphate from glycogenolysis and gluconeogenesis to glucose, which can enter the bloodstream.

Given its central role in metabolism, the liver is subject to a number of pathological conditions based on excessive

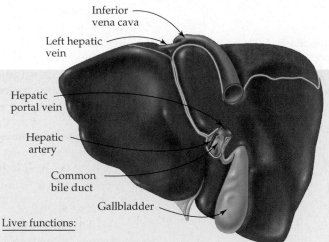

Liver functions:

- Balances level of circulating glucose
- Balances levels of circulating triacylglycerol, fatty acid, and cholesterol
- Removes excess amino acids from circulation; converts their nitrogen to urea for excretion
- Stores reserves of fat-soluble vitamins and iron
- Removes drugs from circulation and breaks them down

▲ **Anatomy of the liver. Blood carrying metabolites from the digestive system enters the liver through the hepatic portal vein. The gallbladder is the site for storage of bile.**

accumulation of various metabolites. One example is *cirrhosis*, the development of fibrous tissue that is preceded by excessive triacylglycerol buildup. Cirrhosis occurs in alcoholism, uncontrolled diabetes, and metabolic conditions in which the synthesis of lipoproteins from triacylglycerols is blocked. Another example is *Wilson's disease*, a genetic defect in copper metabolism. In Wilson's disease, copper accumulates in the liver rather than being excreted or recycled for use in coenzymes. Chronic liver disease, as well as brain damage and anemia, are symptoms of Wilson's disease. The disease is treated by a low-copper diet and drugs that enhance the excretion of copper.

See Chemistry in Action Problems 24.68 and 24.69 at the end of the chapter.

In a person who is well fed and healthy, skeletal muscles derive a small portion of their daily energy needs from acetoacetate, and heart muscles use it in preference to glucose when fatty acids are in short supply. But consider the situation when energy production from glucose is inadequate due to starvation or because glucose is not being metabolized normally due to diabetes (Section 22.9). The body must respond by providing other energy sources in what can become a precarious balancing act. Under these conditions, the production of ketone bodies accelerates because acetoacetate and 3-hydroxybutyrate can be converted to acetyl-CoA for oxidation in the citric acid cycle.

During the early stages of starvation, heart and muscle tissues burn larger quantities of acetoacetate, thereby preserving glucose for use in the brain. In prolonged starvation, even the brain can switch to ketone bodies to meet up to 75% of its energy needs.

The condition in which ketone bodies are produced faster than they are utilized (*ketosis*) occurs in diabetes. It is indicated by the characteristic odor of acetone (a highly volatile ketone) on the patient's breath and the presence of ketone bodies in the urine (*ketonuria*) and the blood (*ketonemia*).

Ketoacidosis Lowered blood pH due to accumulation of ketone bodies.

Because two of the ketone bodies are carboxylic acids, continued ketosis such as might occur in untreated diabetes leads to the potentially serious condition known as **ketoacidosis**—acidosis resulting from increased concentrations of ketone bodies in the blood. The blood's buffers are overwhelmed and blood pH drops. An individual experiences dehydration due to increased urine flow, labored breathing because acidic blood is a poor oxygen carrier, and depression. Ultimately, if untreated, the condition leads to coma and death.

PROBLEM 24.8

Why is the liver referred to as the clearinghouse for metabolism in your body? (See Chemistry in Action: The Liver, Clearinghouse for Metabolism on p. 767.)

PROBLEM 24.9

Which of the following classifications apply to the formation of 3-hydroxybutyrate from acetoacetate?

(a) Condensation   (b) Hydrolysis

(c) Oxidation   (d) Reduction

PROBLEM 24.10

Consider the reactions of ketogenesis.

(a) What role does acetyl-CoA play?

(b) How many acetyl-CoA molecules are used in the production of the ketone bodies?

(c) What is the essential role of ketone bodies during prolonged starvation?

24.8 Biosynthesis of Fatty Acids

Lipogenesis The biochemical pathway for synthesis of fatty acids from acetyl-CoA.

The biosynthesis of fatty acids from acetyl-CoA, a process known as **lipogenesis**, provides a link between carbohydrate, lipid, and protein metabolism. Because acetyl-CoA is an end product of carbohydrate and amino acid catabolism, using it to make fatty acids allows the body to divert the energy of excess carbohydrates and amino acids into storage as triacylglycerols.

Fatty acid synthesis and catabolism are similar in that they both proceed two carbon atoms at a time and in that they are both recursive, spiral pathways. But, as is usually the case, the biochemical pathway in one direction is not the exact reverse of the pathway in the other direction because the reverse of an energetically favorable pathway is energetically unfavorable. This principle applies to β oxidation of fatty acids and its reverse, lipogenesis. Furthermore, catabolism of fatty acids occurs in the mitochondria and anabolism is located in the cytoplasm. The two pathways are compared in Table 24.1.

TABLE **24.1** Comparison of Fatty Acid Oxidation and Synthesis	
Oxidation	**Synthesis**
Occurs in mitochondria	Occurs in cytosol
Enzymes different from synthesis	Enzymes different from oxidation
Intermediates carried by coenzyme A	Intermediates carried by acyl carrier protein
Coenzymes: FAD, NAD^+	Coenzyme: NADPH
Carbon atoms removed two at a time	Carbon atoms added two at a time

The stage is set for lipogenesis by two separate reactions: (1) transfer of an acetyl group from acetyl-CoA to a carrier enzyme in the fatty acid synthase complex (S-enzyme-1) and (2) conversion of acetyl-CoA to malonyl-CoA in a reaction that requires the investment of energy from ATP, followed by transfer of the malonyl group to the acyl carrier protein (ACP) and regeneration of coenzyme A :

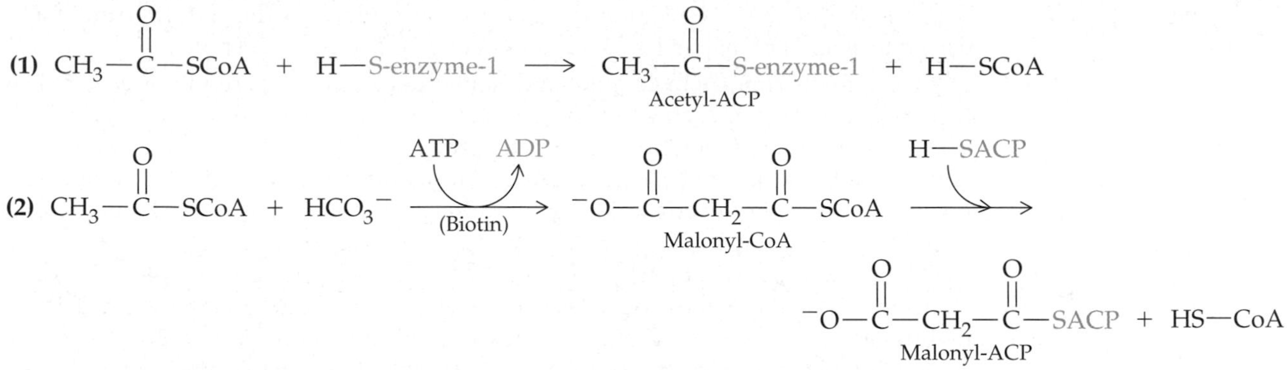

(1) $CH_3-\overset{\overset{\displaystyle O}{\|}}{C}-SCoA$ + H—S-enzyme-1 $\longrightarrow$ $CH_3-\overset{\overset{\displaystyle O}{\|}}{C}-S\text{-enzyme-1}$ + H—SCoA

Acetyl-ACP

(2) $CH_3-\overset{\overset{\displaystyle O}{\|}}{C}-SCoA$ + HCO_3^- $\xrightarrow[\text{(Biotin)}]{ATP \quad ADP}$ $^-O-\overset{\overset{\displaystyle O}{\|}}{C}-CH_2-\overset{\overset{\displaystyle O}{\|}}{C}-SCoA$ $\xrightarrow{\text{H—SACP}}$

Malonyl-CoA

$^-O-\overset{\overset{\displaystyle O}{\|}}{C}-CH_2-\overset{\overset{\displaystyle O}{\|}}{C}-SACP$ + HS—CoA

Malonyl-ACP

(*Fatty acid synthase* is a multienzyme complex that contains all six of the enzymes needed for lipogenesis, with a protein called *acyl carrier protein* [ACP] anchored in the center of the complex. Enzyme-1 is also part of the complex.) The malonyl group of reaction (2) carries the carbon atoms that will be incorporated two at a time into the fatty acid.

Once malonyl-ACP and the acetyl group on S-enzyme-1 have been readied, a series of four reactions lengthens the growing fatty acid chain by two carbon atoms with each repetition (Figure 24.8). Fatty acids containing up to 16 carbon atoms (palmitic acid) are produced by this route.

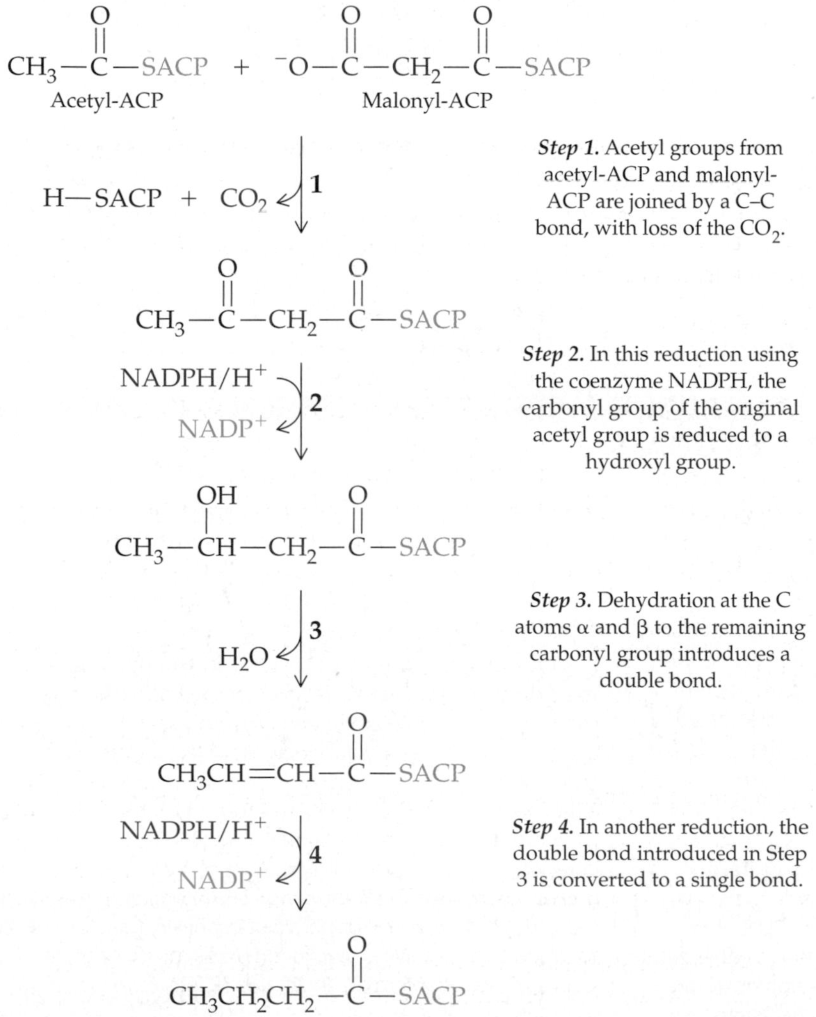

$CH_3-\overset{\overset{\displaystyle O}{\|}}{C}-SACP$ + $^-O-\overset{\overset{\displaystyle O}{\|}}{C}-CH_2-\overset{\overset{\displaystyle O}{\|}}{C}-SACP$

Acetyl-ACP Malonyl-ACP

$\Big\downarrow$ 1   H—SACP + CO_2

Step 1. Acetyl groups from acetyl-ACP and malonyl-ACP are joined by a C–C bond, with loss of the CO_2.

$CH_3-\overset{\overset{\displaystyle O}{\|}}{C}-CH_2-\overset{\overset{\displaystyle O}{\|}}{C}-SACP$

NADPH/H$^+$ $\Big\}$ 2   NADP$^+$

Step 2. In this reduction using the coenzyme NADPH, the carbonyl group of the original acetyl group is reduced to a hydroxyl group.

$CH_3-\overset{\overset{\displaystyle OH}{|}}{CH}-CH_2-\overset{\overset{\displaystyle O}{\|}}{C}-SACP$

$\Big\downarrow$ 3   H$_2$O

Step 3. Dehydration at the C atoms α and β to the remaining carbonyl group introduces a double bond.

$CH_3CH{=}CH-\overset{\overset{\displaystyle O}{\|}}{C}-SACP$

NADPH/H$^+$ $\Big\}$ 4   NADP$^+$

Step 4. In another reduction, the double bond introduced in Step 3 is converted to a single bond.

$CH_3CH_2CH_2-\overset{\overset{\displaystyle O}{\|}}{C}-SACP$

◄ **Figure 24.8**
Chain elongation in the biosynthesis of fatty acids.
The steps shown begin with acetyl acyl carrier protein (acetyl-ACP), the reactant in the first spiral of palmitic acid synthesis. Each new pair of carbon atoms is carried into the next spiral by a new malonyl-ACP. The growing chain remains attached to the carrier protein from the original acetyl-ACP.

Chain Elongation of Fatty Acid

STEP 1: Condensation The malonyl group from malonyl-ACP transfers to acetyl-ACP with the loss of CO_2. The loss of the CO_2 that was added in the endothermic, ATP-driven formation of malonyl-ACP releases energy to drive the reaction.

STEPS 2–4: Reduction, Dehydration, and Reduction These three reactions accomplish the reverse of Steps 3, 2, and 1 in the β oxidation of fatty acids shown in Figure 24.7. The carbonyl group is reduced to an —OH group, dehydration yields a carbon–carbon double bond, and the double bond is reduced by addition of hydrogen. Both reductions involve the coenzyme nicotinamide adenine dinucleotide phosphate, in its reduced form, NADPH.

The result of the first cycle in fatty acid synthesis is the addition of two carbon atoms to an acetyl group to give a 4-carbon acyl group still attached to the carrier protein in fatty acid synthase. The next cycle then adds two more carbon atoms to give a 6-carbon acyl group by repeating the four steps of chain elongation shown here:

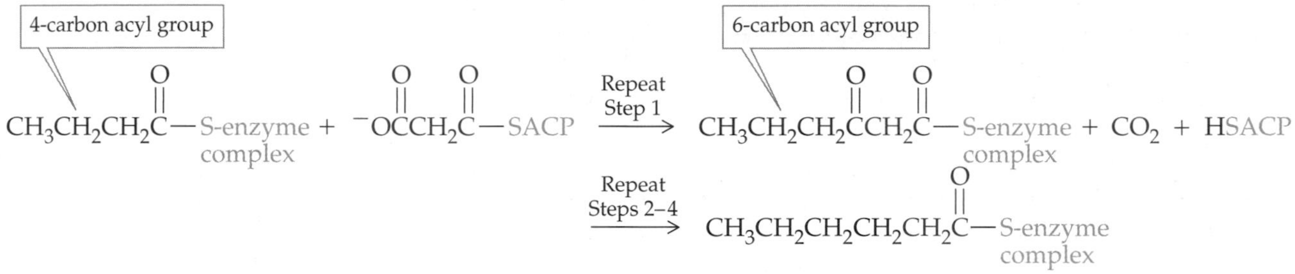

After seven trips through the elongation spiral, a 16-carbon palmitoyl group is produced and released from the fatty acid synthase. Larger fatty acids are synthesized from palmitoyl-CoA with the aid of specific enzymes in the endoplasmic reticulum.

PROBLEM 24.11
Starting with acetyl-S-enzyme-1 and malonyl-CoA, how many molecules of acetyl-CoA are needed to synthesize an 18-carbon fatty acid (C18:0)? How many molecules of CO_2 are released in this process?

SUMMARY: REVISITING THE CHAPTER GOALS

1. What happens during the digestion of triacylglycerols? *Triacylglycerols* from the diet are broken into droplets in the stomach and enter the small intestine, where they are emulsified by *bile acids* and form micelles. Pancreatic lipases partially hydrolyze the triacylglycerols in the micelles. Small fatty acids and glycerol from triacylglycerol hydrolysis are absorbed directly into the bloodstream at the intestinal surface. Insoluble hydrolysis products are carried to the lining in micelles, where they are absorbed and reassembled into triacylglycerols. These triacylglycerols are then assembled into *chylomicrons* (which are *lipoproteins*) and absorbed into the lymph system for transport to the bloodstream (*see Problems 1, 20–25, 70, 71*).

2. What are the various roles of lipoproteins in lipid transport? In addition to chylomicrons, which carry triacylglycerols from the diet into the bloodstream, there are VLDLs (*very-low-density lipoproteins*), which carry triacylglycerols synthesized in the liver to peripheral tissues for energy generation or storage; LDLs (*low-density lipoproteins*), which transport cholesterol from

the liver to peripheral tissues for cell membranes or steroid synthesis; and HDLs (*high-density lipoproteins*), which transport cholesterol from peripheral tissues back to the liver for conversion to bile acids that are used in digestion or excreted (*see Problems 2, 13, 26–29, 60–61, 79, 80, 82*).

3. What are the major pathways in the metabolism of triacylglycerols? Dietary triacylglycerols carried by chylomicrons in the bloodstream undergo hydrolysis to fatty acids and glycerol by enzymes in capillary walls. Triacylglycerols in storage are similarly hydrolyzed within adipocytes. The fatty acids from either source undergo *β oxidation* to acetyl-CoA or resynthesis into triacylglycerols for storage. Acetyl-CoA can participate in resynthesis of fatty acids (*lipogenesis*), formation of *ketone bodies* (*ketogenesis*), steroid synthesis, or energy generation via the citric acid cycle and oxidative phosphorylation. Glycerol can participate in glycolysis, gluconeogenesis, or triacylglycerol synthesis (*see Problems 3, 8, 14, 16, 17, 68, 69*).

4. How are triacylglycerols moved into and out of storage in adipose tissue? Synthesis of triacylglycerols for storage is activated by insulin when blood glucose levels are high. The synthesis requires dihydroxyacetone phosphate (from glycolysis or glycerol) for conversion to glycerol 3-phosphate, to which fatty acyl groups are added one at a time to yield triacylglycerols. Hydrolysis of triacylglycerols stored in adipocytes is activated by glucagon when glucose levels drop (*see Problems 4, 29, 30, 33–35, 63–68, 82*).

5. How are fatty acids oxidized, and how much energy is produced by their oxidation? Fatty acids are activated (in the cytosol) by conversion to fatty acyl coenzyme A, a reaction that requires the equivalent of two ATPs in the conversion of ATP to AMP. The fatty acyl-CoA molecules are transported into the mitochondrial matrix and are then oxidized two carbon atoms at a time to acetyl-CoA by repeated trips through the β-oxidation spiral (*see Problems 5–7, 12, 15, 32, 33, 37–42, 44–51, 72, 78, 81*).

6. What is the function of ketogenesis? The ketone bodies are 3-hydroxybutyrate, acetoacetate, and acetone. They are produced from two acetyl-CoA molecules. Their production is increased when energy generation from the citric acid cycle cannot keep pace with the quantity of acetyl-CoA available. This occurs during the early stages of starvation and in unregulated diabetes. Ketone bodies are water-soluble and can travel unassisted in the bloodstream to tissues where acetyl-CoA is produced from acetoacetate and 3-hydroxybutyrate. In this way, acetyl-CoA is made available for energy generation when glucose is in short supply (*see Problems 9, 10, 18, 74–77*).

7. How are fatty acids synthesized? Fatty acid synthesis (lipogenesis), like β oxidation, proceeds two carbon atoms at a time in a four-step pathway. The pathways utilize different enzymes and coenzymes. In synthesis, the initial four carbons are transferred from acetyl-CoA to the malonyl carrier protein. Each additional pair of carbons is then added to the growing chain bonded to the carrier protein, with the final three steps of the four-step synthesis sequence the reverse of the first three steps in β oxidation (*see Problems 11, 19, 43, 52–59*).

KEY WORDS

β-**oxidation pathway,** *p. 762*

Bile, *p. 754*

Bile acids, *p. 754*

Ketoacidosis, *p. 768*

Ketogenesis, *p. 765*

Ketone bodies, *p. 765*

Lipogenesis, *p. 768*

Lipoprotein, *p. 754*

Mobilization (of triacylglycerols), *p. 761*

UNDERSTANDING KEY CONCEPTS

24.12   Oxygen is not a reactant in the β oxidation of fatty acids. Can β oxidation occur under anaerobic conditions? Explain.

24.13   Identify each lipoprotein described below as either chylomicron, HDL, LDL, or VLDL.

(a) Which lipoprotein has the lowest density? Why?

(b) Which lipoprotein carries triacylglycerols from the diet?

(c) Which lipoprotein removes cholesterol from circulation?

(d) Which lipoprotein contains "bad cholesterol" from a vascular disease risk standpoint?

(e) Which lipoprotein has the highest ratio of protein to lipid?

(f) Which lipoprotein carries triacylglycerols from the liver to peripheral tissues? How are triacylglycerols used?

(g) Which lipoprotein transports cholesterol from the liver to peripheral tissues?

24.14   Lipid metabolism, especially triacylglycerol anabolism and catabolism, is closely associated with carbohydrate (glucose) metabolism. Insulin and glucagon levels in blood are regulated by the glucose levels in blood. Draw lines from the appropriate phrases in column A to appropriate phrases in columns B and C.

A	B	C
High blood glucose	High glucagon/ low insulin	Fatty acid and triacylglycerol synthesis
Low blood glucose	High insulin/ low glucagon	Triacylglycerol hydrolysis; fatty acid oxidation

24.15   One strategy used in many different biochemical pathways is an initial investment of energy early on and a large payoff in energy at the end of the pathway. How is this strategy utilized in the catabolism of fats?

24.16   When oxaloacetate in liver tissue is being used for gluconeogenesis, what impact does this have on the citric acid cycle? Explain.

24.17   Why is it more efficient to store energy as triacylglycerols rather than as glycogen?

24.18   Explain the rationale for the production of ketone bodies during starvation.

24.19   Compare the differences between β oxidation and fatty acid synthesis (lipogenesis). Are these pathways the reverse of each other?

ADDITIONAL PROBLEMS

DIGESTION AND CATABOLISM OF LIPIDS

24.20 Why do lipids make you feel full for a long time after a meal?

24.21 Where does digestion of lipids occur?

24.22 What is the purpose of bile acids in lipid digestion?

24.23 Where are bile acids synthesized, and what is the starting molecule?

24.24 Write the equation for the hydrolysis of a triacylglycerol composed of stearic acid, oleic acid, and linoleic acid by pancreatic lipase.

24.25 Lipases break down triacylglycerols by catalyzing hydrolysis. What are the products of this hydrolysis?

24.26 What are chylomicrons, and how are they involved in lipid metabolism?

24.27 What is the origin of the triacylglycerols transported by very-low-density lipoproteins?

24.28 How are the fatty acids from adipose tissue transported?

24.29 How is cholesterol transported around the body? When it leaves the liver, what is its destination and use?

24.30 The glycerol derived from lipolysis of triacylglycerols is converted into glyceraldehyde 3-phosphate, which then enters into Step 6 of the glycolysis pathway. What further transformations are necessary to convert glyceraldehyde 3-phosphate into pyruvate?

24.31 If the conversion of glycerol to glyceraldehyde 3-phosphate releases 1 molecule of ATP, how many molecules of ATP are released during the conversion of glycerol to pyruvate?

24.32 How many molecules of ATP are released in the overall catabolism of glycerol to acetyl-CoA? How many molecules of ATP are released in the complete catabolism of glycerol to CO_2 and H_2O?

24.33 How many molecules of acetyl-CoA result from catabolism of 1 molecule of glyceryl trilaurate?

24.34 What is an adipocyte?

24.35 What is the primary function of adipose tissues, and where in the body are they located?

24.36 Which tissues carry out fatty acid oxidation as their primary source of energy?

24.37 Where in the cell does β oxidation take place?

24.38 What initial chemical transformation takes place on a fatty acid to activate it for catabolism?

24.39 What must take place before an activated fatty acid undergoes β oxidation?

24.40 Why is the stepwise oxidation of fatty acids called β oxidation?

24.41 Why is the sequence of reactions that catabolize fatty acids described as a *spiral* rather than a *cycle*?

24.42 Which coenzymes are required for β oxidation?

24.43 Are these the same coenzymes necessary for fatty acid synthesis?

24.44 How many moles of ATP are produced by one cycle of β oxidation?

24.45 How many moles of ATP are produced by the complete oxidation of 1 mol of myristic acid?

24.46 Arrange these four molecules in increasing order of their biological energy content (per mole):

(a) Sucrose

(b) Myristic acid, $CH_3(CH_2)_{12}COOH$

(c) Glucose

(d) Capric acid, $CH_3(CH_2)_8COOH$

24.47 Arrange these four molecules in increasing order of their biological energy content per mole:

(a) Mannose

(b) Stearic acid, $CH_3(CH_2)_{16}COOH$

(c) Fructose

(d) Palmitic acid, $CH_3(CH_2)_{14}COOH$

24.48 Show the products of each step in the fatty acid oxidation of hexanoic acid:

(a) $CH_3(CH_2)_4\overset{\displaystyle O}{\overset{\displaystyle \|}{C}}SCoA \xrightarrow[\substack{\text{Acetyl-CoA} \\ \text{dehydrogenase}}]{\text{FAD} \quad \text{FADH}_2}$?

(b) Product of (a) $+ H_2O \xrightarrow[\text{hydratase}]{\text{Enoyl-CoA}}$?

(c) Product of (b) $\xrightarrow[\substack{\beta\text{-Hydroxyacyl-CoA} \\ \text{dehydrogenase}}]{\text{NAD}^+ \quad \text{NADH/H}^+}$?

(d) Product of (c) $+ HSCoA \xrightarrow[\text{transferase}]{\text{Acetyl-CoA}}$?

24.49 Write the equation for the final step in the catabolism of any fatty acid with an even number of carbons.

24.50 How many molecules of acetyl-CoA result from complete catabolism of the following compounds?

(a) Myristic acid, $CH_3(CH_2)_{12}COOH$

(b) Caprylic acid, $CH_3(CH_2)_6COOH$

24.51 How many cycles of β oxidation are necessary to completely catabolize myristic and caprylic acids?

FATTY ACID ANABOLISM

24.52 Name the anabolic pathway that synthesizes fatty acids.

24.53 Explain why β oxidation cannot proceed backward to produce triacylglycerols.

24.54 Name the starting material for fatty acid synthesis.

24.55 Why are fatty acids generally composed of an even number of carbons?

24.56 How many rounds of the lipogenesis cycle are needed to synthesize stearic acid, $C_{17}H_{35}COOH$?

24.57 How many molecules of NADPH are needed to synthesize stearic acid, $C_{17}H_{35}COOH$?

24.58 How does the cell keep the processes of fatty acid synthesis and degradation separated?

24.59 Describe two differences in the reactions for fatty synthesis and the reactions for fatty acid degradation.

CHEMISTRY IN ACTION

24.60 What are desirable goals for fasting levels of total cholesterol, HDL, and LDL values? [*Lipids and Atherosclerosis, p. 757*]

24.61 What is atherosclerosis? [*Lipids and Atherosclerosis, p. 757*]

24.62 What are the differences between the roles of LDL and HDL? [*Lipids and Atherosclerosis, p. 757*]

24.63 Explain the significance of cholesterol/HDL ratios of 3.5, 4.5, and 5.5. [*Lipids and Atherosclerosis, p. 757*]

24.64 What diseases are obese people at high risk of developing? [*Fat Storage: A Good Thing or Not?, p. 760*]

24.65 What role is leptin thought to play in fat storage? [*Fat Storage: A Good Thing or Not?, p. 760*]

24.66 What factors contribute to storage of excess energy as triacylglycerols? [*Fat Storage: A Good Thing or Not?, p. 760*]

24.67 Propose a reason for why excess weight, once gained and stored as fat, is so difficult to lose. [*Fat Storage: A Good Thing or Not?, p. 760*]

24.68 Give some reasons why the liver is so vital to proper metabolic function. [*The Liver, Clearinghouse for Metabolism, p. 767*]

24.69 What is cirrhosis of the liver, and what can trigger it? [*The Liver, Clearinghouse for Metabolism, p. 767*]

GENERAL QUESTIONS AND PROBLEMS

24.70 Consuming too many carbohydrates causes deposition of fats in adipose tissue. How can this happen?

24.71 Why are extra calories consumed as carbohydrates stored as fat and not as glycogen?

24.72 Are any of the intermediates in the β-oxidation pathway chiral? Explain.

24.73 What three compounds are classified as ketone bodies? Why are they so designated? What process in the body produces them? Why do they form?

24.74 What is ketosis? What condition results from prolonged ketosis? Why is it dangerous?

24.75 What causes acetone to be present in the breath of someone with uncontrolled diabetes?

24.76 Individuals suffering from ketoacidosis have acidic urine. What effect do you expect ketones to have on pH? Why is pH lowered when ketone bodies are present?

24.77 Diets that severely restrict carbohydrate intake often result in ketosis for the dieter. Explain why this occurs.

24.78 Compare fats and carbohydrates as energy sources in terms of the amount of energy released per mole, and account for the observed energy difference.

24.79 Lipoproteins that transport lipids from the diet are described as exogenous. Those that transport lipids produced in metabolic pathways are described as endogenous. Which of the following lipoproteins transport exogenous lipids and which transports endogenous lipids?

   (a) Low-density lipoprotein (LDL)

   (b) Chylomicrons

24.80 High blood-cholesterol levels are dangerous because of their correlation with atherosclerosis and consequent heart attacks and strokes. Is it possible to eliminate all cholesterol from the bloodstream by having a diet that includes no cholesterol? Is it desirable to have no cholesterol at all in your body?

24.81 Behenic acid (C22:0) is present in peanut butter.

   (a) How many molecules of acetyl-CoA are produced by β-oxidation of behenic acid?

   (b) How many molecules of ATP are produced in (a)?

   (c) How many molecules of CO_2 arc produced by complete oxidation of the acetyl-CoA produced in (a)?

   (d) How many molecules of ATP are produced in (c)?

   (e) How many total molecules of ATP are produced by the complete oxidation of behenic acid to CO_2?

24.82 In the synthesis of cholesterol, acetyl-CoA is converted to 2-methyl-1,3-butadiene. Molecules of 2-methyl-1,3-butadiene are then joined to give the carbon skeleton of cholesterol. Draw the condensed structure of 2-methyl-1,3-butadiene. How many carbon atoms does cholesterol contain? What minimum number of 2-methyl-1,3-butadiene molecules is required to make one molecule of cholesterol?

24.83 A low-fat diet of pasta, bread, beer, and soda can easily lead to an increase in weight. The increase is stored triacylglycerols in adipocytes. Explain the weight increase and why the excess carbohydrate is stored as fat.

Nucleic Acids and Protein Synthesis

◄ The symmetrical beauty of the DNA molecule has inspired more than just scientific research, as demonstrated by this sculpture of the double helix.

CHAPTER GOALS

1. **What are the compositions of the nucleic acids, DNA and RNA?**
   THE GOAL: Be able to describe and identify the components of nucleosides, nucleotides, DNA, and RNA. (◀◀◀ B, D.)

2. **What is the structure of DNA?**
   THE GOAL: Be able to describe the double helix and base pairing in DNA. (◀◀◀ A, B, D.)

3. **How is DNA reproduced?**
   THE GOAL: Be able to explain the process of DNA replication. (◀◀◀ A, B.)

4. **What are the functions of RNA?**
   THE GOAL: Be able to list the types of RNA, their locations in the cell, and their functions. (◀◀◀ A, B.)

5. **How do organisms synthesize messenger RNA?**
   THE GOAL: Be able to explain the process of transcription. (◀◀◀ A, B.)

6. **How does RNA participate in protein synthesis?**
   THE GOAL: Be able to explain the genetic code, and describe the initiation, elongation, and termination steps of translation. (◀◀◀ A, B, C.)

CONCEPTS TO REVIEW

◀◀◀

A. Hydrogen Bonding
(Section 8.2)

B. Phosphoric Acid Derivatives
(Section 17.8)

C. Protein Structure
(Sections 18.7, 18.8)

D. Carbohydrate Structure
(Section 21.4)

How does a seed know what kind of plant to become? How does a fertilized egg know how to grow into a human being? And as that fertilized egg grows into a developing embryo, how does any given cell know to become part of a finger, a liver, or a heart? The answers to these and a multitude of other fundamental questions about all living organisms reside in the biological molecules known as *nucleic acids*.

Nucleic acids are the chemical carriers of an organism's genetic information. Coded in an organism's *deoxyribonucleic acid (DNA)* is all the information that determines the nature of the organism, be it a dandelion, goldfish, or human being. DNA contains the blueprint for every protein in the body. As you saw in Chapters 18 and 19, proteins have a wide array of structures and functions, and nearly all reactions in the body are catalyzed by enzymes, which are proteins. An organism's proteins determine the nature of the organism.

25.1 DNA, Chromosomes, and Genes

The terms *chromosome* and *gene* were coined long before the chemical nature of these cell components was understood. A *chromosome* (which means "colored body") was a structure in the cell nucleus thought to be the carrier of genetic information—all the information needed by an organism to duplicate itself. A *gene* was presumed to be the portion of a chromosome that controlled a specific inheritable trait such as brown eyes or red hair.

Our knowledge of cell biology and biochemistry has increased remarkably since these terms were introduced. We now understand the molecular structure of chromosomes and genes. We can describe the sequence of events in which genetic information is reproduced when a cell divides. The relationship of genes to the synthesis of proteins is no longer a mystery. These concepts are described in this chapter. The story continues in the next chapter with an introduction to genomics and molecular biology, the study of biology and biochemistry at the DNA level. The achievements of molecular biology have led to a revolution in science and technology, with the biggest development of all being that a complete map of the genetic information passed along during cell division is now available for numerous organisms, including humans.

When a cell is not actively dividing, its nucleus is occupied by *chromatin*, which is a compact, orderly tangle of **DNA (deoxyribonucleic acid)**, the carrier of genetic information, twisted around organizing proteins known as *histones*. During cell division, chromatin becomes even more compact and organizes itself into **chromosomes**. Each chromosome contains a different DNA molecule, and all the DNA is duplicated so that each new cell receives a complete copy.

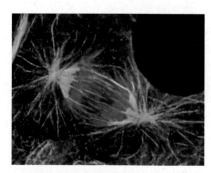

▲ Chromosomes (red) during cell division.

DNA (deoxyribonucleic acid) The nucleic acid that stores genetic information; a polymer of deoxyribonucleotides.

Chromosome A complex of proteins and DNA; visible during cell division.

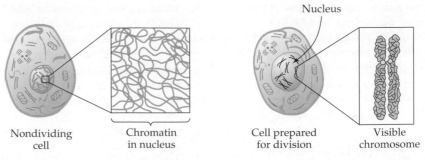

| Nondividing cell | Chromatin in nucleus | Cell prepared for division | Visible chromosome |

Gene Segment of DNA that directs the synthesis of a single polypeptide.

Each DNA molecule, in turn, is composed of many **genes**—individual segments of the DNA molecule containing the instructions that direct the synthesis of a single polypeptide. Interestingly, not all genes coded for by an organism's DNA are expressed as protein. As we will see later in this chapter, some genes code for *functional RNA* molecules.

Organisms differ widely in their numbers of chromosomes. A horse, for example, has 64 chromosomes (32 pairs), a cat has 38 chromosomes (19 pairs), a mosquito has 6 chromosomes (3 pairs), and a corn plant has 20 chromosomes (10 pairs). A human has 46 chromosomes (23 pairs).

25.2 Composition of Nucleic Acids

Nucleic acid A polymer of nucleotides.

Nucleotide A 5-carbon sugar bonded to a cyclic amine base and a phosphate group; the monomer for nucleic acids.

Like proteins and carbohydrates, nucleic acids are polymers. Proteins are polypeptides, carbohydrates are polysaccharides, and **nucleic acids** are *polynucleotides*. Each **nucleotide** has three parts: a five-membered cyclic monosaccharide, a nitrogen-containing cyclic compound known as a *nitrogenous base*, and a phosphate group ($-OPO_3^{2-}$).

A nucleotide

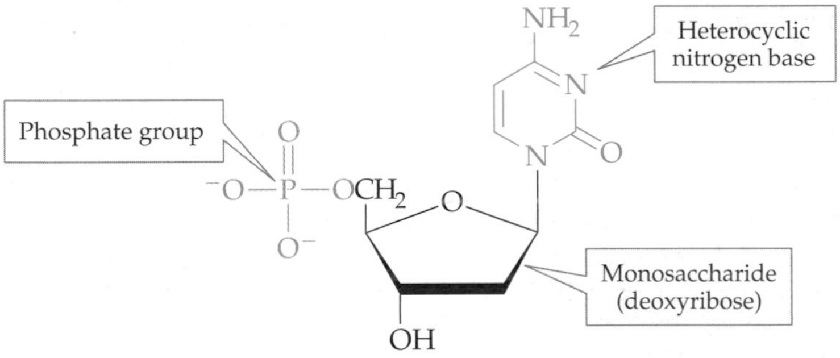

Phosphate group

Heterocyclic nitrogen base

Monosaccharide (deoxyribose)

RNA (ribonucleic acid) Nucleic acids responsible for putting the genetic information to use in protein synthesis; a polymer of ribonucleotides. Includes messenger, transfer, and ribosomal RNA.

There are two classes of nucleic acids, DNA and **RNA (ribonucleic acid)**, with RNA coming in different types. The function of one type of RNA is to put the information stored in DNA to use. Other types of RNA assist in the conversion of the message a specific RNA carries into protein. Before we discuss how the nucleic acids fulfill their functions, we need to understand how their component parts are joined together and how DNA and RNA differ from each other.

The Sugars

One difference between DNA and RNA is found in the sugar portion of the molecules. In RNA, the sugar is D-ribose (Sections 21.4 and 21.5; hereafter simply referred to as ribose), as indicated by the name *ribonucleic acid*. In DNA, the sugar is 2-*deoxy*ribose, giving *deoxyribonucleic acid*. (The prefix *2-deoxy-* means that an oxygen atom is missing from the C2 position of ribose.)

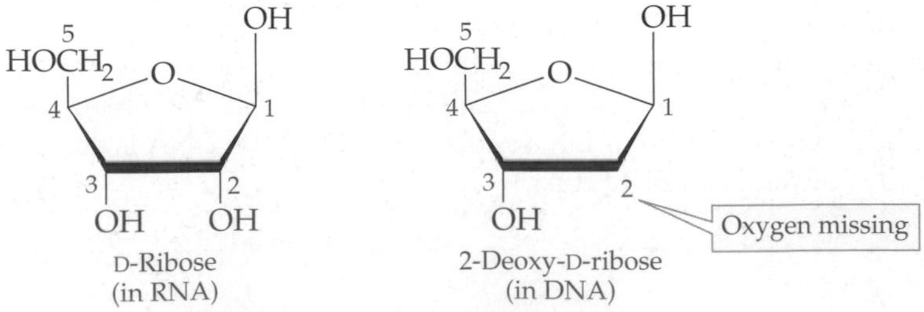

D-Ribose (in RNA)

2-Deoxy-D-ribose (in DNA)

Oxygen missing

The Bases

There are five different kinds of nitrogenous bases found in DNA and RNA, and they are all derived from two parent compounds, purine and pyrimidine. The five nitrogenous bases are shown highlighted in gray in Table 25.1, along with the two parent bases. The nitrogenous bases that are purine derivatives, adenine and guanine, contain two fused nitrogen-containing rings. The bases that are pyrimidine derivatives—cytosine, thymine, and uracil—contain only one nitrogen-containing ring.

TABLE 25.1 Bases in DNA and RNA

PURINE BASES IN NUCLEIC ACIDS			PYRIMIDINE BASES IN NUCLEIC ACIDS			
Purine (Parent)	Adenine (DNA, RNA)	Guanine (DNA, RNA)	Pyrimidine (Parent)	Cytosine (DNA, RNA)	Thymine* (DNA)	Uracil (RNA)

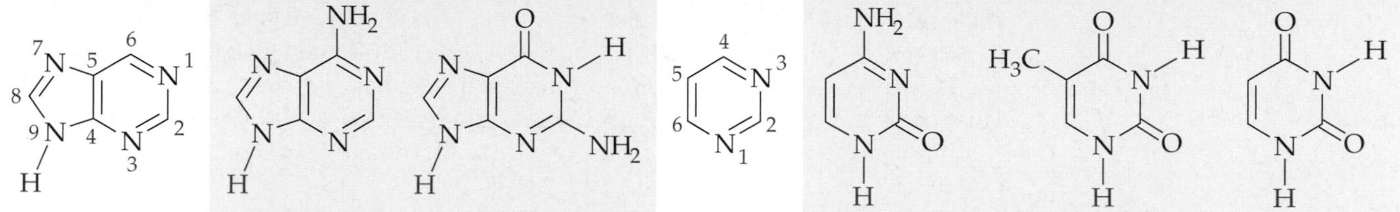

Thymine occurs in a few cases of RNA.

In addition to differing in the sugars they contain, RNA and DNA differ in their bases. As Table 25.1 notes,

- Thymine is present only in DNA molecules (with rare exceptions).
- Uracil is present only in RNA molecules.
- Adenine, guanine, and cytosine are present in both DNA and RNA.

Sugar + Base = Nucleoside

A molecule composed of either ribose or deoxyribose and one of the five nitrogenous bases found in DNA and/or RNA is called a **nucleoside**. The combination of ribose and adenine, for example, gives the nucleoside known as adenosine, which you should recognize as the parent molecule of adenosine triphosphate (ATP) (p. 632):

Nucleoside A 5-carbon sugar bonded to a cyclic amine base; like a nucleotide but with no phosphate group.

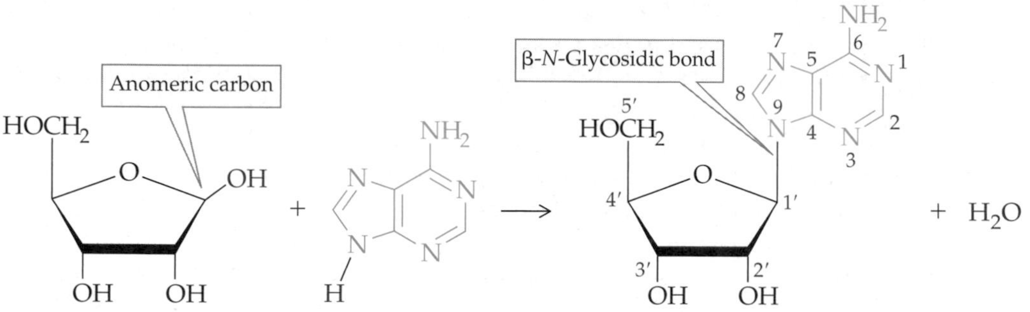

The sugar and base are connected by a bond between one of the nitrogen atoms in the base and the anomeric carbon atom (the one bonded to two oxygen atoms) of the sugar. This bond is a β-N-glycosidic bond. Notice that this linkage (the $1'$ position of the sugar to the nine-position nitrogen atom of the adenine) is closely related to an acetal (Section 16.7).

In each of the nucleic acid bases in Table 25.1, the hydrogen atom lost in nucleoside formation is shown in red.

Nucleoside names are the nitrogenous base name modified by the suffix -*osine* for the purine bases (as we just saw for adenosine) and the suffix -*idine* for the pyrimidine bases. No prefix is used for nucleosides containing ribose, but the prefix *deoxy*- is added

▶▶▶ Recall from Chapter 21 that a glycosidic bond is the bond between the anomeric carbon atom of a sugar and an —OR or —NR group. β Bonds point above the sugar ring, and α bonds point below it.

for those that contain deoxyribose. Therefore the four nucleosides found in RNA are named adenosine, guanosine, cytidine, and uridine, and the four found in DNA are named deoxyadenosine, deoxyguanosine, deoxycytidine, and deoxythymidine.

To distinguish between atoms in the sugar ring of a nucleoside and atoms in the base ring (or rings), numbers without primes are used for atoms in the base ring (or rings), and numbers with primes are used for atoms in the sugar ring.

Worked Example 25.1 Naming a Nucleic Acid Component from Its Structure

Is the compound shown here a nucleoside or a nucleotide? Identify its sugar and base components, and name the compound.

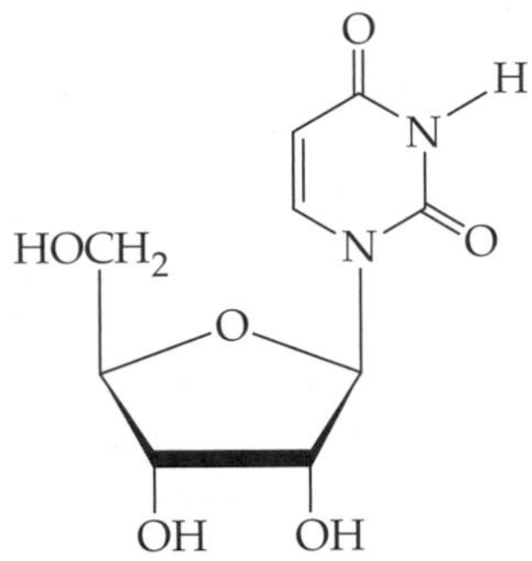

ANALYSIS The compound contains a sugar, recognizable by the oxygen atom in the ring and the —OH groups. It also contains a nitrogenous base, recognizable by the nitrogen-containing ring. The sugar has an —OH in the 2′ position and is therefore ribose (if it were missing the —OH in the 2′ position, it would be a *deoxy*ribose). Checking the base structures in Table 25.1 shows that this is uracil, a pyrimidine base, requiring its name to end in *-idine*.

SOLUTION
The compound is a nucleoside, and its name is uridine.

🔑 KEY CONCEPT PROBLEM 25.1

Name the nucleoside shown here. Copy the structure, and number the C and N atoms (refer to Table 25.1).

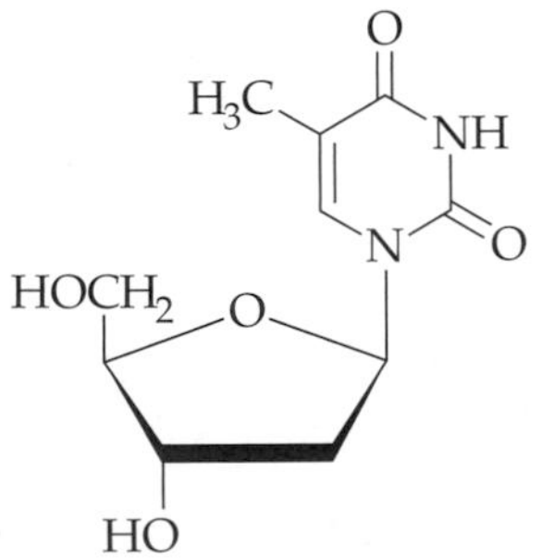

PROBLEM 25.2
Write the molecular formulas for the sugars D-ribose and 2-deoxy-D-ribose. Exactly how do they differ in composition? Can you think of one chemical property that might differ slightly between the two?

Nucleoside + Phosphate = Nucleotide

Nucleotides are the building blocks of nucleic acids; they are the monomers of the DNA and RNA polymers. Each nucleotide is a 5′-monophosphate ester of a nucleoside:

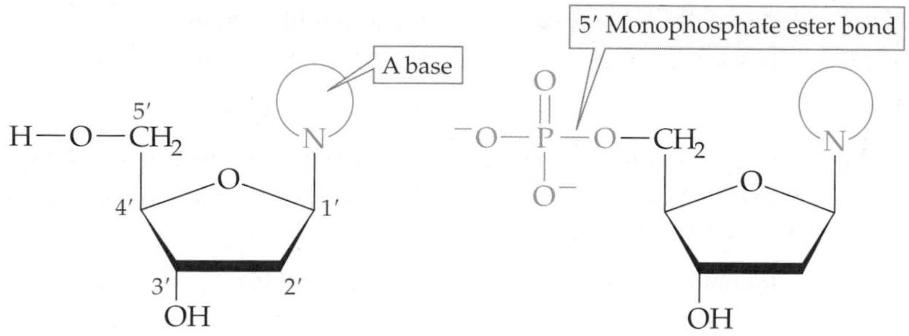

A deoxyribonucleoside

A deoxyribonucleotide

Nucleotides are named by adding 5′-*monophosphate* at the end of the name of the nucleoside. The nucleotides corresponding, for example, to adenosine and deoxycytidine are thus adenosine 5′-monophosphate (AMP) and deoxycytidine 5′-monophosphate (dCMP). Nucleotides that contain ribose are classified as **ribonucleotides** and those that contain 2-deoxy-D-ribose are known as **deoxyribonucleotides** (and are designated by leading their abbreviations with a lower case "d"). For example:

Ribonucleotide A nucleotide that contains D-ribose.

Deoxyribonucleotide A nucleotide that contains 2-deoxy-D-ribose.

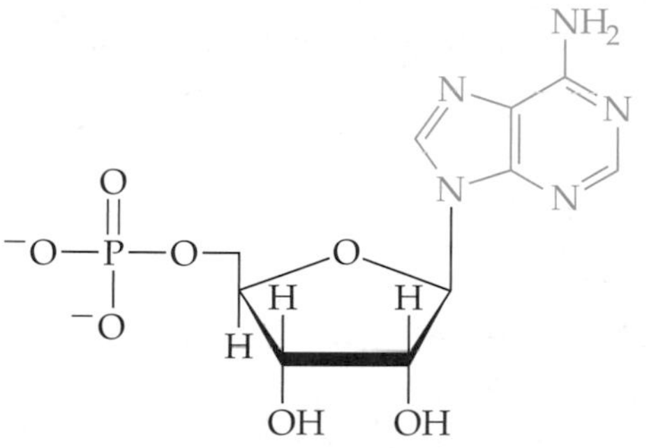

Adenosine 5′-monophosphate (AMP)
(a ribonucleotide)

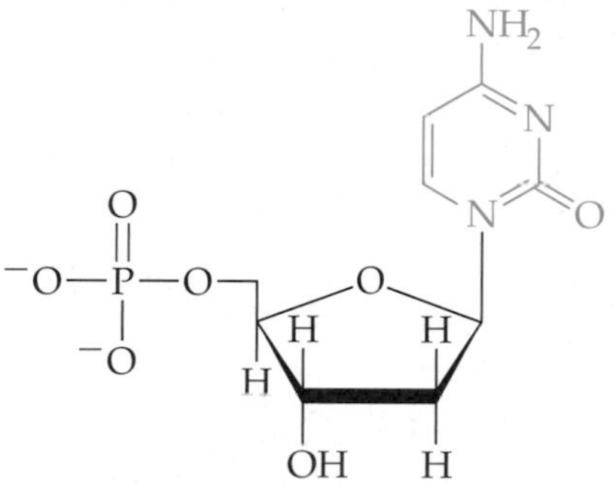

Deoxycytidine 5′-monophosphate (dCMP)
(a deoxyribonucleotide)

Phosphate groups can be added to any of the nucleotides to form diphosphate or triphosphate esters. As illustrated by *adenosine triphosphate (ATP)*, these esters are named with the nucleoside name plus *diphosphate* or *triphosphate*. In preceding chapters, you have seen that adenosine triphosphate (ATP) plays an essential role as a source of biochemical energy (Section 20.5), which is released during its conversion to adenosine diphosphate (ADP).

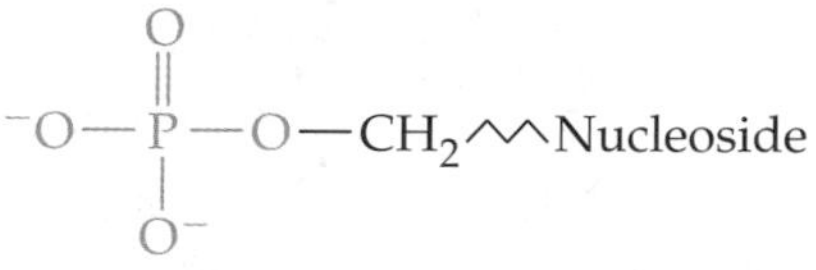

Nucleoside monophosphate

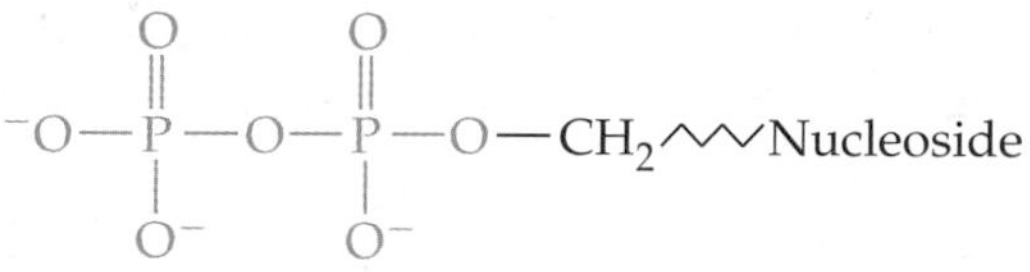

Nucleoside diphosphate

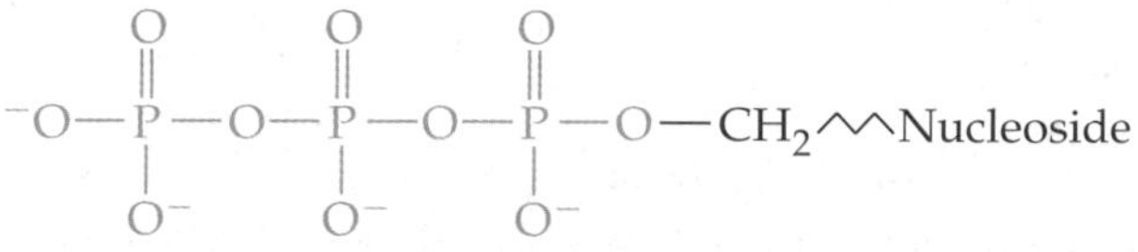

Nucleoside triphosphate

The names of the bases, nucleosides, and nucleotides are summarized in Table 25.2 together with their abbreviations, which are commonly used in writing about biochemistry.

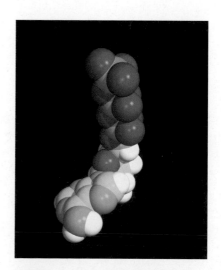

▲ **ATP is the triphosphate of the adenosine nucleotide.**

TABLE **25.2** Names of Bases, Nucleosides, and Nucleotides in DNA and RNA

Bases	Nucleosides	Nucleotides*
DNA		
	Deoxyribonucleosides	**Deoxyribonucleotides**
Adenine (A)	Deoxyadenosine	Deoxyadenosine 5′-monophosphate (dAMP)
Guanine (G)	Deoxyguanosine	Deoxyguanosine 5′-monophosphate (dGMP)
Cytosine (C)	Deoxycytidine	Deoxycytidine 5′-monophosphate (dCMP)
Thymine (T)	Deoxythymidine	Deoxythymidine 5′-monophosphate (dTMP)
RNA		
	Ribonucleosides	**Ribonucleotides**
Adenine (A)	Adenosine	Adenosine 5′-monophosphate (AMP)
Guanine (G)	Guanosine	Guanosine 5′-monophosphate (GMP)
Cytosine (C)	Cytidine	Cytidine 5′-monophosphate (CMP)
Uracil (U)	Uridine	Uridine 5′-monophosphate (UMP)

The nucleotides are also named as, for example, deoxyadenylate and adenylate.

Summary—Nucleoside, Nucleotide, and Nucleic Acid Composition

Nucleoside
- A sugar and a base

Nucleotide
- A sugar, a base, and a phosphate group $(-OPO_3^{2-})$

DNA (deoxyribonucleic acid)
- A polymer of deoxyribonucleotides
- The sugar is 2-deoxy-D-ribose
- The bases are adenine, guanine, cytosine, and *thymine*

RNA (ribonucleic acid)
- A polymer of ribonucleotides
- The sugar is D-ribose
- The bases are adenine, guanine, cytosine, and *uracil*

Worked Example 25.2 Drawing a Nucleic Acid Component from Its Name

Draw the structure of the nucleotide represented by dTMP.

ANALYSIS From Table 25.2 we see that dTMP is deoxythymidine 5′-monophosphate. Therefore, the nitrogen base in this nucleotide is thymine, whose structure is shown in Table 25.1. This base must be bonded (by replacing the H that is red in Table 25.1) to the 1′ position of the deoxyribose, and there must be a phosphate group in the 5′ position of the deoxyribose.

SOLUTION
The structure is

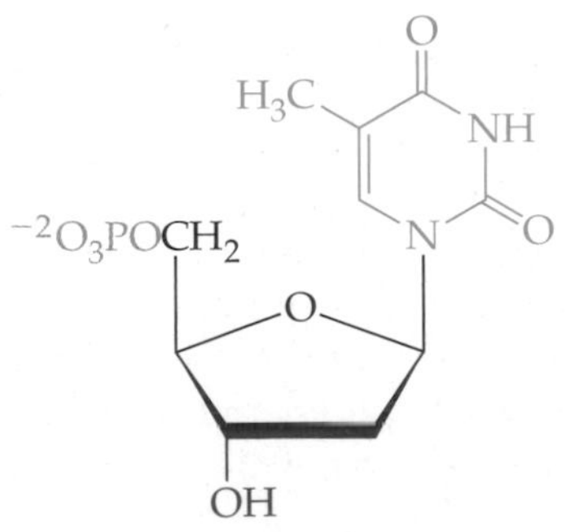

⚷ KEY CONCEPT PROBLEM 25.3

Draw the structure of 2′-deoxyadenosine 5′-monophosphate, and use the primed-unprimed format to number all the atoms in the rings.

PROBLEM 25.4
Draw the structure of the triphosphate of guanosine, a triphosphate that, like ATP, provides energy for certain reactions.

PROBLEM 25.5
Write the full names of dUMP, UMP, CDP, AMP, and ATP.

25.3 The Structure of Nucleic Acid Chains

Keep in mind that nucleic acids are polymers of nucleotides. The nucleotides in DNA and RNA are connected by phosphate diester linkages between the —OH group on C3′ of the sugar ring of one nucleotide and the phosphate group on C5′ of the next nucleotide:

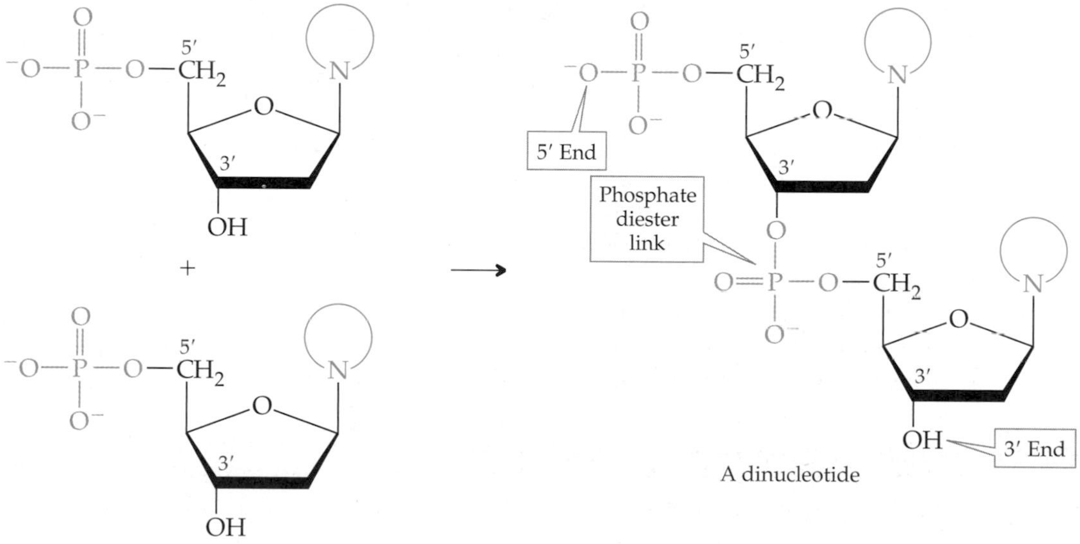

A dinucleotide

A nucleotide chain commonly has a free phosphate group on a 5′ carbon at one end (known as the 5′ *end*) and a free —OH group on a 3′ carbon at the other end (the 3′ *end*), as illustrated in the dinucleotide just above and in the trinucleotide in Figure 25.1. Additional nucleotides join by forming additional phosphate diester linkages between these groups until the polynucleotide chain of a DNA molecule is formed.

Just as the structure and function of a protein depend on the sequence in which the amino acids are connected (see Section 18.7), the structure and function of a nucleic acid depend on the sequence in which the nucleotides are connected. With a nucleic acid, however, we have a second detail to consider: structure and function both depend on the *direction* in which the nucleic acid is read by enzymes involved in making gene products. Like proteins, nucleic acids have backbones that do not vary in composition. The differences between different proteins and between different nucleic acids result from the *order* of the groups bonded to the backbone—amino acid side chains in proteins and bases in nucleic acids.

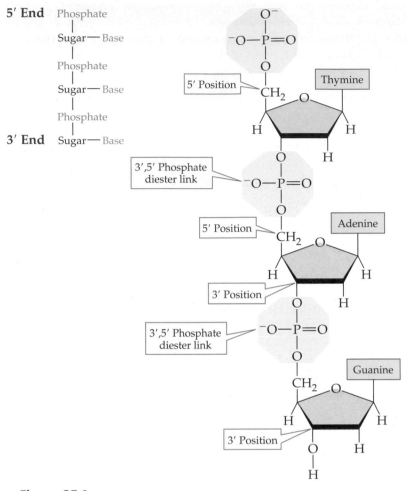

▲ **Figure 25.1**
A deoxytrinucleotide.
In all polynucleotides, as shown here, there is a phosphate group at the 5′ end; there is a sugar
—OH group at the 3′ end; and the nucleotides are connected by 3′, 5′-phosphate diester links.

Comparison of protein and nucleic acid backbones and side chains

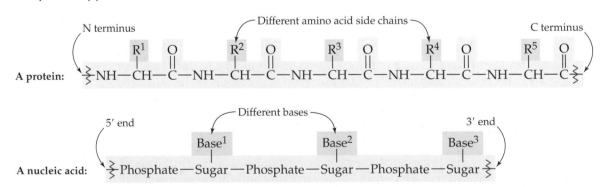

The sequence of nucleotides in a nucleic acid chain is read by starting at the 5′ end and identifying the bases in the order of occurrence. Rather than writing the full name of each nucleotide or each base, one-letter abbreviations of the bases are commonly used to designate the order in which they are attached to the sugar–phosphate backbone: A for adenine, G for guanine, C for cytosine, T for thymine, and U for uracil in RNA. The trinucleotide in Figure 25.1, for example, would be represented by T-A-G or TAG.

PROBLEM 25.6
Name the bases in the pentanucleotide with the sequence G-A-U-C-A. Does this come from RNA or DNA? Explain.

PROBLEM 25.7
Draw the full structure of the DNA dinucleotide C-T. Identify the 5′ and 3′ ends of this dinucleotide.

25.4 Base Pairing in DNA: The Watson–Crick Model

Analysis of the nitrogenous bases in many DNA samples from many different species revealed that in any given species, the amounts of adenine and thymine were always equal, and the amounts of cytosine and guanine were always equal (A = T and G = C). It was also found that the proportions of each (A/T:G/C) vary from one species to another. For example, human DNA contains 30% each of adenine and thymine, and 20% each of guanine and cytosine, whereas the bacterium *Escherichia coli* contains 24% each of adenine and thymine, and 26% each of guanine and cytosine. Note that in both cases, A and T are present in equal amounts and G and C are present in equal amounts. This observation, known as Chargaff's rule (named for Erwin Chargraff, who discovered these base ratios in 1950), suggests that the bases occur in discrete pairs. Why should this be?

In 1953, James Watson and Francis Crick proposed a structure for DNA that not only accounts for the pairing of bases but also accounts for the storage and transfer of genetic information. According to the Watson–Crick model, a DNA molecule consists of *two* polynucleotide strands coiled around each other in a helical, screw-like fashion. The sugar–phosphate backbone is on the *outside* of this right-handed **double helix**, and the heterocyclic bases are on the *inside*, so that a base on one strand points directly toward a base on the second strand. The double helix resembles a twisted ladder, with the sugar–phosphate backbone making up the sides and the paired bases, the rungs.

Double helix Two strands coiled around each other in a screw-like fashion; in most organisms the two polynucleotides of DNA form a double helix.

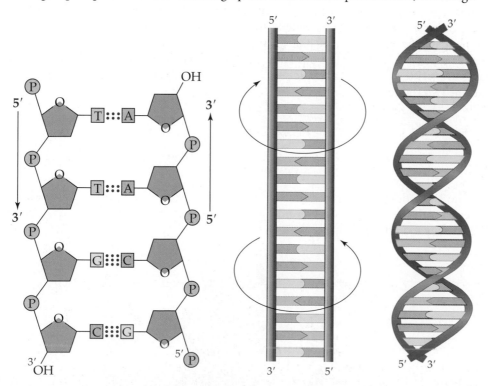

The two strands of the DNA double helix run in opposite directions—one in the 5′ to 3′ direction, the other in the 3′ to 5′ direction (the strands are said to be *antiparallel* to each other). The stacking of the hydrophobic bases in the interior and the alignment of the hydrophilic sugars and phosphate groups on the exterior provide stability to the structure. Hydrogen bonding also enhances DNA stability. Each pair of bases in the center of the double helix is connected by hydrogen bonding. As shown in Figure 25.2, adenine and thymine (A-T) form two hydrogen bonds to each other, and cytosine and guanine (C-G) form three hydrogen bonds to each other. Although individual hydrogen bonds are not especially strong, the thousands upon thousands along a DNA chain collectively contribute to stability of the double helix.

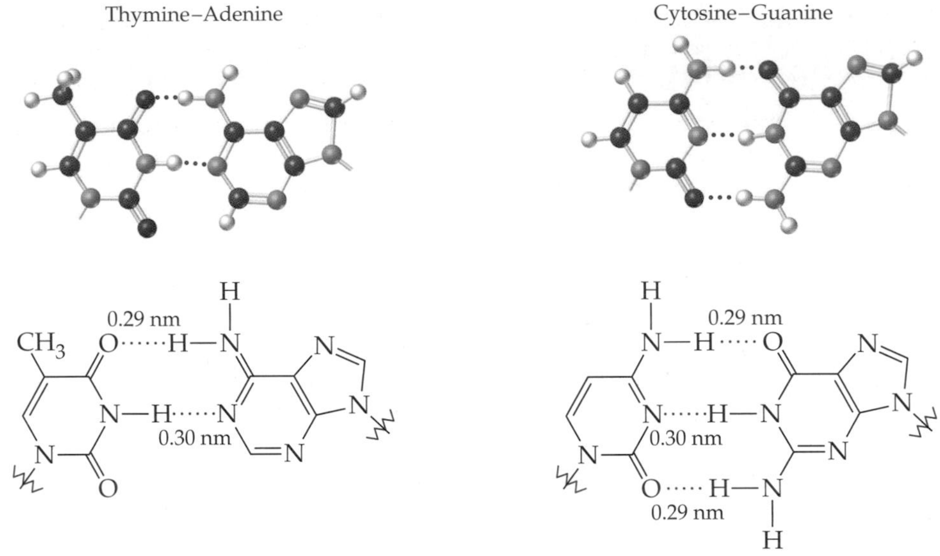

▶ **Figure 25.2**
Base pairing in DNA.
Hydrogen bonds of similar lengths connect the pairs of bases; thymine with adenine, cytosine with guanine.

Thymine–Adenine   Cytosine–Guanine

The pairing of the bases linearly ordered along the two polynucleotide strands of the DNA double helix is described as *complementary*. Wherever a thymine occurs in one strand, an adenine falls opposite it in the other strand; wherever a cytosine occurs in one strand, a guanine falls opposite it on the other strand. This **base pairing** explains why A and T occur in equal amounts in double-stranded DNA, as do C and G.

Base pairing The pairing of bases connected by hydrogen bonding (G-C and A-T), as in the DNA double helix.

To remember how the bases pair up, note that if the symbols are arranged in alphabetical order, the first and last ones pair, and the two middle ones pair. (Or, since the bases are written as block capital letters remember that the two straight ones pair, AT, and the two round ones pair, CG.)

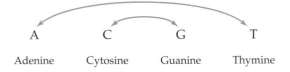

A   C   G   T

Adenine   Cytosine   Guanine   Thymine

The DNA double helix is shown in Figure 25.3. Both its strength and its shape depend on the fit and hydrogen bonding of the bases. As you will see, base pairing is also the key to understanding how DNA functions.

▶ **Figure 25.3**
A segment of DNA.
(a) In this model, notice that the base pairs are nearly perpendicular to the sugar–phosphate backbones.
(b) A space-filling model of the same DNA segment. (c) An abstract representation of the DNA double helix and base pairing.

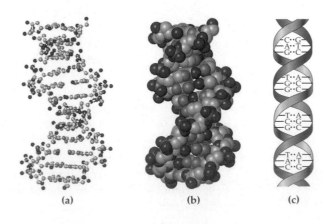

(a)   (b)   (c)

Worked Example **25.3** Writing Complementary Nucleic Acid Sequences

What sequence of bases on one strand of DNA (reading in the 3′ to 5′ direction) is complementary to the sequence 5′ T-A-T-G-C-A-G 3′ on the other strand?

ANALYSIS Remembering that A always bonds to T and C always bonds to G, go through the original 5′ to 3′ sequence, replacing each A by T, each T by A, each C by G, and each G by C. Keep in mind that when a 5′ to 3′ strand is matched in this manner to its complementary strand, the complementary strand will be oriented 3′ to 5′ when read from left to right. (If the direction in which a base sequence is written is *not* specified, you can assume it follows the customary 5′ to 3′ direction when read left to right.)

SOLUTION

Original strand   5′ T-A-T-G-C-A-G 3′
Complementary strand   3′ A-T-A-C-G-T-C 5′

PROBLEM 25.8

Write the complementary sequence of bases for each DNA strand shown below.

(a) 5′T-A-T-A-C-T-G 3′

(b) 5′G-A-T-C-G-C-T-C-T 3′

PROBLEM 25.9

Draw the structures of adenine and uracil (which replaces thymine in RNA), and show the hydrogen bonding that occurs between them.

PROBLEM 25.10

Is a DNA molecule neutral, negatively charged, or positively charged? Explain.

🔑 KEY CONCEPT PROBLEM 25.11

(a) DNA and RNA, like proteins, can be denatured to produce unfolded or uncoiled strands. Heating DNA to what is referred to as its "melting temperature" denatures it (the two strands of the double helix become separated). Why does a longer strand of DNA have a higher melting temperature than a shorter one? (b) The DNA melting temperature also varies with base composition. Would you expect a DNA with a high percentage of G:C base pairs to have a higher or lower melting point than one with a high percentage of A:T base pairs? How do you account for your choice?

25.5 Nucleic Acids and Heredity

Your heredity is determined by the DNA in the fertilized egg from which you grew. A sperm cell carrying DNA from your father united with an egg cell carrying DNA from your mother. Their combination produced the full complement of chromosomes and genes that you carry through life. Each of your 23 pairs of chromosomes contains one DNA molecule copied from that of your father and one DNA molecule copied from that of your mother. Most cells in your body contain copies of these originals. (The exceptions are red blood cells, which have no nuclei and no DNA, and egg or sperm cells, which have 23 single DNA molecules, rather than pairs.)

Cell division is an ongoing process—no single cell has a life span equal to that of the organism in which it is found. Therefore, every time a cell divides, its DNA must be copied. The double helix of DNA and complementary base pairing make this duplication possible. Because of how bases pair, each strand of the double helix is a blueprint for the other strand. The copying process is an awesome aspect of how DNA functions—a process that we discuss in Section 25.6.

But first, we need to answer two related questions: How do nucleic acids carry the information that determines our inherited traits? And how is that stored information interpreted and put into action?

Genetic information is conveyed not just in the numbers and kinds of bases in DNA, but in the *sequence* of bases along the DNA strands; any mistakes in either copying or reading a given DNA sequence can lead to changes in the DNA code (called *mutations*), which may have disastrous consequences for the resulting daughter cells. Every time a cell divides, the information is passed along to the daughter cells, which ultimately pass this genetic information to their daughter cells. Within cells, the genetic information encoded in the DNA directs the synthesis of proteins, a process known as the *expression* of genes.

The duplication, transfer, and expression of genetic information occur as the result of three fundamental processes: *replication*, *transcription*, and *translation*.

Replication The process by which copies of DNA are made when a cell divides.

Transcription The process by which the information in DNA is read and used to synthesize RNA.

Translation The process by which RNA directs protein synthesis.

- **Replication** (Section 25.6) is the process by which a replica, or identical copy, of DNA is made when a cell divides, so that each of the two daughter cells has the same DNA (Figure 25.4).
- **Transcription** (Section 25.8) is the process by which the genetic messages contained in DNA are read and copied. The products of transcription are specific ribonucleic acids, which carry the instructions stored by DNA out of the nucleus, to the sites of protein synthesis.
- **Translation** (Section 25.10) is the process by which the genetic messages carried by RNA are decoded and used to build proteins.

In the following sections we will look at these important processes. Replication, transcription, and translation must proceed with great accuracy and require participation by many auxiliary molecules to ensure the integrity (or fidelity) of the genetic information. Many enzymes working in harmony with one another, coupled with energy-supplying nucleoside triphosphates (NTPs), play essential roles. Our next goal in this chapter is to present a simple overview of how the genetic information is duplicated and put to work, as the full elucidation of these processes is still in progress.

25.6 Replication of DNA

The Watson–Crick double-helix model of DNA does more than explain base pairing. In the short publication that announced their model, Watson and Crick made the following simple statement, suggesting the significance of what they had just discovered:

> It has not escaped our notice that the specific pairing we have postulated immediately suggests a possible copying mechanism for the genetic material.

DNA replication begins in the nucleus with partial unwinding of the double helix; this process involves enzymes known as *helicases*. The unwinding occurs simultaneously in many specific locations known as *origins of replication* (Figure 25.4). The DNA strands separate, exposing the bases and effectively forming a "bubble" in which the replication process can begin. At either end of the bubble, where double-stranded DNA and single-stranded DNA meet, are branch points known as replication forks. A set of multisubunit enzymes called *DNA polymerases* move into position on the separated strands—their function is to facilitate transcription of the exposed single-stranded DNA. Nucleoside triphosphates carrying each of the four bases are available in the vicinity. One by one, the triphosphates move into place by forming hydrogen bonds with the bases exposed on the DNA template strand. A can only form hydrogen bonds with T, and G can only form hydrogen bonds with C. DNA polymerase then catalyzes covalent bond formation between the 5′ phosphate group of the arriving nucleoside triphosphate

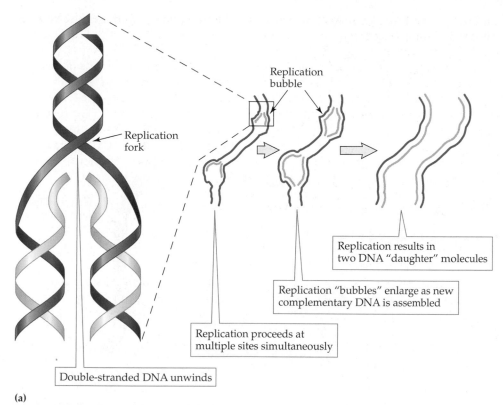

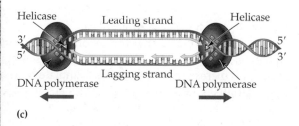

▲ **Figure 25.4**
DNA replication sites.
(a) Replication initiates at sites where the DNA unwinds, exposing single strands. This occurs in multiple locations simultaneously. (b) Electron micrograph of DNA. As DNA unwinds at multiple sites, single-stranded DNA is exposed and replication forks form at the junctions between single- and double-stranded DNA. (c) DNA polymerases at each replication fork travel along the DNA as more and more of it unwinds. The DNA polymerases are responsible for copying of the single-stranded DNA, generating new strands that grow in the 5′ to 3′ direction. One single strand, the leading strand, is copied continuously; the other single strand, called the lagging strand, is copied in segments. (For simplicity, only one replication fork is shown.)

and the 3′—OH at the end of the growing polynucleotide strand, as the two extra phosphate groups are removed:

Bond formation in DNA replication

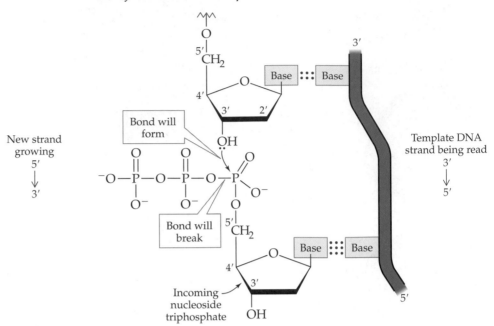

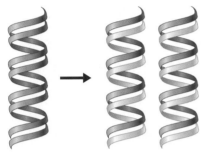

▲ **Semiconservative replication produces a pair of DNA double helixes in which one strand (dark green) is the original strand and the other (light green) is the strand that has been copied from the original.**

DNA polymerase catalyzes the reaction between the 5′ phosphate on an incoming nucleotide and the free 3′—OH on the growing DNA strand. Therefore, the template strand can only be read in the 3′ to 5′ direction, and the new DNA strand can grow only in the 5′ to 3′ direction.

Since each new strand is complementary to its template strand, two identical copies of the DNA double helix are produced during replication. In each new double helix, one strand is the template and the other is the newly synthesized strand. We describe the result as *semiconservative* replication (one of the two parent strands is conserved in each of the two new DNA molecules).

Note in Figure 25.5 that the incoming nucleoside triphosphate is added to the 3′ end of the new strand. In other words, new DNA is synthesized in the 5′ to 3′ direction as the polymerase travels along the template strand in the 3′ to 5′ direction. Because the original DNA strands are antiparallel, only one new strand, known as the *leading strand*, is able to grow continuously as the point of replication (the *replication fork*) moves along. For the leading strand the DNA polymerase, traveling along the template in the 3′ to 5′ direction, is moving in the *same* direction as the replication fork. On the other strand, movement of the DNA polymerase along the template strand in the 3′ to 5′ direction means that the DNA polymerase is moving in the *opposite direction* as the replication fork. As a consequence this other strand, called the *lagging strand*, is replicated in short segments called *Okazaki fragments* (after the Japanese scientist who discovered them). The directions of growth are shown in Figure 25.5, where the leading strand is the continuously growing strand of the new DNA and the lagging strand is the one composed of the short Okazaki fragments. To form the lagging strand from the Okazaki fragments, these short DNA segments are joined together by the action of an enzyme known as *DNA ligase*.

Consider the magnitude of the job in replication. The total number of base pairs in a human cell—the human **genome**—is 3 *billion* base pairs. Yet the base sequences of these huge DNA molecules are faithfully copied during replication, and a random error occurs only about once in each 10 billion to 100 billion bases. The complete copying process in human cells takes several hours. To replicate a huge molecule such as human DNA at this speed requires not one, but many replication forks, producing many segments of DNA strands that are ultimately joined to produce a faithful copy of the original.

Genome All of the genetic material in the chromosomes of an organism; its size is given as the number of base pairs.

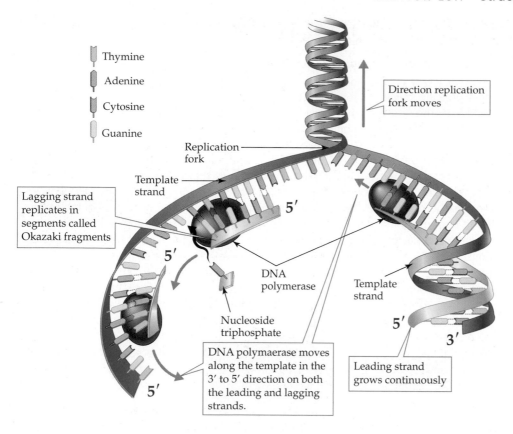

Thymine

Adenine

Cytosine

Guanine

Direction replication
fork moves

Replication
fork

Template
strand

Lagging strand
replicates in
segments called
Okazaki fragments

5'

5'

5'

DNA
polymerase

Template
strand

Nucleoside
triphosphate

DNA polymaerase moves
along the template in the
3' to 5' direction on both
the leading and lagging
strands.

Leading strand
grows continuously

5'

3'

5'

◄ **Figure 25.5**
DNA replication.
Because the new polynucleotide chain
must grow in the 5′ to 3′ direction, the
leading strand (shown at the right, in
light green) grows continuously toward
the replication fork while the lagging
strand (at the left in light green) grows
in segments as the fork moves. The segments are later joined by a DNA ligase
enzyme.

PROBLEM 25.12
What are Okazaki fragments? What role do they serve in DNA metabolism?

25.7 Structure and Function of RNA

RNA is similar to DNA—both are sugar–phosphate polymers and both have nitrogen-containing bases attached—but there are important differences (Table 25.3). We have already seen that RNA and DNA differ in composition (Section 25.2): the sugar in RNA is ribose rather than deoxyribose, and the base uracil in RNA pairs up with adenine rather than with thymine. RNA and DNA also differ in size and structure—RNA strands are not as long (that is, they have lower total molar masses) as DNA molecules. The RNAs are almost always single-stranded molecules (as distinct from DNA, which is almost always double-stranded); RNA molecules also often have complex folds, sometimes folding back on themselves to form double helices in some regions.

TABLE 25.3 Comparison of DNA and RNA

	Sugar	Bases	Shape and Size	Function
DNA	Deoxyribose	Adenine Guanine Cytosine Thymine	Paired strands in double helix; 50 million or more nucleotides per strand	Stores genetic information
RNA	Ribose	Adenine Guanine Cytosine Uracil	Single-stranded with folded regions; <100 to about 50,000 nucleotides per RNA	**mRNA**—Encodes a copy of genetic information ("blueprints" for protein synthesis) **tRNA** Carries amino acids for incorporation into protein **rRNA**—Component of ribosomes (sites of protein synthesis)

CHEMISTRY IN ACTION

It's a Ribozyme!

What is involved in protein synthesis but is not a protein enzyme, not a tRNA, and not exactly mRNA? Why, it is a **ribozyme**, which is RNA acting as an enzyme by catalyzing a chemical reaction.

Any RNA that acts as an enzyme (a term used for protein catalysts) is called a ribozyme. For example, the reaction that removes unneeded sections from newly synthesized mRNA is accomplished by the mRNA itself acting as the reaction catalyst. The mRNA loops back on itself and rearranges the ester bonds (a transesterification reaction) between nucleotides, neatly excising the unneeded sections. The slicing out of unneeded bases (introns) and splicing together of the rest of the mRNA is termed *spliceosome activity* and was originally attributed to a protein that researchers were unable to isolate. In the 1970s Thomas Cech discovered that spliceosome activity was due to mRNA acting on itself; Sidney Altman later confirmed the observation with his work on tRNA and an enzyme named RNaseP. In 1989, Cech and Altman were awarded the Nobel Prize in Chemistry for their discovery of the catalytic (ribozymal) function of RNA.

Since then more than 500 ribozymes in different organisms have been identified. One class, the viroids, are small, circular RNA molecules that infect plants. Viroids are self-splicing and direct the plant host cell to synthesize new viroids in long, repeated strands that then splice themselves out of the strand into individual infective particles. Viroids cause diseases in economically important plants, such as flowers.

Perhaps the largest, best-known ribozyme is the 23S RNA molecule, which is one part of the structure of ribosomes. Structural evidence shows that during protein synthesis in a ribosome, 23S RNA catalyzes the formation of the peptide bond between amino acids in the growing protein molecule. The associated proteins, all 31 of them, appear to provide the necessary structure to maintain the correct three-dimensional relationship among the molecules involved in protein synthesis.

Basic research into the nature and functions of ribozymes continues. However, applied research is directed toward their use in medical treatments. One such undertaking, intended as a treatment for cancer, targets the mRNA responsible for the cell surface receptor *vascular endothelial growth factor*. The hope is that breaking up the mRNA for this receptor will allow fewer blood vessels to grow to supply a tumor with nutrients, thereby slowing tumor growth.

See Chemistry in Action Problems 25.71 and 25.72 at the end of the chapter.

Ribozyme RNA that acts as an enzyme.

Ribosome The structure in the cell where protein synthesis occurs; composed of protein and rRNA.

Ribosomal RNA (rRNA) The RNA that is complexed with proteins in ribosomes.

Messenger RNAs (mRNA) The RNA that carries code transcribed from DNA and directs protein synthesis.

Transfer RNA (tRNA) The RNA that transports amino acids into position for protein synthesis.

Cell nucleus

DNA

Transcription

mRNA

There are also different kinds of RNA, each type with its own unique function in the flow of genetic information, whereas DNA has only one function—storing genetic information. Working together, the three types of RNA make it possible for the encoded information carried by DNA to be put to use in the synthesis of proteins:

- **Ribosomal RNAs** Outside the nucleus but within the cytoplasm of a cell are the **ribosomes**—small granular organelles where protein synthesis takes place. (Their location in the cell is shown in Figure 20.3, p. 628.) Each ribosome is a complex consisting of about 60% **ribosomal RNA (rRNA)** and 40% protein, with a total molecular mass of approximately 5,000,000 amu.
- **Messenger RNAs** The **messenger RNAs (mRNA)** carry information transcribed from DNA. They are formed in the cell nucleus and transported out to the ribosomes, where proteins will be synthesized. They are polynucleotides that carry the same code for proteins as does the DNA.
- **Transfer RNAs** The **transfer RNAs (tRNA)** are smaller RNAs that deliver amino acids one by one to protein chains growing at ribosomes. Each tRNA carries only one amino acid.

25.8 Transcription: RNA Synthesis

Ribonucleic acids are synthesized in the cell nucleus. Before leaving the nucleus, all types of RNA molecules are modified in various ways that enable them to perform their different functions. We focus here on messenger RNA (mRNA; in eukaryotes) because its synthesis (transcription) is the first step in transferring the information carried by DNA into protein synthesis.

In transcription, as in replication, a small section of the DNA double helix unwinds, the bases on the two strands are exposed, and one by one the complementary nucleotides are attached. rRNA, tRNA, and mRNA are all synthesized in essentially the same manner. Only one of the two DNA strands is transcribed during RNA synthesis. The DNA strand that is transcribed is the *template strand*; its complement in the original helix is the *informational strand*. The mRNA molecule is complementary to the template strand, which makes it an exact RNA-duplicate of the DNA informational strand, with the exception that a U replaces each T in the DNA strand. The relationships are illustrated by the following short DNA and mRNA segments:

DNA informational strand	5′ ATG CCA GTA GGC CAC TTG TCA 3′
DNA template strand	3′ TAC GGT CAT CCG GTG AAC AGT 5′
mRNA	5′ AUG CCA GUA GGC CAC UUG UCA 3′

The transcription process, shown in Figure 25.6, begins when RNA polymerase, an enzyme that synthesizes RNA, recognizes a control segment in DNA that precedes the nucleotides to be transcribed. The *genetic code*, which we will discuss in Section 25.9, consists of triplets of consecutive bases known as *codons*. The nucleotide triplets carried by mRNA code for amino acids to be assembled into proteins (Section 25.10). The sequence of nucleic acid code that corresponds to a complete protein is known as a *gene*. RNA polymerase moves down the DNA segment to be transcribed, adding complementary nucleotides one by one to the growing RNA strand as it goes. Transcription ends when the RNA polymerase reaches a termination sequence that signals the end of the sequence to be copied.

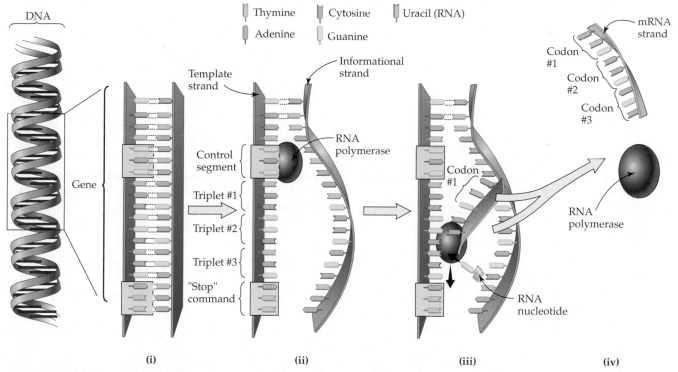

▲ **Figure 25.6**
Transcription of DNA to produce mRNA.
The transcription shown here produces a hypothetical three-codon mRNA. From left to right, (i) the DNA unwinds; (ii) the RNA polymerase connects with the control, or start, segment on the template strand; (iii) the mRNA is assembled as the polymerase moves along the template strand; and (iv) transcription ends when the polymerase reaches the stop command, releasing both the new mRNA strand and RNA polymerase.

At the end of transcription, the mRNA molecule contains a matching base for every base that was on the informational DNA strand, from the site of transcription initiation to the site of transcription termination. Some of these bases, however, do not code for genes. It turns out that genes occupy only about 10% of the base pairs in DNA. The code

Exon A nucleotide sequence in a gene that codes for part of a protein.

Intron A nucleotide sequence in mRNA that does not code for part of a protein; removed before mRNA proceeds to protein synthesis.

Heterogeneous nuclear RNA (hnRNA) The initially synthesized mRNA strand containing both introns and exons.

for a gene is contained in one or more small sections of DNA called an **exon** (exons carry code that is *expressed*). The code for a given gene may be interrupted by a sequence of bases called an **intron** (a section that *intervenes* or *interrupts*), and then resumed farther down the chain in another exon. Introns are sections of DNA that do not code for any part of the protein to be synthesized. The initial mRNA strand (the "primary transcript"), like the DNA from which it was synthesized, contains both exons and introns, and is known as **heterogeneous nuclear RNA (hnRNA)**. Further steps are necessary before the mRNA can direct protein synthesis. In the final mRNA molecule released from the nucleus, the intron sections have been cut out and the remaining pieces (consisting of the exons) are spliced together through the action of a structure known as a *spliceosome* (a protein–RNA complex that removes introns from nuclear RNA).

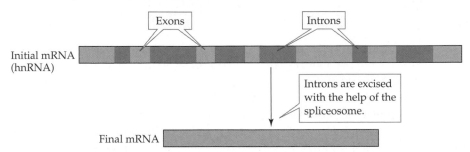

The possible functions of introns, which are noncoding DNA, are the subject of great speculation and study. Thus far, no clear-cut function has been assigned to introns. One intriguing possibility is that they are leftovers from an earlier stage in evolution. An interesting observation is that the exon portions of different genes often code for protein segments of similar structure and function. It has been suggested that introns might separate exons that can be mixed and matched to create new genes, or that the intron portions of one gene may actually be the exon portion of another gene. It has also been postulated that in DNA, introns may act as regulatory sites for other genes or somehow help to stabilize the genome; in any case, introns undoubtedly play an important, not yet fully understood, role in an organism's genetic construction.

Worked Example 25.4 Writing Complementary DNA and RNA Strands from Informational DNA Strands

The nucleotide sequence in a segment of a DNA informational strand is given below. What is the nucleotide sequence in the complementary DNA template strand? What is the sequence transcribed from the template strand into mRNA?

5′AAC GTT CCA ACT GTC 3′

ANALYSIS Recall:

1. In the informational and template strands of DNA, the base pairs are A-T and C-G.

2. Matching base pairs along the informational strand gives the template strand written in the 3′ to 5′ direction.

3. The mRNA strand is identical to the DNA informational strand except that it has a U wherever the informational strand has a T.

4. Matching base pairs along the template strand produces the mRNA strand written in the 5′ to 3′ direction.

SOLUTION
Applying these principles gives

*DNA **informational strand***	5′AAC GTT CAA ACT GTC 3′
*DNA **template strand***	3′TTG CAA GTT TGA CAG 5′
mRNA	5′AAC GUU CAA ACU GUC 3′

PROBLEM 25.13

Both spliceosome activity and ribosomal activity result in the production of biopolymers. What do the spliceosomes synthesize and what do the ribosomes synthesize? What kind of enzyme is used in each instance?

PROBLEM 25.14

What mRNA base sequences are complementary to the following DNA template sequences? Be sure to label the 5′ and 3′ ends of the complementary sequences.

(a) 5′CAT GCT CTA CAG 3'   **(b)** 3′TAT TAG CGA CCG 5′

25.9 The Genetic Code

The ribonucleotide sequence in an mRNA chain is like a coded sentence that spells out the order in which amino acid residues should be joined to form a protein. Each "word" consists of a triplet of ribonucleotides, or **codon**, in the mRNA sentence, which in turn corresponds to a specific amino acid. That is, a series of codons spells out a sequence of amino acids. For example, the series uracil-uracil-guanine (UUG) on an mRNA transcript is a codon directing incorporation of the amino acid leucine into a growing protein chain. Similarly, the sequence guanine-adenine-uracil (GAU) codes for aspartate.

Of the 64 possible three-base combinations in RNA, 61 code for specific amino acids and 3 code for chain termination (the *stop codons*). The "meaning" of each codon—the **genetic code** universal to all but a few living organisms—is given in Table 25.4. Note that most amino acids are specified by more than one codon and that codons are always written in the 5′ to 3′ direction.

Codon A sequence of three ribonucleotides in the messenger RNA chain that codes for a specific amino acid; also a three-nucleotide sequence that is a stop codon and stops translation.

Genetic code The sequence of nucleotides, coded in triplets (codons) in mRNA, that determines the sequence of amino acids in protein synthesis.

TABLE 25.4 Codon Assignments of Base Triplets in mRNA

First Base (5′ end)	Second Base	Third Base (3′ end) U	C	A	G
U	U	Phe	Phe	Leu	Leu
	C	Ser	Ser	Ser	Ser
	A	Tyr	Tyr	*Stop*	*Stop*
	G	Cys	Cys	*Stop*	Trp
C	U	Leu	Leu	Leu	Leu
	C	Pro	Pro	Pro	Pro
	A	His	His	Gln	Gln
	G	Arg	Arg	Arg	Arg
A	U	Ile	Ile	Ile	Met
	C	Thr	Thr	Thr	Thr
	A	Asn	Asn	Lys	Lys
	G	Ser	Ser	Arg	Arg
G	U	Val	Val	Val	Val
	C	Ala	Ala	Ala	Ala
	A	Asp	Asp	Glu	Glu
	G	Gly	Gly	Gly	Gly

The relationship between the DNA informational and template strand segments illustrated earlier is repeated here, along with the protein segment for which they code:

DNA informational strand	5′ ATG CCA GTA GGC CAC TTG TCA 3′
DNA template strand	3′ TAC GGT CAT CCG GTG AAC AGT 5′
mRNA	5′ AUG CCA GUA GGC CAC UUG UCA 3′
Protein	Met Pro Val Gly His Leu Ser

Notice that the 5′ end of the mRNA strand codes for the N-terminal amino acid, whereas the 3′ end of the mRNA strand codes for the C-terminal amino acid. (Remember, proteins are written N-terminal to C-terminal, reading left to right.)

Worked Example 25.5 Translating RNA into Protein

In Worked Example 25.4, we derived the mRNA sequence of nucleotides shown below. What is the sequence of amino acids coded for by the mRNA sequence?

5′ AAC GUU CAA ACU GUC 3′

ANALYSIS The codons must be identified by consulting Table 25.4. They are

5′ AAC GUU CAA ACU GUC 3′
Asn Val Gln Thr Val

SOLUTION
Written out in full, the protein sequence is

asparagine-valine-glutamine-threonine-valine

CHEMISTRY IN ACTION

Viruses and AIDS

Viruses are submicroscopic infectious agents that can replicate only inside living cells. They are ubiquitous in the environment and are the most abundant type of biological entity. Thousands of viruses are known, each of which can infect a particular plant or animal cell. Virus particles consist of only a few biomolecules: some nucleic acid (either DNA or RNA, which can be either single-stranded or double-stranded), and a protein coating (capsid) consisting of just a few proteins. Some viral classes also have a lipid coating over the capsid. How can something so small and with so few components cause diseases like AIDS?

Are viruses living or nonliving? The answer is that they are neither, exactly; they are in between, because a virus particle cannot make copies of itself without a host cell providing the necessary cellular machinery. Once a virus enters a living cell, it takes over the host cell and forces it to produce virus copies, which then leave the host and spread the infection to other cells.

The replication of DNA viruses is straightforward. The virus particle enters the cell, sheds its protein coat, and the cell replicates the viral DNA, producing many copies. The viral DNA is transcribed to RNA and many copies of the capsid proteins

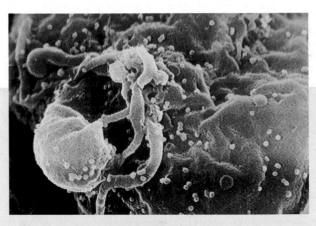

▲ **HIV viruses (green) emerging from an infected lymphocyte.**

are made. Then the new viral DNA copies are packed into the new capsid envelopes, producing new virus particles that are released from the cell to infect other cells.

Most viruses are RNA viruses; their replication is more involved. After an RNA virus infects a cell, either the cell must transcribe and produce proteins directly from the viral RNA template, or else it must first produce DNA from the viral RNA by *reverse transcription*. Reverse transcription is the process by which viral RNA in a host cell is transcribed into a complementary DNA sequence (this is the reverse of the normal DNA to RNA process, hence the name). The enzyme that accomplishes this feat is called *reverse transcriptase* and is provided by the virus itself. Without reverse transcriptase, the viral genome could not become incorporated into the genome of the host cell, and the virus could not reproduce. Viruses that follow the reverse transcription route are known as *retroviruses*.

The *human immunodeficiency virus (HIV-1)* responsible for most cases of AIDS (*Acquired Immune Deficiency Syndrome*) is a retrovirus. As shown in the accompanying diagram, *reverse transcriptase* first produces single DNA strands complementary to the HIV RNA and then produces double-stranded DNA that inserts itself into a host cell chromosome. There, the cell's normal transcription and translation machinery produce RNA and proteins that are assembled into new virus particles.

Unlike bacterial infections, viral infections, whether HIV infections or the common cold, are difficult to treat with chemical agents. The challenge is to design a drug that can act on viruses within cells without damaging the cells themselves and their genetic material. Development of drugs for the treatment of AIDS is especially challenging because HIV has the highest mutation rate of any known virus. Drugs active against one strain of HIV may soon encounter a mutant they cannot combat.

The best success with AIDS drugs thus far has been with a three-drug therapy, the first therapy that allows HIV-infected individuals to survive. Two of the drugs (AZT, azidothymidine; 3TC, lamivudine) are false nucleosides.

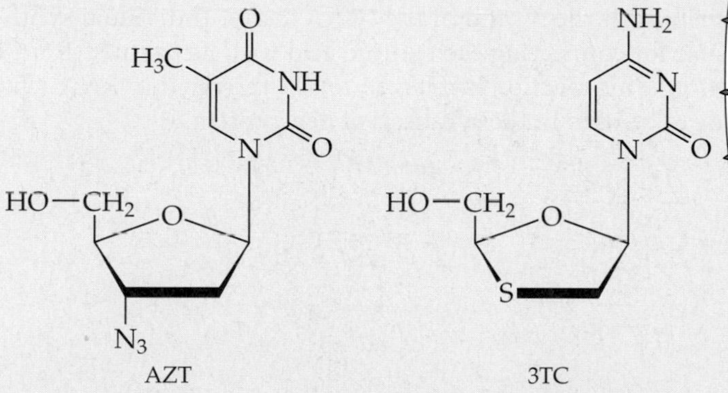

AZT

3TC
(Lamivudine)

The viral reverse transcriptase incorporates them into the viral DNA, and they then slow down production of new viral RNA. The third drug (saquinavir) inhibits an enzyme (protease) that is necessary for production of proteins coded for by the viral genes. Taken together, these three drugs can reduce the

amount of HIV in a patient's body to undetectable levels. This therapy, although successful, is complicated to follow and very expensive. Also, the virus will eventually develop resistance to this therapy as it has to other drugs in the past.

One new approach is the development of a vaccine, as has been successfully done for the viruses responsible for diseases such as smallpox (which has been eradicated) and polio, which now has a very low incidence rate. Some trials of AIDS vaccines have shown promise, but no effective vaccine has yet been developed.

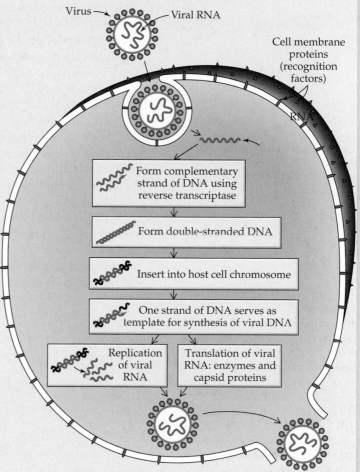

See Chemistry in Action Problems 25.73 and 25.74 at the end of the chapter.

PROBLEM 25.15

List possible codon sequences for the following amino acids.

(a) Val   (b) Phe   (c) Asn   (d) Gly   (e) Met

PROBLEM 25.16

Name the base represented by the codon GAG and identify the amino acid for which this codon codes.

PROBLEM 25.17

What amino acids do the following sequences code for?

(a) AUC   (b) GCU   (c) CGA   (d) AAG

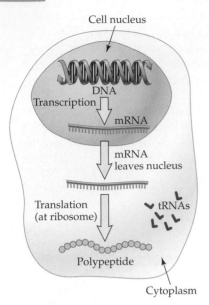

Cell nucleus

DNA

Transcription

mRNA

mRNA leaves nucleus

Translation (at ribosome)

tRNAs

Polypeptide

Cytoplasm

▲ **Overview of protein synthesis. The codons of mature mRNA are translated in the ribosomes, where tRNAs deliver amino acids to be assembled into proteins (polypeptides).**

▶ **Figure 25.7**
Structure of tRNA.
(a) Schematic, flattened tRNA molecule. The cloverleaf-shaped tRNA contains an anticodon triplet on one "leaf" and a covalently bonded amino acid at its 3′ end. The example shown is a yeast tRNA that codes for phenylalanine. All tRNAs have similar structures. The nucleotides not identified (blank circles) are slightly altered analogs of the four normal ribonucleotides. (b) A computer-generated model of the serine tRNA molecule. The serine binding site is shown in yellow and the anticodon in red. (c) The three-dimensional shape (the tertiary structure) of a tRNA molecule. Note how the anticodon is at one end and the amino acid is at the other end.

PROBLEM 25.18
A hypothetical tripeptide Leu-Leu-Leu could be synthesized by the cell. What three different base triplets in mRNA could be combined to code for this tripeptide?

PROBLEM 25.19
How do viruses differ from living organisms? (See Chemistry in Action: Viruses and AIDS.)

25.10 Translation: Transfer RNA and Protein Synthesis

How are the messages carried by mRNA translated, and how does the translation process result in the synthesis of proteins? Protein synthesis occurs at ribosomes, which are located outside the nucleus in the cytoplasm of cells. First, mRNA binds to the ribosome; then, amino acids, which are available in the cytosol, are delivered one by one by transfer RNA (tRNA) molecules to be joined into a specific protein by the ribosomal "machinery." All of the RNA molecules required for translation were synthesized from DNA by transcription in the nucleus and moved to the cytosol for translation.

First, let us examine the structure of the tRNAs. Every cell contains more than 20 different tRNAs, each designed to carry a specific amino acid, even though they are all similar in overall structure. A tRNA molecule is a single polynucleotide chain held together by regions of base pairing in a partially helical structure something like a cloverleaf (Figure 25.7a). In three dimensions, a tRNA molecule is L-shaped, as shown in Figures 25.7b and c.

At one end of the L-shaped tRNA molecule, an amino acid is bonded to its specific tRNA by an ester linkage between the —COOH of the amino acid and an —OH group on the last ribose at the 3′ end of the tRNA chain. Individual synthetase enzymes are responsible for connecting each amino acid with its partner tRNA in an energy-requiring reaction. This reaction is referred to as *charging* the tRNA. Once charged, the tRNA is ready to be used in the synthesis of new protein.

At the other end of the tRNA "L" is a sequence of three nucleotides called an **anticodon** (Figure 25.7). The anticodon of each tRNA is complementary to an mRNA codon—*always the one designating the particular amino acid that the tRNA carries.* For example, the tRNA carrying the amino acid leucine, which is coded for by 5′ CUG 3′ in mRNA, has the complementary sequence 3′ GAC 5′ as its anticodon on the tRNA. This is how the genetic message of nucleotide triplets, the codons, is translated into the sequence of amino acids in a protein. When the tRNA anticodon pairs off with its complementary mRNA codon, leucine is delivered to its proper place in the growing protein chain.

Anticodon A sequence of three ribonucleotides on tRNA that recognizes the complementary sequence (the codon) on mRNA.

The three stages in protein synthesis are *initiation, elongation,* and *termination.* As you read the descriptions, follow along in the diagram of translation in Figure 25.8.

Translation Initiation

Each ribosome in a cell is made up of two subunits of markedly different sizes, called, logically enough, the *small subunit* and the *large subunit.* Each subunit contains protein enzymes and ribosomal RNA (rRNA). Protein synthesis begins with the binding of an mRNA to the small subunit of a ribosome, joined by the first tRNA. The first codon on the 5′ end of mRNA, an AUG, acts as a "start" signal for the translation machinery and codes for a methionine-carrying tRNA. Initiation is completed when the large ribosomal subunit joins the small one and the methionine-bearing tRNA occupies one of the two binding sites on the united ribosome. (Not all proteins have methionine at one end. If it is not needed, the methionine from chain initiation is removed by *post-translational modification* before the new protein goes to work.)

Translation Elongation

Next to the first binding site on the ribosome is a second binding site where the next codon on mRNA is exposed and the tRNA carrying the next amino acid will be attached. All available tRNA molecules can approach and try to fit, but only one with the appropriate anticodon sequence can bind. Once the tRNA with amino acid 2 arrives, a ribozyme in the large subunit catalyzes formation of the new peptide bond and breaks the bond linking amino acid 1 to its tRNA. These energy-requiring steps are fueled by the hydrolysis of GTP to GDP. The first tRNA then leaves the ribosome, and the entire ribosome shifts one codon (three positions) along the mRNA chain. As a result, the second binding site is opened up to accept the tRNA carrying the next amino acid.

The three elongation steps now repeat:

- The next appropriate tRNA binds to the ribosome.
- Peptide bond formation attaches the newly arrived amino acid to the growing chain and the tRNA carrying it is released.
- Ribosome position shifts to free the second binding site for the next tRNA.

A single mRNA can be "read" simultaneously by many ribosomes. The growing polypeptides increase in length as the ribosomes move down the mRNA strand.

Translation Termination

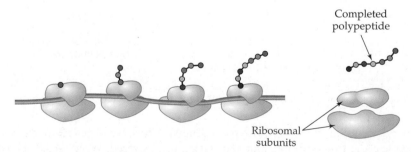

Completed polypeptide

Ribosomal subunits

When synthesis of the protein is completed, a "stop" codon signals the end of translation. An enzyme called a *releasing factor* then catalyzes cleavage of the polypeptide chain from the last tRNA; the tRNA and mRNA molecules are released from the ribosome, and the two ribosome subunits separate. This step also requires energy from GTP. Overall, to add one amino acid to the growing polypeptide chain requires 4 molecules of GTP, excluding the energy needed to charge the tRNA.

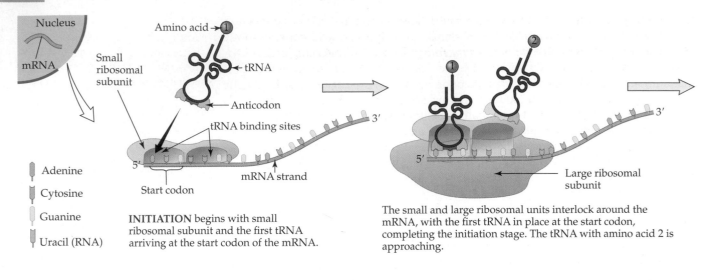

Adenine

Cytosine

Guanine

Uracil (RNA)

INITIATION begins with small ribosomal subunit and the first tRNA arriving at the start codon of the mRNA.

The small and large ribosomal units interlock around the mRNA, with the first tRNA in place at the start codon, completing the initiation stage. The tRNA with amino acid 2 is approaching.

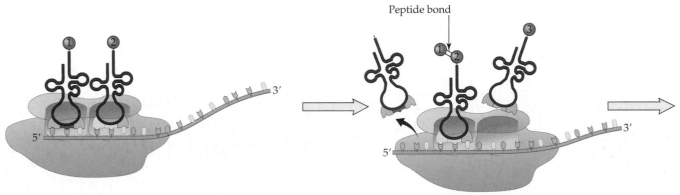

ELONGATION begins as the tRNA with amino acid 2 binds to its codon at the second site within the ribosome.

A peptide bond forms between amino acid 1 and 2, the first tRNA is released, the ribosome moves one codon to the right, and the tRNA with amino acid 3 is arriving.

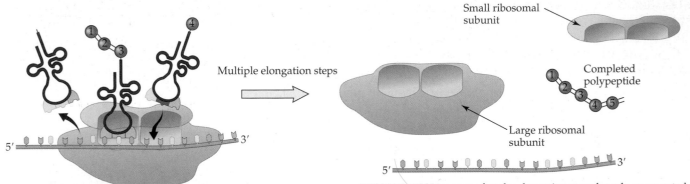

Elongation continues with three amino acids in the growing chain and the fourth one arriving with its tRNA.

TERMINATION occurs after the elongation steps have been repeated until the stop codon is reached. The ribosomal units, the mRNA, and the polypeptide separate.

▲ **Figure 25.8**
Translation: The initiation, elongation, and termination stages in protein synthesis.

In our discussion in this and the preceding sections, we have left many questions about replication, transcription, and translation unanswered. What tells a cell when to start replication? Are there mechanisms to repair damaged DNA or correct random errors made during replication? (There are.) Keep in mind that synthesis of mRNA is the beginning of synthesis of a protein. How are proteins modified, and where does this modification occur? Since each cell contains the entire genome and since cells differ widely in their function, what keeps genes for unneeded proteins from being transcribed? What determines just when a particular gene in a particular cell is transcribed? What indicates the spot on DNA where transcription should begin? How is hnRNA converted into mRNA? How are transcription and the resulting protein synthesis regulated? You will see that steroid hormones function by directly entering the nucleus to activate enzyme synthesis (Section 28.5). This is just one mode of gene regulation. It can also occur by modification of DNA during transcription and during translation. Much is known beyond what we have covered (and if you are curious, take a genetics course!). There are also many questions that we cannot yet fully answer because scientists do not know the answers yet, although research is continuing.

PROBLEM 25.20

What amino acid sequence is coded for by the mRNA base sequence CUC-AUU-CCA-UGC-GAC-GUA?

PROBLEM 25.21

What anticodon sequences of tRNAs match the mRNA codons in Problem 25.20?

PROBLEM 25.22

Why is it difficult to develop a universal influenza vaccine? (See Chemistry in Action: Influenza—Variations on a Theme.)

CHEMISTRY IN ACTION

Influenza—Variations on a Theme

When we talk of "the flu," we take for granted that it is solely a human condition. Flu is caused by the influenza virus, of which there are three major types—A, B, and C—with many subtypes of each one. Influenza A and B viruses cause human flu epidemics almost every winter. In the United States, these seasonal epidemics can cause illness in 10% to 20% of the human population and are associated with an average of 36,000 deaths and 114,000 hospitalizations per year.

Getting a flu shot can prevent illness from types A and B influenza. Influenza type C infections cause a mild respiratory illness and are not thought to cause epidemics. Flu shots do not protect against type C influenza. Unfortunately one shot does not protect you from influenza for life; you have to be re-immunized yearly because the influenza virus mutates rapidly, especially the protein coat. Since influenza viruses are ubiquitous, flu can cause either an epidemic or a pandemic. A disease that quickly and severely affects a large number of people and then subsides is an *epidemic*. A *pandemic* is a widespread epidemic that may affect entire continents or even the world. Both have occurred.

Can animals get the flu? The answer is yes. Many subtypes of influenza A viruses are also found in a variety of animals, including ducks, chickens, pigs, whales, horses, and seals. Certain strains (subtypes) of influenza A virus are specific only to certain species. Unlike other animals, however, birds are susceptible to all known subtypes of the influenza A virus and serve as reservoirs.

Influenza viruses that infect birds are called *avian influenza viruses;* first identified in Italy more than 100 years ago, these viruses occur naturally among birds worldwide. Wild birds,

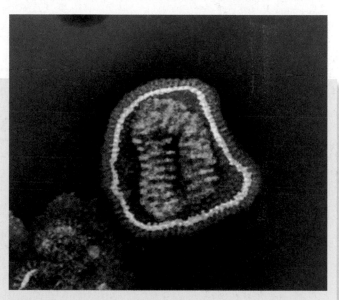

▲ A tranmission electron micrograph of negatively stained influenza A virus particles.

most notably migratory waterfowl such as wild ducks, carry the viruses in their intestines. Avian influenza is very contagious among birds; If infection does occur, domesticated birds, such as chickens, ducks, and turkeys, are particularly susceptible to infection, which either makes them very sick or kills them.

Humans also are susceptible to influenza A viruses, but avian influenza viruses do not usually infect humans due to subtype differences. However, several cases of human infection with avian influenza viruses have occurred since 1997. These viruses may be transmitted to humans directly from birds, from an environment contaminated by avian virus, or through an intermediate host, such as a pig. Because pigs are susceptible to infection by both avian and human viruses, they can serve as a "mixing vessel" for the scrambling of genetic material from human and avian viruses, resulting in the emergence of a novel viral subtype. For example, if a pig is infected with a human influenza virus and an avian influenza virus at the same time, the viruses can re-assort genes and produce a new virus that has most of the genes from the human virus, but surface proteins from the avian virus. This process is known as an *antigenic shift*. This is how a new virus is formed, a virus against which humans will have little or no immunity and that may result in sustained human-to-human transmission and ultimately an influenza epidemic. Conditions favorable for the emergence of antigenic shift have long been thought to involve humans living in close proximity to domestic poultry and pigs. However, recent events suggest humans themselves can serve as the "mixing vessel." This scenario has frightening consequences; so frightening that the Centers for Disease Control and Prevention (CDC) considers the control of avian influenza to be a top priority. Luckily, the bird flu outbreak in 2006 was limited, although serious, and the swine flu pandemic of 2009 was not as virulent a strain as was first thought. That particular influenza A virus mixed genes from human, avian, and swine viruses, resulting in a novel virus to which humans had no immunity. The 2009 viral strain has some genetic similarities to an older influenza virus that had an alarmingly high mortality rate.

In 1918, a strain of influenza that became known as *Spanish flu* killed an estimated 20–50 million people worldwide. Most of those who died were not in the highly fragile groups of very young and very old but rather were healthy adults between 20 and 40 years old. Analysis and reconstruction of the 1918 influenza virus showed it was Type A, variant H1N1. The avian influenza virus we are seeing today is also a type A virus, but a different variant than the virus that caused the 1918 pandemic. However, research has shown that the hemagglutinin genes and gene products (protein) of the avian flu virus are closely similar to those of the 1918 flu virus, suggesting an explanation for why the avian flu is able to infect humans.

Scientists continue to monitor viral sub-strain shifts and drug companies prepare seasonal influenza vaccine based on predictions of what the next season's predominant viral strains will be. Work is also moving forward on a universal vaccine so that you can avoid the yearly shot and be immunized against influenza like you are against other common viral diseases such as measles.

See Chemistry in Action Problems 25.75 and 25.76 at the end of the chapter.

SUMMARY: REVISITING THE CHAPTER GOALS

1. What are the compositions of the nucleic acids, DNA and RNA? *Nucleic acids* are polymers of *nucleotides*. Each nucleotide contains a sugar, a base, and a phosphate group. The sugar is D-ribose in *ribonucleic acids (RNAs)* and 2-deoxy-D-ribose in *deoxyribonucleic acids (DNAs)*. The C5—OH of the sugar is bonded to the phosphate group, and the anomeric carbon of the sugar is connected by an *N*-glycosidic bond to one of five heterocyclic nitrogen bases (Table 25.1). A *nucleoside* contains a sugar and a base, but not the phosphate group. In DNA and RNA, the nucleotides are connected by phosphate diester linkages between the 3'—OH group of one nucleotide and the 5' phosphate group of the next nucleotide. DNA and RNA both contain adenine, guanine, and cytosine; thymine occurs in DNA and uracil occurs in RNA (*see Problems 1–5, 23, 29–32, 47–50*).

2. What is the structure of DNA? The DNA in each *chromosome* consists of two polynucleotide strands twisted together in a *double helix*. The sugar–phosphate backbones are on the outside, and the bases are in the center of the helix. The bases on the two strands are complementary—opposite every thymine is an adenine, opposite every guanine is a cytosine. The base pairs are connected by hydrogen bonds (two between T and A; three between G and C). Because of the *base pairing*, the DNA strands are *antiparallel*: One DNA strand runs in the 5' to 3' direction and its complementary partner runs in the 3' to 5' direction (*see Problems 6–11, 24, 26, 37–44, 51, 52, 72, 81*).

3. How is DNA reproduced? *Replication* (Figure 25.5) requires DNA polymerases and deoxyribonucleoside triphosphates. The DNA helix partially unwinds and the enzymes move along the separated DNA strands, synthesizing a new strand with bases complementary to those on the unwound DNA strand being copied. The enzymes move only in the 3' to 5' direction along the template strand (and thus new DNA strands only grow in the 5' to 3' direction), so that one strand is copied continuously and the other strand is copied in segments as the replication fork moves along. In each resulting double helix, one strand is the original template strand and the other is the new copy (*see Problems 11, 22, 25, 28, 35, 36, 45, 46, 54, 55, 71*).

4. What are the functions of RNA? *Messenger RNA (mRNA)* carries the genetic information out of the nucleus to the *ribosomes* in the cytosol, where protein synthesis occurs. *Transfer RNAs (tRNAs)* circulate in the cytosol, where they bond to amino acids that they then deliver to ribosomes for protein synthesis. *Ribosomal RNAs (rRNAs)* are incorporated into ribosomes (*see Problems 13, 14, 33, 34, 71–74*).

5. How do organisms synthesize messenger RNA? In *transcription* (Figure 25.6), one DNA strand serves as the template and the other, the informational strand, is not copied. Nucleotides carrying bases complementary to the template bases between a control segment and a termination sequence are connected one by one to form mRNA. The primary transcript mRNA (or hnRNA) is identical to the matching segment of the informational strand, but with uracil replacing thymine. *Introns*, which are base sequences that do not code for amino acids in the protein, are cut out before the final transcript mRNA leaves the nucleus (*see Problems 15–17, 27, 53, 75, 76*).

6. How does RNA participate in protein synthesis? The genetic information is read as a sequence of codons—triplets of bases in DNA that give the sequence of amino acids in a protein.

Of the 64 possible codons (Table 25.4), 61 specify amino acids and 3 are stop codons. Each tRNA has at one end an *anticodon* consisting of three bases complementary to those of the mRNA codon that specifies the amino acid it carries. Initiation of *translation* (Figure 25.8) is the coming together of the large and small subunits of the ribosome, an mRNA, and the first amino acid–bearing tRNA connected at the first of the two binding sites in the ribosome. *Elongation* proceeds as the next tRNA arrives at the second binding site, its amino acid is bonded to the first one, the first tRNA leaves, and the ribosome moves along so that once again there is a vacant second site. These steps repeat until the stop codon is reached. The termination step consists of separation of the two ribosome subunits, the mRNA, and the protein (*see Problems 19–21, 56–70, 77–80*).

KEY WORDS

Anticodon, *p. 797*

Base pairing, *p. 784*

Chromosome, *p. 775*

Codon, *p. 793*

Deoxyribonucleotide, *p. 779*

DNA (deoxyribonucleic acid), *p. 775*

Double helix, *p. 783*

Exon, *p. 792*

Gene, *p. 776*

Genetic code, *p. 793*

Genome, *p. 788*

Heterogeneous nuclear RNA (hnRNA), *p. 792*

Intron, *p. 792*

Messenger RNA (mRNA), *p. 790*

Nucleic acid, *p. 776*

Nucleoside, *p. 777*

Nucleotide, *p. 776*

Replication, *p. 786*

Ribonucleotide, *p. 779*

Ribosome, *p. 790*

Ribosomal RNA (rRNA), *p. 790*

Ribozyme, *p. 790*

RNA (ribonucleic acid), *p. 776*

Transcription, *p. 786*

Transfer RNA (tRNA), *p. 790*

Translation, *p. 786*

UNDERSTANDING KEY CONCEPTS

25.23   Combine the structures below to create a ribonucleotide. Show where water is removed to form an *N*-glycosidic linkage and where water is removed to form a phosphate ester. Draw the resulting ribonucleotide structure, and name it.

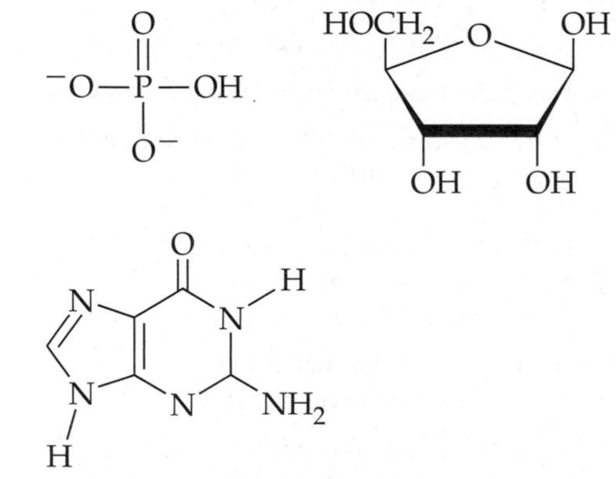

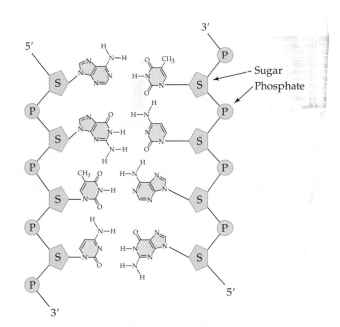

25.24   Copy the following diagram and use dotted lines to indicate where hydrogen bonding occurs between the complementary strands of DNA. What is the sequence of each strand of DNA drawn (remember that the sequence is written from the 5′ to 3′ end)?

25.25   Copy this simplified drawing of a DNA replication fork:

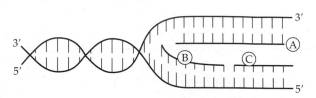

(a) On the drawing, indicate the direction of synthesis of the new strand labeled A and the location of DNA polymerase on the strand.

(b) On the drawing, indicate the direction of synthesis of the new strand labeled B and the location of DNA polymerase on the strand.

(c) How will strand C and strand B be connected?

25.26 What groups are found on the exterior of the DNA double helix? In the nucleus, DNA strands are wrapped around proteins called histones. Would you expect histones to be neutral, positively charged, or negatively charged? Based on your answer, which amino acids do you expect to be abundant in histones, and why?

25.27 In addition to RNA polymerase, transcription of DNA for the synthesis of mRNA requires (a) a control segment of DNA (also called an initiation sequence), (b) an informational strand of DNA, (c) a template strand of DNA, and (d) an end of the sequence (termination sequence). Determine the direction of RNA synthesis on the RNA strand in the following diagram. Draw in the locations of elements (a)–(d).

25.28 Gln-His-Pro-Gly is the sequence of a molecule known as progenitor thyrotropin-releasing hormone (pro-TRH). If we were searching for pro-TRH genes, we would need to know what sequence of bases in DNA we should be looking for. Use the boxes below to indicate answers to parts (a)–(d).

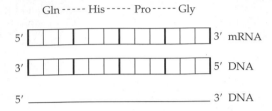

(a) What RNA sequence could code for these four amino acids?

(b) What double-stranded DNA sequence (gene) could code for these amino acids?

(c) Which strand of DNA is the template strand, and which is the informational strand?

(d) How many possible DNA sequences are there?

ADDITIONAL PROBLEMS

STRUCTURE AND FUNCTION OF NUCLEIC ACIDS

25.29 For the following molecule:

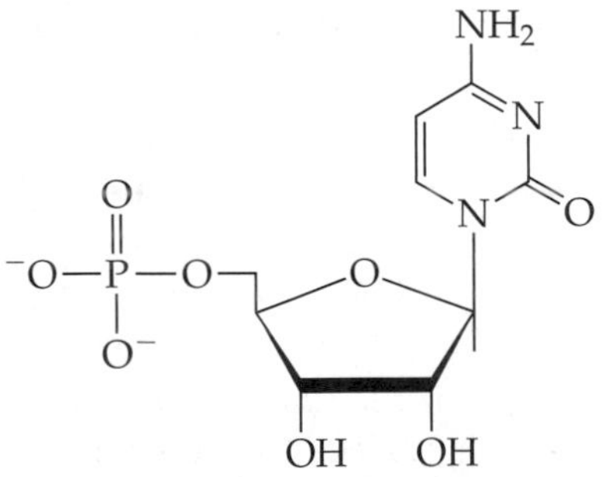

$$NH_2$$

(a) Label the three nucleic acid building blocks it contains.

(b) Draw a box around the nucleoside portion of the molecule.

(c) Draw a circle around the nucleotide portion of the molecule.

25.30 What are the sugars in DNA and RNA, and how do they differ?

25.31 (a) What are the four major heterocyclic bases in DNA?

(b) What are the four major heterocyclic bases in RNA?

(c) Structurally, how do the heterocyclic bases in RNA differ from those in DNA? (See Table 25.1.)

25.32 What are the two structural types of bases in DNA and RNA? Which bases correspond to each type?

25.33 What are the three main kinds of RNA, and what are their functions?

25.34 Rank the following in order of size: tRNA, DNA, mRNA.

25.35 (a) What is meant by the term *base pairing*?

(b) Which bases pair with which other bases?

(c) How many hydrogen bonds does each base pair have?

25.36 How are replication, transcription, and translation similar? How are they different?

25.37 What is the difference between a gene and a chromosome?

25.38 What are the two major components of chromatin?

25.39 What genetic information does a single gene contain?

25.40 How many chromosomes are present in a human cell?

25.41 What kind of intermolecular attraction holds the DNA double helix together?

25.42 What does it mean to speak of bases as being *complementary*?

25.43 The DNA from sea urchins contains about 32% A and about 18% G. What percentages of T and C would you expect in sea urchin DNA? Explain.

25.44 If a double-stranded DNA molecule is 22% G, what is the percentage of A, T, and C? Explain.

25.45 What is the difference between the 3′ end and the 5′ end of a polynucleotide?

25.46 Are polynucleotides synthesized 3′ to 5′, or 5′ to 3′?

25.47 Draw structures to show how the phosphate and sugar components of a nucleic acid are joined. What kind of linkage forms between the sugar and the phosphate?

25.48 Draw structures to show how the sugar and heterocyclic base components of a nucleic acid are joined. What small molecule is formed?

25.49 Draw the complete structure of uridine 5′-phosphate, one of the four major ribonucleotides.

25.50 Draw the complete structure of the RNA dinucleotide U-C. Identify the 5′ and 3′ ends of the dinucleotide.

25.51 The segment of DNA that encompasses a gene typically contains *introns* and *exons*. Define each of these terms.

25.52 What are some possible roles introns might have? What roles do exons have?

NUCLEIC ACIDS AND HEREDITY

25.53 Transcribed RNA is complementary to which strand of DNA?

25.54 Why is more than one replication fork needed when human DNA is duplicated?

25.55 Why do we say that DNA replication is semiconservative?

25.56 What is a codon, and on what kind of nucleic acid is it found?

25.57 What is an anticodon, and on what kind of nucleic acid is it found?

25.58 What is the general shape and structure of a tRNA molecule?

25.59 There are different tRNAs for each amino acid. What is one major way to differentiate among the tRNAs for each amino acid?

25.60 Which amino acid(s) have the most codons? Which amino acid(s) have the fewest codons? Can you think of a reason why multiple codons code for certain amino acids but other amino acids are coded for by very few codons?

25.61 Look at Table 25.4 and find codons for the following amino acids:

  (a) Val   **(b)** Arg   **(c)** Ser

25.62 What amino acids are specified by the following codons?

  (a) C-C-C   **(b)** G-C-G   **(c)** U-U-A

25.63 What anticodon sequences are complementary to the codons listed in Problem 25.62? (Remember that the anticodons are opposite in direction to the codons, so label the 3′ and 5′ ends!)

25.64 What anticodon sequences are complementary to the codons for the amino acids given in Problem 25.61? (Remember that the anticodons are opposite in direction to the codons, so label the 3′ and 5′ ends!)

25.65 If the sequence T-A-C-C-C-T appears on the informational strand of DNA, what sequence appears opposite it on the template strand? Label your answer with 3′ and 5′ ends.

25.66 Refer to Problem 25.65. What sequence appears on the mRNA molecule transcribed from the DNA sequence T-A-C-C-C-T? Label your answer with 3′ and 5′ ends.

25.67 Refer to Problems 25.65 and 25.66. What dipeptide is synthesized from the informational DNA sequence T-A-C-C-C-T?

25.68 What tetrapeptide is synthesized from the informational DNA sequence G-T-C-A-G-T-A-C-G-T-T-A?

25.69 Metenkephalin is a small peptide found in animal brains that has morphine-like properties. Give an mRNA sequence that could code for the synthesis of metenkephalin: Tyr-Gly-Gly-Phe-Met. Label your answer with 3′ and 5′ ends.

25.70 Refer to Problem 25.69. Give a double-stranded DNA sequence that could code for metenkephalin. Label your answer with 3′ and 5′ ends.

CHEMISTRY IN ACTION

25.71 What is a ribozyme? What is unusual about the function of a ribozyme? [*It's a Ribozyme!*, p. 790]

25.72 Some scientists think that an "RNA world" preceded our current cellular reactions dominated by protein enzymes. What would lead them to assert this? [*It's a Ribozyme!*, p. 790]

25.73 Explain the process of reverse transcription. What is the name given to viruses that use this process? [*Viruses and AIDS*, p. 794]

25.74 How do vaccines work? Why is it so difficult to design drugs effective against AIDS? [*Viruses and AIDS*, p. 794]

25.75 Describe how the avian influenza virus is transmitted to humans. [*Influenza—Variations on a Theme*, p. 799]

25.76 The influenza virus H1N1 can infect both humans and other animals. Use the Internet to collect information that allows you to describe some of the similarities and some of the differences between the H1N1 virus and the virus responsible for avian influenza. [*Influenza—Variations on a Theme*, p. 799]

GENERAL QUESTIONS AND PROBLEMS

25.77 A normal hemoglobin protein has a glutamic acid at position 6; in sickle-cell hemoglobin, this glutamic acid has been replaced by a valine. List all the possible mRNA codons that could be present for each type of hemoglobin. Can a single base-change result in a change from Glu to Val in hemoglobin?

25.78 Insulin is synthesized as preproinsulin, which has 81 amino acids. How many heterocyclic bases must be present in the informational DNA strand to code for preproinsulin (assuming no introns are present)?

25.79 Human and horse insulin are both composed of two polypeptide chains with one chain containing 21 amino acids and the other containing 30 amino acids. Human and horse insulin differ at two amino acids: position 9 in one chain (human has serine and horse has glycine) and position 30 on the other chain (human has threonine and horse has alanine). How must the DNA differ to account for this? Identify the 5′ and 3′ ends of the four trinucleotide complementary DNA sequences.

25.80 If the initiation codon for proteins is AUG, how do you account for the case of a protein that does not include methionine as its first amino acid?

25.81 Suppose that 22% of the nucleotides of a DNA molecule are deoxyadenosine and during replication the relative amounts of available deoxynucleoside triphosphates are 22% dATP, 22% dCTP, 28% dGTP, and 28% dTTP. What deoxynucleoside triphosphate is limiting to the replication? Explain.

Genomics

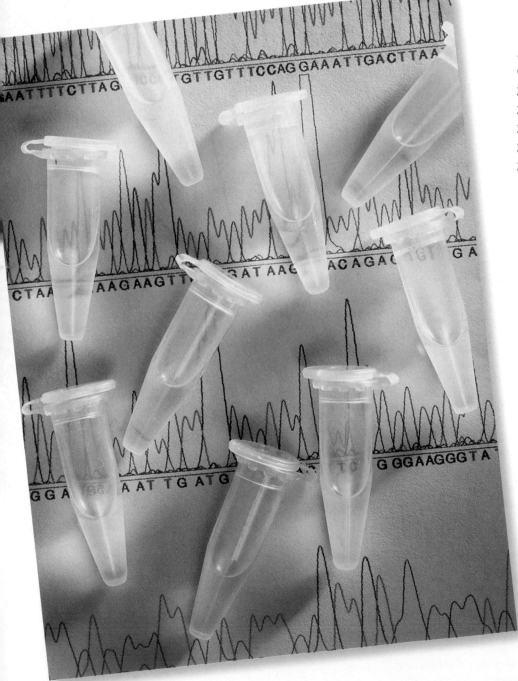

CONTENTS

◄ The vials hold DNA samples dissolved in an aqueous buffer. Behind the vials is the printout from an automatic DNA-sequencing machine.

1. **What is the working draft of the human genome and the circumstances of its creation?**
   THE GOAL: Be able to describe the genome-mapping projects and the major accomplishments of their working drafts. (◀◀ D.)

2. **What are the various segments along the length of the DNA in a chromosome?**
   THE GOAL: Be able to describe the nature of telomeres, centromeres, exons and genes, and noncoding DNA. (◀◀ D.)

3. **What are mutations?**
   THE GOAL: Be able to define mutations, identify what can cause them, and also identify their possible results. (◀◀ B, C, D.)

4. **What are polymorphisms and single-nucleotide polymorphisms (SNPs), and how can identifying them be useful?**
   THE GOAL: Be able to define polymorphisms and SNPs, and explain the significance of knowing the locations of SNPs. (◀◀ A, B.)

5. **What is recombinant DNA?**
   THE GOAL: Be able to define recombinant DNA and explain how it is used for production of proteins by bacteria. (◀◀ B, C.)

6. **What does the future hold for uses of genomic information?**
   THE GOAL: Be able to provide an overview of the current and possible future applications of the human genome map. (◀◀ C, D.)

A. Structure, Synthesis, and Function of DNA
(Sections 25.2–25.3)

B. Base Pairing and Heredity
(Sections 25.4–25.5)

C. Replication of DNA
(Section 25.6)

D. Transcription, Translation, and the Genetic Code
(Sections 25.8–25.10)

I n Chapter 25 we described the fundamentals of DNA structure and function, the biosynthesis of DNA, and its role in making proteins from amino acids. Out of this work on DNA has come a scientific revolution: the sequencing of the entire genome for many organisms. The crowning achievement of this endeavor is that an almost complete and accurate map of human DNA is now available. Creation of this map has been compared to such landmark achievements as harnessing nuclear power and flight into outer space. In significance for individual human beings, there has never been anything like it.

This chapter begins with a description of how this genomic map was obtained. We then explore variations in the content of the DNA in each chromosome and a technique for manipulating DNA. Finally, we look briefly at ways in which genomic information can be put to use.

26.1 Mapping the Human Genome

How to Map a Genome

What does it mean to "map" a genome? For that matter, what exactly is a genetic "map?" Many people tend to think of mapping the genome of a given organism as like reading a novel: you start at the first page and continue until you reach the end. Applying this approach to a genome, you would start at one end of a chromosome and, proceeding base by base, record each nucleotide until you reached the end. Although this would result in an enormous amount of sequence data, it would tell you nothing about what the nucleotides may signify or where things are located with respect to each other. In reality, a genetic map is more like a map you get when you visit a large amusement park. You may see the scary mansion in one corner of the map, the death-defying roller coaster in another, the kiddie-ride area in another, and so on, with all the paths that lead to them shown. The typical map of this type is made up of landmarks and where they are located with respect to each other. A genetic map is no different, with one huge exception: we don't know exactly what many of the landmarks represent. For example, one genetic landmark (or *marker*) might represent a gene for a known trait, or might be a specific pattern of repeating nucleotides. So, in effect, a genomic map is a physical representation of all the landmarks in a genome and where they are with respect to one another.

▲ A sample of DNA ready for analysis.

Mapping the genes on a eukaryotic chromosome is no easy feat. When you consider that the nucleotides that code for proteins (the *exons*) are interrupted by noncoding nucleotides (the *introns*) (see Section 25.8), it should be clear what mapping challenges exist for any organism whose genome contains only a few dozen genes. These challenges are greatly magnified for the human genome, which contains between twenty and twenty-five *thousand* genes! Another challenge to consider is that there is neither spacing between "words" in the genetic code, nor any "punctuation." Using the English language as an analogy, try to find a meaningful phrase in this:

sfdggmaddrydkdkdkrrrsjfljhadxccctmctmaqqqoumlittgklejagkjghjoailambrsslj

The phrase is "mary had a little lamb":

sfdgg**maddry**dkdkdkrrrsjflj**had**xccctmctmaqqqoum**littgkle**jagkjghjoai**lambr**sslj

Now consider how hard finding meaning would be if the phrase you were looking for was in an unfamiliar language! It has been estimated that the string of C's, G's, T's, and A's that make up the human genome would fill 75,490 pages of standard-size type in a newspaper like the *New York Times*.

Two organizations led the effort to map the human genome: the Human Genome Project (a collection of 20 groups at not-for-profit institutes and universities) and Celera Genomics (a commercial biotechnology company). These two groups used different approaches to taking DNA apart, analyzing its base sequences, and reassembling the information. The Human Genome Project created a series of maps of finer and finer resolution (think of a satellite map program such as Google Earth, where you can progress from a satellite photo of the United States to a map of your state to a map of the city where you live to the street you live on and, ultimately, to a picture of the house you live in). Celera followed a seemingly random approach in which they fragmented DNA and then relied on instrumental and computer-driven techniques to establish the sequence (think of breaking a piece of glass into thousands of shards and then piecing them back together). It was believed that data obtained via the combination of these two approaches would speed up the enormous task of sequencing the human genome.

In 2001 the stunning announcement was made that 90% of the human genome sequence had been mapped in 15 months instead of the originally anticipated four years. By October 2004, an analysis of the Human Genome Project reported that 99% of the gene-containing parts of the genome were sequenced and declared to be 99.999% accurate. Additionally, the mapped sequence reportedly correctly identifies almost all known genes (99.74% of them, to be exact). At a practical level, this "gold-standard" sequence data allows researchers to rely on highly accurate sequence information, priming new biomedical research.

The strategy utilized by the Human Genome Project for generating the complete map is shown in Figure 26.1. Pictured at the top is a type of chromosome drawing, known as an ideogram (pronounced id-**ee**-*uh*-gram), for human chromosome 21. The light- and dark-blue shadings represent the location of banding visible in electron micrographs. Chromosome 21 is the smallest human chromosome, with 37 million base pairs (abbreviated 37 Mb) and was the second chromosome to be mapped (chromosome 22 was the first).

In the first step, a *genetic map* was generated. The genetic map showed the physical location of *markers*, identifiable DNA sequences (some within genes, some within noncoding DNA) that were known to be inherited. The markers were an average of 1 million nucleotides apart. This is known as a genetic map because the order and locations of the markers are established by genetic studies of inheritance in related individuals.

The next map, the *physical map*, refines the distance between markers to about 100,000 base pairs. The physical map includes markers identified by a variety of experimental methods, most notably the use of *restriction enzymes* (discussed in Section 26.4).

Chromosome 21 (37 Mb)

◀ **Figure 26.1**
Human Genome Project mapping strategy.

Genetic map:
1 Mb resolution

Genetic map of markers spaced about 1,000,000 base pairs apart

Physical map:
100 kb resolution

Physical map with markers spaced about 100,000 base pairs apart

Overlapping clones

Set of overlapping ordered clones covering 100 kb

Nucleotide sequence

ATGCCCGATTGCAT

Each overlapping clone will be sequenced, sequences assembled into the entire genomic sequence of 3.2×10^9 nucleotides, 37 Mb of which will be from chromosome 21

To proceed to a map of finer resolution, a chromosome was cut into large segments and multiple copies of the segments were produced. The segment copies are called **clones**, a term that refers to identical copies of organisms, cells, or in this case, DNA segments. The overlapping clones, which covered the entire length of the chromosome, were arranged in order to produce the next level of map (see Figure 26.1).

In the next step, each clone was cut into 500 base-pair fragments, and identity and order of bases in each fragment was determined. There is a variety of sequencing methods available, but a common one involves copying the 500 base-pair fragment many times to generate a *nested set* of DNA molecules (a molecule that is one nucleotide long, another that is two nucleotides long, another that is three nucleotides long . . . up to 500 nucleotides long). Each molecule in the nested set ends in a C, G, T, or A, and each of these end nucleotides is fluorescently labeled in a different color. The fluorescently labeled molecules are then separated by size using gel electrophoresis, and the order of colors seen on the gel represent the order of nucleotides in the original 500 base-pair fragment. In the final step, all the different 500 base-pair sequences are assembled into a completed nucleotide map of the chromosome.

Clones Identical copies of organisms, cells, or DNA segments from a single ancestor.

▶▶▶ In Chapter 18 we saw how electrophoresis is used as a technique to separate proteins by charge or size (Chemistry in Action: Protein Analysis by Electrophoresis). Gel electrophoresis is also routinely used with DNA, to separate DNA molecules by size.

◀ **A researcher loads samples into a genome sequencer. The results obtained will appear on the monitor in the colored boxes shown.**

CHEMISTRY IN ACTION

One Genome To Represent Us All?

One might wonder whose genome provided the standard against which those of all other human beings will be evaluated. What individual symbolizes all of us? A star athlete? A brilliant scientist? A truly average person?

It does not take more than a moment's thought to realize that using the DNA of a single individual to represent the entire human genome is a bad idea. What if the person chosen had a genetic aberration? How does a project of this importance deal with ethnic differences? Since no two individuals, other than identical twins, have exactly the same base sequences in their genomes, some sort of normalized average is needed.

To avoid this, the path chosen by both genome mapping groups was to employ DNA from a group of anonymous individuals. In the Human Genome Project, researchers collected blood (female) or sperm (male) samples from a large number of donors of diverse backgrounds. After removing all identifying labels, only a randomly selected few of the many collected samples were used for sequencing, so that neither donors nor scientists could know the origins of the DNA being sequenced. The ultimate map comes from a composite of these random samples.

The Celera project relied on anonymous donors as well. DNA from five individuals (the leader of the Celera team, Craig Venter, has since acknowledged being one of these individuals)

▲ **From the four nucleotides that compose DNA comes the incredibly diverse population that makes up the human race.**

was collected, mixed, and processed for sequencing. The anonymous donors were of European, African, American (North, Central, and South), and Asian ancestry. As a result, one of the most frequently asked questions about the human genome, "Whose DNA was sequenced?" can never truly be answered because the DNA sequenced is a composite of the DNA of many anonymous individuals. The question of whether this one genomic map is indeed randomized enough to allow its general use is still debatable, but it does provide an excellent place from which to start.

See Chemistry in Action Problem 26.58 at the end of the chapter.

The approach taken by Celera Genomics was much bolder. In what has come to be known as their "shotgun approach," Celera broke the human genome into fragments without identifying the origin of any given fragment. The fragments were copied many times to generate many clones of each area of the genome; ultimately they were cut into 500-base-long pieces and modified with fluorescently labeled bases that could be sequenced by high-speed machines. The resulting sequences were reassembled by identifying overlapping ends. At Celera, this monumental reassembly task was carried out using the world's largest non-governmental supercomputing center.

PROBLEM 26.1
Decode the following sequence of letters to find an English phrase made entirely out of three-letter words. (Hint: First look for a word you recognize, then work forward and backward from there.)

uouothedttttrrfatnaedigopredsldjflsjfxxratponxbvateugfaqqthenqeutbadpagfratmeabrrx

26.2 A Trip Along a Chromosome

In this section we take a trip along the major regions and structural variations in the DNA folded into each chromosome. Understanding how DNA is structured should give you some insight into the biotechnology revolution ushered in by the Human Genome Project.

Telomeres and Centromeres

At both ends of every linear chromosome are specialized regions of DNA called **telomeres**. Each telomere in human DNA is a long, noncoding series of a repeating sequence of nucleotides, $(TTAGGG)_n$. Telomeres act as "endcaps," or "covers," protecting the ends of the chromosome from accidental damage that might alter the more important DNA-coding sequences. Telomeres also prevent the DNA ends from fusing to the DNA in other chromosomes or to DNA fragments.

Another chromosomal region that contains large repetitive base sequences that do not code for proteins is the **centromere**. As the DNA in each chromosome is duplicated in preparation for cell division, the two copies remain joined together at a constricted point in the middle of the chromosome; this is the centromere. The duplicated chromosomes bound together at the centromere are known as *sister chromatids*.

Because of the repetitive nature of their sequences, neither telomeres nor centromeres were sequenced in the mapping projects described in Section 26.1.

Each new cell starts life with a long stretch of telomeric DNA on each of its chromosome ends, with over 1000 copies of the repeating group; in humans and other mammals this sequence is usually TTAGGG. Some of this repeating sequence is lost with each cell division, so that as the cell ages, the telomere gets shorter and shorter. A very short telomere is associated with the stage at which a cell stops dividing (known as *senescence*). Continuation of shortening beyond this stage is associated with DNA instability and cell death.

Telomerase is the enzyme responsible for adding telomeres to DNA. It is active during embryonic development. In adults, telomerase is only active in the germ cells destined to become egg and sperm. Under normal, healthy conditions, telomerase is not active in other adult cells (the *somatic* cells). There is widespread speculation that telomere-shortening plays a role in the natural progression of human aging. Some support for this concept comes from experiments with mice whose telomerase activity has been destroyed ("knocked out" in genetic research vernacular). These mice age prematurely, and if they become pregnant, their embryos do not survive.

What would happen if telomerase remains active in a cell rather than declining in activity with age? With the length of its telomeres constantly being replenished by telomerase, the cell would not age and instead would continue to divide. Consider that such continuing division is one characteristic of cancer cells; in fact, the majority of cancer cells are known to contain active telomerase, which is thought to confer immortality on these tumor cells. Where this activity stands in relation to the presence of cancer-causing genes and environmental factors is not yet understood because neither amplification nor mutation of the telomerase gene has been identified in tumors; it is simply active when normally it would not be. As a result, a causal role for telomerase in tumorigenesis has yet to be established. Current research suggests that it is the genes responsible for regulating telomerase expression that are altered in cancer cells. As you might suspect, there are ongoing experiments on the consequences of telomerase inactivation on cancer cells. Additionally, scientists are examining the role that telomerase might play in achieving a sort of human "immortality," at least from a cellular standpoint.

Noncoding DNA

In addition to the noncoding telomeres, centromeres, and introns along a chromosome, there are noncoding promoter sequences, which are regulatory regions of DNA that determine which of its genes are turned on. All of your cells (except red blood cells) contain all of your genes, but only the genes needed by any individual cell will be activated in that cell. At the onset of the Human Genome Project, most scientists believed that humans had about 100,000 genes; as of 2010, researchers have confirmed the existence of approximately 23,000 protein-coding genes in the human genome and identified another approximately 2000 DNA segments that are

Telomeres The ends of chromosomes; in humans, telomeres contain long series of repeating groups of nucleotides.

Centromeres The central regions of chromosomes.

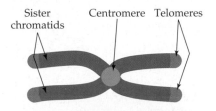

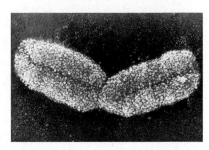

▲ Top: **A duplicated chromosome immediately prior to cell division showing the locations of the telomeres and the centromere.** Bottom: Color-enhanced electron microscope image showing the constriction of the centromere during metaphase.

predicted to be protein-coding genes. This current data suggests that only about 2% of all DNA in the human genome actually codes for protein. It is interesting to note that the human genome has much more noncoding DNA (once referred to as "junk" DNA) than do the genomes known for other organisms. This evidence raises the question of the role played by the vast amount of noncoding DNA present in our genome. The question arises out of the observation that genome size does not correlate with organismal complexity, with one example being that many plants have larger genomes than humans. Some scientists have suggested that the segments of noncoding DNA are needed to accommodate the folding of DNA within the nucleus, others think these segments may have played a role in evolution, while still others argue that the segments are functional but the functions are not yet understood. The function of noncoding DNA remains to be discovered; meanwhile the debate over its role continues to this day.

Genes

In learning about transcription (Section 25.8), you saw that the nucleotides of a single gene are not consecutive along a stretch of DNA, but have coding segments (the *exons*) that alternate with noncoding segments (the *introns*). As an example of what must be dealt with in mapping the human genome, consider a "small," 2900-nucleotide sequence found in a much simpler organism (corn) that codes for the enzyme triose phosphate isomerase:

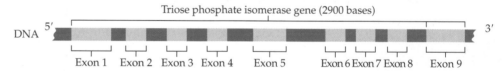

This gene consists of nine exons that account for 759 of the 2900 nucleotides (26%), with the eight introns accounting for the remaining bases. Now imagine the human genome, which is much more complex; it is estimated that somewhere between just 1–3% of our genetic material is coding sequence. Take, for example, chromosome 22. It is one of the smaller human chromosomes and was the first to have all of its nonrepetitive DNA sequenced and mapped. The chromosome map identified 49 million bases containing approximately 693 genes, with an average of eight exons and seven introns per gene. Chromosome 22 is of medical interest because it carries genes known to be associated with the immune system as well as disorders such as congenital heart disease, schizophrenia, leukemia, various cancers, and many other genetically related conditions. The map also revealed several hundred previously unknown genes. With the signal (exon) to noise (intron) ratio being so low (meaning more noise to hide the signal) in the human genome, it will be challenging to completely identify all the coding sequences present.

26.3 Mutations and Polymorphisms

The base-pairing mechanism of DNA replication and RNA transcription provides an extremely efficient and accurate method for preserving and using genetic information, but it is not perfect. Occasionally an error occurs, resulting in the incorporation of an incorrect base at some point.

An occasional error during the transcription of a messenger RNA molecule may not create a serious problem. After all, large numbers of mRNA molecules are continually being produced, and an error that occurs perhaps one out of a million times would hardly be noticed in the presence of many correct mRNAs. If an error occurs during the replication of a DNA molecule, however, the consequences can be far more damaging. Each chromosome in a cell contains only *one* kind of DNA, and if it is miscopied during replication, then the error is passed on when the cell divides.

▲ An error in nucleic acid composition that occurs once in 3–4 million lobsters is responsible for the beautiful color of this crustacean.

An error in base sequence that is carried along during DNA replication is called a **mutation**. Mutation commonly refers to variations in DNA sequence found in a very small number of individuals of a species. Some mutations result from spontaneous and random events. Others are induced by exposure to a **mutagen**—an external agent that can cause a mutation. Viruses, chemicals, and ionizing radiation can all be mutagenic. The most common types of mutations are listed in Table 26.1.

Mutation A rare DNA variant; an error in base sequence that is carried along in DNA replication and passed on to offspring.

Mutagen A substance that causes mutations.

Table **26.1** Types of Mutations

Type	Description
Point mutations	A single base change
Silent	A change that specifies the same amino acid; for example, GUU → GUC, gives Val → Val
Missense	A change that specifies a different amino acid; for example, GUU → GCU gives Val → Ala
Nonsense	A change that produces a stop codon, for example, CGA → UGA gives Arg → Stop
Frameshift	An insertion or deletion of one or more bases where the number of inserted or deleted bases is not a multiple of 3, so that all triplets following the mutation are read differently
Insertion	Addition of one or more bases
Deletion	Loss of one or more bases

The biological effects of incorporating an incorrect amino acid into a protein range from negligible to catastrophic, depending on both the nature and location of the change. The effect might result in a hereditary disease, like sickle-cell anemia or a birth defect. There are thousands of known human hereditary diseases. Some of the more common ones are listed in Table 26.2. Mutations, or sometimes the combination of several mutations, can also produce vulnerability to certain diseases, which may or may not develop in an individual.

Table **26.2** Some Common Hereditary Diseases, Their Causes, and Their Prevalence

Name	Nature and Cause of Defect	Prevalence in Population
Phenylketonuria (PKU)	Brain damage in infants caused by the defective enzyme phenylalanine hydroxylase	1 in 40,000
Albinism	Absence of skin pigment caused by the defective enzyme tyrosinase	1 in 20,000
Tay-Sachs disease	Mental retardation caused by a defect in production of the enzyme hexosaminidase A	1 in 6000 (Ashkenazi Jews); 1 in 100,000 (General population)
Cystic fibrosis	Bronchopulmonary, liver, and pancreatic obstructions by thickened mucus; defective gene and protein identified	1 in 3000
Sickle-cell anemia	Anemia and obstruction of blood flow caused by a defect in hemoglobin	1 in 185 (African-Americans)

Polymorphisms are also variations in the nucleotide sequence of DNA, but here the reference is to variations that are common within a given population. Most polymorphisms are simply differences in the DNA sequence between individuals due to geographical and ethnic differences and are part of the biodiversity exhibited by life on earth. While the vast majority of polymorphisms recorded have neither advantageous nor deleterious effects, some do and have been shown to give rise to various disease states. The location of polymorphisms responsible for some inherited human diseases are shown in Figure 26.2.

Polymorphism A variation in DNA sequence within a population.

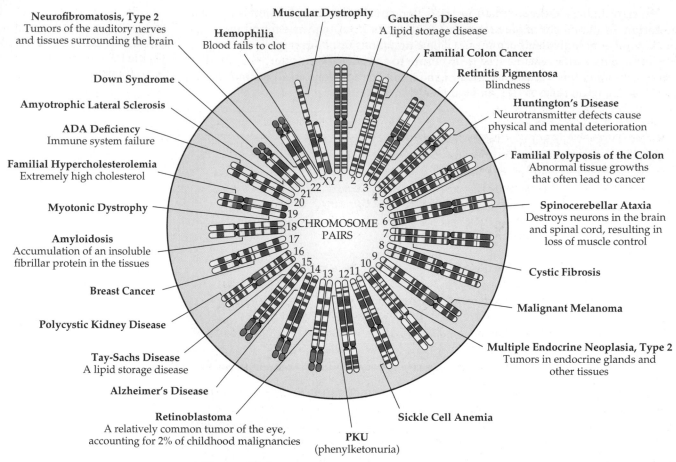

▲ **Figure 26.2**

A human chromosome map.

Regions on each chromosome that have been identified as responsible for inherited diseases are indicated.

Single-nucleotide polymorphism (SNP) Common single-base-pair variation in DNA.

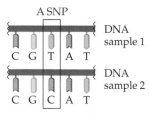

The replacement of one nucleotide by another in the same location along the DNA sequence is known as a **single-nucleotide polymorphism** (SNP, pronounced "snip"). In other words, two different nucleotides at the same position along two defined stretches of DNA are SNPs. A SNP is expected to occur in at least 1% of a specific population and therefore provides a link to a genetic characteristic of that population.

The biological effects of SNPs can be wide ranging, from being negligible to being normal variations such as those in eye or hair color, to being genetic diseases. *SNPs are the most common source of variations between individual human beings.* Most genes carry one or more SNPs, and in different individuals most SNPs occur in the same location.

Imagine that the sequence A-T-G on the informational strand of DNA is replaced with the sequence A-C-G (an SNP); now the messenger RNA produced will have the codon sequence A-C-G rather than the intended sequence A-U-G. Because A-C-G codes for threonine, whereas A-U-G codes for methionine, threonine will be inserted into the corresponding protein during translation. Furthermore, every copy of the protein will have the same variation. The seriousness of the outcome depends on the function of the protein and the effect of the amino acid change on its structure and activity.

In addition to producing a change in the identity of an amino acid, a SNP might specify the same amino acid (for example, changing GUU to GUC, both of which code for valine), or it might terminate protein synthesis by introducing a stop codon (like changing CGA to UGA).

Concurrent with the work of the Human Genome Project, an international team of industrial and academic scientists is compiling a catalog of SNPs. As of 2010, the exact locations in the human genome of over 5 million SNPs had been recorded. Their frequency is roughly one SNP for about every 2000–5000 bases, with many of them in coding regions. These are considered but a fraction of the total that will eventually be identified.

We have described the single amino acid change that results in sickle-cell anemia. It took years of research to identify the SNP responsible for that disease. Had a computerized catalog of SNPs been available at the time, it might have been found in a few hours. Another known SNP is associated with the risk of developing Alzheimer's disease. Not all SNPs create susceptibility to diseases; for example, there is also one that imparts a resistance to HIV and AIDS. Most SNPs have neither advantageous nor deleterious effects on the organism.

▶▶▶ The mutation leading to sickle-cell anemia is described in Section 18.7.

The SNP catalog, although far from complete, has been valuable from the start. Early in its development it was used to locate SNPs responsible for 30 abnormal conditions, including total color blindness, one type of epilepsy, and susceptibility to the development of breast cancer. For example, the catalog has been used to find 15 SNPs in a gene that affects testosterone levels. Examination of the DNA from prostate cancer patients showed that these SNPs occur in four combinations in these people. The next step is to hunt down the role of each of those four genetic variations in the disease. It is hoped that this information will inspire the development of new treatments for diseases.

The search for disease-related SNPs is not easy, although as the SNP catalog expands and the related proteins are understood, this is expected to change. One research group set out to identify SNPs associated with Type II diabetes. Eventually they sequenced a 66,000-nucleotide sequence in a stretch of DNA implicated in diabetes. It contained 180 SNPs. Comparing these sequences for 100 diabetics and 100 nondiabetic controls turned up a combination of three SNPs that signal a susceptibility to diabetes. As of 2011, the SNP catalog maintained by the National Human Genome Research Institute contains over 5700 entries for a variety of disease-related SNPs.

The cataloging of SNPs has ushered in the era of genetic medicine. Ultimately, the SNP catalog may allow physicians to predict for an individual the potential age at which inherited diseases will become active, their severity, and their reactions to various types of treatment. The therapeutic course will be designed to meet the distinctive genomic profile of the person.

Worked Example 26.1 Determining the Effect of Changes in DNA on Proteins

The severity of a mutation in a DNA sequence that changes a single amino acid in a protein depends on the type of amino acid replaced and the nature of the new amino acid. (a) What kind of change would have little effect on the protein containing the alternative amino acid? (b) What kind of change could have a major effect on the protein that contains the alternative amino acid? Give an example of each type of mutation.

ANALYSIS The result of exchanging one amino acid for another depends on the change in the nature of the amino acid side chains. To speculate on the result of such a change requires us to think again about the structure of the side chains, which are shown in Table 18.3. The question to consider is whether the mutation introduces an amino acid with such a different side chain character that it is likely to to alter the structure and function of the resulting protein.

SOLUTION

(a) Exchange of an amino acid with a small nonpolar side chain for another with the same type of side chain (for example, glycine for alanine) or exchange of amino acids with very similar side chains (say, serine for threonine) might have little effect.

(b) Conversion of an amino acid with a nonpolar side chain to one with a polar, acidic, or basic side chain could have a major effect because the side-chain interactions that affect protein folding may change (see Figure 18.4). Some examples of this type include exchanging threonine, glutamate, or lysine for isoleucine.

> 🔑 **KEY CONCEPT PROBLEM 26.2**
>
> Consider that a SNP alters the base sequence in an mRNA codon by changing UGU to UGG. Speculate on the significance of this change.

PROBLEM 26.3

In Chemistry in Action: One Genome to Represent Us All? the issue of what DNA samples to use for the genome mapping project was addressed. If you were part of the original team and it was suggested that you use samples obtained from patients in a local hospital for the mapping project, what problems might you see with this approach?

26.4 Recombinant DNA

Recombinant DNA DNA that contains two or more DNA segments not found together in nature.

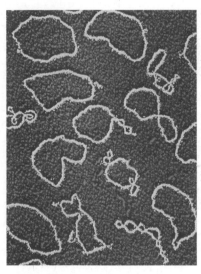

▲ **Plasmids from the bacterium** *Escherichia coli,* **hosts for recombinant DNA.**

In this section, we describe a technique for manipulating, altering, and reproducing pieces of DNA. The technique requires the creation of **recombinant DNA**—DNA that joins two or more DNA segments not found together in nature. Progress in all aspects of genomics has built upon information gained in the application of recombinant DNA. The two other techniques that play major roles in DNA studies are the polymerase chain reaction (PCR) and electrophoresis. PCR is a method by which large quantities of identical pieces of DNA can be synthesized (see Chemistry in Action: Serendipity and the Polymerase Chain Reaction). Electrophoresis, which can be carried out simultaneously on large numbers of samples, separates proteins or DNA fragments according to their size (see Chemistry in Action: Protein Analysis by Electrophoresis in Chapter 18).

Using recombinant DNA technology, it is possible to cut a gene out of one organism and splice it into (*recombine* it with) the DNA of a second organism. Bacteria provide excellent hosts for recombinant DNA. Bacterial cells, unlike the cells of higher organisms, contain part of their DNA in small circular pieces called *plasmids,* each of which carries just a few genes. Plasmids are extremely easy to isolate, several copies of each plasmid may be present in a cell, and each plasmid replicates through the normal base-pairing pathway. The ease of isolating and manipulating plasmids plus the rapid replication of bacteria create ideal conditions for production of recombinant DNA and the proteins whose synthesis it directs in bacteria.

To prepare a plasmid for insertion of a foreign gene, the plasmid is cut open with a bacterial enzyme, known as a *restriction endonuclease* or *restriction enzyme,* that recognizes a specific sequence in a DNA molecule and cleaves between the same two nucleotides in that sequence. For example, the restriction endonuclease *Eco*RI recognizes the sequence G-A-A-T-T-C and cuts between G and A. This restriction enzyme makes its cut at the same spot in the sequence of both strands of the double-stranded DNA when read in the same 5′ to 3′ direction. As a result, the cut is offset so that both DNA strands are left with a few unpaired bases on each end. These groups of unpaired bases are known as *sticky ends* because they are available to match up with complementary base sequences.

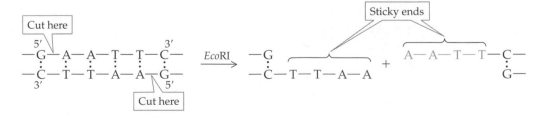

Recombinant DNA is produced by cutting the two DNA segments to be combined with the same restriction endonuclease. The result is DNA fragments with sticky ends that are complementary to each other.

Consider a gene fragment that has been cut from human DNA and is to be inserted into a plasmid. The gene and the plasmid are both cut with the same enzyme, one that

CHEMISTRY IN ACTION

Serendipity and the Polymerase Chain Reaction

Before the 1980s, studying DNA involved the frustration of working with very small, hard-to-obtain samples. Everyone wished there were a way to copy DNA, to make millions of copies of a sample. Their wish was granted one evening by Kary B. Mullis, a young biochemist who was mentally attacking a different problem—how to identify the sequence of nucleotides in DNA. In his own words, here is what happened:

> "Sometimes a good idea comes to you when you are not looking for it. Through an improbable combination of coincidences, naiveté and lucky mistakes, such a revelation came to me one Friday night in April 1983 as I gripped the steering wheel of my car and snaked along a moonlit road into northern California's redwood country. . . . I liked night driving; every weekend I went north to my cabin and sat still for three hours in the car, my hands occupied, my mind free. On that particular night I was thinking about my proposed DNA sequencing experiment."*

Mullis drove along, in his mind trying out and then rejecting various ways to approach the experiment, which required combining DNA polymerase, natural DNA (the target DNA), nucleoside triphosphates, and short synthetic nucleotide chains (*oligonucleotides*) in just the right way. Then,

> "I was suddenly jolted by a realization: The strands of DNA in the target and the extended oligonucleotides would have the same base sequences. In effect, the mock reaction would have doubled the number of DNA targets in the sample! . . . Excited, I started running powers of two in my head: 2, 4, 8, 16, 32—I remembered vaguely that 2 to the 10th power was about 1000 and that therefore 2 to the 20th was around a million."*

The outcome of this night drive was development of the *polymerase chain reaction (PCR)*, now carried out automatically by instruments in every molecular biology lab. In 1993 Mullis shared the Nobel Prize in chemistry for this work. Today, PCR is so common and so simple a technique that it is routinely taught and carried out in undergraduate lab courses.

The goal of PCR is to produce many copies of a specific segment of DNA. The DNA might be part of a genome study, it might be from a crime scene or a fossil, or it might be from a specimen preserved as a medical record. The raw materials required for the reaction are a DNA sample that contains the nucleotide sequence to be amplified, *primers* (short synthetic oligonucleotides with bases complementary to the sequences flanking the sequence of interest), the deoxyribonucleoside triphosphates that carry the four DNA bases, and a DNA polymerase enzyme that will create a copy of the DNA between the primers.

The reaction is carried out in three steps:

STEP 1: Heating of the DNA sample to cause the helix to unravel into single strands:

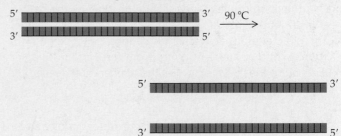

STEP 2: Addition of primers complementary to the DNA flanking the single-stranded DNA sequence to be amplified. It is necessary to create double-stranded DNA at the point where copying is to start, because DNA polymerase needs a free existing 3' end to which it adds nucleotides. The primers indicate this starting point:

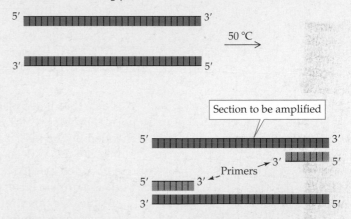

STEP 3: Extension of the primers by DNA polymerase to create double-stranded DNA identical to the original. The DNA polymerase adds nucleotides to the ends of the primers so that the new DNA segment includes the primer DNA:

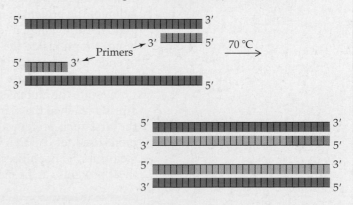

The reactants are combined in a closed container and the temperature cycled from about 90 °C for Step 1, to about 50 °C for Step 2, and to about 70 °C for Step 3. The temperature cycle requires only a few minutes and can be repeated over and over again for the same mixture. The first cycle produces 2 molecules of DNA; the second produces 4 molecules; and so on, with doubling at each cycle. Just 25 amplification cycles yield over 30 million copies of the original DNA segment.

Automation of the PCR was made possible by the discovery of a heat-stable polymerase (*Taq polymerase*) isolated from a bacterium that lives in hot springs (see Chemistry in Action: Extremozymes—Enzymes from the Edge in Chapter 19). Because the enzyme survives the temperature needed for

separating the DNA strands, it is not necessary to add fresh enzymes for each three-step cycle.

The quotations above are from "The Unusual Origin of the Polymerase Chain Reaction," Kary B. Mullis, Scientific American, April 1990, p. 56, which gives an extended account of the thought processes that led to the discovery.

See Chemistry in Action Problems 26.59 and 26.60 at the end of the chapter.

produces sticky ends. Thus, the sticky ends on the gene fragment are complementary to the sticky ends on the opened plasmid. The two are mixed in the presence of DNA ligase, an enzyme that joins them together by re-forming their phosphodiester bonds and reconstitutes the now-altered plasmid.

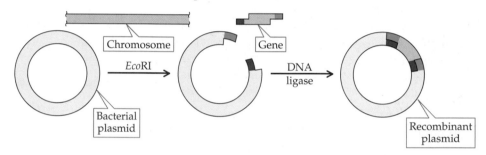

Once the altered plasmid is made, it is inserted back into a bacterial cell, where the normal processes of transcription and translation take place to synthesize the protein encoded by the inserted gene. Since bacteria multiply rapidly, there are soon a large number of them, all containing the recombinant DNA and all manufacturing the protein encoded by the recombinant DNA. Huge numbers of the bacteria can be put to work as a protein factory.

As ideal as this strategy sounds, there are tremendous technical hurdles that have to be overcome before a protein manufactured in this way can be used commercially. One hurdle is getting the recombinant plasmid back into a bacterium. Another is finding a host organism that does post-translationally modify the protein you are trying to make; for example, yeast cells are known to attach carbohydrates to various amino acids in a protein, rendering the protein inactive. The most serious hurdle of all is isolation of the protein of interest from unwanted endotoxins. *Endotoxins* are potentially toxic natural compounds (usually structural components released when bacteria are lysed) found inside the host organism. Because the presence of even small amounts of endotoxins can lead to serious inflammatory responses, rigorous purification and screening protocols are necessary before the protein can be used in humans.

Despite the aforementioned obstacles, proteins manufactured in this manner have already reached the marketplace, and many more are on the way. Human insulin was the first such protein to become available. Others now include human growth hormone used for children who would otherwise be abnormally small, and blood-clotting factors for hemophiliacs. A major advantage of this technology is that large amounts of these proteins can be made, thus allowing their practical therapeutic use.

PROBLEM 26.4

A restriction enzyme known as *Bgl*II cuts DNA in the place marked below.

$$5'-A-//-G-A-T-C-T-3'$$

Draw the complementary 3' to 5' strand and show where it is cut by the same enzyme.

CHEMISTRY IN ACTION

DNA Fingerprinting

A crime scene does not always yield fingerprints. It may, instead, yield samples of blood, semen or bits of hair. DNA analysis of such samples provides a new kind of "fingerprinting" for identifying criminals or proving suspects innocent.

DNA fingerprinting relies on finding variations between two or more DNA samples; for example, DNA isolated from a crime scene can be examined to determine if its variations match those of a suspect or victim. The naturally occurring variability of the base sequence in DNA is like a fingerprint. It is the same in all cells from a given individual and is sufficiently different from that of other individuals that it can be used for identification.

In the human genome there are regions of noncoding DNA that contain repeating nucleotide sequences. The repetitive patterns used in DNA fingerprinting are known as *variable number tandem repeats (VNTRs)*. As the name suggests, a VNTR is a short DNA sequence that is repeated multiple times in a tandem array (end to end to end). The key feature that makes VNTRs useful in fingerprinting is that *for any given VNTR, the number of copies of the repeated sequence varies between individuals*. One person may have a sequence repeated 15 times, while another may have the sequence repeated 40 times. For statistical significance, lab technicians examine several of the known VNTRs across multiple chromosomes to create a DNA fingerprint. The probability of a DNA-fingerprint match with someone other than the correct individual is estimated at 1 in 1.5 billion.

There are two common techniques used for DNA fingerprinting today: the restriction fragment length polymorphism (RFLP) approach and the polymerase chain reaction (PCR) method.

RFLP relies on use of a restriction endonuclease (an enzyme used to cut DNA) that recognizes and cuts sequences on either side of a given VNTR. The general procedure is as follows:

- Digest the DNA sample with the restriction endonuclease.
- Separate the resulting DNA fragments according to their size by gel electrophoresis.
- Transfer the fragments to a nylon membrane (a *blotting* technique).
- Treat the blot with a radioactive DNA probe complementary to the repeating VNTR sequence, so that the probe binds the fragment containing the VNTR sequence.
- Identify the locations of the now-radioactive fragments by exposing an X-ray film to the blot. (The film result of this procedure is known as an *autoradiogram*.)

An autoradiogram resembles a bar code, with dark bands arrayed in order of increasing molecular size of the DNA fragments. To compare the DNA of different individuals, the DNA samples are run in parallel columns on the same electrophoresis gel. In this way, the comparison is validated by having been run under identical conditions. While this method is very accurate, it requires a significant amount of DNA and can take two to four weeks to carry out; it is used primarily for genetic screening.

A more recent method for DNA fingerprinting involves the use of PCR (see Chemistry in Action: Serendipity and the Polymerase Chain Reaction, p. 815). In this method, one can use primers directed toward regions of the DNA that are known to contain variations; these can then be copied using PCR. This amplification process is repeated about 30 times (about 4 minutes per cycle) so that in two hours more than a billion copies are produced. These fragments can then be separated according to size by gel electrophoresis, stained using a blue dye that binds to DNA, and compared against other samples. Unlike the RFLP method, the PCR system, from amplification to analysis, can be carried out in about 24 hours. It can be performed on small amounts of DNA, and even on DNA that has begun to degrade, and is successful with almost every sample. This method has become the primary technique used in crime scene forensic analysis.

How useful is DNA fingerprinting? The illustration below shows hypothetical DNA-fingerprint patterns of six members of a family, where three of the children share the same mother and father and the fourth has been adopted. As you can see, even individuals in the same family will have distinguishably different DNA fingerprints; only identical twins have identical DNA fingerprints. There are always some similarities in the DNA patterns of offspring and their parents, making such fingerprints valuable in proving or disproving paternity.

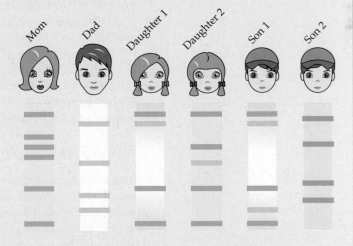

See Chemistry in Action Problems 26.61 and 26.62 at the end of the chapter.

PROBLEM 26.5

A restriction enzyme known as *EcoR*I cuts DNA in the place marked below.

$$5'-G-//-A-A-T-T-C-3'$$

Draw the complementary 3′ to 5′ strand and show where it is cut by the same enzyme.

PROBLEM 26.6

Are the following base sequences "sticky" (complementary) or not? All sequences are written 5′ to 3′.

(a) A-C-G-G-A and T-G-C-C-T   **(b)** G-T-G-A-C and C-A-T-G-G

(c) G-T-A-T-A and A-C-G-C-G

PROBLEM 26.7

In automated PCR experiments, why is *Taq* polymerase used instead of the DNA polymerase found in humans? (See Chemistry in Action: Serendipity and the Polymerase Chain Reaction.)

PROBLEM 26.8

In Chemistry in Action: DNA Fingerprinting, the chances of two people having the same DNA fingerprint was discussed. In 2011 the population of the world was estimated to be about 7 billion. How many people in the world could theoretically have the same DNA fingerprint?

26.5 Genomics: Using What We Know

Genomics The study of whole sets of genes and their functions.

Genomics has a simple and straightforward definition: it is the study of whole sets of genes and their functions. Genomics is inspiring studies that reach into all aspects of plant and animal life. For example, the study of bacterial genomics has been instrumental in linking the three domains of life—Archaea (formerly archeabacteria), Bacteria, and Eukarya—to one another from an evolutionary standpoint. The study of bacterial genomics is not only giving us a better understanding of how bacteria cause disease, it is also helping in the development of new therapies. Plant genomics is enhancing the value and utility of agricultural crops. The genomic study of farm animals is improving their health and availability. Humans will benefit from all of these studies, as well as those that contribute to their own health.

To glimpse where genomics is headed, we have provided descriptions of some of its applications in Table 26.3. These descriptions are not quite definitions; many of these fields are so new that their territory is viewed differently by different individuals. At the opening of this chapter, we noted that we stand at the beginning of a revolution. You may well encounter some of the endeavors listed in Table 26.3 as the revolution proceeds.

Genetically Modified Plants and Animals

The development of new varieties of plants and animals has been proceeding for centuries as the result of natural accidents and occasional success in the hybridization of known varieties. The techniques for mapping, studying, and modifying human genes apply equally as well to the genomes of plants and other animals. The mapping and study of plant and animal genomes can greatly accelerate our ability to generate crop plants and farm animals with desirable characteristics and lacking undesirable ones.

Some genetically modified crops have already been planted in large quantities in the United States. Each year millions of tons of corn are destroyed by a caterpillar (the European corn borer) that does its damage deep inside the corn stalk and out of reach of pesticides. To solve this problem, a bacterial gene (from *Bacillus thuringiensis*, Bt) has been transplanted into corn. The gene causes the corn to produce a toxin that kills the caterpillars. In 2000, one-quarter of all corn planted in the United States was Bt corn. Soybeans genetically modified to withstand herbicides are also widely grown. The soybean crop remains unharmed when the surrounding weeds are killed by the herbicide.

Table 26.3 Genomics-Related Fields of Study

Biotechnology

A collective term for the application of biological and biochemical research to the development of products that improve the health of humans, other animals, and plants.

Bioinformatics

The use of computers to manage and interpret genomic information and to make predictions about biological systems. Applications of bioinformatics include studies of individual genes and their functions, drug design, and drug development.

Functional genomics

Use of genome sequences to solve biological problems.

Comparative genomics

Comparison of the genome sequences of different organisms to discover regions with similar functions and perhaps similar evolutionary origins.

Proteomics

Study of the complete set of proteins coded for by a genome or synthesized within a given type of cell, including the quest for an understanding of the role of each protein in healthy or diseased conditions. This understanding has potential application in drug design and is being pursued by more than one commercial organization.

Pharmacogenomics

The genetic basis of responses to drug treatment. Goals include the design of more effective drugs and an understanding of why certain drugs work in some patients but not in others.

Pharmacogenetics

The matching of drugs to individuals based on the content of their personal genome in order to avoid administration of drugs that are ineffective or toxic and focus on drugs that are most effective for that individual.

Toxicogenomics

A newly developing application that combines genomics and bioinformatics in studying how toxic agents affect genes and in screening possibly harmful agents.

Genetic engineering

Alteration of the genetic material of a cell or an organism. The goals may be to make the organism produce new substances or perform new functions. Examples are introduction of a gene that causes bacteria to produce a desired protein or allows a crop plant to withstand the effects of a pesticide that repels harmful insects.

Gene therapy

Alteration of an individual's genetic makeup with the goal of curing or preventing a disease.

Bioethics

The ethical implications of how knowledge of the human genome is used.

Tests are under way with genetically modified coffee beans that are caffeine-free, potatoes that absorb less fat when they are fried, and "Golden Rice," a yellow rice that provides the vitamin A desperately needed in poor populations where insufficient vitamin A causes death and blindness.

Fish farming is an expanding industry as natural populations of fish diminish. There are genetically engineered salmon that can grow to 7–10 pounds, a marketable size, in up to one-half the time of their unmodified cousins. Similar genetic modifications are anticipated for other varieties of fish, and there is the prospect of cloning leaner pigs.

Will genetically modified plants and animals intermingle with natural varieties and cause harm to them? Should food labels state whether the food contains genetically modified ingredients? Might unrecognized harmful substances enter the food supply? These are hotly debated questions and have led to the establishment of the Non-GMO Project, where the GMO stands for genetically modified organism. The goal of this project is to offer consumers a non-GMO choice for organic and natural products that are produced without genetic engineering or recombinant DNA technologies. Many foods found in stores are labeled "Non-GMO."

▲ "Golden Rice" has been genetically modified to provide vitamin A.

But genetic modifications can also be used to produce previously unseen beauty. Consider the blue rose, a flower that is currently produced by dyeing white roses. Suntory Limited, in a joint venture with Florigene, has recently been able to successfully implant into roses a gene from petunias that leads to the synthesis of blue pigments; these roses are currently being grown in test batches in Japan. Even more exciting is the expectation that the introduction of blue pigments into roses will lead to an explosion in the variety of possible rose colors available to the average consumer.

Gene Therapy

Gene therapy, to put it simply, is the use of DNA to treat disease. It is based on the premise that a disease-causing gene within an individual's cells can be corrected or replaced by inserting a functional, healthy gene into the cells. The most clear-cut expectations for gene therapy lie in treating *monogenic* diseases, those that result from defects in a single gene.

The focus has been on using non-pathogenic viruses as *vectors,* the agents that deliver therapeutic quantities of DNA directly into cell nuclei. The expectation was that this method could result in lifelong elimination of an inherited disease, and many studies have been undertaken. Unfortunately, expectations remain greater than achievements thus far. Investigations into the direct injection of "naked DNA" have begun, with one early report of success in encouraging blood vessel growth in patients with inadequate blood supply to their hearts. The Food and Drug Administration (FDA) has, as of July 2011, not yet approved any human gene therapy product for sale. Current gene therapy is still experimental and has not proven to be widely successful in clinical trials. Although little progress has been made since the first gene therapy clinical trial began in 1990, vigorous research into this area continues as new approaches continue to be examined.

A Personal Genomic Survey

Suppose that prior to diagnosis and treatment for a health problem that a patient's entire genome could be surveyed. What benefits might result? One possibility is that the choice of drugs could be directed toward those that are most effective for that individual. It is no secret that not everyone reacts in the same manner to a given medication. Perhaps the patient lacks an enzyme needed for a drug's metabolism. It is known, for example, that codeine is ineffective as a pain killer in people who lack the enzyme that converts codeine into morphine, which is the active analgesic (see Section 15.6). Perhaps the patient has a monogenic defect, a flaw in a single gene that is the direct cause of the disease. Such a patient might, at some time in the future, be a candidate for gene therapy.

In cancer therapy there may be advantages in understanding the genetic differences between normal cells and tumor cells. Such knowledge could assist in chemotherapy, where the goal is use of an agent that kills the tumor cells but does the least possible amount of harm to noncancerous cells.

Another application of having human genomic information may arise from genetic screening of infants. The immediate use of gene therapy might eliminate the threat of a monogenically based disease. Or perhaps a lifestyle adjustment would be in order for an individual with one or more SNPs that predict a susceptibility to heart disease, diabetes, or some other disease that results from combinations of genetic and environmental influences. And consider that once done, an individual's genetic map would be available for the rest of his or her life. Perhaps someday we may even carry a wallet card encoded with our genetic information. With this knowledge, however, also come ethical dilemmas that have made this use of genomics a hotly debated topic.

Snips and Chips

Our understanding of SNPs is already at work in screening implemented by *DNA chips*. A *DNA chip* is a solid support bearing large numbers of short, single-stranded bits of DNA of known composition. The DNA is organized on the chip in whatever manner is best for a particular type of screening, for example, to identify the presence or absence of polymorphisms. A sample to be screened is labeled with a fluorescent tag and applied to the chip. During an incubation period, sample DNA and chip DNA with complementary nucleic

▲ **A DNA chip used for genetic screening.**

acid sequences will bond to each other. After excess sample of DNA is washed away, the fluorescence remaining on the chip is read to discover where the bonding has occurred and thus what DNA variations are present in the sample DNA. A chip can be used, for example, to screen for the polymorphism that wipes out the analgesic effect of codeine. Or consider a gene with several polymorphisms that codes for an enzyme responsible for metabolizing a cardiovascular agent, antipsychotic, or some other drug. Different individuals may have no effect from a drug, the expected effect, or perhaps have a greater-than-normal response to the drug. Genomic screening can determine whether particular polymorphisms are linked to a patient's ability to respond to the medication. Once such connections have been established, screening tests for polymorphisms of this enzyme could be a diagnostic test carried out by a DNA chip in a doctor's office. The results would aid in choosing the right drug and dosage.

DNA-chip screening has already revealed the genetic variations responsible for two types of pediatric leukemia, a distinction that could not be made by examining diseased cells under the microscope. Because the two leukemias require quite different therapies, use of the chip to identify the types is a valuable development.

Bioethics

We can mention only briefly an area of major concern that arises from the revolution in genomics. This concern is not chemical, nor is it directly related to curing and preventing disease. The existence of this concern is recognized in the ELSI program of the National Human Genome Research Institute. ELSI deals with the Ethical, Legal, and Social Implications of human genetic research. The scope of ELSI is broad and thought-provoking. It deals with many questions such as the following:

- Who should have access to personal genetic information and how will it be used?
- Who should own and control genetic information?
- Should genetic testing be performed when no treatment is available?
- Are disabilities diseases? Do they need to be cured or prevented?
- Preliminary attempts at gene therapy are exorbitantly expensive. Who will have access to these therapies? Who will pay for their use?
- Should we re-engineer the genes we pass on to our children?

If you are interested in the ELSI program, their web page is an excellent resource (http://www.genome.gov/10001618).

PROBLEM 26.9

Classify the following activities according to the fields of study listed in Table 26.3.

(a) Identification of genes that perform identical functions in mice and humans

(b) Creation of a variety of wheat that will not be harmed by an herbicide that kills weeds that threaten wheat crops

(c) Screening of an individual's genome to choose the most appropriate pain-killing medication for that person

(d) Computer analysis of base-sequence information from groups of people with and without a given disease to discover where the disease-causing polymorphism lies

---

SUMMARY: REVISITING THE CHAPTER GOALS

1. What is the working draft of the human genome and the circumstances of its creation? The Human Genome Project, an international consortium of not-for-profit institutions, along with Celera Genomics, a for-profit company, have both announced completion of working drafts of the human genome. With the exception of large areas of repetitive DNA, the DNA base sequences of all chromosomes have been examined. The Human Genome Project utilized a series of progressively more detailed maps to create a collection of DNA fragments with known location. Celera began by randomly fragmenting all of the DNA without first placing it within the framework of a map. In both groups the fragments were cloned, labeled, ordered, and the individual sequences assembled by computers. The results of the two projects are

Protein and Amino Acid Metabolism

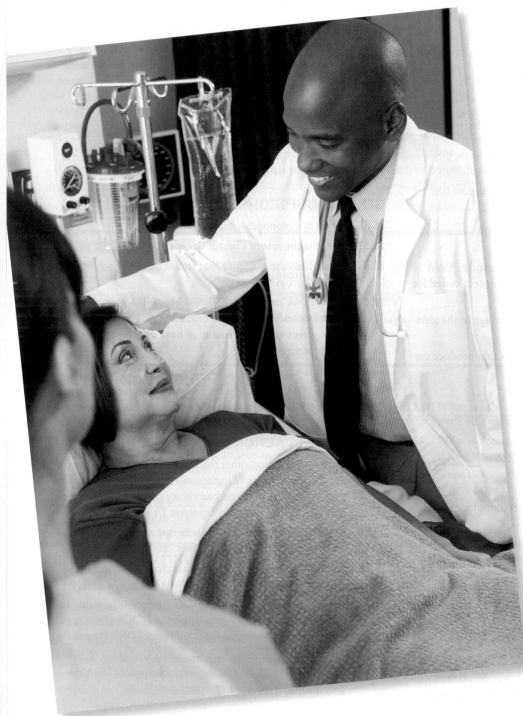

◄ **Understanding the metabolic basis of disease can lead to new and more effective treatments in medicine.**

1. **What happens during the digestion of proteins, and what are the fates of the amino acids?**
   THE GOAL: Be able to list the sequence of events in the digestion of proteins, and describe the nature of the amino acid pool. (◀◀◀ A, B, C.)

2. **What are the major strategies in the catabolism of amino acids?**
   THE GOAL: Be able to identify the major reactions and products of amino acid catabolism and the fate of the products. (◀◀◀ A.)

3. **What is the urea cycle?**
   THE GOAL: Be able to list the major reactants and products of the urea cycle. (◀◀◀ A, C.)

4. **What are the essential and nonessential amino acids, and how, in general, are amino acids synthesized?**
   THE GOAL: Be able to define essential and nonessential amino acids, and describe the general strategy of amino acid biosynthesis. (◀◀◀ A.)

CONCEPTS TO REVIEW
◀◀◀

A. Amino Acids
(Sections 18.3, 18.4)

B. Primary Protein Structure
(Section 18.7)

C. Overview of Metabolism
(Section 20.4)

Before discussing protein and amino acid metabolism, a review of what we have already covered on proteins and amino acids is in order. We discussed the structures of the amino acids and the various levels of protein structure in Chapter 18; the essential function of proteins as enzymes in Chapter 19; and their function within cell membranes in Section 23.8. The biosynthesis of proteins as directed by the genetic code was examined in Chapter 25. We now turn to the remaining aspect of protein biochemistry, which is the metabolic fate of proteins and ultimately amino acids. Although we have the biochemical machinery necessary to make them, the hydrolysis of dietary protein is our major source for amino acids.

27.1 Digestion of Proteins

The end result of protein digestion is simple—the hydrolysis of all peptide bonds to produce a collection of amino acids:

Hydrolysis of peptide bonds

Dietary protein → (Hydrolysis, Protease enzymes) → Amino acids

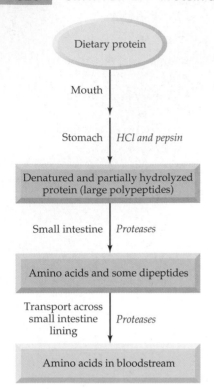

▲ **Figure 27.1**
Digestion of proteins.

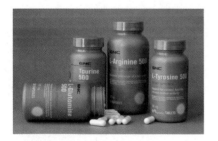

▲ Individual amino acids are promoted for a variety of unproven health benefits. Because amino acids are classified as foods, they need not undergo the stringent testing for purity, safety, and efficacy required for FDA approval.

Amino acid pool The entire collection of free amino acids in the body.

For example:

Alanine   Serine   Phenylalanine

Figure 27.1 summarizes the digestive processes involved in the conversion of protein to amino acids. The breakdown of protein begins in the mouth, where large pieces of food are converted (by chewing) into smaller, more digestible portions. Although no chemical digestion of the protein has begun, this step is necessary to increase the surface area of the food to be digested. The chemical digestion of dietary proteins begins with their denaturation in the strongly acidic environment of the stomach (pH 1–2), where the tertiary and secondary structures of consumed proteins begin to unfold. In addition to hydrochloric acid, gastric secretions include pepsinogen, a zymogen that is activated by acid to give the enzyme pepsin. Unlike most proteins, pepsin is stable and active at pH 1–2. Protein hydrolysis begins as pepsin breaks some of the peptide bonds in the denatured proteins, producing polypeptides.

The polypeptides produced by pepsin then enter the small intestine, where the pH is about 7–8. Pepsin is inactivated in this less acidic environment, and a group of pancreatic zymogens is secreted. These activated enzymes (proteases such as trypsin, chymotrypsin, and carboxypeptidase) then take over to further hydrolyze peptide bonds in the partially digested proteins.

The combined action of the pancreatic proteases in the small intestine and other proteases in the cells of the intestinal lining completes the conversion of dietary proteins into free amino acids. After active transport across cell membranes lining the intestine, the amino acids are absorbed directly into the bloodstream.

The active transport of amino acids into cells is managed by several transport systems devoted to different groups of amino acids. For this reason, an excess of one amino acid in the diet can dominate the transport and produce a deficiency of others. This condition usually arises only in individuals taking large quantities of a single amino acid dietary supplement, such as those often sold in health food stores.

27.2 Amino Acid Metabolism: An Overview

The entire collection of free amino acids throughout the body—the **amino acid pool**—occupies a central position in protein and amino acid metabolism (Figure 27.2). All tissues and biomolecules in the body are constantly being degraded, repaired, and replaced. Cells throughout the body have the enzymes for hydrolysis of waste protein, and a healthy adult turns over about 300 g of protein every day. Thus, amino acids are

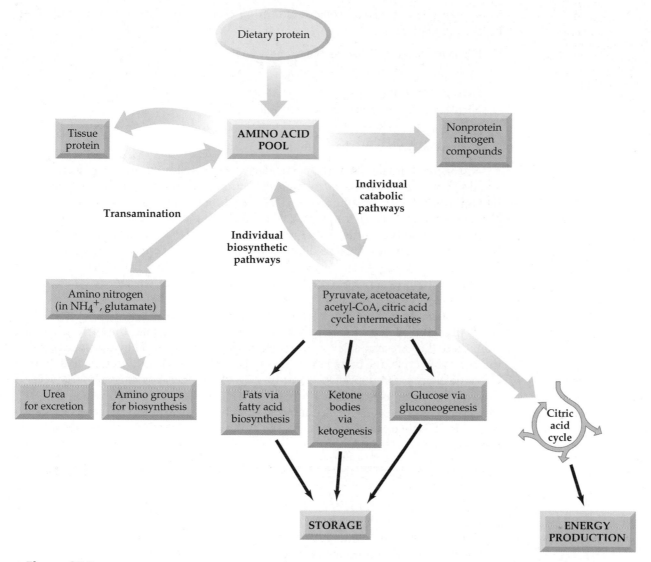

▲ **Figure 27.2**

Protein and amino acid metabolism.
Amino acids move in and out of the amino acid pool as shown. Amino acids and their catabolic products are used for synthesis of other biomolecules as well as for production of energy.

continuously entering the pool, not only from digestion but also from the breakdown of old proteins, and are continuously being withdrawn for synthesis of new nitrogen-containing biomolecules.

Each of the 20 amino acids is degraded via its own unique pathway. The important point to remember is that the general scheme is the same for each one.

General Scheme for Amino Acid Catabolism:

- Removal of the amino group (Section 27.3)
- Use of nitrogen in synthesis of new nitrogen compounds (Section 27.3)
- Passage of nitrogen into the urea cycle (Section 27.4)
- Incorporation of the carbon atoms into compounds that can enter the citric acid cycle (Section 27.5)

Our bodies do not store nitrogen-containing compounds, and ammonia is toxic to cells. Therefore, the amino nitrogen from dietary protein has just two possible fates. Amino nitrogen must either be incorporated into urea and excreted or be used

▶▶▶ Hormones and neurotransmitters are chemical messengers discussed in Chapter 28; Figure 19.10 highlights the nicotinamide group on NAD^+; view the chemical structure of heme in Figure 20.11; purine and pyrimidines can be seen in Table 25.1.

in the synthesis of new nitrogen-containing compounds, including the following types of biomolecules:

Nitric oxide (NO, a chemical messenger)

Hormones

Neurotransmitters

Nicotinamide (in coenzymes NAD^+ and $NADP^+$)

Heme (as part of hemoglobin in red blood cells)

Purine and pyrimidine bases (for nucleic acids)

Nitrogen monoxide (NO) is a particularly interesting molecule: chemically, it has an odd number of electrons (a *free radical*; Section 13.7) and is therefore very reactive. Biologically, it lowers blood pressure, kills invading bacteria, and enhances memory. Nitrogen monoxide (NO) is synthesized in the linings of blood vessels and elsewhere from oxygen and the amino acid arginine. In blood vessels, NO activates reactions in smooth muscle cells that cause dilation and a resulting decrease in blood pressure. Drugs such as nitroglycerin release NO, which explains their usefulness in treating angina, the pain experienced during exertion by individuals with partially blocked blood vessels.

The carbon portion of the amino acid has a much more varied fate. The carbon atoms of amino acids are converted to compounds that can enter the citric acid cycle; from there they are available for several alternative pathways. They continue through the citric acid cycle (the body's main energy-generating pathway; Section 20.8) to give CO_2 and energy stored in ATP. About 10–20% of our energy is normally produced in this way from amino acids. If not needed immediately for energy, the carbon-carrying intermediates produced from amino acids enter storage as triacylglycerols (via lipogenesis) or glycogen (via gluconeogenesis and glycogen synthesis). They can also be converted to ketone bodies.

▶▶▶ Lipogenesis and ketone body synthesis were discussed in Chapter 24. Review gluconeogenesis and glycogen synthesis in Chapter 22.

PROBLEM 27.1

Decide whether each of the following statements is true or false. If false, explain why.

(a) The amino acid pool is found mainly in the liver.

(b) Nitrogen-containing compounds can be stored in fatty tissue.

(c) Some hormones and neurotransmitters are synthesized from amino acids.

(d) Amino groups can be stored in fatty tissue.

(e) Glycine is an essential amino acid because it is present in every protein.

🗝 KEY CONCEPT PROBLEM 27.2

Serotonin is a monoamine neurotransmitter. It is formed in the body from the amino acid tryptophan (Figure 28.6, p. 857). What class of enzyme catalyzes each of the two steps that converts tryptophan to serotonin?

27.3 Amino Acid Catabolism: The Amino Group

Transamination The interchange of the amino group of an amino acid and the keto group of an α-keto acid.

The first step in amino acid catabolism is removal of the amino group. In this process, known as **transamination**, the amino group of the amino acid and the keto group of an α-keto acid change places:

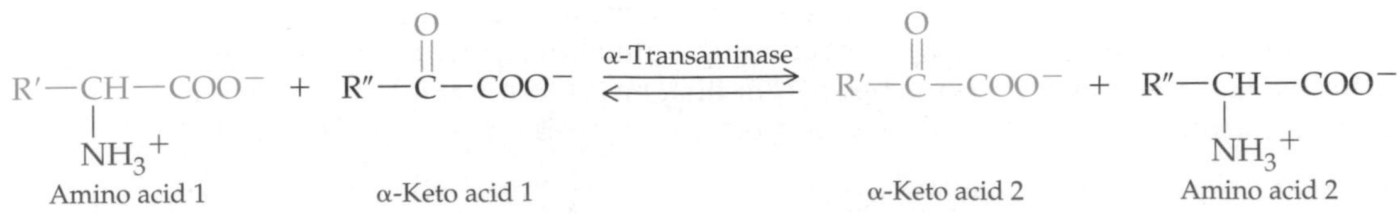

$$R'-\underset{\underset{NH_3^+}{|}}{CH}-COO^- + R''-\overset{\overset{O}{||}}{C}-COO^- \underset{}{\overset{\alpha\text{-Transaminase}}{\rightleftharpoons}} R'-\overset{\overset{O}{||}}{C}-COO^- + R''-\underset{\underset{NH_3^+}{|}}{CH}-COO^-$$

Amino acid 1　　　　　α-Keto acid 1　　　　　　α-Keto acid 2　　　　　Amino acid 2

A number of transaminase enzymes are responsible for "transporting" (hence the prefix "trans") an amino group from one molecule to another. Most are specific for α-ketoglutarate as the amino-group acceptor and can deaminate several different amino acids. The α-ketoglutarate is converted to glutamate, and the amino acid is converted to an α-keto acid. For example, alanine is converted to pyruvate by transamination:

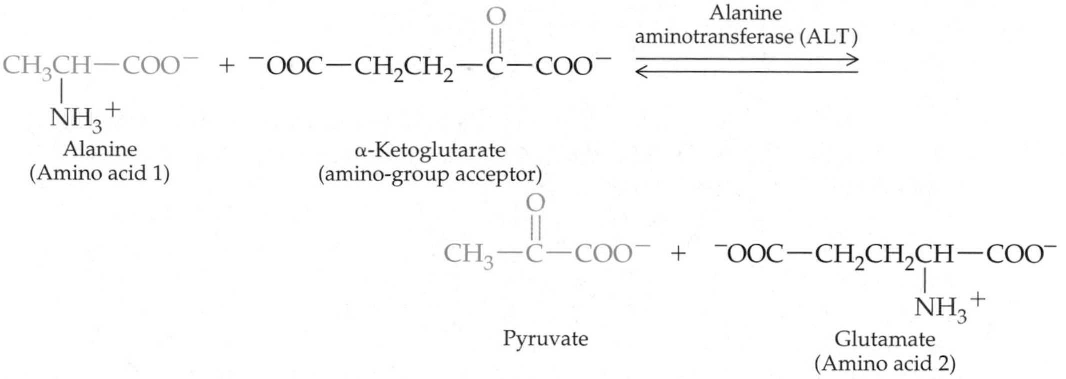

$$CH_3CH-COO^- + {}^-OOC-CH_2CH_2-\overset{\overset{\displaystyle O}{\|}}{C}-COO^- \underset{}{\overset{\text{Alanine}\atop \text{aminotransferase (ALT)}}{\rightleftharpoons}}$$
$$\underset{NH_3{}^+}{|}$$

Alanine
(Amino acid 1)

α-Ketoglutarate
(amino-group acceptor)

$$CH_3-\overset{\overset{\displaystyle O}{\|}}{C}-COO^- + {}^-OOC-CH_2CH_2\underset{\underset{NH_3{}^+}{|}}{CH}-COO^-$$

Pyruvate

Glutamate
(Amino acid 2)

The enzyme for this conversion, alanine aminotransferase (ALT), is especially abundant in the liver, and above-normal ALT concentrations in the blood are taken as an indication of liver damage that has allowed ALT to leak into the bloodstream.

Transamination is a key reaction in many biochemical pathways, where it interconverts amino acid amino groups and carbonyl groups as necessary. The transamination reactions are reversible and go easily in either direction, depending on the concentrations of the reactants. In this way, amino acid concentrations are regulated by keeping synthesis and breakdown in balance. For example, the reaction of pyruvate with glutamate (the reverse of the preceding reaction) is the main synthetic route for alanine.

The glutamate from transamination serves as an amino-group carrier. Glutamate can be used to provide amino groups for the synthesis of new amino acids, but most of the glutamate formed in this way is recycled to regenerate α-ketoglutarate. This process, known as **oxidative deamination**, oxidatively removes the glutamate amino group as ammonium ion to give back α-ketoglutarate:

Oxidative deamination Conversion of an amino acid $-NH_2$ group to an α-keto group, with removal of $NH_4{}^+$.

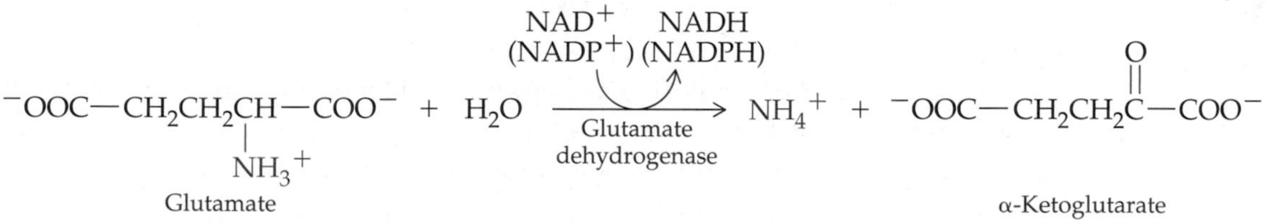

$$\underset{\underset{\underset{\text{Glutamate}}{NH_3{}^+}}{|}}{{}^-OOC-CH_2CH_2CH-COO^-} + H_2O \xrightarrow[\substack{\text{Glutamate} \\ \text{dehydrogenase}}]{\overset{NAD^+ \quad NADH}{(NADP^+)(NADPH)}} NH_4{}^+ + \underset{\alpha\text{-Ketoglutarate}}{{}^-OOC-CH_2CH_2\overset{\overset{\displaystyle O}{\|}}{C}-COO^-}$$

The ammonium ion formed in this reaction proceeds to the urea cycle where it is eliminated in the urine as urea. The pathway of nitrogen from an amino acid to urea is summarized in Figure 27.3.

Worked Example 27.1 Predicting Transamination Products

The blood-serum concentration of the heart-muscle transaminase, aspartate aminotransferase (AST), is used in the diagnosis of heart disease because the enzyme escapes into the serum from damaged heart cells. AST catalyzes transamination of aspartate with α-ketoglutarate. What are the products of this reaction?

ANALYSIS The reaction is the interchange of an amino group from aspartate with the keto group from α-ketoglutarate. We know that α-ketoglutarate always gives glutamate in transamination, so one product is glutamate. The product from the amino acid will have a keto group instead of the amino group; we need to consider various amino acid structures to identify a candidate.

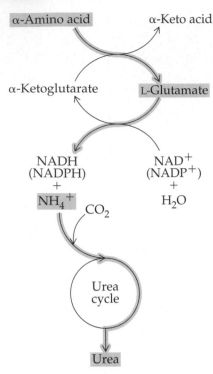

▲ **Figure 27.3**
Pathway of nitrogen from an amino acid to urea.
The nitrogen-bearing compounds and their pathway are highlighted in orange.

Consulting Table 18.3 (which lists the structures of the 20 amino acids), we see that the structure of aspartate (aspartic acid) is

$$^-OOC-CH_2\overset{\alpha}{C}H-COO^-$$
$$\overset{|}{NH_3{}^+}$$

Aspartate

Removing the $-NH_3{}^+$ and $-H$ groups bonded to the α carbon and replacing them by a $=O$ gives the desired α-keto acid, which in this case happens to be oxaloacetate:

$$^-OOC-CH_2-\overset{O}{\underset{\|}{C}}-COO^-$$

Oxaloacetate

SOLUTION
The overall reaction is therefore

$$\text{Aspartate} + \alpha\text{-Ketoglutarate} \longrightarrow \text{Oxaloacetate} + \text{Glutamate}$$

PROBLEM 27.3
What are the structure and the IUPAC name of the α-keto acid formed by transamination of the amino acid threonine? (Refer to Table 18.3.)

PROBLEM 27.4
What is the product of the reaction

$$CH_3-S-CH_2CH_2CH-COO^- \xrightarrow{\;\;\alpha\text{-Ketoglutarate}\quad\text{Glutamate}\;\;} \; ?$$
$$\overset{|}{NH_3{}^+}$$

PROBLEM 27.5
Explain how the conversion of alanine to pyruvic acid (pyruvate) can be identified as an oxidation reaction.

PROBLEM 27.6
Unlike most amino acids, branched-chain amino acids are broken down in tissues other than the liver. Using Table 18.3, identify the three amino acids with branched-chain R groups. For any one of these amino acids, write the equation for its transamination.

27.4 The Urea Cycle

Urea cycle The cyclic biochemical pathway that produces urea for excretion.

Ammonia (as well as the ammonium ion, $NH_4{}^+$) is highly toxic to living things and must be eliminated in a way that does no harm. Fish are able to excrete ammonia through their gills directly into their watery surroundings where it is immediately diluted and its toxic effects effectively neutralized. Since mammals do not live in an environment where this immediate dilution is feasible, they must find other ways to get rid of ammonia. Direct excretion of ammonia in urine is not feasible for mammals, because the volume of water needed to accomplish this safely would cause dehydration. Mammals must first convert ammonia, in solution as ammonium ion, to nontoxic urea via the **urea cycle**.

The conversion of ammonium ion to urea takes place in the liver. From there, the urea is transported to the kidneys and transferred to urine for excretion. Like many other biochemical pathways, urea formation begins with an energy investment. Ammonium ion (from oxidative deamination of amino acids), bicarbonate ion (from carbon dioxide produced in the citric acid cycle), and ATP combine to form carbamoyl phosphate. This reaction takes place in the mitochondrial matrix. Two ATPs are invested and 1 phosphate is transferred to form the carbamoyl phosphate (an energy-rich phosphate ester, like ATP):

$$NH_4^+ + HCO_3^- \xrightarrow[\substack{\text{Carbamoyl} \\ \text{phosphate synthetase I}}]{\substack{\text{2 ATP} \quad \text{2 ADP}}} \underset{\text{Carbamoyl phosphate}}{H_3\overset{+}{N}-\overset{\overset{\displaystyle O}{\|}}{C}-O-PO_3^{2-}} + HOPO_3^{2-} + H_2O$$

Carbamoyl phosphate next reacts in the first step of the four-step urea cycle, shown in Figure 27.4.

STEPS 1 AND 2 OF THE UREA CYCLE: Building Up a Reactive Intermediate The first step of the urea cycle transfers the carbamoyl group, $H_2NC=O$, from carbamoyl phosphate to ornithine, an amino acid not found in proteins, to give citrulline, another nonprotein amino acid. This exergonic reaction introduces the first urea nitrogen into the urea cycle.

In Step 2, a molecule of aspartate combines with citrulline in a reaction driven by conversion of ATP to AMP and pyrophosphate $(P_2O_7^{4-})$, followed by the additional exergonic hydrolysis of pyrophosphate. Both nitrogen atoms destined for elimination as urea are now bonded to the same carbon atom in argininosuccinate (red C atom in Figure 27.4).

STEPS 3 AND 4 OF THE UREA CYCLE: Cleavage and Hydrolysis of the Step 2 Product Step 3 cleaves argininosuccinate into two pieces: arginine, an amino acid, and fumarate, which you may recall is an intermediate in the citric acid cycle (Figure 20.9). Now all that remains, in Step 4, is hydrolysis of arginine to give urea and regenerate the reactant in Step 1 of the cycle, ornithine.

Net Result of the Urea Cycle

$$HCO_3^- + NH_4^+ + 3\,ATP + {}^-OOC-CH_2-\underset{\underset{NH_3^+}{|}}{CH}-COO^- + 2\,H_2O \longrightarrow$$
$$\underset{\text{Aspartate}}{}$$

$$\underset{\text{Urea}}{H_2N-\overset{\overset{\displaystyle O}{\|}}{C}-NH_2} + 2\,ADP + AMP + 4\,HOPO_3^{2-} + \underset{\text{Fumarate}}{{}^-OOC-CH=CH-COO^-}$$

We can summarize the results of the urea cycle as follows:

- Formation of urea from the carbon of CO_2, NH_4^+, and one nitrogen from the amino acid aspartate, followed by biological elimination through urine
- Breaking of four high-energy phosphate bonds to provide energy
- Production of the citric acid cycle intermediate, fumarate

Hereditary diseases associated with defects in the enzymes for each step in the urea cycle have been identified. The resulting abnormally high levels of ammonia in the blood (*hyperammonemia*) cause vomiting in infancy, lethargy, irregular muscle coordination (*ataxia*), and mental retardation. Immediate treatment consists of transfusions, blood dialysis (*hemodialysis*), and use of chemical agents to remove ammonia. Long-term treatment requires a low-protein diet and frequent small meals to avoid protein overload.

▲ Fish do not need to convert ammonia to urea for elimination because it is quickly diluted in the surrounding water; this is why the water in fish tanks must be constantly monitored to ensure that the ammonia concentration does not reach toxic levels.

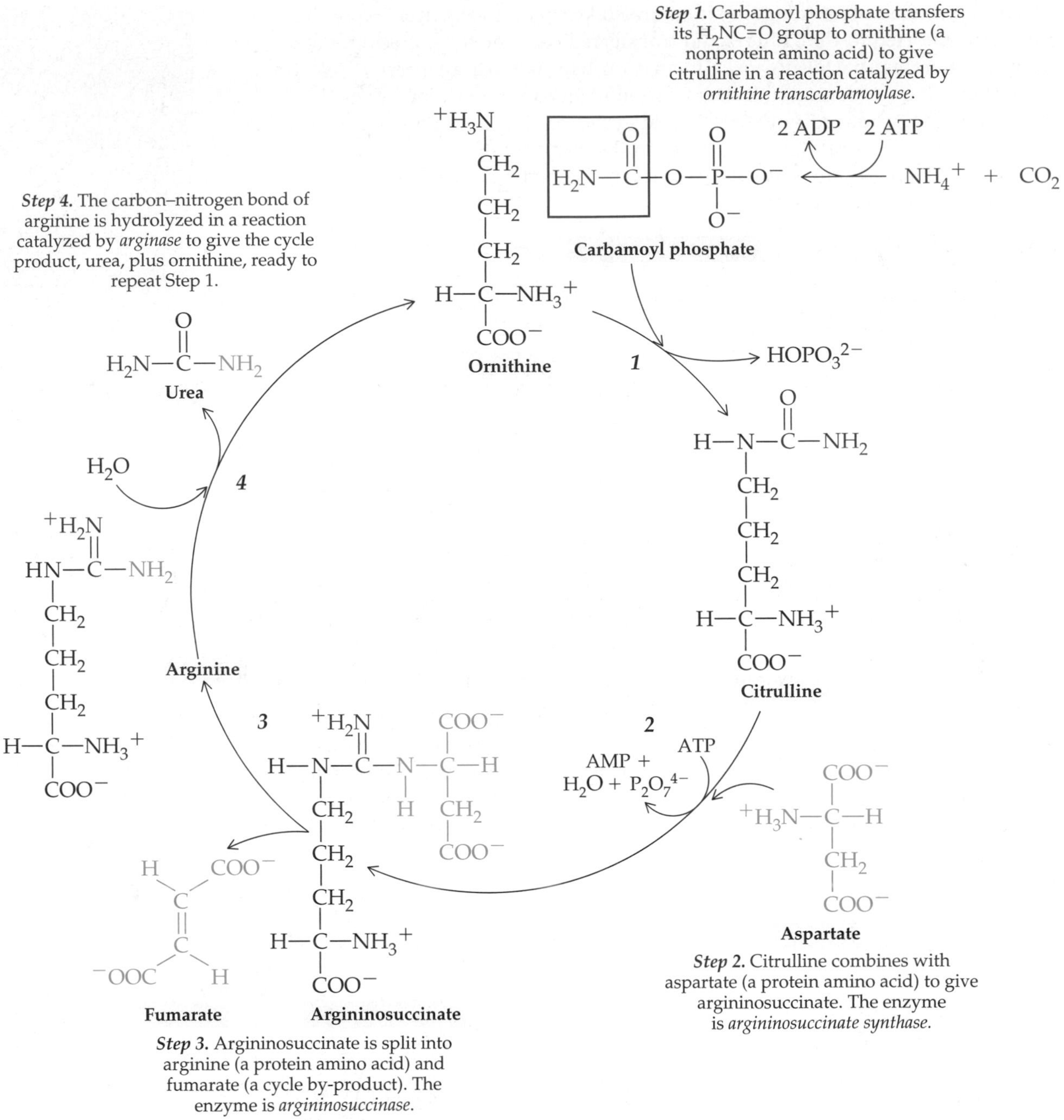

Step 1. Carbamoyl phosphate transfers its $H_2NC{=}O$ group to ornithine (a nonprotein amino acid) to give citrulline in a reaction catalyzed by *ornithine transcarbamoylase.*
2 ADP 2 ATP
NH_4^+ + CO_2
Carbamoyl phosphate
Ornithine
1
$HOPO_3^{2-}$
Citrulline
Step 4. The carbon–nitrogen bond of arginine is hydrolyzed in a reaction catalyzed by *arginase* to give the cycle product, urea, plus ornithine, ready to repeat Step 1.
Urea
H_2O
4
Arginine
3
2
ATP
AMP + H_2O + $P_2O_7^{4-}$
Aspartate
Step 2. Citrulline combines with aspartate (a protein amino acid) to give argininosuccinate. The enzyme is *argininosuccinate synthase.*
Fumarate
Argininosuccinate
Step 3. Argininosuccinate is split into arginine (a protein amino acid) and fumarate (a cycle by-product). The enzyme is *argininosuccinase.*

▲ **Figure 27.4**
The urea cycle.
The formation of carbamoyl phosphate and Step 1, the formation of citrulline, take place in the mitochondrial matrix. Steps 2–4 take place in the cytosol. The carbamoyl group is shown boxed in red at the top of the figure.

PROBLEM 27.7

As Figure 27.4 shows, arginine (a) is converted to ornithine (b) in the last step of the urea cycle. To ultimately enter the citric acid cycle, ornithine undergoes transamination at its terminal amino group to give an aldehyde (c), followed by oxidation to glutamate (d) and conversion to α-ketoglutarate (e). Write the structures of the five molecules (a–e) in the pathway beginning with arginine and ending with α-ketoglutarate. Circle the region of structural change in each.

CHEMISTRY IN ACTION

Gout: When Biochemistry Goes Awry

Gout is a severely painful condition caused by the precipitation of sodium urate crystals in joints. A small amount of our waste nitrogen is excreted in urine and feces as urate rather than urea. Because the urate salt is highly insoluble, any excess of the urate anion causes precipitation of sodium urate. The pain of gout results from a cascade of inflammatory responses to these crystals in the affected tissue.

Even though it has been known for a very long time that the symptoms of gout are caused by urate crystals, understanding the many possible causes of the crystal formation is far from complete, even with modern medicine and all its sophisticated technology. Looking at a few of the pathways to gout illustrates some of the many ways that the delicate balance of our biochemistry can be disrupted.

Uric acid is an end product of the breakdown of purine nucleosides, and loss of its acidic H (in red) gives urate ion. Adenosine, for example, undergoes a number of enzymatic steps to produce xanthine, which is eventually converted to uric acid:

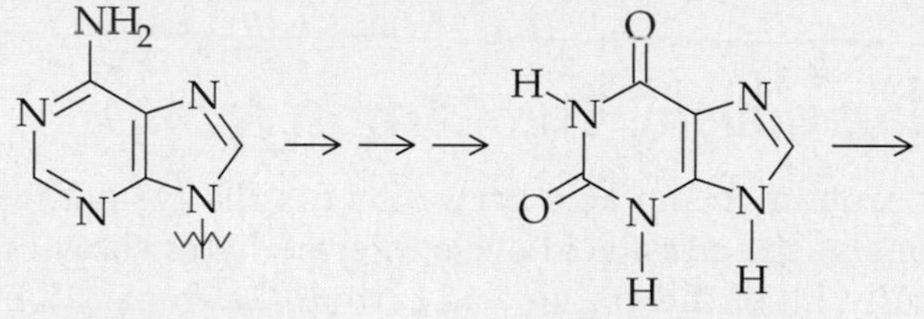

Anything that increases the production of uric acid or inhibits its excretion in the urine is a possible cause of gout. For example, several known hereditary enzyme defects increase the quantity of purines and therefore of uric acid. Sometimes, gouty attacks follow injury or severe muscle exertion. Complicating matters is the observation that the presence of crystals in a joint is not always accompanied by inflammation and pain.

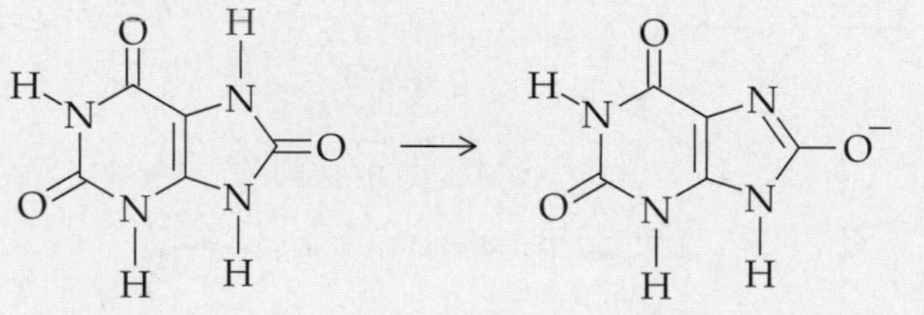

One significant cause of increased uric acid production is accelerated breakdown of ATP, ADP, or the production of AMP. For example, alcohol abuse generates acetaldehyde that must be metabolized in the kidney by a pathway that requires ATP and produces excess AMP. Inherited fructose intolerance, glycogen-storage diseases, and circulation of poorly oxygenated blood also accelerate uric acid production by this route. With low oxygen, ATP is not efficiently regenerated from ADP in mitochondria, leaving the ADP to be disposed of.

Conditions that diminish excretion of uric acid include kidney disease, dehydration, hypertension, lead poisoning, and competition for excretion from anions produced by ketoacidosis.

One treatment for gout relies on allopurinol, a structural analog of hypoxanthine, which is a precursor of xanthine in the formation of urate. Allopurinol inhibits the enzyme for conversion of hypoxanthine and xanthine to urate. Since hypoxanthine and xanthine are more soluble than sodium urate, they are more easily eliminated.

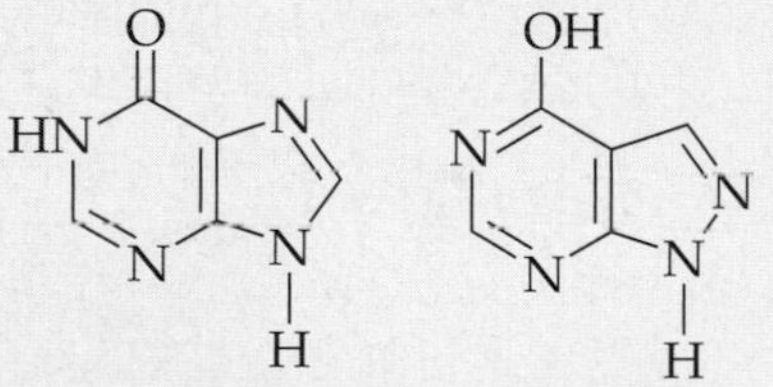

Adenosine   Xanthine

Uric acid   Urate ion

Hypoxanthine   Allopurinol

See Chemistry in Action Problems 27.55 and 27.56 at the end of the chapter.

PROBLEM 27.8

In Chemistry in Action: Gout: When Biochemistry Goes Awry, adenosine is shown to convert to xanthine, the direct precursor to uric acid. Starting with adenosine, list all the changes that occurred on its conversion to xanthine.

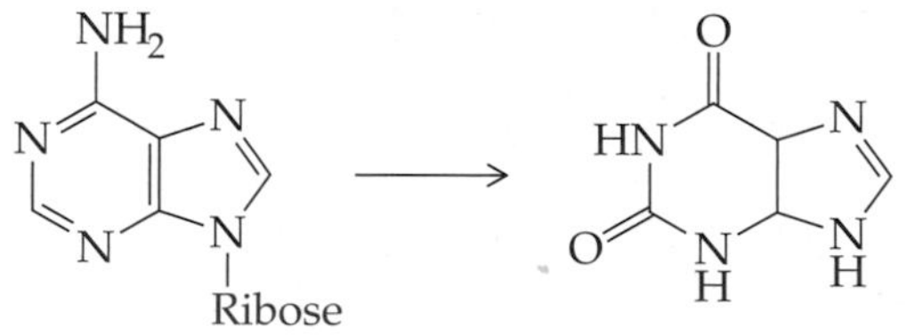

Adenosine   Xanthine

🔑 KEY CONCEPT PROBLEM 27.9

Fumarate from Step 3 of the urea cycle may be recycled into aspartate for use in Step 2 of the cycle. The sequence of reactions for this process is

(a) $^-O-\overset{O}{\overset{||}{C}}-CH=CH-\overset{O}{\overset{||}{C}}-O^-$ $\xrightarrow{H_2O}$ $^-O-\overset{O}{\overset{||}{C}}-\underset{OH}{\overset{|}{CH}}-CH_2-\overset{O}{\overset{||}{C}}-O^-$

　　　　　　Fumarate　　　　　　　　　　　　　Malate

(b) $^-O-\overset{O}{\overset{||}{C}}-\underset{OH}{\overset{|}{CH}}-CH_2-\overset{O}{\overset{||}{C}}-O^-$ $\xrightarrow{NAD^+\ NADH/H^+}$ $^-O-\overset{O}{\overset{||}{C}}-\overset{O}{\overset{||}{C}}-CH_2-\overset{O}{\overset{||}{C}}-O^-$

　　　　　　　　　　　　　　　　　　　　　　　　Oxaloacetate

(c) $^-O-\overset{O}{\overset{||}{C}}-\overset{O}{\overset{||}{C}}-CH_2-\overset{O}{\overset{||}{C}}-O^-$ $\xrightarrow{Glu\ \ \alpha\text{-Ketoglutarate}}$ $^-O-\overset{O}{\overset{||}{C}}-\underset{NH_3^+}{\overset{|}{CHCH_2}}-\overset{O}{\overset{||}{C}}-O^-$

　　　　　　　　　　　　　　　　　　　　　　　　　　　Asparate

Classify each reaction as one of the following:

(1) Oxidation　　　　(2) Reduction　　　　(3) Transamination
(4) Elimination　　　 (5) Addition

27.5 Amino Acid Catabolism: The Carbon Atoms

The carbon atoms of each protein amino acid arrive, by distinctive pathways, at pyruvate, acetyl-CoA, or one of the citric acid cycle intermediates shown in blue type in Figure 27.5. Eventually, all of the amino acid carbon skeletons can be used

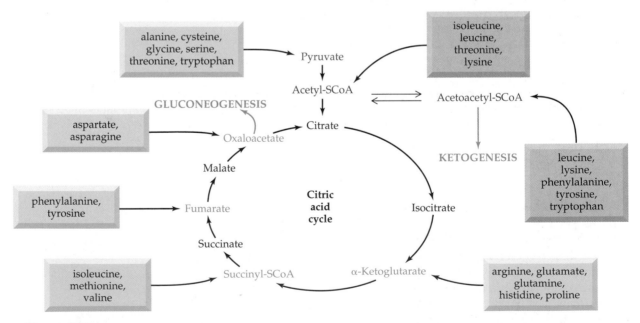

▲ **Figure 27.5**
Fate of amino acid carbon atoms.
The carbon atoms of the amino acids are converted to the seven compounds shown here in red and blue type, each of which is either an intermediate in the citric acid cycle or a precursor to citrate. The amino acids in the blue boxes are glucogenic—they can form glucose via the entry of oxaloacetate into gluconeogenesis. Those in the pink boxes are ketogenic—they are available for ketogenesis.

to generate energy, either by passing through the citric acid cycle and into the gluco-neogenesis pathway to form glucose or by entering the ketogenesis pathway to form ketone bodies.

Those amino acids that are converted to acetoacetyl-CoA or acetyl-CoA then enter the ketogenesis pathway and are called *ketogenic amino acids*.

Those amino acids that proceed by way of oxaloacetate to the gluconeogenesis pathway (Section 22.11) are known as *glucogenic amino acids* (Table 27.1). Both ketogenic and glucogenic amino acids are able to enter fatty acid biosynthesis via acetyl-CoA (Section 24.8).

PROBLEM 27.10
In Chemistry in Action: The Importance of Essential Amino Acids and Effects of Deficiencies, p. 836, the term "conditional amino acids" is discussed with respect to histidine and arginine. Why are they considered such?

27.6 Biosynthesis of Nonessential Amino Acids

Humans are able to synthesize about half of the 20 amino acids found in proteins. These are known as the **nonessential amino acids** because they do not have to be supplied by our diet. The remaining amino acids—the **essential amino acids** (Table 27.2)—are synthesized only by plants and microorganisms. Humans must obtain the essential amino acids from food (see Chemistry in Action: Proteins in the Diet in Chapter 18). Meats contain all of the essential amino acids. The foods that do not have all of them are described as having *incomplete amino acids*, and dietary deficiencies of the essential amino acids can lead to a number of health problems (see Chemistry in Action: The Importance of Essential Amino Acids and Effects of Deficiencies, p. 836). Food combinations that together contain all of the amino acids are *complementary* sources of protein. It is interesting to note that we synthesize the nonessential amino acids in pathways containing only one to three steps, whereas synthesis of the essential amino acids by other organisms is much more complicated, requiring many more steps and a substantial energy investment.

TABLE 27.1 Glucogenic and Ketogenic Amino Acids

Glucogenic	
Alanine	Glycine
Arginine	Histidine
Aspartate	Methionine
Asparagine	Proline
Cysteine	Serine
Glutamate	Threonine
Glutamine	Valine

Glucogenic and Ketogenic
Isoleucine
Lysine
Phenylalanine
Tryptophan
Tyrosine

Ketogenic
Leucine

Nonessential amino acid One of 11 amino acids that are synthesized in the body and are therefore not necessary in the diet.

Essential amino acid An amino acid that cannot be synthesized by the body and thus must be obtained from the diet.

TABLE 27.2 Essential Amino Acids

Amino acids essential for adults		
Histidine	Lysine	Threonine
Isoleucine	Methionine	Tryptophan
Leucine	Phenylalanine	Valine

Some foods with incomplete amino acids
Grains, nuts, and seeds: High in methionine, low in lysine
Legumes: High in lysine, low in methionine
Corn: High in methionine, low in lysine and tryptophan

Some examples of complementary sources of protein

Peanut butter on bread	Nuts and soybeans
Rice and beans	Black-eyed peas and corn bread
Beans and corn	

CHEMISTRY IN ACTION

The Importance of Essential Amino Acids and Effects of Deficiencies

Remember when your mother told you to "eat all your vegetables if you want to grow up big and strong"? Although you may not have appreciated it at the time, she was doing nothing more than ensuring that you got your daily intake of essential vitamins and minerals. Regardless of the amazing numbers of biomolecules our bodies can synthesize, there are some nutrients we need but cannot make. These molecules, called "essential" nutrients, must be harvested daily from the foods we eat. Although there are no known essential carbohydrates, there are essential fatty acids and essential amino acids. We have previously discussed the two essential fatty acids, linoleic and linolenic (Section 23.2).

In Chapter 18 you learned there are nine essential amino acids: histidine, isoleucine, leucine, lysine, methionine, phenylalanine, threonine, tryptophan, and valine. Histidine's classification as essential is argued by some biochemists; although it is essential in growing children, it is considered a nonessential amino acid for adults, as healthy adults are capable of synthesizing enough to meet their biochemical requirements except under physiological requirements imposed by certain stress or disease situations. Some nutritionists also place arginine on the essential list, not because there is no mammalian biochemical pathway for its synthesis but because it is synthesized by cells at an insufficient rate to meet the growth needs of developing mammals. Since the majority of arginine is synthesized as part of the urea cycle (see Figure 27.4), and as such is cleaved to form urea and ornithine, a certain amount must still be taken in daily, especially for men of reproductive age, since 80% of the amino acid composition of male seminal fluid is made of arginine. Both arginine and histidine are sometimes called *conditional amino acids*, as they are truly essential only under certain conditions.

But what would happen if you did not heed your mother's advice? What if your diet was such that one or more of the essential amino acids was missing? Among other topics of research, nutritional biochemists seek to understand what physiological fate will befall someone whose diet is deficient in one of the essential amino acids. This challenging research requires tight controls over the food given to the animal models under study. For example, to determine the effect of a valine deficiency on a mouse, researchers must ensure that its diet contains very little (if any) valine, while not lacking in any other nutrient. Studies like this, as well as observations in humans, have given rise to a number of conclusions concerning the functions of individual essential amino acids and the effects a deficiency may cause:

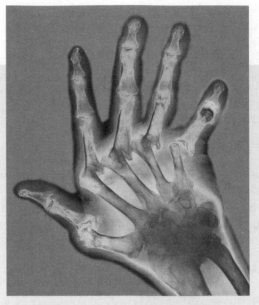

▲ **Colored X ray of the deformed hand of a patient suffering from rheumatoid arthritis. Joint damage (shown in red) has caused the fingers to bend abnormally.**

Histidine: An essential amino acid during the period of growth and conditionally essential in adults, this amino acid may also be required in the diet during old age and in those suffering from degenerative diseases. A deficiency of histidine can cause pain in bony joints and may have a link to rheumatoid arthritis.

Isoleucine, Leucine, and Valine: These three hydrophobic amino acids are essential for the production and maintenance of body proteins; in addition, leucine and valine have been reported to increase mental alertness. It is difficult to tell exactly what are the true effects of the deficiency of any of these three amino acids. Since leucine is especially important in controlling the net synthesis of protein, its deficiency may severely limit regeneration of protein, which, for example, could affect healing after surgery. Valine deficiency has been reported to cause sensitivity to touch and sound.

Lysine: This extremely important amino acid plays a role in absorption of calcium; formation of collagen for bones, cartilage, and connective tissues; and the production of antibodies, hormones, and enzymes. Lysine deficiency can lead to a poor appetite, reduction in body weight, anemia, and a reduced ability to concentrate. Lysine deficiency in the body has also been associated with pneumonia, kidney disease (nephritis), and acidosis, as well as with malnutrition and rickets in children (due to the decreased calcium absorption).

Methionine: The most important metabolic role of this amino acid is as a primary source of sulfur; it is really only necessary when cysteine intake is limited. Methionine seems to play a role in lowering cholesterol and reducing liver fat, protecting kidneys, and promoting hair growth. Methionine deficiency may ultimately lead to chronic rheumatic fever in children, hardening of the liver (cirrhosis), and nephritis.

Phenylalanine: As a starting material for the synthesis of tyrosine, phenylalanine is the primary source of the aromatic rings needed for a whole array of biomolecules, most notably the neurotransmitters (Section 28.4). Deficiency of phenylalanine can lead to behavioral changes such as psychotic and schizophrenic behavior (presumably due to its being needed for the synthesis of tyrosine, dopamine, and epinephrine).

Threonine: This amino acid is key in the formation of collagen, elastin, and tooth enamel. Its deficiency can result in irritability in children and has been suggested by some as being essential in the prevention and treatment of mental illness.

Tryptophan: Considered to be a natural relaxant, it has been used to help relieve insomnia. Tryptophan has also been recommended for the treatment of migraines and mild depression (as it is the metabolic starting material for serotonin) and as such has been called "nature's Prozac®." A deficiency of tryptophan can lead to serotonin deficiency syndrome, which in turn can lead to a broad array of emotional and behavioral problems such as depression, PMS, anxiety, alcoholism, insomnia, violence, aggression, and suicide.

See Chemistry in Action Problems 27.57 and 27.58 at the end of the chapter.

All of the nonessential amino acids derive their amino groups from glutamate. As you have previously seen, this is the molecule that picks up ammonia in amino acid catabolism and carries it into the urea cycle. Glutamate can also be made from NH_4^+ and α-ketoglutarate by **reductive amination**, the reverse of oxidative deamination (Section 27.3). The same glutamate dehydrogenase enzyme carries out the reaction:

Reductive amination Conversion of an α-keto acid to an amino acid by reaction with NH_4^+.

$$NH_4^+ + {}^-OOC-CH_2CH_2\underset{\substack{\| \\ O}}{C}-COO^- \xrightarrow[\substack{\text{Glutamate} \\ \text{dehydrogenase}}]{\text{NADH(NADPH)} \quad \text{NAD}^+(\text{NADP}^+)} {}^-OOC-CH_2CH_2\underset{\substack{| \\ NH_3^+}}{CH}-COO^- + H_2O$$

α-Ketoglutarate   Glutamate

Glutamate also provides nitrogen for the synthesis of other nitrogen-containing compounds, including the purines and pyrimidines that are part of DNA.

The following four common metabolic intermediates, which you have seen play many roles, are the precursors for synthesis of the nonessential amino acids:

Precursors in synthesis of nonessential amino acids

$$CH_3\underset{\substack{\| \\ O}}{C}-COO^- \qquad {}^-OOC-\underset{\substack{\| \\ O}}{C}CH_2-COO^- \qquad {}^-OOC-CH_2CH_2\underset{\substack{\| \\ O}}{C}-COO^- \qquad {}^{-2}O_3POCH_2\underset{\substack{| \\ OH}}{CH}-COO^-$$

Pyruvate   Oxaloacetate α-Ketoglutarate   3-Phosphoglycerate

Glutamine is made from glutamate, and asparagine is made by reaction of glutamine with aspartate:

$${}^-OOC-CH_2CH_2-\underset{\substack{| \\ NH_3^+}}{CH}-COO^- + NH_4^+ \xrightarrow{\text{ATP} \quad \text{ADP}} H_2N-\underset{\substack{\| \\ O}}{C}-CH_2CH_2-\underset{\substack{| \\ NH_3^+}}{CH}-COO^-$$

Glutamate   Glutamine

$${}^-OOC-CH_2-\underset{\substack{| \\ NH_3^+}}{CH}-COO^- \xrightarrow[\substack{ATP \quad AMP}]{\text{Glutamine} \quad \text{Glutamate}} H_2N-\underset{\substack{\| \\ O}}{C}-CH_2-\underset{\substack{| \\ NH_3^+}}{CH}-COO^-$$

Aspartate   Asparagine

The amino acid tyrosine is classified as nonessential because we can synthesize it from phenylalanine, an essential amino acid:

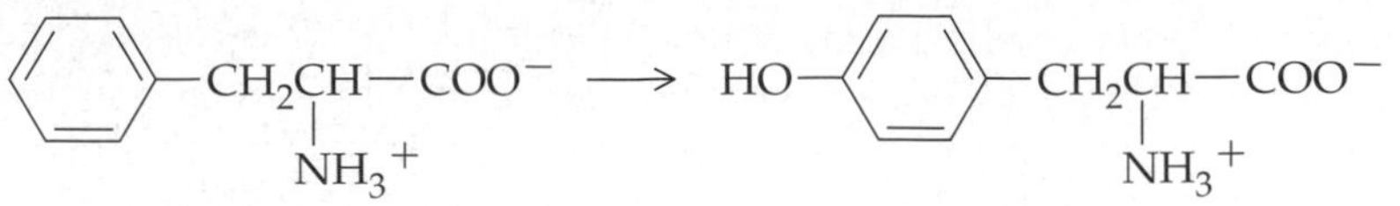

Whatever the classification, we have a high nutritional requirement for phenylalanine, and several metabolic diseases are associated with defects in the enzymes needed to convert it to tyrosine and other metabolites. The best known of these diseases is phenylketonuria (PKU), the first inborn error of metabolism for which the biochemical cause was recognized. In 1947 it was found that failure to convert phenylalanine to tyrosine causes PKU.

PKU results in elevated blood-serum and urine concentrations of phenylalanine, phenylpyruvate, and several other metabolites produced when the body diverts phenylalanine to metabolism by other pathways. Undetected PKU causes mental retardation by the second month of life. Estimates are that, prior to the 1960s, 1% of those institutionalized for mental retardation were PKU victims. Widespread screening of newborn infants is the only defense against PKU and similar treatable metabolic disorders that take their toll early in life. In the 1960s a test for PKU was introduced, and virtually all hospitals in the United States now routinely screen for it. Treatment consists of a diet low in phenylalanine, which is maintained in infants with special formulas and in older individuals by eliminating meat and using low-protein grain products. Individuals with PKU must be on alert for foods sweetened with aspartame (Nutrasweet, for example), which is a derivative of phenylalanine.

🔑 **KEY CONCEPT PROBLEM 27.11**

In the pathway for synthesis of serine,

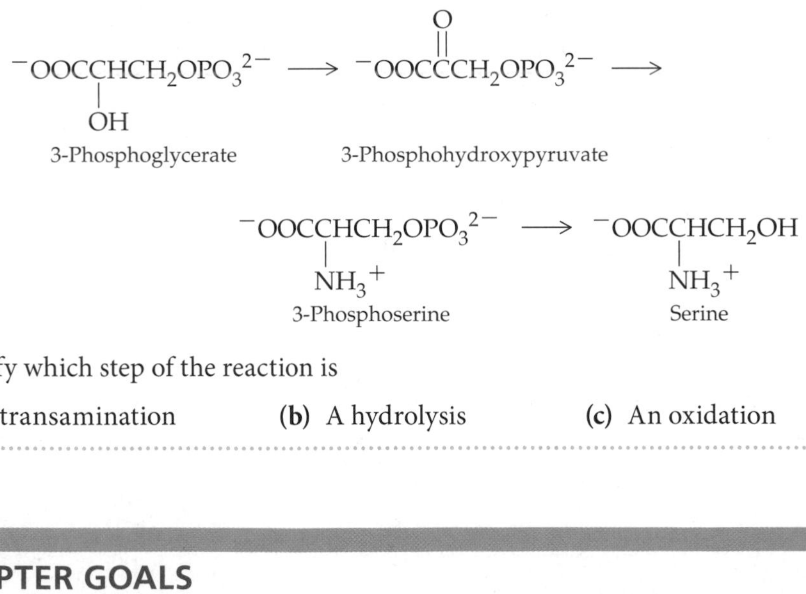

$$^-OOCCHCH_2OPO_3{}^{2-} \longrightarrow {}^-OOCCCH_2OPO_3{}^{2-} \longrightarrow$$

3-Phosphoglycerate (with OH group) 3-Phosphohydroxypyruvate (with C=O group)

$$^-OOCCHCH_2OPO_3{}^{2-} \longrightarrow {}^-OOCCHCH_2OH$$

3-Phosphoserine (with $NH_3{}^+$) Serine (with $NH_3{}^+$)

identify which step of the reaction is

(a) A transamination   (b) A hydrolysis   (c) An oxidation

SUMMARY: REVISITING THE CHAPTER GOALS

1. What happens during the digestion of proteins, and what is the fate of the amino acids? Protein digestion begins in the stomach and continues in the small intestine. The result is virtually complete hydrolysis to yield free amino acids. The amino acids enter the bloodstream after active transport into cells lining the intestine. The body does not store nitrogen compounds, but amino acids are constantly entering the amino acid pool from dietary protein or broken down body protein and being withdrawn from the pool for biosynthesis or further catabolism (see *Problems 12–13, 18–19, 48–49, 51*).

2. What are the major strategies in the catabolism of amino acids? Each amino acid is catabolized by a distinctive pathway, but in most of them the amino group is removed by *transamination* (the transfer of an amino group from an amino acid to a keto acid), usually to form glutamate. Then, the amino group of glutamate is removed as ammonium ion by *oxidative deamination*. The ammonium ion is destined for the *urea cycle*. The carbon atoms from amino acids are incorporated into compounds that can enter the *citric acid cycle*. These carbon compounds are also available for conversion to fatty acids or glycogen for storage, or for synthesis of ketone bodies (*see Problems 14–15, 17, 20–31, 44–47, 50, 52*).

3. What is the urea cycle? Ammonium ion (from amino acid catabolism) and bicarbonate ion (from carbon dioxide) react to produce carbamoyl phosphate, which enters the urea cycle. The first two steps of the urea cycle produce a reactive intermediate in which both of the nitrogens that will be part of the urea end product are bonded to the same carbon atom. Then arginine

is formed and split by hydrolysis to yield urea, which will be excreted. The net result of the urea cycle is reaction of ammonium ion with aspartate to give urea and fumarate (*see Problems 32–35, 47*).

4. What are the essential and nonessential amino acids, and how, in general, are amino acids synthesized? *Essential amino acids* must be obtained in the diet because our bodies do not synthesize them. They are made only by plants and microorganisms, and their synthetic pathways are complex. Our bodies do synthesize the so-called *nonessential amino acids*. Their synthetic pathways are quite simple and generally begin with pyruvate, oxaloacetate, α-ketoglutarate, or 3-phosphoglycerate. The nitrogen is commonly supplied by glutamate (*see Problems 16, 36–42, 54, 57–58*).

KEY WORDS

Amino acid pool, *p. 826*

Essential amino acids, *p. 835*

Nonessential amino acid, *p. 835*

Oxidative deamination, *p. 829*

Reductive amination, *p. 837*

Transamination, *p. 828*

Urea cycle, *p. 830*

UNDERSTANDING KEY CONCEPTS

27.12   In the diagram shown here, fill in the sources for the amino acid pool.

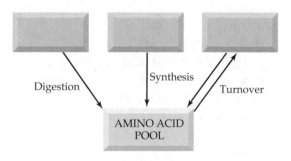

27.13   What are the fates of the carbon and nitrogen atoms in a catabolized amino acid?

27.14   A treatment for hyperammonemia (excess NH_4^+ in the blood) is to administer pyruvate. What two enzymes are necessary to detoxify the ammonium ion in the presence of pyruvate? What is the product?

27.15   Three metabolites that can result from the breakdown of the carbon skeleton of amino acids are ketone bodies, acetyl-CoA, and glucose. Briefly describe how each of these metabolites can be produced from amino acid catabolism.

27.16   Define what an "essential" nutrient is and explain how it differs from a "nonessential" nutrient.

27.17   In the liver, the relative activity of ornithine transcarbamylase is high, that of argininosuccinate synthetase is low, and that of arginase is high. Why is it important that ornithine transcarbamylase activity be high in the liver? What might be the consequence if arginase activity is low or defective?

ADDITIONAL PROBLEMS

AMINO ACID POOL

27.18   Where is the body's amino acid pool?

27.19   In what part of the digestive tract does the digestion of proteins begin?

27.20   What glycolytic intermediates are precursors to amino acids?

27.21   What citric acid cycle intermediates are precursors to amino acids?

AMINO ACID CATABOLISM

27.22 What is meant by transamination?

27.23 Pyruvate and oxaloacetate can be acceptors for the amino group in transamination. Write the structures for the products formed from transamination of these two compounds.

27.24 What is the structure of the α-keto acid formed from transamination of the following amino acids?

(a) Glutamic acid

(b) Alanine

27.25 What is the structure of the α-keto acid formed from transamination of the following amino acids?

(a) Tyrosine

(b) Threonine

27.26 In general, how does oxidative deamination differ from transamination?

27.27 What coenzymes are associated with oxidative deamination?

27.28 Write the structure of the α-keto acid produced by oxidative deamination of the following amino acids:

(a) Leucine

(b) Tryptophan

27.29 What other product is formed in oxidative deamination besides an α-keto acid?

27.30 What is a ketogenic amino acid? Give three examples.

27.31 What is a glucogenic amino acid? Give three examples.

UREA CYCLE

27.32 Why does the body convert NH_4^+ to urea for excretion?

27.33 What is the source of carbon in the formation of urea?

27.34 What are the sources of the 2 nitrogens in the formation of urea?

27.35 Where does aspartate enter the urea cycle and what compound does it eventually leave as? What metabolic cycle does this compound then enter?

AMINO ACID BIOSYNTHESIS

27.36 How do essential and nonessential amino acids differ from each other in the number of steps required for their synthesis in organisms that synthesize both?

27.37 Which amino acid serves as the source of nitrogen for synthesis of the other amino acids?

27.38 If you were diagnosed as having a diet low in lysine, what foods might you include in your diet to alleviate this problem?

27.39 How is tyrosine biosynthesized in the body? What disease prevents this biosynthesis, thereby making tyrosine an essential amino acid for those who have this condition?

27.40 PKU is an abbreviation for what disorder? What are the symptoms of PKU? How can PKU be treated for a nearly normal life?

27.41 Diet soft drinks that are sweetened with aspartame carry a warning label for phenylketonurics. Why?

27.42 Which of the following biomolecules contain nitrogen from an amino acid?

(a) Glycogen

(b) Nitric oxide

(c) Collagen

(d) Epinephrine

(e) Stearic acid

(f) Fructose

GENERAL QUESTIONS AND PROBLEMS

27.43 What energy source is used in the formation of urea?

27.44 Write the equation for the transamination reaction that occurs between isoleucine and pyruvate.

27.45 Name the four products (carbon skeletons) of amino acid catabolism that can enter the citric acid cycle, and show where in the cycle they enter.

27.46 Can an amino acid be both glucogenic and ketogenic? Explain why or why not.

27.47 Where in the body does the conversion of ammonium ion to urea occur? Where is the urea that is formed ultimately transported?

27.48 Consider all of the metabolic processes we have studied. Why do we say that tissue biochemistry is dynamic? Describe some examples of these dynamic relationships.

27.49 Two major differences between the amino acid pool and the fat and carbohydrate pools in the body center on storage and on energy. Discuss these major differences.

27.50 When some of the carbons of glutamate are converted to glycogen, what is the order of the following compounds in that pathway?

(a) Glucose

(b) Glutamate

(c) Glycogen

(d) Oxaloacetate

(e) α-Ketoglutarate

(f) Phosphoenolpyruvate

27.51 The pancreatic proteases are synthesized and stored as zymogens. They are activated after the pancreatic juices enter the small intestine. Why is it essential that these enzymes be synthesized and stored in their inactive forms?

27.52 What is the general scheme by which amino acids are catabolized?

27.53 The net reaction for the urea cycle shows that 3 ATPs are hydrolyzed; however, the total energy "cost" is 4 ATPs. Explain why this is true.

27.54 Why might it be a bad idea to take large quantities of a single amino acid dietary supplement?

CHEMISTRY IN ACTION

27.55 Your grandfather complains of pain in his swollen and inflamed big toe, and the doctor indicates that it is caused by gout. [*Gout: When Biochemistry Goes Awry, p. 833*]

  (a) How would you explain to him what gout is and its biochemical cause?

  (b) What can you suggest to him to prevent these gouty attacks?

27.56 Allopurinol is a drug often used to assist in the control of gout. At which step(s) in the catabolism of purines is allopurinol effective? What is its effect? Compare the structure of allopurinol with the structures of hypoxanthine and xanthine. Where does allopurinol differ in structure from hypoxanthine? Is this the site on the molecule that corresponds to the site where hypoxanthine or xanthine is oxidized? [*Gout: When Biochemistry Goes Awry, p. 833*]

27.57 What medical problems might arise if your diet was found to be low in methionine? [*The Importance of Essential Amino Acids and Effects of Deficiencies, p. 836*]

27.58 What essential amino acid has been called "nature's Prozac"? What are some of the symptoms seen if deficiencies of it occur? [*The Importance of Essential Amino Acids and Effects of Deficiencies, p. 836*]

CHAPTER 28

Chemical Messengers: Hormones, Neurotransmitters, and Drugs

CONTENTS

◄ Floods of chemical messengers help these athletes keep up the physical effort needed to complete the match.

1. **What are hormones, and how do they function?**
   THE GOAL: Be able to describe in general the origins, pathways, and actions of hormones. (◀◀ A, B, E, F.)

2. **What is the chemical nature of hormones?**
   THE GOAL: Be able to list, with examples, the different chemical types of hormones. (◀◀ A, D, F.)

3. **How does the hormone epinephrine deliver its message, and what is its major mode of action?**
   THE GOAL: Be able to outline the sequence of events in epinephrine's action as a hormone. (◀◀ A, D.)

4. **What are neurotransmitters, and how do they function?**
   THE GOAL: Be able to describe the general origins, pathways, and actions of neurotransmitters. (◀◀ C, D.)

5. **How does acetylcholine deliver its message, and how do drugs alter its function?**
   THE GOAL: Be able to outline the sequence of events in acetylcholine's action as a neurotransmitter and give examples of its agonists and antagonists. (◀◀ B, D.)

6. **Which neurotransmitters and what kinds of drugs play roles in allergies, mental depression, drug addiction, and pain?**
   THE GOAL: Be able to identify neurotransmitters and drugs active in these conditions. (◀◀ C, F.)

7. **What are some of the methods used in drug discovery and design?**
   THE GOAL: Be able to explain the general roles of ethnobotany, chemical synthesis, combinatorial chemistry, and computer-aided design in the development of new drugs. (◀◀ B, D.)

CONCEPTS TO REVIEW

◀◀

A. Amino Acids
(Sections 18.3, 18.4)

B. Shapes of Proteins
(Section 18.8)

C. Tertiary and Quaternary Protein Structure
(Sections 18.10, 18.11)

D. How Enzymes Work
(Section 19.4)

E. Sterol Structure
(Section 23.6)

F. Amines
(Chapter 15)

A t this point, you have seen a few of the hundreds of enzyme-catalyzed reactions that take place in cells. How are these individual reactions tied together? Clearly, the many thousands of reactions taking place in the billions of individual cells of our bodies do not occur randomly. There must be overall control mechanisms that coordinate these reactions, keeping us in chemical balance.

Two systems share major responsibility for regulating body chemistry—the *endocrine system* and the *nervous system*. The endocrine system depends on *hormones*, chemical messengers that circulate in the bloodstream. The nervous system relies primarily on a much faster means of communication—electrical impulses in nerve cells, triggered by its own chemical messengers, the *neurotransmitters*. Neurotransmitters carry signals from one nerve cell to another and also from nerve cells to their targets, the ultimate recipients of the messages.

Given the crucial role of hormones and neurotransmitters in the functioning of our bodies, it should not be surprising to find that many drugs act by mimicking, modifying, or opposing the action of chemical messengers.

28.1 Messenger Molecules

Coordination and control of your body's vital functions are accomplished by chemical messengers. Whether the messengers are hormones that arrive via the bloodstream or neurotransmitters released by nerve cells, such messengers ultimately connect with a *target*. The message is delivered by interaction between the chemical messenger and a **receptor** at the target. The receptor then acts like a light switch, causing some biochemical response to occur—the contraction of a muscle, for example, or the secretion of another biomolecule.

Noncovalent attractions draw messengers and receptors together, much as a substrate is drawn into the active site of an enzyme (Sections 18.8, 19.4). These attractions hold the messenger and receptor together long enough for the message to be delivered, but without any permanent chemical change to the messenger or the receptor. The results of this interaction are chemical changes within the target cell.

Receptor A molecule or portion of a molecule with which a hormone, neurotransmitter, or other biochemically active molecule interacts to initiate a response in a target cell.

▶▶▶ Figure 18.4 shows the various types of noncovalent forces that govern the shape of protein molecules. These same types of interactions mediate substrate–enzyme binding, as described in Section 19.4.

Hormone A chemical messenger secreted by cells of the endocrine system and transported through the bloodstream to target cells with appropriate receptors, where it elicits a response.

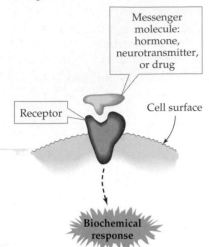

▲ A general representation of the interaction between a messenger molecule and a cellular receptor.

Neurotransmitter A chemical messenger that travels between a neuron and a neighboring neuron or other target cell to transmit a nerve impulse.

Endocrine system A system of specialized cells, tissues, and ductless glands that secretes hormones and shares with the nervous system the responsibility for maintaining constant internal body conditions and responding to changes in the environment.

Hormones are the chemical messengers of the endocrine system. These molecules are produced by endocrine glands and tissues in various parts of the body, often at distances far from their ultimate site of action. Because of this, hormones must travel through the bloodstream to their targets, and the responses they produce can require anywhere from seconds to hours to begin. The action or actions they elicit, however, may last a long time and can be wide-ranging. A single hormone will often affect many different tissues and organs—any cell with the appropriate receptors is a target. Insulin, for example, is a hormone secreted by the pancreas in response to elevated blood glucose levels. At target cells throughout the body, insulin accelerates uptake and utilization of glucose; in muscles it accelerates formation of glycogen, a glucose polymer that is metabolized when muscles need quick energy; and in fatty tissue it stimulates storage of triacylglycerols.

The chemical messengers of the nervous system are a set of molecules referred to as **neurotransmitters**. The electrical signals of the nervous system travel along nerve fibers, taking only a fraction of a second to reach their highly specific destinations. Most nerve cells, however, do not make direct contact with the cells they stimulate. A neurotransmitter must carry the message across the tiny gap separating the nerve cell from its target. Because neurotransmitters are released in very short bursts and are quickly broken down or reabsorbed by the nerve cell, their effects are short-lived. The nervous system is organized so that nearly all of its vital switching, integrative, and information-processing functions depend on neurotransmitters. Neurotransmitters are typically synthesized and released very close to their site of action.

In this chapter, we first discuss hormones and the endocrine system and include a detailed description of how one hormone—epinephrine (also known as adrenalin)—performs its functions. Next we discuss neurotransmitters, using the action of acetylcholine to illustrate how neurotransmitters act. It is essential to recognize that hormones and neurotransmitters play a fundamental role in maintaining your health by their influence on metabolic processes. (See Chemistry in Action: Homeostasis.) Finally, we briefly explore the discovery and design of drugs as chemical messengers.

PROBLEM 28.1

In humans, approximately 12% of all genes are regulatory genes necessary to maintain homeostasis within cells (see Chemistry in Action: Homeostasis). Health check-ups often include a blood panel; common compounds measured include blood glucose and triacylglycerols. Based on your knowledge of metabolism, why would these compounds be included in the blood test? What might that have to do with regulatory genes?

28.2 Hormones and the Endocrine System

The **endocrine system** includes all cells that secrete hormones into the bloodstream. Some of these cells are found in organs that also have non-endocrine functions (for example, the pancreas, which also produces digestive enzymes); others occur in glands devoted solely to hormonal control (for example, the thyroid gland). It is important to note, however, that hormones do *not* carry out chemical reactions. Hormones are simply messengers that alter the biochemistry of a cell by signaling the inhibition or activation of an existing enzyme, by initiating or altering the rate of synthesis of a specific protein, or in other ways.

The major endocrine glands are the thyroid gland, the adrenal glands, the ovaries and testes, and the pituitary gland (found in the brain). The hypothalamus, a section of the brain just above the pituitary gland, is in charge of the endocrine system. It communicates with other tissues in three ways:

- **Direct neural control** A nervous system message from the hypothalamus initiates release of hormones by the adrenal gland. For example,

$$\text{Hypothalamus} \xrightarrow{\text{Nerve message}} \text{Adrenal gland} \longrightarrow \text{Epinephrine}$$

Epinephrine is targeted to many cells; it increases heart rate, blood pressure, and glucose availability.

CHEMISTRY IN ACTION

Homeostasis

Homeostasis—the maintenance of a constant internal environment in the body—is as important to the study of living things as atomic structure is to the study of chemistry. The phrase "internal environment" is a general way to describe all the conditions within cells, organs, and body systems. Conditions such as body temperature, the availability of chemical compounds that supply energy, and the disposal of waste products must remain within specific limits for an organism to function properly. Throughout our bodies, sensors track the internal environment and send signals to restore proper balance if the environment changes. If oxygen is in short supply, for example, a signal is sent that makes us breathe harder. When we are cold, a signal is sent to constrict surface blood vessels and prevent further loss of heat.

At the chemical level, homeostasis regulates the concentrations of ions and many different organic compounds so that they stay near normal levels. The predictability of the concentrations of such substances is the basis for *clinical chemistry*—

the chemical analysis of body tissues and fluids. In the clinical lab, various tests measure concentrations of significant ions and compounds in blood, urine, feces, spinal fluid, or other samples from a patient's body. Comparing the lab results with "norms" (average concentration ranges in a population of healthy individuals) shows which body systems are struggling, or possibly failing, to maintain homeostasis. To give just one example, urate (commonly known as uric acid) is an anion that helps to carry waste nitrogen from the body. A uric acid concentration higher than the normal range of about 2.5–7.7 mg/dL in blood can indicate the onset of gout or signal possible kidney malfunction.

A copy of a clinical lab report for a routine blood analysis is shown in the figure below. (Fortunately, this individual has no significant variations from normal.) The metal names in the report refer to the various cations, and the heading "Phosphorus" refers to the phosphate anion.

See Chemistry in Action Problems 28.86 and 28.87 at the end of the chapter.

TEST	RESULT	NORMAL RANGE	TEST	RESULT	NORMAL RANGE
Albumin	4.3 g/dL	3.5–5.3 g/dL	**SGOT***	23 U/L	0–28 U/L
Alk. Phos.*	33 U/L	25–90 U/L	**Total protein**	5.9 g/dL	6.2–8.5 g/dL
BUN*	8 mg/dL	8–23 mg/dL	**Triglycerides**	75 mg/dL	36–165 mg/dL
Bilirubin T.*	0.1 mg/dL	0.2–1.6 mg/dL	**Uric Acid**	4.1 mg/dL	2.5–7.7 mg/dL
Calcium	8.6 mg/dL	8.5–10.5 mg/dL	**GGT***	23 U/L	0–45 U/L
Cholesterol	227 mg/dL	120–250 mg/dL	**Magnesium**	1.7 mEq/L	1.3–2.5 mEq/L
Chol., HDL*	75 mg/dL	30–75 mg/dL	**Phosphorus**	2.6 mg/dL	2.5–4.8 mg/dL
Creatinine	0.6 mg/dL	0.7–1.5 mg/dL	**SGPT***	13 U/L	0–26 U/L
Glucose	86 mg/dL	65–110 mg/dL	**Sodium**	137.7 mEq/L	135–155 mEq/L
Iron	101 mg/dL	35–140 mg/dL	**Potassium**	3.8 mEq/L	3.5–5.5 mEq/L
LDH*	48 U/L	50–166 U/L			

▲ **A clinical lab report for routine blood analysis. The abbreviations marked with asterisks are for the following tests (alternative standard abbreviations are in parentheses): Alk. Phos., alkaline phosphatase (ALP); BUN, blood urea nitrogen; Bilirubin T., total bilirubin; Chol., HDL, cholesterol, high-density lipoproteins; LDH, lactate dehydrogenase; SGOT, serum glutamic oxaloacetic transaminase (AST); GGT, γ-glutamyl transferase; SGPT, serum glutamic pyruvic transaminase (ALT).**

- **Direct release of hormones** Hormones move from the hypothalamus to the posterior pituitary gland, where they are stored until needed. For example,

Hypothalamus ⟶ Antidiuretic hormone

Antidiuretic hormone, which is stored in the posterior pituitary gland, targets the kidneys and causes retention of water and elevation of blood pressure.

- **Indirect control through release of regulatory hormones** In the most common control mechanism, *regulatory hormones* from the hypothalamus stimulate or inhibit the release of hormones by the anterior pituitary gland. Many of these pituitary hormones in turn stimulate release of still other hormones by their own target tissues. For example,

Hypothalamus $\xrightarrow{\text{Releasing factor}}$ Pituitary gland $\longrightarrow$

Thyrotropin (a regulatory hormone) $\longrightarrow$

Thyroid gland $\longrightarrow$ Thyroid hormones

Thyroid hormones are targeted to cells throughout the body; they affect oxygen availability, blood pressure, and other endocrine tissues.

Chemically, hormones are of three major types: (1) amino acid derivatives, small molecules containing amino groups; (2) polypeptides, which range from just a few amino acids to several hundred amino acids; and (3) steroids, which are lipids with the distinctive molecular structure based on four connected rings common to all sterols (see Section 23.6).

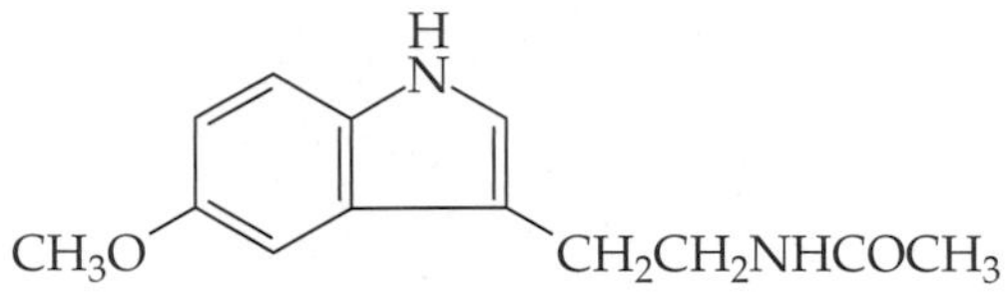

Melatonin, an amino acid derivative
(regulates day–night cycle)

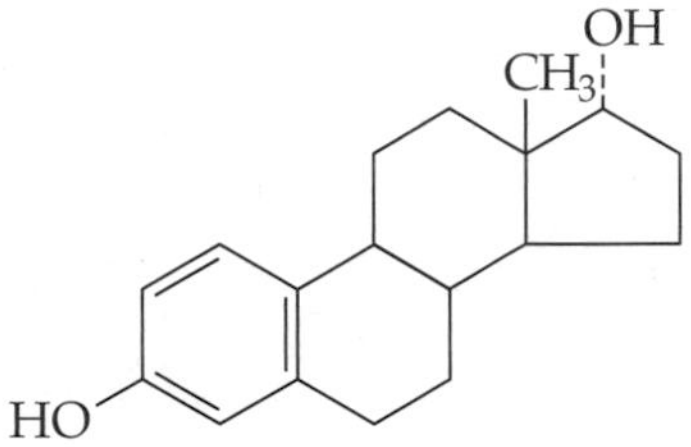

Estradiol, a steroid
(an estrogen that acts in ovulation)

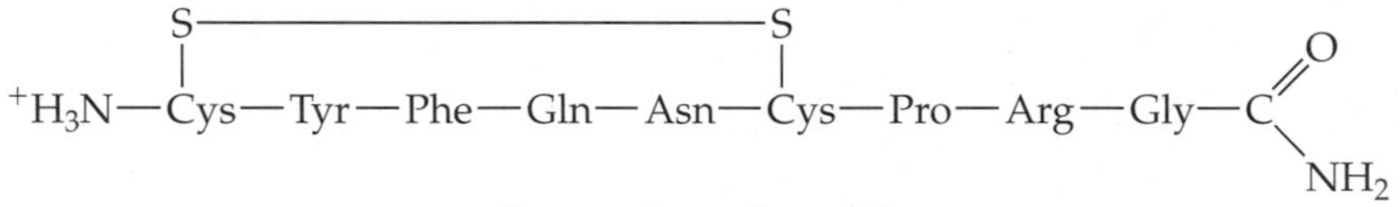

^+H_3N—Cys—Tyr—Phe—Gln—Asn—Cys—Pro—Arg—Gly—C

Vasopressin, a polypeptide
(controls urine volume)

Examples of the targets and actions of some hormones of each type are given in Table 28.1.

TABLE 28.1 Examples of Each Chemical Class of Hormones

Chemical Class	Hormone Examples	Source	Target	Major Action
Amino acid derivatives	Epinephrine and norepinephrine	Adrenal medulla	Most cells	Release glucose from storage; increase heart rate and blood pressure
	Thyroxine	Thyroid gland	Most cells	Influence energy use, oxygen consumption, growth, and development
Polypeptides (regulatory hormones)	Adrenocorticotropic hormone	Anterior pituitary	Adrenal cortex	Stimulate release of glucocorticoids (steroids), which control glucose metabolism
	Growth hormone	Anterior pituitary	Peripheral tissues	Stimulate growth of muscle and skeleton
	Follicle-stimulating hormone, luteinizing hormone	Anterior pituitary	Ovaries and testes	Stimulate release of steroid hormones
	Vasopressin	Posterior pituitary	Kidneys	Cause retention of water, elevation of blood volume and blood pressure
	Thyrotropin	Anterior pituitary	Thyroid gland	Stimulates release of thyroid hormones
Steroids	Cortisone and cortisol (glucocorticoids)	Adrenal cortex	Most cells	Counteract inflammation; control metabolism when glucose must be conserved
	Testosterone; estrogen, progesterone	Testes; ovaries	Most cells	Control development of secondary sexual characteristics, maturation of sperm and eggs

Upon arrival at its target cell, a hormone must deliver its signal to create a chemical response inside the cell. The signal enters the cell in ways determined by the chemical nature of the hormone (Figure 28.1). Because the cell is surrounded by a membrane composed of hydrophobic molecules, only nonpolar, hydrophobic molecules can move across it on their own. The steroid hormones are nonpolar, so they can enter the cell directly by diffusion; this is one of the ways a hormone delivers its message. Once within the cell's cytoplasm, a steroid hormone encounters a receptor molecule that carries it to its target, DNA in the nucleus of the cell. The result is some change in production of a protein governed by a particular gene.

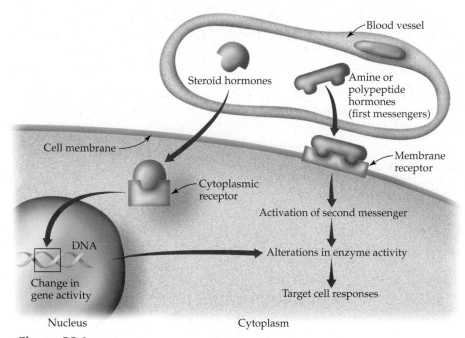

▲ **Figure 28.1**
Interaction of hormones and receptors at the cellular level.
Steroid hormones are hydrophobic and can cross the cell membrane to find receptors inside the cell. Amine and polypeptide hormones are hydrophilic and, because they cannot cross the cell membrane, act via second messengers.

In contrast, the polypeptide and amine hormones are water-soluble molecules and cannot cross the hydrophobic cell membranes. Rather than entering cells, they deliver their messages by bonding noncovalently with receptors on cell surfaces. The result is release of a **second messenger** within the cell. There are several different second messengers, and the specific sequence of events varies. In general, three membrane-bound proteins participate in release of the second messenger: (1) the receptor and (2) a *G protein* (a member of the guanine nucleotide-binding protein family) that transfer the message to (3) an enzyme. First, interaction of the hormone with its receptor causes a change in the receptor (much like the effect of an allosteric regulator on an enzyme; Section 19.7). This stimulates the G protein to activate an enzyme that participates in release of the second messenger. The action of epinephrine by way of a second messenger is described in Section 28.3. Further examples of amino acid, polypeptide, and steroid hormones are given in Sections 28.4 and 28.5.

Second messenger Chemical messenger released inside a cell when a hydrophilic hormone or neurotransmitter interacts with a receptor on the cell surface.

Worked Example **28.1** Classifying Hormones Based on Structure

Classify the following hormones as an amino acid derivative, a polypeptide, or a steroid.

(a)

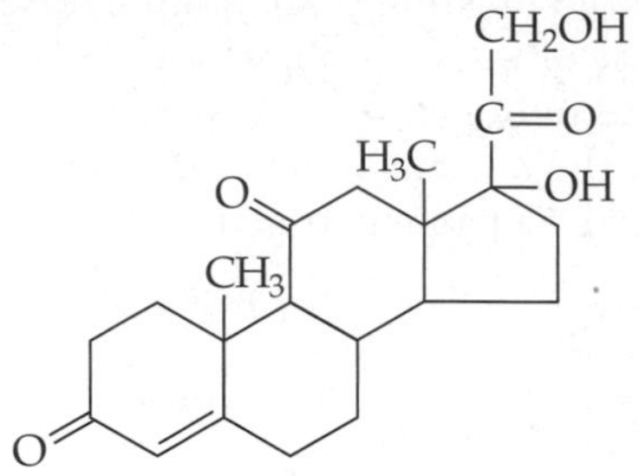

(b)

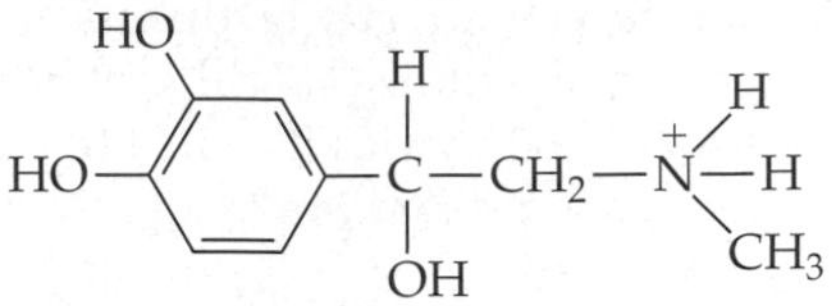

(c) $^+H_3N-His-Ser-Glu- \cdots Thr-COO^-$

ANALYSIS Hormones that are amino acid derivatives are recognized by the presence of amino groups. Those that are polypeptides are composed of amino acids. Steroids are recognizable by their distinctive four-ring structures.

SOLUTION
Compound (a) is a steroid, (b) is an amino acid derivative, and (c) is a polypeptide.

28.3 How Hormones Work: Epinephrine and Fight-or-Flight

Epinephrine (pronounced ep-pin-**eff**-rin), also known as *adrenaline*, is often called the *fight-or-flight hormone* because it is released from the adrenal glands when we need an instant response to danger.

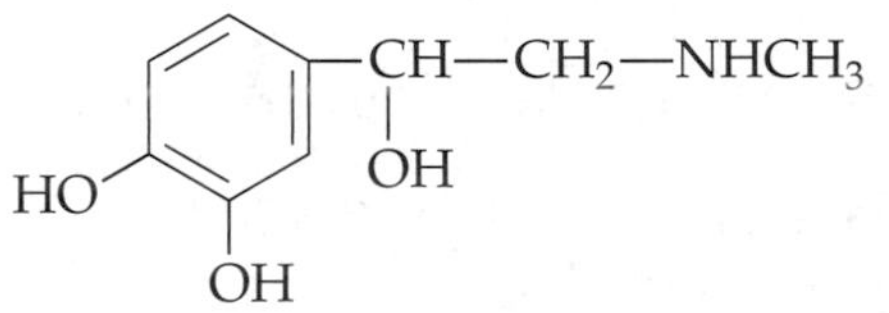

Epinephrine
(Adrenaline)

We have all felt the rush of epinephrine that accompanies a near-miss accident or a sudden loud noise. The main function of epinephrine in a "startle" reaction is a dramatic increase in the availability of glucose as a source of energy to deal with whatever stress is immediate. The time elapsed from initial stimulus to glucose release into the bloodstream is only a few seconds.

Epinephrine acts via *cyclic adenosine monophosphate* (*cyclic AMP*, or *cAMP*), an important second messenger. The sequence of events in this action, shown in Figure 28.2 and described below, illustrates one type of biochemical response to a change in an individual's external or internal environment.

- Epinephrine, a hormone carried in the bloodstream, binds to a receptor on the surface of a cell.
- The hormone–receptor complex activates a nearby G protein embedded in the interior surface of the cell membrane.
- GDP (guanosine disphosphate) associated with the G protein is exchanged for GTP (guanosine triphosphate) from the cytosol.

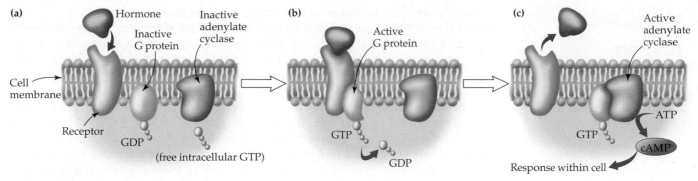

▲ **Figure 28.2**

Activation of cyclic AMP as a second messenger.
(a) The hormone receptor, inactive G protein, and inactive adenylate cyclase enzyme reside in the cell membrane. (b) On formation of the hormone–receptor complex, an allosteric change occurs in the G protein, resulting in the guanosine diphosphate (GDP) of the G protein being replaced by a free intracellular guanosine triphosphate (GTP). (c) The active G protein–GTP complex activates adenylate cyclase, causing production of cyclic AMP inside the cell, where it initiates the action called for by the hormone.

- The G protein–GTP complex activates *adenylate cyclase*, an enzyme that also is embedded in the interior surface of the cell membrane.
- Adenylate cyclase catalyzes production within the cell of the second messenger— *cyclic AMP*—from ATP, as shown in Figure 28.3.
- Cyclic AMP initiates reactions that activate glycogen phosphorylase, the enzyme responsible for release of glucose from storage. (Interaction of other hormones with their specific receptors results in initiation by cyclic AMP of other reactions.)
- When the emergency has passed, cyclic AMP is converted back to ATP.

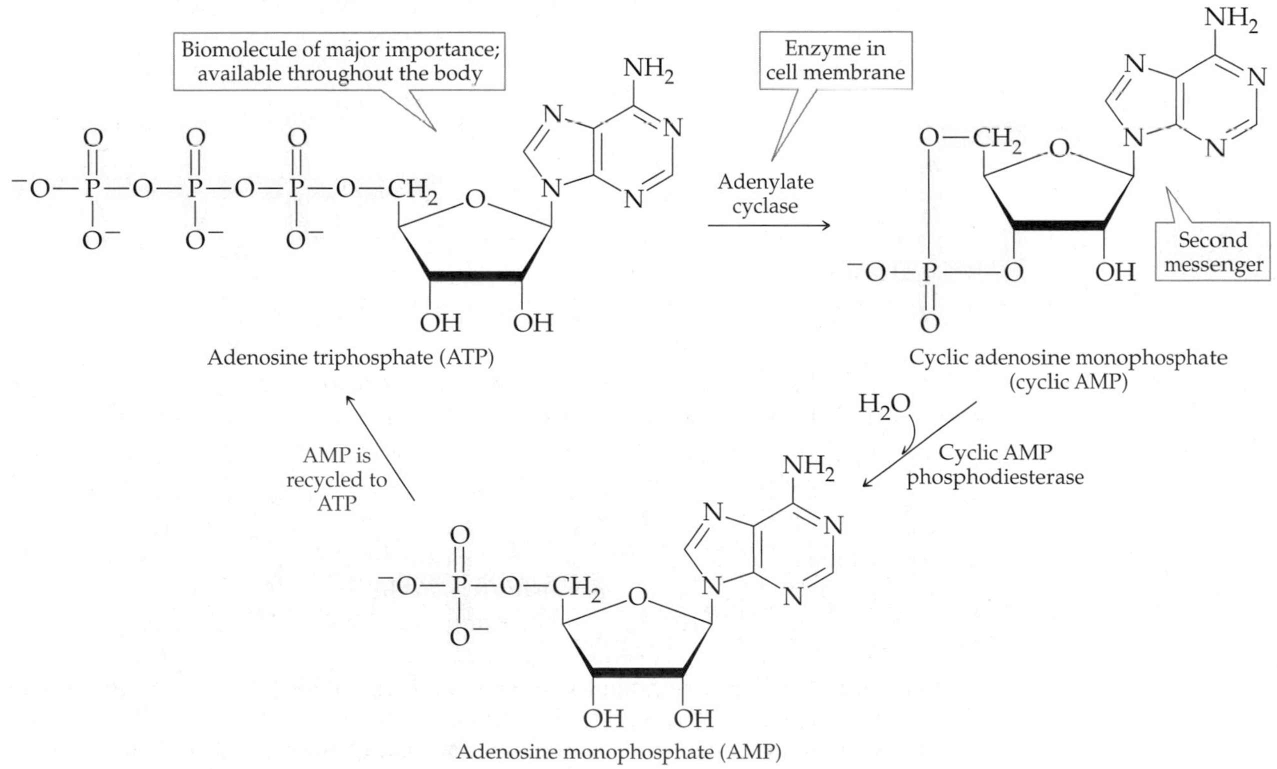

▲ **Figure 28.3**

Production of cyclic AMP as a second messenger.
The reactions shown take place within the target cell after epinephrine or some other chemical messenger interacts with a receptor on the cell surface. (The major role of ATP in providing energy for biochemical reactions was discussed in Section 20.5.)

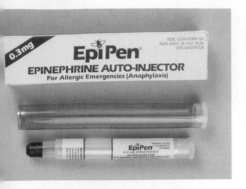

▲ **An epinephrine autoinjection pen. Such devices are carried by individuals at risk of an anaphylactic reaction to an allergen.**

In addition to making glucose available, epinephrine reacts with other receptors to increase blood pressure, heart rate, and respiratory rate; decrease blood flow to the digestive system (digestion is not important during an emergency); and counteract spasms in the respiratory system. The resulting combined and rapid effects make epinephrine the most crucial drug for treatment of *anaphylactic shock.* Anaphylactic shock is the result of a severe allergic reaction, perhaps to a bee sting, a drug, or even to something seemingly as benign as peanuts; it is an extremely serious medical emergency. The major symptoms include a severe drop in blood pressure due to blood vessel dilation and difficulty breathing due to bronchial constriction. Epinephrine directly counters these symptoms. Individuals who know they are susceptible to these life-threatening allergic responses carry epinephrine with them at all times (typically in the form of an autoinjector known as an "EpiPen®").

PROBLEM 28.2

A phosphorus-containing anion is removed from ATP in its conversion to cyclic AMP, as shown in Figure 28.3. The anion is often abbreviated as PP_i. Which of the following anions is represented by PP_i?

(a) $P_3O_{10}^{5-}$ **(b)** $P_2O_7^{4-}$ **(c)** PO_4^{3-} **(d)** $H_2PO_4^-$

KEY CONCEPT PROBLEM 28.3

Caffeine and theobromine (from chocolate) act as stimulants. They work by altering the cAMP signal. Refer to Figure 28.3 and decide how these molecules might interact with an enzyme in the cAMP pathway to enhance the effect of cAMP.

Caffeine   Theobromine

28.4 Amino Acid Derivatives and Polypeptides as Hormones

Amino Acid Derivatives

The biochemistry of the brain is an active area of research. As our understanding of chemical messages in the brain grows, the traditional distinctions between hormones and neurotransmitters are vanishing. Several amino acid derivatives classified as hormones because of their roles in the endocrine system are also synthesized in neurons and function as neurotransmitters in the brain. (Because a barrier—the *blood–brain barrier*—limits entry into the brain of chemicals traveling in the bloodstream, the brain cannot rely on a supply of chemical messengers synthesized elsewhere; see Section 29.4.) Epinephrine, the fight-or-flight hormone, is one of the amino acid derivatives that is both a hormone and a neurotransmitter. The pathway for the synthesis of epinephrine is shown in Figure 28.4; several other chemical messengers are also formed in this pathway.

Thyroxine, another amino acid derivative, is also a hormone. It is one of two iodine-containing hormones produced by the thyroid gland, and our need for dietary iodine is due to these hormones. Unlike other hormones derived from amino acids,

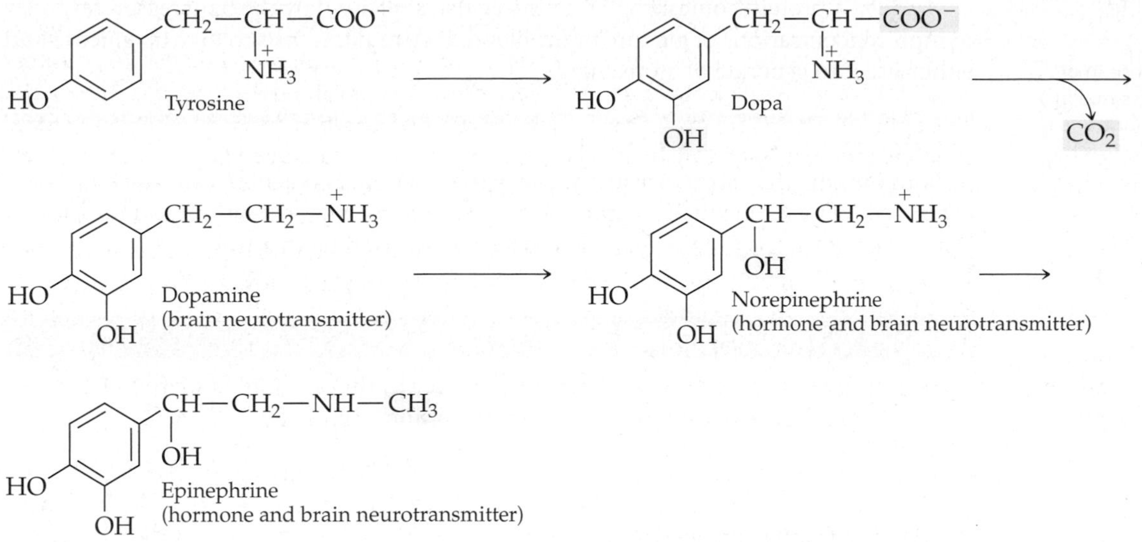

▲ **Figure 28.4**
Synthesis of chemical messengers from tyrosine.
The changes in each step are highlighted in gold for additions and in green for losses.

thyroxine is a nonpolar compound that can cross cell membranes and enter cells, where it activates the synthesis of various enzymes. When dietary iodine is insufficient, the thyroid gland compensates by enlarging in order to produce more thyroxine. Thus, a greatly enlarged thyroid gland (a *goiter*) is a symptom of iodine deficiency. In developed countries, where iodine is added to table salt, goiter is uncommon. In some regions of the world, however, iodine deficiency is a common and serious problem that results not only in goiter but also in severe mental retardation in infants (*cretinism*).

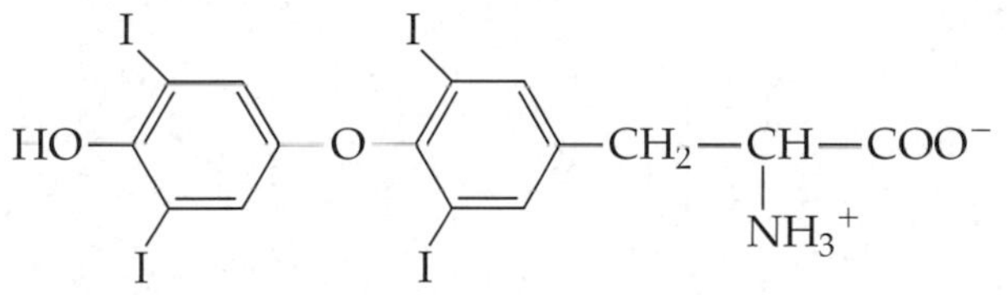

Thyroxine

Polypeptides

Polypeptides are the largest class of hormones. They range widely in molecular size and complexity, as illustrated by two hormones that control the thyroid gland, *thyrotropin-releasing hormone (TRH)* and *thyroid-stimulating hormone (TSH)*. TRH, a modified tripeptide, is a regulatory hormone released by the hypothalamus. At the pituitary gland, TRH activates release of TSH, a protein that has 208 amino acid residues in two chains. TSH in turn triggers release of amino acid derivative hormones from the thyroid gland.

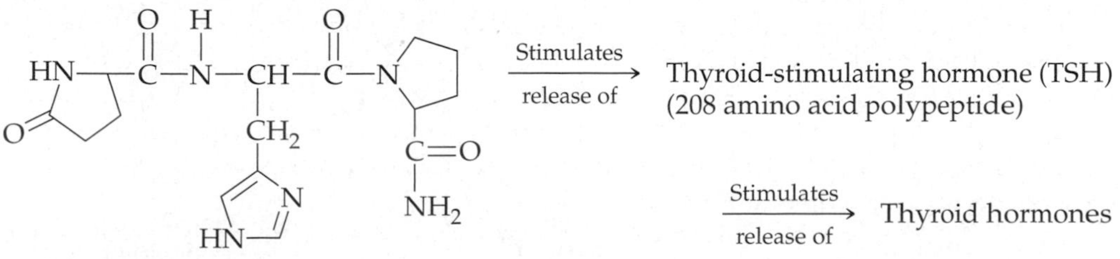

Thyrotropin-releasing hormone
(TRH)

Insulin, a protein containing 51 amino acids, is released by the pancreas in response to high concentrations of glucose in the blood. It stimulates cells to take up glucose and either use it to generate or store energy.

▶▶▶ Because of its importance in glucose metabolism and diabetes mellitus, the function of insulin as a hormone is described in Chapter 22 as part of the discussion of glucose metabolism.

PROBLEM 28.4

Examine the TRH structure and identify the three amino acids from which it is derived. (The N-terminal amino acid has undergone ring formation, and the carboxyl group at the C-terminal end has been converted to an amide.)

🗝️ **KEY CONCEPT PROBLEM 28.5**

Look at the structure of thyroxine shown earlier in this section. Is thyroxine, an amino acid derivative, hydrophobic or hydrophilic? Explain.

28.5 Steroid Hormones

Sterols have in common a central structure composed of the four connected rings you saw in Chapter 23 (see p. 738). Recall that because they are soluble in hydrophobic solvents and not in water, sterols are classified as lipids. Sterol hormones, referred to as steroids, are divided according to function into three types: mineralcorticoids, glucocorticoids (these were discussed in Chapter 23), and the sex hormones, responsible for male and female hormonal and physical characteristics.

The two most important male sex hormones, or androgens, are testosterone and androsterone. These steroids are responsible for the development of male secondary sex characteristics during puberty and for promoting tissue and muscle growth.

Male sex hormones (androgens)

Testosterone 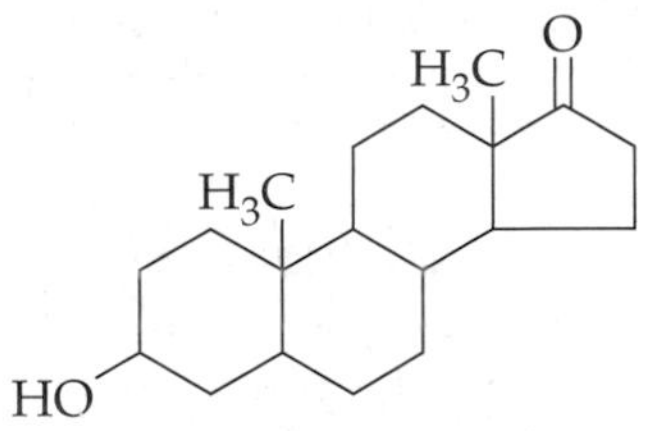   Androsterone

Estrone and *estradiol*, the female steroid hormones known as *estrogens*, are synthesized from testosterone, primarily in the ovaries but also to a small extent in the adrenal cortex. Estrogens govern development of female secondary sex characteristics and participate in regulation of the menstrual cycle. The *progestins*, principally *progesterone*, are released by the ovaries during the second half of the menstrual cycle and prepare the uterus for implantation of a fertilized ovum should conception occur.

Female sex hormones

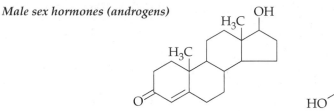

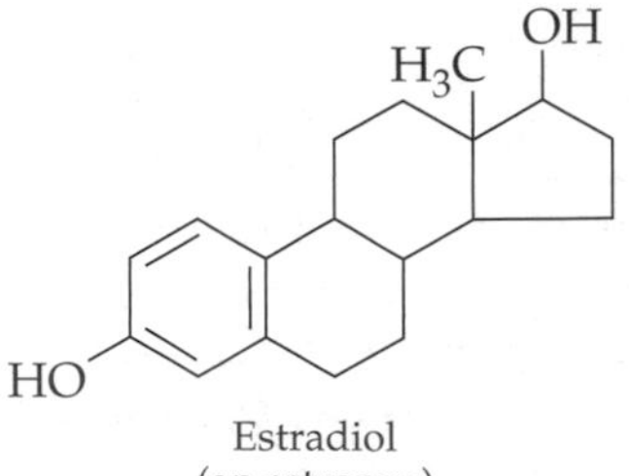

Estradiol
(an estrogen)

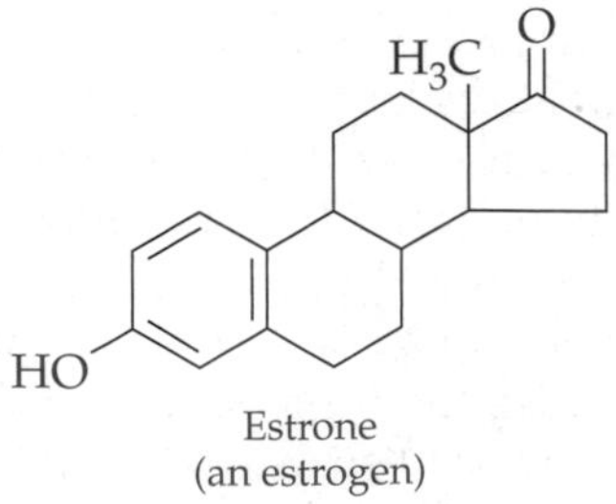

Estrone
(an estrogen)

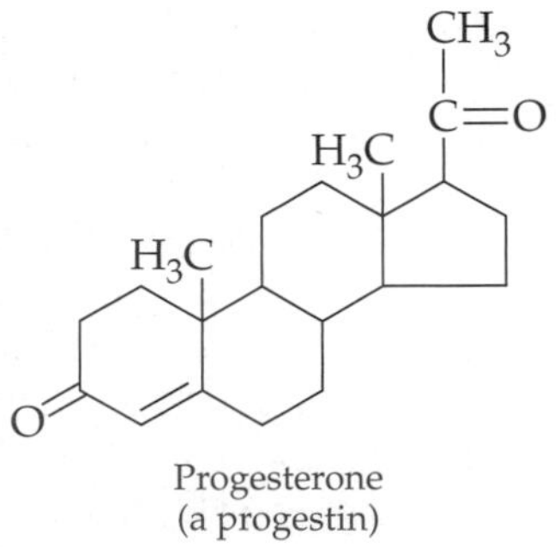

Progesterone
(a progestin)

In addition to the several hundred known steroids isolated from plants and animals, others have been synthesized in the laboratory in the search for new drugs. Most birth control pills are a mixture of the synthetic estrogen *ethynyl estradiol* and the synthetic progestin *norethindrone*. These steroids function by tricking the body into a false pregnant state, making it temporarily infertile. The compound known as *RU-486*, or *mifepristone*, is effective as a "morning after" pill. It prevents pregnancy by binding strongly to the progesterone receptor, thereby blocking implantation in the uterus of a fertilized egg cell. The morning after pill is available in the United States, but must be dispensed by a physician.

Ethynyl estradiol
(a synthetic estrogen)

Norethindrone
(a synthetic progestin)

RU-486
(Mifepristone)

Anabolic steroids, which have the ability to increase muscle mass and consequently strength, are drugs that resemble androgenic (male) hormones, such as testosterone. These steroids have been used by bodybuilders for decades to change their body shape to a more muscular, bulky form; some professional and semiprofessional athletes (both men and women) have used them in the hope of gaining weight, strength, power, speed, endurance, and aggressiveness. Unfortunately, many serious side effects can arise from this abuse of anabolic steroids. Stunted bone growth in adolescents; cancer of the liver, prostate, and kidney; high blood pressure; aggressive behavior; liver damage; irregular heartbeat; and nosebleeds (arising out of blood coagulation disorders) are but a few of the short- and long-term side effects of these agents. Today, most organized amateur and professional sports have banned the use of these and other "performance-enhancing" drugs.

Despite bans, the use of "roids" is widespread in sports. For example, so many baseball players have apparently used anabolic steroids that several congressional hearings have been held on this topic in recent years. Several trainers and players from baseball and other sports have testified, and as a result some individual records are now in question. One of the first athletes outside of baseball to be investigated was Marion Jones, a high-profile track star. She pled guilty in 2007 to using steroids while training for and during her Olympic medal events. She has been stripped of her medals, as have her relay teammates. The list of anabolic steroid users is long and includes cyclists, shot putters, and sprinters. Bulgaria's weightlifters did not participate in the 2008 Summer Olympic Games because routine testing revealed the presence of a banned steroid in every team member.

Did you know that it is legal to treat race horses with anabolic steroids in nearly every state? However, this use has been curtailed in some states, as it has been in humans, spurred by the events of the 2008 Kentucky Derby, when the horse Eight Belles collapsed at the finish line and had to be destroyed. The consensus of racing officials and horse owners is that because Eight Belles was given anabolic steroids, her muscle growth far outpaced bone growth. The combined stress of disproportionately high muscle mass and running the race caused both front ankles to break at the finish line.

To enforce the ban on anabolic steroids, athletes are subjected to random drug screening, but some athletes attempt to get around the screenings by using *designer steroids*—steroids that cannot be detected with current screening methods because identification depends on knowing the compound's structure. However, analysis of a synthetic steroid to determine its structure is easily done. For example, in October 2003, chemists announced that they had identified a new performance-enhancing (and previously undetectable) synthetic steroid. The illegal use of this new compound, tetrahydrogestrinone (THG), was discovered when an anonymous coach sent a spent

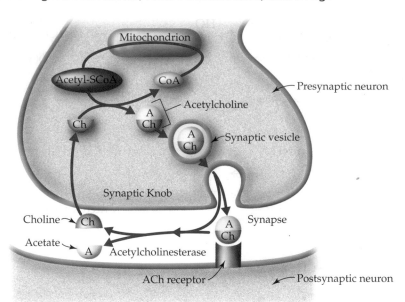

▶ **Figure 28.7**

Acetylcholine release and re-uptake. Acetylcholine is stored in vesicles in the presynaptic neuron. After it is released into the synapse and connects with its receptor, it is broken down by hydrolysis into acetate and choline in a reaction catalyzed by acetylcholinesterase. The choline is taken back into the synaptic knob and reused to synthesize acetylcholine, which is then stored in the vesicles until needed.

PROBLEM 28.9

Propranolol (trade name, Inderal®) is an antagonist for certain epinephrine receptors and is a member of the class of drugs known as beta blockers (because they block what are known as beta receptors). Circle the functional groups in propranolol and name them. Compare the structure of propranolol with the structure of epinephrine and describe the differences.

Propranolol
(Inderal®)

Epinephrine
(adrenaline)

Drugs and Acetylcholine

Many drugs act at acetylcholine synapses, where the tip of a neuron that releases acetylcholine and its target cell lie adjacent to each other. A **drug** is any molecule that alters normal functions when it enters the body from an external source. The action is at the molecular level, and it can be either therapeutic or poisonous. To have an effect, many drugs must connect with a receptor just as a substrate must bind to an enzyme or as a hormone or neurotransmitter must bind to a receptor. In fact, many drugs are designed to mimic a given hormone or neurotransmitter and in so doing elicit either an enhanced or attenuated effect.

Pharmacologists classify some drugs as **agonists**—substances that act to produce or prolong the normal biochemical response of a receptor. Other drugs are classified as **antagonists**—substances that block or inhibit the normal response of a receptor. Many agonists and antagonists compete with normal signaling molecules for interaction with the receptor, just as inhibitor molecules compete with substrate for the active site in an enzyme. To illustrate the ways in which drugs can affect our biochemical activity, we next describe the action of a group of drugs. These drugs are all members of the same drug family in the sense that their biochemical activity occurs at acetylcholine synapses in the central nervous system. The locations of their actions can be seen in Figure 28.7.

Drug Any substance that alters body function when it is introduced from an external source.

Agonist A substance that interacts with a receptor to cause or prolong the receptor's normal biochemical response.

Antagonist A substance that blocks or inhibits the normal biochemical response of a receptor.

- *Botulinus toxin (an antagonist) blocks acetylcholine release and causes botulism.* The toxin, which is produced by bacterial growth in improperly canned food, binds irreversibly to the presynaptic neuron, where acetylcholine would be released. It prevents this release, frequently causing death due to muscle paralysis. Commercially, this toxin (marketed as Botox®) has found use in cosmetic surgery, where carefully controlled doses of it are used to temporarily tighten up wrinkled skin without the need for invasive surgical procedures. Recent experiments have shown that Botox® does not stay at the injection site but migrates along neurons to the brain, far from the original injection.

- *Black widow spider venom (an agonist) releases excess acetylcholine.* In the opposite reaction from that of botulism toxin, the synapse is flooded with acetylcholine, resulting in muscle cramps and spasms.

- *Organophosphorus insecticides (antagonists) inhibit acetylcholinesterase.* All of the organophosphorus insecticides (a few examples are shown below) prevent acetylcholinesterase from breaking down acetylcholine within the synapse. As a result, the nerves are overstimulated, causing a variety of symptoms including muscle contraction and weakness, lack of coordination, and at high doses, convulsions. Recently, the death of thousands of honeybees was attributed to clothianidin dust released from the protective coating on corn seeds during planting. Many organophosphorus compounds are also used as nerve gasses, which is why agriculturists receive special safety training before using these insecticides on crops.

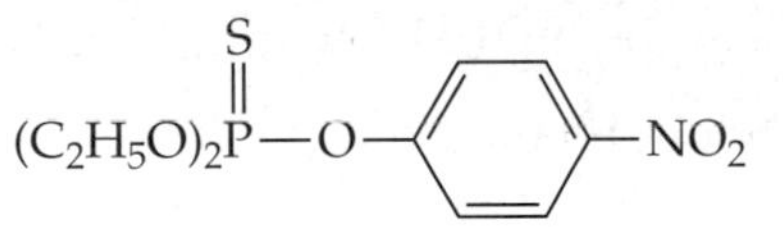

Parathion 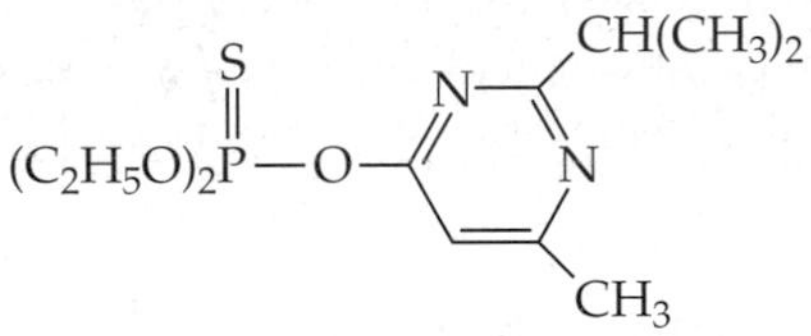   Diazinon 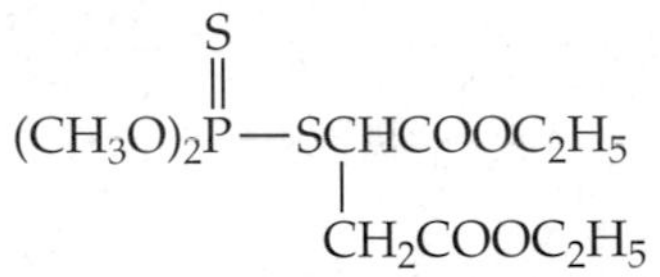   Malathion

- *Nicotine binds to acetylcholine receptors.* *Nicotine* at low doses is a stimulant (an agonist) because it activates acetylcholine receptors. The sense of alertness and well-being produced by inhaling tobacco smoke is a result of this effect. At high doses, nicotine is an antagonist. It irreversibly blocks the acetylcholine receptors and can cause their degeneration. Nicotine has no therapeutic use in humans other than in overcoming addiction to smoking. Nicotine transdermal patches, which release a small, controlled dose of nicotine through the skin, and chewing gum containing nicotine are used to help smokers overcome nicotine addiction. Nicotine (along with its sulfate salt) is one of the most toxic botanical insecticides known and has been used since the 1600s as a contact poison.

- *Atropine (an antagonist) competes with acetylcholine at receptors.* Atropine, found naturally in the nightshade plant, is an alkaloid that is a poison at high doses. At controlled doses, its therapeutic uses include acceleration of abnormally slow heart rate, paralysis of eye muscles during surgery, and relaxation of intestinal muscles in gastrointestinal disorders. Most importantly, it is a specific antidote for acetylcholinesterase poisons such as organophosphorus insecticides. By blocking activation of the receptors, it counteracts the excess acetylcholine created by acetylcholinesterase inhibitors.

▶▶▶ Alkaloids are naturally occurring, nitrogen-containing compounds isolated from plants; usually basic, bitter, and poisonous (see Section 15.6).

- *Tubocurarine (an antagonist) competes with acetylcholine at receptors.* Purified from curare, a mixture of chemicals extracted from a plant found in South America, the alkaloid tubocurarine is used to paralyze patients in conjunction with anesthesia drugs prior to surgery. In the last 30 years, researchers have developed safer, more easily purified synthetic derivatives that have the same mode of action. These molecules have nearly replaced use of tubocurarine in medical procedures.

PROBLEM 28.10

The LD_{50} values (lethal dose in mg/kg, for rats; see Chemistry in Action: How Toxic Is Toxic? p. 499) for the three organophosphorus insecticides listed in this section are parathion, 3–13 mg/kg; diazinon, 250–285 mg/kg; and malathion, 1000–1375 mg/kg. (a) Which would you choose for use in your garden and why? (b) Which is most dangerous for mammals to ingest? Why?

🔑 **KEY CONCEPT PROBLEM 28.11**

Some drugs are classified as agonists whereas others are classified as antagonists.

(a) Sumatripan, sold as Imitrex®, is effective in treating migraine headaches. It acts as an agonist at the serotonin receptor. Explain the effect Imitrex® has on the serotonin receptor.

(b) Ondansetron, sold as Zofran®, acts on a subclass of serotonin receptors to inhibit nausea and vomiting; it is frequently prescribed to patients in chemotherapy. It acts as an antagonist at these receptors. Explain the effect Zofran® has on these receptors.

28.8 Histamine and Antihistamines

Histamine is the neurotransmitter responsible for the symptoms of the allergic reaction so familiar to hay fever sufferers or those who are allergic to animals. It is also the chemical that causes an itchy bump when an insect bites you. In the body, histamine is produced by decarboxylation of the amino acid histidine:

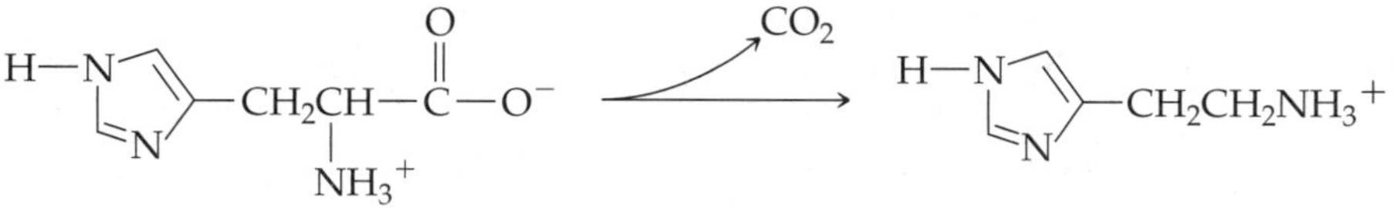

Histidine   Histamine

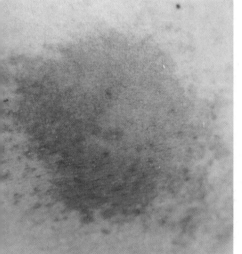

▲ The swelling and inflammation surrounding this insect bite are due to a histamine response.

The *antihistamines* are a family of drugs that counteract the effect of histamine because they are histamine-receptor antagonists. They competitively block the attachment of histamine to its receptors. Members of this family all have in common a disubstituted ethylamine side chain, usually with two *N*-methyl groups. As illustrated by the examples below, the R′ and R″ groups at the other end of the molecule tend to be bulky and aromatic.

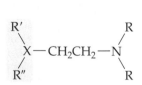

General antihistamine structure

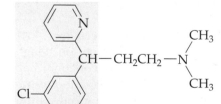

Chlorpheniramine
(an antihistamine)

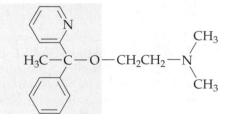

Doxylamine
(an antihistamine)

Histamine also activates secretion of acid in the stomach. Development of an antagonist for this function of histamine was accomplished by what is today commonly known as *rational drug design*. After synthesis of about 200 different compounds with systematic variations on the histamine structure, the goal of attaining a histamine antagonist was achieved. The result was *cimetidine*, widely publicized as a treatment for heartburn under its trade name of Tagamet®. Today many other histamine antagonists exist, including ranitidine, sold under its trade name of Zantac®.

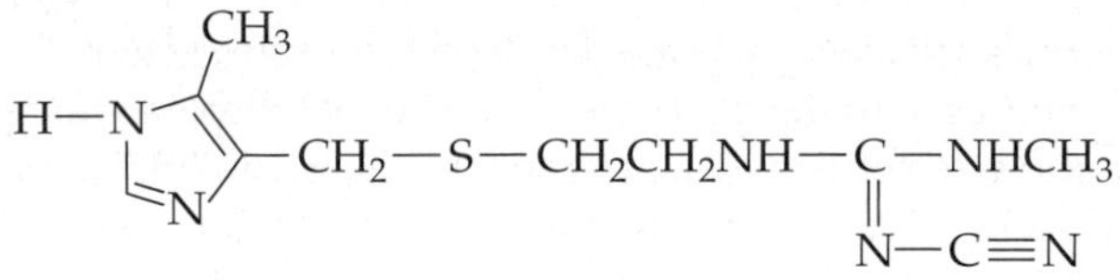

Cimetidine
(Tagamet®)

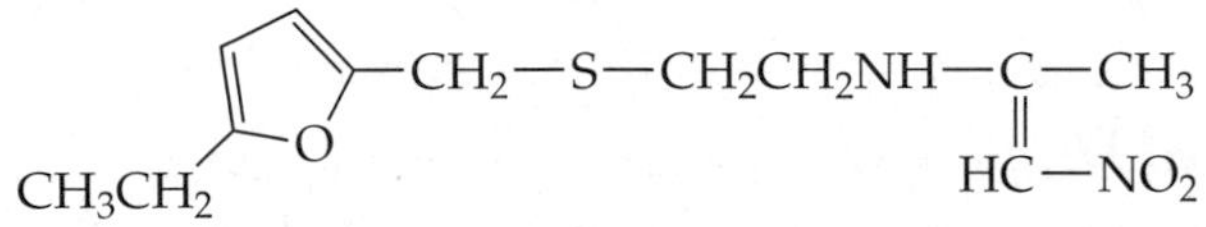

Ranitidine
(Zantac®)

28.9 Serotonin, Norepinephrine, and Dopamine

The Monoamines and Therapeutic Drugs

Serotonin, norepinephrine, and dopamine could be called the "big three" of neurotransmitters. Regular news reports appear as discoveries about them accumulate. Collectively, serotonin, norepinephrine, and dopamine are known as *monoamines*. (Their biochemical syntheses are shown in Figures 28.4 and 28.6.) All are active in the brain and all have been identified in various ways with mood, the experiences of fear and pleasure, mental illness, and drug addiction. Needless to say, chemistry plays a central role in mental illness—that has become an inescapable conclusion.

One well-established relationship is the connection between major depression and a deficiency of serotonin, norepinephrine, and dopamine. The evidence comes from the different modes of action of three families of drugs used to treat depression. Amitriptyline, phenelzine, and fluoxetine are representative of these three types of drugs. Each in its own way increases the concentration of the neurotransmitters at synapses.

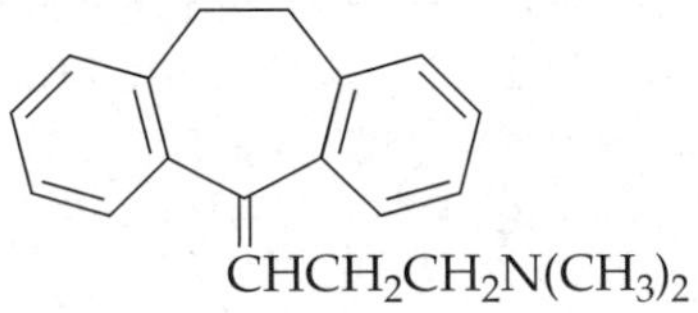

Amitriptyline, a tricyclic antidepressant
(Elavil®)

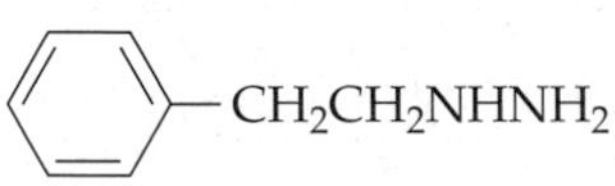

Phenelzine, an MAO inhibitor
(Nardil®)

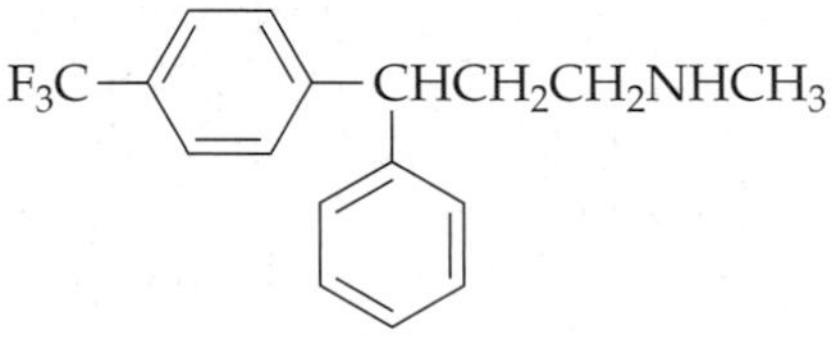

Fluoxetine, an SSRI
(Prozac®)

- Amitriptyline is representative of the *tricyclic antidepressants*, which were the first generation of these drugs. The tricyclics prevent the re-uptake of serotonin and norepinephrine from within the synapse. Serotonin is important in mood-control pathways and functions more slowly than other neurotransmitters; slowing its re-uptake often improves mood in depressed patients.
- Phenelzine is a *monoamine oxidase (MAO) inhibitor*, one of a group of medications that inhibit the enzyme that breaks down monoamine neurotransmitters. This inhibition of *monoamine oxidase* allows the concentrations of monoamines at synapses to increase.
- Fluoxetine represents the newest class of antidepressants, the *selective serotonin re-uptake inhibitors (SSRI)*. They are more selective than the tricyclics because they inhibit only the re-uptake of serotonin. Fluoxetine (Prozac®) has rapidly become the most widely prescribed drug for all but the most severe forms of depression. Most antidepressants cause unpleasant side effects; fluoxetine does not, a major benefit.

It is important to note that the relief of the symptoms of depression by these drugs is not evidence that either the chemical basis of depression is fully understood or that increasing neurotransmitter concentration is the only action of these drugs. The brain still holds many secrets. As one of the pharmacologists who developed fluoxetine put it, "If the human brain were simple enough for us to understand, we would be too simple to understand it."

The complex and not yet fully understood relationships between neurotransmitter activity and behavior are illustrated by the use of fluoxetine for conditions other than depression. It is used to treat obsessive compulsive disorder, bulimia, obesity, panic disorder, body dysmorphic disorder, teen depression, and premenstrual dysphoric disorder (formerly known as PMS). New uses for this class of drugs are constantly being explored.

Dopamine and Drug Addiction

Dopamine plays a role in the brain in processes that control movement, emotional responses, and the experiences of pleasure and pain. It interacts with five different kinds of receptors in different parts of the brain. An oversupply of dopamine is associated with schizophrenia, and an undersupply results in the loss of fine motor control in Parkinson's disease (see Chemistry in Action: The Blood–Brain Barrier, p. 878). Dopamine also plays an important role in the brain's reward system. An ample supply of brain dopamine produces the pleasantly satisfied feeling that results from a rewarding experience—a "natural high." Herein lies the role of dopamine in drug addiction: the more the dopamine receptors are stimulated, the greater the high.

Experiments show that cocaine blocks re-uptake of dopamine from the synapse, and amphetamines accelerate release of dopamine. Studies have linked increased brain levels of dopamine to alcohol and nicotine addiction as well. The higher-than-normal stimulation of dopamine receptors by drugs results in tolerance. In the drive to maintain constant conditions (see Chemistry in Action: Homeostasis, p. 845), the number of dopamine receptors decreases and the sensitivity of those that remain decreases. Consequently, brain cells require more and more of a drug for the same result, a condition that contributes to addiction.

Marijuana also creates an increase in dopamine levels in the same brain areas where dopamine levels increase after administration of heroin or cocaine. The most active ingredient in marijuana is tetrahydrocannabinol (THC). The use of marijuana medically for chronic pain relief has become a controversial topic in recent years, as questions about its benefits and drawbacks are debated.

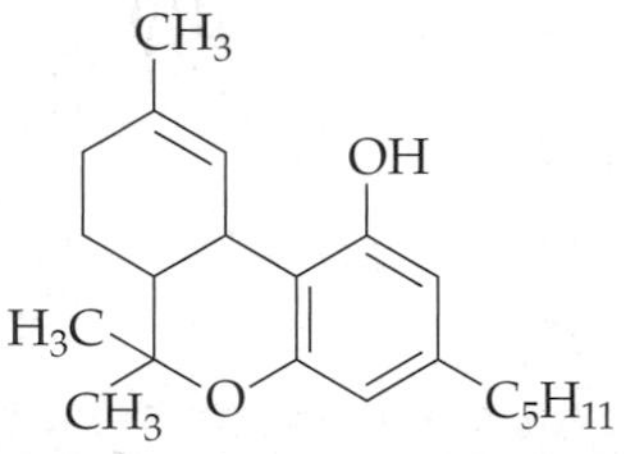

Tetrahydrocannabinol (THC)

🔑 KEY CONCEPT PROBLEM 28.12

Identify the functional groups present in THC. Is the molecule likely to be hydrophilic or hydrophobic? Would you expect THC to build up in fatty tissues in the body, or would it be readily eliminated in the urine?

Worked Example 28.2 Predicting Biological Activity Based on Structure

The relationship between the structure of a molecule and its biochemical function is an essential area of study in biochemistry and the design of drugs. Terfenadine (Seldane®) was one of the first of the new generation of "nondrowsy" antihistamines (it was removed from the market due to potential heart toxicity). Based solely on what you have learned so far, suggest which of its structural features make it an antihistamine.

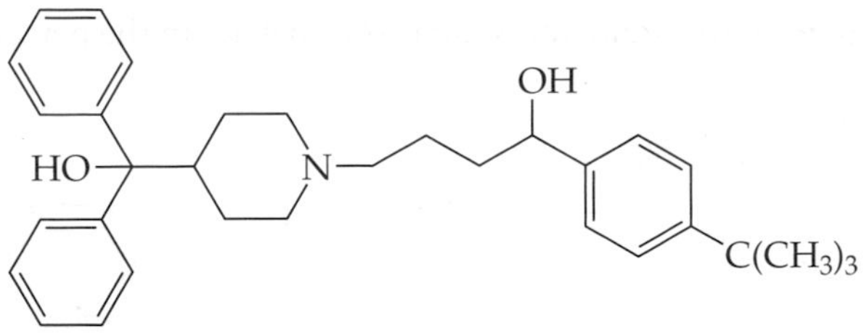

Terfenadine

ANALYSIS From Section 28.8, we see that members of the antihistamine family have in common the general structure shown here: an X group (usually a CH) to which two aromatic groups (noted as *aryl* in the drawing) are attached. The X is also attached to a disubstituted nitrogen by a carbon chain:

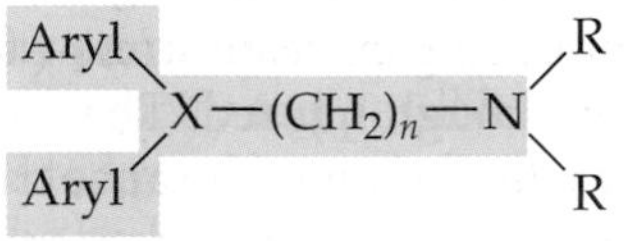

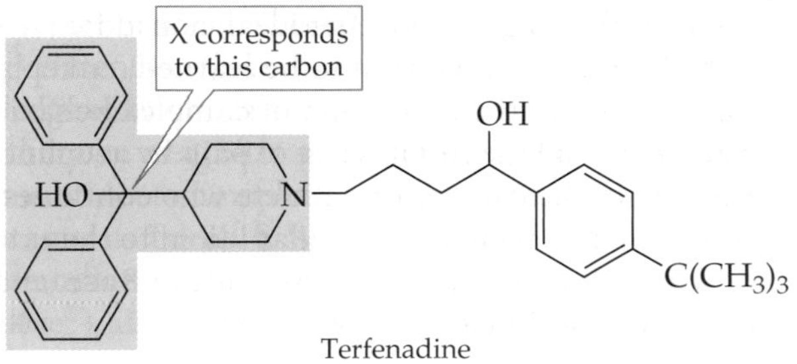

Terfenadine

SOLUTION
Since terfenadine contains the same basic structure as a general antihistamine, its biological function should be similar.

🔑 **KEY CONCEPT PROBLEM 28.13**

Predict which of the following compounds is an antihistamine and which is an antidepressant.

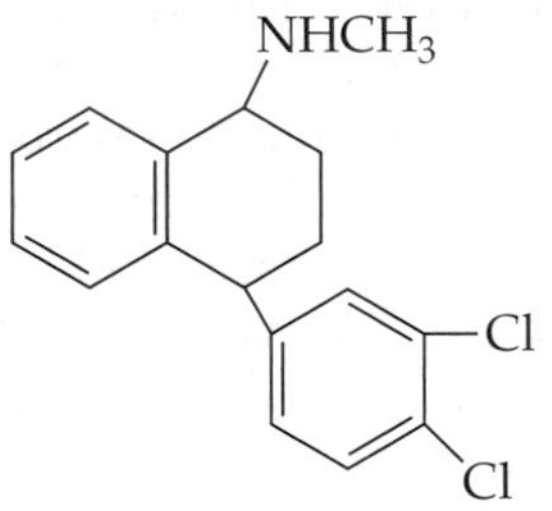

28.10 Neuropeptides and Pain Relief

Studies of morphine and other opium derivatives in the 1970s revealed that these addictive but effective pain-killing substances act via their own specific brain receptors. This raised some interesting questions: why are there brain receptors for chemicals from a plant? Could it be that there are animal neurotransmitters that act at the same receptors?

The two pentapeptides *Met-enkephalin* and *Leu-enkephalin* (Met and Leu stand for the carboxy terminal amino acids, Section 18.3) were discovered in the effort to answer these questions.

Met-enkephalin: Tyr-Gly-Gly-Phe-Met
Leu-enkephalin: Tyr-Gly-Gly-Phe-Leu

HOW HORMONES WORK: EPINEPHRINE

28.34 In what gland is epinephrine produced and released?

28.35 Under what circumstances is epinephrine released?

28.36 How does epinephrine reach its target tissues?

28.37 What is the main function of epinephrine at its target tissues?

28.38 In order of their involvement, name the three membrane-bound proteins involved in transmitting the epinephrine message across the cell membrane.

28.39 What is the "second messenger" inside the cell that results from the epinephrine message? Is the ratio of epinephrine molecules to second messenger less than $1:1$, $1:1$, or greater than $1:1$? Explain.

28.40 What role does the second messenger play in a cell stimulated by epinephrine?

28.41 What enzyme catalyzes hydrolysis of the second messenger to terminate the message? What is the product called?

28.42 Epinephrine is used clinically in the treatment of what life-threatening allergic response?

28.43 People susceptible to anaphylactic shock due to insect stings or certain food allergies must be prepared to treat themselves in case of exposure. How are they prepared and what must they do?

HORMONES

28.44 Give an example of a polypeptide hormone. How many amino acids are in the hormone? Where is the hormone released? Where does the hormone function? What is the result of the hormone message?

28.45 Give an example of a steroid hormone. What is the structure of the hormone? Where is the hormone released? Where does the hormone function? What is the result of the hormone message?

28.46 What do the three major classes of steroid hormones have in common?

28.47 What molecule are the steroid hormones derived from? How does that make the physical properties of steroid hormones different from the other hormones?

28.48 Name the two primary male sex hormones.

28.49 Name the three principal female sex hormones.

28.50 Until relatively recently, the use of androgens by athletes was a common, legal practice. What are the advantages of using androgens during athletic training and competition?

28.51 The use of androgens during athletic training and competition has been banned in national and international sports. What are the disadvantages of using androgens during athletic training and competition?

28.52 List two hormones that also function as neurotransmitters.

28.53 Explain why epinephrine can act as both a neurotransmitter and a hormone without "crossover" between the two functions.

28.54 Identify the class to which each of these hormones belongs:

(a)

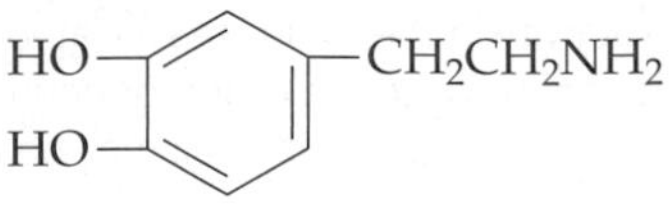

(b) Insulin

(c)

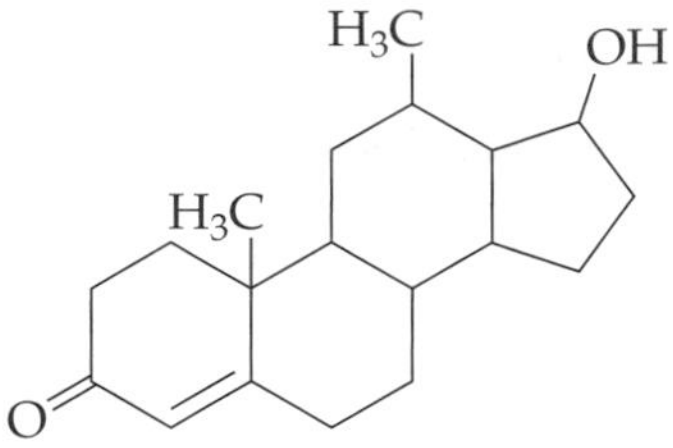

28.55 Identify the class to which each of these hormones belongs:

(a) Glucagon

(b)

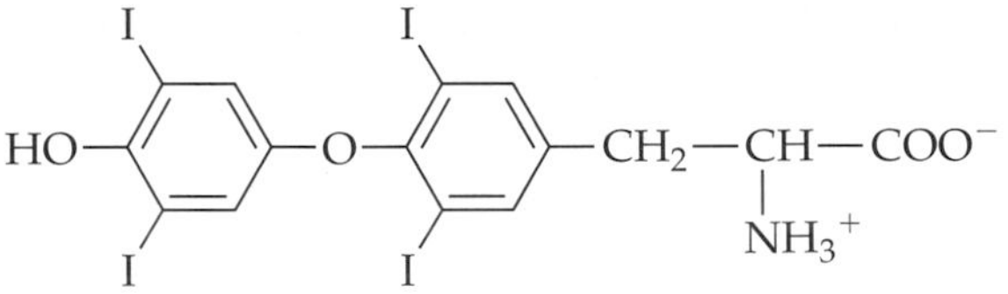

Thyroxine

(c)

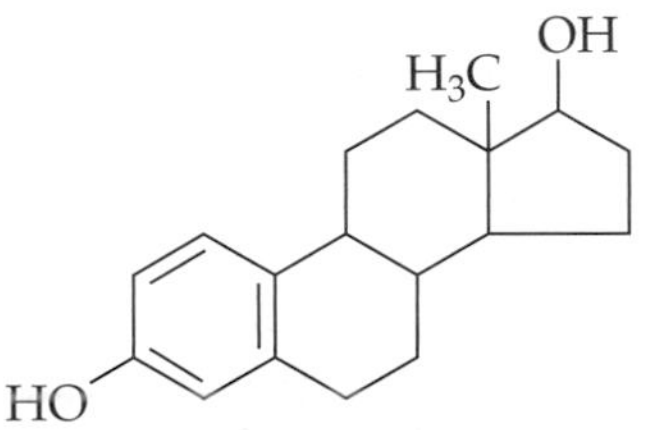

Estradiol

NEUROTRANSMITTERS

28.56 What is a synapse, and what role does it play in nerve transmission?

28.57 What is an axon, and what role does it play in nerve transmission?

28.58 List three cell types that might receive a message transmitted by a neurotransmitter.

28.59 What kinds of cellular or organ actions would you expect to be influenced by neurotransmitters?

28.60 Describe in general terms how a nerve impulse is passed from one neuron to another.

28.61 What are the two methods for removing the neurotransmitter once its job is done?

28.62 List the three steps in chemical transmission of the impulse between a nerve cell and its target.

28.63 Write an equation for the reaction that is catalyzed by acetylcholinesterase.

28.64 Why are enkephalins sometimes called *neurohormones*?

28.65 Outline the six steps in cholinergic nerve transmission.

CHEMICAL MESSENGERS AND DRUGS

28.66 Describe the difference between drugs that are agonists and those that are antagonists.

28.67 Give an example of a drug that acts as an agonist for acetylcholine receptors and one that acts as an antagonist for these receptors.

28.68 Give examples of two histamine antagonists that have very different tissue specificities and functions.

28.69 Give an example of a drug from each family in Problem 28.68.

28.70 Name three families of drugs used to treat depression.

28.71 Name the "big three" monoamine neurotransmitters.

28.72 What is the impact and mode of action of cocaine on dopamine levels in the brain?

28.73 What is the impact and mode of action of amphetamines on dopamine levels in the brain?

28.74 How is the tetrahydrocannabinol of marijuana similar in action to heroin and cocaine?

28.75 Why do we have brain receptors that respond to morphine and other opium derivatives from plants?

28.76 In schizophrenia, the neurons affected by dopamine are overstimulated. This condition is treated with drugs like chlorpromazine (Thorazine®), which bind to the affected receptors and inhibit the dopamine signal. Does chlorpromazine act as an agonist or antagonist?

28.77 Methamphetamine "highs" often are accompanied by behavioral changes that resemble schizophrenia. Does methamphetamine act as an agonist or antagonist?

28.78 What are endorphins? Where in the body are they found?

28.79 "Runner's high," sexual excitement, and other complex behaviors are believed to involve which neuropeptides?

28.80 Enkephalins and endorphins are referred to as "nature's opiates." Explain this saying.

28.81 Why might it be an advantage for an animal to produce its own pain suppressing molecules?

28.82 What does an ethnobotanist do?

28.83 Combinatorial chemistry has added hundreds of drugs to the pharmaceutical market in recent years. What is the basis of the combinatorial approach to drug design? What advantages might the combinatorial approach have for the pharmaceutical industry?

28.84 In what ways are studies of the exact size and shape of biomolecules (such as enzymes, receptors, signal transducers, and so on) leading to the development of new drugs to treat disease?

28.85 How are computers used in the development of new drugs to treat disease?

CHEMISTRY IN ACTION

28.86 One of the responsibilities of the endocrine system is maintenance of homeostasis in the body. Briefly explain what is meant by the term *homeostasis*. [*Homeostasis, p. 845*]

28.87 What is the goal of the measurements of clinical chemistry? [*Homeostasis, p. 845*]

28.88 In animals, hormones are produced by the endocrine glands and tissues in various parts of the body. Why is it necessary for plants to synthesize the hormones in the cells where they are needed rather than in specialized cells? [*Plant Hormones, p. 855*]

28.89 How does 2,4-D, a weed killer, take advantage of the function of a plant hormone? [*Plant Hormones, p. 855*]

GENERAL QUESTIONS AND PROBLEMS

28.90 Suppose you are hiking in the Alaskan wilderness when your path crosses that of a bear. What hormone is responsible for your immediate response?

28.91 How do curare-treated arrows work?

28.92 What characteristics in their mechanism of action does thyroxine share with the steroid hormones?

28.93 List and describe the functions of the three types of proteins involved in transmission of a hormone signal.

28.94 The cyclic AMP (second messenger) of signal transmission is very reactive and breaks down rapidly after synthesis. Why is this important to the signal-transmission process?

28.95 We say that there is signal amplification in the transmission process. Explain how signal amplification occurs and what it means for transmission of the signal to the sites of cellular activity.

28.96 The phosphodiesterase that catalyzes hydrolysis of cyclic AMP is inhibited by caffeine. What overall effect would caffeine have on a signal that is mediated by cAMP?

28.97 Compare the structures of the sex hormones testosterone and progesterone. What portions of the structures are the same? Where do they differ?

28.98 When you compare the structures of ethynyl estradiol to norethindrone, where do they differ? Where is ethynyl estradiol similar to estradiol? Where is norethindrone similar to progesterone?

28.99 Anandamides have been isolated from brain tissues and appear to be the natural ligand for the receptor that also binds tetrahydrocannabinol. Anandamides have also been discovered in chocolate and cocoa powder. How might the craving for chocolate be explained?

An anandamide structure

28.100 Identify the structural changes that occur in the first two steps in the conversion of tyrosine to epinephrine (Figure 28.4). To what main classes and subclasses of enzymes do the enzymes that catalyze these reactions belong?

28.101 Look at the structures of the two male sex hormones shown on p. 852. Identify the type of functional group change that interconverts testosterone and androsterone. To which class of chemical reactions does this change belong?

28.102 Look at the structures of the three female sex hormones shown on p. 852. Identify the type of functional group change that interconverts estradiol and estrone. To which class of chemical reactions does this change belong?

CHAPTER 29

Body Fluids

CONTENTS

◄ Blood and other body fluids help maintain the delicate balance between life and death often faced during medical emergencies.

CHAPTER GOALS

1. **How are body fluids classified?**
   THE GOAL: Be able to describe the major categories of body fluids, their general composition, and the exchange of solutes between them. (◀◀ A, B.)

2. **What are the roles of blood in maintaining homeostasis?**
   THE GOAL: Be able to explain the composition and functions of blood. (◀◀ B, C.)

3. **How do blood components participate in the body's defense mechanisms?**
   THE GOAL: Be able to identify and describe the roles of blood components

that participate in inflammation, the immune response, and blood clotting.

4. **How do red blood cells participate in the transport of blood gases?**
   THE GOAL: Be able to explain the relationships among O_2 and CO_2 transport, and acid–base balance. (◀◀ D.)

5. **How is the composition of urine controlled?**
   THE GOAL: Be able to describe the transfer of water and solutes during urine formation and give an overview of the composition of urine. (◀◀ B, C.)

CONCEPTS TO REVIEW

A. Solutions
(Sections 9.1, 9.2, 9.10)

B. Osmosis and Osmotic Pressure
(Section 9.12)

C. Dialysis
(Section 9.13)

D. pH
(Sections 10.7, 10.8)

We have chosen to put this chapter as the last one in your text because just about every aspect of chemistry you have studied so far applies to the subject of this chapter—body fluids. Electrolytes, nutrients and waste products, metabolic intermediates, and chemical messengers flow through your body in blood and in lymph fluid and exit as waste in the urine and feces. The chemical compositions of blood and urine mirror chemical reactions throughout the body. Fortunately, samples of these fluids are easily collected and studied. Many advances in understanding biological chemistry have been based on information obtained from analysis of blood and urine. As a result, studies of blood and urine chemistry provide information essential for the diagnosis and treatment of disease.

29.1 Body Water and Its Solutes

All body fluids have water as the solvent; in fact, the water content of the human body averages about 60% (by weight). Physiologists describe body water as occupying two different "compartments"—the *intracellular* and the *extracellular* compartments. We have looked primarily at the chemical reactions occurring in the **intracellular fluid** (the fluid inside cells), which includes about two-thirds of all body water (Figure 29.1). We now turn our attention to the remaining one-third of body water, the **extracellular fluid**, which includes mainly **blood plasma** (the fluid portion of blood) and **interstitial fluid** (the fluid that fills the spaces between cells).

To be soluble in water, a substance must be an ion, a gas, a small polar molecule, or a large molecule having many polar, hydrophilic (water-loving) or ionic groups on its surface. All four types of solutes are present in body fluids. The majority are inorganic ions and ionized biomolecules (mainly proteins), as shown in the comparison of blood plasma, interstitial fluid, and intracellular fluid in Figure 29.2. Although these fluids have different compositions, their **osmolarities** are the same; that is, they have the same number of moles of dissolved solute particles (ions or molecules) per liter. The osmolarity is kept in balance by the passage of water across cell membranes by osmosis, which occurs in response to osmolarity differences.

Inorganic ions, known collectively as *electrolytes* (Section 9.9), are major contributors to the osmolarity of body fluids and they move about as necessary to maintain charge balance. Water-soluble proteins make up a large proportion of the solutes in blood plasma and intracellular fluid; 100 mL of blood contains about 7 g of protein.

Intracellular fluid Fluid inside cells.

Extracellular fluid Fluid outside cells.

Blood plasma Liquid portion of the blood: an extracellular fluid.

Interstitial fluid Fluid surrounding cells: an extracellular fluid.

Osmolarity Amount of dissolved solute per volume of solution.

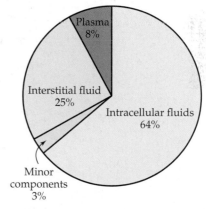

▲ **Figure 29.1**
Distribution of body water.
About two-thirds of body water is intracellular—within cells. The extracellular fluids include blood plasma, fluids surrounding cells (interstitial), and such minor components as lymph, cerebrospinal fluid, and the fluid that lubricates joints (synovial fluid).

▶▶ In osmosis, water moves across a semipermeable membrane from the more dilute solution to the more concentrated solution (see Section 9.12).

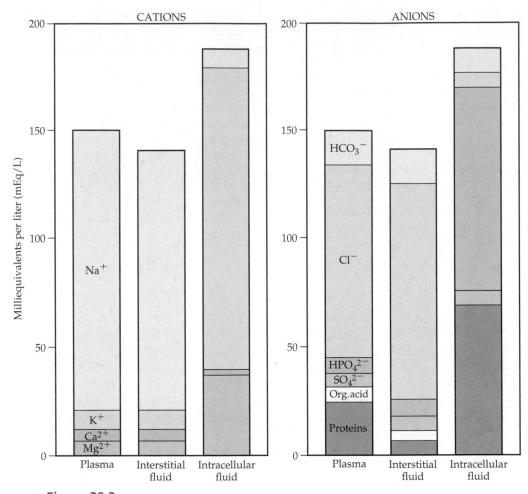

▲ **Figure 29.2**

The distribution of cations and anions in body fluids.

Outside cells, Na^+ is the major cation and Cl^- is the major anion. Inside cells, K^+ is the major cation and HPO_4^{2-} is the major anion. Note that at physiological pH, proteins are negatively charged.

Blood proteins are used to transport lipids and other molecules, and they play essential roles in blood clotting (Section 29.5) and the immune response (Section 29.4). The blood gases (oxygen and carbon dioxide), along with glucose, amino acids, and the nitrogen-containing by-products of protein catabolism, are the major small molecules in body fluids.

Blood travels through peripheral tissue in a network of tiny, hair-like capillaries that connect the arterial and venous parts of the circulatory system (Figure 29.3). Capillaries are where nutrients and end products of metabolism are exchanged between blood and interstitial fluid. Capillary walls consist of a single layer of loosely spaced cells. Water and many small solutes move freely across the capillary walls in response to differences in fluid pressure and concentration (see Figure 29.3).

Solutes that can cross membranes freely (passive diffusion) move from regions of high solute concentration to regions of low solute concentration. On the arterial ends of capillaries, blood pressure is higher than interstitial fluid pressure and solutes and water are pushed into interstitial fluid. On the venous ends of the capillaries, blood pressure is lower, and water and solutes from the surrounding tissues are able to reenter the blood plasma. The combined result of water and solute exchange at capillaries is that blood plasma and interstitial fluid are similar in composition (except for protein content; see Figure 29.2).

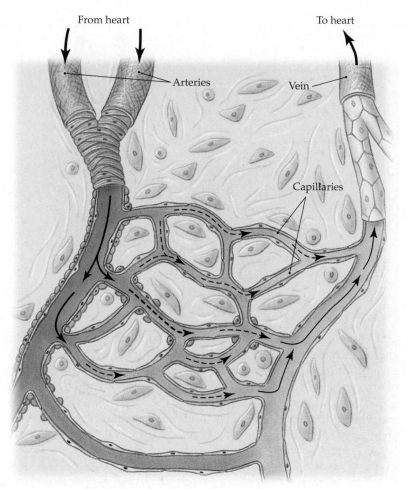

From heart

To heart

Arteries

Vein

Capillaries

◀ **Figure 29.3**
The capillary network.
Solute exchange between blood and interstitial fluid occurs across capillary walls.

In addition to blood capillaries, peripheral tissue is networked with lymph capillaries (Figure 29.4). The lymphatic system collects excess interstitial fluid, debris from cellular breakdown, and proteins and lipid droplets too large to pass through capillary walls. Interstitial fluid and the substances that accompany it into the lymphatic system are referred to as *lymph*, and the walls of lymph capillaries are constructed so that lymph cannot return to the surrounding tissue. Ultimately, lymph enters the bloodstream at the thoracic duct.

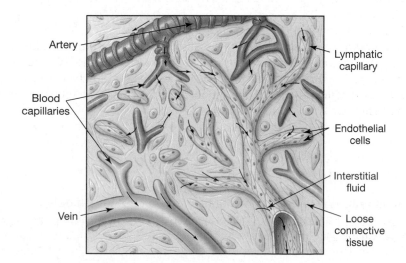

Artery

Blood capillaries

Vein

Lymphatic capillary

Endothelial cells

Interstitial fluid

Loose connective tissue

◀ **Figure 29.4**
Blood and lymph capillaries.
The arrows show the flow of fluids in and out of the various components of peripheral tissue.

▶ **Figure 29.5**
Exchange among body fluids.
Water exchanges freely in most tissues, with the result that the osmolarities of blood plasma, interstitial fluid, and intracellular fluid are the same. Large proteins cross neither capillary walls nor cell membranes, leaving the interstitial fluid protein concentration low. Concentration differences between interstitial fluid and intracellular fluid are maintained by active transport of Na^+ and K^+.

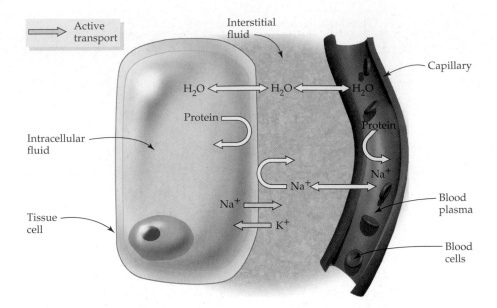

Exchange of solutes between the interstitial fluid and the intracellular fluid occurs by crossing cell membranes. Here, major differences in concentration are maintained by active transport (transport requiring energy) *against* concentration gradients (from regions of *low* concentration to regions of *high* concentration) and by the impermeability of cell membranes to certain solutes, notably the sodium ion (Figure 29.5). Sodium ion concentration is high in extracellular fluids and low in intracellular fluids, whereas potassium ion concentrations are just the reverse: high inside cells and low outside cells (see Figure 29.2).

🔑 **KEY CONCEPT PROBLEM 29.1**

The drug cisplatin is used to treat various forms of cancer in humans. As with many other drugs, the difficult part in designing the cisplatin molecule was to have a structure that ensures transport into the cell. The equilibrium reaction that takes place in the body when cisplatin is administered is

$$\begin{bmatrix} Cl & & NH_3 \\ & Pt & \\ Cl & & NH_3 \end{bmatrix} (aq) + H_2O(l) \rightleftharpoons \begin{bmatrix} Cl & & NH_3 \\ & Pt & \\ H_2O & & NH_3 \end{bmatrix}^{+} (aq) + Cl^-(aq)$$

Cisplatin   Monoaquacisplatin

(This is an example of *ligand exchange.*) Which form of cisplatin would you expect to exist inside the cell (where chloride concentrations are small)? Which form of cisplatin would you expect to exist outside the cell (where chloride concentrations are high)? Which form—cisplatin or monoaquacisplatin—enters the cell most readily? Why?

29.2 Fluid Balance

As you might imagine, preserving fluid balance—a constant amount of fluid in the body—is crucial in maintaining physiological homeostasis. One way we accomplish this is by ensuring that our daily intake of water is roughly enough to equal our daily output of water. Consider the following average intake/output water data for an adult human under normal environmental conditions, shown in Table 29.1.

Table 29.1 Adult Human Daily Average Water Intake/Output

Water Intake	(mL/day)	Water Output	(mL/day)
Drinking water	1200	Urine	1400
Water from food	1000	Skin	400
Water from metabolic oxidation of food	300	Lungs	400
		Sweat	100
		Feces	200
Total	2500		2500

What are the physiological effects if this delicate balance is not maintained? This question is especially important to endurance athletes such as marathon runners and cyclists. During the course of a typical endurance event, especially when performed in the heat, much fluid loss occurs with minimal fluid intake to counter it. This typically results in a loss of body mass during the event and makes it easy to monitor performance versus fluid loss. This has been studied and the results can be summarized as shown in Table 29.2.

Table 29.2 Effects of Body Mass Loss During Athletic Endurance Events

% Loss of Body Mass	Symptoms and Performance
0%	Normal heat regulation and performance
1%	Thirst is stimulated, heat regulation during exercise is altered, performance begins to decline
2–3%	Further decrease in heat regulation, increased thirst, worsening performance
4%	Exercise performance cut by 20–30%
5%	Headache, irritability, "spaced-out" feeling, fatigue
6%	Weakness, severe loss of thermoregulation
7%	Collapse is likely unless exercise is stopped

Exercise physiologists consider 4% body mass loss and above to be the "danger zone." In fact, the sports drink Gatorade® was developed in 1965 for just this reason. Doctors at the University of Florida developed the original formula to solve a serious problem for the school's football team: dehydration. This formula was so successful that by 1868 Gatorade® had become the official sports drink of the National Football League and today commands a major share of the sports-drink market, with gross sales of over 800 million dollars per year. One can see why research into hydration strategies has led to the plethora of "sports drinks" that are now available in your local supermarket. (See Chemistry in Action: Electrolytes, Fluid Replacement, and Sports Drinks, on p. 276.)

Physiologically, the intake of water and electrolytes is regulated, but not closely. However, the output of these substances is *very* closely controlled. Both the intake and output of water are controlled by hormones. Receptors in the hypothalamus monitor the concentration of solutes in blood plasma, and as little as a 2% change in osmolarity can cause an adjustment in hormone secretion. For example, when a rise in blood osmolarity indicates an increased concentration of solutes and therefore a shortage of water, secretion of *antidiuretic hormone* (ADH; also known as *vasopressin*) increases. One key role of the kidneys is to keep water and electrolytes in balance by increasing or decreasing the amounts eliminated. In the kidney, antidiuretic hormone causes a decrease in the water content of the urine. At the same time, osmoreceptors in the hypothalamus and baroreceptors in the heart and blood vessels activate the thirst mechanism, triggering increased water intake.

Antidiuretic hormone (ADH) is so tightly regulated that both oversecretion and undersecretion of this hormone can lead to serious disease states. Excess secretion can lead to what physicians refer to as the *syndrome of inappropriate antidiuretic hormone secretion (SIADH).* Two of the many causes of SIADH are regional low blood volume arising from decreased blood return to the heart (caused by, for example, asthma, pneumonia, pulmonary obstruction, or heart failure) and misinterpretation by the hypothalamus of osmolarity (due, for example, to central-nervous-system disorders, barbiturates, or morphine). When ADH secretion is too high, the kidney excretes too little water, the water content of body compartments increases, and serum concentrations of electrolytes drop to dangerously low levels.

The reverse problem, inadequate secretion of antidiuretic hormone, is often a result of injury to the hypothalamus, and causes *diabetes insipidus.* In this condition (unrelated to diabetes mellitus), up to 15 L of dilute urine is excreted each day. Administration of synthetic hormone can control the problem.

29.3 Blood

Blood flows through the body in the circulatory system, which in the absence of trauma or disease, is essentially a closed system. About 55% of blood is plasma, which contains the proteins and other solutes shown in Figure 29.6; the remaining 45% is a mixture of red blood cells (**erythrocytes**), platelets, and white blood cells (**leukocytes**).

The plasma and cells together make up **whole blood**, which is what is usually collected for clinical laboratory analysis. The whole blood sample is collected directly into evacuated tubes that contain an anticoagulant to prevent clotting (which would normally occur within 20-26 minutes at room temperature). Typical anticoagulants include heparin (which interferes with the action of enzymes needed for clotting) and citrate or oxalate ion (either of which form precipitates with calcium ion, which is also needed for blood clotting, thereby removing it from solution). Plasma is separated from blood cells by spinning the sample in a centrifuge, which causes the blood cells to clump together at the bottom of the tube, leaving the plasma at the top.

Many laboratory analyses are performed on **blood serum**, the fluid remaining after blood has completely clotted. Blood serum composition is not the same as that of blood plasma—as we'll see in Section 29.5, blood clots are not simply clumps of cells, but also include networks of protein that originated from the plasma. When a serum sample is desired, whole blood is collected in the presence of an agent that hastens clotting. Thrombin, a natural component of the clotting system, is often used for this purpose. Centrifugation separates the clot and cells to leave behind the serum.

Major Components of Blood:

- **Whole blood**

    Blood plasma—fluid part of blood containing water-soluble solutes
    Blood cells—red blood cells (carry gases)
    　　　　　　—white blood cells (part of immune system)
    　　　　　　—platelets (help to initiate blood clotting)

- **Blood serum**—fluid portion of plasma left after blood has clotted

The functions of the major protein and cellular components of blood are summarized in Table 29.3. These functions fall into three categories.

Major Functions of Blood:

- **Transport** The circulatory system is the body's equivalent of an interstate highway network, transporting materials from where they enter the system to where they are used or disposed of. Oxygen and carbon dioxide are carried to and from by red blood cells. Nutrients are carried from the intestine to the sites of their catabolism. Waste products of metabolism are carried to the kidneys. Hormones from endocrine glands are delivered to their target tissues.
- **Regulation** Blood redistributes body heat as it flows along, thereby participating in the regulation of body temperature. It also picks up or delivers water and

Erythrocytes Red blood cells; transporters of blood gases.

Leukocytes White blood cells.

Whole blood Blood plasma plus blood cells.

Blood serum Fluid portion of blood remaining after clotting has occurred.

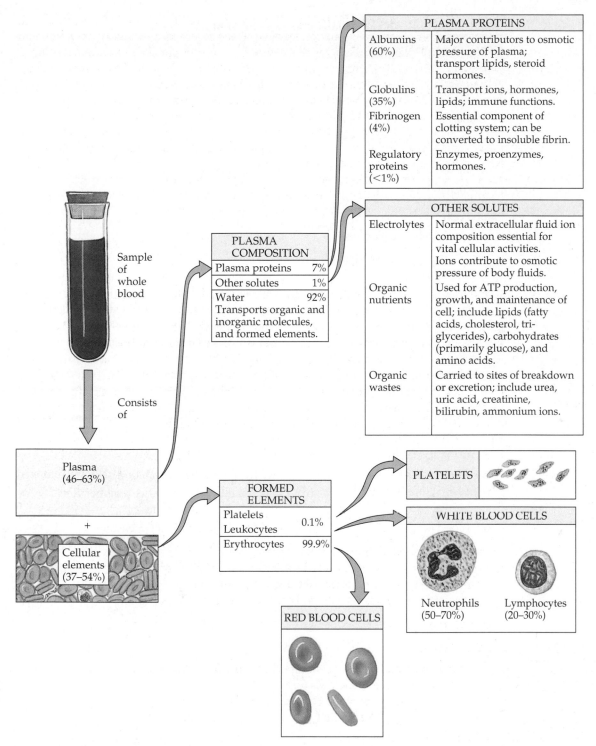

PLASMA PROTEINS	
Albumins (60%)	Major contributors to osmotic pressure of plasma; transport lipids, steroid hormones.
Globulins (35%)	Transport ions, hormones, lipids; immune functions.
Fibrinogen (4%)	Essential component of clotting system; can be converted to insoluble fibrin.
Regulatory proteins (<1%)	Enzymes, proenzymes, hormones.

OTHER SOLUTES	
Electrolytes	Normal extracellular fluid ion composition essential for vital cellular activities. Ions contribute to osmotic pressure of body fluids.
Organic nutrients	Used for ATP production, growth, and maintenance of cell; include lipids (fatty acids, cholesterol, triglycerides), carbohydrates (primarily glucose), and amino acids.
Organic wastes	Carried to sites of breakdown or excretion; include urea, uric acid, creatinine, bilirubin, ammonium ions.

Sample of whole blood

PLASMA COMPOSITION	
Plasma proteins	7%
Other solutes	1%
Water	92%
Transports organic and inorganic molecules, and formed elements.	

Plasma (46–63%)

Consists of

+

Cellular elements (37–54%)

FORMED ELEMENTS	
Platelets Leukocytes	0.1%
Erythrocytes	99.9%

PLATELETS

WHITE BLOOD CELLS
Neutrophils (50–70%) Lymphocytes (20–30%)

RED BLOOD CELLS

▲ **Figure 29.6**
The composition of whole blood.

electrolytes as they are needed. In addition, blood buffers are essential to the maintenance of acid–base balance.

- **Defense** Blood carries the molecules and cells needed for two major defense mechanisms: (1) the immune response, which destroys foreign invaders; and (2) blood clotting, which prevents loss of blood and begins the healing of wounds.

We will take a closer look at the defense functions of blood—the immune response and blood clotting and then finish our discussion by examining the transport of blood gases (Section 29.6). (Lipid transport was discussed in Chapter 24.)

Table 29.3 Protein and Cellular Components of Blood

Blood Component	Function
Proteins	
Albumins	Transport lipids, hormones, drugs; major contributor to plasma osmolarity
Globulins	
Immunoglobulins (γ-globulins, antibodies)	Identify antigens (microorganisms and other foreign invaders) and initiate their destruction
Transport globulins	Transport lipids and metal ions
Fibrinogen	Forms fibrin, the basis of blood clots
Blood cells	
Red blood cells (erythrocytes)	Transport O_2, CO_2, H^+
White blood cells (leukocytes)	
Lymphocytes	Defend against specific pathogens and foreign substances (T cells and B cells)
Phagocytes	Carry out phagocytosis—engulf foreign invaders (neutrophils, eosinophils, and monocytes)
Basophils	Release histamine during inflammatory response of injured tissue
Platelets	Help to initiate blood clotting

PROBLEM 29.2

Match each term in the **(a)–(e)** group with its definition from the **(i)–(v)** group:

(a) Interstitial fluid   **(i)** Fluid that remains when blood cells are removed

(b) Whole blood   **(ii)** Fluid, solutes, and cells that together flow through veins and arteries

(c) Blood serum   **(iii)** Fluid that fills spaces between cells

(d) Intracellular fluid   **(iv)** Fluid that remains when blood clotting agents are removed from plasma

(e) Blood plasma   **(v)** Fluid within cells

CHEMISTRY IN ACTION

The Blood–Brain Barrier

Nowhere in human beings is the maintenance of a constant internal environment more important than in the brain. If the brain were exposed to the fluctuations in concentrations of hormones, amino acids, neurotransmitters, and potassium that occur elsewhere in the body, inappropriate nervous activity would result. Therefore, the brain must be rigorously isolated from variations in blood composition.

How can the brain receive nutrients from the blood in capillaries and yet be protected? The answer lies in the unique structure of the *endothelial cells* that form the walls of brain capillaries. Unlike the cells in most other capillaries, those in

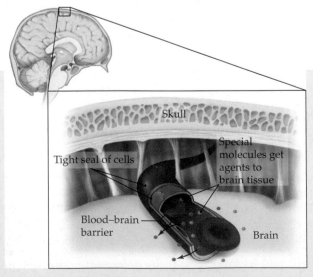

▲ **The blood–brain barrier.**

brain capillaries form a series of continuous tight junctions so that nothing can pass between them. To reach the brain, therefore, a substance must cross this blood–brain barrier (BBB) by crossing the endothelial cell membranes. The BBB serves as internal protection for the brain just as the skull serves as the brain's external protection.

The brain, of course, cannot be completely isolated or it will die from lack of nourishment. Glucose, the main source of energy for brain cells, and certain amino acids the brain cannot manufacture are recognized and brought across the cell membranes by transport mechanisms specific to each nutrient. Similar specific transporters move surplus substances out of the brain.

An asymmetric (one-way) transport system exists for glycine, a small amino acid that is a potent neurotransmitter. Glycine inhibits rather than activates transmission of nerve signals, and its concentration must be held at a lower level in the brain than in the blood. To accomplish this, there is a glycine transport system in the cell membrane closest to the brain, but no matching transport system on the other side. Thus, glycine can be transported out of the brain but not into it.

The brain is also protected by the "metabolic" blood–brain barrier. In this case, a compound that gets into an endothelial cell is converted within the cell to a metabolite that is unable to enter the brain. A striking demonstration of the metabolic brain barrier is provided by *dopamine*, a neurotransmitter, and L-*dopa*, a metabolic precursor of dopamine.

L-Dopa can both enter and leave the brain because it is recognized by an amino acid transporter. However, the brain is protected from an entering excess of L-dopa by its conversion to dopamine within the endothelial cells. Like glycine, dopamine, which is also produced from L-dopa within the brain, can leave the brain but cannot enter it. The dopamine deficiency that occurs in Parkinson's disease is therefore treated by administration of L-dopa.

Since crossing the endothelial cell membrane is the route into the brain, substances soluble in the membrane lipids readily breach the blood–brain barrier. Among such substances are nicotine, caffeine, codeine, diazepam (Valium®, an antidepressant), and heroin. Heroin differs from morphine in having two nonpolar acetyl groups where the morphine has polar hydroxyl groups (Section 15.6). The resulting difference in lipid solubil-

L-Dopa

Dopamine

ity allows heroin to enter the brain much more efficiently than morphine. Once heroin is inside the brain, enzymes remove the acetyl groups to give morphine, in essence trapping it in the brain, a general strategy many medicinal chemists try to capitalize upon. Finding ways to breach the blood–brain barrier is of major concern to medicinal chemists. For example, brain tumors are currently treated with either radiation or surgery, as the chemical agents used to typically treat cancer cannot cross the BBB. Researchers at the St. Louis University School of Medicine have been studying compounds that can sneak past the barrier, a discovery that could help doctors better treat a range of invasive brain malignancies. "The bottom line is, if you can get drugs into the brain, you can cure brain cancer," states Dr. William Banks, a member of the St. Louis research team. The St. Louis team has also been examining compounds that can be used to treat Alzheimer's disease; the key here also being how to get them to cross the BBB. Researchers at UCLA have begun to examine *chimeric therapeutics*, materials that are half drug (which do not cross the BBB) and half "molecular Trojan horse" (genetically engineered proteins that do cross the BBB). As our understanding of this crucial barrier unfolds, we can expect many advances in the treatment of diseases of the brain that thus far have been treatable by only the most invasive of techniques.

See Chemistry in Action Problems 29.63 through 29.66 at the end of the chapter.

29.4 Plasma Proteins, White Blood Cells, and Immunity

An **antigen** is any molecule or portion of a molecule recognized by the body as a foreign invader. An antigen might be a molecule never seen before by the body or a molecular segment recognized as an invader (for example, a protein on the surface of a bacterium or virus). Antigens can also be small molecules, known as *haptens*, that are only recognized as antigens after they have bonded to carrier proteins. Haptens include some antibiotics, environmental pollutants, and allergens from plants and animals.

The recognition of an antigen can initiate three different responses. The first, the **inflammatory response**, is a non-specific, localized response to a given antigen.

Antigen A substance foreign to the body that triggers the immune response.

Inflammatory response A nonspecific defense mechanism triggered by antigens or tissue damage.

▶ **Figure 29.7**
The immune response.
The attack on antigens
occurs by cell-mediated
and antibody-mediated
immune responses.

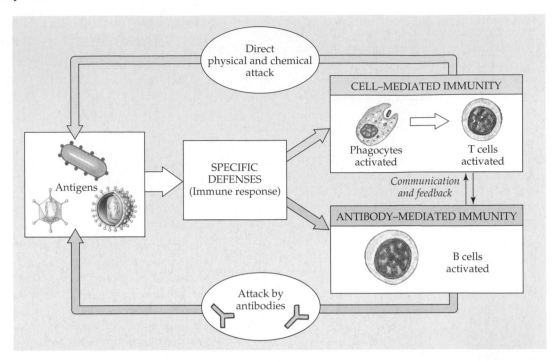

▶ **Figure 29.7**
The immune response.
The attack on antigens
occurs by cell-mediated
and antibody-mediated
immune responses.

Immune response Defense mechanism of the immune system dependent on the recognition of specific antigens, including viruses, bacteria, toxic substances, and infected cells; either cell-mediated or antibody-mediated.

Antibody (immunoglobulin) Glycoprotein molecule that identifies antigens.

The two remaining types of **immune response** (cell-mediated response and antibody-mediated response) do depend on recognition of *specific* invaders (such as viruses, bacteria, toxic substances, or infected cells; Figure 29.7). At the molecular level, the invading antigen is detected by an interaction very much like that between an enzyme and its substrate. Noncovalent attraction allows a spatial fit between the antigen and a defender that is specific to that antigen. The *cell-mediated immune response* depends on white blood cells known as *T cells*. The *antibody-mediated immune response* depends on **antibodies** (or **immunoglobulins**) produced by the white blood cells known as *B cells*.

Both inflammation and the immune responses require normal numbers of white blood cells to be effective (5 to 10 million white blood cells per milliliter). If the white blood cell count falls below 1000 per milliliter of blood, any infection can be life-threatening. The devastating results of white blood cell destruction in AIDS is an example of this condition (see Chemistry in Action: Viruses and AIDS on p. 794).

Inflammatory Response

Inflammation Result of the inflammatory response; includes swelling, redness, warmth, and pain.

Cell damage due to infection or injury initiates **inflammation**, a nonspecific defense mechanism that produces swelling, redness, warmth, and pain. For example, the swollen, painful, red bump that develops around a splinter in your finger is an inflammation (generally known as a *wheal-and-flare reaction*). Chemical messengers released at the injured site direct the inflammatory response. One such messenger is histamine, which is synthesized from the amino acid histidine and is stored in cells throughout the body. Histamine release is also triggered by an allergic response.

Histamine sets off dilation of capillaries and increases the permeability of capillary walls. The resulting increased blood flow into the damaged area reddens and warms the skin, and swelling occurs as plasma carrying blood-clotting factors and defensive proteins enters the intercellular space. At the same time, white blood cells cross capillary walls to attack invaders.

Bacteria or other antigens at the inflammation site are destroyed by white blood cells known as *phagocytes*, which engulf invading cells and destroy them by enzyme-catalyzed hydrolysis reactions. Phagocytes also emit chemical messengers that help to direct the inflammatory response. An inflammation caused by a wound will heal completely only after all infectious agents have been removed, with dead cells and other debris absorbed into the lymph system.

Cell-Mediated Immune Response

The cell-mediated immune response is under the control of several kinds of *T lymphocytes*, or *T cells*. The cell-mediated immune response principally guards against abnormal cells and bacteria or viruses entering the normal cells; it also guards against the invasion of some cancer cells and causes the rejection of transplanted organs.

A complex series of events begins when a T cell recognizes an antigenic cell. The result of these events is production of *cytotoxic*, or *killer*, T cells that can destroy the invader (for example, by releasing a toxic protein that kills the antigenic invaded perforating cell membranes) and *helper* T cells, which enhance the body's defenses against the invader. Thousands of *memory* T cells are also produced; they remain on guard and will immediately generate the appropriate killer T cells if the same pathogen reappears.

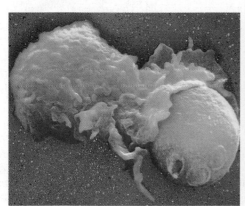 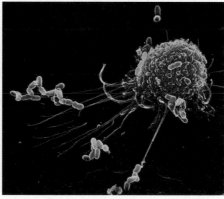

◄ **White blood cells. (left) A lymphocyte phagocytizing a yeast cell. (right) A lymphocyte reaches out to snare several *E. coli* bacteria.**

Antibody-Mediated Immune Response

The white blood cells known as *B lymphocytes* or *B cells*, with the assistance of T cells, are responsible for the antibody-mediated immune response. Unlike T cells, which identify only antigenic cells, B cells identify antigens adrift in body fluids. A B cell is activated when it first binds to an antigen and then encounters a helper T cell that recognizes the same antigen. This activation can take place anywhere in the body, but it often occurs in lymph nodes, tonsils, or the spleen, which have large concentrations of lymphocytes.

Once activated, B cells divide to form plasma cells that secrete antibodies specific to the antigen. The antibodies are *immunoglobulins*. The body contains up to 10,000 different immunoglobulins at any given time, and we have the capacity to make more than 100 million others. The immunoglobulins are glycoproteins composed of two "heavy" polypeptide chains and two "light" polypeptide chains joined by disulfide bonds, as shown in Figure 29.8. The variable regions are sequences of amino acids that will bind a specific antigen. Once synthesized, antibodies spread out to find their antigens.

▶ **Figure 29.8**
Structure of an immunoglobulin, which is an antibody.
(a) The regions of an immunoglobulin. The disulfide bridges that hold the chains together are shown in orange. (b) Molecular model of an immunoglobulin; the heavy chains are gray and blue and both light chains are red.

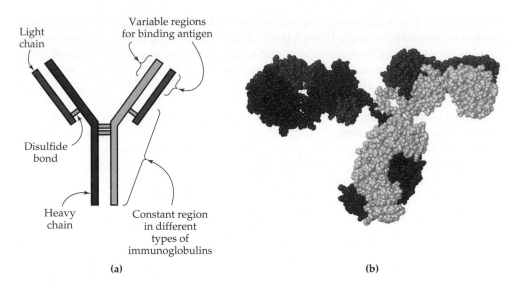

(a)

(b)

Formation of an antigen–antibody complex (Figure 29.9) inactivates the antigen by one of several methods. The complex may, for example, attract phagocytes, or it may block the mechanism by which the invader connects with a target cell.

▶ **Figure 29.9**
Antigen–antibody complexes.
(a) Antigens bind to antigenic-determinant sites on the surface of, for example, a bacterium. (b) Because each antibody has two binding sites, the interaction of many antigens and antibodies creates a large immune complex.

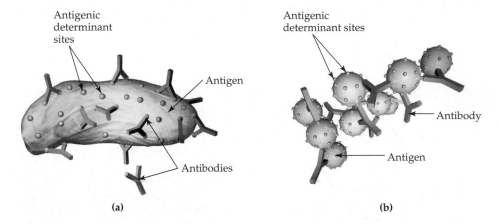

(a)

(b)

Activated B-cell division also yields memory cells that remain on guard and quickly produce more plasma cells if the same antigen reappears. The long-lived B and T memory cells are responsible for long-term immunity to diseases after the first illness or after a vaccination.

Several classes of immunoglobulins have been identified. *Immunoglobulin G antibodies* (known as *gamma globulins*), for example, protect against viruses and bacteria. Allergies and asthma are caused by an oversupply of *immunoglobulin E*. Numerous disorders result from the mistaken identification of normal body constituents as foreign and the overproduction of antibodies to combat them. These **autoimmune diseases** include attack on connective tissue at joints in rheumatoid arthritis, attack on pancreatic islet cells in some forms of diabetes mellitus, and a generalized attack on nucleic acids and blood components in systemic lupus erythematosus.

Autoimmune disease Disorder in which the immune system identifies normal body components as antigens and produces antibodies to them.

Fibrin Insoluble protein that forms the fiber framework of a blood clot.

Vitamin K
(Phylloquinone)

29.5 Blood Clotting

A blood clot consists of blood cells trapped in a mesh of the insoluble fibrous protein known as **fibrin**. Clot formation is a multiple-step process requiring participation of 12 clotting factors; calcium ion is one of the clotting factors. Others, most of which are glycoproteins, are synthesized in the liver by pathways that require vitamin K as a coenzyme. Therefore, a deficiency of vitamin K, the presence of a competitive inhibitor of vitamin K, or a deficiency of a clotting factor can cause excessive bleeding, sometimes from even minor tissue damage. Hemophilia is a disorder caused by an inherited genetic defect that results in the absence of one or more of the clotting factors. Hemophilia occurs in 1 in 10,000 individuals, with 80–90% of people with hemophilia being male.

The body's mechanism for halting blood loss from even the tiniest capillary is referred to as **hemostasis**. The first events in hemostasis are (1) constriction of surrounding blood vessels and (2) formation of a plug composed of the blood cells known as *platelets* at the site of tissue damage.

Next, a **blood clot** is formed in a process that is triggered by two pathways: (1) The *intrinsic pathway* begins when blood makes contact with the negatively charged surface of the fibrous protein collagen, which is exposed at the site of tissue damage. Clotting is activated in exactly the same manner when blood is placed in a glass tube, because glass is also negatively charged. (2) The *extrinsic pathway* begins when damaged tissue releases an integral membrane glycoprotein known as *tissue factor*.

The result of either pathway is a cascade of reactions that is initiated when an inactive clotting factor (a zymogen, Section 19.9) is converted to its active form by cleavage of specific polypeptide sequences on its surface. Commonly, the newly activated enzyme then catalyzes the activation of the next factor in the cascade. The two pathways merge and, in the final step of the common pathway, the enzyme *thrombin* catalyzes cleavage of small polypeptides from the soluble plasma protein fibrinogen. Negatively charged groups in these polypeptides make fibrinogen soluble and keep the molecules apart. Once these polypeptides are removed, the resulting insoluble fibrin molecules immediately associate with each other by noncovalent interactions. Then they are bound into fibers by formation of amide cross-links between lysine and glutamine side chains in a reaction catalyzed by another of the clotting factors:

Hemostasis The stopping of bleeding.

Blood clot A network of fibrin fibers and trapped blood cells that forms at the site of blood loss.

▲ **Colorized electron micrograph of a blood clot. Red blood cells can be seen enmeshed in the network of fibrin threads.**

$$\underset{\text{Gln}}{\text{Gln}}-CH_2CH_2-\overset{\overset{\displaystyle O}{\|}}{C}-NH_2 \; + \; \overset{+}{H_3N}CH_2CH_2CH_2CH_2-\underset{\text{Lys}}{\overset{\text{Protein chain}}{\text{Lys}}} \; \longrightarrow$$

$$\underset{\text{Gln}}{\text{Gln}}-CH_2CH_2-\overset{\overset{\displaystyle O}{\|}}{C}-\underset{\text{Cross-link between protein chains}}{NHCH_2CH_2CH_2CH_2}-\underset{\text{Lys}}{\text{Lys}} \; + \; NH_4^+$$

Once the clot has done its job of preventing blood loss and binding together damaged surfaces as they heal, the clot is broken down by hydrolysis of its peptide bonds.

29.6 Red Blood Cells and Blood Gases

Red blood cells, or erythrocytes, have one major purpose: to transport blood gases. Erythrocytes in mammals have no nuclei or ribosomes and cannot replicate themselves. In addition, they have no mitochondria or glycogen and must obtain glucose from the surrounding plasma. Their enormous number—about 250 million in a single drop of blood—and their large surface area provide for rapid exchange of gases throughout the body. Because they are small and flexible, erythrocytes can squeeze through the tiniest capillaries one at a time.

Of the protein in an erythrocyte, 95% is hemoglobin, the transporter of oxygen and carbon dioxide. Hemoglobin (Hb) is composed of four polypeptide chains with the quaternary structure shown earlier in Figure 18.8. Each protein chain has a central heme molecule in a crevice in its nonpolar interior, and each of the four hemes can combine with one O_2 molecule.

Oxygen Transport

The iron(II) ion, Fe^{2+}, sits in the center of each heme molecule and is the site to which O_2 binds through one of oxygen's unshared electron pairs. In contrast to the

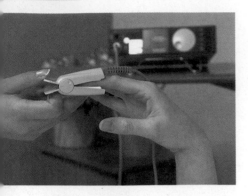

▲ **Figure 29.10**

A pulse oximetry sensor for continuous monitoring of blood oxygen. One side of the sensor contains two light-emitting diodes (LEDs), one that emits in the visible red range (better absorbed by dark-red deoxygenated blood) and one that emits in the infrared range (better absorbed by oxygenated blood, which is bright red). On the opposite side of the sensor, a photodetector measures the light that passes through and sends the signal to an instrument that computes the percent oxygen saturation of the blood and also records the pulse. Normal oxygen saturation is 95–100%. Below 85%, tissues are at risk, and below 70% is typically life-threatening.

cytochromes of the respiratory chain, where iron cycles between Fe^{2+} and Fe^{3+}, heme iron must remain in the reduced Fe^{2+} state to maintain its oxygen-carrying ability. Hemoglobin (Hb) carrying four oxygens (oxyhemoglobin) is bright red. Hemoglobin that has lost one or more oxygens (deoxyhemoglobin) is dark red-purple, which accounts for the darker color of venous blood. Dried blood is brown, because exposure to atmospheric oxygen has oxidized the iron (think of rust). The color of arterial blood carrying oxygen is used in a clinically valuable method for monitoring oxygenation (known as *pulse oximetry*, Figure 29.10).

At normal physiological conditions, the percentage of heme molecules that carry oxygen, known as the *percent saturation*, is dependent on the partial pressure of oxygen in surrounding tissues (Figure 29.11). The shape of the curve indicates that binding of oxygen to heme is allosteric in nature (see Section 19.7). Each O_2 that binds causes changes in the hemoglobin quaternary structure that enhance binding of the next O_2, and releasing each oxygen enhances release of the next. As a result, oxygen is more readily released to tissue where the partial pressure of oxygen is low. The average oxygen partial pressure in peripheral tissue is 40 mmHg, a pressure at which Hb remains 75% saturated by oxygen, leaving a large amount of O_2 in reserve for emergencies. Note, however, the rapid drop in the curve between 40 mmHg and 20 mmHg, which is the oxygen pressure in tissue where metabolism is occurring rapidly.

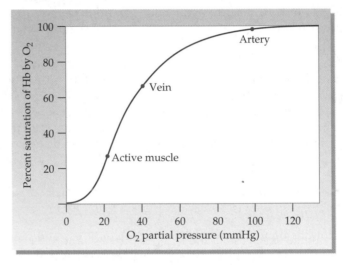

▲ **Figure 29.11**

Oxygen saturation of hemoglobin at normal physiological conditions. Oxygen pressure is about 100 mmHg in arteries and 20 mmHg in active muscles. Note the large release of oxygen as the partial pressure drops from 40 mmHg to 20 mmHg.

Carbon Dioxide Transport, Acidosis, and Alkalosis

Oxygen and carbon dioxide are the "blood gases" transported by erythrocytes. By way of the bicarbonate ion/carbon dioxide buffer, the intimate relationships among H^+ and HCO_3^- concentrations and O_2 and CO_2 partial pressures are essential to maintaining electrolyte and acid–base balance:

$$\underbrace{CO_2(aq) + H_2O(l)}_{\text{Controlled by the lungs}} \Longleftrightarrow H_2CO_3(aq) \Longleftrightarrow \underbrace{HCO_3^-(aq) + H^{+(aq)}}_{\text{Controlled by the kidneys}}$$

In a clinical setting, "monitoring blood gases" usually refers to measuring the pH of blood as well as the gas concentrations. Carbon dioxide from metabolism in peripheral cells diffuses into interstitial fluid and then into capillaries, where it is transported in the blood three ways: (1) as dissolved $CO_2(aq)$, (2) bonded to Hb, or (3) as HCO_3^- in solution. About 7% of the CO_2 produced dissolves in blood plasma. The rest enters erythrocytes, where some of it binds to the protein portion of hemoglobin by reaction with the nonionized amino acid $-NH_2$ groups present:

$$Hb-NH_2 + CO_2 \rightleftharpoons Hb-NHCOO^- + H^+$$

Most of the CO_2 is rapidly converted to bicarbonate ion within erythrocytes, which contain a large concentration of carbonic anhydrase. The resulting water-soluble HCO_3^- ion can leave the erythrocyte and travel in the blood to the lungs, where it will be converted back to CO_2 for exhalation. To maintain electrolyte balance, a Cl^- ion enters the erythrocyte for every HCO_3^- ion that leaves, and the process is reversed when the blood reaches the lungs:

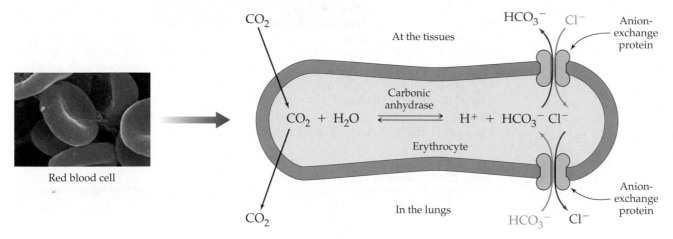

A cell-membrane protein controls this ion exchange, which is passive, as the ions move from higher to lower concentrations.

Without some compensating change, the result of hemoglobin reacting with CO_2 and the action of carbonic anhydrase would be an unacceptably large increase in acidity. To cope with this, hemoglobin responds by reversibly binding hydrogen ions:

$$Hb \cdot 4\,O_2 + 2\,H^+ \rightleftharpoons Hb \cdot 2\,H^+ + 4\,O_2$$

The release of oxygen is enhanced by allosteric effects when the hydrogen ion concentration increases, and oxygen is held more firmly when the hydrogen ion concentration decreases.

The changes in the oxygen saturation curve with CO_2 and H^+ concentrations and with temperature are shown in Figure 29.12. The curve shifts to the right, indicating

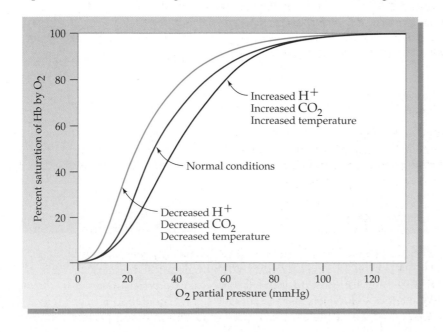

◀ **Figure 29.12**
Changes in oxygen affinity of hemoglobin with changing conditions.
The normal curve of Figure 29.11 is shown in red here.

decreased affinity of Hb for O_2, when the H^+ and CO_2 concentrations increase and when the temperature increases. These are exactly the conditions in muscles that are working hard and need more oxygen. The curve shifts to the left, indicating increased affinity of Hb for oxygen, under the opposite conditions of decreased H^+ and CO_2 concentrations and lower temperature.

Homeostasis requires a blood pH between 7.35 and 7.45. A pH outside this range results in either **acidosis** or **alkalosis**.

Acidosis The abnormal condition associated with a blood plasma pH below 7.35; may be respiratory or metabolic.

Alkalosis The abnormal condition associated with a blood plasma pH above 7.45; may be respiratory or metabolic.

Acidosis	Normal	Alkalosis
Blood pH Below 7.35	Blood pH 7.35–7.45	Blood pH Above 7.45

The wide variety of conditions that cause acidosis or alkalosis can be divided between respiratory malfunctions and metabolic malfunctions. Examples of each are given in Table 29.4. *Respiratory* disruption of acid–base balance can result when carbon dioxide generation by metabolism and carbon dioxide removal at the lungs are out of balance. *Metabolic* disruption of acid–base balance can result from abnormally high acid generation or failure of buffer systems and kidney function to regulate bicarbonate concentration.

Table 29.4 Causes of Acidosis and Alkalosis

Type of Imbalance	Causes
Respiratory acidosis	CO_2 buildup due to:
	Decreased respiratory activity (hypoventilation)
	Cardiac insufficiency (for example, congestive failure, cardiac arrest)
	Deterioration of pulmonary function (for example, asthma, emphysema, pulmonary obstruction, pneumonia)
Respiratory alkalosis	Loss of CO_2 due to:
	Excessive respiratory activity (hyperventilation, due, for example, to high fever, nervous condition)
Metabolic acidosis	Increased production of metabolic acids due to:
	Fasting or starvation
	Untreated diabetes
	Excessive exercise
	Decreased acid excretion in urine due to:
	Poisoning
	Renal failure
	Decreased plasma bicarbonate concentration due to:
	Diarrhea
Metabolic alkalosis	Elevated plasma bicarbonate concentration due to:
	Vomiting
	Diuretics
	Antacid overdose

KEY CONCEPT PROBLEM 29.3

Carbon dioxide dissolved in body fluids has a pronounced effect on pH.

(a) Does pH go up or down when carbon dioxide dissolves in these fluids? Does this change indicate higher or lower acidity?

(b) What does a blood gas analysis measure?

PROBLEM 29.4

Classify the following conditions as a cause of respiratory or metabolic acidosis or alkalosis (consult Table 29.4).

(a) Emphysema

(b) Kidney failure

(c) Overdose of an antacid

PROBLEM 29.5

Classify the following conditions as a cause of respiratory or metabolic acidosis or alkalosis (consult Table 29.4).

(a) Severe panic attack

(b) Congestive heart failure

(c) Running a marathon

PROBLEM 29.6

In Chemistry in Action: The Blood–Brain Barrier, the fact that heroin was better able to cross the blood–brain barrier than morphine was discussed. Looking at the structures of these two molecules (refer to Section 15.6), circle the areas where they differ and why this explains the difference between the potencies of heroin and morphine as analgesics.

29.7 The Kidney and Urine Formation

The kidneys bear the major responsibility for maintaining a constant internal environment in the body. By managing the elimination of appropriate amounts of water, electrolytes, hydrogen ions, and nitrogen-containing wastes, the kidneys respond to changes in health, diet, and physical activity.

About 25% of the blood pumped from the heart goes directly to the kidneys, where the functional units are the *nephrons* (Figure 29.13). Each kidney contains over a million of them. Blood enters a nephron at a *glomerulus* (at the top in Figure 29.13), a tangle of capillaries surrounded by a fluid-filled space. **Filtration**, the first of three essential kidney functions, occurs here. The pressure of blood pumped into the glomerulus directly from the heart is high enough to push plasma and all its solutes except large proteins across the capillary membrane into the surrounding fluid, the **glomerular filtrate**. The filtrate flows from the capsule into the tubule that makes up the rest of the nephron, and the blood enters the network of capillaries intertwined with the tubule.

About 125 mL of filtrate per minute enters the kidneys, and they produce 180 L of filtrate per day. This filtrate contains not only waste products but also many solutes the body cannot afford to lose, such as glucose and electrolytes. Since we excrete only about 1.4 L of urine each day you can see that another important function of the kidneys is **reabsorption**—the recapture of water and essential solutes by moving them out of the tubule.

Reabsorption alone, however, is not sufficient to provide the kind of control over urine composition that is needed. More of certain solutes must be excreted than are present in the filtrate. This situation is dealt with by **secretion**—the transfer of solutes *into* the kidney tubule.

Reabsorption and secretion require the transfer of solutes and water among the filtrate, the interstitial fluid surrounding the tubule, and blood in the capillaries. Some of the substances reabsorbed or secreted are listed in Table 29.5. Solutes cross the tubule and capillary membranes by passive diffusion in response to concentration or ionic charge differences, or by active transport. Water moves in response to differences in the osmolarity of the fluids on the two sides of the membranes. Solute and water movement is also controlled by hormone-directed variations in the permeability of the tubule membrane.

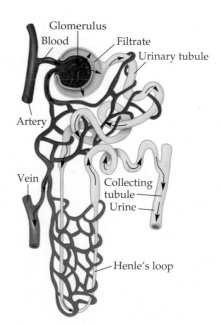

▲ Figure 29.13

Structure of a nephron.
Water moves out of the urinary tubule and the collecting tubule. The concentration of solutes in urine is established as they move both in and out along the tubules.

Filtration (kidney) Filtration of blood plasma through a glomerulus and into a kidney nephron.

Glomerular filtrate Fluid that enters the nephron from the glomerulus; filtered blood plasma.

Reabsorption (kidney) Movement of solutes out of filtrate in a kidney tubule.

Secretion (kidney) Movement of solutes into filtrate in a kidney tubule.

Table 29.5 Reabsorption and Secretion in Kidney Tubules

Reabsorbed
Ions
Na^+, Cl^-, K^+, Ca^{2+}, Mg^{2+}, PO_4^{3-}, SO_4^{2-}, HCO_3^-
Metabolites
Glucose
Amino acids
Proteins
Vitamins
Secreted
Ions
K^+, H^+, Ca^{2+}
Wastes
Creatinine
Urea
Ammonia
Various organic acids and bases (including uric acid)
Miscellaneous
Neurotransmitters
Histamine
Drugs (penicillin, atropine, morphine, numerous others)

29.8 Urine Composition and Function

Urine contains the products of glomerular filtration, minus the substances reabsorbed in the tubules, plus the substances secreted in the tubules. The actual concentrations of these substances in urine at any time are determined by the amount of water being excreted, which can vary significantly with water intake, exercise, temperature, and state of health. (For identical quantities of solutes, concentration *decreases* when the quantity of solvent water *increases*, and concentration *increases* when the quantity of water *decreases*.)

About 50 g of solids in solution are excreted every day—about 20 g of electrolytes and 30 g of nitrogen-containing wastes (urea and ammonia from amino acid catabolism, creatinine from breakdown of creatine phosphate in muscles, and uric acid from purine catabolism). Normal urine composition is usually reported as the quantity of each solute excreted per day, and laboratory urinalysis often requires collection of all urine excreted during a 24-hour period.

The following paragraphs briefly describe a few of the mechanisms that control the composition of urine.

Acid–Base Balance

Respiration, buffers, and excretion of hydrogen ions in urine combine to maintain acid–base balance. Metabolism normally produces an excess of hydrogen ions; a portion of these must be excreted each day to prevent acidosis. Very little free hydrogen ion exists in blood plasma, and therefore very little enters the glomerular filtrate. Instead, the H^+ to be eliminated is produced by the reaction of CO_2 with water in the cells lining the tubules of the nephrons:

$$CO_2 \ + \ H_2O \ \xrightarrow{\text{Carbonic anhydrase}} \ H^+ \ + \ HCO_3^-$$

To bloodstream

To filtrate

CHEMISTRY IN ACTION

Automated Clinical Laboratory Analysis

What happens when a physician orders chemical tests of blood, urine, or spinal fluid? The sample goes to a clinical chemistry laboratory, often in a hospital, where most tests are done by automated clinical chemistry analyzers. There are basically two types of chemical analysis, one for the quantity of a chemical (a natural biochemical, a drug, or a toxic substance) and the other for the quantity of an enzyme with a specific metabolic activity.

The quantity of a given chemical in the blood is determined either directly or indirectly. Many chemical components are measured directly by mixing a reagent with the sample—the *analyte*—and noting the quantity of a colored product formed by using a photometer, an instrument that measures the absorption of light of a wavelength specific to the product. For each test specified, a portion of the sample is mixed with the appropriate reagent and the photometer is adjusted to the exact wavelength necessary.

When it is not possible to utilize this direct technique, other indirect methods that produce a detectable product have been devised. Many analytes are substrates for enzyme catalyzed reactions, and analysis of the substrate concentration is therefore often made possible by treating the analyte with appropriate enzymes. Glucose is determined in this manner by utilizing a pair of enzyme-catalyzed reactions: the glucose is converted to glucose 6-phosphate using its hexokinase-catalyzed reaction with ATP; the glucose 6-phosphate is then oxidized by $NADP^+$; and the quantity of NADPH produced is measured photometrically.

The second type of analysis, determination of the quantity of a specific enzyme or the ratio of two or more enzymes, is invaluable in detecting organ damage that allows enzymes to leak into body fluids. For example, elevation of both ALT (alanine aminotransferase) and AST (aspartate aminotransferase) with an AST/ALT ratio greater than 1.0 is characteristic of liver disease. If, however, the AST is greatly elevated and the AST/ALT ratio is higher than 1.5, a myocardial infarction (heart attack) may likely have occurred. When the substance being analyzed is an enzyme, its presence is detected, monitored, and quantified with an assay that employs a substrate of the enzyme in question; levels of the enzyme are measured by monitoring the substrate's appearance or disappearance. ALT, for example, is determined by photometrically monitoring the disappearance

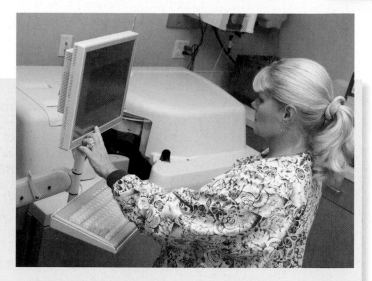

of NADH in the following pair of coupled reactions (where LD = lactate dehydrogenase):

$$\text{L-Alanine} + \alpha\text{-Ketoglutarate} \xrightarrow{\text{ALT}} \text{Pyruvate} + \text{L-Glutamate}$$
$$\text{Pyruvate} + \text{NADH/H}^+ \xrightarrow{\text{LD}} \text{Lactate} + \text{NAD}^+$$

As ALT causes pyruvate to form, LD causes the pyruvate to react with NADH to form lactate and NAD^+. By knowing how fast this reaction will occur with a given amount of LD, and by knowing how fast a given amount of ALT carries out the first reaction, the amount of ALT can be directly quantified in the sample being examined.

Automated analyzers rely on premixed reagents and automatic division of a fluid sample into small portions for each test. A low-volume analyzer that provides rapid results for a few tests accepts a bar-coded serum or plasma sample cartridge followed by bar-coded reagent cartridges. The instrument software reads the bar codes and directs an automatic pipette (which removes small samples of precisely measured volumes) to transfer the appropriate volume of sample to each test cartridge. The instrument then moves the test cartridge along as the sample and reagents are mixed, the reaction takes place for a measured amount of time, and the photometer reading is taken and converted to the test result.

A high-volume analyzer with more complex software randomly accesses 40 or more tests and runs over 400 tests per hour at a cost of less than 10 cents per test. The end result is a printed report on each sample listing the types of tests, the sample values, and a normal range for each test.

See Chemistry in Action Problems 29.67 through 29.69 at the end of the chapter.

The HCO_3^- ions return to the bloodstream, and the H^+ ions enter the filtrate. Thus, the more hydrogen ions there are to be excreted, the more bicarbonate ions are returned to the bloodstream.

The urine must carry away the necessary quantity of H^+ without becoming excessively acidic. To accomplish this, the H^+ is tied up by reaction with HPO_4^{2-} absorbed at the glomerulus, or by reaction with NH_3 produced in the tubule cells by deamination of glutamate:

$$H^+ + HPO_4^{2-} \longrightarrow H_2PO_4^-$$
$$H^+ + NH_3 \longrightarrow NH_4^+$$

When acidosis occurs, the kidney responds by synthesizing more ammonia, thereby increasing the quantity of H^+ eliminated.

A further outcome of H^+ production in tubule cells is the net reabsorption of the HCO_3^- that entered the filtrate at the glomerulus. The body cannot afford to lose its primary buffering ion, HCO_3^-. If HCO_3^- were to be lost, the body would have to produce more; the result would be production of additional acid from carbon dioxide by reaction with water. Instead, H^+ secreted into the filtrate combines with HCO_3^- in the filtrate to produce CO_2 and water:

$$H^+ + HCO_3^- \longrightarrow CO_2 + H_2O$$

In the filtrate　　　　　　　　↳ To bloodstream

Upon returning to the bloodstream, the CO_2 is reconverted to HCO_3^-.

In summary, acid–base reactions in the kidneys have the following results:

- Secreted H^+ is eliminated in the urine as NH_4^+ or $H_2PO_4^-$.
- Secreted H^+ combines with filtered HCO_3^-, producing CO_2 that returns to the bloodstream and again is converted to HCO_3^-.

Fluid and Na$^+$ Balance

The amount of water reabsorbed is dependent on the osmolarity of the fluid passing through the kidneys, the antidiuretic hormone–controlled permeability of the collecting duct membrane, and the amount of Na^+ actively reabsorbed. Increased sodium reabsorption means higher interstitial osmolarity, greater water reabsorption, and decreased urine volume. In the opposite condition of decreased sodium reabsorption, less water is reabsorbed and urine volume increases. "Loop diuretic" drugs such as furosemide (trademarked as Lasix®), which is used in treating hypertension and congestive heart failure, act by inhibiting the active transport of Na^+ out of the region of the urinary tubule called Henle's loop. Caffeine acts as a diuretic in a similar way.

The reabsorption of Na^+ is normally under the control of the steroid hormone aldosterone. The arrival of chemical messengers signaling a decrease in total blood plasma volume accelerates the secretion of aldosterone. The result is increased Na^+ reabsorption in the kidney tubules accompanied by increased water reabsorption.

SUMMARY: REVISITING THE CHAPTER GOALS

1. How are body fluids classified? Body fluids are either intracellular or extracellular. *Extracellular fluid* includes *blood plasma* (the fluid part of blood) and *interstitial fluid*. *Blood serum* is the fluid remaining after blood has clotted. Solutes in body fluids include blood gases, electrolytes, metabolites, and proteins. Solutes are carried throughout the body in blood and lymph. Exchange of solutes between blood and interstitial fluid occurs at the network of blood and lymph capillaries in peripheral tissues. Exchange of solutes between interstitial fluid and intracellular fluid occurs by passage across cell membranes (*see Problems 7, 14–16, 19–20, 24, 27–28, 55–59*).

2. What are the roles of blood in maintaining homeostasis? The principal functions of blood are (1) transport of solutes and blood gases, (2) regulation, such as regulation of heat and acid–base balance, and (3) defense, which includes the *immune*

response and *blood clotting*. In addition to plasma and proteins, blood is composed of red blood cells (*erythrocytes*), which transport blood gases; white blood cells (*leukocytes*), for defense functions; and *platelets*, which participate in blood clotting (Table 29.3) (*see Problems 8, 16–18, 26*).

3. How do blood components participate in the body's defense mechanisms? The presence of an *antigen* (a substance foreign to the body) initiates (1) the inflammatory response, (2) the cell-mediated immune response, and (3) the antibody-mediated immune response. The *inflammatory response* is initiated by histamine and accompanied by the destruction of invaders by *phagocytes*. The *cell-mediated response* is effected by *T cells* that can, for example, release a toxic protein that kills invaders. The *antibody-mediated response* is effected by *B cells*, which generate *antibodies* (*immunoglobulins*), proteins that complex with antigens and destroy them. Blood clotting occurs in a cascade of reactions in which a series of zymogens are activated, ultimately resulting in the formation of a clot composed of *fibrin* and platelets (*see Problems 8, 10–13, 23, 25, 29, 30–40*).

4. How do red blood cells participate in the transport of blood gases? Oxygen is transported bonded to Fe^{2+} ions in hemoglobin. The percent saturation of hemoglobin with oxygen (Figure 29.12) is governed by the partial pressure of oxygen in surrounding tissues and allosteric variations in hemoglobin structure. Carbon dioxide is transported in blood as a solute, bonded to hemoglobin, or in solution as bicarbonate ion. In peripheral tissues, carbon dioxide diffuses into red blood cells, where it is converted to bicarbonate ion. Acid–base balance is controlled as hydrogen ions generated by bicarbonate formation are bound by hemoglobin. At the lungs, oxygen enters the cells, and bicarbonate and hydrogen ions leave. A blood pH outside the normal range of 7.35–7.45 can be caused by respiratory or metabolic imbalance, resulting in the potentially serious conditions of *acidosis* or *alkalosis* (*see Problems 9, 23, 25–29, 41–52, 60–62*).

5. How is the composition of urine controlled? The first essential kidney function is *filtration*, in which plasma and most of its solute cross capillary membranes and enter the *glomerular filtrate*. Water and essential solutes are then reabsorbed, whereas additional solutes for elimination are secreted into the filtrate. Urine is thus composed of the products of filtration, minus the substances reabsorbed, plus the secreted substances. It is composed of water, nitrogen-containing wastes, and electrolytes (including $H_2PO_4^-$ and NH_4^+) that are excreted to help maintain acid–base balance. The balance between water and Na^+ excreted or absorbed is governed by the osmolarity of fluid in the kidney, the hormone aldosterone, and various chemical messengers (*see Problems 13, 22, 53–54, 60*).

KEY WORDS

Acidosis, *p. 886*

Alkalosis, *p. 886*

Antibody (immunoglobulin), *p. 880*

Antigen, *p. 879*

Autoimmune disease, *p. 882*

Blood clot, *p. 883*

Blood plasma, *p. 871*

Blood serum, *p. 876*

Erythrocytes, *p. 876*

Extracellular fluid, *p. 871*

Fibrin, *p. 882*

Filtration (kidney), *p. 887*

Glomerular filtrate, *p. 887*

Hemostasis, *p. 883*

Immune response, *p. 880*

Inflammation, *p. 880*

Inflammatory response, *p. 879*

Interstitial fluid, *p. 871*

Intracellular fluid, *p. 871*

Leukocytes, *p. 876*

Osmolarity, *p. 871*

Reabsorption (kidney), *p. 887*

Secretion (kidney), *p. 887*

Whole blood, *p. 876*

UNDERSTANDING KEY CONCEPTS

29.7 Body fluids occupy two different compartments, either inside the cells or outside the cells.

    (a) What are body fluids found inside the cell called?

    (b) What are body fluids found outside the cell called?

    (c) What are the two major subclasses of fluids found outside the cells?

    (d) What major electrolytes are found inside the cells?

    (e) What major electrolytes are found outside the cells?

29.8 In the diagram shown here, fill in the blanks with the names of the principal components of whole blood:

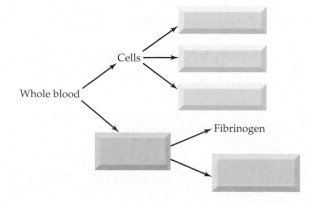

29.9 Fill in the blanks to identify some of the major functions of blood:

    (a) Blood carries _____ from lungs to tissues.

    (b) Blood carries _____ from the tissues to lungs.

    (c) Blood transports _____ from the digestive system to the tissues.

    (d) Blood carries _____ from the tissues to the site of excretion.

    (e) Blood transports _____ from the endocrine glands to their site of binding.

    (f) Blood transports defensive agents such as _____ to destroy foreign material and to prevent blood loss.

29.10 List four symptoms of inflammation.

29.11 Explain how the chemical messenger histamine is biosynthesized and how it elicits each symptom of inflammation.

29.12 Differentiate between cell-mediated immune response and antibody-mediated immune response.

29.13 How does the composition of urine help to maintain a healthy physiological acid–base balance?

ADDITIONAL PROBLEMS

BODY FLUIDS

29.14 What are the three principal body fluids and the approximate percentage of total body water accounted for by each?

29.15 What characteristics are needed for a substance to be soluble in body fluids?

29.16 Give an example of a substance found in tissues that is not soluble in blood. How are components that are not normally soluble in blood transported?

29.17 What effects do the differences in pressure between arterial capillaries, interstitial fluids, and venous capillaries have on solutes crossing cell membranes?

29.18 How does blood pressure compare with the interstitial fluid pressure in arterial capillaries? With the interstitial fluid pressure in venous capillaries?

29.19 What is the purpose of the lymphatic system?

29.20 Where in the body does the lymph enter the bloodstream?

29.21 What is vasopressin?

29.22 What happens when excess secretion of antidiuretic hormone occurs? State two causes of this.

29.23 What is the difference between blood plasma and blood serum?

29.24 At what percent of body-mass loss is collapse very likely to occur?

29.25 What are the three main types of blood cells?

29.26 What is the major function of each of the three types of blood cells?

29.27 What solutes in body fluids are referred to as electrolytes?

29.28 What are the major electrolytes inside cells and outside cells?

29.29 What is an antigen, and what are the three types of responses the body makes upon exposure to an antigen?

29.30 Antihistamines are often prescribed to counteract the effects of allergies. Explain how these drugs work. (Hint: See also Section 9.9.)

29.31 How are specific immune responses similar to the enzyme–substrate interaction?

29.32 What class of plasma proteins is involved in the antibody-mediated immune response?

29.33 What kinds of cells are associated with the antibody-directed immune response, and how do they work?

29.34 State the three major functions of T cells.

29.35 T cells are often discussed in conjunction with the disease AIDS, in which a virus destroys these cells. How do T cells work to combat disease?

29.36 What are memory cells, and what is their role in the immune response?

29.37 What is a blood clot? What is it composed of?

29.38 What vitamin and what mineral are specifically associated with the clotting process?

29.39 Describe the intrinsic pathway in blood clotting.

29.40 Why, do you suppose, are many of the enzymes involved in blood clotting secreted by the body as zymogens?

29.41 How many O_2 molecules can be bound by each hemoglobin tetramer?

29.42 What must be the charge of the iron in hemoglobin for it to perform its function?

29.43 What color is deoxyhemoglobin? Why?

29.44 How does the degree of saturation of hemoglobin vary with the partial pressure of O_2 in the tissues?

29.45 Oxygen has an allosteric interaction with hemoglobin. What are the results of this interaction as oxygen is bonded and as it is released?

29.46 What are the three ways of transporting CO_2 in the body?

29.47 Use Figure 29.11 to estimate the partial pressure of O_2 at which hemoglobin is 50% saturated with oxygen under normal conditions. Dry air at sea level is about 21% oxygen. What would be the percentage saturation of your hemoglobin under these conditions?

29.48 When an actively metabolizing tissue produces CO_2, the H^+ concentration of blood increases. Explain how this happens using a chemical equation.

29.49 Do the following conditions cause hemoglobin to release more O_2 to the tissues or to absorb more O_2?

  (a) Raising the temperature

  (b) Increased production of CO_2

  (c) Increasing the H^+ concentration

29.50 What are the two types of acidosis? How do they differ?

29.51 Ketoacidosis is a condition that can arise in an individual with diabetes due to excessive production of ketone bodies. Is this condition classified as metabolic acidosis or respiratory acidosis? Explain.

29.52 What are the two types of alkalosis? How do they differ?

29.53 Kidneys are often referred to as filters that purify the blood. What other two essential functions do the kidneys perform to help maintain homeostasis?

29.54 Write the reactions by which HPO_4^{2-} and HCO_3^- absorb excess H^+ from the urine before elimination.

GENERAL QUESTIONS AND PROBLEMS

29.55 What is the chemical basis for ethanol's solubility in blood?

29.56 Nursing mothers are able to impart some immunity to their infants. Why do you think this is so?

29.57 Many people find they retain water after eating salty food, evidenced by swollen fingers and ankles. Explain this phenomenon in terms of how the kidneys operate.

29.58 How does active transport differ from osmosis?

29.59 When is active transport necessary to move substances through cell membranes?

29.60 Discuss the importance of the CO_2/HCO_3^- equilibrium in blood and in urine.

29.61 We have discussed homeostasis throughout this text. But what is *hemostasis*? Is it related to homeostasis?

29.62 When people panic, cry, or have a high fever, they often begin to hyperventilate. Hyperventilation is abnormally fast or deep respiration, which results in the loss of carbon dioxide from the blood. Explain how hyperventilation changes the blood chemistry. Why can breathing into a paper bag alleviate hyperventilation?

CHEMISTRY IN ACTION

29.63 How do endothelial cells in brain capillaries differ from those in other capillary systems? [*The Blood–Brain Barrier, p. 879*]

29.64 What is meant by an asymmetric transport system? Give one specific example of such a system. [*The Blood–Brain Barrier, p. 879*]

29.65 What type of substance is likely to breach the blood–brain barrier? Would ethanol be likely to cross this barrier? Why or why not? [*The Blood–Brain Barrier, p. 879*]

29.66 What is the metabolic blood–brain barrier? [*The Blood–Brain Barrier, p. 879*]

29.67 How are photometers used in automated analysis? [*Automated Clinical Laboratory Analysis, p. 889*]

29.68 Why is automated analysis useful to test for enzyme levels in body fluids? [*Automated Clinical Laboratory Analysis, p. 889*]

29.69 In analyzing body fluids for medical diagnoses, what are some advantages of using automated analyzers rather than technicians? [*Automated Clinical Laboratory Analysis, p. 889*]

Scientific Notation

What Is Scientific Notation?

The numbers that you encounter in chemistry are often either very large or very small. For example, there are about 33,000,000,000,000,000,000,000 H_2O molecules in 1.0 mL of water, and the distance between the H and O atoms in an H_2O molecule is 0.000 000 000 095 7 m. These quantities are more conveniently written in *scientific notation* as 3.3×10^{22} molecules and 9.57×10^{-11} m, respectively. In scientific notation (also known as *exponential notation*), a quantity is represented as a number between 1 and 10 multiplied by a power of 10. In this kind of expression, the small raised number to the right of the 10 is the exponent.

Number	Exponential Form	Exponent
1,000,000	1×10^6	6
100,000	1×10^5	5
10,000	1×10^4	4
1,000	1×10^3	3
100	1×10^2	2
10	1×10^1	1
1		
0.1	1×10^{-1}	-1
0.01	1×10^{-2}	-2
0.001	1×10^{-3}	-3
0.000 1	1×10^{-4}	-4
0.000 01	1×10^{-5}	-5
0.000 001	1×10^{-6}	-6
0.000 000 1	1×10^{-7}	-7

Numbers greater than 1 have *positive* exponents, which tell how many times a number must be *multiplied* by 10 to obtain the correct value. For example, the expression 5.2×10^3 means that 5.2 must be multiplied by 10 three times:

$$5.2 \times 10^3 = 5.2 \times 10 \times 10 \times 10 = 5.2 \times 1000 = 5200$$

Note that doing this means moving the decimal point three places to the right:

$$5200.\underset{123}{}$$

The value of a positive exponent indicates *how many places to the right the decimal point must be moved* to give the correct number in ordinary decimal notation.

Numbers less than 1 have *negative exponents,* which tell how many times a number must be *divided* by 10 (or multiplied by one-tenth) to obtain the correct value. Thus, the expression 3.7×10^{-2} means that 3.7 must be divided by 10 two times:

$$3.7 \times 10^{-2} = \frac{3.7}{10 \times 10} = \frac{3.7}{100} = 0.037$$

Note that doing this means moving the decimal point two places to the left:

$$0.037\underset{21}{}$$

The value of a negative exponent indicates *how may places to the left the decimal point must be moved* to give the correct number in ordinary decimal notation.

Representing Numbers in Scientific Notation

How do you convert a number from ordinary notation to scientific notation? If the number is greater than or equal to 10, shift the decimal point to the *left* by n places until you obtain a number between 1 and 10. Then, multiply the result by 10^n. For example, the number 8137.6 is written in scientific notation as 8.1376×10^3:

$$8137.6 = 8.1376 \times 10^3$$

Shift decimal point to the left by 3 places to get a number between 1 and 10

Number of places decimal point was shifted to the left

When you shift the decimal point to the left by three places, you are in effect dividing the number by $10 \times 10 \times 10 = 1000 = 10^3$. Therefore, you must multiply the result by 10^3 so that the value of the number is unchanged.

To convert a number less than 1 to scientific notation, shift the decimal point to the *right* by n places until you obtain a number between 1 and 10. Then, multiply the result by 10^{-n}. For example, the number 0.012 is written in scientific notation as 1.2×10^{-2}:

$$0.012 = 1.2 \times 10^{-2}$$

Shift decimal point to the right by 2 places to get a number between 1 and 10

Number of places decimal point was shifted to the right

When you shift the decimal point to the right by two places, you are in effect multiplying the number by $10 \times 10 = 100 = 10^2$. Therefore, you must multiply the result by 10^{-2} so that the value of the number is unchanged. $(10^2 \times 10^{-2} = 10^0 = 1.)$

The following table gives some additional examples. To convert from scientific notation to ordinary notation, simply reverse the preceding process. Thus, to write the number 5.84×10^4 in ordinary notation, drop the factor of 10^4 and move the decimal point 4 places to the *right* $(5.84 \times 10^4 = 58,400)$. To write the number 3.5×10^{-1} in ordinary notation, drop the factor of 10^{-1} and move the decimal point 1 place to the *left* $(3.5 \times 10^{-1} = 0.35)$. Note that you don't need scientific notation for numbers between 1 and 10 because $10^0 = 1$.

Number	Scientific Notation
58,400	5.84×10^4
0.35	3.5×10^{-1}
7.296	$7.296 \times 10^0 = 7.296 \times 1$

Mathematical Operations with Scientific Notation

Addition and Subtraction in Scientific Notation

To add or subtract two numbers expressed in scientific notation, both numbers must have the same exponent. Thus, to add 7.16×10^3 and 1.32×10^2, first write the latter number as 0.132×10^3 and then add:

$$
\begin{array}{r}
7.16 \times 10^3 \\
+0.132 \times 10^3 \\
\hline
7.29 \times 10^3
\end{array}
$$

The answer has three significant figures. (Significant figures are discussed in Section 2.4.) Alternatively, you can write the first number as 71.6×10^2 and then add:

$$\begin{array}{r} 7.16 \times 10^2 \\ + \ 1.32 \times 10^2 \\ \hline 72.9 \ \times 10^2 = 7.29 \times 10^3 \end{array}$$

Subtraction of these two numbers is carried out in the same manner.

$$\begin{array}{r} 7.16 \ \times 10^3 \\ -0.132 \times 10^3 \\ \hline 7.03 \ \times 10^3 \end{array} \quad \text{or} \quad \begin{array}{r} 7.16 \times 10^2 \\ -1.32 \times 10^2 \\ \hline 70.3 \times 10^2 = 7.03 \times 10^3 \end{array}$$

Multiplication in Scientific Notation

To multiply two numbers expressed in scientific notation, multiply the factors in front of the powers of 10 and then add the exponents. For example,

$$(2.5 \times 10^4)(4.7 \times 10^7) = (2.5)(4.7) \times 10^{4+7} = 10 \times 10^{11} = 1.2 \times 10^{12}$$

$$(3.46 \times 10^5)(2.2 \times 10^{-2}) = (3.46)(2.2) \times 10^{5+(-2)} = 7.6 \times 10^3$$

Both answers have two significant figures.

Division in Scientific Notation

To divide two numbers expressed in scientific notation, divide the factors in front of the powers of 10 and then subtract the exponent in the denominator from the exponent in the numerator. For example,

$$\frac{3 \times 10^6}{7.2 \times 10^2} = \frac{3}{7.2} \times 10^{6-2} = 0.4 \times 10^4 = 4 \times 10^3 \ (1 \text{ significant figure})$$

$$\frac{7.50 \times 10^{-5}}{2.5 \times 10^{-7}} = \frac{7.50}{2.5} \times 10^{-5-(-7)} = 3.0 \times 10^2 \ (2 \text{ significant figures})$$

Scientific Notation and Electronic Calculators

With a scientific calculator you can carry out calculations in scientific notation. You should consult the instruction manual for your particular calculator to learn how to enter and manipulate numbers expressed in an exponential format. On most calculators, you enter the number $A \times 10^n$ by (i) entering the number A, (ii) pressing a key labeled EXP or EE, and (iii) entering the exponent n. If the exponent is negative, you press a key labeled $+/-$ before entering the value of n. (Note that you do not enter the number 10.) The calculator displays the number $A \times 10^n$ with the number A on the left followed by some space and then the exponent n. For example,

$$4.625 \times 10^2 \quad \text{is displayed as} \quad 4.625 \ 02$$

To add, subtract, multiply, or divide exponential numbers, use the same sequence of keystrokes as you would in working with ordinary numbers. When you add or subtract on a calculator, the numbers need not have the same exponent; the calculator automatically takes account of the different exponents. Remember, though, that the calculator often gives more digits in the answer than the allowed number of significant figures. It's sometimes helpful to outline the calculation on paper, as in the preceding examples, to keep track of the number of significant figures.

PROBLEM A.1

Perform the following calculations, expressing the results in scientific notation with the correct number of significant figures. (You don't need a calculator for these.)

(a) $(1.50 \times 10^4) + (5.04 \times 10^3)$

(b) $(2.5 \times 10^{-2}) - (5.0 \times 10^{-3})$

(c) $(6.3 \times 10^{15}) \times (10.1 \times 10^{3})$

(d) $(2.5 \times 10^{-3}) \times (3.2 \times 10^{-4})$

(e) $(8.4 \times 10^{4}) \div (3.0 \times 10^{6})$

(f) $(5.530 \times 10^{-2}) \div (2.5 \times 10^{-5})$

ANSWERS

(a) 2.00×10^{4} (b) 2.0×10^{-2} (c) 6.4×10^{19}

(d) 8.0×10^{-7} (e) 2.8×10^{-2} (f) 2.2×10^{3}

PROBLEM A.2

Perform the following calculations, expressing the results in scientific notation with the correct number of significant figures. (Use a calculator for these.)

(a) $(9.72 \times 10^{-1}) + (3.4823 \times 10^{2})$

(b) $(3.772 \times 10^{3}) - (2.891 \times 10^{4})$

(c) $(1.956 \times 10^{3}) \div (6.02 \times 10^{23})$

(d) $3.2811 \times (9.45 \times 10^{21})$

(e) $(1.0015 \times 10^{3}) \div (5.202 \times 10^{-9})$

(f) $(6.56 \times 10^{-6}) \times (9.238 \times 10^{-4})$

ANSWERS

(a) 3.4920×10^{2} (b) -2.514×10^{4} (c) 3.25×10^{-21}

(d) 3.10×10^{22} (e) 1.925×10^{11} (f) 6.06×10^{-9}

Conversion Factors

Length SI Unit: Meter (m)

 1 meter = 0.001 kilometer (km)

   = 100 centimeters (cm)

   = 1.0936 yards (yd)

 1 centimeter = 10 millimeters (mm)

   = 0.3937 inch (in.)

 1 nanometer = 1×10^{-9} meter

 1 Angstrom (Å) = 1×10^{-10} meter

 1 inch = 2.54 centimeters

 1 mile = 1.6094 kilometers

Volume SI Unit: Cubic meter (m^3)

 1 cubic meter = 1000 liters (L)

 1 liter = 1000 cubic centimeters (cm^3)

   = 1000 milliliters (mL)

   = 1.056710 quarts (qt)

 1 cubic inch = 16.4 cubic centimeters

Temperature SI Unit: Kelvin (K)

 0 K = −273.15 °C

  = −459.67 °F

 °F = (9/5) °C + 32°; °F = (1.8 × °C) + 32°

 °C = (5/9) (°F − 32°); $°C = \dfrac{(°F - 32°)}{1.8}$

 K = °C + 273.15°

Mass SI Unit: Kilogram (kg)

 1 kilogram = 1000 grams (g)

   = 2.205 pounds (lb)

 1 gram = 1000 milligrams (mg)

   = 0.03527 ounce (oz)

 1 pound = 453.6 grams

 1 atomic mass unit = 1.66054×10^{-24} gram

Pressure SI Unit: Pascal (Pa)

 1 pascal = 9.869×10^{-6} atmosphere

 1 atmosphere = 101,325 pascals

   = 760 mmHg (Torr)

   = 14.70 lb/in^2

Energy SI Unit: Joule (J)

 1 joule = 0.23901 calorie (cal)

 1 calorie = 4.184 joules

 1 Calorie (nutritional unit) = 1000 calories

   = 1 kcal

13.68

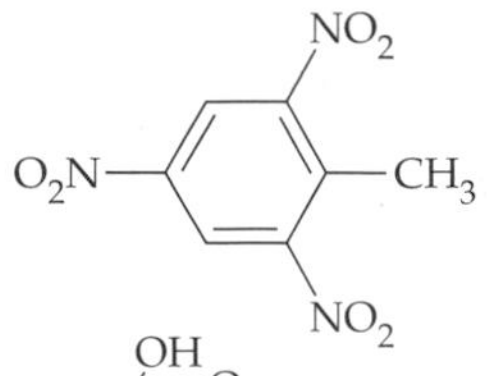

TNT

13.70

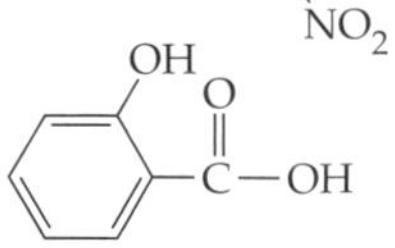

Salicylic acid

13.72 (a) 5-methyl-2-hexene (b) 4-methyl-2-heptyne (c) 2,3-dimethyl-1-butene (d) 1,2,4-trinitrobenzene (e) 3,4-dimethylcyclohexene (f) 3-methyl-1,3-pentadiene **13.74** Br_2 reacts only with cyclohexene.

13.76

13.78

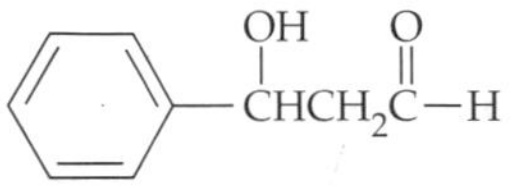

13.80

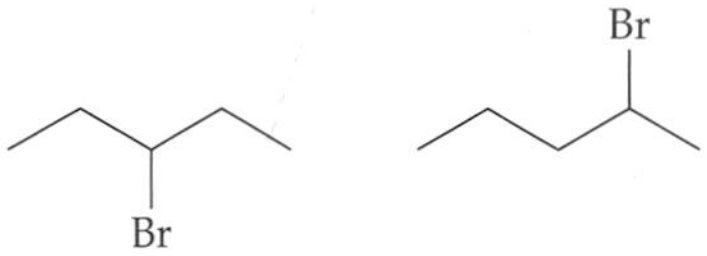

Both ends of the double bond have the same number of hydrogens, and both products can form.

13.82

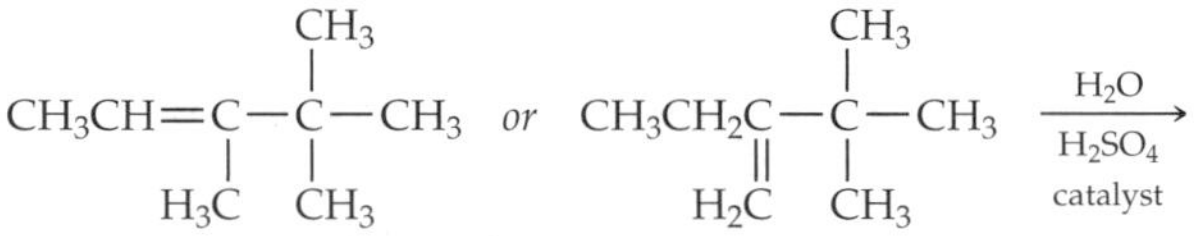

13.84 Rod cells are responsible for vision in dim light; cone cells are responsible for color vision. **13.86** ultraviolet range **13.88** a compound that has two or more benzene-like rings that share a common bond **13.90** $(CH_3)_3C^+$ **13.92** *See below for answer.*

Chapter 14

14.1 (a) alcohol (b) alcohol (c) phenol (d) alcohol (e) ether (f) ether
14.2 The ether oxygen can form hydrogen bonds with water.
14.3 (a)

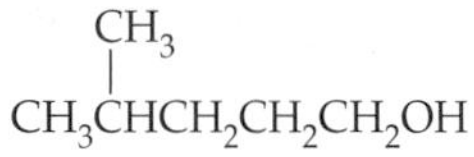

primary alcohol

(b)

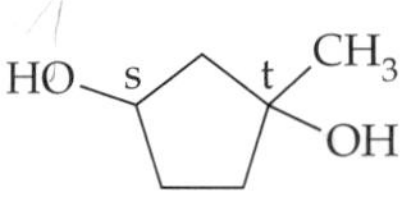

secondary, tertiary alcohol

(c)

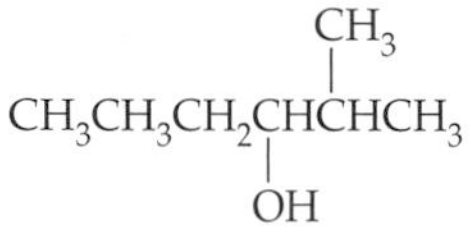

secondary alcohol

(d)

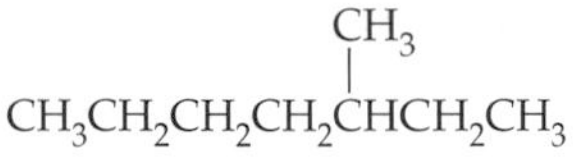

secondary alcohol

(e)

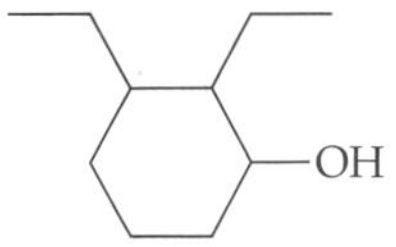

secondary alcohol

14.4 (a) 2-methyl-2-propanol (*tert*-butyl alcohol), tertiary (b) 3-methyl-2-pentanol,

secondary (c) 5-chloro-2-ethyl-1-hexanol, primary (d) 1,2-cyclopentanediol, secondary **14.5** See 14.3 and 14.4 **14.6** highest (d), (b), (a), (c) lowest **14.7** most soluble (b), (c), (a) least soluble **14.8** (a) propene (b) cyclohexene (c) 4-methyl-1-pentene (minor) and 4-methyl-2-pentene (major) **14.9** (a) 2-methyl-2-butanol or 3-methyl-2-butanol (b) 1,2-dimethylcyclopentanol (c) 1,2-diphenylethanol

14.10

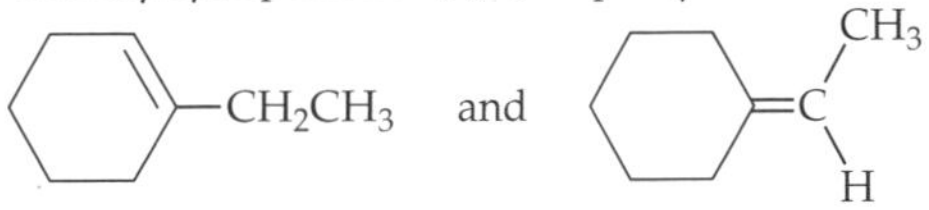

and

14.11 (a)

(b)

(c)

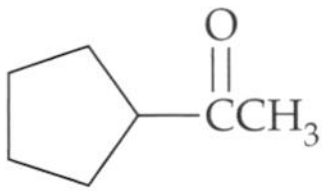

14.12 (a) 2-propanol (b) cycloheptanol (c) 3-methyl-1-butanol
14.13 (a)

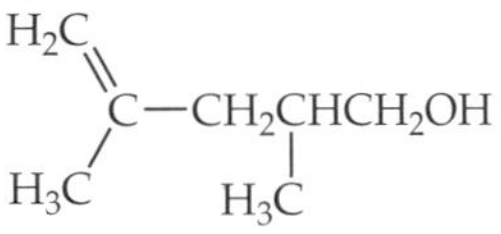

(b)

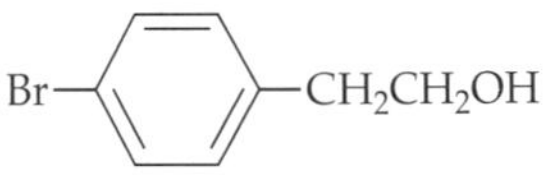

14.14 (a)

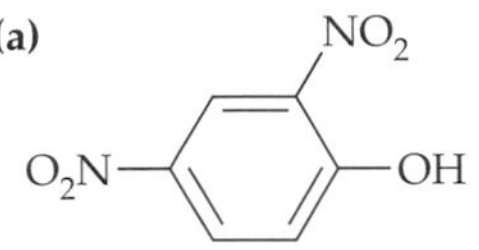

(b)

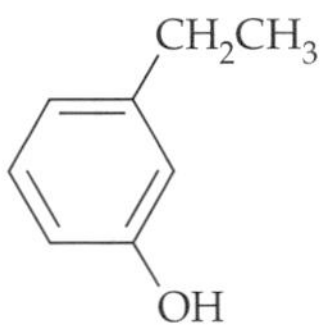

14.15 (a) 2,4-dibromophenol (b) 3-iodo-2-methylphenol
14.16

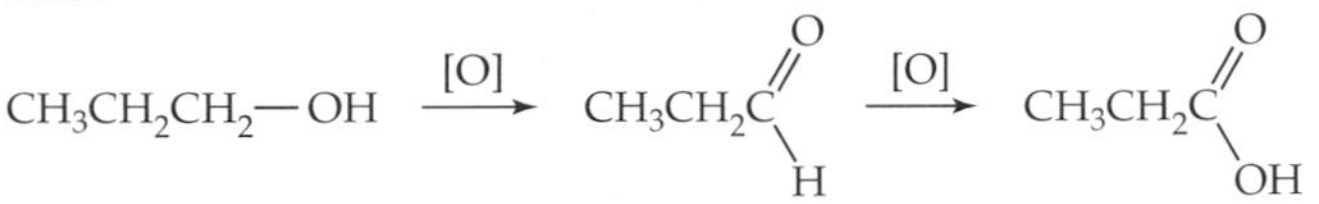

14.17 (a) 1,2-dimethoxypropane (b) *p*-methoxynitrobenzene (c) *tert*-butyl methyl ether **14.18** They inhibit free-radical chain reactions in unsaturated fats. **14.19** (a) $CH_3CH_2CH_2S\!-\!SCH_2CH_2CH_3$ (b) $(CH_3)_2CHCH_2CH_2S\!-\!SCH_2CH_2CH(CH_3)_2$
14.20 (a) 1-chloro-1-ethylcyclopentane (b) 3-bromo-5-methylheptane
14.21 (a) 5-methyl-3-hexanol (b) *m*-methoxytoluene (c) 3-methylcyclohexanol
14.22

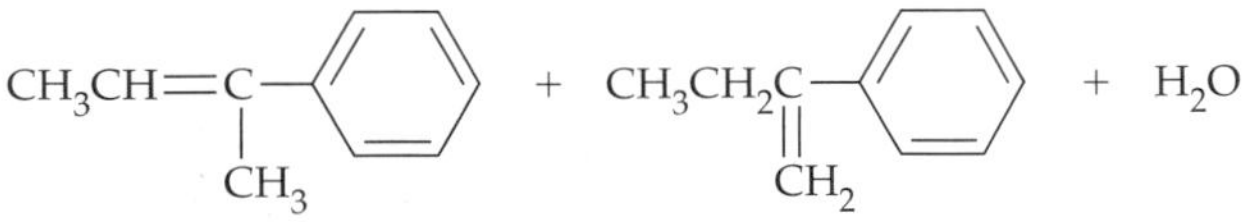

14.23 $(CH_3)_2CHCH_2CH_2CHO$, $(CH_3)_2CHCH_2CH_2CO_2H$
14.24

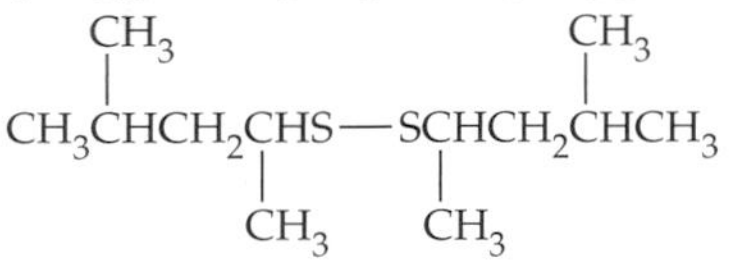

14.25

(a)

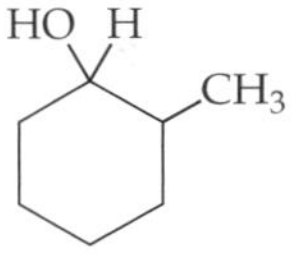

b)

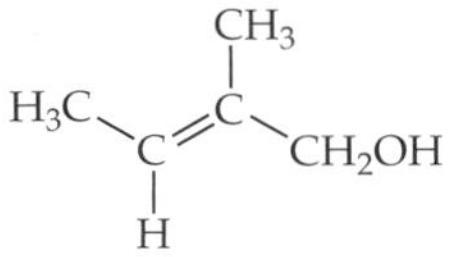

(c)

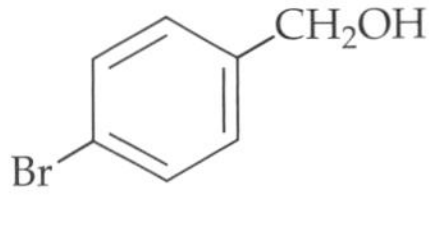

14.26 Alcohols have an —OH group bonded to an alkane-like carbon atom; ethers have an oxygen atom bonded to two carbon atoms; and phenols have an —OH group bonded to a carbon of an aromatic ring.

13.92

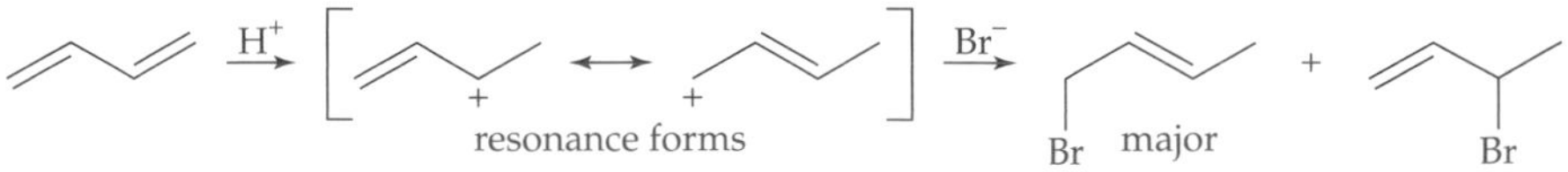

Addition of H^+ produces a carbocation that can be represented as two resonance forms. Br^- adds to produce the observed alkene.

14.28 Alcohols form hydrogen bonds. **14.30** ketone, carbon–carbon double bond, alcohol **14.32** (a) 2-methyl-2-propanol (*tert*-butyl alcohol) (b) 2-methyl-1-propanol (c) 1,2,4-butanetriol (d) 2-methyl-2-phenyl-1-propanol (e) 3-methylcyclohexanol (f) 3-ethyl-3-methyl-2-hexanol

14.34 (a)

(b)

(c)

(d)

(e)

(f)

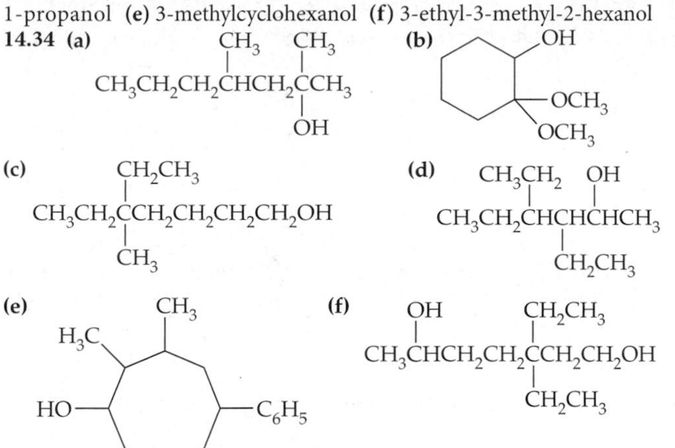

14.36 (a) tertiary (b) primary (c) primary, secondary (d) primary (e) secondary (f) secondary
14.38 lowest (a) < (c) < (b) highest
14.40 a ketone **14.42** a carboxylic acid
14.44 Phenols dissolve in aqueous NaOH; alcohols don't.
14.46
(a)

(b)

(c)

(d)

(e)

HOCH$_2$CH$_2$CH$_2$CH$_2$CH$_2$OH

(f)

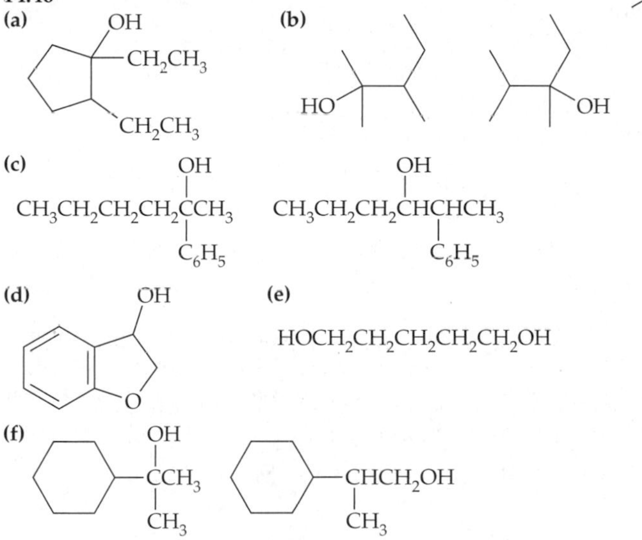

14.48
(a)

(b)

(c)

(d) NR (e) NR (f)

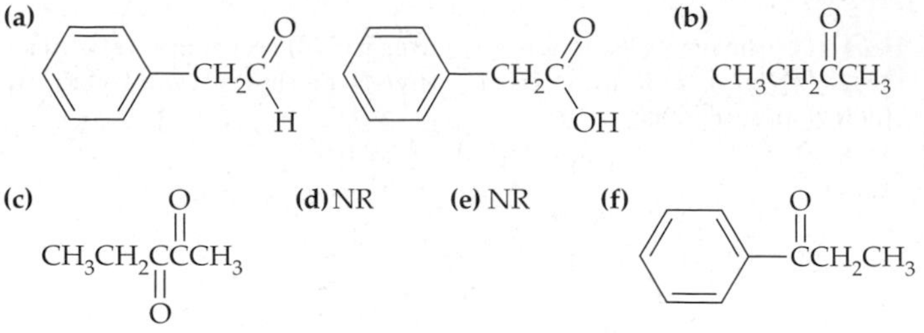

14.50 odor
14.52

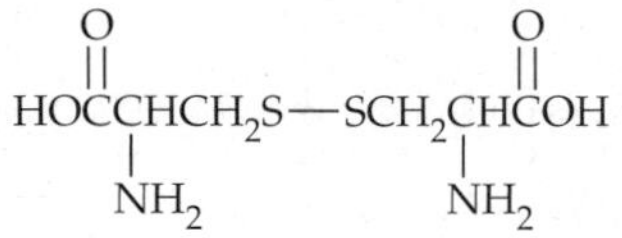

14.54 Alcohols can form hydrogen bonds; thiols and alkyl chlorides can't.
14.56

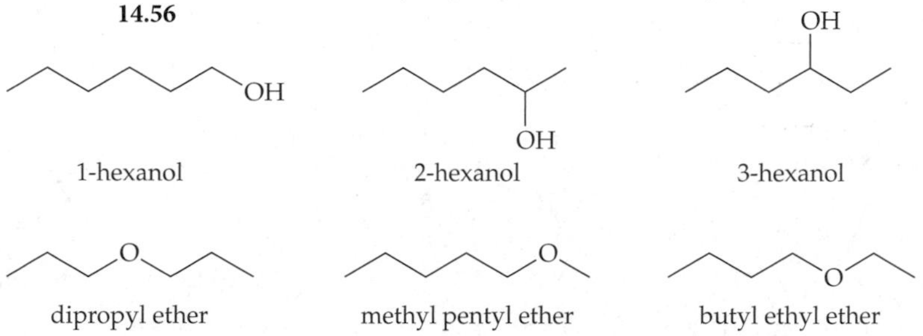

1-hexanol   2-hexanol   3-hexanol

dipropyl ether   methyl pentyl ether   butyl ethyl ether

14.58 Alcohols become less soluble as their nonpolar part becomes larger.
14.60 An antiseptic kills microorganisms on living tissue; a disinfectant is used on nonliving matter. **14.62** (a) *p*-dibromobenzene (b) 1,2-dibromo-1-butene (c) *m*-propylanisole (d) 1,1-dibromocyclopentane (e) 2,4-dimethyl-2,4-pentanediol (f) 4-methyl-2,4,5-heptanetriol (g) 4-bromo-6,6-dimethyl-2-heptyne (h) 1-chloro-2-iodocyclobutane
14.64 3,7-Dimethyl-2,6-octadiene-1-ol

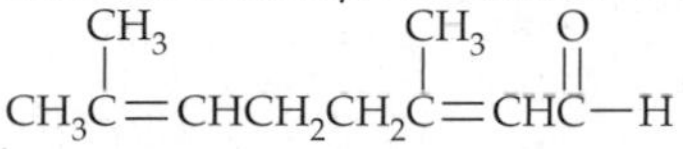

14.66 C$_2$H$_6$O + 3 O$_2$ → 2 CO$_2$ + 3 H$_2$O **14.68** slurred speech: 300–400 mg/dL lethal concentration: 600 mg/dL **14.70** A person breathes into a tube containing potassium dichromate (yellow-orange). If there is alcohol in the breath, it is oxidized by dichromate, which is reduced to Cr(lll) (blue green). **14.72** Vitamin E **14.74** the concentration of anesthetic that results in anesthesia in 50% of patients

14.76 (a)

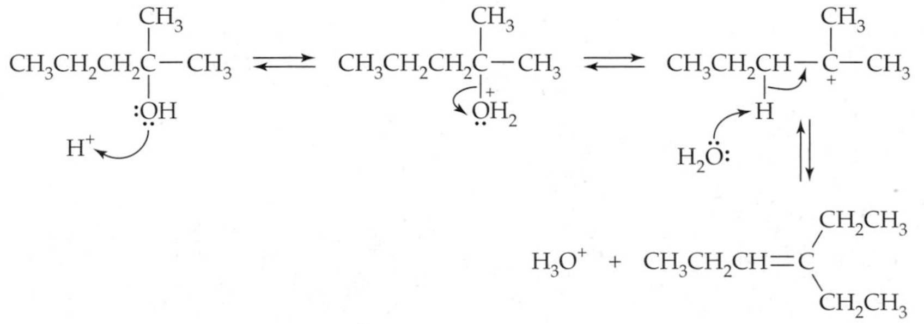

(b)

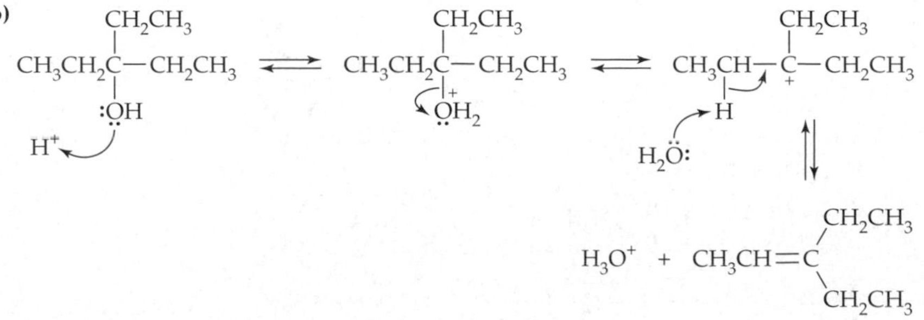

Chapter 15

15.1 (a) primary (b) secondary (c) primary (d) secondary (e) tertiary
15.2 (a) tripropylamine (b) N-ethyl-N-methylcyclopentylamine
(c) N-isopropylaniline
15.3 (a) $CH_3CH_2CH_2CH_2CH_2CH_2CH_2CH_2NH_2$

(b)  $CH_3CH_2CH_2CH_2CH_2\overset{\displaystyle CH_3}{\overset{|}{N}H}$

(c) 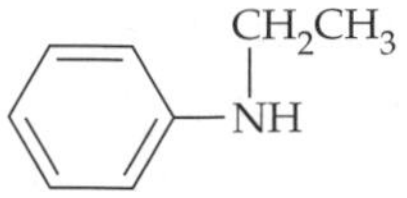 [cyclohexyl]—NH—CH_2CH_3 (d) 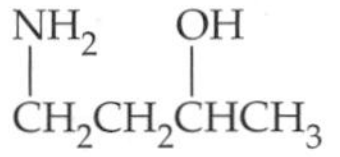 $\overset{\quad NH_2 \quad OH}{CH_2CH_2CHCH_3}$

15.4 pharmaceuticals. Manufacturers don't make their MSDS available to avoid patient confusion.
15.5 The ion has one less electron than the neutral atoms.

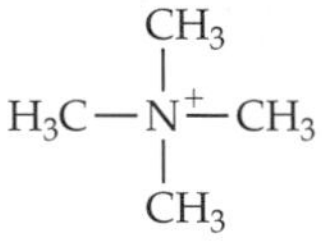

$$H_3C-\overset{\displaystyle CH_3}{\underset{\displaystyle CH_3}{\overset{|}{\underset{|}{N^+}}}}-CH_3$$

15.6 $CH_3CH_2CH_2CH_2NHCH_2CH_3$ N-ethylbutylamine **15.7** Compound
(a) is lowest boiling; (b) is highest boiling (strongest hydrogen bonds).
15.8 (a) 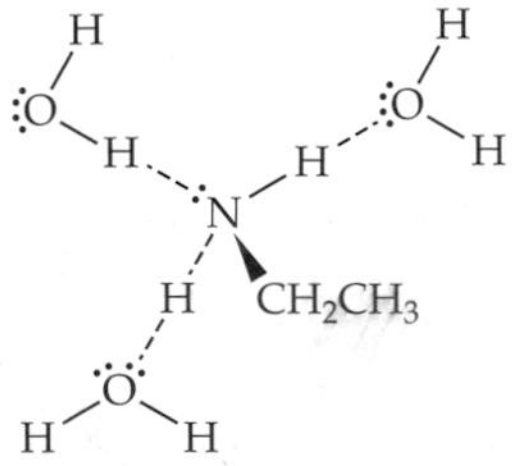 [structure] (b) 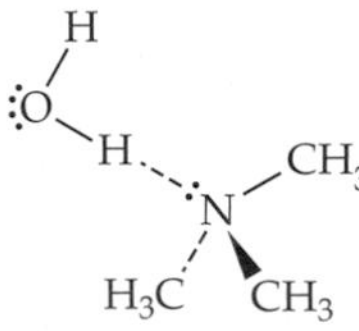 [structure]

15.9 (a) methylamine, ethylamine, dimethylamine, trimethylamine
(b) pyridine (c) aniline **15.10** (a) pyrimidine: $C_4H_4N_2$ (b) purine:
$C_5H_4N_4$ **15.11** (a) and (d)
15.12

(a) 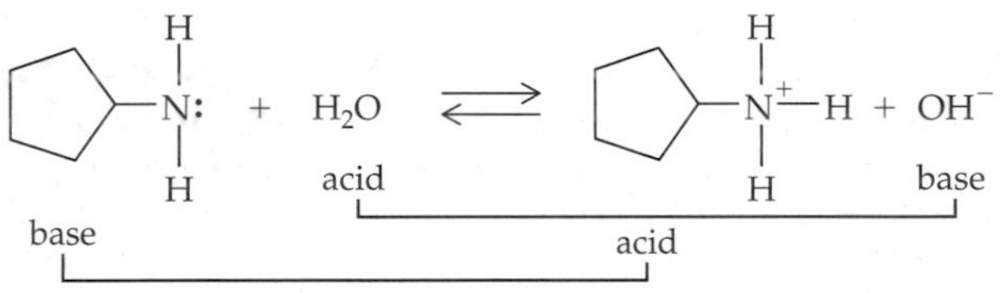 [equilibrium structure] N: + H₂O ⇌ N⁺—H + OH⁻
base   acid   acid   base

(b) 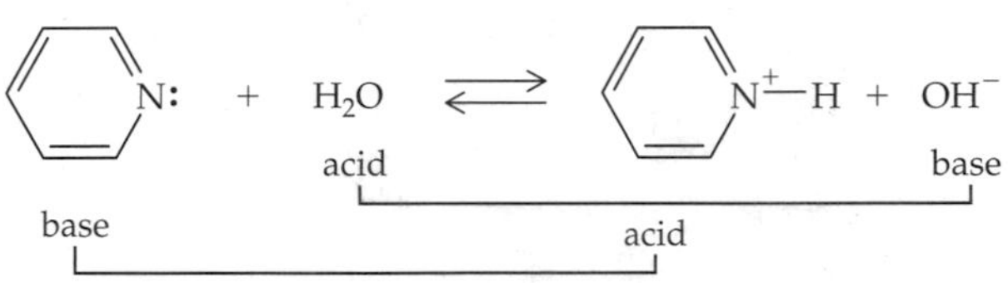 [pyridine] N: + H₂O ⇌ N⁺—H + OH⁻
base   acid   acid   base

15.13

(a) 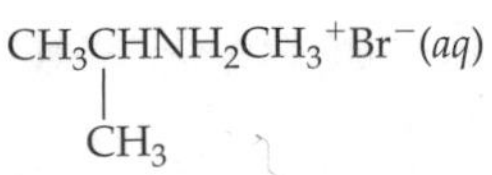 $CH_3CHNH_2CH_3{}^+Br^-(aq)$ (b) 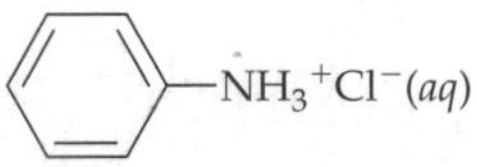 [phenyl]—$NH_3{}^+Cl^-(aq)$
     $\overset{|}{CH_3}$

(c) 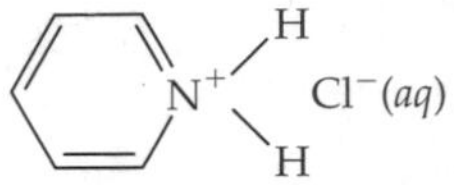 [pyridine]—N^+—H $Cl^-(aq)$ (d) $(CH_3)_3CNH_2 + H_2O\,(l) + Na^+(aq)$

15.14 (a) N-methylisopropylammonium bromide (b) anilinium chloride
(c) piperidinium chloride **15.15** (a) ethylamine (b) triethylamine

15.16
(a) 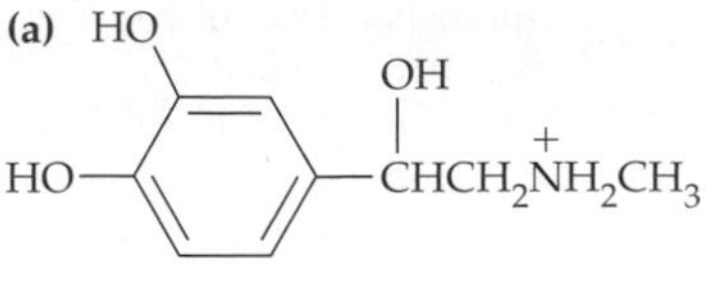 [structure] HO, OH ... —CHCH₂NH₂CH₃   (b) 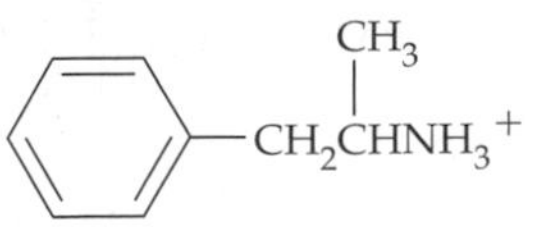 [structure] —CH₂CHNH₃⁺ with CH₃

15.17–15.18

(a) 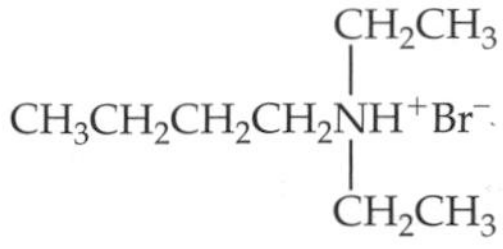 $CH_3CH_2CH_2CH_2\overset{\displaystyle CH_2CH_3}{\underset{\displaystyle CH_2CH_3}{\overset{|}{\underset{|}{N}}}}H^+Br^-$
   (b) $(CH_3CH_2CH_2CH_2)_4N^+OH^-$

Butyldiethylammonium bromide   Tetrabutylammonium hydroxide
or N,N–Diethylbutylammonium bromide   salt of a quaternary amine
salt of a tertiary amine

(c) $CH_3CH_2CH_2NH_3{}^+I^-$ (d) $CH_3\overset{\displaystyle CH_3}{\underset{\displaystyle CH_3}{\overset{|}{\underset{|}{CH}}}}NH_2{}^+Cl^-$

Propylammonium iodide   Isopropylmethylammonium chloride
salt of a primary amine   salt of a secondary amine

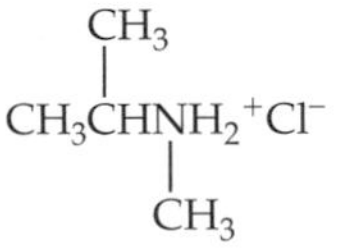

15.19 $CH_3CH_2CH_2CH_2NH_3^+Cl^-(aq) + NaOH(aq) \rightarrow$
$CH_3CH_2CH_2CH_2NH_2 + H_2O(l) + NaCl(aq)$
15.20 Benadryl has the general structure. In Benadryl, R = —CH₃, and
R′ = R" = C_6H_5—.
15.21

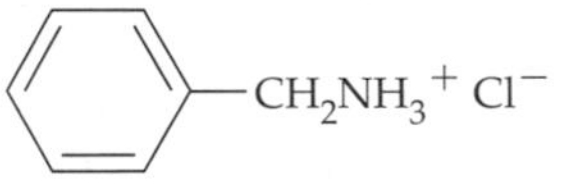

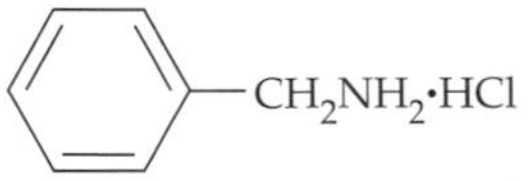

[phenyl]—$CH_2NH_3{}^+$ Cl^- [phenyl]—$CH_2NH_2\cdot HCl$

Benzylammonium chloride

15.22 carboxylic acid/carboxylate; amine/ammonium group; phosphate/
diphosphate
15.23

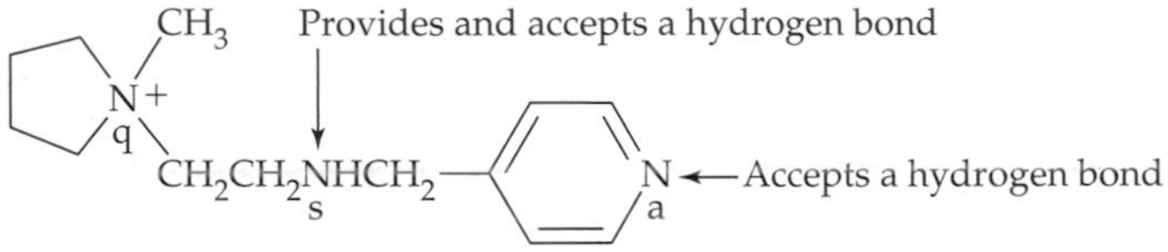

[structure] Provides and accepts a hydrogen bond
N⁺ ... $CH_2CH_2NHCH_2$— ... N ← Accepts a hydrogen bond

15.24 (a) Both amine groups can participate in hydrogen bonding.
(b) Lysine is water-soluble because it can form hydrogen bonds with water.
15.25 (a) 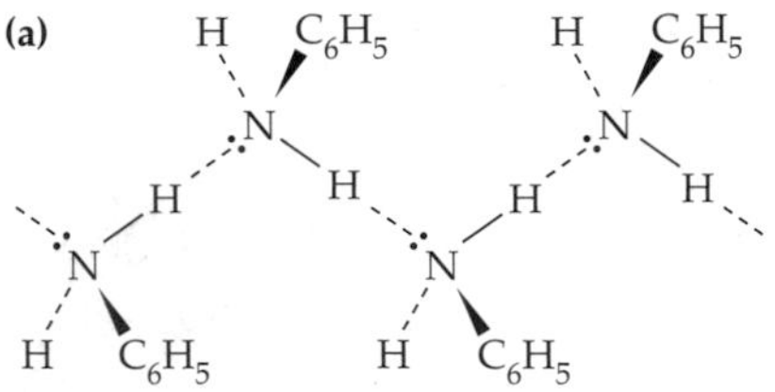 [hydrogen bonding structures]

(b) 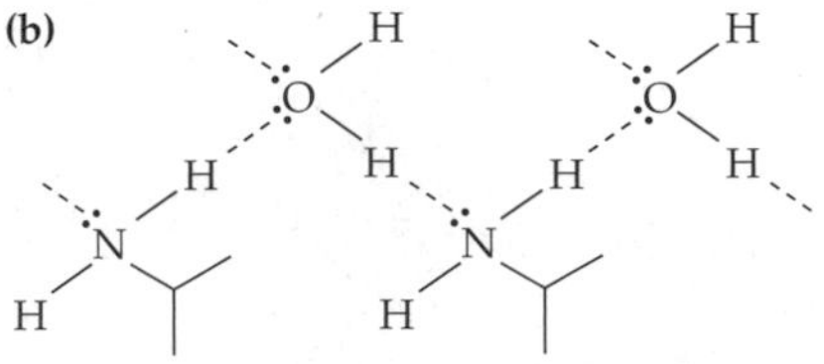 [hydrogen bonding structures]

(c) 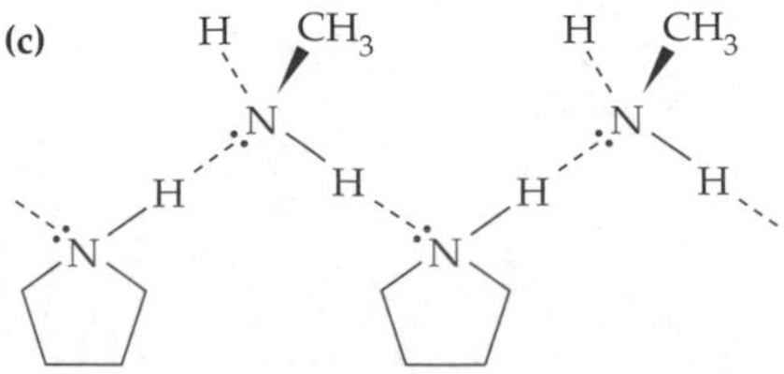 [hydrogen bonding structures]

15.26

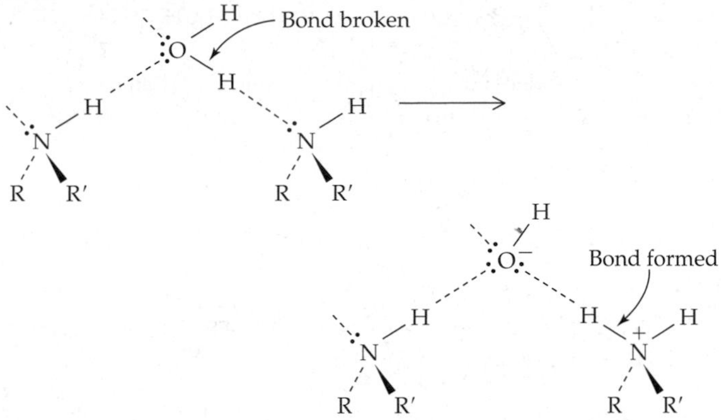

15.27 strongest base:$(CH_3)_2NH$ weakest base:$C_6H_5NH_2$

15.28 (a) 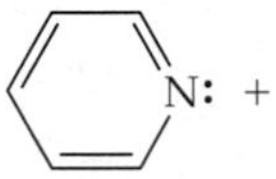 $N: + H_2O$ **(b)** $(CH_3)_2CHNH_3^+ + OH^-$

(c) $(CH_3CH_2)_3NH^+ Br^-$ **(d)** 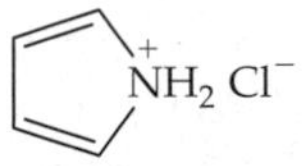 $NH_2^+ Cl^-$

15.30 (a) $CH_3CH_2CH_2CH_2CH_2NCH_3$ (with H on N)   **(b)** 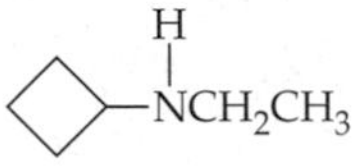 $-NCH_2CH_3$ (with H on N)

(c) 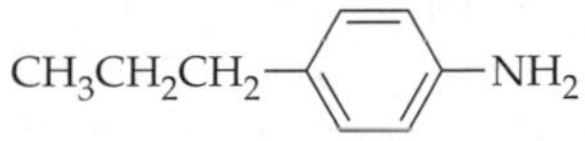 $CH_3CH_2CH_2-$ $-NH_2$

15.32 (a) N-ethylcyclopentylamine (secondary) **(b)** cycloheptylamine (primary)   **15.34** diethylamine

15.36

(a) N-methyl-2-butylammonium nitrate (salt of a secondary amine).

(b) 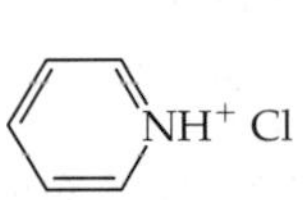 $NH^+ Cl$
(salt of a heterocyclic amine)

(c) 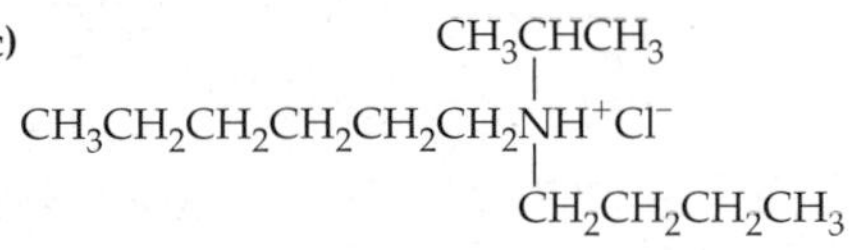 $CH_3CH_2CH_2CH_2CH_2CH_2NH^+Cl^-$ with CH_3CHCH_3 group above and $CH_2CH_2CH_2CH_3$ group below
(salt of a tertiary amine)

15.38

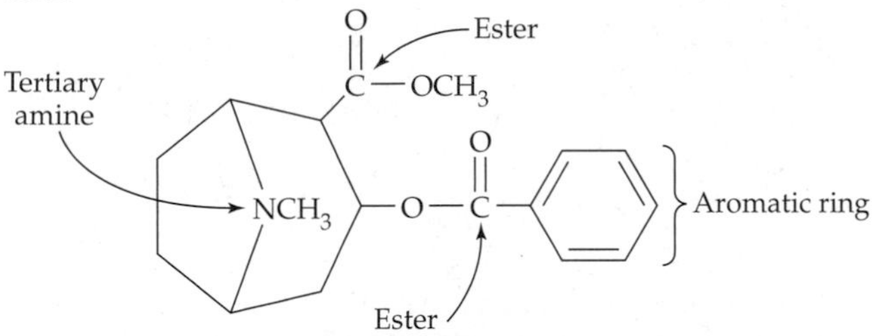

Cocaine

15.40

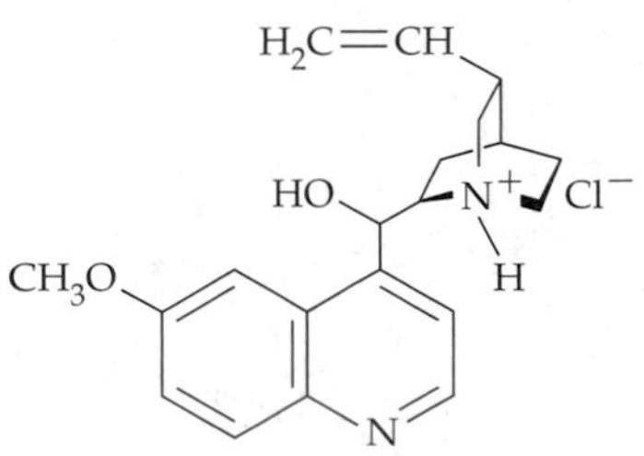

Quinine hydrochloride

15.42 (a) 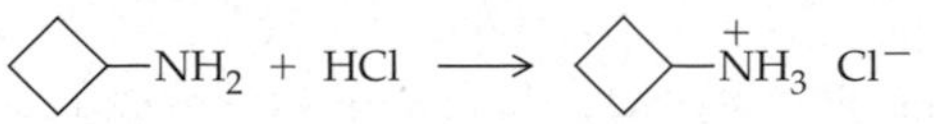 $-NH_2 + HCl \longrightarrow$ $-NH_3^+ Cl^-$

(b) $CH_3CH_2CH_2NCH_3 + H_2O \rightleftharpoons CH_3CH_2CH_2NCH_3^+ + OH^-$ (with H on nitrogen)

(c) 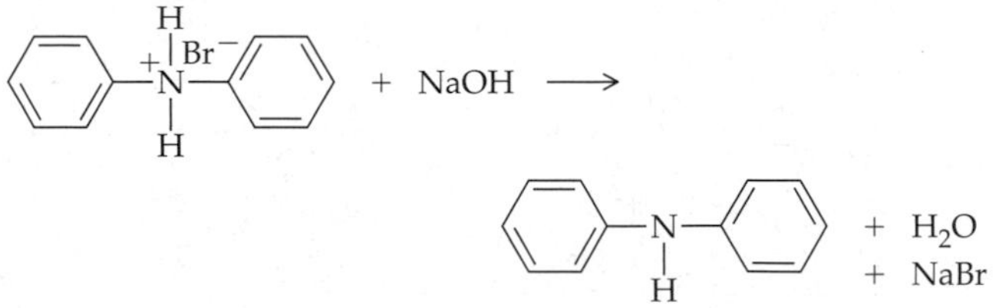 $+ NaOH \longrightarrow$ $+ H_2O + NaBr$

15.44 Choline doesn't react with HCl because its nitrogen isn't basic.
15.46 Its large hydrocarbon region is water-insoluble.
15.48

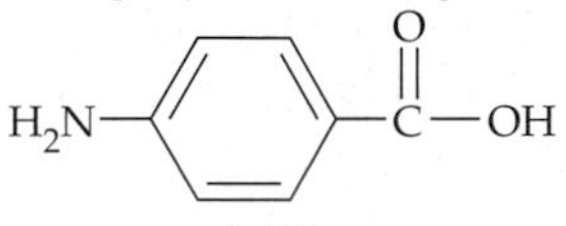

PABA

15.50

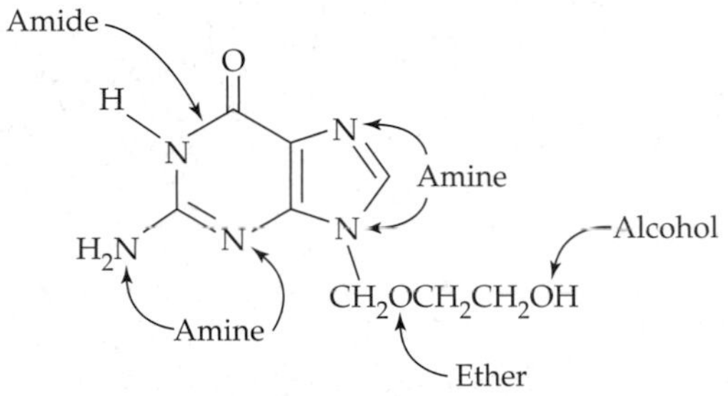

Acyclovir—related to purine

15.52 Amines: foul-smelling, somewhat basic, lower boiling(weaker hydrogen bonds) Alcohols: pleasant-smelling, not basic, higher boiling (stronger hydrogen bonds)   **15.54 (a)** 6-methyl-2-heptene **(b)** p-isopropylphenol **(c)** dibutylamine   **15.56** Molecules of hexylamine can form hydrogen bonds to each other, but molecules of triethylamine can't.   **15.58** Baeocystin is related to indole.   **15.60** Pyridine forms H-bonds with water; benzene doesn't form H-bonds.   **15.62** OSHA requires MSDS for occupational use of hazardous chemicals. You might need a MSDS for NaCl if your job involved working with large amounts of NaCl on a daily basis.
15.64

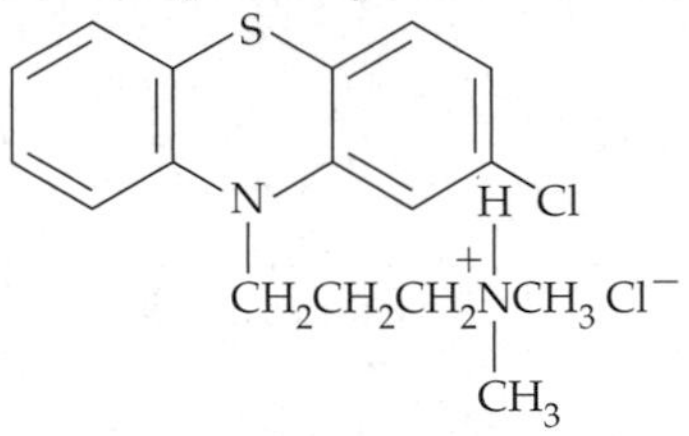

15.65 (a) A forensic toxicologist deals with criminal cases involving drug abuse and poisoning. **(b)** the structure of the toxin, its mode of action, a mechanism to reverse its effects

Chapter 16

16.1 (a)

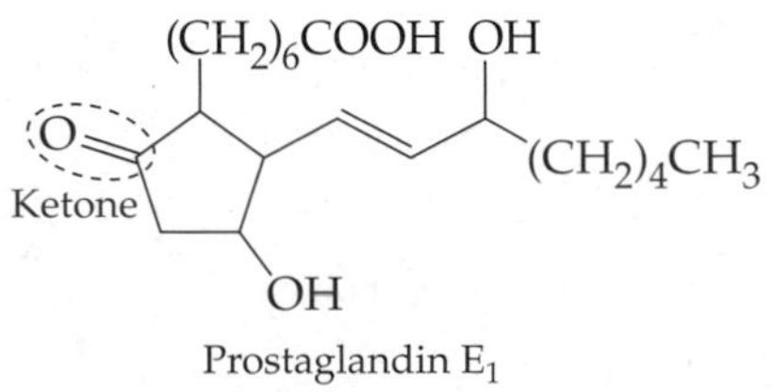

Prostaglandin E$_1$

(b)

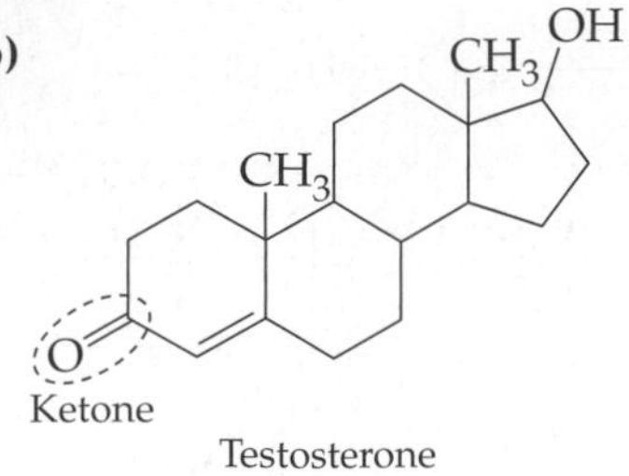

Ketone
Testosterone

(c)

Vanillin

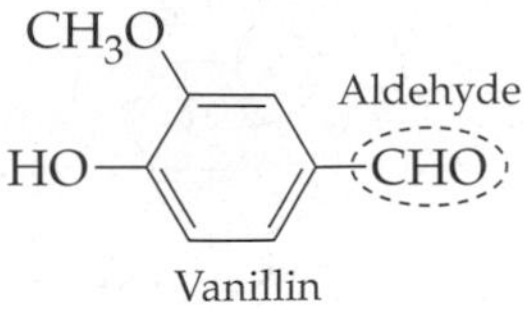

(d) $C_4H_9COCH_3$
Ketone

(e) C_4H_9CHO
Aldehyde

16.2 (d)

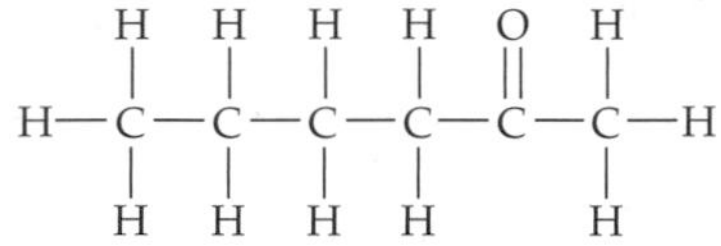

(e)

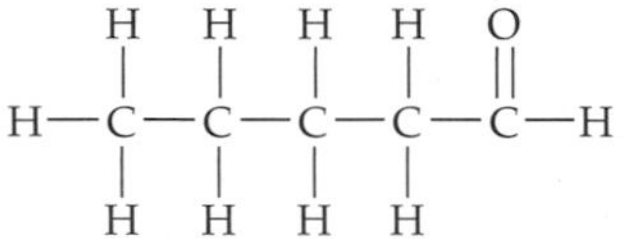

16.3 (a)

$$CH_3CH_2CH_2CH_2CH_2CH_2CH_2CH$$ with =O

(b)

(c)

$$CH_3CH_2CHCH_2CH_2CH$$ with CH_3 and =O

(d)

$$CH_3C-CCH_3$$ with H_3C, CH_3, and =O

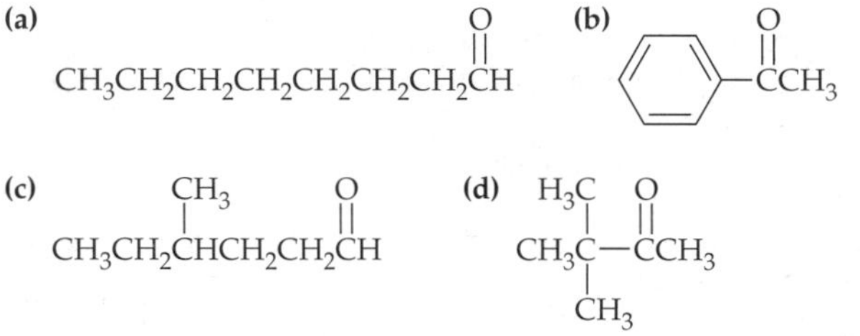

16.4 (a) pentanal **(b)** 3-pentanone **(c)** 4-methylhexanal **(d)** 4-heptanone

16.5

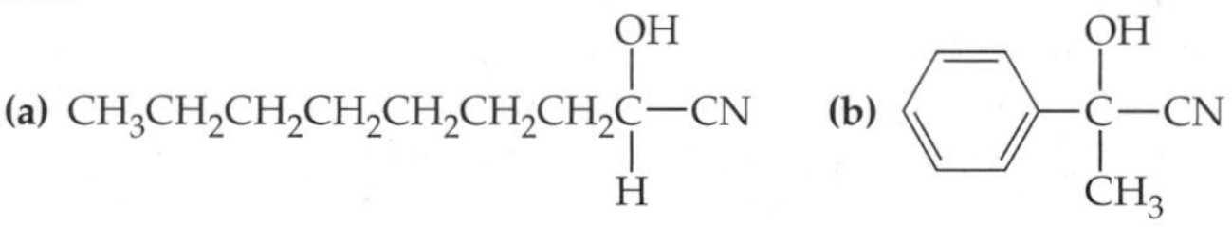

(a) $CH_3CH_2CH_2CH_2CH_2CH_2CH_2C-CN$ with OH and H

(b)

16.6 (a)

$$CH_3CHCH_2CCH_2CH_3$$ with CH_3 and =O
$C_7H_{14}O$
5-Methyl-3-hexanone
A ketone

(b)

$$CH_3CHCH_2CH_2CH$$ with CH_3 and =O
$C_6H_{12}O$
4-Methylpentanal
An aldehyde

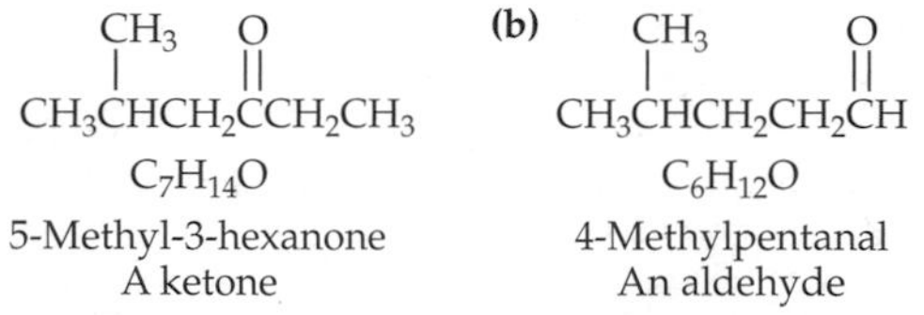

16.7 (a) polar, flammable, liquid, b.p. $< 150°C$ **(b)** polar, flammable, liquid, b.p. $< 150°C$ **(c)** nonpolar, flammable, liquid, b.p. $< 150°C$ **16.8** Alcohols form hydrogen bonds, which raise their boiling points. Aldehydes and ketones have higher boiling points than alkanes because they are polar.

16.9 (a)

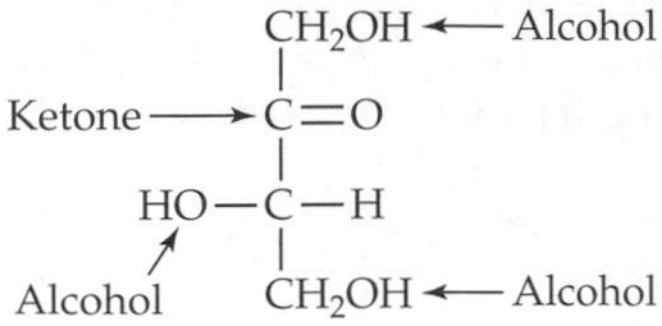

(b)

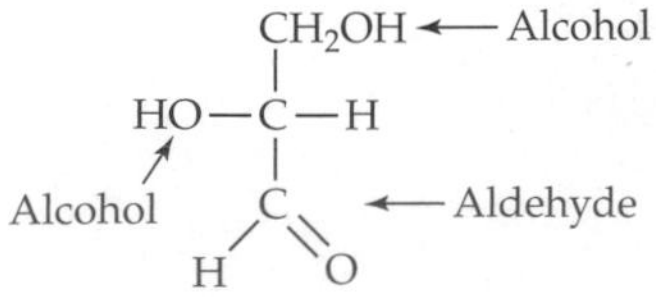

(c)

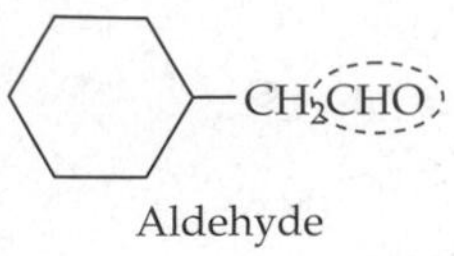

Aldehyde

(d)

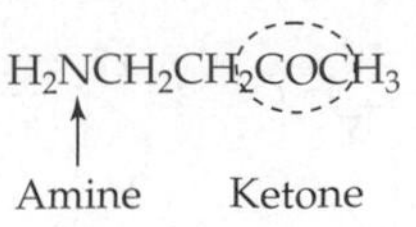

$$H_2NCH_2CH_2COCH_3$$
Amine   Ketone

16.10 (a)

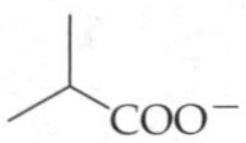

(b) NR **(c)**

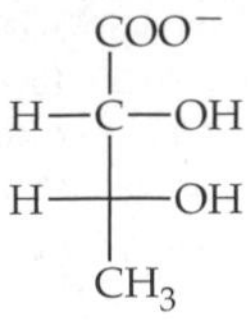

(d) NR

16.11

(a)

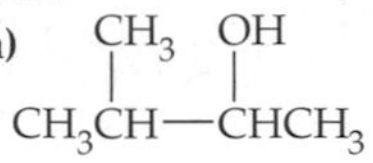

$$CH_3CH-CHCH_3$$ with CH_3 and OH

(b)

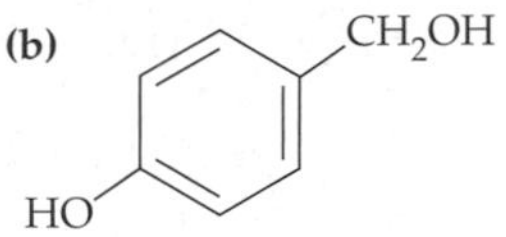

(c)

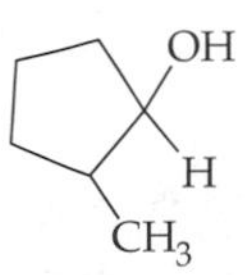

16.12

(a)

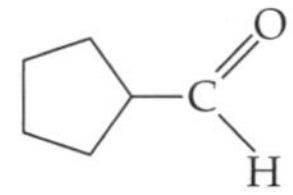

(b)

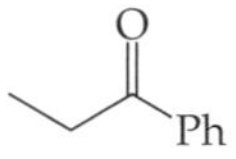

(c)

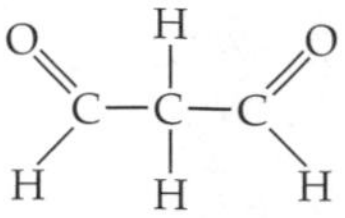

16.13 Compounds (a), (d)

16.14 (a)

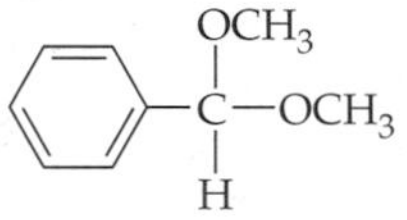

(b)

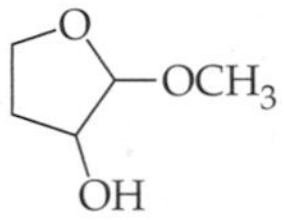

16.15 (a)

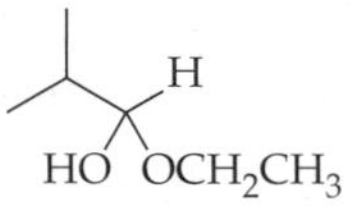

(b)

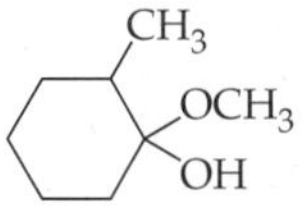

16.16 (a)

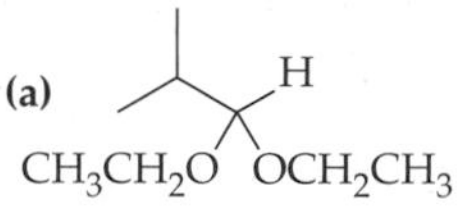

(b)

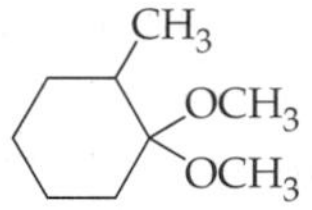

16.17 (a) neither **(b)** neither **(c)** acetal **(d)** hemiacetal **16.18** two caps

16.19 (a)

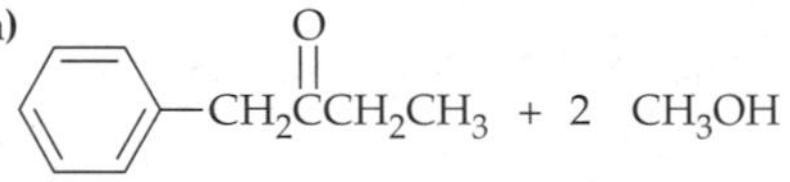

(b)

$$CH_3CH_2OH + 2 \ CH_3CH_2CH_2OH$$

(c)

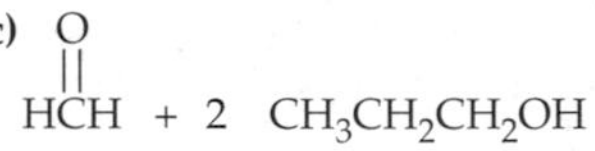

$+ 2 \ CH_3CH_2CH_2OH$

16.20. (a) Hydride adds to the carbonyl carbon. **(b)** The arrow to the right represents reduction, and the arrow to the left represents oxidation. **16.21** Aldehydes can be oxidized to carboxylic acids. Tollens' reagent differentiates an aldehyde from a ketone.

16.22

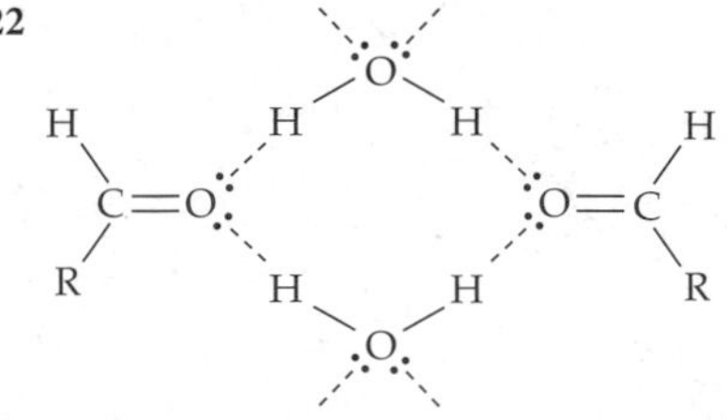

16.23 (a) Under acidic conditions, an alcohol adds to the carbonyl group of an aldehyde to form a hemiacetal, which is unstable and further reacts to form an acetal.

(b)

$$R-\overset{\overset{\displaystyle O\!\!=\!\!H}{|}}{\underset{\underset{\displaystyle H}{|}}{C}}-O-R' \longrightarrow R-\overset{\overset{\displaystyle O-H}{|}}{\underset{\underset{\displaystyle H}{|}}{C}}-O-R'$$

--- Bonds broken
— Bonds formed

16.24 In solution, glucose exists as a cyclic hemiacetal because this structure is more stable.   **16.25** In addition to the two oxygens, an acetal carbon of a ketone is bonded to two carbons. The acetal carbon of an aldehyde is bonded to a carbon and a hydrogen.

Ketone   Aldehyde

16.26 (a)
$$CH_3\overset{\overset{\displaystyle O}{\|}}{C}\overset{}{\underset{\underset{\displaystyle CH_3}{|}}{CH}}CH_3$$

(b)
$$CH_3CH_2CH_2\overset{\overset{\displaystyle O}{\|}}{C}H$$

(c)
$$CH_3CH_2CH_2\overset{\overset{\displaystyle O}{\|}}{C}H$$

(d)
$$HOCH_2CH_2\overset{\overset{\displaystyle O}{\|}}{C}CH_3$$

16.28 Structure (c) has an aldehyde group, and structures (a), (b), and (f) have ketone groups.

16.30 (a)
$$CH_3CH_2\underset{\underset{\displaystyle CH_3}{|}}{CH}CH\overset{\overset{\displaystyle O}{\|}}{C}H$$

(b)
$$\underset{\underset{\displaystyle Cl}{|}}{CH_2}CH_2\underset{\underset{\displaystyle OH}{|}}{CH}\overset{\overset{\displaystyle O}{\|}}{C}H$$

(c)
$$H_3C-\!\!\!\bigcirc\!\!\!-\overset{\overset{\displaystyle O}{\|}}{C}H$$

(d)

(e)

(f)

16.32 (a) 2,2-dimethylbutanal **(b)** 2-hydroxy-2-methylpentanal
(c) 3-methylbutanal **(d)** 4-methyl-3-hexanone
(e) 3-hydroxy-2-methylcyclohexanone
16.34 For **(a)**, a ketone can't occur at the end of a carbon chain. For **(b)**, the methyl group receives the lowest possible number. For **(c)**, numbering must start at the end of the carbon chain closer to the carbonyl group.
16.36 A hemiacetal is produced.
16.38 (a) NR; cyclopentanol

(b)
$$CH_3CH_2CH_2CH_2CH_2\overset{\overset{\displaystyle O}{\|}}{C}OH \; ; \; CH_3CH_2CH_2CH_2CH_2CH_2OH$$

(c)
$$CH_3-\underset{\underset{\displaystyle H}{|}}{\overset{\overset{\displaystyle OH}{|}}{C}}-\underset{\underset{\displaystyle H}{|}}{\overset{\overset{\displaystyle OH}{|}}{C}}-\overset{\overset{\displaystyle O}{\|}}{C}-OH \qquad CH_3-\underset{\underset{\displaystyle H}{|}}{\overset{\overset{\displaystyle OH}{|}}{C}}-\underset{\underset{\displaystyle H}{|}}{\overset{\overset{\displaystyle OH}{|}}{C}}-\underset{\underset{\displaystyle H}{|}}{\overset{\overset{\displaystyle OH}{|}}{C}}-H$$

16.40 (a)
$$H_3C-\!\!\!\bigcirc\!\!\!-CHO \qquad H_3C-\!\!\!\bigcirc\!\!\!-CH_2OH$$

(b)
$$CH_3CH_2\underset{\underset{\displaystyle CH_3}{|}}{\overset{\overset{\displaystyle CHO}{|}}{CH}}CH_2CHCH_3 \qquad CH_3CH_2\underset{\underset{\displaystyle CH_3}{|}}{\overset{\overset{\displaystyle CH_2OH}{|}}{CH}}CH_2CHCH_3$$

(c) $CH_3CH=CHCHO \qquad CH_3CH=CHCH_2OH$

16.42
(a)
$$CH_3CH_2\underset{\underset{\displaystyle CH_3}{|}}{\overset{\overset{\displaystyle OH}{|}}{C}}OCH_2CH_2CH_3$$

(b)
$$CH_3CH_2CH_2\underset{\underset{\displaystyle H}{|}}{\overset{\overset{\displaystyle OH}{|}}{C}}OCH(CH_3)_2$$

(c)
$$CH_3CH_2CH_2\overset{\overset{\displaystyle O}{\|}}{C}H \; + \; CH_3CH_2OH \; + \; CH_3OH$$

(d)
$$\overset{\displaystyle H_3C}{\underset{\displaystyle H_3C}{}}C=O \; + \; HOCH_2CH_2OH$$

16.44 $CH_3\underset{\underset{\displaystyle OH}{|}}{CH}CH_2CH_2CH_2\overset{\overset{\displaystyle O}{\|}}{C}H$ 5-Hydroxyhexanal
16.46 $HOCH_2CH_2CH_2OH$ and CH_2O (formaldehyde).
16.48

Aldosterone

Hemiacetal — Alcohol — Ketone — Ketone — C—C double bond

16.50 p-methoxybenzaldehyde   **16.52** Aldehydes are easily oxidized.
16.54 (a) 2-methyl-3-pentanone **(b)** 1,5-hexadiene **(c)** m-bromotoluene
(d) 4,5,5- trimethyl-3-hexanone
16.56
(a)
$$O_2N-\!\!\!\bigcirc\!\!\!\overset{\displaystyle NO_2}{}-\overset{\overset{\displaystyle O}{\|}}{C}CH_3$$

(b)

(c)
$$CH_3\underset{\underset{\displaystyle OCH_3}{|}}{\overset{\overset{\displaystyle CH_3}{|}}{C}}-CH_3$$

(d)
$$CH_3CH-\underset{\underset{\displaystyle OH}{|}}{\overset{\overset{\displaystyle CH_3}{|}}{CH}}-CHCH_3$$
$$\underset{\displaystyle CH_3}{} \qquad \underset{\displaystyle CH_3}{}$$

16.58
(a) $CH_3CH_2CH(CH_3)_2$
(b) $(CH_3)_2CHCCH_3$ (with $\overset{O}{\|}$)
(c) $HOCH_2CH_2CH_2CH_3$

(d)

16.60 Tollens' reagent reacts with hexanal but not with 3-hexanone.
16.62 2-Heptanone is less soluble in water because it has a longer hydrocarbon chain.   **16.64** The cyanohydrin that decomposes to form HCN is nontoxic and is stable inside the millipede's body.   **16.66 (a)** Advantages: inexpensive, no need to sacrifice animals, **(b)** Disadvantage: results of tests on cultured cells may not be reliable for more complex organisms.
16.68 30 mg

16.70

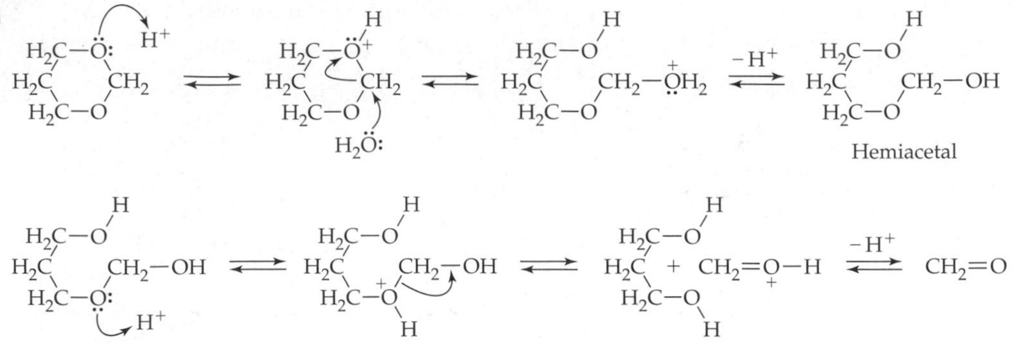

Hemiacetal

Chapter 17

17.1 carboxylic acid: (c) amides: (a) (f) (h) ester: (d) none: (b) (e) (g)

17.2 (a)

$$CH_3CH_2CH_2\underset{\underset{CH_2CH_3}{|}}{CH}\overset{OH}{\underset{|}{CH}}\overset{O}{\underset{||}{C}}OH$$
6 5 4 3 2 1

(b)

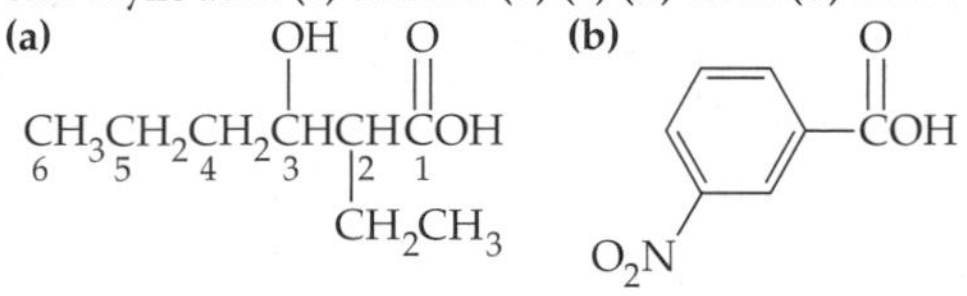

17.3

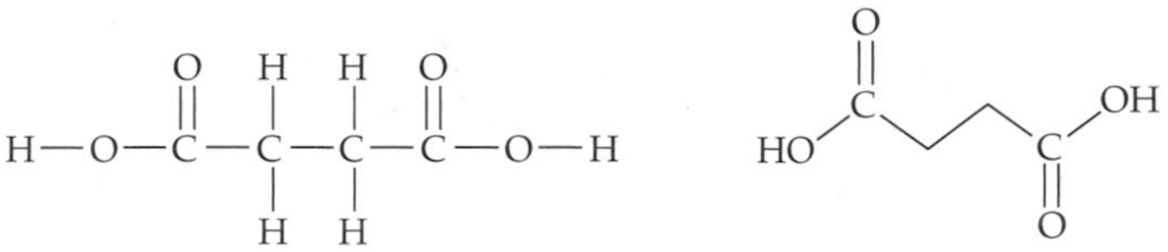

17.4

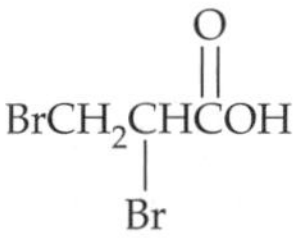

$$BrCH_2\underset{\underset{Br}{|}}{CH}\overset{O}{\underset{||}{C}}OH \quad \text{2,3-Dibromopropanoic acid}$$

17.5 (a)

(b) HCOCH₃ **(c)** CH₂=CHCOCH₂CH₃

17.6 CH₃COOH is highest boiling (most H-bonding). CH₃CH₂CH₃ is lowest boiling (nonpolar). **17.7 (a)** C₃H₇COOH is more soluble (smaller —R group). **(b)** (CH₃)₂CHCOOH is more soluble (carboxylic acid).

17.8
(a)

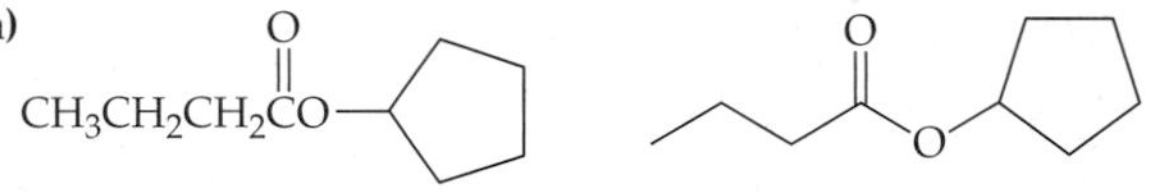

CH₃CH₂CH₂CO— (cyclopentyl)

(b)

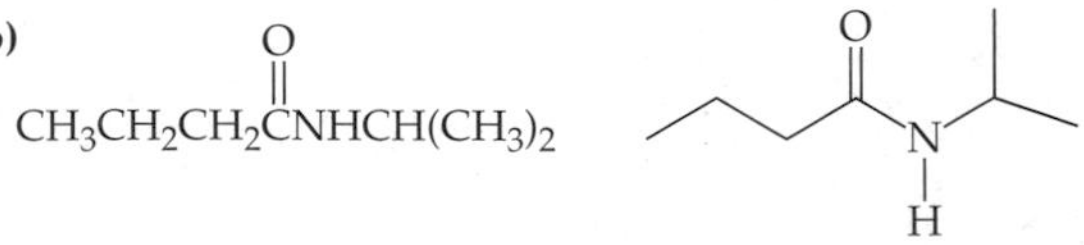

CH₃CH₂CH₂CNHCH(CH₃)₂

(c)

CH₃CH₂CH₂CN(CH₂CH₃)₂

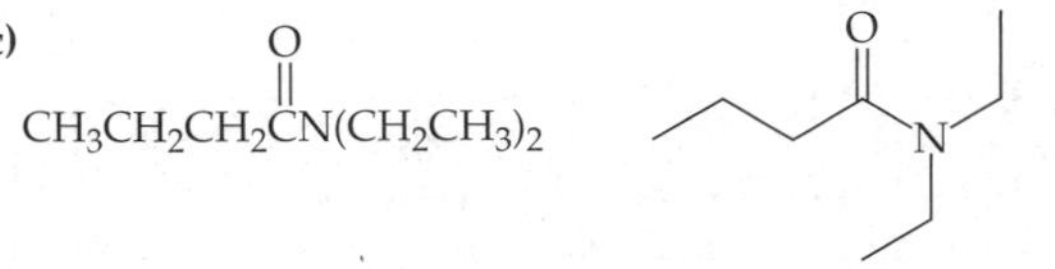

(d) cyclopentyl butyrate N-isopropylbutyramide N,N-diethylbutyramide
17.9 (a) tert-butyl 2-bromobutanoate **(b)** N,N-dimethyl-o-nitrobenzamide
17.10 (a)

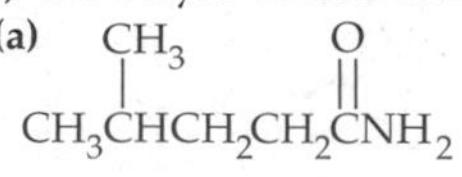

$$CH_3\underset{\underset{CH_3}{|}}{CH}CH_2CH_2\overset{O}{\underset{||}{C}}NH_2$$

(b)

$$CH_3CH_2\overset{O}{\underset{||}{C}}N\underset{\underset{CH_3}{|}}{CH_2CH_3}$$

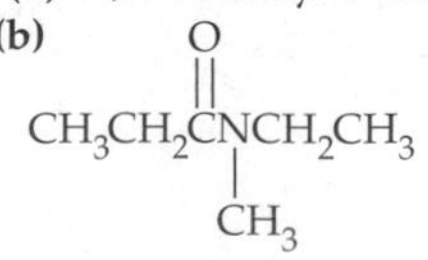

17.11

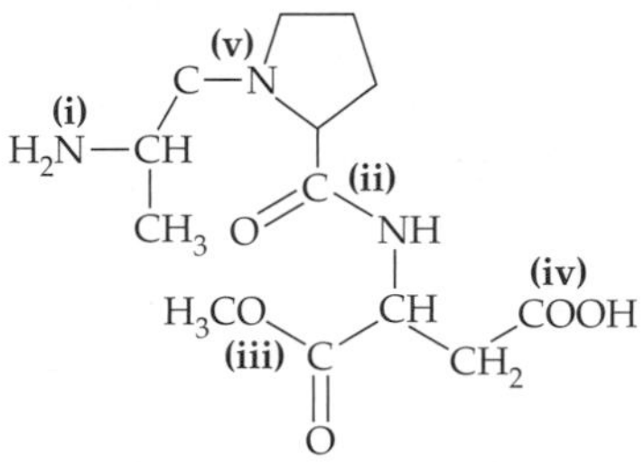

17.12 (a) (ii) **(b)** (i) **(c)** (iii) **(d)** (i) **(e)** (i) **(f)** (iii)

17.13

(a) C₆H₅CNH₂ **(b)** CH₃CH₂COH **(c)** CH₃COCH₂CH₃
amide (C₇H₇NO)   carboxylic acid (C₃H₆O₂)   ester (C₄H₈O₂)

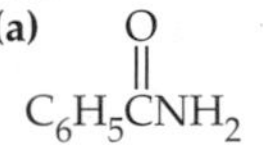

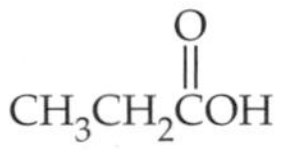

17.14 (a)

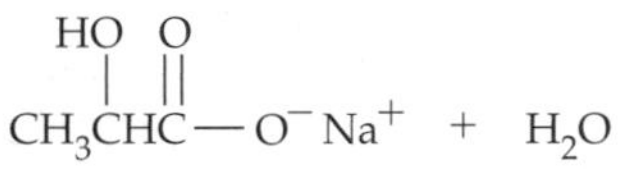

$$CH_3\underset{\underset{OH}{|}}{CH}\overset{O}{\underset{||}{C}}-O^- Na^+ \quad + \quad H_2O$$

(b)

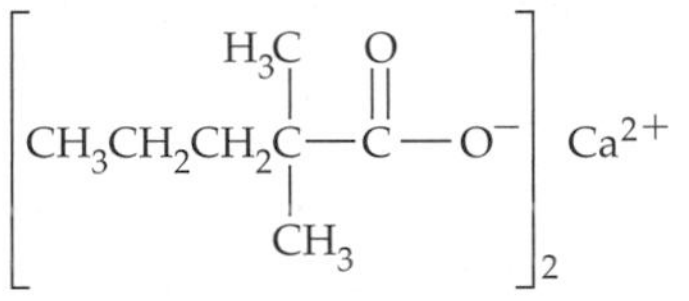

$$\left[CH_3CH_2CH_2\underset{\underset{CH_3}{|}}{\overset{\overset{H_3C}{|}}{C}}\overset{O}{\underset{||}{C}}-O^- \right]_2 Ca^{2+}$$

17.15 (a) (o-substituted benzene with) COO⁻K⁺ and OH **(b)** Na⁺ ⁻OOCCOO⁻ Na⁺

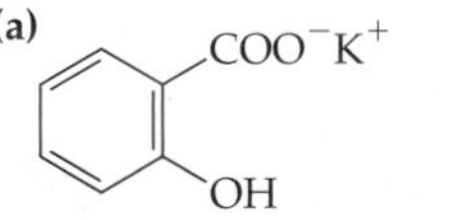

17.16 CH₃COO⁻   ⁻OOCCH₂CH₂CH₂COO⁻   **17.17** hydroxyacetic acid (glycolic acid); 2-hydroxypropionic acid (lactic acid); o-hydroxybenzoic acid (salicylic acid)   **17.18** HCOOCH₂CH(CH₃)₂

17.19 (a)

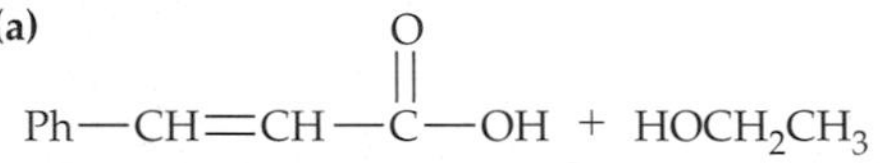

Ph—CH=CH—C(=O)—OH + HOCH₂CH₃

(b)

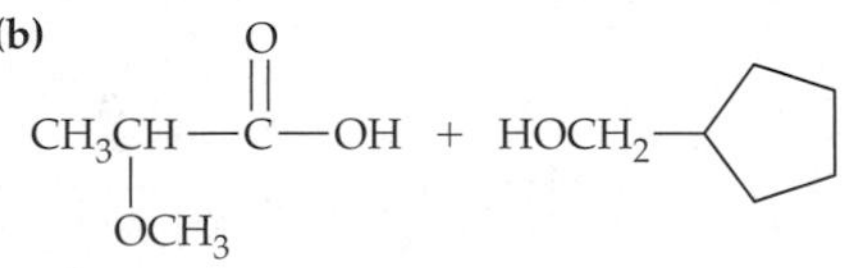

$$CH_3\underset{\underset{OCH_3}{|}}{CH}-\overset{O}{\underset{||}{C}}-OH + HOCH_2-\text{(cyclopentyl)}$$

17.20
(a)

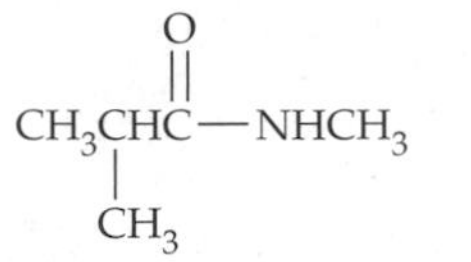

$$CH_3\underset{\underset{CH_3}{|}}{CH}\overset{O}{\underset{||}{C}}-NHCH_3$$

(b)

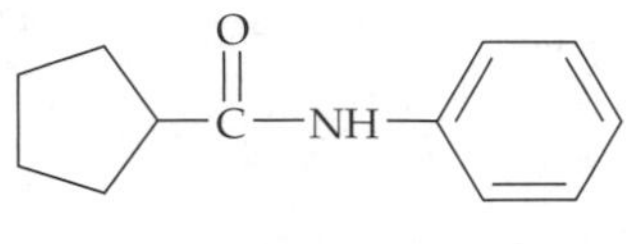

(cyclopentyl)—C(=O)—NH—(phenyl)

17.21 CH₃CH₂O—(phenyl)—NH₂ + HOOCCH₃

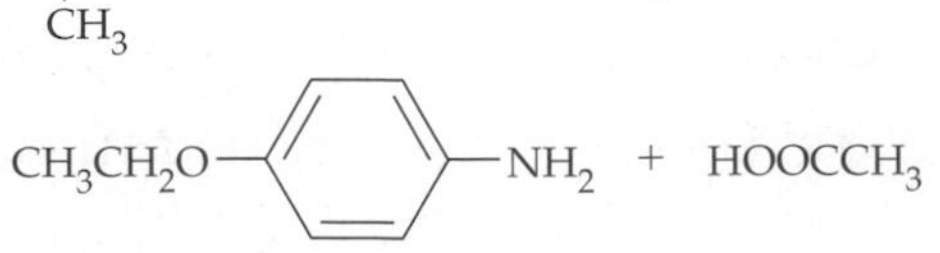

17.22

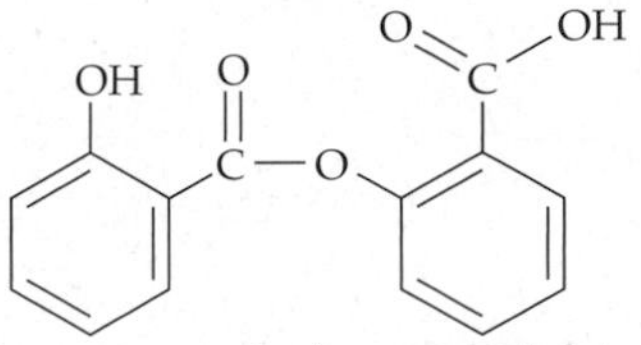

17.23 Aspirin is acidic ($-$COOH), lidocaine is basic (amine), benzocaine is weakly basic (aromatic amine), acetaminophen is weakly acidic (phenol).

17.24 Moisture in the air hydrolyzes the ester bond.

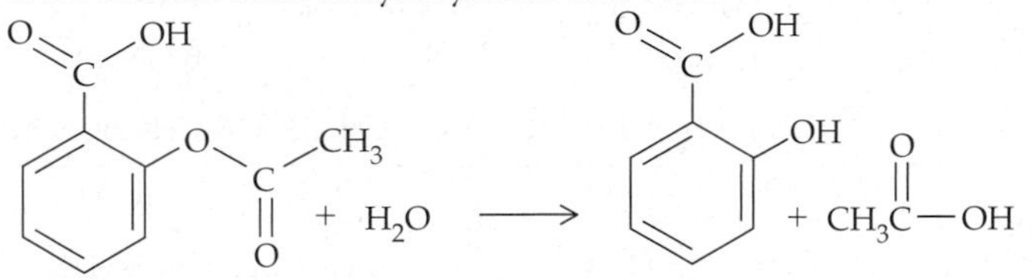

$$+ \ H_2O \longrightarrow + \ CH_3\overset{O}{\underset{}{C}}-OH$$

17.25 (a) *p*-nitrobenzoic acid + 2-propanol (b) phenol + 2-cyclopentene-carboxylic acid (c) 2-aminopropionic acid + ethanol

17.26 (a) 2-butenoic acid + methylamine
(b) *p*-nitrobenzoic acid + dimethylamine

17.27

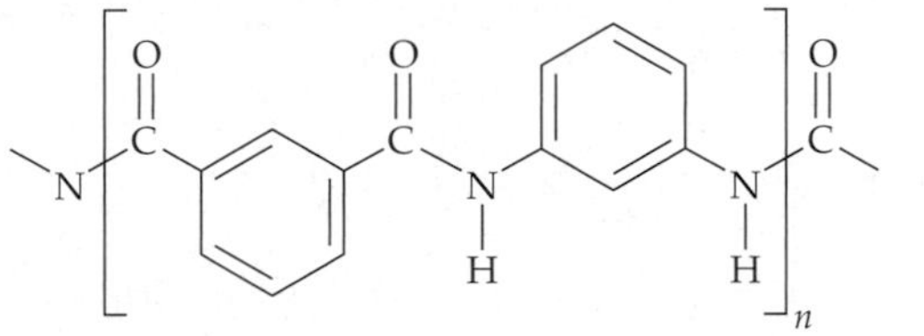

Nomex

17.28 (a)

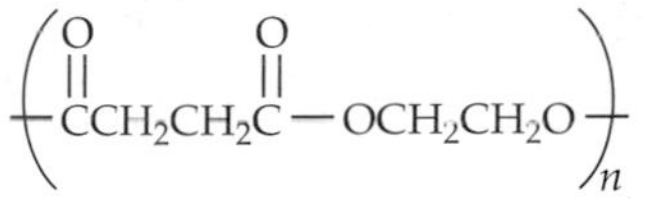

$$\left(\underset{}{\overset{O\quad\quad O}{CCH_2CH_2C}}-OCH_2CH_2O\right)_n$$

(b)

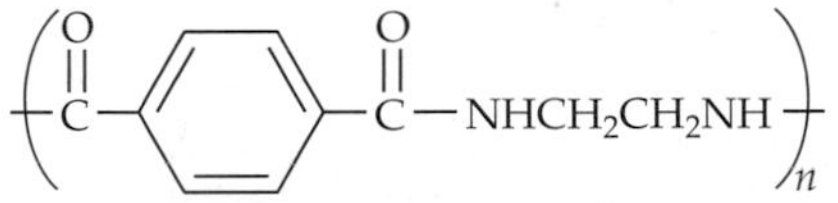

$$\left(\underset{}{\overset{O\quad\quad\quad O}{C}}-NHCH_2CH_2NH\right)_n$$

17.29

$$HO-\underset{OH}{\overset{O}{\underset{|}{\overset{||}{P}}}}-O\underset{}{\overset{CH_3}{\underset{|}{CH}}}CH_3 \qquad {}^-O-\underset{O^-}{\overset{O}{\underset{|}{\overset{||}{P}}}}-O\underset{}{\overset{CH_3}{\underset{|}{CH}}}CH_3$$

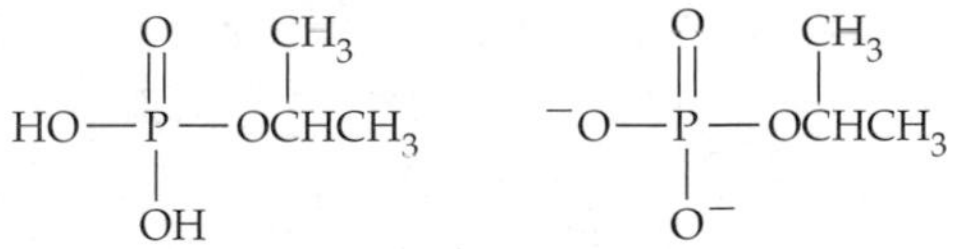

17.30 (a) amide + $H_2O \longrightarrow CH_3COOH + NH_3$
(b) phosphate monoester + $H_2O \longrightarrow CH_3CH_2OH + HOPO_3^{2-}$
(c) carboxylic acid ester + $H_2O \longrightarrow CH_3CH_2COOH + HOCH_3$

17.31

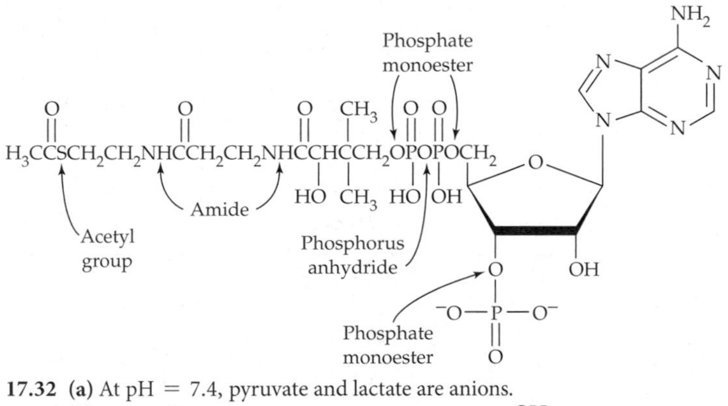

Acetyl group

Amide

Phosphate monoester

Phosphorus anhydride

Phosphate monoester

17.32 (a) At pH = 7.4, pyruvate and lactate are anions.
(b)

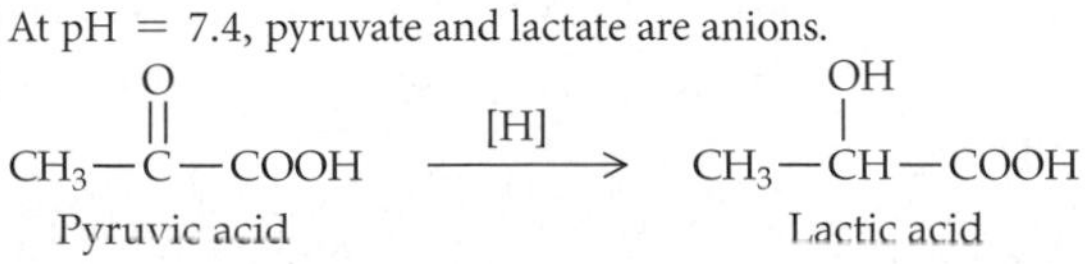

$$CH_3-\underset{}{\overset{O}{\overset{||}{C}}}-COOH \xrightarrow{[H]} CH_3-\underset{}{\overset{OH}{\underset{|}{CH}}}-COOH$$
$$\text{Pyruvic acid} \qquad\qquad \text{Lactic acid}$$

(c) Pyruvate and lactate have similar solubilities in water.

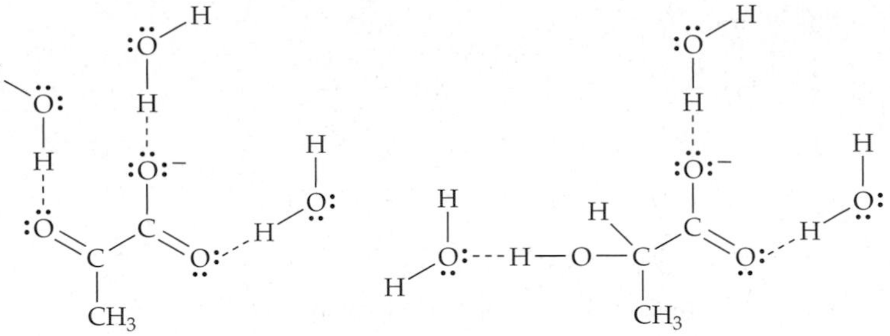

17.33 (a) H_2O + acid or base
(b)

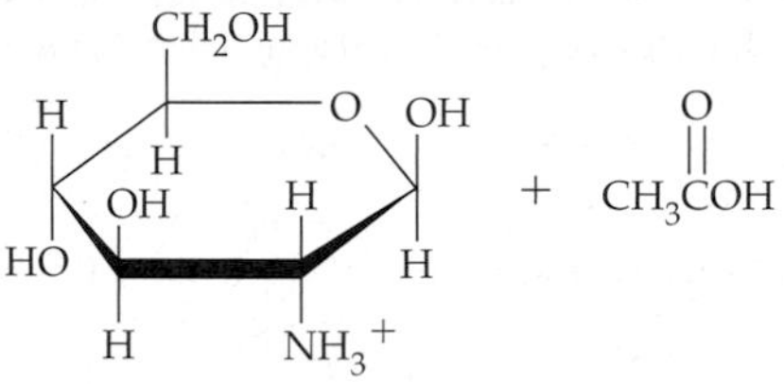

$$+ \ CH_3\overset{O}{\overset{||}{C}}OH$$

17.34 (a) a phosphate ester linkage
(b)

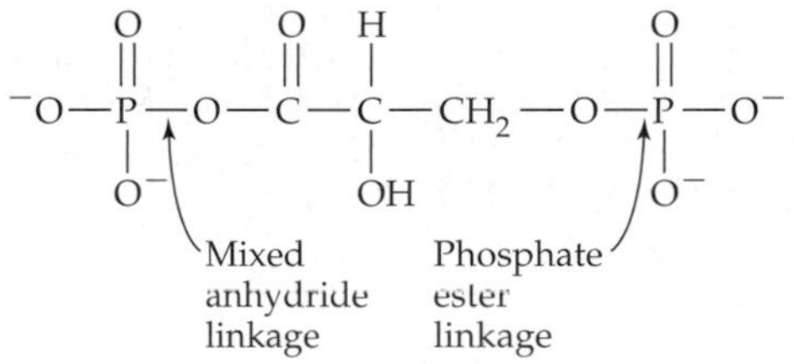

$${}^-O-\overset{O}{\overset{||}{P}}-O-\overset{O}{\overset{||}{C}}-\overset{H}{\underset{OH}{C}}-CH_2-O-\overset{O}{\overset{||}{P}}-O^-$$

Mixed anhydride linkage

Phosphate ester linkage

17.35

${}^-OOCCOO^-$ oxalate ${}^-OOCCH_2COO^-$ malonate ${}^-OOCCH_2CH_2COO^-$ succinate ${}^-OOCCH_2CH_2CH_2COO^-$ glutarate

${}^-OOCCH_2CH_2CH_2CH_2COO^-$ adipate ${}^-OOCCH_2CH_2CH_2CH_2CH_2COO^-$ pimelate

17.36 (a)

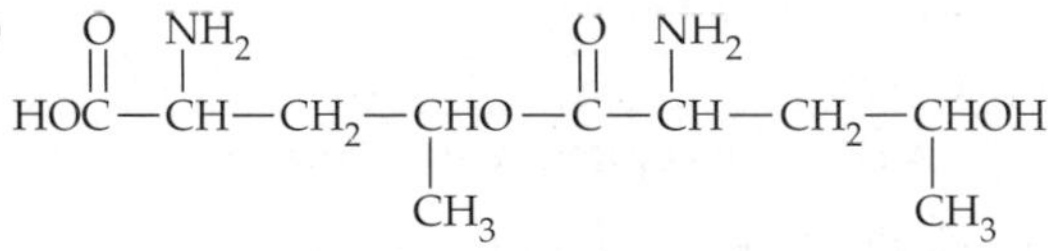

$$HO\overset{O}{\overset{||}{C}}-\overset{NH_2}{\underset{|}{CH}}-CH_2-CHO-\overset{O}{\overset{||}{C}}-\overset{NH_2}{\underset{|}{CH}}-CH_2-\underset{CH_3}{\overset{}{CHOH}}$$

(b)

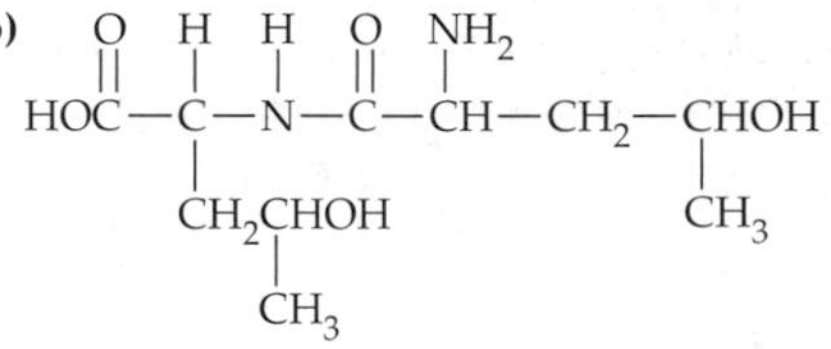

$$HO\overset{O}{\overset{||}{C}}-\overset{H}{\underset{CH_2CHOH}{\overset{|}{C}}}-\overset{H}{\underset{CH_3}{\overset{|}{N}}}-\overset{O}{\overset{||}{C}}-\overset{NH_2}{\underset{CH_3}{\overset{|}{CH}}}-CH_2-CHOH$$

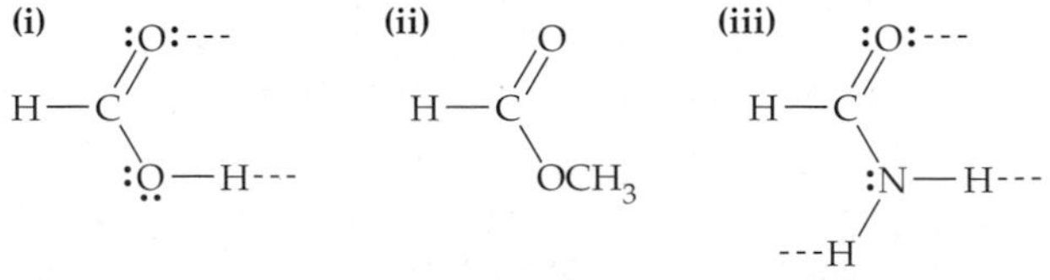

(c)

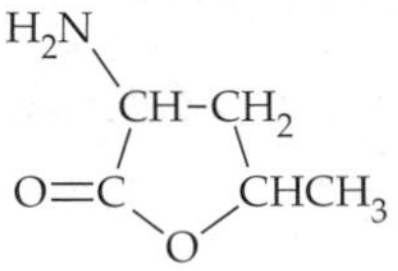

17.37
(a) (i)

$$H-\overset{:O:---}{\overset{||}{C}}$$
$$\overset{}{\underset{:O:}{}}-H---$$
Formic acid

(ii)

$$H-\overset{O}{\overset{||}{C}}$$
$$\overset{}{OCH_3}$$
Methyl formate

(iii)

$$H-\overset{:O:---}{\overset{||}{C}}$$
$$\overset{}{\underset{---H}{:N}}-H---$$
Formamide

(b) Methyl acetate is lowest boiling (no hydrogen bonds); acetamide is highest boiling

17.38

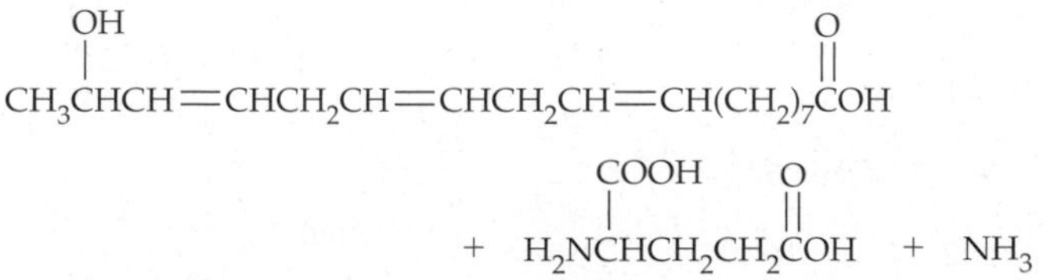

$$\underset{}{\overset{OH}{CH_3CHCH}}=CHCH_2CH=CHCH_2CH=CH(CH_2)_7\overset{O}{\overset{||}{C}}OH$$

$$+ \ H_2N\overset{COOH}{\underset{|}{CH}}CH_2CH_2\overset{O}{\overset{||}{C}}OH \ + \ NH_3$$

17.39 (a) *N*-ethyl acetamide (b) diethylglutarate (c) methyl 2-chlorocyclopentanecarboxylate (d) *N*-ethyl-*N*-methylformamide.

17.40

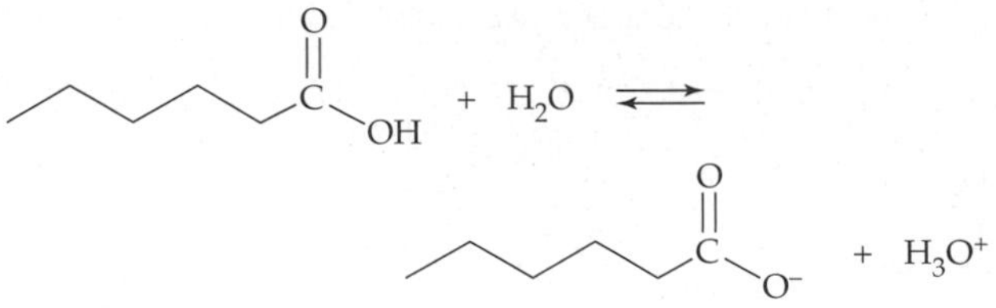

17.42

$CH_3CH_2CH_2COOH$ — Butanoic acid

$CH_3CH(CH_3)COOH$ — 2-Methylpropionic acid

17.44 **(a)** 3-hydroxy-4-methylpentanoic acid **(b)** nonanedioic acid (azelaic acid) **(c)** 4-chlorocyclohexanecarboxylic acid **(d)** *p*-aminobenzoic acid

17.46 **(a)** potassium 3-ethylpentanoate **(b)** ammonium benzoate **(c)** calcium propanoate

17.48 **(a)** $CH_3CH_2CH(CH_3)CH(CH_3)CH_2COOH$

(b)

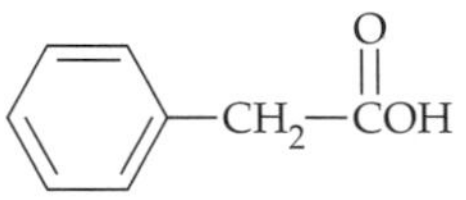

(c)

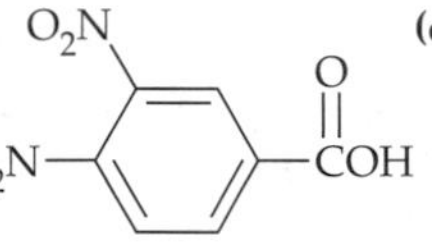

(d) $CH_3CH_2CH_2CO_2^-\ ^+NH(CH_2CH_3)_3$

17.50 $HOOCCH_2CH(OH)COOH$

17.52 $NH_4^+\ ^-OOCCH{=}CHCOO^-\ NH_4^+$

17.54 **(a)** $CH_3CH_2CH_2CH_2CONH_2$ Pentanamide; $CH_3CH_2CONHCH_2CH_3$ *N*-Ethylpropanamide; $HCON(CH_2CH_3)_2$ *N,N*-Diethylformamide

(b) $CH_3CH_2CH_2CH_2COOCH_3$ Methyl pentanoate; $CH_3CH_2COOCH_2CH_2CH_3$ Propyl propanoate; $HCOOCH_2CH_2CH_2CH_2CH_3$ Pentyl formate

17.56 **(a)** 3-methylbutyl acetate **(b)** methyl 4-methylpentanoate

(c)

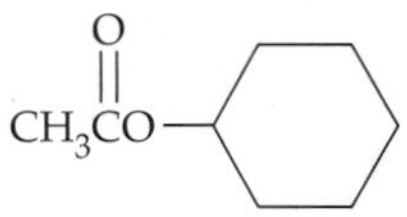

(d)

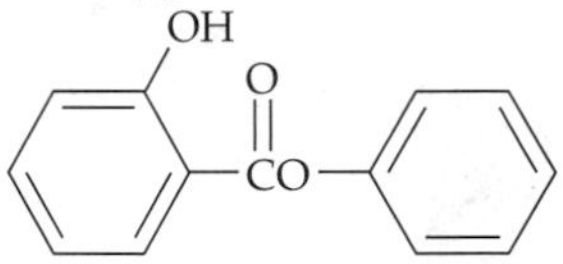

17.58 **(a)** $CH_3COOH + HOCH_2CH_2CH(CH_3)_2$
(b) $(CH_3)_2CHCH_2CH_2COOH + HOCH_3$

(c)

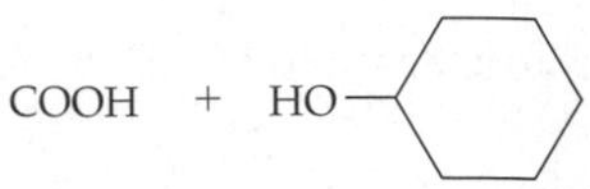

(d)

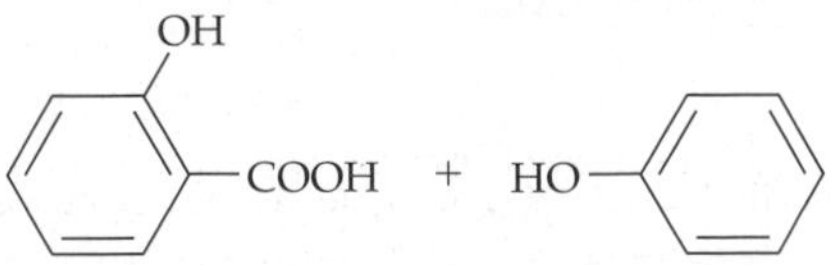

17.60 **(a)** 2-ethylbutanamide **(b)** *N*-phenylbenzamide

(c)

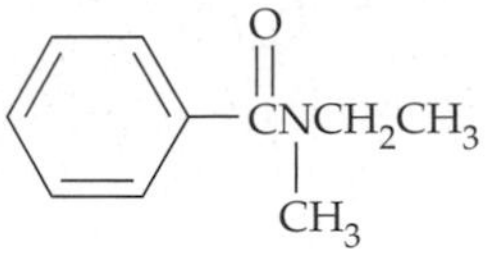

(d) $CH_3CH_2CH_2CHBrCHBrCONH_2$

17.62 **(a)** 2-ethylbutanoic acid + ammonia **(b)** benzoic acid + aniline **(c)** benzoic acid + *N*-methylethylamine **(d)** 2,3-dibromohexanoic acid + ammonia

17.64

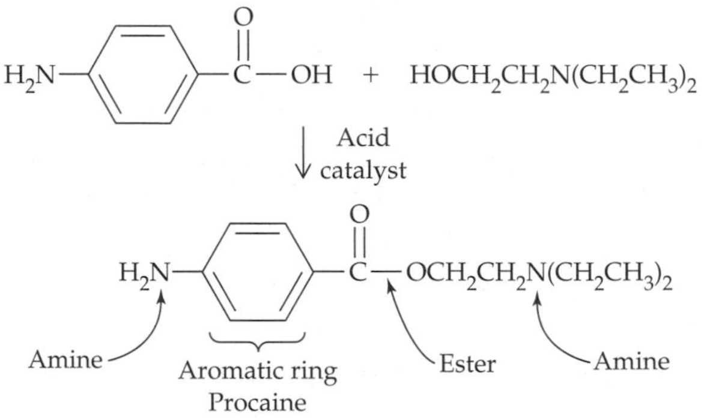

17.66 $HOCH_2CH_2CH_2COOH$

17.68 *See below for answer.*

17.70

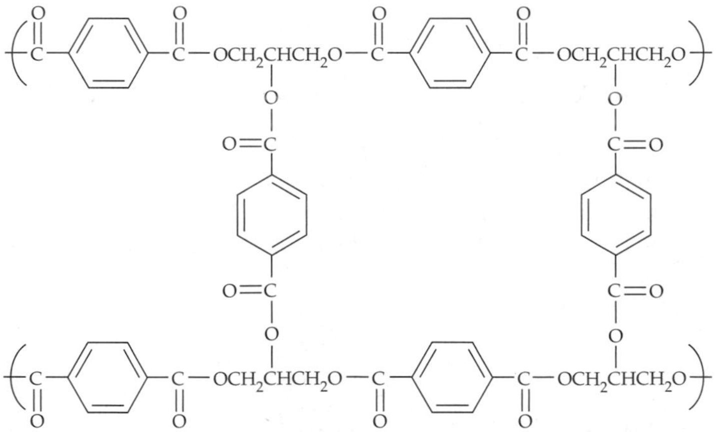

17.68

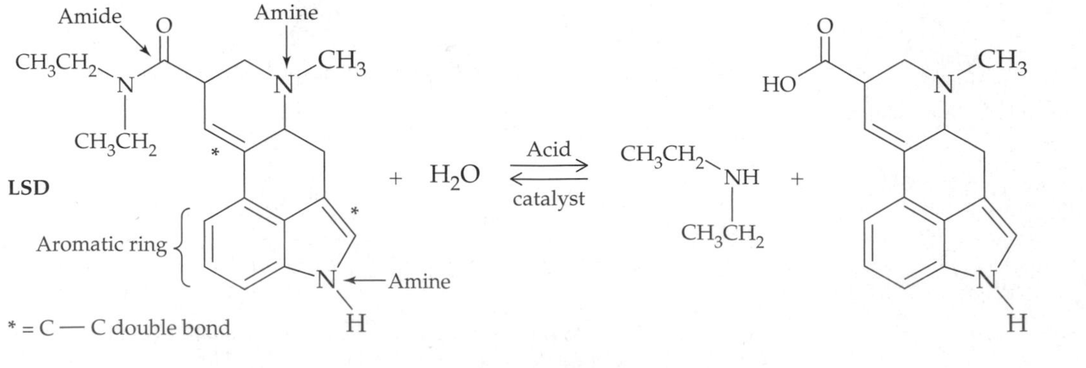

17.72 Dihydroxyacetone and hydrogen phosphate anion.

17.74

$$HO-\overset{\displaystyle O}{\underset{\displaystyle OH}{\overset{\|}{P}}}-O-\overset{\displaystyle O}{\overset{\|}{C}}-CH_3$$

17.76 A cyclic phosphate diester is formed when a phosphate group forms an ester with two hydroxyl groups in the same molecule.   **17.78** N, N-Dimethylformamide is lowest boiling because it doesn't form hydrogen bonds. Propanamide is highest boiling because it forms the most hydrogen bonds.   **17.80** Both propanamide and methyl acetate are water-soluble because they can form hydrogen bonds with water. Propanamide is higher boiling because molecules of propanamide can form hydrogen bonds with each other.

17.82

$$\begin{aligned}&CH_2O-\overset{\displaystyle O}{\overset{\|}{C}}(CH_2)_{16}CH_3\\&CHO-\overset{\displaystyle O}{\overset{\|}{C}}(CH_2)_{16}CH_3 \qquad \text{Glyceryl tristearate}\\&CH_2O-\overset{\displaystyle O}{\overset{\|}{C}}(CH_2)_{16}CH_3\end{aligned}$$

17.84 Trichloroacetic acid: used for chemical peeling of the skin. Lactic acid: used for wrinkle removal and moisturizing.   **17.86** strong acids and bases.

Chapter 18

18.1 Aromatic ring: phenylalanine, tyrosine, tryptophan Contain sulfur: cysteine, methionine
Alcohols: serine, threonine, tyrosine (phenol) Alkyl side chain: alanine, valine, leucine, isoleucine

18.2

$$\begin{array}{c} COOH \\ | \\ \overset{H}{\underset{H_3C}{\diagdown}}C\diagup NH_2 \end{array}$$

18.3

$$\begin{array}{cc} COOH & COOH \\ | & | \\ \overset{H}{\underset{HOCH_2}{\diagdown}}C\diagup NH_2 & \overset{H}{\underset{(CH_3)_2CH}{\diagdown}}C\diagup NH_2 \\ \text{Serine} & \text{Valine} \end{array}$$

The serine side chain has a polar hydroxyl group; the valine side chain has a nonpolar isopropyl group.

18.4 α-amino acids: (a), (d)

18.5 (b) Asn, Ser (c) Thr, Tyr

Asn HC—CH$_2$C—N—H------:O—CH$_2$—CH Ser

Tyr HC—CH$_2$—⟨ring⟩—Ö—H------:O—CH—CH Thr

18.6

Amino group → H$_2$N — C — C ← Carboxylic acid group, "R" group (HC, H, H$_3$C, CH$_3$)

Valine

18.7

$$\begin{array}{cc}
\overset{+}{H_3N}-\overset{\underset{\displaystyle CH_2}{|}}{\underset{\underset{\displaystyle O}{\overset{\|}{C}-OH}}{\underset{\displaystyle CH_2}{|}}}CH-\overset{\displaystyle O}{\overset{\|}{C}}-OH & H_2N-\overset{\underset{\displaystyle CH_2}{|}}{\underset{\underset{\displaystyle O}{\overset{\|}{C}-O^-}}{\underset{\displaystyle CH_2}{|}}}CH-\overset{\displaystyle O}{\overset{\|}{C}}-O^- \\ \text{at low pH} & \text{at high pH} \end{array}$$

18.8 In the zwitterionic form of an amino acid, the —NH$_3^+$ group is an acid, and the —COO$^-$ group is a base.   **18.9** chiral: (a), (b), (d)

18.10 Handed: wrench, corkscrew, jar lid Not handed: thumbtack, pencil, straw   **18.11** 2-Aminobutane has a carbon with 4 different groups bonded to it.   **18.12** chiral: (b), (c)

18.13

$$\begin{array}{cc}
COOH & COOH \\
H_2N-\overset{*}{C}-H & H_2N-\overset{*}{C}-H \\
H-\overset{*}{C}-OH & H_3C-\overset{*}{C}-H \\
CH_3 & CH_2CH_3 \\
\text{Threonine} & \text{Isoleucine}
\end{array}$$

18.14

$$\begin{array}{cc}
H \quad H & H \quad H \\
H-C-C-H & H-C-\overset{*}{C}-Br \\
Br \quad Cl & H \quad Cl
\end{array}$$

18.15

$$\begin{array}{cc}
H_2N-CH-\overset{\displaystyle O}{\overset{\|}{C}}-NH-CH-\overset{\displaystyle O}{\overset{\|}{C}}-OH \\
\quad CH_2OH \qquad\qquad CH(CH_3)_2 \\
\text{Serine} \qquad\qquad \text{Valine}
\end{array}$$

$$\begin{array}{cc}
H_2N-CH-\overset{\displaystyle O}{\overset{\|}{C}}-NH-CH-\overset{\displaystyle O}{\overset{\|}{C}}-OH \\
\quad CH(CH_3)_2 \qquad\qquad CH_2OH \\
\text{Valine} \qquad\qquad \text{Serine}
\end{array}$$

18.16 (a) Gly—Ser—Tyr   Tyr—Ser—Gly   Ser—Tyr—Gly
  Gly—Tyr—Ser   Tyr—Gly—Ser   Ser—Gly—Tyr
  (b)

$$\overset{+}{H_3N}-CH_2-\overset{\displaystyle O}{\overset{\|}{C}}-NH-\underset{\underset{\displaystyle CH_2OH}{|}}{CH}-\overset{\displaystyle O}{\overset{\|}{C}}-NH-\underset{\underset{\displaystyle CH_2}{|}}{CH}-\overset{\displaystyle O}{\overset{\|}{C}}-O^-$$

Gly–Ser–Tyr (CH$_2$ to ring with OH)

$$\overset{+}{H_3N}-CH_2-\overset{\displaystyle O}{\overset{\|}{C}}-NH-\underset{\underset{\displaystyle CH_2}{|}}{CH}-\overset{\displaystyle O}{\overset{\|}{C}}-NH-\underset{\underset{\displaystyle CH_2OH}{|}}{CH}-\overset{\displaystyle O}{\overset{\|}{C}}-O^-$$

Gly–Tyr–Ser (CH$_2$ to ring with OH)

18.17 Ile—Arg—Val   Arg—Ile—Val   Val—Arg—Ile
  Ile—Val—Arg   Arg—Val—Ile   Val—Ile—Arg

18.18 (a) Leu-Asp (nonpolar, polar) **(b)** Tyr-Ser-Lys (all polar)

18.19

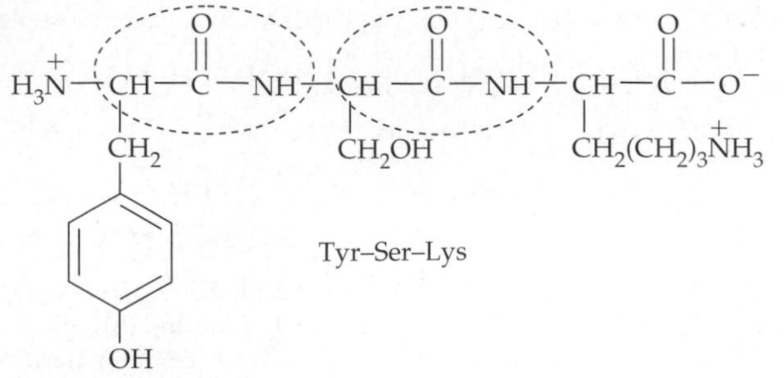

Tyr–Ser–Lys

18.20 Asp-Tyr + Phe + Glu-Asn-Cys-Pro-Lys-Gly

18.21 (a) hydrogen bond (b) hydrophobic interaction (c) salt bridge (d) hydrophobic interaction **18.22** (a) Tyr, Asp, Ser (b) Ala, Ile, Val, Leu

18.23 eleven backbone atoms **18.24** (a) hydrogen bonding (b) Hydrogen bonding takes place between an amide hydrogen and an amide carbonyl oxygen on an adjacent chain. **18.25** Secondary structure: stabilized by hydrogen bonds between amide nitrogens and carbonyl oxygens of polypeptide backbone. Tertiary structure: stabilized by hydrogen bonds between amino acid side-chain groups. **18.26** In a-keratin, pairs of a-helixes twist together into small fibrils that are twisted into larger bundles. In tropocollagen, three coiled chains wrap around each other to form a triple helix.

18.27 (a) tertiary; (b) secondary; (c) quaternary **18.28** At low pH, the groups at the end of the polypeptide chain exist as —NH₃⁺ and —COOH. At high pH, they exist as —NH₂ and —COO⁻. In addition, side chain functional groups may be ionized as follows: (a) no change (b) Arg positively charged at low pH; neutral at high pH: (c) Tyr neutral at low pH, negatively charged at high pH: (d) Glu, Asp neutral at low pH, negatively charged at high pH: (e) no change: (f) Cys neutral at low pH, negatively charged at high pH. **18.29** (a) 1, 4 (b) 2, 4 (c) 2

18.30 See below for answer.

18.31 *Fibrous Proteins:* structural proteins, water-insoluble, contain many Gly and Pro residues, contain large regions of α-helix or β-sheet, few side-chain interactions. Examples: Collagen, α-Keratin, Fibroin. *Globular Proteins:* enzymes and hormones, usually water-soluble, contain most amino acids, contain smaller regions of α-helix and β-sheet, complex tertiary structure. Examples: Ribonuclease, hemoglobin, insulin.

18.32 (a) Leu, Phe, Ala or any other amino acid with a nonpolar side chain. (b), (c) Asp, Lys, Thr or any other amino acid with a polar side chain.

18.33

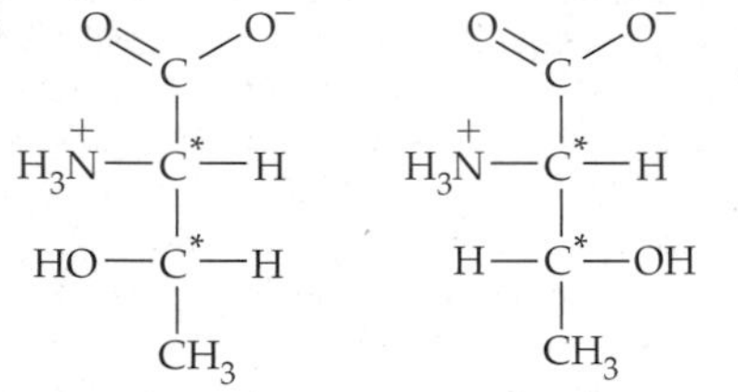

The upper chiral carbon is responsible for the **D, L** configuration.

18.34 (a)

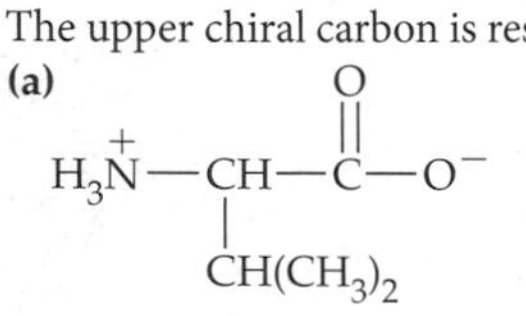

(b)

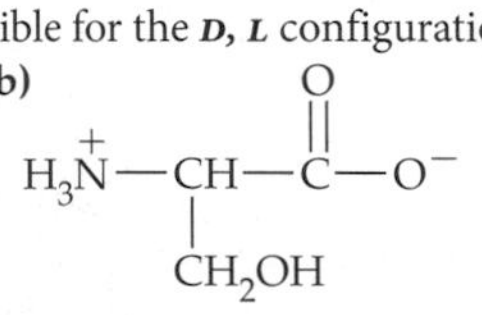

(c)

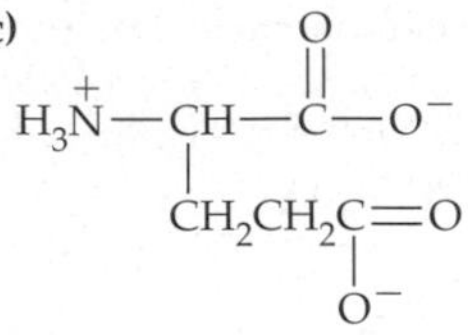

18.36 (a)

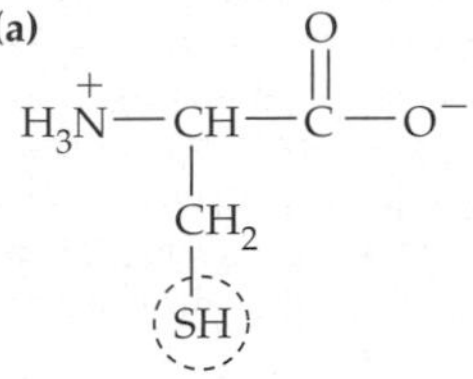

Cysteine (Cys)

(b)

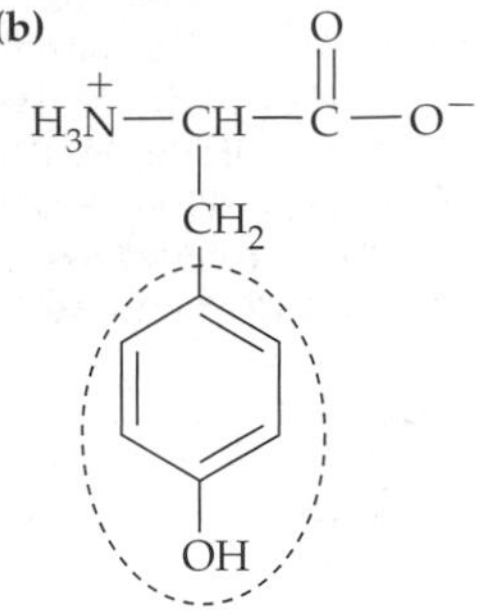

Tyrosine (Tyr)

18.38 neutral: (a), (c); positive charge: (b)
18.40 (a), (c) low pH; (b) high pH
18.42 A chiral object is handed. Examples : glove, car.
18.44 (a), (b)
18.46 (a)

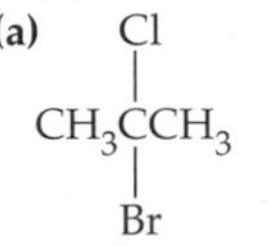

Achiral

(b)

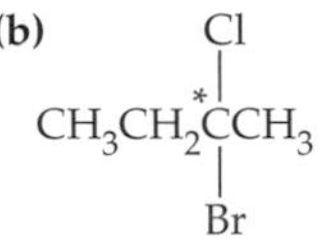

Chiral

(c)

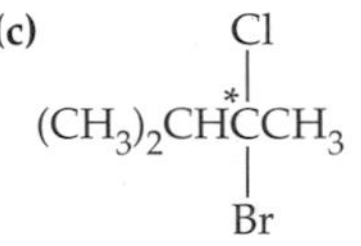

Chiral

18.48

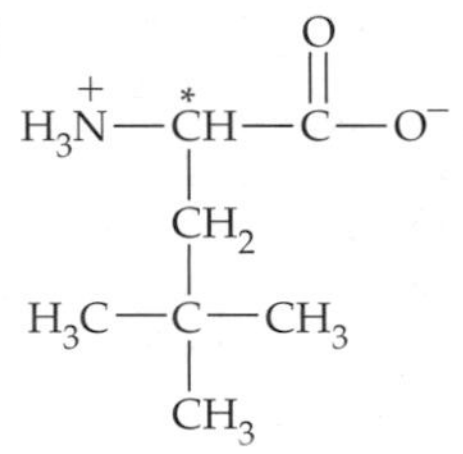

18.50 A simple protein is composed only of amino acids. A conjugated protein consists of a protein associated with one or more nonprotein molecules.

18.52

Type of protein	Function	Example
Enzymes:	Catalyze biochemical reactions	Ribonuclease
Hormones:	Regulate body functions	Insulin
Storage proteins:	Store essential substances	Myoglobin
Transport proteins:	Transport substances through body fluids	Serum albumin
Structural proteins:	Provide shape and support	Collagen
Protective proteins:	Defend the body against foreign matter	Immunoglobulins
Contractile proteins:	Do mechanical work	Myosin and actin

18.30

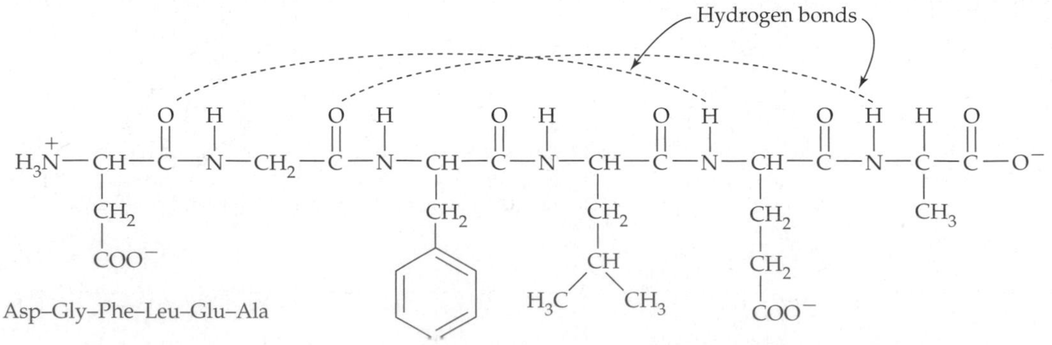

Asp–Gly–Phe–Leu–Glu–Ala

18.54 (a) *Primary structure:* the sequence of connection of amino acids in a protein. **(b)** *Secondary structure:* the orientation of segments of the protein chain into a regular pattern, such as an α-helix or a β-sheet, by hydrogen bonding between backbone atoms. **(c)** *Tertiary structure:* the coiling and folding of the entire protein chain into a three-dimensional shape as a result of interactions between amino acid side chains. **(d)** *Quaternary structure:* the aggregation of several protein chains to form a larger structure. **18.56** Disulfide bonds stabilize tertiary structure. **18.58** In *hydrophobic interactions,* hydrocarbon side chains cluster in the center of proteins and make proteins spherical. Examples: Phe, Ile. *Salt bridges* bring together distant parts of a polypeptide chain. Examples: Lys, Asp. **18.60** When a protein is denatured, its nonprimary structure is disrupted, and it can no longer catalyze reactions. **18.62** Val—Met—Leu, Met—Val—Leu, Leu—Met—Val, Val—Leu—Met, Met—Leu—Val, Leu—Val—Met. **18.64** *Outside:* Asp, His (They can form H-bonds.) *Inside:* Val, Ala (They have hydrophobic interactions.)

18.66 N-terminal   C-terminal

18.68 (a) $H_3\overset{+}{N}CH_2COOH$ **(b)** $H_3\overset{+}{N}CH_2COOCH_3$ **18.70** N-terminal: Val—Gly—Ser—Ala—Asp C-terminal **18.72** A peptide rich in Asp and Lys is more soluble, because its side chains are more polar and can form hydrogen bonds with water. **18.74** People need a daily source of protein in the diet because the human body doesn't store the protein or the amino acids needed for its continuous synthesis of proteins. The body does store fats and carbohydrates. **18.76** Food from animal sources is more likely to contain complete protein than food from plant sources because the proteins in animals contain all of the common amino acids. **18.78** At pH = 6.6, collagen (pI = 6.6) has as many positive charges as negative charges and does not migrate. Bovine insulin (pI = 5.4) is negatively charged and migrates to the positively charged electrode. Human hemoglobin (pI = 7.1) is positively charged and migrates to the negative electrode. **18.80** People were unable to find fresh fruit and vegetables to eat. Fresh produce contains vitamin C, which is necessary for the synthesis of collagen. Without vitamin C, collagen is defective, and scurvy results. **18.82** A change in protein secondary structure from α-helix to β-pleated sheet alters the shape of the prion and causes groups that were close together in the normal prion to be farther apart in the altered prion. This change disrupts hydrogen bonds and salt bridges that were present in the normal protein and results in the formation of new tertiary interactions. **18.84** Protein digestion = hydrolysis of peptide bonds to form amino acids. Protein denaturation = disruption of secondary, tertiary, or quaternary structure without disrupting peptide bonds. **18.86 (a)** *See below for answer.*

(b) Proline rings introduce kinks and bends and prevent hydrogen bonds from forming.

18.88

18.90 Arg, Asp, Asn, Glu, Gln, His, Lys, Ser, Thr, Tyr

18.92 On the outside of a globular protein: Glu, Ser. On the outside of a fibrous protein: Ala, Val. On the outside of neither: Leu, Phe. **18.94** Asp is similar in size and function to Glu. **18.96** Canned pineapple has been heated to inactivate enzymes. **18.98** Enzymes would hydrolyze insulin. **18.100** A combination of grains, legumes, and nuts in each meal provides all of the essential amino acids.

Chapter 19

19.1 ribonuclease **19.2** The enzyme might catalyze reactions within the eye; saline is sterile and isotonic. **19.3** iron, copper, manganese, molybdenum, vanadium, cobalt, nickel, chromium **19.4 (a)** NAD$^+$, coenzyme A, FAD; **(b)** The remaining cofactors are minerals. **19.5 (a)** catalyzes the removal of two —H from an alcohol, **(b)** catalyzes the transfer of an amino group from aspartate to a second substrate, **(c)** catalyzes the synthesis of tyrosine–tRNA from tyrosine and its tRNA, coupled with ATP hydrolysis. **(d)** catalyzes the isomerization of a phosphohexose. **19.6 (a)** urease **(b)** cellulase **19.7** transferase. It catalyzes the transfer of a phosphoryl group to a hexose. **19.8** Water adds to fumarate (substrate) to give L-malate (product). **19.9** Reaction **(a)** **19.10** Acidic, basic and polar side chains take part in catalytic activity. All types of side chains hold the enzyme in the active site. **19.11** Substrate molecules are bound to all of the active sites, **(a)** no effect; **(b)** increases the rate. **19.12** higher at 35°C in both cases **19.13** The rate is much greater at pH = 2. **19.14** Two strategies keep the enzyme active: (1) Use of chaperonins, enzymes that return a protein to its active form; (2) The protein itself is rigid and resists heat denaturation. **19.15** CPK, AST, and LDH$_1$ leak from damaged heart vessels. **19.16 (a)** E1 **(b)** no **19.17** molecule **(b)**, because it resembles the substrate **19.18** a product that resembles the substrate **19.19** irreversible inhibition **19.20 (a)** competitive inhibition **(b)** covalent modification or feedback control **(c)** covalent modification **(d)** genetic control **19.21** Vitamin A-long hydrocarbon chain. Vitamin C-polar hydroxyl groups.

18.86 (a)

Arg——Pro——Pro——Gly——Phe——Ser——Pro——Phe——Arg

19.22 Retinal - aldehyde. Retinoic acid - carboxylic acid. **19.23** enzyme cofactors; antioxidants; aid in absorption of calcium and phosphate ions; aid in synthesis of visual pigments and blood clotting factors. **19.24** Vitamins C and E, β-carotene; These vitamins scavenge damaging free radicals. **19.25** copper, selenium; Both have a biological function and are toxic only in excess.

19.26

19.27 (a) oxidoreductase (b) dehydrogenase (c) L-lactate (d) pyruvate (e) L-lactate dehydrogenase **19.28** No. An enzyme usually catalyzes the reaction of only one isomer. D-Lactate might be a competitive inhibitor. **19.29** NAD$^+$ is an oxidizing agent and includes the vitamin niacin. **19.30** (a) Rate increases when [substrate] is low, but max. rate is soon reached; max. rate is always lower than max. rate of uninhibited reaction. (b) Rate increases. **19.31** (a) Addition or removal of a covalently bonded group changes the activity of an enzyme (b) Hormones control the synthesis of enzymes. (c) Binding of the regulator at a site away from the catalytic site changes the shape of the enzyme. (d) Feedback inhibition occurs when the product of a series of reactions serves as an inhibitor for an earlier reaction. **19.32** (a) feedback inhibition (b) irreversible inhibition (c) genetic control (d) noncompetitive inhibition **19.33** From left to right: aspartate (acidic), serine, glutamine, arginine (basic), histidine (basic). **19.34** (a) removal of two —H from a substrate to form a double bond; (b) replacement of a carboxyl group by —H; (c) hydrolysis of ester groups in lipids **19.36** (a) amylase (b) peroxidase (c) DNAse **19.38** An enzyme is a large three-dimensional molecule with a catalytic site into which a substrate can fit. Enzymes are specific in their action because only one or a few molecules have the appropriate shape and functional groups to fit into the catalytic site. **19.40** (a) hydrolase (b) lyase (c) oxidoreductase **19.42** (a) loss of H$_2$O from a substrate to give a double bond; (b) transfer of a methyl group between substrates; (c) reduction of a substrate **19.44** hydrolase **19.46** (a) riboflavin (B$_2$) (b) pantothenic acid (B$_5$) (c) niacin (B$_3$) **19.48** Lock-and-key: An enzyme is rigid(lock) and only one specific substrate(key) can fit in the active site. Induced fit: An enzyme can change its shape to accommodate the substrate and to catalyze the reaction. **19.50** No. Protein folding can bring the residues close to each other.

19.52 In the stomach, an enzyme must be active at an acidic pH. In the intestine, an enzyme needs to be active at a higher pH and need not be active at pH = 1.5. **19.54** At a high substrate concentration relative to enzyme concentration, the rate of reaction triples if the concentration of enzyme is tripled. **19.56** (a) (b) lowers rate; (c) denatures the enzyme and stops reaction **19.58** *Uncompetitive inhibition:* Inhibitor binds reversibly and noncovalently away from the active site and changes the shape of the site to make it difficult for the enzyme to catalyze reactions. *Competitive inhibition:* Inhibitor binds reversibly and noncovalently at the active site and keeps the substrate from entering. *Irreversible inhibition:* Inhibitor irreversibly forms a covalent bond at the active site and destroys the catalytic ability of the enzyme. **19.60** diagram B **19.62** (1) displacing an essential metal from an active site; (2) bonding to a cysteine residue (irreversible) **19.64** Papain catalyzes the hydrolysis of peptide bonds and partially digests the proteins in meat. **19.66** One site is for catalysis, and one site is for regulation. **19.68** The end product of a reaction series is an inhibitor for an earlier step. **19.70** A zymogen is an enzyme synthesized in a form different from its active form because it might otherwise harm the organism. **19.72** Vitamins are small essential organic molecules that must be obtained from food. **19.74** Vitamin C is excreted, but Vitamin A is stored in fatty tissue. **19.76** Bone is composed of both calcium and phosphorus. **19.78** Reactions can be run at higher temperatures, increasing the rate. **19.80** earliest: CPK; after several days: LDH **19.82** A mild inhibitor allows closer control of blood pressure. A modification to pit viper protein might be to introduce an —SH residue near proline. **19.84** Vitamin A: 0%; Vitamin C 0%; Calcium: 4%; Iron: 6% This food is not a good source of vitamins and minerals. **19.86** They are the most important for maintaining good health. **19.88** *See below for answer.* **19.90** 11 L apple juice **19.92** Because competitive inhibition is reversible, addition of a large amount of the normal substrate will reverse the binding of the inhibitor, and the rate of reaction of the normal substrate will return to its usual value. The effects of uncompetitive inhibition can't be reversed by addition of excess substrate. **19.94** Serine to valine would destroy catalytic activity, since the serine —OH group is essential for catalysis. Aspartate to glutamate might or might not affect catalytic activity since both amino acids have the same functional groups.

Chapter 20

20.1 exergonic: (a), (c); endergonic: (b); releases the most energy: (a) **20.2** Both pathways produce the same amount of energy. **20.3** (a) exergonic: oxidation of glucose; endergonic: photosynthesis (b) sunlight **20.4** (a)

Carbohydrates $\xrightarrow{\text{digestion}}$ Glucose, sugars $\xrightarrow{\text{glycolysis}}$ Pyruvate → Acetyl-CoA $\xrightarrow[\text{cycle}]{\text{citric acid}}$ Reduced coenzymes $\xrightarrow[\text{transport}]{\text{electron}}$ ATP

(b) pyruvate, acetyl-CoA, citric acid cycle intermediates.

19.88

Vitamin E

20.5

$$H_3C-\overset{\overset{O}{\|}}{C}-O-\overset{\overset{O}{\|}}{\underset{\underset{O^-}{|}}{P}}-O^- + H_2O \longrightarrow$$

$$H_3C-\overset{\overset{O}{\|}}{C}-O^- + \ ^-O-\overset{\overset{O}{\|}}{\underset{\underset{OH}{|}}{P}}-O^- + H^+$$

20.6 Energy is produced only when it is needed.
20.7

$$HOCH_2CHCH_2OH \xrightarrow[\text{ATP}\quad\text{ADP}]{} HOCH_2CHCH_2O-\overset{\overset{O}{\|}}{\underset{\underset{O^-}{|}}{P}}-O^-$$

(with OH groups shown)

20.8 If a process is exergonic, its exact reverse is endergonic and can't occur unless it is coupled with an exergonic reaction in a different pathway.
20.9 66 min. **20.10** favorable ($\Delta G = -3.0$ kcal/mol; -12.3 kJ/mol).
20.11 (b), (c), (d) FAD has five heterocyclic rings (three in the ADP part, and two in the site of reaction on the left).
20.12 (a)

$$^-OOC-\overset{|}{\underset{|}{C}}-CH-CH_2COO^-$$
(with H, O, H circled)

$$^-OOC-CH-CH-COO^-$$
(with H, H circled)

$$^-OOC-CH_2-\overset{|}{\underset{|}{C}}-COO^-$$
(with O-H, H circled)

(b) oxidoreductases
20.13 Citric acid, isocitric acid. **20.14** steps 3, 4, 6, 8. **20.15** Succinic dehydrogenase catalyzes the removal of two hydrogens from succinate to yield fumarate, and FAD is the coenzyme associated with dehydrogenations.
20.16 citrate (tertiary); isocitrate (secondary); malate (secondary)
20.17 isocitrate **20.18** Steps 1–4 correspond to the first stage, and steps 5–8 correspond to the second stage. **20.19** Mitochondrial matrix
20.20 *Similarities*: both involve the reaction of glucose, oxygen, carbon dioxide, and water; both take place in organelles (chloroplasts, mitochondria); both involve large, metal-ion-containing molecules (chlorophyll, heme); both involve electron transfer; both involve similar coenzymes. *Differences*: photosynthesis captures energy, whereas electron transport releases energy; photosynthesis requires light, whereas oxidative phosphorylation doesn't. **20.21** O_2. Movement of H^+ from a region of high $[H^+]$ to a region of low $[H^+]$ releases energy that is used in ATP synthesis.
20.22 (a) Succinyl phosphate + $H_2O \longrightarrow$
$\qquad\qquad$ Succinate + $HOPO_3^{2-}$ + H^+
$\quad$ (b) ADP + $HOPO_3^{2-}$ + $H^+ \longrightarrow$ ATP + H_2O
$\qquad\qquad \Delta G = +7.3$ kcal/mol ($+30.5$ kJ/mol)
20.23 (a) Stage 1 (digestion) (b) Stage 4 (ATP synthesis) (c) Stage 2 (glycolysis) (d) Stage 3 (citric acid cycle). **20.24** Endergonic; coupled reactions **20.25** NAD^+ accepts hydride ions; hydrogen ions are released to the mitochondrial matrix, and ultimately combine with reduced O_2 to form H_2O. **20.26** (a) Step A (NAD^+) (b) Step B (c) product of A (d) oxidoreductase **20.27** Step 1: lyase Step 2: isomerase Step 3: oxidoreductase Step 4: oxidoreductase, lyase Step 5: ligase Step 6: oxidoreductase Step 7: lyase Step 8: oxidoreductase **20.28** Metals are better oxidizing and reducing agents. Also, they can accept and donate electrons in one-electron increments. **20.30** An endergonic reaction requires energy, and an exergonic reaction releases energy. **20.32** Enzymes affect only the rate of a reaction, not the size or sign of ΔG. **20.34** exergonic: (a), (b); endergonic: (c). Reaction (b) proceeds farthest toward products. **20.36** prokaryote: (b), (e); eukaryote: (a), (b), (c), (d) **20.38** Organelles are subcellular structures that perform specialized tasks within the cell. **20.40** Cristae, the folds of the inner mitochondrial membrane, provide extra surface area for electron transport and ATP production to take place. **20.42** Metabolism refers to all reactions that take place inside cells. Digestion is the process of breaking food into small organic molecules prior to cellular absorption. **20.44** acetyl-CoA **20.46** An ATP molecule transfers a phosphoryl group to another molecule in exergonic reactions. **20.48** $\Delta G = -4.5$ kcal/mol (-18.8 kJ/mol). **20.50** not favorable (positive ΔG) **20.52** (a) NAD^+ is reduced, (b) NAD^+ is an oxidizing agent, (c) NAD^+ participates in the oxidation of a secondary alcohol to a ketone, (d) $NADH/H^+$
(e)

$$H-\overset{|}{\underset{|}{C}}-OH \xrightarrow[\text{NAD}^+ \quad \text{NADH/H}^+]{} \ C=O$$

20.54 mitochondria **20.56** Both carbons are oxidized to CO_2. **20.58** 3 NADH, one $FADH_2$. **20.60** Step 3 (isocitrate $\rightarrow \alpha$-ketoglutarate), Step 4 (α-ketoglutarate $\rightarrow$ succinyl $-$ SCoA) and Step 8 (malate $\rightarrow$ oxaloacetate) store energy as NADH. **20.62** One complete citric acid cycle produces four reduced coenzymes, which enter the electron transfer chain and ultimately generate ATP. **20.64** H_2O, ATP, oxidized coenzymes **20.66** (a) FAD = flavin adenine dinucleotide; (b) CoQ = coenzyme Q; (c) $NADH/H^+$ = reduced nicotinamide adenine dinucleotide, plus hydrogen ion; (d) Cyt c = Cytochrome c **20.68** NADH, coenzyme Q, cytochrome c **20.70** The citric acid cycle would stop. **20.72** In oxidative phosphorylation, reduced coenzymes are oxidized, and ADP is phosphorylated. **20.74** H^+ ions pass through a channel that is part of the ATP synthase enzyme, where they release energy that drives oxidative phosphorylation. **20.76** Oxygen consumption increases because the proton gradient from ATP production dissipates. **20.78** A seal has more brown fat because it needs to keep warm. **20.80** Bacteria use H_2S because no light is available for the usual light-dependent reaction of H_2O that provides O_2 and electrons. **20.82** (no answer) **20.84** Daily activities such as walking use energy, and thus the body requires a larger caloric intake than that needed to maintain basal metabolism. **20.86** The light reaction produces O_2, NADPH, and ATP. The dark reaction produces carbohydrates from water and CO_2. **20.88** Refrigeration slows the breakdown of carbohydrates by decreasing the rate of respiration.
20.90

$$CoAS-\overset{\overset{O}{\|}}{C}-CH_3 \ + \ \overset{\overset{COO^-}{|}}{\underset{\underset{\underset{\underset{COO^-}{|}}{CH_2}}{|}}{C=O}} \xrightarrow{\text{condensation}}$$

$$CoAS-\overset{\overset{O}{\|}}{C}-CH_2-\overset{\overset{COO^-}{|}}{\underset{\underset{\underset{\underset{COO^-}{|}}{CH_2}}{|}}{C}}-OH$$

20.92 oxidoreductases **20.94** FAD; oxidoreductases **20.96** Energy from combustion is released to the surroundings as heat and is wasted. Energy from metabolic oxidation is released in several steps and is stored in each step so that is available for use in other metabolic processes. **20.98** The enzymes superoxide dismutase and catalase and vitamins E, C, and A can inactivate these species. **20.100** adipose tissue, skin cells, skeletal muscle, heart muscle. **20.102** mitochondrial matrix **20.104** *least oxidized*: succinate; fumarate; malate; oxaloacetate; *most oxidized*

Chapter 21

21.1 (a) aldopentose (b) ketotriose (c) aldotetrose
21.2

$$HOCH_2-\overset{\overset{OH}{|}}{CH}-\overset{\overset{OH}{|}}{CH}-\overset{\overset{OH}{|}}{CH}-\overset{\overset{O}{\|}}{CH}$$

An aldopentose

$$HOCH_2-\overset{\overset{OH}{|}}{CH}-\overset{\overset{OH}{|}}{CH}-\overset{\overset{OH}{|}}{CH}-\overset{\overset{O}{\|}}{C}-CH_2OH$$

A ketohexose

21.3 32 stereoisomers   **21.4** (d)   **21.5** The bottom carbon is not chiral. The orientations of the hydroxyl groups bonded to the chiral carbons must be shown in order to indicate which stereoisomer is pictured.

21.6 (a)

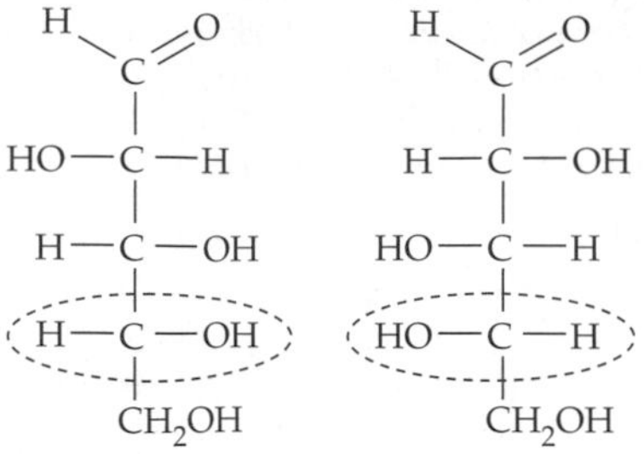

A D-aldopentose   An L-aldopentose

(b)

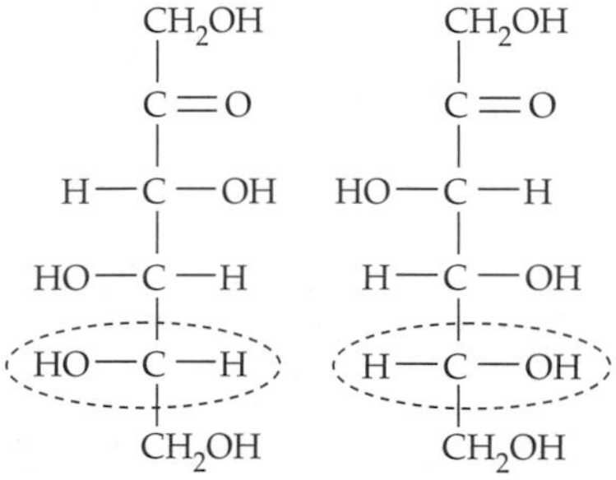

An L-ketohexose   A D-ketohexose

21.7 An enzymatic path would produce only the desired enantiomer. This would provide the desired product without need for separation of enantiomers and would eliminate the need to test both enantiomers.

21.8

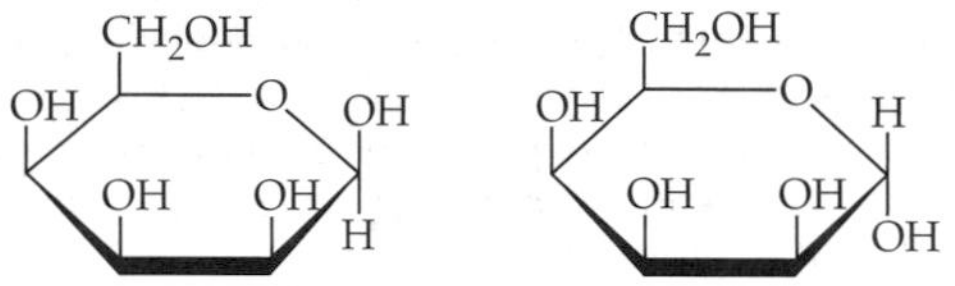

β-anomer   α-anomer

21.9

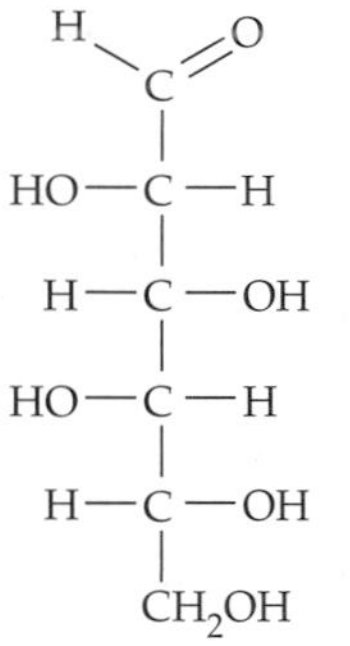

D-Idose

21.10 (a) Rings **1** and **4** (5 carbons) are amino sugars, **(b)** Ring **3** (4 carbons) is an unmodified sugar, **(c)** Ring **2** (6 carbons) is a nonsugar.

21.11

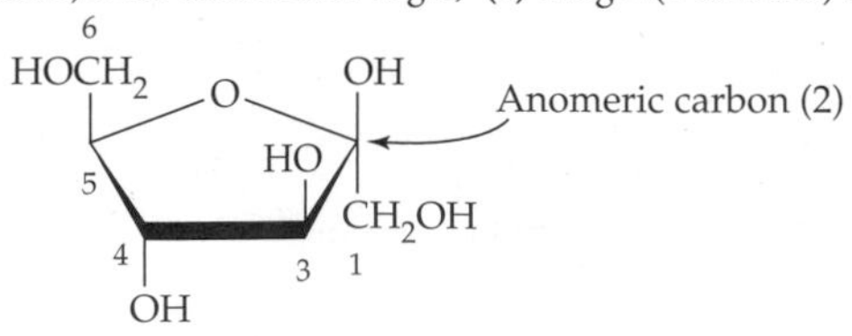

β-anomer

Anomeric carbon (2)

21.12
(a)   **(b)**

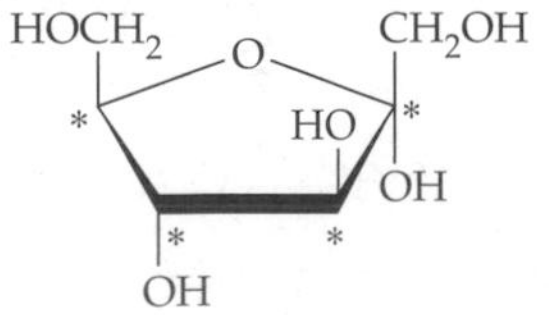

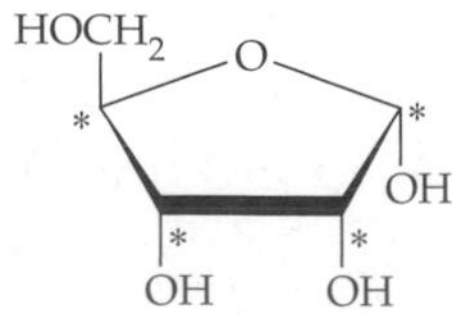

(c)

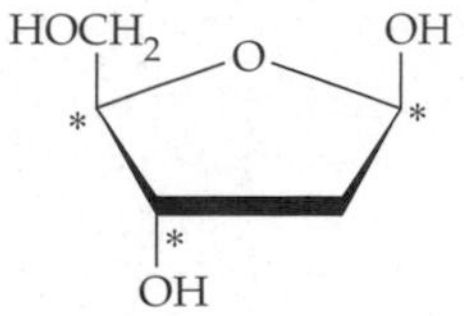

21.13 (a) an α anomer **(b)** carbon 6 **(c)** Groups that are below the plane of the ring in D-galactose are above the plane of the ring in L-fucose. Groups that are above the plane of the ring in D-galactose are below the plane of the ring in L-fucose. **(d)** yes   **21.14** N-acetyl-D-glucosamine, D-galactose, and L-fucose are found in all blood types.

21.15

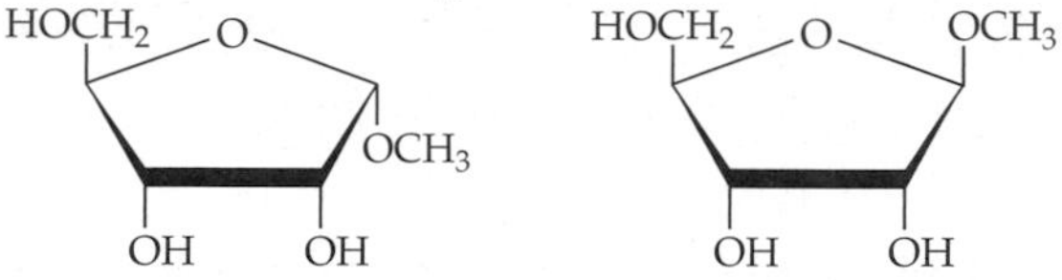

Methyl α-D-riboside   Methyl β-D-riboside

21.16 a β-1,4 glycosidic link   **21.17** β-D-Glucose + β-D-Glucose
21.18 (a) maltose; fermenting grain **(b)** sucrose; sugar beets **(c)** lactose; milk   **21.19** Glucose and fructose are simple carbohydrates; starch is a complex carbohydrate. Soluble and insoluble fiber are complex carbohydrates that are not digestible by humans.   **21.20** glutamine, asparagine
21.21 an α-1,4 glycosidic link   **21.22** No. There are too few hemiacetal units to give a detectable result.   **21.23** The spherical particles of glycogen are compact and easily available as a source of glucose. The chains of cellulose serve as structural components of plants.   **21.24** irreversible inhibition; permanently inactivates an enzyme's active site; inhibits the synthesis of bacterial cell walls; modified sugar polymers, peptidoglycans

21.25   Starch $\xrightarrow{\text{Amylase}}$ Maltose $\xrightarrow{\text{Maltase}}$ Glucose
polysaccharide   disaccharide   monosaccharide

21.26 (a) diastereomers, anomers **(b)** enantiomers **(c)** diastereomers
21.27 (a) (b)

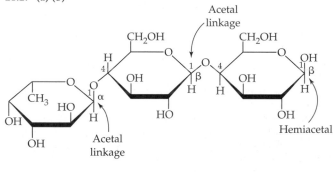

A   B   C
α-anomer   β-anomer   β-anomer

(c) α-1,4 linkage between C4 of B and C1 of A **(d)** β-1,4 linkage between C4 of C and C1 of B   **21.28 (a) (b)** No monosaccharides are identical, and none are enantiomers. **(c) (d)**

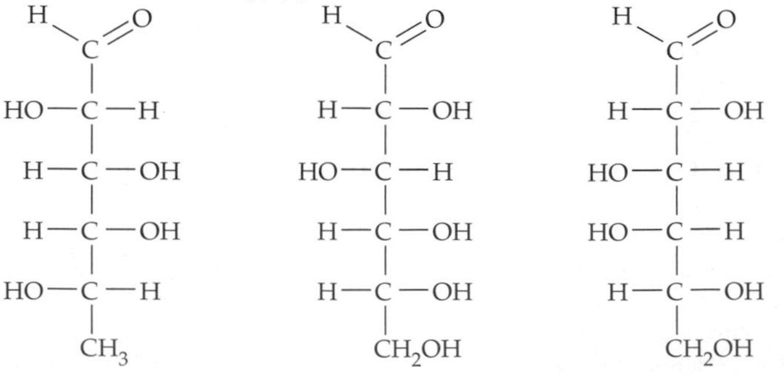

L-Fucose   D-Glucose   D-Galactose

21.29 Monosaccharide C is oxidized. Identification of the carboxylic acid also identifies the terminal monosaccharide.

```
        ⁻O     O
          \   //
           C
           |
      H — C — OH
           |
     HO — C — H
           |
     HO — C — H
           |
      H — C — OH
           |
         CH₂OH
```

21.30 No

21.31

Polysaccharide	Linkage	Branching?
Cellulose	β-1,4	no
Amylose	α-1,4	no
Amylopectin	α-1,4	yes: α-1,6 branches occur ~ every 25 units
Glycogen	α-1,4	yes: even more α-1,6 branches than in amylopectin

21.32 Glucose is in equilibrium with its open-chain aldehyde form, which reacts with an oxidizing agent.
21.34 -ose **21.36** (a) aldotetrose (b) ketopentose (c) aldopentose (d) ketohexose **21.38** right part = 4 chiral carbons; left part = 5 chiral carbons; total = nine chiral carbons

21.40

```
     H    O
      \  //
       C
       |
      CH₂  ←— Oxygen missing here
       |
  H — C — OH        A four-carbon deoxy sugar
       |
     CH₂OH
```

21.42 glucose—energy source; galactose—brain tissue, fructose—energy source; ribose—nucleic acids, coenzymes **21.44** They are mirror images (enantiomers). **21.46** The reduction product of D-erythrose is achiral. **21.48** A polarimeter measures the degree of rotation of plane-polarized light by a solution of an optically active compound. **21.50** Equimolar solutions of enantiomers rotate light to the same degree but in opposite directions. **21.52** A reducing sugar contains an aldehyde or ketone group. **21.54** An anomer is one of a pair of hemiacetal stereoisomers formed when an open-chain sugar cyclizes. Anomers differ in the orientation of the hydroxyl group at the anomeric carbon. **21.56** the α form

21.58

```
      H  H  H  H  OH O
      |  |  |  |  |  ||
 HO — C— C— C— C— C— C— H   =
      |  |  |  |  |
      H  OH OH OH H
```

β-D-Altrose and α-D-Altrose ring structures

21.60

```
         CH₂OH
          |
    HO — C — H
          |
    HO — C — H
          |
     H — C — OH
          |
     H — C — OH
          |
         CH₂OH
```

21.62

```
    HO     O
      \   //
       C
       |
   H —— OH
       |
   H —— OH
       |
   H —— OH
       |
     CH₂OH
```

22.64 A glycoside is an acetal that is formed when the hemiacetal —OH group of a carbohydrate reacts with an alcohol.

21.66

Disaccharide structure with labeled Hemiacetal carbon

The hemiacetal carbon in this problem is in equilibrium with an open-chain aldehyde that is a reducing sugar.

21.68 Sucrose has no hemiacetal group. **21.70** Amylose and amylopectin are both components of starch and both consist of long polymers of α-D-glucose linked by α-1,4 glycosidic bonds. Amylopectin is much larger and has α-1,6 branches every 25 units or so along the chain. **21.72** Gentiobiose contains both an acetal grouping and a hemiacetal grouping. Gentiobiose is a reducing sugar. A β-1,6 linkage connects the two monosaccharides. **21.74** Trehalose is a nonreducing sugar because it contains no hemiacetal linkages. The two D-glucose monosaccharides are connected by an α-1,1 acetal link. **21.76** Starch is the storage form of glucose in plants; glycogen serves the same purpose in animals. **21.78** Enzyme-catalyzed reactions usually produce only one enantiomer. **21.80** People with type O blood can receive blood only from other donors that have type O blood. People with type AB blood can give blood only to other people with type AB blood. **21.82** pectin and vegetable gum: found in fruits, barley, oats and beans. **21.84** glucose; cellulose in a matrix of pectin, lignin, and cellulose **21.86** Penicillin inhibits the enzyme that synthesizes bacterial cell walls. Mammals don't have this synthetic pathway. **21.88** No. they are not mirror images.

21.90

Raffinose structure with Acetal labels

21.92

```
              OH  O
              |   ||
      HOCH₂ — *C — C — CH₂OH      1,3,4-Trihydroxy-2-butanone
              |
              H
```

1,3,4-Trihydroxy-2-butanone has one chiral carbon and exists as a pair of enentiomers.
21.94 Enzymes produced by the bacteria in yogurt predigest most of the lactose, making it possible for lactose-intolerant people to eat yogurt without symptoms.

21.96

Dulcitol ------------------------ Plane of symmetry

Dulcitol is optically inactive because it has a plane of symmetry and thus doesn't have an enantiomer.   **21.98** 170 kcal (710 kJ)   **21.100** fructose: fruit; lactose: milk; amylose: wheat starch   **21.102** Cellulose is rigid and is insoluble in water; glycogen coils up, is flexible, and dissolves in water.

Chapter 22

22.1 (a) glycogenesis (b) glycogenolysis (c) gluconeogenesis   **22.2** glycogenesis, pentose phosphate pathway, glycolysis   **22.3** (a) steps 6 and 7 (b) steps 9 and 10   **22.4** Isomerizations: steps 2, 5, 8

22.5

22.6 (a) pyruvate (b) Step 6: glyceraldehyde 3-phosphate is oxidized; NAD^+ is the oxidizing agent   **22.7** Table sugar (sucrose) promotes the growth of bacteria that cause tooth decay; honey (glucose + fructose) does not.

22.8

Fructose 6-phosphate enters glycolysis at Step 3.

22.9 Glucose and galactose differ in configuration at C4.   **22.10** (a) The energy is lost as heat. (b) The reverse of fermentation is very endothermic; loss of CO_2 drives the reaction to completion in the forward direction.   **22.11** in preparation of bread, yogurt, cheese, beer, and wine   **22.12** Insulin decreases; blood glucose decreases, the level of glucagon increases. Glucagon causes the breakdown of liver glycogen and the release of glucose. As glycogen is used up, the level of free fatty acids and ketone bodies increases.   **22.13** fasting blood sugar check, glucose tolerance test

22.14

Sorbitol

Sorbitol can not form a cyclic acetal because it does not have a carbonyl group.

22.15 (a) The increase in $[H^+]$ drives the equilibrium shown in Section 22.9 to the right, causing the production of CO_2. (b) Le Châtelier's Principle.   **22.16** Creatine phosphate, stored in muscles, is an immediate source of ATP. ATP from glucose and glycogen metabolism is a slower process.   **22.17** phosphorylation, oxidation   **22.18** hydrolases   **22.19** (a) when the supply of glucose is adequate and the body needs energy. (b) when the body needs free glucose. (c) when ribose 5-phosphate or NADPH are needed. (d) when glucose supply is adequate, and the body doesn't need to use glucose for energy production.   **22.20** Phosphorylations of glucose and fructose 6-phosphate produce important intermediates that repay the initial energy investment. Fructose 1,6-bisphosphate is cleaved into two three-carbon compounds, which are converted to pyruvate.   **22.21** (a) when the body needs energy, in mitochondria; (b) under anaerobic conditions, in yeast; (c) under anaerobic conditions, in muscle, red blood cells; (d) when the body needs free glucose, in the liver   **22.22** Step 1: transferase Step 2: isomerase Step 3: transferase Step 4: lyase Step 5: isomerase Step 6: oxidoreductase, transferase Step 7: transferase Step 8: isomerase Step 9: lyase Step 10: transferase. transferases (because many reactions involve phosphate transfers). Ligases are associated with reactions that synthesize molecules, not with reactions that break down molecules.   **22.23** (g), (c), (b), (e), (f), (a), (d)   **22.24** Sources of compounds for gluconeogenesis: pyruvate, lactate, citric acid cycle intermediates, many amino acids. Gluconeogenesis takes place when glucose levels are low.   **22.25** Germinating seeds need to synthesize carbohydrates from fats; humans obtain carbohydrates from food.   **22.26** (a) No (b) Molecular oxygen appears in the last step of the electron transport chain, where it combines with water, H^+ and electrons (from electron transport) to form H_2O.   **22.28** glucose + galactose; in the lining of the small intestine

22.30

Type of Food Molecules	Products of Digestion
Proteins	Amino acids
Triacylglycerols	Glycerol and fatty acids
Sucrose	Glucose and fructose
Lactose	Glucose and galactose
Starch, maltose	Glucose

22.32 acetyl-CoA; lactate; ethanol + CO_2 **22.34** glycogenesis: synthesis of glycogen from glucose; glycogenolysis: breakdown of glycogen to form glucose   **22.36** ribose 5-phosphate, glycolysis intermediates   **22.34** (a) all organs; (b) liver; (c), (d) muscle, liver   **22.40** None of steps of glycolysis require oxygen.   **22.42** (a) steps 1, 3, 6, 7, 10; (b) step 6; (c) step 9   **22.44** (a) Substrate-level phosphorylation: 2 mol ATP; oxidative phosphorylation (ideal): 6 ATP (b) Oxidative phosphorylation: 3 mol ATP (c) Substrate- level phosphorylation: 1 mol ATP; oxidative phosphorylation: 11 mol ATP. Substrate-level phosphorylation is formation of ATP as a by-product of a reaction; oxidative phosphorylation is formation of ATP as a byproduct of electron transport.

22.46

22.48 4 mol acetyl-CoA   **22.50** *Hypoglycemia*: low blood sugar; weakness, sweating, rapid heartbeat, confusion, coma, death *Hyperglycemia*: high blood sugar; increased urine flow, low blood pressure, coma, death   **22.52** ketone bodies   **22.54** In Type 2 diabetes, insulin is in good supply, but cell membrane receptors fail to recognize insulin.   **22.56** Excess glucose is converted to sorbitol, which can't be transported out of cells. This buildup changes osmolarity and causes cataracts and blindness.   **22.58** muscle cells   **22.60** Glycogenolysis uses less energy because it is a hydrolysis reaction.   **22.62** pyruvate, lactate   **22.64** Several steps in the reverse of glycolysis are energetically unfavorable.   **22.66** Steps 1, 3, 10 of glycolysis; all involve phosphate transfers   **22.68** when muscle glucose is depleted and oxygen is in short supply   **22.70** glycoproteins, bacteria, dextran, polysaccharide storage granules   **22.72** In an environment rich in sucrose, bacteria secrete an enzyme that transfers glucose units from digested sucrose to the dextran polymer. The residual fructose is metabolized to lactate, which lowers pH. The resulting acidic environment in the mouth dissolves minerals in teeth, leading to cavities. **22.74** beer, wine, cheese, yogurt, sour cream, and buttermilk **22.76** 140 g/dL vs 90 g/dL **22.78** The curve lies between the curve for a diabetic person and a nondiabetic person **22.80** *First used* → *Last used* ATP, creatine phosphate, glucose, glycogen, fatty acids from triacylglycerols **22.82** phosphoryl group transfers **22.84** Glucose obtained from the hydrolysis of glycogen is phosphorylated by reaction with inorganic phosphate ion and enters the glycolysis pathway as glucose 6–phosphate. Thus, one fewer ATP is needed (at Step 1), and one more ATP is produced. **22.86** In the absence of oxygen, pyruvate from catabolism of glucose in wine was fermented by yeast enzymes to ethanol and CO_2, which increased the pressure in the bottle and popped the cork. **22.88** (a) consumes energy (b) yields energy **22.90** (1) Lactate can only be converted to glucose in the liver; (2) Lactate lowers the pH in muscle cells and must be removed. **22.92** (a) when glucose is abundant and the body needs energy; (b) when glucose is in short supply, as in starvation or fasting

Chapter 23

23.1 (a) eicosanoid (b) glycerophospholipid (c) wax
23.2

$$CH_3(CH_2)_{18}\overset{O}{\overset{\|}{C}}-OCH_2(CH_2)_{30}CH_3$$

23.3

$$CH_2OC(CH_2)_7CH=CH(CH_2)_7CH_3$$
$$CHOC(CH_2)_7CH=CH(CH_2)_7CH_3$$
$$CH_2OC(CH_2)_7CH=CH(CH_2)_7CH_3$$

23.4 cookies (lower in both total fat and saturated fat) **23.5** (a) butter (b) soybean oil (c) soybean oil **23.6** *See below for answer.*
23.7 When two different fatty acids are bonded to C1 and C3 of glycerol, C2 is chiral. **23.8** London forces; weak; hydrogen bonds between water molecules are stronger than London forces.
23.9 The resulting acyl groups are from stearic acid.

$$CH_2OC(CH_2)_7CH=CH(CH_2)_7CH_3$$
$$CHOC(CH_2)_7CH=CH(CH_2)_7CH_3$$
$$CH_2OC(CH_2)_7CH=CH(CH_2)_7CH_3$$

$$\xrightarrow{3\,H_2}$$

$$CH_2OC(CH_2)_{16}CH_3$$
$$CHOC(CH_2)_{16}CH_3$$
$$CH_2OC(CH_2)_{16}CH_3$$

23.10 Both soaps and detergents consist of ionic heads and hydrophobic tails, and both clean by forming micelles around greasy dirt. Unlike detergents, soaps can form soap scum when used in hard water.

23.11

$$CH_2OC(CH_2)_{16}CH_3$$
$$CHOC(CH_2)_{16}CH_3$$
$$CH_2OC(CH_2)_7CH=CH(CH_2)_7CH_3$$

$$\xrightarrow{\text{NaOH, } H_2O}$$

or the isomer

$$CH_2OH$$
$$CHOH$$
$$CH_2OH$$

$$+ \quad 2\,CH_3(CH_2)_{16}COO^-\,Na^+$$
$$CH_3(CH_2)_7CH=CH(CH_2)_7COO^-\,Na^+$$

23.12 Lecithins emulsify fats in the same way as soaps dissolve grease: The fats are coated by the nonpolar part of a lecithin, and the polar part of lecithins allows fats to be suspended in aqueous solution. **23.13** (a) glycerol, phosphate ion, choline, $RCOO^-Na^+$, $R'COO^-Na^+$, (b) sphingosine, phosphate ion, choline, sodium palmitate

23.14

$$(CH_3)_3\overset{+}{N}CH_2CH_2O-\overset{O}{\overset{\|}{P}}-O-CH_2$$
with O^-, $CHNH-\overset{O}{\overset{\|}{C}}(CH_2)_{12}CH_3$ (Myristic acid), $CHOH$, $CH=CH(CH_2)_{12}CH_3$

Choline Phosphate — Hydrophobic tail
Hydrophilic head — Hydrophobic tail

23.15

Stearic acid acyl group
$$CH_2-O-\overset{O}{\overset{\|}{C}}-(CH_2)_{16}CH_3$$
Oleic acid acyl group
$$CH-O-\overset{O}{\overset{\|}{C}}-(CH_2)_7CH=CH(CH_2)_7CH_3$$
$$CH_2-O-\overset{O}{\underset{O^-}{\overset{\|}{P}}}-OCH_2CH_2NH_3^+$$
Phosphate Ethanolamine

23.16 (a), (c), (e), (f) **23.17** in butter: cholesterol; in margarine: trans fatty acids **23.18** They must be hydrophobic, contain many amino acids

23.6

$$H_3C-CH_2-CH_2-CH_2-CH_2-CH=CH-CH_2-CH=CH-CH_2-CH=CH-CH_2-CH=CH-CH_2-CH_2-\overset{O}{\overset{\|}{C}}-OH$$

with nonpolar side chains, and must be folded so that the hydrophilic regions face outward. **23.19** yes **23.20** Glucose 6-phosphate has a charged phosphate group and can't pass through the hydrophobic lipid bilayer. **23.21** The surfaces are in different environments and serve different functions. **23.22** carboxylic acid (most acidic), alcohol, C — C double bonds, ethers. The molecule has both polar and nonpolar regions. Form hydrogen bonds: —COOH, —OH. **23.23** A has the highest melting point. B and C are probably liquids at room temperature. **23.24** 12.2% palmitic acid, 87.5% stearic acid; more like C

23.25

$$CH_2OC(CH_2)_{14}CH_3$$
$$CHOC(CH_2)_7CH=CH(CH_2)_7CH_3$$
$$CH_2O-P-OCH_2CH_2$$
$$O^-\quad NH_3^+$$

A glycerophospholipid

23.26 Because the membrane is fluid, it can flow together after an injury. **23.27** C_{16} saturated fatty acids. The polar head lies in lung tissue, and the hydrocarbon tails protrude into the alveoli. **23.28** A lipid is a naturally-occurring molecule that dissolves in nonpolar solvents. **23.30** $CH_3(CH_2)_{16}COOH$: straight chain **23.32** *Saturated fatty acids* are long-chain carboxylic acids that contain no carbon–carbon double bonds. *Monounsaturated fatty acids* contain one carbon–carbon double bond. *Polyunsaturated fatty acids* contain two or more carbon–carbon double bonds. **23.34** An essential fatty acid can't be synthesized by the human body and must be part of the diet. **23.36 (a)** The double bonds in an unsaturated fatty acid (linolenic acid) make it harder for them to be arranged in a crystal. **23.38** Fats: saturated and unsaturated fatty acids, solids; Oils: mostly unsaturated fatty acids, liquids.

23.40

$$CH_2-O-C-CH_2(CH_2)_9CH_3$$
$$CH-O-C-CH_2(CH_2)_9CH_3$$
$$CH_2-O-C-CH_2(CH_2)_9CH_3$$

23.42 a protective coating

23.44

$$CH_3(CH_2)_{13}CH_2C-OCH_2(CH_2)_{14}CH_3$$

Cetyl palmitate

23.46

$$CH_2-O-C-(CH_2)_nCH_3$$
$$CH-O-C-(CH_2)_nCH=CH(CH_2)_nCH_3$$
$$CH_2-O-P-OCH_2CH_2CH_2\overset{+}{N}(CH_3)_3$$
$$O^-$$

23.48 hydrogenation **23.50** saponification **23.52** The product is shown in Problem 23.9 **23.54** Glycerophospholipids have polar heads (point outward) and nonpolar tails that cluster to form the membrane. Triacylglycerols don't have polar heads. **23.56** A sphingomyelin and a cerebroside are similar in that both have a sphingosine backbone. The difference between the two occurs at C1 of sphingosine. A sphingomyelin has a phosphate group bonded to an amino alcohol at C1; a cerebroside has a glycosidic link to a monosaccharide at C1. **23.58** Glycerophospholipids have an ionic phosphate group that is solvated by water. **23.60** In a soap micelle, the polar hydrophilic heads are on the exterior, and the hydrophobic tails cluster in the center. In a membrane bilayer, hydrophilic heads are on both the exterior and interior surfaces of the membrane, and the region between the two surfaces is occupied by hydrophobic tails. **23.62** glycolipids, cholesterol, proteins **23.64** *See below for answer.*

23.66

$$CH_2-O-C-(CH_2)_{14}CH_3 \longleftarrow \text{Palmitic acid}$$
$$CH-O-C-(CH_2)_7CH=CH(CH_2)_7CH_3 \longleftarrow \text{Oleic acid}$$
$$CH_2-O-P-OCH_2CH_2CH_2NH_3^+ \longleftarrow \text{Propanolamine}$$

Glycerol · · · O^- Phosphate group

A glycerophospholipid

23.68 Active transport requires energy because it is a process in which substances are transported across a membrane in a direction opposite to their tendency to diffuse. **23.70 (a)** simple diffusion **(b)** facilitated diffusion **(c)** active transport **23.72** Cholesterol is a component of cell membranes and is the starting material for the synthesis of all other steroids. **23.74** *Male sex hormones:* androsterone, testosterone *Female sex hormones:* estrone, estradiol, progesterone **23.76** They are synthesized near their site of action. **23.78** linolenic acid **23.80** Leukotrienes are responsible for triggering asthmatic attacks, inflammation and allergic reactions. **23.82** By transferring its acetyl group, aspirin inhibits the enzyme that is responsible for the first step in the conversion of arachidonic acid to prostaglandins. **23.84** meat, fish, poultry, dairy products, nuts, seeds, processed foods **23.86** Both soaps

23.64

$$CH_2OH$$
$$\text{OH} \cdots O \cdots O-CH_2 \quad \text{Sphingosine} \quad \text{Myristic acid}$$
$$\text{OH} \quad H$$
$$CH-NH-C-CH_2CH_2CH_2CH_2CH_2CH_2CH_2CH_2CH_2CH_2CH_2CH_2CH_3$$
$$\text{OH} \quad CH-OH \quad O$$
$$\text{D-Galactose}$$
$$CH=CHCH_2CH_2CH_2CH_2CH_2CH_2CH_2CH_2CH_2CH_2CH_2CH_2CH_3$$

A cerebroside

and detergents consist of ionic heads and hydrophobic tails, and both clean by forming micelles around greasy dirt. The polar heads make the cluster soluble.   **23.88** Margarine contains more mono- and polyunsaturated fats but is also more likely to contain trans fats.   **23.90** (b) (c) (e) (f)

23.92

$$CH_2-O-\overset{\displaystyle O}{\overset{\|}{C}}-(CH_2)_{12}CH_3$$
$$CH-O-\overset{\displaystyle O}{\overset{\|}{C}}-(CH_2)_7CH=CHCH_2CH=CHCH_2CH_3$$
$$CH_2-O-\overset{\displaystyle O}{\overset{\|}{C}}-(CH_2)_{12}CH_3$$

or

$$CH_2-O-\overset{\displaystyle O}{\overset{\|}{C}}-(CH_2)_{12}CH_3$$
$$CH-O-\overset{\displaystyle O}{\overset{\|}{C}}-(CH_2)_{12}CH_3$$
$$CH_2-O-\overset{\displaystyle O}{\overset{\|}{C}}-(CH_2)_7CH=CHCH_2CH=CHCH_2CH_3$$

23.94 (a) beef fat (b) plant oil (c) lard   **23.96** It is saponifiable.   **23.98** sphingomyelins, cerebrosides, gangliosides   **23.100** multiple sclerosis   **23.102** (a) (d)   **23.104** 11.5 g

Chapter 24

24.1 Cholate has 4 polar groups on its hydrophilic side that allow it to interact with an aqueous environment; its hydrophobic side interacts with TAGs. Cholate and cholesterol can't change roles.   **24.2** Arterial plaque is made up of cholesterol and other lipid-containing materials. HDL removes cholesterol, whereas LDL delivers cholesterol to tissues.   **24.3** Dihydroxyacetone phosphate is isomerized to glyceraldehyde 3-phosphate, which enters glycolysis.   **24.4** Storage of excess fat is linked to increased risk of developing type II diabetes, stroke, heart attacks, and colon cancer. **24.5** (a), (b) *Step 1;* a C=C double bond is introduced; FAD is the oxidizing agent. *Step 3;* an alcohol is oxidized to a ketone; NAD⁺ is the oxidizing agent. (c) *Step 2;* water is added to a carbon-carbon double bond. (d) *Step 4;* HSCoA displaces acetyl-CoA, producing a chain-shortened acyl-SCoA fatty acid   **24.6** (a) 8 acetyl-CoA, 7 β oxidations (b) 12 acetyl-CoA, 11 β oxidations   **24.7** step 6, step 7, step 8   **24.8** It is the largest reservoir of blood in the body; it is the site of numerous metabolic processes; it is the site of storage of many biomolecules   **24.9** (d)   **24.10** (a) Acetyl-CoA provides the acetyl groups used in synthesis of ketone bodies, (b) 3 (c) The body uses ketone bodies as an energy source during starvation. **24.11** 7 additional acetyl-CoA; 8 additional CO_2 **24.12** Oxygen is needed to reoxidize reduced coenzymes, formed in β oxidation, that enter the electron transport chain.   **24.13** (a) chylomicrons; because they have the greatest ratio of lipid to protein (b) chylomicrons (c) HDL (d) LDL (e) HDL (f) VLDL; used for storage or energy production (g) LDL   **24.14** high blood glucose → high insulin/low glucagon → fatty acid and triacylglycerol synthesis: low blood glucose → low insulin/high glucagon → triacylglycerol hydrolysis; fatty acid oxidation   **24.15** Formation of a fatty acyl-CoA is coupled with conversion of ATP to AMP and pyrophosphate. This energy expenditure is recaptured in β oxidation. **24.16** Less acetyl-CoA can be catabolized in the citric acid cycle, and acetyl-CoA is diverted to ketogenesis.   **24.17** Catabolism of fat provides more energy per gram than does catabolism of glycogen, and thus fats are a more efficient way to store energy.   **24.18** Ketone bodies can be metabolized to form acetyl-CoA, which provides energy.   **24.19** No. Although both these processes add or remove two carbon units, one is not the reverse of the other. The two processes involve different enzymes, coenzymes and

activation steps.   **24.20** They slow the rate of movement of food through the stomach.   **24.22** Bile emulsifies lipid droplets.   **24.24** products are mono- and diacylglycerols, stearic acid, oleic acid, linoleic acid, glycerol **24.26** Acylglycerols, fatty acids, and protein are combined to form *chylomicrons*, which are lipoproteins used to transport lipids from the diet into the bloodstream.   **24.28** by serum albumins   **24.30** Steps 6–10 of the glycolysis pathway.   **24.32** 9 molecules ATP; 21 molecules ATP **24.34** An adipocyte is a cell, almost entirely filled with fat globules, in which triacylglycerols are stored and mobilized.   **24.36** heart, liver, muscle cells **24.38** A fatty acid is converted to its fatty acyl-CoA in order to activate it for catabolism.   **24.40** The carbon β to the thioester group (two carbons away from the thioester group) is oxidized in the process.   **24.42** FAD, NAD⁺ **24.44** 17 ATP   **24.46** *Least* glucose, sucrose, capric acid, myristic acid *Most* **24.48**

(a)
$$CH_3CH_2CH_2CH=\overset{\displaystyle O}{\overset{\|}{CHCSCoA}}$$

(b)
$$CH_3CH_2CH_2\overset{OH}{\overset{|}{CH}}CH_2\overset{O}{\overset{\|}{C}}SCoA$$

(c)
$$CH_3CH_2CH_2\overset{O}{\overset{\|}{C}}CH_2\overset{O}{\overset{\|}{C}}SCoA$$

(d)
$$CH_3CH_2CH_2\overset{O}{\overset{\|}{C}}SCoA \quad + \quad CH_3\overset{O}{\overset{\|}{C}}SCoA$$

24.50 (a) 7 acetyl-CoA, 6 cycles (b) 4 acetyl-CoA, 3 cycles   **24.52** lipogenesis   **24.54** acetyl-CoA   **24.56** 8 rounds   **24.58** Fatty acid synthesis takes place in the cytosol; fatty acid degradation takes place in mitochondria. **24.60** Total cholesterol: 200 mg/dL or lower. LDL: 130 mg/dL or lower. HDL: 40 mg/dL or higher.   **24.62** LDL carries cholesterol from the liver to tissues; HDL carries cholesterol from tissues to the liver, where it is converted to bile and excreted.   **24.64** type II diabetes, colon cancer, heart attacks, stroke   **24.66** calorie-dense food, lack of exercise   **24.68** The liver synthesizes many important biomolecules, it catabolizes glucose, fatty acids and amino acids, it stores many substances, and it inactivates toxic substances.   **24.70** The excess acetyl-CoA from catabolism of carbohydrates is stored as fat. The body can't resynthesize carbohydrate from acetyl-CoA. **24.72** The alcohol intermediate is chiral.   **24.74** Ketosis is a condition in which ketone bodies accumulate in the blood faster than they can be metabolized. Since two of the ketone bodies are carboxylic acids, they lower the pH of the blood, producing the condition known as ketoacidosis. Symptoms of ketoacidosis include dehydration, labored breathing, and depression; prolonged ketoacidosis may lead to coma and death.   **24.76** Ketones have little effect on pH, but the two other ketone bodies are acidic, and they lower the pH of urine.   **24.78** The energy yield from fats is almost twice the energy yield from carbohydrates. A carbohydrate has fewer carbons than a fat of similar molar mass, and 1/3 of the carbons of a carbohydrate are lost as CO_2.   **24.80** The body synthesizes cholesterol when no cholesterol is present in the diet. The body needs cholesterol for membrane function and for synthesis of steroid hormones.   **24.82** $H_2C=CHC(CH_3)=CH_2$. Since cholesterol has 27 carbons, at least 6 2-methyl-1,3-butadiene molecules are needed.

Chapter 25

25.1

2'-Deoxythymidine

25.2 D-Ribose ($C_5H_{10}O_5$) has one more oxygen atom than 2-deoxy-D-ribose ($C_5H_{10}O_4$), and thus can form more hydrogen bonds.

25.3

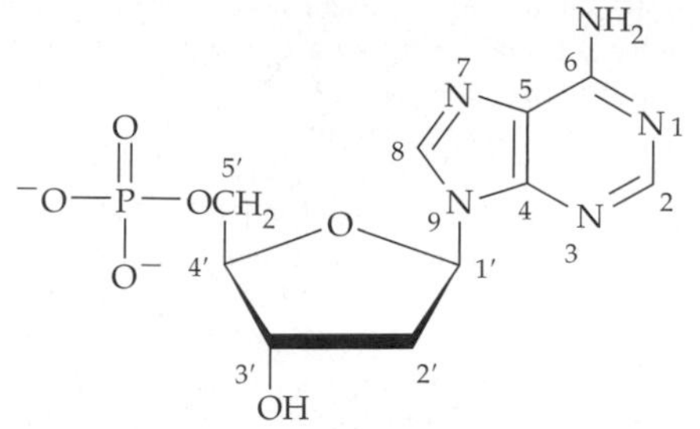

2'-Deoxyadenosine 5'-monophosphate

25.4

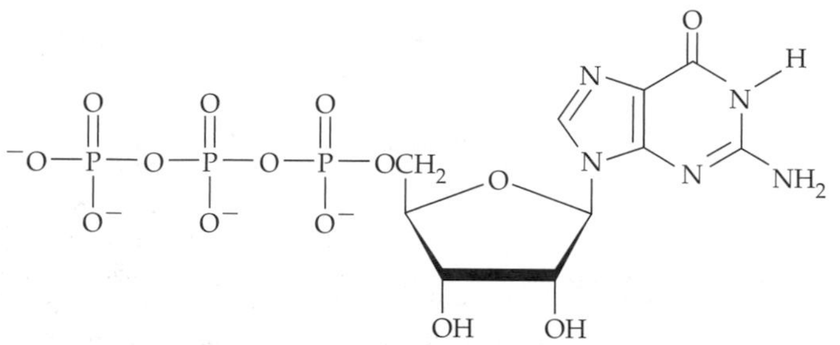

Guanosine 5'-triphosphate (GTP)

25.5 dUMP–2'-Deoxyuridine 5'-monophosphate; UMP–Uridine 5'-monophosphate; CDP–Cytidine 5'-diphosphate; AMP–Adenosine 5'-monophosphate; ATP–Adenosine 5'-triphosphate **25.6** guanine–adenine–uracil–cytosine–adenine. The pentanucleotide comes from RNA because uracil is present.

25.7

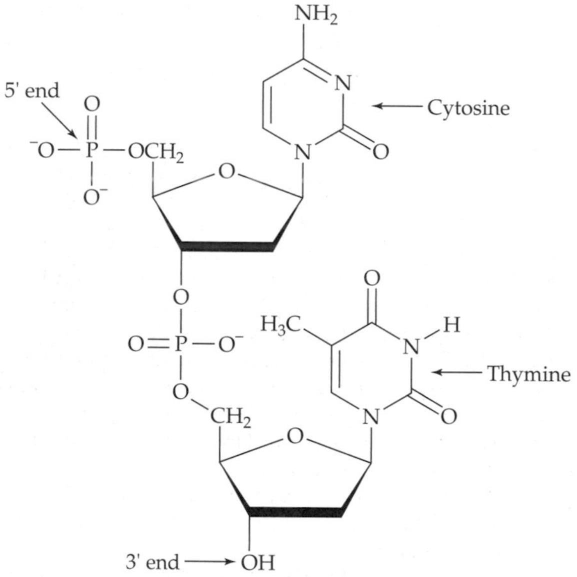

25.8 (a) 3' A-T-A-T-G-A-C 5' (b) 3' C-T-A-G-C-G-A-G-A 5'

25.9

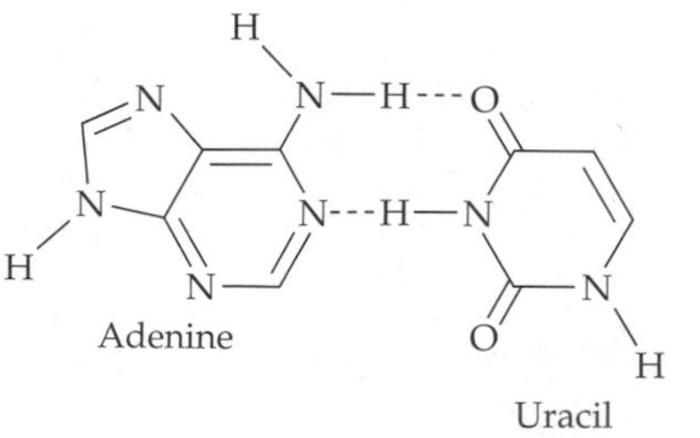

25.10 negatively charged (because of the phosphate groups) **25.11** (a) A longer strand has more hydrogen bonds, (b) A chain with a higher percent of G/C pairs has a higher melting point, because it has more hydrogen bonds.

25.12 Okazaki fragments are segments of DNA synthesized by using the lagging strand as a template. The fragments are later joined by a DNA ligase enzyme. **25.13** In spliceosomes, introns from hnRNA are removed to yield mRNA; in ribosomes, proteins are synthesized, using mRNA as a template. Each process uses a different RNA enzyme. **25.14** (a) 3' G-U-A-C-G-A-G-A-U-G-U-C 5' (b) 5' A-U-A-A-U-C-G-C-U-G-G-C 3' **25.15** (a) GUU GUC GUA GUG (b) UUU UUC (c) AAU AAC (d) GGU GGC GGA GGG (e) AUG **25.16** The sequence guanine-adenine-guanine codes for glutamate. **25.17** (a) Ile (b) Ala (c) Arg (d) Lys **25.18** Six mRNA triplets can code for Leu: UUA, UUG, CUU, CUC, CUA, CUG if no codons are duplicated. Among the possible combinations:

5'UUAUUGCUU 3'	5' UUAUUGCUC 3'	5' UUAUUGCUA 3'
5'UUAUUGCUG 3'	5' UUACUUCUC 3'	5' UUACUUCUA 3'

25.19 Viruses consist of a strand of nucleic acid wrapped in a protein coat; viruses can't replicate or manufacture protein independent of a host cell.

25.20–25.21

mRNA sequence: 5'   CUC—AUU—CCA—UGC—GAC—GUA 3'

Amino-acid sequence: L e u—I l e—P r o—C y s—A s p—V a l

tRNA anticodons: 3' GAG   UAA   GGU   ACG   CUG   CAU 5'

25.22 The influenza virus mutates rapidly.

25.23

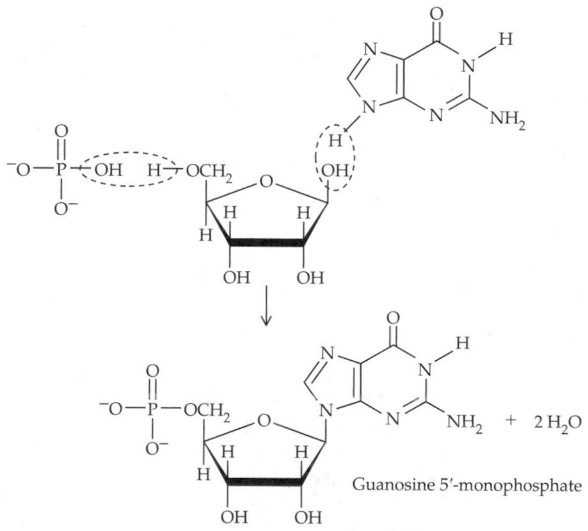

Guanosine 5'-monophosphate

25.24

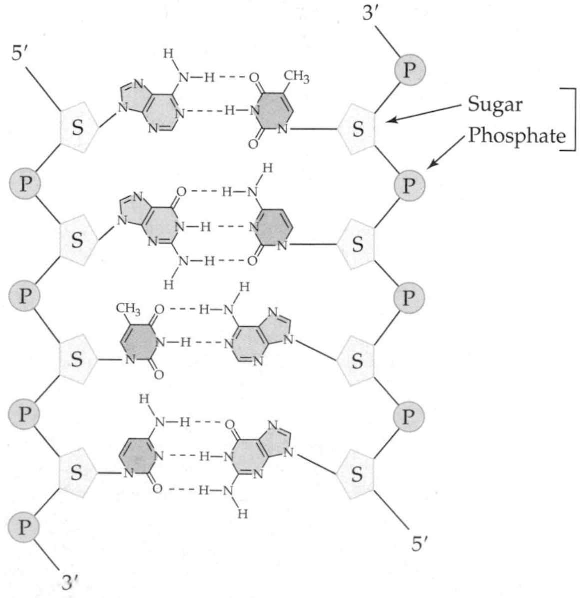

Sequence of the left chain: 5' A-G-T-C 3'
Sequence of the right chain: 5' G-A-C-T 3'

25.25

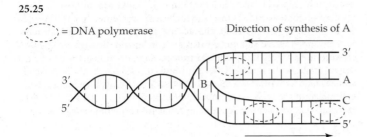

25.26 The sugar-phosphate backbone is found on the outside of the DNA double helix. Histones are positively charged; they contain groups such as Lys, Arg and His.

25.27

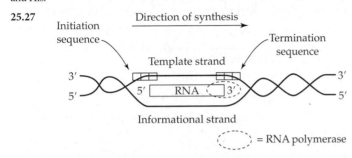

25.28 More than one codon can code for each amino acid. Only one possibility is shown.

(a) 5′ | C | A | A | C | A | C | C | C | C | G | G | G | 3′ mRNA

(b) 3′ | G | T | T | G | T | G | G | G | G | C | C | C | 5′ DNA template strand

(c) 5′ | C | A | A | C | A | C | C | C | C | G | G | G | 3′ DNA informational strand

(d) 64 possible sequences

25.30 2-deoxyribose (DNA); ribose (RNA). 2-Deoxyribose is missing an —OH group at C2.   **25.32** The purine bases (two fused heterocyclic rings) are adenine and guanine. The pyrimidine bases (one heterocyclic ring) are cytosine, thymine (in DNA) and uracil (in RNA).   **25.34** DNA is largest; tRNA is smallest.   **25.36** *Similarities:* All are polymerizations; all use a nucleic acid as a template; all use hydrogen bonding to bring the subunits into position. *Differences:* In replication, DNA makes a copy of itself. In transcription, DNA is used as a template for the synthesis of mRNA. In translation, mRNA is used as a template for the synthesis of proteins. Replication and transcription take place in the nucleus of cells, and translation takes place in ribosomes.   **25.38** DNA, protein   **25.40** 46 chromosomes (23 pairs)   **25.42** They always occur in pairs: they always H-bond with each other.   **25.44** 22% G, 22% C, 28% A, 28% T. (%G = %C; %A = %T: %T + %A + %C + %G = 100%)   **25.46** 5′ to 3′

25.48

25.50

Uridine

Cytidine

25.52 Introns may be parts of other genes, they may regulate genes, they may stabilize the genome. Exons carry the code for a gene.   **25.54** to increase the speed of replication of DNA   **25.56** A codon is a sequence of three nucleotides on mRNA that codes for a specific amino acid in protein synthesis.   **25.58** A tRNA molecule is cloverleaf-shaped. The tRNA anticodon triplet is on one "leaf," and an amino acid bonds covalently to the 3′ end.   **25.60** Ser, Arg, and Leu each have six codons; Ala, Gly, Pro, Val, and Thr each have four. Met and Trp each have only one codon. These numbers are somewhat correlated with the relative abundance of these amino acids in proteins.   **25.62 (a)** proline **(b)** alanine **(c)** leucine

25.64 Codons are written (5′ → 3′), and anticodons are written (3′ → 5′)

(a)	Val	Codons:	GUU	GUC	GUA	GUG		
		Anticodons:	CAA	CAG	CAU	CAC		
(b)	Arg	Codons:	CGU	CGG	CGA	CGC		
		Anticodons:	GCA	GCC	GCU	GCG		
(c)	Ser	Codons:	UCU	UCC	UCA	UCG	AGU	AGC
		Anticodons:	AGA	AGG	AGU	AGC	UCA	UCG

25.66 (5′ → 3′) UACCCU   **25.68** Val–Ser–Thr–Leu

25.70 Informational strand (5′ → 3′): TAT–GGT–GGT–TTT–ATG–TAA

Template strand (3′ → 5′):   ATA–CCA–CCA–AAA–TAC–ATT

Other sequences are possible   **25.72** Ribozyme activity is common among the simplest and most primitive life forms, such as viroids, leading scientists to speculate that ribozyme catalysis might have preceded enzyme catalysis.   **25.74** To be effective, a drug must be powerful enough to act on viruses within cells without damaging the cells and their genetic material.   **25.76** Influenza A viruses are described by a code that describes the hemagglutinins (H) and the neuraminidases (N) in the virus. The H1N1 virus was responsible for the 1918 influenza pandemic, and the H5N1 virus is present in avian flu. Since these viruses can undergo antigenic shift in host animals, there is concern when infected birds and animals harbor influenza viruses.   **25.78** 249 bases   **25.80** Met is removed after synthesis is complete.

Chapter 26

26.1 "the fat red rat ate the bad rat"   **26.2** As a result of the SNP, the base sequence codes for Trp, instead of Cys. This change would probably affect the functioning of the protein.   **26.3** The sample might not be random; the donors might not be anonymous; issues of informed consent might arise.   **26.4** 3′ –T–C–T–A–G– //–A– 5′   **26.5** 3′ –C–T–T–A–A– //–G– 5′   **26.6 (a)** sticky **(b) (c)** not sticky   **26.7** Taq polymerase can withstand high temperatures and doesn't need to be replaced for each PCR cycle.

26.8 4 people **26.9** (a) comparative genomics (b) genetic engineering (c) pharmacogenetics (d) bioinformatics **26.10** (1) A genetic map, which shows the location of markers one million nucleotides apart, is created. (2) Next comes a physical map, which refines the distance between markers to 100,000 base pairs. (3) The chromosome is cleaved into large segments of overlapping clones. (4) The clones are fragmented into 500 base pieces, which are sequenced. **26.11** The variations are only a small part of the genome; the rest is identical among humans. A diverse group of individuals contributed DNA to the project. **26.12** *telomeres* (protect the chromosome from damage, involved with aging), *centromeres* (involved with cell division), *promoter sequences* (determine which genes will be replicated), *introns* (function unknown) **26.13** Similarities: both are variations in base sequences. Differences: A mutation is an error that is transferred during replication and affects only a few people; a polymorphism is a variation in sequence that is common within a population. **26.14** Recombinant DNA contains two or more DNA segments that do not occur together in nature. The DNA that codes for a specific human protein can be incorporated into a bacterial plasmid using recombinant DNA technology. The plasmid is then reinserted into a bacterial cell, where its protein-synthesizing machinery makes the desired protein. **26.15** Major benefits of genomics: creation of disease-resistant and nutrient-rich crops, gene therapy, genetic screening. Major negative outcomes: misuse of an individual's genetic information, prediction of a genetic disease for which there is no cure. **26.16** Celera broke the genome into many unidentified fragments. The fragments were multiplied and cut into 500 base pieces, which were sequenced. A supercomputer was used to determine the order of the bases. This approach allowed for faster sequencing of the human genome. **26.18** 50% **26.20** (a) Approx. 200 genes are shared between bacteria and humans. (b) A single gene may produce several proteins. **26.22** The clones used in DNA mapping are identical copies of DNA segments from a single individual. In mapping, it is essential to have a sample large enough for experimental manipulation. **26.24** The youngest cells have long telomeres, and the oldest cells have short telomeres. **26.26** It is the constriction that determines the shape of a chromosome during cell division. **26.28** A silent mutation is a single base change that specifies the same amino acid. **26.30** random and spontaneous events, exposure to a mutagen **26.32** A SNP can result in the change in identity of an amino acid inserted into a protein a particular location in a polypeptide chain. The effect of a SNP depends on the function of the protein and the nature of the SNP. **26.34** A physician could predict the age at which inherited diseases might become active, their severity, and the response to various types of treatment. **26.36** a change in the type of amino acid side chain **26.38** (a) Both codons code for Ala (b) Substitution of Ile for Thr is more serious because the amino acids have very different side chains. **26.40** Proteins can be produced in large quantities. **26.42** Sticky ends are unpaired bases at the end of a DNA fragment. Recombinant DNA is formed when the sticky ends of the DNA of interest and of the DNA of the plasmid have complementary base pairs and can be joined by a DNA ligase. **26.44** (a) sticky (b) not sticky **26.46** Pharmacogenomics is the study of the genetic basis of responses to drug treatment. Pharmacogenomics helps doctors prescribe the most effective medicine for a patient, based on the patient's genetic makeup. **26.48** corn, soybeans **26.50** a DNA chip **26.52** A monogenic disease is caused by the variation in just one gene. **26.54** ATACTGA **26.56** A restriction endonuclease is an enzyme that recognizes a specific DNA sequence and cleaves the DNA between two particular nucleotides in that sequence. **26.58** If the DNA from an individual or a single ethnic group had been used, it would have been impossible to map traits due to genetic variability. **26.60** (1)A solution of DNA

that is to be copied is heated so that the DNA separates into two strands. (2) Two oligonucleotide primers, which are complementary to the ends of the segment of DNA to be copied, are attached to the DNA strands. (3) DNA polymerase and nucleotides are added, and the segment of DNA between the primers is copied. The process is repeated many times until a large amount of the desired DNA is produced. **26.62** A VNTR (variable number tandem repeat) is a region of noncoding DNA that contains repeating nucleotide sequences. Comparing the VNTRs on several genes of an individual allows scientists to create a DNA fingerprint of that, person.

Chapter 27

27.1 (a) false (b) true (c) true (d) false (e) false **27.2** oxidoreductase; lyase

27.3

OH   O
| ||
$CH_3CHCH_2CCOO^-$
4-Hydroxy-α-ketopentanoate

27.4

OH   O
| ||
$CH_3CHCH_2CCOO^-$
4-Hydroxy-α-ketopentanoate

27.5 by the loss of two hydrogens to either NAD^+ or $NADP^+$

27.6 valine, leucine, isoleucine

H_3C NH_3^+
| |
$CH_3CHCHCOO^-$ + $^-OOCCH_2CH_2CCOO^-$
Valine α-Ketoglutarate

H_3C O
| ||
$CH_3CHCCOO^-$ + $^-OOCCH_2CH_2CHCOO^-$
                                 |
                            NH_3^+
α-Keto-3-methylbutanoate   Glutamate

27.7

27.8 *See below for answer.* **27.9** (a) 5 (b) 1 (c) 3
27.10 They are essential only under certain conditions.

27.8

(1) oxidative deamination; (2) hydrolysis; (3) oxidation

27.11 3-Phosphoglycerate → 3-Phosphohydroxypyruvate (oxidation)
3-Phosphohydroxypyruvate → 3-Phosphoserine (transamination)
3-Phosphoserine → Serine (hydrolysis)

27.12

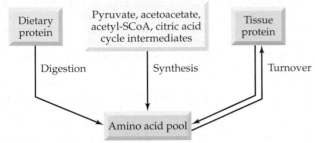

27.13 (1) Catabolism of an amino acid begins with a transamination reaction that removes the amino nitrogen. (2) The resulting α-keto acid, which contains the carbon atoms, is converted to a common metabolic intermediate. (3) The amino group of glutamate (from the amino acid) is removed by oxidative deamination. (4) The amino nitrogen is transformed to urea in the urea cycle and is excreted. **27.14** glutamate dehydrogenase; alanine aminotransferase. Alanine is the product. **27.15** The carbon atoms from ketogenic amino acids can be converted to ketone bodies or to acetyl-SCoA. The carbon atoms from glucogenic amino acids can be converted to compounds that can enter gluconeogenesis and can form glucose, which can enter glycolysis and also yield acetyl-CoA. **27.16** All amino acids are necessary for protein synthesis. The body can synthesize only some of them; the others must be provided by food and are thus essential in the diet. **27.17** to quickly remove ammonia from the body; buildup of urea and shortage of ornithine **27.18** throughout the body **27.20** pyruvate, 3-phosphoglycerate **27.22** In transamination, a keto group of an α-keto acid and an amino group of an amino acid change places.

27.24

(a)

$$^-O-\overset{\overset{\displaystyle O}{\|}}{C}-CH_2CH_2-\overset{\overset{\displaystyle O}{\|}}{C}-COO^-$$

(b)

$$CH_3-\overset{\overset{\displaystyle O}{\|}}{C}-COO^-$$

27.26 An $-NH_3^+$ group of an amino acid is replaced by a carbonyl group, and ammonium ion is eliminated. Oxidative deamination is an oxidation, rather than a transfer.

27.28

(a)

$$\overset{\overset{\displaystyle CH_3}{|}}{CH_3CHCH_2}-\overset{\overset{\displaystyle O}{\|}}{C}-COO^-$$

(b)

$$CH_2-\overset{\overset{\displaystyle O}{\|}}{C}-COO^-$$ (indole ring structure)

27.30 A ketogenic amino acid is catabolized to acetoacetyl-CoA or acetyl-CoA. Examples: leucine, isoleucine, lysine **27.32** Ammonia is toxic. **27.34** One nitrogen comes from carbamoyl phosphate, which is synthesized from ammonium ion by oxidative deamination. The other nitrogen comes from aspartate **27.36** Nonessential amino acids are synthesized in humans in 1–3 steps. Essential amino acids are synthesized in microorganisms in 7–10 steps. **27.38** legumes, meat **27.40** phenylketonuria; mental retardation; restriction of phenylalanine in the diet **27.42** (b) (c) (d) **27.44** isoleucine + pyruvate → α-keto-3-methylpentanoate + alanine **27.46** yes. Some amino acids yield two kinds of products—those that can enter the citric acid cycle and those that are intermediates of fatty acid metabolism. **27.48** Tissue is dynamic because its components are constantly being broken down and reformed **27.50** (b) → (e) → (d) → (f) → (a) → (c). **27.52** (1) The amino group is removed; (2) Nitrogen is either used in synthesis of new nitrogen—containing compounds or excreted as urea; (3) The remaining carbon atoms are converted into compounds that can enter the citric acid cycle. **27.54** An excess of one amino acid might overwhelm a transport system that other amino acids use, resulting in a deficiency of those amino acids. **27.56** Oxidized allopurinol inhibits the

enzyme that converts xanthine to uric acid. The more soluble intermediates are excreted. The nitrogen at position 7 of hypoxanthine is at position 8 in allopurinol, where it blocks oxidation of xanthine. **27.58** tryptophan; emotional and behavioral problems

Chapter 28

28.1 Both compounds reflect homeostasis. The glucose level is regulated by an endocrine hormone. **28.2** (b) **28.3** The molecules resemble the heterocyclic part of cAMP, and they might act as inhibitors to the enzyme that inactivates cAMP. **28.4** Glu-His-Pro **28.5** The hydrophobic part of the structure is larger than the polar, hydrophilic part. **28.6** Testosterone has a $-CH_3$ group between the first two rings; nandrolone doesn't. Otherwise, their structures are identical. **28.7** Brassinolide has a core structure that resembles a steroid framework. **28.8** (a) 3 (b) 1 (c) 2 **28.9** Similarities: both structures have aromatic rings, secondary amine groups, alcohol groups. Differences: propranolol has an ether group and a naphthalene ring system; epinephrine has two phenol hydroxyl groups; the compounds have different side-chain carbon skeletons. **28.10** (a) Malathion: it's the least toxic, (b) Parathion is most toxic (smallest LD_{50}). **28.11** (a) prolongs the effect of serotonin (b) blocks the response at the receptor **28.12** phenol hydroxyl group, ether, carbon–carbon double bond, aromatic ring. THC is hydrophobic and is likely to accumulate in fatty tissue. **28.13** (a) antihistamine (b) antidepressant **28.14** (a) polypeptide hormone (produced in the anterior pituitary gland) (b) steroid hormone (produced in ovaries) (c) Progesterone-producing cells have LH receptors, (d) Progesterone is lipid-soluble and can enter cells. **28.15** Adenylate cyclase can produce a great many molecules of cAMP, which phosphorylate kinase enzymes. These enzymes can cause the breakdown of glycogen to yield glucose. **28.16** (a) insulin (polypeptide hormone) (b) pancreas (c) in the bloodstream (d) Insulin doesn't enter cells directly because it can't pass through cell membranes. Instead, it binds with a cell surface receptor. **28.17** binding to receptors; activating second messengers **28.18** Enzymatic inactivation; reuptake by presynaptic neuron. **28.19** These substances increase dopamine levels in the brain. The brain responds by decreasing the number and sensitivity of dopamine receptors. Thus more of the substance is needed to elevate dopamine levels, leading to addiction. **28.20** A *chemical messenger* is a molecule that travels from one part of the body to another location, where it delivers a signal or acts to control metabolism. The *target tissue* is the cell or group of cells whose activity is regulated by the messenger. A *hormone receptor* is the molecule with which the chemical messenger interacts if it is a hormone. **28.22** A vitamin is usually an enzyme cofactor, whereas a hormone regulates enzyme activity. **28.24** Neither a hormone nor its receptor is changed as a result of binding to each other. The binding forces between hormone and receptor are noncovalent. **28.26** The endocrine system manufactures and secretes hormones. **28.28** polypeptide hormones, steroid hormones, amino acid derivatives **28.30** Enzymes are proteins; hormones may be polypeptides, proteins, steroids or amino acid derivatives. **28.32** Polypeptide hormones travel through the bloodstream and bind to cell receptors, which are on the outside of a cell. The receptors cause production within cells of "second messengers" that activate enzymes. **28.34** the adrenal medulla **28.36** through the bloodstream **28.38** In order of involvement; the hormone receptor, G protein, and adenylate cyclase. **28.40** It initiates reactions that release glucose from storage. Termination occurs when phosphodiesterase converts cAMP to AMP. **28.42** anaphylaxis **28.44** Insulin contains 51 amino acids, is released from the pancreas, and acts at cells, causing them to take up glucose. **28.46** Mineralocorticoids (aldosterone), glucocorticoids (cortisone), and sex hormones (testosterone, estrone) all have the four-fused-ring skeleton. **28.48** androsterone, testosterone **28.50** Androgens increase muscle mass and strength. **28.52** epinephrine, norepinephrine, dopamine **28.54** (a) amino acid derivative (b) polypeptide hormone (c) steroid hormone **28.56** A synapse is the gap between two nerve cells that neurotransmitters cross to transmit their message. **28.58** nerve cell, muscle cell, endocrine cell **28.60** A nerve impulse arrives at the presynaptic end of a neuron. The nerve impulse stimulates the movement of a vesicle, containing neurotransmitter molecules, to the cell membrane. The vesicle fuses with the cell membrane and releases the neurotransmitter, which crosses the synaptic cleft to a receptor site on the postsynaptic end of a second neuron. After reception, the cell transmits an electrical signal down its axon and passes on the impulse. Enzymes then deactivate the neurotransmitter so that the neuron can receive the next impulse. Alternatively, the neurotransmitter may be returned to the presynaptic neuron. **28.62** (1) Neurotransmitter molecules are released from a presynaptic neuron. (2) Neurotransmitter molecules bind to receptors on the target cell. (3) The neurotransmitter is deactivated. **28.64** They are secreted in the central nervous system and have receptors in brain tissue. **28.66** Agonists prolong the response of a receptor. Antagonists block the response of a receptor. **28.68** Antihistamines such as doxylamine counteract allergic responses caused by histamine by blocking histamine receptors in mucous membranes. Antihistamines such as cimetidine block receptors for histamine that stimulate production of stomach acid. **28.70** *Tricyclic antidepressant:* Elavil™ *MAO inhibitor:* Nardil™ *SSRI:* Prozac™ **28.72** Cocaine increases dopamine levels by blocking reuptake. **28.74** Tetrahydrocannabinol (THC) increases dopamine levels in the same brain areas where dopamine levels increase after administration of heroin and cocaine. **28.76** antagonist **28.78** Endorphins are polypeptides with morphine-like activity. They are produced by the pituitary gland and have receptors in the brain. **28.80** They interact with the same receptors as opioids. **28.82** An ethnobotanist discovers what indigenous people have learned about the healing power of plants. **28.84** Scientists who know about the exact size and shape of enzymes and receptors can design drugs that interact with the active sites of these biomolecules. **28.86** Homeostasis is the maintenance of a constant internal environment. **28.88** Plants don't have endocrine systems or a circulatory fluid like blood. **28.90** epinephrine **28.92** Both have large nonpolar regions and can cross cell membranes to activate the synthesis of enzymes. **28.94** (1) Once the message has been delivered, cyclic AMP is no longer needed. (2) The precursor to cyclic AMP must be ready for the next signal. **28.96** The response to a hormonal signal is prolonged. **28.98** Ethynyl estradiol and norethindrone differ only in the ring on the far left: the ring is a phenol in ethynyl estradiol and is an enone in norethindrone. Ethynyl estradiol and estradiol differ only in the five-membered ring: a —C≡CH group is present in ethynyl estradiol and absent in estradiol. Norethindrone is similar to progesterone in all but two respects: progesterone has a methyl group between the first two rings, and has an acetyl group in the five-membered ring, instead of the two groups of norethindrone. **28.100** substitution of —OH for —H (oxidoreductase); loss of CO_2 (lyase) **28.102** oxidation of —OH to a ketone

Chapter 29

29.1 In the cell: the charged form. Outside the cell: the uncharged form. The uncharged form enters the cell more readily. **29.2** (a) iii (b) ii (c) iv (d) v (e) i **29.3** (a) pH goes down; more acidic (b) $[O_2]$, $[CO_2]$, $[pH]$ **29.4** (a) respiratory acidosis (b) metabolic acidosis (c) metabolic alkalosis **29.5** (a) respiratory alkalosis (b) respiratory acidosis (c) metabolic acidosis **29.6** Heroin has two acetyl groups in the same location as the two hydroxyl groups of morphine. These nonpolar acetyl groups make heroin soluble in the membrane lipids of endothelial cells and more able to pass into these cells. **29.7** (a) intracellular fluid (b) extracellular fluid (c) blood plasma, interstitial fluid (d) K^+, Mg^{2+}, HPO_4^{2-} (e) Na^+, Cl^-
29.8

29.9 (a) O_2 (b) CO_2 (c) nutrients (d) waste products (e) hormones (f) white blood cells, platelets **29.10** swelling, redness, warmth, pain **29.11** Histamine is synthesized by the enzymatic decarboxylation of histidine. Histamine dilates capillaries, increasing blood flow that reddens and warms the skin. Blood-clotting factors and defensive proteins cause pain and swelling. **29.12** *Cell-mediated immune response:* under control of T cells; arises when abnormal cells, bacteria or viruses enter cells; invaders killed by T cells. *Antibody-mediated immune response:* under control of B cells, assisted by T cells; occurs when antigens enter cells; B cells divide to produce plasma cells, which form antibodies; an antibody-antigen complex inactivates the antigen. **29.13** Excess hydrogen ions are excreted by reaction with NH_3 or HPO_4^{2-}. H^+ ions also combine with bicarbonate, producing CO_2 that returns to the bloodstream. **29.14** intracellular fluid (64%), interstitial fluid (25%), plasma (8%) **29.16** Substances not soluble in blood, such as lipids, are transported by blood proteins. **29.18** Blood pressure in arterial capillaries is higher than interstitial fluid pressure, and blood pressure in venous capillaries is lower than interstitial fluid pressure. **29.20** the thoracic duct **29.22** An excess of antidiuretic hormone causes a decrease in the water content of the urine. This excess may be caused by pulmonary or central nervous system disorders. **29.24** 7% **29.26** *Red blood cells* transport blood gases. *White blood cells* protect the body from foreign substances. *Platelets* assist in blood clotting. **29.28** *Inside cells:* K^+, Mg^{2+}, HPO_4^{2-}; *Outside cells:* Na^+, Cl^- **29.30** Antihistamines block attachment of the neurotransmitter histamine to its receptors. **29.32** immunoglobulins **29.34** Killer T cells destroy the invader; helper T cells enhance defenses; memory T cells can produce new killer T cells if needed. **29.36** Memory cells "remember" an antigen and are capable of producing antibodies to it for a long time. **29.38** Vitamin K, Ca^{2+} **29.40** They are released as zymogens in order to avoid undesirable clotting in noninjured tissues. **29.42** +2 **29.44** If pO_2 is below 10 mm Hg, hemoglobin is unsaturated. If pO_2 is greater than 100 mm Hg, hemoglobin is completely saturated. Between these pressures, hemoglobin is partially saturated. **29.46** a dissolved gas, bound to hemoglobin, bicarbonate ion

29.48 $$CO_2 + H_2O \underset{}{\overset{\text{Carbonic anhydrase}}{\rightleftharpoons}} HCO_3^- + H^+$$

29.50 *Respiratory acidosis* occurs when there is buildup of CO_2 in the blood; *Metabolic acidosis* is due to increased production of metabolic acids.
29.52 *Respiratory alkalosis* occurs when there is a loss of CO_2; *Metabolic alkalosis* occurs when there is elevated plasma bicarbonate concentration.

29.54 $$H^+ + HCO_3^- \rightleftharpoons CO_2 + H_2O$$
$$H^+ + HPO_4^{2-} \rightleftharpoons H_2PO_4^-$$

29.56 A nursing mother's antibodies can be passed to her baby in breast milk. **29.58** Active transport is the movement of solutes from regions of low concentration to regions of high concentration, a process that requires energy. Osmosis is the movement of water through a semipermeable membrane from a dilute solution to a more concentrated solution, a process that requires no energy. **29.60** In the blood, CO_2 from metabolism reacts to form $HCO_3^- + H^+$. The H^+ is bound to hemoglobin, which releases O_2, and is carried to the lungs. There, the H^+ is released and O_2 is bound to hemoglobin. In the urine, CO_2 reacts to form HCO_3^- and H^+. The HCO_3^- returns to the bloodstream, and the H^+ is neutralized by reaction with HPO_4^{2-} or NH_3. Whenever excess HCO_3^- accumulates in blood or urine, it can react with H^+ to form $H_2O + CO_2$. **29.62** When blood CO_2 level drops, the following reaction occurs to restore CO_2 supply:

$$H^+ + HCO_3^- \longrightarrow H_2CO_3 \longrightarrow CO_2 + H_2O$$

This reaction uses up H^+ ions and leads to alkalosis. Breathing into a paper bag recaptures the expired CO_2 and restores the blood CO_2 level. **29.64** Substances can either be transported into a cell or be transported out of a cell, but not both. **29.66** The metabolic blood-brain barrier is a pathway in which a substance is converted in an epithelial cell to a metabolite that can't enter the brain. **29.68** Automated analysis can reproducibly detect changes in enzyme levels that might indicate organ damage.

Credits

Text and Art Credits

Chapter 8: 219, Adapted from NASA, Goddard Institute for Space Studies, Surface Temperature Analysis (GIS Temp), http://data.giss.nasa.gov/gistemp.

Chapter 15: 465, Content was copied from MSDS of *Fisher Chemical* brand product, with permission.

Chapter 16: 489, Adapted from *Introduction to Ecological Biochemistry*, 2/e by J.B. Harborne. Academic Press, Inc., 1982.

Photo Credits

Chapter 1: 2, imagebroker.net/SuperStock; 5, Richard Megna/Fundamental Photographs; 8, PhilSigin/iStockphoto; 12(a) top, Norov Dmitriy/iStockphoto; 12(b) top, Ben Mills; 12(c) top, Shutterstock; 12(a) middle, Andraž Cerar/Shutterstock; 12(b) middle, Leeuwtje/iStockphoto; 12(c) middle, Ben Mills; 12(a) bottom, Russell Lappa/Photo Researchers, Inc.; 12(b) bottom, Texas Instruments Inc.; 14(a), Richard Megna/Fundamental Photographs; 14(b), Richard Megna/Fundamental Photographs; 14(c), Richard Megna/Fundamental Photographs; 15, eROMAZe/iStockphoto; 16, Centers for Disease Control; 17, Richard Megna/Fundamental Photographs; 19, Pearson Education/McCracken Photographers; 21, artkamalov/Shutterstock; 22, Pearson Education/Eric Schrader; 24, Pearson Education/Eric Schrader; 25, tdbp/Alamy; 28, Pearson Education/Michal Heron; 30, Richard Megna/Fundamental Photographs; 31, Stockbyte/Photolibrary; 33, Claire VD/Shutterstock; 35, Ivica Drusany/iStockphoto; 36, BD Adams; 38, Pearson Education/Eric Schrader.

Chapter 2: 44, Katie Dickinson/Shutterstock; 46, AP Photo/Donna Carson; 48, IBM Research, Almaden Research Center; 52, Richard Megna/Fundamental Photographs; 54, Richard Megna/Fundamental Photographs; 56, NASA, ESA and H.E. Bond (STScI); 57, Michael Neary Photography/iStockphoto; 66, James Benet/iStockphoto.

Chapter 3: 72, Juan Jose Rodriguez Velandia/Shutterstock; 74, Pearson Education/Eric Schrader; 76(a), Richard Megna/Fundamental Photographs; 76(b), Richard Megna/Fundamental Photographs; 77 top, NASA; 77 bottom, Richard Megna/Fundamental Photographs; 78 both, Dimitris S. Argyropoulos; 83, Daniella Zalcman/Shutterstock; 93, Steve Gschmeissner/SPL/Photo Researchers, Inc.

Chapter 4: 98, David R. Frazier Photolibrary, Inc./Alamy; 100, Martin Barraud/Alamy; 113, Upsidedowndog/iStockphoto; 118, Claudia Veja/Alamy; 125, Yakobchuk Vasyl/Shutterstock.

Chapter 5: 132, Harald Sund/Brand X Pictures/Getty Images; 137, David R. Frazier/Photo Researchers, Inc.; 138, Richard Megna/Fundamental Photographs; 140, Dr. P. Marazzi/Photo Researchers, Inc.; 143 left, Richard Megna/Fundamental Photographs; 143 right, Richard Megna/Fundamental Photographs; 147 top, Luca DiCecco/Alamy; 147 bottom, David Young-Wolff/PhotoEdit.

Chapter 6: 158, AFP/Getty Images/Newscom; 160, Richard Megna/Fundamental Photographs; 164 left, Library of Congress; 164 right, Science Photo Library/Photo Researchers, Inc.; 172, Jane Norton/Shutterstock.

Chapter 7: 178, Ron Lewis/Icon SMI/Newscom; 181, Richard Megna/Fundamental Photographs; 185, discpicture/Shutterstock; 186, GeoStock/Getty Images; 187 left, Aaron Amat/Shutterstock; 187 right, Samuel Perry/Shutterstock; 194, AC/General Motors/Peter Arnold Images/Photolibrary; 195, Reuters/Vladimir Davydov; 196, Photolibrary/Indexopen; 204, Myles Dumas/iStockphoto.

Chapter 8: 212, Tony Waltham/AGE Fotostock; 221, NASA; 227, Stephen Sweet/iStockphoto; 228, Laura Stone/Shutterstock; 238, Richard Megna/Fundamental Photographs; 239 top, Alexei Zaycev/iStockphoto; 239 middle, Harry Taylor/Dorling Kindersley; 239 bottom, AGE Fotostock; 240 left, Jens Mayer/Shutterstock; 240 right, Jonny Kristoffersson/iStockphoto.

Chapter 9: 252, Phil Schermeister/NGS Images; 256, Pearson Education/Tom Bochsler; 259, Richard Megna/Fundamental Photographs; 263, AP Photo/Gurinder Osan; 265(a), Richard Megna/Fundamental Photographs; 265(b), Richard Megna/Fundamental Photographs; 265(c), Richard Megna/Fundamental Photographs; 273(a), Richard Megna/Fundamental Photographs; 273(b), Richard Megna/Fundamental Photographs; 276, Jason Getz/Atlanta Journal-Constitution/MCT/Newscom; 281(a), Sam Singer; 281(b), Sam Singer; 281(c), Sam Singer; 284 left, Martin Dohrn/SPL/Photo Researchers, Inc.; 284 right, Lev Dolgachov/Shutterstock.

Chapter 10: 290, Liga Lauzuma/iStockphoto; 292, Pearson Education/Eric Schrader; 299, Gastrolab/Photo Researchers, Inc.; 308(a), Richard Megna/Fundamental Photographs; 308(b), Pearson Education/Tom Bochsler; 308 left, Pearson Education/Tom Bochsler; 312, Robert Caplin/Newscom; 316, Pearson Education/Eric Schrader; 318(a), Richard Megna/Fundamental Photographs; 318(b), Richard Megna/Fundamental Photographs; 320 top, RMAX/iStockphoto; 320 bottom, National Atmospheric Deposition Program.

Chapter 11: 328, P. Berndt/Custom Medical Stock Photo/Newscom; 338 top, Simon Fraser/RVI/SPL/Photo Researchers, Inc.; 338 bottom, Media Minds/Alamy; 343, Stanford Dosimetry, LLC; 344, Mark Kostich/iStockphoto; 345, Tony Freeman/PhotoEdit; 347, Stephen Uber/iStockphoto; 348, Custom Medical Stock Photo.

Chapter 12: 356, Kevin Burke/Corbis; 359, Xinhua News Agency/Newscom; 385, Chloe Johnson/Alamy.

Chapter 13: 394, Larry Hales/iStockphoto; 409(a), Richard Megna/Fundamental Photographs; 409(b), Richard Megna/Fundamental Photographs; 417(a), Pearson Education/Eric Schrader; 417(b), Pearson Education/Michal Heron; 419, kryczka/iStockphoto; 420, Denis Tabler/Shutterstock.

Chapter 14: 432, davidf/iStockphoto; 446, Pearson Education/Eric Schrader; 448, norcon/iStockphoto; 449, Pearson Education/Eric Schrader; 451, Rod Planck/Photo Researchers, Inc.; 452, Coleman515/iStockphoto; 453, Prisma Archivo/Alamy.

Chapter 15: 460, Tim Messick/iStockphoto; 474, Pearson Science/Eric Schader; 477 top, Pearson Science/Eric Schader; 477 bottom, Allan Rosenberg/Getty Images–Photodisc; 478, aaM Photography, Ltd./iStockphoto.

Chapter 16: 484, Elke Dennis/Shutterstock; 489, Paul Marek; 493, Baloncici/iStockphoto; 495(a), Richard Megna/Fundamental Photographs; 495(b), Richard Megna/Fundamental Photographs; 499, Dušan Zidar/iStockphoto.

Chapter 17: 514, Warren Photographic Ltd.; 520, RedHelga/iStockphoto; 528, Pearson Education/Eric Schrader; 529, Andrei Rybachuk/Shutterstock; 532, Drug Enforcement Administration; 538, Pearson Education/Tom Bochsler; 539, Pearson Education/Eric Schrader.

Chapter 18: 548, Fresh Food Images/Photolibrary; 558 top, sunnyfrog/iStockphoto; 558 bottom, sturmwarnung/iStockphoto; 562, Centers for Disease Control; 564, swalls/iStockphoto; 565, USDA; 571 top, Natalia Clarke/Shutterstock; 571 bottom, Larry Ye/Shutterstock; 573(a), Pearson Education/Kim M Gernert; 573(b), Pearson Education/Kim M Gernert;

574(a) top, Pearson Education; 574(a) bottom, Pearson Education/ Richard J. Feldmann; 574(b) bottom, Molecular Graphics and Modelling, Duke University/Pearson Education/PH College; 576 top, St. Mary's Hospital Medical School/Photo Researchers, Inc.; 576 bottom, NMSB/ Custom Medical Stock Photo; 578, Woldee/iStockphoto.

Chapter 19: 586, Jeff J Daly/Alamy; 588(a), Richard Megna/ Fundamental Photographs; 588(b), Richard Megna/Fundamental Photographs; 588(c), Richard Megna/Fundamental Photographs; 595, Galyna Andrushko/Shutterstock; 608, David Goodsell; 610, voylodyon/Shutterstock; 613, Elena Aliaga/Shutterstock.

Chapter 20: 622, Joel Saget/AFP/Getty Images/Newscom; 627, AFP Photo/Fisheries and Oceans Canada/UVIC-Verena Tunnicliffe/ Newscom; 634, ooyoo/iStockphoto; 636, Joao Virissimo/Shutterstock; 646, David Goodsell; 649, formiktopus/Shutterstock.

Chapter 21: 656, YinYang/iStockphoto; 662, SergioKSV/iStockphoto; 670(a), Corbis Premium RF/Alamy; 670(b), Pearson Education/Eric Schrader; 670(c), Olga Langerova/iStockphoto; 677, Pearson Education/ Eric Schrader; 679, Igor Negovelov/iStockphoto; 680, NH/Shutterstock.

Chapter 22: 692, Olga Miltsova/Shutterstock; 693, Science Photo Library/Alamy; 700 left, Elena Elisseeva/iStockphoto; 700 middle, David Crockett/iStockphoto; 700 right, Luca Manieri/iStockphoto; 702, Pearson Education/Andrea Mattevi and Wim G.J. Hol; 709, FreezeFrameStudio/iStockphoto; 712, Peter Kirillov/Shutterstock.

Chapter 23: 720, Sandra vom Stein/iStockphoto; 725, Wim Claes/ Shutterstock; 728, Pearson Education/Eric Schrader; 729, Science Photo Library/Alamy; 732, Anne Stahl/iStockphoto; 734, C Squared Studios/ Getty Images–Photodisc; 740, Steve Lupton/Corbis.

Chapter 24: 752, Arco Images GmbH/Alamy; 757, Biophoto Associates/Photo Researchers, Inc.; 760, John Sholtis/Amgen, Inc.; 764, Tobias Helbig/iStockphoto.

Chapter 25: 774, Roy Kaltschmidt/Lawrence Berkeley National Laboratory; 775, Thomas Deerinck, NCMIR/Photo Researchers, Inc.; 779, Prof. K. Seddon & Dr. T. Evans, Queen's University, Belfast/Photo Researchers, Inc.; 787, David S. Hogness; 794, Centers or Disease Control; 799, Centers for Disease Control.

Chapter 26: 804, James King-Holmes/Photo Researchers, Inc.; 805, BSIP/Ermakoff/Photo Researchers, Inc.; 807, Roy Kaltschmidt/ Lawrence Berkeley National Laboratory; 808, RexRover/iStockphoto; 809, Biophoto Associates/Photo Researchers, Inc.; 810, Splash News/ Newscom; 814, Dr. Gopal Murti/Photo Researchers, Inc.; 819, Syngenta; 820, AP Photo/Maye-e Wont.

Chapter 27: 824, Monkey Business Images/Shutterstock; 826, Pearson Education/Eric Schrader; 831, craykeeper/Shutterstock; 836, CNRI/ Photo Researchers, Inc.

Chapter 28: 842, Diego Barbieri/Shutterstock; 850, Pearson Education/ Michal Heron; 855, Serhiy Shullye/Shutterstock; 856, Synaptek/SPL/ Photo Researchers, Inc.; 860, Borut Trdina/iStockphoto; 864, Garden Row Foods; 865, National Institute of Standards and Technology.

Chapter 29: 870, Vladm/Shutterstock; 881 left, Biology Media/ Science Source/Photo Researchers, Inc.; 881 right, Lennart Nilsson/ Boehringer Ingelheim/SCANPIX; 883, Volker Steger/Peter Arnold/ Photolibrary; 884, Pearson Education/Michal Heron; 885, Janice Carr/ Centers for Disease Control; 889, Joseph Abbott/iStockphoto.

Index

Note: Page numbers in **boldface** type indicate definitions of terms.

1,4 link, **676**
3TC (lamivudine), 795

Absolute alcohol, 435
ACE (angiotensin-converting enzyme) inhibitors, 607
Acetaldehyde
  in acetal formation, 501
  in ethyl alcohol metabolism, 446
  in hemiacetal formation, 500
  properties, 490, 493
  structure, 109, 488, 493
  uses, 125, 493
Acetal hydrolysis, 504–506, 507
Acetals, **501**–506, 674
Acetaminophen, 865
Acetanilide, 865
Acetic acid
  acidity, 293, 448
  carbonyl derivatives, 522
  naming of, 525
  properties, 520, 525
  structure, 525
  uses, 292
Acetoacetate, 765, 766, 767
Acetone
  in acetal formation, 501
  in hemiacetal formation, 500
  as ketone body, 765, 766
  odor on breath, 708, 767
  as product of *Clostridium* fermentation, 703
  properties, 216, 493–494, 499
  structure, 488, 493
  uses, 493–494
Acetyl acyl carrier protein (acetyl-ACP), 769
Acetylcholine
  breakdown of, 606
  drug interactions with, 858–859
  in irreversible inhibition, 606
  mechanism of, 857–858
  in neurotoxin mechanisms, 478
  structure, 478
  synthesis, 857
Acetylcholinesterase, 606
Acetyl-CoA, **630**
  breakdown in citric acid cycle, 641
  conversion of glucose into, 694
  conversion of pyruvate into, 701, 702, 704–705
  conversion to ketone bodies, 707, 759, 765
  in energy generation, 631, 758–759, 764
  in lipid metabolism, 759
  in lipogenesis, 768–769
  production of, 630, 631
Acetyl-coenzyme A. *See* Acetyl-CoA

Acetylene, 105, 398, 399
Acetyl groups, **518**, 640–641. *See also* Acetyl-CoA
Acetylsalicylic acid (ASA), 8
Achirality, **557**–559
Acid anhydrides, 516, 523
Acid–base balance, 884–886, 888–890
Acid–base indicators, **308**
Acid–base reactions
  carboxylic acids in, 526–527
  common reactions, 316–317
  definition of, 294–295
  neutralization reactions, 138, **141**–142, 318
Acid–base titration, 317–319
Acid dissociation constants (K_a), **301**, 526
Acid equivalents, 313–315
Acidity
  of aqueous solutions, 302–303
  of denaturation agents, 578
  determination of, 303–305, 308
  of salt solutions, 321–322
Acidosis, 312–313, **886**, 890
Acid rain, 320–321
Acids, **92**, 291–322. *See also* Acid–base reactions; Acidity; pH; Strong acids; Weak acids
  acid equivalents, 313–315
  anions derived from, 92
  in aqueous solution, 291–292
  basic concepts, 91–92
  buffer solutions, 308–311
  common, 292
  concentrations of, 317–319
  conjugate, 295
  corrosiveness of, 296
  definitions, 291–292, 293
  diprotic, 293, 315
  examples, 92
  in neutralization reactions, 141–142
  normality of, 314
  as proton donors, 293
  strength of, 296–300
  titration, 317–319
  unsaturated, 517–518, 519
  water as, 302
ACP (acyl carrier protein), 769
Acquired Immunodeficiency Syndrome (AIDS), 607, 795. *See also* HIV-1
Actinides, 53
Activation, enzyme, **602**
Activation energy (E_{act}), **191**–192, 193, 594
Active sites, **588**, 596, 603
Active transport, **743**, 744, 826
Actual yield, **169**–171
Acute toxicity, 499
Acyclic alkanes, 383, 384
Acyl carrier protein (ACP), 769
Acyl-CoA, 758, 762
Acyl-CoA acetyltransferase, 763

Acyl-CoA dehydrogenase, 762–763
Acylglycerols, 754
Acyl groups, **516**, 753
Acyl transferase, 761
Acyl transfer reactions, 516
Addition reactions, **403**
  alcohols, 500
  aldehydes, 500–506
  alkenes, 407–408, 409, 413, 414–415
  alkynes, 407–408
  carbonyls, 506–507
  ketones, 500–507
  Markovnikov's rule, 410–412, 415
Adenine
  base pairing of, 783–785
  in nucleotide chains, 782
  as purine derivative, 777
  structure, 421, 470
Adenosine, 637, 777, 778
Adenosine diphosphate (ADP), 632–634, 696, 697, 699. *See also* ATP–ADP conversion
Adenosine monophosphate (AMP), 697
Adenosine triphosphate (ATP), **629**. *See also* ATP–ADP conversion
Adenylate cyclase, 849
ADH (antidiuretic hormone), 845, 875–876, 890
Adipic acid, 538
Adipocytes, 759, 760, 761
Adipose tissue, 727, 728, 729, 755, 756
ADP (adenosine diphosphate), 632–634, 696, 697, 699. *See also* ATP–ADP conversion
ADP–ATP conversion. *See* ATP–ADP conversion
Adrenaline. *See* Epinephrine
Aerobic conditions, **701**, 702
Agglutination, 672
Agitation, mechanical, as denaturation agent, 578
Agonists, **858**–859
AIDS (Acquired Immunodeficiency Syndrome), 607, 795. *See also* HIV-1
α-Keratins, 571
Alanine, 557–558
Alanine aminotransferase (ALT), 829
Alanine transaminase (ALT), 601
Albumins, 755, 756, 759
Alcohol dehydrogenase, 446, 591
Alcohol family, 360
Alcoholic beverages, 195
Alcoholic fermentation, 435, 703–**704**
Alcoholism, 767, 862
Alcohols, **433**
  acidity, 448–450
  common, 434–436
  drawing, 451
  functional groups, 362
  hydrophilic/hydrophobic parts, 439

monosaccharide reactions with, 674–675
  naming, 436–438
  as organic molecule family, 361, 362
  phosphate esters of, 675–676
  primary, 437, 441, 496
  properties, 433–434, 439–440
  reactions of, 440–445, 528–529
  secondary, 437, 441, 444, 496
  tertiary, 437, 441
Aldehydes, **486**
  aromas, 485
  carbonyl groups in, 485
  common, 492–493
  functional groups, 362
  in monosaccharides, 658
  naming, 488
  as organic molecule family, 361, 362
  as products of alcohol oxidation, 444
  properties, 484, 490–492
  reactions of, 494–498, 500–506, 673–674
  structure, 486–487
  testing for, 495–496
  toxicity, 492
Aldohexose, 663
Aldolase, 696, 698
Aldoses, **658**, 674
Aldosterone, 739, 890
Aldotetrose, 660
Aleve®, 865
Alkali metals, **54**
  cation formation by, 75, 81
  compounds with halogens, 73–74
  electron-dot symbol, 79
  properties, 54
  as reducing agents, 144
  valence-shell electron configurations, 63, 79
Alkaline batteries, 147
Alkaline earth metals, **55**, 63, 81, 144
Alkaline phosphatase (ALP), 601
Alkalinis, 312–313, **886**
Alkaloids, **476**–477
Alkalosis, 312–313, **886**
Alkanes, 357–387
  acyclic, 383, 384
  cycloalkanes, **383**–384, 386–387
  isomers, 364–366
  naming, 374–380
  as organic molecule family, 360–362
  physiological effects of, 381
  properties, 380–381
  reactions of, 381–383
  saturated, 395–396
  structure, 364–366
  thermal "cracking," 396
Alkene families, 360
Alkene polymers, 415–418